WORLD CONGRESS ON NEURAL NETWORKS- SAN DIEGO

1994 International
Neural Network Society
Annual Meeting

Town & Country Hotel
San Diego, California USA
June 5-9, 1994

VOLUME 1

Lawrence Erlbaum Associates, Inc., Publishers
365 Broadway
Hillsdale, New Jersey 07642

ISBN 0-8058-1745-X

Books published by Lawrence Erlbaum Associates are printed on acid-free paper, and their bindings are chosen for strength and durability.

Printed in the United States of America

WCNN '94 ORGANIZING COMMITTEE

Paul Werbos, Chairman, *National Science Foundation*

Harold Szu, *Naval Surface Warfare Center*

Bernard Widrow, *Stanford University*

WCNN '94 SPECIAL SESSION CHAIRS

BIOMEDICAL APPLICATIONS OF NEURAL NETWORKS
David G. Brown, *Center for Devices and Radiological Health,*
US Food and Drug Administration
John N. Weinstein, *National Cancer Institute, US National Institutes of Health*

COMMERCIAL AND INDUSTRIAL APPLICATIONS OF
NEURAL NETWORKS
Bernard Widrow, *Stanford University*

FINANCIAL AND ECONOMIC APPLICATIONS OF
NEURAL NETWORKS
Guido J. Deboeck, *World Bank*

APPLICATION OF NEURAL NETWORKS IN THE
CHEMICAL PROCESS INDUSTRIES
Thomas McAvoy, *University of Maryland*

MIND, BRAIN, AND CONSCIOUSNESS
John G. Taylor, *King's College London*

WCNN '94 PROGRAM COMMITTEE

Daniel Alkon, *National Institutes of Health*
Shun-ichi Amari, *University of Tokyo*
Richard A. Andersen, *Massachusetts Institute of Technology*
James A. Anderson, *Brown University*
Kaveh Ashenayi, *University of Tulsa*
Andrew Barto, *University of Massachusetts*
Horacio Bouzas, *Geoquest*
David G. Brown, *Center for Devices and Radiological Health, US FDA*
Gail Carpenter, *Boston University*
David Casasent, *Carnegie Mellon University*
Ralph Castain, *Los Alamos National Laboratory*
Chris Darken, *Siemens Corporate Research*
Joel Davis, *Office of Naval Research*
Judith Dayhoff, *University of Maryland*
Guido J. Deboeck, *World Bank*
David Fong, *Photon Dynamics, Inc.*
Judy Franklin, *GTE Laboratories*
Walter J. Freeman, *University of California at Berkeley*
Kunihiko Fukushima, *Osaka University*
Michael Georgiopoulos, *University of Central Florida*
Lee Giles, *NEC Research Institute*
Stephen Grossberg, *Boston University*
Dan Hammerstrom, *Adaptive Solutions, Inc.*
Robert Hecht-Nielsen, *HNC, Inc.*
Robert Jannarone, *University of South Carolina*
Jari Kangas, *Helsinki University of Technology*
Christof Koch, *California Institute of Technology*
Teuvo Kohonen, *Helsinki University of Technology*
Bart Kosko, *Signal and Image Processing Institute*
Clifford Lau, *Office of Naval Research*
Soo-Young Lee, *Korea Advanced Institute of Science and Technology*
George Lendaris, *Accurate Automation Corporation*
Daniel Levine, *University of Texas - Arlington*
Alianna Maren, *Accurate Automation Corporation*
Kenneth Marko, *Ford Motor Company*

WCNN '94 PROGRAM COMMITTEE

Thomas McAvoy, *University of Maryland*
Thomas McKenna, *Office of Naval Research*
Larry Medsker, *American University*
Erkki Oja, *Lappeenranta University of Technology*
Robert Pap, *Accurate Automation Corporation*
Barak Pearlmutter, *Siemens Corporate Research*
Richard Peterson, *Georgia Tech Research Institute*
Gerhardt Roth, *Brain Research Institute*
David Rumelhart, *Stanford University*
Mohammad Sayeh, *Southern Illinois University*
Dejan Sobajic, *Electric Power Research Institute*
Harold Szu, *Naval Surface Warfare Center*
John G. Taylor, *King's College London*
Brain Telfer, *Naval Surface Warfare Center*
Shiro Usui, *Toyohashi University of Technology*
John N. Weinstein, *National Cancer Institute*
Paul Werbos, *National Science Foundation*
Bernard Widrow, *Stanford University*
Takeshi Yamakawa, *Kyushu Institute of Technology*
Lotfi A. Zadeh, *University of California at Berkeley*
Mona Zaghloul, *George Washington University*

CONGRESS SPONSOR

The International Neural Network Society (INNS) is the sponsor of WCNN '94 - San Diego.

PRESIDENT   **Walter J. Freeman**, *University of California at Berkeley*
PRESIDENT-ELECT   **John G. Taylor**, *King's College London*
PAST PRESIDENT   **Harold Szu**, *Naval Surface Warfare Center*
SECRETARY   **Gail Carpenter**, *Boston University*
TREASURER   **Judith Dayhoff**, *University of Maryland*

BOARD OF GOVERNORS:

Shun-ichi Amari, *University of Tokyo*
James A. Anderson, *Brown University*
Andrew Barto, *University of Massachusetts*
David Casasent, *Carnegie Mellon University*
Leon Cooper, *Brown University*
Rolf Eckmiller, *University of Bonn*
Kunihiko Fukushima, *Osaka University*
Stephen Grossberg, *Boston University*
Mitsuo Kawato, *Advanced Telecommunications Research Institute*
Christof Koch, *California Institute of Technology*
Teuvo Kohonen, *Helsinki University of Technology*
Bart Kosko, *University of Southern California*
Christoph von der Malsburg, *University of Southern California*
Alianna Maren, *Accurate Automation Corporation*
Paul Werbos, *National Science Foundation*
Bernard Widrow, *Stanford University*
Lotfi A. Zadeh, *University of California at Berkeley*

ORDER OF APPEARANCE

TECHNICAL AREAS   continued

TABLE OF CONTENTS

Presenting author is listed first.

VOLUME 1

Plenaries

Special Session: Biomedical Applications of Neural Networks

Oral

TABLE OF CONTENTS   continued

Special Session: Commercial and Industrial Applications of Neural Networks

Oral

Special Session: Application of Neural Networks in the Chemical Process Industries

Oral

Special Session: Mind, Brain, and Consciousness

Oral

Applications

Oral

TABLE OF CONTENTS   continued

TABLE OF CONTENTS   continued

Machine Vision

Oral

Neural Fuzzy Systems

Oral

Poster

TABLE OF CONTENTS   continued

VOLUME 2

Neurocontrol and Robotics

Oral

TABLE OF CONTENTS   continued

Prediction and System Identification

Oral

Poster

Mathematical Foundations

Oral

TABLE OF CONTENTS   continued

Hardware Implementations

TABLE OF CONTENTS   continued

Biological Neural Networks

Oral

Poster

TABLE OF CONTENTS continued

VOLUME 3

TABLE OF CONTENTS   continued

Supervised Learning

Oral

xxviii

TABLE OF CONTENTS   continued

TABLE OF CONTENTS continued

VOLUME 4

Associative Memory

Oral

Poster

TABLE OF CONTENTS   continued

Unsupervised Learning

Oral

Biological Vision

Circuits and System Neuroscience

Oral

Links to Cognitive Science & Artificial Intelligence

Oral

Speech and Language

Oral

TABLE OF CONTENTS continued

Cognitive Neuroscience

Oral

Neurodynamics and Chaos

Oral

TABLE OF CONTENTS   continued

Plenaries

Fuzzy Logic and Soft Computing: Issues, Contentions and Perspectives

Lotfi A. Zadeh*

Abstract

The past few years have witnessed a rapid growth in the number and variety of applications of fuzzy logic, ranging from consumer products and industrial process control to medical instrumentation, information systems and decision analysis. The foundations of fuzzy logic have become firmer and its impact within the basic sciences — and especially in mathematical and physical sciences — has become more visible and more substantive.

The other side of the picture is that the successes of fuzzy logic have also generated a skeptical and sometimes hostile reaction. The crux of the position of skeptics is that fuzzy logic is overrated or wrong and that anything that an be achieved through the use of fuzzy logic can also be achieved through the use of conventional techniques.

Most of the criticisms directed at fuzzy logic are rooted in a misunderstanding of what it is and/or a lack of familiarity with it. In many cases, what is not recognized is that the term fuzzy logic (FL) is actually used in two different senses. In a narrow sense, fuzzy logic (FLn) is a logical system which is an extension of multivalued logic and is intended to serve as a logic of approximate reasoning. But in a wider sense, fuzzy logic (FLw) is more or less synonymous with the theory of fuzzy sets (FST), that is, a theory of classes with unsharp boundaries. In this perspective, FL = FLw, and FLn is merely a branch of FL. What is important to recognize is that today the term fuzzy logic is used predominantly in its wider sense. It is in this sense that any field X can be fuzzified — and hence generalized — by replacing the concept of a crisp set in X by a fuzzy set. In application to basic fields such as arithmetic, topology, graph theory, probability theory and logic, fuzzification leads to fuzzy arithmetic, fuzzy topology, fuzzy graph theory, fuzzy probability theory and FLn. Similarly, in application to applied fields such as neural network theory, stability theory, pattern recognition and mathematical programming, fuzzification leads to fuzzy neural network theory, fuzzy stability theory, fuzzy pattern recognition and fuzzy mathematical programming. What is gained through fuzzification is greater generality, higher expressive power, an enhanced ability to model real-world problems and, most importantly, a methodology for exploiting the tolerance for imprecision — a methodology which serves to achieve tractability, robustness and lower solution cost.

Although there has been a great deal of progress in our understanding of fuzzy logic and its potentialities, there are many issues that remain to be addressed. One such issue is that of the induction of fuzzy rules from observations. Although some successes have been achieved through the use of neural network techniques and genetic algorithms, there are many problems in this realm that remain to be solved. Other important issues relate to the problems of interpolation, commonsense knowledge

*Computer Science Division and the Electronics Research Laboratory, Department of EECS, University of California, Berkeley, CA 94720; Telephone: 510-642-4959; Fax: 510-642-5775; E-mail: zadeh@cs.berkeley.edu.

March 10, 1994

Self-organization in a simple brain model

Dimitris Stassinopoulos and Per Bak

Brookhaven National Laboratory
Upton NY 11973 USA

Preben Alstrøm

The Niels Bohr Institute
Copenhagen 2100, Denmark

Abstract. Simulations on a simple model of the brain are presented. The model consists of a set of randomly connected neurons. Inputs and outputs are also connected randomly to a subset of neurons. For each input there is a set of output neurons which must fire in order to achieve success. A signal giving information as to whether or not the action was successful is fed back to the brain from the environment. The connections between firing neurons are strengthened or weakened according to whether or not the action was successful. The system learns, through a self-organization process, to react intelligently to input signals, i. e. it learns to quickly select the correct output for each input. If part of the network is damaged, the system relearns the correct response after a training period.

How does the brain work?

Two points of view as to where to look for the "secret" are often expressed:

1). The truth is in the detail. The brain consists of neurons. Once we understand the mechanism of the single neuron, we understand in principle everything. Thus, we must put emphasis on measuring the properties including the flow of chemicals, electrical potentials and pulses etc. at the synapses, axons etc. This traditional view has been very successful in science, most noticeably in particle physics where all matter has been reduced to a few quarks and gluons.

2) The truth is in the complexity. The brain has billions of neurons, each connected to thousands of other neurons. Once you have enough neurons, properly connected, intelligent behavior emerges by some magic. It has even been said that the brain must necessarily be so complicated that it can not possibly be understood by the brain. How then can we possibly generate a theory which deals with all these elements? Even to write down the map of the brain would require libraries of books.

Let us look into these two point of views. Let us compare with the way we would "understand" a man-made object, namely a computer.

First, following the strategy of looking into the details, we would take the computer apart and study its smallest parts. We would measure the characteristics of the transistors, that is, how the various currents and potentials depend on each other. We would have to understand the quantum mechanical properties of the materials, silicon etc, on which the transistor is based. Clearly, this will lead nowhere. Without any idea about the function that the transistors perform, no insight emerges. The computer engineer couldn't care less about how the transistor works - it is irrelevant for his purposes.

Second, although it is a popular view that a computer works because of its vast number of circuits, it is not so. The world's largest computers work the same way as the smallest pocket calculator. It simply has more storage, more processors, more input-output devices etc.

Thus, neither of the two points of views are correct for the computer, and most certainly they are not correct for the brain either. In order to understand the computer, one has to understand the principles by which the elements are put together. Whether the elements are of one type or another, whether they are of electrical, optical, or mechanical nature is irrelevant as long as they perform the correct function, that is for instance to carry out a simple logical operation such as an "AND" or "OR" logical operation on two bits. One does not have to explain the complete system with its myriads of connection to understand the computer. The truth is not in the intricacies. A computer is basically a simple device, sending numbers or bits from one location to another, and performing trivial operations with pairs of those numbers.

The same, we argue, goes for the brain. The goal must be to understand the principles by which the neurons interact. This doesn't mean that the study of the hardware, such as the flow of Ca^{++} and Na^+ ions at the synapses and axons, is irrelevant, in the same sense that the feasibility of constructing transistors is not irrelevant for the computer, but simply that this study can be decoupled from a general study of the mechanisms of the brain.

There is, however, one major conceptual difference between understanding the computer and understanding the brain. The computer was built by design. An engineer put together all the circuits etc. and made it work. In other words, with no engineer, we have no computer. However, there is no engineer around to connect all the synapses of the brain. One might imagine that the brain is ready and hard-wired at birth, with its connections formed by biological evolution and coded into the DNA. This does not make any sense. Evolution is efficient, but not that efficient. The amount of information contained in the DNA is vastly insufficient to specify all neural connections. The structure has to be *self-organized* rather than by design.

Thus, in order to understand the brain, we must understand the principles by which it organizes itself, presumably through its interaction with the environment. In order to be biologically feasible, those principles have to be simple and robust. In analogy with the computer, once those principles are understood there might be little qualitative difference between the smallest lobster brain and the human brain. If we are lucky, the difference is quantitative rather than qualitative. This "evolutionary" conjecture has not gained much acceptance; not because of lack of plausibility but because it failed to meet the immediate challenge it raises: to prove by demonstration the existence of such a simple and plausible model.

Conventional attractor neural network models (For reviews see Amit[1] and Hertz et al[2]) work in two modes: a learning mode where the strengths of the neural connections are computed and a retrieving mode where the network recognizes input signals, i. e. provides the same pattern for several similar input patterns. More advanced models use complicated back-propagation algorithms which continuously update the connections by a computation not performed by the neural network itself. These models have been important in constructing technologies for pattern recognition, and emphasis has been on maximizing their capacity for learning, without regards to questions raised in realistic modelling of brain function. From its birth, a real brain is "on its own" in an environment that constantly changes with no outside agent to turn switches between learning mode and retrieval mode.

Recently, Alstrøm and Stassinopoulos[3] addressed some of these points in a new class of neural networks, denoted *adaptive performance networks*. The central idea is the introduction of a global evaluative feedback signal, a dynamic threshold, and a reinforcement rule with no need of further computation. Here, we address the question of how can we get intelligent behaviour not through engineering but through self-organization. We shall demonstrate that this type of network can be trained to react "intelligently" to external sensory signals. In a fashion analogous to the behaviorist techniques used in the training of animals we introduce our system with a set of external signals each of which rewards a specific action. The system learns to recognize all signals and choose the corresponding rewarding action. "Learning" and "retrieving" are two aspects of the same dynamical process. It must be. Individual neurons don't know what is globally going on; they perform their thing automatically, without concern to whether they contribute to a learning or a retrieving task. Only an outside observer is able to identify what is going out as "learning" or "retrieving" by inspecting its behavior.

The goal of any scientific theory or model is to capture the essential elements of experiments or observations in nature. Here we wish to model intelligent behavior at its simplest. To be concrete, consider the situation in which a system provides food to a "monkey" if the correct button is pressed. Which button is correct depends on whether a red or a green light is on. This signal, which is shown to the monkey, is all the information the monkey has in order to figure out which is the right button at every instant. The monkey learns the correct reaction after a "learning" period of trial and error. If the outside world changes, i. e. the "correct" buttons are switched, the monkey should be able to modify its behavior. The monkey is able to learn progressively more complicated patterns. The ability of a model to mimic this process of learning "intelligent" responses (leading to satisfaction) to outside signals is denoted "artificial intelligence".

We start by visualizing our model-brain in its embryonic state: a network of neurons with random connections. Little genetic information is needed to construct such random networks. Sensory signals are fed into the brain randomly. The neural output, such as stimulation of muscle fibers, is also sent randomly. The environment responds to the action directed by the brain's output by rewarding (or not rewarding) it. The result is fed back to the brain through a global signal, which could be a change in the level of a hormone or an increase in the blood-sugar content. There is no mechanism by which the information can be fed back selectively to the individual neurons.

In our picture the interplay with the environment is essential in organizing the brain's ability to explore and become more experienced, allowing it to react intelligently. In order to represent this, our model interacts with the "outer world" in three different ways (Fig. 1). There is i) an input signal giving information about the state of the outer world; ii) a resulting action by the system toward the environment; iii) a global feedback signal indicating whether this action was successful or not in accomplishing the goal. Our model is necessarily grossly oversimplified; its sole purpose is to demonstrate certain simple general principles.

We have studied two network topologies: a layered one and a random one. In the latter model, both *inputs*, *outputs*, and *internal connections* are completely random. N neurons are each connected randomly to C other neurons. The neurons can be either in a firing state, $n_i = 1$, or a non-firing state, $n_i = 0$. The input to the i'th neuron from other neurons is $h_i = \sum J_{i,j} n_j$, where the summation is over the C interacting neighbors. Initially, the j's are randomly chosen in the interval $0 < J < 1$. The neuron fires if the input exceeds a threshold T. The interactions with the environment are implemented as follows.

i) The sensory signal is represented by an additional contribution, h' to the input signal of a number of random neurons. These various branches can be thought of as different features of the input signal such as sound, shape, color, smell, position, size, etc. Different inputs are represented by different sets of random input neurons (see Fig. 1). ii) The output signal is the firing state of a set of randomly selected output neurons. For each input signal, the action is considered successful if one or more specific but randomly selected neurons, belonging to the set of output neurons, are all firing. iii) If the action is successful, a positive reinforcing signal $r \ll 1$ is fed back to all firing neurons. If the action is unsuccessful a negative signal is fed back. The reinforcement modifies all connections between firing neurons $J_{i,j} \rightarrow J_{i,j} + [r J_{i,j}(1 - J_{i,j}) + h] n'_i n_j$, where n'_i denotes the state of the i'th neuron at the next time step and h is a random noise between $-h_0$ and h_0. The inputs are normalized, $J_{i,j} \rightarrow J_{i,j} + J_{i,j} / \sum_j J_{i,j}$.

Thus, if the action is successfull, all connections between firing neurons are reinforced, whether or not they participated in delivering the correct output; if the action is unsuccessful, the connections between firing neurons is weakened.

In addition to the above input-output functions, the model has a global control mechanism for the activity (Alstrøm and Stassinopoulos) for the total number of firing output neurons, A. It is important that this be kept to a minimum. If A exceeds a value A_0 the threshold T is reduced, while if A is smaller than A_0 the threshold is increased, $T \rightarrow T + \delta \text{sgn}(A - A_0)$. Thus, if there is no output, or the output is too low, the system is "thinking", that is its sensitivity is increased until an appropriate output is achieved. If the system is "confused", i. e. there is too much output, the sensitivity is lowered. Modulatory chemicals released into the brain help performing this function for the real brain, in addition to participating in the formation of the synapses, the J's discussed above.

At each time step the system is updated in parallel following the algorithm above. The performance P of the network is defined as the average success rate over 250 successive time steps. Figs 2-6 show the results for a number of different tasks.

In the layered version, the neurons are arranged in rows, with each neuron firing to the three nearest neighbors in the next row. Inputs are random, but output neurons are those in the bottom row. At each time step the system is updated in parallel following the algorithm above.

First, the "monkey" experiment defined above was simulated. A layered network with 256 neurons was studied, with $C = 3$ ($\eta_0 = 0.01, r = 0.1$). Two input signals, each with 16 random input neurons, were chosen. For each input, a pair of output cells was defined in the bottom row. The input signals were switched every 2000 time steps (or when complete success, meaning that the selected output neurons were active while all other neurons were not, has been achieved over 250 consecutive steps). Figure 2a shows the performance versus time. First, there is a period which we can identify as a learning period in which the success rate is low and oscillating. Eventually the networks locks into a state where success is obtained very quickly in response to the switching of inputs. In this phase, the system reacts intelligently to the input signal. It switches quickly back and forth between the two correct outputs. The transition from the learning phase to the retrieval phase is quite abrupt. We emphasize that no outside switch was activated at this point. Figure 2b shows a similar curve for the random-topology case. Again a sharp, self-organized transition from a learning mode to a retrieval mode is observed.

What happens inside the network during the learning phase? Through a complicated self-organization process, the system creates internal contacts or connections between selected parts of the input signal and the correct output cell(s). The process can be thought of as the formation of a river network connecting output with input. When the output is incorrect, the river flow is reduced at existing connections. When the flow is correct, the flow is reinforced. When there is too little output, the river beds are widened.

The state of the system after completion of the learning phase cannot be calculated by means of a simple algorithm. (The synapses are formed by self-organization rather than design). The "fast" dynamical switching between one connection pattern and another under switching of the outside signal in the "retrieval" phase following the long learning phase is quite complicated. Figure 3a,b shows the firing patterns for the red and green responses, respectively. Figure 4 shows a movie of the switching process from the "red" response to the "green" response. The switching takes place through ten intermediate steps. We doubt that any engineer would come up with such a solution. If we were free to construct the network "by design" we could obviously come up with a much simpler and efficient solution. The memory lies in the conservation of parts of the river beds from previous correct connections.[7]

The system has self-organized into a state where the change of "water supply" at random positions causes a fast conversion to the correct output. In the learning phase the system is very sensitive to the relative small changes in input- in that sense it is chaotic. No such dynamical switching takes place in conventional neural networks where connections are essentially hard-wired in the retrieval mde.

Figure 5 shows the response to "damage" of the network. After $\sim$150000 time steps, a block of 30 neurons was removed from the network. After a transient period the network has relearned the correct response, carving new connections in the network. In other words, instead of using some features of the input signal the system learns to use other features. Think of this as replacing "vision" with "smell". The memory is distributed and robust,[8] as it should be in order to represent real brain function. The new firing patterns are shown in figure 3c,d.

Figure 6 shows the situation where a third input (and corresponding pair of output cells) was added after the first two responses had been learned. After a transient period where the system is confused and the success rate is low, the network eventually learns the three appropriate responses. Figure 3e,f,g shows the firing patterns after the three inputs have been learned.

A brain working according to the principles illustrated here requires a minimum of biological complexity - it is a relatively simple organ without much structure. Little information is needed to construct the simple network with essentially arbitrary connections. The correlations that control the switching behavior of the system hint to the fact that 'it is not only the well developed "riverbeds", and where most of the activity takes place, that are important for the function of the network but also the relatively silent regions in between'. Evidence of this can be seen in the rather complicated landscape of the $J_{i,j}$s (Fig. 3h,i). The landscape is strikingly rugged. This is somewhat counterintuitive. One might have expected well-carved riverbeds and isolated switches. Seemingly, this configuration which from an engineering point of view is more efficient, it is not compatible with the self-organization process.

In conclusion, we have constructed a simple model simulating aspects of brain function. The build-up of the $J_{i,j}$ landscape is due to a self-organization process. We suggest that simple robots performing "intelligent" tasks can be constructed following the principles outlined here.

References

1. Amit, D. J. *Modelling Brain Function: The World of Attractor Neural Networks* (Cambridge University Press, Cambridge, 1989).

2. Hertz, J., Krogh A., & Palmer, R. G. *Introduction to the Theory of Neural Computation* (Addison-Wesley, Redwood, 1991).

3. Alstrøm, P. & Stassinopoulos, D., submitted to Phys. Rev. Lett. (1994).

5. McCulloch, W. S. & Pitts, W. Bull. Math. Biophys. 5, 115 (1943).

6. The original AS-model[3] is "blind" in the sense that it operates with a fixed input signal at the upper layer.

7. A more detailed study of the dynamics of this learning mechanism is in progress.

8. To check for robustness we tested the performance of the system when signals were presented randomly and for an arbitrary duration of time.

Figure captions

Figure 1. Block diagram of brain model. Each signal is represented by random inputs to a number of neurons. For each signal, here red or green, there is a combination of one or more output neurons (shaded circles) which must fire in order to achieve success. The environment feeds back a signal indicating whether or not success was achieved. a) Layered network; b) Random network.

Figure 2. a) Performance vs. time for layered system with two input signals which are switched every 2000 time units or when the system is consistently successfull. After a training period during which the network self-organizes, the system enters an intelligent state with fast switching between the correct outputs. b) Same for random network.

Figure 3. Firing patterns. a,b) The two sets of input neurons are colored red and green, respectively. For the red input, output cells 10 and 15 of the bottom row must be triggered simultaneously to achieve success; for the green input the output cells 7 and 12 must be triggered. The yellow squares indicate neurons which are firing for the two inputs in the fast switching mode. c,d) The same as above but in the case where the system has relearned the correct response after removal of a block of 30 neurons (shaded area). Note the difference from the original response. e,f,g) Same as above, but with three inputs. The response of the two original inputs (e,f) is different from the original one (a,b). h,i) The configurations of $J_{i,j}$s pointing to the right, for the two cases discussed above (a-b, c-d). The different values are depicted with a rainbow-color map ranging from black and dark blue for the lowest values to red for the highest.

Figure 4. Movie showing the "fast" switching between the "red" response and the "green" response. The transition takes place through ten complicated steps.

Figure 5. Performance for the layered system, but with 30 neurons damaged after 150000 time steps. The system has relearned the correct response after 210000 time steps.

Figure 6. Same system as shown in figure 2a, with a third input added after 150000 steps. After a confused learning period, the correct output for all three inputs is learned after 450000 time steps.

(a)

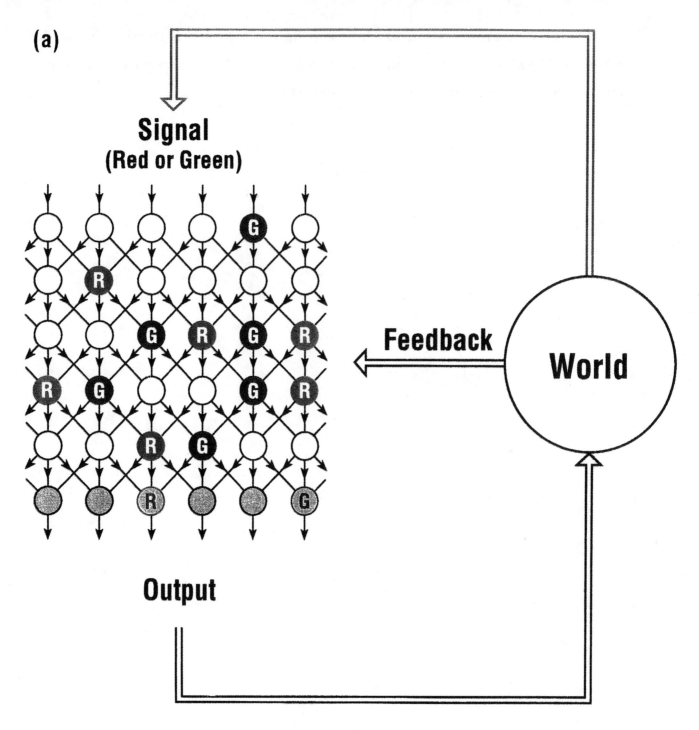

Figure 1
Stassinopoulos D., Bak P. and Alstom P.

(b)

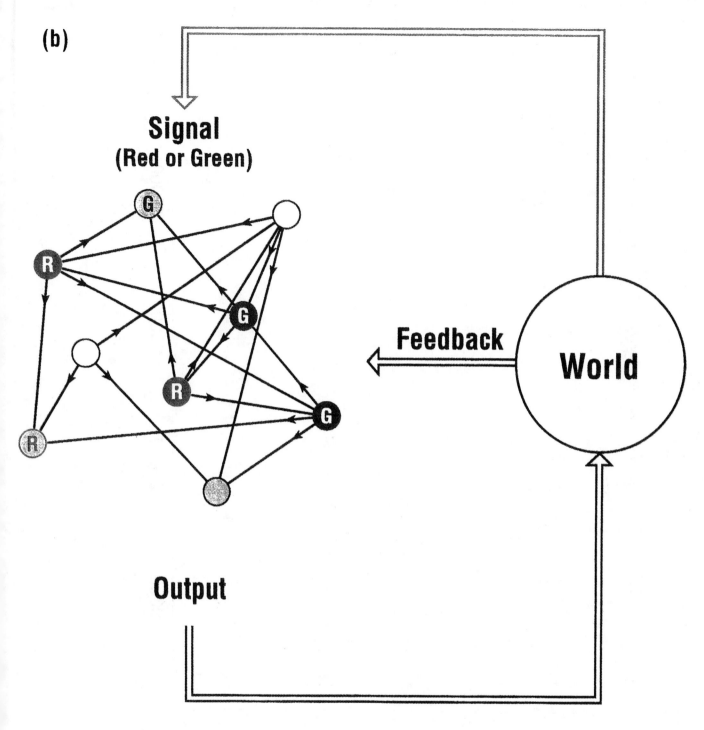

Figure 1
Stassinopoulos D., Bak P. and Alstrom P.

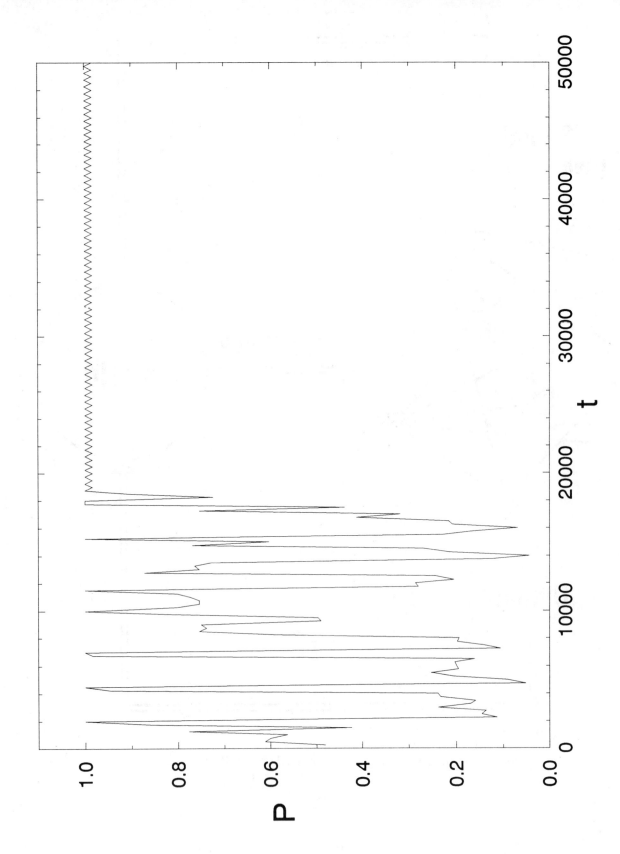

Figure 2a

I-18

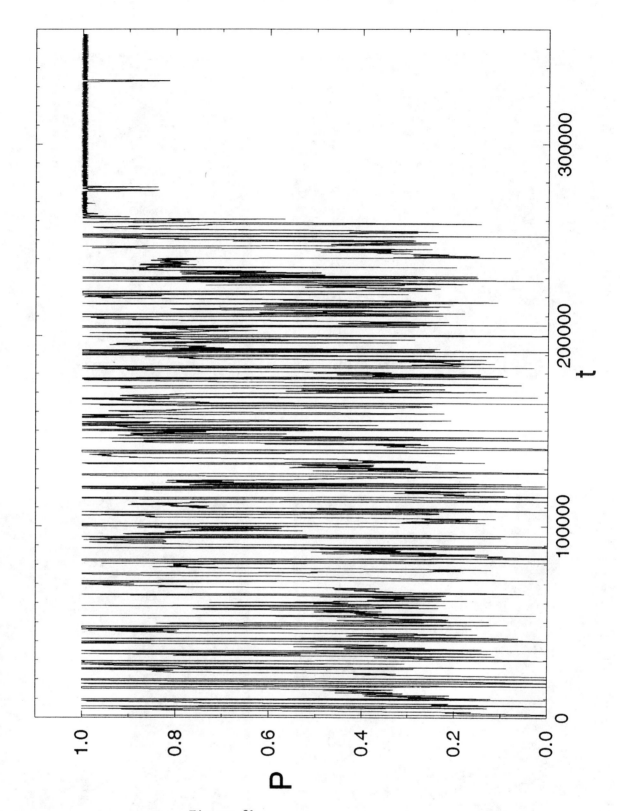

Figure 2b

I-19

(a)

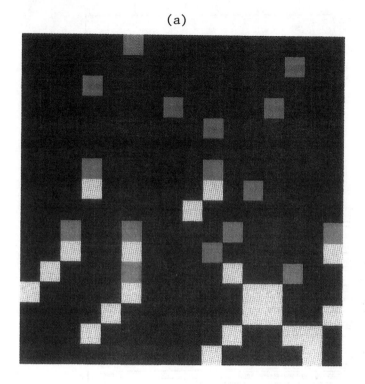

(b)

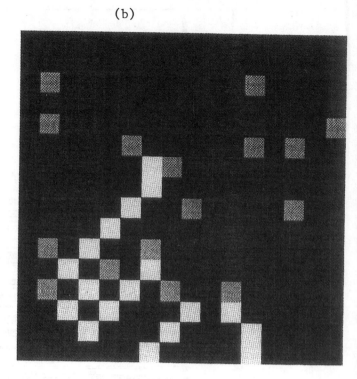

(c)

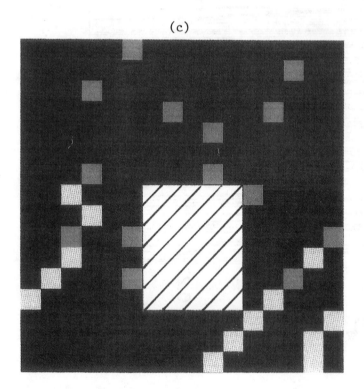

(d)

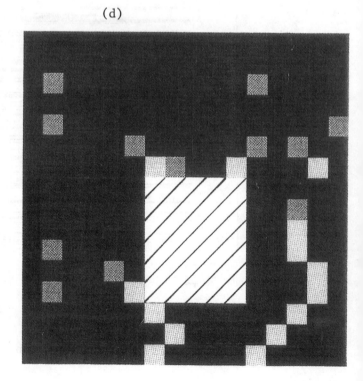

Figure 3

(e)

(f)

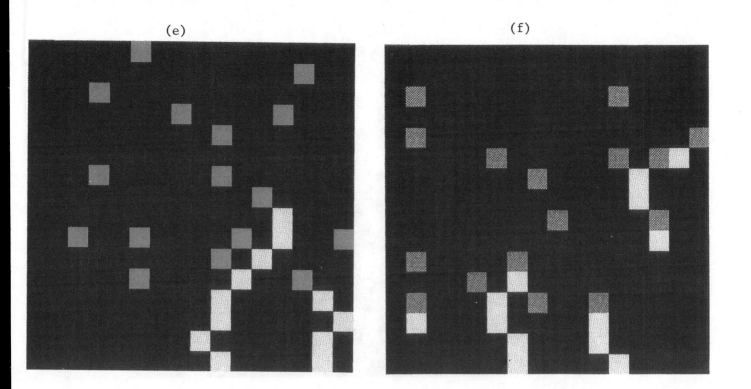

(g)

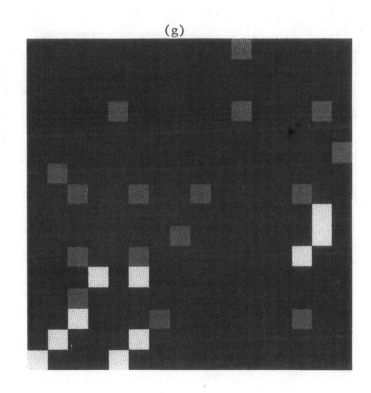

Figure 3

(h)

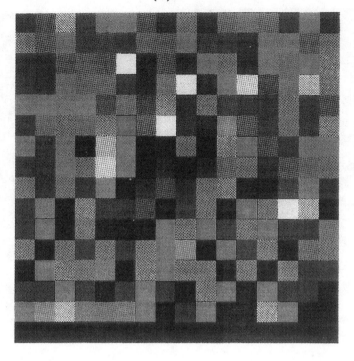

(i)

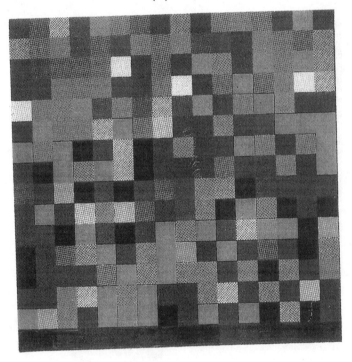

Figure 3

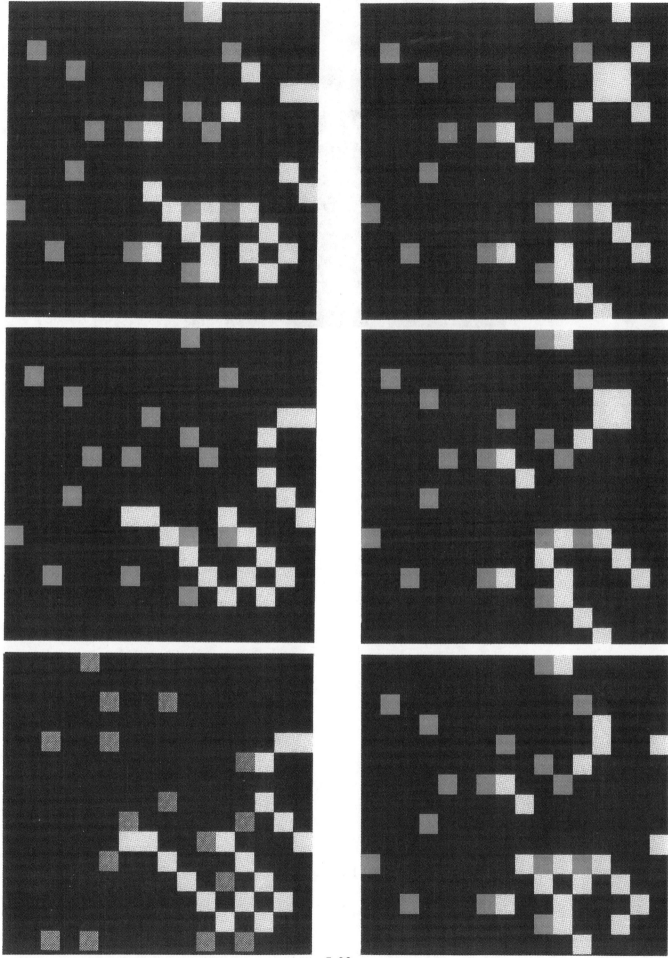

Figure 4

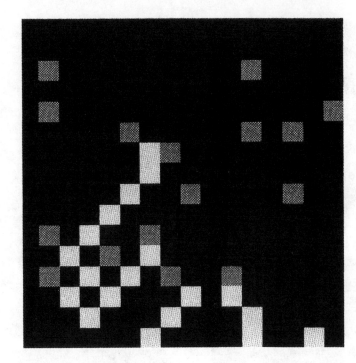

Figure 4

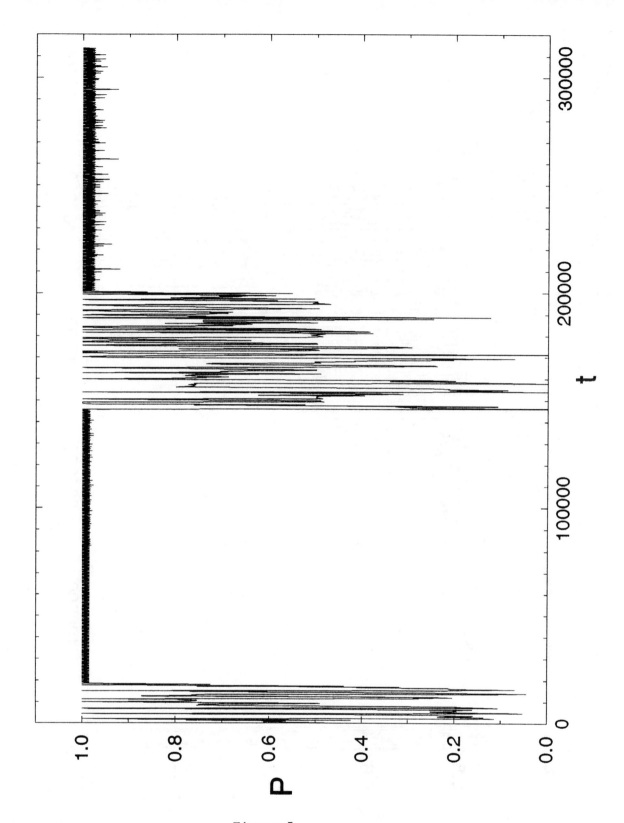

Figure 5

I-25

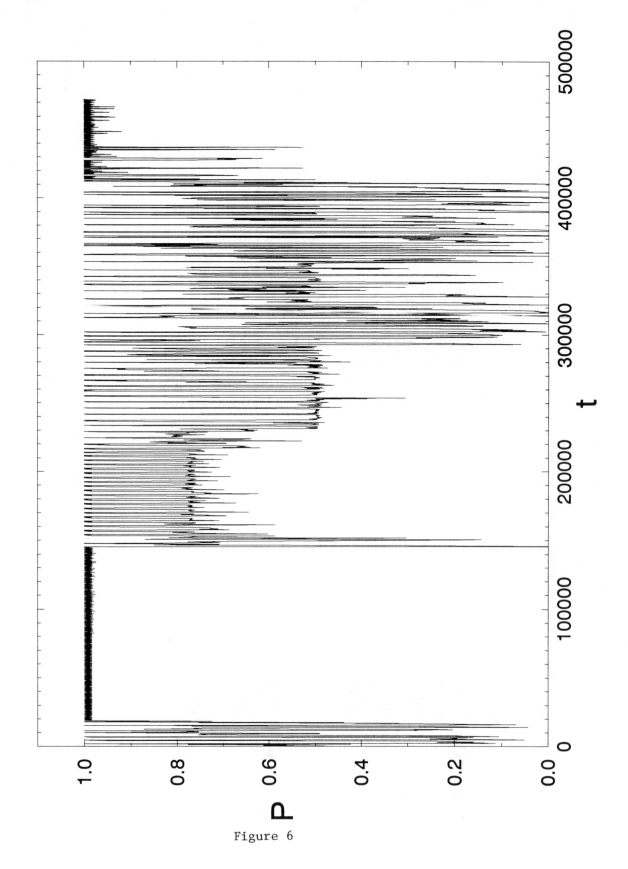

Figure 6

I-26

New Progress Towards Truly Brain-Like Intelligent Control

Roberto A. Santiago
BehavHeuristics, Inc. (BHI)
335 Paint Branch Drive, College Park, MD 20742
(301)585-9220

Paul J. Werbos
Room 675, National Science Foundation
Arlington, VA 22230
(703)306-1339

Abstract

This paper gives the details on an unpublished portion of the WCNN plenary given by the second author. The talk will review the reasons why the brain is a neurocontroller [1-3].

Neural network designs of practical use in control engineering can serve as subsystems of other control designs, implicitly clone experts or existing controllers, track a desired trajectory or reference model, and optimize performance over time[2,4,5]. Optimization provides the most general and powerful capabilities, across a wide range of applications, even for tracking. Industry use of optimization designs has expanded greatly, and includes some very crucial applications; however, the designs used until now were either limited to batch, off-line learning, or were limited to small or medium engineering problems, around 10 controls, to be used efficiently. Other designs which do not account for delayed impacts of action are even more limited. All of these function unlike the human brain which routinely handles large complex control problems.

This paper reports the first simulations of Dual Heuristic Programming (DHP), the first of a family of real-time optimization architectures explicitly designed to scale to very large numbers of controls. These first tests use an old benchmark problem, the cart-pole balancer, which does not test the scaling capabilities; however, they do show that DHP works as well or better than older designs on small problems, and they offer practical experience which supplements the design in [4]. The next tests, now started, involve a hybrid electric car at the University of Maryland, important to the "Clean Car" Initiative currently being pursued by the Clinton Administration.

Introduction and Context

Neural network control designs for optimization have seen a tremendous expansion in industry in the past two or three years. Industry has long known how to solve simple tracking problems, such as how to keep a chemical plant working without blowing up, how to design a car capable of running, and so forth. The big challenges now involve reducing energy use or waste or pollution or cost, even while continuing to track a dynamic process; and developing control for very tricky systems, mainly nonlinear systems with complex delayed effects of actions. The first of these goals can be met by using optimization techniques, applied to minimizing a performance measure which combines tracking error plus measures of cost or pollution, etc. Both goals can be met by using optimization designs, like DHP, which account for the delayed effects of action, and allow for noise and non-linearity.

As an example, Neurodyne[4] has recently developed a medium-scale optimization design for electronic fuel injection in cars. This design is far more advanced and brain-like than the usual state of the art. Based on preliminary data, Arthur D. Little predicts this design will yield ultra-low emissions and a significant improvement in fuel economy, with a simple retrofit of existing cars. Real tests on a GM Saturn are planned for this year.

The switch to more advanced cars, which do not require gasoline or internal combustion engines, the main theme of the President's "Clean Car" initiative, will also require better control. Even today, the main reason why car companies say they cannot easily accommodate proposed laws requiring the sale of electric cars is the problem of cost. High-efficiency AC or brushless DC motors are easy to get, for about $1,000, but existing controllers have unacceptable losses (circa 25%) and cost about $7,000. Optimal neurocontrol can reduce these losses, and allow the use of high-throughput-per-dollar neural chips, such as, perhaps, the Motorola chip, designed with the car market in mind.

Working neural net designs for optimization fall into two categories: direct optimization, as in Model-Predictive Control[4], widely used in the chemical industry; and approximate dynamic programming (ADP), which includes "reinforcement learning" designs as a special case. Direct optimization is usually based on some form of backpropagation. Some authors simply calculate derivatives through a plant model at one time, without adding in the cross-time terms required to calculate the exact, total gradient. This sometimes works on simple tracking problems, but it breaks down on problems like the benchmark biomass or ecological management problems, or on other problems which essentially require planning[7]. To calculate the cross-time terms <u>exactly</u>, one must either use true backpropagation through time, which is essentially an off-line method, or use forward methods whose costs do not scale well for large problems[7]. Nevertheless, Feldkamp's group at Ford has achieved impressive results using direct optimization[7], as has Hrycej at Daimler-Benz.

The reinforcement learning designs most popular in academia do not scale well to medium-size engineering problems; however, Neurodyne and Accurate Automation Corporation have developed medium-scale ADP-based designs which have had a recent explosion in applications this past year, including flight tests proving improved thrust in an F15, semiconductor fabrication in collaboration with Texas Instruments, the first prototype for an airplane capable of flying to earth orbit, clean car work, and so forth. A large-scale method in the same family could permit even better performance and a wider range of applications, after the details are worked out.

DHP is the highest member of the ADP family under real development (GDHP is more capable but is currently not in any real world development or application). DHP answers the need for even better performance on a wide range of problems, especially large scale problems. At BehavHeuristics, work is underway to develop DHP for real world applications varying from the financial markets to real-time optimal control for large problems[8]. The remainder of this paper will describe the simulations to date, starting out by defining the test problem in detail. These simulations do not represent an optimal implementation of DHP but are the first real working examples.

Definition of the Pole Balancer Problem

The Cart Pole Balancer (CPB) problem provides a unique dynamic for testing adaptive control systems. While it does not test the scaling properties of DHP it does offer a foundation from which to exploit these scaling properties, having proven its performance is up to par or better for current standards. Equations for a CPB emulator are widely available [e.g. 9], so they will not be discussed here.

For sake of clarity we will define the problem as follows:

1. Let C = an adaptive controller
2. Let P1 = a pole of length l1, weight w1, and radius r1
3. Let P2 = a pole of length l2, weight w2, and radius r2
4. Let E represent the environment (in this case the track)
5. Let X represent the cart on the track
6. C controls X in E so that P1 is balanced upright on X starting from an unbalanced position
7. Let C converge.
8. Replace P1 with P2 and start from an unbalanced position.
9. Let C converge.
10. Return to P1 and start from an unbalanced position.

Success with the CPB problem is defined as the ability to generalize across the domain of the problem so that C can remember how to control X to balance P1 in step 10 without having to train again. The dynamics of changing the pole in the environment provide a non-linear property which has posed a challenge to neural and classic controllers alike.

To approach the CPB problem from the viewpoint of DHP we must define the control signal $\mathbf{u}(t)$, the state vector $\mathbf{R}(t)$, and a generalized utility function U.

The control signal $\mathbf{u}(t)$ is a single value which represents an acceleration in the positive or negative direction of X on E. The components of $\mathbf{R}(t)$ can be summed up as follows.

Position of X	-1.1 to +1.1	meters	$R_1(t)$
Velocity of X	-1 to + 1	meters/second	$R_2(t)$
Acceleration of X	-.5 to + .5	meters/second^2	$R_3(t)$
Position of P	-P/2 to +P/2	radians	$R_4(t)$
Velocity of P	-P/4 to +P/4	radians/second	$R_5(t)$
Acceleration of P	-P/4 to +P/4	radians/second^2	$R_6(t)$

The measurements of P are with respect to the pole standing straight up on X. Notice that at no point is there any information given concerning the nature of the pole. An important stipulation of the problem is to create this controller without giving it the length, weight, and radius of the pole. The controller may only learn and adapt to a dynamic system by making inferences from its behavior.

Finally, a utility function, U, must be defined. Thought was given to the choice of utility measure to be used with this problem. DHP does not require that U be finely crafted, to the degree required for Lyapanov functions but it is important that it express a desired performance. The lead author first consulted with a friend experienced with juggling and other balancing tricks who provided some useful insights. Though large velocities are generally unacceptable in balancing tricks, large accelerations are, so long as the acceleration comes in small spurts. In other words a juggler will use small accelerations of his palm to keep a broom balanced on end. Also, in observing the broom, the juggler never takes time to measure a broom; instead, he observes the top of the broom in order to get the feedback he needs. These factors come together to provide the following utility function.

$$U(t) = \ - a*abs(R_1(t))/1.1 + \ b*(1-abs(R_2(t))/(2*abs(R_3(t)) - c*sin(R_4(t) + P/2) + d*(1-sin(2*R_5(t) + P/2)/sin(2*R_6(t) + P/2)$$

The variables a-d are weighting components for the utility function. The utility function above varies from previous approaches to this problem where a utility of some sort was passed only when failure was reached. This definition of the problem is much too constraining and bears little resemblance to brain-like learning. With R(t), u(t) and U in hand we are ready to start designing and implementing the DHP controller.

Dual Heuristic Programming
To understand adaptive critics we must first step back and understand the components of dynamic programming, the goal of adaptive critics. Dynamic programming in the general sense is a function that is supplied a model and a utility function for some system to be controlled. A value, J, for every time, t, is output. The nature of J is such that maximization of J over a short horizon insures maximization of utility over the long horizon. In other words this J is a secondary utility function which makes the job of optimizing over an infinite time horizon much simpler[4].

The problem with pure dynamic programming centers around the complexity of the equations to calculate J. J in large problems can take massive amounts of computational power to calculate. For this reason the adaptive critic architecture was designed to approximate a J function (or some part of a J function). This can be done efficiently and effectively by neural networks. In essence, this is the core of all adaptive critic architectures.

The simple approach to the adaptive critic would be to directly approximate a J function with a neural network and maximize it for J(t) to J(t+1). This is the strategy behind HDP[4]. This is similar to backpropagation of utility except the adaptive critic as stated above provides a more accurate target for adapting the action network. In this case the action network is adapted to maximize J. This is not done directly but by propagating changes first through a model and then back to the action network. This will become clearer in the section on implementation of DHP to this problem.

The drawback to HDP is that the critic only outputs a single J value that correlates to utility. This value when propagated back tells us how badly we did, and therefore allows us to change our weights in the action network to maximize it, but it makes no reference to which u(t) from the action needs to be changed and how. For a controller with numerous controls, above 10 that is, the action network becomes more difficult to converge.

DHP is designed to approximate the derivative of the Bellman equation[4], used in dynamic programming to calculate J, with respect to $R(t)$ as understood by the model. The model is then used to calculate the change in each control component to maximize J. This is quite different from HDP whose critic outputs an approximated J value. Instead the DHP critic outputs the derivative value of J with respect to each $R(t)$. This value will be referred to in this paper as $L(t)$. $L(t)$ indirectly provides information about each component of $u(t)$.

The DHP Architecture

The DHP controller is made up of four components: a critic network, a model network, an action network, and a utility function. Notice that the first three components are networks while the last one is just a discrete function for measuring utility which we defined above. Each network can be adapted using any supervised learning method. The important functional component of DHP is the ability to backpropagate values from the output to the input. In other words, given a certain output what is the required input to the network. For convenience, dual subroutines have been developed which provide a generalized way of doing this backpropagation across many systems. These methods can be found in Chapter 10 of [4].

Each component of DHP has a very specific purpose. The action network outputs a $u(t)$ which is the control signal that is adapted to maximize J. The critic network is adapted to output $L(t)$ values which maximize U over the long or infinite horizon. The model network is meant to accurately predict the state of the system at t+1, $R(t+1)$, given $R(t)$ and $u(t)$. U is used as the source for modifying the critic network. The way each of the networks is adapted is the core functionality of DHP.

The next three sections are devoted to the detailed explanation of how to adapt each network. Once these are understood the application of DHP to the CPB problem becomes trivial. The following diagram and set of equations which have been slightly modified from Chapter 13 of [4] are presented to help the reader with this discussion. Note that the F_ notation regards a feedback calculation. Details of this notation can be found in [4] as well.

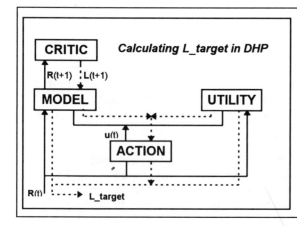

Calculating L_target in DHP

Implementation of DHP

1. Obtain $R(t)$, $u(t)$ and $R(t+1)$
2. Obtain $L(t+1)$
3. Calculate $F\_u(t) = F\_U_u(R(t),u(t)) + F\_f_u(R(t),u(t),L(t+1))$
4. Calculate $L\_target = F\_f_R(R(t),u(t),L(T+1)) + F\_U_R(R(t),u(t)) + F\_A_R(R(t),F\_u(t))$
5. Adapt critic network with L_target
6. Adapt model network using the observed $R(t+1)$
7. Adapt action network using $F\_u(t)$

It is the hope of both authors that this explanation will promote the development of new applications of DHP for real world problems.

Adapting the Action Network

1. Generate an action $u(t)$ based on $R(t)$ through the action network
2. Generate a prediction $R(t+1)$ with the model network using $R(t)$ and $u(t)$
3. Generate $L(t)$ by inputing $R(t+1)$ to the critic network
4. Use a dual subroutine through the model network to calculate the changes to $u(t)$ that would produce the changes in $R(t+1)$ suggested by $L(t)$, these changes are also known as $F\_u(t)$

5. If your utility function uses any **u**(t) to calculate a utility value it is then necessary to calculate the derivative of U with respect to each component of **u**(t). From this calculation a change in **u**(t) can be determined. Add that to the F_u(t) as generated above.
6. Using these changes to **u**(t), adapt the weights in your action network

Adapting the Model Network

The main inputs to the model network are **R**(t) which is the current state of the system and **u**(t) the control signals that are taken in response to **R**(t). Adaptation of the model network is based on predicting **R**(t+1) and then observing the state and correcting for errors. Having a very robust model network is key to a good DHP architecture. If a complete model is available it is possible to use a system of equations instead of a neural network. If this is the case, which in reality it rarely is, you can apply the chain rule for ordered derivatives to that system of equations to make the same calculation as is being made with backpropagation.

Adapting the Critic Network

The plan to change the adaptive critic is such that when we predict we are going to see this state **R**(t) we return the proper values with respect to J. Technically speaking we want to make calculations for **R**(t-1) such that when the model network sees **R**(t-1), it outputs an **R**(t), which the critic network has been adapted this time to output **L**(t+1). By waiting and watching the resulting state from **u**(t), we can observe our error in optimization. More importantly, the critic network will learn to make changes the previous step to arrive at the utility and J value found at t+1. The analogy would be "Now that I know that taking the first left gets me home faster than the second left, when I come down this street again I will get over to the left so I will be prepared to take the quicker route." We do the following calculations to adapt the critic network. These steps are the equivalent of 4 and 5 in the diagram above.

1. Use **R**(t) adjusted by **L**(t), which was calculated using **R**(t+1), and using a dual subroutine to calculate the changes in the values of **R**(t). We will call these changes in **R**(t), **L**_target1
2. Calculate the change **R**(t) with respect to utility (in other words take into account how utility changed) and treat these values as **L**_target2.
3. Calculate the change in **R**(t) with respect to F_u as calculated above and treat these values as **L**_target3.
4. Calculate **L**_target = **L**_target1 + **L**_target2 + **L**_target3
5. Use this as the target for training the critic network. The condition under which this network is being trained can be stated " When the critic is input an **R** that matches this **R**(t) I will respond with the changes as specified in **L**_target".

The Application of DHP to the Cart-Pole Problem

Application of DHP to the CPB problem should be straightforward at this point. The utility function has been specified and the components of **u**(t) and **R**(t) have been described which will set up the architecture of each network. There are several tricks involved in training a DHP network. These tricks, for lack of space, will not be described here but can be discussed with the primary author.

The largest concern with this implementation was the model network. The model network needs to be robust enough to learn the behavior. Time lagged recurrence was used along with several other training methods including the adaptive learning rate. These methods are spelled out in chapters 3 and 10 of [4].

Results

The results of the experiment were conclusive. The DHP controller was able to handle the dynamics of the CPB problem. The following chart is a report of the results. A simple backpropagation network and a backpropagation of utility network were also tried on the same set of poles. The first number represents the amount of times the pole fell before success was found. Success was defined as balancing the pole for 30 minutes. The second number represents the average cycle count for all the iterations that failed. One cycle is equivalent to one second on the problem.

Pole	Backpropagation Through Time	Backpropagation of Utility	Dual Heuristic Programming
P1	40/925	42/821	43/866
P2	36/913	46/857	47/861
P1	35/896	41/879	37/943
P2	42/901	36/913	36/1007
P3	40/853	32/842	39/1095
P1	38/941	29/985	28/1121
P2	41/1002	28/1003	27/1219
P3	39/944	23/921	26/1311
P4	39/883	44/831	30/1269
P1	43/872	30/947	16/1327
P4	41/885	42/833	21/1211
AVG	39.5/910.5	35.7/893.8	31.8/1111.8

As can be seen the DHP controller had much more success. The trend in the data suggests that the controller was converging upon an optimal strategy for all types of poles. In fact, further poles were tested with the DHP controller and the failures continued to decrease and the amount of time the controller could keep the pole balanced increased on those trials. These results are not included in the table because this data was not collected from the other two networks.

Overall, the DHP network showed much improved performance on this problem when compared to other network architectures. The average failures were much smaller and the average balance time was much higher than the other two architectures. Further expansion with the scaling properties in DHP will be used on the University of Maryland project. If this performance can be maintained as the controller is scaled to larger problems it will mean a great advancement in real-time control technology.

Conclusion

More robust learning was found using the adaptive critic technique. In particular DHP offers the insight into a problem that other control strategies have lacked. Its adaptability for changing situation needs seems to be far more abundant than other architectures. Obviously this was a first-of-its-kind experiment and further research is necessary. Regardless, the performance of this DHP experiment shows that great possibilities exist in controlling and optimizing highly non-linear parallel systems.

An extension of this project is being made to apply the DHP architecture to a hybrid electric vehicle at the University of Maryland. The car uses an electric motor supported by an internal combustion engine. Optimization of this type of car to get the most mileage out of its fuel would mean substantially lowered emissions and fuel consumption without loss of performance.

In closing, the adaptive critic family of neural networks has just started to be explored. With higher and higher demands being made in industry for optimization for anything from profit to purity of product, DHP promises to deliver in many industries. With the rise of faster computers and specializing in efficient and accurate networks, it is easy to surmise that the new era of efficient, adaptive, and optimal controllers are just around the corner.

1. P.Werbos, The brain as a neurocontroller, in K.Pribram, ed, *Origins*, Proc. of the 2nd Appalachian Conf., INNS Press, 1994.

2. P.Werbos, *The Roots of Backpropagation: From Ordered Derivatives to Neural Networks and Political Forecasting*, Wiley, 1994.

3. P.Werbos, Neural networks, consciousness, ethics and the soul, *WCNN94 Proc.*, INNS Press,Erlbaum,1994.

4. D.White & D.Sofge, eds, *Handbook of Intelligent Control: Neural, Fuzzy and Adaptive Approaches*, Van Nostrand, 1992

5. P.Werbos, Elastic fuzzy logic,*J. of Intelligent and Fuzzy Systems* (Wiley), Vol.1,No.4,1993.

6. *Small Business Innovation Research 1994*, NSF Program Announcement

7. P.Werbos, How we cut prediction errors in half by using a different training method,*WCNN94 Proc.*,INNS Press, Erlbaum, 1994.

8. K. Otwell, S. Hormby, W. Hutchinson, A Large-Scale Neural Network Application for Airline Seat Application,*WCNN94 Proc.*,INNS Press, Erlbaum, 1994.

9. A. Wieland, Evolving Controls for Unstable Systems, IEEE

10. P. Werbos, Backpropagation Through Time: What It Does and How To Do It, Proc. of the IEEE, Vol. 78, No. 10, 1990

*The views herein are those of the authors, and do not in any way represent NSF or BHI.

**BHI holds patents pending for DHP, Elastic Fuzzy Logic[5], and many related techniques developed by Werbos for the first time in [4], as well as a corrected version of GDHP, a "next step" beyond DHP.

Biomedical Applications of Neural Networks

Session Chairs: David G. Brown
John Weinstein

APPLICATION OF ARTIFICIAL NEURAL NETWORKS TO MEDICAL IMAGE PATTERN RECOGNITION

Shih-Chung B. Lo, Jyh-Shyan J. Lin, Matthew T. Freedman, and Seong K. Mun
Radiology Department, Georgetown University Medical Center, Washington, D.C. 20007

ABSTRACT

Three neural network models were employed to test our databases in the experiment. The first method was a pattern match neural network. The second one was a conventional backpropagation neural network. The third method was a "backpropagation trained neocognitron" in which the signal propagation is operated with convolution calculation from one layer to the next. In the convolution neural network (CNN) experiment, several output association methods and trainer imposed driving functions in conjunction with convolution neural network are proposed for general medical image pattern recognition. An unconventional method of applying rotation and shift invariance is also used to enhance the neural net performance.

We have tested these methods for the detection of microcalcifications on mammograms and lung nodules on chest radiographs. Pre-scan methods were previously described elsewhere. The artificial neural networks act as final detection classifiers to determine if a disease pattern is present on the suspected image area. We found that the convolution neural network, which internally performs feature extraction and classification, achieves the best performance among the three neural network models. These results show that some processing associated with disease feature extraction is a necessary step before a classifier can make an accurate determination.

I. INTRODUCTION

Various image processing techniques have been proposed for the detection of disease patterns. With each of these methods there is a trade-off between increased sensitivity and decreased specificity. By setting less stringent criteria on the above algorithms, the sensitivity of the detecting programs can be increased. However, when using any of these methods to detect subtle diseases, we must use addition methods to decrease the number of false positives. For this reason, several investigators have attempted to use various advanced image processing and artificial classifiers to improve the disease detection [1-5].

Many artificial neural network models have recently been applied to diagnostic imaging research [6-7]. The main tasks of these research efforts are aimed at assisting radiologists either in the accuracy improvement of quantitative measures or in the improvement of sensitivity and specificity for a disease detection. In diagnostic imaging, the neural network techniques incorporated with image processing methods have become a major research trend in the field of computer-aided diagnosis. Medical diagnoses involve very sophisticated decision-making processes. We will limit our studies to the recognition of image patterns. In this paper, we will also discuss characteristics of some disease patterns in clinical images and their implications on the neural network classifications.

II. MATERIAL AND METHODS

A. Disease Patterns on Projection X-Ray Images

Projection radiographs shown on films are generated by the transmission of x-ray beams through a patient. The resulting x-rays, of varying intesity, form a radiographic image. For many years, this technique has been used as a diagnostic procedure for initial or primary examination of a disease associated with physical tissue changes. The major drawback of projection radiography is that x-ray beams project the original anatomical three-dimensional objects onto a two-dimensional image. In other words, each pixel intensity on the image represents a total x-ray attenuation integrated from a line passing through the patient. Bone and soft tissue, and many abnormal changes of tissue can be distinguished from one another in an x-ray image because they attenuate x-rays differently. However, subtle abnormalities superimposed on various normal tissues and bones are difficult to discover. The disease pattern recognition on these images, which requires a professional training, is quite different from that of the character recognition or other image pattern recognition. The degree of difficulty is not easy to measure. Qualitatively speaking, the ratio of signal and structure noise in the task of disease pattern recognition can be very small. Consider a local suspected area that may or may not contain a disease pattern, $s(x,y) \in S$. This local area often contains some background information resulting from normal tissues, $b(x,y) \in B$. The total intensity function denoted as $f(x,y)$ is given by:

$$f(x,y) = s(x,y) + b(x,y) \quad \quad \text{... (1)}$$

In general, four situations are possible in a suspected area: (i) high signal to background ratio (s/b) representing an obvious case, (ii) $s(x,y) << b(x,y)$ representing a subtle case, (iii) $s(x,y) = 0$ and $b(x,y) \approx s'(x,y)$, where $s' \in S$, and (iv) $s(x,y) = 0$ and $b(x,y)$ is not similar to any disease pattern. Most cases falling in situation (ii) result in true-negatives. Cases associated with situation (iii) may produce a false-positive determination by a classifier.

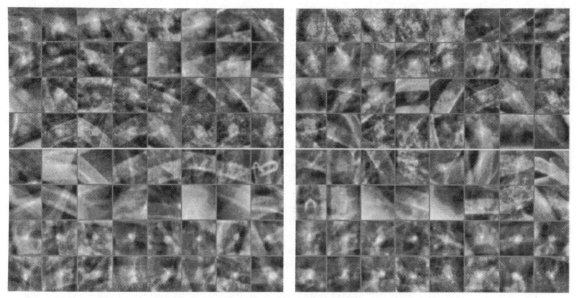

Figure 1. Left 64 patches were used for the training and right 64 patches were used for the testing.
Each patch on the upper 4 rows contains a nodule. Each patch on the bottom 2 rows contains an end-on vessel.
The remaining patches contain image profile from other lung and rib structures.

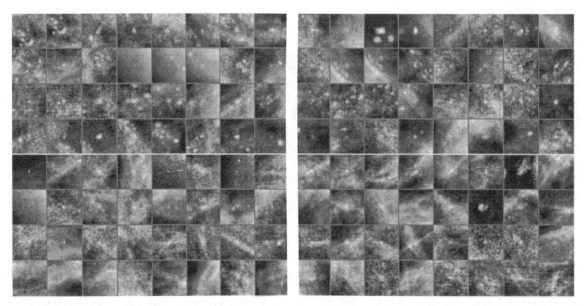

Figure 2. Left 64 patches were used for the training and right 64 patches were used for the testing. Only center portion of
each patch, 16x16 out of 32x32 pixels, was used in the study. Each patch on the upper 4 rows contains at least a
microcalcification. Each patch on the bottom 4 rows contains at least a local maximum spot.
Patches at block numbers (1,5), (5,5), (7,5), (9,5), and (2,7) contain a film defect in each block.

Pattern match and backpropagation, two commonly used pattern classifiers, were employed to compare the performance on the detection of clustered microcalcifications selected from mammograms and the detection of lung nodules extracted from chest radiographs. Regions of interest, formatted at 32x32x12 bit, normal or abnormal, were extracted by the corresponding methods previously described [3-4]. Both geometrical pattern and relative intensity of a local area on a radiographic image are important information in a radiographic reading. The background trend of each ROI was removed to eliminate low frequency variation. However, the background structures (i.e., radiographic image of bone on chest image, vessels, and large soft tissue differences) remain in each ROI. No normalization procedure was taken, because normalization can mix a disease pattern with a non-disease pattern. For example, (a) small nodules and end-on vessels and (b) microcalcifications and film defects will not be distinguishable. Since many disease patterns are superimposed on background structures, supervised training was chosen for the study. (So far, we have not experienced a successful unsupervised training technique with our database.)

A.1. Disease Pattern Characteristics of Microcalcifications and Lung Nodules
One must realize that the larger the nodule the higher the contrast of the nodule profile on the radiograph. Small rounded

objects possessing high contrast are most likely end-on vessels. On the other hand, film defects are highly contrast independent of size. However, the gray value differences between the peak of microcalcifications and local background tissue are somewhat proportional to the size of the calcifications on mammograms. See Figure 1 for examples of end-on vessels and true nodules. Several image blocks shown on Figure 2 demonstrate the difference between microcalcifications and film defects. All image blocks are randomly selected from our database and processed by a histogram expansion for the display purpose. It is essential to use a sufficiently small digitization to preserve the disease pattern. Potential problems of using a large digitization spot for acquiring mammographic images are: (a) the edge of a small film defect can be blurred and (b) very small microcalcifications are not actually digitized.

B. Neural Networks

B.1 Associated Memory Based Pattern Match Neural Networks for Disease Detection

A classifier takes a feature vector and produces a classification. The core portion of pattern match classifier searches for the close pattern in the memory. If no pattern match is found in the memory, a new pattern is created and stored for that particular classification in the memory during the training. Several neural networks belong to this type of pattern match: (a) adaptive resonance theory (ART) and its extensions (i.e., ART-2, ARTMAP, etc), (b) learning vector quantization (LVQ), (c) restricted coulomb energy (RCE), and (d) Dynamically Stable Associate Learning (DYSTAL) [8].

We used the processed image block (i.e., patch) as the input feature vector. Feature vectors of this kind were "highly contaminated" by background structures, which are difficult to be separated from disease patterns. It is obvious that this was not an optimal way of using pattern match. Extracted features representing various aspects of disease patterns, if there is a way to extract them, are desirable for a pattern match technique. Since DYSTAL was originally designed with image input, we tested it on our database in comparison to other neural networks of which some internally possess feature extraction procedures.

B.2. Backpropagation Neural Network Technique for Disease Pattern Recognition

Sometimes it is difficult to compare one type of neural network to another. In this subsection, we would like to use the well-known backpropagation (BP) neural network to investigate its performance with (BP/1H) and without (BP/0H) a hidden layer. We expect that the hidden layer would serve as a feature extractor. The same training and testing data sets, which again were "highly contaminated" and used in the pattern match neural network, were entered into the BP neural network.

B.3. Convolution Neural Network for Disease Pattern Recognition

The above BP neural network arrangements did not emphasize the local signal interactions, which are more important than non-local interaction in a general image pattern recognition. We, therefore, included a convolution neural network (CNN) in the experiment. The structure of the CNN is a simplified version of the neocognitron [9-10]. We used only a 2-level structure and eliminated all the complex-cell layers. Nets between two adjacent layers were selectively interconnected across groups. We modified the neocognitron network structure and used a convolution constrained backpropagation method for the training. Figure 3 shows the fundamental structure of this neural network.

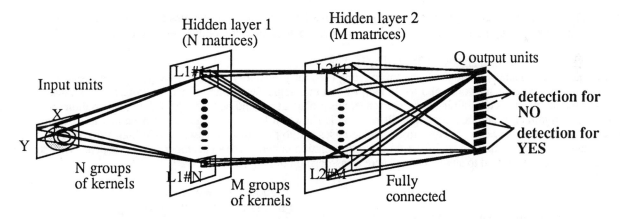

Figure 3. Artificial convolution neural network for disease pattern recognition

In the CNN signal processing, each group in the receiving layer gets signals from a group of weights (e.g., kernels). For the forward signal propagation, the resultant of the weighting factors of the kernel convoluting the element values of the front layer is collected onto the corresponding matrix elements of the receiving layer. This operation accounts for the major difference between convolution type neural network and regular fully connected neural network. We used a 7×7 convolution kernel for each layer. Each hidden layer consists of 10 groups. The output layer has 10 nodes (2 categories) which were fully connected to the second hidden layer.

C. Training of Neural Networks

C.1. Classification Invariance of Matrix Operations

In general, medical image patterns possess either a circular symmetric shape (e.g., nodule) or lack a fixed geometric pattern (e.g., calcification). In such cases, image pattern recognition does not call on top-down or left-right as classification criterion. Therefore, we can take advantage of this characteristic as an invariance. In other words, we can rotate and/or shift the input vector two-dimensionally and maintain the same output assignments for the training. This method may have two effects on the neural network: (i) to instruct the neural network that the rotation and shift of the input vector would receive the same classification result; and (ii) to increase the total number of training samples which is expected to enhance the performance of the neural network. In this study, we only rotated each suspected image block 8 times for input to test our hypothesis. Four of the rotations are: 0°, 90°, 180°, 270°. In addition, we also flipped over (left-right) the original image matrix and used the same rotations again to obtain 4 additional rotations.

C.2. Modification of Backpropagation Training for the CNN

As indicated in section A.1, a high signal of a feature can result from a negative object. Therefore, we used a Gaussian-like activation function for the cumulated signal propagation between input layer and the first hidden layer. The purpose of this activation function is to treat both low and high cumulated signals as false features that would eventually facilitate the calcification process in the following layers. This Gaussian-like activation function would not be appropriate for the BPNN using an image block as the vector described in B.2. In the conventional BPNN, fully connected rather than locally connected networks were implemented.

We used the sigmoid activation function for the forward signal propagation for all layers other than the first hidden layer and applied backpropagation training for the adjustment of weights between any two adjacent layers. The main difference between conventional weights and kernel weights is that the former are independent and the latter are constrained by grouping. By looking at the CNN processing, one may find that signals are filtered and modulated as in a circuit system. Signal propagation from one layer to the next is composed of: (a) an adaptive convolution combiner and (b) activation functions (Gaussian-like - eq. (2) - and sigmoid - eq. (3) functions for the first hidden layer and for other layers, respectively) which are given below:

$$S_x(i,j; n) = \frac{4 \times \exp\left\{-\sum_{u,v,m \Leftrightarrow n}\left[k_x(u,v; n) \times S_{x-1}(i-u,j-v; m)\right]\right\}}{1 + \exp\left\{-\sum_{u,v,m \Leftrightarrow n}\left[k_x(u,v; n) \times S_{x-1}(i-u,j-v; m)\right]\right\}} \qquad ...(2)$$

$$\text{and } S_x(i,j; n) = \frac{1}{1 + \exp\left\{-\sum_{u,v,m \Leftrightarrow n}\left[k_x(u,v; n) \times S_{x-1}(i-u,j-v; m)\right]\right\}} \qquad ...(3)$$

where $S_X((i,j); n)$ represents signal at node (i, j), nth group, and x layer. $k_x((u,v); n)$ denotes a weighting factor value at net (u, v), nth group, and connecting from x-1 to x layer. $m \Leftrightarrow n$ represents those in group m that connect to group n.

C.3. Backpropagation Neural Network Trained by Radiologists

In the study, we modeled radiologists' diagnostic rating (i.e., the probability of a disease existing in a suspected area.) and incorporated it into the neural network training. In fact, when a radiologist determines a specific probability of a disease pattern in an image area based on his/her training and experience, this probability would be accompanied with a variation (or a standard deviation). An asymmetric output association distribution is shown in Figure 4. The use of asymmetric fuzzy assignment attempted to instruct non-disease cases toward low value nodes and to push disease cases toward high value nodes. With this fuzzy assignment for the output nodes in the training, the relation between adjacent nodes is established. This supervised training can be generally applied to any situation where an association of outputs is necessary.

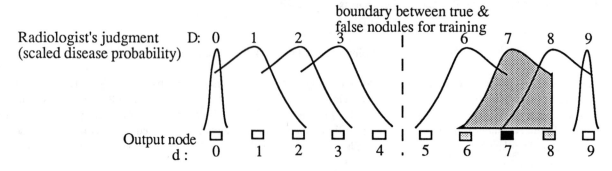

Figure 4. Fuzzy output association is constructed by a Gaussian and a trainer imposed repulsive function

D. Classification of Output Values in the Testing

Corresponding to the grading system arranged in the training, a polarized (linearly weighted) function is given as an indication. In practice, we can define a normalized disease detection index (NDDI) for the judgment of a suspected area:

$$NDDI = \frac{\sum_{n \in \text{true nodes}} \left[O_n \times \left(n - n_o + \frac{1}{2} \right) \right]}{\sum_{n \in 0}^{N-1} \left[O_n \right] \times \frac{N-1}{2}} \qquad ...(4)$$

where n denotes the node in the output layer, n_o is the node number of the least likely true node, O_n is the output value at node n, and N is the total number of output nodes. Hence a nodule detection index of 0 indicates a definite non-nodule and a nodule detection index of 1 or greater implies a definite nodule case determined by the neural network. The calculated NDDIs were evaluated by the receiver operating characteristic (ROC) analysis to measure the performance of the neural network.

III. RESULTS

A. Detection of Clustered Microcalcifications

After the pre-scan process by the computer program, 38 digital mammograms provide 220 true and 1132 false subtle microcalcifications. For the neural network studies, we divided the mammograms into two sets: 19 images (containing 108 true and 583 false image blocks) for training and another set of 19 images (containing 112 true and 549 false image blocks) for test. We did not ask radiologists to rate image blocks in the training set. Therefore, only 2 output nodes with 8 rotated input patches were used. Neither output association nor trainer imposed function was employed. In this study, we also found that the use of a small image block of 16x16 resulted in the best accuracy in the detection of clustered microcalcifications .

Table I. Performance of neural networks in the detection of clustered microclacifications.

Neural Networks	DYSTAL	BP/0H	BP/1H	BP/CNN
Az (Area under the ROC curve)	0.78	0.75	0.86	0.97
Detection Accuracy (% true-positive detection)	70	70	75	90
(# false- positive per image)	4.3	4.5	3.5	0.5

Table I shows the results of using three neural networks. DYSTAL and BP/0H, acting as classifiers, receives the lowest performance. The best performance index (Az) was 0.90 when the determination was based on individual microcalcifications and was improved to 0.97 when the determination was based on the clustered microcalcifications using CNN. In the latter method, suspected clusters including 1 or 2 spots were rejected and the average NDDI taken from the clustered spots was used for the ROC evaluation. This is because the detection of clustered microcalcifications is more clinically significant than individual calcifications, since the clustered microcalcifications (3 or more) are a strong indication of breast carcinoma in radiological diagnosis.

B. Detection of Lung Nodules

Our training image blocks were extracted from 13 chest radiographs containing multiple nodules. The pre-scan process was performed first to locate the center of the island and isolate the image block for training. A senior radiologist selected 51 true nodules, 54 end-on vessels and 60 non-nodules areas. Each original and its 7 "brother" image blocks share the same score vector (probability of a disease and output association) pre-determined by the radiologist. During the training, the original and its 7 "brother" image blocks are entered as a group in the same sequence.

The test set was collected from 31 images containing 95 nodules and 258 non-nodules and was confirmed by biopsy or by follow-up showing growth of the nodule. Table II shows the performance of using different neural network techniques and corresponding enhancement methods (i.e., Fuzzy output training).

Table II. Performance of neural networks in the detection of lung nodules.

Neural Networks	DYSTAL	BP/0H	BP/1H	BP/CNN	BP/CNN/FUZZY
Az (Area under the ROC curve)	0.56	0.58	0.68	0.82	0.88
Detection Accuracy (% true-positive detection)	60	60	70	80	80
(# false-positive per image)	7	6.8	5	4	2.5

These comparison studies in the of both diseases imply that pattern classifiers such as DYSTAL and BP/0H can not function alone to analyze "highly contaminated" image blocks (patches). Once the feature extraction procedure was added, the performance of the neural network increased as evidenced in the results of BP/1H, BP/CNN, and BP/CNN/FUZZY in Tables I and II. We also learned that the convolution for two-dimensional feature extraction and fuzzy training guided by radiologists' determination were successful methods to improve the disease detection. With the neural network used in this studies, we could not isolate which procedure, the feature extraction or the final classification, in the CNN was improved by the training.

IV. DISCUSSION AND CONCLUSIONS

Medical image pattern recognition using extracted features for input has been proposed in the detection of disease patterns [6]. Since only a small number of inputs are used (as compared to 16×16 input signals for CNN), computation can be much less for the training. As long as the features of a disease pattern are well-defined and can be quantified as values or vectors, many neural network techniques should be able to classify the features. On the other hand, the CNN can internally extract features of disease patterns and is capable of distinguish non-disease from disease patterns. A potential advantage of using the CNN is that once we are able to analyze the trained kernels, feature extraction can be specifically defined not only by the users' experience but also by the confirmation of the CNN.

In this study we have utilized CNN in conjunction with several effective training methods: (i) providing a radiologist rating scale for the training of neural nets, (ii) introducing the neural network with the classification invariance of input matrix operations, (iii) use of output association functions to fuzzify the radiologists' determination and to establish the relationship between adjacent output nodes, and (iv) rendering trainer imposed functions to enhance the performance of the neural network. We found that the performance of CNN in detecting both diseases improved significantly by administering these training methods.

This paper has demonstrated that feature extraction from disease patterns is a necessary procedure before a finial determination can be made by a classifier. Pattern classifier including newly developed neural networks would not be able to distinguish "highly contaminated" feature vectors.

ACKNOWLEDGMENTS

The work is support in part by a US Army Grant (DAMD17-93-J-3007). The content of this information does not necessarily reflect the position or the policy of the government.

Database for the studies of microcalcifications was supplied by Dr. Heang-Ping Chan of University of Michigan, Ann Arbor. The LABROC program was written by Dr. Charles Metz and his colleagues at The University of Chicago. The authors are also grateful to Dr. Walid Tohme and Ms. Susan Kirby for their editorial assistance.

REFERENCES

1. Doi, K, (1989). Feasibility of computer-aided diagnosis in digital radiography. Japanese Journal of Radiological Technology, **45**, 653-663.
2. Doi, K., Giger, ML, MacMahon, H, et al, (1992). Potential usefulness of real-time computer output to radiologists' interpretations. Scientific Exhibit, Space 10-001, Presented at RSNA 1992 Chicago Ill.
3. Chan, HP, Doi, K, & Galhotra, S, (1987). Image feature analysis and computer-aided diagnosis in digital radiography: 1. Automated detection of microcalcifications in mammography. Medical Physics, **14**, 538-548.
4. Giger, ML, Doi, K, & MacMahon, H, (1988). Image feature analysis and computer-aided diagnosis in digital radiography: 3. Automated detection of nodules in peripheral lung field. Medical Physics, **15**, 158-166.
5. Giger, ML, Ahn, N, Doi, K, MacMahon, H, & Metz, CE, (1990). Computerized detection of pulmonary nodules in digital chest images: Use of morphological filters in reducing false-positive detections. Medical Physics Journal, **17**, 861-865.
6. Lo, SB, Freedman, MT, Lin, J, & Mun, SK, (1993). Automatic lung nodule detection using profile matching and back-propagation neural network techniques. J. Digital Imaging, **6**(1), 48-54.
7. Wu, Y, Doi, K, Giger, ML, & Nishikawa, RM, (1992). Computerized detection of clustered microcalcification in digital mammograms: Applications of artificial neural networks. Medical Physics, **19**, 555-560.
8. Alkon, DL, Blackwell, KT, Barbor, GS, Rigle, AK, and Vogl, TP, (1991). Pattern-recognition by an artificial network derived from biologic neuronal systems, Biol. Cybern, **62**, 363.
9. Fukushima, K, Miyake, S, & Ito, T,(1983). Neocognitron: A neural network model for a mechanism of visual pattern recognition. IEEE Transactions on Systems, Man, and Cybernetics, **13**(5), 826-834.
10. Fukushima, K, and Wake, N, (1991). Handwritten alphanumeric character recognition by the neocognitron. IEEE Trans. on Neural Networks, **2**, 355-365.

Application of Artificial Neural Networks to the Task of Merging Feature Data in Computer-aided Diagnosis Schemes

Maryellen L. Giger, Ping Lu, Zhimin Huo, Wei Zhang

Kurt Rossmann Laboratories for Radiologic Image Research
Department of Radiology, The University of Chicago
5841 S. Maryland Avenue, Chicago, Illinois 60637

Abstract

We have been developing methods for the computerized detection and classification of lesions in digital mammographic images. In general, the methods involve preprocessing of the image data, extraction of suspected lesions from the background surround, extraction of features of each suspected lesion, and then a merging of the features into a decision regarding the suspected status of the potential lesion. We have investigated artificial neural networks (ANN) for use in merging the feature data. In our detection scheme for mass lesions, the ANN is used to merge the features in order to distinguish true-positive detections (actual lesions) from false-positive detections. In our classification scheme, the ANN is used to merge the features into a decision on the likelihood of malignancy (i.e., likelihood of being cancerous). This paper provides a brief overview of the detection and classfication schemes along with application of ANN in merging the image feature data.

Introduction

Mammography is currently the imaging examination used in the early detection of breast cancer. The task of radiologists in breast cancer diagnosis includes the visual localization of potential abnormalities on mammograms and the classification of them with respect to malignancy. In the detection task, 10% - 20% of cancers are missed by current mammographic interpretation methods (1). With regard to the classification task, although general rules for the differentiation between benign and malignant breast lesions exist, only 10 to 20% of masses referred for surgical breast biopsy are actually malignant (2-4). In addition, it has been reported that second reading of mammograms does improve sensitivity for cancer detection (5). Thus, there exists a potential role for computerized image analysis, in the early detection of breast cancer, as an aid to supplement the human observer (radiologist), allowing the final diagnostic decision to be made by the radiologist -- thus the term "computer-aided diagnosis" (6-9).

Various investigators have been developing computerized schemes for the analysis of mammographic images (10). These schemes combine computer vision methods with artificial intelligence techniques in their attempts to detect clustered microcalcifications and masses.

Methods

a) Computerized detection of mass lesions

We are developing a computerized scheme for the detection of masses in digital mammograms (11-14). Based on the deviation from the normal architectural symmetry of the right and left breasts, a bilateral-subtraction technique is used to enhance the conspicuity of possible masses. The scheme employs two pairs of conventional screen-film mammograms (the right and left MLO views and CC views), which are digitized. After the right and left breast images in each pair are aligned, a nonlinear bilateral-subtraction technique is employed that involves linking multiple subtracted images to locate initial candidate masses. Various features are then extracted and merged using an artificial neural network in order to reduce false-positive detections resulting from the bilateral subtraction.

The features extracted from each suspected mass lesion include geometric measures, gradient-based measures and intensity-based measures. The geometric measures are lesion size, lesion circularity, margin irregularity, and lesion compactness. The gradient-based measures are the average gradient (based on a 3 by 3 Sobel operator) and its standard deviation calculated within the specified region of interest. The intensity-based measures are local contrast, average gray value, standard deviation of the gray values within the lesion, and the ratio of the average to the standard deviation (15). The features were normalized between 0 and 1 and input to the a back-propagation, feed-forward neural network (16). The ANN's structure consisted of 10 input units, one hidden layer with 7 hidden units and one output unit. In this task, the output unit ranged from 0 to 1, where 1 corresponded to the suspected lesion being an actual mass (i.e., a true-positive detection) and 0 corresponded to the suspected lesion being a false-posiitve detection (and thus, allowed to be eliminated as a suspect lesion-candidate). Based on the performances of the ANN as a function of iteration, in terms of self-consistency and round robin analyses, the optimal number of training iterations was determined.

ROC (receiver operating characteristic) analysis (17,18) was applied to evaluate the output of the ANN in terms of its ability to distinguish between actual mass lesions and false-positive detections. The output values from the ANN for actual masses and for false positive detections were used in the ROC analysis as the decision variable. Basically, the ROC curve represents the true-positive fraction and the false-positive fraction at various thresholds of the ANN output. In ROC analysis, the area under the ROC curve (Az) can be used to indicate the performance of the measure in question with respect to the specified task. A larger area under the ROC curve (to a maximum of one) corresponds to better performance. ROC analysis was used a an index of performance in determining the "optimal" number of input features, the "optimal" number of hidden units, and the "optimal" number of training iterations of the ANN.

b) Computerized classification of mass lesions

Our earlier work (19) showed that a back-propagation, feed-forward artificial neural network could merge human-extracted features of mammographic lesions into a likelihood of maliganncy at a similar level of that of an expert mammographer. In the study presented in this paper, however, ANN is used to merge computer-extracted features of mass lesions into a likelihood of malignancy.

The method takes as input the center location of a mass lesion in question. Next, the lesion is segmented from the breast parenchyma (background) using an automatic region growing technique and various features of the lesion are extracted (20). The automatic lesion segmentation involves the analysis of the size of the grown region as a function of the gray-level interval used for the region growing (21). Many of the extracted features are determined from a cumulative edge-gradient-orientation histogram analysis (21), modified for orientation relative to a radial angle (20). Input to an ANN consists of four features from the gradient analysis along with the average gray value within the grown lesion. The gradient measures include the FWHM (full width at half max) of the cumulative edge-gradient-orientation histogram calculated from pixels within the lesion and its neighboring surround, and from just pixels along the lesion margin. These measures correspond to the presence of spiculation, which is a sign of malignancy in the visual interpretation of mammographic masses. The ANN's structure consisted of 5 input units, one hidden layer with 4 hidden units and one output unit. In this task, the output unit ranged from 0 to 1, where 1 corresponded to the lesion being malignant and 0 corresponded to the lesion being benign. Use of ROC analysis with self-consistency testing and round-robin testing was employed as discussed in the previous section.

Results

For the detection scheme, each clinical mammogram was digitized into a matrix, approximately 2K by 2K in size with 10-bit quantization, and then spatially averaged to a 512 by 512 matrix for input to the detection algorithm (pixel size of approximately 0.5 mm). In the self-consistency analysis, the ANN achieved an Az of 1.0 and in the round-robin analysis, the ANN achieved an Az of 0.92 in distinguishing actual masses (true positives) from false-positive detectios. In an evaluation study using the 154 pairs of clinical mammograms (90 pairs with masses and 64 pairs without), the detection scheme yielded a sensitivity of 95% at an average of 2.5 false-positive detections per image.

The classification method was evaluated using a pathologically-confirmed database of 95 masses (57 malignant and 38 benign), of which all but one had been sent to biospy. The mammograms in the database had been digitized to a pixel size of 0.1 mm. Using the five input features, an Az (area under to the ROC curve) of 0.83 was obtained in the task of distinguishing benign from malignant masses using a round-robin method for evaluation. However, we found that by using a rule-based decision on one of the features (FWHM) based on its correspondence to visual interpretation methods, prior to use of the ANN, the performance increased yielding an Az of 0.90.

Summary

We have found the conventional back-propagation, feed-forward artificial neural network to be useful in the merging of mammographic image feature data into decisions concerning true-positive vs. false-positive detections and malignant vs. benign status. It is necessary though to appropriately structure and train the ANN including analysis of individual features, optimization of the number of hidden units, use of an optimal number of training iterations to avoid loss of generalizability and appropriate means for evaluation (such as ROC analysis).

We are currently incorporating the ANN into an intelligent mammography workstation, which we are developing for use as a "second opinion" in breast cancer screening.

Acknowledgments

The authors are grateful to Kunio Doi, Ph.D., Charles E. Metz, Ph.D., Robert Nishikawa, Ph.D., Carl Vyborny, M.D., Ph.D., and Robert A. Schmidt, M.D. for their discussions. This work is being done as part of the National Digital Mammography Development Group (NDMDG), which was established and funded in part by the NCI/NIH. The research was supported in parts by the American Cancer Society (FRA-390), USPHS grants CA48985 and CA24806, and the U.S. Army Medical Research and Development Command grant 92153010. The contents of this paper are solely the responsibility of the authors and do not necessarily represent the official views of any of the supporting organizations.

References

1. Tabar L. Dean PB: Basic principles of mammographic diagnosis. Diagn. Imag. Clin. Med. 54: 146-157, 1985.
2. Tabar L, Dean PB: Teaching Atlas of Mammography, Georg Thieme Verlag (Studdgart, New York 1983).
3. Bassett LW, Gold RH: Breast cancer detection: Mammography and other methods in breast imaging. (Grune & Stratton, New York, 1987).
4. Moskowitz M: Screening for breast cancer: How effective are our tests? A critical review. Ca-A Cancer Journal for Clinicians 33:26-39, 1983.

5.   Bird RE. Professional quality assurance for mammography screening programs. Radiology 177:587, 1990.

6.   Chan HP, Doi K, Vyborny CJ, et al. Improvement in radiologists' detection of clustered microcalcifications on mammograms: the potential of computer-aided diagnosis. Invest Radiol 25:1102-111, 1990.

7.   Doi K, Giger ML, Nishikawa RM, Hoffmann KR, MacMahon H, Schmidt RA, Chua KG: Digital radiography: A useful clinical tool for computer-aided diagnosis by quantitative analysis of radiographic images. Acta Radiologica 34: 426-439, 1993.

8.   Giger ML, Doi K, MacMahon H, Nishikawa RM, Hoffmann KR, et al.: An "intelligent" workstation for computer-aided diagnosis. RadioGraphics 13: 647-656, 1993.

9.   Vyborny CJ, Giger ML: Artificial intelligence in mammography. AJR 162: 699-708, 1994.

10.   Giger ML: Computer-aided Diagnosis. In RSNA Categorical Course on TEchnical Aspects of Breast Imaging syllabus pp. 283-298, 1993.

11.   Giger ML, Yin F-F, Doi K, Metz CE, Schmidt RA, Vyborny CJ: Investigation of methods for the computerized detection and analysis of mammographic masses. Proc. SPIE 1233: 183-184, 1990.

12.   Yin F-F, Giger ML, Doi K, Metz CE, Vyborny CJ, Schmidt RA: Computerized detection of masses in digital mammograms: Analysis of bilateral-subtraction images. Medical Physics 18: 955-963, 1991.

13.   Yin F-F, Giger ML, Vyborny CJ, Doi K, Schmidt RA: Comparison of bilateral-subtraction and single-image processing techniques in the computerized detection of mammographic masses. Invest Radiol 28: 473-481, 1993.

14.   Nishikawa RM, Giger ML, Doi K, Vyborny CJ, Schmidt RA, Metz CE, Wu Y, et al.: Computer-aided detection and diagnosis of masses and clustered microcalcifications from digital mammograms. Proc. SPIE 1905: 422-432, 1993.

15.   Lu P, Giger ML, Schmidt RA, Vyborny CJ, Doi K, Bick U, et al.: Computer-aided detection of masses on digital mammograms: Processing and feature extraction with multiple-gray-level resolution. Radiology 189(P): 186, 1993

16.   Rumelhart DE, Hinton GE, Williams RJ: Learning internal representations by error propagation. In: Rumelhart DE, McClelland JL, PDP Research Group. Parallel distributed processing: Explorations in the microstructure of cognition. Cambridge: MIT Press 1: 318-362, 1986.

17.   Metz CE: ROC methodology in radiologic imaging. Invest Radiol 21: 720-733, 1986.

18.   Metz CE: Some practical issues of experimental design and data analysis in radiological ROC studies. Invest Radiol 24: 234-245, 1989.

19.   Wu Y, Giger ML, Doi K, Vyborny CJ, Schmidt RA, Metz CE: Application of neural networks in mammography: Applications in decision making in the diagnosis of breast cancer. Radiology 187:81-87, 1993.

20.   Huo Z, Giger ML, Vyborny CJ, Schmidt RA, Doi K, Lu P: Computer-aided diagnosis in mammography: Classification of malignant and benign masses. Radiology 189(P): 318, 1993.

21.   Matsumoto T, Yoshimura H, Doi K, et al. Image feature analysis of false-positive diagnoses produced by automated detection of lung nodules. Invest Radiol 27:587-597, 1992.

Application of a shift-invariant artificial neural network for detection of breast carcinoma in digital mammograms

Wei Zhang, Maryellen L. Giger, Robert M. Nishikawa, Kunio Doi
Kurt Rossmann Laboratories for Radiologic Image Research
Department of Radiology, The University of Chicago
5841 South Maryland Avenue, Chicago, Illinois 60637

ABSTRACT

A computer-aided diagnosis (CAD) scheme has been developed in our laboratory for the detection of clustered microcalcifications in digital mammograms. In this study, we apply a shift-invariant neural network to eliminate false-positive detections reported by the CAD scheme. The shift-invariant neural network is a multilayer back-propagation neural network with local, shift-invariant interconnections. The advantage of the shift-invariant neural network is that the result of the network is not dependent on the locations of the clustered microcalcifications in the input layer. The neural network is trained to detect each individual microcalcification in a given region of interest (ROI) reported by the CAD scheme. A ROI is classified as a positive ROI if the total number of microcalcifications detected in the ROI is greater than a certain number. The performance of the shift-invariant neural network was evaluated by means of a *jack-knife* (or *holdout*) method and ROC analysis using a database of 112 ROIs as reported by the CAD scheme when applied to 34 mammograms. The analysis yielded an average area under the ROC curve (A_z) of 0.92. Approximately 55% of false-positive ROIs were eliminated without any loss of the true-positive ROIs. The result is considerably better than that obtained in our previous study using a conventional three-layer, feed-forward neural network. The effect of the network structure on the performance of the shift-invariant neural network is also studied.

I. INTRODUCTION

Breast cancer causes 44,000 deaths per year in the United States. Mammography has been proven to be the primary diagnostic procedure for the early detection of breast cancer.[1] Between 30% and 50% of breast carcinomas demonstrate microcalcifications on mammograms, and between 60% and 80% of the carcinomas reveal microcalcifications upon histologic examination.[2-4] Therefore, clustered microcalcifications on mammograms are an important sign in the detection of breast carcinoma. To give radiologists a "second opinion" in detecting clustered microcalcifications on mammograms, a computer-aided diagnosis (CAD) scheme based on filtering and feature extracting techniques has been developed in our laboratory.[5,6] The CAD scheme identifies small regions of potential clustered microcalcifications that are then indicated on the digitized mammogram. In an analysis of 78 mammograms, 85% of the true clusters were detected with 2.5 false-positive detections per image, (false-positives are those which do not actually contain clustered microcalcifications). Generally, it is desirable to improve the sensitivity of the CAD scheme in order to detect the most subtle cases. However, as the sensitivity increases with the current CAD scheme, the false-positive detection rate will also increase. To improve the overall performance, therefore, we have applied an artificial neural network to eliminate some of the false-positive detections indicated by the CAD scheme.[7] The neural network used in our previous study was a conventional three-layer, feed-forward neural network with a single output unit. The power spectra of the regions of interest (ROI) indicated by the CAD scheme were used as the input to the neural network. The neural network was trained to classify positive or negative ROIs with its output value of 1 or 0, respectively. In our previous study, about 20% of the false-positive detections could be eliminated by the neural network without any loss of the positive detections.

In this study, we attempt to improve the reduction of the number of the false-positive detections of the CAD scheme by applying a novel shift-invariant neural network[8,9] which contains higher generalizing ability than the conventional neural network. The performance of the shift-invariant neural network is evaluated quantitatively by means of a *jack-knife* (or *holdout*)[10] method and receiver operating characteristic (ROC) analysis[11,12] using the same database used in our previous study.[7]

II. METHOD

In this study, the ROIs indicated by the CAD scheme are first preprocessed with background-trend correction and normalization, and are then entered to the shift-invariant neural network. The shift-invariant neural network is trained to detect each individual microcalcification in a given ROI. A ROI is classified as a positive ROI if the total number of microcalcifications detected in the ROI is greater than a certain number; otherwise the ROI is classified as a negative ROI. Finally, the performance of the shift-invariant neural network is evaluated.

A. Shift-invariant neural network

1. General concept

Our shift-invariant neural network is a layered feed-forward neural network with local, spatially-invariant interconnections as illustrated in Figs. 1(a) and (b).[8,9] The basic structure of the shift-invariant neural network is similar to that of the Neocognitron model developed by Fukushima *et al.*[13,14] However, the shift-invariant neural network developed by Zhang *et al*[8,9] for image processing is a feed-forward neural network without the lateral interconnections and feedback loops that are included in the Neocognitron. Furthermore, error backpropagation (EBP) is used as the training algorithm in the shift-invariant neural network. The shift-invariant neural network has been shown to be a powerful tool for pattern recognition and image processing.[8,9]

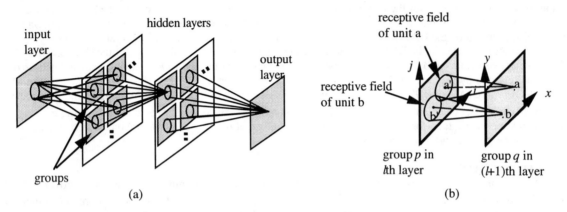

Fig. 1. Illustration of (a) shift-invariant neural network; (b) shift-invariant interconnection between two groups.

In Fig. 1(a), units in the input layer and output layer correspond to pixels of the input and output "images", respectively. Units in any single hidden layer are divided into groups as has been employed in the Neocognitron. Each unit in a subsequent layer is connected with the units of a small region in each group in the preceding layer. Each small circle shown in Fig. 1(a) illustrates a small predefined region called the receptive field for the unit in the subsequent layer.[13] To obtain the shift-invariant responses, connection weights between any two groups in two layers are constrained to be shift-invariant.[8,9] Figure 1(b) illustrates the shift-invariant interconnections between two groups in two layers. As shown in Fig. 1(b), each unit (unit a or b for example) in one group of the subsequent layer receives input from the small region centered at the corresponding unit (unit a' or b'). The distributions (or patterns) of connection weights for any units within a group are identical for all units in that group. In general, if $W(i,j;x,y)$ denotes the connection weight between the unit at the location (i, j) in the preceding layer and the unit at (x, y) in the subsequent layer, the shift-invariant connection weights can be formulated as follows:

$$W(i,j;x,y) = W(i-x, j-y) \tag{1}$$

Consequently, the interconnection between the units in two groups can be considered to represent a spatial filter with the connection weights as its elements and with a size corresponding to that of the receptive field.

In the case of multigroup and multilayer neural networks as shown in Fig. 1(a), units in the same layer but belonging to different groups have the same size of receptive field, but different patterns of connection weights.[8, 9] To avoid the effect of edges in input images, the number of units in each group of subsequent layer is reduced depending on the size of the receptive field. Assume that the number of units of a group in the lth layer is $N \times N$ and the receptive field size in the $(l + 1)$th layer is $M \times M$, the number of the units of the group in the $(l + 1)$th layer will then be[9]

$$\text{No. of units} = (N - M + 1) \times (N - M + 1). \tag{2}$$

We define the input of the unit (x, y) by $N^l_p(x,y)$, the connection weights by $W^l_{p,q}(x,y)$ and the output of the unit by $O^l_p(x,y)$, where

$l = (1,2,...L)$, the layer number,

$p = (1,2,...P^l)$, the group number in the lth layer, and

$q = (1, 2, ... P^{l+1})$, the group number in the $(l+1)$th layer.

With the feed-forward propagations of signals in the network, the outputs in the subsequent layer are given by summation of "filtered" patterns, which are obtained by convolution of the patterns in different groups of the preceding layer with a number of filters (or connection weights), followed by pointwise thresholding,[9] namely,

$$N^{l+1}_q(x,y) = \sum_{p=1}^{P^l} O^l_p(x,y) * W^l_{p,q}(x,y), \tag{3}$$

$$O^{l+1}_q(x,y) = f(N^{l+1}_q(x,y) + b^{l+1}_q), \tag{4}$$

where the symbol * denotes the operation of convolution and $f(x)$ is the sigmoid-like activation function to denote the pointwise thresholding. b^{l+1}_q is a constant (or the bias of the sigmoid-like function). In this study, except for units in the input layer, we use a bipolar sigmoid-like function given by

$$f(x) = \frac{2}{1+\exp(-x)} - 1. \tag{5}$$

The activation function of units in the input layer is linear function.

The conventional error-back-propagation algorithm[15] (EBP) is modified for training with the shift-invariant interconnections.[8,9] The training error related to the differences between the desired outputs and the actual outputs for all the input training images is determined by

$$E = \sum_i \sum_{x,y} (T^i(x,y) - O^i(x,y))^2, \tag{6}$$

where $T^i(x,y)$ denotes the desired output image and $O^i(x,y)$ denotes the actual output image, of the neural network for the training input image i.

2. Training for detection of individual microcalcifications

The shift-invariant neural network is trained to detect each individual microcalcification. For an input ROI containing microcalcifications, the desired output image (of the ROI) of the network was given such that the output of a unit in the output layer is 1, only if the corresponding unit in the input layer is at the center of a microcalcification, a "training free" zone around the center of the microcalcification, and -1 otherwise (see the input and desired output images shown in Fig. 2). The pixel values of pixels in these training-free areas will not be forced to learn a certain value during the training procedure. In other words, the neural network will be allowed to produce any output values within these regions. This method makes training of the neural network easier and faster, because we have found in our initial study[16] that it is difficult to enforce the neural network to make the same output value for various microcalcifications that are different in sizes and shapes.

In this study, a cross-validation technique for training and testing of the neural network is employed in order to avoid overtraining problem occured in our initial study.[16] Using this technique, image data in the database are divided into two randomly selected groups, namely, the training and the validating (or testing) sets. The network is trained by the training set and tested by the validating or testing set at intervals of a certain number of iterations. The training of the network is terminated just before the performance of the network for the validating set decreases.

B. Database

The digitized mammograms used in this study were obtained by digitizing conventional screen-film (Kodak Min R/OM) mammograms using a Fuji drum scanner system with a pixel size of 0.1x0.1 mm^2 and a 10-bit gray scale. ROIs used in this experiment were the same as those employed in our previous study.[7] A total of 112 ROIs of 55x55 pixels (about 5.5x5.5mm^2) were selected from 34 digitized mammograms. Among them were 56 positive

ROIs, i.e., ROIs that contained clustered microcalcifications and 56 false-positive ROIs that contained false-positive clusters as reported by the CAD scheme.

All of the locations of the centers of microcalcifications, which were used as "desired output images" in the training of the neural network, were identified by an expert mammographer.

C. Classification of clustered microcalcifications

The output image of the shift-invariant neural network for a given input ROI image is first thresholded to yield a binary image at a certain threshold pixel value. The borders of "white" areas in the binary output image is then traced using a four-connectivity-region growing technique. Once borders are traced, "white" areas are segmented from each other. Each isolated "white" area is counted as one "detected microcalcification". If the number of "detected microcalcifications" in the output image is equal to or greater than a certain number (cluster criterion), the input ROI is considered to be a positive ROI, i.e., a ROI with clustered microcalcifications; otherwise, the ROI is considered to be a negative ROI. Both the optimal threshold pixel value and the cluster criterion were determined empirically using ROC analysis as described later in Section III.

D. Evaluation

The performance of the neural network was evaluated using a *jack-knife* method and ROC analysis.[11] In order to compare the performance of the shift-invariant neural network to that of the conventional neural network used in our previous study, the same holdout ratio for training and testing were used as in our previous study. For each category, i.e., positive or false positive ROIs, one half of the cases were selected randomly from the database for training, and the other half were used for testing of the trained network. This evaluation method was repeated several times by randomly changing the cases for training and testing to examine the effect of case selection on the overall performance. In this study, since training is very time-consuming, only five repetitions of training and testing were performed. For each of the five testing data, the true-positive fraction (TPF) and the false positive fraction (FPF) of the classification decisions of the trained network were calculated at various threshold pixel values, while the cluster criterion was assigned to two. ROC analysis[20] was used to analyze independently the results obtained from the five testing data sets. ROC curves were obtained by fitting the TPF and FPF data using ROCFIT program developed by Metz *et al.*[11,12]

The average area under the ROC curve, A_z, and the average minimum FPF at the TPF of 1.0 for the five data sets are employed as measures of the performance of the network. In addition, the standard deviations of the A_z and the minimum FPF (at TPF=1.0) are considered as indicators of the generalization of the result. Generally, larger A_z and smaller standard deviation indicate greater overall performance of a network. Also note that the lower the FPF (at TPF=1.0), the larger the number of false-positive ROIs that can be eliminated by the network while preserving all of the positive ROIs.

III. RESULTS

The effect of the structure of the neural network (i.e., the number of layers, groups and the size of the filter in each layer) on the overall performance was studied. Eight different structures were investigated in our experiments. For simplicity, we kept the filter size constant throughout all of the layers within each network. In order to compare the results of our previous study,[7] the output image size of the shift-invariant neural network was chosen to be 31x31 pixels (odd number of pixels is preferred for the determination of a "center" pixel of a ROI) while the input ROI size is determined by the structure of the network based on Eq. 2.

All of the structures were trained and tested with the five different combinations of the 56 positive and 56 false-positive ROIs in our database. Table I gives the average A_z values and their standard deviations as well as the minimum FPF at the TPF of 1.0 for the various structures evaluated. Here we use codes to describe the network structures. The code 1211_7, for example, indicates that it is a four layer network with one group in the input layer, two in the second layer, one in the third layer, one in the output layer, and that the filter size in each layer is 7x7. It should be noted in Table I that the structure 1211_7 has the largest A_z and the smallest standard deviation among all of the structures investigated. In Table I, the structure 1211_7 has the lowest FPF (at TPF=1.0) except for the structure 1211_5. However, since the difference between the FPFs (at TPF=1.0) obtained with 1211_7 and 1211_5 is very small and the difference between A_z values is considerably larger, the network structure 1211_7 was considered the best structure for our further studies.

Input layer   1st hidden layer   2nd hidden layer   Output layer

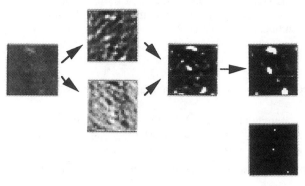

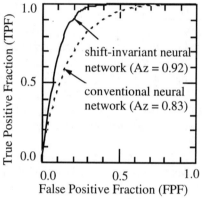

"truth"

Fig. 2 Illustration of input testing ROI, output image, responses in hidden layers and the desired output image.

Network	groups	Filter size	A_z	FPF
11_7	1,1	7x7	0.85 ± 0.03	0.64 ± 0.08
111_7	1,1,1	7x7	0.89 ± 0.05	0.44 ± 0.21
121_7	1,2,1	7x7	0.88 ± 0.03	0.54 ± 0.15
1111_7	1,1,1,1	7x7	0.91 ± 0.03	0.58 ± 0.13
1211_7	1,2,1,1	7x7	0.92 ± 0.02	0.42 ± 0.10
1211_5	1,2,1,1	5x5	0.89 ± 0.03	0.41 ± 0.10
1211_9	1,2,1,1	9x9	0.87 ± 0.03	0.63 ± 0.21
1321_7	1,3,2,1	7x7	0.89 ± 0.04	0.45 ± 0.20

Table I Performance the neural networks with various structures.

Figure 3. Comparison of ROC curves.

As an illustration of how the 1211_7 network works after training, Fig. 2 shows a ROI from the testing set as detected by the CAD scheme, the corresponding desired output image, and the actual responses of the units in each layer. It appears in Fig. 2 that microcalcifications in the processed images in groups 1 and 2 of the second layer are enhanced and suppressed, respectively. Microcalcifications appear to be clearly identifiable in the third layer, and are further enhanced in the final output layer.

Figure 3 shows the comparison of the average ROC curves for distinguishing positive ROIs from false positive ROIs obtained in this study and our previous study. It is apparent that the shift-invariant neural network performs noticeably better than the general neural network approach used in our previous study. With the shift-invariant neural network approach, about 55% of false-positive ROIs identified by the automated computer scheme can be eliminated without any loss of true-positive ROIs. With the conventional neural network used in our previous study, however, only about 20% of false positive ROIs can be eliminated while preserving all of the positive ROIs.

By using the "training free" zone and the cross-validation techniques, the performance of the shift-invariant neural network is also improved comparing to the results reported in our initial study.[16]

IV.   DISCUSSION AND CONCLUSION

The improved performance of the shift-invariant neural network approach compared with that of the conventional neural network used in our previous study is related to the following facts. First, the original ROI is used as the input (i.e., spatial domain analysis), so there is no loss of information before input to the neural network if the preprocessing can be ignored. Second, the connection of units in the shift-invariant neural network are localized, i.e., an unit is only connected with the units within a small region in the preceding layer. Therefore, a local variation, such as artifacts in the input image, does not affect the output of the units whose receptive fields do not include the local variation.[8,9,13,14] In addition, the final decision of classifying an input ROI as positive or negative is based on whether the number of detected microcalcifications is above a given criterion, regardless of the exact number and the distribution of microcalcifications within a cluster. Therefore, the shift-invariant neural network approach to the detection of clustered microcalcifications is independent on the shape of the clustered microcalcifications.

REFERENCES

[1] S. A. Feig, "Decreased cancer mortality through mammographic screening: Results of clinical trials," Radiology **167**, 659-665 (1988).

[2] J. N. Wolfe, "Analysis of 462 carcinomas," Am. J. Radiol. **121**, 846-853 (1974).

[3] R. R. Mills, R. Davis, and A. J. Stacey, "The detection and significance of calcifications in the breast: A radiological and pathological study," Br. J. Radio. **49**, 12-26 (1976).

[4] E. A. Sickels, "Mammographic features of 300 consecutive noninvasive breast cancers," Am. J. Radio. **146**, 661-663 (1986).

[5] H. -P. Chan, K. Doi, C. J. Vyborny, R. A. Schmidt, C. E. Metz, K. L. Lam, T. Ogura, Y. Wu, and H. MacMahon, "Improvement in radiologists' detection of clustered microcalcifications on mammograms: The potential of computer-aided diagnosis," Invest. Radiol. **25**, 1102-111- (1990).

[6] Nishikawa RM, Giger ML, Doi K, Vyborny CJ, Schmidt RA, Metz CE, Wu Y, Yin F-F, Jiang Y, Huo Z, et al.: Computer-aided detection and diagnosis of masses and clustered microcalcifications from digital mammograms. Proc. SPIE 1905: 422-432 1993.

[7] Y. Wu, K. Doi, M. L. Giger, and R. M. Nishikawa, "Computerized detection of clustered microcalcifications in digital mammograms: Applications of artificial neural networks," Med. Phys. **19**, 555-560 (1992).

[8] W. Zhang, K Itoh, J. Tanida, and Y. Ichioka, "Parallel distributed processing model with local space-invariant interconnections and its optical architecture," Appl. Opt. **29**, 4790-4797 (1990).

[9] W. Zhang, A. Hasegawa, K Itoh, and Y. Ichioka, "Image processing of human corneal endothelium based on a learning network," Appl. Opt. **30**, 4211-4217 (1991).

[10] K. Fukunaga, Introduction to Statistical Pattern Recognition, Second ed. (Academic press, Inc., New York, 1990).

[11] C. E. Metz, "Current problems in ROC analysis," Proc. Chest Imaging Conference (WW Peppler and AA Alter eds), Madison, Wisconsin, 315-336 (1988).

[12] C. E. Metz, "Some practical issues of experimental design and data analysis in radiological ROC studies," Invest. Radiol. **24**, 234-245 (1989).

[13] K. Fukushima, S. Miyake, T. Ito, "Neocognitron: A neural network model for a mechanism of visual pattern recognition," IEEE Trans. Systems Man and Cybernetics SMC-13, 826-843 (1983).

[14] K. Fukushima, "A neural network for visual pattern recognition," Computer 21, 65-76 (1988).

[15] D. E. Rumelhart and J. L. McClellend, Eds., *Parallel Distributed Processing* (MIT, Cambridge, MA, 1986), pp. 318-362.

[16] W. Zhang, K. Doi, M. Giger, Y. Wu, R. Nishikawa, R. Schmidt, "Computerized detection of clustered microcalcificaitons in digital mammograms using a shift-invarinat artificial neural network", Medical Physics, (1993, submitted).

ARTIFICIAL NEURAL NETWORKS FOR OUTCOME PREDICTION IN CANCER

Harry B. Burke, M.D., Ph.D., Philip H. Goodman, M.D., David B. Rosen, Ph.D., Department of Medicine, University of Nevada School of Medicine, Washoe Medical Center, 77 Pringle Way, Reno, Nevada 89520

Abstract

Background. The TNM staging system has been used since the early 1960's to predict breast cancer patient outcome. In an attempt to increase prognostic accuracy, many putative prognostic factors have been identified. Because the TNM stage model can not accommodate these new factors, the proliferation of factors in breast cancer has led to clinical confusion. What is required is a new computerized prognostic system that can test putative prognostic factors and integrate the predictive factors with the TNM variables in order to increase prognostic accuracy.

Methods. Using the area under the curve (AUC) of the receiver operating characteristic, I compare the accuracy of the following predictive models: pTNM staging system, principal component analysis, classification and regression trees, logistic regression, cascade correlation neural network, conjugate gradient descent neural network, probabilistic neural network, and backpropagation neural network.

Results. The pTNM staging system's accuracy is .720. Logistic regression (LR) and both the probabilistic neural network (PNN) and the backpropagation neural network (BPNN) are significantly more accurate than the pTNM staging system, using just the TNM variables (.762, .759, and .768, respectively). Adding variables further increases the prediction accuracy of LR and both PNN and BPNN (.776, .777, .779, respectively). Adding the new prognostic factors p53 and HER-2/neu increases the backpropagation neural network's accuracy to .850. These results generalize across breast cancer data sets and to a colorectal cancer data set.

Conclusions. Computerized prediction systems are more accurate than the current look-up table system. The backpropagation neural network is consistently more accurate than the best conventional statistical models. Artificial neural networks are able to combine prognostic factors to further improve prognostic accuracy. Artificial neural networks are robust across data bases and cancer sites, they can perform as well as the best traditional prediction methods, and they can capture the power of nonmonotonic predictors and discover complex interactions.

INTRODUCTION

For over thirty years measuring cancer outcome has been based on the TNM staging system (tumor size, number of lymph nodes with metastatic disease, and distant metastases). There are several problems with this model. First, it is not very accurate, for breast cancer it is 44% accurate. Second its accuracy can not be improved because predictive variables can not be added to the model. Third, it does not apply to all cancers. In this paper I compare the most powerful computerized prediction models, including artificial neural networks.

Artificial neural networks (ANN) are a class of nonlinear regression and discrimination models. They do not have a priori biological reality. ANNs are being used in many areas of medicine, with several hundred articles published in the last year. Representative areas of research include anesthesiology, radiology, cardiology, psychiatry, and neurology. ANNs are being used in cancer research including image processing, analysis of laboratory data for breast cancer diagnosis, and the discovery of chemotherapeutic agents.

It should be pointed out that the analyses in this paper rely upon previously collected prognostic factors. These factors were selected for collection because they were significant in a generalized linear model such as the linear or logistic models. There is no predictive model that can improve upon linear or logistic prediction models when the predictor variables meet the assumptions of these models and there are no interactions. Therefore the objective of this paper is not to outperform linear or logistic models on these data. Rather, our objective is to show that, with variables selected by generalized linear models, artificial neural networks can perform as well as the best models .

There is no a priori reason to believe that future prognostic factors will be binary or linear, and that there will not be complex interactions between prognostic factors. In fact, we will present evidence that suggests that cancer is a complex system; that future prognostic factors will be nonmonotonic and they will exhibit complex interactions. A further objective of this paper is to demonstrate that artificial neural networks are likely to outperform the conventional models when there are unanticipated nonmonotonic factors or complex interactions.

METHODS

Data

The Patient Care Evaluation (PCE) data set is collected by the Commission on Cancer of the American College of Surgeons (ACS). The ACS, in October 1992, requested cancer information from hospital tumor registries in the United States. The ACS asked for the first 25 cases of breast cancer seen at that institution in 1983, and it asked for follow up information on each of these 25 patients through the date of the request. These are only cases of first diagnosis of breast cancer. Follow up information includes known deaths. The PCE data set contains, at best, eight year follow-up. We chose to use a five year survival end-point. This analysis is for death due to breast cancer, not all cause mortality.

For this analysis cases with missing data and those who are censored before five years, are not included so that the prediction models can be compared without putting any prediction model at a disadvantage. We randomly divided the data set into training/testing and validation subsets of 5,169, and 3,102 cases, respectively.

Models

In this study we are examining the relative prognostic accuracy in predicting five year survival of the most important predictive models. The goal is not to try to determine the maximum predictive accuracy obtainable for a specific cancer site (that is the subject of a future work). The TMN stage model used in this analysis is the pathologic model (pTNM) based on the 1992 American Joint Committee on Cancer's Manual for the Staging of Cancer. The pathologic model relies upon pathologically determined tumor size and lymph nodes. This contrasts with clinical staging which relies upon the clinical examination to provide tumor size and lymph node information. To determine the overall accuracy of the TNM stage model I compared the model's prediction for each patient, where the individual patient's prediction is the fraction of all the patients in that stage who survive, to each patient's true outcome.

Principal component analysis is a data reduction technique based on the linear combinations of predictor variables that minimizes the variance across patients. The logistic regression analysis is performed in a stepwise manner, without interaction terms, using the statistical language S-plus, with the continuous variable age modeled with a restricted cubic spline to avoid assuming linearity. We will show that logistic regression is identical to a two layer neural network with a logistic transfer function and a maximum likelihood criterion function. Two types of Classification and Regression Tree (CART) analyses are performed using S-plus. The first was a 9-node pruned tree (with 10-fold cross validation on the deviance), and the second was a shrunk tree with 13.7 effective nodes.

There are many types of neural networks. The most commonly used neural networks in medical research are multilayer perceptrons that use backpropagation training. Backpropagation training consists of fitting the parameters (weights) of the model by a criterion function, usually square error, using the gradient descent optimization function. In backpropagation neural networks the error (the difference between the true outcome and the predicted outcome) is propagated back from the output to the connection weights in order to adjust the weights in the direction of minimizing the error. The first practical multilayer perceptron trained with backpropagation was developed by Werbos, independently derived by Parker, and further developed by Rumelhart, Hinton, and Williams and Sejnowski and Rosenberg. We have used three neural networks that differ in their method of training. One neural network is simple gradient descent by the delta rule, where the weights are updated after each epoch (an epoch is one presentation of all the patients). The second neural network is stochastic gradient descent, where the weights are updated after each case is presented rather than after each epoch. The third neural network, called Quickprop (S.E. Fahlman), is one of a number of methods that backpropagates the second derivative of the error through the network, i.e., it uses the rate of change of the change in error. All the multilayer perceptron neural network training in this paper is based on the squared error criterion function unless otherwise stated, and backpropagation refers to gradient descent.

All outcome analyses, except for PCA, CART, cascade correlation, and conjugate gradient descent, were performed twice. The second analysis was performed independently by a different researcher who did not know the first researcher's results. There were no significant differences between the two researcher's results. All results are based on the validation data set.

Accuracy

Predictive accuracy depends on three factors: the quality of the data, the predictive power of the prognostic factors, and the prognostic model's ability to capture the power of the prognostic factors. This work focuses on the prognostic model's ability to capture the power of the prognostic factors.

The measure of comparative accuracy is the area under the curve (AUC) of the receiver operating characteristic (ROC). Generally, the AUC is a nonparametric measure of discrimination. Square error summarizes how close each patient's predicted value is to its true outcome. The AUC measures the relative goodness of the set of predictions as a whole by comparing the predicted probability of each patient with that of all other patients. The computational approach to the AUC that employs the trapezoidal approximation to the area under the receiver operating characteristic curve for binary outcomes was first reported by Bamber, and later in the medical literature by Hanley and McNeil. This was extended by Harrell to continuous outcomes.

The AUC is calculated for the predictive scores of each algorithm in order to compare their average accuracy in predicting outcome. The AUC is independent of both the prior probability of each outcome and the threshold cutoff for categorization and its computation requires only that the algorithm produce an ordinally-scaled relative predictive score. With n levels of outcome, the AUC estimates the average probability, over all possible n-tuples of patients with differing outcome levels, that an algorithm will assign sequentially higher scores in the proper order. In terms of mortality, the AUC estimates the average probability, over all possible pairs of patients with differing outcome, that an algorithm will assign a higher mortality score to those who died compared to those who survived. The AUC varies from zero to one. When the prognostic score is unrelated to survival time the AUC is .5, representing chance. The further the AUC is from .5 the more correct the prediction model is at predicting which of two patients will live longer. The AUC is calculated in the following manner. All pairs of predictions are examined.

Pairs with different outcomes and different predictions are tested for concordance or discordance of outcome with prediction, pairs with different outcomes and the same prediction are "ties", and pairs with the same outcome are not counted, regardless of prediction. The area under the curve of the receiver operating characteristic can be interpreted as the sensitivity averaged over all specificities, alternatively it can be interpreted as the specificity averaged over all sensitivities.

RESULTS

All results are based on the independent variable sample not used for training/testing (i.e., the validation data set), and all analyses employ the same validation data set. Using the PCE breast cancer data set, we can assess the accuracy (AUC) of the pTNM stage model in terms of five year survival (Table 1).

Table 1. PCE 1983 Breast Cancer Data: 5 year Survival Prediction Accuracy, TNM Variables.

PREDICTION MODEL	ACCURACY[*]	SPECIFICATIONS
pTNM Stages	.720	Ø,I,IIA,IIB,IIIA,IIIB,IV
Stepwise Logistic Regression	.762	no interactions
Probabilistic Neural Network	.759	bandwidth = 6s
Backpropagation Neural Network	.768	3-8-1[**]

[*] The area under the curve of the receiver operating characteristic. The standard error for all methods is less than .01.
[**] The number of input nodes, hidden nodes, and output nodes, respectively.

The probabilistic neural network is slightly less accurate than logistic regression, the backpropagation neural network was slightly more accurate than logistic regression, and all three models are significantly more accurate than the pTNM stage model, using just the TNM variables (all SEs are less than .01, p < .01 for all models compared to pTNM model).

We can examine the accuracy of several prediction models using the most powerful of the predictor variables available in the data set. Table 2 shows the accuracy results for each model.

Table 2. PCE 1983 Breast Cancer Data: 5 Year Survival Prediction, 54 Variables.

PREDICTION MODEL	ACCURACY[*]	SPECIFICATIONS
pTNM Stages	.720	Ø,I,IIA,IIB,IIIA,IIIB,IV
Principal Component Analysis	.714	one scaling iteration
CART, pruned	.753	9 nodes
CART, shrunk	.762	13.7 nodes
Stepwise Logistic regression	.776	with cubic splines
Fuzzy ARTMAP Neural Network	.738	54-F2a, 128-1
Cascade correlation Neural Network	.761	54-21-1
Conjugate gradient descent Neural Network	.774	54-30-1
Probabilistic Neural Network	.777	bandwidth = 16s
Backpropagation Neural Network	.779	54x40x1

[*] The area under the curve of the receiver operating characteristic. The standard error for all methods is less than .01.

Adding variables to the prediction models does improve accuracy. Principal component analysis, with one scaling iteration, has an accuracy of .714. Two types of classification and regression trees (CART), pruned and shrunk, demonstrate accuracies of .753 and .762, respectively. Logistic regression with cubic splines for age has an accuracy of .776. In addition to the backpropagation neural network and the probabilistic neural network, three types of neural networks are tested. Fuzzy ARTMAP's accuracy is the poorest at .738. Cascade-correlation and conjugate gradient descent have the potential to do as well as backpropagation. The PNN increases its accuracy to .777 and the backpropagation neural network's accuracy increases to .779. All models except PCA are significantly more accurate than the TNM stage model (SEs are less than .01, p < .01 for all models compared to the pTNM model)

DISCUSSION

For predicting five year survival, several computerized prediction models are more accurate than the TNM stage model using just the TNM variables. The backpropagation neural network is consistently more accurate than the best prediction models, and adding additional variables does increase its accuracy.

We will not present a detailed statistical analysis of these predictive models in this paper. Rather, we will focus on their ability to discover new prognostic factors, especially those that are either nonmonotonic (not constantly increasing or constantly decreasing), or whose prognostic value (the ability to improve predictive accuracy) depends on their interaction with other factors.

There is no reason to believe that all future prognostic factors will be monotonic. Thus, we would like the new prognostic system to be able to capture the predictive power of nonmonotonic prognostic factors. Because the models used in the past to test putative prognostic factors for prognostic value can not discover nonmonotonic factors without knowing in advance the shape of the nonmonotonic factor and adjusting for that nonmonotonic factor prior to the analysis, we must illustrate the features of a nonmonotonic prognostic factor rather than describe an existing nonmonotonic prognostic factor. An example of a very simple nonmonotonic prognostic factor is a laboratory value such as white blood cell count that predicts death at both its low and high values. Table 3 shows a comparison of the accuracy of four prediction models when a simple artificially generated nonmonotonic prognostic factor is added to the TNM variables in the PCE data set.

Table 3. PCE 1983 Breast Cancer Data: 5 year Survival Prediction Accuracy, Nonmonotonic Variable Added to TNM Variables.

PREDICTION MODEL	ACCURACY[*]	SPECIFICATIONS
pTNM Stages	.720	Ø,I,IIA,IIB,IIIA,IIIB,IV
Logistic Regression	.762	no interactions
Probabilistic Neural Network	.935	band width = 0.1s
Backpropagation Neural Network	.948	4-20-1

[*] The area under the curve of the receiver operating characteristic. The standard error for all methods is less than .01.

Since the pTNM stage system can not, by definition, be expanded we have included its accuracy only for comparison. Logistic regression does not capture the predictive power of this simple nonmonotonic prognostic factor, its AUC is .762. Both the PNN and the backpropagation neural network are able to capture the predictive power of the nonmonotonic factor, their AUCs are .935 and .948, respectively.

We can use these data to demonstrate the fact that a multilayer perceptron neural network without a hidden layer, with a logistic transfer function and using as its criterion function maximum likelihood is identical to logistic regression. In the above four variable analysis the logistic regression model has an AUC of .762, a two layer neural network using the maximum likelihood criterion function has a AUC of .761. It should be noted that a two layer neural network using square error as its criterion function, rather than maximum likelihood, produces a result that is very close to, but not identical with, that produced by logistic regression. The AUC for the two layer neural network using square error is .754. It is also the case that a two layer neural network with a linear transfer function is identical to linear regression. Neural networks can do everything that linear and logistic regression can do, and they can do much more.

A good method for determining if there are important nonmonotonic variables or complex interactions is to compare the results of a two layer neural network (or logistic regression) with those of a three layer neural network; if the three layer neural network is significantly more accurate then there are either nonmonotonic variables or complex interactions, or both.

Complex systems are typically dominated by nonmonotonicity or interactions between their components. Cancer is primarily a genetic disease, and it is a complex system. Cancer genes do not act in isolation; oncogenes, suppresser genes, and genetic mutations cause cancer though the complex interaction of the genes and their products. A cascade of genes is required to produce a cancer. Thus, we can not assume that a gene or its product will have an independent prognostic value before it is combined with other genes and/or their products, or that gene interactions are binary, or that there will only be a few simple genetic interactions. Further, we can not specify in advance of the analysis what complex genetic interactions will occur. We need to capture these complex interactions because the prognostic value of the genes and their products can depend on their interactions. Because neural networks with sufficient hidden units can approximate any continuous function to any degree of accuracy, they can, without a priori specification of the important variables, discover these complex interactions and learn the variables that are important.

Neural networks are able to capture the power of nonmonotonic prognostic factors and they are efficient discoverers of complex interactions; thus they are appropriate for the description of complex systems and for the characterization of their effects.

Neural networks often have a large number of parameters (weights), but overfitting (loss of generalization by fitting the patterns in the test data too precisely) can be prevented by keeping the weights small, which reduces the effective number of degrees of freedom. Methods for accomplishing this include penalizing large weights, or stopping the iterative fitting algorithm before the weights have grown to their full size. It is often the case that, when one of these methods is used, predictive accuracy is better than it would be if we simply used a smaller model and fit the data without restriction. When a method is used that reduces the weights that are not being increased by the input variables, the weights to the hidden layer shrink, and when there are only linear relationships present, the hidden layer weights approach zero and the neural network approximates a linear model.

ARTIFICIAL NEURAL NETWORK FOR PATTERN RECOGNITION IN MAMMOGRAPHY

Baoyu Zheng *, Wei Qian, and Laurence P. Clarke

Department of Radiology, College of Medicine and H. Lee Moffitt Cancer & Research Institute
at the University of South Florida, Tampa, FL 33612

ABSTRACT

A novel multistage artificial neural network (MSANN) is proposed for detecting micro-calcification clusters (MCCs) in digital mammography. Two algorithms with Kalman filtering are used for training the MSANN. A new nonlinear decision method is introduced to improve further the performance of the classification. The experimental results show that the sensitivity of this classification / detection is 100% with the false positive (FP) detection rate of less than 1 MCCs per image for limited database of images with biopsy proven MCCs, and show that the ANN detector has the different ability of detection by changing its architecture and parameters. . The proposed methods are automatic or operator independent and provide realistic image processing times as required for breast cancer screening programs. Full clinical analysis is planned using large databases.

1. INTRODUCTION

The importance of mammography for early detection of breast cancer has been well demonstrated in clinical trials and mammography currently offers the best cancer control strategy since the cause of breast cancer is still unknown. The aims of computer assisted diagnosis (CAD) methods are the automatic extraction or detection of suspicious areas in digital mammogram such as micro-calcification clusters (MCCs). These methods serve as a "second opinion" to assist radiologists in performing a clinical diagnosis [1-2].

CAD methods previously reported for digital mammography includes both statistical and non-statistical approaches. Bayesian classifiers, back-propagation (BP) artificial neural networks (ANNs), binary decision trees and asymmetry measures have used for either MCC or mass detection. The reported results on MCC detection from digitized screen film mammograms do not exceed 85% sensitivity for less than 1 FP cluster per image [5].

In this work, a novel multistage ANN with the improving nonlinear detection is presented which consists of two stages, the "detail network" stage and the "feature network" stage. Two algorithms with Kalman filtering (KF): the back-propagation algorithm (BP) with KF [6] and the augment-Lagrange-programming based algorithm (ALP) with KF [7], were employed in training the network. In addition, the function and performance of the ANN are also discussed. The preliminary ANN classification results for twenty images (512*512 pixels) indicate that this pattern recognition (PR) method yielded 100% sensitivity with less than 1 FP clusters per image.

2. MULTISTAGE NEURAL NETWORK AND ITS TRAINING

2.1 Multistage Neural Network with the Nonlinear detection [8]

The Multistage Neural Network is depicted in Figure 1. In this architecture, the first stage is called the "detail network" where all pixel values of a original image is used as its input; while the second is known as a "feature network" where the actual output from the first stage of network and a set of features extracted from the

----

* Baoyu Zheng is with the Department of Telecommunication Engineering, Nanjing University of Posts & Telecommunications, P. R. China; At present, is a visiting Professor at the H. Lee Moffitt Cancer research center at the University of South Florida.

original image are used as its inputs. In our study these features including average, variance, average-energy and energy variance of input image-blocks, of which the variance and the energy-variance are defined by:

$$var = [\frac{1}{M \times N} \sum_{i=1}^{M} \sum_{j=1}^{N} [x(i,j) - avg]^2]^{1/2}$$ (1)

and

$$evar = [\frac{1}{M \times N} \sum_{i=1}^{M} \sum_{j=1}^{N} [x(i,j)^2 - eavg]^2]^{1/2}$$ (2)

respectively, where avg and eavg are the average and the average-energy of a input image-block $x(i,j)$, $i=1,2,...,M, j=1,2,...,N$, respectively. Two of these features, such as average and energy-variance, are used as inputs of the second stage of ANN, other features are then used as detection parameters which will be discussed later.

In this multistage architecture, each stage is three layer feed-forward ANN with a hidden layer, in which the output of a neuron (unit or node) is an integrated sum of weighted inputs. Its output is shaped by a sigmoid-like function and servers as input to the next layer of neurons. By use of training algorithms the neural network can be trained to certain states. The output is given by the following equation:

$$output = \frac{1 - \exp(-\sum_{i} w_i x_i)}{1 + \exp(-\sum_{i} w_i x_i)}$$ (3)

where x_i and w_i are the input and its weight. It has been shown that this structure can form a good approximation to any continuous boundary. The output of the second stage of the ANN can be used as the decision value for classification. In order to improve the reliability and the accuracy of the detection, when we apply the MSANN for the detection of MCCs, the output of ANN at the second stage is modified as

$$output2 = \frac{1 - \exp(-\sum_{i} w_i x_i + v)}{1 + \exp(-\sum_{i} w_i x_i + v)}$$ (4a)

for v>t, and

$$output2 = \frac{1 - \exp(-\sum_{i} w_i x_i)}{1 + \exp(-\sum_{i} w_i x_i)} \frac{1 - \exp(-v)}{1 + \exp(-v)}$$ (4b)

for v<t, where t is threshold value and v is the variance or the energy-variance. The variance is known as the detection parameter because it affects the detection reliability. If the variance is used as the input of the "feature network", we select the energy-variance as the detection parameter; alternatively, if the energy-variance is used as the input of the network, the variance is taken as the detection parameter.

The above modification is based on the fact that in digital mammogram, the areas with micro-calcification clusters and their surrounding normal tissues have the different intensity such as their average, variance, energy and its variance in which the variance or energy-variance potentially plays a more significant role. Generally, the variance (or energy-variance) of the former is more than that of the latter.

2.2 Network Training [6][7]

Two algorithms, the back-propagation algorithm with Kalman filtering (KF) [6] and augment Lagrange programming (ALP) with KF [7], were employed for training the proposed multistage neural network. The former is based on a generalized delta learning rule. And in the latter the training algorithm is regarded as an augmented Lagrange programming problem (an equality-constrained optimization problem) in which the back-propagation of errors is replaced by iteration of state variables (outputs of neurons) corresponding to Lagrange-multipliers. Updating of weights and state-variables can be performed in parallel. As a result, its convergence rate is very fast. Another attractive feature of the ALP-based algorithms is that in training different layers of the ANN are totally mutual-independent. Therefore, it is specially suitable for parallel processing and has significantly better convergence properties than conventional BP algorithms.

Using the above algorithms, the first-stage and the second-stage of the network are sequentially trained. The input, which can be the original image or an enhanced image, is provided to the input layer of the first-stage neural network. The actual output of the first-stage neural network, which has been trained, and a set of features such as variance and energy from the original image, are provided to the input layer of the second-stage neural network. Its output corresponds to the output of whole network. The desired output is provided to the output layer at each stage during the training process.

In both the BP algorithm with KF and the ALP-based algorithm with KF, the update for the weights is based on the following equations[6]:

Output layer weight:

$$W_o(t) = W_o(t-1) + k_o(t)(d_o - y_o) \tag{5}$$

and hidden layer weight

$$W_j(t) = W_j(t-1) + k_j e_j u_j \tag{6}$$

with the Kalman gain vector :

$$k_j(t) = \frac{R^{-1}(t-1) X_{j-1}(t)}{b + x_{j-1}^T(t) R_j^{-1}(t-1) X_{j-1}(t)} \tag{7}$$

and the update equation for the inverse matrix :

$$R_j^{-1}(t) = [I - k_j(t) x_{j-1}^T(T)] R_j^{-1}(t-1) / b_j$$

$$\tag{8}$$

where I is an identity matrix, x is the input at each layer, d_o is the desirable output, and y_o is the actual output. b_j is a "forgetting" factor, u_j is the convergence rate , and e_j is the back-propagation error which is replaced by iteration of state variables corresponding to Lagrange-multipliers in the ALP-based algorithm.

Contrary to the standard BP algorithm which minimizes the mean-squared error with respect to the weights, we minimize the mean-squared error between the desired output and the actual output with respect to the summation outputs (inputs to the nonlinearities) in our study. Error signals, generated by the BP algorithm or state variables corresponding to different Lagrange-multipliers created by the ALP algorithm , are used to estimate values at the summation outputs that will improve the total network error. These estimates along with the input vectors to the respective nodes, are used to produce an updated set of weights through a system of linear equations at each node. These systems of linear equations are solved using a Kalman filter at each layer. Training patterns are run through the network until convergence is reached. The advantages of the above algorithms are:

*Rapid convergence property.
*Low training error(high training accuracy).
*More suitable to large scale networks.
*More suitable to parallel processing.

The last two properties are more promising for the ALP-based algorithm. Table I shows the parameters and the convergence performance of the above approach. As a comparison, the recent results of Wu [4].

Table I Parameters of networks for the classification of micro-calcification

Type of approaches	Number of input units	Number of hidden units	Number of output units	Number of iterations		
				BP [4]	BP with KF	ALPwithKF
Spatial domain	64 (8x8)	5	1	>5000	640	560
	1024(32x32)	15	1	1000	160	120
	4096(64x64)	50	1	------	80	80

The above results are obtained without taking into account parallel processing. If the parallel processing is considered, the ALP-based algorithm will have better performance. Also according to our experiments, when number of input units is larger such as 64 (8*8) pixels, the BP algorithm will have very poor convergence performance, while our algorithm still have good performance for a set of random-selected weights even when number of input units is 4096 (64*64) pixels.

3. RESULTS AND DISCUSSION

3.1 Experimental Results

We first select two types of regions-of-interest (ROIs) from the enhanced mammogram where a hybrid filter with nonlinear filtering and wavelet transform was used to enhance the micro-calcifications [3]: one which includes calcification and one which includes only normal tissue. Once input data are normalized to the range of 0 to 1, the image are processed by the ANN with the nonlinear decision. The "decision" of whether there are or not MCCs in a given region of the image depends on the output of the ANN with the nonlinear decision. In the detection of MCCs, a moving-window, whose size is the same as the training block, is moved one by one on a give image. If the output is more than a given threshold, emperimently selected, the output is identified as MCCs.

A preliminary evaluation of the proposed methods was performed on twenty subimages (512x512 pixels) selected from full digitized mammograms, containing biopsy proven MCCs, perform . The location and geometry of each clusters were determined by an expert mammographer based on visual readings and biopsy results. A truth file was thus established for each of the twenty images, which was used to determine the true-positive (TP) and false-positive (FP) rates of the algorithms. A cluster of three or more calcifications per cm^3 (areas of about 95x95 pixels on the digital images) was a FP, if it was not identified in the truth file.

The ANN classification results indicate that this PR method yielded 100% sensitivity of less than 1 FP clusters per image. The classification time for a 512x512 image less than one minute on a SUN SPARC station 2 computer. The advantage of using two stage ANN was demonstrated by also using single stage ANN. The sensitivity of the classifier with the single stage dropped to about 85 % for the same FP detection rate of MCCs per image. Representative results for two clinical cases are shown in Figs. 2: (a) the original mammogram, (b) the MCC detection result for the two stage ANN, which is the best detection result corresponding to (a), (c) the detection result for the single ANN, and (d) the detection result without the ANN. The second stage ANN structure therefore plays a significant role in this classification scheme.

The advantage of using enhanced data as inputs to the ANN was demonstrated by also using the unprocessed images as inputs to the network. The sensitivity of the later dropped to 81% for the same FP detection rate as the enhanced images. So, the enhancement also plays a significant role in this classification scheme.

3.2 Discussion on the Function and Performance of ANN

Artificial neural networks (ANN) have been shown to be very useful and effective alternatives for implementing intelligent systems in Biology and Medicine, such as adaptive pattern classification and recognition. It has been proved that they perform better and quicker than conventional methods in situations where noise and uncertainty is present. A crucial aspect concerning the network performance is the ability of the network to classify correctly input data, which were not included in its training set. Good ability is a result of appropriate network design. A small number of interconnection weights should be generally used for this purpose, and any priori knowledge about the problem should be included in the network architecture. In our study, the variance (or energy-variance) in (4a) and (4b) just provides such a critical information.

Our recent studies concerning ANN design, indicate that structured neural network classifiers are especially useful when applied not only to a set of features extracted from images, but also to image pixel values, and indicate that the detection accuracy of ANN is strongly dependent on architecture of the neural network and its parameters, specially for the second stage of network. This is because the sensitivity of the different network architecture to parameters is different and the network parameters are obtained for a specified training set. The effect of the network parameter and its parameters upon the detection performance is also shown in Fig. 2, in which (b) and (e) show the detection accuracy for the different network architecture, (b) and (f) show the detection accuracy corresponding the different network parameters for the same training accuracy. It is obvious that their performance is very different for both different network parameters and the different network architecture.

4. CONCLUSION

In this study, a novel multistage ANN with the improving nonlinear decision was applied to enhanced images in order to recognize patterns that may include micro-calcification in digital mammogram. Experimental results have shown that the new approach has the higher sensitivity of classification and the lower FP detection rate than previously reported [6], and indicated that the ANN detector have the different ability of detection by changing its architecture and parameters.

It is the intent to apply these methods to the full digitized images, for both diagnostic and screening image databases, for full clinical evaluation using standard receiver operating characteristic (ROC) analysis [4]. The practical impact of the proposed methods is the fact that they are fully automatic or operator independent with realistic training/classification times or real-time analysis if parallel hardware is used.

REFERENCES

[1] L. P. Clarke, W. Qain, and et al, "Nonlinear filtering techniques for improved classification of mammographic parenchymal patterns in cancer screening," Proc. of the 34th Annual Meeting of AAPM, Calgary, Alberta, Canada, Aug. 1992.

[2] W. Qain, L. P. Clarke, and et al, "Detail preserving tree structured nonlinear filters in mammography," IEEE Trans. Med. Imag., to be published, March 1994

[3] W. Qian, L. P. Clarke, and et al, "Tree-structured nonlinear filter and wavelet transform for micro-calcification segmentation in mammography," Proc. of the SPIE IS&T Conf., San Jose, CA, Jan. 1992.

[4] Y.Wu, et al, "Computerized detection of clustered micro-calcification in digital mammogram Applications of artificial neural networks," Med. Phys. 19 (3), May/June 1992.

[5] W. Zhang, and et al, "Computerized detection of clustered macro-calcification in digital mammogram using a shift-invariant artificial neural network (abstr). Med. Phys. 20:881, 1993.

[6] R. S. Scalero and N. Tepedelenlioglu, "A fast new algorithm for training feed-forward neural networks," IEEE Trans. Signal Processing, vol. 40, no. 1, pp.202- 210, Jan. 1992.

[7] Baoyu Zheng, Wei Qian, and Laurence P. Clarke, " Augment-Lagrange-programming based feed-forward neural networks with application to pattern recognition in mammography," IEEE Trans. Neural Networks, to be submitted, March 1994.

[8] Baoyu Zheng, Wei Qian, and Laurence P. Clarke," Multistage neural network for pattern recognition in mammogram screening," IEEE Int. Conf. Neural Network (ICNN'94), submitted, Dec. 1993.

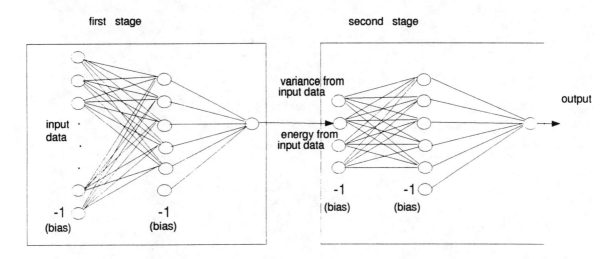

Fig. 1 The multistage neural network architecture for pattern recongniton in mammograms

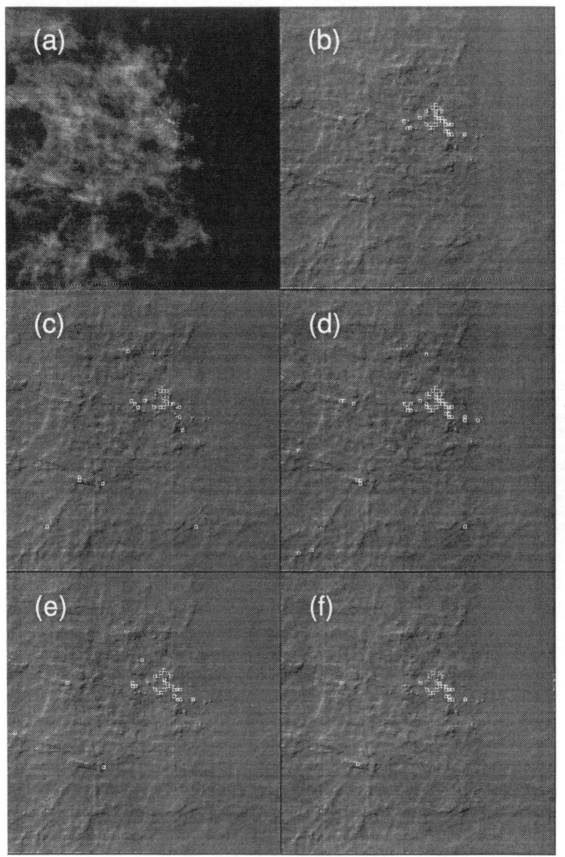

Fig. 2. (a) The original mammograms, (b)the detection result for the two stage ANN, (c) the detection result for the single ANN, (d) the detection result without the ANN, (e) the detection result with the different hidden-layer structure from (b), and (f) the detection result with the different parameters from (b).

Biomedical Application of Neural Networks in JAPAN

Shiro USUI and Naohiro TODA

Physiological Engineering Lab.,
Department of Information and Computer Sciences,
Toyohashi University of Technology,
Tempaku, Toyohashi 441, JAPAN

Abstract

Trends of activities in biomedical application of neural networks in Japan are overviewed. Many efforts are being made in various levels and ares in field of biomedical engineering to realize intelligent medical systems using the neural networks.

1. Introduction

Neural networks as a new technology have been utilized to make applications of real world problems. This new technology is based on parallel distributed processing and regarded as an alternative approach to artificial intelligence (AI) among conventional rule-based approaches. It is well known that the rule-based approach suffers from some problems such as 'the explosion of number of cases'. Because of such problems, the artificial intelligence in biomedical engineering field has not yet been employed for practical use sufficiently, especially in the medical diagnosis.

Neural networks are expected to make a breakthrough for such bottleneck problems, and many efforts are being made in various levels and fields towards the creation of the true intelligent machines.

In this article, such recent activities in field of biomedical engineering in Japan are summarized. First, activities of related Japanese institutes and societies are introduced, and then, issues are classified into the several groups and described respectively.

2. Activities on neural networks in Japanese biomedical engineering

Japanese Neural Network Society (JNNS) already held the 4th annual conference where the wide varieties of advanced applications and neural networks theories were discussed. The Institute of Electronics, Information and Communication Engineers (IEICE) has the group societies on Neuro-Computing, and Medical Electronics and Bio-Cybernetics, and each has more than ten meetings per a year. Furthermore, the Institute of Electrical Engineers of Japan (IEEJ) has systematically investigated on Vision Neural System Engineering under the special group (chaired by S.Usui) for the last three years.

Particularly, two years ago, Japanese Society of Medical and Bio-Engineering organized a professional group on Neuro-Information Processing in Medical Engineering (chaired by S.Usui), which treats applications of the artificial neural networks in medical and bioengineering areas, and they also hold bimonthly meetings on related fields. The issues enumerated in the following sections are taken mainly from the papers reported in NIPME meeting of JSMBE, because they cover most of important neural network related applications in Japanese Biomedical Engineering.

3. Biomedical engineering applications

One of the aims of biomedical engineering is to provide a complete automatic medical system (medical tests, diagnosis, therapy, care etc.). To achieve this, there are so many problems to be observed and solved. Consequently, it is natural that the field of biomedical engineering includes both scientific and technological aspects. From scientific point of view, it is ordinary way to construct and improve models of the phenomena in order to elucidate an interesting natural one. On the other hand, in the technological and engineering viewpoints, it is required to concentrate on making applications using such models. In general, achieved level of the application has tightly been related to the plausibility of the model. Therefore, the situation where researchers in both sides work and publish their results in the same field, is important for higher progress. Especially in the field of biomedical engineering, the situation is different from other fields because the artificial neural networks themselves are one of the biological organism models, called nervous system. These models are not imported from other fields but produced within the field.

Generally, we can say that the areas of interest in Japan can be divided into the three categories : 1) artificial neural networks, 2) artificial organs and 3) diagnosis. We will review them in the following sections.

4. Artificial neural networks

Although the neural networks are expected to make a breakthrough, as mentioned above, the principles of parallel distributed processing on which the neural networks are based, and/or the properties of the neural networks have not been established firmly. Therefore, various theoretical problems are investigated as much as application studies. In biomedical fields in Japan, many researchers also publish their theoretical works. However, attention is not only focused on the theoretical exploration. Wide scale of the neural network architectures and learning techniques gives possibility of a practical use. Let us briefly list some well-known activities in this sphere.

Neocognitron, the artificial neural network proposed by Fukushima, is constructed for a specific task such as image pattern recognition. Through unsupervised learning process, neocognitron gets ability to recognize the input pattern. Neocognitron has been investigated with inputs represented only two gray-levels, and examined how it responses to the multi-level input images (Miura, Takeuchi, Suzuki), and further, to the fractal images (Murata, Wakabayashi, Matsui).

Multilayer feed-forward neural networks which are trained by back-propagation supervised learning algorithm, have ability to approximate arbitrary continuous nonlinear mapping. Due to the universal property, this type of the networks is most widely accepted in Japan. However, some problems have been remained such as requiring of long time for learning, local minima, difficulties in determining the network structures, implementation of variable weight on hardware. To produce useful applications, these problems should be overcome, and the properties of this type of the network should be clarified in practical use.

For example, the fluctuated-threshold effects in the multilayered neural networks are observed (Iwami, Tanaka, Matsui). The Kick Out learning algorithm (Ochiai, Toda, Usui) of neural network is widespread in use to construct a forward dynamics model of human arm (Kawato), prediction model for carp's EEG (Toda, Usui) and so on. It is pointed out that use of AIC (Akaike Information Criterion) for determining network structure has no reasons (Hagiwara, Toda, Usui). Simulation analysis was made on shapes of local minimum (Horikawa). A method for estimating AR(autoregressive) parameters by the neural network referring to the preceding time-course was proposed (Hatakeyama, Uosumi, Ono).

Other types of the networks are also in investigation such as : nonlinear mapping approximation with radial basis function(RBF) (Suzuki et al.), a hysteresis associative memory with ideal information storing-recalling function (Jinno, Saito, Yana), genetic algorithm generated medical data examples (Hasegawa, Arakawa, Kishi).

5. Artificial organs

5.1 Artificial densory systems

Sensory organs of human or animals are entrances to a huge information processing system such as the brain and thus have highly sophisticated organizations. Researchers in this area are concentrated to construct the models for each organ. In this subsection we will introduce the studies classified into the two categories: the visual system and other systems.

5.1.1 Visual system

Visual system is understood to treat more than 80% of total amount of information in sensory inputs to the brain. In this area, many studies elucidate this significant information processing system from the early stages up to the higher central stage.

The classical apparent motion is analyzed using the neural network model (Kita, Sekine, Nishikawa). A feature extracting model on brightness perception with lateral inhibition are constructed (Tsukada, Sasaki, Yagi). There is a proposal of the neural network model of a motion detection taking recruitment into account (Unno, Uchida, Shimodaira). Further, mechanisms of information integration in the middle vision are investigated (Inui, Yamashita).

5.1.2 Other sensory systems

The evidence that on the current level of knowledge the visual system represents the largest information source did not decrease the interest of researchers in other sensory systems. We can also find exciting works related to this domain : the function of extracting inter-aural time difference(ITD) and inter-aural level difference(ILD) in auditory nervous system described by a pulse neuron model (Kuroyanagi, Iwata), the artificial neural network model of the taste nervous system in rats (Katayama et al.), an expression of the odor sensory quantity by the neural networks (Sakuraba, Nakamoto, Moriizumi).

5.2 Artificial prothesis

Artificial legs, arms and other prothesis for handicapped people play very important role in these days. There are several papers on artificial prothesis using the neural networks : a learning control method of a biped locomotive robot (Murai, Kurematsu, Kitamura), an electromyogram pattern recognition system for hand control (Hiraiwa et al.), a control system of optic axis by automatic selection of control laws (Kuwano, Wakamatsu, Suda), identification and control of circulatory system driven by artificial heart (Kondo et al.).

6. Medical diagnosis

Medical diagnosis totally depends on reliable measurement for medical tests. Since every step of diagnosis requires intelligent processes, the neural network approach is mostly used in these areas.

6.1 Measurements
6.1.1 Data compression, restoring and inversion

Multilayer neural networks are utilized for a data compression system of electrocardiogram (Ngasaka, Iwata), and for noise elimination of heart rates data acquired by central monitoring system in a neonatal intensive care unit (Kishi et al.).

The restoration of positron density distribution (the images obtained from positron emission CT) (Kinoshita et al.), or damaged simple X-ray images (Doushita et al.) with the multilayer neural network are discussed. Scattered photon in single photon emission CT is also estimated by the neural networks (K.Ogawa).

Multilayer neural networks or the network inversion techniques are shown to be efficient for the certain inverse problems such as source localization in actual magnetic encephalogram(MEG) data (Kiyuna et al.), and positional estimation in multi-sensor systems (Ogawa, Sase, Kosugi).

6.1.2 Measurement and recognition of images

Since medical images contain much useful information for diagnosis, the machines are required to recognize the images as well as medical doctors. That is one of the wide range of neural network applications which takes an important place in the current research. It can be denoted by the number of related studies such as : segmentation of internal organs (Sakamoto) or extracting 3D shapes of vocal tract and nasal cavity from magnetic resonance images(MRI) (Matsumura et al.), characterization of parenchymal patterns for MR images of patients with liver disease (Yoshino et al.), topographic measurements of the retinal fundus and the neural information processing (Yoshimura), classification of white blood corpuscle (Oshino, Yamamoto), extracting features of stained cell images (Okii, Kaneki, Ono).

Furthermore, the several authors developed the methods for classification of human faces : a self-producing classification method applied for a large number of human faces (Inaba, Kato, Akazawa) and a correlation analysis of human face (Kimura, Nakayama).

6.1.3 Classification of biological signal

There are many kind of biological signals for medical diagnosis, such as electroencephalogram(EEG), electromyogram(EMG), electrocardiogram(ECG) etc. These signals are used for estimating of the states of alive organs, and adequately classified signals are required for diagnosis. Let us introduce some recent works :

- A certain hybrid neural network for classification of time series data (Fujimoto et al.).
- A pattern association network for recognition of mental activity by EEG (Ivanisuky).
- A multilayer feature mapping for recognition of sleep states by EEG analysis (Shimada, Shiina, Saitou).
- A pattern classification for EMG by neural networks (Mori, Tsuji, Ito).
- Spectral analysis and neural network analysis of abnormal ECG (Uosumi, Suzuki, Ono).
- Recognition of ECG using Self-organizing neural network (Suzuki).
- Recognition of P-, QRS-, and T-wave in ECG by neural network (Motoki, Suzuki).
- A personal computer system for ST-segment recognition using neural networks (Suzuki et al.).
- A new parameter for diagnosis, a nonlinear measure of time series using neural network is proposed, and carp's EEG is analyzed by the nonlinear measure (Toda, Usui).
- Estimation of the fetal weight using multilayer neural network (Shigemitsu, Inaba, Kubo).
- Constructing a nonlinear model of the P_{co_2} control system by neural network (Fukuoka et al.).
- Analysis of amino acid sequence by neural network (Iida, Mamitsuka).

6.2 Integrative Diagnosis

Generally, the final diagnosis is established by integrating of the test results. However, highly complicated decision making processes are required through processing of enormous number of medical data. Neural networks have a capability to be powerful tools in these situations.

Neural networks are used for real-time diagnosis whose specific character is structural convertibility to descriptive rules and learning personality (Iida). There is an integrative evaluation method of awake EEG based on quantitative EEG interpretation by means of neural network (Nakamura et al.).

Several practical researchers have constructed diagnosis support systems on workstations or personal computers; for motor functional disorders in upper limb using the neural networks (Motoki et al.), also for mental medicine using probabilistic logic neural networks: mSDN versus AI and Bayesian statistics (Iida et al.), and for chronic liver disease using the artificial neural networks (Oguri et al.).

7. Conclusion

Trends of activities in field of biomedical application of the neural networks in Japan were overviewed. As can be seen in these reviewed studies, the neural networks, also in Japan, are prevailing in sphere of biomedical engineering. One of the remarkable properties of the neural networks is that they can treat so wide class of data, such as binary, categorical, time series, images etc., while other conventional models do not have such a property. Since biomedical engineering usually treats such data, it can be said that the field conquests a good position to make the neural networks more fruitful.

Biomedical Applications of Neural Networks:

VEP's, Cardiology, Neurology

by

Evangelia Micheli-Tzanakou
Rutgers University Biomedical Engineering
Piscataway, NJ 08855-0909 USA
(908)932-2037/3155
e-mail: etzanako@galdalf.rutgers.edu

Introduction

Computer assisted modeling and simulation of complex systems is of growing importance in biomedical engineering. To construct models of multi-dimensional non-linear systems is, in many areas, an extremely difficult and time consuming task. Analytical models have, more than often, to be based on highly simplified assumptions and they often exclude a large number of other factors because the dependencies and relationships are not always clearly apparent. Because of these difficulties scientists and engineers often employ simulations based on observations, clinical data, physiological measurements and other types of data. Neural Networks (NNs) and Fuzzy logic offer an important alternative to analytical approaches. In general one expects NNs to learn their alloted tasks independently — simply by use of examples or training data. As training data previously observed values of different physiological measurements such as brain waves, cardiovascular functions and neurological disorders are used. In classification tasks, measured values are graded either as normal or faulty.

Another method of handling multi-dimensional non-linear systems is fuzzy logic. With fuzzy logic non-linear interrelations can be formulated explicity and in a familiar way. Fuzzy logic is used extensively in control engineering. Fuzzy logic, like NNs, can be used for modeling and for classification purposes. While the emphasis with NNs lies on a system's own discovery of interrelations on the basis of training data, fuzzy logic concentrates on the use of existing statistical knowledge rather than exact data. Fuzzy NNs combine these two approaches.

In order to further simplify computational expertise, some preprocessing of data may be used, where characteristic features of the signals are used as imputs instead of the signals as a whole. Methods that can be used for preprocessing include Fourier Transforms, Wavelet transforms and Karhunen-Loeve expansion. In this paper, work on Visual Evoked Potentials, cardiac infarction detected by echocardiography and its prediction of mortality are examined, as well as the role that education plays in future neurological disorders such as Alzheimer's disease.

I. Detection of Multiple Sclerosis from Visual Evoked Potentials

Most of the NNs training methods are supervised in nature. A supervised system must rely on an accurate and quantifiable label of any input pattern, and generally requires a significant number (at least several hundred) of training example patterns. In using neural networks for the analysis of medical signals there is usually not available a certain pattern label, and if available, the degree of abnormality cannot easily be specified. Perhaps more importantly, there is usually not the luxury of a large volume of training data.

An unsupervised training method does not rely on the accuracy of any external experts, but analyzes only the statistics of the patterns and how they relate to one another. It is therefore not sensitive to errors from a clinical diagnosis. Consequently, it is expected that an unsupervised system will be able to provide a more accurate generalization with fewer training patterns. In this application, both a feature extracting and a clusterining module were trained through the control of the optimization routine ALOPEX [1]-[5]. Upon convergence, the feature extractor implements a Karhunen-Loeve feature extraction [6] and the clustering module performs a modified version of Fuzzy c-Means clustering [7]. For a more detailed discussion of the methods of design of the system, the reader should refer to other works [8].

Multiple Sclerosis is a chronic progressive disease of the central nervous system, the symptoms of which vary greatly from person to person. One of the most commonly afflicted areas is the visual system, with manifestations of varying degrees of blindness, nystagmus, strabismus, ptosis, and hemianopia, and problems with night and color vision (usually blue/yellow and red/green).

A Visual Evoked Potential (VEP) can be described as the resultant electrical signal of a large section of the brain arising from a visual stimulus. Most data collection systems average the signals from many stimulus presentations to improve this signal to noise ratio.

The original 512 point sampled waveform was reduced to a 6 feature set by a feature extraction network. The value of 6 features was chosen by plotting the converged neuronal output variance of each cell in the feature extraction network against the number of features chosen. When this is done, as in Figure 1, the curve shows diminishing information return when using more than 6 features. Interestingly, this value agrees with another study using the Karhunen-Loeve expansion with VEP signals [9]. When the patterns are clustered with the ALOPEX modified Fuzzy c-Means (FCM) algorithm, the use of an entropy cluster validity measure showed an optimal solution for separation of the patterns into two clusters (Figure 2).

With an appropriate selection of a threshold, the entire population of definite MS (DMS) patients can be separated from the control subjects. The unsupervised system is contructed with linear feedforward elements. This simplifies the reconstruction of cluster centers which were determined by the ALOPEX modified FCM routine as input patterns. In this way, the reasoning of the system can be analyzed. Figure 3 illustrates the cluster prototype centers reconstructed as input patterns for each of the Black/White patterns. It is clear that there are significant differences between the waveforms which are identified by each cluster, and many of these discrepancies are from portions of the waveforms which up to now were largely ignored or considered irrelevant in clinical diagnosis with VEP. This could aid physician training if additional experiments are conducted to deduce whether these discrepancies are real and diagnostically relevant.

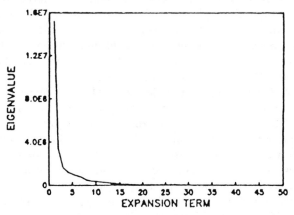

Figure 1 - The eigenvalue (or feature cell output variance) as a function of the number of the feature for the Black/White VEP patterns.

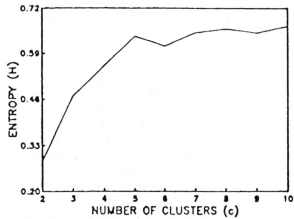

Figure 2 - The entropy cluster validity measure for the VEPs generated by Black/White Checkerboard stimulation as it aries with the number of clusters.

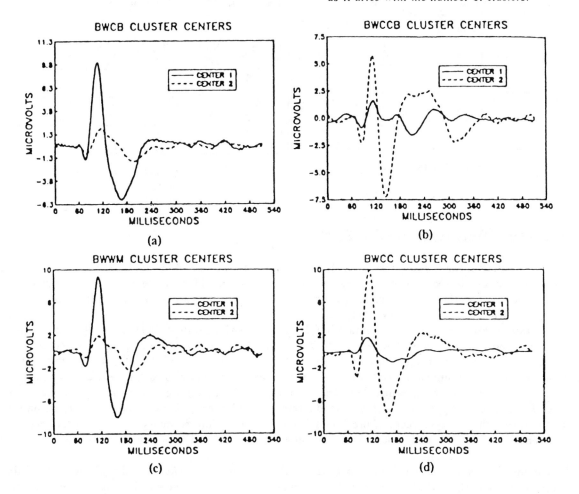

Figure 3 - The cluster centers reconstructed as pattern waveforms for the clustering results of the Black/White (a) Checkerboard, (b) Circular Checkerboard, (c) Windmill, and (d) Concentric Circle.

II. Reflected Ultrasound for Myocardial Infarction

Myocardial infarction is the No. 1 cause of adult mortality in the USA. Patients who suffer acute myocardial infarction develop a scar in the left ventricle, which is located on a portion of the left ventricular wall. It is possible to study the scar using modalities such as X-ray, CT and MRI imaging, but these modalities are not as practical since they cannot image in real-time. Ultrasound imaging is more commonly available and is noninvasive. However, it is often difficult to obtain satisfactory tissue images from these patients. One reason is that there is excessive scatter of ultrasound when it travels through heart and lungs. At present, ultrasound imaging equipment is built to get pleasing images. During the processing of ultrasonic signals and imaging some useful information is lost. Ultrasonic tissue characterization uses all the information before it is lost [10]-[13]. In this study we use the myocardial echogram to study myocardial infarction by modifying the structure of a perceptron combined with a feedback algorithm ALOPEX, which is used in the analysis of distribution of gray levels of M-mode ultrasonic images. An area of interest is selected on the anterior or posterior wall of the septum of the left ventricle during a whole cardial cycle. This area is then normalized to the size of 30 * 10 and sent into the neural network. After training the neural network with subjects having myocardial infarction, normal subjects and subjects having very noisy images, we test it with unknown subjects. This neural network can be updated with new data continuously. The ALOPEX algorithm is used in the feedback. ALOPEX shows a very strong convergence. During the retraining it has shown powerful flexibility. It overcomes local minima very easily due to an added random noise.

In this study we use a multilayer perceptron with nonexclusive outputs, and we also use noisy images to train our neural network in order to eliminate human-preprocessing. 35 normal subjects, 18 scar subjects and 16 noisy subjects (total of 189 templates) are used in the training and 55 subjects are used in the testing. The testing results are shown in Tables 1 and 2. For different cutoff values (0.2 and 0.3) these results show that the method works well, but not so well for scar patients. The reason is that there are not enough scars in the training set.

Cutoff 0.2	Normal 177	Hypoki- netic 14	Akinetic 7	Diskine- tic 0	Scar 15
Testing Scar	7	2	1	0	7
Testing Normal	122	5	4	0	4
Testing Unknown	48	7	2	0	5

Table I   Testing Table with 0.2 Cutoff Value

Cutoff 0.3	Normal 177	Hypoki- netic 14	Akinetic 7	Diskine- tic 0	Scar 15
Testing Scar	9	2	2	0	7
Testing Normal	128	6	4	0	4
Testing Unknown	40	6	1	0	4

Table 2   Testing Table with 0.3 Cutoff Value

III. Vital Status after Myocardial Infarction

Patients who survive the acute phase of a myocardial infarction (heart attack) have an increased risk of mortality persisting up to 10 years or more. Estimation of the probability of being alive at a given time is important to the patients and their physicians, and is usually ascertained by the use of statistical methods. We have employed artificial neural networks to achieve this goal.

A large database MIDAS (Myocardial Infarction Data Acquisition System) including all 49,250 myocardial infarctions that occurred in the state of New Jersey in 1986 and 1987, with follow-up as long as five years, was used in the development and testing of the neural networks. Nineteen variables of the MIDAS database that were associated with vital status, by univariate statistics, were chosen as input variables to the network. These were: sex, age, diabetes mellitus, arrhythmia (irregular heartbeat) congestive heart failure (weak heart), stroke, peripheral vascular disease (of the legs), hypertension (high blood pressure), pulmonary disease, liver disease, chronic kidney disease, anemia, cancer, obesity, occurrence of previous myocardial infarction, coronary bypass surgery, percutaneous transluminal coronary angioplasty, and two insurance classifications associated with low resource utilization (self-pay and Medicaid).

Single and multi-layer neural networks, using ALOPEX with input patient variables of the MIDAS data set were used to predict six month mortality. Because the information included in the database is not sufficient to allow the exact prediction of vital status (dead or alive) in all patients with 100% accuracy, we developed a neural network able to categorize patients according to the probability of dying within a given period of time, rather than predicting categorically whether a patient will be dead or alive at a given time in the future.

We observed that there were many instances where two or more patients had identical input characteristics while some were dead and some alive at the end of the study period. For this reason, it is difficult to train a standard neural network. Since there is no unique output value for all input cases, the network has difficulty converging to a unique set of solutions.

To alleviate this problem, a conflict resolution algorithm was developed. The algorithm takes templates with identical input vectors and averages each of their input characteristics to produce a single case. Their output values of vital status are averaged, producing, in effect, a percent probability of mortality for the particular set of input characteristics. In addition, 10 output nodes were used in the final layer, each corresponding to a range of percent-chance of mortality. (E.g. Node 1: 0 - 10%, Node 2: 10 - 20%, etc.). The output node containing the correct probability value was set to a value of 1.0, the others to 0.0. In this manner, the network should be able to provide percent-probability of mortality, and also resolve input case conflicts.

The neural networks constructed to predict vital status of patients with acute myocardial infarction were able to categorize cases with a fair degree of success. Although their accuracy was not 100% this probably cannot be achieved with the limited information contained in the database. On the other hand, this method of classification of patients was based on easily and cheaply obtainable information that is routinely collected on all patients who are hospitalized for heart attacks. A formal comparison of the accuracy of neural networks and standard statistical techniques [14] may ascertain the practical usefulness of neural networks in these applications.

Further improvement of the performance of the neural networks may be obtained by additional training and the use of different network architectures.

This work has implemented two new modifications to the standard neural network methodology, i.e., conflict resolution by averaging the expected outputs corresponding to identical input cases and assignment of a measure of reliability to the output based on the number of cases with a given input vector that were used in training the network.

IV. Educational Effects on Future Neurological Disorders

Recently the concept of brain reserve capacity (BRC) as an explanation of threshold theory [15] has come under much study. While there is no direct measure of BRC, it is assumed to be indirectly associated and proportional to general intelligence and educational level. Threshold theory attempts to explain observed instances of the brain's robustness to central nervous system disease and aging. A study by Zhang, et al. [16] linked low education levels to an increased prevalence of dementia. The possible protective effect of higher education on symptom progression in Alzheimer's Disease was also reported by Stern [17]. Many other studies support a quantitative threshold at which clinical symptoms are manifested, yet little is known about this threshold. It is believed that brain reserve capacity may alter the threshold level.

Much of our knowledge about biological systems is derived from the study of simple models, a practice applied to several fields of engineering and is applicable to the study of the brain as well. A neural network model capable of reproducing some aspects of brain function, namely pattern recognition and classification, is presented. The model is studied in both unimpeded and increasingly impaired states, representing normal and aged effects. The performance of each of the networks, representing various levels of education or BRC, are compared.

In order to mimic the effect of education, a neural network was trained (or educated) to various levels of response. Testing of each network's performance occurred under identical test conditions. Each network was presented noisy images and correct recognition was examined. Figure 4 shows the results averaged over 100 trials. The four curves represent the various levels of training; that is, with 50%, 60%, 70% and 80% maximal learning. The x-axis corresponds to the amount of gaussian distributed noise applied to the input patterns, while the ordinate reveals the number of targets correctly identified. Input training patterns were binary vectors of length eight.

While the plot of Figure 4 clearly shows that increased training improves the network's ability to recognize noisy patterns, how does increased training effect a network's susceptibility to a progressive decline, as that seen in aging, and presumably dementia? Progressive deterioration of the network was modeled as a random noise disruption of the stored weights. Gaussian noise added to the weights, with increasing standard deviations, represent this progression. The greater the amount of noise applied to the learned sets of weights, the more inaccurate they become. Note that initial constraints restricted the learned set of weights to values between -1 and 1. It was found that this damage reduced the networks' robustness by degrading its ability to perform the same recognition task.

Figures 5 and 6 show these results for two different standard deviations of the Gaussian noise imposed on the weights of the trained network. Notice that for higher education levels, the network is more resistant to damage. These results show that lower education levels suffer more from degradation of weights, than do the higher trained networks (Compare starting points of Figs. 5 and 6).

The plots of Figures 5 and 6 show the progressive impairment. By comparing these results to Figure 5 (undamaged) it is evident that higher "education" makes the system more robust to this type of damaging. All curves demonstrate loss of recognition ability with increasing impairment, yet the 50% and 60% curves show a markedly sharper decline that do the 70% and 80% networks. From these results, there appears to be a threshold training level, between 60% - 70% where the system suddenly becomes more robust.

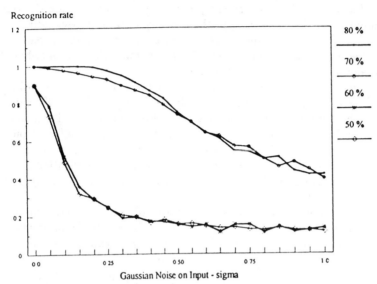

Figure 4 Recognition vs. Noise on Input Patterns

Network Damaged with Gaussian Noise

Sigma = 0.01

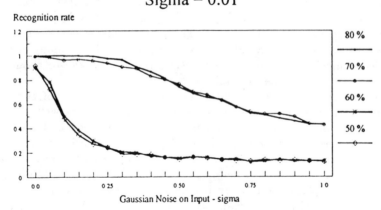

Figure 5 Progressive Impairment Model---Early Stage

While the network is simple, it is by studying the simple that we learn more about the complex. Our ability to show that the level of training can act as a deterrent for memory loss in a progressive deterioration is potentially important. Our results support those of Zhang [16] in a study of The Prevalence of Alzheimer's Disease in China.

The model presented here seems to indicate that there exists a minimum threshold education that is necessary to gain this benefit. The results show little or no difference among 50% or 60% training, nor is there a great difference among 70% and 80% trained. However, there is a large difference between the 60% and 70% trained network under progressive deterioration. Further work includes finding if there is indeed a threshold within this region, and to study what happens at that point and why we see a great increase in the robustness of the system.

Network Damaged with Gaussian Noise
Sigma = 0.05

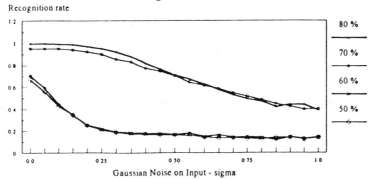

Figure 6. Progressive Impairment Model---Middle Stage

References:

[1] Harth E. and E. Micheli-Tzanakou, 1974. "A Stochastic Method for Determining Visual Receptive Fields", Vision Research 12: 1475-1482.

[2] Melissaratos and E. Micheli-Tzanakou, 1990. "The Parallel Character of the ALOPEX Process." J. of Med Syst. 13(5):243-252.

[3] Micheli-Tzanakou, E. 1990. "When a Feature Extractor Becomes a Feature Generator." IEEE EMBS Mag. Special Issue on Neural Networks, pp. 19-22, (Sept.).

[4] Dasey T. J. and E. Micheli-Tzanakou, 1989. "A Pattern Recognition Application of the ALOPEX Process with Hexagonal Arrays". Proc. IEEE Intern. Joint Conf. on Neural Networks, Vol. II: 119-125.

[5] Micheli-Tzanakou, E., T. J. Dasey and T.-S. Chon, 1989. "ALOPEX - Pattern Recognition and Probability Receptive Fields using Rectangular and Hexagonal Arrays." In Medicon '89, 296-297.

[6] Fukanaga, K. and Koontz, W.L.G., 1970. "Application of the Karhunen-Loeve Expansion to Feature Selection and Ordering". IEEE Trans. on Computers C-19(4), 311-318.

[7] Bezdek, J.C., Ehrlich, R. and Fell, W,: 1984. "FCM: The Fuzzy c-Means Clustering Algorithm: Computers and Geosciences, 10(2):191-203.

[8] Micheli-Tzanakou, E. and Dasey, T.J.: "Unsupervised global optimization: applications on classification of handwritten digits and visual evoked potentials", IEEE Intern. Conf. on Systems, Man and Cyber. 737-744 (1992).

[9] Urbach, D., Gur, M., Pratt, H. and Peled, R. 1986. "Time domain analysis of VEP's: Detection of Waveform Abnormalities in Multiple Sclerosis", Invest. Ophthalmol. Sci. 27:1379-1384.

[10] Popp, R.L., "Recent Experience with Ultrasonic Tissue Characterization", The American J. of Cardiology, Vol. 69, pp 112H-120H, Jun 18, 1992.

[11] Thomas, L.J. III, S. Wickline, J. Petez, B. Sobel and J. Miller, "A Real Time Integrated Backscatter Measurement Systm for Quantitative Cardiac Tissue Characterization," IEEE Trans. on Ultrasonics, Ferroelectrics and Frequency Control, Vol. UFFC-33, No. 1, pp. 27-32, Jan. 86.

[12] Weng, L., J. Reid, P. Shankar, K. Soetanto, and X. Lu, "Nonuniform Phase Distribution in Ultrasound Speckle Analysis-Part I: Background and Experimental Demonstration," IEEE Trans. on Ultrasonics, Ferroelectrics and Frequency Control, Vol. 39, No. 3, pp. 352-359, May 1992.

[13] Sleefe, G.E. and Lele, P. "Tissue Characterization Based on Scatterer Number Density Estimation", IEEE Trans. on Ultrasonics, Ferroelectrics, and Frequency Control, Vol. 35, No. 6, pp. 749-757, Nov. 1988.

[14] Schlant, R.C., Forman, S., Stamler, J., Canner, P.L., "The natural history of coronary heart disease: prognostic factors after recovery from myocardial infarction in 2789 men. The 5 year findings of the coronary drug project", Circulation, Vol. 66, pp. 401-414, 1982.

[15] Satz, P. 1993. "Brain Reserve Capacity on Symptom Onset After Brain Injury: A Formulation and Review of Evidence for Threshold Theory", Neuropsychology, Vol. 7, No. 3 273-295.

[16] Zhang, M., Katzman, R., Salmon, D., Jin, H., Cai, G., Wang, Z., Qu, G., Grant, I., Yu, E., Levy, P., Klauber, M. R., and Liu, T. "The Prevalence of Dementa and Alzheimer's Disease in Shanghai, China: Impact of Age, Gender and Education", Annals of Neurology, 27, 428-437, 1990.

[17] Stern, Y., Alexander, G., Prohovnik, I., and Mayeux, R. "Education provides a cognitive reserve against the clinical manisfestations of Alzneimer's disease: Evidence from regional cerebral blood flow. Soc. of Neuroscience Abs. 17, 1258, (1991).

Computational schemes and neural network models of human arm trajectory control

Tamar Flash* and Michael I. Jordan[+]

* Department of Applied Mathematics and Computer Science, The Weizmann Institute of Science, Rehovot, Israel, 76100.

+ Department of Brain and Cognitive Sciences, Massachusetts Institute of Technology, Cambridge, MA, 02139.

Abstract

The control of multi-joint arm movements requires of the central nervous system (CNS) to perform complicated transformations from the desired behavioral goals into appropriate neural commands to the muscles. Although, little is known about the control algorithms used by the brain in performing these transformations- the picture emerging from a series of behavioral and modeling studies is that of a hierarchically organized system whereby higher levels are involved in planning desired spatial hand trajectory plans while lower levels are concerned with their execution. Here we discuss evidence for this view provided by several recent studies of motor adaptation to various kinds of external perturbations unexpectedly introduced during arm reaching movements. To further investigate the nature of the internal motor representations subserving human arm trajectory formation a neural network model was developed and its main underlying hypotheses and predictions are described. Finally, the implications of these two studies with regard to the internal organization of arm movement generation processes will be discussed.

1   Introduction

Traditionally, motor control studies have focused on anatomical and physiological questions and on single-joint movements. Over the last decade, however, it has become increasingly clear, that to gain deeper insight into motor control, the problems underlying the generation of multi-joint movements and the "computations" performed by the brain in the solution of such problems must also be investigated. Since motor behavior is fundamentally multi-dimensional and might be alternatively represented in muscle, joint, or end-effector spaces, two fundamental questions in motor control research are in what space(s) or coordinate frame(s) are motor behaviors represented and what rules govern the selection of particular movements among the infinite number of possible ones.

Experimental observations of human unconstrained point-to-point reaching movements have indicated that these movements are characterized by straight hand paths and symmetric bell-shaped velocity profiles that tend to remain invariant, despite variations in movement direction, speed, and initial position (Morasso, [17]; Hollerbach & Flash, [14]). These kinematic features of reaching movements were accounted for based on optimization theory (Flash & Hogan, [8]). Following an idea originally suggested by Hogan [12] in the single-joint case, the smoothness of multi-joint arm movements was quantified in terms of the integral of squared jerk of the hand in space as follows:

$$C_J = \frac{1}{2} \int_0^{t_f} \left(\left(\frac{d^3x}{dt^3}\right)^2 + \left(\frac{d^3y}{dt^3}\right)^2 \right) dt \tag{1}$$

where $\vec{r}(t) = (x(t), y(t))$ is the vector of hand position and t_f is the movement duration. It was then suggested that among all possible hand trajectories that join some specified initial and final positions, the motor system selects to generate those trajectories that minimize the above cost function. Such trajectories follow spatial straight hand paths and have symmetric, bell–shaped velocity profiles. The minimum-jerk model was also shown to successfully account for curved, obstacle-avoidance and drawing movements (Flash and Hogan [8]; Viviani and Flash [21]. The main tenet of the model was, however, that arm motions are planned in terms of hand trajectories in extrapersonal space.

To execute any desired motion plan, appropriate joint torques and muscle activation patterns must be generated. One possible way that this can be done is by first transforming the desired hand trajectory plans into appropriate joint rotations by solving the inverse kinematics problem. Then, the necessary joint torques can be derived by solving the "inverse dynamics" problem. Given the complicated dynamic interactions existing between the moving skeletal segments during multi-joint movements, and the complexities involved in the need to distribute the necessary joint torques among a highly redundant set of muscles, it was hypothesized that the motor system must have developed alternative means and control schemes for motor execution that do not involve explicit joint torque and muscle force computations. One such scheme is the so called equilibrium trajectory model (Feldman,[4]; Hogan, [13], Flash, [5], Bizzi et al., [2]). According to this model, the viscoelastic properties of muscles might play an important role in allowing the motor system to bypass the need for explicit torque computations. Thus, movements are generated by gradually shifting the limb equilibrium position, along the desired motions while the equilibrium positions are internally coded by specifying the appropriate neural activities to sets of agonist and antagonist spring- like muscles. Alternatively, the recent progress in neural network research, has led to a renewed interest in the possibility that while the motor system may not solve from scratch the inverse kinematics and dynamics computations each time a new movement is about to be generated, successful solutions to these problems are embedded into the synaptic connections between the elements of biological cortical and subcortical networks which are enrolled in various motor functions. (e.g, Alexander et al.,[1]). According to the "hierarchical approach" to human arm trajectory control expressed above and elsewhere (e.g., Flash [6]), the motor system is hierarchically organized and desired behavioral goals are gradually transformed into actual movements following a step-by-step transformation whereby higher motor levels specify the desired motion plans while lower levels are concerned with their execution. Recently, an alternative view was suggested (Uno et al., [20]). Thus, while it was again postulated that the motor commands are directly calculated from the goal of the movement, represented by some performance index, by contrast to the minimum-jerk model, Uno et al. ([20]) have postulated that the underlying criterion for movement selection involves the optimization of the rate of change of joint torques. This latter objective of performance is critically dependent on the dynamics of the musculoskeletal system. Thus, while according to the minimum-jerk model, kinematic motion plans are selected independently of the movement dynamics or external load conditions, according to this alternative model, substantially different hand trajectories are expected to be generated for movements performed in different regions of the workspace, or under different load conditions. These two alternative classes of models would also have substantially different predictions with respect to the characteristics of the movement output following load adaptation.

Motor adaptation studies

In a recent study (Flash and Gurevich, [10]; Gurevich, [11]), the question of what is learned during load adaptation was examined. For this purpose an experimental paradigm was used whereby static elastic loads were unexpectedly introduced during human reaching toward visual targets. While the first few movements immediately after the application of the load were misdirected and missed the final target, following a relatively small number of practice trials (5-7) in the presence of the load, the movements tended to converge toward the ones seen in the unperturbed case, i.e., to follow straight hand paths with symmetric velocity profiles (Flash and Gurevich, [7]). These observations have therefore indicated that human arm trajectories tend to obey the same kinematic plan independently of the external force conditions thus supporting the idea of separate levels of trajectory planning and execution. Similar conclusions were arrived at in another recent study (Shadmehr and Mussa-Ivaldi, In Press) whereby velocity-dependent force fields were used to perturb the movements and the perturbed trajectories performed in the presence of the new force fields were again found to converge toward the ones seen in the unloaded case. In a third related study, Wolpert et al. ([10]) have used altered visual feedback conditions that caused an increase in the perceived curvature of aiming movements achieved through computer manipulations. The increase in the perceived curvature of the unconstrained point-to-point movements led to significant corrective adaptation in the curvature of the actually produced movements; the hand movements became curved, thereby reducing the visually perceived curvature. These results have therefore again suggested that arm trajectories are planned in extrinsic visual space and are incompatible with assumptions of the minimum-torque change model or similar models assuming movement generation based on the optimization of dynamics-based objectives of performance or ones which are based on intrinsic coordinates (e.g., joint angles, muscle forces, etc.).

2 Learning from spatial deviations: a neural network model

In a recent study (Jordan, Flash and Arnon, In Press) a somewhat different approach to modeling point-to-point reaching movements than the one used in the minimum-jerk [8] model was taken. The motor control system was assumed to prefer motions of the hand along straight paths in space. In attempting, however, to account for the temporal aspects of the movements, the characteristic velocity profiles were hypothesized to implicitly arise from the dynamical properties of the hardware subserving the generation of reaching movements, namely the arm and muscle dynamics, including muscle activation–contraction properties, and the dynamics of the neural networks that transform movement commands into muscle activations. The model was implemented as a neural network that learns to perform movements by correcting errors between the desired and actual performance, the errors being the spatial deviations of the hand from straight paths. The network was based on a general approach to motor learning known as "distal supervised learning" (Jordan and Rumelhart, [16]).

A fundamental problem in motor learning theory concerns the nature of the corrective feedback that is available to the learner. In many motor learning problems corrective information is not provided directly to the learner in terms of motor command errors. Rather, desired behavior is specified in terms of the outcome of movement as assessed by various sensors. This general problem has been referred to as the problem of the "distal teacher" in motor learning. One possible way for transforming a distal sensory error (e.g., in the limb spatial position) into signals for correcting the proximal motor commands is by making use of forward models of the kinematics and dynamics of the controlled plant ([16]). The role of the forward models is essentially that of providing a mechanism for transforming distal sensory errors into proximal motor errors. The forward models must themselves be learned by correcting the error between predicted sensory outcomes and actual sensory outcomes. Once those models have been partially trained they can be used to train the controller. The composite system, composed of the controller and the forward models is trained based on the difference between the desired sensation and the actual sensation. While the composite system is being trained the forward models are held fixed and only the controller is altered.

Modeling and simulation

The model that we implemented ([9]) generated neural inputs to a set of muscles, thereby producing joint torques for the arm. The model consisted of a cascade of neural networks, beginning with the *central controller* which received as inputs the initial and the desired final hand positions. The outputs of the central controller were fed to a *muscle dynamics network* which provided a forward model of the muscle activation–contraction dynamics. The outputs of the muscle network, which represented predicted muscle forces, were then fed into the network representing an internal forward model of the two–joint arm dynamics. The outputs of this *forward dynamics network* corresponded to the predicted joint accelerations. They then were integrated once to yield joint velocities and twice to yield joint positions, which were then fed to the network designated as the *forward kinematics network*, which transformed predicted joint positions and velocities into predicted hand positions and velocities. Finally, the hand position outputs were fed back to the central controller network, thus providing recurrent feedback that drove the network forward in time based on recurrent algorithms developed by Jordan ([15]) to deal with trajectory formation problems. The overall network was provided with inputs only at the first time step and was allowed to run for the entire duration of the movement. Additionally, outputs of several of the forward models were fed back either to other forward models or to the central controller.

All of the forward models in the chain, with the exception of the muscle model, were trained separately prior to the training of the controller using the backpropagation algorithm ([18]). The muscle model was designed based on the form of the differential equations describing biological muscles. Various architectures were tested for the central controller. In the final design, however, the network was composed of one layer of input units, one layer of output units, and two layers of hidden units. The inputs to the central controller consisted of the initial hand position and the desired final hand position. The latter inputs were set at the start of each movement and remained fixed throughout the movement. The former inputs were updated via the recurrent feedback by the output of the entire composite network. Each hidden unit was provided with a recurrent loop onto itself, and there were direct connections from the input layer and from both hidden layers to the output layer. This internal connectivity provided additional dynamics to the controller and was found to be important in the simulation studies. Finally, there were four outputs of the central controller network which provided neural inputs to the four muscles.

Because the controller and the musculoskeletal system are dynamical systems, errors at the final time step can be caused by poor choices of actions at any of the earlier time steps. To deal with this temporal credit assignment problem, the "backpropagation–in–time" algorithm was used (Rumelhart, Hinton, & Williams,[18]). The existence of the forward models did not alter the manner in which the backpropagation–in–time was performed. Errors were passed backward through the forward models and the controller at each time step and only the weights in the controller were actually changed at the end of this process. That is, only the controller was adjusted so as to minimize the performance error.

The effects of using several types of performance errors were tested. We found that requiring of the arm to reach the target with prescribed end-point position, velocity and acceleration is inadequate for the purpose of generating human–like trajectories in the case of two–joint planar movements. Thus, an algorithm whereby errors in the path of motion of the hand were utilized in the training of the network was developed. A desired movement was assumed to be specified as a path in Cartesian space. The continuous path was approximated by a sequence of equally-spaced via points. Errors were then generated as spatial discrepancies between these via points and the path of the actual motion of the hand. These errors were provided continuously to the network during the course of the movement. Our goal in developing this via point algorithm was to avoid making assumptions that the learner has prior knowledge of the specific times that the via points should be reached. This is consistent with our assumption that the training data specifies the desired *paths* of movements, not their *trajectories*.

The via point algorithm which we developed is closely related to the "elastic net" algorithm of Durbin and Willshaw ([3]). The algorithm associated to each via point a window in space. During the course of motion, when the hand passes through the window associated with a given via point, an error vector is generated. The window dropped off smoothly as a Gaussian function in space, thus the magnitude of the error vector was modulated as a function of the distance in space of the hand from the center of the window. Moreover, the spatial dimension of the window was decreased over the course of learning. Specifically, the modulated error vector at time t was given by the following expression:

$$\mathbf{e}(t) = \sum_{i \in via} s(t) e^{-\frac{1}{2\sigma^2} \|\mathbf{x}_i^* - \mathbf{x}(t)\|^2} (\mathbf{x}_i^* - \mathbf{x}(t)), \qquad (2)$$

where $\mathbf{x}_i^*$ is the spatial center of the window associated with the ith via point, $s(t)$ is a temporal modulation function, and σ is a scale factor. The sum in this expression is taken across all of the via points defining a given movement. Note that the via point centers are not indexed by time—the position of the hand ($\mathbf{x}(t)$) is compared to all via points at each moment in time. We assume that the spatial scale factor σ decreases during learning, starting from a large value and decreasing as the performance improves. We also assume that the modulation function $s(t)$ is a triangular–shaped function that activates the via point windows (synchronously) at the beginning of a movement and turns them off at the end of a movement. All of the via points are allowed to pull the hand toward the desired path at each moment in time. The magnitude of the pull diminishes for via points that are far away. In the central region of the path there are essentially equal numbers of via points on both sides of the hand position, thus the pull from far–away via points and tend to cancel. Away from the central region, however, there are either more via points ahead of or behind the hand position. Consequently, the via point algorithm has an effect of either accelerating or decelerating the hand in the direction of the target. Thus, the via point algorithm has a natural and sensible effect on both the spatial and temporal aspects of the motion.

In the experiments conducted to examine the network performance, the network was trained to generate 32 trajectories, 16 for each of two initial positions. After the performance reached a criterion on these training trajectories, the weights of the controller network were fixed and its generalization performance was evaluated on a novel set of trajectories. The network was trained to perform reaching movements towards static targets with small final errors and small spatial deviations from the straight line connecting the initial and final targets. The model was then used to predict the internal neural commands and muscle activation patterns that might be involved in the generation of the smooth ("minimum-jerk") movements observed in humans and monkeys while reaching towards visual targets. At its final design stage and following training it was found that the entire network generates smooth biological-like movements and that the neural commands to the muscles obey the same temporal activation patterns to those experimentally observed in human subjects during reaching movements.

These results have therefore indicated that rather than utilizing explicit smoothness costs, trajectories resembling minimum jerk trajectories might result from the inherent smoothing properties of the neural controller, the muscles and the arm mechanics. Such smoothing properties arise from the time constants of these systems and tend to regularize the trajectories acquired by the controller. The via point algorithm also smoothed the motions. This occurred because the error vector provided by the algorithm changed smoothly at nearby points in space. We also relied on the via point algorithm to constrain the spatial properties of the movements, in particular to yield quasi–straight line movement. Our hypothesis was that these two constraints alone are sufficient to produce human–like movement. That is, we hypothesized that the temporal properties of trajectories are constrained by two factors: the explicit constraint of producing straight–line paths of motion in conjunction with the implicit smoothing properties of the dynamical systems underlying the movement.

3 Summary

In this article, two recent studies dealing with motor learning and adaptation in the context of human arm reaching movements were discussed. The result from our load adaptation study [7]) and those of others ([19], [10]) have indicated that in the performance of the motor task of reaching toward visual targets, the motor system aims at achieving very particular kinematic plans for the movement trajectories regardless of the external load conditions. A neural network for reaching movements was then presented. Given that the model was shown to successfully predict realistic arm trajectories and muscle activation patterns, this may provide evidence in support of idea that during unconstrained reaching movements the motor system aims at achieving straight paths for the hand and that the typical observed bell-shaped velocity profile is an emergent feature of the control system. Moreover, the neural network modeling work has emphasized the significance that internal models of arm kinematics and dynamics may play in motor learning and adaptation. Finally, neural network models of the kind presented here may subserve further investigations aimed at probing into the internal motor representation underlying the control of multi-joint motor behavior and might be useful in various biomedical applications such as the development of adaptive control methods for neuroprostheses.

References

[1] Alexander G.E., DeLong M.R., and Crutcher M.D. Do cortical and basal ganglionic motor areas use "motor programs" to control movement? *Behavioral and brain sciences*, 15:656–665, 1992.

[2] Bizzi E., Hogan N., Mussa-Ivaldi F.A., and Giszter S. Does the neurvous system use equilibrium-point control to guide single and multiple joint movements. *Behavior and Brain Science*, 15:603 –613, 1992.

[3] Durbin R. and Willshaw D. An analog approach to the travelling salesman problem using an elastic net method. *Nature*, 326:689–691, 1987.

[4] Feldman A.G. Once more on the equilibrium-point hypothesis (λ model) for motor control. *Journal of Motor Control*, 18:17–54, 1986.

[5] Flash T. The control of hand equilibrium trajectories in multi-joint arm movements. *Biological Cybernetics*, 57:257–274, 1987.

[6] Flash T. The organization of human arm trajectory control. In Winters J.M. and Woo S.L.Y, editors, *Multiple Muscle Systems. Biomechanics and Movement Organization*, pages 283–301. Springer-Verlag, 1990.

[7] Flash T. and Gurevich I. Human motor adaptation to external loads. Technical Report 2, Annual International Conference of the IEEE Engineering in Medicine and Biology Society., 1991.

[8] Flash T. and Hogan N. The coordination of the arm movements: an experimentally confirmed mathematical model. *Journal of Neuroscience*, 7:1688–1703, 1985.

[9] Flash T. Jordan M.I. and Arnon Y. Learning arm trajectories from spatial deviations. *Journal of Cognitive Neuroscience*, In Press.

[10] Ghahramani Z. Wolpert D.M. and Jordan M.I. On the role of extrinsic coordinates in arm trajectory planning: Evidence from an adaptation study. *submitted*, 1994.

[11] Gurevich I. *Strategies Strategies of motor adaptation to external loads during planar two-joint movement.* PhD thesis, Dept. of Applied Mathematics & Computer Sc., The Weizmann Institute of Science, 1993.

[12] Hogan N. An organizing principle for a class of voluntary movements. *Journal of Neuroscience*, 4(11):2745–2754, 1984.

[13] Hogan N. The mechanics of multi-joint posture and movement. *Biological Cybernetics*, 52:315–331, 1985.

[14] Hollerbach J.M. and Flash T. Dynamic interactions between limb segments during planar arm movement. *Biological Cybernetics*, 44:67–77, 1982.

[15] Jordan M.I. Motor learning and the degrees of freedom problem. In Jeannerod M., editor, *Attention and Performance, XIII*, pages 796–836. Hillsdale, NJ:Erlbaum, 1990.

[16] Jordan M.I. & Rumelhart D.E. Forward models: Supervised learning with a distal teacher. *Cognitive Science*, 16:307–354, 1992.

[17] Morasso P. Spatial control of arm movements. *Experimental Brain Research*, 42:223–227, 1981.

[18] Rumelhart D.E., Hinton G.E., and Williams R.J. Learning representations by back-propagating errors. *Nature*, pages 533 – 536, 1986.

[19] Shadmehr R. and Mussa-Ivaldi F.A. Geometric structure of the adaptive controller of the human arm. Technical report, Massachusetts Institute of Technology, 1993.

[20] Uno Y., Kawato M., and Suzuki R. Formation and control of optimal trajectory in human multijoint arm movement - minimum torque-change model -. *Biological Cybernetics*, 61:89–101, 1989.

[21] Viviani P.& Flash T. Minimum-jerk, two-thirds power law and isochrony: converging approaches to the study of movement planning. *Journal of Experimental Psychology: Perception and performance*, In press.

Computer-assisted Pap Smear Screening Using Neural Networks

Laurie J. Mango, M.D., Robert Tjon, and James M. Herriman

Neuromedical Systems, Inc.
Two Executive Boulevard
Suffern, NY 10901

Abstract

The PAPNET® Cytological Screening System is designed to increase both the accuracy and efficiency of screening cytological specimens, in particular the cervical (or "Pap") smear. The system provides a semi-automated means of detecting cervical smear abnormalities which can be missed by conventional manual screening methods. The PAPNET system includes both image processing and neural network classifiers to select 128 of the most abnormal cellular scenes from each smear. These scenes are evaluated by a trained cytologist who makes the final diagnosis.

The paper describes current medical practice and the challenges in automating this process. The PAPNET system's architecture and major functional elements are described. Special considerations for training and evaluating the neural networks used to classify the complex scenes found on Pap smears also are discussed.

The Pap Smear and Cervical Cancer Detection

The Papanicolaou-stained cervical smear has long been recognized as one of the greatest advancements in cancer prevention. Since its introduction 40 years ago as a method of screening for abnormalities of the uterine cervix, the "Pap" smear has been instrumental in reducing cervical cancer mortality by more than 70% in the United States[1]. These smears are screened in pathology laboratories by trained cytologists who microscopically examine slides to detect evidence of this disease or its precursors. Such evidence is found through morphological changes in some cells on the smear. The pre-cancerous phase progresses slowly and if found early usually can be treated effectively.

Manually screening Pap smears is a fatiguing, tedious and error-prone task. Up to 100 smears, each containing 50,000 to 400,000 cells, can be examined by a cytotechnologist each day. Habituation is difficult to avoid, as over 90% of all smears are normal. On a smear which does contain evidence of disease, a very small number (typically 1/10th of 1% or less) are actually diagnostic. Screening is akin to searching for a needle in a haystack where most haystacks have no needles. These factors contribute to a false-negative rate (proportion of true positives called negative) estimated to be from 20% to 40%.

---

[1] *Cancer Facts and Figures 1993.* American Cancer Society, p13

The nature of Pap smear screening and its ubiquity (an estimated 70 million taken in the U.S. annually), make automating some or all of the process an attractive option. Historically, computerized classification of the cells found on Pap smears has proven to be a difficult task. It is difficult even to reliably segment objects (cells and clusters) in the complex and overlapping scenes intrinsic to these smears. In practice, smear preparations vary greatly in staining, thickness, background and the presence of artifacts.[2] Finally, many stages and degrees of abnormality exist which must be reliably distinguished from the overwhelming number of "normal" cells which suffuse even "positive" smears. For these reasons, development of automated systems has been a great challenge.

The PAPNET Cytological Screening System

The PAPNET System serves as an adjunct to current medical practice by automating the search for potentially abnormal cells on the smear. These selected cells are then interpreted by a trained cytologist. The complete system includes two units: a Scanner which is located in a central processing facility and a Review Station located in the pathology laboratory. The Scanner uses both conventional image processing techniques and neural networks to identify 128 of the most abnormal appearing cellular scenes on each slide. Digital color images of each scene are recorded by the Scanner. These images are then viewed on the Review Station by a cytologist who "triages" each slide as either "Negative" or "Review", with the later indicating the need for microscopic examination.

The Scanner includes an automated microscope with a robotic arm for loading and unloading slides. After loading, the image processor is used during the low magnification pass over the slide to produce a map identifying areas of cellularity. Next, during the medium magnification pass over the mapped areas, the centers of suspicious cells and clusters are marked by the image processor so that the neural network can assign a score to each marked object. The score reflects its resemblance to the "abnormal" objects used to train the network. During the final, high magnification pass, color images are stored of the 64 single and 64 cluster cell scenes with the highest neural network scores.

The image processor uses size, shape and color to identify suspicious cells and clusters while eliminating those which look "normal" or are deemed to be artifacts. Separate neural networks are used to score single cells and clusters. Both are feed-forward, back-propagation networks created through supervised training on positive (abnormal) and negative (normal) libraries. The libraries consist of gray-scale images which are used as inputs for the networks.

The PAPNET system is currently in use in the United States as part of several clinical investigations. Abroad, it is being used for the routine screening of cervical smears.

---

[2]Mango LJ,: *Computer-assisted Cervical Cancer Screening Using Neural Networks.* Cancer Letters, In Press 1994.

PAPNET System Design Objectives

The PAPNET system addresses three major design objectives:

1. Use the conventionally stained Pap smear
2. Maintain sensitivity to the variety of diagnostic cells encountered
3. Maintain the throughput rate required for practical use

The conventionally stained Pap smear presents severe challenges for computerized analysis. As described above, the typical smear contains hundreds of thousands of cells, may of which overlap or are massed into dense clusters. A wide variety of cell types, artifacts and debris are frequently present. The age of the patient, unrelated disease states, as well as how and when the sample was taken can have a substantial effect on the number and type of cells on the smear. Staining can vary greatly from laboratory to laboratory and from batch to batch within a laboratory. Such highly variable, natural scenes present tremendous difficulties for standard algorithmic pattern classifiers.

The progression and presentation of the disease states themselves are also highly variable. Disease progression is usually a relatively slow process with cells evolving from normal to atypical to dysplastic to pre-invasive and then invasive states. In the early stages of this process, the size and darkness of the nuclei increase. Also, the ratio of the nuclear to cytoplasmic area increases. As the disease develops, the nucleus progressively fills the cell, while the cell size decreases. In the final stages, the nucleus can be easily mistaken at typical screening power for debris or white blood cells. An automated system should be sensitive at each step in the disease progression. Such nonlinear changes can easily confound simple classification schemes.

Most fundamentally, the interpretation of cytological abnormality cannot be defined absolutely by a standard set of rules. Many types, stages, and degrees of abnormality exist representing a disjoint set of morphologies. In many cases, equally well-trained and experienced cytologists can arrive at different diagnoses which cannot be adjudicated by any *objective* analysis of the available data. This *subjectivity* is a very problematic aspect of cytology, presenting many gray areas which cannot be precisely defined. But such definition has been a prerequisite for developing useful automated cytological systems. [3]

For a practical system, there is a limit to the scale and complexity of processing applied to solve these problems. There are many sophisticated image processing and classification techniques developed for research environments which can be useful for such difficult subject matter. Unfortunately the computational load imposed makes them unsuitable at the present time for practical application. Digitizing a Pap smear at a useful resolution can yield many gigabytes of image data. Even with special purpose hardware, processing resources must be husbanded and directed at the most likely targets.

---

[3]Mango LJ, and Herriman JH: *The PAPNET Cytological Screening System*. Compendium on the Computerized Cytology and Histology Laboratory, In Press 1994.

Hierarchical Classification

The PAPNET system architecture includes a series of classifiers, which work together to meet the objectives of the application. These are:

1. Primary Classifier - Algorithmic image processor
2. Secondary Classifier - Neural network
3. Ultimate Classifier - Cytologist

Because of the inherent difficulty of completely automating the process, the cytologist must remain the system's ultimate classifier. The objective thus becomes automating the search for abnormality, not making an automated diagnosis. By directing the cytologist's attention to the most likely areas of abnormality, the effects of habituation are minimized while the (still unmatched) abilities of the trained human interpreter are enhanced. The productivity of the cytologist can be greatly increased, since the 128 cellular scenes chosen can be reviewed in about 1 minute vs. 5 minutes for conventional microscopic screening.

Owing to the difficult job the automated portion of the system must perform, neural networks were chosen for use as the secondary classifier. They excel at robust pattern recognition and are ideally suited for the highly variable nature of the Pap smear. Neural networks "learn" the same way cytologists do - by generalizing from "training sets". The non-linear relationship between cell morphology and disease state can be accommodated much more easily with neural networks than traditional algorithmic or rule-based systems. The neural networks use gray-scale images as inputs, as these were found to be more effective for classification than image feature sets.

Conventional image processing algorithms were chosen for use in the primary classifier for reasons of efficiency. Neural network algorithms are computationally intensive and would require prohibitive resources to analyze every area (or even each object) on a slide. Since most objects on the slide are not diagnostic (even on a "positive" slide), the image processor is used to focus the neural networks where they are most efficiently used. Since image processing algorithms can be readily accelerated with available hardware, this is a practical approach. The image processor reduces the hundreds of thousands of objects on the slide by an order of magnitude or more by eliminating objects which can be confidently classified as "normal" (i.e. non-diagnostic).

Neural Network Development

The performance in a given application of a neural network depends on the type of network used, the libraries used for training and the training methodology. Through experimentation, it was found that a standard back-propagation architecture yielded the best results.

Because of the highly variable nature of both the positive and negative universes encountered by the neural networks, large libraries were used for training. They were initially built by cytologists from example cells culled from several different laboratories' slides. Once the first libraries were completed, the supervised method was used to train the network. During the training session care was taken to avoid overtraining the neural network by constantly monitoring its performance against a test library.

Test set performance, in conjunction with statistical error measurement served to assess the balance between minimizing the classification error rate and maximizing generalization. Once it completed training, the neural network would be used on actual slides and its performance evaluated. If the results were unsatisfactory, misclassified objects from the test slides were added to the negative libraries. The positive libraries were expanded by adding correctly classified objects from the test slides and or by manually adding positive examples from the slide which were missed. The final libraries contained many thousands of cells taken from hundreds of slides.

The system test process was difficult and time consuming because many slides had to be scanned, with the results accumulated and interpreted. Because of the nature of the application, this interpretation was largely subjective in many cases. During development, it was often found that "improvements" to the neural networks that made them sensitive to certain "difficult to find" cells made the networks much less sensitive to other cells which were correctly classified before. Fine-tuning the networks was an empirical and heuristic process. This is probably not a unique situation for neural network developers.

The great imbalance between the number of positive and negative cells in a positive smear poses special concerns for the PAPNET system's automated classifiers. Even "obviously" positive smears frequently contain over 1000 negative objects for each diagnostic cell. Since diagnostic cells can vary so much in their morphology, a danger exists in "losing" all of the cells by making the neural networks too specific. On the other hand, since a trained cytologist reviews all of the 128 images produced by the system, only a few (as little as one) of the images presented need to be diagnostic for the system to be successful.

The solution to this somewhat unusual set of sensitivity and specificity constraints is to present examples across the entire range of abnormality. The classification cascade's is designed such that no stage could unintentionally block out all of the diagnostic cells. The neural classifiers are not trained to maximize the number of positive cells, but to accommodate the cost of rejecting fewer negative objects by preserving diversity.

Clinical Trial Results

The PAPNET Cytological Screening System is currently being used to analyze conventionally prepared cervical smears in a variety of investigational studies. Several large clinical trials, involving a total of more than 60,000 smears have been completed or are currently in progress.

The system may be particularly useful in rescreening cervical smears because of its sensitivity to the types of cytologic abnormalities typically missed by manual screening. Such cases usually contain few abnormal cells, the very small cells characteristic of advanced disease or abnormality manifested exclusively as clusters or fragments.

For example, in a recently published study from the Netherlands[4] the system was shown to detect cancer cells in smears which were repeatedly misdiagnosed during manual screening. Ten archived false-negative smears from patients with histologically proven invasive cervical carcinoma were selected for rescreening by two pathologists; 10 smears, which were true-positive for invasive carcinoma, were used as controls in addition to 10 true-negative smears. Boon *et al* showed that during PAPNET-assisted rescreening, all false-negative cases were detected by PAPNET, displaying abnormal cells or abnormal epithelial fragments, and all of the smears studied were subsequently reclassified by both pathologists as suspicious or carcinomas.

---

[4]Boon ME, Kok, LP: *Neural Network Processing Can Provide Means to Catch Errors That Slip Through Human Screening of Pap Smears.* Diag. Cytopath. 1993

Data Compression for Long Time ECG Recording Using Neural Networks
– Clinical Evaluation and Hardware Design –

Yasunori NAGASAKA   Akira IWATA

Dept. of Electrical and Computer Engineering,
Nagoya Institute of Technology, Showa, Nagoya, 466 Japan
E-Mail: tako@mars.elcom.nitech.ac.jp, iwata@mars.elcom.nitech.ac.jp

Abstract

Data compression system using neural networks for long time ECG recording has been designed. BPNN (neural network trained by back propagation) and PCANN (neural network which computes principal component analysis) are used for data compression. We have compared their performances with existing methods SAPA and TOMEK in our previous study. MIT/BIH Arrythmia database was used for evaluation. Observing the reproduced waveforms, BPNN and PCANN had almost the same performance, and they were superior to SAPA and TOMEK concerning the accuracy of reproduction. The reproduced waveforms were clinically eveluated by 10 cardiologists. 10 kinds of waveforms, which were selected by a cardiologist, were presented to the cardiologists. They gave the score 1 to 5 to each reproduced waveform according to whether the waveform had serious problems which will influence diagnosis. We summed up the scores and investigated the relationship between the summed scores and PRD, CC and the compression rate. Finally we discuss the design of the hardware implementation utilizing a DSP.

1 Introduction

Holter monitoring system provides the function of long time ECG recording and is useful to detect cardiac disorders and arrhythmia, which are often hard to detect by usual short time ECG recording. Existing Holter monitoring systems are utilizing an analog magnetic tape for storing ECG data. However the use of an electronic device like an IC memory card is expected instead of the magnetic tape in the future. By replacing the magnetic tape with the electronic device, improvement of stability, durability, reliability and ease of maintenance can be realized. However, some data compression technique is still required to use the IC memory card, due to the large volume of digitized ECG data.

We proposed a data compression technique using neural networks. In the previous papers[1][2], we evaluated the performances of BPNN (neural network trained by back propagation) and PCANN (neural network which computes principal component analysis) in our system from several points of view. We compared their performances with the existing methods. Both BPNN and PCANN showed better results than the others. They showed 1.1 to 1.4 times higher compression rates than the others to achieve the same accuracy of the reproduction (13.0% of PRD (Percent Root-Mean-Square Difference) and 99.0% of CC (Correlation Coefficient)). Observing the reproduced waveform (RW), BPNN and PCANN had almost the same performance, and they were superior to the others. But one question was remained through the experiments. When we observed the RWs which processed by different methods, we noticed the extremely different RWs even though their estimated accuracy by PRD and CC were almost equal. So our question is whether the criteria for evaluation like PRD, CC really reflect the error rate which will influence diagnosis.

Here we try to give one answer to the question. We mainly discuss the clinical evaluation of the RWs reproduced from the compressed data processed by some compression methods. To evaluate objectively, we asked 10 cardiologists to judge the accuracy of the reproduction. They gave the score 1 to 5 to each RW regarding whether the RW had serious problems which will influence diagnosis or not. We summed up the scores and investigated the relationship between the summed scores and PRD, CC and the compression rate. Finally we discuss the design of the hardware implementation utilizing a DSP.

2 Neural Network Model and Principle of Data Compression

The architecture of BPNN is shown in the left part of Fig. 1. This network consists of 3 layers (input, output and 1 hidden layer). The point of this architecture is the hidden layer where the neurons are limited to very few number than that of input and output layer. The input and the output layer have the same number of neurons. BP[3] is used as the learning rule. PCANN has quite similar shape to BPNN except for the bias neuron. PCANN has no bias neuron. The connection weights between hidden and output layer w_{jk} are the duplication of w_{ij}. Learning algorithm of PCANN is described in Ref.[4].

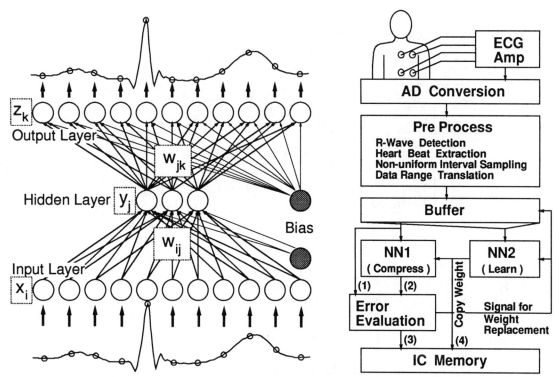

Figure 1: (Left) Architecture of BPNN. (Right) Functional block diagram of the ECG data compression system.

In BPNN and PCANN, the data compression principle is the same. Both input and output layers deal with one heart beat period of the ECG waveform. Learning is carried out to give the network the ability to reproduce the same waveform as the input one on the output layer. Before the compression starts, w_{jk} are recorded for later reproduction. By recording the activation levels of the hidden neurons instead of input data (which are equal to original waveform) while processing, data compression is carried out. The input waveform can be reproduced only from the recorded connections and activation levels of the hidden neurons. The compression rate is approximately given by the ratio of number of neurons in the hidden layer to that of the input layer.

3   ECG Data Compression System Using NN

The functional block diagram of the ECG data compression system is shown in the right part of Fig. 1. The detail of the algorithm is described in Ref.[2]. The important feature of the system is that the system has 2 NNs which work in parallel. While NN1 is compressing the data, NN2 continues to learn with the current data in the buffer and keeps the latest connection weights, which follow the latest changes of the waveform.

Data compression process is progressed as follows. The well-trained connection weights of NN2 are duplicated on NN1 and are also stored to the IC memory before the compression starts (4). After the compression work starts, if the accuracy of RWs is kept, the activation levels of hidden neurons are recorded ((2)→(3)) instead of the original waveform (1). Sudden disturbed waveforms may appear, and in that case the original waveform is recorded ((1)→(3)). When the waveform changes and the changes are continuously appeared, RW's error may increase and the signal for the weight replacement is generated. As a result, the connection weights of NN1 are replaced by those of NN2, and the new connection weights are stored to the IC memory again (4). The replaced new connection weights are well-trained by NN2 and can follow the latest change of waveform. Thus NN1 can keep the accurate reproduction and a proper data compression is always carried out.

Table 1: 10 symptoms list included in test data sets.

No.	Symptom	Datafile	Time
S-1	Paced beat	MIT102	01:00
S-2	Isolated QRS-like artifact	MIT105	17:58
S-3	Left bundle branch block beat	MIT109	01:00
S-4	Aberrated artial premature beat	MIT113	08:29
S-5	Premature ventricular contraction	MIT119	01:00
S-6	Normal beat	MIT119	01:30
S-7	Right bundle branch block beat	MIT124	01:00
S-8	Nodal (junctional) premature beat	MIT124	05:08
S-9	Fusion of ventricular and normal beat	MIT124	10:30
S-10	Ventricular flutter wave	MIT207	00:45

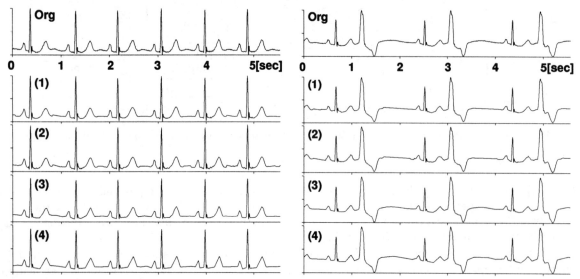

Figure 2: Comparison of the original waveform and the reproduced waveforms. Org: original, (1): BPNN-2, (2): PCANN-5, (3): SAPA-8, (4): TOMEK-11. Numbers after the name of method correspond to the index in Fig. 3.

4   Clinical Evaluation

4.1   Method

We used MIT/BIH Arrhythmia Database for evaluation. This database includes 48 sets of various ECG waveform from the normal one to many kinds of arrhythmia. We asked the cardiologist to choose the typical waveform examples which represent the usual case of Holter recording. As a result 10 examples were selected. Table 1 shows the 10 symptoms included in the examples.

For each example, 12 RWs (4 methods: BPNN, PCANN, SAPA[5] and TOMEK[6], × 3 different error thresholds) were generated. One set of data which were presented to the cardiologists for evaluation consisted of 10 sheets. Each sheet included 1 symptom and consisted of 13 waveforms, where first one was the original waveform and the others were the RWs. The RWs were randomly arranged and presented to the cardiologists. The examples of the original and the RWs are shown in Fig. 2. Figure 2(Left) shows the examples of normal beat and Fig. 2(Right) shows the examples of arrhythmia.

When we asked the cardiologist to choose the typical examples, we also asked how accurate the RWs were so that they will aid in proper diagnosis. According to the answer to our question, we could know that the

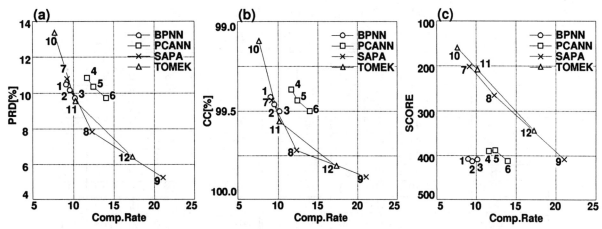

Figure 3: Compression rates versus PRD, CC, Score in BPNN, PCANN, SAPA and TOMEK.

cardiologist's requirement was high, and changed the error threshold to the smaller value than the one in the previous study. As a result almost all the RWs achieved under 11.0% of PRD and over 99.3% of CC.

Figure 3(a) shows the relationship between the compression rate and PRD. Similarly Fig. 3(b) shows the relationship between the compression rate and CC. Each curve indicates a different method, and each point on one curve is the average of 10 symptoms and indicates the result with different error threshold. If the points and the curve of one method are closer to the origin of the graph, the results of the method are better than the others. It can be seen from the results that BPNN, SAPA and TOMEK have the same level of performance. That is, they are placed on almost the same curve. PCANN showed slightly bad performance. It is placed above the others.

To evaluate the RWs clinically, we asked 10 cardiologists to judge the accuracy of the reproduction. One set of data which consisted of 10 symptoms were presented to the cardiologists. For each symptom, one original waveform and 12 RWs were presented, as described before. We randomly presented the RWs to avoid the cardiologists' preconception, so that they could not know by which method each RW was processed. We asked them to give the score 1 to 5 to each RW depending on how serious problems which would influence diagnosis were found in the RW. Each score's meaning was as follows.

5 : No problem which influence diagnosis, acceptable.

3 : Minor problems are seen, acceptable or not, depending on the case.

1 : Serious problems which influence diagnosis, not acceptable.

Scores 2 and 4 were only used in the case that the cardiologists hesitated to make a decision of 5 or 1. They meant that the RW was a little better or worse than score 3. We also requested them to leave the comments on the data sheets regarding the points which they evaluated as good, bad, insufficient, not acceptable, or must be improved. From those comments, we can know the cardiologists' way of thinking and their requirements.

4.2 Result

We summed up the scores for each RW. Table 2 shows the result. One RW can get the score 10 to 50. "Total" in the table shows the summed score of 10 symptoms, and means the total performance of the method with a certain error threshold. The number 1 to 3 added to the name of method, for example B"1" or P"2", means different error threshold. The Number 1 is the case of large error threshold, and in that case the compression rate become high but the score is low. Number 3 is the opposite case. Figure 3(c) shows the relationship between the summed scores and the compression rate. Difference of the results was considerably large between PRD, CC and the cardiologists' score. That is, according to PRD and CC, BPNN and PCANN were evaluated as the same level to the middle range of the result of SAPA and TOMEK. On the other hand, the cardiologists evaluated that BPNN and PCANN were equal to the highest level of accuracy of SAPA and TOMEK. Regarding this result, we can say that PRD and CC evaluate one side of the waveform, and they are not completely the same to the cardiologists' evaluation. In the cardiologists' evaluation, BPNN and PCANN were superior to SAPA and TOMEK.

Analyzing the comments for the RWs, the cardiologists' evaluation about each method became clear. From their comments, BPNN and PCANN have similar characteristic about reproduction and SAPA and TOMEK

Table 2: Scores for each reproduced waveform.

Symptom	B1	B2	B3	P1	P2	P3	S1	S2	S3	T1	T2	T3
S-1	47	46	43	40	37	39	17	22	40	13	17	29
S-2	37	42	38	42	42	42	12	20	28	12	13	23
S-3	42	42	43	41	42	45	14	15	29	12	13	17
S-4	40	39	39	45	42	45	18	37	39	15	29	42
S-5	41	42	42	39	40	37	25	30	44	21	27	48
S-6	39	41	40	32	37	44	18	22	48	14	14	37
S-7	40	39	39	32	34	35	18	25	41	13	22	34
S-8	35	40	39	35	40	40	27	32	41	22	25	33
S-9	45	40	44	43	34	44	19	21	48	19	19	38
S-10	41	41	41	41	40	41	33	41	50	19	29	43
Total	407	412	408	390	388	412	201	265	408	160	208	344

Note: B1–B3: BPNN, P1–P3: PCANN, S1–S3: SAPA, T1–T3: TOMEK.

are also similar about reproduction. All methods can completely reproduce the peak amplitude of R wave and R–R interval. The difference mainly appears on P wave or T wave or sometimes QRS complex, and the delicate shape or curve of those waves were pointed out. In BPNN and PCANN, the typical opinions were about P wave, for example "lack of P wave", "faked P wave", "hard to find the start and end point of P wave", "change of P wave's shape", and so on. However this result means that no serious problem exists on the other part. The accuracy of P wave should be improved in BPNN and PCANN. In SAPA and TOMEK, the typical opinions were about poligonal shape, for example "not curved ST–T", "hard to find P or T wave", "different starting of QRS complex", and so on. P wave and ST–T were pointed out many times. They need delicate curves to be reproduced, and hence the poligonal shape may especially stand out.

5 Hardware Design

We are designing the hardware implementation. Figure 4 shows the fundamental design of the ECG Data Compression System. We planned to use the DSP designed for cellular phone as the processing unit. This type of DSP requires low electrical power consumption and includes an A/D converter. We will utilize the A/D converter for the preprocessing of the digitized data. The system consists of 3 boards, which are the main board, the analog board and the display board. The main board has the DSP, ROM, SRAM, IC memory card interface, and such, on it. The analog board has an ECG amplifier and a DC power supply. The display board has an LCD display module and switches. The system can transfer the data to a computer via serial interface. The DSP works continuously when the system is turned on. The total requirement of the electrical power is not small, even if we use a model with low power consumption. The life of the existing battery is not so long. It will be difficult to make the system work the whole day at the present time. The development of long life and compact battery is expected.

6 Conclusion

We presented the result of clinical evaluation and the hardware design of ECG data compression system using neural networks. BPNN and PCANN are used for data compression. We generated the RWs by BPNN, PCANN, SAPA and TOMEK. The RWs were clinically eveluated by 10 cardiologists. 10 kinds of waveforms, which were selected by a cardiologist, were presented to the cardiologists. They gave the score 1 to 5 to each RW regarding whether it had serious problems which will influence diagnosis or not. We summed up the scores and investigated the relationship between the scores and PRD, CC. Regarding the result, we can say that PRD and CC evaluate one side of the RW, and they are not completely the same to the cardiologists' evaluation. In the cardiologists' evaluation, BPNN and PCANN were superior to SAPA and TOMEK. Analyzing the cardiologists' comments, the characteristics of each method became clear. They pointed out that the problem of BPNN and PCANN is about the P wave, and the problem of SAPA and TOMEK is about their poligonal shape. Finally we discussed the design of the hardware implementation utilizing a DSP.

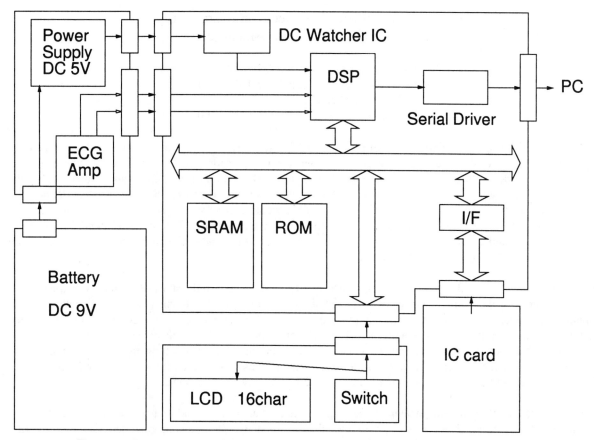

Figure 4: Design of the ECG Data Compression System Using Neural Networks.

Acknowledgement

We thank Prof. Kazunobu YAMAUCHI, Dr. Makoto HIRAI, and other cardiologists of Nagoya University Hospital for the evaluation of the ECG waveforms.

References

[1] Nagasaka,Y., Iwata,A. : "Data Compression of Long Time ECG Recording Using BP and PCA Neural Networks", *IEICE Trans. Inf. & Syst.*, Vol.E76-D, No.12, pp.1434–1442, Dec., 1993.

[2] Nagasaka,Y., Iwata,A. : "Performance Evaluation of BP and PCA Neural Networks for ECG Data Compression", *Proc. Int. Joint Conf. Neural Networks*, Nagoya, Vol.1, pp.1003–1006, 1993.

[3] Rumelhart,D.E., Hinton,G.E. and Williams,R.J. : *Parallel Distributed Processing*, Vol.1,2, MIT Press, 1986.

[4] Oja,E., Ogawa,H. and Wangviwattana,J. : "Principal component analysis by homogeneous neural networks, Part I: the weighted subspace criterion", *IEICE Trans. Inf. & Syst.*, Vol.E75-D, No.3, pp.366–375, Mar., 1992.

[5] Ishijima,M., Shin,S., Hostetter,G.H. and Sklansky,J. : "Scan-Along Polygonal Approximation for Data Compression of Electrocardiograms", *IEEE Trans. Biomed. Eng.*, Vol.BME-30, No.11, Nov., pp.723–729, 1983.

[6] Tomek,I. : "Two Algorithms for Piecewise-Linear Continuous Approximation of Functions of One Variable", *IEEE Trans. Comput.*, Vol.C-23, No.5, pp.445–448, 1974.

Finite training sample size effects on neural network pattern classification in low-dimensional feature space

D.G. Brown, M.P. Anderson, R.F. Wagner, A.C. Schneider[*]
Center for Devices and Radiological Health, FDA
Rockville, MD 20857
[*]Stanford University, Stanford, CA 94309

ABSTRACT: Clinical applications of neural networks are frequently hampered by a paucity of available data. In this study we examine the effect of training set size on network performance for a simple classification task. Following the work of Wagner et al.[1] for classical statistical (likelihood-ratio) classifiers, this is done within the context of adding a new, perhaps very noisy or highly correlated feature to an existing input data set. Results are similar to that of the previous study, demonstrating that for small data sets, additional noisy/correlated features degrade network performance. Sophisticated statistical resampling techniques including the "jackknife," Fukunaga-Hayes group jackknife, and "bootstrap" to remove small-sample bias and estimate performance variation are examined and found to offer significant advantages.

INTRODUCTION: Limited patient number often is a significant constraint in the study of medical decision making for a particular clinical condition. Especially in the initial stage of algorithm development, insufficient data is usually a significant problem. Two approaches to improving decision performance are to seek additional features from the existing patients--even though these features may be much noisier or be highly correlated with the original features-- and to use more sophisticated statistical techniques to wring further information from the data at hand. These approaches have been studied by Wagner et al. for conventional statistical decision rules[1,2] and have been extended in a recent paper[3] and the present investigation to include neural network techniques.

Shortage of patients leads to both incomplete training and incomplete testing--and to a conflict with regard to how best divide the patient population between these two phases of a study. We are concerned here only with the first phase: Given a training population of size N (denoted 2N in references 1 and 2) divided equally between the two classes, how close to ideal performance can be achieved?

METHODOLOGY: The type of detection task used in this study is illustrated in figure 1. Two feature vectors are to be separated, one centered at the origin, $\mathbf{0}$ $(0,...,0)$, and the other at the unit vector, $\mathbf{1}$ $(1,...,1)$. The original feature vector is two dimensional, and a third feature is added to "improve" performance. The vectors are Gaussian distributed with equal covariance matrices and therefore are ideally separated by a linear surface (line, plane--or hyperplane for a higher dimensionality task).[4] Notice in figure 1 that the perceived improved separation of the two Gaussian clouds for the 3D case is accomplished because the length of the $\mathbf{1}$ vector is $\sqrt{n}$, where n is the number of dimensions (In this and the following similar 3D figures, the ordinate is the third feature dimension, and the abscissa is the positive diagonal between the other two dimensions). For the equal-variance, zero-correlation case (covariance matrix $\mathbf{C} = \mathbf{I}$ in figure 1) the ideal decision surface is the plane perpendicularly bisecting the line segment joining the centers of gravity of the two clouds (or more accurately, the family of planes perpendicular to that line corresponding to decision surfaces that generate the entire receiver operating characteristic (ROC) curve for this task).

Five different cases were considered. The first two of these, cases A and B, are the 2D and 3D identity matrix covariance cases shown in figure 1. Cases C and D exemplify the addition of correlated features, where $C_{13} = C_{31} = .75$ and $-.75$ respectively, and case E represents addition of a very noisy feature, with variance $C_{33} = 10$.

Two types of neural networks were used in this study. The first is a standard back propagation (BP) neural network with either of two architectures: a simple two layer (3-1 nodes) "perceptron" and a slightly more complicated network with 10 nodes in a hidden layer (3-10-1 nodes). The BP network has been described by many sources.[5] It was run without a momentum term and with target goals of .1 and .9 rather than 0.0 and 1.0 in order to increase the "fluidity" of the weights during training. Values surpassing the target goals were not allowed, however, to contribute to the sum of squares error. The second type of neural network is called DYSTAL. It is a vector quantization scheme in which class vectors or "patches" are determined during the training phase.[6] The class of whichever patch is most similar to a given test vector is assigned to that test vector. A simple least squares similarity measure was used both in the training phase to control the number of patches and in the test phase to determine class assignment.

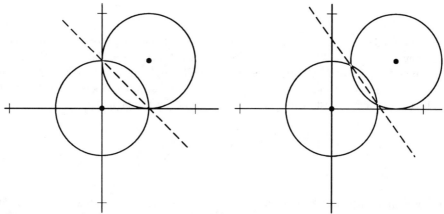

Figure 1. One standard deviation surface of Gaussian clouds for 2D case A (left) and 3D case B (right). Ideal decision surface indicated by dashed line. For the 3D case, the figure is a cross section in the feature 1 = feature 2 plane.

The area under the ROC curve, A_z, was used as the measure of observer performance. The most obvious way of calculating A_z would be to use the decision function on the test data many times, varying the decision function threshold to change the operating point (values of sensitivity and specificity) and tracing out and integrating under the ROC curve. Instead, we use the fact that the percentage correct for a 2 alternative forced choice (2AFC) experiment is directly equal to A_z.[4] The test set of 10,000 "patients" is divided into 5000 pairs of normals and positives, and a 2AFC experiment is performed on these 5000 pairs to obtain the percent correct and hence A_z.

For comparisons between observers, relative efficiency is a useful concept. To obtain efficiency, A_z is transformed to a corresponding detectability index d_a through the relationship

$$d_a = \sqrt{2}\, \Phi^{-1}(A_z)$$

where Φ^{-1} is the inverse Gaussian distribution function. The efficiency is calculated as the ratio of the squares of the d_a values of the two observers. Because the simple signal-known-exactly (SKE) task used here can be solved exactly, we are privy to the ideal observer solution, so efficiencies are given relative to that optimal observer.

Three statistical techniques were used to estimate the small-sample bias and measurement variance of A_z. These are the jackknife, the Fukunaga-Hayes, and the bootstrap techniques. The first and third of these are described in a cogent work by Bradley Efron,[7] and the second is given in a paper by the named authors.[8]

The jackknife is a technique which uses the results for N patients and the set of N results for N-1 patients (leaving one out each time) to predict the asymptotic behavior of a curve--assumed to have a 1/N dependent bias term. Thus, denoting the value of A_z for N patients as A_N, we easily derive the expression $A_z = NA_z-(N-1)\overline{A}_{N-1}$, where the overbar on A_{N-1} indicates that we are using the average of the N estimates of A_{N-1}. The variance estimate is given by the following formula:

$$\hat{\sigma}_J^2 = \left(\frac{N-1}{N}\right)\sum_{i=1}^{N}\left(A_{N-1(i)} - \overline{A}_{N-1}\right)^2$$

The Fukunaga-Hayes technique estimates the asymptotic results from values at N and N/2 rather than at N and N-1. In this technique both the normal and positive classes are arbitrarily divided into two groups, resulting in four normal/positive pairings. It could also be referred to as a "group" jackknife, except that only four of the many possible ways of grouping N things N/2 at a time are used. The 1/N bias dependence is also still assumed, yielding $A_z = 2A_N - \overline{A}_{N/2}$.

The bootstrap technique takes the given data set as an estimate of the true probability distribution of the data. Additional patients are then generated by selecting, with replacement, from this data pool. Thus up to N^N different data sets of size N may be generated. Of course N of these will simply have the same patient N times, and many of them will only have members of one class. Bizarre as that may seem, the bootstrap technique has been found to give remarkably good results for estimating the variance of the desired statistic:

$$\hat{\sigma}_B^2 = \frac{1}{M-1} \sum_{i=1}^{M} (A_{B(i)} - \overline{A}_B)^2$$

where M is some large number (here 100) of data sets of size N drawn with replacement from the data pool, and $\overline{A}_B$ is the average of the $A_{B(i)}$ values.

RESULTS: Values of ROC area A_z and efficiency relative to the ideal observer were obtained for networks trained on 200 separate realizations of N patients and tested on the 10,000 patient test set. Results for cases A and B are shown in figure 2, along with data from reference 1 for the classical statistical decision function. The best neural network results were for a single patch for each class for DYSTAL and for the simple perceptron architecture for BP. The agreement among the three techniques is remarkable. Note that the classical method involves explicit matrix inversion and therefore could not be carried out for very small numbers of patients, whereas the neural network appeared to experience no difficulty even when network parameters (BP) were far underdetermined. We believe that pseudoinverse techniques could be used to extend the domain of the classical method into this area as well. Of course the variance for small numbers of patients becomes extremely large.

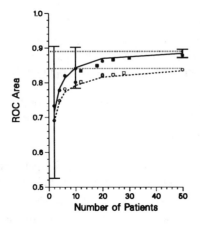 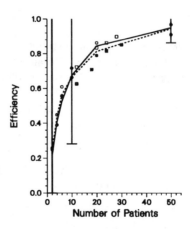

Figure 2. ROC Area (left) and Efficiency (right) estimates as a function of number of patients. 2D Case A: dotted line - BP network, open circle - DYSTAL, open square - classical statistical decision rule of reference 1. 3D Case B: solid line - BP, solid circle - DYSTAL, solid square - classical result. The horizontal dotted lines are the asymptotic ideal results for each case.

Figure 3 displays the performance of the two BP architectures for case B. It is noteworthy that the best performance is obtained for quite small reductions in the error term, further reductions being associated with overtraining "to fit the noise" and reduction in observer performance. The figure also illustrates how for the vastly underconstrained training of the second network, the BP solution serendipitously converges to nearly the correct solution before gradually degrading.

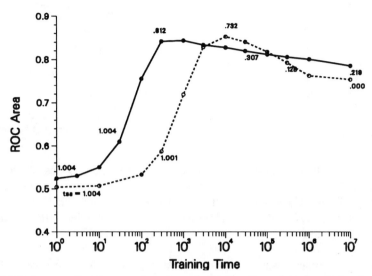

Figure 3. ROC Area estimates as a function of training time (iterations) for the 3-1 node BP network (solid curve) and the 3-10-1 network (dotted curve). Total sum of squares error (tss) normalized to 1 for the "chance" observer (output = 0.5 for all input).

Results for highly correlated and anticorrelated features, cases C and D, were also calculated and found to follow a similar pattern. The neural network results were somewhat better than the classical results (lower bias) for the positive correlation case and worse for the negative correlations. It is noteworthy how much difference the sign of the correlation makes, with the ideal observer results lying at A_z = .85 and .98 respectively. This at first appears very surprising; however, the relationship between the respective Gaussian clouds is very different in the two cases, as shown in figure 4.

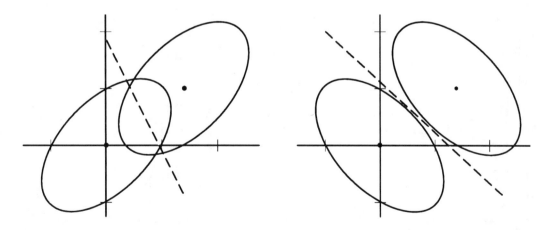

Figure 4. Representation of one standard deviation surface of Gaussian clouds for positive correlation Case C (left) and negative correlation Case D (right). Ideal decision surface indicated by dashed line.

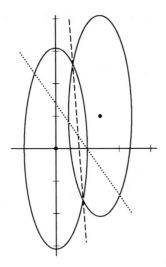
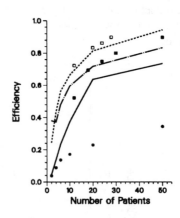

Figure 5. Left: One standard deviation surface for Gaussian clouds of 3D Case E. Ideal decision surface indicated by dashed line. Dotted line indicates plane perpendicular to line connecting cloud centers. Right: Efficiency estimates as a function of number of patients. 2D Case A: dotted line - BP network, open square - classical statistical result. 3D Case E: solid line - BP, interrupted line - modified DYSTAL, solid square - classical result, solid circle - DYSTAL.

Figure 5 illustrates network performance when a very noisy feature is added to the first two "clean" ones. For this case (E) the networks perform less well than the classical technique, and DYSTAL with our simple least squares similarity measure appears to fail badly. BP is significantly depressed and does not give convincing evidence of approaching the 2D result let alone surpassing it for the very modest gain envisaged by the ideal observer. An indication of why DYSTAL is failing is given in the depiction of the Gaussian clouds for that case. Note that the ideal observer decision surface is no longer nearly perpendicular to the line connecting the centers of the two clouds. This difficulty is resolved by modifying the similarity measure by dividing each squared term by the estimated variance for the respective feature. As shown in figure 5, with this modified similarity measure, DYSTAL's performance is greatly enhanced.

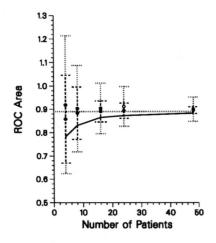
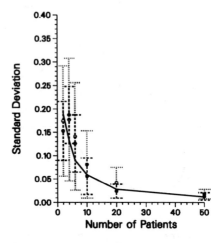

Figure 6. A_z and its standard deviation for Case B. Left: solid line - BP, open circle - jackknife estimate, closed circle - Fukunaga-Hayes estimate. Right: solid line - simulation results, open circle - jackknife estimate, closed circle - bootstrap estimate.

Figure 6 contrasts the performance of the jackknife and Fukunaga-Hayes techniques for elimination of the bias. Both seem to give quite good results on average for even very small numbers of patients. The error bars for a single realization, however, are quite large, especially for the jackknife technique. Both techniques are essentially extrapolation techniques, and there is much more error involved in extrapolating from two points which are very close together than from two widely separated points.

For the variance estimates from the jackknife and bootstrap methods a very similar situation exists. Both methods on average give good results for the variance (or its square root as shown in figure 5); however, the single measurement error in these estimates are very large. Once again, the jackknife gives a variation in the standard deviation of a factor of 2 or more greater than that of the bootstrap technique.

SUMMARY: For simple detection tasks neural networks can give quite good performance, even in regimes for which the classical decision function can't be calculated--and even when their weights and biases are severely underconstrained by the available data. The addition of very noisy features is evidently detrimental to network performance, however, more than for the classical methods.

Of the three statistical techniques studied here, the Fukunaga-Hayes method appeared to be superior to the jackknife for estimating the value of A_z. Similarly, the bootstrap gave better results than the jackknife for estimating the variance of A_z. These appear to be promising methods for small sample bias elimination and variance estimation, respectively.

REFERENCES:

1. R.F. Wagner, D.G. Brown, J-P. Guedon, K.J. Myers, K.A. Wear, "Multivariate Gaussian pattern classification: effects of finite sample size and the addition of correlated or noisy features on summary measures of goodness," Information Processing in Medical Imaging, Proceedings IPMI '93, pp. 507-524, 1993.
2. R.F. Wagner, D.G. Brown, J-P. Guedon, K.J. Myers, and K.A. Wear, "On combining a few diagnostic tests or features," Proc. of the SPIE 2167 (to be published: 1994).
3. D.G. Brown, M.P. Anderson, R.F. Wagner, and A.C. Schneider, "Finite training sample size effects on neural network pattern classification," Proc. of the SPIE 2167 (to be published: 1994).
4. D.M. Green and J.A. Swets, Signal Detection Theory and Psychophysics, Robert E. Krieger, Huntington, NY, 1974.
5. D.E. Rummelhart, J.L. McClelland, and the PDP research group, Parallel Distributed Processing Vol. 1: Explorations in the Microstructure of Cognition, MIT Press, Cambridge, MA, 1986.
6. T.P. Vogl, K.T. Blackwell, J.M. Irvine, G.S. Barbour, S.D. Hyman, and D.L. Alkon, "DYSTAL: A neural network architecture based on biological associative learning," Progress in Neural Networks, Vol. III, C.L. Wilson and O.M. Omidvar ed., Ablex Publishing Corp., Norwood, NJ, 1992.
7. B. Efron, The Jackknife, the Bootstrap and Other Resampling Plans, Society for Industrial and Applied Mathematics, Philadelphia, 1982.
8. K. Fukunaga and R. R. Hayes, "Effects of sample size in classifier design," IEEE Trans. Pattern Anal. Machine Intell., PAMI-11, 873-885, 1989.

MEDICAL STUDENTS' AND EXPERIENCED IMMUNOLOGISTS' PROBLEM-SOLVING STRATEGIES CAN BE DISTINGUISHED BY ARTIFICIAL NEURAL NETWORKS

Ronald H. Stevens, Ph.D.
Peter Wang, MS.
Alina Lopo, MD, Ph.D.
Noah Bogan, MS.
Department of Microbiology and Immunology
UCLA School of Medicine
Los Angeles, California 90024-1747

ABSTRACT

The sequence of actions that medical students performed while solving computer-based problems in immunology were electronically captured and used to train artificial neural networks for the rapid classification of subsequent students' strategies on these problems. Such networks could categorize problem solutions of other students as successful or non-successful >85% of the time. These same neural networks however, performed poorly when classifying experienced immunologists' successful problem solutions, suggesting an ability to distinguish novice from expert performances. These results indicate that appropriately trained neural networks can be useful tools which, based on performance, can distinguish levels of expertise in a knowledge domain and perhaps provide new evaluation opportunities in education and training

1. INTRODUCTION

Most medical and other educational curricula currently contain non-lecture learning experiences which emphasize active, self-directed learning that are presented to the students in a variety of small group and problem-solving formats[1,2]. In evaluation, however, the multiple-choice question format often dominates and efforts to develop innovative learning experiences have not always been paralleled by the development of comparable evaluation tools which more closely mirror alternative forms of learning.

The IMMEX Project at UCLA has focused on developing electronic learning and evaluation tools for revealing the strategies of students while engaged in problem-solving. We have constructed computer-based problems in immunology, infectious disease, surgery and other disciplines based on the general problem-solving paradigm of a starting condition, a goal condition, and the resources to transit between these states[3,4]. We have started from the premise that while it is relatively easy to determine whether or not students solve problems, it is more difficult to evaluate student strategies during the problem-solving process, particularly when large numbers of student performances are being collected.

One source of this difficulty is the variability of problem-solving strategies. Such strategies at the student and physician level can be very diverse. In our problem setting, in over 6,000 student problem performances, few (0.1-0.5%) of the students have employed the same strategy to solve a problem. This variability presumably depends on the knowledge, the representation of the problem and the experience of the problem solver. In the latter regard, it is well documented that experts recognize features of problem situations that novices do not and this results in a different process of understanding and search of the problem state[5].

However, despite this strategic diversity at the individual student level, when the performances of large numbers of students are viewed on a series of problems, subtle, more general features can be associated with successful performance of any particular problem[4,6]. We have recently shown that artificial neural networks trained on a large number of student performances can recognize these subtle features of problem solutions[7], and can classify new student performances as successful or non-successful ~90% of the time. More importantly, the use of this software approach can begin to reveal the learning processes of students in complex domains.

In this study we wished to determine how artificial neural networks trained on novice problem performances, which presumably consist of basic forward and backward chaining strategies, would classify the performances of expert immunologists which presumably would be more schema driven.

2. The IMMEX Problem-Solving Format

The approach is based on the cognitive principles of having a starting condition (i.e. Case History), a goal condition (i.e., Diagnosis) and the access to the information (i.e. patient laboratory tests) needed to transit these conditions[8]. While this is a simple form of problem-solving, it is also powerful in that it is applicable to a broad number of disciplines and educational levels and can function as a useful prototype for other problem-solving situations.

Each problem starts with a patient history that contains sufficient information for the generation of hypotheses regarding the possible immune defect involved. Students performing these problems then may access additional information and laboratory tests from 50-70 different menu items which can be used to verify/reject hypotheses. When they are confident of the patient's immune defect a diagnosis can be made. The details of the software and its implementation have been described in detail[6,9].

3. Analysis of Pooled Student Performances by Search-path Mapping

During the problem-solving, a transaction database records the student's selection of information, time, score, diagnosis, etc. This can be accessed by search-path mapping software which displays each student's sequential requests for more information. Therefore, each individual (Figure 1) or group (Figure 2) problem-solving performances may be reconstructed. In reconstructing the problem-solving process the search-path mapping software displays rectangles which represent the potential test selections available to the students and then lines interconnect the sequence of tests selected. In determining the criteria for display, Structured Query Language (SQL) queries are made to this database in the form "Select choices from tests where case = "IMMUNOLOGY #23" and name="J11" for an individual search-path map or "Select choices from tests where case="IMMUNOLOGY #1" and solved=TRUE" for group search-path maps. In response to these queries, lines connect the tests selected with the lines originating from the upper left hand corner of the 'from' test and extending to the lower center of the 'to' test. For group search-path maps, the thickness of the lines is proportional to the number of students making that selection.

The search-path maps of groups of students who successfully solve problems reveal elaborate patterns of test selections which are different for each problem.

4. Construction and Training of Artificial Neural Networks with Student Performances

Multi-layer feed-forward artificial neural networks were trained to recognize these group problem-solving patterns using over 400 performances of students who successfully solved one or more of seven different problems. The training data for the backpropagation neural networks[10] was obtained from individual student problem-solving performances which for the most part were collected under examination conditions.

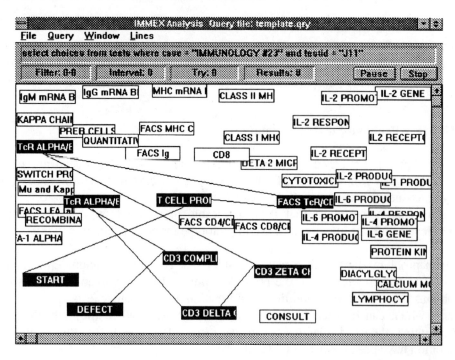

Figure 1. Reconstruction of Individual Problem Performances by Search-path Mapping using IMMEX::ANALYSIS Software[5].

Individual search-path maps connect the sequence of tests chosen by a student while solving a problem. This student started the problem (lower left), selected T-Cell Proliferation as the first test, FACS TcR/CD3 as the second test, etc. until the completion of the problem (DEFECT).

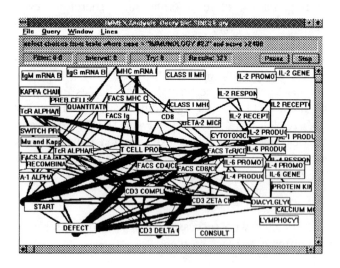

Figure 2 Group Search-path Map for 63 Students Solving the CD3 Complex Problem. Group search-path maps display the test selections made by all the students satisfying a particular query to the database, e.g. whether or not a problem was solved. In this analysis, the identity of the individual student is lost, but the pattern of what it means to correctly solve a problem emerges. This pattern is different for correct solutions for each problem and forms the basis of the neural network approach for analyzing students' successful and non-successful solutions

As students progress through the problems the sequence of their test selections is recorded in the form of classifying characteristics. For instance, in Figure 1A, the classifying characteristics would be "Start To T-Cell Proliferation", "T-Cell Proliferation To FACS TcR/CD3", "FACS TcR/CD3 To TcR Alpha/Beta Chains" etc. All training data were drawn from the test selections of students who successfully solved a problem, and these were obtained for each of seven immunology case simulations. This process resulted in a total of 533 classifying characteristics.

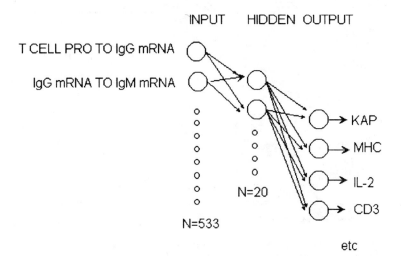

Figure 3. Architecture of the Neural Network. The neural network constructed consisted of 533 input neurons (one for each classifying characteristic), 40 hidden neurons, and seven case-specific output neurons, which were fully interconnected by weighted links; the momentum was 0.9, the learning rate was 0.6, and the network was trained to a 0.005 sum of errors[7]

During testing, an individual student's test selection is presented to the neural network and the output weights collected. The output weights range from 0 (condition is absent) to 1 (condition is present). This process is repeated for each test selection made by the student until the completion of the problem, resulting in a series of output weights for each problem which can be displayed as histograms. Test selections made by a student that are not represented in the 533 classifying characteristics are skipped by the analysis. Successful performances are indicated by high output weights for the relevant problem and low for the other problems. Unsuccessful, and false negative performances are indicated by low output weights across all problems. The correspondence between the search-path mapping and the output weights from the artificial neural network trained to recognize successful problem-solving performances across 7 problems is shown in Figure 4.

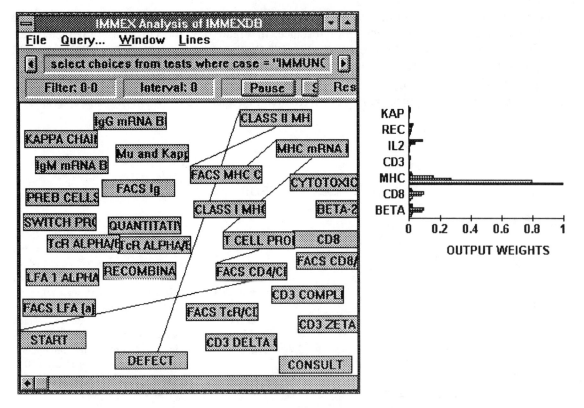

Figure 4. Comparison of the outputs of IMMEX::ANALYSIS search-path mapping and IMMEX::NEURAL which provides an interpretation of the analysis output. These figures follow the progression of one student as tests were selected during problem-solving. The lines connecting the boxes show the sequence of the student's tests. The histograms show the cumulative output weights returned from a trained neural network as each of these test selections were presented to the network.

5. Artificial Neural Networks Trained with Successful Performances of UCLA Students Poorly Predict the Performance of Experts, but Accurately Predict the Performance of Other Students

Anonymous problem performances by experienced immunologists were collected over a 3-day period at the 1993 American Association of Immunologists meeting. Requests for additional information by workshop attendees indicated that 76% held the title Assistant Professor or higher and provides an indication of the level of expertise. During the workshop, 224 problem performances were collected. Forty-six of these performances were not completed and these data were not further analyzed. Of completed problems, there were 123 performances resulting in correct solutions and 55 instances in which the diagnosis was missed. This frequency of solutions (69%) was slightly higher than that of UCLA second-year medical students under testing conditions (302/450 or 67%) this past year. Of these 178 immunologists' performances, 87 were on problems in which student performances were used to train artificial neural networks. These performances constitute the experimental data for this study.

CONTINGENCY TABLES

| | STUDENTS' PERFORMANCE | |
	TRUE +	TRUE -
NETWORK CLASSIFICATION +	46	2
NETWORK CLASSIFICATION −	17	47

| | IMMUNOLOGISTS' PERFORMANCE | |
	TRUE +	TRUE -
NETWORK CLASSIFICATION +	23	1
NETWORK CLASSIFICATION −	43	20

Table 1. Contingency Tables of Student and Immunologists Problem Performances as Classified by Student-Trained Artificial Neural Network Classification of These Performances.

The sensitivity for the individual problems performed by the immunologists was: Bare Lymphocyte Syndrome (27%), CD3 Complex Deficiency (13%), Beta-2 Microglobulin Defect (25%), Recombinase Defect (27%), and IL-2 Promoter Defect (75%). Varying the neural network output weight decision threshold values between 0.45 and 0.65 for the true positive performances did not produce significant differences in the above classifications. The student and immunologist distribution of true positive and false negative performances were significantly different (Pearson χ^2 = 18.46 P<0.0005).

True negative performances of both the students (47/49) and immunologists (20/21) were accurately detected by the artificial neural networks trained with student performances (Table 1). The neural networks identified 33/44 (75%) true positive performances of second-year UCLA medical students and 18/26 (69%) true positive performances of first-year George Washington University medical students, all of which were obtained under testing conditions. Thus subsequent student performances when presented to the trained neural networks, were correctly classified as having solved or not solved a particular problem >85% of the time.

In contrast, only 23/66 (35%) of the immunologists' true positive performances were identified by the student trained neural networks. These results indicate that the sequence of actions employed by immunologists in solving the same problems are not well encapsulated by neural networks trained on students' successful problem performances.

6. CONCLUSIONS

These studies indicate that appropriately trained artificial neural networks may be useful educational tools which can be used not only for routine (and rapid) evaluation of student problem-solving performances, but also which can be used to discriminate between novice and expert performances.

This introduces the concept of performance-based evaluation for complex problem-solving situations and suggests approaches which can encompass many disciplines, capitalizing upon the advances in technology and information science. As one future extension, with acquisition of a sufficient number of immunologists' problem performances it may be possible to train artificial neural networks based on these experts' performances. In an evaluation setting then, student "passing" would consist not only of solving a series of problems, but by solving them with a strategy better represented in the expert neural network rather than the novice-trained neural network.

REFERENCES

[1.]   Muller, S. (Chairman). Physicians for the twenty-first century. Report of the project panel on the general professional education of the physician and college preparation for medicine. *Journal of the American Medical Association* 1988; 260:367-372.

[2.]   Science for All Americans; A Project 2061 Report on Literacy Goals in Science, Mathematics and Technology, *American Association for the Advancement of Science,* Washington, DC, 1989.

[3.]   Stevens, R.H., Kwak, A.R., McCoy, J.M. Evaluating preclinical medical students by using computer-based problem-solving examinations. *Academic Medicine* 1989; 64:685-687.

[4.]   Stevens, R.H. Search-path mapping: A versatile approach for visualizing problem-solving behavior. *Academic Medicine* 1991; 66:S73-75.

[5.]   Schmidt, H.G., Norman, G.R., Boshuizen, H.P.A. A Cognitive Perspective on Medical Expertise: Theory and Implication. *Academic Medicine* 1990, 65:611-616.

[6.]   Stevens, R.H., McCoy, J.M., Kwak, A.R. Solving the problem of how medical students solve problems. *MD Computing.* 1991; 8:13-20.

[7.]   Stevens, R.H., Najafi, K. Artificial neural networks as adjuncts for assessing medical students' problem-solving performances on computer-based simulations. *Computers & Biomedical Research* 1993; 26:172-187.

[8.]   Newell, A. *Unified Theories of Cognition.* Harvard University Press, 1990.

[9.]   Kwak, A.R., Stevens, R.H. Administering a microcomputer-based problem-solving examination. *Journal of Biological Computing* 1990;17(3):9-13.

[10.]   Rumelhart, D.E., Hinton, G.E., & Williams, R.J. Learning Internal Representations by Error Propagation. In D.E. Rumelhart and J.L. McClelland (Eds.) *Parallel Distributed Processing* (Vol 1). Cambridge, Ma; MIT Press.

ACKNOWLEDGMENTS

Supported in part by funding from the United States Public Health Services, Bureau of Health Professions. Special thanks to Drs. Phyllis Kind, Barbara Dau and Ann Linton at GWU for providing student performances, and to the immunologists who participated in the IMMEX Problem-Solving Software Workshop at the 1993 AAI meeting in Denver

NEURAL FILTERS AND HYBRID NEURAL NETWORKS FOR GAMMA CAMERA-BREMSSTRAHLUNG IMAGE RESTORATION

Wei Qian, Laurence P. Clarke, Maria Kallergi and Michael Abernathy

Department of Radiology, College of Medicine and H. Lee Moffitt Cancer Center & Research Institute at the University of South Florida, Tampa, FL 33612

ABSTRACT

A new class of filters called neural filters and hybrid neural networks (NFHNN) is proposed for the restoration of of bremmstrahlung radiation from pure beta emitters of different beta particle energies (Y-90, P-32), as required for quantitative measurement and in-vivo management of antibody therapy. The neural filtering (NF) can perform optimal noise removal and the hybrid neural networks (HNN) are well suited to solve the image restoration schemes in nuclear medicine. Order statistic neural network hybrid filters (OSNNH) is a special case of the NFHNN. Its restoration performance is quantitatively evaluated by investigating the relationship between the externally measured counts from sources of P-32 and Y-90 at various depths in water. Evaluation of phantom and patient filtered images demonstrates that the proposed new class of filters avoids ring effects observed in other restoration filters for both radionuclides.

I. INTRODUCTION

The use of HNN's for gamma camera image restoration is proposed to partly compensate for image degradation due to photon scattering and photon penetration effects through the camera collimator. The particular clinical model involved is the quantitative measurement of bremmstrahlung radiation from pure beta emitters (Y-90, P-32), as required for the in-vivo management of antibody therapy. The restoration problem of bremstrahlung detection is particularly difficult because of: (a) the enhanced scatter and penetration effects due the wide energy range of bremstrahlung photons and (b) the poor conversion efficiency for beta emitters that degrades signal to noise ratio of the images. Image restoration filters have been proposed for single photon detection to partly compensate for image degradation and have met with limited success. Methods proposed have included the Wiener filter, the Metz filter and constrained Least Squares filter that generally require an *a priori* knowledge of the system' s response function and an estimate of the noise power spectrum [1]. These filters generally involve two components, a low pass filter for noise suppression and an inverse filter for deconvolution. These filters have had limited success because the inverse operation often makes the restoration an ill conditioned, unstable, or singular problem. When the Wiener filter is applied to bremsstrahlung images, the combined influence of the degraded system response and the high noise content introduces greater instability in the deconvolution that results in ringing artifacts and an over-compensation of the system response function [1, 2]. Alternative methods for image restoration are therefore necessary for imaging beta emitters using a gamma camera.

II. THE ALGORITHM OF NEURAL FILTERS AND HYBRID NEURAL NETWORKS

The architecture of the NFHNN is based on the motivation that NF can perform optimal noise removal and a HNN can be used for deconvolution. Virtually all image restoration schemes can be posed as the solution to some particular optimization problem. Hopfield neural network is often used to solve the problem [2-5]. The difficulty in using Hopfield neural network for this purpose is that the iteration procedure may often be trapped into a local minimum, which usually corresponds to an invalid solution. Moreover, the values assigned to the parameters of an energy function can greatly affect the convergence rate of the iteration. The hybrid neural networks are better suited to solve the optimization problem [7].

In nuclear medicine, the blurred image Y can be considered as the sum of the operation of the 2-dimensional blur matrix H on the object X and the statistical noise n:

$$Y = HX + n \tag{1}$$

where Y, X, and n are lexicographically ordered 1-dimensional vectors and H is the matrix resulting from the point spread function samples. In the ideal case of zero noise ($n=0$), the problem of image restoration corresponds to the existence and uniqueness of an inverse transformation. Both existence and uniqueness are important. If the inverse transformation does not exist, then there is no mathematical basis for asserting that X can be exactly recovered from Y. Problems for which there is no inverse transformation, i.e., H^{-1} does not exist, are said to be *singular*. On the other hand, H^{-1} may exist but not be unique; i.e., there may be more than one H^{-1}. Finally, even if H^{-1} exists and is unique, it may be *ill-conditioned*, by which it means that a trivial perturbation in Y can produce nontrivial perturbation in X. That is, there exists ε, which can be made arbitrarily small such that

$$H^{-1}\{ H + \varepsilon \} = X + \beta \tag{2}$$

when $\beta >> \varepsilon$, β is not arbitrarily small and is not negligible. Thus, an ill-conditioned problem is one in which inherent data perturbations can result in undesirable effects in the solution by inverse transformation. Note that image restoration problems of this class are at best and are frequently singular. However, gamma camera images, and bremsstrahlung images in particular, are contaminated by various kinds of noise processes. The presence of noise means that a "proper" solution for the object distribution must be selected from within an infinite family of candidate solutions. In reality, there is no proper solution but only solutions derived from various combinations of available *a priori* information and desired performance criteria. One of the most essential problems is the fact that image restoration is an ill-conditioned problem at best and a singular problem at worst. In the proposed NFHNN filter, the neural filter removes the noise before the HNN performs image restoration. The hybrid neural networks are then well suited to solve the optimization problem [7]

A. Neural Filters

The neural filter, shown in Fig. 1, is defined as follows:

$$H(\underline{X}) = \sum_{m-1}^{M-1} \sigma \left(W^m x^m - W_0^m \right) \qquad (3)$$

where x^m is the input array on threshold level m defined as follows:

$$X^m_i = T^m(X_i) = \begin{cases} 1, & \text{if } X_i \geq 1 \\ 0, & \text{otherwise} \end{cases} \qquad (4)$$

for m=1,2, $\cdots$, M-1.

W^m and W_0^m are the weight matrix and the threshold of the neuron on threshold level m, respectively. W^m is defined as

$$W^m = \begin{bmatrix} W^m_{-l,1} & W^m_{-l,2} & \cdots & W^m_{-l,N} \\ W^m_{-l+1,1} & W^m_{-l+1,2} & \cdots & W^m_{-l+1,N} \\ \cdot & \cdot & \cdots & \cdot \\ \cdot & \cdot & \cdots & \cdot \\ W^m_{l,1} & W^m_{-l,2} & \cdots & W^m_{l,N} \end{bmatrix} \qquad (5)$$

Although the neuron function $\sigma(.)$ could be any function, we will focus on a sigmoidal function in this work. According to the mapping property of a neural network with sigmoidal functions [6], a sigmoidal function can approximate all filters, such as weighted order statistic (WOS) filters, stack filters and linear FIR filters. One intuitive explanation for this is that for large incoming weights, the sigmoidal function is at "high gain" state and can approximate the unit step function. For small weights, by using a sigmoidal function, one can get an approximation to linear functions. Any neural filter with a sigmoidal function which has the same neuron with linear activation function on each threshold level reduces to a linear FIR filters. The adaptive neural filtering under the mean absolut error (MAE) criterion and under the least mean square (LMS) criterion, the adaptive LMS generalized stack filtering algorithm and the adaptive LMS generalized weighted order statistic filtering algorithm were derived elsewhere [6]. The smoothing order statistic nonlinear filtering, as an example of neural filters, was succesfully used in [2].

B. Hybrid Neural Networks

Given the view of the infinite family of solutions that can be generated from a noisy, ill-conditioned solution, the selection of a specific solution from the family must be guided by some criterion or a set of criteria. Analysis and numerical formulation of a criterion is a topic discussed in *optimization theory*. Virtually all image restoration schemes can be posed as the solution to some particular optimization problem. In the hybrid neural network model, shown in Fig.2, the optimization problem which minimizes a discrete objective function is converted into an optimization problem which minimizes an energy function of the network. The HNN presented here contains two parts: one is a *Goal network* and another one is a *Constraint network*. The *Constraint network* models the constraints of an optimization problem and computes the updating value of each neuron such that the energy function monotonically converges to satisfy all constraints of the problem. The *Goal network* points out the direction of convergence for finding an optimal value for the cost criteria. These two subnets ensure that the hybrid neural network finds a feasible as well as an optimal solution. Based on the model of the hybrid neural network, the image restoration problem in nuclear medicine can be considered as

$$\text{Minimize} \quad X^T R X \tag{6}$$
$$\text{Subject to} \quad (Y - HX)^T (Y - HX) \leq e \tag{7}$$

where R is a linear operator defined in [2]. The *goal network* corresponds to Eq.(6) and the constraint network corresponds to Eq.(7), which is also a hybrid restoration process that is both a deterministic and stochastic optimization problem. The structure of the neural network given in [2] is a sub-section of the hybrid neural networks.

III. EXPERIMENTAL RESULTS

Volume sources of P-32 and Y-90, each 3.75 cm diameter, were imaged at 10 cm depth in a water tank, with a 5 cm air gap between the tank and the collimated gamma camera. The two beta particle energies of P-32 and Y-90 generate a bremsstrahlung energy spectrum with different photon energy ranges and varying degrees of image degradation and image noise level as shown in Figure 3 (a) and (d), respectively. Y-90 shows greater image degradation due to its higher energy beta particles, and a smaller Signal-To-Noise ratio due to a lower level of activity in the source..

The restored images of P-32 and Y-90 are shown in Figure 3 (c) and (f), respectively. Stable restoration was obtained for both beta emitters with improvement in resolution indices for the volume source but the extent of restoration was dependent upon both the SNR and the radionuclide, as observed for the weaker Y-90 source. Alternative filters such as the Metz or Weiner filters are unstable for highly degraded images such as those found with bremsstrahlung imaging [2]. Further work using Y-90 sources is planned.

IV. CONCLUSIONS

The preliminary data suggests that the NFHNN may be potentially useful for quantitative measurements of beta emitters proposed for antibody therapy. More experimental data are required to determine differences in the effective linear attenuation coefficient for both isotopes and the stability of segmentation with different source strengths and depths in water [2]. The NFHNN should also prove to be useful for imaging of single photon emitters at high photon energy to compensate for the image degradation due to photon scattering or photon penetration through the collimators of the detectors used.

REFERENCES

[1]. B. C. Penney, M. A. King, R. B. Schwinger, S. P. Baker and P. W. Doherty " Modifying constrained least-squares restoration for application to single photon emission computed tomography projection images" Med. Phys. vol. 15, pp 334-342, 1988.

[2]W. Qian, M. Kallergi, L. P. Clarke, "Order-Statistic Neural-Network Hybrid Filters for Gamma Camera Bremsstrahlung Image Restoration," *IEEE Transactions on Medical Imaging, March 1993, Vol.12, No.1, pp58-65.*

[3]Y-T. Zhou, R. Chellappa, A. Vaid, and B.K Jenkins, " Image Restoration Using a Neural Network," *IEEE Trans. ASSP*, vol.36, pp. 1141-1151, 1988.

[4]. H. D. Li, W. Qian, L. P. Clarke, and M. Kallergi. "Neural Network for Maximum Entropy Restoration of Nuclear Medicine Images." *Proceedings of the International Conference on Acoustics, Speech, and Signal Processing*, Minneapolis, Minnesota; April 27-30, 1993.

[5]J. B. Abbiss, B. J. Brames, and M. A. Fiddy, "Superresolution Algorithms for a Modified Hopfield Neural Network," *IEEE Trans. Signal Proc.*, vol.39, pp. 1516-1523, 1991.

[6]. Lin Yin, Jaako Astola and Yrjo Neuvo " A New Class of Nonlinear Filters - Neural Filter" IEEE Trans. on Signal Processing, Vol. 41, No. 3 March, 1993

[7]. K.T. Sun and H.C. Fu " A Hybrid Neural Network Model for Solving Optimization Problems" IEEE Trans. on Computers. Vol. 42, No. 2 Feb. 1993

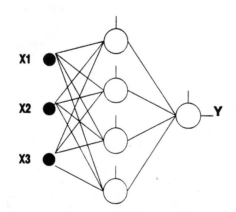

Fig1. The structure of Neural Filter

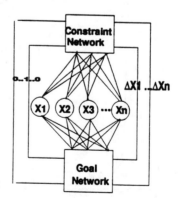

Fig2. The structure of Hybrid Neural Network

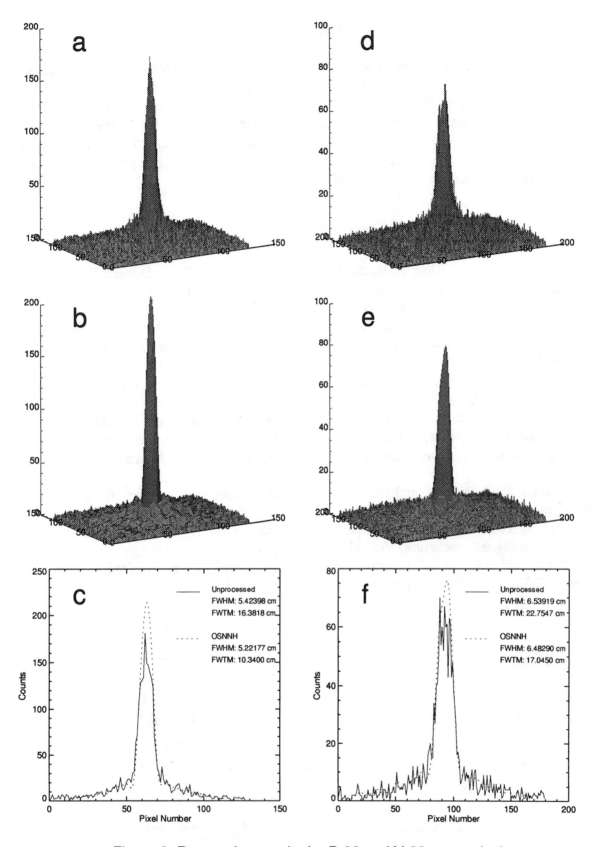

Figure 3: Restoration results for P-32 and Y-90 respectively
(a) and (d), raw data; (b) and (e), restored data; (c) and (f), cross section

A Neural Network Approach to the Efficient Control of Neuromuscular System with Big Variance — Toward Further Improvement of the FES —

Nozomu HOSHIMIYA   Toshiyuki NAKAMURA   Ryoko FUTAMI
Yasunobu HANDA†

Department of Electronic Engineering, Faculty of Engineering, Tohoku University,
Aobayama, Sendai 980, Japan
†Department of Anatomy, Tohoku University School of Medicine, Sendai 980, Japan
Email: toshi@hoshimiya.ecei.tohoku.ac.jp

Abstract—Functional Electrical Stimulation (FES) is efficient for the restoration of the paralyzed muscular faculties. For the fine control, however, stimulation parameters should be adjusted for each electrode-muscular system because of their big variance in characteristics. This paper, focussing on these problems, shows an artificial neural network approach for this type of problem.

1. Introduction

Functional Electrical Stimulation (FES) is an efficient and powerful method for the restoration of the motor functions of the paralyzed upper and lower extremities, and is also widely used in several fields, for example, the restoration of the motor function of the upper extremity function (which has not been realized by usual medical method) of the quadriplegic patient [1] [2]. Percutaneous electrode was used to localize specific electrical stimulation to individual muscles. There were serious problems. Typical one is that there is no effective general solution for obtaining suitable stimulation patterns for multi-channel neuromuscular system because of the big variance in the input(stimulation)-output(response) characteristics. We could make good clinical success in the FES application by using an approximation method based on the measured multi-channel electromyography (EMG signals) of the normal volunteers [1] [2]. But this was not a fundamental solution for this problem.

In this paper, another basic approach for fine control of muscle system by artificial neural networks will be discussed as a promising new strategy toward further improvement of the multi-channel FES system.

The characteristics of neuromuscular system are non-linear and have big variance. Actual muscle is the congregation of multiple motor units, and the maximum tension and the threshold of each motor unit are variant. How can we control each motor unit ?

Thoma et al. reported on the method to stimulate fascicles selectively by using the "epineural fixation"(1987) [3]. Grill and Mortimer reported on the selective stimulation for the medial gastrocnemius and lateral gastrocnemius/soleus muscles by using a single multiple contact nerve cuff electrode(1993) [4]. So we assume here it is able to activate motor units selectively. On such assumption, we think that the control object constituted of the elements which have big variance had better be controlled by the neural network constituted of many neurons. One of such basic neural network structure may be CMAC (Cerebellar Model Arithmetic Computer) which was proposed by Albus(1981) [5]. In this paper, we apply it to the control model of the neuromuscular system with big variance. This neural network is trained so that the desired tension is observed at the output of muscle which is constituted of motor units with big variance. In this training we introduce a new cost function to maximize the number of recruited motor units. By this maximization, small muscle tension can be generated by small motor units which are considered to have comparatively large controllabilities and fatigue resistant characteristics.

2. Control of Object Constituted of Multiple Motor Units

2.1 Model and Learning Algorithm

Figure 1 is the simulated model with the control object constituted of the elements which have big variance. Here, G, P, M units are the first layer, the second layer and the motor units, respectively. The input is the desired tension Td ($0 \leq Td \leq 100$). The number of G cell is 100, and the input-output characteristics of j-th G cell Gj ($0 \leq j \leq 99$) is defined as

$$Y_{Gj} = \phi(0.1(Td - j)) \tag{1}$$

where $\phi(x) = min(max(x, 0), 1)$ (see *Fig. 2*).

The number of P cell is 100, and the input-output characteristics are sigmoid type.

The number of the motor unit M is 100, and the input-output characteristics of the k-th motor unit Mk ($0 \leq k \leq 99$) are

$$Y_{Mk} = Tmax_k f_M(Y_{Pk} - \theta_k) \tag{2}$$

where Y_{Mk} is the output of the k-th motor unit, $Tmax_k$ is the maximum tension of the k-th motor unit ($0.3 \leq Tmax_k \leq 3.0$), θ_k is the threshold of the k-th motor unit ($0.4 \leq \theta_k \leq 0.6$), and $f_M(x) = 1/1 + exp(-30x)$ (see *Fig. 3*).

On the other hand, we defined as follows the cost function E to be reduced.

$$E = E_1 + rE_2 \tag{3}$$

$$E_1 = \frac{1}{2}(T - Td)^2 \tag{4}$$

$$E_2 = -\sum_{i=0}^{99} Y_{Pi} \tag{5}$$

where r is the positive constant, and $T = \sum_{k=0}^{99} Y_{Mk}$. To reduce E_1 means to reduce the error between input and output. To reduce E_2 means to increase the total quantity of electrical stimulation, i.e., to maximize the number of recruited motor units.

We used the back-propagation algorithm for the learning of the network assuming that the characteristics of all electrode-motor unit pairs had already been measured.

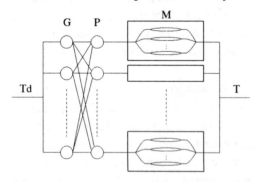

Figure 1. Model with the control object constituted of the elements which have big variance.

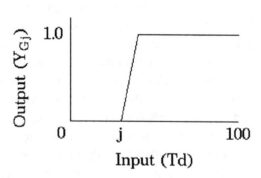

Figure 2. Input-output characteristics of j-th G cell.

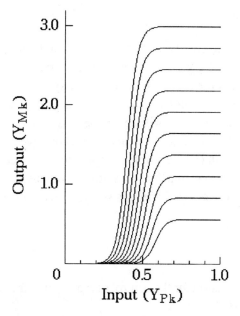

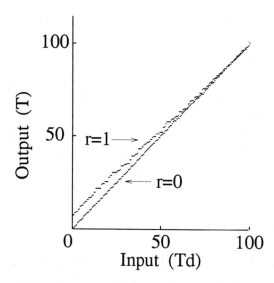

Figure 3. Input-output characteristics of the motor units(M). The characteristics of the 10 motor units are shown in figure.

Figure 4. Input-output characteristics after learning for each value of 'r'.

2.2 Simulation Result

Figure 4 and *5* are the simulation results for each value of r. *Fig. 4* shows the input-output characteristics after learning, and *Fig. 5* shows the firing pattern of motor units for each input Td.

It can be seen from *Fig. 4* that the muscle output T equals to the desired tension Td except for the case of $r = 1$ and small Td. On the other hand, it can be seen from *Fig. 5* that in case of $r = 1$, motor unit with small maximum tension tend to fire mainly for small desired tension (this can be partially observed also in the case for $r = 0$). The reason is that if only a few motor units with large maximum tension were recruited, the input-output characteristics would result in sigmoid type.

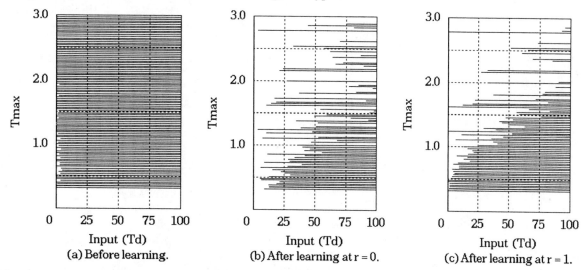

Figure 5. Firing pattern of motor units. Solid line shows the area of input (Td) that caused the motor unit activated above 80% of its $Tmax$. (a)Before learning. The value of the weight is random value between 0.0 and 1.0. (b),(c)After learning. In figure, a line indicate that a motor unit fire for each input Td.

I-117

3. Conclusion

In this paper, we assumed to be able to activate motor units selectively, and proposed a neural network approach for efficient control of the neuromuscular system with big variance toward further improvement of the FES. We considered the static motor control, and applied the idea of CMAC to this system. We used the error between input and output and the quantity of electrical stimulation as the cost function, and could activate mainly the motor units with small maximum tension. But there will be another cost function applicable. Besides, to use the back-propagation algorithm for the learning of the neural network, we assumed that we have known the characteristics of all motor units. So in case of using our approach, it is necessary to examine the characteristics of motor units by local stimulation. In actual muscle control, muscle fatigue and tonic/phasic characteristics are also important, which were neglected in this study. These problems on muscle dynamics should be further studied.

References

[1] Y. Handa and N. Hoshimiya: "Functional electrical stimulation for the control of the upper extremities", *Medical Progress through Technology*, vol.12, pp.51-63 (1987)

[2] N. Hoshimiya, A. Naito, M. Yajima and Y. Handa: "A multichannel FES system for the restoration of motor functions in high spinal cord injury patients: A respiration-controlled system for multijoint upper extremity", *IEEE Transactions on BME*, vol.36, pp.754-760 (1989)

[3] H. Thoma, M. Frey, J. Holle, H. Kern, W. Mayr, G. Schwanda and H. Stoehr: "Functional neurostimulation to substitute locomotion in paraplegia patients", *Artificial Organs*, VHC Publishers Inc., pp.515-529 (1987)

[4] Warren M. Grill and J. Thomas Mortimer: "Functional control of joint torque with a cuff electrode", *Proc. 15th Annual International Conference of the IEEE-EMBS*, pp.1328-1329 (1993)

[5] James S. Albus: "Brains, Behavior, and Robotics", McGraw-Hill (1981)

Neural Networks for Biomedical Prediction Tasks

Judith E. Dayhoff, Daw-Tung Lin, and Panos A. Ligomenides
Institute for Systems Research
University of Maryland
College Park, MD 20742

Abstract

Neural networks show promise in prediction tasks where a time-history of one or more parameters is used to predict future measurements of a system. Prediction tasks arise in biomedical engineering as well as domains such as systems control, signal processing, and financial analysis. Neural networks allow close matching of system properties without the requirement to know the underlying physical and mathematical equations that govern the system to be predicted. Dynamic networks with time-delays and recurrent loops are especially appropriate for time-series predictions. We have researched applications and properties of an adaptive time-delay neural network (ATNN) with an adaptation scheme for both weights and internal time-delays as well as configurations with recurrent loops from output to input units. The high performance of this network on sample problems indicates that it is appropriate and promising for biomedical applications.

1 Introduction

Time-series prediction is a task that is highly applicable to a variety of problems in biomedical engineering. Situations where one or more parameters are monitored over a period of time are common, and typically a prediction of the future values of those parameters is highly useful. For example, patient monitoring is done to alert doctors of changes in measured parameters such measurements associated with breathing, brain activity, or heart beat. A cogent prediction paradigm could potentially alert doctors that a dangerous situation is about to arise before the actual measured parameters show the danger signs explicitly. A neural network that can detect a combination of shifts in parameters that are not detectable by eye would be highly useful in such a situation.

We have selected a neural network for time-series prediction that has a configuration and learning rule that is highly appropriate to prediction problems. This neural network, called the Adaptive Time-Delay Neural Network (ATNN), has a feed-forward architecture with time-delays on its interconnections [1-3]. The time-delays can have arbitrary values and the lengths of the delays are adapted during training. The weights are also adapted according to a schedule that alternates changes in weights with changes in time-delays so as to learn the prediction problem from a time history of data.

We have tested this neural network configuration on a set of alternative data types, including a chaotic series and a smooth trajectory. In some cases the network was configured in a feed-forward manner, with the output being a function solely of a time-history of data. In other cases, a recurrent connection was allowed from the output units to the input units, so that a past history of the network's own predictions was used in future prediction scenarios. Prediction performance was high on both types of problems.

We conclude that the ATNN is a promising approach to time-series prediction problems, including those that occur in biomedical engineering. With its ability to adapt time delays, information from particular points in the past can be brought to bear on a prediction of future scenarios. Prediction of parameters that are monitored in patients can be of use in clinical situations as well as in researching and understanding the complexity of the underlying physiological subsystems.

2   References

1. S. P. Day and M. R. Davenport, 1993. Continuous-time temporal back-propagation with adaptive time delays. IEEE Trans. on Neural Networks 4: 348-354. Also appeared in Neuroprose Technical Report Archive, Internet ftp archive.cis.ohio-state.edu, August 1991.

2. D.-T. Lin, J. E. Dayhoff, and P. A. Ligomenides, 1994. Spatiotemporal topology and temporal sequence identification with an adaptive time-delay neural network. SPIE Intelligent Robots and Computer Vision XII: Algorithms and Techniques 2055: 536-545.

3. D.-T. Lin, J. E. Dayhoff, and P. A. Ligomenides, 1994. Prediction of chaotic time series and resolution of embedding dynamics with the ATNN. In WCNN-94 Proceedings.

3   Acknowledgements

This work was supported by the Systems Research Center of the University of Maryland, the National Science Foundation (NSF BIR 9309169 and NSFD CD 8803012), the Applied Physics Laboratory of Johns Hopkins University (APL), the Ballistic Missile Defense Organization (BMDO) and the Naval Research Laboratory (N00014-93-K-2019).

Neural Networks in the Biomedical Sciences:
A Survey of 386 Publications Since the Beginning of 1991

John N. Weinstein*, Timothy Myers, Joseph J. Casciari,
John Buolamwini, and Krishnamachari Raghavan

Laboratory of Molecular Pharmacology, Developmental Therapeutics Program (DTP), Division of Cancer Treatment (DCT), National Cancer Institute (NCI), Bethesda, MD 20892

* To whom correspondence should be directed.

ABSTRACT

We survey and classify 386 articles published since the beginning of 1991 on artificial neural networks in the biomedical sciences. Many of the studies address clinical problems; others address issues in laboratory research, particularly in neurophysiological modeling. Among the clinical subspecialties, oncology, cardiology, respiratory medicine, infectious diseases, neurology, and psychology are well-represented. Applications to medical imaging include analysis of the images themselves and analysis of descriptors derived from those images. Likewise, applications to electroencephalograms (EEGs) and electrocardiograms (EKGs) sometimes take as input the signal itself, sometimes derived parameters. The molecular biological applications include numerous methods for predicting recognition motifs in nucleic acids and secondary or tertiary structures in proteins. The diversity is impressive, but we are still groping for guidelines that can help us decide when an artificial neural network is really the best available technology for the problem at hand.

INTRODUCTION

In the last few years, the literature on artificial neural networks in biomedical science has literally exploded. To survey that literature, we did a combination of keyword and mesh heading searches in Index Medicus and in the UnCover database of the Colorado Alliance of Research Libraries (CARL Systems, Inc., Denver, CO). The resulting databases were consolidated in a library under Endnote Plus (Niles and Associates, Inc., Berkeley, CA). Extraneous references were deleted to arrive at a final compilation of 386 articles. Not captured by this approach are books and many meeting publications (including those from WCNN). A classification scheme was developed organically in Excel spread-sheet form as we went through the abstracts and/or publications. Then, to achieve uniformity in classification between entries examined at the beginning and end of the process, we went through them all a second time. Table 1 shows the first and last parts of the final working spread-sheet. The categories we generated have several characteristics worth noting:

(1) They are grouped thematically;
(2) They are not mutually exclusive;
(3) They are highly subjective.

Endnote Reference	A Reviews	A Letters, editorials	B Cancer	B Cancer drugs	C Cardiovascular	C EKG analysis	C Clinical Neurology	D Neurophysiol (model)	D Vision	D Speech	D EEG	D Cognitive Science	D Psychology	E Respiratory	E Veterinary medicine	E Infection Disease	F Clinical Diagnosis	F Clinical (in broad sense)	F Using Clinical Data	G Clinical chemistry	G cytology, pathology	G Medical imaging	G Image proc. (not imaging)	G MRI imaging	G x-ray, CT scan	H Drugs	H QSAR	I Molecular Biology	I Protein structure	I Nuc acid seq, structure	I Circ dichro spectra	J Mass spectrometry	J Physiology (non-neuro)	J Immunology	J Endocrinology	J Biochemistry	J Biology	K Biotechnol. Processing	K Med Education	K Robotics	K Forensics	L Statistics	L vs Statistical methods	L Receiver operator char.	M Network Innovation	M Physiological learning	M Genetic algorithm	M Biol. nets for comput.	M Chemical NNets	N History	N Other	Comment
1 Abeyratne* 1991 #346							1	1									1	1																																		brain source localization
2 Adelsberger* 1992 #240							1																																				1									neuro, reducing statistical dependence
3 Agyei* 1992 #199															1		1	1																																		dx of sexually transmitted diseases
4 Ajay* 1993 #18			1	1																						1	1																1									QSAR on DHFR, rank regress, std regress
5 Akay* 1992 #250					1												1	1	1																																	dx of coronary artery dis. from heart sounds
6 Akay* 1993 #1					1												1	1	1																																	dx of coronary artery dis. from heart sounds
7 Allen* 1993 #141					1												1	1	1																																	periph vasc dis dx from photelect plthysmog
8 Alvager* 1993 #37																	1	1	1							1																										dx of adverse drug reactions
9 Anastasio* 1992 #314							1	1																																												vestibular compensation
10 Andrade* 1993 #109																												1		1																					protein 2o struc fromm UV circ. dichroism
11 Andrea* 1991 #377			1	1																							1																									DHFR QSAR
12 Andreou* 1991 #354		1																																																		Electronic art imitates life
13 Arnold* 1992 #218							1	1																																												vestib-coul reflex
14 Ashutosh* 1992 #246														1			1	1	1																																	weaning from respiratory support
15 Astion* 1992 #227	1																	1		1	1																															clinical lab,pathology
16 Astion* 1992 #340			1														1	1	1	1																								1								cancer dx from clin. lab (vs quadratic discrim)
372 Wu* 1992 #126																												1																	1							protein sub-family id; n-gram hashing
373 Wu* 1992 #256			1														1	1	1																									1								dx of calcific. in breast digital mammog.
374 Wu* 1992 #307					1		1										1	1	1																																	on-line cerebral blood flow monitor
375 Wu* 1993 #101							1			1							1	1	1																																	EEG auditory evoked potentials
376 Wu* 1993 #106																	1	1	1			1																							1							NNets for imaging analysis
377 Wu* 1993 #167			1														1	1	1							1																										mammography decision-making
378 Wu* 1993 #420					1		1										1	1	1																																	on-line cerebral bld flow monitor
379 Xing* 1993 #79							1	1									1	1	1																																	vision model, Gabor filter
380 Xue* 1992 #302					1	1																																												1		EKG analysis
381 Yee* 1993 #421																																																				1	optimiz of lab animal growth
382 Zadak* 1993 #117							1	1										1																																		NNet in cochlear implant
383 Zajicek* 1992 #232		1																																																		Artificial life
384 Zelicoff* 1992 #324		1			1																																															myocard. infarction prediction
385 Zipser* 1992 #306								1																																												Neurol models and identification theory
386 Zipser* 1993 #99								1																																												Spiking NNet model of short term memory
Total:	22	17	40	5	39	10	140	31	34	14	12	21	28	12	5	91	167	106	19	13	24	18	9	7	19	6	13	32	9	7	13	8	3	3	2	13	8	3	2	4	25	11	29	3	3	2	3	5	2	5		

Table 1. First and last segments of the classification table for 386 references. A - General; B - Cancer; C - Cardiovasc.; D - Neurosci.; E - Other diseases; F - Clinical; G - Clin. labs & imaging; H - Drugs; I - Molec. studies; J - Physiol., biochem., etc.; K - Other applications; L - Statistical comparisons, validation; M - Innovations; N - Other

RESULTS AND DISCUSSION

This is a polyglot literature -- written in mixtures of medical jargon, computer-speak, cognitive theory, and various other dialects. Included are occasional dollops of psychobabble, neurobabble, and sociobabble. Contributions runs the gamut from the highly sophisticated and innovative to those that represent little more than classroom learning exercises that somehow found their way into print. Each biomedical subspecialty seems to be entitled to one editorial that asks the rhetorical question "What are neural networks?" followed up by a full-length paper that answers the question in tutorial form. We count 25 contributions that seriously attempt to compare the outcome of neural network analysis with that from one or more statistical methods. There are 29 that, in our subjective opinion, develop innovative neural network architectures, learning strategies, or statistical analyses.

Table 2 lists some totals for overall categories. Given the origins and continued associations of the field, it comes as no surprise that almost half of the publications (176) relate to the neurosciences. Of those, 32 focus on clinical neurology, and 141 involve neurophysiological modeling. (In the latter category are some that simply invoke connectionist paradigms; these could have been omitted from the review if we had taken a strict-constructionist view of what constitutes an artificial neural network.) Forty publications relate to cancer and 40 to cardiovascular disease but, astoundingly, only 1 to AIDS. In all, 169 involve clinical aims broadly construed; of those, 108 are based on actual clinical data.

Table 2. Highlights of a classification of 386 publications since the beginning of 1991 on artificial neural networks in the biomedical sciences. Categories are not mutually exclusive.

Oncology	40	Clinically-oriented	169
Cardiology (including vascular)	40	Using clinical data	108
Respiratory medicine	12	Cytology, pathology, clinical lab	54
Infectious diseases	5	Imaging (MRI, CT, ultrasound, etc.)	44
Clinical neurology	32	Protein structure analysis	32
Psychology	28	Nucleic acid sequence analysis	9
Cognitive sciences	22	QSAR studies	7
Neurosciences (as models)	141	EEG analysis	12
		EKG analysis	10

Abbreviations: MRI, magnetic resonance imaging; CT, computerized tomography; QSAR, quantitative structure-activity relationship (among small chemical compounds); EEG, electro-encephalogram; EKG, electrocardiogram.

Applications in molecular biology are booming: 32 studies use artificial neural networks to predict protein secondary or tertiary structure; 9 predict nucleic acid sequence motifs or secondary structures. Molecular biology is an arena in which the networks appear quite often to outpace the competing methodologies tried. In some of the 44 publications on medical imaging, networks process the images themselves; in others, descriptors of the images constitute the input. Similarly, the 12 studies on EEG analysis and 10 on EKG analysis are divided between those in which networks analyze the tracings and those in which the analyses are done on derivative quantities.

A loaded question -- that will not be answered here: "In how many of these studies were neural networks used to address biological problems, and in how many were biomedical problems used to develop or demonstrate neural networks?" And linked to that: "In how many studies did neural networks achieve better results than could be achieved by other statistical techniques (linear, non-linear, or non-parametric)." In our own research, we often find ourselves asking the latter question.

REFERENCES

It would not be possible to give references for the whole database here, so, reflecting our own research interests, only those related to cancer are listed. The entire database will be presented elsewhere.

Cancer Pathology, Cytology

1. Molnar B, Szentirmay Z, Bodo M, Sugar J, Feher J. Application of multivariate, fuzzy set and neural network analysis in quantitative cytological examinations. Anal Cell Pathol 1993;5:161-75.
2. Boon ME, Kok LP. Neural network processing can provide means to catch errors that slip through human screening of pap smears. Diagn Cytopathol 1993;9:411-6.
3. Dawson AE, Austin RJ, Weinberg DS. Nuclear grading of breast carcinoma by image analysis. Classification by multivariate and neural network analysis. Am J Clin Pathol 1991;.
4. McGuire WL, Tandon AK, Allred DC, Chamness GC, Ravdin PM, Clark GM. Treatment decisions in axillary node-negative breast cancer patients. Monogr Natl Cancer Inst 1992;1992:173-80.
5. Nafe R, Choritz H. Introduction of a neuronal network as a tool for diagnostic analysis and classification based on experimental pathologic data. Exp Toxicol Pathol 1992;44:17-24.
6. O'Leary TJ, Mikel UV, Becker RL. Computer-assisted image interpretation: use of a neural network to differentiate tubular carcinoma from sclerosing adenosis. Mod Pathol 1992;5:402-5.
7. Tsai DY, Fujita H, Horita K, Endo T, Kido C, Sakuma S. Breast tumor classification by neural networks fed with sequential-dependence factors to the input layer. IEICE Trans. on Info. and Systems 1993;E76D:956-962.
8. Ricketts IW. Cervical cell image inspection - a task for artificial neural networks. Network: Computation in neural systems 1992;3:15.
9. Schaberg ES, Jordan WH, Kuyatt BL. Artificial intelligence in automated classification of rat vaginal smear cells. Anal Quant Cytol Histol 1992;14:446-50.

Cancer Clinical Chemistry

10. Astion ML, Wilding P. Application of neural networks to the interpretation of laboratory data in cancer diagnosis [see comments]. Clin Chem 1992;38:34-8.
11. Cohen ME, Hudson DL, Banda PW, Blois MS. Neural network approach to detection of metastatic melanoma from chromatographic analysis of urine. Proc Annu Symp Comput Appl Med Care 1991;1991:295-9.
12. Schweiger CR, Soeregi G, Spitzauer S, Maenner G, Pohl AL. Evaluation of laboratory data by conventional statistics and by three types of neural networks. Clin Chem 1993;39:1966-71.

Cancer Imaging (Except X-ray)

13. Tourassi GD, Floyd CJ. Artificial neural networks for single photon emission computed tomography. A study of cold lesion detection and localization. Invest Radiol 1993;28:671-7.
14. Dhawan AP, Arata L. Segmentation of medical images through competitive learning. Comput Methods Programs Biomed 1993;40:203-15.
15. Goldberg V, Manduca A, Ewert DL, Gisvold JJ, Greenleaf JF. Improvement in specificity of ultrasonography for diagnosis of breast tumors by means of artificial intelligence. Med Phys 1992;19:1475-81.
16. Maclin PS, Dempsey J. Using an artificial neural network to diagnose hepatic masses. J Med Syst 1992;16:215-25.
17. Piket MM, Taflove A, Lin WC, Katz DS, Sathiaseelan V, Mittal BB. Initial results for automated computational modeling of patient-specific electromagnetic hyperthermia. Ieee Trans Biomed Eng 1992;39:226-37.

18. Prater JS, Richard WD. Segmenting ultrasound images of the prostate using neural networks. Ultrason Imaging 1992;14:159-85.

19. Ostrem JS, Valdes AD, Edmonds PD. Application of neural nets to ultrasound tissue characterization. Ultrason Imaging 1991;13:298-9.

Cancer X-ray Imaging (including Mammography)

20. Lo SC, Freedman MT, Lin JS, Mun SK. Automatic lung nodule detection using profile matching and back-propagation neural network techniques. J Digit Imaging 1993;6:48-54.

21. Piraino DW, Amartur SC, Richmond BJ, Schils JP, Thome JM, Belhobek GH, Schlucter MD. Application of an artificial neural network in radiographic diagnosis. J Digit Imaging 1991;4:226-32.

22. Wu Y, Doi K, Giger ML, Nishikawa RM. Computerized detection of clustered microcalcifications in digital mammograms: applications of artificial neural networks. Med Phys 1992;19:555-60.

23. Wu Y, Giger ML, Doi K, Vyborny CJ, Schmidt RA, Metz CE. Artificial neural networks in mammography: application to decision making in the diagnosis of breast cancer. Radiology 1993;187:81-7.

24. Boone JM, Seshagiri S, Steiner RM. Recognition of chest radiograph orientation for picture archiving and communications systems display using neural networks. J Digit Imaging 1992;5:190-3.

Cancer Molecular Biology (including Karyotyping)

25. Malet P, Benkhalifa M, Perissel B, Geneix A, Le CB. Chromosome analysis by image processing in a computerized environment. Clinical applications. J Radiat Res (Tokyo) 1992;.

26. Graham J, Errington P, Jennings A. A neural network chromosome classifier. J Radiat Res (Tokyo) 1992;.

27. Guthrie C, Gregor J, Thomason MG. Constrained Markov networks for automated analysis of G-banded chromosomes. Comput Biol Med 1993;23:105-14.

Cancer Drug Quantitative Structure-Activity Relationships (QSAR)

28. Ajay. A unified framework for using neural networks to build QSARs. J Med Chem 1993;36:3565-71.

29. Andrea TA, Kalayeh H. Applications of neural networks in quantitative structure-activity relationships of dihydrofolate reductase inhibitors. J Med Chem 1991;34:2824-36.

30. So SS, Richards WG. Application of neural networks: quantitative structure-activity relationships of the derivatives of 2,4-diamino-5-(substituted-benzyl)pyrimidines as DHFR inhibitors. J Med Chem 1992;35:3201-7.

31. Tetko IV, Luik AI, Poda GI. Applications of neural networks in structure-activity relationships of a small number of molecules. J Med Chem 1993;36:811-4.

Other Clinical Cancer Diagnosis

32. Maclin PS, Dempsey J, Brooks J, Rand J. Using neural networks to diagnose cancer. J Med Syst 1991;15:11-9.

33. Ravdin PM, Clark GM. A practical application of neural network analysis for predicting outcome of individual breast cancer patients. Breast Cancer Res Treat 1992;22:285-93.

34. Ravdin PM, Clark GM, Hilsenbeck SG, Owens MA, Vendely P, Pandian MR, McGuire WL. A demonstration that breast cancer recurrence can be predicted by neural network analysis. Breast Cancer Res Treat 1992;21:47-53.

35. Ravdin PM, Clark GM, Hough JJ, Owens MA, McGuire WL. Neural Network Analysis of DNA flow cytometry histograms. Cytometry 1993;14:74-80.

36. Bartels PH, Thompson D, Weber JE. Diagnostic decision support by inference networks. In Vivo 1993;7:379-85.

Miscellaneous:

37. Weinstein JN, Kohn KW, Grever MR, Viswanadhan VN, Rubinstein LV, Monks AP, Scudiero DA, Welch L, Koutsoukos AD, Chiausa AJ, et al. Neural computing in cancer drug development: predicting mechanism of action. Science 1992;258:447-51.

38. Howells SL, Maxwell RJ, Peet AC, Griffiths JR. An investigation of tumor 1H nuclear magnetic resonance spectra by the application of chemometric techniques. Magn Reson Med 1992;28:214-36.

39. Howells SL, Maxwell RJ, Howe FA, Peet AC, Stubbs M, Rodrigues LM, Robinson SP, Baluch S, Griffiths JR. Pattern recognition of 31P magnetic resonance spectroscopy tumour spectra obtained in vivo. Nmr Biomed 1993;6:237-41.
40. Prideaux JA, Mikulecky DC, Clarke AM, Ware JL. A modified neural network model of tumor cell interactions and subpopulation dynamics. Invasion Metastasis 1993;13:50-6.

Prediction of Breast Cancer Malignancy for difficult cases using an Artificial Neural Network

Carey E. Floyd Jr*, A. Joon Yun, Joseph Y. Lo, Georgia Tourassi,
Daniel C. Sullivan, Phyllis J. Kornguth
Department of Radiology, Duke University Medical Center,
Durham, NC 27710
* also Department of Biomedical Engineering , Duke University,
Durham, NC 27710

Abstract

An Artificial Neural Network was developed to predict breast cancer from mammographic findings. Radiologists read the mammograms and filled out a list of eight findings. These findings were encoded as features for an Artificial Neural Network (ANN). Results from biopsy were taken as truth in the diagnosis of malignancy. The ANN was trained on a set of patient records and was tested on a set for which the radiologists' diagnosis was indeterminate. Performance for the network was evaluated in terms of sensitivity and specificity over a range of decision thresholds and was expressed as an ROC curve. The trained network was evaluated on a subset of patients for which the radiologists' diagnosis was indeterminate. With an optimal threshold, the neural network performed with a diagnostic accuracy of 0.84. This performance suggests that an artificial neural network may be used as a diagnostic aid for prediction of breast cancer.

Introduction

Breast cancer is a serious health problem with an estimated 182,000 new cases diagnosed in the US this year. An estimated 46,000 women will die from this disease in 1993[1]. Mammography remains the most sensitive technique for early detection of breast cancer. While mammography alone is a sensitive test, a significant fraction of those patients referred to biopsy do not have a malignancy. While specific, biopsy is an invasive, costly, and emotionally stressful procedure. In an effort to reduce the number of benign cases which are sent to biopsy, we have investigated an artificial intelligence technique to predict the outcome of biopsy from radiographic findings.

A variety of medical tasks have been successfully performed using such networks including analysis of EKG patterns[2], decision-making in pathology[3], texture analysis in ultrasound[4], lesion detection in SPECT images[5], image boundary detection[6], differential diagnosis from chest radiographs [7, 8], prediction of pulmonary embolism[9, 10], breast cancer analysis[11], and decision-making in mammography[12]. Here we present an ANN which has been trained to predict breast malignancy from mammographic findings for indeterminate (difficult) cases.

MATERIALS AND METHODS

The ANN for malignancy prediction was implemented as a backpropagation architecture with one hidden layer and a sigmoid activation function. Input feature values were the radiographic findings assigned by the radiologists. These findings were assigned numerical values as described below. The network was trained to predict biopsy results.

Training

The network was trained using a backpropagation supervised training algorithm. The training set included examples which represented the full range of possible inputs so that the network will correctly classify any new input set.

Case Selection

The training and testing sets were selected from mammograms with corresponding biopsies. The pool of cases consisted of 203 cases (62 malignant, 141 benign) randomly selected from those examinations which were verified by surgical biopsy during the interval between January 1991 through May 1992. Craniocaudal, mediolateral oblique, and (optional) magnification views had been obtained by x-ray screen-film technique. Radiologists read the films and entered the radiographic findings on forms. Malignant or benign outcome from surgical biopsy was also recorded.

Defining the Features List

The checklist findings entry form consisted of a list of eight radiographic features. Numerical values were assigned to these features such that a radiographic finding which was known to have strong correlation with malignancy was given a high numerical value. In addition, the radiologist assigned an overall impression of malignancy on a scale from one to five (1=benign; 2=probably benign; 3=indeterminate; 4=probably malignant; 5=malignant).

Constructing the Neural Network

A backpropagation neural network (fig. 1) with one hidden layer was created for the classification task.
The input layer consisted of 8 nodes which represented the eight (numerically ordered) radiographic features from the data entry form (excluding the overall radiological impression): mass size, mass margin, asymmetric density, architectural distortion, calcification number,

calcification morphology, calcification density, and calcification distribution.

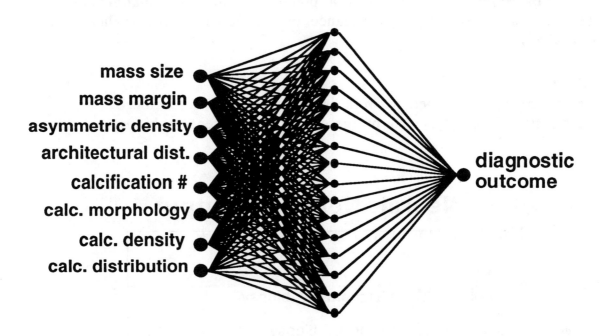

INPUT LAYER   HIDDEN LAYER   OUTPUT LAYER

mass size
mass margin
asymmetric density
architectural dist.
calcification #
calc. morphology
calc. density
calc. distribution

diagnostic outcome

Fig. 1 Architecture of neural network for predicting biopsy results from radiographic findings.

The hidden layer consisted of 16 nodes. The number of hidden nodes was chosen by trial and error from the range between 5 and 25 nodes. The output layer consisted of a single node representing diagnostic outcome; 0.0 for benign and 1.0 for malignant. After a series of trials the training parameters were optimized: number of nodes in the hidden layer=16, learning coefficient=0.5, momentum coefficient=0.4, and training interval=300 iterations. The network was implemented on a desktop computer (Macintosh Quadra 950: Apple Computer Inc., Cupertino Ca) using commercial software (Neural Ware Inc., Pittsburgh PA).

Training and Testing the Network

The performance of the network for indeterminate cases was examined. First, a testing set of 32 difficult cases that the radiologist had called "indeterminate" (25 actual benign, 7 malignant) was selected from the original 203 cases. Next, the network was trained on a set with equal population of benign and malignant cases (55 malignant; 55 benign). This training set was sampled from the 171 remaining cases (203 total - 32 testing) by using all 55 of the malignant cases plus 55 randomly selected benign cases. The training was "supervised"; for each case the network was provided with both the input of radiographic findings and the corresponding biopsy diagnosis. For training, the value of the output node was 0.0 if the biopsy pathology was benign and 1.0 if the result was malignant. The network was presented with the testing set after 300 iterations of training and produced a predictive value for malignancy between 0.0 and 1.0. The performance of the network was evaluated by ROC analysis.

Results

A histogram for the trained network is shown in fig. 2 for the 32 indeterminate cases only. All of these cases were sent to biopsy.

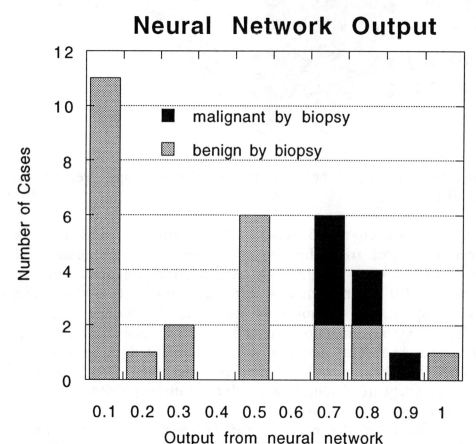

Fig. 2. Histogram for the output values of the trained network for the indeterminate category.

An ROC curve for the performance of the trained network on the indeterminate cases shows good performance for the ANN (fig. 3) with an ROC area index of 0.86.

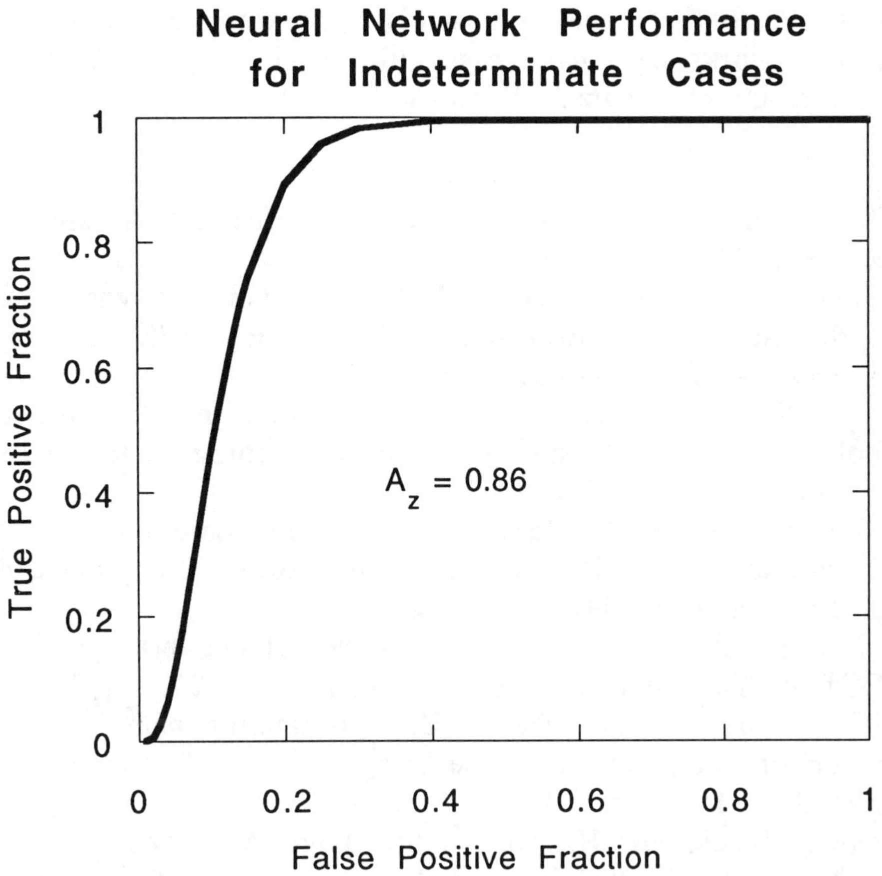

Neural Network Performance for Indeterminate Cases

Fig. 3 Performance of network for the indeterminate category.

Discussion

The radiologists' estimate of probability for malignancy determines the recommendation of biopsy for a patient. Indeterminate lesions are sent to biopsy depending on the presence of other patient factors such as previous history of breast cancer or positive family history. To use the results from a neural network, a decision threshold must be set. In breast cancer prediction, The cost of a false negative prediction is much larger than the cost of a false negative. With a threshold of 0.6, this network would have sent all 7 of the malignant cases to biopsy but only 5 of the 25 benign cases (Sensitivity = 1.0, Specificity = 0.80). With this optimal threshold, the neural network performed with a diagnostic accuracy of 0.84. It is important to note that these indeterminate cases are the very difficult cases. This difficulty adds to the significance of the network's high accuracy[13].

Our study suggests that numerical decision-making techniques such as artificial neural networks may have a useful role in improving the accuracy and consistency of medical diagnosis.

References

1.   Boring CC, Squires TS, and Tong T. Cancer Statistics. CA A cancer journal for clinicians 1993; 43:   7-26.
2.   Cios KJ, Chen K, and Langenderfer RA. Use of neural networks in detecting cardiac diseases from echocardiographic images. IEEE Eng. in Medicine and Biology 1990; 9:   58-60.
3.   Dytch HE and Wied GL. Artificial neural networks and their use in quantitative pathology. Analytical and Quantitative Cytology and Histology 1990; 12:   379-393.
4.   DaPonte JS and Sherman P. Classification of ultrasonic image texture by statistical discriminant analysis and neural networks. Computerized Medical Imaging and Graphics 1991; 15:   3-9.
5.   Floyd CE Jr and Tourassi GD. An artificial neural network for lesion detection in SPECT images. Investigative Radiology 1992; 27:   667-672.
6.   Amartur SC, Piraino D, and Takefuji Y. Optimization neural networks for the segmentation of magnetic resonance images. IEEE Transactions on Medical Imaging 1992; 11:   215-220.
7.   Asada N, Doi K, MacMahon H, Montner SM, Giger ML, Abe C, and Wu Y. Potential usefulness of an artificial neural network for differential diagnosis of interstitial lung diseases: pilot study. Radiology 1990; 177: 857-860.
8.   Gross GW, Boone JM, Greco-Hunt V, and Greenberg B. Neural networks in radiologic diagnosis: II. interpretation of neonatal chest radiographs. Investigative Radiology 1990; 25:   1017-1023.
9.   Scott JA and Palmer EL. Neural network analysis of ventilation-perfusion lung scans. Radiology 1993; 186:   661-664.
10.   Tourassi G, Floyd C, Sostman H, and Coleman R. An Artificial Neural Network Approach for the Diagnosis of Acute Pulmonary Embolism. Radiology 1993; 189:   555-558.
11.   Dawson AE, Austin RE, and Weinberg DS. Nuclear Grading of Breast Carcinoma by Image Analysis: Classification by Multivariate and Neural Network Analysis. Am. J. Clin. Pathology 1991; 95:   S29-S37.
12.   Wu Y, Giger ML, Doi K, Vyborny CJ, Schmidt RA, and Metz CE. Artificial neural networks in mammography: application to decision making in the diagnosis of breast cancer. Radiology 1993; 187:   81-87.
13.   Nishikawa RM, Giger ML, Doi K, Metz CE, Yin F-F, Vyborny CJ, and Schmidt RA. Effect of case selection on the performance of computer-aided detection schemes. Medical Physics 1994; 21:   265-269.

Neural Network Recognition of Multiple Mammographic Lesions

Philip Downes
E-Systems, Inc.
P.O. Box 6056, CBN24
Greenville, Tx   75403

ABSTRACT

Neural network recognition of mammographic lesions are studied. Digitized mammograms containing circumscribed and stellate lesions are used for training an ART II network. Texture quantification via fractal analysis method provides a data representation for lesion detection and classification enhancement.

Introduction

The primary of goal of any radiological service is to process cases in the most accurate and efficient way. Most types of cases in radiology are difficult to automate due to the usual problems associated with machine vision: translation-rotation invariance, inconsistent image brightness and inconsistent quality of radiographs. Mammography provides a class of case which can take a board certified radiologist 15-20 minutes to arrive at a diagnosis from viewing the six radiographs associated with each case. The cost, however, is fixed and the task tedious. Any aid that provides lesion detection or recognition would be a asset in a clinical setting. From the machine vision standpoint, mammography provides some positive points by having high quality x-rays and the multiplicity of views. Mammography provides a tractable, self-contained problem in that other medical aspects of the subject do not affect the differential diagnosis, only the choice of treatment. Mammographic surveys require three radiographs at different angles on both sides. These six views are inspected and cross-correlated for possible lesions. When a particular type of lesion is hypothesized, other radiographic indicators are sought to determine if the lesion is benign or malignant. These indicators may not be on the same radiograph or at the same scale as the lesion. A frequent indicator of malignancy are micro-calcifications. These are often hidden in the "noise" of the overlying tissue or in lesions themselves and by their nature require magnification to ascertain their cluster density. This search for micro-calcifications and their evaluation slows the diagnostic process. The neural network approach to micro-calcification classification will be addressed elsewhere.

Previous work [1] [2] [3] has demonstrated recognition and texture quantification of mammographic lesions of both the benign and malignant types. In [2] a texture quantification scheme was implemented using fractal analysis. In [3] ART II was used to recognize gray scale images of individual lesions. It's limitation was the collapsing of categories for types of lobular lesions. Specifically, lobular lesions of the circumscribed and uncircumscribed type were place in the same category. This limitation is overcome here by the inclusion of the *symmetric adaptive thresholding* scheme of Ryan and Winter to the *F2* activity equation of ART II. In addition, fractal analysis is used with ART II for detection and classification of lesions. The texture of a lesion is often proportional to the malignancy. Here, the texture is quantified by the fractal dimension.

The possible classifications of breast masses are numerous, the most common being abscesses, duct ectasia, fat necrosis and fibrocystic disease such as epithelial cysts; adenosis of various types, intralobular or extralobular fibrosis and tumors. Mammographic lesions fall into several basic categories that are used in this study: lobular and stellate. These two categories occur in a range of sizes and shapes and must be recognized in a variety of overlying parenchymal structure. However, they are sufficiently consistent in shape, density and scale as to provide a trackable problem for first steps in neural classification of breast morphology. It should be noted that much of the literature for automated diagnosis of mammograms is concerned with finding only the microcalcifications: the primary mammographic signature of cancer. An automated mammographic system will also need to classify all the morphological aspects of each case in order to discount a possible differential diagnosis.

The process of lesion detection proceeds by placing left and right mammograms side by side and scanning downward, comparing left and right views. Both views are compared on a region by region basis with the texture differences driving the saccade. Differences in the parenchyma (breast structure) must be considered and often complicate the search for lesions. Figures 1 and 2 show a case with multiple lesions on the left and the opposing null mammogram on the right. The texture quality of both views, including the ductal pattern is often inconsistent with the presence of pathology. This basic method is used here. The inspection system scans in the comparable region from both views and then computes the fractal dimension and the fractal histogram. These distributions are inspected for significant differences and provide the first indication for tagging as an area of interest. Areas of interest are then scanned by ART II/SAT for lesion classification.

The lobular and stellate lesions considered here are typical in mammography. A class of lobular lesion is the fibroadenoma which is homogeneous in density with a contour that is ovoid to lobular. A stellate lesion may or may not have a central mass but conveys itself on the mammogram as have wisps in a radial pattern from the central point of the lesion. Mammograms containing circumscribed and stellate lesions of different scales were digitized for use in this study. Examples of cases are shown below with Figure 1 containing two stellate lesion in the upper half and a lobular lesion just below center. The defining morphology is more apparent in the edge detection view of Figure 3.

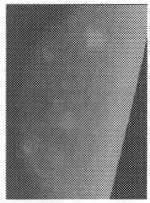

Fig. 1 Left view showing stellate and lobular lesions.

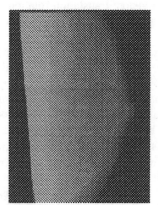

Fig. 2 Right view null.

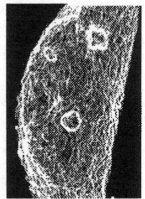

Fig 3. Edge detection of Fig 1 showing stellate stellate wisps outside the two masses.

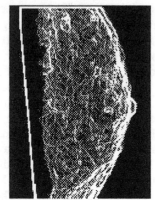

Fig 4. Edge detection of Fig 2.

Fractal Analysis

Neural networks often perform better with data representations other than the raw data. Radiological assessments are often driven by textures that the radiologist has correlated through training to pathology. This is also true of mammographic analysis where the texture of a structure is often indicative of malignancy and a trigger to closer visual inspection. To investigate the ability of texture as a data representation for an ART II network, a fractal analysis was performed.

Mandelbrot has developed a novel class of functions know as fractals whose dimension provides a good estimate of surface roughness. A fractal is defined as a set for which the Hausdorff-Besicovich dimension is strictly larger than the topological dimension. For example, a smooth surface has fractal dimension that is equal to the topological dimension and a "hilly" surface has a fractal dimension >> topological dimension. Fractal are an appropriate mathematical framework to study the nonuniform and complex shapes found in radiographs. Pentland [4] presents findings that support that most natural surfaces are spatially isotropic fractals and the intensity image of these surfaces are also fractals. In addition, Pentland [4][5] has outlined a method of performing fractal analysis and discussed it as a path for texture analysis. Lundahl et. al. [6] has applied a slightly different method of calculating the fractal dimension to images of healing human calcaneous. Mammographic lesions exhibit varying degrees of texture which are an aid in their classification. In addition, the mammographic diagnosis of malignancy is related to the edge roughness of a lesion.

The method used for calculating the fractal dimension of digitized images is based upon the relationship between the fractal dimension and the power spectral density. Pentland's technique consists of first finding the power spectral density (PSD) and then use the relation $PSD = kf\,e^{-2H-1}$ to calculate $D=2-H$ for the fractal dimension. The power spectral density is calculated and a least squares fit of $\log(PSD)$ vs. $\log(f)$ is performed to determine the slope H and the dimension D. Thus each location of the image is assigned a dimension which is rotation invariant. The fractal dimension $D=2-H$ is then plotted as a 64 gray level image. Pentland's approach also supplies a degree of scale invariance (8:1). This is supposed to provide a texture scale-invariant representation of objects in the scene such as lesions. Hence, an ART II/SAT could perform lesion identification utilizing the fractal analysis data representation. To implement Pentland's algorithm here the digitized mammograms (256x256x64) pixel images used here, the power spectral density is calculated for 8x8 patches.

In addition to scale invariance, the fractal model provides texture edge detection. This occurs when the dimension at a location is less the topological dimension. Hence, areas of uniform fractal dimension represent uniform textures and appear as a constant a gray level in the fractal image. Hence, scenes having subtle differences in their boundary, such as between a smooth desert and a lake, have a recognizable edge in the fractal image.

For the mammogram problem fractal analysis was done in two parts. First on whole views containing lobular and stellate lesions and then on magnified sections of the areas containing these lesions. The fractal histogram of all cases were inspected and a pattern found. In the null lesion cases, the histogram shifted to above dimension 2.0. When a single or multiple lesions were present the histogram centered around dimension 2.0. This pattern held for multiple scales as indicated by Figures 5 and 6. Figure 5 concerns the histograms of the entire view for both lesion presence and null cases. Tmam10 contains a large fibroadenoma while Tmam12 contains smaller fibroadenoma. In contrasting the histograms of the lesion and null cases it is seen that the undisturbed parenchymal of the null cases produce the higher fractal dimensions. Hence, lesions in this study are simply displacing the more complex textures. Figure 6 displays the histogram for magnified areas of interest containing lesions and the same respective region in the opposing mammogram. The clear differences suggest using the histogram as a lesion detector for determining areas of interest for classification or for driving a saccade for finding other areas of interest.

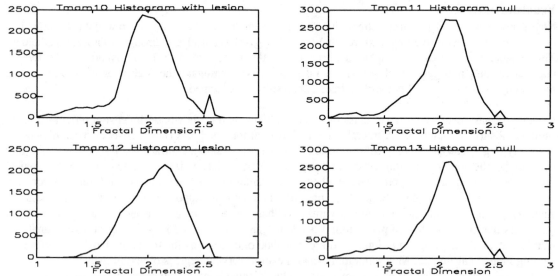

Fig.5. Fractal histograms of whole mammograms with lesions and null conditions.

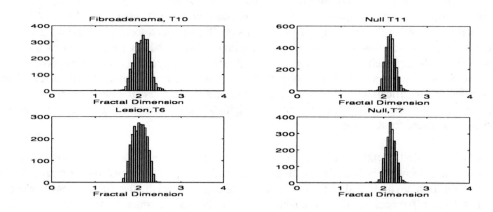

Fig. 6. Fractal Histograms for magnified views of lesions and null areas.

ART II Modifications with Symmetric Adaptive Thresholding

Previous use of ART II to classify lesions produced mixed results and often misclassified types of stellate lesions into the fibroadenoma category [3]. The problem was traced to the standard ART II model recoding category nodes to smaller input patterns. To alleviate this problem the work of Ryan and Winter's symmetric adaptive thresholding modification of ART I was adapted. In short, the F2 equation of ART II was changed to:

$$dy/dt = -Ay + (1-y)[g(y)+\Sigma piZij - \lambda u|I-q|] - (C-y)\Sigma g(y)$$

where the $- \lambda u|I-q|$ is the symmetric adaptive thresholding that is added to the excitatory term. Here, λ is the parameter that controls the category size, I is the normalized magnitude of the input, q is the pattern size and u is the time that the node i is activated. With this modification the network was able to distinguish all stellate lesions from fibroadenomas.

Classification System

The flow of detection and classification was divided among two ART II/SAT networks: one for classifying the fractal histogram of a local region acting as the lesion detector and the other to classify the region for lesions if an appropriate histogram had been detected.

In the simulation program a conditional statement decides whether to activate the lesion classifier or not.. For a fully integrated neural architecture a gated dipole could be used. This system worked effectively for the 6 cases studied here. The images of these cases were digitized as 256x256x64 grey levels for both the whole mammogram and the magnified lesions. For lesion sizes considered here (1-2cm) this was adequate for both the fractal analysis and classification. However, it is inadequate for microcalcification studies. Further results concerning the classification of microcalcification clusters in relation to morphology using 1024x1024x256 grey levels in 14 complete cases will be reported elsewhere.

References

[1]Downes, P.T., Oldham, W.J.B., and V. Hunter, MD, *Neural Network Recognition of Mammographic Lesions*, Radiological Society of North America Conference, 1987

[2] Oldham, W.J.B., Downes, P.T., V. Hunter, MD., *Fractal Image Analysis of Mammograms*, Radiological Society of North America Conference, 1987

[3] Downes, P.T. and V. Hunter, MD, *ART II Recognition of Mammographic Lesions*, Radiological Society of North America Conference, 1988

[4] Pentland, A., *Fractal-Based Description of Natural Scenes*, IEEE Transaction on Pattern Analysis and Machine Intelligence, Vol. PAMI=6, No. 6, Nov 1984

[5] Pentland, A., *Shading into Texture*, Artificial Intelligence 29, 1986, pp. 147-170

[6] Lundahl, T. Ohley, W.J., Kay, S., Siffert, R., *Fractional Brownian Notion: A Maximum Likelihood Estimater and Its Application to Image Texture*, IEEE Trans. on Medical Imaging, Vol. MI-5, No. 3 Sept. 1986

QRS Complex Recognition Using NLD and Neural Networks

Philip Downes
E-Systems, Inc.
P.O. Box 6056, CBN24
Greenville, Tx   75403

ABSTRACT

Automated recognition of QRS complexes of electrocardiograms (ECG) has been a focus in medical equipment development for a number of years. Preprocessing of these often noisy time series has been subjected to the standard linear techniques before submission to a pattern recognition algorithm. Here, methods from nonlinear dynamics are applied to noisy electrocardiograms of different pathology before submission to two neural architectures. A radial basis function network with adaptive center allocation is used to learn cases of ECG. In addition, an ART II - Masking Field architecture is used to scan and classify ECG to recognize changes in the QRS complex.

1.0 Introduction

Automated recognition of electrocardiograms (ECG) is a concern in the both the intensive care and long time care of cardiac patients. Patient requirements include detection and recognition of ECG transients and changes in cardiac pathology. Detection is often based on previous knowledge of a stable patient's ECG and distinguishing new characteristics occurring in the time series. These characteristics can be indicative of transient or permanent pathology requiring immediate clinical attention. The frequency and trend of a particular sequence of complexes is also relevant. Here, two networks are used to perform these separate functions. A standard radial basis function network and RBF network modified for adaptive assignment of centers is used to learn the ECG time series and act as a state change detector. A scanning ART II-Masking Fields architecture is used to learn patient's ECG. The Masking Field architecture is modified with the symmetric adaptive threshold method of Ryan and Winter for enhanced subset recognition. The intra-inter cluster competition of Masking Fields is able to recognize the combinations of waveforms present in the QRS complex which indicate distinct pathologies.

Recent characterization methods of time series analysis from nonlinear systems have been applied to ECG. The initial focus was to relate observed nonlinearities to cardiac pathology. This included studies of the occurrence and sequence of *bifurcations* before and after fibrillation. Some of these nonlinear signal processing methods have import to efficient RBF network input vector construction. Previous experience has shown that using time delay vectors used to reconstruct attractors from a scalar time series as input produces faster training and prediction of RBF networks. That is, the network is learning the attractor. In addition the appropriate embedding dimension for the attractor reconstruction from an often noisy time series must be determined. The methods to provide the choice of time delay, embedding dimension and noise reduction are discussed below.

2.0 Attractor Reconstruction Using SVD

Attractor reconstruction from a time series is done via Taken's theorem. This method recontructs the attractor by plotting time delay vectors in phase space with $x=[x(t), x(t+\tau), x(t+2\tau)]$ begin the vector. Each element of the vector is taken from the scalar time series and incorporates the time delay τ to create the embedding vector. This method requires choosing a time delay interval for sampling the time series. This choice of time delay can be determined by using Fraser's mutual information method [1] [2]. The mutual information is calculated over a range of delay values and the delay corresponding to the first minima of the mutual information is chosen for the reconstruction. This assures that the points of the attractor are maximally independent. In addition the attractor reconstruction must be done in the appropriate dimension representing the dynamics. The embedding dimension can be determined by inspecting the singular spectrum of the system. This approach, due to Broomhead and King [4], calculates the singular value decomposition of the covariance matrix $x^T x$ whose entries are the time delay vectors. The number of singular values above the noise floor represents the appropriate dimension for attractor reconstruction. An additional befenit is the noise reduction performed by using the new basis vectors determined by the largest singular vectors and reploting the attractor.

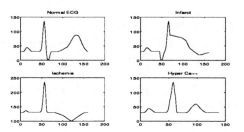

Fig. 1. Four type of ECG waveforms studied.

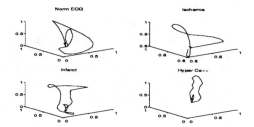

Fig. 2. Takens embedding of time series in Fig 1

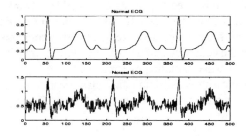

Fig.3. Normal and noisy ECG.

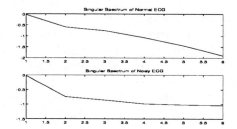

Fig 4. Singular values of ECG of Fig 3.

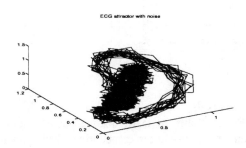

Fig. 5 Attractor of normal ECG with noise.

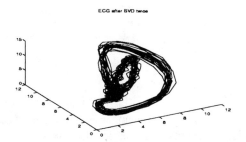

Fig. 6. Attractor after SVD applied twice.

3.0 RBF Network

Two RBF architectures were tried for learning the various ECG states: the standard RBF of Moody and Darken [6] and the adaptive RBF network outlined by Mel and Omohundro [7]. These networks have had success in learning various nonlinear time series. The RBF network is a connectionist type gradient descent network consisting of two layers. The first layer consists of radial basis functions (termed centers) to which an input vector is submitted. The basic idea is to modify the network such that the centers *cover* the input space where the high frequency components occur. In this way the network as learns the attractor of the dynamical system in the most efficient manner. Both networks were trained on a time series containing 100 QRS complexes of the same pathology. A separate RBF network is trained for each pathology.

Both networks were able to learn the various ECG's with mean predictive error of 5.0E-3 for a covering of 100 centers. There was little gain in the adaptive network in its ability to lower the prediction error. Prediction intervals from 1 to 20 where tried with corresponding adjustments of the learning parameters. With these results, a hardware implementation seems feasible with the caveat that a network for each pathology would have to be used. The exception to this would be the long term monitoring in which a patient's ECG was initially learned and only the detection of an abnormal situation is sought.

4.0 ART II - Masking Fields

An alternative to learning the dynamics of the time series is to use a network architecture that classifies according to patterns of subset waveforms. Normally, in evaluating an ECG the clinical setting by scanning the ECG time series and noting the subpatterns the PQRST complexes. The occurrence of a single form for a short period of time can indicate a transient pathology such as an infarct. A network architecture should be able to provide a translation invariant classification. This can be done by an ART II network that scans the ECG, building up categories of subpatterns of the PQRST complexes. Such a scan pattern is seen in Fig. 7. The $F2$ output pattern can then be feed into a Masking Fields network for classification. The advantage of this network combination is clear: a change in subset pattern of an ECG can be classified immediately as opposed to having to wait for a cumulative prediction error comparison between RBF networks. In this way alarms can be set for the occurrence of a clinically relavant transition. An example would be the decrease of the amplitude of the T wave signaling hypercalcemia.

The ART II-Masking Fields approach relies on the reliable subset detection amd classification. ART II merely has to classify the subset patterns to provide category node pattern as input to Masking Fields. This is easily done for the ECG cases studied here.

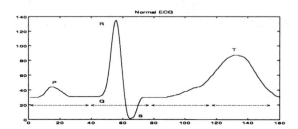

Fig. 7 Subset scanning intervals

Howvere, a design problem arose with the Masking Fields ability to learn distinct subset patterns. Individual patterns could be learned but the inter-cluster and intra-cluster competition blocks out the learning of multiple patterns. Hence, the required recognition of different subset combinations could not be realized. Various methods were tried to rectify this until the adaptation of Ryan and Winter's *symmetric adaptive thresholding* scheme produced stable learning. In short, the normal $F2$ activity equation is modified by adding the term: $-\lambda_i u_i (I - q_i)$ to the excitatory term of equation (A25) of [8]. Here, λ is the parameter that controls the cluster size, I is the normalized magnitude of the input, q is the pattern size and u is the time that the node i is activated. Once the modification was implemented, Masking Fields could learn combinations of ECG subsets whose number is limited only by the size of the network. Below is an example of how three common conditions are classified by first subset classification then Masking Fields. The three Masking Field inputs are easily separated even though there exists common subsets.

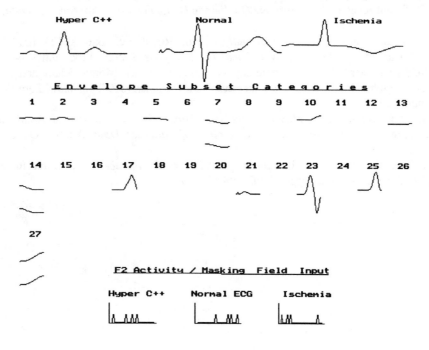

5.0 Summary

Methods of nonlinear dynamics provide the appropriate dimension and input vector size for RBF networks. The proper time delay τ is determined from the first minima of the mutual information. The time delay then becomes the appropriate choice for constructing the input vector to an RBF network or any network whose role is to learn the dynamics of the system. In addition the ability of ART class models were studied and found to be an effective classifier within the scope of a stable ECG. It should be noted that this study was not done for a sufficient range of noise levels such that a firm conclusion to its utility. However, the ECG in a typical ICU situation utilizes a three lead system. This produces little noise except with patient movement.

References

[1] Fraser, A.M. and Swinney, H.L., Phys. Rev., 33A, 1134 (1986)

[2] Fraser, A.M., IEEE Trans. on Info. Theory, 35, 245, (1989)

[3] Takens, F., *Detecting Strange Attractors in Turbulence*, In: Dynamical Systems and Turbulence, (ed. D. A. Rand and L. S. Young, Springer, Berlin

[4] Broomhead, D. S. and King, G. P., *Extracting Qualitative Dynamics from Experimental Data*, Physica D, 20, 217-39

[5] Broomhead, D. S., and Jones, R , *Time Series Analysis*, Proc. Royal Soc. Lond. A, 423, 103-21

[6] Moody, J. and Darken, C., *Learning with Localized Receptive Fields*, Proceedings of the 1988 Connectionist Models Summer School, ed. Touretzky, Hinton , Sejnowski , Morgan Kaufmann

[7] Mel, B. W., and Omohundro, S. M., *How Receptive Field Parameters Affect Neural Learning*, NIPS 3, Morgan Kaufmann, 1991

[8] Cohen, M.A., and Grossberg, S., *Masking Fields: A Massively Parallel Neural Architecture for Learning, Recognizing, and Predicting Multiple Groupings of Patterned Data,* Applied Optics, 26(10), 1866-1891, 1987

[9] Ryan, T. W. and Winter, C. L., *Variations on Adaptive Resonance*, IEEE First International Conference on Neural Networks, San Diego: IEEE, 1987, 767-775

Commercial and Industrial Applications of Neural Networks

Session Chair: Bernard Widrow

A Large-Scale Neural Network Application for Airline Seat Allocation

Ken Otwell, Sharon Hormby,
and William Hutchison, Ph.D.
BehavHeuristics, Inc.
335 Paint Branch Drive
College Park, MD 20742
U.S.A.

Abstract

A large-scale neural network application for airline seat inventory management has been developed by BehavHeuristics, Inc., and is in daily use at USAir, Inc. on 150 user workstations. This paper discusses a variety of issues related to the application, including knowledge engineering, scale-up, non-stationary domains, multi-network architectures, and the requirement for improved algorithms such as have been developed at BehavHeuristics.

Introduction

BehavHeuristics has pioneered the application of neural networks in the field of airline "yield management," or seat inventory control, implementing systems for airlines from Europe to Australia and integrating with a variety of reservation systems over the past several years. BehavHeuristics' current generation *Airline Marketing Assistant*™ (AMA) product integrates two neural networks for forecasting passenger demand and "no-shows" with mathematical optimization and analysis algorithms, an advanced graphic user interface, and a networked relational database. The system, which is heavily customized for each airline and has been twice redesigned from the ground up, is in daily use by as many as 150 revenue analysts on networked 486 PC workstations at USAir, the largest such installation to date by any vendor.

This paper focuses on a sophisticated, large-scale application of advanced neural network technology. Therefore, knowledge of general feed-forward neural network concepts and processing, as well as alternate statistical, econometric and process control models, is assumed. Advanced neural network techniques, such as recurrent networks and multi-net architectures, are described thoroughly in the references. Proprietary algorithms developed by BehavHeuristics are discussed in terms of their capabilities in comparison to standard techniques. This paper details some of BehavHeuristics' proprietary advancements, characteristics of the yield management problem and how they relate to a neural network solution, and plans for further technology development and deployment.

Technology Overview

BANKET™ (BehavHeuristics' Adaptive Network Knowledge Engineering Technology) embodies a set of proprietary neural network algorithms to learn non-linear mappings between independent and dependent variables via supervised learning, as well as to discover optimal responses to input data via reinforcement learning.[1] The underlying functionality provided by BANKET is conceptually similar to that provided by backpropagation, with significant differences in performance with regard to learning dynamics and processing time.

BANKET has been under development since 1983 and has been tested and enhanced extensively during development of a variety of business-decision applications including flight crew training scheduling, credit risk scoring, stock portfolio selection, and optimal seat allocation, as well as passenger demand and no-show forecasting. In contrast to the prevalent practice of providing generic toolkits and consulting services, BehavHeuristics has developed and marketed high-end, vertical applications based on neural network technology, thus gaining corporate experience in how to scale-up, enhance, exploit, and integrate the strengths of the technology to achieve success in the marketplace. The most recent release of BANKET provides the following capabilities:

- Standard representations for boolean, categorical, continuous, bounded-continuous, and periodic input data,

- Uni-directional functional mappings that can be arbitrarily non-linear,

- Learning algorithms which generate minimal network architectures, including the dynamic addition and deletion of both nodes and arcs, while simultaneously adjusting weights,

- Output in the form of both mean and standard deviation (expected process error) at each network firing,

- Continuous adaptation to non-stationary dynamics without the necessity of refitting historical data,

- An integrated Temporal Differences technique for utilizing incremental information for training prior to output target availability,[2]

- Learning algorithms which are not gradient-based and are not subject to problems of local minima when used in standard feedforward mode,

- Learning rates based solely on noise rejection and generalization requirements, rather than approximating the infinitesimal learning rate required by pure gradient descent methods,

- A training process which requires a minimal number of data samples — 7 passes to reliably learn the exclusive-or mapping — and does not require even a single pass over all of the available airline daily booking data to achieve forecast accuracy,

- Configurations for minimizing any one of a predefined set of error measures, loss functions, or inverted utility functions when learning (custom functions are easily implemented),

- Internal node and weight structures which are easily interpreted and directly manipulable by the application customer without the need for post-hoc sensitivity analysis,

- Adaptations to multi-scale periods during historical random sampling which can then be locked against drift during on-line adaptation in non-stationary domains,

- Sparse matrix efficiency for very large networks in software only — the USAir application uses a 70,000 node/250,000 weight network and fires in less than one-half second on a 486 PC.

BANKET also incorporates a number of capabilities that are not used in the current airline application, but have been used in other applications and are being investigated for use in AMA, including:

- Time-Lagged Recurrence for adding full NARMEX (Non-linear AutoRegressive Moving-average with EXogenous variables) and Kalman filter modeling performance,

- Multi-Network configurability (HDP, DHP, and their variations[3],[4]) for providing "approximate dynamic programming" capabilities for optimization of control decisions over time.

A prototype version of AMA contained an adaptive critic-style network, in combination with a model network, to generate the values for each of a fixed set of discrete seat allocation actions. While successful in an early prototype, this technique is not in the current version but is being redesigned for inclusion in future releases. These issues are discussed further in the context of the problem domain below.

Airline Yield Management

Airline yield management is the allocation of passenger seats to different fare categories on individual flight departures. This field concentrates on maximizing revenue by reserving a sufficient number of seats for late-booking, high-fare passengers while attempting to fill the remainder of the available capacity with earlier-booking, discount-fare passengers. Fare categories, or classes, are used to segment the market and can number as few as three and as many as 26. They usually include a variety of restrictions such as 7 or 21-day advance purchase and overnight or over-weekend requirements. The non-linearity of the booking patterns and the non-stationary nature of the air travel market require sophisticated forecasting and optimization approaches to gain the maximum possible revenue. The criticality of the forecasting module in these systems cannot be overstated. Saving one extra seat for a last minute full-fare passenger per flight (who actually shows up) can provide incremental revenue in the tens of millions of dollars per year, with negligible incremental expense.

The BANKET forecast accuracy has been proven in several data trials and overall revenue benefits from an early version of the AMA system were greater than 5% in a controlled test against expert analysts at a European airline during a 6-month period — despite the market instability caused by the Desert Storm military operation.[5]

Inventory Optimization Process

The seat inventory optimization process, regardless of the specific technical approaches used, consists of a forecasting process followed by a seat reallocation process. The forecast approaches and measures are discussed below, followed by an intuitive analysis of the industry standard Expected Marginal Seat Revenue (EMSR) algorithm for setting seat allocations.

Passenger Forecasting

Unconstrained demand to come: This refers to the mean raw demand which is yet to materialize, irrespective of seat allocation constraints. That is, how many passengers will make reservations in a fare class given an unlimited availability of seats, and who haven't already done so.

Variability of demand to come: This measure is necessary to specify the process error, or the normal variation in bookings assigned to noise and not predictable by any available indicators. AMA generates a specific variance forecast for each separate mean forecast (which does not presume a normal distribution.)

No-show bookings: This refers to the number of passengers who have purchased tickets but will not claim their seats at departure. AMA generates net no-show forecasts by individual fare class as a percentage of bookings.

Variability of no-show bookings: This measure is in the same scale as the no-show forecast and provides a measure of process error in the no-show behavior.

There are a variety of forecasting approaches in use in the airline industry for these purposes. Most use sophisticated time series models to isolate the trends and patterns in the data and to extract from these patterns a forecast of future market behavior. These techniques are limited due to their requirement that booking histories for each flight must always be available, their inaccuracy in times of rapid change (the air travel market is notoriously non-stationary) as well as their inability to generalize these changes across similar markets. In contrast, a causal method (or a process identification model as formulated in control theory) can be used to develop a mathematical relationship between the series being projected and the actual independent variables that impact it. As well established in control theory, a stationary process model can theoretically be converted to an equivalent input-output model (i.e., pure time series), however, the implied assumption of a stationary market makes this translation invalid. In addition, airlines constantly modify their flight schedule, inhibiting the usefulness of any technique which requires extrapolations from past booking behavior on the same flight.

In contrast, a causal model seeks to understand why the demand is occurring by quantifying the relationship between demand and any factors that might explain its movements. Since correlations do not necessarily imply causality, domain knowledge is necessary to determine which independent variables are appropriate to use. A major strength of a causal model is that it can immediately adjust its estimates based on changes in the predictive factors, prior to any observed effect. A well-designed causal model can also provide a forecasting tool and a simulation environment in the same system, which is ideal for airline revenue analysts. This approach lends itself to prediction of new markets before any actual flight data is available, where time series techniques require pre-existing schedules. The most widely used causal modeling techniques in airline forecasting are multiple regression and, to a lesser extent, the more powerful Box-Jenkins techniques which combines regression, time-series information, and past model performance. At least one airline is known to use a Kalman filter technique on a mainframe, which reportedly took two years to develop.

One of the main drawbacks of the explicit modeling techniques is that they require the model builder to know a priori which factors will influence demand and how those factors will interact with each other. While model builders can make an educated guess as to the factors influencing airline demand (day of week, time of day, city-pair, business or leisure market, competition, season, special events, etc.), they may not be able to build a realistic model that accurately reflects how these factors interact. Identifying the non-linear combinations is very difficult since they change over time and each market (origin-destination pair) has unique dynamics. The neural approach, while still requiring extensive knowledge engineering to determine the relevant causal factors which are cost-effective to capture, alleviates the airline analyst from having to build (and continually rebuild) the model by hand.

Where the flight schedules are relatively stable, the most powerful and complex traditional techniques, e.g., NARMEX methods and Kalman filters, can — in the hands of a skilled practitioner — make optimal use of both time-series and causal independent variables. The recently popularized advances in time-lagged recurrent networks (which actually have been around but misunderstood and under-appreciated since Werbos originally discovered them in the early 70's[6]), combine the automatic learning of neural networks with the computational power of these techniques, providing the best of both worlds. However, whether the incremental accuracy provided in the time series data, which is frequently non-existent anyway, is worth the cost of obtaining it in this application is not clear at this time.

Expected Marginal Seat Revenue Algorithm

The EMSR algorithm is an industry standard for calculating optimal seat allocations given the ticket price and the set of forecasts for each fare class. The algorithm starts with all seats unassigned (except any which are currently booked), computes the expected marginal seat revenue (fare times the probability of booking the next seat) for the next seat in each class, and assigns a seat to the class with the highest value; repeating until no seats remain unassigned. There are additional costs associated with overbooking (when predicted no-shows do show), and additional complexities with overlapping flight segments, which are also factored in.

The original AMA prototype used a neural network to learn to predict the value of adding each incremental seat to each fare class. This network was very similar to an adaptive critic network trained by the temporal differences technique as originally defined by Barto, Sutton, and Anderson.[7] There was no need for a network to generate a control action, since each of a limited number of actions were explicitly evaluated. After this system was trained, the weights were examined and found to provide behavior virtually identical to the EMSR algorithm, albeit somewhat more robustly. Because of issues regarding user acceptance of such a novel technology (AMA was first marketed in 1987 and first installed in 1989), and the unclear benefits of the neural approach in that form, an EMSR optimization algorithm was substituted instead.

However, there is an implicit assumption in the EMSR approach which prevents it from achieving true optimal seat allocations over time. That is, each optimization assumes that no reoptimizations will occur before departure, even though individual flights are actually reoptimized 15 to 30 times during the booking cycle. A true time-dynamic solution, as provided by dynamic programming, would learn the expected materialization rates and set more aggressive allocations knowing that they could be adjusted later. For example, more seats might be allocated for high-fare passengers early in the booking cycle, if it were known that they could be reallocated later when the danger of rejecting needed low-fare passengers became too great. The original network implementation did not capture the complete time dynamics since it too implicitly assumed that each allocation was final. However, BehavHeuristics is currently researching a multi-network, DHP-class neural network architecture to directly implement an approximate dynamic programming solution for this problem. This example illustrates the domain understanding that usually develops only after years of working within an application area.

Performance and Scale-up

The USAir application has several characteristics which effect performance in convergence and processing time. It has, for example, an average of over 2 segments (one stop) per flight, 10 booking classes, 4 forecasts per class, 70,000 nodes, and 250,000 connection weights. We have found, with our sparse matrix neural network algorithms implemented in software and with no custom hardware acceleration, that AMA on a 486 PC can achieve the processing speeds and converge during the training regimen illustrated in Table 1.

Based on the implementation of continuous daily training, the AMA forecast model can be recalibrated nightly to maintain currency. This has enabled the forecasts to adjust, in days rather than weeks, to such dramatic market shifts as those caused by the Desert Storm operation, competitors going out of business and changes in industry or carrier fare structures. The daily training data is a random sample (without replacement) of the previous weeks booking data. The weights which are effected by inputs from cycles longer than one week (i.e., seasonality) are locked after historical training and not allowed to drift during on-line training. Thus, historical retraining must be performed on a periodic basis.

How would this compare to standard backpropagation? For comparison purposes, we can assume the same network size and processing speeds for a traditional backpropagation system implemented in software. While we have not seen any published research suggesting that backpropagation systems having such large volumes of data available will require fewer than 500 or so passes through the data set, if we assume that only 10 passes will be required, *over one-year of processing time* will be required for historical training. Unless every parameter and option is specified perfectly the first time, several years (or decades) of processing time will be required to calibrate and train the backpropagation system. BANKET's ability to converge after processing only 50 to 80% of a large data set in a single pass is crucial to its feasibility for real-world applications. Additionally, the data I/O accounts for over 20 percent of total processing, forcing a strong lower bound on processing speeds, especially for algorithms which require dozens of passes through the data.

Table 1: AMA Processing and Training Speeds

On-line Forecast Process per Flight	~ Processing Time
Forecast demand, no-shows, and variances	1 second
Forecast, optimize, perform various booking and statistical calculations, read from and write to the database	9 seconds
Training Process	**~Data Trials**
2 years historical data for 5,000 flight segments per day	500,000 trials
Most Recent 6 months	1,200,000 trials
Ongoing Daily Calibration	16,000 trials per day
Training Process	**~Processing Time**
Basic Training (non-epoch)	1.1 seconds per trial
Historical & Recent Learning	3 weeks
Ongoing Daily Calibration	4.5 hours per day

Summary

Large-scale decision-support applications of advanced neural network technology are demonstrably feasible and marketable. However, as with any advanced technology, skillful application and a thorough understanding of the requirements of both the users' needs and the problem domain are required.

---

[1] Barto, A.G. (1992). Reinforcement Learning and Adaptive Critic Methods, in *The Handbook of Intelligent Control*, D. White & D. Sofge, eds., Van Nostrand, pp 469-492.

[2] Sutton, R.S., (1987). *Learning to Predict by the Methods of Temporal Differences*. GTE Technical Report TR87-509.1.

[3] Werbos, P.J. (1992). Approximate Dynamic Programming for Real-Time Control and Neural Modeling, in *The Handbook of Intelligent Control*, D. White & D. Sofge, eds., Van Nostrand, pp 493-526.

[4] Santiago, R.A., Werbos, P.J. (1994). New Progress Toward Truly Brain-Like Intelligent Control, in *Preceedings of the World Congress on Neural Networks*, San Diego, CA.

[5] Hormby, S.S., (1991). Yield Management Operational Trials at DAN-Air Services. in *Proceedings of the Airline Group of the International Federation of Operational Research Societies (AGIFORS) Yield Management Study Group*, Minneapolis, MN.

[6] Werbos, P.J. (1974). *Beyond regression: New tools for prediction and analysis in the behavioral sciences*. Unpublished Doctoral Dissertation, Harvard University.

[7] Barto, A.G., Sutton, R.S., & Anderson, C.W. (1983). Neuronlike elements that can solve difficult learning control problems, in *IEEE Transactions on Systems, Man, and Cybernetics*, SMC-13, pp 834-846.

Neural Control for Hydrocarbon Processing

by

Tim Graettinger and Jeff Buck
NeuralWare, Inc.
Penn Center West 4, Suite 227
Pittsburgh, PA 15276

Abstract

In this presentation, we describe NeuCOP, the Neural Control and Optimization Package. It combines nonlinear, neural network process models with nonlinear optimization techniques to achieve multivariable, adaptive, closed-loop control. This controller first determines economically optimal, steady-state operating levels for the process. It then drives the process to these levels and maintains them in the presence of measured and unmeasured disturbances.

We describe the process of modeling, simulating, and commissioning NeuCOP for control of an industrial, hydrocarbon processing unit. The results we present demonstrate the control action as NeuCOP optimizes production objectives, satisfies operating constraints, and reduces the overall variability of the process responses.

PREDICTION AND CONTROL OF PAPER MACHINE PARAMETERS USING NEURAL NETWORK MODELS

John B. Rudd, P.E.

Senior Consultant

Pavilion Technologies, Inc.
3500 W. Balcones Center Drive
Austin, TX 78759

ABSTRACT

The control of paper machine quality parameters is a multi-faceted problem that the machine tender has faced since paper making became a continuous process. When the stock preparation and paper machine are taken as a whole, the dynamics and chemistry of the control problem are high-dimensional and highly nonlinear. In addition, the controls exhibit an inherent sensitivity to external perturbations such as consistency variations, broke rates, recycle addition, etc. Coupled with these continuous control problems is the fact that many of the final parameters associated with product quality are measured in the laboratory using samples that are only collected at reel turn-up.

This paper demonstrates the use of adaptive process modeling techniques to develop a robust process control model that operates in real time and addresses all of the issues mentioned above. Data collected during a two month period, June 1- August 1, 1993 on the No. 4 Paper Machine at Packaging Corporation of America's Tomahawk, WI mill was used to build the model. A standard software package was used to generate the control model that provides continuous values, for control purposes, of both CMT (a paper crush property) and porosity over the entire time span of building each paper machine reel. The model produced by the software package embodies a Focused Attention Neural Network (FANN), which provides a way to take into account the case of correlated inputs and unmeasured external influences by projecting attention onto the control variables by implementing an intermediate model of the state variable dynamics. Figure 1 shows a simplified schematic of the process from which measured values were taken to build this model

BACKGROUND

The control of paper machine quality parameters is a problem that traditionally has fallen into two categories: indirect control and model-based control.

In the first case, laboratory measurements are made using samples taken from a reel after turn-up. Adjustments are then made to certain regulatory controllers in an attempt to affect these final quality parameters. There are inherent problems with this type of control in that the samples taken to the lab are from a small portion of the reel (the last 50-100 wraps) and it is assumed that the laboratory results are constant for the entire reel. When changes are made to the regulatory controls, the chosen manipulated variables are those that each machine tender considers to be key to controlling the particular quality parameters. This is normally done based upon the machine tenders experience and his own best guess.

The second approach is to use first-principles and/or statistical modeling [1-3] techniques. However, many processes (continuous and batch) exhibit characteristics that make these modeling and control techniques difficult [4]:

1. Non linearity or uncertainty in the first-principles model.
2. High-dimensional multivariate sensory inputs and control variables that may display complicated or detrimental interactions.
3. Inherent, variable time-delays.
4. Inadequate and uncertain measurements.
5. Plant safety and environmental constraints.
6. Unmeasured or uncontrollable changes in external variables such as feed consistency variation, outside temperature, barometric pressure, etc.

First principles modeling is most appealing because it is based upon applied mathematics, chemistry and physics. However, basic development of this type of model requires an extensive understanding of the process along with the capability to reduce that understanding to a comprehensive mathematical representation. Even when employing broad simplifications to make the mathematics tractable, this approach often requires man-years to develop an adequate model. Because of the limited fidelity of such models, they often do not work well in practice due to idiosyncrasies in the real-world machine dynamics. Even though, in many cases, first principles models have proven to be effective in their operation and results, the maintenance of the complex mathematical models demands the same level of capability and understanding as needed to develop the original models.

Statistical modeling is another methodology that requires specialized knowledge. An in depth knowledge of statistical methods along with a good understanding of the techniques for the design of experiments is necessary to successfully build models of this type. These experiments are usually required to gather data for the statistical model and can be very expensive and time consuming. In most cases they require that the process be perturbed over wide ranges of operations. Also, with the statistical models, a high level of support is required for the long term maintenance and support of the model.

Both of the above modeling approaches necessitate a long range commitment on the part of the user. This is a requirement if the life of the model is to last past the transfer or retirement of the developer.

The use of existing historical data to gain insights into the process dynamics before doing design experiments can be a much better approach. In fact, in many cases the experiments may not be necessary.

NEW APPROACHES TO CONTROL
Artificial neural networks [5-7,11-13] represent a set of powerful mathematical techniques for modeling, control and optimization that "learns" process dynamics directly from historical data. The features that make neural networks ideal for exploiting historical data can be summarized as follows: Neural networks are non linear regression algorithms that can model high-dimensional systems and have a very simple, uniform user interface; they work well for both batch and continuous processes; and, they can be used in either static or dynamic modeling.

Recent advances in the mathematics and understanding of the mechanisms of learning, coupled with the power of modern inexpensive computers, allows the building of artificial neural networks to be used for adaptive modeling and control of manufacturing processes.

NEURAL NETWORKS FOR PREDICTION
The process of training a neural network to predict, optimize and control processes can be divided into two stages: model building and optimization control. The first stage is equivalent to the classic prediction (or forecasting) prob-

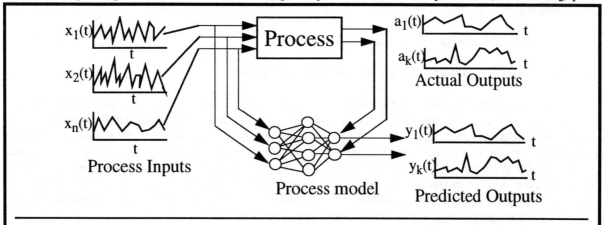

Figure 1. Neural network for predictive model of process dynamics. It is assumed that there is a physical process that has multiple inputs $x_1(t)$, $x_2(t)$,…, $x_n(t)$ (such as pressures, temperatures, flow-rates, etc.) and one or more interesting output parameters $a_1(t)$,…,$a_k(t)$ (such as yield, impurity, etc.). The neural network learns the process dynamics from historical data so as to predict outputs $y_1(t)$,…,$y_k(t)$ that closely match the actual outputs $a_1(t)$,…,$a_k(t)$

lems. As an example for this paper, the problem is to predict quality parameters for a paper machine reel from the past historical data of the process variables as shown in Figure 1. To test how well the prediction scheme works, a portion of the historical data is used to train the model. When the model has finished learning on this data set, it is tested using the remaining data to determine how well it can perform on data it has never seen. The measure used to determine how well a model is trained is a term called Relative Error. Train Relative Error is the total error for a complete pass through the training data and the Test Relative Error is the total error for a complete pass throughout the test data. The lower these errors are, the better the model is. A Relative Error of 0.0 indicates that the model predicts the data perfectly. A Relative Error greater than 1.0 indicates that the model is worse than a model that constantly predicts the mean of the data. R-squared is a standard error measure commonly used in linear regression. The relationship between Relative error and R-squared is:

$$R\text{-Squared} = 1 - (Relative\text{-}Error)^2$$

After training is complete, if the Train and Test Errors are close, relatively low and the model predicts accurately on the test data, the model is said to be generalized. This method has already been demonstrated in the past for brown stock washer systems [8], TMP refiners [9] and paper machines[10].

ADVANTAGES OF THE NEURAL NETWORK APPROACH FOR PREDICTION

The neural network "learns" a fully nonliner high-dimensional response surface of the machine dynamics from the process data. The reader is directed to several articles in the literature on the use of neural networks and the back propagation algorithm [11] that describe the main function. It is assumed at this point that there is some familiarity with the neural network approach.

The neural network uses very simple functions in the hidden layers (typically sigmoidal), but it combines these functions in a multi-layer nested structure, and it has been shown that any function can be approximated by the neural network [12]. The main advantages of the neural network approach are:

1. Neural networks require little human expertise; the same neural network algorithm will work for many different systems.

2. Neural networks have nonlinear dependence on parameters, allowing a nonlinear, more realistic mode.

3. Neural networks can save manpower by moving most of the work to the computer.

4. Neural networks typically work much better than traditional rule-based expert systems on these types of problems because the important relationships and rules are difficult to discern, or the number of rules can be overwhelming.

5. Neural networks are relatively insensitive to noise.

CONTROL AND OPTIMIZATION OF THE MACHINE DYNAMICS

Once the predictive model is constructed and trained, the model is used to extract useful information about the process. The model can be used for predicting future behavior of the process to determine when it will go outside acceptable ranges, to determine the most sensitive variables for affecting the outputs, for gaining process understanding, or for establishing new setpoint recommendations. However, to make the correct set point recommendations the model has to do more than predict -- it has to learn the causal relationships within the process, which is a more difficult task. For example, if CMT (a paper cruch property) is the control parameter, it is important to learn the effects of time, consistency variations, broke rates, recycle addition,, etc. on the prediction of CMT, but it is just as important to learn how consistency variations, broke rates, recycle addition, etc. affect time.

Several methods have been proposed on how to "invert" the plant dynamics, i.e. predict the inputs required to achieve the desired output. These include direct inversion, or learning an inverse of the process by placing the outputs as inputs to the model and the inputs as outputs to the model. Except for the most trivial linear non-redundant systems,

I-154

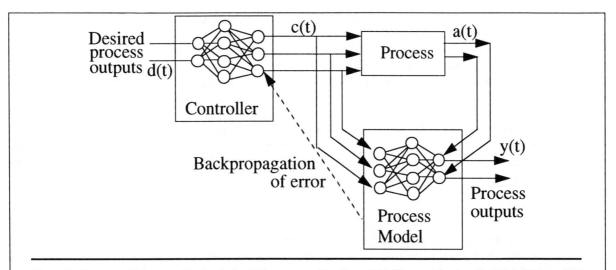

Figure 2. Structure of the neural network controller proposed by Barto [10]. The neural network model of Figure 2 is trained by backpropagation to minimize the error between the output of the net $y(t) = y(c(t),W)$ and the output of the process $a(t)$ by adjusting the weights W, then the weights are "frozen" to fix the model of the process. The desired output, $d(t)$ of the process then entered into a control error function, $E = \Sigma \, (d(t) - y(t))^2$ and the control network learns how to adjust the process control parameters to achieve the desired output by performing gradient descent to the control variables $c(t)$ in the model $y(c(t),W)$.

this direct inversion method is not recommended due to the non-invariability of a multi-variate process [13]. Other authors have suggested a more traditional approach to control using the predictive model generated by the network in a predictive feed-forward loop. For example, Barto [13] suggests back propagation of the errors through the trained model to generate targets for training a control model as shown in Figure 2.

Although the strategy proposed by Barto is useful in special circumstances, it has been found to be inadequate for real-world applications for several reasons. First of all, in real world applications, there are always correlations in the input data. For example, one variable, rush drag, is highly correlated to a number of other variables (slice opening, flow and reel speed). If there is a perfect correlation, then the model will learn to pay attention to one variable or a combination at random depending on the initial (randomly chosen) weights of the neural network. In this case eliminating the dependent variable resulted in a more accurate model. Second, and perhaps more important, even if the variables are not highly correlated, the model may learn to pay attention to a variable that is not controllable. Many of the variables in a process are measured, or "state," variables that are dependent on the settings of the actual controlled variables. It is commonly found that the neural network may pay attention to these state variables instead of the control variable. It doesn't do any good to have a control model that recommends that one of these state variables be controlled to a prescribed value if there is no direct control to achieve that value. Third, most of the standard paradigms available do not take into account time delays, dead times or other critical factors in process dynamics that are essential to a proper control strategy. Nor do they take into account constraints that may be put on the variable ranges.

To surmount the problems of correlated inputs and control problems that include state variables, a more comprehensive paradigm that focuses attention of the state variables onto the control variables while taking into account real constraints was used. Figure 3 shows the structure of a Focused Attention

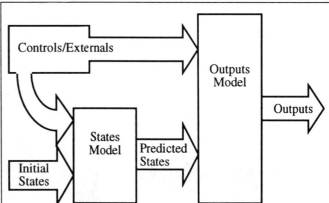

Figure 3. Control strategy showing an intermediate prediction of the state variations as a function of the control variables to give a faithful representation of the plant dynamics and focusing attention on the controls.

Neural Network (FANN)[14] that projects attention onto the control variables by building an intermediate model of the state variable dynamics on the control variables. When the FANN is used, the model faithfully represents the behavior of the state variables as the controls are changed. This is essential for modeling the causal effects in the plant and to achieve the proper control strategy. Figure 4 demonstrates a recent case on a paper machine where CMT was predicted and controlled. Plotted are the actual measured values for CMT and the CMT value as it would be under direct control.

In this case, the model is even able to operate under the influence of unmeasured external perturbations. This is possible because the state variables contain inherent information about the external perturbations, and, as long as the perturbations are slow with respect to the process dynamics, the controls can be changed so as to compensate for the perturbations. A good example would be the effect of chip moisture.

CONCLUSIONS

This paper discusses a very important principle that needs to be incorporated into control strategies using neural networks to achieve proper results. The standard approach proposed in many cases does not account for the case of correlated inputs or control problems including state (dependent) variables. However, the Focused Attention Neural Network (FANN) solves this problem by projecting attention onto the control variables by building an intermediate model of the state variable dynamics on the control variables. Where as most of the variables in a real-world application are measured rather than directly manipulated, this is an extremely important consideration in real world problems. The added benefit of this approach is that the effects of unmeasured external influences can be inferred from the state variable information and compensated for by appropriate changes in control settings. This can be done because the state variables contain inherent information about these external influences, and, as long as the perturbations of the external variables are slow with respect to the process dynamics, the controls can be changed to compensate for the disturbances.

It should be noted that the models created here are fully dynamic nonlinear models that learn without any first-principles information; the models learn to predict and control directly from the data.

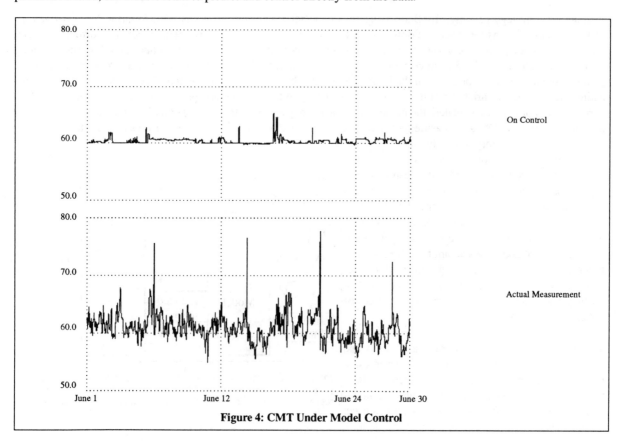

Figure 4: CMT Under Model Control

REFERENCES

1. K.J. Astrom, *Automatica*, "Expert Control," 13, 277-286 (1986).

2. B.B. Kuo, <u>Automatic Control Systems</u>, 4ed, Englewood Cliffs, NJ: Printice-Hall (1982)

3. W.L. Brogan, <u>Modern Control Theory</u> , 2ed, Englewood Cliffs, NJ: Printice-Hall (1985)

4. J.D. Keeler, *1993 CAIPEP*, "Prediction and Control of Chaotic Chemical Reactions Via Neural Network Models" (1993).

5. J. Moody and C. Darken, *Neural Computation*, "Fast Learning in Networks of Locally-Tuned Processing Units" 1, 281-294 (1989).

6. E. Hartman and J.D. Keeler, Neural Computation, "Predicting the Future: Advantages of Semi-local Units" 3, 566-579 (1991).

7. A.S. Weigend, B.A. Huberman, D.E. Rumelhart, *Intl. J. Neural Systems*, "Predicting the Future: A Connectionist Approach" 1, 193 (1990).

8. J.B. Rudd, *Proceedings TAPPI 1991 Engineering Conference*, "Using a Neural Network Controller for Advanced Control Applications" 101-113, (1991).

9. S.B.L. Kooi and K. Khorasani, *Tappi Journal*, "Control of the Woodchip Refiner Using Neural Networks" Vol.75 No. 6, 156-162, (1992).

10. C.A. Schweiger, J.B. Rudd, Proceedings TAPPI 1993 Process Control Conference, "Prediction and Control Of Paper Machine Parameters Using Adaptive Technologies in Process Modeling," (1993).

11. D.E. Rumelhart, G.E. Hinton and R.J. Williams, "Learning Internal Representations by Error Propagation," in D.E. Rumelhart, J.L. McCelland and the PDP Research Group, <u>Parallel Distributed Processing: Explorations in the Microstructure of Cognition. Volume 1: Foundations</u>, Cambridge, MA: MIT Press/Bradford (1986).

12. E. Hartman, J.D. Keeler and J. Kowalski, *Neural Computation*, "Layered Neural Networks With Gaussian Hidden Units as Universal Approximators" 2, 210-215 (1990).

13. W.T. Miller, R.S. Sutton and P.J. Werbos (Eds.), <u>Neural Networks for Control</u>, MIT Press (1990).

14 J.D. Keeler and E. Hartman, Pavilion Technology, Inc. Technical Report, "Focused Attention Neural Networks" (in progress).

Application of Neural Networks in the Chemical Process Industries

Session Chair: Thomas McAvoy

Sensor Data Analysis Using Autoassociative Neural Nets

Dong Dong and Thomas J. McAvoy*

Department of Chemical Engineering and Institute of System Research

University of Maryland, College Park, MD 20742

Abstract

Autoassociative neural nets have many potential applications. In this paper, a new structure for an autoassociative neural net is proposed. The new structure is based on nonlinear principal component analysis . The use of autoassociative neural nets with the new structure for sensor validation and missing sensor replacement in a distillation example is discussed.

1 Introduction

All advanced control applications relys on having valid sensor data. When flawed data are used, the results can be bad performance and even unsafe operations. This raises the problem of sensor validation. From time to time certain sensors may become unavailable because of sensor failures or maintenance activities. If the data provided by a sensor are essential for process operation or control, it is important to have an estimated value if the sensor becomes unavailable. Such problems of sensor data analysis have grown in importance because in recent years chemical processes have been more tightly designed. A first principle model of a process combined with statistical methods and optimization techniques can be used to estimate sensor values. But, in practice a first principle model is very difficult to get, and such methods have the disadvantages of being computationally intensive and as a result often they are not used in on-line applications.

Autoassociative neural nets provide an alternative method for sensor data analysis. An autoassociative neural net is a multi-layer feed-forward neural network whose input and output layers have the same dimensions. An autoassociative network uses the identity mapping as its objective function. Usually, at least one of its hidden layers is smaller in dimension than either the input or output layer, and this small dimension layer is called the "bottleneck layer". Kramer (1992) discussed autoassociative neural nets, and pointed out that five layers are necessary for such nets in order to be able to model nonlinear processes. The application of autoassociative neural nets in monitoring process conditions has also been reported (Peel et al., 1991). Since there are five layers in an autoassociative neural net, the training can be very difficult. Another problem for an autoassociative neural net is that the theoretical meaning of the outputs of its bottleneck layer is not clear. Nonlinear Principal Component Analysis (NPCA) (Dong & McAvoy, 1993) solves these two problems. Since autoassociative neural nets based on NPCA consist of two three layer neural nets, training is easy. The outputs of the bottleneck layer are nonlinear principal components, and they have a clear interpretation in theory.

---

*To whom all correspondence should be addressed

In this paper, the method of using an autoassociative neural net based on NPCA for sensor validation and missing sensor replacement is discussed. The organization of the paper is as follows. We first briefly introduce the concepts of Principal Component Analysis (PCA) and NPCA, and discuss the relationship between PCA, NPCA, and autoassociative neural nets. Then the techniques of sensor validation and missing sensor replacement using autoassociative neural nets based on NPCA are illustrated. The techniques are applied to a distillation process.

2 PCA, NPCA, and Autoassociative Neural Nets

The concepts of linear and nonlinear principal components can be best illustrated in Fig.1. The data points are two dimensional so they may be more easily visualized. Fig.1a shows the concept of a linear principal component. The linear principal component line minimizes the sum of all the orthogonal deviations between the straight line and the data. A data set X which contains n samples of m variables can be expressed in terms of l linear principal components with $l \leq m$ as

$$X = TP' + E \tag{1}$$

where $T = [t_1, t_2, ..., t_l]$ is defined as principal component scores, P is defined as principal component loadings, and E is the residual data. The principal loadings determine the directions of principal component lines, and the principal scores are the coordinates of the respective points on the principal component lines. Fig.1b shows the concept of a nonlinear principal component. The nonlinear approach is the same as the linear principal component approach, except that it summarizes the data with a smooth curve which is determined by nonlinear relationships among all the variables. This smooth curve minimizes the orthogonal deviations between the data and the curve. A data set X which contains n samples of m variables can be expressed in terms of l nonlinear principal components with $l \leq m$ as

$$X = F(T) + E \tag{2}$$

where $T = [t_1, t_2, ..., t_l]$ is defined as the nonlinear principal component scores, and F is defined as the nonlinear principal component loading function.

There is a close connection between principal components and autoassociative neural networks. The key point of an autoassociative neural network is the "bottleneck layer" , which a layer of hidden nodes smaller in dimension than either the input or output layer. The concept of an autoassociative neural network is similar to principal components : using a lower dimension to explain maximum information. For a linear autoassociative neural network which has linear nodes and three layers , it has been proven that if the outputs of its bottleneck layer are the PCA scores, this autoassociative neural network is optimal (Baldi & Hornik, 1989; Bourlard & Kamp, 1988). Here optimal means that this autoassociative neural network keeps maximum information among all networks with the same structure. It is very interesting that the best linear autoassociative neural net is just like a linear PCA filter, and the dimension of its hidden layer is the number of principal components. In the NPCA method proposed by Dong and McAvoy (1993), the neural network NPCA models form a nonlinear autoassociative neural net. Its structure is shown in Fig. 2. There are two three layer neural networks. The first three layer network maps from the data space to the nonlinear principal component score space, and the second three layer network maps from the nonlinear principal component score space to the data space corrected by the nonlinear principal components. If we put them together, they form a five layer autoassociative neural net. This autoassociative neural net works like a nonlinear PCA filter, and the dimension of its bottleneck layer is the number of nonlinear principal components.

3 Autoassociative Neural Nets for Sensor Data Analysis

The two neural networks in the new autoassociative network structure can be trained separately, so the training is straightforward. Any appropriate algorithm, e.g. backpropagation (Werbos, 1977; Rumelhard et al., 1986) can be used for training. In this work we use the conjugate gradient learning method (Leonard & Kramer, 1990; Fletcher & Powell, 1963) to train the neural network because of two nice features of this method: (1) the learning speed of the conjugate method is much faster than that of general backpropagation; and (2) the learning rate constants are calculated automatically and adaptively. Another issue is to determine how many hidden units are required for each three layer network. In this work, a cross-validation scheme (Stone, 1978; Stone & Brooks, 1990) is employed.

After determining the architecture and appropriately training an autoassociative neural net, the network can be used for sensor validation and missing sensor replacement. Our approach is the same as that proposed by Kramer (1992). We assume that the training data set contains enough information to cover the range of good process operation. The resulting autoassociative neural net is an appropriate model for all good sensor data. If there is no faulty sensor the output X' should be close to the input X. If the ith sensor fails, then x'_i will differ significantly from the x_i. Sensor validation can be accomplished by monitoring the differences between the inputs and the outputs and using them to check for sensor failure. Sensor validation with gross errors is more complicated than sensor failure. We will discuss this case in Section 5. If the important sensor data become unavailable due to sensor failures or maintenance activities, missing sensor replacement is necessary for the continuity of operations. Because the process variables expressed by sensor data are correlated , an autoassociative neural net contains information that allows replacement of missing sensors with values estimated from remaining sensors. As discussed above there are two mappings in an autoassociative neural net. The first is from high dimensional data space to lower dimensional score space , and the second is from lower dimensional score space to high dimensional corrected data space while keeping the maximum variation of the original data space. So for a missing sensor in the data space, the most likely value for this sensor is the value that minimizes the squared difference between the input data space and the corrected data space. Let X be an input vector, X' the output of the autoassociative neural net, and X_k is the value of the missing sensor. The missing sensor replacement involves finding the value of x_k that:

$$\min_{x_k}(X - X')^2 \qquad (3)$$

The problem given by eq. 3 is a univariate optimization problem. During the optimization, the values of the remaining sensors are fixed at their measured values. If there is more than one missing sensor at a time the problem becomes a multivariable optimization problem. The solution is still straightforward.

4 Application to a Chemical Process

A distillation column is used for studying the method proposed in this paper. The column is a high purity column which separates an ideal mixture with 41 trays and with the feed on tray 21. The characteristics of the column are : relative volatility=1.5, reflux ratio=4.29 , feed composition=0.50, top composition=0.99, bottom composition=0.01. A solution for distillation rating is obtained by using the Smoker equation (Tolllver & Waggoner, 1982). In many distillation control schemes tray temperatures are used to estimate top and bottom compositions (Mejdell & Skogestad, 1990) , in a so-called inferential control. If some sensors are unavailable, missing sensor replacement can be used for controlling product purity. Further, the tray temperatures are highly correlated. Therefore, this process is a good candidate for applying autoassociative neural net techniques.

In this work we assume there are six temperature measurements at trays 5, 10, 15, 24, 30, 36. For the feed concentrations varying between 0.4 and 0.6, top composition varying between 0.981 and 0.999, and bottom composition between 0.001 and 0.019, we get 100 temperature samples. The NPCA method is used to analyze the data, and two nonlinear principal components can explain 98.96% of the variation of the data set. By means of the NPCA analysis , we get tabular data which consist of the original data set, the nonlinear principal component scores, and the data corrected by the two nonlinear principal components. The detailed procedure can be found in (Dong & McAvoy, 1993). The tabular data are used to train the two three-layer networks. Cross-validation is used for determining the number of the hidden nodes in the two three layer networks. Nine hidden nodes are best for both two three layer networks. So the final autoassociative neural net is 6:9:2:9:6 architecture.

We use the Squared Prediction Error (SPE) to monitor the difference between the input and the output of the autoassociative neural net. The SPE is given by :

$$SPE(i,j) = (x(i,j) - x(i,j)')^2 \tag{4}$$

where i is the sampling time, j is the number of process variables, $x(i,j)$ is j process variables at time i, and $x(i,j)'$ is a prediction of the autoassociative neural net. If the Lth sensor fails, then $SPE(i,L)$ will have an abnormal change. For a failure sensor, its output is usually zero, or a drifting signal. If we simulate sensor two as the failed sensor, then $SPE(i,2)$ is around 10^5, while the SPEs of other variables are only around 10^1. After the failed sensor is detected, the next step is missing sensor replacement. The objective function for missing sensor replacement is given by :

$$OBJ(i) = (\sum_{j=1}^{n}(x(i,j) - x(i,j)')^2)^{0.5} \tag{5}$$

where n is the total number of process variables. At every sampling time we estimate the value of missing sensors using :

$$\min_{x(i,k)}(OBJ(i)) \tag{6}$$

where $x(i,k), k = k_1, k_2, ...$ are missing sensor inputs. The multivariate optimization is implemented using a quasi-Newton method and a finite-difference gradient method (Dennis & Schnabel, 1983). Because we can get estimated values at every sampling time, the method can be easily used on-line. Fig.3 shows the results for one missing sensor. Fig.3.a is the result when sensor 2 fails and Fig.3.b is the result for sensor 5. Fig.4 shows the result for two missing sensors at the same time. Fig.4.a is for sensor 1, and Fig4.b is for sensor five. The results for both one missing sensor and two missing sensors are very good. Fig.5 shows the result of three missing sensors at same time, where the three missing sensors are sensor one , three and four. Even when three sensors are missing at the same time, the result is still acceptable.

5   Discussion and Conclusions

A new structure of an autoassociative neural network based on NPCA is presented, and its application for sensor validation and missing sensor replacement is discussed. The work presented here has been restricted to steady-state only. The work of sensor validation in this paper is just for the simplest case, where the sensor fails totally. Sensor validation with gross error is more complicated than this simplest case. For gross error detection and removal, a robust autoassociative neural net approach (Kramer, 1992) is applicable. The detailed procedure for robust autoassociative neural nets based on NPCA is currently being studied. The results on a distillation column show that the proposed method gives excellent results for on-line sensor replacement.

Fletcher, R. & Powell, M. J. D. (1963). "A rapid descent method for minimization." *Comput. J.*, **6**, 163–167.

Kramer, M. A. (1992). "Autoassociative neural networks." *Computers Chem. Engng.*, **16**:(4), 313–328.

Leonard, J. & Kramer, M. K. (1990). "Improvement of the backpropagation algorithm for training neur al networks." *Computers Chem. Engng.*, **14**, 337–341.

Mejdell, T. & Skogestad, S. (Nov., 1990). "Composition control of distillation columns using multiple temperature measurements." In *AIChE Annual Meeting*, Chicago IL.

Peel, C., Morris, A. J., & Kiparissides, C. (1991). "Process condition monitoring and neural network feature detection." In *Proc. of 1993 IFAC World Congress*, volume 4, 65–70.

Rumelhard, D., Hinton, G., & Williams, R. (1986). *Parallel Distributed Processing*, Chapter Learning Internal Representations by Error Propagation, 318–362. MIT Press, Cambridge, MA.

Stone, M. (1978). "Cross-validation: a review." *Math. Operationsforsch. Statist., Ser. Statistics*, **9**:(1).

Stone, M. & Brooks, R. (1990). "Continuum regression: cross-validated sequentially constructed prediction embracing ordinary least squares, partial least squares and principal component regression." *J. Roy. Statist. Soc., Series B*, **52**:(2), 237–269.

Tolllver, L. T. & Waggoner, R. C. (1982). "Approximate solutions for distillation rating and operating problems using the smoker equations." *Ind. Eng. Chem. Fundam.*, **21**, 422–427.

Werbos, P. (1977). *Beyond Regression: New Tols for Prediction and Analysis in the behavioral Sciences*. Ph.D. thesis, Harvard University.

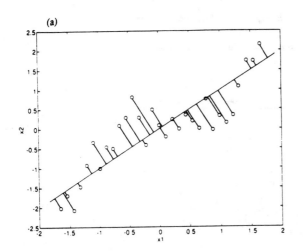 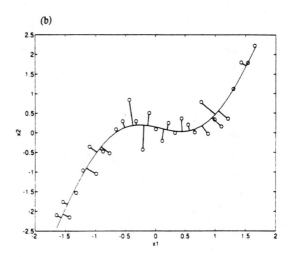

Figure 1: *(a) The linear principal component minimizes the sum of squared orthogonal deviations using a straight line. (b) The nonlinear principal component minimizes the sum of squared orthogonal deviations using a smooth curve.*

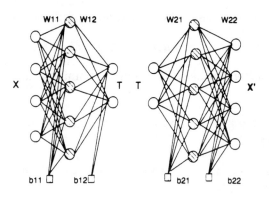

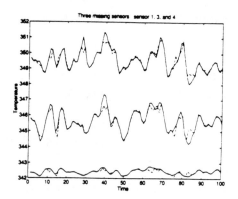

Figure 2: *The new structure of an autoassociative neural network*

Figure 5: *The results for three missing sensors.*

(Solid line : actual value, dotted line : estimated value)

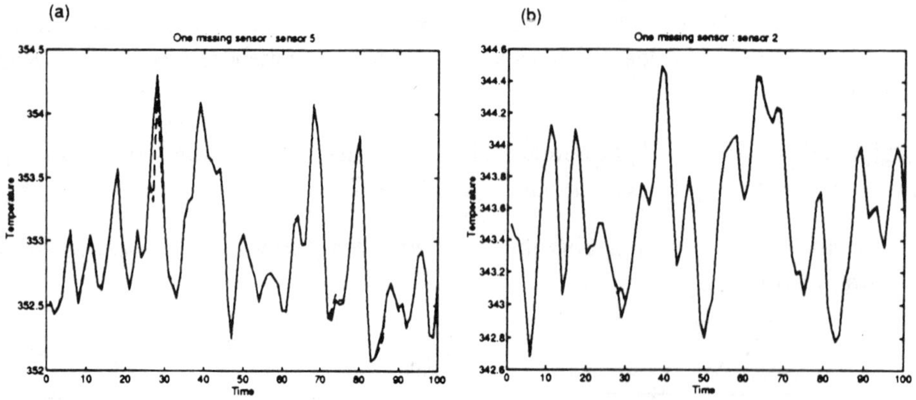

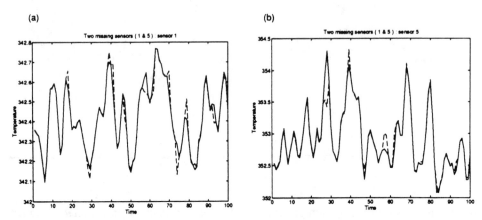

Figure 3: *The results for one missing sensor, (a) sensor 2 (b) sensor 5. (Solid line : actual value, dotted line : estimated value)*

Figure 4: *The results for two missing sensors, (a) sensor 1 (b) sensor 5. (Solid line : actual value, dotted line : estimated value)*

I-166

Rectification of Packed Distillation Column Data via Subset Identification

Randall S. Barton and David M. Himmelblau

Dept. of Chemical Engineering, University of Texas, Austin, TX 78712

Abstract

Internally recurrent neural networks (IRN) are used to rectify simulated noisy process data from a dynamic, nonlinear packed distillation column. IRN's are shown to be capable of rectifying relevant subsets of the process measurements, as well as the full vector of process measurements. Experimental results are presented to demonstrate that IRN's are able to model the deterministic dynamics of a complicated process using noisy measurements, and reduce the uncertainty in those measurements significantly.

1. Introduction

Studies in data rectification are concerned with developing techniques for obtaining an accurate estimate of the true state of a process from the often noisy, corrupted measurements taken from that process. The rectified process data, or possibly rectified subsets of process data, are hopefully better suited for making decisions which directly or indirectly affect the performance of the plant or a process, such as occur in control. This paper applies IRN's to the rectification of dynamic data from a realistic, nonlinear process (a packed distillation column), and investigates the feasibility of rectifying relevant subsets of measurements from this process.

2. Background

Techniques for rectifying steady-state process data are well developed and are not reviewed in this paper [5]. However, processes that are characterized as "steady-state" in practice continually fluctuate about a nominal steady-state operating point. Therefore, the potential utility of rectification techniques which take into account process dynamics is obvious. For a dynamic, nonlinear process, traditional approaches to solving the rectification problem recast the steady-state formulation as:

$$\text{Minimize: } \Phi(\mathbf{y}_t, \hat{\mathbf{y}}_t, \mathbf{y}_{t-1}, \hat{\mathbf{y}}_{t-1}, \cdots) \qquad \text{Subject to: } \begin{aligned} \mathbf{f}(\dot{\mathbf{x}}_t, \mathbf{x}_t, \mathbf{u}_t, t) &= 0 \\ \mathbf{h}(\mathbf{x}_t, t) &= 0 \\ \mathbf{g}(\mathbf{x}_t, t) &\geq 0 \end{aligned} \qquad (1)$$

where Φ is a generalized objective function, $\mathbf{x}_t$ is a vector of state variables at time t, $\mathbf{y}_t$ and $\hat{\mathbf{y}}_t$ are the actual measurements and rectified measurements respectively, $\mathbf{f}$ is a dynamic process model, $\mathbf{g}$ is a vector of inequality constraints (including bounds on the variables), and $\mathbf{h}$ is a vector of known equality constraints. The model constraint equations $\mathbf{f}$ are typically dynamic differential equations. Almost all previous methods proposed in this area rely on an accurate model of the physical system which may not be available and/or may be too expensive to develop.

3. Data Rectification using Artificial Neural Networks

Because of their abilities (1) to realize complex nonlinear functional mappings from inputs to outputs, (2) to "learn" these mappings from examples of historical process data, (3) to incorporate process dynamics, and (4) to make use of relatively low development costs, certain neural network architectures have shown promise as tools for dynamic process modeling and system identification. Karjala et al., 1992, were the first to propose the use of recurrent neural networks for dynamic data rectification and to compare the ANN approach to more traditional methods of rectifying dynamic data [3]. They demonstrated that recurrent networks were capable of learning process dynamics in the presence of noise and of making significant reductions in the noise level of their predictions given noisy inputs. In fact, for a simple nonlinear system (a draining tank), an internally recurrent (Elman) neural network was shown to perform better than more traditional dynamic data rectification methods [1].

In this work Gaussian transfer functions were used in the hidden layer of the IRN. As shown in Fig. 1, the IRN uses internal feedback from the hidden layer to itself to incorporate process dynamics. This feedback, in effect, integrates the signal to the hidden nodes providing the network with internal states and a form of memory. This allows a single input vector of process variables at time t to be used to predict the process variables at time $t+1$ (or further into the future). For real plant data, the true values of the measured variables are not known and, thus, optimal target patterns for network training are not available. By reposing the problem as a time series prediction problem and using an IRN to predict the current set of measurements based on past measurements, the lack of optimal target patterns can be avoided.

Figure 1: Internally Recurrent Neural Network

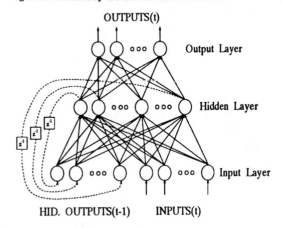

Figure 2: Packed Distillation Column

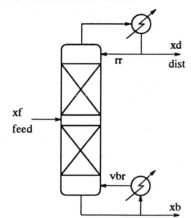

4. The Deterministic Process Model

A dynamic model of a packed distillation tower called the VE model was used as the "true" process in this study. A. A. Patwardhan developed this simplified dynamic model from first principles to simulate the separation of binary chemical mixtures [6]. The VE model consists of five differential equations and nine algebraic equations. We considered the deterministic VE model to be an exact description of the real process states at any given time so that the rectified data values could be compared with the "true" data values, an end that cannot be accomplished for a real process. This is the easiest way to demonstrate that the proposed rectification procedure is effective, and thus, build confidence that the procedure will work on actual process data.

Fig. 2 indicates the six variables which were deemed to be "measured" and were to be used for rectification. The feed composition, x_f, and flow rate, *feed*, are assumed to be measured disturbances. The manipulated variables are the vapor boil-up rate, *vbr*, and the distillate rate, *dist*. The distillate composition, x_d, and the bottoms composition, x_b, are the controlled variables, and they are considered to be the most important ones for the purposes of data rectification in this work.

5. Experimental Methods

The VE model of the packed distillation column was used to generate simulated process data in a highly nonlinear operating region. The training and testing sets for this work each consisted of ~7500 points sampled at intervals of four minutes [4]. The deterministic inputs and outputs from the column were corrupted with zero-mean Gaussian noise to simulate noisy process data to be rectified, and the IRN's used for rectification were trained and tested on this corrupted data as would be required in any real situation.

For data rectification of all six variables simultaneously, the network input is a vector of all the process measurements y_t, both inputs and outputs, at time t. The network outputs a prediction of the same process measurements $\hat{y}_{t+1}$ one time step into the future (at time $t+1$). Thus, the neural network rectifier acts as a one step ahead predictor of all the process inputs and outputs. In this work, the networks were trained to rectify all of the process measurements simultaneously as well as various subsets of the process measurements.

6. Experimental Results and Discussion

To present our results, we need to define three types of residuals: the measurement residual, the apparent residual, and the true residual. The *measurement residual vector* evaluated at time $t+1$ is defined in Eqn. 2:

$$\text{Measurement Residual Vector:} \quad \mathbf{m}_{t+1} = \mathbf{y}_{t+1} - \mathbf{d}_{t+1} \tag{2}$$

where $\mathbf{y}_{t+1}$ is the vector of simulated process measurements and $\mathbf{d}_{t+1}$ is the vector of "true" values obtained via the VE Model. The *simulated measurements* $\mathbf{y}$ to be rectified were produced by adding noise to the deterministic *"true"* values $\mathbf{d}$. In this work, additive, zero-mean, Gaussian noise was used to approximate actual process measurement noise. Two different noise levels were examined, 3% and 10%, as defined by:

$$\% \text{ Noise Level}_i = \left[\left(\sigma_{m_i} * \text{Range}_i^{-1}\right) * 100\right] \tag{3}$$

where Range_i is the range of the ith process variable. σ_{mi} is the standard deviation of the *measurement residuals* m_i between the simulated process measurements y_i and the "true" values d_i for the ith process variable, evaluated over the entire data record, as shown in Eqn. 4:

$$\sigma_{m_i} = \left(\frac{1}{T}\sum_{t=1}^{T} m^2_{i,t}\right)^{\frac{1}{2}} \tag{4}$$

The m_i's can be thought of as measurement errors and form the components of the measurement residual vector $\mathbf{m}_{t+1}$ at each time step with $i = 1, ..., p$, where p is the number of process variables being rectified and T is the total number of time steps in the data record.

The network was trained using the noisy simulated measurements $\mathbf{y}$. The network input was $\mathbf{y}_t$ and the target output for the network was $\mathbf{y}_{t+1}$. The network outputs a prediction $\hat{\mathbf{y}}_{t+1}$ of the process variables one time step ahead and $\hat{\mathbf{y}}_{t+1}$ is deemed the vector of rectified process measurements. The differences between the elements in the *vector of rectified values* $\hat{\mathbf{y}}_{t+1}$ and the respective elements in the simulated process measurement vector $\mathbf{y}_{t+1}$ are called the elements in the *apparent residual vector* $\mathbf{a}_{t+1}$, and are the network prediction errors that are minimized during network training:

$$\text{Apparent Residual Vector:} \quad \mathbf{a}_{t+1} = \mathbf{y}_{t+1} - \hat{\mathbf{y}}_{t+1} \tag{5}$$

The difference between the predictions from the network $\hat{\mathbf{y}}_{t+1}$ and the "true" values of the deterministic process variables $\mathbf{d}_{t+1}$ are defined as the vector of *true residuals* $\mathbf{r}_{t+1}$, and are error measures which are useful for evaluating network performance:

$$\text{True Residual Vector:} \quad \mathbf{r}_{t+1} = \hat{\mathbf{y}}_{t+1} - \mathbf{d}_{t+1} \tag{6}$$

The standard deviation of the true residuals for the ith process variable evaluated over the entire length T of the data record was used for evaluating network performance, and is defined in Eqn. 7:

$$\sigma_{r_i} = \left(\frac{1}{T}\sum_{t=1}^{T} r^2_{i,t}\right)^{\frac{1}{2}} \tag{7}$$

A comparison of σ_{mi} and σ_{ri} provides a quantitative measure of network rectification performance as is defined in Eqn. 8:

$$p_i = \left[\left(\sigma_{r_i} - \sigma_{m_i}\right) * \sigma_{m_i}^{-1}\right] * 100 \tag{8}$$

where p_i, is the percentage change in the standard deviation of the "measurement" error in the ith process variable as a result of data rectification.

We are interested in obtaining unbiased estimates of the process variables and achieving a reduction in uncertainty (variance) by rectification. The results for the estimation of the true values of the process variables by several rectification experiments are given in Figs. 3 - 6. Each plot shows the "true" values d_i, the simulated process measurements y_i, and the rectified process measurements $\hat{y}_i$ determined by the neural network plotted against time at 4 minute intervals, for the ith process variable. The code for the networks in Figs. 3 - 6 indicates the number of nodes in the first (input) layer, the second (hidden) layer, and the third (output) layer.

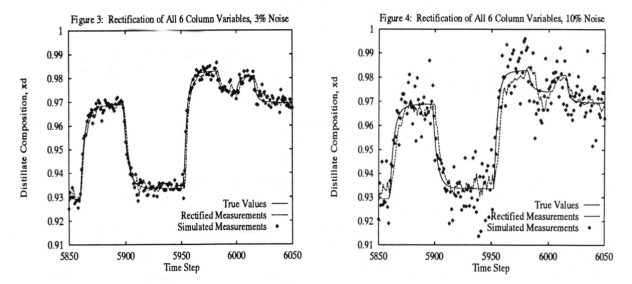

Figs. 3 and 4 show the rectification of the distillate composition measurements (x_d) when all six column variables were rectified simultaneously. The noise in the simulated measurements was at the 3% level in Fig. 3 and the 10% level in Fig. 4. Figs. 5 and 6 show the rectification of the distillate composition measurements (x_d) when a subset of only the two control variables (x_d, x_b) were rectified. The noise in the simulated measurements was at the 3% level in Fig. 5 and the 10% level in Fig. 6.

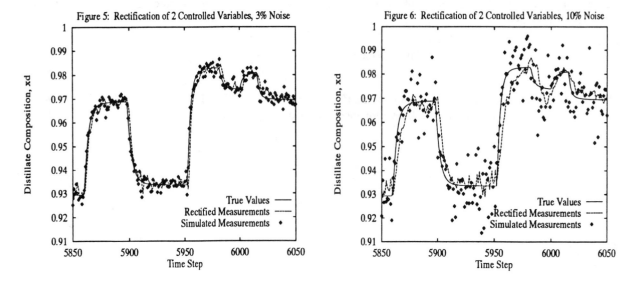

Table 1 summarizes the results for the reduction in uncertainty (variance) found in this study. Cols. 2 and 3 represent rectification of all six process variables simultaneously using a 6-9-6 IRN. Cols. 4 and 5 represent rectification of a subset of three process variables (x_d, *dist*, *vbr*) using a 3-9-3 IRN. Cols. 6 and 7 show the results of rectifying a subset of the two control variables (x_d, x_b) with a 2-4-2 IRN.

Table 1: **Percentage Change in Standard Deviation of "Measurement" Errors, p_i**

Variable	6-9-6 IRN		3-9-3 IRN		2-4-2 IRN	
	3% Noise	10% Noise	3% Noise	10% Noise	3% Noise	10% Noise
x_d	-18.1	-51.9	-13.8	-48.3	-12.4	-50.6
dist	-23.3	-62.2	-4.4	-52.3		
vbr	+0.2	-49.6	+1.3	-48.9		
x_b	-29.2	-56.6			-24.4	-55.2
feed	+43.8	-36.3				
x_f	+2.0	-50.7				

Table 1 draws attention to three important results. First, the measurement noise in the two control variables, x_d and x_b, was significantly reduced in all cases, including rectification of only subsets of variables. The reduction is highest when all of the column measurements are rectified together, and decreases slightly as smaller subsets of measurements are rectified. Second, it is difficult to rectify the inputs to the process because the inputs were step changes. The network cannot predict a random step change as is clearly illustrated by the performance on the feed variables, *feed* and x_f, at the 3% noise level. This behavior has been reported before and is common to all dynamic rectification techniques attempting to rectify random step changes in process variables [2], [3]. The performance is better for the two manipulated variables, *dist* and *vbr*. These variables are subject to rate of change constraints. They undergo only approximate step changes which provide the network with more information and facilitates better network performance for these variables. Third, the measurement noise reduction was greater at the 10% noise level than at the 3% noise level. However, higher measurement noise levels in the simulated process measurements used to train the networks tend to increase the bias in the network estimates ŷ of the true process variables **d**. This bias is most evident as a time delay between the actual process and the network estimates. As the process measurements become noisier, it becomes more difficult for the IRN to distinguish actual dynamics from random fluctuations. The network has to delay prediction until the evidence indicates that the process is actually changing.

7. Correlation Analysis

An examination of the correlations among the true residuals **r** and the apparent residuals **a** can be useful in determining the adequacy of the neural network models. With an ideal model, the following properties should hold:

$$\frac{E[r_{i,t-\tau} * r_{i,t}]}{E[r_{i,t}^2]} \begin{matrix} = 0 \; ; \; \tau \neq 0 \\ = 1 \; ; \; \tau = 0 \end{matrix} \quad ; \quad \frac{E[a_{i,t-\tau} * a_{i,t}]}{E[a_{i,t}^2]} \begin{matrix} = 0 \; ; \; \tau \neq 0 \\ = 1 \; ; \; \tau = 0 \end{matrix} \tag{9}$$

where E is the expectation operator and τ is the integer time step difference. Eqn. 9 defines two normalized autocorrelation functions for the true residuals and the apparent residuals. They indicate that the residuals for the ith process variable at each time step should be uncorrelated with the residuals at any other time step. Normalized autocorrelation functions for x_d and *dist* were calculated using Eqn. 10:

$$\phi_{\Psi_i}(\tau) = \left(\sum_{t=1}^{T-\tau} \Psi_{i,t} * \Psi_{i,t-\tau} \right) * \left(\sum_{t=1}^{T} \Psi_{i,t}^2 \right)^{-1} \tag{10}$$

where Ψ_i are the residuals of interest (true r_i or apparent a_i) for the ith process variable and $0 \leq \phi_\Psi(\tau) \leq 1$. Again, T is the total number of time steps in the data record and τ is the integer time step difference.

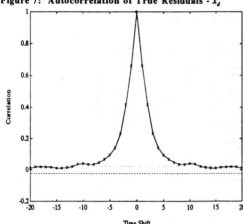

Figure 7: Autocorrelation of True Residuals - x_d Figure 8: Autocorrelation of Apparent Residuals - x_d

Figs. 7 and 8 show the normalized autocorrelation functions of the true residuals and the apparent residuals, respectively, for x_d when all six column variables were rectified simultaneously at the 3% noise level. There is significant correlation of the true residuals r_i out to ~5 time steps as shown in Fig. 7. This indicates that the network is not modeling the true process exactly. This is because the network has not been trained on the true values **d** as they would not be available in practice. In Fig. 8, the autocorrelation function of the apparent residuals indicate very little significant correlation between residuals at different time steps, and is much closer to the hoped for ideal than are the autocorrelation function of the true residuals. This outcome demonstrates that the autocorrelation function of the apparent residuals can give a misleading indication that the network is modeling the process well. However, this is the best that can be done given the noisy simulated measurements used for training the network.

8. Acknowledgement

The authors wish to acknowledge the financial support of Texaco Inc.

9. References

[1] Elman, J. L., "Finding Structure in Time," *Cognitive Science*, **14**(2), 179-211 (1990).

[2] Karjala, T. W. and D. M. Himmelblau, "A Comparison of Dynamic Data Reconciliation using Recurrent Artificial Neural Networks with Traditional Methods," submitted to *AIChE Journal*, (1993).

[3] Karjala, T. W., D. M. Himmelblau, and R. Miikkulainen, Data Rectification using Recurrent (Elman) Neural Networks, In *Proceedings of the IEEE-IJCNN*, Baltimore (1992).

[4] MacMurray, J. C., "Modeling and Control of a Packed Distillation Column Using Artificial Neural Networks," M. S. Thesis, The University of Texas at Austin, (1993).

[5] Mah, R. S. H., *Chemical Process Structures and Information Flows*, Butterworth's Publishers, Stoneham, MA, (1990).

[6] Patwardhan, A. A., "Modeling and Control of a Packed Distillation Column," Ph.D. Dissertation, The University of Texas at Austin, (1991).

The Application of Neural Networks in the Development of an On-line Model for a Semi-Regenerative Catalytic Reformer

C. Chessari, B. McKay, O. Agamennoni, G. Barton, and J. Romagnoli
Department of Chemical Engineering
The University of Sydney
NSW 2006, Australia

P. Watson
Caltex Refining Co. Pty. Limited
Kurnell NSW 2230, Australia

ABSTRACT

This paper outlines the development of an on-line predictive model of a complex industrial unit using a neural network approach. This work was the result of a collaborative project between the Department of Chemical Engineering, University of Sydney, and a local oil refinery. The final implemented model of the catalytic reformer was developed through a number of phases. The initial phase comprised the identification of the important process variables from an original set which were expected to be of significance to the catalytic deactivation process. This step reduced the dimensionality of the modelling task. The final model was a multilayer feedforward network with adaptive capabilities and an input structure providing "process memory" capabilities. The modelling system was developed as an on-line strategy with an interface to a commercial distributed control system (DCS) to obtain real-time plant data, and to present results to operations personnel. Preliminary performance of the model has been very encouraging.

1. INTRODUCTION

The development of accurate mechanistic models of industrial processes can be a difficult endeavour. In practice, most systems encountered in industry are non-linear to some extent and the development of a "first principles" model based on a detailed knowledge of the physics and chemistry of the process is generally time consuming, and in some cases impossible where unknown or changing mechanisms exist. An alternative approach to model building is to employ only plant input/output data. Neural networks, (Rumelhart and McClelland, 1986) which have a well established ability to learn complex non-linear functional relationships, provide one promising method of developing "black box" models for complex industrial processes.

A reforming unit changes the molecular structure of the heavy straight run naphtha (HSR) feed stock, which has a low octane rating, producing a high octane reformate suitable for petrol manufacture. A catalytic reforming unit consists of a number of reactors and heaters, together with a product separator. A semi-regenerative reformer processes feed stock for a time and then shuts down for regeneration of the catalyst which can retain its usefulness over multiple regenerations and has an ultimate life of some seven to ten years.

A model for the catalyst deactivation in a reforming unit can be used as the basis for an on-line optimisation strategy, determining the required operational parameters to achieve desired end of run deactivation at the scheduled time. Such a scheme would ensure that maximum performance is achieved from the catalyst for each regeneration performed. There is substantial economic benefit in the successful implementation of such a model-based scheme. A typical flowsheet for a reforming unit is illustrated in Figure 1.

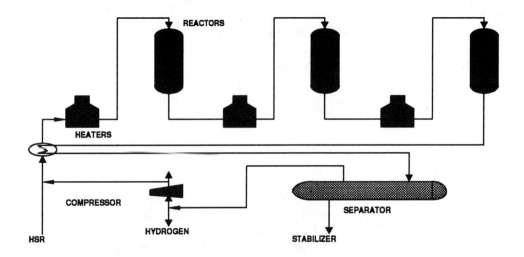

Figure 1: Reforming unit flowsheet.

2. PROCESS ANALYSIS

The initial phase of the model development involved the analysis of historical plant data to ascertain what variables were important, and whether the results of the various data analyses reflected what was known about the plant from operating experience. Over 700 sets of data were available for analysis.

The overall process constitutes two distinct dynamic systems. Firstly, the dynamics of the reactors which have time constants of the order hours, and secondly the long-term dynamics of the catalyst deactivation. The focus of the desired model is on the long-term effects of catalyst deactivation.

A number of sampling frequencies were trialled and that which gave the optimum compromise between performance and practical limitations turned out to be daily sampling. The data obtained and used in model development thus represented the daily steady-state condition of the plant. The collected data was daily averaged data from the control system (combined with spot sampling from laboratory results). The data is not dynamic in terms of short-term behaviour, but in terms of the catalyst deactivation which is of the order months, daily data adequately reflects this longer term dynamics. In effect, this stage attempted to find an adequate sampling rate which resulted in minimal information loss with respect to observed process behaviour. Too fast a rate could introduce spurious behaviour while too slow a sampling rate could result in loss of process information.

Conventional linear correlation techniques, (Manly, 1986), as well as non-linear sensitivity analyses and non-linear principal component analyses using neural networks, were used to evaluate the relative importance of the original set of process variables. This step reduced the dimensionality of the modelling task by establishing the most important process variables.

The process analysis began with a set of thirteen possible input variables thought likely to be of significance to the single output which was required to be predicted.

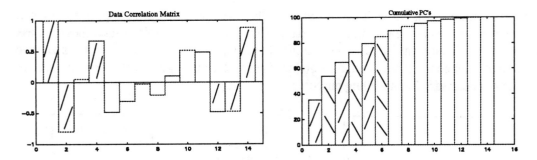

Figure 2: Data correlation and principal component analysis results.

Typical results from the linear analyses performed are shown in Figure 2. The data correlation matrix shown as the left bar graph in Figure 2 suggests that approximately half the variables are strongly linearly related with the designated output which is the first variable in the bar graph. Similarly, the cumulative principal components shown in the right bar graph of Figure 2 show that six principal components account for over 80% of the total variance, which suggests that a reduced set of variables are able to adequately describe the process behaviour. The linear results suggested that a reduced number of variables, approximately half the original input set, accounted for most of the variation in the data and thus would be the most appropriate to employ in any model building.

Both non-linear analysis techniques used rely on neural network technology for their implementation. Non-linear principal component analysis (NLPCA) was implemented by training a feedforward neural network to learn the identity mapping, (Kramer, 1991). The network comprises input and output layers, and three hidden layers. The first hidden layer maps the inputs into a lower dimension which is the output of the second hidden layer. The third hidden layer attempts to reconstruct the original inputs from the lower dimensional output of the second hidden layer. The main difference between PCA and NLPCA is that the latter involves non-linear mappings between the original and reduced dimension spaces. If any non-linear correlations between variables exist, NLPCA will describe the data with greater accuracy and/or by fewer factors than PCA.

The NLPCA analysis showed that only two principal components were required to reconstruct the inputs to the same accuracy as the PCA analysis. This implied that non-linear correlations existed between the variables.The significance of individual process variables on the non-linear principal components extracted by the NLPCA was evaluated by obtaining the first-order partial derivatives (ie the Jacobian matrix) of the feedforward neural network model of the input-output feature space. The Jacobian obtained from this neural network model is a scaled version of the true Jacobian and, therefore, needs to be "unscaled". To compare the effects on a consistent basis, the relative change of each process variable on the output was calculated. Subsequent scaling by maximum values allows the relative importance of the variables to be tracked as a percentage, the Relative Perturbation Value (RPV), throughout a run (Van Der Walt et al, 1993).

Additionally, sensitivity analyses can be undertaken by first training a feedforward network to develop an input-output model of the process, from which first order partial derivatives can be obtained. The inputs to the network are all possible variables affecting the process and there is a single designated output. In an analogous fashion to that used for the NLPCA, the Jacobian is unscaled and calculated with respect to the relative change in the inputs, to compare the effects of the inputs on the output on a consistent basis.

The non-linear analyses were consistent with the results from the linear analyses, with approximately half the variables accounting for most of the variation in the data. However, some variables which showed weak linear correlations displayed large non-linear interactions. Figure 3 shows the relative effects of two variables on the output throughout a run. Variables giving rise to no significant effect over a number of runs were regarded as unnecessary for modelling purposes.

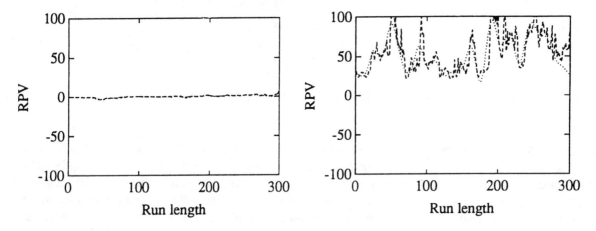

Figure 3: Unscaled Jacobian sensitivities of the output with respect to relative inputs.

3. MODEL DEVELOPMENT

From the process data analysis it was determined that use of just six of the original thirteen variables should be sufficient to provide an accurate model of the reformer.

As noted previously, the process is dynamic in the long-term as a consequence of the deactivation of the catalyst. This changes the reformer response to identical process inputs throughout the life of a run. This time dependent behaviour presents a modelling problem, as similar inputs are required to yield dissimilar outputs at different times. Therefore, some estimate or measure of "catalyst quality" was required to effectively set the level of catalyst activity within the model. In effect, the model required the ability to exhibit "process memory" to estimate the current extent of catalyst deactivation. In order to evaluate various candidate models for this required behaviour, a pulse input change was introduced into each model. After the pulse, the system output should lie above its unperturbed response. A number of different model types were investigated - linear and non-linear (linear in its parameters) regression models, as well as multilayer feedforward, tapped delay feedforward, and recurrent neural networks.

The linear models were unable to display the required process memory type behaviour. Their response to pulses resulted in behaviour qualitatively quite different to that observed on the plant. Figure 4 illustrates the behaviour of the linear model when subjected to an input step pulse starting at run length 100 and finishing at run length 200. Also shown, as a reference, is the unperturbed behaviour.

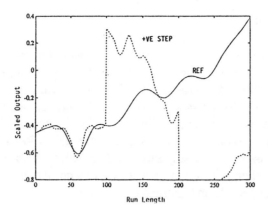

Figure 4: Linear model response to an input step pulse and unperturbed response - REF.

Both recurrent neural network models and feedforward networks with extra inputs consisting of past values of the inputs (ie tapped delay feedforward networks) were also developed in an attempt to incorporate some memory of the catalyst condition into the model. Neither of these models performed in a manner consistent with known plant behaviour. Problems caused by longer training times and local minima were also encountered for these models.

The final model framework was a multilayer feedforward network with adaptive capabilities and an input structure providing process memory capabilities. As well as the identified key process variables in the model input space, integrated terms developed from a mechanistic knowledge of catalyst deactivation were also included as model inputs, the latter effectively permitting the model to estimate the level of catalyst activity. It is important to note that the neural network itself was used to determine the relative importance of the integrated variable contributions.

The behaviour of the final model with respect to an input step pulse starting at run length 100 and finishing at run length 200 is shown in Figure 5, as is the unperturbed response of the model.

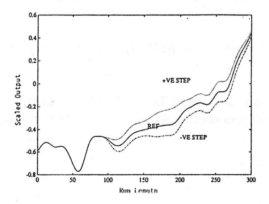

Figure 5: Final model behaviour subject to an input step pulse and unperturbed response - REF.

4. MODEL IMPLEMENTATION

Initially, the model was tested off-line to evaluate its behaviour with respect to available historical data and with what experienced plant personnel would expect. Finally, it was implemented as an on-line strategy with an interface to a commercial distributed control system (DCS) to obtain real-time plant data, and also as a means of presenting results to operations personnel. The model is continuously adapted to conform to the latest process information. Extensive checking and filtering are performed on all DCS data. A method for the determination of the relative importance of plant data to be included in the model training set has also been developed to deal with the issue of long sequences of data with little variation, which can lead to model degradation with time. This method relies on the calculation of a norm between successive points and the comparison of current points with those in an historical data buffer.

5. CONCLUSIONS

This work clearly demonstrated that a successful industrial application of neural network technology is as much about detailed data analysis, correct model structure selection, the right choice of development tools (this project made extensive use of the Matlab package) and how best to integrate the final model with commercial DCS hardware, as it is about the actual development of the network model itself.

ACKNOWLEDGEMENTS

The enthusiasm, support and constructive input of CALTEX Refining Ltd personnel in this collaborative project are gratefully acknowledged.

REFERENCES

Kramer, M.A., (1991). Nonlinear Principal Component Analysis Using Autoassociative Neural Networks, *AIChE Journal*, **37**(2), 233-243.

Manly, B.F.J., (1986). *Multivariate Statistical Methods: A Primer*. Chapman and Hall, London, England.

Rumelhart, D.E., and McClelland, J.L. (1986). *Parallel Distributed Processing*, MIT Press, Cambridge, Mass.

Van Der Walt, T.J., Van Deventer. J.S.J., and Banard, E. (1993). The Dynamic Modelling of Ill-Defined Processing Operations Using Connectionist Networks. *Chemical Engineering Science*, **48**(11), 1945-1958.

USING PRESSURE SENSOR PATTERN ANALYSIS FOR PRECISION INJECTION MOLDED PARTS

Douglas J. Cooper[†] and Suzanne L. B. Woll
Chemical Engineering Department
University of Connecticut
Storrs, CT 06269-3222

Blair Souder
Plastics Processing Development
United Technologies Research Center
East Hartford, CT 06108

ABSTRACT

This work explores the use of artificial neural networks (ANN's) as an online tool for quality monitoring of parts produced from an injection molding process. The method of approach is to train a back propagation network (BPN) to associate part quality with the measurement profile, or pattern, produced from a pressure sensor placed in the mold cavity. In this study, part quality is defined as final part length. Results presented show that the ANN is successful in predicting part quality based on pressure sensor pattern analysis. Further, these results show that the ANN outperformed the statistical technique now widely practiced by the injection molding process industry for predicting part quality.

INTRODUCTION

Injection molding is a high volume, low cost manufacturing process in which plastic pellets are formed into useful components. As shown in Figure 1, plastic pellets are drawn into the barrel of an injection molding machine via a rotating screw. Plastication occurs through shear forces imparted by the screw combined with thermal energy from surrounding heater bands. The screw retracts during plastication and is then driven forward to inject the plastic melt into a mold at the end of the barrel. The screw continues to hold pressure for a period of time while the melt packs and cools in the mold. When the part or parts are sufficiently cool, the mold opens and they are ejected. This cycle, which ranges from less than a minute to several minutes depending on the size of the parts, then repeats.

Difficulties in producing precision parts in large volumes arise because slight variations in processing conditions can cause significant changes in part quality. Detecting deviations in part quality based on process data and then adjusting conditions to restore desired quality are complex tasks due to the multivariable, nonlinear nature of the injection molding process.

Although it is true that many production molding machines operate under closed loop control with regard to individual process parameters such as barrel temperature and injection velocity, there is no automatic feedback with regard to the quality of the parts produced. The part quality feedback which does exist is from routine product sampling and inspection following traditional statistical process control (SPC) methods. Quality control via set point adjustments is then left to operator experience.

[†] Author to whom correspondence should be addressed

Recent trends to improve manufacturing capability include SPC of discrete process parameters such as peak mold cavity pressure, plastic melt temperature and injection time. Applying SPC methods to measured process parameters permits the development of automated online methods, and as a result, the quality of injection molded parts continues to improve.

This work seeks to facilitate this continuous improvement by developing improved methods for online part quality monitoring and control. The method of approach is to train a BPN to associate part quality, defined in this work as part length, with the measurement pattern produced from a mold cavity pressure sensor.

PART QUALITY MONITORING

Online quality monitoring and control requires the determination of part quality from measurable process parameters. SPC methods assume that if the process parameters being monitored are all within a specified number of standard deviations from a mean value, then the part being produced is of acceptable quality. One disadvantage to this approach is that only discrete data samples, collected at a few specific points in time during injection, are used to predict the part quality. A second disadvantage is that parameter interactions are not considered, resulting in false part rejections or acceptances.

A more comprehensive approach would be to develop a mathematical model incorporating machine settings, polymer properties and mold geometry and then to predict part quality characteristics using this model. While sophisticated models which describe the injection molding process do exist, they are far too computationally expensive to be used on the plant floor for monitoring and control purposes.

An alternative approach is to develop a neural network model which is trained to predict part quality from measured process data. By training the neural network on real data, the nonidealities of the process are included in the part quality model without requiring extensive analysis and mathematical modeling. In addition, once the network is trained, real-time operation can be achieved as a result of the relatively low computational load of this type of model.

Recently, Haeussler and Wortberg (1993) developed a neural network that relates discrete sensor information to part quality. However, since there is a great deal of evidence that suggests that complete data profiles contain significantly more information about part quality than do a few discrete values (Frech and Meyer, 1982; Wu and Chen, 1990), this work explores the application of ANN's to the pattern recognition of compete data profiles.

For this investigation, mold cavity pressure profile is used for predicting part quality. Cavity pressure is known to be directly related to part quality and, in fact, one of the simplest and most effective SPC techniques uses peak cavity pressure to predict part quality. As shown in Figure 2, which contains actual pressure profiles used in this study, the mold cavity pressure sensor trace consists of an initial rise, a peak value, a transitional region, a packing pressure plateau, a "knee" bend and, finally, a pressure decay. These features correspond to mold filling, completion of fill, transition to mold packing, mold packing, gate freezing and mold cooling. Indeed, the complexity of the pressure profile alone suggests that the entire pattern should be considered as a complete picture or snapshot rather than selecting one or two discrete values from the profile to represent the injection behavior.

GENERATING THE TRAINING/TEST PATTERNS

In this work, a BPN was trained for the pattern recognition task. To produce the training and test mold cavity pressure patterns, three experiments were conducted on a Toyo Ti55G$_2$, which is a production quality injection molding machine.

Experiment 1 was a Box-Behnken designed experiment (e.g. Mason *et al.*, 1989) in which the ram velocity was varied between 20, 40 and 60% of machine capability, the hydraulic hold pressure was varied between 1.73, 2.75 and 3.45 MPa and the barrel temperature was varied between 293, 299 and 304 $^{\circ}$C. The middle values for each sequence are considered the baseline conditions. A three parameter designed experiment with three values for each parameter, when using the Box-Behnken approach, results in 15 combinations or experimental conditions. Three of these 15 are repeated experiments at the baseline conditions.

Ten pressure trace pattern were collected at each of the 15 conditions of Experiment 1. Cavity pressure data was collected at a rate of 25 Hz over a period of 14 seconds beginning at the start of injection for each shot using a high speed data acquisition system. A portion of the resulting pressure profiles are shown in Figure 2. The length of the parts were measured using a hand caliper.

Experiments 2 and 3 were designed to gather information on transient process behavior caused by typical process disturbances such as variations in material characteristics. The baseline plastic was a mineral reinforced nylon sold commercially as Minlon 10B40. The first disturbance material introduced was a 100% first generation regrind, created by grinding parts molded from virgin material back into pellet form and then using that material as feed to the process.

Other disturbances included a 50/50 virgin/first generation regrind mixture and a virgin material contaminated with non-reinforced nylon. During an experiment, virgin material was introduced before and after each disturbance to return the process to steady state. 161 and 192 pattern sets were collected from Experiments 2 and 3, respectively. The primary difference between these experiments was the sequence in which the disturbance materials were introduced.

The input patterns for the BPN were created from this data using a multi-step procedure. First, the patterns were shifted in time to locate the maximum cavity pressure for each shot at 0.12 sec. This normalizes the data by eliminating lag variability introduced from the hydraulic actuation system. Second, unscaled pressure transducer data ranging from 0-10 volts were used directly rather than scaling the signals between 0 and 77 MPa. Finally, every point between 0 and 0.25 seconds and every tenth point thereafter up to 9 seconds was used, thereby reducing the number of points in a given profile from 350 to 28. The resulting patterns were "front-loaded" in this manner to focus on significant features found during the relatively short injection period.

The BPN outputs were generated from the part length measurements corresponding to the input patterns. Surface finish and part thickness are a few examples of other quality parameters that could have been evaluated. Part lengths were reduced to values between -1 and 1 to correspond to a sigmoidal network output. To do this, the maximum, minimum and mean values of the part length training data were determined. Then, using algebraic transformations, the part length data was centered around a mean of 0 and scaled between -0.5 and 0.5 such that the farthest point did not exceed a distance of 0.5 from the mean.

BPN TRAINING

Once the network pattern space was defined, a 28-4-1 BPN was constructed (Caudill, 1988; Rumelhart and McClelland, 1986). The 28-4-1 network consists of 28 input nodes, 4 hidden nodes and 1 output node. The initial weights for the network were randomly generated values between -0.01 and 0.01. The nonlinear activation function chosen for this network was the hyperbolic tangent function with limits [-1,1]. In addition, the more efficient conjugate gradient technique was used during training to determine weight adjustments rather than the generalized delta rule. For more details on BPN construction, see Cooper *et al.* (1992).

The network was trained using every other pattern obtained during Experiments 1 and

2, and the complement was used as the test set to monitor BPN convergence. That is, the sum of squared error (SSE) of the test set was evaluated along with, but independently of, the training set. When a point was reached where improvements in training set SSE did not result in corresponding improvements in the test set SSE, no additional BPN weight adjustments were made and the BPN was considered converged.

Convergence occurred at approximately 2000 iterations. Further training would only have resulted in memorization of the training set and a loss in generalization of the input/output relationship. Data from Experiments 1 and 2 were used in an effort to develop a model well-suited to both steady state and transient conditions. An independent evaluation of the network performance was then made using data from Experiment 3.

Since the value of this approach depends on the BPN's diagnostic performance as compared to current monitoring techniques, the network performance was compared to an SPC model based on the current industrial approach of using peak cavity pressure. The SPC statistical model was generated from the data collected at the baseline conditions.

A given part was considered acceptable if, in the SPC model, the peak pressure for a particular sample was within the specified pressure range or if, in the neural network model, the part length predicted was within the specified length range. The actual part length was then used to determine the fraction of defects correctly identified by each method.

ONLINE QUALITY MONITORING

Figure 3 shows part length predictions for Experiment 3 data plotted along with actual part length. As shown, the BPN predicted the data quite accurately. Discrepancies are visible in the contaminated region; however, the model did predict the correct trend of shorter part lengths and it is assumed that these parts would still be rejected, regardless of the error in this region. Sample 54 is an outlier. The input pattern was shaped differently from any of the training patterns. A pre-screening procedure may have prevented this error from occurring.

The only other significant model mismatch occurred in the region of 100% regrind. This mismatch may have been caused by insufficient representation of this disturbance type in the training set. The sample of regrind used in Experiment 2 (150 g instead of the usual 500 g) was too small to generate the same response as a full barrel of regrind. Once again though, the direction of the trend was correct. BPN's are very capable of interpolating between known input patterns but, as evidenced here, are not reliably in extrapolating outside these patterns. In general, however, the BPN model performed very well.

Figure 4 shows the result of the benchmark test. As shown, the BPN outperformed the SPC peak cavity pressure model in terms of correctly accepting and rejecting parts. In the ± 1 to ± 4 standard deviation range where typical production limits are set, the BPN model identified a higher percentage of defects than was observed with the SPC model. Beyond the ± 4 standard deviation range where only distinct outliers are detected with such loose limits, the BPN performed similarly to the SPC model.

CONCLUSION AND FUTURE GOALS

The BPN trained in this work was successful in predicting part length based on mold cavity pressure profiles. In addition, the BPN demonstrated superior part quality prediction capabilities when compared to SPC. This suggests that ANN's based on complete data profiles can be applied effectively in the injection molding industry to improve quality monitoring. Future work will focus on demonstrating the capabilities of this monitoring technique online and on incorporating the technique into a viable closed loop quality control scheme.

ACKNOWLEDGEMENTS

The authors gratefully acknowledge the support of the University of Connecticut Precision Manufacturing Center for their support of this work.

REFERENCES

Cooper, D. J., L. Megan and R. F. Hinde, Jr., "Comparing Two Neural Networks for Pattern Based Adaptive Process Control, AIChE Journal, **38**, 41 (1992).

Caudill, M., "Neural Networks Prime," *AI Expert*, **3**, 53 (1988).

Frech, F. and U. Meyer, "Measuring and Interpreting the Mold Cavity Pressure in Injection Molding," *Industrial Application of Piezoelectric Pressure Measurement*, 3 (1992).

Haeussler, J. and J. Wortberg, "Quality Assurance in Injection Molding with Neural Networks," *SPE ANTEC*, 123 (1993).

Mason, R. L., R. F. Gunst and J. L. Hess, Statistical Design of Experiments, Wiley and Sons, New York (1989).

Rumelhart, D. E. and J. L. McClelland, Parallel Distributed Processing: Exploration in the Microstructure of Cognition: 1. Foundations, MIT Press, Cambridge (1986).

Wu, J.-L. and S. J. Chen, "Pattern Analysis of Injection Molding Process: Statistical Correlation Study," *SPE ANTEC*, 233 (1990).

Wong, A. J., "Recognition of General Patterns Using Neural Networks," *Biological Cybernetics*, **58**, 361 (1988).

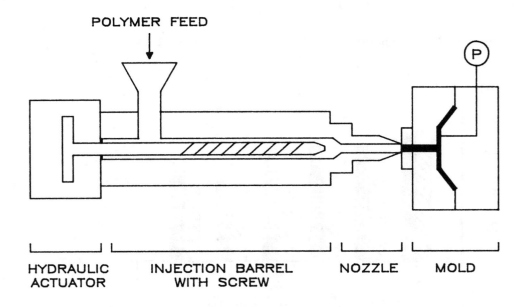

Figure 1: The injection molding process

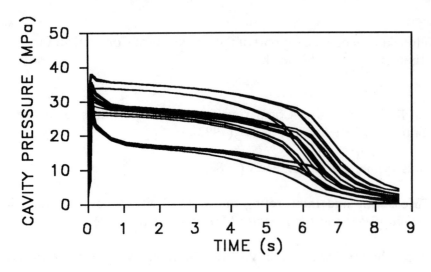

Figure 2: Sample mold cavity pressure profiles used to train BPN

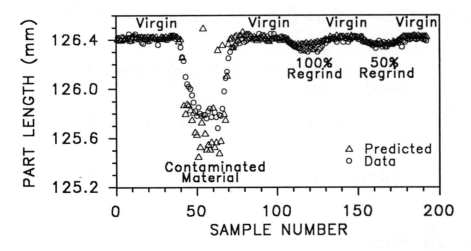

Figure 3: BPN prediction of part length for Experiment 3 data

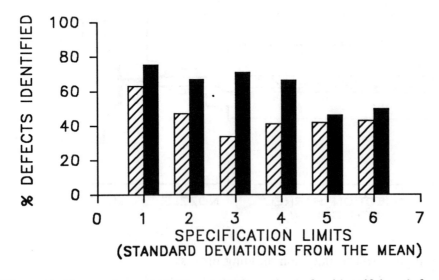

Figure 4: Comparison of BPN and SPC methods for identifying defective parts

IDENTIFICATION OF A WASTE WATER NEUTRALIZATION PROCESS USING NEURAL NETWORKS

Bernd EIKENS and M. Nazmul KARIM

Department of Agricultural and Chemical Engineering,
Colorado State University, Fort Collins, Colorado 80523, USA

Abstract. This paper addresses the issue related to the modeling of a nonlinear process using neural networks. Three network architectures, namely the multilayer perceptron (MLP), the resilient propagation network (Rprop) and the radial basis function network (RBFN) are applied to real-time identification of a waste water neutralization process. The results of these identification methods are presented and compared for each neural network model. In addition these networks are implemented in a model predictive control environment and their performance is discussed. The results show that the network structures are applicable for modeling the system, the radial basis function model improves the approximation and the control task.

Key Words. Identification; neural nets; pH control; predictive control.

1. INTRODUCTION

System identification can be described as the art and science of building mathematical models of dynamical system and signals based on observed inputs and outputs. An expression for the examined system's behavior has to be derived. During the last decade identification of dynamical nonlinear systems based on observed input-output data has become important (Ljung, 1993). Conceptually this approach results in learning a certain pattern from the training set and then applying that pattern to new data. Modeling a system can be posed as the problem of learning an input-output mapping. The system involved may be nonlinear and complex. The identification or prediction of time series of these systems is the leading application area for neural nets to control problems. For the neural network two different types of mapping structures are available: global mappings and local mappings. Two network structures both belonging to the class of feedforward networks are considered here. The multilayer perceptron (MLP) belonging to the first class has proven to be suitable for these problems. In general, the learning speed for networks using global mappings is slow since they are normally based on a backpropagation which is an iterative error-gradient learning algorithm. The backpropagation algorithm is capable of training a MLP on nonlinear mappings, but convergence is not guaranteed due to the local minima embedded in a typical error surface. In order to speed up the training procedures, several other training methods for the feedforward architecture have been developed (e.g. resilient propagation, quickpropagation).

An alternative architecture for implementing nonlinear multivariate input-output mapping is the radial basis function network (RBFN) which belongs to the group of local mappings. In this case, the input space is divided in localized receptive fields around center points. The architecture of a RBFN is similar to the feedforward neural network. It consists of three layers of nodes: the input, the hidden and the output layer. The activation of the hidden units is computed by applying a radial basis function to the Euclidian distance between the input pattern and the center vector. The performance of a radial basis function network is determined by the two parameters associated with each RBF: the proper selection of the RBF centers based on the available data points and the width controlling the amount of overlapping.

In this paper, these neural network based models are used for the identification of a pH neutralization process and their abilities to predict nonlinear time-series are shown. A chemical plant effluent is simulated by mixing two components, sodium bicarbonate and sodium hydroxide, with time-varying amounts. Sulfuric acid is used to neutralize the feed stream in a continuous stirred tank reactor. The control goal is to add the exact amount of H_2SO_4 in order to neutralize process waste stream by knowing only the pH of the stream.

2. SYSTEM REPRESENTATION

2.1. Feedforward Neural Network

The multilayer perceptron (MLP) consists of interconnected processing units that are organized in layers. After summation of the weighted inputs, a nonlinear function, in this case the sigmoid function is used as the activation in each node. The structure of a three layer feedforward neural network consisting of three input and one output units is shown in Figure 2.1. In this research two different algorithms have been applied for training of the feedforward neural network using the sigmoid function as the nonlinearity. The goal of the training procedure is to find proper weights of the network that minimizes the sum of the squared errors between the network prediction $\hat{\mathbf{y}} = [\hat{y}_1, \ldots, \hat{y}_N]^T$ and the desired output $\mathbf{y} = [y_1, \ldots, y_N]^T$. First, an enhanced backpropagation algorithm including batching and step size optimization is utilized (Leonard and Kramer, 1990). It has been shown that feedforward neural networks with one layer of hidden nodes and trained with backpropagation are universal function approximators (Hornik *et al.*, 1990). For the second learning procedure an algorithm called resilient propagation is used (Braun and Riedmiller, 1992). Resilient propagation (Rprop) is an adaptive learning algorithm taking the local topology of the error function into account. An update value Δ_{ij} is calculated for each weight adjustment according to the following equation:

$$
\Delta_{ij}(t) = \begin{cases} \alpha \cdot \Delta_{ij}^{(t-1)} & \text{if } \frac{\partial E}{\partial w_{ij}}^{(t-1)} > 0 \\ \beta \cdot \Delta_{ij}^{(t-1)} & \text{if } \frac{\partial E}{\partial w_{ij}}^{(t-1)} < 0 \\ 0 & \text{else} \end{cases}
\tag{1}
$$

where α and β are constants such that $0 < \beta < 1 < \alpha$. The update value is provided with a sign depending on the gradient $\frac{\partial E}{\partial w_{ij}}^t$. In this case the weight step is determined simply by the sequence of the sign of the error function derivative. This turns out to be a reliable information about the local error function. In case of a sign change of the partial derivative the previous update step of the weight is reverted. The update values and the weights are changed in a batch mode, i.e. after each cycle of presenting the whole data set. The resilient propagation algorithm can be characterized as a very robust and fast learning algorithm (Braun and Riedmiller, 1993).

2.1. Radial Basis Function Network

Radial basis functions (RBF) have been proposed as an alternative architecture for generating multivariate, nonlinear input-output mappings. They are traditional techniques for strict interpolation in multidimensional space. The generalized form of radial basis function is applicable to the network structure. The radial basis function network (RBFN) uses local mappings to construct the input-output space. It can be regarded as a feedforward neural network with three layers, namely an input, a hidden layer with the RBF nonlinearity and a linear output layer. With each node of the hidden layer a parameter vector, the center, is defined. Instead of evaluating just the weighted sum of the inputs, the Euclidian distance between the input pattern $\mathbf{x}$ and the center vector $\mathbf{c}$ is computed. The possible choices for input and activation functions for FNN and RBFN are shown in Table 2.1. The input of the hidden node is defined as q, $\varphi(q)$ denotes the nonlinearity associated with each hidden node and σ is the width or spread parameter for the Gaussian function.

Table 2.1: Comparison of a multilayer perceptron and radial basis function network

Network	Node input	Activation
MLP (sigmoid)	$q = \mathbf{x}^T \mathbf{w}$	$\varphi(q) = (1 + e^{-q})^{-1}$
RBF (general)	$q = \|\mathbf{x} - \mathbf{c}\|$	$\varphi(q)$
RBF (Gaussian)	$q = \|\mathbf{x} - \mathbf{c}\|$	$\varphi(q) = e^{-q/\sigma}$
RBF (thin-p.-s.)	$q = \|\mathbf{x} - \mathbf{w}\|$	$\varphi(q) = q^2 \log q$

Besides the Gaussian and the thin-plate-spline function shown in the table, other possible choices are the multiquadratic and the inverse multiquadratic functions. The performance of a radial basis function network is determined by the parameters associated with each RBF. The proper selection of the RBF centers based on the available data points is very important in order to reflect the whole input space. If the Gaussian function is selected as the nonlinearity, a second parameter associated with each center is the width σ, which controls the amount of overlapping. An optimal mapping of the input to the output space would be the one that maps the probability density distribution (PDF) in the most accurate manner trying to preserve the local structures.

In this research two different methods for the placement of the RBF centers are compared. In the first approach, the initialization is done by choosing the centers evenly spaced over the whole input space. During the training procedure the centers are adjusted based on a gradient descent method. For the second procedure we selected a cluster analysis on the basis of Euclidian distance. Several clustering algorithms are available and applicable for the selection of the center vectors: k-means clustering, medoid and centroid methods (Kaufman and Rousseeuw, 1990). The clustering procedure applied in this research is based on the k-means method. The initial centers $\mathbf{x}_c$ are selected based on the mean values of the input data. The center vectors represent the mean of value of each cluster. For each data-vector $\mathbf{x}_j$ of the input space, the dissimilarity d_{jc} to each temporary center $\mathbf{x}_c$ is calculated. The vector $\mathbf{x}_j$ is assigned to the nearest cluster and the mean of that cluster is updated. For the identification procedure in this paper, the thin-plate-spline function has been chosen as the basis function. The weights between the hidden and output layer are calculated using the gradient descent method.

3. WASTE WATER pH NEUTRALIZATION

The previously described neural network structures have been applied to the identification of a pH neutralization process. This operation is very challenging with respect to identification and control since the process is of nonlinear nature and shows time-variant process gains. The described behavior is generated by sudden changes in the chemical decomposition of the waste water. Using this system the identification performance of the previously described networks structures are compared. In the following, the radial basis function network trained with the clustering procedure is called RBFN-1, the second approach is called RBFN-2.

3.1. Identification Results

The pH waste water neutralization process is simulated using the model described by Pröll and Karim (1993a). A training set consisting of 700 input-output data pairs has been created by varying the feed concentration according to a pseudo random with random amplitude sequence. Additionally, a test set of 300 data pairs has been generated in order to evaluate the learning and generalization abilities of the networks. The input vector $\mathbf{x}$ in this neutralization process consists of the pH value of the feed, $d(t) = pH_{feed}$, the pH value of the tank $y(t) = pH_{tank}$ and the manipulated variable at each time step $u(t) = V_{H_2SO_4}$. Several tests suggested that the input vector $\mathbf{x} = [y(t-1), y(t-2), y(t-3), d(t-1), u(t-1)]^T$ is the most appropriate choice. This result was also obtained using the cross-correlation and the auto-correlation tests. For the multilayer perceptron the number of hidden nodes was set to 8 based on the crossvalidation procedure described by Werbos et al. (1992). A satisfactory solution as shown in Figure 3.1 was achieved after 15 training cycles. For strong gradient changes of the function small deviations are present at low and high pH values. For the second neural network structure based on the RPROP learning algorithm the identification result is shown in Figure 3.2. As can be seen in this case also, the error variance increases for local maxima and minima. The overall performance of the resilient propagation network is surprisingly good keeping in mind the simplicity of this learning algorithm.

The radial basis function networks - RBFN-1 and RBFN-2 - have been trained with the same data set using the aforementioned training procedures. For both cases the number of hidden nodes N_h has been varied and the optimal solution with respect to the training procedure and the approximation accuracy has been found as $N_h = 15$. The first RBF based network has been trained using the clustering procedure for the centers and the gradient descent algorithm for the weights connecting the hidden and the output layer. The overall performance is comparable to the FNN and RPROP method. According to Figure 3.3, the RBFN-1 model is more accurate in regions of low and high pH values. For the last identification procedure the centers are initially evenly spaced and then adapted based on the gradient descent method. The result is shown in the next Figure 3.4. Compared to the previously shown results the overall error has been reduced significantly. To achieve this accuracy, a more time consuming learning algorithm compared to the RBFN-1 and RPROP has to be adopted.

Algorithms based on gradient descent are known to be extremely slow and tedious especially if they are applied for the entire weight space. Both radial basis function networks show more appropriate approximation abilities than the feedforward neural network using the sigmoid function. This is not surprising since the RBFNs have a guaranteed learning procedure, while backpropagation can get stuck in local minima (Broomhead and Lowe, 1988). The resilient propagation has similar problems dealing with the nonlinearity of the input space, but has the advantage of a short learning time. The standard square error (SSE) of all four modeling methods is shown in Table 3.1. While the SSE for the MLP, RPOP and RBFN-1 is of the same order of magnitude, it has been reduced significantly for the RBFN-2. The error for the radial basis function based on gradient descent training method is shown Figure 3.5. The autocorrelation function applied to the modeling error shows an acceptable white noise signal which indicates the quality of the model.

Table 3.1: Comparison of the standard squared error

Network	RBFN-1	RBFN-2	MLP	RPROP
SSE	0.05098	0.02602	0.05575	0.05865

4. MODEL PREDICTIVE CONTROL

In order to control the neutralization process the in the previous section described neural network models are implemented in a model predictive control environment (Pröll and Karim, 1993b). The structure is shown in the Figure 4.1. As in conventional MPC, a nonlinear programming problem (NLP) has to be solved every time step. This NLP is given by the multistep, quadratic cost function

$$\min_{\mathbf{u}(t),\mathbf{u}(t+1),..,\mathbf{u}(t+N_c-1)} J = \left[\sum_{j=\tau_d+1}^{N_p} \left(\mathbf{e}_j^T \mathbf{\Gamma}_e \mathbf{e}_j \right) + \sum_{j=0}^{N_c-1} \left(\triangle \mathbf{u}(t+j)^T \mathbf{\Gamma}_u \triangle \mathbf{u}(t+j) \right) \right] \qquad (2)$$

where $\mathbf{e}_j$ is the error vector at time $(t+j)$, N_p is the prediction horizon, N_c the control horizon, and τ_d is the estimated maximum time delay of the process. $\mathbf{\Gamma}_e$ and $\mathbf{\Gamma}_u$ are weighting matrices. A detailed description of the neural network based model predictive controller is given by Pröll and Karim (1993b). The solution to the nonlinear programming problem is based on the modified Marquardt algorithm which incorporates boundary constraints by penalizing the objective function.

4.2. Closed loop control

Exemplary the multilayer perceptron and the radial basis function network (RBFN-1) have been implemented into the MPC environment. The feasibility of using FNN and RBFN in nonlinear time-varying closed-loop control systems are verified and the performance are evaluated. For the closed-loop operation 1000 discrete time steps have been used. The control horizon was set to 1 and the prediction horizon equal to 6. On the pH measurement a noise with zero mean and a standard deviation of 0.03 pH units has been superimposed. The weighting factors were obtained by a heuristic rule. For both neural network models oscillations are visible at time step $t = 250$ and $t > 800$. These are due to the shift of a very steep titration curve ($t > 700$, no buffer in the feed stream). Comparing Figures 4.5 and 4.6 it is noticed that RBFN based MPC shows a slightly superior performance than the multilayer perceptron based MPC. The SSE of the offset between the setpoint and the real output is less for RBFN than for MPC using MLP. The manipulative input for the RBFN based MPC controller is shown in Figure 4.7. The figure for the manipulated variable in the case of MLP is similar.

5. CONCLUSIONS

In this paper, four different neural networks have been applied for the identification of a waste water neutralization. These identified models have been implemented into a model predictive controller. It has been shown how these networks can be used to estimate and implement nonlinear mappings applied to time series. The performance of the RBFNs for the presented system is superior compared to the multilayer perceptron. The effect on the closed-loop control experiments has been shown. However, both model structures have been trained off-line. An opportunity to update the networks with respect to the parameters and the network structure is desirable and is addressed in future work.

Acknowledgement: The authors wish to acknowledge the financial support from the National Science Foundation (BCS – 9118955) for this research.

6. REFERENCES

Braun, H., M. Riedmiller (1992). Rprop: A fast adaptive learning algorithm. *Proc. of the Int. Symposium on Computer and Information Science VII.*

Braun, H., M.Riedmiller (1993). Rprop: A fast and robust backpropagation learning strategy *Proc. of the ACNN.*

Chen, S., S.A. Billings and P.M. Grant (1992). Recursive hybrid algorithm for non-linear system identification using radial basis function networks. *Int. J. of Control*, **5**, Vol. 55, 1051–1070.

Hornik, K. (1991). Approximation capabilities of multilayer feedforward networks. *Neural Networks*, **4**, 251-257.

Kaufman, L., P.J. Rousseeuw (1990). *Finding Groups in Data - An Introduction to Cluster Analysis.* John Wiley & Sons, New York.

Leonard J., M.A. Kramer (1990). Improvement of the backpropagation algorithm for training neural networks. *Computers Chem. Engng.*, **14**, 337–341.

Ljung, L., J. Sjöberg (1993). A system identification perspective on neural nets. *Proc. IEEE Workshop on Neural Networks of Signal Processing*, IEEE Science Center, New York.

Pröll, T. and M.N. Karim (1993a). Model predictive control using real-time NARX approach. in press *AIChE Journal.*

Pröll, T. and M.N. Karim (1993b). Real-time predicitive control based on nonlinear autoregressive and neural network models. *Submitted to Chemical Engineering Science.*

Werbos, P., T. McAvoy and T. Su (1992). Neural networks, system identification and control in the chemical process industries. in *Handbook of Intelligent Control* (D.A. White, D.A. Sofge, Ed), Van Nostrand Reinhold, New York.

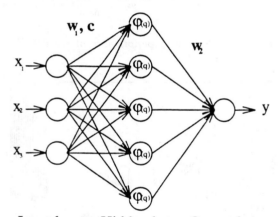

Fig. 2.1.: Neural Network structure

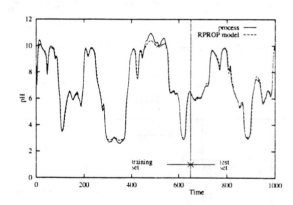

Fig. 3.2: Process output and RPROP model output

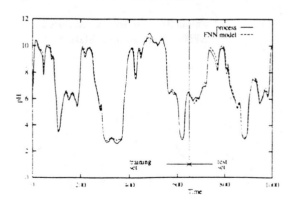

Fig. 3.1: Process output and FNN model output

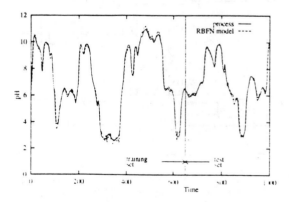

Fig. 3.3: Process output and RBFN-1 model output

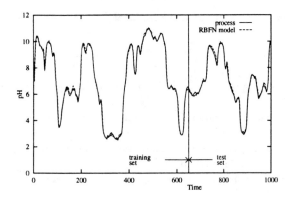

Fig. 3.4: Process output and RBFN-2 model output

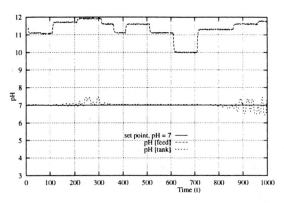

Fig. 4.2: Closed loop performance of the FNN model

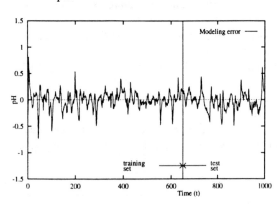

Fig. 3.5: Modeling error of the RBFN-2 model

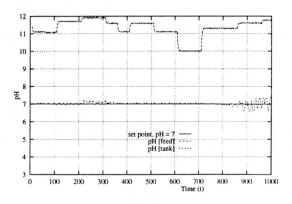

Fig. 4.3: Closed loop performance of the RBFN model

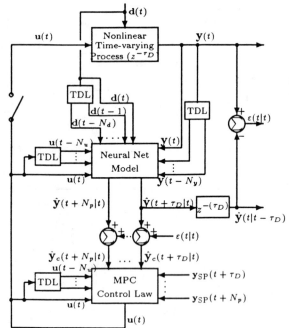

Fig. 4.1: Proposed adaptive MPC structure

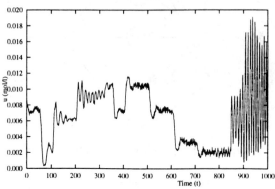

Fig. 4.4: Manipulated variable u for closed loop RBFN model based simulation

Neural Networks as Generic Nonlinear Controllers

Tariq Samad and Wendy Foslien
Honeywell Technology Center, Minneapolis, MN 55418
samad@htc.honeywell.com, foslien@htc.honeywell.com

Abstract

Currently popular neurocontrol approaches exhibit one common problem: substantial application-specific development is involved with each. Neural networks must be trained, essentially from scratch, for every application. Retraining or adaptation is also necessary for handling process drifts and changes in performance criteria. We discuss an approach for generic neurocontrol: the same, pre-developed neural network can be used for a wide range of applications. No application-specific training or adaptation is necessary; instead, application-specific aspects are provided as input to the network. We refer to these neurocontrollers as "Parametrized Neurocontrollers." Some results are presented for a PNC that includes a dynamic (recurrent) neural network.

Introduction

A common shortcoming of most neural network applications to control systems is the need for extensive application-specific development. This is true for both neural network modeling approaches (e.g., [2]), in which case a network must be trained on appropriate data gathered from the process, and for the use of neural networks as controllers, which require the optimization of the neural network controller based on a process model (e.g., [5]), the actual process (e.g., [1]), or an existing controller (e.g., [6]).

The attendant expense in time and computation is a significant barrier to widespread implementation of neurocontrol systems, and compares unfavorably to the implementation cost for conventional control. For example, with the multiple-input multiple-output linear controllers that are now widely used in the chemical process industries, once the (linear) model is identified, the controller design is straightforward. Also, simple SISO linear control schemes such as PID controllers enable the use of the same control law in domains as diverse as building, process, and flight control systems.

The number of successful neurocontrol applications is growing, but the overall impact of the technology is still small. We assert that the high implementation cost of current approaches is a primary factor. In principle, nonlinear control systems—we believe nonlinearity is the key feature that distinguishes neural from conventional control—can benefit innumerable applications, but a considerable increase in development time and effort will often be an unacceptable price.

We describe a "generic" neurocontrol approach: neural network controllers that are developed off-line and can subsequently be used for a variety of applications—both different processes and performance criteria. No application-specific training or adaptation is required. We refer to these controllers as "Parametrized Neurocontrollers" (PNCs). The concept has been presented before [8—suggested for supplementary reading]. Here we provide further elaboration and further, although still limited, experimental results, in this case with PNCs based on dynamic (recurrent) neural networks.

Parametrized Neurocontrollers

The key to the PNC concept are external inputs that inform the neurocontroller about specifics of the process and control criterion. Thus relevant aspects of the application are provided as input to a PNC (Fig. 1). These inputs are parameters that relate to parametrized process models and control criteria and are in addition to dynamic inputs such as the setpoint, error signals, and meaured or estimated process states. The two types of external inputs make PNCs generic in two distinct ways: the process model parameter estimates $\hat{p}_p$ facilitate application to different processes and the control parameters p_c allow different performance criteria to be accommodated.

The convenience of application of PNCs is obtained at significant, but off-line, computational cost. Where current neurocontrol approaches require the training of a neural network for an individual application (a process or process model and a performance criterion), PNCs are trained for a family of applications (Fig. 2). For each weight vector w generated by the training algorithm (a nonlinear optimization algorithm), a number of closed-loop simulations are conducted. These simulations sample spaces of process models P_M, control performance criteria, input signals, and process model parameter estimation errors. The cost function $J(w)$ that the training algorithm attempts to minimize is computed as some function (e.g., the average or the maximum) of individual cost function evaluations from each simulation (see [8,9] for some details).

The computationally intensive development buys on-line simplicity. Once optimized, the neural network can be implemented as a hardwired module in a controller which can then be installed and used on any process, and for any criterion, within its design space. The memory and processing requirements imposed by PNCs are minimal: on the order of 100 weights and 100 arithmetic operations respectively for the admittedly simple experiments we have conducted so far.

Nonlinear Control for Linear Processes

To develop a PNC for a variety of processes, an appropriate space of process models must first be identified. This space determines the class of applications for the PNC. Where the target processes are sufficiently similar in terms of the physical phenomena involved, and where these phenonmena are well-understood, a parametrized first-principles nonlinear model can be used. But such cases are rare and cannot form the basis of a truly generic control design approach. In most of our work, we have adopted a simpler and more broadly applicable solution. In ignorance of known common nonlinearities, we assume none: PNCs designed for linear process models are likely to be the most generic.

The wisdom of developing neural network controllers for linear process models may appear questionable, but in fact nonlinear control can provide significant benefits even for this seemingly simple case. We note two in particular:
1. Enhanced robustness. A nonlinear controller can provide less sensitivity to process changes such as due to equipment wear, changes in operating points, and disturbances. For robust performance, the optimal controller for a linear process is known to be linear only for some special cases [3,7].
2. Control of Arbitrary Response Features. Linear controllers are often designed to minimize cost functions, but synthesis procedures are limited to quadratic or other analytically convenient forms. Thus performance parameters such as weightings on output tracking and control energy can be used to adjust system response. In practice, however, control engineers and operators are often concerned with practical response features such as settling times, rise times, and maximum overshoots. A nonlinear controller can allow direct control of such features.

Dynamic Neural Networks as PNCs

All but the simplest feedback controllers are dynamic devices: the control output is a function of historical information and not just the current process output. With neurocontrollers, dynamics are often handled externally by providing, as input to the network, past samples of the process output or some history-sensitive features of the output such as the integral or derivative error; the neural network itself is a conventional feedforward architecture that implements an algebraic mapping.

Dynamic neural network (DNN) models—neural networks with built-in dynamic elements—are an attractive alternative to such preprocessing solutions. An appropriately designed dynamic neural network controller would not require the prior determination of the number of process output samples that must be presented or the relevant dynamic features that must be computed.

Here we present some preliminary experimental results with hybrid SISO PNCs that consist of a fixed PI (proportional-integral) controller and a dynamic neural network. The process space the PNCs are designed for are linear first-order models. The PNCs allow direct control of the closed-loop settling time through a "desired settling time" input d_{ST}. The overall controller output u is the summation of the PI output and the DNN output:

$u = u_{PI} + u_{NN}.$

The PI controller is described by the linear dynamical equation

$u_{PI} = K_C e + K_I \int e \, dt$

where K_C and K_I are the proportional and integral gains respectively of the PI controller and e is the error between the setpoint and the current process output. For the neural network, we have adopted a continuous-time dynamic model [4]. The network consists of n internal dynamic units with outputs y_i, and the neural network output is a linear weighted sum of the unit outputs:

$$u_{NN} = \sum_{i=1}^{i \leq n} q_i y_i + q_0.$$

The y_i's are sigmoidal functions of the states x_i of the units. We have chosen a computationally more efficient sigmoidal form than the logistic curve or the hyperbolic tangent:

$$y_i = \frac{x_i}{1 + |x_i|}.$$

Each unit evolves according to a first-order dynamic equation with external inputs e and d_{ST}:

$$T_j \frac{dx_j}{dt} = -x_j + \sum_{i=1}^{i \leq n} w_{ji} y_i + w_{j0} + p_1 e + p_2 d_{ST},$$

from some given initial conditions $x(0)$. The network parameters to be optimized thus consist of the output weights q_i, the inter-unit weights w_{ji}, the input weights p_i, and the unit time constants T_i. In these experiments we used five unit DNNs; the total number of modifiable parameters was 51.

The optimization criterion was the average squared error between the desired settling time and the actual settling time (i.e., as observed in closed-loop simulation). Both quantities were scaled between 0 and 1 over a range of reasonable values. The average was computed over 200 closed-loop simulations with different randomly determined d_{ST} values, setpoint changes, controller initial conditions, and parameter estimation errors. For a more realistic PNC, the simulations would also cover a space of process model parameters. With a linear first-order process however, generality in process model space can be more simply achieved by appropriately scaling the dynamics and the output of a controller that is designed assuming a single process model.

To calculate an accurate settling time, the simulated closed-loop has to be in steady-state when the setpoint change is made. With the nonlinear controller in the loop, steady-state can only be ensured by running the simulation. The random initial conditions constitute a disturbance to the closed-loop. We require the closed-loop to settle to the original setpoint within a certain duration (1000 time steps in the experiments reported here), at which time the setpoint is changed and the settling time can be computed. The design procedure thus imposes a constraint on disturbance rejection while regulating the settling time. A prohibitively high cost function value is returned if the disturbance is not rejected.

We designed PNCs under two conditions: a nominal design in which the PNC had perfect parameter estimates available, and a robust design for which parameter estimation errors of up to 10 percent were injected. The performance of the optimized PNCs was then evaluated over a range of estimation errors. As shown in Fig. 3, the nominal design is superior for low estimation errors but degrades less gracefully. The robustness is manifested in higher values of estimation error, not in the design range—in fact, the nominal design performs better until around 15%. Figure 4 shows sample time responses for the robust PNC for low, intermediate, and high settings of d_{ST} (with perfect parameter estimates). Both disturbance rejection and setpoint tracking responses are shown.

As is apparent from the figure, effective control of the settling time is achieved with the one tuning knob. However, the responses shown are unsatisfactory in one important respect. In general, settling time and response overshoot are complementary features. Overshoot is the cost typically paid for fast settling, and PID controllers allow—indirectly—for reducing the overshoot by increasing the settling time. The PNC shows the opposite correlation: the overshoot increases with increased settling time.

This observation highlights one aspect of our approach. The PNC concept permits a flexibility in control design that has not hitherto been attempted to our knowledge. This flexibility has some adverse implications. The design procedure, coupled with the near-universal nonlinear dynamical system modeling capabilities of neural networks, can lead to controllers that satisfy all explicitly specified requirements but in unexpected and non-intuitive ways. PNC design imposes more of a burden on appropriate problem specification than conventional control design. In the example above, the cost function should incorporate a weighted overshoot penalty. When this is done, the desired inverse relation between settling time and overshoot is obtained.

References

[1] Barto, A.G., Sutton, R.S., and C. Anderson (1983). Neuronlike elements that can solve difficult learning control problems. *IEEE Trans. on Systems, Man, and Cybernetics, 13.*

[2] Bhat, N. and T.J. McAvoy (1989). Use of neural nets for dynamic modeling and control of chemical process systems. *Proc. American Control Conf.*

[3] Khargonekar, P., T. Georgiou, and A. Pascoal (1987). On the robust stabilizability of linear time invariant plants with unstructured uncertainty. *IEEE Trans. on Automatic Control. AC-32.*

[4] Konar, A.F. and T. Samad (1992). *Dynamic Neural Networks.* Technical Report SSDC-92-I4152-2, Honeywell Technology Center, 3660 Technology Drive, Minneapolis, MN 55418.

[5] Nguyen, D. and B. Widrow (1990). The truck backer-upper: an example of self-learning in neural networks. In *Neural Networks for Control*, W.T. Miller et al. (eds.), MIT Press.

[6] Pomerleau, D.A. (1991). Neural network-based vision processing for autonomous robot guidance. *Appl. of Artificial Neural Networks II*, S.K. Rogers (Ed.), Proc. SPIE 1469, pp. 121-128.

[7] Poolla, K. and T. Ting (1987). Nonlinear time-varying controllers for robust stabilization. *IEEE Trans. on Automatic Control, AC-32.*

[8] Samad, T. and W. Foslien (1993). Parametrized neurocontrollers. *Proc. of the Eighth IEEE Int. Symp. on Intelligent Control.*

[9]. Samad, T. and T. Su (1994). Neural networks as process controllers—optimization aspects. *Proc. American Control Conference.*

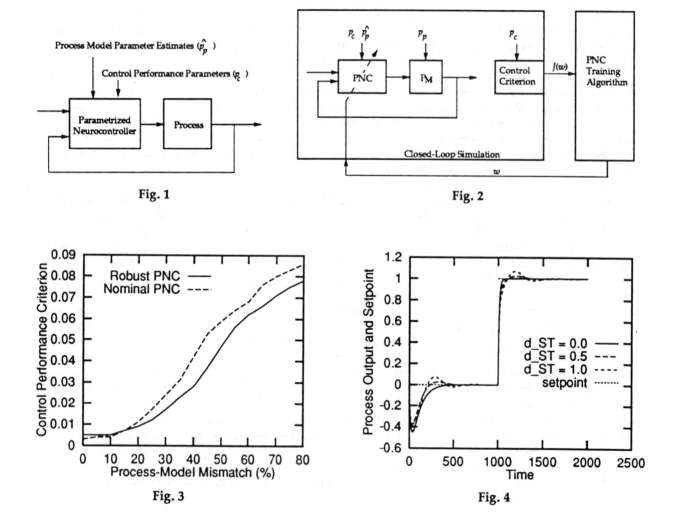

Fig. 1   Fig. 2

Fig. 3   Fig. 4

A Neural Network Based Prediction Scheme
For An Industrial Propathene Reactor

O. Agamennoni, C. Chessari, J.A. Romagnoli, G.W. Barton and K. Bourke[1]

Chemical Engineering Department
The University of Sydney, NSW 2006, Australia

(1) ICI Australia Operations
16-20 Beauchamp Rd
Matraville, NSW 2036, Australia

Key words: Neural network, application, prediction.

ABSTRACT

In this paper, we present the development of a neural network (NN) based model to predict the Melt Flow Index (MFI) on a propathene reactor, from other available measurements. The MFI is a measure of the average molecular weight of a polymer and represents an important product quality specification.

1. INTRODUCTION

The work reported in this paper is one of the projects being undertaken as part of a collaboration between ICI (Australia and the UK), and the Universities of Sydney (Australia) and Newcastle (UK) into the potential for applying neural network technology within ICI worldwide. The eventual aim of this work is to provide a prediction of the MFI that is robust enough to be used as part of a closed-loop control scheme. Attempts by previous workers to produce a mechanistic model of this reactor have been singularly unsuccessful.

There are two main potential advantages to the use of neural networks for such model development. Firstly, they can provide an accurate approximation to most dynamic systems (Narendra and Parthasarathy, 1991). In addition, the available computer hardware and network training algorithms are now such that a fit to the available training data can be achieved in a reasonable time (Hush and Horne, 1993).

Data preprocessing and NN structural analysis pertinent to this plant have been presented in previous papers (Agamennoni et al., 1993 and 1994). The NN prediction scheme was developed to predict the MFI variation one hour into the future. Two different schemes were studied for this purpose. The difference between the two schemes is in the number of input variables considered. In the first scheme, four input variables together with an averaged present value of the MFI form the input set. In the second scheme, six inputs are used, with a special data compressor being employed for four of the inputs in order to reduce the number of tapped delay inputs.

2. PREDICTION SCHEME

The NN based prediction scheme was developed to predict an averaged MFI variation, which may be mathematically expressed as follows,

$$\Delta \text{MFI}(t) = \sum_{k=-1}^{1} \text{MFI}(t+60+10*k) - \sum_{k=0}^{2} \text{MFI}(t-10*k) \qquad (1)$$

where t is time in minutes and ∆MFI is an incremental change between the actual MFI and the MFI one hour ahead. The sampling time used was 10 minutes and averages of three samples were used to reduce the effects of measurement noise.

A prediction error E(t) may be defined as the difference between the ∆MFI value and the NN output:

$$E(t) = \Delta MFI(t) - NN(t) \qquad (2)$$

2.1 Prediction Scheme 1

Figure 1 shows the architecture of the first prediction scheme. The average of the last three MFI measurements, as well as the feed flowrate to the reactor, the average temperature (ie the average of all available temperature measurements in the reactor), the reactor hydrogen concentration and the central probe temperature (ie the single most representative available temperature) are used to predict the average of three MFI values one hour into the future.

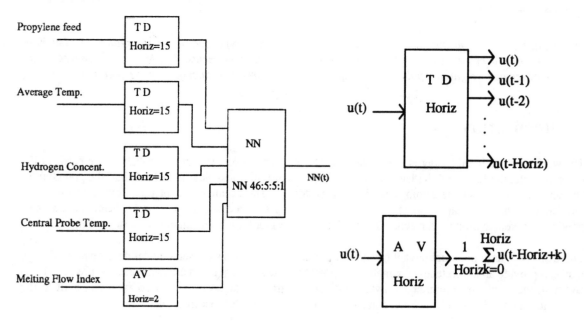

TD is a tapped delay unit and **Horiz** the number of samples backward, while **AV** is an averaging unit.
NN 46:5:5:1 is a feedforward network with 62 inputs (4*15+2), 5 neurons in the input layer, 5 neurons in the hidden layer and 1 output.

Figure 1: Prediction Scheme 1.

The data set available had 1170 sample points. The first 870 sample points were used for training and the remainder for testing. The network was trained using a backpropagation based algorithm with the following features:

(a)   Random selection of a subset of the training patterns. A new training set of 400 sample points was randomly selected from the first 870 available samples every 30th epoch.

(b)   Individually adapted learning rates (Jacobs, 1988). Each parameter ω_i (ie both weights and biases) has its own adaptive learning rate, lr_i and in each epoch k is adjusted as follows,

$$lr_i(k+1) = \begin{cases} lr_i(k)*lr_{inc} & \text{if } \dfrac{\partial e}{\partial \omega_i} \text{ doesn't change sign.} \\[2ex] lr_i(k)*lr_{dec} & \text{if } \dfrac{\partial e}{\partial \omega_i} \text{ changes sign.} \end{cases}$$

where e is the sum of squares error E(t) defined in eqn. (2). The learning factor was automatically adjusted between 0 and 1 with lr_{inc} = 1.05 and lr_{dec} = 0.75, while the momentum factor was fixed at 0.95. Different size neural networks were tried, with that shown in Figure 1 being the smallest that allowed us to achieve an acceptably accurate approximation.

Figure 2 shows the measured MFI and the output from the NN. It is important to note that the NN output is very close to the measured value for the first 130 testing samples, that is up to a sample number of 1000. Beyond this point, it should be realised that the prediction scheme is being asked to predict MFI values in a range considerably above the levels seen by the network during training.

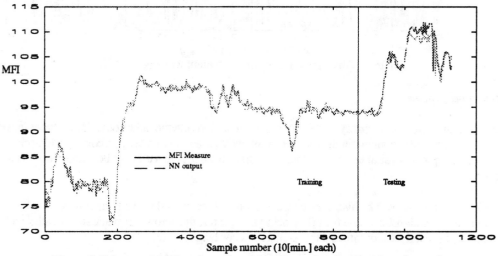

Figure 2: Measured MFI and predicted (one hour ahead) value for scheme 1.

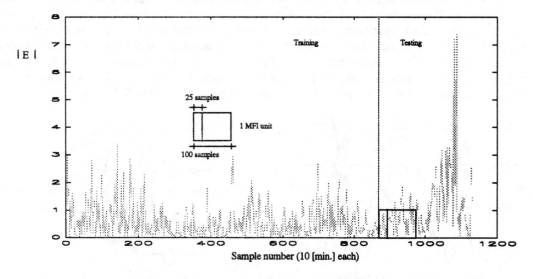

Figure 3: Absolute error (|E|) between the measured and (one hour ahead) predicted MFI values.

Figure 3 shows the absolute value of the prediction error, as defined in Equation 2. During the first 150 test samples (ie 25 hours of operation]), the error in the prediction is always below 2 MFI units, while the absolute value of ΔMFI, as defined in Equation 1, reachs values close to 4 MFI units in the first half of test samples and 8 MFI units in the second half of test samples (see Figure 4).

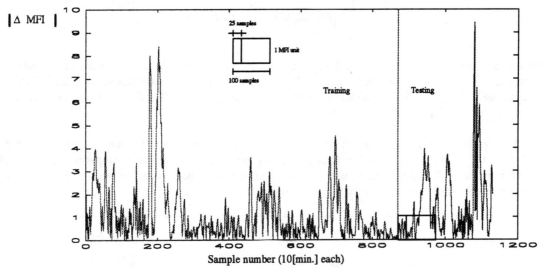

Figure 4: Absolute value of the incremental change ΔMFI.

2.2 Prediction Scheme 2

In an attempt to improve the accuracy of the NN based prediction scheme, additional inputs were introduced into the model. However, to maintain the number of inputs at an acceptable level, a compression scheme was implemented. The process variables that are known to directly affect the MFI may be classified into two groups:

(a) High level relationships: The hydrogen concentration and the central probe temperature.
(b) Medium level relationships: The feed flowrate to the reactor, the amount of reaction activator added to the reactor, the catalyst shot rate and the average reactor temperature.

Inputs belonging to the first group (along with the average of the last three MFI measurements) were fed directly to the NN as before, while inputs in the second group were 'compressed' using an auto-associative network (see Figure 5) before being fed to the predictive NN (see Figure 6). Auto-associative networks use an architecture composed of an input layer, a number of hidden layers and an output layer in the manner of a typical feedforward network. The hidden layer in the middle is called the *bottleneck layer*. The network is trained to produce the identity matrix, that is, to produce identical input and output patterns. In this way, a compression of the information is produced in the bottleneck layer. The size of the bottleneck layer may be considered as the number of nonlinear principal components required to describe the system.

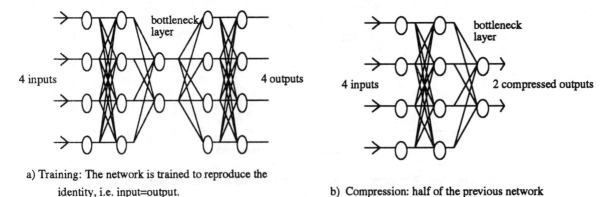

a) Training: The network is trained to reproduce the identity, i.e. input=output.

b) Compression: half of the previous network

Figure 5: Auto-associative networks for (a) training, and (b) data compression.

I-198

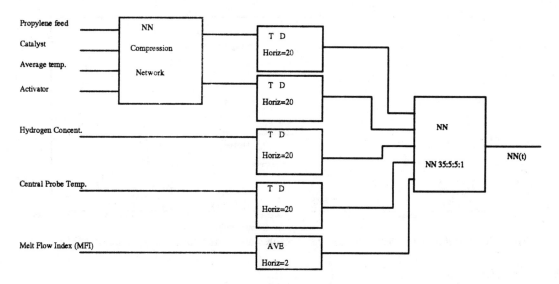

Figure 6: Prediction scheme 2.

Use of the second scheme allowed us to improve the approximation of the MFI dynamics during the training phase (see Figures 7 and 8 for sample points up to 870, and compare with Figures 2 and 3). For the first 25 test samples (about 4 hours of operation), the second scheme also shows better performance than the first scheme. However, the test results beyond this point are not as good as those obtained with the previous scheme. Overfitting of the training data appears to be degrading the behavior of the network with respect to long-term prediction. As with the first scheme, the second approach fails to predict the largest changes during the test phase where the network is being exposed to MFI values beyond those seen during training.

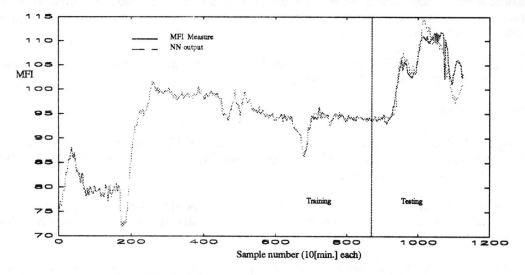

Figure 7: Measured MFI and predicted (one hour ahead) value for scheme 2.

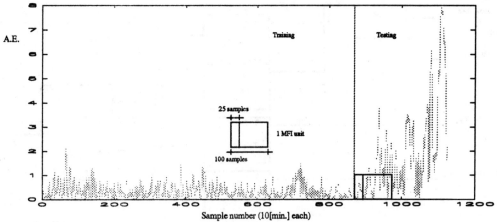

Figure 8: Absolute error ($|E|$) between the measured and (one hour ahead) predicted MFI values.

3. CONCLUSIONS

The results of a study regarding the possible development of a neural network based model to predict the MFI of the product from a propathene reactor one hour into the future, from measured operating variables, have been presented.

Two schemes were used to provide a prediction of the MFI into the near future. Both schemes showed that it is possible to produce a good prediction of the MFI behaviour one hour ahead. With the first scheme, it was possible to predict the variation of the averaged MFI, within an acceptable error, during a one day test period without having to retrain the network. It should be noted that during this day's prediction, the MFI gradually increased to values considerably above those seen during the training period. However, to maintain prediction accuracy over longer periods of time, it is felt that an adaptive scheme (rather than periodic retraining) would be a more practical option.

ICI Australia operations personnel are currently considering the practicalities of employing such an estimator for the MFI in both open and closed-loop modes.

4. REFERENCES

Agamennoni O., Romagnoli J., Barton G. and Bourke K., "Inferential Measurement Through a Neural Network Model. Application to an Industrial Unit", 21th Australasian Chemical Engineering Conference, CHEMECA '93, Sept. 1993, Melbourne, Australia.

Agamennoni O., Romagnoli J., Barton G. and Bourke K., "Neural Network Based Inferential Measurement On An Industrial Propathene Reactor", To be presented at the Fifth International Symposium on Process System Engineering, PSE' 94, Seoul, South Korea.

Hush D.R. and Horne B.G., "Progress in Supervized Neural Networks", IEEE Signal Processing Magazine, January 1993.

Jacobs R.A., "Increased Rates of Convergence Through Learning Rate Adaptation", Neural Networks, 1, 295-307, 1988.

Narendra K. and Parthasarathy K., "Gradient Methods for the Optimization of Dynamical Systems Containing Neural Networks", IEEE Transactions on Neural Networks, Vol. 2, No. 2, March 1991.

5. ACKNOWLEDGMENTS

The authors wish to thank ICI Australia Operations for their technical assistance during this project and for permission to publish these results.

An Inferential Approach Using Neural Network Models for Controlling Chemical Processes

Nan Ye and Thomas J. McAvoy,* Dept. of Chemical Engineering, University of Maryland, College Park, MD 20742

Karlene A. Kosanovich and Michael J. Piovoso, E.I. Du Pont & Company, Wilmington, Delaware 19880

Abstract In this paper an earlier inferential approach is extended to nonlinear systems. A statistically based neural network modeling approach, NNPLS (neural network partial least squares), is used to develop the inferential models. Application of the inferential approach to the Tennessee Eastman industrial test process is investigated. Control of both the product flow and compositions is improved with the inferential control.

1 Introduction

The Tennessee Eastman Control Problem is a realistic and complicated plant-wide process control test problem (Downs & Vogel, 1993). With 41 measurements, 12 manipulated variables and a large range of operation, the Tennessee Eastman process can be used to study many topics in basic and advanced control. A number of studies have be carried out on the Tennessee Eastman process (Ricker, 1993a; Ricker, 1993b; Lyman & Georgakis, 1993; Banerjee & Arkun, 1993; McAvoy & Ye, 1993; Ye et al., 1993b; Ye et al., 1993a). A base decentralized PID control system has been designed for the process which can stablize the system, reject all disturbances, follow all setpoint changes, and which also can move the process to different operation regimes (McAvoy & Ye, 1993). Control for the process can be improved by adding advanced control on top of the base control system. One problem for the process is that due to some unmeasurable disturbances the product flow rate and compositions have large variations under the base control. How to improve the control of nonlinear systems for unmeasurable disturbances is a general problem in chemical plants.

This work will provide a method for reducing the variation of the product properties, or the key controlled variables, for nonlinear systems with unmeasurable disturbances and apply the proposed control approach to the Tennessee Eastman test plant. An inferential control structure was proposed by Ye et al (1993b) which used PLS (Partial Least Squares) models and applied them to the Tennessee Eastman process at one operation point. With the inferential control approach the variations of the product flow rate and compositions were decreased for some unmeasurable disturbances. In that work linear models were used for the single operation point. This work is an extension of the above work to nonlinear systems in which multiple operation points are considered and nonlinear neural network modeling techniques are applied. In another project, Ye el al. (1993a) applied an optimal averaging level control approach to the Tennessee Eastman process. The optimal averaging level control made significant reduction in the variation of the product flow.

Recent research has shown the powerful function of neural networks in nonlinear systems modeling (Bhat et al., 1990; Piovoso & Owens, 1991; Billings et al., 1992; Qin & McAvoy, 1992). Qin and McAvoy (1992) proposed a method combining neural networks with PLS named NNPLS (Neural Network Partial Least Squares). In neural network modeling the preselected input and output variables are often correlated. By integrating statistical analysis methods and neural neural networks as is done in NNPLS, input and output data are analyzed before the data are used to train neural networks. In this way, the training time is reduced and model accuracy is improved. NNPLS will be used for modeling in this work.

In the next section, the Tennessee Eastman process and the base control system will be introduced first, and then the optimal operation points for different product ratios and optimal averaging level control will be discussed. After that, the inferential feedforward/feedback control with the NNPLS models is presented. The results of the inferential control for the Tennessee Eastman process at the different optimal operation points are given and compared with the results of the base control and the optimal averaging level control.

---

*To whom all correspondence should be addressed.

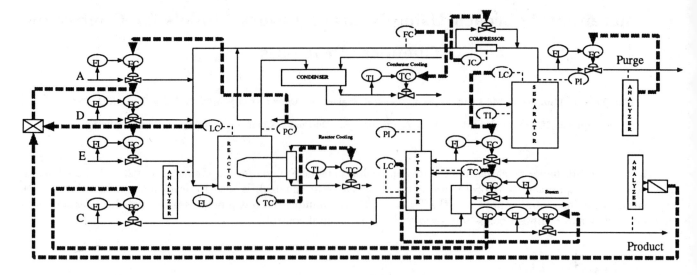

Figure 1: *The Tennessee Eastman process and the base control system*

2   Overview of the Tennessee Eastman Problem

2.1   Tennessee Eastman process and base control system

Fig. 1 is a schematic of the Tennessee Eastman process with the designed base control system. The are five unit operations involved in the process, the reactor, separator, stripper, condenser and compressor. Two main reactions take place in the process to produce liquid products H and G from gaseous reactants A, C, D and E. There are three operating modes for G/H ratios at 50/50, 90/10 and 10/90.

A systematic approach was used to design the base control system (McAvoy & Ye, 1993). The base control system has 1 single loop, 9 cascade loops and 1 cascade ratio loop. A selector control system, which is not shown in Fig. 1, is also designed for rejecting a disturbance which shuts down one of the key manipulated variables, the A feed stream.

2.2   Optimal operation points

In the Tennessee Eastman test problem (Downs & Vogel, 1993) only one base operation is given for G/H ratio at 50/50. Ricker (1993b) calculated the optimal steady state operation minimizing the total cost of the plant for different product ratios with G/H at 90/10, 50/50 and 10/90. However one problem with his results is that some valves are at there low or high limits, which decreases the degrees of freedom of the system. Another problem is that at the optimal operation points, the purge stream is too small for the process to meet the material balance at steady state for some disturbances.

In order to get optimal operation points at which the base control system still can reject all the disturbances, the optimization was done differently with some constraints employed. It was found that the stripper steam cost in the test problem is almost three times higher than a reasonable steam cost, which results in the steam valve always being at its low limit at optimal points. Because the steam flow with a reasonable cost has a small effect on the total cost of the process , the steam valve is fixed at 50% open. Another constraint is that the recycle valve is fixed at 20% open. In this way at the optimal points the loop pairings of the base control system are still appropriate according to relative gain analysis (McAvoy, 1983). The last constraint for the optimization is that the steady state value of the B composition in the purge is small enough for the process to satisfy a material balance when it undergoes a step reduction in the B composition in the C feed from 0.005% to 0.002%. The number 0.002% is determined based on the disturbance size given in the test problem. With all the constraints, the optimal operation points for G/H at 90/10, 50/50 and 10/90 are calculated. [1]

---

[1]The optimal operation points (steady state values and valve positions) are available in electronic form. Contact by E-mail: nyycl@eng.umd.edu.

2.3 Optimal averaging level control

An optimal averaging level control approach was applied to the Tennessee Eastman process and control of the product flow rate was improved significantly (Ye et al., 1993a). Similar results are obtained when the optimal averaging level control is applied at the optimal operation points. The variation of product flow rate is greatly reduced. However it is found that the variation of the product compositions is increased when the optimal averaging level control is added to the process. In other words, the improvement for the product flow rate is achieved at the expense of the product compositions. The inferential control presented in this paper will improve the control for both the product flow rate and product compositions.

3 Inferential Model Development

The random disturbances of the compositions in the C feed flow cannot be measured and they have large effect on the product properties. Unmeasurable disturbances causing large changes in product properties is a very common problem in chemical processes.

Often these unmeasurable disturbances affect some other variables, such as pressures, temperatures and valve positions in a plant faster than they affect the products, which are the variables one really wants to control. If one can build a steady state model to predict the unmeasurable disturbances from the pressures and temperature etc. and another steady state model to predict product properties, the controller moves for the product properties can be calculated based on the two models by compensating for the disturbances while keeping the product properties constant. The model for predicting the disturbances can be written as

$$\hat{d} = F_1(y_m, u_1) \tag{1}$$

where $\hat{d}$ is the predicted disturbance vector, y_m represents the measurement vector which involves temperatures and pressures and u_1 consists of the controller moves which include valve positions and the setpoints of the cascade inner loops except the controllers for the product properties. The model for predicting the product properties is

$$\hat{y} = F_2(u_2, \hat{d}) \tag{2}$$

where $\hat{y}$ are the predicted product properties, u_2 are the manipulated variables of the product properties. From Eq. (1) and Eq. (2), one can calculate values of u_2 to keep $\hat{y}$ constant for the predicted disturbances $\hat{d}$.

In earlier work (Ye et al., 1993b), an approach is proposed to use one model to directly predict the controller moves, u_2, for eliminating the disturbances and keeping the product properties at their setpoints. The model is

$$u_2 = G(y_m, u_1) \tag{3}$$

The output of Eq. (3) is equivalent to the results calculated from Eq. (1) and Eq. (2). However it is much simpler to just build one model and use one model to directly calculate u_2.

For a linear system, Eq. (3) can be a linear model. For nonlinear systems, nonlinear modeling techniques should be used. Another aspect which has to be considered during modeling is the correlation among the input variables in Eq. (3). The dimension of y_m and u_1 is usually very large and the variables in y_m and u_1 are highly correlated. The NNPLS modeling approach (Qin & McAvoy, 1992) combines neural networks with partial least squares. It is a nonlinear modeling approach and at the same time deals with the correlation problem in the input and output variables. For the Tennessee Eastman process with G/H at 50/50, 10/90 and 90/10, a nonlinear model is needed for predicting the controller moves. The NNPLS models are used in this work instead of the linear PLS models used in (Ye et al., 1993b).

3.1 Input and output variables

For the Tennessee Eastman process with the base control system, the model outputs u_2 are the D and C feed setpoints which are manipulated variables for the product flow and product composition ratio. y_m involves the total feed to the reactor, separator temperature, separator pressure and stripper pressure, which are the measurements not being used by the base control system. u_1 consists of the A feed flow setpoint, E feed flow setpoint, purge rate setpoint, separator underflow setpoint, stripper steam flow setpoint, reactor cooling temperature setpoint, separator cooling temperature setpoint and compressor recycle valve. The setpoint of the G/H ratio is added as another input variable representing different operating conditions.

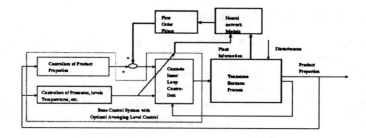

Figure 2: *The inferential feedforward/feedback control with neural network models*

	G/H = Flow	90/10 G	G/H = Flow	50/50 G	G/H = Flow	10/90 G
Base control	0.393	0.0676	0.537	0.113	0.522	0.0336
Base + Averaging level control	0.184	0.131	0.205	0.227	0.214	0.0887
Base + Averaging Level + Inferential control	0.0660	0.0470	0.118	0.129	0.126	0.0363

Table I: *Standard deviation of product properties with different control schemes*

3.2   Data for modeling

Input and output data are collected for training and testing the NNPLS models. Disturbances with different sizes are added to the process when all the loops in the base control system are closed. For each disturbance, the process converges to a steady state and the input and output variables of the model are recorded. Data are generated at the three optimal operation points with different G/H ratios. A total of 720 data points are calculated.

3.3   Model training and testing

Two separate models are used for predicting the D feed and C feed setpoints. For the D feed setpoint, all 13 input variables are used. For the C feed setpoint, the inputs are the A feed setpoint and G/H ratio setpoint only. Analysis was carried out for selecting the input variables for the C feed (Ye et al., 1993b). It is still true for the NNPLS models that the A feed setpoint is the dominant variable affecting the C feed. The G/H ratio, which is retained as a input for the C feed, reflects the different operating modes.

One third of the data are used for training and the rest for testing. Both the models have three factors. Adding more factors does not have much effect on model accuracy. The model for the D feed has 8 hidden nodes and for the C feed 3 hidden nodes. Both models can capture more than 80% of the total variance in the training and testing data.

4   Inferential Feedforward/Feedback Control

The developed inferential models are added to the base control system. This forms an inferential steady state feedforward control system. A diagram of the feedforward/feedback control for the Tennessee Eastman process is given in Fig. 2. Since the D and C feed setpoints calculated by the steady state models could have relatively fast changes, first order filters are used to slow down the changes. In the statement of the Tennessee Eastman problem, constraints on the rate of change for both the C feed and D feed were given. The C feed could not have significant frequency content in the range 12 to 80 hr^{-1} while the D feed could not have significant frequency content in the range 8 to 16 hr^{-1}. The first order filters are designed according to their constraints. The transfer function of the first order filter for the D feed is $1/(0.56(hr)s+1)$ and for the C feed is $1/(0.36(hr)s+1)$.

5   Results

The inferential feedforward/feedback control is implemented on the Tennessee Eastman process together with the optimal averaging level control (Ye et al., 1993a). The process is operated at the three optimal operation points. The disturbances considered during modeling are the random fluctuations of compositions in the C feed flow. Control results for the product flow rate and product compositions G are shown in Fig. 3 and Fig. 4, in which the results of the inferential control are contrasted with the results of the base control and optimal averaging level control. Comparison of the standard deviation of the product flow rate and product compositon G among different control schemes is given in Table I.   For product flow rate the standard deviation is reduced 78% from the base control to the inferential control, and 42 % from the optimal averaging level to the inferential control at 50/50 G/H. The corresponding results are

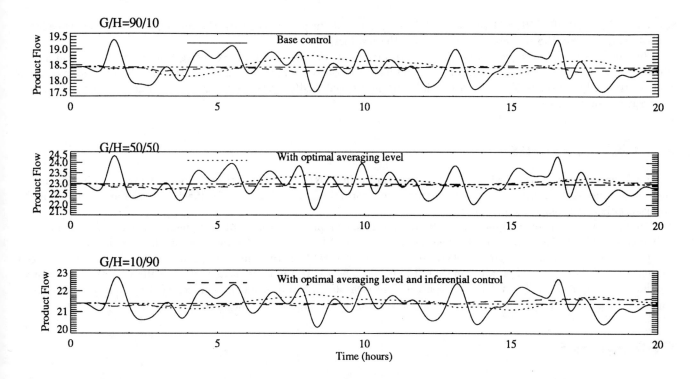

Figure 3: *Product flow with inferential feedforward/feedback control for random composition disturbances in C feed flow*

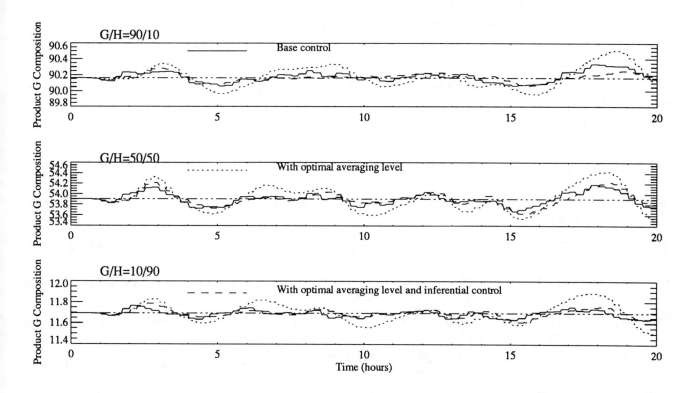

Figure 4: *Product G composition with inferential feedforward/feedback control for random composition disturbances in C feed flow*

83% and 64% at 90/10 G/H, and 74% and 41% at 10/90 G/H. Improvement with the inferential feedforward/feedback control using the NNPLS models is significant for the product flow.

Fluctuations in the product composition G are increased with the optimal averaging level control. By adding the inferential feedforward loop, variation in the product composition is reduced. This is because the optimal averaging level control only considers the flow rate, while the inferential feedforward/feedback control takes both the flow and compositions into account.

6 Conclusions

An inferential feedforward/feedback control structure using NNPLS neural network models is proposed in this paper. These neural network models can capture disturbance information faster than the feedback loop can and control for the unmeasurable disturbances is improved.

The inferential control is applied to the Tennessee Eastman process at the optimal operation points for the product G/H ratios at 90/10, 50/50 and 10/90. The inferential control has reduced the variation in the product flow rate over that produced by optimal averaging level control. The unmeasurable disturbances, the random fluctuation in the C feed compositions, only cause very small changes in the product flow with the inferential control, while with the base control the change is significant. The inferential control approach also has improved the control of the product compositons which was degraded when the optimal averaging level control was applied to the process.

References

Banerjee, A. & Arkun, Y. (1993). "Control configuration design applied to the tennessee eastman plant-wide control." In *AIChE Annual Meeting*, St. Louis, Missouri.

Bhat, N. V., Minderman, P. A. J., McAvoy, T. J., & Wang, N. S. (1990). "Modeling chemical process systems via neural computation." *IEEE Control System Magazine*, 24.

Billings, S. A., Jamaluddin, H. B., & Chen, S. (1992). "Properties of neural networks with applications to modeling non-linear dynamical systems." *International Journal of Control*, 55:(1), 193.

Downs, J. J. & Vogel, E. F. (1993). "A plant-wide industrial process control problem." *Computers Chem. Engng.*, 17:(3).

Lyman, P. R. & Georgakis, C. (1993). "Plant-wide control of the tennessee eastman problem." Submit to Computers and Chemical Engineering.

McAvoy, T. J. (1983). *Interaction analysis: principles and applications*. Monograph Series. Instrument Society of America.

McAvoy, T. J. & Ye, N. (1993). "Base control for the tennessee eastman problem." To be appear in Computers and Chemical Engineering.

Piovoso, M. J. & Owens, A. J. (1991). "Sensor data analysis using artificial neural networks." In *Proc. of Int. Conf. Chem. Process Control*, Texas.

Qin, S. J. & McAvoy, T. (1992). "Nonlinear PLS modeling using neural networks." *Computers Chem. Engng.*, 16:(4), 379.

Ricker, N. L. (1993a). "Model-predictive control of a continuous, nonlinear, two-phase reactor." Submit to Journal of Process Control.

Ricker, N. L. (1993b). "Optimal steady-state operation of the tennessee eastman challenge process." Submit to Computers and Chemical Engineering.

Ye, N., McAvoy, T. J., Kosanovich, K. A., & Piovoso, M. J. (1993a). "Plant-wide control using an inferential approcah." In *Proc. of 1993 ACC*, 1900, San Francisco, CA.

Ye, N., McAvoy, T. J., Piovoso, M. J., & Kosanovich, K. A. (1993b). "Optimal averaging level control for the tennessee eastman problem." In *Presented at the 1993 Annual AIChE Meeting*, St. Louis, Missouri, USA.

Mind, Brain, and Consciousness

Session Chair: John G. Taylor

Computer Simulation of Conscious Sensory Experiences

F. N. Alavi & J. G. Taylor

February 1994

Centre for Neural Networks
King's College London
The Strand
London WC2R 2LS

We consider a simplified (one–dimensional) version of the coupled Thalamus–Nucleus Reticularis Thalamus–Cortex system. We simulate on computer the injection of current into selected columnar portions of this system. We propose a model for the control of conscious sensory awareness, and show that the results of our simulations are consistent with the experimental predictions of Libet (1982) on the study of neuronal functions for conscious sensory experiences.

1   Introduction

Recently, consciousness and the control of consciousness have become an important topic of study in the cognitive sciences. We find in the neurobiological literature, however, that these topics have been the subject of attention by neurophysiologists for some time now. Primarily, in this paper, we are interested in the important set of results obtained by Libet (1982).

It is known that much of the activities and responses of the waking human brain proceed without conscious effort on the part of the individual, and without subjective experiences being directly associated with them. To study conscious sensory experiences (and, generally, subjective experiences) with respect to neural actions that ultimately determine them therefore requires an ability on the part of the experimenter to be able to manipulate neuronal dynamic activity in a controlled manner. Libet (1982) stipulates that direct intracranial electrical simulation of neurons in a conscious human subject is one of the very few approaches available for such purposes. Even then, the risks inherent in such an approach, as well as the different responses that electrical stimuli can elicit, restrict the possible scope of such experiments. Furthermore, any direct electrical stimulation of neurons has to be acceptably brief, thereby further restricting the scope and effectiveness of the experiment to only those neuronal activities that were initiated within this brief duration of the stimulus.

One finds that electrical stimuli, in general, initiate (or alter) three distinct types of cortical cerebral functions:

- The "excitable" effect in the cortex, where some overt functional response is elicited. Examples include the electrically recordable primary evoked potential of the primary cortex, which is followed by slower event-related potentials over wider cortical regions, which are related to cognitive aspects of the sensory response.

- The "interference" effect observed in the excitable cortex, e.g. the masking of normal peripheral sensory inputs when electrical stimuli are applied to the primary sensory cortex. Typically, it is observed that interference requires a larger electrical stimulus than that needed to initiate a sensory experience (which has a definite threshold).

- The "modularity" effect, e.g. enhancement of somatic sensation or complex psychological changes occuring as a result of electrical stimulation.

In the next section, we describe the results obtained by Libet (1982) in the light of these identifiable cortical cerebral functions. We also give a mathematical analysis of his results and propose a model base on this and earlier work by us that justifies Libet's observations. In Section 3, we present results obtained by us by computer simulation that give credence to our model.

2   Relationship between injected current and sensory responses

It has been possible to study the responses identified in the previous section and identify some of the important parameters that elicit a conscious sensory experience following direct neuronal stimulation. Specifically, we are interested here in the temporal factors that govern the relationship between such sensory experiences and their underlying neural activity. The relevant parameters in this case turn out to be the peak current (the intensity I) and the train duration (τ_D) of a train of pulsed stimuli of some brief period ≤ 0.5 milliseconds. Libet's work involved the application of I at just the threshold level needed to produce conscious awareness (e.g. of skin being touched). When I is adjusted for each τ_D, it is found that there is a minimum intensity $I_{\min}$ below which no sensation is reported no matter how long τ_D is made. Conversely, $I_{\min}$ elicits no response at all unless it is repeatedly pulsed for at least an average of 0.5 seconds. This large value of τ_D was termed by Libet the "utilisation τ_D", and was observed to be independent of changes in the pulse frequency ν or other stimulation parameters. For τ_D smaller than the utilisation τ_D, the required $I_{\min}$ begins to grow rapidly (see Figure 1 in Libet (1982)).

Libet's empirical observations have been subjected to their first (as far as we know) mathematical analysis in Taylor (1993). Consider Figure 1, which shows the qualitative behaviour of the relationship between I and τ_D, as observed by Libet. We can identify two distinct regions in Figure 1, namely region A and region B.

In region A, we see that the minimum time for conscious awareness (τ_D) decreases as I increases. For fixed firing frequency ν, the quantitative results obtained by Libet show that

$$I^2 \tau_D = \text{constant}. \tag{1}$$

For varying ν, this is modified to

$$\nu I^2 \tau_D = \text{constant}, \tag{2}$$
$$\propto E,$$

where E is the total electrical energy being delivered.

In region B (for $\tau_D \geq 0.5$ seconds), we have

$$I \propto \nu^{-\frac{1}{2}}, \tag{3}$$

or, equivalently,

$$\nu I^2 = \text{constant}, \tag{4}$$
$$\propto P,$$

where P is the electrical power supplied.

We conclude, as in Taylor (1993), that consciousness requires a minimum *energy* to be switched on, but a minimum *power* for its continuation. The condition on E (consistent with the 'time on' proposition of Libet) to achieve consciousness is, simply,

$$E \geq \Theta, \tag{5}$$

where Θ is an appropriate threshold. This, together with earlier work on the global control and growth of activity on the cortex modulated by the underlying nucleus reticularis thalamus (NRT) acting as a Fourier filter (Taylor & Alavi 1993), enables us to present a model with the above property. Qualitatively, we propose that:

The uniqueness of consciousness arises from competition between areas of cortical activity controlled by a sheet of (inhibitory) NRT neurons.

We do not intend to repeat here the mathematical analysis of our model, details of which can be found in Taylor & Alavi (*op.cit.*), nor the anatomical or more general description of it, first presented in Taylor (1992).

3   Simulation Results

3.1   The Simulation Model

The simulation model we investigated is illustrated in Figure 2. It is essentially one–dimensional, which corresponds to *lines* of thalamic, NRT and cortical neurons. It is useful for simulation purposes to think of the boxed subsystem in Figure 2 as a single module that can be linearly replicated (with bidirectional lateral links among the NRT units). This allows the size of the simulation to be scaled to suit the available computing power.

Within each module, we have inter–unit signal flow as specified by the arrow–tipped curves. Every tip labelled with a '+' signifies an excitatory signal, while every '−' corresponds to an inhibitory signal. Within every module, the time evolution of each neural unit's voltage is determined by integrating the following set of equations (they were described in more detail in Taylor & Alavi (1993)) with the notation $\dot{u} = \partial u / \partial t$:

$$\dot{u}_C(\mathbf{r}) = -\frac{1}{\tau_C}u_C(\mathbf{r}) + \frac{1}{\tau_C}\sum_{\mathbf{r}'} W_{CT}^{EE}(\mathbf{r},\mathbf{r}')f_T(u_T(\mathbf{r}')) \tag{6a}$$

$$\dot{v}_N(\mathbf{r}) = -\frac{1}{\tau_N}v_N(\mathbf{r}) + \frac{1}{\tau_N}\sum_{\mathbf{r}'}\left[W_{NC}^{EI}(\mathbf{r},\mathbf{r}')f_C(u_C(\mathbf{r}')) + W_{NI}^{EI}(\mathbf{r},\mathbf{r}')f_T(u_T(\mathbf{r}')) \right.$$
$$\left. +W_{NN}^{II}(\mathbf{r},\mathbf{r}')g_N(v_N(\mathbf{r}')) \right] + \text{ dendro–dendritic terms} \tag{6b}$$

$$\dot{v}_T(\mathbf{r}) = -\frac{1}{\tau_T'}v_T(\mathbf{r}) + \frac{1}{\tau_T'}\sum_{\mathbf{r}'} W_{TN}^{II}(\mathbf{r},\mathbf{r}')g_N(v_N(\mathbf{r}')) + \frac{1}{\tau_T}W_{TO}I(\mathbf{r}) \tag{6c}$$

$$\dot{u}_T(\mathbf{r}) = -\frac{1}{\tau_T}u_T(\mathbf{r}) + \frac{1}{\tau_T}\sum_{\mathbf{r}'}\left[W_{TC}^{EE}(\mathbf{r},\mathbf{r}')f_C(u_C(\mathbf{r}')) + W_{TT}^{EI}(\mathbf{r},\mathbf{r}')g_T(v_T(\mathbf{r}')) \right] + \frac{1}{\tau_T}I(\mathbf{r}) \tag{6d}$$

Excitatory neurons are assumed to be at a coordinate position $\mathbf{r}$ (using the same coordinate frame for thalamus, NRT and cortex) on the thalamic and cortical sheets and to have membrane potentials labelled $u_T(\mathbf{r})$ and $u_C(\mathbf{r})$, and sigmoidal outputs $f_i(u_i)$, ($i = T$ and C, respectively), with threshold θ_i and temperature T_i. Inhibitory neurons in the thalamus and on the NRT (with the same coordinate positions) have membrane potentials denoted by $v_T(\mathbf{r})$, $v_N(\mathbf{r})$, with similar sigmoidal outputs g_T, g_N to the other neurons. Connection weights from the j'th excitatory (inhibitory) neuron at $\mathbf{r}'$ to the i'th excitatory (inhibitory) neuron at $\mathbf{r}$ are denoted by $W_{ij}^{EE}(\mathbf{r},\mathbf{r}')$, $W_{ij}^{EI}(\mathbf{r},\mathbf{r}')$, $W_{ij}^{IE}(\mathbf{r},\mathbf{r}')$, $W_{ij}^{II}(\mathbf{r},\mathbf{r}')$.

Within a computing context, of course, a discretised version of these equations has to be integrated over some suitable small time step (we used the Runge–Kutta fourth–order integration routine). Such a scheme entails in practice that we replace the hard–limiting non-linearity by a smooth analytical function. We adopted (in the actual simulation code) the following form, as used by La Berge *et al.*(1992):

$$f(x_A) = h_A Y(x_A - \theta_A)\left[1 - \exp\left\{-\beta_A(x_A - \theta_A)\right\}\right], \tag{7}$$

where h_A is a scaling parameter, $Y(\circ)$ is the step function, θ_A is the threshold for unit A and β_A is its inverse temperature.

3.2 Simulation Results

In Figure 3, we plot the results of one of our actual simulation runs. The x–axes of these plots represent the spatial positions of a line of 100 neurons. The y–axes represent $\mathrm{OUT}(u_T)$ and $\mathrm{OUT}(v_T)$ for the cases of the thalamic excitatory and inhibitory neurons respectively, and user–scaled[1] raw voltage output from the U_N and U_C excitatory neurons in the NRT and cortex respectively. Time delays for signal propagation between neurons were set to zero. The simulation was allowed to proceed as follows: a small input (of critical height[2] $h_c = 7.33$) is first allowed to propagate from the thalamus to the cortex from neuronal columns 60 to 90. The cortex is allowed to settle down into its stable state of activity (which represents a stable sensory experience). At this point (within t_0 steps of integration), a stronger input (of height $h_{\mathrm{in}} > 7.33$) is injected in the neuronal columns 20 to 50. This corresponds to an injected electrical stimulus. The stimulus was observed to destroy the established stable activity on the cortex and replace it with new activity representative of the new stimulus. The time taken to destroy the original activity completely, T, is recorded. Figure 4 shows this process diagramatically. In Figure 5, we plot the values of T obtained against h_{in}. The qualitative agreement with Libet's experimental observation (cf. Figure 1) is clear.

4   Conclusions

The thalamus–NRT–cortex comples model is in agreement with the results of Libet and his colleagues (1982) that conscious awareness, produced by application of electric current by direct cortical stimulation satisfies electrical energy (to turn on) and power laws (to stay on). We interpret such agreement as itself experimental support for the thalamus–NRT–cortex model of consciousness. This model is part of the 'relational mind' approach to consciousness of one of us (Taylor 1991, 1992), and needs to be augmented by activity in other areas, such as working memories, etc. However, the part of the model involved with the thalamus–NRT–cortex complex not only seems supported by what is the most relevant available quantitative data, but also can be extended to include further data on timing assessments associated with the phenomenon of 'bacward referral of time', also associated with Libet. Both the original data and the extension to temporal features lead to extensive predictions of further experimental features; these may be able to be tested in the near future (Villa 1993).

5   References

La Berge, D., Carter, E. and Brown, V. (1992), A Network Simulation of Thalamic Circuit Operations in Selective Attention, *Neural Computation*, **4**, 318–331.

Libet, B. (1982), Brain Stimulation in the Study of Neuronal Functions for Conscious Sensory Experiences, *Human Neurobiol.*, **1**, 235–242.

Taylor, J. G. (1991), Can Neural Networks ever be made to think?, *Neural Network World*, **1**, 4–12.

Taylor, J. G. (1992), Towards a Neural Network Model of the Mind, *Neural Network World*, **6**, 797–812.

Taylor, J. G. (1993), A Competition for Sensory Awareness, KCL preprint (submitted for publication).

Taylor, J. G. and Alavi, F. N. (1993). Mathematical Analysis of a Competitive Network for Attention, in *Mathematical Approaches to Neural Networks*, ed. J. G. Taylor, North–Holland, Amsterdam.

Villa, A. (1993), private communication.

---

[1] As a result, the vertical scales in any of the plots are not in proportion. This, however, is not a concern, since we are interested in the general behaviour of the system rather than particular values of output voltages.

[2] Note that the height of the input is proportional to the incoming current. The critical height is simply the smallest input that survives the journey to the cortex.

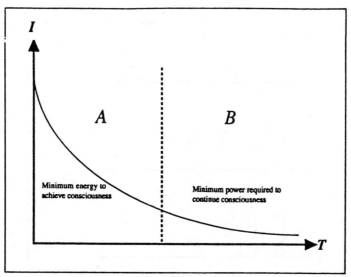

Figure 1. Libet's experimental results for the variation of injected current as a function of the conscious awareness time. The partitioning of the graph into regions A and B, which identifies the activation energy and continuation power for consciousness, is ours.

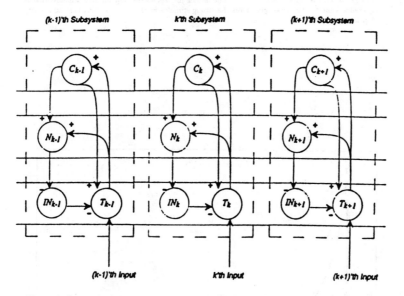

Figure 2. Schematic of the one–dimensional thalamus–NRT–cortex system used in our computer simulations.

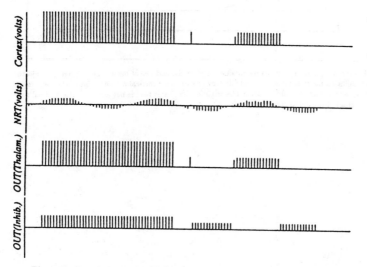

Figure 3. An actual output from our simulation. The x-axes here represent lines of 100 neurons. The plot was taken at an instance when a strong input h_{in} had been injected and allowed to propagate to the cortex. The weak activity on the cortex (towards the right) is already beginning to break down.

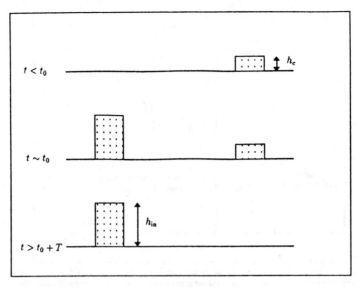

Figure 4. Diagrammatic explanation of the procedure we used to evaluate the time taken for the injected stimulus to destroy existing cortical activity. The upper line represents existing activity of height h_c on the cortex for time $< t_0$. The middle line shows the new injected stimulus that is injected at time t_0. The lower line shows the strong stimulus as the sole surviving cortical activity after a time $t_0 + T$.

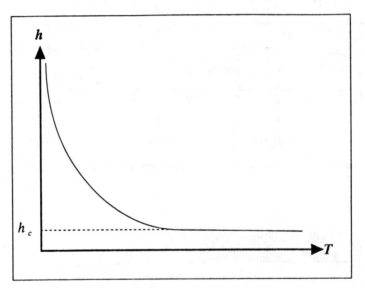

Figure 5. Qualitative results we obtained to show dependence of height (i.e. strength) of injected stimulus on the time taken to totally destroy any previous cortical activity. The qualitative resemblance to Figure 1 should be noted. The origin of the T axis here is not zero, but the minimal time for onset of the initial cortical activity.

Steps Toward a Neural Theory of Self-Actualization

Daniel S. Levine

Department of Mathematics, University of Texas at Arlington, Arlington, TX 76019-0408

Abstract

The qualitative psychological notion of self-actualization, due to Maslow, is understood mechanistically as an optimal state that is available to, but not always reached by, a neural network. This is described in terms of a Lyapunov (energy) function for a submodule of the network, combined with a supervising node that sends a signal if the energy function for the submodule's current state is higher than the energy function for other imagined states. Suggestions are made for parametric variations that determine to what extent the network will change its state if the current state is found not to be globally optimal, even if it is optimal for a smaller subnetwork. Speculative analogies are drawn between parts of the network and functions of the amygdala, prefrontal cortex, and midbrain noradrenergic system.

The Problem

As neural network models increase their power to explain human cognition, it is natural that neural network theory will incorporate some great insights of qualitative psychologists. Werbos [32], for example, traced the origin of the network notion of back propagating errors to insights of Sigmund Freud about cause and effect, and others have noted that Freud also anticipated Hebbian learning. Other researchers [14, 28] have developed schemes for sensory-motor coordination that incorporate Jean Piaget's notion of circular reaction. Along these lines, the purpose of this article is to suggest ways to understand in neural network contexts the idea of *self-actualization* due to Abraham Maslow (e.g., [25, 26]). This term was intended by Maslow to mean human functioning at the highest possible level. He devoted much detail to characteristics of self-actualizing people — and those of average people in temporary episodes of self-actualization known as *peak experiences* — and space does not permit a comprehensive list of these characteristics here. We will deal with one of the most important, namely, that such people tend to resolve ambiguities in a way that synthesizes conflicting interests within the mind rather than deciding between them; hence, typical dichotomies such as serious versus playful, masculine versus feminine, strong versus generous, rational versus emotional, are bridged by innovative solutions to problems.

Maslow is among those who believe that human behavior is not necessarily, or even much of the time, optimal. How much behavior is in fact optimal by some criterion is a source of lively debate in the social as well as biological sciences; for implications of that debate in neural network theory, see [19], Chapter 7, or the book in progress edited by Levine and Elsberry [20]. Yet even apart from that debate, a mechanistic *description* of what constitutes optimal behavior (in the broad sense, including concepts and beliefs) is becoming possible. The dynamical systems language of local and global energy minima, and perhaps some variant of simulated annealing, affords insight into the nature of optimality in the brain and mind. The heterogeneity of the database about self-actualization or its absence means that the discussion herein will largely be abstract. It will, however, make some very tentative suggestions about involvement of specific brain areas and transmitter systems in the processes discussed.

Global Versus Local and Part Versus Whole

Simulated annealing [13] is widely used to move a system out of a suboptimal local minimum of an energy function, and closer to an optimal global minimum. In Fig. 1, I propose an alternative to simulative annealing, one that seems related to human introspection. The basic needs of the organism are encoded by a competitive (on-center off-surround module) as in Cohen and Grossberg [3]. By the Cohen-Grossberg theorem, that network has a Lyapunov function V and always approaches a steady state that is at least a local minimum of that function. My proposal is to supervise this competitive module by a "world modeler" module, possibly analogous to part of the prefrontal cortex (cf. [12]). The world modeler makes "copies" of various possible states of the need subsystem and calculates the Lyapunov function for each. If V of the current state is larger than V of some other project state, this sends a signal to a "negative affect" module that in turn sends random noise back to the need subnetwork, that can move it out of an unsatisfying local minimum in much the same manner as in a Boltzmann machine.

The scheme of Fig. 1 is a first approximation, but must be expanded to include context-dependent biases among needs. Another of Maslow's ideas is the *hierarchy of needs*. Basic survival needs like safety or food tend to be satisfied first, then needs for love or belonging, and finally needs for development of full potential. A homeless person, for example, tends to be less bothered by a job that stifles his or her creative potential than is an affluent person. Hence, there must be a scheme whereby a few overwhelming needs suppress perception of mismatch from a global energy minimum in the state of other needs. Maslow [25, p. 26] says, and Hofstede [11] confirms, that this hierarchy is not a strict all-or-none progression. Some personalities and cultures can more easily than others accept dissatisfaction in a lower-level need in order to try to resolve the "whole picture." Leven [15] states there are three major styles of problem solvers: "Dantzig" or direct solvers who try simply to achieve an available solution; "Bayesian" solvers who play the percentages and try to maximize a measurable criterion, and "Godelians" who use both intuition and reason to arrive at innovative solutions. Hence, any neural model of self-actualization and the hierarchy of needs is subject to immense parametric variations representing personality differences. But an overall schema for selective attention to a subclass of needs — that is, limited capacity consciousness — is within our reach.

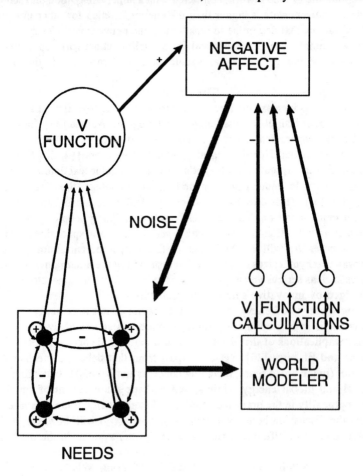

Fig. 1. Alternative scheme for simulated annealing. If the current state of the Cohen-Grossberg-based needs module has a larger energy function than some alternative state detected by the world model module, this generates an error signal at the negative affect module, which in turn sends noise to perturb the needs module.

Selective enhancement among drives is used in a network model [17, 21] for simulating mood changes in consumer preference. There are many possible neural network schemes for selective enhancement of nodes in a module via neuromodulation from a source outside the module. The idea of an unsatisfying *local minimum* may at times need to be reconfigured as a minimum for an energy function over part, but not all, of the needs module. If a subset B of the need set N suppresses the other needs excessively, the contribution of nodes in $N-B$ to the calculation of the energy function V is also weakened. This is because, in [3], V has the form

$$V(\vec{x}) = -\sum_{i=1}^{n} \int_{0}^{x_i} b_i(y) d_i'(y) dy + \frac{1}{2} \sum_{j,k=1}^{n} c_{jk} d_j(x_j) d_k(x_k),$$

where the c_{jk} are positive constants and the d_j are monotone nondecreasing differentiable functions. This equation shows that if the system is in a state the primarily differs from an optimal state in those node activity variables v_i for which $i \in N\text{-}B$, the affective error signal from this mismatch will be weakened.

The system of Fig. 1 is subject to regulation on many levels. The two main processes to be regulated are (1) the competitive needs module itself, in which tonic signals can move the module's behavior toward either "winner-take-all" or stable coexistence; (2) the gain from the negative affect error signal to the production of "simulated annealing" noise. Detailed neuroanatomical identification of the nodes and their various controllers and modulators is premature, but some provocative suggestions can be made. Either the needs module or the error signal may be identifiable with a part of the amygdala, an area of the limbic system that has been implicated in calculations of emotional valuation [6, 29]. The prefrontal cortex has extensive feedback connections with the amygdala. The effects of fronto-amygdalar connections, in addition to those arising from the "world modeler" module of Fig. 1, could include control of the gain of the "noise" signal from the "negative affect" module. This suggestion comes from the clinical suggestion (e.g., [27]) that frontally damaged individuals can express frustration when their actions are ineffective, but this frustration does not lead them to change their actions.

The amygdala (particularly its central and basolateral portions) is also heavily innervated by noradrenergic (NA) projections from the locus ceruleus [7]. In addition to enhancing novel or significant or significant inputs [10], NA plays a role in generating cognitive attributions and beliefs. Individuals that are generally deficient in this transmitter tend toward learned helplessness and lowered confidence in their ability to affect events [16, 30]. A milder form of learned helplessness, with an intermediate NA level, could generate a passivity about satisfying the needs in the set $N\text{-}B$ (see above) if those in B are already met. In other words, the person may feel *confident* only about satisfying a limited set of needs. In the network of Fig. 1, NA signals could directly affect the competitive needs module, making its dynamics more winner-take-all with a low NA level, more coexistent with a high NA level. Grossberg [9] showed that tonic excitatory signals can have a uniformizing effect on activities in a competitive on-center off-surround network. The NA signal could similarly tonically arouse the needs module, as shown in Fig. 2. Larger NA moves this module toward equilibria that satisfy a greater number of needs.

Self-actualization and Information Processing

Now that a tentative theory of interactions and choices between drives (Maslow's "hierarchy of needs") has been outlined, let us look further at what constitutes satisfaction of a "self-actualization drive." The discussion in this part continues and extends that in Levine, Leven, & Prueitt [23]. We return to the point of Maslow [25, 26] that self-actualization[1] involves creative synthesis of previously conflicting concepts or beliefs. Fig. 3 depicts a continuum of human behavior from the most "disintegrated" to the most "integrated." Decisions based on winner-take-all choices to act strong or generous, playful or serious, and so forth, are more effective than decisions made by people with frontal lobe damage. Also, choices are based on rational judgment are more effective than choices based on entrenched habits. But if the claims of both conflicting entities (e.g., "strength" and "generosity") are strong enough, still more effective choices (even if riskier ones) are available from syntheses of the two alternatives. This leads to new ways of acting and thinking, such as combining generosity and strength into being powerful so as to empower others, or playfulness and considerateness into "an it harm none, do as you will." Since these high-level syntheses involve a blend of rational, intuitive, and instinctive processes, that is, all of MacLean's "three brains" [24], they should, as Fig. 3 suggests, engage the prefrontal cortex which is the chief communicator between the three brains.

Different degrees of self-actualization lead to different ways to resolve ambiguity. Wegner and Vallacher [31, p. 124 ff.], for example, report studies of general impressions people formed about women who "acted innocent" and yet were known to be sexually promiscuous. Most people adopted either the univalent strategy of resolution (she's "good" or "bad," not both), the aggregative strategy (she's "a bit of each"), or the integrative strategy (she's "confused" — an answer which ties the paradox together). The integrative strategy involves an ability, and decision, to transfer to a higher level in conceptual space if no decision made at a lower level is satisfactory. Levine [18] described one possible way to implement ambiguity-dependent interlevel switching in an adaptive resonance theory (ART) network. The original ART [2] always comes to a decision as to which of several categories an input pattern belongs to, regardless of the ambiguity in the arriving information. This is based on a parameter called *vigilance* that

---

[1] Maslow's abbreviation for self-actualization, SA, is also the abbreviation for simulated annealing! Since this is a synchronicity, we owe a debt to Carl Jung as well as to Maslow.

measures how closely an input must match a stored prototype to be considered part of the category that prototype encodes. Levine's extension, shown in Fig. 4, includes two separate vigilance parameters, one for "certain match" and one for "possible match." If "possible match" occurs to more than one category but certain match to none, control is transferred to a different level. Such a transfer also occurs in the mortgage underwriter simulations in [3].

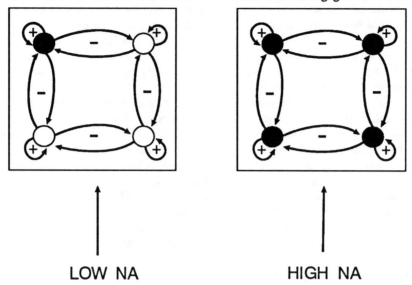

LOW NA   HIGH NA

Fig. 2. Effect of noradrenaline (NA) level on an on-center off-surround module, such as the needs module of Fig. 1. Dark circles indicate nodes with positive asymptotic activity.

Previous models [5, 23] posited rule-coding neurons in the prefrontal cortex. The choices between rules in those networks, however, were within one level (e.g., sorting cards on the basis of color versus shape of design). The prefrontal cortex also seems to make choices *between levels*, that is among *types* of rules. Examples of rules which need intact frontal lobes to be learned effectively are (1) choose whichever object is the most novel [23]; (2) alternate moving to the left and right [8]; and (3) press each one of several panels once, regardless of order [1]. The greater the level of self-actualization, in general, the higher the level of rules that will tend to be chosen. This depends on the lower vigilance levels r_{min} (the numbers that connote probable, but not certain, match) in Fig. 4. These vigilances in turn, I believe, depend on complex interactions between the neurotransmitters noradrenaline and serotonin; these are beyond the scope of this article but related experimental results are found in [10].

Acknowledgment
Many ideas in this article arose from eight years of stimulating discussions with Sam Leven, who also brought to my attention several of the references (Hofstede, Ingvar, Samson et al., and Wegner and Vallacher).

References
[1] Bapi, R. S., & Levine, D. S. (submitted). Modeling the role of the frontal lobes in performing sequential tasks. I. Basic structure and primacy effects.

[2] Carpenter, G. A., & Grossberg, S. (1987). *Computer Vision, Graphics, and Image Processing*, **37**, 54-115.

[3] Cohen, M. A., & Grossberg, S. (1983). *IEEE Transactions on Systems, Man, and Cybernetics* **13**, 815-826.

[4] Collins, E., Ghosh, S., & Scofield, C. (1988). *IEEE International Conference on Neural Networks*, Vol. II.

[5] Dehaene, S., & Changeux, J.-P. (1991). *Cerebral Cortex*, **1**, 62-79.

[6] Eichenbaum, H., & Buckingham, J. (1991). In M. Gabriel & J. Moore (Eds.), *Learning and Computational Neuroscience: Foundations of Adaptive Networks*. Cambridge, MA: MIT Press.

[7] Foote, S. L., Bloom, F. E., & Aston-Jones, G. (1983). *Physiological Reviews*, **63**, 844-914.

[8] Goldman, P. S., & Rosvold, H. E. (1970). *Experimental Neurology*, **27**, 291-304.

[9] Grossberg, S. (1973). *Studies in Applied Mathematics* **52**, 213-257.

[10] Hestenes, D. O. (1992). In D. S. Levine & S. J. Leven (Eds.), *Motivation, Emotion, and Goal Direction in Neural Networks*. Hillsdale, NJ: Erlbaum.

[11] Hofstede, G. (1980). *Culture's Consequences: International Differences in Work-related Values.* Beverly Hills, CA: Sage.

[12] Ingvar, D. (1985). *Human Neurobiology,* **4,** 124-136.

[13] Kirkpatrick, S., Gelatt, C. D., Jr., & Vecchi, M. P. (1983). *Science,* **220,** 671-680.

[14] Kuperstein, M. (1988). *Science,* **239,** 1308-1311.

[15] Leven, S. J. (1987). Choice and neural process. Unpublished dissertation, University of Texas at Arlington.

[16] Leven, S. J. (1992). In D. S. Levine & S. J. Leven (Eds.), *Motivation, Emotion, and Goal Direction in Neural Networks.* Hillsdale, NJ: Erlbaum.

[17] Leven, S. J., & Levine, D. S. (submitted). Multiattribute decision making in context: A dynamic neural network methodology.

[18] Levine, D. S. (1989). In W. Webster (Ed.), *Simulation and AI — 1989.* San Diego: Society for Computer Simulation.

[19] Levine, D. S. (1991). *Introduction to Neural and Cognitive Modeling.* Hillsdale, NJ: Erlbaum.

[20] Levine, D. S., & Elsberry, W. R. (Eds.) (1995). *Optimality in Biological and Artificial Networks?* Hillsdale, NJ: Erlbaum.

[21] Levine, D. S., & Leven, S. J. (1993). In World Congress on Neural Networks, Portland, OR, Vol. I.

[22] Levine, D. S., & Leven, S. J. (in press). In F. Abraham & A. Gilgen (Eds.), *Chaos Theory in Psychology.* Westport, CT: Greenwood.

[23] Levine, D. S., Leven, S. J., & Prueitt, P. S. (1992). In Levine, D. S. & Leven, S. J. (Eds.), *Motivation, Emotion, and Goal Direction in Neural Networks.* Hillsdale, NJ: Erlbaum.

[24] MacLean, P. D. (1970). In F. Schmitt (Ed.), *The Neurosciences Second Study Program.* New York: Rockefeller University Press.

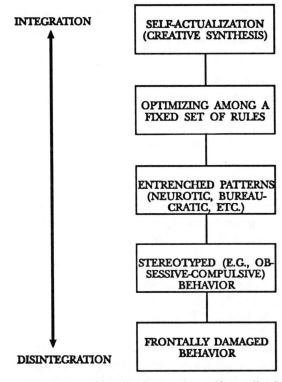

Fig. 3. Continuum of behavioral patterns from frontally damaged to self-actualized, with stereotyped or entrenched behavior in between. (Adapted from Levine & Leven [22], with permission of Greenwood Publishing Group.)

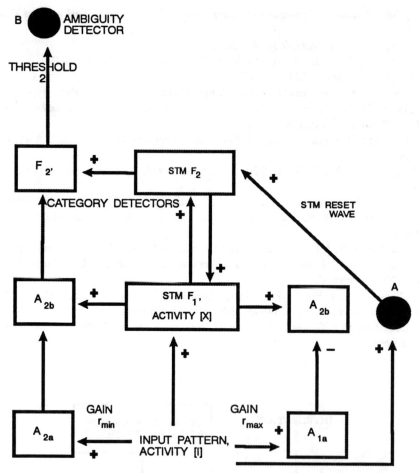

Fig. 4. Ambiguity detection network. In ART 1, input and prototype are said to match if the ratio of total STM activity [X] at F_1 to input pattern activity [I] exceeds *vigilance, r*. Here r is replaced by two values, r_{min} for possible match and r_{max} for certain match. A_{2b} is activated if $[X]/[I] > r_{min}$. Each category node at F_2 has a copy at $F_{2'}$ that is activated by combined signals from the same F_2 node and from A_{2b}. The ambiguity detector fires if two or more $F_{2'}$ nodes are active. (From Levine, 1989; reprinted with permission of the Society for Computer Simulation.)

[25] Maslow, A. H. (1968). *Toward a Psychology of Being*. New York: Van Nostrand.

[26] Maslow, A. H. (1972). *The Farther Reaches of Human Nature*. New York: Viking.

[27] Milner, B. (1964). In J. Warren & K. Akert (Eds.), *The Frontal Granular Cortex and Behavior*. New York: McGraw-Hill.

[28] Ogmen, H., & Prakash, R. V. (1992). Self-organization via active exploration in robotics. Technical Report, Department of Electrical Engineering, University of Houston.

[29] Pribram, K. H. (1991). *Brain and Perception*. Hillsdale, NJ: Erlbaum.

[30] Samson, J. A., Mirin, S. M., Hauser, S. T., Fenton, B. T., & Schildkraut, J. J. (1992). *American Journal of Psychiatry*, **146**, 806-809.

[31] Wegner, D., & Vallacher, R. (1977). *Implicit Psychology*. New York: Oxford University Press.

[32] Werbos, P. J. (1993). Freud, the mind, and approximate dynamic programming. Talk for panel of SIG on Mental Function and Dysfunction, World Congress on Neural Networks, Portland, OR.

Neural Nets, Consciousness, Ethics and the Soul

Paul J. Werbos[*]
8411 48th Avenue, College Park, Maryland, USA 20740

ABSTRACT

The problem of consciousness -- like other questions about the nature of mind and the purpose of life -- has been with us for millennia, and a serious effort to understand this problem must draw on what has been learned in many disciplines, many cultures, and many centuries. Neural net research does provide something new and critical here: it is a novel effort, already showing success, to develop a more complete understanding of the phenomenon of intelligence and mind, precise enough to be replicated on electronic computers, yet fully consistent with what we see in the brain and in experiments on overt behavior. A deeper understanding of intelligence and the mind has immediate implications for the problem of consciousness, and related psychological issues.

This paper provides a global summary of these implications, as seen from the viewpoint of existentialism, Confucianism, and linguistic analysis -- established philosophical traditions which should not be ignored here. Among the six issues discussed are the subjective sense of existence, the levels of intelligence, the foundations of ethics, alternative states of consciousness, the soul, and the role of quantum theory. In all cases, the paper presents candid personal views which may be regarded as heresies by a significant fraction of the community. The paper argues that neural network research can indeed yield important insights into all of these questions, but that it does not provide a basis for overthrowing earlier views in philosophy or for resolving the debate about the existence of the soul; instead, it may help us to understand, unify, sharpen and deepen some very ancient insights.

INTRODUCTION

In 1992, a prominent speaker at the annual conference of the European Neural Network Society declared "an open season on the problem of consciousness." The "problem of consciousness" is a very old problem, and one may legitimately ask why we would suddenly spend so much energy in revisiting it at this time. There are at least two legitimate answers to that question: (1) that fundamentally new insights, developed by the neural network community in interdisciplinary research, let us address the problem of consciousness at a higher level; (2) that a relaxation of certain academic taboos -- restricting analysis to overt behavior only (as in classical behaviorism) or to linguistic analysis only (as in some university philosophy departments in the US and UK) may now permit us to face up to issues which it was hard to address ten or twenty years ago. These answers lead, however, to further questions: (1) If insights from neural network research are so useful, then why are so many of the new manifestoes on consciousness written by people with limited knowledge of the real frontiers of the field (i.e., of those aspects which are most relevant to higher intelligence?); (2) Where is there serious philosophical depth in this discussion, above and beyond the classical Anglo-American approach?; (3) Just what is the problem of consciousness anyway?

This paper will draw heavily on current neural network research, as one might expect, but it will also draw on traditions like existentialism and Confucianism, which have critical contributions to make. I do not have enough space here to explain all the vicissitudes and varieties of existentialism or Confucianism; however, these traditions are very important as an antidote to some of the more extreme and parochial approaches to philosophy which have existed in the past in some American universities. Twenty years ago, the leading theory of ethics in the Anglo-American philosophy departments was a theory attributed to Rawls which proceeded entirely by performing a semantic analysis of the word "justice" and of what it should mean (based on assorted assumptions about what good definitions for a word should be), building up to strong recommendations for what policy makers should do all across the board. (Bear in mind that the problem of ethics refers to the problem of purpose and goals in human life; it requires a lot more than just coming up with a formula to keep lawyers happy.) This episode reminds me of a meeting I once attended at the Census Bureau, where famous world-class statisticians proposed to develop a measure of value or utility, for use in allocating federal funds, by simply doing a factor analysis of a complete set of available

---

*The views herein are purely my personal views, oversimplified in places to make a point. They certainly do not in any way represent the views of any of my employers past and present, one of whom remains a close friend and supporter even though he is totally aghast at section 5.

data series collected by the Bureau. This situation would have been very amusing, except that billions of dollars of federal funds have actually been allocated on the basis of formulas derived in such ways. See [2] for a discussion of assorted ways that value measurements have been developed in the government.

Nevertheless, I would agree with the Anglo-American school on at least two basic points: (1) that it is foolish to invest too much energy in worrying about words like "consciousness" until we develop some sort of clear idea of what it is that we are worrying about, an idea of what the word is supposed to mean; (2) that language, in general, does play a deep and central role in philosophy[1].

So what, then, is the "problem of consciousness"? There are at least 6 different kinds of questions that people appear to be asking under this general rubric:

1. How is it possible -- objectively -- that human beings meet the dictionary definition of "consciousness" -- a basic sense of awareness, which allows them to respond to what they are aware of?

2. How is it possible that human beings have a subjective feeling that we do in fact <u>exist</u>, given that we have the various capabilities discussed under questions 1 and 3?

3. How is it possible that human beings show <u>additional</u> capabilities, such as intelligence or emotions or creativity, which we commonly tend to associate with our consciousness?

4. What is it in the brain that distinguishes between states of "consciousness" versus states of "unconsciousness" like sleep?

5. Can the human mind -- in its widest scope -- be explained entirely in terms of atoms and neurons, or do we need to invoke some sort of "soul" to explain the full range of our experience?

6. Can the human mind be fully explained in terms of algorithms or Turing-machine concepts (generalized to include continuous variables), or must we invoke concepts of quantum computing[3]?

This paper will present my personal opinions on these questions. The reader should be reassured that I am aware of the idiosyncratic nature of my views, and that my strategic goals in the neural network field [4-7] are sufficiently explicit that they leave no room at all for any kind of bias against anyone who can advance those goals, regardless of their views on these questions. Because of page limits, this paper will simply explain what my views <u>are</u>, and cite other papers which explain the critical details.

1. THE OBJECTIVE QUESTION OF AWARENESS

Question number one is hardly a problem at all, from an objective point of view -- even though it is probably the most semantically correct interpretation of the "problem of consciousness." Not only human beings, but all animals on earth show some degree of awareness of their environment. Awareness -- in a literal, objective interpretation of the word -- simply refers to the ability of organisms to input and respond to data from the environment. There is no great mystery in explaining why that phenomenon should evolve (i.e. can confer an advantage to survival), and no great mystery in seeing that there are neural circuits capable of providing that simple capability.

2. THE SUBJECTIVE SENSE OF EXISTENCE

From a very strict existentialist point of view, it is nonsense to try to "explain" our own subjective sense of existence. Our subjective sense of existence or awareness is <u>our starting point</u>, the foundation on which we build everything else. This question is analogous to a question which novices ask of physicists:"Dr. Einstein, can you explain why R=T in general relativity? What underlying phenomena give rise to that equation? What kind of ether do electromagnetic waves travel in?" The point is that Einstein was looking for the lowest level of physical description, that level which inherently cannot be explained as the working out of something more fundamental. Both Einstein and the existentialists were very active in questioning and revising their views of what exists at the most fundamental level, but they still maintained an effort to build everything else up from that level.

From an objective point of view, we may twist the question around, and ask how it is that organisms could <u>evolve</u> a sense of their own existence as such. Marvin Minsky answered this years ago, by simply pointing out that there are evolutionary advantages in organisms developing models of the self and insights to describe their own thinking. Once again, there is no real problem here from an objective point of view. When we ask whether <u>other</u> human beings have a sense of their own existence, we are essentially just asking the objective question; the answer is obviously "yes." (It would still be "yes" even if other humans were actually just programs in a vast virtual reality game, so long as those programs demonstrated the pertinent objective capabilities.) From an objective point of view, one may go further and argue that sane, self-aware organisms will naturally tend to accept the existentialist view of taking their own existence and awareness as a starting point, because this is an honest reflection of how their natural thought-processes work. (See section 3.)

From a strict Anglo-American point of view, neither of these answers is entirely satisfactory, because they seem to assume that there really do exist organisms on earth, that there is such a thing as biological evolution, etc. If we limit our thinking to nothing but the manipulation of words, without ever grounding ourselves in any sort of direct perception of reality, then we can in principle permit any fantastic combination of words to emerge from our mouths. From such a viewpoint, we could just as well worry deeply about issues like why the sun appears to rise every day; after all, can we be <u>really</u> sure that the earth revolves about the sun. Even if we accept that there is always some distant degree of uncertainty here (as is appropriate, from an existentialist point of view), it would seem silly to invest a huge amount of emotional energy on quirky little hypothetical contingencies which are poorly integrated into the rest of our concerns and which we have no way to account for in any case.

I do not believe that all American philosophers adhere to the extreme viewpoint I am arguing against here; in fact, I will not spend any further time on that particular species of philosophy here. Also, I do not mean to downplay the issue of how we <u>know</u> that the sun is likely to rise tomorrow; studying that issue is quite different from actually worrying about what to do (or how to answer intellectual questions) in case the sun actually does not rise to tomorrow. See section 10.4.6.4 of [8] for a discussion of how old questions, like the question of the sun rising tomorrow, do in fact get assimilated into more far-ranging theory in the neural network field.

3. INTELLIGENCE, EMOTIONS, CREATIVITY AND ETHICS

In most of my research, I have found it preferable to address the issue of "intelligence," rather than the issue of "consciousness," because it expresses more exactly where the hard-core scientific issues really lie. My view of intelligence is itself somewhat controversial, and some psychologists would argue that it is far too narrow; however, even my view requires us to include creativity as an attribute of intelligence.

For technical reasons, the existence of emotions turns out to be necessary as part of any system which possesses even a crude modicum of intelligence[1]. This is one case where neural net theory does indeed have something to say about conventional views of the mind: <u>contrary</u> to popular wisdom, as expressed in Star Trek etc., intelligent androids and the like cannot be devoid of emotional systems, because emotional systems are a necessary component of intelligent systems [1,9]. Backpropagation itself originated in 1974 as a surprisingly direct <u>translation</u> of Freud's concept of "emotional energy" or "psychic energy" into mathematics; those concepts are also the basis of the most powerful neurocontrol systems in engineering applications today[5].

In a formal sense, I would define an "intelligent system" as a system capable of <u>maximizing</u> some kind of measurement of utility or reinforcement or performance or goal-satisfaction (with or without prior knowledge of how that measure is defined as a function of other variables) <u>over time</u>, in an environment whose dynamics are not known in advance, so that the system must <u>learn</u> both the dynamics and a strategy of action in real time through experience. It must be a <u>generalized</u> system, capable of adapting to "any" noisy, nonlinear environment, if given enough time to adapt. (See [8, chapter 10] for more precise concepts to replace the word "any.") This definition <u>implicitly</u> includes the ability to solve complex problems which, in turn, implies some degree of creativity.

Neural net designs now exist, on paper, which appear fully capable of meeting this definition [1,8] (though there are a few points where the approach is clear but the details have yet to be worked out[6,7]). Some psychologists would complain that human beings are not totally rational or optimal; however, realistic neural net designs have imperfections which are similar in many ways to those of humans, and very simple reinforcement learning designs can fit both "operant" and ""classical" conditioning[4].

Classical views of intelligence have often assumed that intelligence is either a binary variable (either you have it or you don't) or a continuous variable (everything from microbes to superhumans has a certain degree of it). A careful examination of the real-time optimization designs now available[8] suggests, instead, that intelligence is more like a <u>quantized</u> or <u>discrete</u> variable. (Continuous variables like brain size and metabolic level also have some significance, contrary to what is politically correct; if they were irrelevant, evolution would have settled on a zero-cost zero-weight brain.) For example, even with simple supervised learning networks -- which probably exist as local circuits in the brain[4] -- there are fundamental, qualitative differences between local designs based on fixed preprocessors, feedforward designs with adaptable hidden units, and simultaneous-recurrent networks adapted by simultaneous backpropagation; these yield distinct quantum levels of capability in approximating functions[6].

At a more global level, Bitterman[10] demonstrated years ago that there are basic, qualitative differences between intelligence in different classes of vertebrates. These differences have clearcut links to the qualitative differences in the gross cellular architecture between brains from different classes of vertebrates. These differences, in turn, can be related to clearcut differences which exist between different levels of design in artificial neural networks; for example the "error critic" design in [8, chapter 13] requires something like a merger of limbic (critic) cortex and general (neuroidentification) cortex, which does in fact underlie the historical evolution of neocortex in the mammal, whose removal (according to Bitterman) generates the removal of processing capabilities which happen to be related to error critics. To an engineer, it is astonishing that anyone would simply assume qualitatively equivalent behavior from well-designed systems with radically different components and structures; however, behaviorist dogma historically made it very difficult to study these basic realities. (A cynic might argue that the behaviorists were trying to defend themselves against the charge that experiments with animals might not tell us directly about humans. Another explanation is that behaviorists were trying to save the world from the dangers of racism -- including racism against snails and microbes.)

What would it take to achieve a quantum level of intelligence which can truly adapt to "any" environment, up to the full potential of the universal Turing machine? In [8, chapter 13] and [11], I argued that full Turing machine capabilities require the use of explicit symbolic reasoning. The naive next step is to conclude that human beings -- who seem capable of symbolic reasoning -- represent a quantum step in the evolution of intelligence, above other mammals. From the viewpoint of everyday experience, this would seem highly probable, at first.

On the other hand, formal symbolic reasoning is a reasonably recent phenomenon. Jim Anderson, in analyzing how humans learn arithmetic, has argued that humans possess "two" learning mechanisms: (1) a highly developed and fine-tuned "sensory" system, shared with other mammals; (2) a "buggy alpha test version" of formal symbolic reasoning. After all, if symbolic reasoning is the foundation of human technology and civilization, how do we explain the fact that human technology and civilization is only a few thousand years old? The obvious answer (elaborated on in [1]) is that humans represent a recent, unstable transitional life-form, which has only recently evolved just enough capability for symbolic reasoning to let it muddle through a few technological design problems, on a one-in-a-million basis (which is still enough to start a technological civilization, when there is a culture available to disseminate new ideas, as has been observed even in chimpanzees). We ourselves are the "missing link" between the mammalian and the symbolic levels of intelligence. Perhaps there will never be such a thing as a fully perfected symbolic reasoner, but it is clear that humans have not exhausted whatever potential does exist.

One might then pose the problem of consciousness as follows: Are human beings really "conscious" or "intelligent"? Perhaps not, in the larger scheme of things.

In [1], I suggest that simple wiring changes, related to the balance between the waking state and the dreaming state, might be central to human abilities in symbolic reasoning. (These, in turn, might be related to the unique wiring of the human NRTP[12] as discussed by John Taylor.) If so, there is little doubt that such capabilities could be wired into a computer as well. Computers could be made "conscious" or "intelligent" at a level beyond that of human brains today, if we were crazy and suicidal enough to want to do this.

In my view, the biggest single symptom of our lack of evolution is our inability to master the most fundamental aspects of symbolic reasoning: the ability to accurately articulate our true goals and values, in a way which is totally in harmony with the presymbolic aspects of our thought, and allows us to master symbols instead of being mastered by them. In crude language, the problem is that we lie to ourselves. (In psychiatrists' terms, we overuse denial as a defense mechanism.) We lack the ability to simply articulate -- in a direct, honest way -- the information coming to us from all of our feelings and our everyday experience of life. My examples of Anglo-American philosophers and statisticians, in the Introduction, are not isolated examples. To use symbols effectively, humans must learn even the most basic things, the hard way, like dogs learning to walk on two feet. It is natural for humans to learn symbolic reasoning, when they have enough time and help and intelligence, but the process can be very difficult. The basic foundation of Confucian ethics -- to learn to know oneself, and to be "true" to oneself -- may be viewed as a remarkably clear expression of (and aid to) that learning process. In this view, the mark of a sane human being is an attitude towards life which includes a kind of total openness to the empirical data which comes to us from our senses and from our emotionally-charged feelings, and an easy two-way communication and harmony between the symbolic and nonsymbolic aspects of our intelligence. This is very close, of course, to the Freudian ideal of "sanity."

From a more formalistic point of view, Confucian ethics may be justified as follows. As Bertrand Russell pointed out long ago, there can be no logical, operational answer to questions like "What should we do with our lives?," because the word "should" does not have any operational, objective content. However, there can be an operational answer to the question:"What <u>would</u> I do if I were wise? What 'answers' to the problems of ethics would <u>satisfy me</u> -- put me in a state of stable mental equilibrium in accepting these 'answers' -- if I fully understood myself, my feelings, and my environment?" These questions are inherently meaningful and operational because they address the <u>I</u>, the self, which <u>can</u> be understood -- in part because of neural network research[1]. Using <u>these</u> questions as the foundations of ethics leads one directly to the pursuit of "integrity," as defined by Confucius.

This section should not be interpreted as an endorsement of all the secondary ideas which have evolved in Confucianism over the years. Confucianism -- like Christianity, Marxism, Islam, Buddhism, and Western science -- has accumulated its share of obnoxious barnacles, due to the universal existence of power-seekers, opportunists masquerading as zealots, gullible followers and groupthink.

4. STATES OF "CONSCIOUSNESS" VERSUS "UNCONSCIOUSNESS"

There is a radical difference between the concept of consciousness as "wakefulness" and the concept of consciousness as "intelligence."

Neural network theory already provides some insight into the reasons why <u>intelligent</u> organisms must have <u>multiple</u> states of consciousness. For example, in [8,13], I argue that some form of "dreaming" or "simulation" is essential to the efficient adaptation (or effective foresight) of advanced reinforcement learning systems. After Sutton and I had long discussions of that paper (cited by Sutton) at GTE in 1987, Sutton actually performed simulations (described in [14]) demonstrating this point empirically. This interpretation of dreaming is basically equivalent to the theory developed independently by LaBerge[15], who is arguably the leading dream researcher in the world today.

As noted in the previous section, I have also suggested how an intermediate stage of consciousness, linked to hypnosis[1], may be important to human abilities with language. Deep sleep (and its sub-states?) remain a mystery, but there are new possibilities for linking that phenomenon to neural network research[6]. More research is needed here, especially to pin down the link between neural net models and brain circuits, but there is good reason to expect success in this work, if sufficient effort is applied.

5. WHAT ABOUT THE SOUL?

Up to this point, I might hope that any truly rational scientist, reviewing the evidence carefully, would at least respect the views I have expressed. From this point on, I have no such illusions.

Sections 3 and 4 argued that everything we associate most energetically with human consciousness -- intelligence, emotions, creativity, dreams, and so on -- can be fully understood in terms of classical neural network models, consistent with the Turing theory of computation, and consistent with neuroscience[4]. By Occam's Razor, this suggests that the hypothesis of a "soul" is totally unnecessary and should be abandoned. This is clearly a highly rational conclusion to draw, and I remember believing in this conclusion very intensely back at ages 8 through 19. However, on a purely personal basis, I have come around to the view that something like a "soul" -- a part of the mind and the self which cannot be reduced to atoms and neurons -- is in fact necessary in order to explain the full range of human experience.

Based on past experience, I would predict that most readers will feel a fair amount of surprise at seeing that last sentence in print. A good number of readers -- including some very creative and prominent people -- will quietly voice agreement with that sentence, but will wonder where we go from here. A few canny old psychiatrists may even snigger: "So someone else has discovered that you need Jung as well as Freud to come to terms with the full spectrum of human experience. So what else is new?" A few psychologists will immediately leave the room, for fear that the physicists will denounce them as practitioners of voodoo and steal all their federal funding if they are seen consorting with people who express such views. (These fears are not entirely based on fantasy, either.) A very few readers will actually feel honest, subjective uncertainty about the issue, and really seek evidence for and against. (That was my stance in 1969-71, the period when I really first developed backpropagation, ADAC and other backpropagation-based critic designs, though I only published [16] then.) A fair number of very articulate readers -- including many powerful administrators, if any of them still attend INNS meetings -- will instantly think about two question: (1) Has an eccentric lunatic just walked into the room? Is this another Eccles[17]?; (2) If we make room for the discussion of the soul hypothesis on an equal footing with the "standard" alternative, do we risk losing the insights we get from neural net research and unleashing forces of sheer craziness and illogical thinking which could overwhelm us?

There is no way that a paper this brief could seriously resolve the concerns of all these groups. However, I would like to make some comments regarding the last two concerns.

Back in 1964, when I first read Hebb's ideas about this, I found myself in complete agreement with his views. Hebb was trying to explain the idea of Occam's Razor, which we now understand more precisely [8, chapter 10]. He described how prior expectations -- which encourage us not to invoke "expensive" assumptions which complicate our underlying understanding of the universe -- are important in science, above and beyond empirical data as such. As an example, he pointed towards the laboratory work in parapsychology. He argued that most scientists would probably agree with the conclusions of that work, if they judged the statistics as they do with most scientific papers they read. However, because those conclusions have a huge improbability"cost" apriori, we would still tend to disbelieve them, if we take a balanced look at prior and empirical information. Based on section 3, I would take this a step further: I would argue, even now, that all of the laboratory data we have now regarding human abilities, from problem-solving through to parapsychology, is still not convincing enough to justify the soul hypothesis.

In fairness to the parapsychologists, I should confess that I do not know that literature enough to draw strong conclusions. There is an analogy here between parapsychology and the study of ancient history: it requires reliance on a huge body of secondary sources, many of them quite willing to stretch the truth in favor of diverse biases (some in favor and some against), so that it would take a huge effort to make a truly judicious analysis. Even if one did all that work, one should recall the example of Aristotle, who produced a wonderfully judicious resolution of the scientific issues of the time; judicious or not, it was dead wrong. Thus even if the results from parapsychology were very clearcut, the average scientist could not afford to know enough to find a compelling reason to believe them.

Given this situation, how could I -- or any other scientist, thinking for himself or herself -- give any credence at all to the soul hypothesis?

In my own case, the answer lies in direct, personal observation of what I see around me. I do not expect all rational scientists to agree with me, because they do not share the same base of experience. But I do not accept the idea that I myself, in formulating my own views, must discard any personal experience which has not been socialized through the laboratory. I like to believe that my interest in the human mind, and my acceptance of the existentialist/Confucian viewpoint back in 1964, was the real case of my making these observations -- which I did not allow myself to accept for several years.

Just how strange and eccentric is it to be open to the soul hypothesis based on personal experience? Years ago, the National Science Foundation commissioned a major study of the underlying values of the American people, through the National Opinion Research Center (NORC) at the University of Chicago, a leading center of excellence in surveys and sociology and the like[19]. One of the difficult issues they addressed was the nature of beliefs and experience related to the soul hypothesis. They discovered that personal experiences played a far greater role than they had expected beforehand. Even more surprising, they found that the percentage of people claiming such experience increased monotonically with education and other measures of success. The investigators have reported [19] the great surprise they encountered when they presented this result to their review board. A skeptic on the board pointed out that their statistical results would predict that 70% of that very board (composed of PhDs) would have answered "yes" to a highly inflammatory-looking question. After this, 70% of the board did in fact come forward, reluctantly, and validate the prediction -- to the great surprise of everyone in the room. My own views of the soul hypothesis and the relevant experience are considerably more complex and idiosyncratic than what was reported in [19], but the bottom line is still this: whether I am a lunatic or not, I am certainly not such an eccentric one (except perhaps in my willingness to articulate taboo ideas, when my session chair asks me to address a controversial issue). There are many serious, technical people who take the soul hypothesis seriously, and they merit equal time on this issue.

Would these statistics be different for people who -- in addition to being well-trained -- are highly independent, creative thinkers, the kind of people who have demonstrated more than anyone else their ability to ignore conventional wisdom (both parents and peers) and arrive at their own viewpoint? It is interesting to go back and consider the four greatest physicists of this century, the four pioneers who rebuilt the very foundations of modern physics -- Einstein, Schrodinger, Heisenberg and DeBroglie. Einstein often used the word "God," and is often alleged to have been a mystic; however, in what I have seen of his writings, I see no reason to believe that this was anything more than the erudite but firmly "secular" theology I have seen very often, expressed in similar ways, at the local Unitarian church. On the other hand, records of the conversations between Schrodinger and Einstein make it very clear that Schrodinger was deeply interested in things like Sufi mysticism - something which is far more than mere allegory. Heisenberg consistently described his physics in Vedantic terms, and invited well-known yogins to expound their views at the Copenhagen Institute. DeBroglie is said to have been a follower of Bergson's vision of collective intelligence, which would appear to be a close relative of Teilhard de Chardin's views. All in all, the 70% figure would seem to be in the ballpark here.

Would the soul hypothesis per se undermine the effort to understand the mind in a scientific way? On the contrary, one might argue that efforts to totally repress this idea (or to hand it over as a monopoly to television preachers) would be as conducive to sanity as any other kind of gross repression of thought.

The greatest abuse of the soul hypothesis has come from power seekers who try to use it as an excuse for making other people follow their orders in a blind, unthinking manner, without opening themselves to personal experience, to mathematical or scientific efforts to understand that experience, and so on. The formulation I am proposing here would still start out from the Confucian/existentialist point of view; that view clearly argues that we should try to be true to our entire self -- including both the brain and the soul. If neural network mathematics is useful in understanding the general phenomenon of intelligence -- regardless of the hardware that implements this intelligence -- then it should, in principle, be useful even in explaining other forms of intelligence. So far as I can tell, in my own experience, this does appear to be the case. A highly condensed summary of my more specific thoughts along these lines as of early 1993 may be found in [1,20,21]; however, consideration of the sixth and final issue has begun to modify some of the details of my thinking here. It would be impossible to summarize all of that here, and many readers would not be interested in any case; however, I should note that I agree with the classic Bayesian view, that it is sometimes most rational to maintain a set of models of what is going on -- very concrete and coherent models -- and to act on the basis of a probability distribution, which honestly reflects one's uncertainty. If ever there was a situation requiring decision making under uncertainty, it is his one.

6. QUANTUM COMPUTING, MIND AND SOUL

Penrose, in a famous new book[3], argues that the human level of intelligence -- whatever it may be -- cannot be reduced to any sort of Turing-machine algorithm. He argues that quantum-mechanical effects are crucial to how the brain works, and that quantum mechanics cannot be reduced to mere Turing-machine computation.

As discussed in section 3, I do not really see evidence for any specific capabilities in the human brain which require such a hypothesis. The technical literature on quantum computing has indeed proven that quantum systems yield a qualitatively new kind of computing, which leads to a new kind of universal model more general than the Turing model; however, it also includes little basis for confidence that this model of computation buys us anything very useful, or anything relevant to the brain[22]. (The examples found in that literature are mainly inspired by the Copenhagen interpretation or the many-worlds interpretation of quantum mechanics.) Penrose has collaborated with a group looking for quantum effects in the form of coherent photon propagated inside of microtubules[23]; important as the microtubules may be[4,9], even to computing, I am disturbed by some of the puns I have heard, suggesting that "coherent" photons would naturally explain the "coherence" of our sense of self.

Nevertheless, looking more closely at this issue, I can see some real possibilities. There are many different interpretations of the real significance of quantum theory; even if only one interpretation can be objectively true, they are all close enough that they give some valid intuition about the phenomena themselves. One interpretation which I have developed[24] is the idea that quantum effects can be explained by assuming that causality runs forwards and backwards, symmetrically, in quantum experiments. Thus, when people use special crystals to demonstrate basic quantum effects, there is a kind of settling down through a resonance between past and future -- like a Hopfield net or a simultaneous-recurrent net[9], but without the need to wait for convergence through iteration in forwards time. Even if the human brain has no such capabilities, I can imagine a possibility (with 20% probability?) that this could be used to increase the power of optical neural networks. It is questionable that humanity would benefit much from such technology, but the intellectual issue is worth resolving.

One reviewer has asked for a simple example of backwards causality in quantum physics. The simplest example I know was discussed in my 1974 paper on quantum foundations (cited in [25]), based on the account of nuclear exchange reactions in Segre's book *Nuclei and Particles.* Suppose that you could design a cannon which, without any electronic control system could generate the following capability: whenever an enemy rocket is about to come up over the horizon, it will automatically swivel into exactly the right angle, and fire at the exact time, so that it will hit the target exactly when the target first appears over the horizon, even if the target is fired after the cannon must fire to meet it. If anyone ever built such a cannon, one might attribute it to magic or precognition, or suspect over-the-horizon radar and cheating. But neutrons, shooting pi mesons out to oncoming protons, have displayed exactly such a "precognition." The conversion of the oncoming proton to a neutron proves that charged mesons are exchanged. More relevant, but complicated, examples (involving optics and Bell's Theorem) are cited in [25]. Behavior like this may sound mysterious, but it is fully consistent with the model of a universe governed entirely by partial differential equations.

Taking this further, one might even imagine that Penrose's concepts might be relevant to the style of computing used by "soul," even if they are not relevant to the brain. This leads to interesting thoughts concerning the role of time and causality which are far beyond the scope of this paper[24].

REFERENCES

1. P.Werbos, Neural networks and the human mind: new mathematics fits ancient insights, *IJCNN92-Beijing Proceedings*, IEEE, New York, 1992. An updated version appears in [5].

2. P.Werbos, Rational approaches to identifying policy objectives.*Energy*, Vol. 15, No.3/4, 1990. Reprinted in J.Weyant and T.Kuczmowski eds, *Systems Modeling Handbook*, Pergamon, 1994.

3. R.Penrose,*The Emperor's New Mind: Concerning Computers, Minds and the Laws of Physics*, Oxford, 1989.

4. P.Werbos, The brain as a neurocontroller: New hypotheses and new experimental possibilities, in K.Pribram, ed., *Origins...*, Proc. of the Second Appalachian Conference, INNS Press, Erlbaum, 1994.

5. P.Werbos,*The Roots of Backpropagation: From Ordered Derivatives to Neural Networks and Political Forecasting*, Wiley, 1994.

6. P.Werbos,Supervised learning: Can it escape from its local minimum, *WCNN93 Proc.*,INNS Press, Erlbaum, 1993.

7. P.Werbos,How we cut prediction errors in half by using a different raining method, *WCNN94 Proc.*, INNS Press, Erlbaum, 1994.

8. D.White & D.Sofge,*Handbook of Intelligent Control: Neural, Fuzzy and Adaptive Approaches*,Van Nostrand, 1992.

9. P.Werbos,The cytoskeleton:Why it may be crucial to human learning and to neurocontrol,*Nanobiology*, Vol.1,No.1,1992.

10. M.E.Bitterman, Comparative analysis of learning, *Science* 188, p.699-709, 1975. See also The evolution of intelligence, *Scientific American*, January 1965.

11. P.Werbos, Neurocontrol and fuzzy logic: Connections and designs, *International Journal of Approximate Reasoning*, Vol.6, No.2, February 1992.

12. J.G,Taylor, From single neuron to cognition, in I.Aleksander & J.Taylor, eds, *Artificial Neural Networks 2* (ICANN92 Proceedings), North Holland, 1992.

13. P.Werbos, Building and understanding adaptive systems: a statistical/numerical approach to factory automation and brain research, *IEEE Trans. SMC*, Jan/Feb, 1987.

14. W,Miller,R.Sutton & P.Werbos, eds, *Neural Networks for Control*, MIT Press, 1990.

15. S.LaBerge & Rheingold,*Exploring the World of Lucid Dreaming*, Ballantine, 1990.

16. P.Werbos, The elements of intelligence, *Cybernetica* (Namur), No.3, 1968.

17. J.Eccles, Evolution of complexity of the brain with the emergence of consciousness, in K.Pribram,ed, *Rethinking Neural Networks: Quantum Fields and Biological Data*, INNS Press, Erlbaum, 1993.

18. D.O.Hebb, *The Organization of Behavior*, Wiley, 1949.

19. A.M.Greeley & W.C.McCready, Are we a nation of mystics?, *New York Times Magazine*, Jan. 26, 1975.

20. P.Werbos,Quantum theory and neural systems: alternative approaches and a new design, in K.Pribram ed.([17]).

21. P.Werbos, Generalized information requirements of intelligent decision-making systems, *SUGI 11 Proceedings*, SAS Institute, Cary, NC, 1986. A version updated in later 1986 is available from the author.

22. D.Deutsch, Quantum computing, *Physics World*, June 1992.

23. paper(s) on coherent photons, in K.Pribram, ed, [4].

24. P.Werbos, Self-organization: reexamining the basics, and an alternative to the big bang, in K.Pribram ed.[4]. For more mathematical treatments focusing solely on the issue of quantum foundations as such, see [25].

25. P.Werbos, Quantum theory, computing and chaotic solitons, *IEICE Trans. on Fundamentals*, Vol E76-A, No.5, May 1993; Chaotic solitons and the foundations of physics: a potential revolution, *Applied Mathematics and Computation*, Vol 56, No.2/3, July 1993.

Applications

Session Chairs: David Casasent
Robert Pap
Dejan Sobajic

ORAL PRESENTATIONS

ANN DESIGN OF IMAGE PROCESSING CORRELATION FILTERS AND CLASSIFIERS

DAVID CASASENT

Carnegie Mellon University
Department of Electrical and Computer Engineering
Center for Excellence in Optical Data Processing
Pittsburgh, PA 15213

ABSTRACT

Three applications of artificial neural networks (ANNs) are described and their use in image processing is noted. They involve the solution of new constrained optimization problems that arise in distortion-invariant detection filters, the design of the weights for an analog accuracy neural net with noise and non-ideal components, and the use of square-law nonlinearities (that exist in optical detectors) and complex-valued weights to inherently produce higher-order decision surfaces. Emphasis is given to ANN techniques to design shift-invariant and distortion-invariant correlation filters. The specific case detailed is low-level vision detection of all objects in a scene independent of distortions and contrasts.

1. INTRODUCTION

The three applications we discuss employ several of the key properties of artificial neural networks (ANNs): their ability to solve difficult optimization problems, their fault tolerance, and their use of nonlinearities. The examples chosen arise in image processing, but should be of use in other applications also.

The first ANN (Section 2) is used to design correlation filters to locate multiple classes of objects in clutter with distortions and contrast differences present. These are referred to as detection filters. Since shift-invariance is required (the locations of the objects are not known), a correlator is used and the neural net is used to design the filters for this system. This application is given major attention. The second ANN (Section 3) application arises when the ANN hardware can support fast basic operations such as matrix-vector multiplications, but cannot support complex decision making steps or learning algorithms; and when the hardware (and data) has analog accuracy, nonideal components and noise. This situation arises in many analog VLSI and optical neural nets using off-line learning. The third application (Section 4) is only briefly noted. It concerns the use of new nonlinear functions (simple square-law detectors) that are inherently available optically (or digitally) and how they and complex-valued weights can inherently provide more complex decision surfaces that improve recognition rates and learning times, while using fewer hidden layer neurons resulting in better generalization.

2. SHIFT-INVARIANT DISTORTION-INVARIANT CORRELATION FILTER DESIGN

A major use of ANN algorithms, architectures and hardware occurs in image processing. In the initial low-level vision stage, one of the first steps required is to locate the positions of all possible objects of interest in a scene. This is referred to as detection. Each of these regions of interest (ROIs) is subsequently further processed to determine the class of object present in each ROI. This is a formidable problem since the number of objects and their locations are not known (the purpose of this first stage is to estimate these). A conventional neural net approach requires one input neuron for each pixel in the scene (perhaps $N_1 = 500^2$ neurons). Since the locations of the object(s) are not known, shift-invariant interconnections are required. With N_1 input neurons, this requires N_1^4 interconnections (which is quite excessive). The problem is further complicated by the need to handle all distorted versions of each object. This can be trained into the ANN weights (but now a large training set and long learning times are required) or the number of interconnections can be increased (this has significant hardware effects). A preferable hardware architecture, when shift-invariance is required, is the use of a correlator. This is now feasible with digital signal processing chips. To accommodate objects with different distortions, distortion-invariant filter designs are used. When objects in many different classes can be present in clutter, sets of filters and different levels of computer vision are used.

Figure 1 shows a simplified correlator block diagram and a new role for neural net techniques in such scene analysis problems. The 2-D correlation of an input scene f and a filter h is performed by inverse Fourier transforming (FT^{-1}) the product of the Fourier transform (FT) of the input F and the conjugate Fourier transform H* of the filter. The FT and correlation provide the shift-invariance required and such a correlator architecture is in fact a shift-invariant neural net [1]. We consider the use of an ANN to design the filter functions to be used in the correlator.

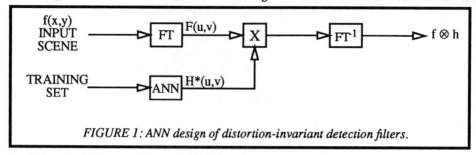

FIGURE 1: ANN design of distortion-invariant detection filters.

For the case considered, the detection filter is comprised of a set of Gabor filter functions. In polar FT format, a Gabor filter function (GF) is [2]

$$G_n(x, y) = \exp[-\pi(x^2/a^2 + y^2/b^2)]\exp[j2\pi\omega r \cos(\theta - \phi)]. \tag{1}$$

The correlation of an input image f with G_n gives a 2-D analog output whose value at each point in f can be viewed as the amount of a given radial frequency ω at orientation ϕ present in a local area, defined by (a,b), about each input pixel in the input scene f. We construct our detection filter from a number of different GFs; each choice of the n = (a,b,ω,ϕ) parameters results in a new G_n. To avoid the need to apply a number of different Gabor filters and analyze a number of separate 2-D analog outputs, we form one composite filter that is a combination of a number of G_n. The problem we consider involves detecting many different classes of objects in a variety of distortions in the presence of clutter. Gabor functions are attractive for this since they provide the best joint space and frequency description [3], because they are excellent texture descriptors [4], and because they are biologically motivated [3]. To formulate the problem for an ANN solution, we consider a set of training images s_T of some of the true class objects and a small set of training images s_C of representative clutter. The detection filter is a macro Gabor function (MGF) that is the sum of a number of different GFs

$$MGF = \sum_n w_n G_n. \tag{2}$$

To solve for the combination coefficients or weights w_n, we develop a criteria function E. The filter is $\underline{G}\underline{w}$, where the columns of the matrix $\underline{G}$ are the G_n and the vector $\underline{w}$ is the weights w_n used to combine several different G_n into one macro filter. The peak value of the correlation of this filter with an input $\underline{s}$ is the vector inner product $\underline{s}^T\underline{G}\underline{w}$. We require this output to be $d_T = 1$ for objects and $d_C = 0$ for clutter. With the different training images $\underline{s}$ as columns of a matrix $\underline{S}$, the criteria function to be minimized is

$$E = 0.5\|\underline{S}^T\underline{G}\underline{w} - \underline{d}\|^2, \tag{3}$$

where the elements of the vector $\underline{d}$ are $d_T = 1$ or $d_C = 0$ depending on the $\underline{s}$.

This is thus a constrained optimization problem. The ANN used is shown in Figure 2. The P_1 input neurons are the training images, the P_1-to-P_2 interconnections are the G_n functions, the number of hidden layer neurons at P_2 equals the number of GFs chosen, the desired value of the P_3 output neuron is 1 or 0. The ANN must select the Gabor function parameters n = (a,b,ω,r), for each G_n and it must select the combination weights $\underline{w}$ to minimize the criteria function. We achieve this by adapting both the P_1-to-P_2 weights (the G_n functions and their parameters) and the P_2-to-P_3 weights (their combination coefficients $\underline{w}$). This is quite different from other ANNs used to calculate the Gabor coefficients used to compactly represent an image for data compression [5].

We initiate the neural net with an approximate set of initial G_n functions [6]. We initially use: four G_n with $\phi = 0°$, $90°$, $45°$ and $135°$, to allow detection of objects in different scales and orientations; one G_n with $\omega = 0$, to allow the dc level of the filters to be adapted to enable detection of low contrast objects and rejection of bright constant background regions; and one G_n with $\omega = 2a/3$ and a = b = 15 pixels, this detects clutter well) and an initial set of weights $\underline{w}$ (chosen to give d = 1 for the broadside view of the largest object and nearly a zero-mean filter). The ANN algorithm then adapts these initial weights and G_n parameters to produce the final filter. We present the training set to the input neurons and adapt the weights $\underline{w}$ from P_2-to-P_3. We then repeat the training set several times and continue to adapt the P_2-to-P_3 weights (for a fixed set of G_n parameters or P_1-to-P_2 weights). We repeat adapting the w_n weights P_2-to-P_3 for K iterations. We then repeat the training set and perform one adaptation of the G_n parameter

I-232

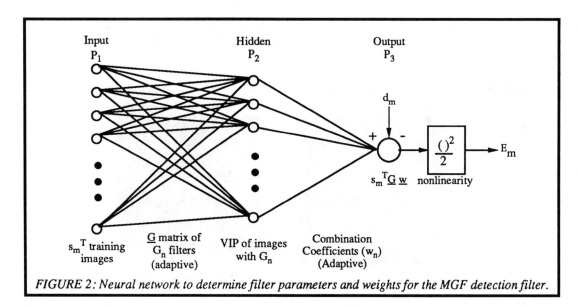

FIGURE 2: Neural network to determine filter parameters and weights for the MGF detection filter.

weights from P_1-to-P_2. We then adapt the $\underline{w}$ weights for another K iterations. For each adaptation of the P_1-to-P_2 weights, we thus perform K adaptations of the P_2-to-P_3 weights and we repeat this cycle L times (for each of L adaptations of the P_1-to-P_2 weights). We then select the set of G_n functions and parameters and the associated set of $\underline{w}$ weights that yields the lowest value for the criteria function and synthesize our filter from the associated G_n and w_n weights.

The P_2-to-P_3 weight update rule we use for the $\underline{w}$ is a conjugate gradient algorithm with periodic restarts [7] (since this is much faster than a gradient descent or delta rule). Since it is monotonically convergent, we perform K adaptive iterations of it for each set of G_n weights from P_1-to-P_2. Adapting the P_1-to-P_2 weights (i.e. selecting the Gabor features to use) is more difficult. We use a similar algorithm and calculation of the step vectors by the chain rule. This involves calculation of the derivatives of G_n with respect to each of the Gabor parameters (a,b,ω,r). We choose the step sizes so that we produce a change in each of the Gabor parameters by about 1% for each of the L iterations. Since this portion of the adaptive algorithm is less numerically stable, we use only one adaptation of the P_1-to-P_2 weights, we then adapt the P_2-to-P_3 weights for K iterations and then return to adapt the P_1-to-P_2 weights for one iteration, etc.

We used K = 40 and L = 100 iterations and found adequate solutions in all cases. Table 1 shows the final five Gabor functions and their parameters (columns 2 to 4) and their combination weights (column 5) chosen by the ANN. The first three G_n have orientations at about 0° (horizontal) and at two diagonals (about 45° and 129°). The fourth G_4 function controls the dc value of the filter and the last G_5 function models the clutter. These choices in Table 1 could not be arrived at by ad hoc methods and thus such ANN design methods appear very attractive for this and similar problems.

Filter	(a,b)	ω	ϕ	w_n
G_1	(21,19)	1.11/80	1.69°	0.009835
G_2	(37,12)	2.04/80	45.51°	0.01657
G_3	(29,15)	1.42/80	128.39°	0.01242
G_4	(85,29)	0	--	-0.005064
G_5	(15,15)	1/10	0°	-0.00007775

Table 1: Optimized parameters and weights for MGF

Figure 3a shows a typical input scene considered. It contains 8 objects in high clutter (the targets lie in the horizontal strip below the clutter region. The objects on the left have much higher contrast than those on the right. The database investigated contained six different classes of objects, with 21 different aspect distorted views of each (covering a full 360° in aspect), in a variety of representations and contrasts. Our initial purpose was to achieve high detection rates P_D. For the 610 objects in 95 scenes tested, we located 604 for an excellent $P_D = 99\%$ detection performance rate from this filter. Fusion with other detection algorithms [8] reduced false alarms. Figure 3b shows the detection output for Figure 3a. As seen all objects are located with only 4 false alarms. This is quite significant given the low contrast, high clutter, and large number of classes and distortions considered.

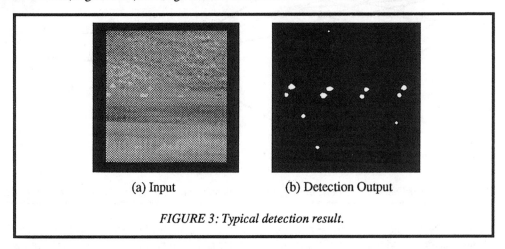

(a) Input   (b) Detection Output

FIGURE 3: Typical detection result.

3. HANDLING ANALOG WEIGHTS, NOISE AND NON-IDEAL COMPONENTS

Brief mention is made of this ANN application. It uses a Ho-Kashyap [9] ANN for pattern recognition. This ANN has the largest storage capacity and yields the best performance in the presence of input noise. Earlier work [10] showed how to select its design parameter σ to provide good results with different bit accuracies in the neuron values and the weights. We have recently modified tis algorithm to involve: training of the ANN on quantized data (of given bit accuracy), calculating weights quantized to a given bit accuracy, and preprocessing the training set to include nonideal input and hidden layer neuron responses. This new ANN synthesis technique yielded even better results. With N input neurons, we were able to store $M > 1.5N$ sets of input vector data (in general position) and to recognize all M input vector data with a $P_c > 95\%$ correct recognition rate. This is quite near the maximum storage possible [11] of $M = 2N$ (which only reached as $N \rightarrow \infty$, thus our results with N = 16 neurons are nearly ideal).

4. NEW NONLINEAR NEURON FUNCTIONS

Different neuron nonlinearities are well-known to significantly improve performance. We have considered a simple square-law detection nonlinear neuron transfer function. When this is used with complex-valued weights $\tilde{w}_{ij} = w_{ij} + jv_{ij}$, we find that each neuron describes a general hyperquadratic decision surface. For the case of three input neurons ($x_1, x_2,$ and $x_3 = 1$), the outputs for two hidden layer neurons are

$$f_1(\underline{x}) = \left\| \tilde{w}_{11}x_1 + \tilde{w}_{12}x_2 + x_3 \right\|^2, f_2(\underline{x}) = \left\| \tilde{w}_{21}x_1 + \tilde{w}_{22}x_2 + x_3 \right\|^2 \qquad (4)$$

and their decision surface $f_1 = f_2$ has the general form

$$ax_1^2 + bx_2^2 + cx_1x_2 + dx_1 + ex_2 + f = 0$$

Thus, such neuron nonlinearities can produce any piecewise hyperquadratic surface. They achieve this inherently and this can significantly reduce training time and the number of hidden layer neurons required, thus improving generalization and the performance of ANN classifiers.

ACKNOWLEDGMENT

The support of various aspects of this research by the Advanced Research Projects Agency (monitored by the Naval Air Warfare Center) and the Office of Naval Research is gratefully acknowledged.

I-234

REFERENCES

1) D. Casasent, "Large capacity neural nets for scene analysis", *Proc. SPIE*, Vol. 1709, pp. 18-32, April 1992.

2) D. Casasent, J.S. Smokelin and A. Ye, "Wavelet and Gabor transforms for detection", *Optical Engineering*, Vol. 31, No. 9, September 1992, pp. 1893-1898.

3) J. Daugman, "Uncertainty relation for resolution in space, spatial frequency, and orientation optimized by two-dimensional visual cortical filters", *J. Opt. Soc. Am.A*, Vol. 2, pp. 1160-1169, July 1985.

4) A. Bovik, M. Clark and W. Geisler, "Multichannel texture analysis using localized spatial filters", *IEEE Trans. on Patt. Anal. and Mach. Intell.*, Vol. 12, pp. 55-73, January 1990.

5) J. Daugman, "Complete discrete 2-D Gabor transforms by neural networks for image analysis and compression", *IEEE Trans. on ASSP*, Vol. 36, pp. 1169-1179, July 1988.

6) D. Casasent and J.S. Smokelin, "Neural net design of Gabor wavelet filters for distortion-invariant object detection in clutter", *Proc. SPIE*, April 1994.

7) M. Powell, "Restart procedures for the conjugate gradient method", *Mathematical Programming*, Vol. 12, pp. 241-254, 1977.

8) D. Casasent, A. Ye, J.S. Smokelin and R. schaefer, "Optical correlation filter fusion for object detection", *Optical Engineering*, April 1994.

9) B. Telfer and D. Casasent, "Ho-Kashyap optical associative processors", *Applied Optics*, Vol. 29, pp. 1191-1202.

10) D. Casasent and B. Telfer, "High capacity pattern recognition associative processors", *Neural Networks*, Vol. 5, No. 4, pp. 687-698, July-August 1992

11) T. Cover, "Geometrical and statstical properties of systems of linear inequalities with applications in pattern recognition", *IEEE Trans. eelec. Comp.*, Vol. EC-14, pp. 326-3234, June 1965.

Invited Paper to be presented on June 6, 1994 at 1994 International Neural Network Society Annual Meeting , San Diego, CA

MATHEMATICAL CONCEPTS UNDERLYING the FUNCTIONAL-LINK APPROACH

YOH-HAN PAO* and BORIS IGELNIK*

Case Western Reserve University
and AI WARE, Inc.
Cleveland, OH 44106

ABSTRACT

Mathematical concepts underlying the Functional-Link approach are described. Motivation, strategy, mathematical ideas and perspectives of the approach are discussed. It is shown that the Functional-Link approach is based on an integral representation of the function to be approximated and on evaluation of the integral by the Monte Carlo method. While the architecture of the Functional-Link allows the use of simple linear learning, the use of Monte Carlo technique provides an opportunity for accurate and efficient representation, with respect to the dimension of the input space. Thus the Functional-Link approach seems to be a reasonable compromise between complexity of learning and efficiency of representation. The approach opens new possibilities for enhancing the efficiency of representation by making use of methods of variance reduction known in the theory of the Monte Carlo method.

1. Introduction

This paper is in the nature of a qualitative discussion of the mathematics of the Functional-Link (FL) net approach to the task of function approximation, in the context of neural-net computing. The purpose of this discussion is

(a) to describe the motivation for developing the FL method,
(b) to state the essence of the strategy of the approach,
(c) to present a sketch of the mathematical proof of the universal approximation capability of the method,
(d) to relate the FL approach to the growing body of works establishing ties between mathematics and neural-net computing, and finally,
(e) to present some conjectures regarding the potential for future developments along the lines of the FL approach.

---
* Supported in part by the Air Force Office of Scientific Research (F33615-90-C-5944) and Wright Laboratory, Materials Directorate (F33615-87-C-5250).

These matters are covered in the following sections of this paper. In addition we present a summary of the results of computations which compare the performance of the FL net with that of the more traditional Backpropagation algorithm [1], demonstrating the vastly improved computational efficiency of the FL approach.

2. Motivation and Strategy

With the help of retrospection, it is possible to explain the motivation and strategy for developing the Functional-Link in simple terms.

To establish context and to provide focus, we concern ourselves with the task of function approximation using a single-hidden-layer Perceptron, the computation of which can be diagrammed as shown in Figure 1 (a). There are two layers of linear links, only the hidden layer nodes are nonlinear, and the nonlinear transformation is specified explicitly to be that of the sigmoidal activation function.

It is known that such a computational net can serve as a universal approximator of continuous functions from $K \in R^d$, K is compact, to R [2]-[4]. However in constructing the approximation, all the parameters β_j, $\mathbf{w}_j$, b_j need to be learned, and that can be a task of high computational complexity, so much so that the learning might not be achievable in practice.

Inspired by the work on high-order nets by Giles and his collaborators [5] and by the earlier work of Nilsson [6] on the benefits of nonlinear preprocessing of pattern space, one of the present authors (Y.-H. Pao [7]) suggested initially that not all of the hidden-layer nodes need be restricted to sigmoidal activation transformation, so that the network of Figure 1 (a) might be modified and augmented to be like that of Figure 1 (b). In addition, the appeal of the new nonlinear functional-links <u>lay in the fact that they did not have to be learned;</u> no parameters had to be learned.

This approach remained an *ad hoc* practice until experience was accumulated with use of the Random-Vector version of the Functional-Link (RVFL) net. An illustration of that net is shown in Figure 1 (c). It appears to be identical to that of Figure 1 (a), the conventional Perceptron, except for the critical differences that in the RFVL net the learning of the upper layer linear weights $\{\beta_j\}$ is separated from the formation of the functional links $g(\mathbf{w}_j\mathbf{x} - b_j)$, and <u>in fact none of the parameter values, $\{\mathbf{w}_j\}, \{b_j\}$, need be learned.</u> Accounts of use of that mode of the FL have been published [8]-[10]. The pragmatic result is that the approach is indeed efficient in learning.

The <u>objective </u>of our work is to increase computational efficiency without sacrificing accuracy. The <u>strategy</u> is to parametrize the functional form of the node transformation and to use a continuous distribution of that transformation, in contrast to a possibly large but discrete number of such nodes. The gain in efficiency comes about through use of statistical evaluation of the resulting integral over the space of hidden-layer parameters. Our work has led us to understand that we are not confined to the traditionally used sigmoidal activation function but can generalize our approach to a wide variety of functional forms. Correspondingly the term "Random-Vector" is to be interpreted quite generally in accordance with the context of the functional form of the link transformations.

Because the central point of our approach is evaluation of a multiple integral by the Monte Carlo method, all techniques for enhancing the efficiency of the Monte Carlo method (for example, through variance reduction) can be used for enhancing the efficiency of the RVFL net, after some modification.

3.   Sketch of Mathematical Proof

In this section we formulate our main result and give a sketch of a mathematical proof for it. The result, stated in the Theorem, says that (1) the RVFL net is a universal approximator and (2) gives an estimate of the error of representation, which tends to zero with $n \to \infty$ (n is number of basis functions) independent of d, dimension of input space. Although the rate with which the error tends to zero can be made sufficiently larger, we avoid optimization over the space of the internal parameters of the activation function, thus attaining a reasonable compromise between complexity of learning and efficiency of representation.

Below we give first a qualitative explanation of our proof and then more detailed description of each step of it.

In the first four steps of our proof we use a product $\prod_{i=1}^{d} g'(w_i(x - y_i))$ instead of sigmoidal function g. The former can be considered as an approximation of a d-dimensional rectangular window located at a point $y = (y_1, \ldots y_d)$ with a resolution determined by a parameter $w = (w_1, \ldots w_d)$. Thus in step 1, a continuous function f is represented as a limit of an integral over the space of parameter y with an integrand which is window transformation of f . Our idea is that summation over discrete set of parameters should be replaced by the integration over continuous parameter space. In accordance with this idea we add integration over parameter w in step 2. Therefore, after the first two steps, we can approximate our function by an integral over space of parameters (y, w). This integral representation gives us opportunity not to include parameters (y, w) in optimization procedure but to choose them randomly using Monte Carlo method to estimate the integral in step 3. An estimate of the error of representation, given by formula (2) of the Theorem, can be made in step 3 as well. Step 4 is a standard step: since we cannot expect to know the value of the function f at all of the points considered in the representation, we replace those values of f by indefinite coefficients which should be

found by optimization. In step 5 and step 6 we replace the window $\prod_{i=1}^{d} g'(w_i(x - y_i))$ by a single unit output $g\left(\sum_{i=1}^{d} w_i(x - y_i)\right)$, traditionally used in neural-net computing. This is done for the cosine-squasher g in step 5 and for any differentiable sigmoidal g in step 6.

The RVFL net is a d-dimensional function $\tilde{f}$ defined on the unit cube I^d, $I = [0;1]$

$$\tilde{f}(\mathbf{x}) = \sum_{j=1}^{n} \beta_j g(\omega_j \mathbf{x} - b_j),$$

where g is a differentiable sigmoidal function, $\beta_j \in R$, $\omega_j \in R^d$ are uniformly distributed in $[-W;W]^d$ for some $W > 0$ and are independent random vectors, $b_j = \omega_j \xi_j$, ξ_j are uniformly distributed in I^d and are independent random vectors, $j = 1, \ldots n$.

Following Leshno *et al.* [11], we denote $\omega = (n, \beta, \omega_1, \ldots \omega_n, b_1, \ldots b_n, W)$, where $\beta = (\beta_1, \ldots \beta_n)$ as a *parameter of the net* and $\Lambda = \{\omega\}$ as a set of all possible parameters of the net. Let $C(I^d)$ is a set of all continuous functions on I^d, $f_\omega = \tilde{f}$. Then our main result can be formulated as a theorem.

THEOREM

For any $f(\mathbf{x}) \in C(I^d)$ and any $\varepsilon > 0$ a RVFL net f_ω, $\omega \in \Lambda$, can be found such that

$$|f(\mathbf{x}) - f_\omega(\mathbf{x})| < \varepsilon, \quad \mathbf{x} \in I^d, \tag{1}$$

and with probability P arbitrarily close to 1

$$|f(\mathbf{x}) - f_\omega(\mathbf{x})| < C_{f,g,d,P} / \sqrt{n}, \quad \mathbf{x} \in I^d. \tag{2}$$

Thus (1) is a statement about the universal approximation capabilities of the RVFL net, while (2) is an estimate of the error of representation which, surprisingly independent of dimension d of the input space, tends to zero with $n \to \infty$, allowing us to avoid considerably the curse of dimensionality. Below we give a sketch of the proof divided in several steps.

STEP 1. We proved [12], that f can be represented in the form

$$f(\mathbf{x}) = \lim_{W_1 \to \infty} \ldots \lim_{W_n \to \infty} \int_{I^d} f(\mathbf{y}) \prod_{i=1}^{d} w_i g'(w_i(x_i - y_i)) d\mathbf{y},$$

where $d\mathbf{y} = dy_1 \ldots dy_n$.

This formula can be considered as a representation of the function f as a sum of d-dimensional windows $\prod_{i=1}^{d} g'(w_i(x_i - y_i))$ with very high resolution, determined by the high values of parameters $w_1, \ldots w_d$. The formula can be easily proved by changing variables y_i to $z_i = w_i(x_i - y_i), i = 1, \ldots d$.

STEP 2. Making use of the l'Hospital rule [13] we transform previous formula to the form

$$f(\mathbf{x}) = \lim_{w_1 \to \infty \ldots w_n \to \infty} \frac{1}{W^d} \int_D d\mathbf{w} \int_{I^d} f(\mathbf{y}) \prod_{i=1}^{d} w_i g'(w_i(x_i - y_i)) d\mathbf{y},$$

where $D = [0, W]^d$.

Thus function f is represented as a sum of windows with a continuous spectrum of locations and resolutions.

STEP 3. We evaluate the integral in STEP 2 using the Monte Carlo procedure[14][15]. This is the central point of our approach. It is well known [16][17] that the Monte Carlo method is one of the most efficient techniques in approximate calculation of multiple integrals. The essence of the method is that integral evaluation is made through calculating the average value of the integrand instead of evaluating a sum of elementary volumes. Thus the curse of dimension can be ameliorated. We then have

$$f(\mathbf{x}) \cong \frac{1}{W^d} \sum_{j=1}^{n} f(\xi_j) \prod_{i=1}^{d} g'(\omega_{ji}(x_i - \xi_{ji})),$$

where $\omega_j = (\omega_{j1}, \ldots \omega_{jd}), \xi_j = (\xi_{j1}, \ldots \xi_{jd}), j = 1, \ldots n,$

with estimate of accuracy given by formula

$$\left| f(\mathbf{x}) - \frac{1}{W^d} \sum_{j=1}^{n} f(\xi_j) \prod_{i=1}^{d} g'(\omega_{ji}(x_i - \xi_{ji})) \right| < C_{f,g,d,P} / \sqrt{n}.$$

STEP 4. We replace $f(\xi_j)/W^d$ by indefinite coefficients a_j, determined by optimization, thereby having formula

$$f(\mathbf{x}) \cong \sum_{j=1}^{n} a_j \prod_{i=1}^{d} g'(\omega_{ji}(x_i - \xi_{ji})).$$

STEP 5. Applying STEP 3 and STEP 4 to a special choice of g, the cosine-squasher function [18], we obtain a representation of the RVFL net in the form

$$f_\omega(\mathbf{x}) = \sum_{j=1}^{n} \beta_j g\left(\sum_{i=1}^{d} \omega_{ji} x_i - b_j \right)$$

with estimate of accuracy of representation of the function f by the RVFL net, given by formula (2). Vectors $\omega_j, j = 1, \ldots d$ are distributed in $[-W; W]^d$ instead of $[0; W]^d$ since we transform product of cosines into a sum.

Thus theorem is proved for this particular choice of sigmoidal function.

STEP 6. Approximating each <u>one-dimensional cosine-squasher</u> by a neural net with any fixed differentiable sigmoidal activation function and predetermined parameters $\{w, b\}$ [12][19] we complete the proof.

4. Relating the Functional-Link Approach to Recent Works on the Mathematics of Feedforward Neural Networks and Some Perspectives

Recently a number of papers have been published expanding on the results of [2]-[4] about the universal approximation capabilities of feedforward neural networks. Among them are [11][12],[19]-[28]. The main direction of these works is to determine the most general conditions on activation function so that one layer feedforward neural network (nonlinear Perceptron) can serve as a universal approximator for continuous functions with different domains and different metrics. At the same time some restrictions were made in order to facilitate the problem of learning. For example Chui and Li [26] proved that the nonlinear Perceptron can be taken in the form

$$\sum_{(\mathbf{i}, k) \in J} c(\mathbf{i}, k) g(\mathbf{i}\mathbf{x} + k),$$

where $\mathbf{i} \in Z^d, k \in Z,$

that is, the internal parameters (parameters of the hidden layer) can be chosen only from the set of integer numbers.

Hornik [27] proved that if g is analytic and nonpolynomial on the degenerate open interval B then the nonlinear Perceptron can be taken in the form

$$\sum_{j=1}^{n} \beta_j g(\mathbf{w}_j \mathbf{x} + b),$$

where $b \in B$ and $g^{(k)}(b) \neq 0, k = 0, 1, 2, \ldots,$

$\mathbf{w}_j \in A, j = 1, \ldots n$ and A should contain a neighborhood of the origin.

Leshno *et al.*[11] proved that if g is locally essentially bounded and not polynomial on the domain Ω then for every compact $K \in \Omega$, $f \in C(K)$ uniform universal approximator for f can be taken in the form

$$\sum_{j=1}^{n} \beta_j g\left(\lambda_j \, \mathbf{w}_j \mathbf{x} + \theta_j\right), \quad \lambda_j, \theta_j \in R, \quad \mathbf{w}_j \in A, \quad j = 1, \dots n,$$

and $A \subseteq R^d$ is such a set that there does not exist a nontrivial homogeneous polynomial vanishing on A.

The last result actually states that the number of internal parameters can be reduced considerably without losing the universal approximation feature. Thus it should be not surprising that in the Functional-Link net we have only two internal parameters(W and the fiducial probability P).

Another direction of research is represented ,for example, by papers of Barron [29], Jones [30],White [31]. In particular in Barron's paper it was shown that neural networks can serve as universal approximators for continuous functions more efficiently than traditional functional approximators, such as polynomials, trigonometric expansions or splines.The error of approximation tends to zero with the rate $O(1/n)$ for specific class of functions in the nonlinear Perceptron compared with $O\left(1/\sqrt{n}\right)$ in the RVFL net. But in the RVFL net we learn only external parameters, while in the nonlinear Perceptron all, external and internal, parameters are subjected to learning. Thus RVFL net seems to be a reasonable compromise between complexity of learning and accuracy (and therefore complexity) of representation.

It should be pointed out again that approach presented here allows us to use numerous techniques of variance reduction known in the approximation of multiple integrals by the Monte Carlo method. Thereby we will be able , after some modification, to reduce constant $C_{f,g,d,P}$ and, therefore, to enhance accuracy of representation without losing simplicity of learning.

5.   Explanation of the Use in Applications

The RVFL method has been used in several tasks by the present authors and their research collaborators, and by other researches, all with favorable results.

As an example, in principle the thickness of film created by Molecular Beam Epitaxy can be monitored through optical ellipsometry. Given the (complex) refractive index of the substrate and the film thickness, it is possible to calculate the values of the ellipsometry measurements. But even when given the requisite ellipsometry measurements, it is very difficult to obtain accurate estimation of the (complex) refractive index of the deposited film and of the film thickness. This task of inversion of a complex functional relationship $\left(\psi_0, \Delta_0, \psi_1, \Delta_1\right) \to \left(n, k, d_0, d_1\right)$ was carried out using a system of RVFL nets with good results. In this task the input variables are two pairs of ψ and Δ angular measurements and there are four outputs, n and k (real and imaginary parts of the refractive index respectively) of the film, and two film thicknesses d_0 and d_1. Each of the nets were trained with 10^4 training patterns (constituting a very sparse set of training patterns in 4D space) and excellent generalization was achieved.

An example of the excellent results attainable is shown in Figure 2, where we compare the refractive index, n, with the actual known values. The error is less than 0.1%.

Training for 10^4 training set patterns with a consultation system error of less than 10^{-4} could usually be achieved in about 6 hours on a SPARC 10 workstation, whereas training was never satisfactorily achieved with Backpropagation.

Our experience with the use of the RVFL approach in dealing with a number of other tasks confirms our judgement that this approach is indeed of high efficiency and of reasonable accuracy. Some features of those tasks and our experiences with those learning tasks are summarized in Table 1.

Table 1. Comparison of Learning Efficiencies of the Functional-Link (RVFL) and Backpropagation (BP) Methods.

TASK	RVFL				BP			
	Vari-ables	Training Patterns	Time	Itera-tions	Vari-ables	Training Patterns	Time*	Itera-tions
Ellipsometry	7	30,000	17 Hrs (SparcII)	5,000	7	30,000	Terminated after 24 Hrs	$> 10^4$
Character Recognition	5	2,000	6 Hrs (PC 486)	250	5	2,000	Terminated after 96 Hrs	$> 10^6$
Chemical Product Formulation	16	2,628	1 Hr (SparcII)	125	16	2,628	Terminated after 12 Hrs	$> 10^4$
Underwater Acoustics	31	385	5 Hrs (PC 486)	1000	31	385	Terminated after 50 Hrs	$> 10^5$

* Ended because of failure to achieve comparable accuracy

References

[1] D. E. Rumelhart, G. E. Hinton, and R. J. Williams, "Learning internal representations by error propagation,: in D. E. Rumelhart, and J. L. McClelland, "Parallel Distributed

processing:explorations in the microstructure of cognition, 1, *Parallel distributed processing*, **1** , pp. 318-362. Cambridge, MA: MIT Press, 1986.

[2] K. Funahashi, "On the approximate realization of continuous mappings by neural networks," *Neural Networks*, vol.2, pp.183-192, 1989.

[3] G. Cybenco, "Approximation by superposition of a sigmoidal function," *Mathematics of Control,Sygnals and Systems*, vol.2, pp. 303-314, 1989.

[4] K. Hornik, M. Stinchcombe, and H. White, "Multilayer feedforward networks are universal approximators," *Neural Networks*, vol.2, pp. 359-366, 1989.

[5] C. L. Giles and T. Maxwell, "Learning, invariance and generalization in higher-order neural networks," *Applied Optics*, vol.26, pp. 4972-4978, 1987.

[6] N. J. Nilsson. *Learning machines: Foundations of trainable classifying systems*. New York: McGraw-Hill, 1965.

[7] Y.-H. Pao. *Adaptive pattern recognition and neural networks*. Reading, MA: Addison-Wesley, 1989.

[8] Y.-H. Pao and Y Takefuji, "Functional-Link computing: Theory, system architecture, and functionalities," *Computer Magazine*, vol.3, pp. 76-79, 1991.

[9] Y.-H. Pao, S. Phillips, and D. J. Sobajic, "Neural-net computing and the intelligent control of systems," *International Journal of Control*, vol.56, pp.263-290, Taylor and Francis, Ltd., London, U.K., 1992.

[10] Y.-H. Pao, G. H. Park, and D. J. Sobajic, "Learning and generalization characteristics of the random vector Functional-Link net," *Neurocomputing*, vol.6, No. 1, Elsevier Press, 1994.

[11] M. Leshno, V.Ya. Lin, A. Pinkus, and S. Schocken, "Multilayer feedforward networks with nonpolynomial activation function can approximate any function," *Neural Networks*, vol.6, pp. 861-867, 1993

[12] B. Igelnik and Y.-H. Pao, "Efficient learning in the functional-Link net;explicit construction of one layer feedforward neural net and estimates of accuracy of approximation," *submitted to IEEE Transactions on Neural Networks*, 1993.

[13] W. Rudin. *Principles of mathematical analysis*. New York: McGraw-Hill, 1964.

[14] J. M. Hammersley and D. C. Handscomb. *Monte Carlo method*. London: Methuen, 1964.

[15] A. H. Stroud. *Approximate calculation of multiple integrals*. Englewood Cliffs, NJ: Prentice-Hall, 1971.

[16] J. F. Traub, G. W. Wasilkowski, and H. Wozniakowski. *Information based complexity*. New York: Academic Press.

[17] J. F. Traub and H. Wozniakowski, "Theory and applications of information-based complexity," in *1990 Lectures in Complex Systems, Santa Fe Institute*. Edited by Lynn Nadel and Daniel L. Stein. Reading, MA: Addison-Wesley, 1991.

[18] A. R. Gallant and H. White, "There exist a neural network that does not make avoidable mistakes," in *IEEE Second International Conference on Neural Networks*, pp. 1:657-664,San Diego: SOS Printing, 1988.

[19] B. Igelnik, Y.-H. Pao, "Additional perspectives on feedforward neural nets and the Functional-Link net," *Proceedings of IJCNN'93-Nagoya*, Japan, vol.3 pp.2284-2287, 1993.

[20] K. Hornik, M. Stinchcombe, and H. White, "Universal approximation of an unknown mappings and its derivatives using multilayer feedforward networks," *Neural Networks,* vol.3, pp.551-560, 1990.

[21] K. Hornik, "Approximation capabilities of multilayer perceptrons," *Neural Networks,* vol.4, pp.251-257, 1991.

[22] V. Kreinovich, "Arbitrary nonlinearity is sufficient to represent all functions by neural networks," *Neural Networks,* vol.4, pp.381-384, 1991.

[23] Y. Ito, "Approximation of continuous functions on R^d by linear combinations of shifted rotations of asigmoid function with and without scaling," *Neural Networks,* vol.5, pp.105-116, 1992.

[24] P. Cardaliaguet and G. Euvrard, "Approximation of a function and its derivative with a neural network," *Neural Networks,* vol.5, pp.207-220, 1992.

[25] V. Kurkova, "Kolmogorov's theorem and multilayer neural networks," *Neural Networks,* vol.5, pp.501-506, 1992.

[26] C. K. Chui and X. Li, "Approximation by ridge functions and neural networks with one hidden layer," *Journal of Approximation Theory,* vol.70, pp.131-141, 1992.

[27] K. Hornik, "Some new results on neural network approximation," *Neural Networks,* vol.6, pp.1069-1072, 1993.

[28] D. A. Sprecher, "A universal mapping for Kolmogorov's superposition theorem," *Neural Networks,* vol.6, pp.1089-1094, 1993.

[29] A. R. Barron, "Universal approximation bounds for superpositions of a sigmoidal function," *IEEE Transactions on Information Theory,* vol.39, pp. 930-945, 1993.

[30] L. K. Jones, "Constructive approximations for neural networks by sigmoidal functions," *Proceedings of the IEEE,* vol. 78, pp.1586-1589, 1990.

[31] H. White, "Connectionists nonparametric regression: Multilayer feedforward networks can learn arbitrary mappings," *Neural Networks,* vol.3, pp. 535-550, 1990.

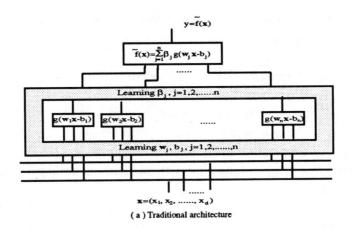

(a) Traditional architecture

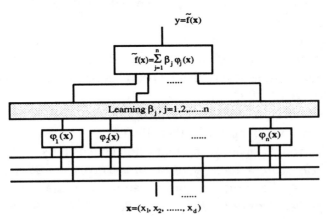

(b) General Functiional-Link, φ_j, j=1,2,...,n are nonlinear functions

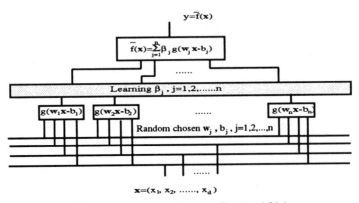

(c) Random vector version of the Functional-Link

Figure 1. Comparison of different architectures
of one-layer feedforward neural networks

I-246

Detecting Ground Clutter Contamination
of Weather Radar Data with Neural Networks

Richard Cornelius
National Center for Atmospheric Research[*]
Atmospheric Technology Division
Remote Sensing Facility
P. O. Box 3000
Boulder, CO 80307

Abstract

This paper describes the application of neural networks to the problem of recognizing ground clutter signatures in WSR-88D weather radars. The motivation is the fact that meteorologists can look at weather radar displays and very quickly recognize ground clutter with high accuracy. Current automatic recognition techniques that perform well rely on large maps that must be updated frequently for best results. An implementation of a local receptive field texture-based feature used in conjunction with standard Doppler moment estimates is described. When implemented with a neural network, the application of this feature set is shown to provide classification performance approaching that of meteorologists, without the high memory overhead or frequent operator intervention of current methods.

1. Introduction

A new generation of Doppler weather radars is currently being installed across the United States — the WSR-88D (Weather Surveillance Radar, 1988 Doppler). The Doppler capability improves the ability of meteorologists to forecast the weather and to more accurately estimate the amount of rain and snow falling on various watersheds. This helps provide more timely flood predictions and accurate water management.

The WSR-88D detects many different targets — for example, precipitation, insect and seed tracers in clear air, clouds, isolated point targets, and ground clutter. These WSR-88D systems have built-in ground clutter filtering which reduces artifacts introduced when radar energy bounces off of buildings and hills. This clutter suppression reduces contamination from stationary objects on the ground, but also causes real meteorological information to be lost when stationary storms are scanned. For this reason, the ground clutter filters are typically only used for the regions close to the radar where fixed ground clutter contamination is a serious problem.

As these systems are being installed across the country, another problem related to ground clutter has become more apparent. When the humidity and air density of layers of the atmosphere vary, the change in refractivity causes the radar beam to bend differently. Sometimes it bends up, which causes confusion about the height of storms.

---

[*] The National Center for Atmospheric Research is operated by the University Corporation for Atmospheric Research, under sponsorship of the National Science Foundation.

The much worse problem is that when the beam bends down it causes ground clutter echoes to appear further away than normal. This "anomalously propagated" (AP) radar beam is responsible for substantial distortions in precipitation estimates.

This AP looks different than "weather" when viewed on a display. Thus, meteorologists can account for the contamination when making their forecasts. Computer algorithms that calculate precipitation rates and give automatic warnings are not currently able to recognize the AP and remove it, so the automatic warning systems produce false warnings and inaccurate precipitation estimates. The problem of ground clutter contamination has been studied before [1, 2, 3], and other approaches to AP detection proposed [5, 6]. [1] compared fixed ground clutter with anomalously propagated ground clutter, and found that their spatial gradients are more similar to each other than either is to precipitation. Thus, we emphasize recognizing fixed ground clutter with the intent of extending the result to AP.

Previous work [3] on seasonally updated static maps of ground clutter residue provides the performance baseline for this analysis. These maps work well for detecting ground clutter residue that results from normal propagation of radar beams. The data storage and processing requirements of that approach motivate this effort to discriminate clutter residue from weather, using only the spectral moment estimates from a patch of range cells, near the cell that is being tested.

Previous work [4] using neural networks for discriminating ground clutter from weather used the spectral moment estimates from one range cell at a time as classification features. See Figures 1 and 2 for plots of SNR vs velocity that show the problem of discriminating clutter residue from weather. The previous result was that obvious weather (wind speed above 3 m/s) and obvious noise (returned signal to noise ratio below 0 dB) were readily detected. It was also found that high-signal, low-velocity weather could not be reliably discriminated from ground clutter. This paper extends the previous work by adding features based on spatial variability along a radar beam radial.

Weather SNR vs Velocity	Clutter Residue SNR vs Velocity
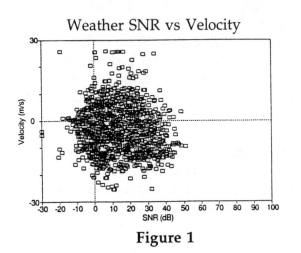	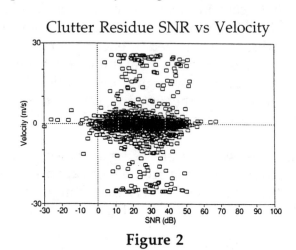
Figure 1	**Figure 2**

Artificial neural networks are used for this study based on the realization that a radar meteorologist examines multiple features like signal strength, Doppler velocity, and

Doppler spectrum width simultaneously (i.e. switching a display quickly between the different moment estimates) in order to make accurate classifications. This ability to combine the influence of multiple features simultaneously over large areas at a glance is difficult to match with current algorithms.

The neural network training process finds multidimensional discrimination thresholds that result in optimum classification performance. Neural networks provide good noise immunity, which is important when dealing with noisy measurements of physical phenomena. The networks can be adapted to varying conditions in the field by adding problematic data samples to the training set and retraining.

2. Radar Data Description

The data obtained from the radar are in the form of spectral moment estimates that are sampled in range, azimuth, and elevation. The data for this project are provided by the Mile High Radar (MHR), which is a prototype of the WSR-88D systems previously described. The range resolution of the Mile High Radar is 225 meters per range cell, and the beam width is just under 1°. The spectral moment estimates are used as follows:

   0th moment -- Signal (in dBM)
   1st moment -- Doppler velocity (in meters/second)
   2nd moment -- Doppler spectral width (in m/s)

This base data is written to 8mm tapes at the rate of about 300 megabytes per hour, or more than 7 gigabytes per day. A very small amount of the available data was used for this analysis. The data for the training and test sets were obtained from 360° scans at a single elevation. Each scan covers a disk with a radius of 148.5 km (660 range cells of 225 meters) with an azimuthal resolution of 1°. This results in a total of 237600 range cells of data per scan. Of the -20 to +80 dB dynamic signal to noise range, only range cells above +6 dB were used. The remainder were thresholded out so the network didn't need to learn about noise. Homogeneous data sets of 9 range cells were chosen at random from the 1000+ sets that passed the 6 dB minimum SNR threshold test.

The clutter training and test sets were obtained on 21 December 1992 (MHR tape M21Dec92) on a clear day (no precipitation) at an elevation of 0.5°. This scan has many range cells contaminated with fixed ground clutter residue with up to 55 dB signal to noise (after removing 55 dB of clutter with narrow bandwidth notch filters). The mountains return very strong echoes affected by weather because of blowing snow.

The weather training and test sets were obtained on 15 June 1992 (MHR tape M92303), on a stormy day with >30 dB SNR weather echoes. These weather samples were chosen because of an unusually large patch of near zero velocity precipitation, and also because there was no anomalous propagation visible in this scan. Other scans from the same day showed enough AP to contaminate the data sets.

The generalization performance of the trained neural network is then tested with samples from MHR tape M93240, which is a 0.5° scan obtained on 30 August 1993, that contain both heavy precipitation (scattered thunderstorms) and strong ground clutter.

The spatial returned power gradients have been proposed as a useful discrimination feature [1]. One measure of the spatial gradients is a quantity we call texture. The texture is a measure of smoothness based on the RMS value of the first difference between range cells separated by the specified spatial lag. Statistical analysis of the textures of both SNR and spectrum width provide significant discrimination between precipitation and fixed ground clutter. See Figure 3 for an example of the texture of spectrum width at lag 2 for weather and clutter residue. The texture of the Doppler velocities is not used because it was found to have very poor discrimination ability.

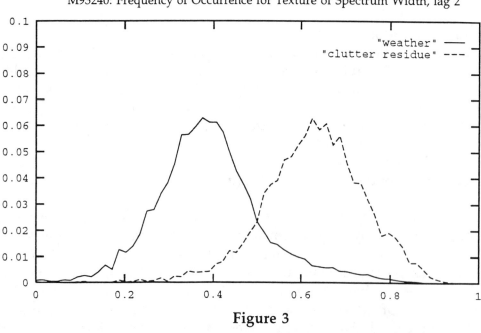

M93240: Frequency of Occurrence for Texture of Spectrum Width, lag 2

Figure 3

The results presented below were obtained by processing the spectral moment estimates from nine adjacent range cells along a radar beam radial to produce multiple statistical features which can then be used as inputs to a neural network. The features that are provided to the neural network are as follows:

    Mean Velocity (m/s)
    Mean Signal to Noise ratio (in dB)
    Texture of Signal to Noise (dB)
    Texture of spectrum width (m/s)

The mean and texture of SNR and spectrum width are calculated with range lags of 1, 2, and 3 range cells, and their discrimination ability is compared with that of single range cell features. All use a window size of nine range cells (2025 m) with the classification determined for the center cell.

3. Neural Network Architecture Description
The neural network to be used in this analysis is based on the Aspirin/MIGRAINES neural network simulator [7, 8]. Given a high level description of the desired network (number of inputs, outputs, hidden units, number of layers, and activation functions),

the Aspirin parser produces 'C' language code that can be trained and tested off-line and then integrated into a production system.

The network that was used has 3 inputs, 15 hidden units, and a single continuous output that is treated as binary. The activation function in the hidden and output layers was a sigmoid.

4. System Implementation

300 samples each of clutter residue and weather were used to form the training set. 1000 samples each of clutter residue and weather were used to form the test set. These samples were drawn from the same scans used to create the training set. Thus, the performance on this data set gives an indication of whether the training process has overfit the network to the training data set, but gives little indication of how the network will perform on different data sets. An additional 10,000 samples each of weather and clutter residue from M93240 were used as a cross-check to verify the generalization performance of the trained network.

5. Results

The occurrence frequency of correctly classified samples is shown in Table 1, with a value of 1.0 being perfect classification (relative to the clutter residue map [3]). The actual score is followed by the possible score (e.g. 270/300). Note the relatively poor generalization on the M93240 weather set for the network trained with the single range cell features as compared with the multi-cell based texture features.

		Clutter	Weather
Single range cell method	Training Set	.84 (251/300)	.94 (283/300)
	Test Set	.83 (763/915)	.94 (913/971)
	M93240 Set	.84 (8428/10000)	.74 (7403/10000)
Nine range cells, lag 1	Training Set	.90 (270/300)	.95 (285/300)
	Test Set	.89 (894/1000)	.94 (945/998)
	M93240 Set	.93 (9277/10000)	.88 (8779/10000)
Nine range cells, lag 2	Training Set	.91 (272/300)	.94 (283/300)
	Test Set	.89 (887/1000)	.94 (941/1000)
	M93240 Set	.91 (9129/10000)	.89 (8912/10000)
Nine range cells, lag 3	Training Set	.90 (271/300)	.94 (283/300)
	Test Set	.88 (876/1000)	.94 (945/1000)
	M93240 Set	.92 (9159/10000)	.88 (8843/10000)

6. Summary

A neural network trained with pure examples of weather and fixed ground clutter residue can correctly classify more than 85% of the samples from a mixed data set. The texture at lag 2 did the best job of correctly classifying weather that the network had not seen during training, and the texture at lag 1 was best at detecting clutter residue. A high rate of correct detection of weather is crucial since there is typically 5 to 10 times as much weather as clutter residue in cases of interest from the Mile High Radar.

Use of this texture feature combined with the seasonal clutter residue maps could be a useful addition to the WSR-88D radars. Future extensions to this work could include adding elevation and azimuth texture information, additional spectral moments, and maps of the terrain slopes that could be illuminated by anomalous propagation.

7. Acknowledgement

This work was prepared under contract to the WSR-88D Operational Support Facility of the National Weather Service and the Forecast Systems Laboratory of the National Oceanic and Atmospheric Administration.

8. References

[1] Sirmans, D., (1987). NEXRAD Suppression of Land Clutter Echo Due to Anomalous Microwave Propagation. National Severe Storms Lab, NOAA/ERL

[2] Andersson, T. (1993). Clutter Suppression with Doppler Radar - A Case Study. Proceedings of the 26th AMS Conference on Radar Meteorology, pp 241-244.

[3] Pratte, F., Gagnon, R., and Cornelius, R. (1993). Ground Clutter Characteristics and Residue Mapping. Proceedings of the 26th AMS Conference on Radar Meteorology, pp 50-52.

[4] Cornelius, R., and Gagnon, R. (1993). Artificial Neural Networks for Radar Data Feature Recognition. Proceedings of the 26th AMS Conference on Radar Meteorology, pp 340-342.

[5] Weber, M., Stone, M., and Cullen, J. (1993). Anomalous Propagation Associated with Thunderstorm Outflows. Proceedings of the 26th AMS Conference on Radar Meteorology, pp 238-240.

[6] Johnson, G., Smith, P., Nathanson, F., Brooks, L. (1975). An Analysis of Techniques for Dealing with Anomalous Propagation. Proceedings of the 16th AMS Conference on Radar Meteorology, pp 374-377.

[7] Leighton, R. (1992). The Aspirin/MIGRAINES Neural Network Software, Release V6.0. The MITRE Corporation.

[8] Wieland, A., Leighton, R., and Morgart, W. (1988). Aspirin for MIGRAINES. Proceedings of the 1988 International Neural Network Society Conference.

TEST AND EVALUATION OF NEURAL NETWORK APPLICATIONS
FOR SEISMIC SIGNAL DISCRIMINATION

Gagan B. Patnaik(*) and Thomas J. Sereno, Jr.

Science Applications International Corp.
10260 Campus Point Drive
San Diego, CA   92121

(*) Advanced Geocomputing Technologies
P.O.Box 927477
San Diego, CA   92192-7477

This report describes operational test and evaluation of two neural network applications that were integrated into the *Intelligent Monitoring System (IMS)* for automated processing and interprepation of regional seismic data. Also reported is the result of a preliminary study on the application of neural networks to regional seismic event identification. The first application is for initial identification of seismic phases (*P* or *S*) recorded by 3-component stations based on polarization data and context. This neural network performed 3-6% better than the current rule-based system when tested on data obtained from the 3-component IRIS stations in the former Soviet Union. This resulted in an improved event bulletin which showed that the number of analyst-verified events that were missed by the automated processing decreased by more than a factor of 2 (about 10 events/week). The second operational test was conducted on the neural network developed by MIT/Lincoln Laboratory for regional final phase identification (e.g., *Pn*, *Pg*, *Sn*, *Lg*, and *Rg*). This neural network performed 3.3% better than the rule-based system in *IMS* station processing. However, for the final phase identifications obtained after network processing (where data from all stations are combined), the gain dropped to about 1.0%. It is likely that this could be regained by using the neural network phase identification confidence factors in the network processing. Finally, our preliminary study on the application of neural networks to identify regional seismic events on the basis of *coda* shape gave about 80% accuracy on data recorded at GERESS. In general, the neural network classifier utilized the *coda* decay rate which was lower for the earthquakes than it was for the explosions, although there was substantial overlap.

Reference: Patnaik, Gagan B., Thomas J. Sereno, Jr. and Richard D. Jenkins. "Test and Evaluation of Neural Network Applications for Seismic Signal Discrimination", Tech. Report: PL-TR-92-2218 (II), Phillips Laboratory Directorate of Geophysics, Air Force Materiel Command, Hanscom Air Force Base, MA   01731-5000, 28 September 1992.

PLASMA SHAPE RECOGNITION IN A TOKAMAK MACHINE.

Francesco Carlo Morabito
Università di Reggio Calabria
Dipartimento Ingegneria Elettronica e Matematica Applicata
Via E.Cuzzocrea,48, 89127 Reggio Calabria (Italy)
Tel.+39 965 875224 , Fax +39 965 875220

Abstract

Nonlinear system identification is one of the major topics of interest in today's neural network research. In this paper we present a special problem of great relevance in the context of nuclear fusion applications: the identification of the plasma boundary in a machine of the tokamak type from the knowledge of magnetic measurements provided by properly located sensors. The problem is not only solved by means of neural networks of different topologies and by introducing suitable criterion functions but also deriving an interpretation of the internal representation of the model. A careful analysis of this model can suggest important consideration about two problems of great interest in nuclear fusion research: the fault tolerance and the minimisation of the number of sensors.

1.INTRODUCTION.

Plasma shape identification is concerned with extracting information about the geometry of a plasma column in the vacuum chamber of a tokamak machine by processing a set of measurements provided by sensors located in the proximity of the chamber walls. As a result, it can be considered a pattern recognition problem.

The tokamak is by far the most common experimental device in nuclear fusion research based on the concept of magnetic confinement. The axisymmetric configuration here analysed is the ASDEX Upgrade [1], however the methods proposed are appliable to other than the considered machine. On the other hand, for the ASDEX-U case several results of identification, by means of other methods, are currently available [2] and useful for comparative analyses. Axisymmetric plasma column are usually described by a number of parameters which can be related to one another.

In the special case of a circular plasma with high aspect ratio the number of parameters defining the equilibrium is restricted to three[3].Furthermore, these conditions enable us to derive formulae describing the equilibrium without knowing the profiles of current and pressure in the plasma cross-section. We have already treated this case with very good results[4,5]. In the more difficult, but also more practically relevant, case of *elongated* plasmas , the number of parameters needed to satisfactorily describe the equilibrium is larger, but always finite. In addition, we have not at our disposal analytic solutions of the equilibrium equations and some relevant parameters are related to the actual current density distribution inside the plasma. Once selected the parameters of interest, the aim of each possible identification procedure is to derive approximate expressions relating shape parameters to measurements. In order to control in real time the evolution of a discharge, the estimation of the parameters has to be carried out in a matter of *ms*. For this reason a neural network (NN) approach seems appealing. The use of NNs for sensory processing presents at least three advantages:

i) the functional form relating the set of plasma parameters to the measurements is defined by the NN model and is implicitly non linear;

ii) a proper topology of NN allows to easily recover parameters linearly related to the measurements;

iii) the regression model can be obtained off-line by means of a proper database and once trained the NN can work in real time. The problem under study is equivalent to that, commonly encountered in computer vision, of approximating a surface from noisy and sparse data [6]. Indeed, we treat an *inverse problem,* ill-posed in the ense of Hadamard that can be stabilized by proper techniques, in particular by restricting the class of solutions to those involving a limited number of free parameters.

The major aim of this work is not to show the reliability of the method, already demonstrated in [7,8], rather to understand how NNs models solve the problem, possibly exploiting the concept of regularization introduced in the model, either implicitly or explicitly.

2.PLASMA SHAPE IDENTIFICATION IN TOKAMAK DISCHARGES.

The identification of the plasma boundary starts from the knowledge of a set of measurements performed in properly located points by means of selected sensors. We limit ourselves to magnetic measurements, i.e. the poloidal flux and/or the θ component of the poloidal field. The sensors (flux loops and magnetic probes) are located along some contour of the vacuum chamber. Actually, in our simulations, the database of patterns needed for the training and the once-off linear regression is generated by means of an equilibrium code which represents a numerical model of the experiment. Each record of this database includes both the values of the physical quantities of interest and the related measurements. The criterion used to generate the sample cases is described in detail in [7], anyway the simulations are carried out aiming to cover the entire range of possible states of the physical system. For this reason a pseudo-random variation of the code parameters has been applied using the Monte Carlo method. A preliminary linear statistical analysis of the database was made by using *NAg* routines in order to compute mean values, standard deviations, maximum and minimum values, self-correlation and cross-correlation matrices and finally a linear regression model. Each record of the database consists in 31 flux measurements and 8 plasma parameters which are supposed well characterising the equilibrium. The only configuration of plasma here treated is the X-point one, where the plasma boundary is defined by the flux line where a null point of the field occurs. A model interpolating all of the possible configurations is now under study. The plasma parameters here considered are the following: R- and Z- coordinates of the X-point, Rxp,Zxp, poloidal beta, Bp,internal inductance, Li , major and minor radius, R,a, elongation, k, and triangularity, Tr. Fig.1 shows a typical lower X-point configuration, the arrangement of magnetic sensors and the geometric plasma parameters for the Asdex-Upgrade machine. It is worth noting, in view of the comments on section 3, that the *elongation* parameter is related to the *(Zup-Zlow/Rout-Rin)* ratio, and the *triangularity* is related to the difference *(R-Rxp)*. The poloidal beta and internal inductance of the plasma are determined by the current density profile.The uncertainties in estimating these parameters are related to the elongation: the prediction can be good for sufficiently elongated plasmas, as those considered in our database. In the next section we explain how to solve these problems using the multilayer NNs.

3.NEURAL REPRESENTATION AND SOLUTION OF THE PROBLEM.

The neural network model that we use is the multilayer feedforward one with a hidden layer of neurons with sigmoidal activation functions and a linear output layer. The number of inputs and outputs is fixed by the problem as formulated in sect.2. The number of hidden neurons is related to the number of cases of the training dataset (700), to the required generalization capabilities measured by means of a test dataset (300 cases), and finally to the complexity of the non linear mapping to be interpolated. In principle one can improve the approximation capabilities of the model increasing the number of terms of the series expansion : this strategy is not appropriate if the number of free parameters of the model is not related to the number of constraints (size of the dataset). Because we use a learning procedure based on gradient descent, a global minimum is unlikely to be found: the local minima generally reached can be consistent with the training data but not always with the actual problem. By considering a fixed network size (in our case 31x12x8), one can ask for the number of training samples required to achieve good generalization. The theoretical response is given by the Vapnik-Chervonenkis dimension (VCdim) [9]. One can roughly relate VCdim to the number of weights of the input-hidden layer in the case of hard-limiting nonlinearities. Our dataset size is larger than the number of weights of the entire network; however, this number seems less than of what required from a theoretical viewpoint. Neverthless, we have found good performance in solving our problem. A cross-validation like technique is here applied to avoid overtraining of the data. The results of the identification procedure are reported in Tab.I.

The reasons of the good performance of the NN model can be related to the regularization techniques implicitly introduced in the model that indeed reduce the effective number of free parameters of the network [10]. First of all, specifying the network architecture introduces *per se* some degree of regularization. Furthermore, by using sigmoidal nonlinearities the degree of smoothness of the solution space is high. *A priori* knowledge of the problem allows to introduce some other constraints, in such a way reducing the ill-posedness of the inverse problem. In this paper, for example, we show that the introduction of a direct link between input and output has a very beneficial effect. Indeed, the accuracy of the estimation of the plasma parameters is better than what given by a standard

NN(see Tab.I). In addition, the linear regression can be preliminarily carried out via statistical analysis, and then the learning step reduces to the determination of only the deviation from the linear behavior[5]. This can be accomplished by a reduced size NN with a hidden layer of only 8 neurons. It is worth noting that this can also reduce the run time of the network in the forward-only operation. The learning algorithm we have used is the standard backpropagation with learning rate, η , starting from η =1, and then decreasing to avoid oscillation around the minimum. The reduction of η is also related to a proper scheduling of the momentum term.

The effect of the introduction of a linear term can easily be understood by analysing the pattern of the weights of two NNs (with and without direct connections). Figs. 2[*] and 3[*] show the so called Hinton diagrams for the trained NNs.We can interpret these maps by considering three kind of hidden neurons (HNs): i) feature detection HNs, ii) fine tuning HNs, iii) features correlating HNs [5]. In short, some HNs detect a special feature in the pattern of input, other HNs tune the estimate inside the *class* selected by feature detection HNs. Finally, features correlating HNs learn relationships among output parameters: let us consider,for example, HN12 in fig.2. HN12 activates high values of elongation, which generally implies low Zxp. Furthermore, HN12 drives very low values of triangularity which derive from Rxp>>R. In the case of fig.3, the linear term is devoted to the feature detection process and to some extent to the features correlating process. The fine tuning process is instead performed by the nonlinear HNs. It is clear that in presence of only negative small weights the activations of HNs are in any case very small as requested by the correction process. Figs. 4[*] and 5[*] show the patterns of activations for two sample cases of the test dataset: the described effect of the regularization via introduction of *a priori* knowledge is here evident.

	Rxp	Zxp	Bp	Li	R	a	K	Tr
Standard NN	2.95	3.42	3.31	2.49	1.97	2.19	2.62	3.47
NN + Linear Connections	2.92	2.41	2.19	2.84	1.40	1.15	2.08	2.15

Tab.I - *Accuracy of the estimation in terms of full scale percent error.*

4.FAULT TOLERANCE VS. MINIMISATION OF THE SENSORS.

Taking a glance to fig.2, it is not surprising that the corresponding NN is anything but fault tolerant. HNs 8 and 12,and inputs 2, 21, 26, 27 and 30 embodies most of the information concerning the plasma position and shape. The NN with direct linear connections is more fault tolerant w.r.t. the HNs having assigned to the linear term the task of rough classification of the input vectors. The role of the inputs is yet unchanged, so the resulting NN is not fault tolerant w.r.t. the inputs. On the other hand, one of the main objectives of current research in tokamak reactor concerns the minimisation of the number of sensors to be placed inside the chamber. In addition, it would be of high interest to have some hints which lead to the possible exclusion of terms not sufficiently significant from the regression. The analysis of the latter point of view is carried out in [7]. In this work we would like to add some considerations about the fault tolerance. In particular, by a proper choice of the error function to be minimised during the training step, one can discourage the learning algorithm from seeking solutions with very large weights and/or weights which deviate too much from the initial weights [11]. Actually, we attempt again to regularize the solution by adding a term to the cost function related to the complexity of the model [12]. In our case we choose the following error function:

$$E\left(\underline{\underline{w}}\right) = \frac{1}{N_0} \sum_{j=1}^{N_0} \left(y_j\left(\underline{\underline{w}}\right) - d_j\right)^2 + \frac{\ell}{2} \sum_{i=1}^{N_w} w_i^2$$

where the first term is the standard squared error criterion measuring the distance from the data, and the ℓ parameter is a small positive constant used to decide the relative importance of the two terms. This technique is simply embodied in the standard backpropagation algorithm and is commonly known as *weight decay method*. The resulting trained NN exhibits better fault tolerance properties (see fig.6[*])

also continuing to perform the estimation satisfactorily. A more skilled technique that ensures uniform fault tolerance is reported in [13]. The rationale behind this approach is to make all HNs equally relevant in the NN. In short, in the NNs framework it is possible to select strategies which match the problem we have to cope with.

5.CONCLUDING REMARKS.

We have discussed the equilibrium parameters recovery for non-circular plasmas using NNs. Special emphasis is given to the interpretation of the NN representation of the problem. Indeed, a suitable analysis allows to exploit NN approach to deal with the problem of optimal selection of magnetic measurements. In particular, a method has been proposed which allows to manage in the training phase the trade-off between fault tolerance and minimisation of sensors. In our case the introduction of measurement noise can be viewed as a regularizing effect in the same way as the one described in sect.4. This improves the robustness of the NN and consequently its fault tolerance.

ACKNOWLEDGMENT

The work reported in this paper was performed under the direction of Professors E. Coccorese and R. Martone, to whom I am very indebted. The author also thank M. Campolo and F. Cirianni for technical assistance.

REFERENCES.

[1] The ASDEX-Upgrade Team, in Fusion Technology, Proc.13th Symp. Varese, Pergamon,Press, 1, 203, 1984.

[2] P.J.McCarthy, "An Integrated Data Interpretation System for Tokamak Discharges",Ph.D.dissertation, Cork University, 1992.

[3] V.S.Mukhovatov, V.D.Shafranov, "Plasma Equilibrium in a Tokamak", Nuclear Fusion, vol.11,p.605,1971.

[4] E.Coccorese, R.Martone, and F.C.Morabito,"On line Plasma Shape Identification in a Tokamak Reactor via Neural Network,Proc.V Italian Workshop on Neural Networks, Word Scientific Publishing, p.349,1992.

[5] F.C.Morabito,"Multilayer Neural Network for Identification of Non-Linear Electromagnetic Systems.", WCNN, I-428, Portland, OR, 1993.

[6] M. Bertero, T.A. Poggio, and V. Torre, "Ill-Posed Problems in Early Vision", Proc. of the IEEE, vol.76, no.8, 1988.

[7] E.Coccorese,R.Martone,and F.C.Morabito,"Identification of Non-Circular Plasma Equilibria using a Neural Network Approach", paper submitted to Nuclear Fusion, Jen 1993.

[8] J.B.Lister, and H.Schnurrenberger,"Fast Non-linear Extraction of Plasma Equilibrium Parameters using a Neural Network Mapping", Nuclear Fusion, vol. 31, 7, p. 1291, 1991.

[9] V.N. Vapnik and A.Y. Chervonenkis, "On the uniform convergence of relative frequencies of events to their probabilities", Theory of Probability and its Applications, vol.16, p.264, 1971.

[10] J. Mao, and A.K. Jain, "Regularization Techniques in Artificial Neural Networks", WCNN, Portland, OR, IV-75, 1993.

[11] S.J. Hanson and L.Y.Pratt, "Comparing Biases for Minimal Network Construction with Back-Propagation", in D.S. Touretzky ed., *Advances in neural Information Processing Systems 1*, p.177, Morgan Kaufmann, 1989.

[12] T.Poggio and F.Girosi, "A Theory of Networks for Approximating and Learning", A.I.Lab. Memo, 1140, MIT, 1989.

[13] C.Neti,M.H.Schneider, and E.D.Young, "Maximally Fault Tolerant Neural Networks", IEEE Trans. on NN,vol.3,1, 1992.

*   Figures drawn by Neural Works Professional II / Plus, Neural Ware Inc. Pittsburg, PA.

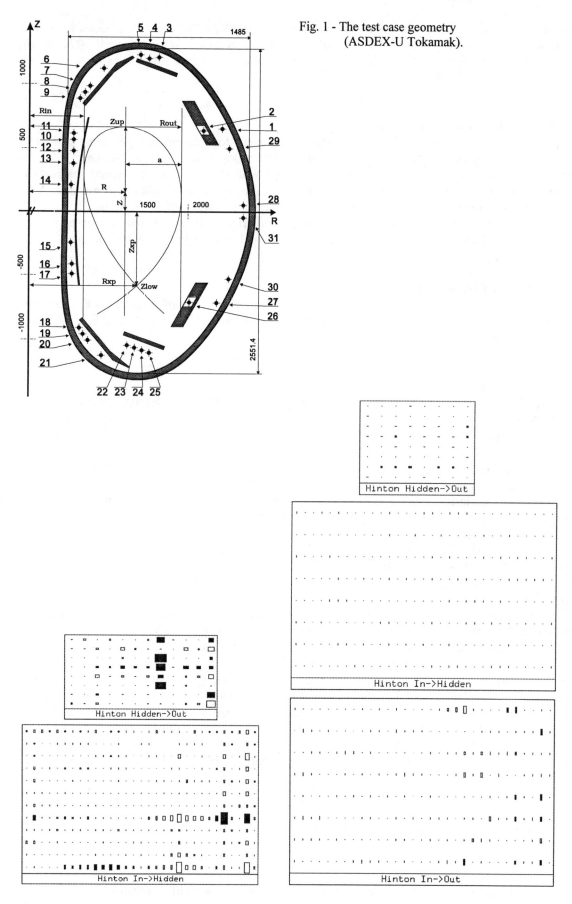

Fig. 1 - The test case geometry
(ASDEX-U Tokamak).

Fig. 2 - Pattern of weights for the standard NN

Fig. 3 - Pattern of weights for the modified NN

I-258

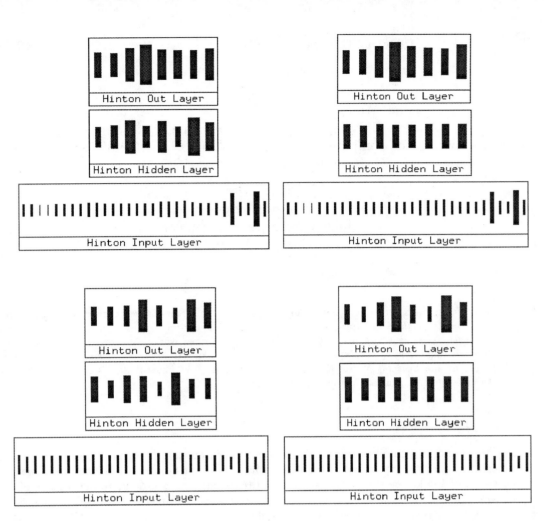

Fig. 4 - Patterns of activations for two test cases (standard NN).

Fig. 5 - Patterns of activations for the same cases (modified NN).

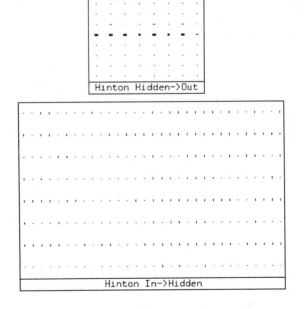

Fig. 6 - Pattern of weights for a *fault tolerant* NN

Robust Multispectral Road Classification in Landsat Thematic Mapper Imagery

James Wolfer
Andrews University
Department of Computer Science
Berrien Springs, MI 49104-0360

James Robergé
Department of Computer Science
Illinois Institute of Technology
Chicago, IL 60616

Thom Grace
Department of Computer Science
Illinois Institute of Technology
Chicago, IL 60616

Abstract

Classifying roads in remotely sensed imagery has been the target of several contemporary research efforts. Detecting these features in Landsat Thematic Mapper imagery is of consequence for both agricultural assessment and urban planning. In our previous work, we showed that road pixels could be distinguished by their spectral signatures in raw Landsat TM images using both Multilayer Perceptrons and Learning Vector Quantization. In this work we show that this ability is robust in harsh environments and seasonal lighting variations.

1   Introduction

In 1982, the Landsat 4 satellite was placed into sun-synchronous orbit around the earth. A primary instrument on board this spacecraft is the Thematic Mapper, or Landsat TM. This instrument scans a ground swath of 185 km perpendicular to the satellite's direction of motion, and is capable of resolving ground areas of 30m on each side. The data is sampled and quantified to 8 bits/pixel in each of seven spectral bands, ranging from infrared to visible light.

While primarily designed for agricultural assessment, Landsat TM imagery has been used to monitor the environmental impact of human activities including the analysis of urban and population growth, identifying regions for urban development, and monitoring the environment. Several of these activities require the identification of human-imposed structural features, such as roads, residential areas, and industrial developments. Changes in these features over time can be used to estimate urban growth, verify census data, and monitor the accuracy of cartographic databases. Since these features are typically smaller than the resolution of the Landsat TM, they present a challenging problem for computer vision systems.

Road discrimination is a subset of the problem of land-cover discrimination. Several investigations have addressed road surface classification either independently, or as a part of a more general classification scheme [1–5]. These efforts focus upon the use of knowledge-based systems to identify roads. The resulting systems typically organize the identification process into several distinct phases, including: image filtering, segmentation, applying inference rules to identify candidate road pixels, using geometric inference to extract linear features, and final candidate classification. The principal focus of these efforts is the identification of structures with linear geometry as potential roads.

These knowledge-based systems perform well at the expense of a considerable investment in the development of application specific image manipulation software, geometric analysis routines, and expert rule bases.

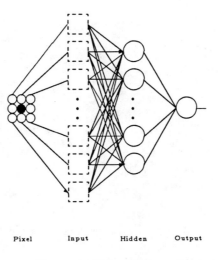

Pixel   Input   Hidden   Output

Figure 1: Network Organization

2   Neural Network Road Identification

Several investigators have explored the strengths and weaknesses of neural networks when specifically applied to remotely sensed land use analysis. Benediktsson et al. [6], McClellan et al. [7], Ryan et al. [8], and more recently Heermann et al. [9] all describe the application of neural networks to Landsat TM imagery. The consensus of these investigations indicates that the neural networks perform at a level competitive with other statistical techniques.

In our previous work [10, 11], we showed that road pixels could be distinguished by their spectral signatures in raw Landsat TM images using both Backpropagation trained Multilayer Perceptrons (MLP) and Learning Vector Quantization (LVQ1 and LVQ2). Since the MLP performed slightly better (see Tables 1 and 2) we chose it for this investigation.

The fact that a single pixel exceeds the width of most roads coupled with the observation that many man-made materials (and some natural phenomena) exhibit spectral characteristics which are similar to roads [9] suggests that the classification process should include not only the spectral characteristics of the pixel being classified, but the spectral characteristics of the surrounding pixels as well. Including this contextual information allows the neural network to train on both the spectral and spatial properties of the input data.

Figure 1 shows a neural network organization that incorporates both spectral and spatial information. In this diagram each box represents seven fully-connected input units, one for each of the seven spectral bands corresponding to a pixel in the Landsat TM image. Based upon an empirical analysis [10, 11], we chose to use twenty hidden units for this investigation.

The training set was selected from Landsat TM imagery for the Joliet, Illinois region shown in Figure 2. This mid-summer image contains a representative selection of both rural and urban features including agricultural, residential, and industrial areas. As a consequence, it also contains a variety of surfaces, ranging from small rural roads to multi-lane highways. The training set consisted of 552 samples selected to incorporate a wide range of image features. A battery of tests, including histogram analysis, Euclidean cluster analysis, Sammon mapping, and Principal Component Analysis were applied to the training set [11]. These tests show no readily apparent segmentation boundaries.

The neural network was trained on a Silicon Graphics Iris 4D 210 and applied to the image. Figure 3 shows the resulting classification. Tables 1 and 2 presents a summary of the results based on manually classifying a typical region [10, 11]. Note that highway intersections and residential streets are identifiable. It should be observed that of the pixels that were misclassified as roads, many were rectangular surfaces such as building roofs and parking lots or areas in which small clouds intersected roads. There

Figure 2: Landsat TM: Joliet, Illinois

were also several pixels that represent private roads, such as driveways. These were considered to be non-road pixels for these experiments.

An analysis of the networks weight and activation values revealed that the network developed a representation for contrast. Figure 4 shows a Hinton diagram of the weights associated with the inputs from the classified pixel (center) and its nine neighbors. In this diagram the columns represent the seven spectral bands, with the last column being the weights to bias units. There is one row per hidden unit. Generally, excitatory weights in the pixel being classified have the corresponding weights in their neighbors inhibited. The relatively large weights in bands one through three (visible) and band four (infrared) suggest that these bands may be the most significant for extracting road information, which is consistent with human observation [12]. For a more detailed analysis of both performance and internal representation see [11].

3 Harsh Environments

A useful technique should also be robust. In this section, we describe the results of applying the neural network to structural environments requiring both spectral and spatial information. We demonstrate that, with minor adaptation, it has the ability to perform under adverse conditions, such as metropolitan Chicago, and to be able to perform across geographic regions and seasonal illumination variations.

3.1 Metropolitan Chicago

Figure 5 shows the Landsat TM image of metropolitan Chicago, Illinois. Since a single pixel typically represents a non-homogeneous ground surface region, the detection of features in a densely homogeneous image is much more difficult for both man and machine. Figure 6 shows the results of applying the neural network trained on the Joliet region to metropolitan Chicago. While most major highways are detected in this image, the ability of this network to discriminate fine detail in this region is limited.

Figure 3: Joliet Roads

To determine if the network's ability to incorporate spatial information depends upon the size of the neighborhood, the spatial context was extend to include both a pixel and its 24 closest neighbors. This network was then retrained using the 552 Joliet sample set and applied to both the Joliet and the metropolitan Chicago images. Figure 7 shows the resulting classification for the Chicago image. Note that major roads are visible, concrete roads and airport runways are not classified as roads, and most buildings are not misclassified as roads.

3.2   Regional Variations

Another indication of robustness is the performance across images from different times and regions. Differences in terrain can render the classifier ineffective (e.g. shadows cast by mountains obscuring road surfaces). Lighting differences can also play a role. While the Landsat TM is sun-synchronous, seasonal changes can cause dramatic differences.

Figure 8 shows the Landsat TM image for Washington D.C., a November image. Note that the overall level of illumination reaching the sensor array is diminished. Since the training set was selected from the Joliet image, we would like to have the Washington D.C histogram match that of Joliet. Applying the standard image processing routine of histogram matching [13–15] results in the image shown in Fig. 9. Histogram matching is an approximation, in this case the resulting image is both brighter than the original and is closer to the Joliet prototype.

Figure 10 shows the result of classifying this histogram matched image with the Joliet trained neural network. The classifier retains much of its ability to distinguish surface properties such as airports and buildings, as well as to reasonably classify road surfaces. Note that the misclassification of the river water can be attributed to density variations visible in Figure 9 possibly due to deposits in the water. This is similar to the phenomenon described by Heerman, who showed that clouds could alias as urban features in Landsat TM imagery [9].

Table 1: Road Identification Results

Architecture	Pixels	Correct	Omitted	%
MLP	791	707	84	89.4
LVQ1	791	596	195	75.4
LVQ2	791	596	195	75.4

Table 2: Non-Road Identification Results

Architecture	Pixels	Correct	Incorrect	%
MLP	15593	15276	317	98.0
LVQ1	15593	14793	800	94.9
LVQ2	15593	14793	800	94.9

4 Summary

We have demonstrated a neural network that can be trained to discriminate road surfaces based on spectral information from raw Landsat TM imagery. This system performed at a level consistent with other contemporary approaches, and has the advantage of operating on raw input without the need to establish an application-specific rule base. Equally important, this discrimination capability is robust across metropolitan regions and seasonal illumination variations.

References

[1] S. W. Wharton, "A spectral-knowledge-based approach for urban land-cover discrimination," *IEEE Transactions on Geoscience and Remote Sensing*, vol. GE-25, May 1987.

[2] F. Wang and R. Newkirk, "A knowledge-based system for highway network extraction," *IEEE Transactions on Geoscience and Remote Sensing*, vol. 26, September 1988.

[3] J. Ton, J. Sticklen, and A. K. Jain, "Knowledge-based segmentation of landsat images," *IEEE Transactions on Geoscience and Remote Sensing*, vol. 29, March 1991.

[4] J. V. Cleynenbreuge, S. Osinga, F. Fierens, P. Suetens, and A. Oosterlinck, "Road extraction from multi-temporal satellite images by an evidential reasoning approach," *Pattern Recognition Letters*, vol. 12, 1991.

[5] Z. Aviad and P. C. Jr., "Road finding for road-network extraction," in *IEEE Conference on Computer Vision and Pattern Recognition*, 1988.

[6] J. A. Benediktsson, P. H. Swain, and O. K. Ersoy, "Neural network approaches versus statistical methods in classification of multisource remote sensing data," *IEEE Transactions on Geoscience and Remote Sensing*, vol. 28, July 1990.

[7] G. McClellan, R. DeWitt, L. Hemmer, N. Matheson, and O. Moe, "Multispectral image-processing with a three-layer backpropagation network," in *Proceedings of the International Joint Conference on Neural Networks*, June 1989.

[8] T. Ryan, P. Sementilli, P. Yuen, and B. Hunt, "Extraction of shoreline features by neural nets and image processing," *Photogrammetric Engineering and Remote Sensing*, vol. 57, p. 947, July 1991.

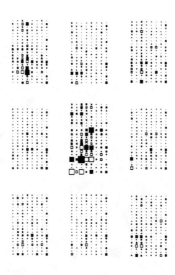

Figure 4: Hinton Diagram: Input to Hidden Units

[9] P. D. Heermann and N. Khazenie, "Classification of multispectral remote sensing data using a back-propagation neural network," *IEEE Transactions on Geoscience and Remote Sensing*, vol. 30, pp. 81–88, Jan. 1992.

[10] J. Wolfer, J. Robergé, and T. Grace, "A comparison between backpropagation and learning vector quantization for multispectral road classification in landsat thematic mapper imagery," in *Proceedings of the Fifth Midwest Artificial Intelligence and Cognitive Science Society Conference*, Apr. 1993.

[11] J. Wolfer, *A Multispectral Approach to the Identification of Human-Imposed Structures in Landsat Thematic Mapper Imagery Using Artificial Neural Networks*. PhD thesis, Illinois Institute of Technology, 1993.

[12] R. ichiro Taniguchi and E. Kawaguchi, "Road network extraction from landsat tm image," in *IEE Third International Conference on Image Processing and its Applications*, July 1989.

[13] R. C. Gonzalez and R. E. Woods, *Digital Image Processing*. Reading, MA: Addison Wesley, 1992.

[14] W. Niblack, *An Introduction to Digital Image Processing*. Englewood Cliffs, NJ: Prentice Hall, 1986.

[15] A. K. Jain, *Fundamentals of Digital Image Processing*. Englewood Cliffs, NJ: Prentice Hall, 1989.

Figure 5: Landsat TM: Metropolitan Chicago, Illinois

Figure 6: Metropolitan Chicago, 9 Neighbors

Figure 7: Metropolitan Chicago, 24 Neighbors

Figure 8: Landsat TM: Washington D.C.

Figure 9: Washington D.C. Histogram Matched

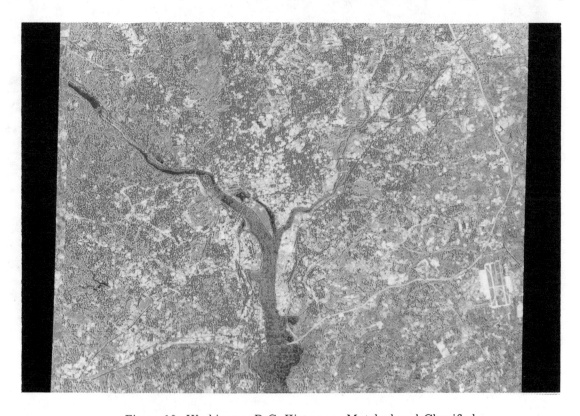

Figure 10: Washington D.C. Histogram Matched and Classified

Neural Network Based Chemical Sensor Systems for Environmental Monitoring

Paul E. Keller, Richard T. Kouzes, Lars J. Kangas
Pacific Northwest Laboratory
P.O. Box 999, K1-87
Richland, WA 99352
pe_keller@pnl.gov, rt_kouzes@pnl.gov, lj_kangas@pnl.gov

Compact, portable systems capable of quickly identifying contaminants in the field are of great importance when monitoring the environment. One of the missions of the Pacific Northwest Laboratory is to examine and develop new technologies for environmental restoration and waste management at the Hanford Site (a former Plutonium production facility). In this paper, three prototype sensing systems are discussed. These prototypes are composed of sensing elements, data acquisition system, computer, and neural network implemented in software and are capable of automatically identifying contaminants. The first system employs an array of tin-oxide gas sensors and is used to identify chemical vapors. The second system employs an array of optical sensors and is used to identify the composition of chemical dyes in liquids. The third system contains a portable gamma-ray spectrometer and is used to identify radioactive isotopes. In these systems, the neural network is used to identify the composition of the sensed contaminant. With a neural network, the intense computation takes place during the training process. Once the network is trained, operation consists of propagating the data through the network. Since the computation involved during operation consists of vector-matrix multiplication and application of look-up tables (activation function), unknown samples can be rapidly identified in the field.

1. INTRODUCTION TO THE PROBLEM

Enormous amounts of hazardous waste were generated by more than 40 years of plutonium production at the Hanford Site. There are an estimated 1700 waste sites distributed around the 560 square miles of southeastern Washington that comprise the Hanford Site.[1] This waste includes nuclear waste (e.g., fission products), toxic chemical waste (e.g., carbon tetrachloride, ferrocyanide, nitrates, etc.), and mixed waste (combined radioactive and chemical waste). The current mission at the Hanford Site is environmental restoration and waste management.

As part of this mission, the Pacific Northwest Laboratory is exploring the technologies required to perform environmental restoration and waste management in a cost effective manner. This includes the development of portable, inexpensive systems capable of real-time identification of contaminants in the field. The objective of our research is to demonstrate the potential information processing capabilities of the neural network paradigm in sensor analysis. The initial portion of this effort involves the development of three prototype systems, where each prototype combines a sensor array with a neural network. These prototypes are discussed in this paper.

Artificial neural networks (ANNs) are used in a wide variety of data processing applications where real-time data analysis and information extraction are required. One advantage of the neural network approach is that most of the intense computation takes place during the training process. Once the ANN is trained for a particular task, operation is relatively fast and unknown samples can be rapidly identified in the field.

2. SENSOR DATA ANALYSIS

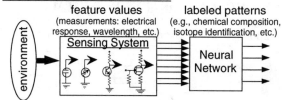

Figure 1. Sensor system combined with an ANN.

There are many real-time (rapid response) and remote sensing applications that require an inexpensive, compact, and automated system for identifying an object (e.g., target, chemical, isotope). Such a system can be built by combining a sensor array with an ANN. A generic system is shown in Figure 1.

The quantity and complexity of the data collected by sensor arrays can make conventional analysis of data difficult. ANNs, which have been used to analyze complex data and for pattern recognition, could be a better choice for sensor data analysis. A common approach in sensor analysis is to build an array of sensors, where each sensor in the array is designed to respond to a specific analyte. With this approach, the number of sensors must be at least as great as the number of ana-

This research was supported by the Northwest College and University Association for Science (Washington State University) under Grant DE-FG06-89ER-75522 with the U.S. Department of Energy.
Pacific Northwest Laboratory is operated for the U.S. Department of Energy by Battelle Memorial Institute under contract DE-AC06-76RLO 1830.

lytes being monitored. When an ANN is combined with a sensor array, the number of detectable analytes is generally greater than the number of sensors.[2]

A sensor array is composed of several sensing elements, where each element measures a different property of the sensed sample. Each object (e.g., target, chemical, isotope) presented to the sensor array produces a signature or pattern characteristic of the object. By presenting many different objects to the sensor array, a data base of signatures can be built up. From this data base, training sets and test sets are generated. These sets are collections of labeled patterns (signatures) representative of the desired identification mapping. The training sets are used to configure the ANNs. The goal of this training is to learn an association between the sensor array patterns and the labels representing the data.

When a chemical sensor array is combined with an automated data analysis system (such as an ANN) to identify vapors, it is often referred to as an artificial nose. Several researchers have developed artificial noses that incorporate ANNs for use in applications including monitoring food and beverage odors,[3] automated flavor control,[4] analyzing fuel mixtures,[5] and quantifying individual components in gas mixtures.[6] Several ANN configurations have been used in artificial noses including backpropagation-trained feed-forward networks, Kohonen's self-organizing networks, Hamming networks, Boltzmann machines, and Hopfield networks.

3. CHEMICAL VAPOR SENSOR SYSTEM

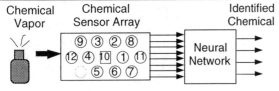

Figure 2. Chemical vapor sensing system.

The first prototype system, shown in Figure 2, identifies and quantifies chemicals vapors. It employs an array of nine tin-oxide gas sensors, a humidity sensor, and two temperature sensors to examine the environment. Although each sensor is designed for a specific chemical, each responds to a wide variety of chemical vapors. Collectively, these sensors respond with unique signatures (patterns) to different chemicals. During the training process, various chemicals with known mixtures are presented to the system. In the initial studies, the backpropagation algorithm was used to train the ANN to provide the correct analysis of the presented chemicals.

The nine tin-oxide sensors are commercially available Taguchi-type gas sensors obtained from Figaro Co. Ltd. (Sensor 1: TGS 109, Sensors 2 and 3: TGS 822, Sensor 4: TGS 813, Sensor 5: TGS 821, Sensor 6: TGS 824, Sensor 7: TGS 825, Sensor 8: TGS 842, Sensor 9: TGS 880). Exposure of a tin-oxide sensor to a vapor produces a large change in its electrical resistance.[7] The humidity sensor (Sensor 10: NH-02) and the temperature

sensors (Sensors 11 and 12: 5KD-5) are used to monitor the conditions of the experiment and are also fed into the ANN.

The prototyped ANN was constructed as a multi-layer feedforward network and was trained with the backpropagation of error algorithm by using a training set from the sensor data base.[8] The parameters used to train this ANN are listed in Table 1. This prototype was initially trained to identify 8 household chemicals: acetone, correction fluid (White Out), Duco cement, glass cleaner, isoproponal alcohol, lighter fluid, rubber cement (Naphtha and Hexane), and vinegar. Another category, "none", was used denote the absence of all chemicals except those normally found in the air. This resulted in 9 output categories from the ANN. Figure 3 illustrates the network layout.

Table 1. ANN Training Parameters

Type:	Backpropagation in batch mode
Architecture:	12-6-9 fccdforward
Activation:	Logistic
Learning Rate:	0.01
Momentum:	0.9
No. of Epochs:	15000

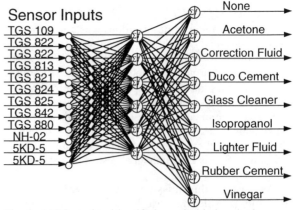

Fig. 3. ANN used to identify household chemicals.

During operation, the sensor array "smells" a vapor, the sensor signals are digitized and fed into a computer, and the ANN (implemented in software) then identifies the chemical. This identification time is limited only by the response of the chemical sensors, but the complete process can be completed within a few seconds. Figure 4 illustrates both the sensor response and the ANN classification of the system for a variety of test chemicals presented to the prototype.

4. OPTICAL SENSOR SYSTEM

The second prototype system, shown in Figure 5, employs an array of optical sensors and identifies the composition of chemical dyes in solution. Light is passed through the dye solution and into an array of seven optical sensors. Each optical sensor consists of a silicon detector covered by a narrow bandpass interference filter and is sensitive to a specific wavelength of

Sensor Values   ANN Output

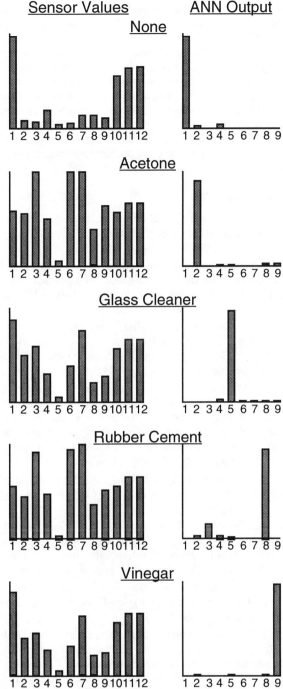

Fig. 4. Sample responses and ANN classifications. The numbers correspond to sensors and ANN outputs that are shown in Figure 3.

light in the visible and near-infrared spectrum. The output of each sensor provides an input to the ANN. By examining the absorption of the liquid at different wavelengths, the ANN is able to identify and quantify the dyes. Initial tests with this system have just begun.

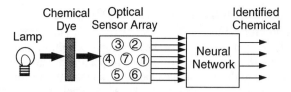

Figure 5. Optical sensor array system.

5. RADIATION SENSOR SYSTEM

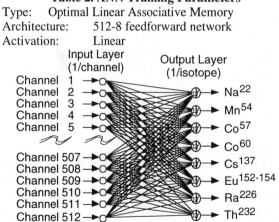

Figure 6. Gamma-ray spectrometer with ANN.

The third prototype system, shown in Figure 6, contains a portable gamma-ray spectrometer and is used to identify and quantify radioactive isotopes. The gamma-ray spectrometer consists of a sodium iodide (NaI) crystal, photomultiplier, pulse height analysis circuit, and multichannel analyzer. There are 512 channels of data produced by the spectrometer. All 512 channels are fed into the ANN. The ANN is configured as an optimal linear associative memory[9] where each neuron implements a linear activation function. There is a single processing layer in the ANN where the number of output neurons is equal to the number of isotopes being identified (8 in this case). This ANN is shown in Figure 7 and described in Table 2.

One feature of this approach to gamma-ray spectral analysis is that the whole spectrum is used in the identification process instead of individual peaks in the spectrum. For this reason, it is potentially more useful for processing data from lower resolution gamma-ray spectrometers (like those employing NaI detectors).[10]

Table 2. ANN Training Parameters
Type: Optimal Linear Associative Memory
Architecture: 512-8 feedforward network
Activation: Linear

Fig. 7. ANN used to identify radioactive isotopes.

This system was trained with the spectra of 8 radioactive isotopes: Sodium (Na^{22}), Manganese

(Mn^{54}), Cobalt (Co^{57}), Cobalt (Co^{60}), Cesium (Cs^{137}), Europium ($Eu^{152-154}$), Radium (Ra^{226}), and Thorium (Th^{232}). The spectra of these isotopes are illustrated in Figure 8. Operation consists of presenting an unknown sample to the system, generating a gamma-ray spectrum, and passing the spectrum to the ANN which produces a classification of the unknown sample. The values on the output neurons are proportional to the quantities of each radioactive isotope found in the sample. Figure 9 illustrates an example of the classification and quantification of a sample composed of equal amounts of $Cobalt^{60}$ and $Cesium^{137}$. The resulting classification by the ANN correctly identifies the composition of the sample as being composed of equal quantities of both isotopes.

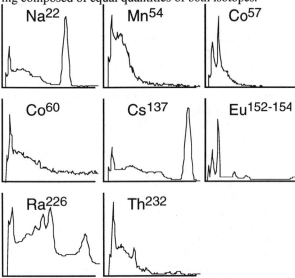

Figure 8. Gamma-ray spectra of each isotope in the training set. There 512 channels per spectrum.

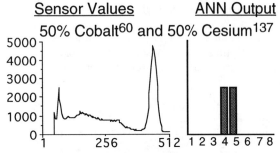

Figure 9. Sample spectra and ANN classification.

6. DISCUSSION

Three prototype systems that employ neural networks for sensor analysis were presented. The first prototype combined an array of tin-oxide gas sensors with a neural network and was used to identify common household chemicals. The second prototype combined an array of optical sensors and was used to identify chemical dyes in solution. The third prototype combined a gamma-ray spectrometer with a neural network and was used to identify radioactive isotopes.

Initial results demonstrated the pattern recognition capabilities of the neural network paradigm in sensor analysis. These prototypes also demonstrated several advantages of this approach over conventional analytical techniques including compactness, portability, real-time analysis, and automation. Further work will involve comparing neural network sensor analysis to more conventional techniques, exploring other neural network paradigms, and evolving the preliminary prototypes to field systems.

7. REFERENCES

1. Barbara Goss Levi, "Hanford seeks short- and long-term solutions to its legacy of waste," *Physics Today*, vol. 45, no. 3, pp. 17-21, March 1992.

2. B.S. Hoffheins, Using Sensor Arrays and Pattern Recognition to Identify Organic Compounds, MS-Thesis, The University of Tennessee, Knoxville, TN, 1989.

3. J.W. Gardner, E.L. Hines and M. Wilkinson., "Application of Artificial Neural Networks to an Electronic Olfactory System," *Measurement Science and Technology*, vol. 1, no. 5, pp. 446-451, May 1990.

4. T. Moriizumi, T. Nakamoto and Y. Sakuraba, "Pattern Recognition in Electronic Noses by Artificial Neural Network Models," in *Sensors and Sensory Systems for an Electronic Nose*, J.W. Gardner and P.N. Bartlett, Eds. Amsterdam, The Netherlands, Kluweer Academic Publishers, 1992, pp. 217-236.

5. R.J. Lauf and B.S. Hoffheins, "Analysis of Liquid Fuels Using a Gas Sensor Array," *Fuel*, vol. 70, pp. 935-940, August 1991.

6. H. Sundgren, F. Winquist, I. Lukkari and I. Lundström, "Artificial Neural Networks and Gas Sensor Arrays: Quantification of Individual Components in a Gas Mixture," *Measurement Science and Technology*, vol. 2, no. 5, pp. 464-69, May 1991.

7. product literature from Figaro USA, Inc., P.O. Box 357, Wilmette, IL 60091, USA.

8. D.E. Rumelhart, G.E. Hinton and R.J. Williams, "Learning internal representations by error propagation," in *Parallel Distributed Processing: Explorations in the Microstructures of Cognition. Vol. 1: Foundations*, D.E. Rumelhart and J.L. McClelland, Eds. Cambridge, MA, MIT Press, 1986, pp. 318-362.

9. Teuvo Kohonen, in *Self Organization and Associative Memoriy*, third ed., New York, NY, Springer-Verlag, 1989.

10. P. Olmos, J.C. Diaz, J.M. Perez, G. Garcia-Belmonte, P. Gomez, V. Rodellar, "Application of neural network techniques in gamma spectroscopy," *Nuclear Instruments and Methods in Physics Research*, vol. A312, pp. 167-173, 1992.

An Automated System for Environmental Monitoring Using a Neural Network Classifier*

Michael J. Larkin and **Michael P. Perrone**
Prometheus Inc.
21 Arnold Ave.
.Newport, RI 02840
larkin@dam.brown.edu
mpp@cns.brown.edu

Abstract

We present a novel method of detecting changes, such as erosion or deforestation, from time sequential pairs of remote images. After preprocessing the images and obtaining a difference image, we use a neural network-based system to adaptively threshold the difference image and resolve areas of pixel intensity with a terrain classifier which combines information in the original images. The result is that we detect precisely the types of changes in which we are interested, without being "distracted" by changes due to noise or natural within-terrain variability of pixel intensity.

1 Introduction

The objective of our research has been to design an automated system for detecting changes in the environment, based upon time sequential remote sensor images of the same area. Our approach was to apply image processing techniques to the original digital images in order to compensate as much as possible for errors due to registration (i.e., a given pixel in the second image does not necessarily correspond to the pixel in the identical position in the first image), as well as variations in pixel intensity due to illumination changes, clouds, and certain natural variabilities inherent in certain types of terrain that are not of importance for analysis purposes. At the same time, it is recognized that preprocessing will not necessarily correct all of these errors, so the system was designed to be robust to errors due to registration or pixel intensity variability, as well as other types of noise.

The basic premise is to take the two images and subtract one from the other, creating a difference image. Ideally, any non-zero pixel intensities in the difference image would indicate that a change in the environment had occurred. Of course, the problems of registration and other types of noise will also result in contributions to the difference image. Also, there will be certain types of changes in the image that are characteristic of certain types of textural terrain (trees or grasses, for instance) that are not of much interest. Thus, the problem is to determine what features in the difference image are representative of meaningful changes in the environment such as deforestation, erosion or pollution; and which features are due to noise or various pixel intensity variabilities.

Our system runs a window over the difference image and computes the average pixel intensity within the window. If the pixel intensity exceeds a given threshold, the corresponding windows in the two preprocessed original images are compared, through the use of a neural network based terrain classifier. As described in the following sections, this system determines if any change has occurred in the window based on the results of the terrain classifier.

---

*This work was performed under Army Contract No. DACA76-93-C-0005, under subcontract to SEA CORP.

2 Overview of Algorithm

This section outlines the basic steps of our algorithm. These steps are detailed in subsequent sections.

- Preprocessing - image registration and normalization

- Generate smoothed difference image

- For each pixel above a fixed threshold, classify the texture in the corresponding regions from both preprocessed images.

- A pixel is interesting if the texture classifications differ.

- If the ratio of interesting to uninteresting pixels in a given region is greater than some threshold, then the region is interesting.

3 Image Preprocessing

This section describes the image preprocessing required to prepare the images for input into our classification algorithm. The goal of preprocessing is to bring the images into registration and to match local pixel intensities. We achieved this with the methods outlined below. We propose to improve upon these preliminary algorithms in our future work.

Before the system can find the changes in two images (we will designate an image obtained at time t_1 by A, and B will be used to denote the subsequent image of the same scene at time t_2), the images must be preprocessed to account for atmospheric effects, differences in illumination, and differences in angle, perspective or altitude of the sensor.

The first problem that the system will have to correct for is *registration*. Two images A and B are said to be in registration if every pair of pixels (a_{ij}, b_{ij}), where a_{ij} is a pixel in the image A and b_{ij} is a pixel with the same coordinates in image B, correspond to the same point in the actual scene. If the sensor is not at precisely the same location when both images are observed, then this will not be the case. Thus, we need to find a mapping $T : B \longmapsto B$, where B is the transformation of B that is in registration with A.

One possible technique, which we would explore in future work, is to take advantage of characteristics that would appear in most of the images that we are likely to observe. Features such as roads, buildings, rivers, borders of fields, in addition to well defined geologic features such as cliffs and ridges, form a set of "landmarks" within an image. These features are readily found by an edge detector algorithm. In this manner, we would reduce A and B to "skeleton" images, consisting only of the edges. Then, we would apply a deformable template matching algorithm to find the values of scale, translation and rotation necessary to bring the images into registration.

In practice, many of the differences between the two images will be a result of sun angle and orientation and overall illumination [Townshend, 1981], and thus these differences must be compensated for to enable the changes of interest to be detected. We examined normalization techniques that could be employed to solve this problem. For example, the pixel intensities of each image could be scaled and translated to fit into the same range, or we could match the mean pixel intensities of the images and scale the image intensities such that both images have the same variance in pixel intensity about the mean. While these global measures may be sufficient, it may be necessary to consider methods which vary over the image if the illumination is uneven or from different directions. It may also be useful to employ smoothing algorithms to remove noise from the images. We have investigated the optimal combination of these techniques to achieve image normalization in various settings.

4 Difference Image

One fundamental aspect of our algorithm is the difference image which, in its simplest form, is the difference between pixel intensities in the overlapping regions of the two images. If the images are identical, the difference image should be all zeroes. We impose the constraint that the algorithm should be insensitive to the order in which the two images are presented; therefore we define the difference image as

$$D_{ij} = |A_{ij} - B_{ij}| \tag{1}$$

where A_{ij} and B_{ij} are the pixel intensities in the ith row and jth column of images A and B respectively. which are invariant to swapping A and B. Note that it is necessary to map the images onto the same grid if any rotation or scale transform is used for registration..

4.1 Image Smoothing

Difference images tend to be very noisy due to natural variations from image to image and "ghosting" that can occur due to poor registration. In order to ameliorate these problems, we convolve our difference images with a square indicator function. Thus the pixel value in the smoothed image is given by

$$D_{ij}^{\text{smoothed}} = \sum_{lm} k(i - l, j - m)D_{lm} \tag{2}$$

where $k(l,m) = 1$ when $|l| < r$ and $|m| < r$ and $k(l,m) = 0$ otherwise. We can adjust the amount of smoothing by varying the radius, r, of k. We can also approximate Gaussian smoothing by repeated convolution with k. Note also, that this smoothing can be applied to the classifications given by the texture classifiers.

4.2 Pixel Intensity Histograms

The amounts of smoothing and thresholding needed for accurate detection of variations within and image can be suggested by examining histograms of the pixel values of a given image. We consider several histograms in our work, including histograms of the preprocessed, differenced, and smoothed images. In the preprocessed images, one typically has a smooth distribution of pixel values which is nearly identical for both images. Smoothing over difference images results in a main peak in the pixel histogram corresponding to zero difference and minor peaks in the tails corresponding to more interesting pixels (See Figure 1).

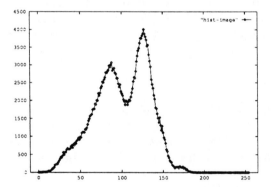
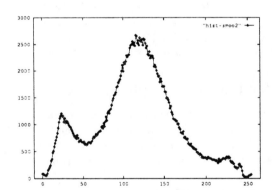

Figure 1: The left graph shows the pixel histogram of an original image. The right graph shows the pixel histogram of the smoothed difference image. Useful information is contained in the tails of the histogram on the right.

5 Adaptive Thresholding

At the heart of our environmental change detection algorithm is the an adaptive threshold which uses information from both the difference image and the texture classifier to filter out uninteresting regions if the images.

5.1 Algorithm for Detecting Differences Between Images

Heuristically, the decision criterion for flagging a windowed region as being interesting can be stated as the following steps:

- If the average pixel intensity (API) of the difference image is very low, the difference is not significant/interesting.

- If the API is high and the classifications from the different images are different, the difference is significant/interesting.

- If the API is high but the classifications are identical, the difference is not significant.

We can improve on the algorithm by including a sensor fusion center (neural net based) that will learn when the three inputs are significant and when they are not. Thus we can make our thresholding nonlinear and more robust.

Ideally, we could say that for all pixels $d_{ij} \in D$, a level of intensity greater than zero indicates a change in the scene being imaged. However, due to natural variations in the imaged objects or terrain a certain level of pixel variability is expected. It is therefore necessary to identify an optimal threshold to determine whether a pixel value in the difference image is significant. Thus we determine these values from images where known changes have been located and quantified.

Because it is unlikely that every region of the image will have the same optimal threshold, we used a neural network approach to identify various classes of regions from a given corpus of images for which different optimal thresholds can be determined. The neural networks were used to determine which "terrains" in the difference image are interesting and which are not. Once the neural networks are trained, they are used to determine what terrain class a particular region belongs to. With this information, we can use a specialized threshold to determine whether an observed variation in the images is of significance. The advantage to this approach is that the system is more sensitive where small variations are important and less sensitive where they are not, resulting in more changes being detected and less "false alarms", or changes that are detected which have no importance.

5.2 Pattern Classifiers

In this section, we consider two image classifiers designed to identify terrain/texture class in subregions of the images: The KNN algorithm and the RCE algorithm. The training input to these algorithms are hand-labelled subimages of a fixed size. We refer to these subimages as data vectors. We note here that there exist other neural network algorithms which could also be applied to the task of terrain classification.

5.2.1 The KNN Algorithm

The K Nearest Neighbor (KNN) algorithm [Duda and Hart, 1973] functions by finding the nearest K vectors from our previously labelled data vectors to a new data vector for which the terrain class is unknown. The classification for the new data vector is given by the majority class of the K nearest neighbors. The distance metric that is used in this algorithm is not essential and for high dimensional spaces an l_1-norm is generally sufficient as well as being faster to calculate than most other norms.

5.2.2 The RCE Algorithm

The Reduced Coulomb Energy (RCE) algorithm [Reilly et al., 1982] creates networks of neurons with bounded activity function given by

$$n_i(\vec{x}) = 1 - \Theta(||\vec{x} - \vec{m}_i||_2 - t_i) \tag{3}$$

where $\Theta(\cdot)$ is a step function. Thus the activity of RCE neuron i is 1 if the input is within a distance t_i of $\vec{m}_i$ and 0 otherwise. Classification of a given input is determined by choosing the class of memories which has the largest total output. In its simplest version, the RCE algorithm builds a network in the following manner. For each memory in the data set:

1) If the classification is correct, make no changes.

2) If the network activity is zero (no classification), add a new neuron to the network using the new memory as the center and set the neuron's threshold equal to the distance to the nearest memory of a different class.

3) If the classification is incorrect or confused,

    a) Shrink the thresholds of the neurons which were responsible for the error.

    b) Pass the memory through the network again.

This process is repeated until the network stops changing. Given enough resources, this algorithm can cover arbitrarily complex boundaries between classes for a deterministic classification problem.

6 Application

A version of the algorithm described in the preceding sections was implemented on real satellite images and the results are presented below. From Figure 2 and Figure 3, it can be see that our algorithm can correctly select the regions of a photographed area which have changed.
This research is continuing. Further results will be presented at the conference on different images and more elaborate classification algorithms.

References

[Duda and Hart, 1973] Duda, R. O. and Hart, P. E. (1973). *Pattern Classification and Scene Analysis.* John Wiley, New York.

[Reilly et al., 1982] Reilly, D. L., Cooper, L. N., and Elbaum, C. (1982). A neural model for category learning. *Biological Cybernetics*, 45:35–41.

[Townshend, 1981] Townshend, J. (1981). *Terrain Analysis and Remote Sensing.* George Allen & Unwin.

Figure 2: The left image shows a small region of an real satellite photograph. The right image shows the same region slightly offset to simulate registration error and with an orchard and field "planted" where houses and streets exist in the left image.

Figure 3: The left image shows the difference image and the right image shows the regions which where labelled "interesting" by our algorithm.

NEURAL NETWORK BASE KNOWLEDGE FUSION IN HYBRID LUNG NODULE DETECTION SYSTEM

Y. S. Peter Chiou[*+], Y. M. Fleming Lure[*] and Panos A. Ligomenides[+]

[*] Caelum Research Corporation, 11229 Lockwood Dr., Silver Spring, MD 20901
(TEL) 301-593-1748, (FAX) 301-593-3951
[+] Cybernetic Research Lab., Electrical Eng. Dept., University of Maryland, College Park, MD 20742
E-mail: yunshu@eng.umd.edu+*

ABSTRACT This paper describes the system architecture of a neural knowledge base object detection system and its application to detection and classification of lung cancerous pulmonary radiology. The configuration of the system includes the following processing phases: (1) pre-processing to enhance the figure-background contrast; (2) Morphology based quick selection of object suspects based upon the most prominent feature of nodules; and (3) feature space determination and neural network based suspect fields reduction; (4) neural network based knowledge fusion processing and final classification of suspect fields. Preliminary results from applying the approach to lung cancerous pulmonary radiology are also reported.

INTRODUCTION

This paper describes a Computer Aided Diagnosis (CAD) system to improve the accuracy and speed of object recognition in cluttered and noisy image background. The detection method is based on a hybrid scheme of digital processing, artificial neural network and knowledge base synergy. This CAD tool was applied to early detection of cancerous pulmonary nodule from X-ray films. The resulting hybrid system is a robust, effective and fast Hybrid Lung Nodule Detection (HLND) System.

Dr. Doi and Dr. Giger of University of Chicago have shown that it is feasible to automate the lung nodule detection process by searching in the chest X-ray radiography for a set of preselected nodule features [1,3-7]. With the help of modern digital computer and digital image processing techniques, some success was obtained in detecting cancerous lung nodules from digitized chest X-ray images [2,8,9,11,12,14]. Although the digital processing method correctly identified cancerous nodules, it also misidentified numerous other anatomic structures in the image as nodules.

Because of its capability to learn and generalize from training data set, artificial neural network (ANN) techniques are chosen for identifying true-positive objects from false-positive objects. By applying ANN techniques, the common features of the true-positive objects and the false-positive objects can be extracted and used internally by the ANN in the learning process to differentiate between true and false objet of interest. The generalization property of the ANN suggest that the features learned from the training data set would be applicable to other data set as well. By applying knowledge base techniques, the logic reasoning of experts' knowledge for making diagnosis can be extracted and simulated during the detection process. In the case of lung nodule detection, the patient's age, history of smoking, living environment and work condition may become a factor in deciding true-positives nodules. Hybrid Lung Nodule Detection (HLND) system is developed to integrate the robustness of ANNs and the logic reasoning of knowledge bases with the accuracy of digital signal/image processing techniques in a single system for shape feature analysis in diagnostic radiology which provides accurate and robust recognition performance [2]. The configuration of the HLND system includes the following processing phases: (1) pre-processing to enhance the figure-background contrast; (2) Morphology based quick selection of nodule object suspects based upon the most prominent feature of nodules; and (3) feature space determination and neural network based suspect fields reduction; (4) neural network based knowledge fusion processing and final classification of nodule suspect fields.

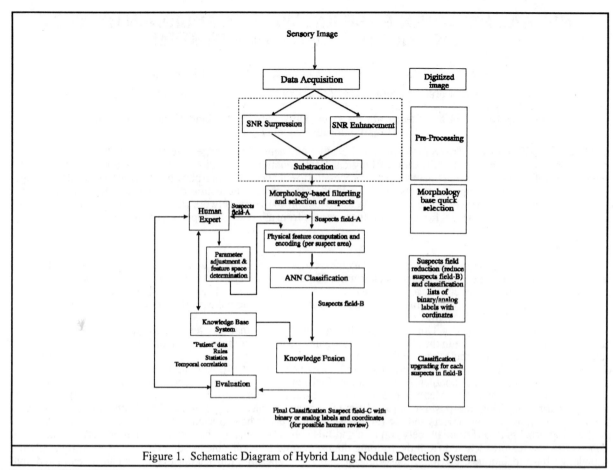

Figure 1. Schematic Diagram of Hybrid Lung Nodule Detection System

PRE-PROCESSING

The digital chest images were obtained from Georgetown University Hospital and University of Maryland Medical Center. Each pulmonary radiograph was digitized to 2000x2048x12 bits where each pixel represents about 200 μm for a 14" by 17" X-ray film. The images are later reduced to 500x512x12 bits image for computational speed. Each image contains at least one nodule. The actual location of the nodules are verified by computed tomography (CT) or followed by radiologists. A reversible contrast scaling function is used to obtain a constant contrast between lung space and the mediastinum area. Potential nodule information in a pulmonary radiograph is enhanced by a differential technique which subtracts a nodule suppressed image (through a median filter) from a nodule enhanced image (through a matched filter with a spherical profile) [2-7]. This approach would reduce the camouflaging anatomic background in

The difference image, containing nodule-enhanced signal, is used for morphology base selection processing phase.

Median filtering technique tends to smooth the image by reducing the intensity of abnormal phenomenon (e.g., nodules). Match filtering technique, which correlates the energy of the synthetical nodule image with original image, generates resultant images with highest values corresponding to the locations of potential nodule suspects. The matched filtering technique involves fast Fourier transform, complex conjugate, and complex matrix multiplication with assumption of white noise (i.e., Fourier spectrum equals constant). A spherical profile with diameter of 3mm is used to synthesize the ideal nodule images. Substraction between the resultant images derived from median and matched filtering methods further enhanced the nodule-to-background information [5].

MORPHOLOGY BASED QUICK SELECTION

A search algorithm is applied for quick (pre-) selection of all possible nodule suspects based mainly upon the most prominent feature of nodule - the spherical profile [4,5,6]. The difference image is processed by locally-adaptively area extraction process using edge and gray value tracking with different gray values for thresholding and morphological operations. It provides an initial determination of features, arising from nodules and arising from anatomic background. Circularity and effective radius of the segmented image block are evaluated at different thresholding levels to determine the location and the size of the nodule suspects. All the suspect areas (blocks) with dense area (high gray values) equivalent to 3 mm of diameter or less are captured in 32x32x12 bits images for further evaluation.

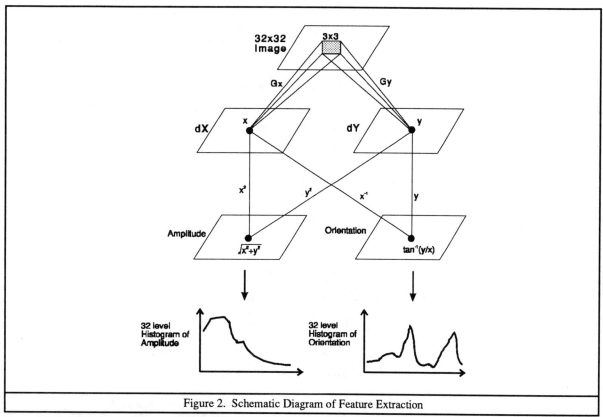

Figure 2. Schematic Diagram of Feature Extraction

Neural Network Based Suspect Reduction

A supervised back-propagation (BP) neural network classifier is developed for classification of each anatomic structure. The BP ANN classifier contains four layers. Input layer consists of 64 neurons corresponding to combination of both amplitude and orientation bins of marginal distribution. Two hidden layers contains 128 and 64 neurons, which are chosen as multiple of eight (pre-determined anatomic structure classes) since the properties of each class are desired to be coded evenly within the network. Finally a two-neuron output layer is used to classify either true positive or false positive nodules.

Since BP ANN **learned** from the training data set presented to it during learning phase (weight adaptation phase), the resulting class samples which presented to the BP ANN should have equal probability among classes. Thus the BP ANN will not biased toward any result classes (in our case, TRUE nodule class and FALSE nodule class). In our case, 87 of the 392 samples (22.5%) are TRUE nodule, while 305 samples (77.8%) are FALSE nodule. The BP ANN will biased toward FALSE nodule class if the data set is applied for training. Therefore the TRUE nodule sample was replicated 7 times and FALSE nodule samples was duplicated twice based upon the statistical properties of the training set. As a result, 609 out of 1219 samples (49.95%) are TRUE nodules and 610 out of 1219 samples (50.05%) are FALSE nodules in the resulting data set. 40% of the data set are used as training set depending on the results of image shape feature analysis [2].

NEURAL NETWORK BASE KNOWLEDGE FUSION

Knowledge fusion processor is designed to integrate different decision from different decision maker to obtain the optimal classification accuracy. As the data fusion processor, which has been used widely in communication theory and satellite remote sensing applications. The knowledge fusion processor fuse classification from ANN classification (suspect B-fields) and expert diagnosis (through knowledge base inference).

The knowledge fusion processor is a combination of a static feed forward network and a dynamic recurrent network. The structure of the knowledge fusion processor is illustrated in Figure 3. The static feed forward network implement a rule-based neural knowledge base. The configuration of the static neural knowledge base is a three-layer feed forward network. First layer is Premises Layer, which accepts encoded premises from expert's observation and diagnosis. Second Layer is the Rule layer where each node in this layer represents a rule in the knowledge base. Every node in Rule layer connected to the nodes in Premises layer only when the premises represented by the nodes will take part in the rule's resolving process. The connections between Premises layer to Rule layer is defined when the rules were first constructed. To add a new rule to the neural knowledge base, a new rule node in the Rule Layer will be introduced to the system, new premises will be introduced to Premises Layer. The connections between the premises and the new rule node will also be determined.

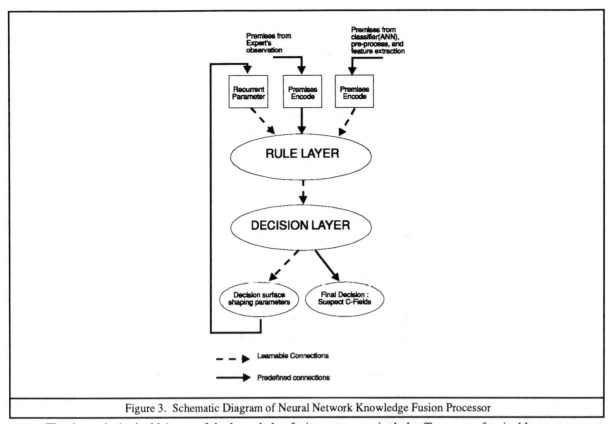

Figure 3. Schematic Diagram of Neural Network Knowledge Fusion Processor

The dynamic (trainable) part of the knowledge fusion processor includes Two part of trainable recurrent networks. One of the dynamic network is the Suspect network which accepts inputs from the suspect B-fields from ANN classifier, pre-processing parameters, and feature space determination parameters to take into account the decision process of the neural-digital classification process of HLND system. The other dynamic network is a decision surface shaping parameters network. The function of this network is to form a decision surface to determine final classification (suspect C-fields).

However, the three part of the knowledge fusion processor is not mutual exclusive. The neural knowledge base might use some of the parameters generated in the process of neural-digital classification. The trainable Suspect network can also use the expert's diagnosis as part of it input pattern. In fact, the only difference between Neural-Knowledge Base and Suspect network is that the connections and weights between Rule layer and Premises layer are determined at time the rules were constructed. Yet the weight and connections of the Suspect network is trained with a backpropagation algorithm. While the weights of the decision surface shaping network is trained with a recurrent network algorithm.

EXPERIMENTAL RESULTS

The knowledge base is still under construction. Therefore, the knowledge fusion process has little effect on the experimental results. The ANN classification result are report herein. It takes around 130 epoches to train the BP ANN classifier to learn up to 100% accuracy of the training data set. With a fully-trained BP ANN, True-positive classification accuracy can reach 93.3% over the overall image base as shown in Table 2. It is found that the trained BP ANN increases the detection accuracy of true nodule up to 93% with around 7% false detection. By examining the weight matrix, the effect due to different feature (either amplitude or orientation) can be determined. Such implementation can also be easily implemented in a highly parallel, reconfigurable, and scalable, neural network co-processor called MNR [15] for fast and real time processing.

		Actual Structure	
		True Nodule	False Nodule
Classified	True Nodule	93.3%	6.7%
	False Nodule	1.3%	98.7%
Table 2. Classification Accuracy for Nodule Detection			

FEATURE DETERMINATION AND SUSPECTS REDUCTION
Image Feature Extraction

Since the quick selection process are based on the general features of lung nodules -- the spherical profile, a classification algorithm based on localize anatomic features is needed. We developed an algorithms for localized feature extraction and classification based on gradient edge analysis of local anatomic structure in the 32x32 image blocks [2,10].

The nodule suspects (A-Fields) passed through the morphology based filtering process, thus they would contain the specific geometric features the quick selection filter was designed for, in this case of lung nodule detection, the spherical profile in the X-ray images. In order to define a feature space in which the ANN architecture can be trained to derive a decision surfaces for separating different classes of anatomic structures, a feature extraction function that can complement the major search algorithm (morphology based filter) is needed. Such feature extraction algorithm should minimize the homogeneous effect among the suspect A-Fields selected from quick selection process, yet maximize the geometric differences among the suspect A-Fields. Therefore we designed a feature extraction algorithm based on sobel operators to respond to the gradient in the image.

After first two processing phases (pre-processing and morphology based quick selection), nodule suspect A-Fields are determined from each image. Typically, there are 15-30 suspects on a radiograph. The nodule suspect is extracted into a 32x32 pixel image (larger than 9 mm in diameter) sufficient for the ANN-based development. After processing 31 radiographs, more than 380 nodule suspects in **original** and **difference** image blocks (32x32 pixel) are obtained for further development of the ANN classification. Among the nodule suspects, 22.2% of them are true positive nodules. Since sufficient data base for various anatomic structures are required for analysis, many false positive nodules are included for further investigation. With properly adjustment of parameters, the success rate in detection of nodule can achieve 70% after first two phases.

Anatomic Class								
	RX	RV	VC	EV	RE	BO	VS	TN
No. of samples	96	40	41	43	28	42	15	87
Total suspect image blocks: 392								
Table 1. Eight Types of Anatomic Classes								

The suspect image blocks are first classified into 8 classes: true nodule (TN), rib crossing (RX), rib-vessel crossing (RV), vessel cluster (VC), end-vessel (EV), rib edge (RE), bone (BO), and vessel (VS), based on the content of the image and previous related works [2, 11]. Generally, the suspect image blocks contains more than one class of information. It is found that among 392 images 24.5% are rib crossing and 22.2% are true, as shown in Table 1. Since eight (8) categories of anatomic classes are obtained from real radiographs, overlapping of several phenomenon in single image block is quite common. The classification is primarily based on the most dominant anatomic structure in the image. Based on these image blocks, several features are analyzed and extracted.

A 1-D histogram of gradient component (either amplitude or orientation) has been applied by Matsumoto et al., [11] for analysis of subtracted image block. In this analysis, we investigated both elements of gradient vector (amplitude and orientation) from original image block. A 3x3 Sobel operator for image edge enhancement is applied to the original image block to obtained two 32 x 32 images: one is amplitude image and another one is orientation image. The orientation angles are within the range between 0 and 360 degree, whereas the amplitude varies from 0 to 1024. Feature vector pairs are generated from histogram of orientation and amplitude. It was found that most non-nodule 32x32 images contain identifiable histogram features in amplitude and orientation gradient image.

By performing the histogram operation on gradient image, two sets of marginal distribution curves are obtained: one for orientation distribution and another one for amplitude distribution. The feature vectors from the nodule curves (both in orientation and amplitude) is quite distinct from rest of other structures. Each distribution is normalized to enhance its variation through performing division by ten, which is the deviation of these curves, and followed by taking its square. These feature vectors are then used for development of supervised neural classifier in this study.

It is found that for true nodules the distribution of orientation angles is relative uniform compared with other false positive cases and the magnitude of gradient amplitude of true nodules is mostly concentrated in smaller magnitude. Most types of false positive nodules demonstrate two peaks separated at around 180 degree in orientation angle axis except for vessel cluster. Because bone is wider than vessel in the 32 x 32 images and the contrast between bone and anatomic background is stronger than that for vessel, one peak at distribution of orientation is typically smaller than another one for bone whereas they are within similar range for vessel class. Each peak in bone gradient images is sharper (i.e., smaller standard deviation) than that in vessel images. Rib-edge gradient image shows one stronger amplitude distribution at certain angle because of the orientation of the rib in the 32 x 32 image. Gradient distribution for rib-vessel crossing also demonstrates one stronger peak with relatively larger standard deviation at orientation axis. Although it is expected to obtain one sharper peak at angle axis, it shows very insignificant effect due to the low contrast of end vessel. Vessel-cluster gradient image shows more rough contour (i.e., larger standard deviation along the amplitude axis) than this from nodule. This type of analysis and classification algorithm perform well in noisy conditions, because the distribution enhancement tends to smooth out the noise contribution to the feature vector. Images containing mixed features will be easily analyzed. Parameters including standard deviation, curtosis, skewness, and other texture information from the feature vectors are currently extracted for further supervised neural network applications.

SUMMARY

A neural-knowledge base analysis and detection algorithms are developed for improvement of the performance of Hybrid Lung Nodule Detection (HLND) system. The configuration of the proposed system includes the following processing phases: (1) pre-processing to enhance the figure-background contrast; (2) Morphology based quick selection of nodule object suspects based upon the most prominent feature of nodules; and (3) feature space determination and neural network based suspect fields reduction; (4) neural network based knowledge fusion processing and final classification of nodule suspect fields. After first processing phases, several suspect image blocks are captured. Extraction of shape features is performed through edge enhancement, evaluation of marginal distribution curves and feature extraction. A pair of feature vectors is determined based on the analysis of image blocks. A supervised back-propagation-trained neural network is developed for recognition of the derived feature curve, a marginal distribution curves. A knowledge fusion processor is under development to include prior information not inherent in the X-ray image into HLND system. Preliminary results show that this feature set is able to identify most true nodule at accuracy of 93% with around 7% false detection. More data set are still needed for further improvement of the HLND system.

ACKNOWLEDGEMENT

This work is supported by grant number 1 R43 CA58116-01 from the National Cancer Institute, National Institute of Health. Its contents are solely the responsibility of the authors and do not necessarily represent the official view of the NCI/NIH.

REFERENCES

[1]   Chan, H.P., Doi, K., Vyborny, C.J., et al.: "Improvement in Radiologists' Detection of Clustered Microcal-cification Mammograms: The Potential of Computer- Aided Diagnosis," Inves. Radio., Vol. 25, 1990, pp. 1102-1110.

[2]   Chiou, Y.-S. P., J.-S. J. Lin, Lure, Y.-M. F., P. A. Ligomenides, M. T. Freedman, and S. Fritz, ''Shape Feature Analysis Using Artificial Neural Networks for Improvements of Hybrid Lung Nodule Detection (HLND) System '', SPIE Medical Imaging 1993 Symposium, Newport Beach, CA.

[3]   Doi, K.: "Feasibility of Computer-Aided Diagnosis in Digital Radiography," Jap. J. Radio. Technol. Vol. 45, 1989, pp. 653-663.

[4]   Doi, K., Giger, M.L., MacMahon, H., et al.: "Clinical Radiology and Computer- Aided Diagnosis: Potential Partner in Medical Diagnosis?," RSNA 1990, Scientific Exhibit, Space 129.

[5]   Giger, M.L., Doi, K., and MacMahon H.: "Image Feature Analysis and Computer-Aided Diagnosis in Digital Radiography. 3. Automated Detection of Nodules in Peripheral Lung Field," Med. Phy. Vol. 15, 1988, pp. 158-166.

[6]   Giger, M.L., Doi, K., and MacMahon, H., et al.: "Pulmonary Nodules: Computer- Aided Detection in Digital Chest Images," RadioGraphics, Vol. 10, 1990, pp. 41- 51.

[7]   Giger, M.L., Ahn, N., Doi, K., MacMahon, H., Metz, C.E.: "Computerized Detection of Pulmonary Nodules in Digital Chest Images: Use of Morphological Filters in Reducing False-Positive Detections" Med. Phys., Vol. 17, 1990, pp. 861-865.

[8]   Heelan, R.T., Flechinger, B.J., Melamed, M.R., et al.: "Non Small Cell Lung Cancer: Results of the New York Screening Program." Radiology, 1984; 151: 289- 293.

[9]   Lin, J.S., Ligomenides, P.A., Lure, Y.M.F., Lo, B.S. and Freedman, M.T.: "Application of Artificial Neural Networks for Improvements of Lung Nodule Detection," Proc. Symposium for Computer Assisted Radiology, S/CAR '92, SCAR, Baltimore, June 14-17, 1992.

[10]   Chiou, Y.S.P., Lure, Y.M.F., et al, "Neural Network Based Hybrid Lung Nodule (HLND) System", IEEE International Conference on Neural Network, San Francisco, CA, March 28-April 1, 1993.

[11]   Matsumto, T., H. Yoshimura, K. Doi, M. L. Giger, A. Kano, H. MacMahon, K. Abe, and S. Montner, "Image Feature Analysis of False-Positive Diagnosis Produced by Automated Detection of Lung Nodules", Investigative Radiology, 1992, pp. 587-597.

[12]   Montain, C.F.: "Value of the New TNM Staging System for Lung Cancer," 5th World Conference on Lung Cancer, CHEST:96/1, 1989, pp. 47s-49s.

[13]   Rumelhart, D.E., McClelland, J.L., Parallel Distributed Processing: Explorations in the Microstructure of Cognition, MIT Press, 1986.

[14]   Stitik, F.P., Tockman, M.S. and Khouri, N.F.: "Chest Radiology," in Miller, A.B. (Ed.): Screening for Cancer, New York, Academic Press, 1985, 163-191.

[15]   Ligomenides, P.A., Jump, L. B. and Chiou, Y-S: "A Reconfigurable Ring Architecture for Large Scale Neural Networks," Conf. Fuzzy and Neual System and Vehi. Appli., 1991, Tokyo, Japan.

[16]   Chiou, Yun-Shu: "A Neural-Knwoeldge Base System for Diagnosis in Noisy Image Background", PhD Dissertation, Dept. of Electrical Engineering, University of Maryland, College, MD. (in progress)

[17]   Chiou, Y.-S. and Lure, Y.-M F., "Hybrid Lung Nodule Detection (HLND) System", To be published in Cancer Letters, Elsevier Scientific Pub. Tre. Ltd., 1994.

[18]   Chiou, Y.S.P., Lure, Y.M.F., Ligomenides, P.A., "Neural-Knwoeldge Base Detection in Hybrid Lung Nodule Detection (HLND) System", Proceedings of Int'l Conf. on Neural Network, IEEE Neural Network Council, Orlando, Florida, June 28-July 2, 1994.

Neural Network Classifier for Hepatoma Detection

Bambang Parmanto[*], Paul W. Munro[*], Howard R. Doyle[+],
Cataldo Doria[+], Luca Aldrighetti[+], Ignazio R. Marino[+], Sandi Mitchel[+], and John J. Fung[+].
[*]Department of Information Science, University of Pittsburgh, Pittsburgh PA 15260
[+]Section of Computational Medicine, Pittsburgh Transplantation Institute, University of Pittsburgh.

Abstract

Detection of hepatoma (liver cancer) prior surgery is very important for liver transplant patients. This is due to the high probability of recurrence in the transplanted liver, which in turn undermines the benefit of transplantation. Our goal was to develop a classifier system that is able to diagnose the existence of hepatoma in patients being evaluated for liver transplantation based on parameters collected routinely, without the need for more expensive and/or invasive procedures. This paper will present the use of neural network classifier for hepatoma detection. Instead of using a single network, this paper will investigate the merit of a neural network ensemble with collective decision making in improving classification performance. Mean-square error (MSE) and Cross-entropy (CE) objective functions in the backpropagation learning procedure will also be investigated in this experiment.

Introduction

Hepatocellar carcinoma (HCC), or hepatoma for short, is a very important clinical problem in patients that are being considered for liver transplantation. This is due to the high probability of recurrence of hepatoma after transplantation, which in turn undermines the benefit of transplantation. If a hepatoma can be identified prior transplantation, patients can be entered into special protocols that may improve their ultimate outlook.

Unfortunately, the diagnosis can be difficult to establish, especially in the presence of cirrhosis. The result of routine screening ultrasonograms in cirrhotic patients is unsatisfactory. There are a number of imaging techniques that are being used to try to improve detection rate such as MRI, angiography, CT portography, etc. Some of these are invasive procedures, with their associated complications, and they all represent an extra expense.

Our goal has been to develop a good detection system with a minimum of imaging, or invasive studies. Neural networks will be used as a classifier system to discriminate patients with and without hepatoma. Previous studies (Dorfner & Porenta, 1993; Bounds et. al., 1990; and Mulsant, 1990 among others) have shown the effectiveness of neural networks in clinical diagnosis environment. This study will take a different approach to the use of neural networks for clinical diagnosis. In order to improve the performance of a neural network classifier, this experiment will explore the idea of simple averaging among a group of neural network ensembles. This experiment will also compare two different cost functions used in the backpropagation learning, namely mean squared error (MSE) and cross-entropy (CE).

The Data and Preprocessing

For this investigation, 200 data items with the associated diagnoses are available. The data were collected from a population of patients who underwent primary orthotopic liver transplantation at the Presbyterian University Hospital in Pittsburgh. The data consist of both positive and negative diagnoses with the proportion of 60 positive and 140 negative, where a positive diagnosis refers to the existence of hepatoma and a negative diagnosis refers to the absence of hepatoma. The diagnosis was established by examining the native liver after transplantation, or from pre-transplant needle biopsies of the liver.

Each data item consists of 16 measurements or demographic of an individual patient (see Table 1), and a diagnosis (positive or negative). This data set is plagued by a number of typical problems, such as noise and missing data. We propose a solution for the missing data problem in the next section (architecture). This particular data set is furthermore characterized by the unfortunate property that some variables range over 3 orders

Table 1. Variables

Demography:	Radiology:	Serology:	Clinical Chemistry:	
Age	Liver ultrasound	Hep. A antibody	Total bilirubin	Prothrombin time
Ethnic Gorup	Abdominal CT scan	Hep. B surf. antigen	Gamma glutamyl trans.	Alfa-fetoprotein
		Hep. B surf. antibody	Glutamic transaminase	
		Hep. B E antigen	Pirufic transaminase	
		Hep. B core antibody	Carcinoembryonic antigen	

of magnitude across the patients; hidden units cannot be sensitive across the entire range. Each variable was scaled according to a power transformation, $y=x^p$, where p is chosen such that the ratio of the maximum value to the minimum value of y equals some prespecified value F (see Figure 1):

$$Y = X^P$$

$$p = \log_r F$$

Y is the transformed data and X is the original data. The basis of log function "r" is the ratio between maximum and minimum of the original data (X_{max}/X_{min}) and F is the ratio between maximum and minimum of the transformed data (Y_{max}/Y_{min}). F is an adjustable parameter that may vary from one variable to another depending on the range of transformed data we want to achieve.

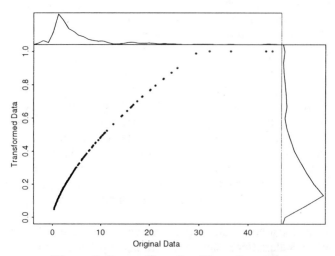

Figure 1. Power Function Transformation.

Data variables were transformed according to the function $y=x^p$, such that the ratio ymax/ymin is 10. The scatterplot shows the transformed values of the bilirubin variable plotted against the corresponding raw data. Density plots on the top and on the right side show data distributions for both representations.

Network Architecture

The network architecture used in this experiment is feedforward, with three effective layers beyond the input layer: an immediate layer to the input layer which we call encoder layer, a hidden layer, and an output layer (figure 2). Each input unit is connected to a bank of encoder units, but no connection with other banks in the encoder layer (not fully connected). The connection from encoder layer to the hidden layer and from the hidden layer to the output layer is fully connected. The encoder layer was used with the hope that each unit in the encoder bank will respond to certain distribution in the input variable.

The networks consist of 16 input units which are the number of variables in the data, 4 units in each encoder bank, 20 hidden units, and 1 output unit (represents the diagnosis). The data in the input units is a continuous value between 0 and 1. The output of the network is also a continuous value between 0 and 1. Because the task of the network is to perform a classification, we can treat the continuous output of the network as a probability or confidence with 0 represent the absent of diagnosis and 1 as the presence. In interpreting the output of the network, the continuous value between 0 and 1 will be "rounded" according the decision threshold being used. For example, if we use threshold of 0.5 the output of greater than 0.5 will be considered as positive and less than 0.5 as negative.

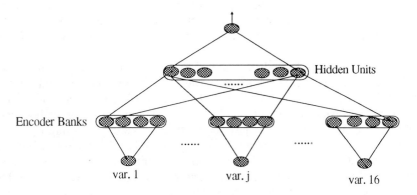

Figure 2. Network Architecture

Each of the 16 variables is represented by a single input unit, that projects to a set of N "encoder" units dedicated to that variable. The 16N encoder units then project to a common set of hidden units that projects in turn to a single output unit.

The network was trained using the backpropagation learning procedures (Rumelhart, Hinton, & Williams, 1986). Two types of objective function in the backpropagation were compared in this experiment: the Mean-Squared Error (MSE) and Cross-Entropy (CE). Suppose we want to train the network to produce a desired output for a set of input vectors. The objective function in the backpropagation procedure compares the actual output activation of the network to the desired output for the given inputs. This function seeks to minimize this difference in order to produce the correct classification for a given input pattern. The MSE is a measure of how poorly the network is performing with its current weights and it seeks to minimize the mean-squared error between the actual output of network's node $O_1, ..., O_n$ and the desired output $D_1, ..., D_n$:

$$MSE = \frac{1}{N}\sum_{j=1}^{N}(O_j - D_j)^2$$

In the CE objective function (Hinton, 1987; Hampshire & Weibel, 1990), we only attach meaning to binary output vectors while a real-valued output vector is treated as the probability that individual components have value of "1". For a given set of training cases, the likelihood of producing the desired output is maximized when the following cross-entropy function CE is minimized:

$$CE = -\sum_{j=1}^{N}D_j\log_2(O_j) + (1 - D_j)\log_2(1 - O_j)$$

In practice, cross-entropy can help avoid the network getting stuck in the extreme (such as 0 or 1) when the desired output is actually on the opposite extreme. Which objective function is more appropriate for a given task depends on the natural interpretation of the output for the task. Since the task in this experiment is detecting the existence of hepatoma, the interpretation of cross-entropy objective function is very appealing. In this case, the actual real-valued output of the network can be interpreted as the probability of a given patient to have hepatoma.

This architecture handles missing values in the data quite nicely. If missing data arrives in the input unit, the encoder will give a zero response to the hidden units. By doing so, the encoders do not map missing value the same way as other values in the data, and map the missing one to a "neutral" value.

Committee of Networks

The ultimate goal of neural networks as a classifier is generalization, it's ability to compose the best parameters out of the data that will be used to predict unseen data. Unfortunately, one of the drawbacks of a neural network classifier is the fact that it suffers from the problem of many local minima. The parameters in a neural network take the form of neuronal weights. Independent runs that may include different starting weights, different set of sampling, or different learning methods will end up at different set of connection weights (Kollen & Pollack, 1991). A collective decision making among a committee of independently trained networks has been proposed to improve the performance of neural networks (Hansen & Salomon 1990, Perrone, 1993, Ghosh et al., 1992).

In this experiment, 11 networks were independently trained to form a committee. All the networks in the committee have exactly the same architecture. Each network was initialized with a different set of random weights. The output of each member of the committee will be used to form a collective decision. We used several variations in making a collective decision, all of them are based on a simple averaging method (Hansen & Salomon, 1990; Perrone, 1993). The first alternative is just taking the average of the committee's response, where each network has equal weight. The second alternative is using "majority rule", where each network has an equal vote. The first one can be extended by taking into account the confidence level of the individuals in the committee. For example, we exclude "indecisive" networks that have response between 0.4 to 0.6, 0.3 to 0.7, and so forth. In the majority rule, each network in the committee has binary yes-no vote (the network has only 1 output) and the output of the committee will be the output that voted by 6 or more networks. While in the average decision, each network has a floating point output.

In measuring the network's performance, we are only concerned with the percent correct in classification. Perrone (1993) measured the performance of neural network in it's mean square error (MSE) and the percent correct in classification. He observed the impact of averaging in both performance measures. Although minimizing the MSE usually also optimize the classification performance, there is no guarantee that minimizing MSE necessarily maximizes classification performance. Since MSE is a continuous measure and classification performance is discrete, it is possible to have a network with a high MSE and yet have a high classification performance. In this experiment, we are only concerned with the use of committee as far as it's improvement to the percent correct in classification.

Experiment

Training set and test set are composed from the data items. We faced the problem of a small data set and imbalance proportion between negative and positive diagnoses. Out of 200 total data that we have, only 60 of them are positive. We use 100 items (out of 200) as a training set with negative and positive diagnoses in an equal proportion. We also drew 20 items with equal proportion as a test set. Using random sampling without replacement, 6 pairs of training set and test sets were composed from the data. The remaining 80 items with negative diagnosis are also used for a test set but are not included as a crossvalidatory stopping criteria. Each network was trained an all the training set. The training was stopped using crossvalidatory criteria: when the error in the test set goes up, the training ended. The performance of the network is measured in the test sets (20 items) and the remaining 80 items. Since we have 6 pairs of training set and test set, the network performance is basically tested on the entire data.

Two different types of networks with MSE and CE objective functions were independently trained in this experiment. Since each type forms a committee with 11 networks as a member, we have 22 networks as a whole. The entire networks were trained and tested in each pair of the training set - test set.

Introducing "white" noise to the training set can improve generalization by obscuring "idiosyncratic" features. In the data that we used, some missing values only exist in the data with a positive diagnosis. Early experiments without introducing noise showed that the network turned out to pick this idiosyncrasy as a clue: every time we gave missing values for that variable, it classified the pattern as positive. In order to mitigate this problem, noise was introduced to the data. During training, we randomly gave missing values to the input. The result showed that the network didn't pick the wrong clue from the data anymore.

Results

We are interested in comparing the performance of the networks with MSE and CE objective function. We are also interested in observing the performance of collective decision making using neural network committee compared to the performance of individual networks. The performance is measured as percent correct in classification using the threshold of 0.5. The summary of these comparisons is shown in Table 2.

First, we compute the average without taking into account the confidence level of the individual network in the ensemble, then take the average of the ensemble after excluding items with output between 0.4 - 0.6, 0.3-0.7, 0.2-0.8, respectively; this excludes 9.5%, 21%, 34% of items for the respective confident intervals.

	Averaging of Network Ensemble					Individual Networks	
	Majority Vote	Confidence I	Confidence II	Confidence III	Confidence IV	Best Indiv.	Average
		(includes all)	(excl. 0.4-0.6)	(excl. 0.3-0.7)	(excl. 0.2-0.8)		
MSE	0.83	0.85	0.86	0.84	0.84	0.85	0.79 +/- 0.03
CE	0.88	0.88	0.88	0.88	0.88	0.88	0.85 +/- 0.02

Table 2.
Comparison of Individual Networks and Committee

The table shows that by any measure, the networks with CE objective function outperform networks with MSE objective function. In the committee setting, CE outperforms MSE by 5% using majority vote and around 3% using simple averaging. While in the individual networks, on the average CE is significantly better than MSE, with 6% difference and the best individual of CE is 3% higher than MSE. The explanation of this result may lie in the fact that the interpretation of network output in this particular task is naturally close to the interpretation of network output in the CE objective function.

The result also shows that averaging can significantly improve the performance. Using MSE, the result of the average ensemble by excluding the indecisive network can reach the performance of 0.86, this is far better than single network with performance of 0.79. The result of averaging of ensemble even better than the best performance that can be reached by individual network, although this seems not always the case. Perrone (1993) has shown that the result of ensemble is always better than the average individual network. This improvement still hold in the CE networks, on the average the performance of committee is 3% higher than the individual. Although the best individual in this case is as good as the committee.

The diagnostic performance, such as the performance that we just discussed, in the clinical test is usually measured in a pair of sensitivity and specificity (Weiss & Kulikowski, 1991). Sensitivity is referred to as the percentage of correctly classifying positive (presence of disease) cases, while specificity is referred to as the percentage of correctly classifying negative case. In a continuous output of the network between 0 and 1, these two values are taken only in one threshold. A more accurate measure of performance should take into account continuous threshold between 0 and 1. Receiver Operating Curves (ROC) that plot sensitivity over 1-specificity are given to asses the interdependence between those two values across continuous threshold. The ROC for this experiment (figure 3) is the result of averaging among ensemble of network.

The curve generated from the ensemble network using CE objective function has an area index of .9526 (from the maximum value of 1.00). This result compares favorably with diagnostic instruments and is consistent with clinical standards. For example, using threshold of 0.32 the output of the network ensemble has sensitivity of 0.89 and specificity of .90.

Discussion

The combination of techniques for training (committee training, power function scaling, and the encoder architecture), show remarkable power in this diagnostic application. In future studies we plan to extend this work by tuning the number of encoders to the variables, analyzing the network solution by analyzing the encoder unit response properties, and experimenting with larger committee sizes.

Aside from performing respectably on a difficult diagnostic task, this approach offers a new tool for enhancing the potential of backpropagation: encoder units to provide a distributed representation for each variable and to give a natural representation for missing data. As a given variable traverses the domain from its minimum to maximum value, the corresponding encoder vector traces a one dimensional manifold. This representation of the variable is presumably tuned to the task, and is likely not to come particularly close to the zero vector. Hence the zero vector can be used to represent missing data, and will not generally correspond to an actual value.

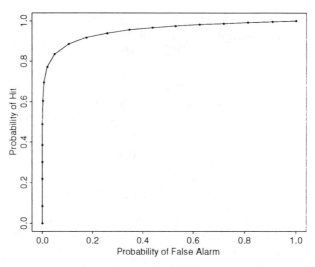

Figure 3. ROC Curve

Figure 3. ROC Curve. As the threshold for positive diagnosis is decreased, the probability of correct positive and incorrect diagnoses both increase. Using this curve, an acceptable point can hopefully be chosen, such that there is a useful probability of correct diagnosis, while the probability of false alarm is acceptably low. The area under the curve is generally an indication of the quality of the diagnostic. A perfect curve would go up the left axis of the box, and across the top, giving an area of 1.

Another technique that we investigated bears description because it illustrates part of the rationale behind the encoder representation. Here, each variable was scaled from 0 to π, and subsequently represented by the sine and cosine (two input units). This gives a 2-D representation where the input variable lies on a semicircle; thus, missing values can be represented by the zero vector, which lies equally distant from all potential input values.

References

Bounds, D.G, Lloyd, P.J., Mathew, B.G. (1990) A comparison of neural network and other pattern recognition approaches to the diagnoses of low back disorders. *Neural Networks*, Vol.3. pp. 583-591.

Dorfner, Georg & Porenta, Gerold (1993) "On Using Feedforward Neural Networks for Clinical Diagnostic Tasks". Research Report, Austrian Research Institute for Artificial Intelligence, 1993.

Ghosh, Jedeep, Deuser, Larry, and Beck, Steven (1992) A Neural network based hybrid system for detection, characterization, and classification of short-duration oceanic signal. *IEEE Journal of Oceanic Engineering*, Vol. 17, No. 4.

Hampshire, John B., Waibel, Alexander H. (1990) A novel objective function for improved phoneme recognition using time-delay neural networks. *IEEE Transactions on Neural Networks*, Vol. 1, No. 2.

Hansen, Lars, Salamon, Peter (1990) Neural network ensembles. *IEEE Transactions on Pattern Analysis and Machine Intelligence.* Vol. 12, No. 10.

Hinton, G.E. (1987) "Connectionist Learning Procedures," Carnegie-Mellon Univ., Pittsburgh, PA, Tech. Report. CMU-CS-87-115 (revised version), December 1987.

Kolen, J.F and Pollack, J.B. (1991) Backpropagation is sensitive to initial conditions. *NIPS 3*. pp. 860-867.

Mulsant, B.H. (1990) A neural network as an approach to clinical diagnosis. *M.D. Computing*, Vol. 7, No.1.

Perrone, Michael (1993) *Improving Regression Estimation: Averaging Methods for Variance Reduction with General Extensions to General Convex Measure Optimization.* PhD Thesis, Department of Physics. Brown University.

Rumelhart, D.E., Hinton, G.E., and Williams, R.J. (1986) Learning internal representations by error propagation. In Rumelhart, D.E., McCleland, J.L., and the PDP Research Group, editors, *Parallel Distributed Processing: Explorations in the Microstructure of Cognition. Volume 1: Foundations*, MIT Press, Cambridge, MA.

Weiss, Sholom, Kulikowski, Casimir (1991) *Computer Systems That Learn: Classification and Prediction Methods from Statistics, Neural nets, Machine Learning, and Expert Systems.* Addison-Wesley: San Mateo, CA.

Hierarchical Neural Networks for Partial Diagnosis in Medicine

Lucila Ohno-Machado and Mark A. Musen
Section on Medical Informatics, Stanford School of Medicine
Medical School Office Building X-215, Stanford University, Stanford, CA 94305
machado@camis.stanford.edu, musen@camis.stanford.edu

Abstract

Various domains require hierarchical classification. In medicine, learning partial diagnoses can be helpful when time and information constraints are present. Hierarchical neural networks provide a good means to perform partial diagnosis. We implemented a hierarchical backpropagation-based model for the domain of thyroid diseases, and compared the results against those of nonhierarchical networks in terms of sensitivities and specificities. In our system, high-level neural networks filter instances that are relevant for use in specialized neural networks. The hierarchical model required fewer epochs to be trained and yielded a higher classification rate in the test set than did the nonhierarchical one. The hierarchical model also had the advantage that fewer data attributes for each instance were required at higher levels. Therefore, using this model decreases the problem of dealing with missing values, and provides a framework to establish a parsimonious sequence of tests for diagnosing thyroid diseases.

1. Background

In most real-life situations, medical decision making is done in absence of complete information. Diagnostic tests may be ordered to decrease uncertainty, but actions take place before all results become available. The actions (which could be ordering of new tests, or prescribing a treatment) may change the course of the disease. Cases that are resolved in this initial phase may never be assigned a final diagnosis. Conversely, further investigation may yield a more precise diagnosis. The diagnostic process is then repeated, until no additional information is necessary. Yet, the decisions made early in the diagnostic process -- usually in the absence of complete information -- play a key role on patient outcomes. These decisions are based on partial diagnoses derived from a limited set of observations. *Partial diagnoses* are key components in medical reasoning [Pople, 1982], usually consisting of syndromic, rather than etiologic, diagnoses.

Thyroid diseases are classified in two major classes: *hypothyroidism* and *hyperthyroidism*. Each of these classes can be further divided according to the etiology of the disease: hypothyroidism can be divided in *primary, secondary*, and so on. We have built a computer program to help physicians decide whether a patient has hypothyroidism, hyperthyroidism, or normal thyroid function by interpreting the results of the patient's laboratory tests, and defining a partial diagnosis. Such a partial diagnosis may be useful in explaining some of the patient's findings, in helping a clinician to make decisions regarding what diagnostic tests to order next, and in helping the physician decide which medications may be appropriate (even though this partial diagnosis may not be sufficient to allow the clinician to decide on the optimal therapy). The system produces useful results early in the course of the investigation, when only scarce information is available. In cases where the system determines that the patient's thyroid function is not normal, further processing occurs, and a final diagnosis is suggested.

Many taxonomies of diseases (nosologies) are structured in a hierarchical fashion [Gara, Rosenberg, and Goldberg, 1992]. This type of classification not only is easier to understand than a flat list of diseases, but also provides a basis that guides the differential diagnosis. It is therefore natural to use a hierarchical classification system to perform medical diagnosis. Several authors have used this approach when building medical expert systems, or rule-based systems [Weiss, Kulikowski, Amarel, and Safir, 1978]. Although performance may be acceptable, problems with expert systems usually occur during the knowledge-acquisition phase, when a great amount of time is spent on extracting information from the expert [Forsythe and Buchanan, 1989]. Furthermore, expert judgment may contain biases [Tversky and Kahneman, 1974], a problem that machine-learning approaches, by extracting information from evidence, may also avoid.

Hierarchies of neural networks are not new. Ballard proposed them as a solution to the problem of building large networks [Ballard, 1990]. He developed a modification of the backpropagation algorithm to be applied to these hierarchies; he reported that preliminary computer experiments showed that his approach resulted in a better performance in large problems in terms of time and accuracy than did the approach that uses the backpropagation algorithm with several internal levels. He did not report specific results of these studies. Our motivation for using hierarchical networks was somewhat different. Although we were concerned with the scaling problem, the objective of our project was to develop a hierarchical network that would perform partial diagnosis accurately and parsimoniously. We applied the backpropagation algorithm to a sequence of networks, so that each network was trained in a supervised way. The first level of this hierarchical system was presented with fewer data attributes than were given to the more specialized level. The purpose of this first network was to establish a partial diagnosis of *hypothyroidism, hyperthyroidism, other conditions*, or *no disease*.

Curry and Rumelhart used hierarchical networks to classify mass spectra [Curry and Rumelhart, 1990]. Our system is based on their architecture, except that we did not incorporate extra units for representing the degree of confidence in the top-level network's results. Curry and Rumelhart did not compare the hierarchical system with its nonhierachical counterpart. Other approaches using neural networks involve preprocessing of data by several statistical techniques, usually in a nonsupervised manner [Hrycej, 1992]. Frean has proposed a method for constructing the hierarchical networks dynamically, but concepts associated with each intermediate level did not have a specific meaning, as they do in our system [Frean, 1990]. Alternatives to building a supervised hierarchical classifier outside the field of neural connectionist systems include piecewise linear machines, as described by Nilsson [1965], and classification trees [Breiman, Friedman, Olshen, and Stone, 1984].

Hierarchical classification in medical domains has been done in a few cases. Ash and Hayes-Roth have studied the use of action-based hierarchies in a surgical intensive-care unit [Ash and Hayes-Roth, 1993], and there are rule-based systems that rely on hierarchical classification [Weiss, Kulikowski, Amarel, and Safir, 1978].

2. Material and Methods

We used the set of cases of thyroid diseases provided by Quinlan [1987], and distributed by the University of California at Irvine [Murphy and Aha, 1992]. It consists of more than 9000 instances, each with 29 attributes. A previous version of this database was used by Quinlan to show the implementation of decision trees [Quinlan, 1986]. There are continuous and discrete values, as well as many missing values. Input consists mainly of values for laboratory-test results. There are 20 classes for output, which can be grouped in at least four superclasses. Data were collected from 1984 to 1987 in an Australian medical institution. Similar data were also used previously in a neural-network implementation [Schiffmann, Joost, and Werner, 1992]. The authors described the difficulty that the system had in learning the patterns. They tried different variations of backpropagation, and studied the variability of learning associated with variation in learning rate and momentum. As in Quinlan's experiments, their problem was just to classify whether or not the patient had hypothyroidism. The authors were not concerned with learning both partial and final diagnoses. Weiss also used a similar set of data to compare different machine-learning algorithms in the domain of thyroid diseases, showing that the smaller error rates in the testing set were associated with neural networks of nine hidden units, trained by a backpropagation variant [Weiss and Kulikowski, 1990].

2.1. Multiple Neural-Network Architecture

Two top-level networks that determined partial diagnoses (triage neural networks) consisted of multilayered perceptrons (MLPs), with inputs provided by the reduced set of data attributes (20 inputs in the case of the first partial networks), or the complete set of data attributes (23 inputs in the case of the other networks). We varied the number of input attributes to measure the importance of the three additional attributes to the determination of the partial diagnosis. The attributes were laboratory values that could be left out in the first clinical assessment of thyroid diseases (T3, T4, and TBG). Figure 1 shows the architecture of the triage networks, and Figure 2 shows the architecture of the specialized network. The complete set of data (23 inputs) was presented to the generic network, in which the final diagnoses corresponded to output units. Figure 3 shows the architecture of the generic network.

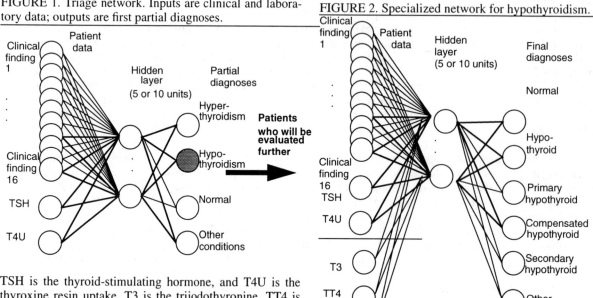

FIGURE 1. Triage network. Inputs are clinical and laboratory data; outputs are first partial diagnoses.

FIGURE 2. Specialized network for hypothyroidism.

TSH is the thyroid-stimulating hormone, and T4U is the thyroxine resin uptake, T3 is the triiodothyronine, TT4 is the total thyroxine, and TBG is the thyroxine-binding globulin.

The triage networks in the hierarchical model were trained to distinguish among four classes of diagnoses: (1) normal, (2) hyperthyroid, (3) hypothyroid, and (4) other conditions. The specialized network was then trained on only those cases considered hypothyroid by the triage network. It was trained to classify instances in the following final diagnoses: (1) hypothyroid, not otherwise specified; (2) primary hypothyroid; (3) compensated hypothyroid; and (4) secondary hypothyroid. In the generic and triage networks, the training set was composed of the first 4000 instances in the database. The test set was composed of the remaining 5000 instances. In the specialized networks, the training set was composed of all training instances considered hypothyroid by the corresponding triage network. The test set was composed of all test instances considered hypothyroid in the corresponding triage network.

FIGURE 3. Generic neural network. Inputs are all laboratory data; outputs are final diagnoses. TSH is the thyroid-stimulating hormone, T4U is the thyroxine resin uptake, T3 is the triiodothyronine, TT4 is the total thyroxine, and TBG is the thyroxine-binding globulin.

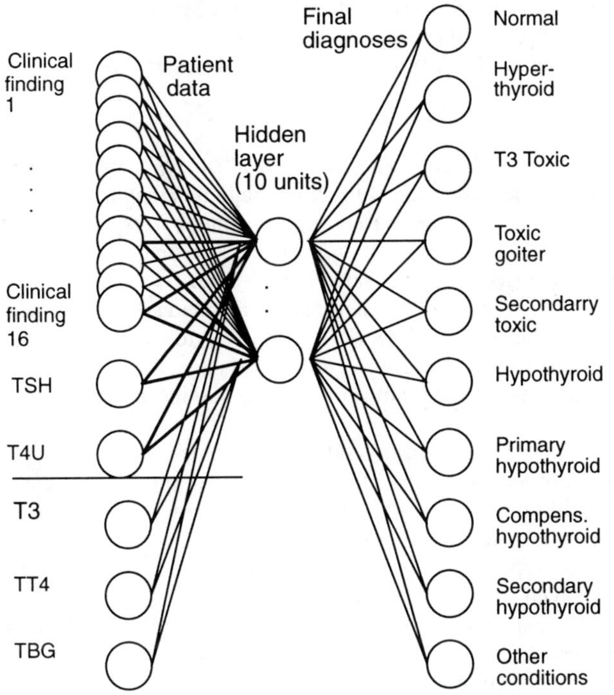

FIGURE 4. Number of epochs required.

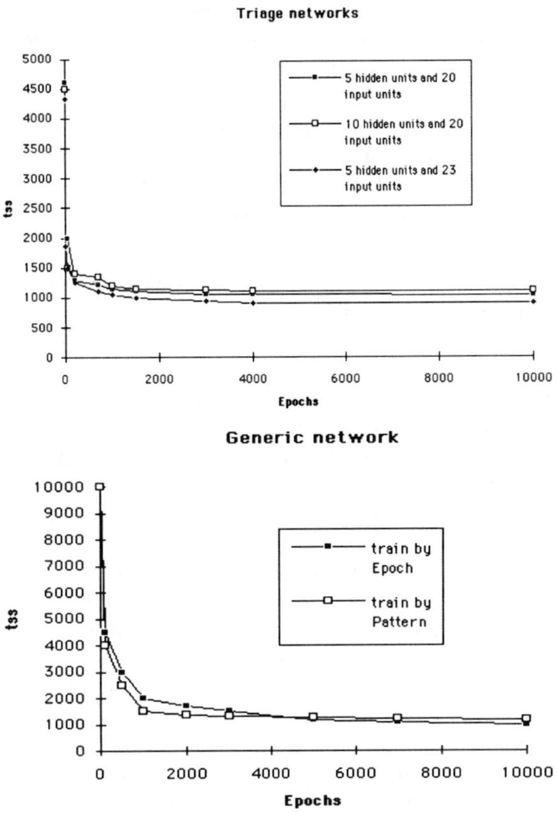

Three triage networks were built in which there were (1) 20 input units and five hidden units, (2) 20 input units and 10 hidden units, and (3) 23 input units and five hidden units. We built specialized networks with five and 10 hidden units, so that we had three systems for the hierarchical model: one with an overall of 20 hidden units, when 20 input units and 10 hidden units were used for the triage network; one with an overall of 10 hidden units, with 20 input units and five hidden units in the triage network; and one with also an overall of 10 hidden units, but with 23 input units and five hidden units in the triage network. The generic network was built with 23 input units, 10 hidden units, and 10 hidden units.

We formatted all input files to provide one output unit for each desired diagnosis in each level of the hierarchies. Continuous values were preserved, and true-false values were assigned "1" and "0," respectively. Missing values were assigned to their means, and scaling was done for continuous values to provide inputs in the order of 100 to 10^{-4}. Of all attributes in Quinlan's set, we did not use those that flagged only whether continuous values were present (e.g., "measurement": true or false), those referring to patients' identification numbers, those determining the referral center, and the FTI (free thyroxine index). The latter is just the ratio between two other inputs, so the network should be able to derive it. The ability of neural networks (as opposed to classification trees and other discriminants) to combine inputs in this way was shown by Reibnegger and associates [Reibnegger, Weiss, Werner-Felmayer, Judmaier, and Wachter, 1991], who dealt with the aminotransferases ratio in a neural net system used to diagnose liver diseases.

Each of the components of the hierarchical system, and the generic network learned using a standard backpropagation algorithm [Rumelhart, Hinton, and Williams, 1986]. We started with a learning rate of 0.5, but we had to decrease it to 0.01 to achieve a reasonable performance in both the training and the test sets. Since it is known that the

I-293

prevalence of hypothyroid cases in the data set is 92 percent [Weiss and Kulikowski, 1990], this rate was a lower bound to our classification-rate goal. The parameter momentum was set to 0. Weight updating was done by epochs, rather than by patterns.The decision about when to stop training was not straightforward. One-hundred percent accuracy in the training set was not obtained even after 10,000 epochs in the generic model, which took approximately 48 hours on a shared SunSparc2. Since the total sum of squares (tss) decreased slowly after 10,000 epochs, we decided to stop training then. By doing so, we could also compare our results to those of Schiffmann. All networks were trained for 10,000 epochs. Performance of the test set (measured by the tss) was decreasing with the tss of the training set, so there was no sign of overfitting at this point.

2.2. Evaluation

Although the goal of learning was to minimize the tss, we could not use this measure to evaluate the networks because a different number of outputs were involved in each system. The classification rate provided a good means to evaluate the percentage of correctly classified cases (or the accuracy of the classifiers), but in fact has little meaning in medical practice. Sensitivities (the proportion of a test's true-positive results to all genuinely positive cases) and specificities (the proportion of a test's true-negative results to all genuinely negative cases) are among the most important measures of performance for a diagnostic test in medicine [Sox, Blatt, Higgins, and Marton, 1988]. It is also usual to compare discriminating power of two tests by comparing the areas under each test's receiver operating characteristic (ROC) curve over the whole range of cut-off values [Centor, 1991]. We compared classification performance using sensitivities and specificities.

3. Results

Table 1 shows the classification rates for performing the partial diagnosis of hypothyroidism. We obtained the numbers corresponding to the generic network by adding the numbers for each of the final diagnoses that can be classified as hypothyroidism. The classification rates for final diagnoses in the hierarchical systems correspond to the results of the specialized networks for hypothyroidism. Table 2 shows the results for the specific final diagnosis of primary hypothyroid. Table 3 shows the results for the final diagnosis of compensated hypothyroid.

Figure 4 shows how the tss decreased with learning in the triage networks, generic networks, and specialized networks. Note that it took more time to go through each epoch in the generic network, as compared to the combination of triage networks and specialized networks, since there are many more diagnoses to be learned in the generic network than in the triage network. The specialized networks were easy to train, since only about 300 instances were filtered in the triage network.

The generic network had the least accuracy in all cases. In fact, this network could indicate compensated hypothyroid correctly in only 248 of 394 hypothyroid cases, and did not recognize any other type of hypothyroidism. Sensitivity to primary hypothyroidism was, therefore, zero. Although not shown in the tables, the generic network could not recognize any case of hyperthyroidism, whereas hierarchical systems with all 23 inputs units provided to the triage network were the most accurate for classifying this superclass (accuracy 96.16 percent, sensitivity 80 percent, and specificity 96.57 percent). The triage network that contained just 20 input nodes was also unable to recognize cases of hyperthyroidism. The reason for these results may be that the three inputs that were left out in the 20-input models were indeed essential to reach a diagnosis of hyperthyroidism.

The generic neural network was unable to learn patterns that were infrequent in the training set. One example of an infrequent diagnosis was primary hypothyroidism, as mentioned above. The generic network usually yielded high specificities (98.63, 99.24, and 96 for *hypothyroidism*, *primary hypothyroidism*, and *compensated hypothyroidism*, respectively), whereas sensitivity for these different categories ranged from zero to 92.53 percent. There was no important change in accuracy, sensitivity, or specificity when the triage and specialized networks were composed of 10 versus five hidden units.

3. Discussion

The degree of uncertainty in diagnosis depends on the penalty for false positives and false negatives. Therefore, an accuracy of 99.99 percent may not mean much when high specificity is coupled with low sensitivity, or vice versa. The sensitivity and specificity have to be considered by the health-care worker when she receives test results. If rare patterns must not be missed (e.g., a treatable important disease), we can improve our results by lowering the threshold of some output units, to ensure higher sensitivity. Preliminary results show that this procedure may be important to calibrate the network to recognize rare, but important, patterns.

We have not considered physician or patient preferences in our system. Also, we have not addressed costs, risks, severity of illness, or any measure of patients' well-being. We present sensitivities and specificities so that the appropriate misclassification penalties can be assigned. It is unrealistic to assume that costs for false positives and false negatives are the same in the medical domain. For example, we can see in Tables 1 and 3 that, although the generic network has a lower accuracy than does a simple "guess" that all patients do not have the disease, its sensitivity is far from zero. Utility measures, although difficult to acquire, may provide additional insight on how to choose the best classifier for this data set.

It is interesting to investigate whether the results conform the literature concerning thyroid diseases. The fact that hierarchical systems could learn almost as well with fewer input units confirms certain guidelines of the American Thyroid Association [Surks, Chopra, Mariash, Nicoloff, and Solomon. 1990] that suggest that few laboratory tests are necessary to diagnose certain thyroid conditions. We are undertaking further research in this area. The use of background knowledge to choose which units to leave out for the triage networks needs further investigation. It speeded up learning, since fewer weights had to be adjusted, yet it did not decrease accuracy. A physician needs to review cases that were misclassified, to check whether they comprised mainly certain conditions that are more difficult to diagnose, as in clinical practice.

TABLE 1. Classification rates for superclass *hypothyroid* (percent)

System	Accuracy train	Sensitivity train	Specificity train	Accuracy test	Sensitivity test	Specificity test
Generic network	95.93	55.34	98.77	95.82	62.94	98.63
Hierarchical system: 20 hidden, 20 + 23 input, units	99.25	96.56	99.43	98.50	91.11	99.13
Hierarchical system: 10 hidden, 20 + 23 input, units	99.12	95.41	99.38	98.54	91.87	99.10
Hierarchical System: 10 hidden, 23 + 23 input, units	99.07	91.22	99.62	98.38	88.57	99.21
No computer-based system: (assigning *not hypothyroid* to all)	93.45	0	100	92.12	0	100

TABLE 2. Classification rates for class *primary hypothyroid* (percent)

System	Accuracy train	Sensitivity train	Specificity train	Accuracy test	Sensitivity test	Specificity test
Generic network	96.55	0	99.38	96.90	0	99.24
Hierarchical system: 20 hidden, 20 + 23 input, units	99.25	85.96	99.64	97.90	68.64	98.61
Hierarchical system: 10 hidden, 20 + 23 input, units	99.27	82.46	99.77	98.38	67.72	99.11
Hierarchical system: 10 hidden, 23 + 23 input, units	98.90	73.68	99.64	98.08	61.86	98.96
No computerized system: (assigning "not hypothyroid" to all)	97.15	0	100	97.64	0	100

TABLE 3. Classification rates for class *compensated hypothyroid* (percent)

System	Accuracy train	Sensitivity train	Specificity train	Accuracy test	Sensitivity test	Specificity test
Generic network	95.92	98.63	95.82	95.82	92.53	96.00
Hierarchical system: 20 hidden, 20 + 23 input, units	99.15	93.88	99.35	97.56	80.22	98.54
Hierarchical system: 10 hidden, 20 + 23 input, units	99.00	94.56	99.17	99.08	80.55	98.56
Hierarchical system: 10 hidden, 23 + 23 input, units	98.60	92.52	98.83	97.72	87.31	98.31
No computer-based system: (assigning *not hypothyroid* to all)	96.33	0	100	94.64	0	100

Another interesting extension would be to use enhancing techniques, such as weight elimination and weight decay, to improve performance. We also need to do rigorous evaluation before determining whether this classifier can be useful in clinical settings. Our classification rates were different from those of previous works. Shiffmann reports a best classification rate of 98.48 percent, whereas Weiss and Kulikowski reported results as good as 98.80 percent. Our best result to diagnose the superclass hypothyroid was 98.54 percent correct classification with the hierarchical system.

Examples of the importance of partial diagnosis in medicine are common. Partial diagnoses that guide the diagnostic and treatment processes are relative. In certain centers, were the constraints on resources are strong, as in primary-care institutions, what is considered a final and specific diagnosis may correspond to a partial diagnosis in a more specialized center. Furthermore, different patients may require different levels of refinement of diagnosis. These issues play an important role in the decision regarding how partial a diagnosis should be. Triage of patients may benefit from the use of hierarchical classification systems. Identifying patients who are suitable for research studies and practice guidelines, for example, requires selecting individuals from a large population of patients. The degree of selection accuracy may have a great influence on patients' satisfaction and on health care financial costs.

4. Conclusion

The hypothesis that hierarchical neural networks would perform more accurately than nonhierarchical ones, because they "filtered" cases to be classified by more refined networks, was confirmed by this experiment. In all cases, the overall accuracy of the hierarchical system with 20 inputs for the triage network, 23 inputs for the specialized network, and five hidden units for both networks was the highest. In one category (compensated hypothyroidism), however, the sensitivity of the hierarchical system was lower than was that of the generic network. The generic network was slower than the combination of triage and specialized networks.

Use of a hierarchical neural network classification system in a medical domain improved classification rates, compared to nonhierarchical neural network system. In the limited domain of thyroid diseases, the system proved to be accurate and practical. More important, results derived from this study may be valid across domains, so hierarchical neural networks may be useful for many diagnostic tasks in which partial diagnoses are necessary.

References

Ash, D., and Hayes-Roth, B. A Comparison of Action-Based Hierarchies and Decision Trees for Real-Time Performance. *Proceedings of the Eleventh National Conference on Artificial Intelligence*, MIT Press, Cambridge, MA, 1993.

Ballard, D. Modular Learning in Hierarchical Neural Networks. In Schwartz, E.L. (ed), *Computational Neuroscience*, Bradford, London, 1990.

Centor, R.M. Signal Detectability: The Use of ROC Curves and Their Analyses. *Medical Decision Making*, 11, 102-6, 1991.

Curry, B., and Rumelhart, D. MSnet: A Neural Network That Classifies Mass Spectra. *Tetrahedron Computer Methodology*, 3, 213-37, 1990.

Frean, M. The Upstart Algorithm: A Method for Constructing and Training Feedforward Neural Networks. *Neural Computation*, 2, 198-209, 1990.

Forsythe, D.E., and Buchanan, B.G. Knowledge Acquisition for Expert Systems: Some Pitfalls and Suggestions. *IEEE Transactions on Systems, Man, and Cybernetics*, 19, 435-42, 1989.

Gara, M.A., Rosenberg, S., and Goldberg, L. DSM-III-R as a Taxonomy. *Journal of Nervous and Mental Disease*, 180, 11-9, 1992.

Hrycej, T. *Modular Learning in Neural Networks*. John Wiley and Sons, Inc, 1992.

Tversky, A., and Kahneman, D. Judgment Under Uncertainty: Heuristics and Biases. *Science*, 185, 1124-31.

Murphy, P.M., and Aha, D.W. *UCI Repository of Machine Learning Databases* (on-line directory), University of California at Irvine, Department of Information and Computer Science, Irvine, CA, 1992.

Nilsson, N. *Learning Machines*. McGraw-Hill, New York, 1965.

Pople, H.E. Heuristic Methods for Imposing Structure on Ill-Structured Problems: The Structuring of Medical Diagnosis. In Szolovits, P. (ed) *Artificial Intelligence in Medicine*. Westview Press, 1982.

Quinlan, J.R. Induction of Decision Trees. *Machine Learning*, 1, 81-106, 1986.

Quinlan, J.R. Simplifying Decision Trees. *International Journal of Man-Machine Studies*, 27, 221-34, 1987.

Reibnegger, G, Weiss, G., Werner-Felmayer, G., Judmaier, G, and Wachter H. Neural Networks as a Tool for Utilizing Laboratory Information: Comparison with Linear Discriminant Analysis and with Classification and Regression Trees. *Proc. Nat. Acad. Sci. USA*, 88, 1146-30, 1991.

Rumelhart, D.E. Hinton, G.E., and Williams, R.J. Learning Internal Representation by Error Propagation. In Rumelhart, D.E., and McClelland, J.L. (eds) *Parallel Distributed Processing*. MIT Press, Cambridge, MA 1986.

Schiffmann, W., Joost, M., and Werner, R. *Optimization of the Backpropagation Algorithm for Training Multilayer Perceptrons*. Universitat Koblenz, Technical Report 15/1992, Fachbericht Physik, 1992.

medicineK.I. *Medical Decision Making*. Butterworth, Stoneham, 1988.

Surks, M.I, Chopra, I.J., Mariash, C.N., Nicoloff, J.T., and Solomon, D.H. American Thyroid Association Guidelines for Use of Laboratory Tests in Thyroid Disorders. *JAMA*, 263, 1529-32, 1990.

Weiss, S.M., Kulinowski, C.A., Amarel, S., and Safir, A. A Model-Based Method for Computer-Aided Medical Decision Making. *Artificial Intelligence* 11, 145-72, 1978.

Weiss, S. M., and Kulikowski, C.A. *Computer Systems That Learn*. Morgan Kaufmann, San Mateo, CA 1990.

Neural Network Models for Quantitative Genetics with Application to Dairy Cattle

David Bisant, Daniel Brown
Stanford University, Program in Neuroscience
Stanford, CA 94305
Email: bisant@decatur.stanford.edu

Abstract

This study applied neural networks to a problem in quantitative genetics, namely, the prediction of offspring given genetic data about both parents. Applied to dairy cattle, the network was to predict whether the offspring would or would not be a good milk producer within a reasonable tolerance level. The breeding of dairy cattle is a very competitive multi-million dollar industry. Artificial insemination centers have been established to facilitate and promote the breeding process. The ability to successfully predict offspring performance is important for these centers since they can avoid wasting resources on matings which are unlikely to produce good milk-producing offspring.

The network performance was compared against current quantitative genetic models coupled with insights from an expert geneticist. This conventional method was able to predict the offspring performance with 50% success. A basic feed-forward network with multiple hidden layers was applied to the problem, and was able to predict offspring performance with a success level of 68%.

This initial success of neural network models applied to the breeding of dairy cattle suggests they could be a useful tool when applied to other areas of quantitative genetics.

Introduction:

Current genetic theory has had a rich history of development and application. The study of discrete characters (e.g. brown eyes versus blue eyes) has fallen into the area of population genetics. Population genetics problems are easily modelled with simple algebra and there has been much success in applying these models to problems in the field. The study of continuous characters (e.g. height and weight) lies in the field of quantitative genetics. The problems in this area are much more complex and often involve the interactions of multiple genes with each other and with the environment. The models used on these problems are much more sophisticated, often employing advanced first order statistics, regression, and multivariate analysis. The models used in both population and quantitative genetics are probabilistic in nature since the underlying physical process is partly random. This underlying physical process is the segregation of one or more genes each of which follows the laws of Mendelian inheritance, and hence independently segregate and assort. Due to the complexity of these genetic and environmental interactions, quantitative genetic models have had limited success when applied to problems in the area.

Faced with stiff competition in a multimillion dollar industry, animal breeders are looking for ways to improve upon the present models. In the Canadian dairy system, artificial insemination centers have been established to promote and facilitate genetic improvement in dairy cattle. Over the last 25 years, the output of high quality milk by the average dairy cow has doubled. Stiff competition is effecting continued improvement. To bring about this improvement, superior animals in one generation must be selected and used to produce the next generation.

Genetic modelling is assisted in this process by a series of metrics developed by the Canadian dairy industry and government. These metrics are an evaluation of a dairy cow according to the following properties:

milk production These rankings are based on milk yield, fat content, protein content, and ratios between protein and fat. These traits are expressed as Breed Class Averages (BCA) which adjust for age, month of calving, and other environmental factors.

conformation These traits include size, shape, normality of various body parts, and others that are associated with the ability of an animal to withstand the stresses of high production and to have a long productive life in the herd. These metrics are adjusted for non-genetic factors such as age and inter-herd variations.

auxiliary traits These include such factors as calving ease, fertility, and milking speed.

These metrics are combined with relative and progeny information to produce an Estimated Transmitting Ability (ETA) score for each trait of interest. The ETA score is adjusted for the genetic merit of an animals mates, differences between sexes, and other genetic information. The ETA scores for an animal are continually updated as new progeny information becomes available. The ETA has been found to be the most accurate predictor of genetics which an animal can pass onto its progeny.

With dairy cattle, an overall index has been developed which incorporates the most important traits related to milk production and which are expected to be the most significant determinants of profitability at the farm level. This Lifetime Profit Index (LPI) emphasizes milk production but also weighs in other characters such as milk quality, mammary system, and feet & legs. The LPI score for an animal is the primary selection tool of all dairy breeders.

With the ETA scores and the LPI for each animal, a geneticist tries to determine which matings are most likely to produce the best offspring. In this case, given both parents, a model would predict the resulting offspring. By using historical data from many different prior matings, a neural network could be trained to predict the offspring of future matings. Such historical data is available. Unfortunately, the neural network is unable to factor in genetic data from several generations of a family. Such information might be useful.

Method:

For this study, the problem of predicting the genetic offspring for a given mating was attacked. This problem is the most important from a commercial standpoint and there exists

COW								BULL							CALF
production			conformation				LPI	production			conformation				LPI	LPI
-11	-8	-9	-1	0	-1	-4	-600	9	14	9	4	5	-14	6	784	-44
2	9	3	2	3	9	-1	518	6	9	7	-2	-2	-4	4	450	70
-1	16	3	2	2	4	-3	664	9	14	9	4	5	-14	6	784	594

Figure 1: Examples of ETA scores and LPI rankings for parents and offspring.

comparative measurements from competing methods. Breeding data for a one year period was obtained. The data consisted of ETA and LPI scores for a cow, a bull, and the resulting male offspring. A portion of the data is given in Figure 1. The goal is to use the ETA and LPI scores for the bull and cow to predict the LPI score for a resulting male offspring. Recall that the LPI is an overall index measurement and serves as the best indicator of future breeding success. Hence, it is this measurement which artificial insemination and breeding centers are most interested in. With this in mind, the neural network models used took the ETA scores and the LPI for both parents and produced the LPI for the resulting male offspring.

A perusal through the data illustrates some of the problems in presenting it to a neural network. Each different type of ETA score and the LPI all have a different range. The final output should be a number between -1000 and 2000. It was unclear how the output should be represented. A first guess was to present the input data directly, and directly predict the output with a linear output unit. This and the other output representation methods which were tried are listed below:

1. single linear output, no scaling

2. single output scaled between 0 and 1

3. 10 outputs discrete mapped between -1000 and 2000 (high=1.0 lo=0.0)

4. 10 outputs thermometer (high units set to 1.0)

5. 4 output discrete mapped between -1000 and 2000 (high=1.0 lo=0.0)

6. 4 output discrete 1000, 500, 500, 1000 (hi=1.0 lo=0.0)

In each case, the data was randomly divided into a training file of 325 matings and a cross-validation or testing file of 124 matings. It is the network performance on the testing files which is reported in the results section.

The best method of output representation was determined empirically. Determining this best method was the most time consuming step in the application process. In addition, a smaller effort was made to determine the optimal network architecture in terms of layers and hidden units. Standard feedforward networks were used in all trials. The LNKnet simulator from the Massachusetts Institute of Technology was used for constructing and training some of the neural networks. Additionally, the CNAPS neural network engine from Adaptive Solutions along with their Buildnet software package was used for the more computationally intensive network training.

Results:

The interpretation of the output results require some analysis. The LPI range in our data set spanned from -1000 to 2000. From a quantitative genetic standpoint, it would be valuable to predict within some reasonable distance of the correct values, say one-tenth of the entire range or 300 LPI units. From a breeding standpoint, it would be more valuable to predict whether the offspring will be a good producer (greater than 500) or whether it would be a bad producer (less than 500). Both of these scores are presented below.

The network used for the first datafile which represented the output with a linear output unit failed to converge. Our next trials with the output scaled between 0 and 1 produced good results. The other methods of data presentation were reasonably close but failed to provide further improvement.

With regard to network architecture, each of the networks tried had 16 input units. The networks architectures which performed the best had two hidden layers of 8—10 sigmoidal units each and the final output layer with a single sigmoidal unit. Other networks were tried by varying the number of layers and hidden units, but no improvement in performance was observed. Convergence was usually achieved after training for 7 or 8 epochs. The performance of the best network on the testing data was 68% accuracy when looking at the ability to predict good milk producers from bad milk producers. The performance was 62% when looking at the quantitative genetic measure where a prediction is considered correct if it is within 300 LPI units of the actual value.

Conclusions:

Previous to this study, the best performance achieved on this data by conventional methods was 50%. This performance was achieved by quantitative genetic models including information spanning many generations and matings. Also necessary to achieve this performance was the application of these models by a geneticist experienced in these areas. Hence, it is a bit of an art. Conventional methods are limited by the modelling power of first order statistics and what little insight the human expert provides.

The neural network approach is a different look at the same problem. Instead of tracking characters over several generations, these models infer the general inheritance pattern of these characters based on observations from random matings. This approach is not able to incorporate information from several generations, but it is able to incorporate second or higher order information into its model. The better performance of networks with more than 1 hidden layer would suggest there is alot of second or higher order information which is important in this problem. The success of this preliminary study suggests that neural networks can contribute significantly to problems in the area of quantitative genetics. Similarly, the accuracy of neural network models could provide significant savings to animal breeding centers by helping to avoid nonproductive matings.

Acknowledgements

The authors wish to thank Jacques Ajenstat and Brian VanDoormaal for their assistance in compiling the data, and David Rumelhart for providing the research environment that makes this type of study possible. They also wish to thank Adaptive Solutions for making available a CNAPS neural network engine.

References

[1] Canadian Association of Animal Breeders, PO Box 817, Woodstock Ontario, Canada N4S8A9. *genetic improvement*, 1993.

[2] D. S. Falconer. *Introduction to Quantitative Genetics*. Longman, Burnt Mill, England, 1989.

Unsupervised Competitive Learning Neural Network Algorithms for Circuit Bipartitioning

M. Kemal Unaltuna* and Vijay Pitchumani**

*Department of Electrical and Computer Engineering
121 Link Hall
Syracuse University, Syracuse, NY 13244

**Intel Corporation, SC3-38
2880 Northwestern Parkway
Santa Clara, CA 95052

Abstract

Circuit bipartitioning is an NP-hard combinatorial optimization problem in the layout synthesis of VLSI circuits, where we wish to find a partition of the circuit elements into two blocks such that the number of signal nets crossing the partition boundary is minimized. We have developed and experimented with several competitive learning neural network algorithms to solve this problem. The algorithms were tested on randomly generated circuits as well as several popular benchmark circuits. The stochastic reward and punishment neural network produced the best results which were comparable to those found by the Ratio Cut algorithm of Wei and Cheng.

1 Introduction

Circuit bipartitioning is a very important combinatorial optimization problem in the layout synthesis of VLSI circuits. It has been proven to be NP-hard. Given a circuit consisting of a set of cells (modules) connected by a set of nets (signals), the circuit bipartitioning (also called mincut partitioning) problem is to find a partition of the cells into two blocks such that the number of nets which have cells in both blocks is minimized.

A circuit netlist naturally defines a hypergraph H, with vertices corresponding to modules and (generalized) edges corresponding to signal nets. Throughout our discussion, we assume that the hypergraph H contains M nodes (modules) $V = \{m_1, m_2, \ldots, m_M\}$, and N edges (signal nets) $E = \{n_1, n_2, \ldots, n_N\}$ where each edge is a subset of V. Each node m_i has an area, or size, of $s(m_i)$. The objective is to partition the M nodes to two nonempty disjoint subsets, or blocks, L and R, $V = L \cup R$, with sizes $size(L)$, and $size(R)$, such that the number of hypergraph edges connecting the two blocks (also called the $cutset$) is minimized. Since the problem is NP-hard, many heuristic algorithms have been proposed, the most popular of which is due to Fiduccia and Mattheyses [1] with a time complexity of $O(P)$ where P is the total number of pins. Generally, the Fiduccia-Mattheyses (FM) algorithm is quite efficient but it needs a predefined restriction on the subset sizes $size(L)$, and $size(R)$, which is usually set such that $size(L) \simeq size(R)$. For hierarchical designs predefining the subset sizes is overly restrictive. Recently, Wei and Cheng introduced the ratio-cut metric to locate the "natural" clusters in the circuit and obtained improved results [2].

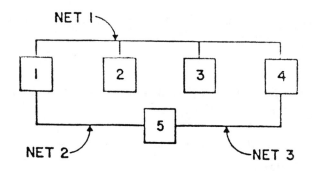

Figure 1: A simple circuit

2 A Competitive Learning Neural Net Model for Circuit Bi-partitioning

Circuit partitioning can be seen as a categorization problem where we want to assign the modules of the circuit to partitions each of which defines a category. This task can be accomplished by a certain class of neural networks called competitive learning or winner-take-all neural networks [4]. The aim of such networks is to cluster or categorize the input data. Similar inputs should be classified as being in the same category, and so should fire the same output unit.

Our task is to code the modules as input vectors to a competitive learning neural network with two output units. This representation scheme should allow the neural network to categorize the modules according to their connectivities such that heavily interconnected modules are grouped together into the same category. This way, we can also minimize the cutset. We could use the representation scheme proposed by Hemani and Postula [3] for the similar placement problem where they used the rows of the connectivity matrix as input vectors to a self-organizing neural network. The connectivity matrix $C = [c_{ij}]$ is derived from the netlist of modules such that c_{ij} represents the connectivity between modules i and j. This transformation however, destroys the hypergraph property of the circuit netlist by mapping it to a weighted graph. For the partitioning problem such a transformation is unnecessary. We can use the netlist directly to represent the modules in terms of the signal nets they are connected to. Consider the MxN matrix $A = [a_{ij}]$. The entry a_{ij} will be one if module m_i is on net n_j, i.e., $m_i \in n_j$, and zero otherwise. This way, row a_i of the matrix A is a binary vector representing module m_i. As an example, consider the circuit shown in Figure 1. We have 5 modules and 3 nets. Module m_1 is on nets n_1 and n_2, but not on net n_3. Thus, the vector a_1 corresponding to module m_1 is equal to $(1,1,0)^T$. For this example, the matrix A is given by:

$$A = \begin{pmatrix} 1 & 1 & 0 \\ 1 & 0 & 0 \\ 1 & 0 & 0 \\ 1 & 0 & 1 \\ 0 & 1 & 1 \end{pmatrix}$$

The representation scheme proposed above is in one-to-one correspondence with the hypergraph model and accurately describes the circuit at hand.

Now consider a neural network with two winner-take-all output units numbered 0 and 1, and the standard competitive learning rule [4]. Let w_{ij} be the weight from input j to output i. Our first neural network algorithm is given as follows:

Algorithm 1:
Initialize weights from N inputs to the 2 output nodes to small random values.
Set the sizes of the partitions to zero, $size_0 = size_1 = 0$.
for each module m_i **do**
    Present its input vector and determine the winner node k^* with minimum
        $d_k = \sum_{j=1}^{N} (a_{ij} - w_{kj})^2$
    Assign module m_i to node k^*.
    Set $size_{k^*} = size_{k^*} + s(m_i)$.
endfor
Initialize gain term $(0 \leq \eta < 1)$. Set iterations = 1.
while Weights did not converge **do**
    Randomly select a module m_i and present its corresponding input vector a_i.
    Compute distances d_k between the input vector and each output node k using
        $d_k = \sum_{j=1}^{N} (a_{ij} - w_{kj})^2 + \alpha * size_k$
    Select winner node k^* as that output node with minimum d_k.
    Update weights to node k^* using
        $\Delta w_{k^* j} = \eta (a_{ij} - w_{k^* j})$
    if iterations mod $M = 0$ **then** $\eta = 0.90\eta$
    Set $size_{k^*} = size_{k^*} + s(m_i), size_{1-k^*} = size_{1-k^*} - s(m_i)$.
    Increment iterations
endwhile
Set $size_0 = size_1 = 0$.
for each module m_i **do**
    Present its input vector and determine the winner node k^* with minimum
        $d_k = \sum_{j=1}^{N} (a_{ij} - w_{kj})^2$
    Assign module m_i to node k^*.
    Set $size_{k^*} = size_{k^*} + s(m_i)$.
endfor
Determine the number of nets cut by the partition boundary.

Note that an extra term, $\alpha * size_k$, is added to the distance calculation during the learning phase to bias the network towards the partition with the smaller size.

While Algorithm 1 performed well on small examples with up to 40 modules, its performance progressively got worse as the problem size increased. The results for even the smallest benchmark problem PrimarySC1 (752 modules, 904 nets) were very bad and the running time became unacceptably high.

3   A Stochastic Reward and Punishment Neural Network

There are several problems with the winning and learning rules used in Algorithm 1. In the minimum distance winning rule, the zero and one entries in the input vector are equally important. But we would like a module to be classified according to the nets that it is connected to and not according to the nets it is not connected to. Consider the following winning rule where the output unit with the largest score is declared the winner. The score of a unit is defined as the normalized scalar product of the input vector and the weight vector plus a normalized balance term, and can be written as

$$score_k = \frac{1}{|a_i|} \sum_{\substack{j \\ a_{ij} \neq 0}} w_{kj} + \alpha \left(1 - \frac{size_k}{total\_size}\right) \tag{1}$$

where $|a_i|$ is the number of 1 entries in the a_i-vector, and $total\_size = \sum_{i=1}^{M} s(m_i)$. Finding the winner is now a $O(|a_i|)$ operation where it was a $O(N)$ operation in Algorithm 1.

The learning rule in Algorithm 1 has a similar problem where the whole weight vector is updated each time, regardless of the corresponding entries in the input vector. We can construct a new rule where only those elements of the weight vectors are updated which correspond to one entries in the input vector. Let node k be the winner and l the loser. The new rule is given by:

$$\Delta w_{kj} = \begin{cases} \eta(1 - w_{kj}) & a_{ij} = 1 \\ 0 & \text{otherwise} \end{cases}$$

$$\Delta w_{lj} = \begin{cases} \eta(0 - w_{lj}) & a_{ij} = 1 \\ 0 & \text{otherwise} \end{cases}$$

In this learning rule, the winner is rewarded and the loser is punished. Note that with the use of the new winning and learning rules, one iteration of the algorithm can be accomplished in $O(|a_i|)$ time. We will refer to the modified algorithm as Algorithm 2.

Although Algorithm 2 performed much better than Algorithm 1, the solutions to the benchmark problems were on average still considerably worse than the ones obtained by the FM algorithm. One reason for this is that very frequently it gets stuck at local minima. To overcome this, we created Algorithm 3 where the winner is determined using a stochastic rather than a deterministic rule. Let the winning probability of a node k be given by

$$p_k = \frac{e^{score_k/T}}{\sum_l e^{score_l/T}} \tag{2}$$

Since we have only two nodes this expression becomes

$$p_k = \frac{1}{1 + e^{(score_l - score_k)/T}} \tag{3}$$

When T is very high, both units have winning probabilities close to 0.5 regardless of their scores. As T approaches zero, the winning probability of the unit with the higher score approaches 1. With this approach (which we will call Algorithm 3) we were able to find solutions as well as or better than the FM algorithm on many initialization instances.

In the next section we describe the experimental setup and give the simulation results.

4   Simulation Results

A simulation algorithm for Algorithm 3 has been implemented in C language on a SUN4 architecture. The parameters were found in the following way.

The balance coefficient α should try to keep a sensible balance between the partitions rather than enforcing a strictly 1:1 balance. Since the scalar product term in equation (1) is normalized, its value is between 0 and 1. We want the balance term to contribute no more than 10 % to the overall score. Since it too is normalized, we set α to 0.1.

Ideally, the starting temperature T_{start} should be set to a value such that the winning probabilities are close to 0.5. In the worst case, the difference between the scores of the winning and losing units can be at most 1.1, since the highest possible score is $1 + 0.1 = 1.1$, and the lowest possible score is 0. Thus we have to set T_{start} such that

$$p_k = \frac{1}{1 + e^{-1.1/T_{start}}} \simeq 0.5 \tag{4}$$

where k is the node with the higher score. For example, setting $T_{start} = 11$ makes $p_k = 0.525$. We could start with this value for T_{start}, however our experiments showed that starting with $p_k \simeq 0.6$ is sufficient for simulation purposes above which the results show very little, if any, improvement. This value of p_k approximately corresponds to $T_{start} = 2.5$ which we used in our simulations.

Similarly, there is no need to cool the network until $T_{end} \simeq 0$. We found a value of 0.001 to be adequate for this purpose. Starting with $T = T_{start}$, T was decreased by 5 % every M iterations until $T < T_{end}$.

A very interesting observation we made is that setting the gain factor $\eta \simeq 1$ and keeping it there for a long time produced much better results than reducing it smoothly over time. This is because the network is better able avoiding local minima and explore a bigger part of the search space when the weight vectors were changed frequently and abruptly. Thus, η was kept at the value 1.0 until $T < T_{end}$ and than reduced rapidly by 15 % every M iterations for $20 * M$ iterations.

The algorithm was tested on six benchmark examples from Microelectronics Center of North Carolina (MCNC): PrimSC1, PrimSC2, Test02, Test03, Test04, and Test05. For each test case the algorithm was run 10 times and the best result was taken. The largest example (PrimSC2) has 3029 nets and 2907 modules. In terms of CPU time, the longest run took about 35 seconds.

Table 1 compares our results with the results of Wei and Cheng [2] where they ran the FM algorithm and their ratio cut algorithm 20 times each and reported the best results. The size ratio was set to 1:3 for each algorithm. In Table 1 the reported ratio cut values are normalized, i.e.

$$RatioCut = \frac{NetCut}{\frac{size_0 * size_1}{total\_size^2}}$$

As can be observed from the table, the neural net algorithm generally outperforms the FM algorithm by as much as 50 % (PrimSC2) except on Test04 and Test05 where the ratio cut values are within 4 %. It also outperforms the ratio cut algorithm on PrimSC2. On average its results are slightly worse than the results of the ratio cut algorithm.

TABLE 1

Circuit	# Nets	# Modules	Fiduccia-Mattheyses		Wei-Cheng		Neural Network	
			Net Cut	Ratio Cut	Net Cut	Ratio Cut	Net Cut	Ratio Cut
PrimSC1	904	752	46	196.9	35	147.3	21	192.2
PrimSC2	3029	2907	166	728.4	77	361.1	77	358.3
Test02	1866	1663	66	287.7	43	189.3	49	213.8
Test03	1699	1607	84	389.1	49	221	61	250.6
Test04	1738	1515	44	176	44	176	46	184
Test05	2910	2595	42	168	42	168	44	176.2

References

[1] C. M. Fiduccia and R. M. Mattheyses, "A linear time heuristic for improving network partitions", *ACM/IEEE Design Automation Conference*, pp. 175-181, 1982.

[2] Y. C. Wei and C. K. Cheng, "Ratio cut partitioning for hierarchical designs", *IEEE Transactions on CAD*, pp. 911-921, July 1991.

[3] A. Hemani and A. Postula, "Cell placement by self organization", *Neural Networks*, Vol.3, pp. 377-383, 1990.

[4] J. Hertz, A. Krough, and R. G. Palmer, *Introduction to the theory of neural computation.* Addison-Wesley, Redwood City, California, pp. 218-219, 1991.

[5] R. P. Lippmann, "An introduction to computing with neural nets", *IEEE ASSP Magazine*, pp. 4-22, April 1987.

Modified Back-Propagation Neural Network Device Characterization for VLSI Circuit Simulation

Pekka Ojala, Jukka Saarinen and Kimmo Kaski

Tampere University of Technology
Microelectronics Laboratory
P.O. Box 692,
FIN-33101 Tampere, Finland

ojala@ee.tut.fi, jukkas@ee.tut.fi, kaski@ee.tut.fi

Abstract

A novel, fast and accurate neural network tool is proposed for efficient technology independent realization of the interface between device modelling and circuit simulation. An enhanced back-propagation neural network based algorithm is applied to the problem of modelling various device characteristics. Simulations show fast convergence or learning rate and an excellent fit of recalled characteristics to the measured device data. The utilized algorithm is robust and capable of presenting the entire device characteristics unaltered even with largely reduced amount of the teaching material. The good monotonicity of the neural network generated device data facilitates the usage of the method in circuit simulation purposes. Possible further applications of implementing circuit level macromodels with this technique are discussed.

1 Introduction

The integration of measured semiconductor device behaviour or data from numerical device simulators into a circuit simulator has been a long standing well known problem for the integrated circuit designer. For digital circuits the requirement of accurate functional modelling include knowledge of device currents together with the internal and external RC-products to facilitate proper timing simulations. For analog circuit designs the simulation has proven more difficult. The linear circuit gain is governed by the small-signal parameters, *transconductance* and *output conductance*, and their frequency behaviour. Therefore, accurate and continuous models for small-signal parameters over the complete operation region are required. The continuity of these models follows if the derivatives of the device current models with respect to terminal potentials are continuous [Tsi87]. Precision modelling of analog circuits also requires accurate presentation of the substrate effects in dc- and ac-operation. Other inaccuracies in simulation have been attributed to poor or non-existent modelling of the subthreshold region, non-linearities in device operation and voltage dependent capacitances. Several approaches are currently available to generate device level behavioural modelling. The numerical solutions of semiconductor equations of the devices have been applied in 2D and 3D to accurately model the physics of ultra small devices. Similarly, by starting from basic semiconductor physics, microscopic or particle level simulation, approaches have provided the device electrical characteristics. These techniques are computationally intensive tasks that are suitable for technology analysis and enhancement. Their capability to provide the device modelling interface for circuit simulation simultaneously as it proceeds is, however, seriously limited by the required CPU-time. Other techniques have been developed for more efficient device modelling interfaces. Typical approaches for the realization of this crucial interface for accurate and fast circuit simulation have included analytical, parameterized semiconductor device models [Ant88,Met90,She83,Tsi84] table look-up models with various interpolation techniques [Rof93,Shi83] and a more atypical method of tensor product splines [Bis85].

The most widely applied approach of using *parameterized analytical models* for presenting electrical characteristics of a device has been plagued with several difficulties. The parameter extraction for these models, itself, presents a difficult problem even if the models are physically sound and include every possible physical phenomena that completely describes the device. Two approaches can be utilized in the device parameter extraction. First, the parameters for physically based models can be defined from the tedious and time consuming extraction of *measurements* for the device.

Some models use non-physical fitting parameters to include device behaviour that can not be explained otherwise. This approach faces difficulties, as in the case of the semi-empirical MOSFET model usually referred as level 3 in SPICE circuit simulator, owing to the difficult estimation of parameters from regression fitting of model to the data. Second, the previously extracted physically sound set of parameters can be *fine-tuned in a general non-linear optimizer* to fit the model to the measured or numerically simulated device data [Dog83,Oja88,Yan83]. This approach is, however, capable of producing highly unphysical interpretations of the device parameters, which in turn may show up as unexpected and detrimental effects during circuit simulation.

As a conclusion the analytical and semi-empirical models, while introducing several fitting parameters for the second order *short* or *narrow channel effects* or *subthreshold conduction*, suffer critically from difficult parameter extraction. The determination of parameters for these models is a tedious numerical task itself. While it is performed only once for the device, the single parameter set is usually not capable of describing multiple sizes of devices.

To overcome the difficulties in parameterized models, a variety of table look-up methods with different interpolation techniques have been used [Rof93]. These models typically store the device current in a table. For a four terminal device such as MOSFET or MESFET, a 3D table is formed as a function of gate, drain and substrate potential. The table size, therefore, grows as the third power of the number of input vectors, and becomes the limiting factor in the modelling accuracy. While efficient interpolation is required to reduce the amount of data in the tables, the continuity of the derivatives between consecutive datapoints is also required for proper presentation of small signal parameters. For digital circuit simulation linear interpolation can be adequate, but with practical table sizes it leads to large error in small signal parameters of analog circuits. The third order interpolation scheme of Ref. [Rof93] is capable of estimating the derivatives with smaller amounts of data, but polynomial fit requires another set of numerical operations. The methods that present the device current with a 2D table of gate and drain potential and add the substrate effect or channel length modulation with a sparse 3D table are capable of further reducing the amount of required data points. These models, however also, require a higher order polynomial fit for interpolated datapoints and will, otherwise, lead to inaccurate small-signal parameters.

In this paper the authors describe a novel, physically and technologically independent methodology for the realization of the device modelling interface for circuit simulation purposes. This interface has been implemented with a modified back-propagation neural network algorithm [Vog88]. The algorithm is programmed with C-programming language in a typical small-scale UNIX workstation, but can also be transferred to any desktop personal computer and it does not require extensive memory capabilities or superfast data processing.

2   Network structure and learning scheme

The network used for this study is a three-layer feedforward network with the error back-propagation learning algorithm [Rum86] that consists of input, hidden, and output layers. Each layer contains several processing elements with sigmoidal nonlinearities. Cybenko [Cyb89] has shown that this net can be used to approximate arbitrary functions, *i.e.* it can model any continuous nonlinear transformation. The significant consequence is that a neural net using sigmoidal nonlinearities and only one hidden layer can form complex disjoint and convex decision regions. In this study, the back-propagation neural network is utilized as a continuous function approximator.

The network is feedforward in the sense that each unit receives inputs only from the units in the preceding layer. The network converts input signals according to connection weights. During learning, connection weights are adjusted in a direction to minimize the sum of squared errors between the desired outputs and the network outputs. The errors are then propagated back to modify each connection weight.

A back-propagation neural network used herein is shown in Fig. 1. In the following, the subscripts k, j and i refer to any unit in the output, hidden, and input layers, respectively. The total inputs to unit j in the hidden layer or unit k in the output layer is

$$net_r = \sum_S w_{rs} O_{s'}, \qquad r = k,j; \quad s = j,i; \tag{1}$$

where w_{rs} is the weight from the sth unit to the rth unit and O_S represents the output of unit s in the hidden and input layers. A sigmoidal nonlinearity is then applied to each unit r to obtain the output as

$$O_r = f\left(net_r\right) = \frac{1}{\exp\left\{-\left(net_r - \theta_r\right)\right\}}, \tag{2}$$

where θ_r serves as a threshold of unit r. Hence, each layer communicates with all successive layers. There is no feedback within the network between layers of individual units and no communication with other units in the same layer.

In the learning process, the network is presented with a pair of patterns, an input pattern, and a corresponding desired output pattern. Learning comprises of changing the connection weights and unit thresholds so as to minimize the mean squared error between the actual outputs and the desired output patterns with the gradient descent method. The activity of each unit is propagated forward through each layer of the network by using (1) and (2). The resulting output pattern is then compared with the desired output pattern, and an error δ_k for each output unit is calculated as

$$\delta_k = (t_k - O_k)\, O_k\,(1 - O_k), \tag{3}$$

where t_k is the desired output and O_k is the actual output. The error at the output is then back-propagated recursively to each lower layer as follows:

$$\delta_j = O_j\left(1 - O_j\right) \sum_k \delta_k w_{kj}. \tag{4}$$

In order for the network to learn, the value of each weight and threshold has to be incrementally adjusted proportionally to the contribution of each unit compared with the total error. The change in each weight and threshold is calculated as

$$\Delta w_{rs}(l+1) = \eta \delta_r O_s + \alpha \Delta w_{rs}(l), \quad r = k, j; \; s = j, i; \tag{5}$$

where η controls the rate of learning and l denotes the number of times for which a set of input patterns have been presented to the network. The parameter α determines the effect of previous weight changes on the current direction of movement in weight space. The connection weights and thresholds of the network are usually initialized to small random values uniformly distributed between -0.5 and 0.5. This initialization prevents the hidden units from acquiring identical weights during learning.

One characteristic of error back-propagation nets is the long learning time. Learning times are typically longer when complex decision regions are required and when networks have more hidden layers. To accelerate the convergence of this standard back-propagation algorithm, we have used the modified back-propagation method presented by Vogl et.al. [Vog88]. This algorithm includes three main modifications.

The first modification is that the network weights are not updated after each learning pattern. Instead, the weights are modified only after all input patterns have been presented. The changes for each weight are summed over all of the input patterns and the sum is applied to modify the weight after each iteration over all the patterns. The updating rule for weights in the network is invoked according to the following rule:

$$\Delta w_{rs}(l+1) = \eta \sum \delta_r O_s + \alpha \Delta w_{rs}(l), \quad r = k, j; \; s = j, i. \tag{6}$$

Further modifications include the altered learning rate η and the momentum factor α. The learning rate η is varied according to whether or not an iteration decreases the total error for all patterns. If an update results in reduced total error, η is multiplied by a factor $\phi > 1$ for the next iteration. If a step produces a network with a total error more than a few percent above the previous value, all changes to the weights are rejected, η is multiplied by a factor $\beta < 1$, α is set to zero, and the step is repeated. When a successful step is taken, α is reset to its original value. For a successful step α resembles momentum as it tends to favour the change of weights to the earlier successful direction.

The modifications to the standard back-propagation algorithm can greatly accelerate the convergence. After the learning, the neural network exhibits extremely low memory and computation requirements during classification. Hence, it is very suitable for real-time processing.

3   Device modelling methodology

For the circuit simulation several characteristic sources of data from the devices are initially required in order to facilitate the variety of analyses of interest, namely the operation point, transient, dc- and ac-analysis. The required data or models for circuit simulation, for example, with FET-devices includes the terminal currents versus bias voltages and terminal non-reciprocal non-linear relationships of capacitances versus bias voltages. Typically, these models also present small-signal parameters analytically for the FET. In Fig. 2 we present the methodology for providing these data sets to the circuit simulation environment by using an enhanced back-propagation algorithm [Vog88] that was described in above.

We have modelled a typical FET drain current dc-curve family by giving the value of drain current data to the processing network as output teaching material. Correspondingly drain bias and gate bias values act as the network input teaching material. Therefore, our back-propagation network consists of two input processing elements and one output processing element. In addition to them, we have chosen to use one hidden layer of processing elements. In the modelling five hidden layer processing elements were used. This was found by trial and error to be a suitable and cost-effective number for the drain current data in question. If we had chosen to seek a solution for the drain current also as a function of substrate bias, we would have included a third input processing element to present the third dimension of the input vector. The addition of the bias processing element for the input layer is expected to enhance the learning capabilities of the network. First, with the 2D model we study the monotonicity and accuracy of the network. An example of 3D modelling will subsequently be given. As our present network consists of eight processing elements and a bias unit, the updating of the network in each iteration cycle is extremely fast even with a modest desktop computer. We have used a fully connected network with all the processing elements in a hidden layer connected to the all input layer elements with weighted connections and also to the sole output layer element similarly with weighted connections.

The training material, *i.e.* input and output data for the network is first scaled linearly to fit between 0 and 1, typically we have used the range [0.15,0.85]. Scaling of input data ensures that a proper section of the sigmoid is used in producing the output of input layer elements. Similarly, scaling of output training set enables the output layer elements to present the data with the sigmoid function. Before teaching of the network can take place the values of the weights are selected randomly within a desired range of values as described in section 2. During the teaching period the scaled input data is fed to the network input nodes and the desired scaled output is presented to the output node. The back-propagation of error between the desired output and network output is used for updating the weights between the processing elements in different layers of the network. This process is iteratively repeated until a desired error level is reached for the modelled output or until no further improvement will take place during a specified number of iterations. The final values of the weights are employed in the recalling of network output for chosen input and finally the output is rescaled to the original scale of data.

4   Results, comparisons and discussions

As the target of our neural network device characteristic modeller, we have chosen a GaAs MESFET technology. This serves as a fairly difficult task because the simulation accuracy of analog GaAs circuits has consistently been worse than for comparable Si MOSFET technology due to less evolved device models [Sho92]. Our proposed approach is also applicable to other difficult device modelling problems, such as Si MOSFETs with small channel lengths. In Fig. 3 we present the modelling results for the drain current curve family of GaAs MESFET's with a geometrical form factor $W/L = 50\mu m/2\mu m$ (data from [Sho92]). The modelling output from the network is marked with 'o' and it is superimposed on the training data that is marked with 'x'. A very good fit with a relative sum of squares error of 1.41 per cent was reached in less than 70000 iteration cycles for the weights during the learning period. The precision modelling of the dc-curve family for GaAs MESFET has been difficult with the analytical models because of the complicated second order phenomena in device physics. These device anomalies include, for example, backgating or sidegating from adjacent devices, impact ionization triggered leakage current to substrate and gate terminal, drain potential induced barrier lowering for short devices and deep level trapping dependent leakage current and subthreshold characteristics [Sho92]. Therefore, even with a set of optimized model parameters the above scale of modelling error has been unreachable. Therefore, this error level presents a remarkably good fit to the measured data for the particular type of device.

The evolution of the modelling error for this data is presented in Fig. 4. Here we have shown the modelling error from 0 to 10 000 iterations, with the inserted figure for iterations between 0-100. Learning can be seen to evolve with some fast leaps between slower paces until finally after 70000 iterations the convergence to the minimum error with this network is reached.

While the magnitude of the relative error for the modelling of the curve family is acceptable, the monotonicity and the interpolation capabilities of the network output have to be verified to ensure proper modelling of the data between the teaching material data points. The monotonicity of the recalled data with optimal weights was tested by creating a fine mesh of input vectors that were fed to the network. The resulting network output presented a well behaved monotonicity. Fig. 5 presents a graphical 3-dimensional view of monotonicity where the data, that the network recalled, is marked with dots while the training set is marked with 'x'.

A more demanding test for the network is performed by reducing the amount of training material to one half of the original data by removing every other gate bias value from the data set and calculating the network weights again for the remaining data. These weights are further used to recall the original data set as a whole, thereby interpolating the curves for every other value of gate bias. Fig. 6 presents the result of modelling the interpolation of data. All the measured data in this particular test is marked with 'x' and the learnt data for the trained points of data set with '*'. The interpolated, recalled data corresponding measured points is marked with 'o' and the recalled mesh data with '.'. While the interpolated data-points do show somewhat larger residual error in modelling, 6.25 per cent compared with 1.81 per cent for the learnt data, the substantial reduction of the teaching material has not lead into a catastrophic modelling failure. Instead, the network is still able to present the intermediate data points with reasonable and adequate accuracy.

To further evaluate the modelling capabilities of the network to a different types of data, we have modelled the temperature dependence of the GaAs MESFET drain current versus gate voltage characteristics. Fig. 7 presents the simulated device data compared with the measured data. Again a remarkably good fit to the data is shown within less than 70000 iterations of learning updates for the network weights. Multidimensionality of the network input is now formed by the temperature parameter together with the gate bias voltage. Similarly, any other variable can be added to further specify the complexity and dimension of input data matrix. The continuity of drain current from the *subthreshold* to above threshold regions of operation is a difficult problem for any analytical model. A smooth transition, which can be seen from Fig. 7 for several temperatures, is assured by the monotonicity of the neural network output. In modelling the drain current destination patterns data was first scaled by taking a logarithm of base ten, which stands for performing a non-linear scaling, in order to ensure an adequate dynamics for the network. Furthermore, the linear scaling within the range [0,1] was performed, as before, for the network input data. In recalling the network output with optimal weights the rescaling procedures were performed in reverse order. The linear scaling was performed first which was followed by the exponential rescaling of base ten. A relative error of 1.77 per cent was reached for this particular modelling. This value presents a very good modelling accuracy when it is compared to the analytical models. The latter cannot adequately estimate the magnitude of the gate leakage currents at elevated temperatures because of the difficulties in estimating the leakage current model parameters [Sho92].

Next, in Fig. 8, we present an example of small-signal parameter modelling, namely the GaAs MESFET output conductance, as it is recalled with the same network topology that was used earlier. Output conductance modelling with analytical models has suffered from discontinuous models between regions of device operation. In comparison, the neural model provides fully continuous and monotonous modelling. The network learnt the teaching material in 70000 iterations after which the final relative error of 2.26 per cent was reached. In comparison the typical accuracy for analytic output conductance modelling with optimized model parameters has remained at 5-10 per cent for analog CMOS technologies [Oja88].

Finally, in order to provide a useful and fast device modelling interface neural network will have to be capable of modelling device data with more than two input dimensions. The 3D table look-up models allow presentation of the FET device data with respect to all four terminal potentials (Vgs, Vds, Vsb). We demonstrate the similar modelling with a back-propagation algorithm by adding a third processing element for the 3D input data-vector in our network. In Fig. 9, recalled GaAs MESFET drain current characteristics is presented with the training set. Fig. 9 a) shows the lower gate bias regime of -1.5 to -0.3 V and Fig. 9 b) the higher regime of 0.0 to 0.3 V, respectively. The 3D input vector for network is formed by adding the substrate or sidegate potential to feed the third input processing element. We use both positive and negative sidegate bias to make the modelling problem even more demanding. In less than 60000 iterations the network converged to a result showing relative error of 2.28 per cent for the entire 3D data. Previously, a 3-4 per cent relative error for short-channel Si MOSFET had been demonstrated with 3D table look-up technique [Rof93].

Since the data that was given to the network was sparse, even better accuracy can be achieved if a finer mesh for input vector is used. We would like to draw attention to some specific characteristics of the device data. Namely, the drain current at high drain to source potential difference has a characteristic increase owing to electron-hole pairs that are generated by impact ionization in the channel. The generated holes will lead to decrease of substrate depletion thickness under the channel and this, together with the generated electrons, tend to increase the drain current. Analytically, it is difficult to model this phenomenon within the accuracy that is presented here. Similarly, the recovery from negative sidegating at high drain bias due to impact ionization is correctly presented with the simulations. The complicated nature of shift from the negative to positive sidegating is correctly modelled by the network which demonstrates high variability of the network transformation of weights to fitted data.

In our example the back-propagation network device modelling interface requires a total of 21 network weights for two dimensional data and a bias unit. If the third input dimension is included in network with five hidden layer elements, total of 26 weights are required. For more than five processing elements in the hidden layer, the number of weights will be higher. These weights will have to be stored in memory for each presentation of data. The amount of stored weights presents a remarkable saving of memory when it is compared to the table look-up method. About 500-1000 datapoints will have to be saved for each channel length, for the table to attain the same accuracy. Therefore, we use only 3-5 per cent of the memory that is used in a typical implementation of the table look-up method.

In terms of the CPU-time the implemented neural network interface is more efficient for circuit simulation than analytical models. The device modelling task is required to be performed only once and circuit simulation is performed sequentially with fast recollection of the model from the stored weight-vector. In comparison, analytical models are evaluated simultaneously with the circuit simulation which leads to longer overall simulation times. Therefore, the implemented neural network device modelling interface is also capable of reducing the time-consumption of circuit simulations.

5 Conclusion

The method of realizing the interface between device modelling and circuit simulation using a neural network algorithm has been shown to produce excellent fit to the measured data. The objective of presenting a general device characteristics in circuit simulator environment is, therefore, reached. Any kind of circuit element can be accurately modelled and represented, and a standard automatable neural network can be set up for the construction of these representations.

The implemented enhanced back-propagation algorithm combines a fast learning rate with efficient and accurate recall of the learnt material. The method is especially suitable for applications where physically justified analytic device models lack the required accuracy. Such is the case of deep submicrometer devices or novel device structures with as of yet unclear physical phenomena. Also the technology independent approach for the modelling facilitates quick adjustment to the new device structures, materials and technologies.

The macromodelling of complex circuit structures with easy neural network parameter presentation vastly simplifies the required simulations for large systems. It reduces efficiently the required memory for the circuit presentation and simulation. The proposed approach for modelling interface facilitates and encourages the user to model complex topologies. In simulation it promotes inclusion of desired behavioural information of general phenomena with easy to extract neural network weights, which are a fully compact and ideal form to present, save and transfer knowledge, such as system level behaviour.

6   Acknowledgements

This work has been supported by the Academy of Finland and Emil Aaltonen Foundation.

References

[Ant88] P. Antognetti and G. Massobrio, Semiconductor Device Modeling with SPICE, McGraw-Hill, New York, 1988.

[Bis85] G. Bischoff and J. P. Krusius, "Technology Independent Device Modeling for Simulation of Integrated Circuits for FET Technologies," *IEEE Transactions on Computer-Aided Design*, vol. CAD-4, no. 1, Jan. 1985, pp. 99-110.

[Cyb89] C. Cybenko, "Approximations by Superpositions of a Sigmoidal Function," *Math. Contr., Signal, Syst.*, vol. 2, 1989, pp. 303-314.

[Dog83] K. Doganis and D. E. Scharfetter, "General Optimization and Extraction of IC Device Model Parameters," *IEEE Transactions on Electron Devices*, vol. ED-30, no. 9, Sep. 1983, pp. 1219-1229.

[Met90] META-Software, Inc., HPICE User's Manual 9001, Campbell, CA 95008, 1990.

[Oja88] P. Ojala, K. Kankaala, H. Tenhunen, and K. Kaski, "Advanced Techniques for Circuit Parameter Extraction", Report 5-88, Tampere University of Technology, Department of Electrical Engineering, Laboratory of Microelectronics, July 1988.

[Rof93] A. Rofougaran and A. A. Abidi, "A Table Lookup FET Model for Accurate Analog Circuit Simulation," *IEEE Transactions on Computer-Aided Design of Integrated Circuits and Systems*, vol. CAD-12, no. 2, Feb. 1993, pp. 324-335.

[Rum86] D. E. Rumelhart, G. E. Hinton, and R. J. Williams, "Learning Internal Representations by Error Propagation in Parallel Distributed Processing," *Explorations in the Microstructures of Cognition, Vol. 1: Foundations*, Cambridge, MA, The MIT Press, 1986, pp. 318-362.

[She83] B. J. Sheu, D. L. Scharfetter, P.-K. Ko, and M.-C. Jeng, "BSIM: Berkeley Short Channel IGFET Model for MOS-Transistors," *IEEE J. Solid-State Circuits*, vol. SC-22, no. 4, Aug. 1983, pp. 558-566.

[Shi83] T. Shima, H. Yamada, and R. L. M. Dang, "Table Look-up MOSFET Modeling System Using a 2-D Device Simulator and Monotonic Piecewise Cubic Interpolation," *IEEE Transactions on Computer-Aided Design of Integrated Circuits and Systems*, vol. CAD-2, no. 2, Apr. 1983, pp. 121-126.

[Sho92] F. S. Shoucair and P. K. Ojala, "High-Temperature Electrical Characteristics of GaAs MESFET's (25-400°C)," *IEEE Transactions on Electron Devices*, vol. 39, no. 7, Jul. 1992, pp. 1551-1557.

[Tsi84] Y. P. Tsividis and G. Masetti, "Problems in Precision Modeling of the MOS Transistor for Analog Applications," *IEEE Transactions on Computer-Aided Design*, vol. CAD-3, no. 1, Jan. 1984, pp. 72-79.

[Tsi87] Y. P. Tsividis, Operation and Modelling of the MOS Transistor, McGraw-Hill, New York, 1987.

[Vog88] T. P. Vogl, J. K. Mangis, A. K. Rigler, W. T. Zink, and D. L. Alkon, "Accelerating the Convergence of the Back-propagation Method," *Biological Cybernetics*, 59, 1988, pp. 257-263.

[Yan83] P. O. A. Yang and P. Chatterjee, "An Optimal Parameter Extraction Program for MOSFET Models," *IEEE Transactions on Electron Devices*, vol. ED-30, no. 9, Sep. 1983, pp. 1214-1219.

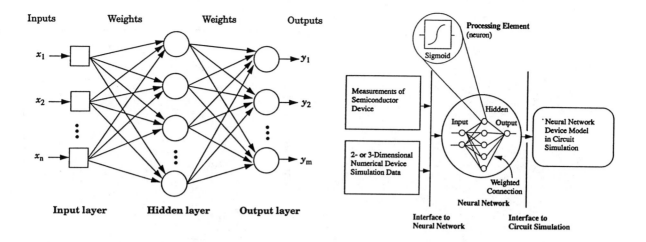

Figure 1. Structure of neural network.

Figure 2. Neural network device modelling methodology.

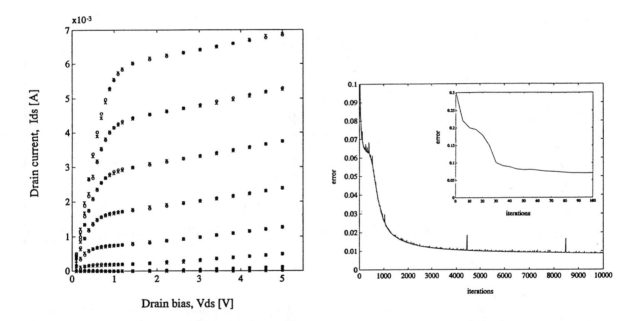

Figure 3. Measured and neural network generated characteristics for GaAs MESFET drain current versus drain and gate voltages, 'x': measured data, 'o': simulated.

Figure 4. Evolution of the modelling absolute error.

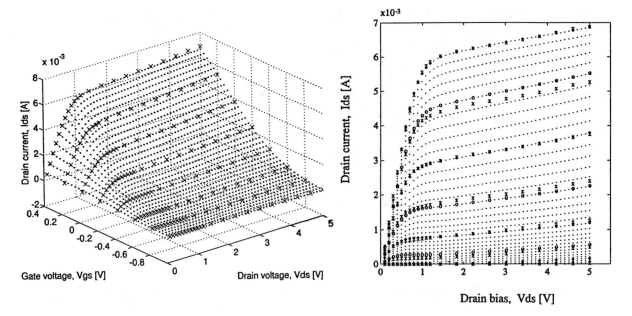

Figure 5. Monotonicity of the neural network generated device data compared to the teaching material after 50000 iterations with 5 hidden neurons, 'x': teaching material, '.': learnt data.

Figure 6. Interpolation capability of the neural network, 'x': measured material, '*': learnt data corresponding teaching points, 'o': interpolated data, '.': mesh data.

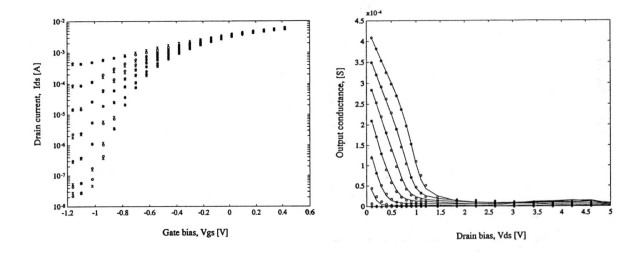

Figure 7. Measured and neural network generated characteristics for GaAs MESFET drain current versus gate voltage in room temperature and above, 'x': measured data, 'o': simulated data.

Figure 8. Continuous GaAs MESFET output conductance modelling with the neural network, solid lines as measured data, 'o': data recalled by network.

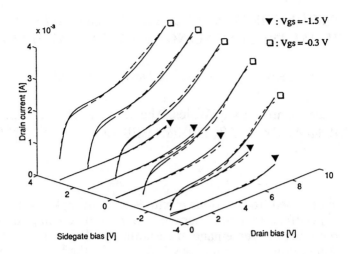

Figure 9. a)

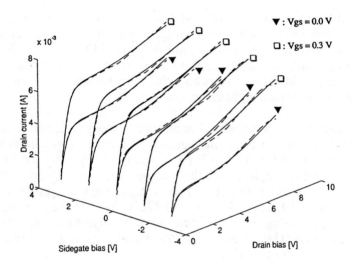

Figure 9. b)

Figure 9. 3D drain current modelling as a function of drain, gate and substrate (sidegate) bias for GaAs MESFET with a feature size of $W/L = 50\mu m/2\mu m$. Measured datapoints (solid lines), data recalled by network (dashed) a) gate bias values -1.5 and -0.3 V b) gate bias values 0.0 and 0.3 V.

ON THE ANALYSIS OF PYROLYSIS MASS SPECTRA USING ARTIFICIAL NEURAL NETWORKS. INDIVIDUAL INPUT SCALING LEADS TO RAPID LEARNING.

Mark J. Neal, Royston Goodacre & Douglas B. Kell

Institute of Biological Sciences, University of Wales, Aberystwyth, Dyfed SY23 3DA, U.K.
MJN@ABER.AC.UK RRG@ABER.AC.UK DBK@ABER.AC.UK Fax: +44 970 622354

Abstract

Pyrolysis mass spectra were obtained from various mixtures containing known amounts of glycogen and casamino acids. Feedforward neural networks were trained using the standard backpropagation algorithm to predict the percentage of casamino acids in unseen mixtures from their pyrolysis mass spectra. By scaling the input nodes *individually*, the variation between the spectra could be maximised and the convergence rate (as judged by the RMS error on test sets) increased by more than 100-fold compared with training runs in which the scaling was over the whole dataset.

INTRODUCTION

There is a continuing need for more rapid, precise and accurate analyses of the chemical composition of fermentor broths and the organisms which they contain. An ideal method would permit the simultaneous estimation of multiple determinands, would have negligible reagent costs, and would run under the control of a PC, to allow flexible operation of the sample handling, instrument calibration, and data analysis and visualisation routines. Our present work is directed towards the development of exactly such an instrument.

Pyrolysis is the thermal degradation of a material in an inert atmosphere, and leads to the production of volatile fragments from non-volatile material such as microorganisms or other biological samples (Irwin 1982). Curie-point pyrolysis is a particularly reproducible and straightforward version of the technique, in which the sample, dried onto an appropriate ferromagnetic metal or alloy, is rapidly heated (0.5s is typical) to the Curie point of the metal, which may itself be chosen (358, 480, 510, 530, 610 and 770°C are common temperatures). The volatile fragments (pyrolysate) resulting from the Curie-point pyrolysis may then be separated and analysed in a mass spectrometer (Meuzelaar *et al* 1982), and the combined technique is then known as pyrolysis mass spectrometry or PyMS.

Almost all biological materials will produce pyrolytic degradation products such as methane, ammonia, water, methanol and H_2S, whose mass:charge (m/z) ratio < 50, and fragments with m/z > 200 are rarely analytically important in microbiology (Berkeley *et al* 1990) unless very special conditions are employed (Smith & Snyder 1992). The analytically useful data are thus constituted by a set of 150 intensities (normalised to the total ion count) versus m/z in the range 51-200.

Within microbiology and biotechnology, PyMS has been used as a taxonomic aid in the *identification* and *discrimination* of different microorganisms (Gutteridge 1987). To this end, the reduction of the multivariate data generated by the PyMS system (and indeed of those generated by other arrays of sensors; Gardner & Bartlett 1991) is normally carried out using principal components analysis (PCA), whihc is a well-known technique for reducing the dimensionality of multivariate data whilst preserving most of the variance. Whilst PCA does not take account of any groupings in the data, neither does it require that the populations be normally distributed, i.e. it is a non-parametric method. (In addition, it permits the loadings of each of the m/z ratios on the principal components to be determined, and thus the extraction of at least *some* chemically significant information.) The closely-related canonical variates analysis technique then separates the samples into groups on the basis of the principal components and some *a priori* knowledge of the appropriate number of groupings (MacFie *et al* 1978). Provided that the data set contains "standards" (i.e. type or centro-strains) it is evident that one can establish the closeness of any unknown samples to a known organism, and thus effect the identification of the former. An excellent example of the discriminatory power of the approach is the demonstration (Goodacre & Berkeley 1990) that one can even use it to distinguish 4 strains of *E. coli* which differ only in the presence or absence of single antibiotic-resistance plasmids.

More recently, we (Goodacre *et al*. 1992, 1993b, 1994a) and others (Chun *et al*. 1993) have exploited artificial neural networks (ANNs) in supervised learning mode for the very successful identification of a variety of biological samples from their pyrolysis mass spectra, training fully interconnected multilayer perceptrons (MLPs) with one hidden layer on known standards using binary-encoded outputs and the standard backpropagation algorithm, and testing on spectra from unseen samples. We have also exploited Kohonen's self-organising feature map (Kohonen 1989) succesfully to carry out unsupervised learning, and hence the classification of microorganisms, from their pyrolysis mass spectra (Goodacre *et al*. 1994a).

Of perhaps more general chemical interest is the ability to use PyMS and ANNs for the *quantification* of substances in complex biological samples. The strategy is to obtain pyrolysis mass spectra from appropriate samples of interest and train ANNs to recognise the relative concentration of a chemical substance (as measured by wet chemistry) from the PyMS. We again demonstrated for the first time that ANNs could indeed be trained to give accurate values for the concentration of indole in *Escherichia coli* cultures (Goodacre & Kell 1993), and for the concentrations of individual compunds in a variety of binary, ternary and more complex mixtures (e.g. Goodacre *et al*. 1993a, 1994b).

Given that any non-volatile biological material can be pyrolysed, and that it has been established that MLPs with sigmoidal activation functions and at least one hidden layer of arbitrary size can effect any nonlinear mapping of a continuous function to an arbitrary degree of accuracy (e.g. Hornik *et al*. 1989), our interest is focussed on improving both the learning speed and the ability to generalise of ANNs trained on pyrolysis mass spectral data. In the case of PyMS data, each input is of a similar *character* (in that they are all chemical fragments), but some inputs may contain more noise than others (in that lower ion counts will have a greater percentage of electronic noise); in the worst case the lowest inputs may simply be noise, whose presence would both harm learning and without a rather robust cross-validation method would likely lead to overtraining. Since the data are normalised to the total ion count, any increase in a given mass is necessarily accompanied by a concomitant decrease in all of the others. However, it is known from the statistical literature (as the 'parsimony principle') that much better predictions can often be obtained when only the most relevant input variables are considered (e.g. Rawlings 1988, Miller 1990, Seasholtz & Kowalski 1993), it was therefore of interest to analyse the effects of varying the methods of scaling the *input* variables on the performance of our ANNs.

There are of course within the connectionist literature a multitude of articles which describe optimal growth or pruning of feedforward networks, designed to effect a sparse representation of the input-to-output mapping and thence improve generalisation (see e.g. LeCun *et al*. 1989, Mozer & Smolensky 1989, Fahlman & Lebiere 1990, Weigend *et al*. 1991, Finoff *et al*. 1993, Hassibi & Stork 1993). However, most of these growth/ skeletonisation algorithms have been devised to work on the creation or destruction of *individual weights*, particularly those to and from the hidden layer(s), and at all events make no attempt to distinguish the physically meaningful inputs from the latent variables represented by the nodes in the hidden layers (cf. Moody 1992). Since obtaining extra variables not only tends to cause overfitting but also normally costs more, it is *more generally* desirable to minimise the number of inputs used in the formation of the connectionist representation. The present study therefore addresses, and serves to illustrate, the substantial importance of optimal scaling of the inputs for the speed of learning and, to some extent, the ability to generalise.

EXPERIMENTAL SYSTEM

The experimental system studied consisted of mixtures of casamino acids and glycogen, as a model for the complex proteins and carbohydrates to be found in typical biological samples. Mixtures containing different percentages of each component were made up gravimetrically, and pyrolysed at 530°C as described (Goodacre *et al* 1993a). Typical pyrolysis mass spectra are shown in Fig 1, where it can be seen that they are not easy to distinguish by eye, and one may construe that such data constitute ideal material for analysis *via* computer/AI/neural methods.

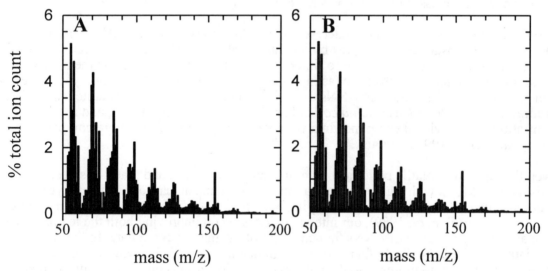

Fig 1. Normalised pyrolysis mass spectra of (A) 20 μg glycogen *plus* 100 μg casmino acids, and (B) 20 μg glycogen *plus* 90 μg casmino acids

The training set consisted of normalised spectra from mixtures containing 20 μg glycogen *plus* 10, 20, 30...100 μg casmino acids whilst the test set were spectra from mixtures containing 20 μg glycogen *plus* 5, 10, 15, 20, 25...100 μg casmino acids. To avoid the well-known problem of the sensitivity of backpropagation to initial conditions (Kolen & Pollack 1990), each run was done in sextuplicate and the data median-averaged. All neural networks were of the fully interconnected feedforward MLP type with a 150-8-1 architecture, and trained using the standard backpropagation algorithm with a logistic activation function, a learning rate of 0.1 and a momentum term of 0.9. Inputs were scaled as described in the text, whilst outputs were scaled between 0.1 and 0.9.

RESULTS AND DISCUSSION

Individual scaling of inputs

Whilst the usual backpropagation methods scale all inputs and outputs to lie between 0 and 1, this leaves open the question of how the scaling is done throughout the (columns of the) *population* of examples of interest. In particular, in the present case, some input columns contribute far more numerically to the inputs to the hidden layer than others (Fig 1). It is common in some other supervised multivariate calibration methods such as partial least squares to normalise the inputs in proportion to the reciprocal of their standard deviations (see e.g. Martens & Næs 1989). We therefore studied the effect of scaling the inputs on the basis of the highest ion counts throughout the entire dataset *versus* scaling the inputs of each m/z independently over the dataset. In the latter case, this means that the range of each input in the population is made equal.

TRAINING SET % RMS ERROR	EPOCHS UNTIL CONVERGENCE TO STATED % RMS ERROR		TEST SET % RMS ERROR	
	Scaled individually	Scaled on whole dataset	Scaled individually	Scaled on whole dataset
2	90	805	2.95	2.61
1	335	9770	2.44	2.02
0.50	725	84060	2.00	2.57
0.25	1470	217640	2.12	2.65
0.125	2240	>500000	2.08	-

Table 1. Effect of scaling inputs individually on the speed of convergence of backpropagation learning on an MLP.

It is evident from the data in Table 1 that *individual* scaling of the input nodes can effect a dramatic speed-up, of more than 100-fold, in the convergence of a neural network learning algorithm. This indicates that when all the scaled inputs to the net are of approximately the same magnitude the error value from a single input is less likely to dominate the error value at a given node, and therefore is less likely to swamp smaller error values associated with other connections to that node. This allows the reduction of error values in many dimensions in the input space to occur simultaneously. Put another way, by scaling the inputs *individually* in this way we are maximising the variance in the training set data, which therefore makes the discriminating features in the data easier (quicker) to learn.

From the data in Table 1 it is clear that although the convergence of the learning algorithm on the training set data is much quicker, there is a slight reduction in the accuracy of the predictions on the unseen data. This can however be improved by allowing the network to train to a slightly lower RMS error on the training set. The trade-off is such that individual scaling is still markedly superior when the criterion of training is the RMS error on the *test* data.

Pruning input variables

Given the dramatic speed-up that could be obtained by scaling the inputs individually, it was also of interest to see whether generalisation could be affected by removing masses whose numerical contribution to the total ion count over the population of samples was the lowest. The results of such a study are shown in Table 2, where it may be seen that removal of the numerically least significant masses had little effect on generalisation and a slightly unfavourable effect on the number of epochs needed for convergence to a given RMS error on the test set. This is consistent with the conclusion above that maximising the overall variance in the dataset leads to faster learning.

NUMBER OF EPOCHS UNTIL STATED % RMS ERROR OF TRAINING SET				
Training set % RMS error	Zero inputs removed	Remove m/z if <0.025%	Remove m/z if <0.05%	Remove m/z if <0.1%
2	90	125	90	95
1	335	280	345	460
0.5	725	850	950	1060
0.25	1470	1785	2105	2670
0.125	2240	2605	3250	4760
% RMS ERROR ON TEST SET				
2	2.95	3.07	3.17	3.02
1	2.44	2.33	2.37	2.18
0.5	2	2.08	2.27	2.44
0.25	2.12	2.21	2.19	2.75
0.125	2.08	2.26	2.43	3.53

Table 2. Effect of removal of masses with the lowest contribution to the total ion count over the population on the speed of learning and generalisation. Input nodes were scaled individually.

CONCLUSION

Individual scaling of the inputs of an artificial neural network maximises the variance in a given dataset and can effect a dramatic speed-up in the rate of convergence to a given RMS error on both training and test data. In the examples displayed, this speed-up could be more than 100-fold.

Acknowledgments

We thank the Biotechnology Directorate of the UK SERC for support of this work, under the terms of the LINK scheme in Biochemical Engineering, in collaboration with Horizon Instruments, Neural Computer Sciences and Zeneca plc.

References

Berkeley, RCW, Goodacre, R, Helyer, R & Kelley, T (1990) *Lab. Pract.* **39** (10) 81-83.

Chun, J, Atalan, E, Ward, AC & Goodfellow, M (1993) *FEMS Microbiol. Lett.* **107**, 321-326.

Fahlman, SE & Lebiere, C (1990) *The cascade-correlation learning architecture.* Report CMU-CS-90-100, Carnegie-Mellon University.

Finoff, W., Hergert, F. & Zimmermann, H.G. (1993) *Neural Networks* **6**, 771-783.

Gardner, JW & Bartlett, PN (1991) in *Techniques & Mechanisms in Gas Sensing*, ed. Mosley, PT, Norris, JOW & Williams, DE, pp. 347-380. Adam Hilger, Bristol.

Goodacre, R & Berkeley, RCW (1990) *FEMS Microbiol. Lett.* **71**, 133-138.

Goodacre, R & Kell, DB (1993) *Anal. Chim. Acta* **279**, 17-26.

Goodacre, R, Kell, DB & Bianchi, G (1992) *Nature* **359**, 594.

Goodacre, R Edmonds, AN & Kell, DB (1993a) *J. Anal. Appl. Pyrol.* **26**, 93-114.

Goodacre, R, Kell, DB & Bianchi, G (1993b) *J. Sci. Food Agric.* **63**, 297-307.

Goodacre, R, Neal, MJ, Kell, DB, Greenham, LW, Noble, WC & Harvey, RG (1994a) *J. Appl. Bacteriol.*, **76**, 124-134.

Goodacre, R, Neal, MJ & Kell, DB (1994b) *Anal. Chem.*, in the press.

Gutteridge CS (1987) *Meth. Microbiol.* **19**, 227-272.

Hassibi, B & Stork, DG (1993) in Hanson, SJ, Cowan, JD & Giles, CL, eds., *Advances in Neural Information Processing Systems 5*, 164-171, Morgan Kaufmann, San Mateo, CA.

Hornik, K, Stinchcombe, M.& White, H (1989) *Neural networks* **2**, 359-366.

Irwin, WJ (1982) *Analytical Pyrolysis: A Comprehensive Guide.* Marcel Dekker, New York.

Kohonen, T. (1989) *Self-Organization and Associative Memory.* Springer-Verlag, Berlin.

Kolen, JF & Pollack, JB (1990) *Complex Systems* **4**, 269-280.

Le Cun, Y., Denker, J.S. & Solla, S.A. (1989) in Touretzky, DS (ed) *Advances in Neural Information Processing Systems* Vol 2, 598-605. Morgan Kaufmann, New York.

MacFie, HJH, Gutteridge, CS & Norris, JR (1978) *J. Gen. Microbiol.* **104**, 67-74.

Martens, H. & Næs, T. (1989) *Multivariate Calibration.* Wiley, New York.

Meuzelaar, HLC, Haverkamp, J and Hileman, FD (1982) *Pyrolysis Mass Spectrometry of Recent and Fossil Biomaterials.* Elsevier, Amsterdam.

Miller, AJ (1990) *Subset selection in regression.* Chapman & Hall, London.

Moody, J. (1992) in Lippmann, RP (ed) *Advances in Neural Information Processing Systems 4*, 847-854. Morgan Kaufmann, San Mateo, CA.

Mozer, MC & Smolensky, P (1989) in Touretzky, DS (ed) *Advances in Neural Information Processing Systems* Vol 1, 107-115. Morgan Kaufmann, New York.

Reed, R (1993) *IEEE Trans. Neural Networks*, **4**, 740-747.

Rawlings, JO (1988) *Applied Regression Analysis.* Wadsworth & Brooks, Pacific Grove, CA.

Seasholtz, MB & Kowalski, BR (1993) *Anal. Chim. Acta* **277**, 165-177.

Smith, PB & Snyder, AP (1992) *J. Anal. Appl. Pyrol.* **24**, 23-38.

Weigend, AS, Rumelhart, DE & Huberman, BA (1991) in Lippmann, RP, Moody, E & Touretzky, DS (Eds.), *Neural Information Processing Systems 3,* pp. 875- 882. Morgan Kaufmann, San Mateo, CA.

Using A Neural Network To Predict Electricity Generation

Ronald L. Capone
Ronald L. Capone & Associates
3134 North Piedmont Street
Arlington, VA 22207
(703) 525-2832

Sue Kimbrough
Air & Energy Environmental Research Laboratory
U.S. Environmental Protection Agency
Research Triangle Park, NC 27711
(919) 541-2612

Abstract

Predicting electricity generation is important to developing forecasts of air pollutant release and to evaluating the effectiveness of alternative policies which may reduce pollution. A neural network model (NUMOD) predicting electricity generation fueled by coal, natural gas, and oil (whose combustion releases air pollutants) was developed to run on a personal computer. NUMOD uses 3 linked, feed-forward neural networks, each trained with the extended delta-bar-delta paradigm. One network predicts coal-fired generation and its output is fed as input to each of the other 2 networks, 1 for gas-fired generation and 1 for oil-fired generation. In addition, all 3 networks use inputs describing electricity demand, fuel prices, generating equipment, climate, and power pooling. Pearson's r calculated at various points during training, out-of-sample tests, and performance evaluation was greater than 0.93 and frequently greater than 0.98.

Background

The search for a simple, accurate, and robust electricity generation model was motivated by federal legislation designed to reduce air pollution. On November 15, 1990 the Clean Air Act Amendments of 1990 (CAAA) were signed into a law requiring that extreme, severe, serious, and multi-state moderate ozone non-attainment areas use photochemical grid modeling to demonstrate future attainment with the ozone national ambient air quality standard (NAAQS) [Section 182(e)(2)(A)]. In addition to photochemical grid modeling, CAAA requires that ozone non-attainment areas submit State Implementation Plans (SIPs) that provide for a 15 percent reduction from baseline emissions by 1996 [Section 182(b)(1)(A)] and that SIPs for serious, severe, and extreme areas must provide for a 3 percent annual reduction (averaged over 3 years) from 1996 until attainment is achieved [Section 182(c)(2)(B)]. These plans are intended to provided for reasonable further progress (RFP) toward attainment.

Section 182(b)(1)(A) specifies that the 15 percent reduction from baseline emissions accounts for any growth in emissions, such as might be caused by combustion of fossil fuels, after 1990. A key component of the RFP and photochemical grid modelling demonstrations is development of credible growth factors for existing pollutant inventories. In turn, credible growth factors require accurate forecasts of economic variables and the activities associated with them, such as electricity generation.

Traditionally, electricity generation has been forecast using linear programming models which are very complex. Although they provide richly detailed output, this comes at the price of simplicity, speed, and economy. They tend to use large, often arcane input files to set up linear programs which are themselves quite large and time-consuming to solve. Moreover, they exhibit behavior typical of linear programs: "knife edge" sensitivity to inputs and large numbers of alternative optimum solutions. Running, for the most part, on main frame computers, these models can be expensive to set up, run, and analyze making extensive sensitivity analysis difficult and exploration of alternative scenarios impractical. These factors among others motivated a search for an alternative approach.

A successful alternative would have to meet the following objectives: 1) It would be less complex and capable of running on a personal computer (PC). 2) It would be robust and its robustness could be demonstrated by sensitivity analysis and accurate backcast of historical results. 3) It would execute rapidly, allowing a larger number of alternative scenarios to be examined within reasonable budget constraints and calendar time. Any model meeting these qualifications could be used in either of 2 ways: as a screening tool for traditional models, selecting scenarios for more detailed simulation via traditional models thereby allowing policy analysts to consider more alternatives without sacrificing detail; or as a stand-alone tool in situations where detail is not needed or where bounding the universe of possible futures is important.

Neural networks were selected as one way of meeting the demand for a simple, fast, accurate, and robust models which could be used either for screening or stand-alone. Among their attractions are their ability to synthesize functional relationships, bypassing the specification problem and avoiding costly development of purpose-built behavioral algorithms. We called our first model the Neural Network Utility Model — NUMOD.

Inputs, Outputs and Model Architecture

NUMOD's inputs include factors known to impinge on short run (fixed capital) electricity generating decisions: end user demand, the price of fuel, climate, generating capacity, and power pool affiliation. Outputs are generation in MWH fueled by coal, oil, and natural gas plus a generation index, or "growth factor", for which 1990 generation = 1.00. Each input vector represents 1 year of state aggregate data for any of the 48 contiguous states plus data for the power pool to which the state belongs. Therefore each output vector represents annual, fuel-specific generation in the state. Inputs are organized into records, each of which is independent of the others and NUMOD executes once for each record in its input file. Similarly, outputs are written to an output file for further analytic or modelling use. This architecture created obstacles which had to be overcome in order to train NUMOD's networks and these are discussed below.

During development, we found that the best results were achieved by building specialized neural networks and linking them together. The best performance resulted from simulating coal-fired generation and using that as one of the inputs to the oil and the gas networks. This has a common-sense basis: utilities usually try to use their large, economical coal-fired units as much as possible and only use their smaller, more expensive oil- and gas-fired units to meet peak and emergency loads. It therefore seemed reasonable to adopt an architecture in which oil- and gas-fired generation was made dependent on coal-fired generation. Along the same lines, NUMOD accounts for nuclear and hydro-electric generation by netting them out, reasoning that these very low expense generating units will be used first whenever possible.

Figure 1 depicts NUMOD's principal parts: a data input module, a pre-processor for the coal network, a preprocessor for the gas/oil networks, 3 neural networks, and a post-processor which calculates index values, writes the output file, and performs housekeeping chores.

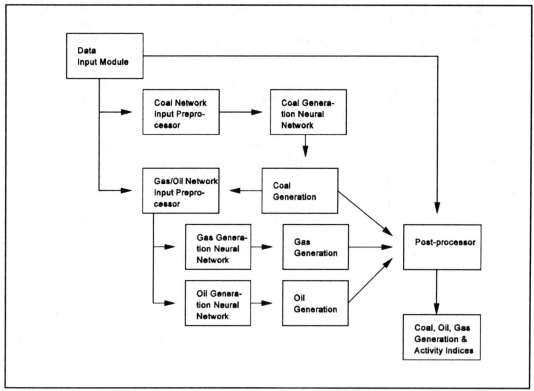

Figure 1 NUMOD Components

Input Normalization

NUMOD only recognizes a geographic state as an input vector. Yet states differ in size, in the amount of electricity purchased by end users, and in the number and size of their generating stations. In short, there are big states and there are small states and NUMOD had to accept inputs from both ends of the spectrum without saturating its transfer functions. The saturation problem becomes somewhat worse when NUMOD is required to predict generation perhaps 20 years in the future. At even modest rates of economic growth, demand, generating capacity, and fuel prices will be much greater in the year 2010 than they are now. Taken all together, inputs had to be normalized to remove skewness, scale, and potential neurode saturation. A 4-step normalization procedure was used:

- Step 1, *remove skewness* by taking natural logs of all real-number inputs.
- Step 2, *remove scale* using a z-transform, i.e. subtracting the mean and dividing the result by the standard deviation. This gave all real-number inputs the same relative magnitude in preparation for step 3.
- Step 3, *map transformed input vectors onto a hypersphere*, ensuring that all input vectors have the same euclidean length and that no element of an input vector can take a value greater than the sphere's radius.
- Step 4, *scale inputs to the domain of a standard hyperbolic tangent function* to prevent neurode saturation by linear scaling the domain of the hyperbolic function to approximately ± 1 radius.

In practice, Step 4 is built into the network development platform (NeuralWare Professional II Plus) using the built-in MinMax table.

A convenient radius was chosen so that for the entire set of input vectors in the data file there were more-or-less equal numbers in each hemisphere. In effect, this procedure maps input vectors into regions, or "patches", on the surface of the hypersphere and the patches tend to occur in each portion of the surface. It is thought that the net effect is a fairly thorough mapping of the hypersphere's surface onto the output space after training is complete. One further consequence of hyperspherical mapping is that the number of inputs to each network is increased by 1 in order to accommodate the so-called augmentation dimension.

Normalization is done twice: once for the coal generation network and then again for the gas and oil generation networks. The coal generation network is solved to produce its output and this is fed to the gas/oil preprocessor and to the post-processor, as shown in Figure 1. Because the gas and oil networks use the same inputs as the coal network *plus* coal generation, their hypersphere has 1 more dimension.

Desired outputs were transformed by taking their natural logs. Two benefits result from this: skewness is reduced and, after post-processing, negative outputs are precluded. During post-processing, base-e exponents of raw output neurode activation levels are taken. Although the magnitude of the result might be small, it is never negative — negative generation makes no sense.

Data for Supervised Training

Data used for supervised training were assembled from publicly available data collected by the U.S. Department of Energy, the U.S. Department of Commerce, the U.S. Department of the Interior, the Edison Electric Institute, and the National Electric Reliability Council (NERC). They consist of state-level generation, generating capacity, fuel price, climate, and economic data for 1980 - 1991. Years before 1980 were not used because they may be atypical. Oil price shocks beginning in 1974, rapid inflation, and economic recession during the late 1970's all acted to make the decade unusual. Data for years after 1991 are not yet complete, although the release of any missing data will probably occur very soon.

All data are aggregated to states and only the 48 contiguous states were considered. Power pools were taken to be contiguous with regions established by NERC. There are 9 such regions and their boundaries were adjusted somewhat to coincide with state boundaries.

Neural Network Architecture and Training

Each of the 3 networks is feed-forward with an input layer connected to 1 hidden layer containing 4 neurodes which is connected to an output layer with only 1 neurode. A single bias neurode is connected to the hidden and output layers. Hyperbolic tangent functions are used for energy transfer and activation levels are simply the sums of incoming energies. Training was accomplished using extended delta-bar-delta with noise injection during early stages of training. The three networks were trained separately with the coal network trained first. Coal network output was manually added to the training data for the gas and oil networks. Thus, they "knew" what the coal network would tell them.

All 3 networks were trained using a 2-phase procedure designed to maximize data use. In Phase 1, the networks were trained with files containing only 75 percent of the data and the remaining 25 percent was held back for an out-of-sample test. Training data was selected randomly. After the out-of-sample tests showed that the networks had learned (rather than just memorizing) and that they had adequately synthesized a function which mapped respective input spaces to the output spaces, the networks were retrained (Phase 2) using all of the available data. The rational for the 2-phase training procedure was this: If no memorization occurs after a given number of presentations using 75 percent of the data, no memorization will probably occur after the same number of presentations using all of the data. Because there is probably more diversity in a complete data set than in any subset, networks will learn somewhat more during Phase 2. The only purpose served by the out-of-sample test is to demonstrate learning without memorization and the ability to generalize. Having passed the test, it serves no further purpose. Table 1 summarizes training results using Pearson's r as a measure of training success.

This table shows that training, measured by Pearson's r, was effective. It also shows that Phase 2 was very helpful in the case of oil-fired generation and certainly did no harm for coal- and gas-fired generation. Note that 20,000 extra presentations were allowed during Phase 2 — largely to accommodate a training file with 33 percent more records.

Table 1 Training Results

| Network | Number of Presentations (Phase 1/Phase 2) | Pearson's r | | Phase 2 |
| | | Phase 1 | | |
		Train-ing	Out-of-Sample Test	
Coal-fired Generation	50,000 / 70,000	0.993	0.992	0.992
Oil-fired Generation	70,000 / 90,000	0.961	0.928	0.970
Gas-fired Generation	70,000 / 90,000	0.983	0.980	0.981

NUMOD Performance

Over-all performance of NUMOD was assessed in several ways, 2 of which are discussed here: backcast for historical years and sensitivity analysis. Figure 2 plots backcast results for 1985 - 1991, which are probably the most important years because electric utility behavior during the last part of the 1980's is more indicative of future behavior than earlier years.

In Figure 2, NUMOD output is plotted on the vertical axis against historical values on the horizontal axis. A 45 degree reference line, which is the locus of perfect backcasts, is also plotted. The amount of vertical deviation from the reference line measures error. It is clear from this plot that NUMOD backcasts reasonably well — outputs are grouped tightly around the reference line.

Limited sensitivity analysis has been completed as of this writing. Several of the most critical inputs were varied by 10 percent above and below the values in the data file and changes in NUMOD output were examined. Variables included end user electricity demand and changes in the shape of the load-duration curve, which measures factors related to the time of day of electricity demand. It was found that NUMOD predicts that generation will increase by less than the amount of increase in demand when demand increases and it will decrease by less than the amount of decrease when demand decreases. A ± 10 percent increase/decrease in demand calls forth a ± 8 percent increase/decrease in generation. This is sensible because increased demand will probably result in more efficient use of generating resources while the opposite is true of lower demand. Results also show that coal, oil, and gas generation behave somewhat differently depending on how peak demand changes relative to total demand — when peak demand increases/decrease more than over-all demand gas and oil generation tend to increase/decrease more than coal generation. In short, NUMOD behavior tends to mimic ways actual electric utilities behave.

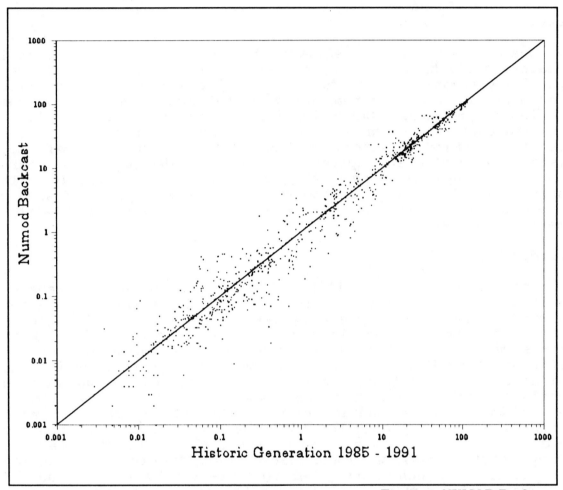

Figure 2 NUMOD Backcast

Conclusions

Our general conclusions are that neural network models are quite capable of playing a part in predicting electricity generation. We were able to design, develop, test, and implement this model with a very small resource expenditure. It runs on a PC very quickly, uses somewhat less than 60 kBytes of memory and its outputs appear to achieve an acceptable level of accuracy.

The Second Method of Lyapunov and Neural Networks in Power Systems Stability Studies

D.R.Marpaka, W.R.Hwang, and Vinay K. Moturi
Department of Electrical Engineering
College of Engineering and Technology
Tennessee State University
Nashville, TN 37209-1561

Key Words: Neural Networks, Backpropagation, Transient Stability Critical Clearing Time, Transient Energy Function.

Abstract:

One of the primary objectives of electric utility industry is to maintain a satisfactory power supply to its customers. In this paper a systematic new method to study the transient stability assessment of power system using neural networks and Lyapunov function is presented. Determination of critical clearing time is of paramount importance for post-fault analysis of an interconnected power system. In this paper the results of different existing methods are compared. The data needed to train neural network are generated from the transient energy function. The results obtained by this method are compared with that of some of the existing methods. This new method is illustrated with a numerical example.

Introduction

The study of the stability of power systems under transient conditions is a tedious task because the differential equations describing even the simplest system are nonlinear. The general approach has been to obtain a time solution and observe if the various machines tend to lose or maintain synchronism [1]. The differential equations, describing the power system dynamics, are nonlinear with constant coefficients under the assumption of constant voltage behind transient reactance and constant input to the machines [2]. A characteristic inherent to electric power systems is that they operate under the presence of disturbances. The disturbances are of external or internal origin. The stability of power systems deals with the character of the electro-mechanical oscillations of synchronous generators created by a disturbance in the power system conditions. Whether the post-disturbance process leads to loss of synchronous operation is the subject of primary concern [3]. Some of the methods to study the transient stability are:
a) equal area criterion, b) phase-plane method, c) energy-integral criterion, d) numerical integration, e) probabilistic methods, f) pattern recognition, g) the second method of Lyapunov, h) transient energy stability analysis, and i) artificial neural networks.

First three methods give identical results, but are applicable to simple two-machine systems. Though numerical integration method gives the time of state transition of the system, it has three main drawbacks: a) each fault must be treated separately, b) stability limits are obtained by separate trials, c) smaller time-step intervals are needed to ensure accuracy and numerical stability. All of these make the integration process very time consuming. It is reported that the procedure using "decomposition-aggregation" integration by Xia and Heydt has resulted smaller integration times. Some of the approaches of probabilistic and pattern recognition methods are briefly discussed by Sobajic and Pao [3].

The basic objective of the second method of Lyapunov is to ascertain the stability characteristics of a dynamic system governed by a set of differential equations, without an explicit knowledge of the solution. This method has limited practical value for the following reasons: a) The method provides sufficient but not necessary conditions for stability and these conditions are often too conservative to be of practical value, b) Computational requirements of the method have made the study of large scale power systems infeasible, c) The method requires a simplified system representation, d) The value of suitably designed Lyapunov function has to be calculated and compared with the critical value of the function previously determined, e) Integration of fault-on system equations is needed to obtain the post-fault initial conditions and the critical clearing time. The first two drawbacks have been eliminated as much as possible by using Transient Energy Stability Analysis (TESA) by Athay & et.al. [4].

The Proposed Method

Dynamic security assessment of electric power systems using artificial neural networks was studied by Sobajic and Pao with changes in system operating conditions and topology while the other parameters are kept unchanged [3].

Our approach takes the advantage of the second method of Lyapunov to determine the domain of stability for a given system configuration and operating conditions. The Lyapunov function for the problem under investigation is constructed by the method presented in [5]. An artificial neural network is trained with the data generated by the Lyapunov function to classify the stability domain into either stable or possibly unstable. The network will be tested for its performance during training. Once the network attains the desired capability, it is presented with the data representing the real-time operating conditions of the system that was not presented earlier.

The distinct advantage of this method is that critical clearing time can be found without computing the value of the Lyapunov function for different values of rotor angles and velocities. Training the neural network under consideration is done off-line.
Search for an optimal architecture for rapid convergence and minimum error is also presented. The numerical example given in [5] is studied to validate the method.

Artificial Neural Networks:

Artificial neural net models or simply "neural nets" or connectionist models or parallel distributed processing models or neuromorphic systems attempt to achieve human-like performance via dense interconnection of simple computational elements [6]. Artificial neural systems, or neural networks are physical cellular systems which can acquire, store, and utilize experimental knowledge. Much of the inspiration for such systems comes from neuroscience.

The proposed method takes the parallel processing capability and fault-tolerance nature of neural networks to determine the critical clearing time in real-time. Neural network is trained using Rumelhart error backpropagation [7] with the input and target output data obtained from the stability domain of the system. The performance of network was evaluated with different sets of random weights for optimal number of neurons in a single-hidden layer for rapid convergence and desired least mean squared error.

For a quick and ready reference, the rule for the adaptation of synaptic weights is given below.

$$W_{ij}(t+1) = W_{ij}(t) + \eta \delta_j X_i + \alpha (W_{ij}(t) - W_{ij}(t-1)) \qquad (1)$$

where $W_{ij}(t)$ is the weight from hidden node i or from an input to node j at time t, X_i is either the output of node i or is an input, η is a gain term, δ_j is an error term for node j, α is a momentum term whose value lies between 0 and one.

Power System Model

To illustrate the proposed method, a synchronous generator with nonzero damping, connected to an infinite bus is considered. The normalized post-fault state can be written as

$$\frac{d^2\delta}{dt^2} + D\frac{d\delta}{dt} = P_i - \sin \delta \qquad (2)$$

The region asymptotic stability is given by equation 3

$$\frac{D}{2}x_1^2 + \frac{(1+D)}{2D}x_2^2 + x_1 x_2 + \frac{(1+D^3)}{D}[2\cos\delta_0 - \cos(x_1+\delta_0) - P_{ix_1}] \langle M_2 \qquad (3)$$

where the right-hand side of the inequality is given by

$$M_2 = \frac{(\pi-2\delta_0)^2 D^4}{2(1+D^3)} + \frac{(1+D^3)}{D}[2\cos \delta_0 - P_i(\pi-2\delta_0)] \qquad (4)$$

I-332

Numerical Example

To illustrate the proposed method numerical example given in [5] is considered. The post-fault system and faulted systems are described by

$$\frac{d^2\delta}{dt^2} + 0.01\frac{d\delta}{dt} = 0.4 - \sin\delta$$

$$\frac{d^2\delta}{dt^2} + 0.01\frac{d\delta}{dt} = 0.4 - 0.2\sin\delta$$

The post-fault system differential equation of the power system under study is solved by numerical integration and phase-plane analysis to determine the transition of the system from stable to unstable. The results are shown in Fig. 1 and 2. The critical clearing time by these methods is 3.1345 seconds.

The training data, the rotor angles and rotor angular velocities are obtained from the asymptotic stability region given by the equation 3. The region outside the stability domain indexed as +1 and inside region as -1 are the desired outputs corresponding to the input vector of rotor angles and rotor angular velocities.

A feedforward multilayer neural network was trained with different sets of random weights to determine the optimum number of processing elements for rapid convergence with bound on least mean squared error as 0.001. The results of the search with a range from two to twenty processing units are shown in Fig.3. As seen in Figure 4, the architecture with eight neurons in a single hidden layer is the optimum one. Perforformance of the proposed network is shown in Figures 5 and 6.

After the network has obtained the desired capability, the network was tested with the data that was not presented earlier during training period. The critical clearing time by this method was found to be between 3.1 - 3.2 seconds.

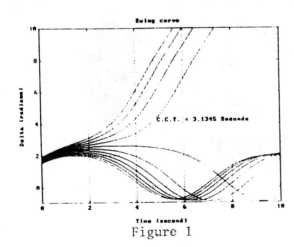

Figure 1

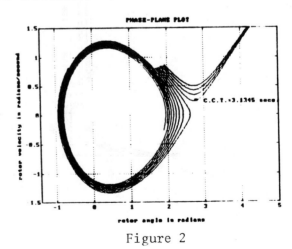

Figure 2

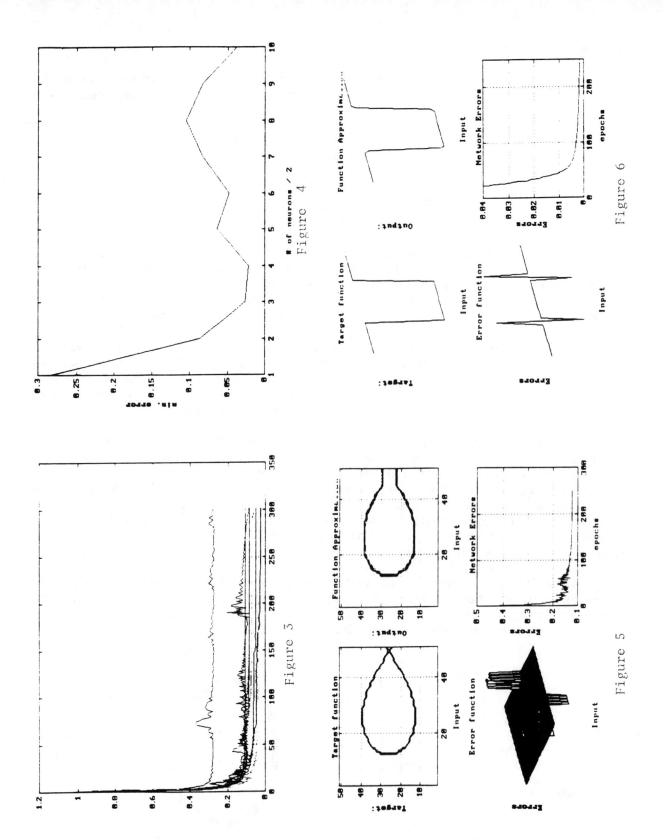

Figure 3

Figure 4

Figure 5

Figure 6

I-334

Results

Critical clearing times obtained by the three methods are

Numerical Integration Method	3.1345 seconds
The Second Method of Lyapunov	3.1345 seconds
Neural Network Approach	3.1 - 3.2 seconds

Conclusions

In this paper an attempt is made to show the combination of the second method of Lyapunov, pattern recognition and neural networks. The distinct advantage of this approach is elimination of need for calculation value of Lyapunov function and comparison with the predetermined critical value. This makes the approach suitable for real-time application. This method naturally inherits the conservativeness though not seen in this example. An important question to be answered is its applicability to large scale systems. Currently, the work with refinements in modeling such as: governor's dynamics, transfer conductances, saliency is in progress and use of self-organizing networks for security assessment is also under investigation.

References

[1] G.E.Gless, " Direct Method of Lyapunov Applied to Transient Power System Stability, " IEEE Transactions on Power Apparatus and Systems, vol. PAS 85, No.2 February 1966, pp 159-168.

[2] El-Abiad and Nagappan, " Transient Stability Regions of Multimachine Power Systems, " IEEE Transactions on Power Apparatus and Systems, vol. 85, No. 2 February 1965, pp 169-179.

[3] Dejan J. Sobajic and Yoh-Han Pao, " Artificial Neural-Net Based Dynamic Security Assessment of Electric Power Systems" IEEE Transactions on Power Systems, Vol. 4, No.1 February 1989, pp 220-228.

[4] T. Athay, " Systems Engineering For Power: Emergency Operating Control, " U.S.Department of Energy, Conf-790904--P1, Section IV, pp 1-113.

[5] M.A.Pai, M. Ananda Mohan and J. Gopala Rao, " Power System Transient Stability Regions Using Popov's Method, " IEEE Transactions on Power Apparatus and Systems,Vol., PAS-89, No.5/6 May/June 1970, pp 788-794.

[6] Lippmann," An Introduction to Computing with Neural Nets," IEEE ASSP Magazine, vol.4, No.2 April 1987, pp 4-22.

[7] D.E.Rumelhart, G.E.Hinton and R.J.Williams, " Learning Internal Representations by Error Propagation in Parallel Distributed Processing," Explorations in the Microstructures of Cognition, Vol. 1: Foundations, pp 318-362, MIT Press 1986.

Using the Hopfield Network with Annealing to Solve the Team Decision Theory Problem

Giridhar Rao
Systems Application Engineering, Inc.
3655 Westcenter Drive
Houston, TX 77042

William J.B. Oldham*
Dept. of Computer Science
Texas Tech University
Lubbock, TX 79409

Abstract

Team Decision Theory is a statistical discipline that has several applications in areas such as decentralized control and distributed computing. In the middle to late 1970's, this area was studied quite extensively. However, there were several limitations to the scope of the study due to the inherent mathematical intractability of the problem. There were severe restrictions on the nature of the system inputs and their probability distribution functions. Unless the underlying probability density functions of the system parameters were Gaussian, it was not possible to derive analytical solutions to the problems.

In recent years, neural networks have become increasingly popular as a means to solve large optimization problems. The high interconnectivity and the nature of neuron layouts and interactions have led to success in mapping large optimization problems to neural networks. In particular the Hopfield Network with annealing has been successful for these problems. Neural networks are not sensitive to the underlying probability distributions of the systems they are trying to solve.

This work ties these vastly different areas of research together by mapping the team decision theory problem to the modified Hopfield network. Two examples of team decision theory problems were mapped to this type of neural network. In one case, the neural network converged to the optimal solution 100% of the time; in the other case, the network converged to the optimal solution more than 50% of the time. The network solutions were compared against the optimal solution found by exhaustive search.

1 Team Decision Theory

Team Decision Theory has been described as the theory of decentralized stochastic decision making [1]. Assume we have a system of decision makers (DM's), where each DM has different information that is correlated to the information that the other DM's possess through a known a priori probability distribution function. Each DM makes a decision based on its information that will lead to the minimization of the expected value of a global loss function. Since the loss function is the same across the entire system, there is no "conflict of interest" [2] between DM's. Furthermore, since the a priori probability distribution function of the correlation between the information of the DM's is the same across the entire system, there is no "difference of opinion" [2] between DM's. In other words, the DM's are working toward a common goal, hence the name Team Decision Theory. The main difference between Team Decision Theory and ordinary Decision Theory is that each DM has to take into account the decisions other DM's could make while making its own decision. Ho [1] characterizes the essentials of a team decision problem as follows:

1. Each DM has *different* but *correlated* information about the underlying problem. The correlation between the DM's information is known at the time the decision is to be made.

2. The DM's need to *coordinate* their actions in order to minimize the system loss function. Each DM has to account for the decisions made by the other DM's while making its own decision.

---

*Author to whom all correspondence should be addressed.

3. Communication between the DM's is allowed before the decision-making process begins. Thus, each DM has an idea of the effect of the other DM's decisions on the system in general, and the loss function in particular. This *beforehand communication* allows the DM to agree on taking their coordinated actions based on the different information they have.

The loss function for such a system is formulated in such a way so as to be dependent on the decisions each DM takes with respect to the others.

2 Modified Hopfield-Tank Network

The modified neural network algorithm suggested by Bout and Miller [3] uses some techniques from simulated annealing and offers improved performance over the regular Hopfield network. Bout and Miller applied their network to the Travelling Salesman Problem with very encouraging results. For the 30-city problem, they were able to achieve solutions that were within 4% of the upper bound of an optimal solution.[1]

The network maintains the same shape and size as the regular network, but, each neuron V_{xi}, now represents a probability that city x will reside in position i of the tour. The probabilities obey a Boltzmann distribution, i.e.,

$$V_{xi} \propto e^{\frac{E_{xi}}{T}} \tag{1}$$

where T is the annealing temperature and E_{xi} is the mean field of a node. The mean field represents the cost of city x occupying position i in the tour. Thus, a higher mean field corresponds to a less favorable occupation position, causing the probability to drop for such a node to occupy that position. The mean field is given by:

$$
\begin{aligned}
E_{xi} = {} & dP1 \sum_{y \neq x} V_{yi} \\
& + dP2 \sum_{y \neq x} d_{xy} \left(V_{y,i+1} + V_{y,i-1} \right).
\end{aligned}
\tag{2}
$$

The first term discourages two cities from occupying the same position on the tour, while the second term encourages cities with the smallest distance between them to occupy adjacent positions on the tour. The energy function to be minimized is given by:

$$
\begin{aligned}
E = {} & \frac{dP1}{2} \sum_{i} \sum_{x} \sum_{y \neq x} V_{xi} V_{yi} \\
& + \frac{dP2}{2} \sum_{x} \sum_{y \neq x} \sum_{i} d_{xy} V_{xi} \left(V_{y,i+1} + V_{y,i-1} \right).
\end{aligned}
\tag{3}
$$

The network iterates as follows:

1. Select a starting temperature.

2. While temperature is greater than a lower bound

   (a) Do until a fixed point is found

      i. Select a city x at random
      ii. Calculate $E_{xi} \forall i$
      iii. Calculate $V_{xi} \forall i$
      iv. Calculate E

---

[1] The upper bound was calculated using the simulated annealing technique described in [4].

3. Update the temperature

The above algorithm, suggested as an improvement to the original Hopfield-Tank network, maintained the high interconnectivity of the original network, and added in a new flavor with the annealing. The annealing process allows the system to move from one trajectory to another, and thus allows the network to converge to better solutions. The main disadvantage of this scheme is that since the network has to anneal to a solution, the convergence time is increased significantly.

3 Two-city B & H Problem

The first step toward determining whether a mapping of the Team Decision Theory Problem to neural networks existed and if so, what this mapping was, was to take a small problem described by Ho [1] and map it to a Hopfield Network. Although the problem defined and used in this section is a little contrived, it served as a good starting place and laid a good foundation upon which to determine if this research was feasible and gave several insights into the nature of the Team Decision Theory Problem and the necessary ingredients required by a Neural Network that would be developed to solve it.

3.1 Problem Definition

Imagine a situation where Mr. B, a Boston resident, and Mr. H, a Hartford resident, have to meet in Worcester for an important meeting. They decide that they will meet at Worcester at a certain time on a given day provided it does not rain. After this communication, there is no further communication between them. Also, there is an uncertainty about the weather, and each man has access to his own local weather information, and only an idea of the probable weather in Worcester based on their respective local weather information. The nature of the meeting and the road conditions are such that going or not going to the meeting when it is raining or shining in Worcester carries with it a certain penalty. The penalty varies based upon whether one or both of the partners make it to the meeting or not, since both need to be at the meeting for there to be any work conducted. Thus, each man has to keep in mind what the other person will do while making his own decision. This is a simple Team Decision Problem with all the ingredients and the decision that each partner has to make is whether or not to go to the meeting based on if it is raining in his city or not. The decisions are to be made in such a way that the total penalty involved in the decision set is minimized.

Table 1 shows one example of a loss table for this system. This table clearly shows how the loss values are a function of the decisions each DM makes (u_B, u_H) and the weather condition at the common location where they are to meet (ξ_W). The joint probability is given in Table 2. This gives the correlation between

Table 1: Loss Function of the System

u_B	u_H	ξ_W	$L(u_B, u_H, \xi_W)$
0	0	0	-10.0
0	0	1	4.0
0	1	0	3.0
0	1	1	2.0
1	0	0	3.0
1	0	1	2.0
1	1	0	0.0
1	1	1	-5.0

the weather conditions of the three cities (ξ_B, ξ_H, ξ_W). The goal is to determine the decision rule set that will minimize the overall expected loss.

This problem was mapped to the regular Hopfield network. The description of that mapping and the results obtained can be found in [5, 6].

Table 2: Probability Distribution Function of ξ

ξ_B	ξ_H	ξ_W	$p(\xi)$
0	0	0	0.25
0	0	1	0.05
0	1	0	0.1
0	1	1	0.1
1	0	0	0.1
1	0	1	0.1
1	1	0	0.05
1	1	1	0.25

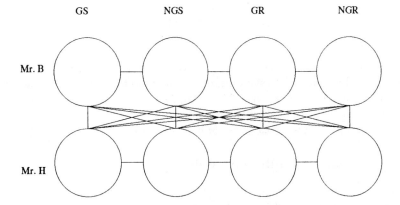

Figure 1: Hopfield-Tank Network for Team Decision Theory

3.2 Modified Hopfield Network

3.2.1 Mapping

The modified Hopfield Network is shown in Figure 1. The neurons in the first row represent the four possible decision rule pairs for Mr. B, while those in the second row represent those for Mr. H. The first column represents "go on shine," the second column represents "don't go on shine," the third column represents "go on rain," and the fourth column represents "don't go on rain." A '1' as the output value of a neuron at network convergence indicates that that decision rule must be adopted, while a '0' indicates that it should not. The node values were set up to follow a Boltzmann distribution, as described in Section 2. The node values were normalized across each mutually exclusive decision pair. The mathematical formulation is given below:

$$U_{i,j} = V_{i,j+1} \forall i, j = 0, 2$$
$$U_{i,j} = V_{i,j-1} \forall i, j = 1, 3 \tag{4}$$

$$E_{i,j} = DP1 \times \sum_{j1=0}^{3} U_{i,j1} + DP2 \times \sum_{j1=0}^{3} \sum_{i2=0, i2 \neq i}^{1} \sum_{j2=0}^{3} V_{i2,j2}$$
$$\times \ (\text{sh\_l}[i, j1, j2] \times \text{sh\_p}[j1, j2] + \text{ra\_l}[i, j1, j2] \times \text{ra\_p}[j1, j2]) \forall i, j \tag{5}$$

$$S_{i,j} = e^{-\frac{E_{i,j}}{T}} + e^{-\frac{E_{i,j+1}}{T}} \forall i, j = 0, 2$$
$$S_{i,j} = e^{-\frac{E_{i,j}}{T}} + e^{-\frac{E_{i,j-1}}{T}} \forall i, j = 1, 3 \tag{6}$$

$$V_{i,j} = \frac{e^{-\frac{E_{i,j}}{T}}}{S_{i,j}} \forall i, j \tag{7}$$

where T is the current annealing temperature. The energy function of the network is given by:

$$
\begin{aligned}
E = & \frac{DP1}{2} \sum_{i=0}^{1} \sum_{j=0}^{1} v_{i,j} \times v_{i,2 \times j+1} \\
& + \frac{DP2}{2} \sum_{i1=0}^{1} \sum_{j1=0}^{3} \sum_{i2=0,i2 \neq i1}^{1} \sum_{j2=0}^{3} V_{i1,j1} \times V_{i2,j2} \\
& \times \quad (\text{sh\_l}[i1,j1,j2] \times \text{sh\_p}[j1,j2] + \text{ra\_l}[i1,j1,j2] \times \text{ra\_p}[j1,j2])
\end{aligned}
\tag{8}
$$

For this system, the constants were set as follows:

$$
\begin{aligned}
DP1 &= 2.0 \\
DP2 &= 10.0.
\end{aligned}
$$

In Equations 5 and 8, the first term ensures that only one of the GO-NOGO pair is activated while the second term ensures that the expected loss is minimized and an optimal solution reached. The network was allowed to anneal from an upper temperature of 10.0 down to a lower temperature of 0.05 in factors of 0.95. The parameter values, as well the annealing temperature limits, were determined throught trial and error. Various values were tried, and these values gave the best results.

3.2.2 Experiments Run and Results Observed

Four sets of loss and probability values were used to test this network mapping. The optimal solution was generated using an exhaustive search for each set of loss and probability values. The network solutions were compared against this optimal solution. The network was able to converge to the correct solution every time, a significant improvement over the performance of the regular Hopfield network. As hypothesized, the annealing was able to force the network out of local minima and push it toward converging to a global minimum. There was, of course, the overhead of the extra execution time that accompanies annealing algorithms.

4 Three-city B, H, & W Problem

This problem was generalized to a case where there were 3 DM's and 3 weather conditions that determined whether the DM's should meet in a common location or not. This increased the problem size considerably; the joint probability table had 81 entries and the loss table 24 entries. The optimal decision rule set had to be chosen out of a total of 512 possible sets. The neural network mapping we developed performed very well, converging to the correct solution over 50% of the time. Details of the implementation and the results can be found in [6].

5 Conclusions

The modified Hopfield network is appropriate to the team decision theory problem. Several different types of team decision theory problems were mapped to the modified Hopfield network with a significant degree of success. For each problem, our neural network was able to iterate to at least a good solution, if not an optimal one. This gives one the confidence that the neural network was able to solve the problems without specific knowledge of the underlying probability distributions of the system parameters. This is a big step toward cracking the inherent intractability of team decision theory problems. The other insight gained from this work was that the system inputs, probability density functions, and most importantly the solution space, had to be discrete. This is not a large limitation since we sample the probability distribution function off a priori measurements. In order for the neural network to solve the team decision theory problem, it had to be able to represent every possible decision in the solution space of the problem, and *pick* the correct decisions as opposed to *calculate* them.

References

[1] Y.C Ho, "Team Decision Theory and Information Structures", *Proceedings of the IEEE*, vol. 68, pp. 644–654, June 1980.

[2] R. Radner, "Team Decision Problems", *Annals of Mathematical Statistics*, vol. 33, pp. 857–881, 1962.

[3] D.E Van den Bout and T.K Miller III, "Improving the Performance of the Hopfield-Tank Neural Network Through Normalization and Annealing", *Biological Cybernetics*, vol. 62, pp. 129–139, 1989.

[4] S Kirkpatrick, C. D Gelatt Jr., and M.P Vecchi, "Optimization by Simulated Annealing", *Science*, vol. 220, pp. 671–680, 1983.

[5] G Rao and W.J.B Oldham, "Mapping the Team Decision Theory Problem to Neural Networks", *in 6th Oklahoma Symposium on Artificial Intelligence*, pp. 41–47, Nov. 1992.

[6] G. Rao, *Mapping the Team Decision Theory Problem to Hopfield-like Neural Networks*, PhD Dissertation, Texas Tech University, Lubbock, Texas, 1993.

Modified Frequency Sensitive Self-Organization Neural Network for Image Data Compression

Lih-Yih Chiou, Jimmy Limqueco, Jun Tian, Chidchanok Lursinsap, Henry Chu
The Center for Advanced Computer Studies
University of Southwestern Louisiana
Lafayette, LA 70504-44330
e-mail: lur@cacs.usl.edu

Abstract-This paper presents a neural network based method for data compression using vector quantization technique. The key element in the vector quantization approach: codebook, is generated via a simulated neural network, by using modified frequency sensitive self-organization algorithms[MFSO 1, 2, 3]. First the concepts involved and learning algorithm are discussed, and then the results are presented and are compared with the results by Linde-Buzo-Gray(LBG) algorithm and FSO algorithm. The proposed methods can achieve good performance and is very effective.

I. INTRODUCTION

Although a classical topic, image data compression becomes more important in the recent years. It reduces significant amount of time and space in the areas such as network transmission, storage of images in a database, etc. A fundamental goal of data compression is to reduce the bit rate for transmission or data storage while maintaining an acceptable fidelity or image quality. Our goal is to use a self-organization neural network to simulate the Vector Quantization method for image data compression.

Vector Quantization(VQ) method[1] is very effective at low to medium compression ratio. The most famous and classical Linde-Buzo-Gray algorithm[2] is excellent in producing the reconstructed image data but is not adaptable to changing data input, as mentioned by Fang[3]. The LBG algorithm requires that data be input in a batch mode so that it can be arranged and rearranged to reduce the distortion function. The LBG method also requires significant amount of computation.

Since the inherent feature of Vector Quantization(VQ) makes it easy to implement it in neural network, various studies have been made on the subject[3,4,8,10]. Fang[3] first introduced the idea of Frequency Sensitive Self-Organization neural network approach to solve the two problems mentioned above. It is very efficient but does not achieve as good result as with LBG method.

In this paper, we incorporate the frequency sensitive approach and force attraction concept to yield a better result in training the neurons. In section II, the proposed algorithm and results are presented. In section III, results by different algorithms are shown and compared.

II. CONCEPTS AND ALGORITHMS

By observing the result from the FSO method, it is noticed that the neurons still can not be fully utilized, which is an inherent problem of self-organization networks[5-9]. The intuitive approach is to involve more neurons during computation[5]. The more code templates are included in a code book, the more accurate image can be reproduced. Therefore, instead of updating the winning neuron only, we also update neurons with the least usage so that they will be drag to the main stream gradually. Then after a certain time of training, the winning frequency will be evenly distributed among the neurons.

Since in general, the image vectors tend to be concentrated at certain area and sparse at the other area, more neurons should be assigned to represent those higher populated area so that more details from the reconstructed image can be obtained. In the mean while, less or no neurons will be assigned to a area if there are only a few image vectors present in that area. And as the concentration of one area grows, the more attraction it will have for the surrounding neurons, which will be dragged toward that area(see the figure 1). The following three methods differ in the way neurons are distributed, each has its advantages and disadvantages in terms of performance and time complexity and VLSI design complexity. We propose three different approaches as follows.

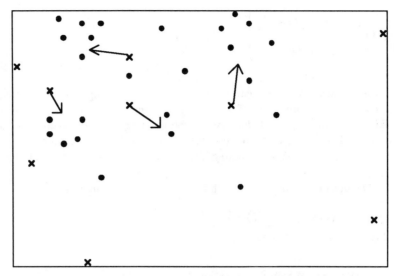

Fig.1 the Concept of Force Attraction

A. Modified Frequency Sensitive Self-Organization 1

In MFSO1, we update the neuron which is winner, and the neuron with the least winning frequency so it will have a better chance to be a winner in the future. The algorithm is listed below:

1. Initialize the code vectors W_i and the winning frequency F_i for each neuron:

$$W_i(0) = R_i$$

$$F_i(0) = 1, \quad i = 1,2,\ldots\ldots\ldots N$$

where R_i is a random vector number generator function. N is the number of code vectors. And $W_i(0) = [W_{i1}(0), W_{i2}(0), \ldots W_{iM}(0)]$. First N input vectors can also be used as initial code vectors instead of random generated code vectors from R_i.

2. Compute the distortion $D_i(t)$ between an input vector and all the code vectors in the code book:

$$D_i(t) = d(X(t), W_i(t)) = \sum_{j=1}^{M}(X_j(t) - W_{ij}(t))^2,$$

where t is the training time index.

3. Select the neuron with the minimum distortion as the winner and set its output $O_i(t)$ a as follows:

$$O_i(t) = \begin{cases} 1 & \text{if } D_i(t) < D_j(t),\ 1 \le i, j \le N, i \ne j \\ 0 & \text{otherwise.} \end{cases}$$

4. Update the code vector with a frequency sensitive training rule and the associated winning frequency:

$$W_i(t+1) = W_i(t) + S(t)O_i(t)(X(t) - W_i(t))$$

$$S(t) = \begin{cases} \dfrac{1}{F_i(t)}, & \text{if } 1 \le F_i(t) \le F_{th} \\ 0 & \text{otherwise} \end{cases}$$

$$F_i(t+1) = F_i(t) + O_i(t),$$

where $S(t)$ is the frequency sensitive learning rate, and F_{th} is the upper threshold frequency. Only the winning code vector is updated. The training rule moves the code vector toward the input vector by a fractional amount, which decreases as the winning frequency increases. If the winning frequency is larger than the $F_{th,}$ no further training is performed ton the neuron.

5. Select a neuron with the smallest winning frequency, F_{min}, and a neuron with maximum frequency, F_{max}

If $F_{min}/F_{max} < D_{th,}$ update the code vector with F_{min} with the following rule:

$$W_{F_{min}}(t+1) = W_{F_{min}}(t) + \eta(W_{F_{max}}(t) - W_{F_{min}}(t))$$

6. repeat step 2 to 5 for all input vectors.

B. Modified Frequency Sensitive Self-Organization 2

MFSO1 yielded far better results than the FSO method. But it is still inferior to the LBG method. One instinctive modification is to attract more than one neurons at a time in order to have a even better utilization of the neurons. The whole procedure is very similar to the MFSO1 methods except step 5, which is listed as follows:

5. Select all the neurons with the smallest winning frequency, F_{min}, and the winner neuron with winning frequency, F_{win}.

If $F_{min}/F_{win} < D_{th,}$ update the code vector with F_{min} with the following rule:

$$W_{F_{min}}(t+1) = W_{F_{min}}(t) + \eta \times (W_{F_{win}}(t) - W_{F_{min}}(t))$$

The least frequently used neuron is replaced by a group of neurons whose usage is below a certain level as compared to the current winning neuron.

During the training process, It was found that eventually the neurons that are attracted to one densely populated area would get closer and closer to a same vector value. Such tendency is highly undesirable and results in another type of underutilization problem. The ideal scenario would be the neurons being distributed like the stars and planets in a galaxy, with its relative distance determined by the attractive force between the two identities, which in term is determined by the relative mass. Yet each star and planet remains to be an individual object no matter how closely they are attracted to each other. In the case of distributing neurons, the winning frequency serves the same purpose as the mass of the stars. That gives rise to the modification in MFSO3.

C. Modified Frequency Sensitive Self-Organization 3

To solve the problem mentioned in MFSO2 above, another modification is made in the updating rule. The step 5 is as follows:

5. Select all the neurons with the smallest winning frequency, F_{min}, and the winner neuron winning frequency, F_{win}.

   If $F_{min}/F_{win} < D_{th}$, update the code vector with F_{min} with the following rule:

$$W_{F_{min}}(t+1) = W_{F_{min}}(t) + \eta \times \rho(t) \times (W_{F_{win}}(t) - W_{F_{min}}(t))$$

$$\rho(t) = \frac{1}{c};$$

$$c = c + 1;$$

c indicates the sequence in which the least winning neurons are updated. c is incremented by 1 as each such neuron is updated. Note that the neurons are attracted to each populated region at different rate because of c.

III. SIMULATION AND ANALYSIS

The distortions using algorithms mentioned above are shown in Fig.2. One of the images and its compressed versions are shown in Fig.3. Each code vector consists of 16 elements, with image size of 256 by 256 and 8-bit gray scale level.

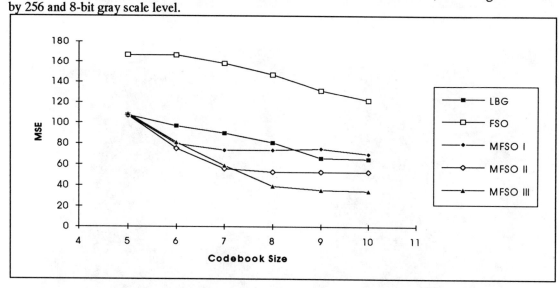

Fig. 2 Distortions(MSE) using LBG, FSO and MFSO1,2,3.

A close inspection of step 5 of MFSO1,2,3 algorithms concludes that all three algorithms have the same time complexity. Yet they are different in VLSI design complexities. It is interesting to notice that for MFSOs algorithm the neurons(i.e., codevectors) are moved around the data while in the LBG method, data are arranged around the current code vectors. Since the number of codevectors are relatively small as compared to the amount of input data, the MFSO algorithms require less computation time than the LBG method. .

IV. CONCLUSION

It is obvious from the images shown in Fig.3 that MFSO methods give better results, and it is comparable in speed to the FSO method. The application of force attraction concept is proved to be very effective in reducing the distortion. The design employing the algorithms above is currently in progress and will soon be presented.

Fig.3 Original & different algorithms

a)Original

b)LBG

c)MFSO1

d)MFSO2

e)MFSO3

I-346

REFERENCES

1. Nasser M. Nasrabdi and Robert A. King, "Image coding using vector quantization: A Review", *IEEE Trans. on Commun.*, Vol.36, Aug. 1988, pp. 957-971.
2. Yosephlinde, Andres Buzo and Robert M. Gray, "An algorithm for vector quantizer Design", *IEEE Trans. on Commun.* Vol. Com-28, Jan. 1980, pp.84-95.
3. Wai-Chi Fang, Bing J. Sheu, Oscal T.-C. and Joongho Choi, "A VLSI neural processor for image data compression using self-organization networks", *IEEE Trans. on Neural Network*, Vol. 3, May 1992, pp. 506-518.
4. Cheng-Chang Lu and Young Ho Shin, "A neural network based image compression system", *IEEE Trans. on Comsumer Electronics*, Vol 38, Feb, 1992, No.1, pp.25-29.
5. John Hertz, Anders Krogh, Rochard G.Palmer, *"Introduction to the theory of neural computation"*, Addison-Wasley, 1991
6. T.Kohonen, *"Self-Organization and Associative Memory"*, Springer-Verlag,1988.
7. R.R.Lippman, "An Introduction to Computing with Neural Nets", *IEEE ASSP Magazine*, Vol3, No.4, pp4-22.
8. S.Grossberg, "Competitive Learning: from interactive activation to adaptive resonance", *Cognitive Sci.*, Vol.11, pp.23-63, 1987.
9. B. Kosko, "Stochastic competitive learning", *Proc. IEEE Int. Joint Conf. Neural Networks*, Vol.II, June 1990, pp.215-226
10 N.M.Nasrabadi, Y.Feng, "Vector quantization of images based upon the Kohonen self-organizing feature maps", *Proc. IEEE Int. Conf. on Neural Networks*, pp.1101-1108,1988.

Modeling Cortical Neuron Responses using Artificial Neural Networks

Mathew J. Palakal[1], Siva K. Chittajallu[2], Donald Wong[3]

[1]Department of Computer Science
[2]Department of Mechanical Engineering
[3]Department of Anatomy
Indiana University - Purdue University at Indianapolis
Indianapolis, IN 46202-5132

Abstract

Bats that echolocate use biosonar to perceive their target as an auditory image by extracting cues from the target-reflected echoes of their emitted pulses. Bats actively control the sound structure and temporal pattern of their sonar emission that includes signal parameters such as pulse duration, pulse repetition rate, amplitude, bandwidth, and harmonics during the search, approach, and terminal phases of a typical hunting cycle. Neurophysiologically, it has been found that a population of delay-sensitive neurons differing in echo delays perform cross correlation for target-range perception and and also these neurons participate in processing other target attributes besides target range. This paper presents a model based on artificial neural networks to learn the delay-tuning properties of the delay-sensitive neurons. This network is then used for generating the delay-tuning curves toward the building of an auditory system framework of an FM bat.

I. Introduction

Echolocating bats perceive their target image by extracting the acoustic cues conveyed in the target-reflected echoes of their emitted biosonar pulses (Busnel and Fish 1980). During echolocation, bats actively control the sound structure and temporal pattern of their sonar emission such as Pulse Duration (PD), Pulse Repetition Rate (PRR) that is likely related to the perceptual demands during target-directed flight (Simmons et al. 1975). Behavioral studies into the echolocation process showed that FM bats exhibit an exceptionally fine delay acuity in discriminating between two sets of echoes differing in delays in the order of microseconds (Simmons et al. 1990b). Correlation is considered to be a possible mechanism underlying this fine delay acuity. Simmons and Chen (1989) suggest that the sharp temporal acuity demonstrated in FM bats may underlie their ability to perceive target shape, as well as target distance.

Cross-correlation processing in the bat auditory system requires a mechanism for the coincidence of the emitted pulse and the temporally delayed echo. Neurophysiological evidence for such a mechanism is provided by delay-sensitive neurons, which have been characterized in the brain of a number of echolocating bats (Suga and O'Neill 1978). These neurons show facilitative responses to artificial pulse-echo pairs at particular echo delays, and are likely to participate in target-range perception.

In the auditory cortex of *Myotis lucifugus*, the species that we are studying, delay-sensitive neurons also mediate other aspects of target perception in addition to target range (Wong et al 1992). This is suggested by the changes in the delay tuning properties of these cortical neurons when such temporal parameters as PRR and/or PD are systematically varied in simulating stimulus conditions found in target approach (Wong et al. 1992; Tanaka et al. 1992). These delay-sensitive neurons play a critical role in an auditory system model for the FM bat, *Myotis lucifugus* (Chittajallu et al. 1994) that we have proposed. A delay-sensitive neuron can be characterized by the variation of its best delay (BD) to the stimulus parameters, PRR and PD. The BD of the neuron is defined as the pulse-echo delay for which there is a maximum response for a specific pulse repetition rate and pulse duration. The specific aim of this study is to model these delay-sensitive neuron's BD response pattern in order to build the delay module as part of the framework for the auditory system. We present a brief overview of the framework in section II of this paper. Section III describes the use of artificial neural networks to develop the delay-tuning networks and section IV presents the results.

II. The Auditory System Framework

Little is currently known about how the neural responses are integrated to generate a unitary acoustic image of the target. An important first step is the development of a modeling framework of the FM bat auditory system (Figure 1a). This framework incorporates several functional aspects of the biological system such that only specific components have direct neurobiological relevance while other components are based upon behavioral results (Simmons 1979; Simmons et al. 1990a) and engineering solutions. Therefore, a signal-processing approach is used to augment behavioral and neurophysiological approaches directed toward understanding the perceptual mechanisms in FM bats. The main components of this framework include pulse and echo channels, a delay module, a correlation module, and higher-level modules for target-feature extraction.

In the auditory system framework, the desired biosonar pulse is created in the arbitrary waveform generator (Figure 1a). It is then emitted through a microphone and is simultaneously passed directly into the pulse channel. It consists of a bank of bandpass filters that span the bat's frequency range used for echolocation. The delayed target-reflected echo enters the echo channel that mimics the peripheral auditory system. The electrical signal from the microphone is amplified by the time-gain control stage and passed through an array of bandpass filters. The mechanism for the coincidence of the pulse and echo, for cross-correlation, is provided in the model by the combination of the pulse channel, the delay module and the correlation module. The delay module serves to delay the signal propagating through the pulse channel to implement the coincidence. In addition, it provides the tuning role necessary for providing the fine delay resolution. The emitted biosonar pulse and the target-reflected echo coincide at the correlation module to yield the frequency-delay map. Higher-level processing of this delay map yields target information such as range, velocity and target class.

An important component of this framework is the delay module. This module consists of a tapped delay line, and a delay-tuning network. A bank of such units with different delay tuning properties operate on the signal propagating through the pulse channel and encode the delay-frequency structure of the pulse. The tapped delay line provides the delayed pulse. The delay tuning network, on the other hand, serves to tune the output of the tapped delay line to provide the desired delay resolution in the delay-frequency map. The inputs to the delay-tuning network are the temporal parameters of the emitted pulse. The dynamic characteristics of the delay-tuning network would mimic that of the biological delay-sensitive neurons in the FM bat cortex to natural sonar signals used in different hunting phases.

The delay-tuning network is an essential component of the auditory-system framework. These networks provide the tuning mechanism necessary to extract the fine delay-frequency map of the target-reflected echoes necessary for target discrimination (Figure 1b). Delay-sensitive neurons that have been identified in neurophysiological studies of the *Myotis* auditory cortex are tuned to specific delays between components in the acoustic stimulus, and thus influence further cortical processing that results in target perception.

Neurophysiological studies show that pulse repetition rate (PRR) and pulse duration (PD) are important temporal parameters in the stimulus that affect the delay-tuning properties of a delay-sensitive neuron. The purpose of this study is to model the delay-tuning network (DTN) using artificial neural networks. The modeling of DTN is based on neurophysiological data on delay-sensitive neurons obtained from a previous study of the auditory cortex of the little brown bat, *Myotis lucifugus* (Tanaka et al. 1992).

Theoretical analyses on thirty-three delay-sensitive neurons from eight animals revealed that there are essentially six different classes of delay-sensitive neurons in the auditory cortex of FM bat, *Myotis lucifugus* (Tanaka et al. 1992; Chittajallu et al. 1994). Neurons from each of these class behave differently for given set of PRR and PD pair. The PRR values ranged from 5/sec. to 99/sec. for PD values 4, 2, and 1ms. The response property of each class of neurons is described below:

Class 1 Units: These units exhibit a constant BD for a range of PDs and PRRs. For example, one of the units in this class showed a constant BD of 3ms for all PRR and PD pair.
Class 2 Units: The BD of these units drops with PD and remains constant over the range of PRR. The drop in the BD with a drop in PD is characteristic of tracking neurons.

Class 3 Units: This class of units exhibits a constant BD with an increase in PRR at short PDs, but they lose their delay-sensitivity at high PRRs and long PDs.

Class 4 Units: This class is the counterpart of class 2. In both instances the BD changed as the PD and PRR are changed. While the PD is the determinant of BD for Class 2 units, it is PRR that is the determinant of BD for Class 4 units. These units show a constant BD for a specific PRR, but show a decreasing BD with increasing PRR.

Class 5 Units: In this class of units, the BD decreases as the PD shortens and the PRR increases. This class exhibits the response properties of the classic tracking neuron. As the bat progresses through the hunting cycle, the BD should drop to match the diminishing distance between the bat and the target. In this class, a relatively long PD and low PRR results in a high BD. As the PD shortens and the PRR increases, stimulus conditions found in hunting cycle, the BD drops steadily to track the target.

Class 6 Units: This class of units exhibits no delay sensitivity under unnatural stimulus conditions (i.e., at high PRRs and long PDs). However, under natural stimulus conditions, the BD of these units decreases when PD and PRR are increased. This class is sensitive to variation of each of the stimulus parameters like Class 5 units. However, Class 6 loses its facilitation at high PRRs.

III. Modeling Delay-Tuning Network

The purpose of the delay-tuning network (DTN) is to generate the tuning property of a given class of neuron for a set of PRR and PD. Therefore, the input to DTN is the stimulus parameter pair (PRR and PD) and the output is a tuning curve for a unit in a given class. However, within a given class, the tuning property can change depending on the magnitude of the input parameter pairs. An interconnection among several such DTNs within a class and across all classes will constitute the delay-tuning network for the entire auditory-system framework. A standard back-propagation neural network (ANN) is used to model the DTN networks. Each class of neurons is modeled separately using different ANN. The purpose of these ANN models are two-fold:

A.   Predicting Neuron Responses for Unknown Stimulus Pairs
Neurophysiological experiments were conducted only on a limited set of PRR and PD values. For example, not all ranges of PRR values were tested for a given neuron. Similarly, for certain neurons PD was tested for only 2ms and 4ms. Other values like 1ms and 3ms were not tested. This is because of experimental conditions during data collection. Therefore, from neurophysiological stand point, a model that can reliably predict the tuning patterns for unknown sets of stimulus parameters is important. Such a model will allow neurophysiologists to better understand the functional properties of these neurons.

B.   Predicting Tuning Curves for the Delay Unit
The output of the ANN is the actual tuning curve. This curve will be used in the delay unit (Figure 1b) as weight vectors in order to perform correlation between the emitted pulse and the echo. However, in order to build the auditory system framework, the tuning property for the entire range of stimulus pairs must be available. Since the bat continuously changes the stimulus parameters during its target directed flight, the model must be capable of generating the tuning property for all sets of stimulus parameters.

The Neural Network Model
The ANN that we used to model the DTN is a back-propagation network with three hidden layers. Inputs to the DTN are pulse repetition rate and pulse duration. There are 12 outputs that corresponds to the delay-tuning curve for the given stimulus parameter set. The training data consisted of electrophysiological experimental data collected from *Myotis lucifugus* for various stimulus parameter pairs. The training data set were normalized between 0 and 1 for each unit. The ANN converged in 12,000 iterations for a global error of 0.0001.

IV. Experimental Results

One representative unit from each class was used to train the ANN. Thus there are six different ANNs corresponding to each class. Each ANN is capable of accepting a range of PRR and PD pairs as input and generate a corresponding tuning curve. Results from two sample tests are given in figures 2 and 3. Figure 2 shows the tuning curves corresponding to a unit from class 2 which is a tracking neuron. Each sub-plot in this figure is a tuning curve for one set of PRR and PD. In figure 2, the DTN was trained on PD values of 1, 2 and 4 ms and PRR values of 5/s, 10/s, 30/s, 50/s, and 70/s. The trained DTN was then tested for the untrained stimulus value, PD = 3ms for PRR values of 5/s, 10/s, 20/s, 30/s, 40/s, 50/s, 60/s, and 70/s as shown in column 3 in bold face. Similarly, the network was also tested for untrained stimulus value for PRR = 20/s, 40/s, and 60/s for all PD values. These are shown across in bold faced rows of figure 2.

It can be seen from figure 2, that the ANN generalized well and captured the essential properties of a tracking neuron. The tracking neuron has the property that the best delay (the highest peak in the tuning curve) drops for small PDs while it stays constant for a wide range of PRR. This property suggests that this class of units is tuned to a specific target range independent of the PD. The network clearly predicted this behavior as seen in figure 2 for PD=3ms and PRR=20/s, 40/s, and 60/s.

Figure 3 shows tuning curves for another sample unit from class 5. This is also a tracking neuron with a different behavior. The best delay of this unit drops as PD drops while PRR increases. Notice in figure 3, the highest peak (the best delay) shifts to the right as PRR increases. This unit was trained with experimental data for PD=1ms, 2ms and 4ms and PRR=5/s, 10/s, 20/s, 40/s, 60/s, and 80/s. The network was then tested for PD=3ms for all PRRs as shown in bold face in column. The network was also tested for PRR=30/s, 50/s, and 70/s. As in the previous case, the network was able to capture the essential features of this tracking unit by correctly responding to a given set of stimulus pairs.

V. Conclusions

We have presented a neural network based model of a delay-tuning network to predict the tuning properties of delay-sensitive neurons. These neurons, found in the auditory cortex of the FM bat *Myotis lucifugus*, play an important role in their target directed flight. These neurons are sensitive to stimulus parameters, pulse repetition rate and pulse duration. The bat actively control these parameters during the various phases of their hunting cycle. The purpose of the ANN model of the delay sensitive neurons is to generate the tuning curve for a given neuron to different set of PRR and PD input pairs. The tuning curve generated by these networks will be used in our auditory system framework to compute the correlation between the pulse and echo for generating the acoustic image of the target. The networks performed well and generalized within a reasonable amount of time.

References

Busnel RG, Fish JF (eds) (1980) Animal Sonar Systems. Plenum Press, New York.
Chittajallu SK, Palakal MJ, Wong D (1994) Analysis and Classification of Delay-sensitive Cortical Neurons Based on Response to Temporal Parameters in Echolocation Signals (in preparation).
Roverud RC, Grinnell AD (1985) Discrimination performance and echolocation signal integration requirements for target detection and distance determination in the CF/FM bat, Noctilio albiventris. J Comp Physiol A 156:447-456.
Simmons JA, Chen L (1989) The acoustic basis for target discrimination by FM echolocating bats. J Acoust Soc Am, 86:1333-1350.
Simmons JA, Howell DJ, Suga N (1975) The information content of bat sonar echoes. Am Sci 63:204-215.
Simmons JA, Ferragamo M, Moss CF, Stevenson SB, Altes RA (1990a) Discrimination of jittered sonar echoes by the echolocating bat Eptesicus fuscus: The shape of target images in echolocaton. J Comp Physiol A 167:589-616.
Simmons JA, Moss CF, Ferragamo M (1990b) Convergence of temporal and spectral information into acoustic images of complex sonar targets perceived by the echolocating bat, Eptesicus fuscus. J Comp Physiol A 166:449-470.
Suga N, O'Neill WE, Kujirai K, Manabe T (1983) Specificity of combination-sensitive neurons for processing of complex biosonar signals in auditory cortex of the mustached bat. J Neurophysiol 49:1573-1626.
Sullivan WE (1982) Neural representation of target distance in auditory cortex of the echolocating bat Myotis lucifugus. J Neurophysiol 48:1011-1032.
Tanaka H, Wong D, Taniguchi I (1992) The influence of stimulus duration on the delay tuning of cortical neurons in the FM bat, Myotis lucifugus. J Comp Physiol A 171:29-40.
Wong D, Maekawa M, Tanaka H (1992) The effect of pulse repetition rate on the delay-sensitivity of neurons in the auditory cortex of the FM bat, Myotis lucifugus. J Comp Physiol A, 170: 393-402.

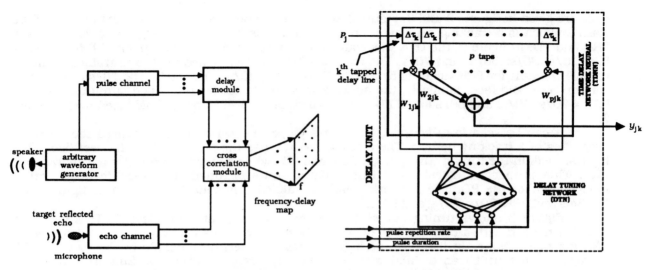

Figure 1 (a): The schematic of the bat auditory system framework and (b) a detailed diagram of the delay unit showing the delay-tuning network

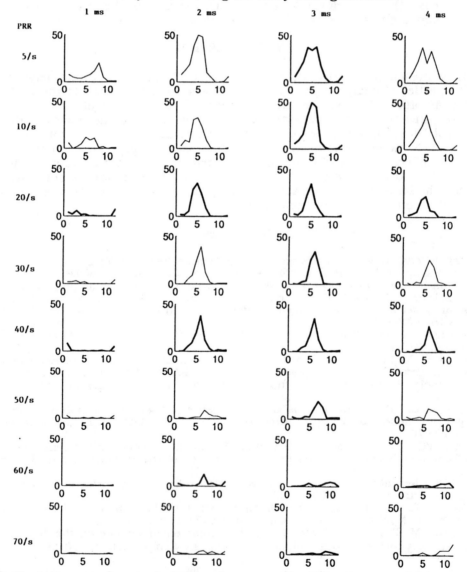

Figure 2. Tuning curves for a typical Class 2 neuron. The Pulse Duration (PD) shown on top ranges from 1 to 4 ms and the Pulse Repetition Rate per second are shown on the left margin

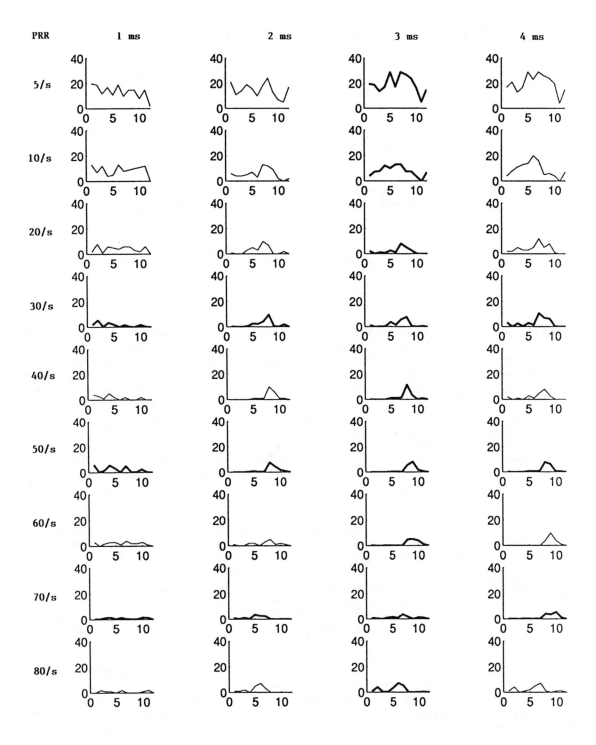

Figure 3. Tuning curves for a typical Class 5 neuron. The Pulse Duration (PD) shown on top ranges from 1 to 4 ms and the Pulse Repetition Rate per second are shown on the left margin

An Improved DNA Encoding Scheme for Neural Network Modeling

Mark F. Russo
Scientific Computing, Sterling Winthrop Pharmaceutical Research Division
9 Great Valley Parkway, Malvern, PA. 19355

Anne C. Huff
Virology and Oncopharmacology, Sterling Winthrop Pharmaceutical Research Division
1250 South Collegeville Road, Collegeville, PA. 19426

Charles E. Heckler
Applied Statistics, Eastman Kodak Company
6 Eastman Avenue, Bldg. 6, Rochester, NY. 14650

Audrey C. Evans
Preclinical and Scientific Statistics, Sterling Winthrop Pharmaceutical Research Division
9 Great Valley Parkway, Malvern, PA. 19355

Abstract

A new scheme is presented for encoding DNA sequences for use in building neural network models. The encoding scheme is useful for data that relates DNA sequences with the presence or absence of some property. The scheme replaces each base with a logarithm of the probability of chance deviation between the observed frequency of base occurrence at a particular position within sequences possessing a particular property and the actual frequency of base occurrence within the entire DNA strand. Neural network models developed using DNA sequence data encoded with the new scheme showed an improved ability to predict the potential of topoisomerase to cleave DNA sequences, compared to neural network models developed using the same DNA sequence data encoded with the popular CODE-4 [1] encoding scheme. The new scheme results in encodings that are only one quarter the size of that obtained using the CODE-4 encoding scheme. It also reduces the number of parameters in the neural network model by approximately 75%. This dramatic reduction in parameters produces a more substantial neural network model using the same DNA sequence data. Subsequent statistical tests on the best neural network model obtained using the new encoding clearly demonstrate the strong significance of the model.

I. Introduction

Artificial Neural Networks have become increasingly popular for building models that correlate nucleotide or amino acid sequences with some property possessed by the sequence [1,2,3,4,5,6,7,8]. This popularity can be attributed to a significant number of successful applications coupled with the ease with which the technique is applied.

Syntactically, DNA sequences are linear strings of four characters, A, C, T or G. Each corresponds to one of the four nucleotides that makes up DNA. Similarly, peptides are linear sequences of 20 characters, each corresponding to one of the 20 possible amino acids. It is widely believed that the linear sequence (or syntax) of a segment of DNA or a peptide is sufficient information to describe its biological behavior. It should be possible therefore to correlate observed biological behavior with an associated sequence.

Several techniques have been investigated for encoding a DNA or amino acid sequence into a vector of numbers appropriate for processing by a neural network. [9,10,11] have developed an encoding scheme for amino acid sequences that captures the physicochemical properties of each amino acid as three distinct numerical values. An amino acid sequence is then encoded with a vector of numbers that is three times as long as the number of amino acids in the sequence. This encoding scheme has been used to develop many successful correlations between amino acid sequence and its properties.

Two popular encoding schemes for DNA sequences are the CODE-4 and CODE-2 schemes. The CODE-4 scheme replaces each nucleotide with a sequence of three zeros and a one. The position of the one in the sequence uniquely identifies the base. For example, if each base in a sequence were replaced according to the substitution set: {C/0001, G/0010, A/0100, T/1000}, the resulting vector of 0's and 1's would be one possible CODE-4 encoding of the sequence. The encoded vector is four times as long as the original sequence. The CODE-2 scheme replaces each of the four nucleotides with a unique two digit binary number. Consider for example the set of substitutions: {A/00, T/01, G/10, C/11}. The resulting encoded vector is two times as long as the original sequence. [1] has found the CODE-4 scheme to be superior to the CODE-2 scheme for representing DNA sequences in neural network models.

A series of experiments was designed to study the mechanism of inhibition of certain antitumor and antibacterial agents on type II DNA topoisomerase (topo II) [12,13,14]. Cleavage assays were performed on pBR322 DNA [18] and the 28 bases surrounding each cleavage site experimentally identified. A neural network technique was used to build a model to predict which sequences are cleaved by topo II in the presence of an additional chemical agent. Initially the CODE-4 scheme was used to encode the 28-base DNA sequences in the data set. The resulting neural network models were unsatisfactory showing a maximum prediction rate of only 50%. In an attempt to improve the performance, we investigated a new encoding scheme for the 28-base DNA sequences. The new scheme replaces each base at each position in a cleaved sequence with the base 10 logarithm (or negative logarithm) of the probability that the occurrence of the particular base at its position is different from the average value seen in the entire DNA sequence. The resulting neural network model built with the new encoding scheme improved prediction capability to 70% with only one quarter the number of parameters. Subsequent statistical analyses provide strong support for the significance of the neural network model.

II. Methods

II.1 Artificial Neural Networks

Neural network models in this investigation were developed using a program of our own design. The program was written in the C programming language [17] and runs on an IBM PC compatible personal computer containing an 80486 microprocessor. All networks were of the fully connected feedforward type and were trained using backpropagation [16]. Computing elements in each network used the squashing function, s(x),

$$s(x) = \frac{1}{1 + e^{-x}} - \tfrac{1}{2} \qquad \text{(Eq. 1)}$$

which has a range of (-0.5,0.5). Data sets were scaled linearly to the same range using a maximum and minimum value computed over all data in the entire training data set. The error function minimized during training was,

$$E = \frac{\left(\sum_{i=1}^{N_v} \sum_{j=1}^{N_e^l} \left(t_j - o_j^l \right)^2 \right)^{\frac{1}{2}}}{N_v N_e^l} \qquad \text{(Eq. 2)}$$

where E is the residual error, t_j is the jth element of the ith target vector, o_j^l is the output of the jth element of the last layer, N_e^l is the number of elements in the last layer and N_v is the number of vector pairs in the training set.

II.2. Data Sets and the Encoding Scheme

A complete data set was obtained by moving a window of size 28 one base at a time down the entire counterclockwise strand of pBR322 DNA. 1061 unique 28-base sequences were obtained; 80 of which were found experimentally to be cleaved by topo II in the presence of an additional chemical agent. Cleavage was indicated in the data set with a "1"; no cleavage was indicated with a "0". For more information on experimental methods and characteristics of the experimental data see [14].

106 (10% 0f 1061) sequences with their corresponding cleavage site indicator values were removed at random from the complete data set and placed into the test data set. The remaining 955 sequences with their corresponding cleavage site indicator values then comprised the training data set.

Data sets were encoded by replacing all DNA sequences in both the training and test data sets with a unique vector of 28 real numbers. Each of the real numbers is a base 10 logarithm of the probability (P) of chance deviation between the expected and observed number of occurrences of the base at the position in the sequence. Probabilities are were computed as follows.

Let : $p_B =$ the frequency of occurrence of a given base (B) within the counterclockwise strand of pBR322 DNA (where: p_A=0.2373, p_T=0.2252, p_C=0.2600, p_G=0.2775)

$n =$ the number of cleavage sites sequenced (n=80)

$pn =$ the expected number of cleavage sites to have a given base at any particular position

$m =$ the observed number of cleavage sites which had a given base at that position.

If the observed was greater than expected (m > pn), then *P* is the probability of a chance occurrence of m or more instances:

$$P = \sum_{i=m}^{n} \frac{n!}{i!(n-1)!} (p_B)^i (1-p_B)^{n-i}$$ (Eq. 7)

In this case the encoding for the given base at that position was computed as the $-\log_{10}(P)$.

If the observed was less than the expected (m < pn), then P is the probability of a chance occurrence of m or fewer instances:

$$P = \sum_{i=0}^{m} \frac{n!}{i!(n-1)!} (p_B)^i (1-p_B)^{n-i}$$ (Eq. 8)

In this case the encoding for the given base at that position was computed as the $+\log_{10}(P)$.

The complete encoding consists of 4 possible numbers (one for each of the bases) for each of the 28 positions in the sequence. When computing the encoding only the data in the training data set was used.

Consider as an example the following computation. After splitting the complete data set into a training and test data set, 70 of the 80 cleaved sequences remained in the training data set. If 25 of the 70 had an A in a particular position in the sequence, then since m = 25 > 16.6 = (0.2373*70),

$$P = \sum_{i=25}^{70} \frac{70!}{i!(70-1)!} 0.2373^i (1-0.2373)^{70-i} = 0.016154$$

and the encoding for an A in that position is $-\log_{10}(0.016154)$= 1.791710. This is repeated for all four bases in each of the 28 sequence positions. To our knowledge this technique has not previously been used to encode DNA sequence data for building neural network models.

III. Results

III.A. Neural Networks

Two series of neural networks were investigated. One series was trained with training data encoded using the $\log_{10}(P)$ encoding just described. The second series was trained with the same training data only this time encoded with the CODE-4 encoding scheme described previously. Corresponding test data sets were also encoded in an identical manner. The neural networks in each series differed primarily by their topologies. All neural network topologies contained one hidden layer but the number of nodes in each hidden layer was varied from 0 to 9. Neural networks trained with the $\log_{10}(P)$ encoded training set had 28 input elements, and those trained with the CODE-4 encoded training data had 4*28=112 input elements.

Each neural network was trained several times with different random initial values for network parameters. The best result was retained in each case. Training of all networks continued until the rate of decrease of the residual network error was lower than 10^{-7} per training cycle. Since the main goal of the investigation was to be able to correctly predict all sequences that would be cleaved under the given experimental conditions, we chose to define the best neural network model as the one that correctly predicted the greatest number of cleaved sequences. This is measured using the corresponding test data set which contained data not previously seen by the neural network model. The ability of all neural networks to correctly predict a lack of cleavage exceeded 90%.

Figure 1 is a bar graph of the percent of correctly predicted cleaved sequences verses the number of computing elements in the hidden layer of the neural network for the $\log_{10}(P)$ and CODE-4 encodings.

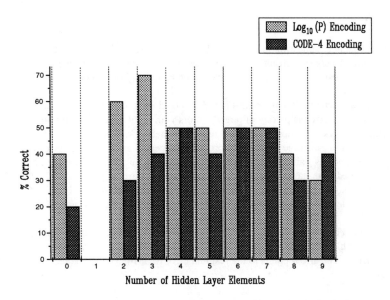

Figure 1: Comparison of predictive performance for $\log_{10}(P)$ and CODE-4 encodings.

We can see from Fig. 1 that as the number of hidden layer computing elements increased in the series of neural networks trained with the $\log_{10}(P)$ encoded data, the percent of correctly predicted cleaved sequences initially increased quickly, peaked at three computing elements, and then began to trail off. The initial rise is due to the increase in complexity of the model due to the increased number of internal computing elements. After three hidden layer computing elements, prediction capability began to decrease. This is most likely due to the onset of overfitting of the data by the neural network. At this point the ability of the model to capture the true relationship in the data diminishes and simple data "memorization" begins.

Prediction performance of the CODE-4 data displayed a different behavior. It increased more slowly and then leveled off at about 50% as the number of computing elements in the hidden layer increased.

In networks with 0 to 3 hidden computing elements, the ones trained with the $\log_{10}(P)$ encoded training set clearly show an improved prediction capability over those trained with the CODE-4 encoded training data. Prediction capability for all networks with 4 or more hidden layer computing elements are comparable.

The number of parameters in the network trained with the CODE-4 encoded data with 9 elements in the hidden layer had 1027 parameters, more than there were vector pairs in the training data set. This is an undesirable situation due to the potential for overfitting the data, therefore no topologies with greater than 9 elements in the hidden layer were investigated. The best neural network obtained with the $\log_{10}(P)$ encoded data had only 91 parameters which is much less than the 955 sequences in the training data set.

These results clearly indicate that changing the encoding scheme for DNA sequence data from the CODE-4 to $\log_{10}(P)$ scheme can improve neural network models. The similar reduction in the number of parameters between neural network topologies resulting from the two encoding schemes is highly desirable since it reduces the number of parameters to a level well below the number of vector pairs in our training data set.

An advantage of the CODE-4 encoding is that it is independent of the data set. Since the $\log_{10}(P)$ encoding is determined through a statistical analysis of the data in the training data set, a new encoding must be computed for each new or modified training data set. Apparent advantages of the $\log_{10}(P)$ encoding is a dramatic reduction in the number of parameters in the model as well as the ability of the neural network to develop a better model with increased predictive capabilities.

III.B. Statistical Analyses

Since only 10% of the sequences appearing in the original data set were actually cleaved, there was a question as to whether the results presented were significantly different from a random result. To further verify the validity of the result, two statistical tests were applied to the best model developed using the $\log_{10}(P)$ encoded data.

A permutation test [15] was performed on the neural network model. In a permutation test (as we have applied it to neural networks) we repeatedly randomize the pairing of target vectors with input vectors in the training set, reassign the parameters in the neural network to random values and retrain the network. The residual error (E) remaining upon completion of training is stored each time. The entire process is repeated as many times as possible. The residual error associated with the model that was trained using the original, non-randomized data set is then compared with the distribution of errors obtained from the models trained using data sets whose target data was randomly paired with input data. If the actual model is significantly better than the models generated with randomly paired data, its residual error is expected to be significantly less than the distribution of errors obtained from the randomized data models.

20 different randomly paired data sets were generated. Each was used to train 20 new neural networks. All 20 networks had the same topology: one hidden layer made up of three computing elements. Figure 2 is a histogram representing the frequency of residual errors. The arrow points to the residual error (0.087435) of the actual neural network model trained with the original data.

The arrow appears far to the left of the "permutation distribution." Due to the large number of observations, the permutation distribution is well-approximated by a normal distribution. We fit a normal distribution to the residual error data using the sample mean (0.19126) and a standard deviation (0.0807). The normal distribution is drawn with a dashed line in Figure 2. The estimated probability that one would observe a residual error of 0.087435 from the permutation distribution under the assumption of normality is 10^{-37} (highly significant).

For our second test we made use of a contingency table [15]. A contingency table can be used to test the hypothesis that one set of data is dependent on another set. A contingency table is appropriate in this case because we consider target and output data to be "bivariate"; the data can indicate or predict the presence (1) or absence (0) of DNA cleavage. We used a contingency table to test for the dependence of the target values in the test data set and the predicted output obtained from the trained neural network fed the input vectors of the test data set.

The null hypothesis of the statistical test is that the two data sets are independent of each other. The alternative hypothesis is that the two data sets are dependent. The null hypothesis is rejected if the test statistic (X^2) exceeds a tabulated value for a chosen level of risk (α).

The test statistic for the results obtained using the $\log_{10}(P)$ encoding was calculated to have a value of 23.94. Using the appropriate table we determine that to reject the null hypothesis (at a risk of $\alpha=0.005$ - taking one chance in 200 of rejecting the null hypothesis when it is true) the X^2 value must exceed 7.88. Clearly this is very much the case and we can therefore conclude that the output of the neural network and the target data are highly dependent. In other words, the neural network model is highly significant.

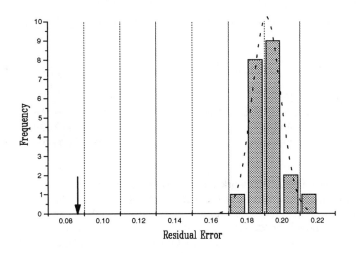

Figure 2: Histogram of permutation test results with a normal distribution.

IV. Conclusion

A new encoding scheme for DNA sequence data to be used when building neural network models is presented. The new encoding scheme is compared to the CODE-4 scheme by observing the performance of two series of feedforward neural network topologies trained with DNA sequence data encoded both ways. Results indicate that a performance gain is possible over the CODE-4 encoding scheme using the new scheme with a dramatic, four-fold decrease in the number of model parameters. Subsequent statistical analyses verify the strong significance of the best neural network model obtained using the new encoding scheme.

References

[1] Demeler, B. and Zhou, G. *Nucleic Acids Research*, Vol. 19, No. 7 pp. 1593-1599, Oxford University Press. 1991.
[2] Brunak, S., Engelbrecht, J. and Knudsen, S.,, *Nucleic Acids Research*, Vol. 18, No. 16 pp. 4797-4801. 1990.
[3] O'Neill, M.C., *Nucleic Acids Research*, Vol. 19, No. 2 pp. 313-318. 1991.
[4] Bohr, H., et al, *FEBS Letters*, Vol. 241, No. 1,2 pp. 223-228. 1988.
[5] Qian, N. and Sejnowski, T.J., *J. Mol. Biol.*, **202**, 865-884. 1988.
[6] McGregor, M.J., Flores, T.P. and Sternberg, M.J.E., *Protein Engineering*, Vol. 2, No. 7, pp. 521-526. 1989.
[7] Holley, L.H., Karplus, M., *Proc. Natl. Acad. Sci.*, Vol. 86, pp. 152-156. 1989.
[8] Bohr, H., et al, *FEBS Letters*, Vol. 261, No. 1 pp. 43-46. 1990.
[9] Hellberg, S., Sjostrom, M. and Wold, S., *Acta Chemica Scandinavica* B 40, pp. 135-140, 1986.
[10] Hellberg, S., Sjostrom, M., Skagerberg, B. and Wold, S., *J. Med. Chem.* No. 30, pp. 1126-1135, 1987.
[11] Wold, S., et al, *Can. J. Chem.*, Vol. 65, pp.1814-1820, 1987.
[12] Huff, A.C., Leatherwood, J.K. and Kreuzer, K.N., *Proc. Natl. Acad. Sci.*, Vol. 86 pp.1307-1311, Feb. 1989.
[13] Huff A.C. and Kreuzer K.N., *The Journal of Biological Chemistry*, Vol. 265, No. 33, pp. 20496-20505, Nov. 1990.
[14] Huff A.C., et al, (in preparation).
[15] Cox, D.R. and Hinckley, D.V., *Theoretical Statistics*, Chapman and Hall. 1979.
[16] Rumelhart, D.E., et al, *Parallel Distributed Processing, Explorations in the Microstructure of Cognition, Volume 1: Foundations*, The MIT Press, Cambridge Mass. 1986.
[17] Kernighan B.W. and Ritchie, D.M., *The C Programming Language*, Prentice Hall, Englewood Cliffs, N.J. 1988.
[18] Maniatis, T., et al, *Molecular Cloning - A Laboratory Manual*, Cold Spring Harbor Laboratory. 1982.

A NEURAL NETWORK TOOL FOR FORECASTING FRENCH ELECTRICITY CONSUMPTION

Corinne MULLER[1], M. COTTRELL[2], B. GIRARD[2], Y. GIRARD[2], Morgan MANGEAS[1,2]

(1) Électricité de France
Direction des Études et Recherches
1, avenue du Général de Gaulle
92141 Clamart - France

(2) SAMOS
Université - Paris 1
90, rue de Tolbiac
75634 Paris cedex 13 - France

Abstract : This paper presents a neural network tool for forecasting half-hour electrical power consumption. This tool allows us to forecast from one half-hour to twenty-four hours in advance. First, we have classified daily consumption curves, using Kohonen self-organizing maps. Secondly, we have developed several neural models, one for each class. These neural models are composed of 48 neural networks, each specialized in the forecasting of one specific half-hour of the day. The initial results show that the neural tool is adaptable and functions well.

Forecasting power loads is a basic and crucial problem for Electricité de France. The difficulty lies in the nature of electricity, which is unstockable. In addition, we have to satisfy consumption at any time and therefore to match production to consumption instantaneously. Given this context, we would like to optimize our use of the cheapest electric power, which is nuclear power, and not to start up expensive production units. Moreover, it is more difficult to modulate the production of nuclear power units quickly than it is for other units. These economic and management problems are an indication of the importance of high-quality forecasts.

Up to now, to forecast electricity consumption, we have used linear models which are called ARMA models (AutoRegressive-Moving Average). Generally, these models give good predictions for ordinary days such as normal weekdays. But for special days, such as public holidays or special tariff days, the forecasts are less satisfactory. Our goal is to improve the quality of the forecasts in both cases: for ordinary and special days. Rather than adopting the usual method, we use several neural models, each specialized in the forecasting of one type of day and one specific hour. To construct such networks, we first made a classification of the daily power curves, and then used it to build the specialized networks. This paper presents first, the data; secondly, the results of the classification; and thirdly, the different neural networks.

I The data

We are studying the half-hour electrical power consumption for metropolitan France. For each day, we have a curve composed of forty-eight half-hour power loads. Our data goes back to 1986. Our ultimate goal is to make forecasts from a half-hour to twenty-four hours in advance. A typical curve of a "normal" day (Figure 1) comprises two peaks: one in the morning, which begins around eight a.m.; and one in the evening, which is sharp in the winter and disappears in the summer.

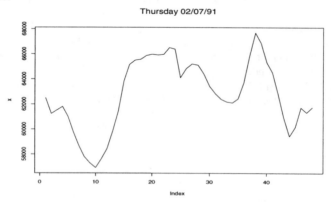

Figure 1 : Daily consumption curve of a normal winter day,
between 12:30 a.m. and 12:00 a.m. (MW)

This series has two periodicities of 1- and 7-day orders (Figure 2). For instance, a Wednesday curve is similar to the previous Tuesday curve (periodicity of order 1) and also similar to the previous Wednesday curve (periodicity of order 7).

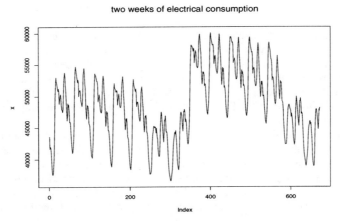

Figure 2 : Evolution of a two-week consumption curve, from Monday to Sunday (MW)

Unfortunately, forecasting can not be based only on these periodicities, because there are different types of perturbations that can deeply change the consumption curve. The most common perturbations are public holidays (Figure 3) and special tariff days. The differences between these curves show that we have to build different forecasting models for the different curve shapes. The goal of classification is to define these different curve shapes.

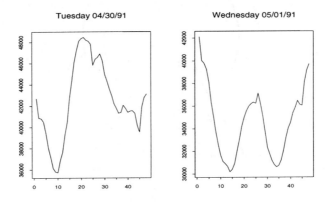

Figure 3 : Consumption curves for Labor Day in France (Wednesday 05/01/91) and the day before (MW)

II Classification

We first tried to build a single neural network to solve the problem. We quickly noticed that the forecasts were inadequate. This was due to two factors. First, a neural network can not work in "loop". Generally, with an ARMA-type linear model, the basic model gives a one-step forecast, and to obtain further steps, for instance step two, the one-step forecast is considered as an input value and the second step forecast is the new model output, and so on. This process works in the case of linear models; in the case of neural networks however, the activation functions are sigmoïdal, and the forecasts obtained with this loop method are not reliable. In addition, there are numerous differences in the curve shapes and a single model cannot give precise forecasts for both an August weekday and a Christmas day.

The first of these problems will be solved in the last part of this paper, *The neural models* To solve the second problem, we made a classification of the consumption curves using Kohonen self-organizing maps. We also used Data Analysis methods (hierarchical clustering and k-means): we obtained nearly the same results in the three cases. The advantage of Kohonen maps is the topology of the classes obtained. That means that a map of the classes is obtained. And two classes that have similar representative curves are close on the map.

We used several different maps (square, circle, line), and obtained similar results. In every case, we discerned two breakdowns. The first is a weekly breakdown that distinguishes two kinds of days: Saturdays, Sundays, public holiday days and special days on the one hand; and Mondays, Tuesdays, Wednesdays, Thursdays and Fridays on the other. This breakdown appears in Figure 2. The second breakdown is annual. The year is divided into 3 parts: the first, from May to September; the second, from October to January; and the third, from February to April. These three periods are more or less homogeneous. The last one is the least so, due to the temperature variations in spring.

The classification we have retained aims at optimum simplicity. In fact, the classes obtained are used to forecast, that is to say that we have to attribute a class to a future daily curve. For instance, today is Wednesday, November 24, and we would like to attribute a class to Thursday, November 25 without knowing the shape of its daily curve. To do this, we have retained a typology of 16 classes as shown in the next figure. In Figure 4, each concentric circle represents a type of day: the external circle - Monday; the second - Tuesday to Friday; the third - Saturday, Monday and Friday on public-holiday weekends; and the fourth - Sunday and public holidays. Each quarter represents a season.

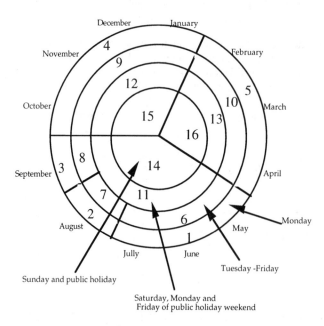

Figure 4 : Classification of daily power consumption curves

In our final neural network forecasting tool, this typology is used as follows. We have defined four large classes which correspond to the weekly breakdown. Consequently, we have built four different neural models. The associated neural networks are different in terms of synaptic weight values, through the architectures are nearly the same. A yearly breakdown is also used. For each large class, we have built several season class input neurons (as many as necessary). For example, every input layer of the Monday neural network is composed of several neurons; among these is one binary input neuron for the season May-June-July, another for August, another for September, another for October-November-December-January and a last one for February-March-April. In fact, there are five season class input neurons for each neural network in the Monday neural model.

III The neural models

As we have already said, the forecasting tool is composed of four different neural models: a Monday model, a Tuesday-Friday model, a Saturday model (also used for Monday and Friday public-holiday weekends) and a Sunday model (also used for public holidays). These four models are built following the same philosophy. We will explain in detail here the Tuesday-Friday model. It is composed of forty-eight neural networks which are multi-layer perceptrons; each neural network is used to forecast one specific half-hour. There is one neural network for 12:30 a.m., one for 1:00a.m.,..., one for 11:30 p.m. and one for 12:00 a.m.. At each time step, we forecast the difference between the consumption value of day d at time t and the consumption value of day d-1 at the same time t. The input is composed of 17 past consumption values, 1 future and 17 past temperature values, 1 future and 17 past nebulosity values, 5 season class values, 4 weekday binary values and 3 special-tariff day binary values. This represents 65 input neurons. There is only one hidden layer composed of 4 neurons. The activation function for the hidden neurons is sigmoïdal; that for the output neuron is linear. This architecture is illustrated in Figure 5. The optimization of the average quadratic error is performed with a second-order method (BFGS) because of its reliability and rapidity.

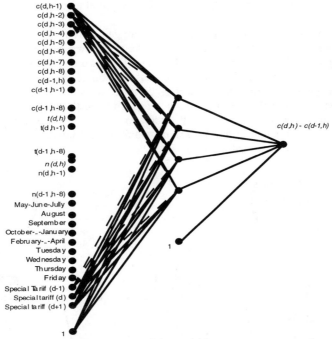

Figure 5 : Architecture of the multi-layer perceptron used
for the Tuesday-Friday forecasting at hour h

To reduce the number of parameters of each neural network and to increase its robustness, we have used a weight elimination method (Statistical Stepwise Method) which we have already explained in detail in previous papers [Cott.,93] [Man.,93]. This has allowed us to reduce the number of parameters from 269 to a value between 114 and 207 depending on the case. In most cases, the quadratic average error has also decreased. To evaluate the performance of theforecasting neural networks, we have calculated the averaged relative error for every time step. The results are shown in the following curve (Figure 6).

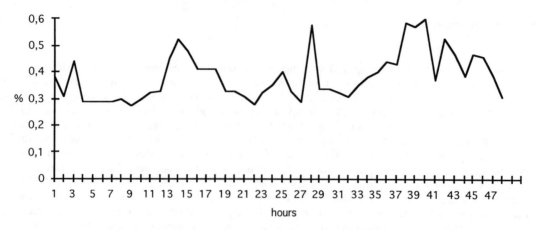

Figure 6 : Averaged relative errors of the 48 Tuesday-Friday neural networks
for the years 1986 to 1992, after weight elimination

Our ultimate goal is not only to forecast one step ahead, but more generally from one step to forty-eight steps and even more. For these forecasts, we use several neural networks as follows. Suppose it is Friday 11:00 a.m., we would like the forecasts from 11:30 a.m. to Saturday 11:00 a.m. First, we will use the Tuesday-Friday 11:30 a.m. forecasting neural network to obtain an estimation of the consumption at 11:30 a.m. based on the previous real values. To obtain an estimation of the consumption at 12:00 p.m., we will use the Tuesday-Friday 12:00 p.m. with, as input, both the estimation of the consumption at 11:30 a.m. and the previous real values, and so on. To forecast Saturday 12:30 a.m., we will use the Saturday 12:30 a.m. forecasting neural network with, as input, both the real values for the consumption before Friday 11:00 a.m. and the estimations of consumption from Friday 11:30 a.m. to 12:00 a.m.. This process is illustrated in Figure 7.

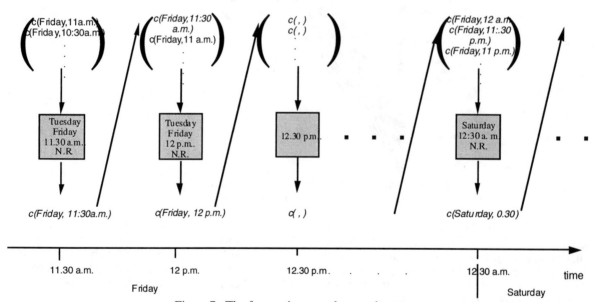

Figure 7 : The forecasting neural network sequence

For one-step forecasting, the neural networks have averaged relative errors between 0.29% and 0.60%. Each week class has nearly the same error. The hours for which there are only small variations in the consumption values are easier to forecast. To illustrate this fact, for the Tuesday-Friday model, at 5:00 a.m. there are small variations and the 5:00 a.m forecasting network has an averaged relative error of 0.30%; on the contrary, at 7:00p.m. there are large variations and the averaged relative error of the 2-hour forecasting network is 0.57%.

I-364

Forecasting further steps is obviously less satisfactory, but performance does not decrease too quickly. For forecasts from one step to forty-eight steps, the averaged relative errors of our first simulations are between 0.03% and 2.00% with any initial forecast hour and day. These first results are in the same range than those of the linear model generally used, whose averaged performance is 2.4%. But further simulations must give better results.

Conclusion

The two most significant properties of this neural network forecasting tool are, first; its good results for both normal days and special days; and second; its adaptability. In fact, it can be used to forecast from any time on any day to any horizon. This is precisely the kind of tool that is useful for a Company like ours.

This forecasting tool is being tested during 1994. We now believe that this tool, or a more advanced one, will be used in an operational way in future years. We think that it should be used not alone but also with the linear model, which is now familiar to dispatchers, and perhaps with other models developed with the aid of new methods such as non-parametric forecasting, wavelets or fuzzy logic.

Bibliography

[Cott.,93]   Cottrell M., Girard B., Girard Y., Mangeas M., *Time series and neural networks: a statistical method for weight elimination*, ESANN-1993 proceedings, Editions Quorum (ISBN 2-9600049-0-6)

[Ginz.,92]]   Ginzberg I., Horn D., *Learning the rule of a time series,* Int. J. of Neural Systems, Vol 3, N2, pp 167-177, 1992

[Groo.,90]   Groot C., Wurst D., *Analysis of Univariate Time Series with connectionnist nets : A case Study of Two Classical Examples*, proceedings of the Munotec Workshop Dublin, Dec. 1990 and Neurocomputing (in press)

[Horn.,91]]   Hornik K., *Approximation capabilities of multilayer feedforward Networks*, Neural Networks, 4, 1991

[Lape.,87]   Lapedes A.S., Farber R., *Nonlinear signal processing using Neural Networks : Prediction and system modeling*, Los Alamos National Laboratory Technical Report, 1987

[Man.,93]   Mangeas M., Cottrell M., Girard B., Girard Y., Muller C., *Advantages of the multilayer perceptron for modeling and forecasting time series : application to the daily electrical consumption in France*, Neuronîmes'93 proceedings, Nîmes, October 25-29, 1993

[Mull.,92]   Muller C., Hatabian G., Caire P., *Progress in forecasting by neural networks*, IJCNN'92 proceedings, Baltimore, June 1992

[Varf.,90]   Varfis A., Versino C., *Univariate Economic Time Series Forecasting by Connectionnist Methods*, INNC-Paris, 1990

[Weig.,90]   Weigend A.S., Huberman B.A., Rumelhart D.E., *Predicting the future   a Connectionnist Approach*, Int. J. Neural Systems, Vol 1, n°3, 1990

Hierarchical Competitive Neural Nets Speed Complex Fluid Flow Calculations

Theresa W. Long, NeuroDyne Inc., 108 Brooks St., Williamsburg, VA 23185
Emil L. Hanzevack, University of South Carolina, Columbia, SC 29208

Abstract

Much research is being done in the area of neural networks, and industry is actively seeking successful application to real world problems. We describe here a successful application. We have used neural networks to model complex coolant flow patterns, such as those encountered in design of hypersonic aircraft. Previous calculation methods, while reasonably accurate, are iterative and extremely time consuming. Our new approach uses a hierarchical neural network architecture to model coolant flow distribution in multiple heat exchanger panels. This method is direct, fast, and accurate.

Coolant System for Hypersonic Aircraft

Development of hypersonic aircraft requires a high degree of system integration. A hypersonic engine may rely on hydrogen for fuel. Since it is stored at cryogenic temperatures, this fuel can also be used as a coolant for aerodynamically heated surfaces [Petley, et al.]. This dual service can potentially lead to very efficient design. However, design tools are needed that can provide rapid, accurate calculations of complex fluid flow patterns. Existing methods are much too slow to allow multiple simulations, spanning a wide range of conditions, needed for efficient design [White, et al.].

Envisioned hydrogen flow patterns and routing schemes incorporate multiple, tiered levels of distribution. We chose the base case of one 6 leg heat exchanger panel, each leg having 3 straight line components, with the necessary associated bends, splits, and merges (Figure 1). Flow is regulated through valved adjustment of inlet and outlet pressures for multiple sets of panels connected in parallel and/or series. Although proper flow control is critical, extensive use of valves is undesirable due to weight, volume, and access considerations. Much of the distribution must therefore be accomplished by constant configuration devices (orifices, restrictors, etc.) that have to operate over a wide range of conditions. Distribution within the panels is further complicated by the nature of the supercritical, gas-like fluid being used as coolant.

Iterative Solution Time Consuming

The basic engineering problem being addressed is as follows: in a gas/gas heat exchanger, given desired inlet pressure ($p1$) and temperature ($T1$), outlet pressure ($p2$), and heat load (Q, broken into 18 different q values, one for each straight segment), what mass flow rate of coolant ($m1$) is required? At first glance, this appears to be a straightforward heat transfer calculation, except that there are a couple complications in this particular application.

The wide range of operating conditions, high pressure, high heat load, and gaseous nature of the coolant result in variable properties (density, viscosity, and specific heat) throughout each leg as well as across the panel. Thus, the heat exchanger must be broken down into small individual components (straight line, bends, splits, and merges) for accurate calculations. Properties are then assumed to be approximately constant in each small component. Furthermore, it is desired to study shock heating loads on small elements of the heat exchanger, as well as relatively uniform heat loads. Therefore, we also need to calculate the split flow fraction at each split component in the heat exchanger (e.g., 5 different split fractions in a typical 6 leg panel).

The previous approach was to write a fluid flow equation, equation of state, loss factor equation, pressure drop equation, and heat transfer equation for each component, and then solve this system of simultaneous equations (Figure 2). Thus there are five equations for each component, so for a typical 6 leg panel, with 3 straight segments per leg along with associated bends, splits, and merges, this yields a system of 160 equations in 160 unknowns. If we were given $p1$, $T1$, and $m1$ (as well as Q, of course), this would still be a straightforward forward dynamics calculation for $p2$. The equations could be solved sequentially, starting with the first component, and marching downstream through the entire heat exchanger, with the outlet conditions calculated from each component serving as the inlet conditions used for the next component.

However, in this application, we are given p1, T1, and **p2** (and Q), and need to determine **m1**. Therefore we have an implicit set of equations, and desire the solution of the inverse dynamics model. Thus, the previous solution method requires an initial guess, not only of m1, but also of the internal flow distribution (i.e., each of the 5 split fractions). Then an iterative calculation must be performed, until the calculated p2 equals the desired p2. Convergence depends on the quality of the initial distribution guesses.

While this can be done, it is extremely time consuming, especially when multiple panels in series and/or parallel are considered. This previous solution method took several hours of computer time, even for relatively simple panel configurations. This would force design to be accomplished after investigation of only a few flight conditions. It is preferable to base design on the wide range of conditions encountered in a complete flight profile. This is the incentive for investigating neural nets for these calculations.

Neural Net Solution Rapid

In this research we first developed and implemented a flow simulation model, using transport equations, for individual coolant system components. The computer code named COOL, written in C language, can do the flow and heat transfer calculations for an individual panel, or for multiple panels in series. For our base case there are 21 inputs (p1, T1, m1, plus heat load of 18 different q values) and 7 outputs (p2, T2, and 5 flow split fractions, s1 to s5). Nevertheless, the calculation in this forward, explicit direction is fast.

We then ran COOL many times in the forward direction (choosing p1, T1, and m1, and calculating p2), using randomly selected values of all input parameters, each spanning their expected operating range. This gave us a training set of data for use in our neural networks. However, for the neural network training and testing, we rearranged the data so that p2 was an input value and m1 was an output, still leaving 21 inputs and 7 outputs, but now arranged to allow for direct calculation of the desired variables, i.e., the inverse dynamics model (Figure 3).

A neural network code named TCOMP was written for this purpose. Using TCOMP, training of an entire 6 leg panel using a 6000 case data set can now be accomplished in approximately 2 hours (on a Sparc2 workstation). This is less than the time that it would take to calculate a single case using the iterative method. Once the net is trained, subsequent calculation on any given set of input values can be accomplished in a fraction of a second. Therefore, we have achieved our goal of an explicit, direct, and fast calculation of the desired variables.

Competitive Net for Coolant Panel

Many neural network architectures have been suggested for various applications. Most of these may be broadly described as global or local learning methods. When a function is highly nonlinear, or when its dynamic characteristics vary in different operating regimes, it is difficult to fit the input-output data with a single global function (or system model) that faithfully describes the system behavior. The piecewise approach of local function approximation is more suitable for this type of system. A neural network can be used for each local curve. We will call these local fitting neural nets the expert nets. A gating net is then used to classify the input data and send it to the appropriate expert net. This constitutes a competitive net. The competitive net architecture, newly developed in this project, is shown in Figure 4.

We have made two modifications to the competitive net architecture originally suggested by Jacobs and Jordan. First, we added a hidden layer to the gating net. This hidden layer is necessary to provide additional connections to ensure that the classification problem is solvable. The second modification is that we used the inner product of the error vector (weighted by the gating net output) as the objective function for each expert net, instead of the mixture density maximum likelihood suggested previously. This feature allows for easier cascading of gating nets. As the complexity of coolant panel configurations is increased, it is anticipated that this cascaded gating net architecture will be better able to handle the complexity.

Figure 5a shows the training results for TCOMP, plotted as average percent error vs. number of training epochs. For comparison, results are also shown for traditional backpropagation nets with one and two hidden layers (LEARN1 and LEARN2, respectively). TCOMP achieves a training error of only 2.5% after 200 epochs, vs. 9.0% and 8.0% for the backprop nets. Furthermore, testing error is 2.3%, showing TCOMP is also able to generalize.

However, the competitive net requires more computer time per epoch. To insure a fair comparison, Figure 5b shows the same training results plotted as average percent error vs. cpu training time. Although many researchers report comparisons based on epochs, we believe that the comparison based on actual training time is more apropos for most practical cases of interest. But for our case, even this more harsh comparison demonstrates that TCOMP learns much more quickly in the first few minutes of training time (note the steep learning curve during the first ten minutes), and that it also attains a significantly lower error at the completion of training (2.8% after two hours, vs. 8.8% or 6.1%).

Hierarchical Net for Multiple Panels

The final technical obstacle to overcome was to find a way to link multiple panels together. The problem can be illustrated by considering the case of two 6 leg panels in series, panels A and B. As discussed above, we have successfully demonstrated a neural net that can take inputs p1, T1, p2, and Q, and accurately determine the desired mass flow rate m1. However, in the two panel case, the given inputs are now p1, T1, and p3 (the outlet pressure from the second panel B, not the first). In this case p2, needed as input for panel A, is not available.

One possible approach to this problem would be to guess an intermediate value of p2 (approximately 2/3 of the way between p1 and p3 would be the best guess for most cases). Then it would be necessary to iterate on this p2 value until the mass flow rate calculated for panel A (mA) and the flow rate for panel B (mB) converged. This approach was attempted, but mainly because of the combination of uniform and shock heat loads in the data set, convergence was neither fast nor certain.

A second approach would be to simply build a bigger neural net, encompassing both panels. However, we rejected this approach because of the increasing dimension problem. For even a two panel case, this would result in a single net with 39 inputs (p1, T1, p3, and 36 q values) and 14 outputs (m1, p2, T2, T3, and 10 flow split fractions). This would be unwieldy for even the two panel case, and clearly impractical for anything larger. A more versatile approach was sought.

The approach chosen, and proven successful, was to use a second level of neural net to predict p2, using a reduced input data set (Figure 6). It was found that p2 could be determined very accurately (only 0.2 - 0.3% error) using only p1, T1, p3, QA, and QB (where QA and QB are the average heat loads over panels A and B respectively, rather than all 36 component q values). Thus this second level "p net" has only 5 inputs and 1 output. Therefore, since this significantly reduced data set was found sufficient for the "p net," extension to multiple panels, without the dimension of the input variable set becoming too large, is entirely feasible.

Thus we have created a hierarchical neural net structure, written in C code named COOLER. The "p net" first estimates the pressure between panels. Then this p2 value is used as an input variable by the "panel net" to calculate mA and T2 for panel A. Next the p2 and calculated T2 values, along with the given p3, are used again by the same "panel net" to calculate mB and T3 for panel B.

The beauty of this approach is that no additional neural net training is needed. Once the "p net" and "panel net" weights are computed and saved, additional calculation of any number of cases is rapid. One thousand test cases were run in only 33 seconds, with average error of less than 7%. Sensitivity analysis has shown that this level of accuracy is reasonable and consistent with the measurement accuracy achievable for a real system. For example, a typical 3% accuracy for pressure measurements in such a system would lead to approximately an 8 - 10% accuracy requirement for the mass flow rate prediction. In addition, we believe that additional accuracy can be obtained in future research in this hierarchical net direction.

We have developed and successfully implemented a hierarchical neural network scheme to link two heat exchanger panels together in series. Although beyond the scope of this project, we now are confident that linking additional panels in series and/or parallel is entirely possible and feasible. We are very pleased with this result, since the possibility of using hierarchical neural networks is often mentioned, but to date there have been few actual successful implementations reported in engineering applications (although different versions of hierarchical net are used in pattern recognition applications).

Conclusions

Rapid, direct solutions of complex fluid flow problems has significant value in design simulations. Neural nets offer a powerful tool for the expedient computation of complex non-linear flow dynamics. This capability would allow a designer to evaluate performance over full mission or multi-mission operating conditions, and to optimize system designs more effectively. Therefore, designs would be accomplished both faster and better. However, the results of this research go beyond this single application. We can now develop and provide a hierarchical method and software for general purpose fluid flow calculations used in a wide variety of chemical processing applications.

There are three innovative aspects to this research. First, we have used training data generated from a set of fluid flow and heat transfer equations in forward dynamics form, then trained a neural net to solve the associated inverse dynamics problem. Second, we developed a new and improved version of a competitive net architecture. Finally, we have developed and successfully implemented a hierarchical neural network scheme to link multiple heat exchanger panels together.

Acknowledgement

We gratefully acknowledge the National Science Foundation for support of this research.

Notation

(in any consistent set of units)
m   mass flow rate [mass/time]
p   pressure [(force/(length*length) or (mass)/(time*time*length)]
Q   heat load, overall [(energy/mass) or (length*length)/(time*time)]
q   heat load, individual segment [(energy/mass) or (length*length)/(time*time)]
s   split fraction for each branch between legs (s1 to s5, i.e., 5 splits for 6 legs) [dimensionless]
T   temperature [degrees]
subscripts:
A   first panel
B   second panel
1   inlet to first panel
2   outlet from first panel
3   outlet from second panel

Literature

[1]   Petley, D., S. Jones, and W. Dziedzic, "Analysis of Cooling Systems for Hypersonic Aircraft," AIAA Third International Aerospace Planes Conference, Orlando, FL, December 1991.
[2]   White, D.A., A. Bowers, K. Iliff, G. Noffz, M. Gonda, and J. Menousek, "Flight, Propulsion, and Thermal Control of Advanced Aircraft and Hypersonic Vehicles," in D.A. White and D.A. Sofge, (eds.), Handbook of Intelligent Control, New York, Van Nostrand Reinhold, 1992.
[3]   Jacobs, R.A., M.I. Jordan, S.J. Nowlan, & G.E. Hinton, "Adaptive Mixtures of Local Experts", Neural Computation, 3, 79-87, 1991.

Theresa W. Long is President of NeuroDyne Inc. (804/229-9957 or 617/252-3360, Fax: 804/229-9957 or 617/252-3359). She holds a Ph.D. in Mechanical Engineering from the University of South Carolina (1988). Previously she was a Research Engineer for Exxon Research & Engineering Co., Westinghouse Savannah River Co., and Lawrence Livermore National Laboratory. She was recently a Visiting Scholar at Massachusetts Institute of Technology. Dr. Long conducts research in the areas of neural networks, optimal control, and robotics.
Emil L. Hanzevack is a Research Professor at the University of South Carolina, and an independent consultant (804/229-9957 or 803/777-4181, Fax: 804/229-9957). He holds a Ph.D. in Chemical Engineering from Northwestern University (1974). Previously he was a Group Head for Exxon Research & Engineering Co. Dr. Hanzevack conducts research in the areas of fluid flow, with specific emphasis on application of neural network and computer vision technology.

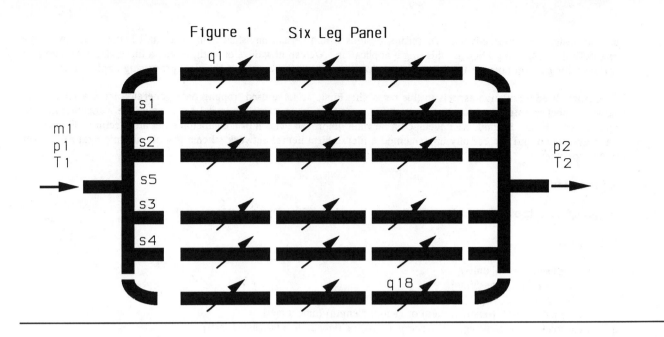

Figure 1   Six Leg Panel

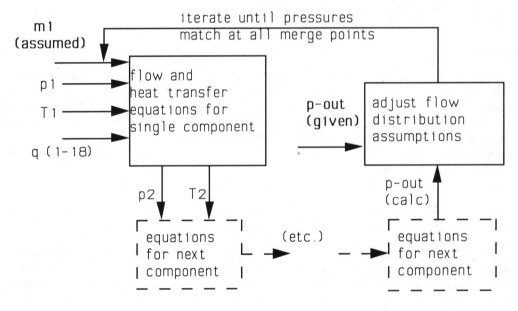

Figure 2   Iterative Marching Solution

Figure 3   Direct Flow Calculation

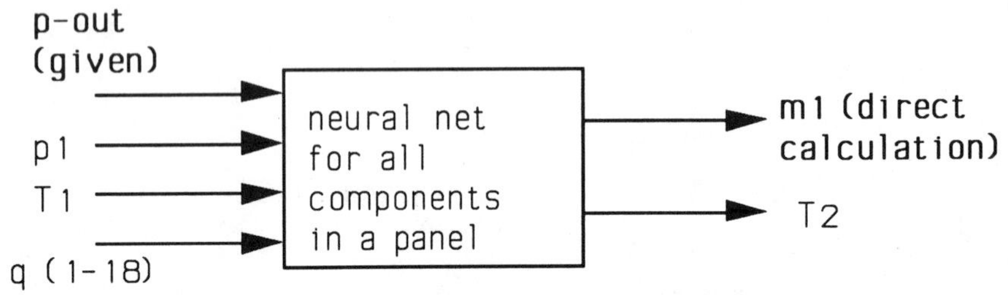

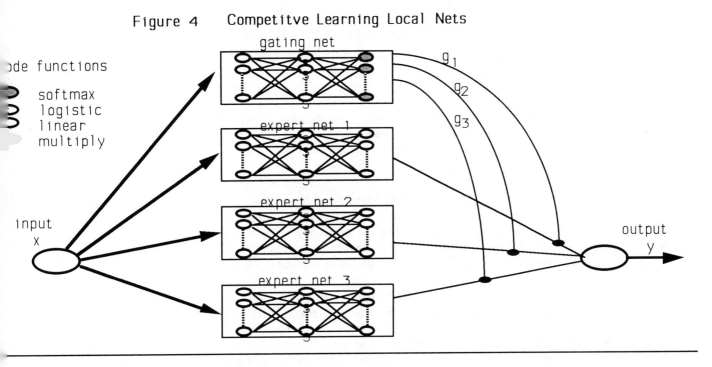

Figure 4   Competitve Learning Local Nets

ode functions

softmax
logistic
linear
multiply

gating net

expert net 1

expert net 2

expert net 3

input
x

g_1

g_2

g_3

output
y

---

tcomp vs. backprop (1 or 2 layers)

Figure 5a

Figure 5b

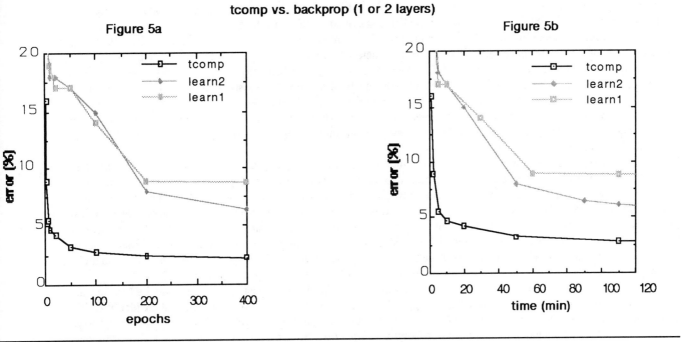

Figure 6   Hierarchical Competitive Nets

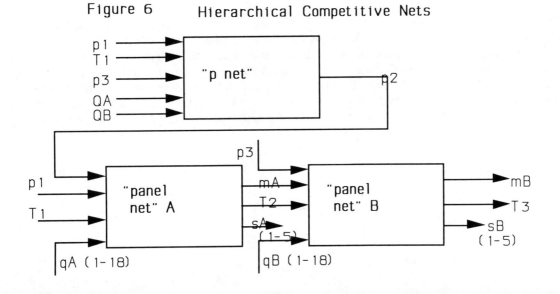

Neural Networks for Steam Boiler MIMO Modeling and Advisory Control

Dr. Kenneth F. Reinschmidt (President)   Dr. Bo Ling

Stone & Webster Advanced Systems Development Services, Inc.
245 Summer Street
Boston, Massachusetts 02210

ABSTRACT

In this paper, neural networks are developed for the modeling and control of a steam boiler. Neural network simulation models are trained using data from the results of a series of step response tests on an actual once-through utility boiler. A Neural network controller is trained to minimize an objective function. A modified back-propagation algorithm is given which includes the effect of an existing model.

I. INTRODUCTION

Artificial Neural network technology is rapidly finding opportunities for applications to the control of power plant systems and equipment. Neural networks can learn the performance characteristics of plants from plant operational data or from plant models, and can be used to simulate plant operations and to control plant parameters. Neural networks can predict system responses for dynamic control purposes. Unlike many types of computer simulation models, even nonlinear neural networks can be readily inverted, to compute the necessary changes in control variables to produce the desired changes in controlled variables.

Many computer methods have been used for the simulation and control of power plants. Statistical time series methods, involving the empirical fitting of parameters to autoregressive-moving average models have been extensively used for plant simulation and for dynamic matrix control, but require considerable competence in statistical methods. Mathematical simulation models can be developed for existing plants, but development of these models requires considerable engineering skill, experience, and detailed knowledge of the physical processes operating in the plant. Neural network technology offers an alternate method for the generation of empirical response surfaces for power plant processes. Using plant monitoring data, neural networks can learn the performance characteristics of existing plants.

Neural networks are not limited to simulation, in the sense of predicting a response for a specified action, but can also be used to generate the action necessary to produce a given response, i.e., to control the plant. This is feasible because even nonlinear neural networks can be readily inverted. Some other types of simulation models cannot be inverted, or must be linearized in order to be numerically inverted. This feature makes neural network models complementary, rather than competitive, to other type of plant models. Also, the development of neural networks does not require detailed knowledge of the physical processes internal to the system being modeled, knowledge of advanced statistical methods, or experience in the development of mathematical models, making neural networks attractive for application to the control of operational power plants.

Artificial neural networks, both feedforward and feedback, have been successfully applied in various areas for control and modeling: truck backer-upper [6], nonlinear system stabilization [4], system identification and control [5], chemical process modeling [1], etc. Various techniques for steam boiler modeling and control have been reported which include: Dynamic Matrix Control [8], Kalman filtering [10], linear regulator [11]. However, due to the varying operating environment, a robust method is required which must be capable of modeling the changing system and generating an optimal control.

In this paper, two different feedforward neural networks are developed to (1) model the steam boiler which has three inputs: throttle valve position (V), fuel firing rate (F) and feedwater flow rate (W); three outputs: power load (L), steam temperature (T) and steam pressure (P); (2) design a controller which, based on the steam boiler simulation model, produces a series of controls. These controls increase the power load to the setpoint as smoothly and fast as possible while maintaining steam temperature and steam pressure varying within certain limit. The neural network boiler simulation model consists of nine independent small models. The neural network controller is trained to minimize an energy function which is of a weighted quadratic form. The basic backpropagation algorithm [9] has been modified to include the effect of the steam boiler neural network model. The same technique can be also applied to various other control cases, e.g., decrease power load, regulate the steam temperature, etc.

This paper is organized as follows: in Section II, the neural network steam boiler model, together with nine small models, are presented; in Section III, the structure of neural network controller is shown; some simulation results are shown in Section IV; the learning algorithm used to train the controller is given in Appendix A.

II. NEURAL NETWORKS FOR STEAM BOILER MODELING

The neural network simulation model is based on the results of a series of step response tests on an actual utility once-through boiler [12]. The objective of the neural network simulation model is to reproduce these experimental step responses, and to predict the responses of the boiler to other inputs. The controlled variables and control variables in the model are shown in Figure 2.1

In the actual plant tests [12], the control variables were given independent step changes to generate nine bivariate records:

- power load L vs. throttle valve position V;
- power load L vs. fuel flow rate F;
- steam pressure P vs. feedwater flow rate W;
- steam temperature T vs. throttle valve position V;
- power load L vs. feedwater flow rate W;
- steam pressure P vs. throttle valve position V;
- steam pressure P vs. fuel flow rate F;
- steam temperature T vs. feedwater flow rate W;
- steam temperature T vs. fuel flow rate F.

The computer data were digitized from the plots in Woo and Anderson [12]. The data from these nine experimental tests were used to train nine neural networks, namely, $f_{LV}(.), f_{LW}(.), f_{LF}(.), f_{PV}(.), f_{PW}(.), f_{PF}(.), f_{TV}(.), f_{TW}(.), f_{TF}(.)$, where $f_{LV}(.)$ represents the model between L and V, etc. As an example, Figure 2.2 shows the configuration of the neural network for $f_{PV}(.)$.

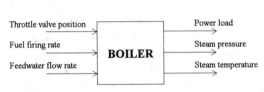

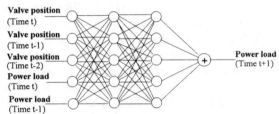

Figure 2.1. The boiler with three control variables and three controlled variables.

Figure 2.2. The neural network modelling power output vs. valve position.

As indicated in [12], the model of power load L vs. F, W, V can be formed in terms of superposition:

$$L_{t+1} = f_{LF}(L_t,...,L_{t-d},F_t,...,F_{t-d}) + f_{LW}(L_t,...,L_{t-d},W_t,...,W_{t-d}) + f_{LV}(L_t,...,L_{t-d},V_t,...,V_{t-d}) \quad (2.1)$$

Similarly,

$$P_{t+1} = f_{PF}(P_t,...,P_{t-d},F_t,...,F_{t-d}) + f_{PW}(P_t,...,P_{t-d},W_t,...,W_{t-d}) + f_{PV}(P_t,...,P_{t-d},V_t,...,V_{t-d}) \quad (2.2)$$

$$T_{t+1} = f_{TF}(T_t,...,T_{t-d},F_t,...,F_{t-d}) + f_{TW}(T_t,...,T_{t-d},W_t,...,W_{t-d}) + f_{TV}(T_t,...,T_{t-d},V_t,...,V_{t-d}) \quad (2.3)$$

where d represents the number of delays. For simplicity of notation, all delays in the above three models are chosen the same. These three models are then put together as one single neural network model to simulate the boiler which has three inputs and three outputs (Fig. 2.1). This single neural network gives the predicted value of all three controlled variables as a function of past values of the control and controlled variables. That is, the neural network simulates the function:

$$x_{t+1} = f(x_t, x_{t-1},...,x_{t-d}) \quad (2.4a)$$

where $x = [P, T, L]^T$, $f: R^m \to R^3$, t is the current time step index, $1 \le t \le$ samples, d the number of lagged time steps which value is determined by error-and-trial, m the dimension of independent variable space. Equivalently,

$$\begin{bmatrix} P_{t+1} \\ T_{t+1} \\ L_{t+1} \end{bmatrix} = \begin{bmatrix} f_{LF}(L_t,...,L_{t-d},F_t,...,F_{t-d}) + f_{LW}(L_t,...,L_{t-d},W_t,...,W_{t-d}) + f_{LV}(L_t,...,L_{t-d},V_t,...,V_{t-d}) \\ f_{PF}(P_t,...,P_{t-d},F_t,...,F_{t-d}) + f_{PW}(P_t,...,P_{t-d},W_t,...,W_{t-d}) + f_{PV}(P_t,...,P_{t-d},V_t,...,V_{t-d}) \\ f_{TF}(T_t,...,T_{t-d},F_t,...,F_{t-d}) + f_{TW}(T_t,...,T_{t-d},W_t,...,W_{t-d}) + f_{TV}(T_t,...,T_{t-d},V_t,...,V_{t-d}) \end{bmatrix} \quad (2.4b)$$

Since all delays are assumed the same, the index of dimension m is $2(d+1)$.

All neural networks for nine models stated above have the same structure: one input layer, two hidden layers and one output layer (Fig.2.2). The activation functions of neurons in both hidden layers are the sigmoidal functions ranging from 0 to 1. The activation function of the neuron in the output layer simply sums up all output signals out of the previous layer. The number of inputs and the number of neurons in both hidden layers are determined by balancing the learning speed and learning error. The learning is performed by the basic back propagation algorithm [9]. Other modified algorithms have been tried, those including back propagation with momentum, adaptive learning rate, etc. [2]. Based on our experience, the basic back propagation algorithm is more robust. The learning speed depends on the system structure. If one chooses a suitable structure, the basic back propagation algorithm leads to an acceptable learning error reasonably fast.

All nine neural network models have fit the original data quite well. Figure 2.4 and 2.5 show the comparison of actual data and neural network results associated with two models. Figure 2.5 shows the combined effect of 4% step increases in all three control variables simultaneously. This figure was obtained by superimposing the actual plant responses from the previous nine figures, as was done in the original paper [12].

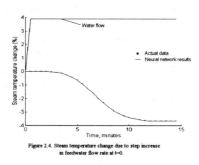
Figure 2.4. Steam temperature change due to step increase in feedwater flow rate at t=0.

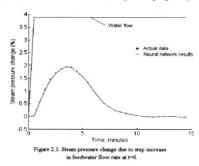
Figure 2.3. Steam pressure change due to step increase in feedwater flow rate at t=0.

III. NEURAL NETWORK CONTROLLER

In the boiler, water and fuel are manipulated at rates needed to balance the requirements of the three controlled variables, i.e., power load, steam pressure, and steam temperature. The demand for power is determined exogenously to the system, and variations in the power load around the specified load should be minimized. To reduce thermal stresses and to maximize the service life of the boiler and turbine, changes in steam pressure and steam temperature should be kept within limits as the load changes. The objective of the boiler control system is to manipulate the control variables to meet the exogenously imposed demands for power while keeping the steam pressure and temperature relatively constant. Transients in pressure, temperature, and power load are to be minimized.

As we stated in Section II, the neural network boiler model consists of nine small neural network models. However, the neural network controller has only one model which structure is shown in Figure 3.1. The activation functions of the neurons in the output layer are nonlinear sigmoidal functions as well.

The control system consists of both the neural network simulation model of Eq. (2.4) and the neural network controller, as diagrammed in Figure 3.2. The approach used here is similar to that used by Nguyen and Widrow[6]. The neural network steam boiler model is exactly the neural network simulation model described in the previous section. The neural network weights for this model were kept constant while neural network controller

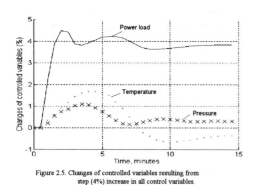
Figure 2.5. Changes of controlled variables resulting from step (4%) increase in all control variables.

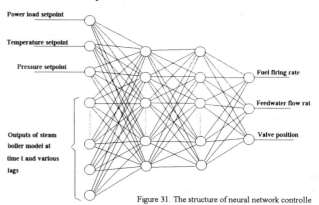
Figure 31. The structure of neural network controlle

is being trained. This was done in a recursive manner. At each time step t, there are two models: the neural network boiler model and the neural network controller. As shown in Figure 3.2, the controller computes the values for the control variables V_t, W_t, and F_t, and the boiler model computes the values of P_{t+1}, T_{t+1}, and L_{t+1}, using V_t, W_t, and F_t, and P_t, T_t, and L_t, as well as the lagged variables.

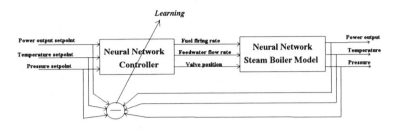

Figure 3.2. Neural network controller model with learning

The performance of the controller is based on the values of the controlled variables, P_{t+1}, T_{t+1}, and L_{t+1}, whereas the controller must be trained to compute values for the control variables V_t, W_t, and F_t. This is accomplished by the use of an energy function:

$$E = \tfrac{1}{2} \sum_{t=1}^{Samples} r_L (L_t^d - L_t)^2 + r_P (P_t^d - P_t)^2 + r_T (T_t^d - T_t)^2 \qquad (3.1)$$

where L_t^d, P_t^d and T_t^d represent the desired power load, steam pressure and steam temperature at time t, and r_L, r_P and r_T are the penalty coefficients for the power load, steam pressure and steam temperature.

In order to train the neural network controller, the basic back-propagation algorithm [9] has been modified to include the effect of the steam boiler model. The modified learning algorithm is given in Appendix A. The block diagram of this learning process is shown in Figure 3.3, where vectors X and Y represent control and controlled variables, D is the operator of one-step delay.

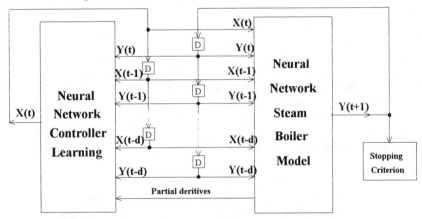

Figure 3.3. Block diagram of recursive learning of neural network controller.

IV. SIMULATION RESULTS

Figure 4.1 shows the control variables V_t, W_t, and F_t computed by the neural network controller trained to produce an increase in power load of +2% at 30 seconds and +4% at one minute. The steam temperature variation is to be limited between -0.8% and +0.8%. This can be done by making the penalty coefficient of the steam temperature term in Eq. (3.1) larger than the other two coefficients. In this way, the steam temperature variation is more highly penalized, relative to the other penalty terms. The system transient responses based on the control strategy in Fig. 4.1 are shown in Fig. 4.2. It is observed that the temperature change is indeed controlled within the limit, -0.8% to +0.8%, although the power load has a somewhat larger swing.

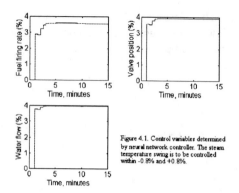

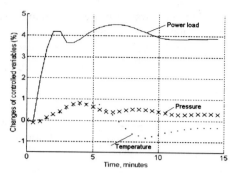

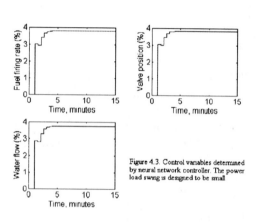

Figure 4.1. Control variables determined by neural network controller. The steam temperature swing is to be controlled within -0.8% and +0.8%.

Figure 4.2. Controlled variables resulting from neural network network controller in Fig. 4.1.

If we want to focus on minimizing the swing in the power load, we can make the corresponding penalty coefficient in the penalty function larger. Fig. 4.3 shows the control strategy which puts less constraint on both steam temperature and steam pressure. Fig. 4.4 shows the transient responses of system with the control variables in Figure 4.3. In this figure, the transient response of power load is faster and more smooth. But the steam temperature change has exceeded the normal limit, -1% to +1%. And the steam pressure change is larger as well.

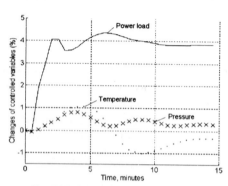

Figure 4.3. Control variables determined by neural network controller. The power load swing is designed to be small

Figure 4.4. Controlled variables resulting form neural network controller in Fig. 4.3.

From all figures above, it is observed that there is a trade-off between power load change and steam temperature change. Smaller changes in power load will result in larger swings in steam temperature. If we limit the steam temperature within a small range, the power load reaches its steady state more slowly. However, the steam pressure changes are relatively small. By properly setting the penalty coefficients in the penalty function, we can balance the requirements on power load and steam temperature. Of course, it is possible to specify constraints that cannot be satisfied with the existing boiler system.

V. CONCLUSION

The above process illustrates some of the potential applications of neural networks in power plant simulation and optimal control. Neural networks can be trained to simulate plant performance directly from plant data, with little operator intervention. With continuous learning, the neural networks can adapt to secular changes in the plant power parameters, such as those caused by slagging, fouling, soot blowing, etc. Clearly neural networks have a wide field for application in improving the performance and extending the life of power plants.

REFERENCES

[1] N.V. Bhat, P.A. Minderman, T. McAvoy, N.S. Wang, "Modeling chemical process systems via neural computation", IEEE Control System Magazine, pp. 24-29, April, 1990.

[2] J. Hertz, A. Krogh, R.G. Palmer, *Introduction to the Theory of Neural Computation*, Addison-Wesley Publishing Company, 1991.

[3] M. Khalil, S. Omatu, "A neural network controller for a temperature control system", IEEE Control System Magazine, pp. 58-64, June 1992.

[4] B. Ling, F.M.A. Salam, "State feedback stabilization of nonlinear systems via the neural network approach", Proc. of American Control Conference, San Francisco, CA, June 1993, pp. 89-92.

[5] K.S. Narendra, K. Parthasarathy, "Identification and control of dynamical systems using neural networks", IEEE Trans. Neural Networks, Vol. 1, pp. 4-27, Mar. 1990.

[6] D. Nguyen, B. Widrow, "The truck backer-upper: an example of self-learning in neural networks", SPIE Vol. 1293 Applications of Artificial Intelligence VIII, pp. 596-602, 1992.

[7] K.F. Reinschmidt, "Neural networks: next step for plant simulation and control", Power Engineering, Nov. 1991.

[8] J.A. Rovnak, R. Corlis, "Dynamic Matrix Based Control of fossil power plants", IEEE Trans. Energy Conversion, Vol. 6, No. 2, June 1991.

[9] D.E. Rumelhart, J.L. McClelland and the PDP Research Group, *Parallel Distributed Processing: Explorations in the Microstructure of Cognition*, MIT Press, 1986.

[10] A. Tysso, J. C. Brembo, K. Lind, "The design of a multivariable control system for a ship boiler", Automatica, Vol. 12, pp. 211-224, 1976.

[11] A. Tysso, "Modelling and parameter estimation of a ship boiler", Automatica, Vol. 17, pp. 157-166, 1981.

[12] R. Woo, G.R. Anderson, "Dynamic response of a supercritical power plant", Instrumentation Technology, July, 1969.

Appendix A: Learning algorithm for training the neural network controller

● **Update weights between output layer and the 2nd hidden layer (next to the output layer):** Let the index f, v and w be associated with the output nodes F, V and W of the controller.

$$\Delta w_{fj}^3 = \eta \delta_f^3 f(h_j^2) \qquad \Delta w_{vj}^3 = \eta \delta_v^3 f(h_j^2) \qquad \Delta w_{wj}^3 = \eta \delta_w^3 f(h_j^2)$$

$$\delta_f^3 = f'(h_f^3)\left(r_L(L_t^d - L_t)\frac{\partial f_{LF}}{\partial F} + r_P(P_t^d - P_t)\frac{\partial f_{PF}}{\partial F} + r_T(T_t^d - T_t)\frac{\partial f_{TF}}{\partial F} \right)$$

$$\delta_v^3 = f'(h_v^3)\left(r_L(L_t^d - L_t)\frac{\partial f_{LV}}{\partial V} + r_P(P_t^d - P_t)\frac{\partial f_{PV}}{\partial V} + r_T(T_t^d - T_t)\frac{\partial f_{TV}}{\partial V} \right)$$

$$\delta_w^3 = f'(h_w^3)\left(r_L(L_t^d - L_t)\frac{\partial f_{LW}}{\partial W} + r_P(P_t^d - P_t)\frac{\partial f_{PW}}{\partial W} + r_T(T_t^d - T_t)\frac{\partial f_{TW}}{\partial W} \right)$$

$$\frac{\partial f_{LF}}{\partial F} = \sum_{j=1}^{M_{LF}} W_{LF_j}^3 f'(H_j^2) \sum_{s=1}^{N_{LF}} W_{LF_{js}}^2 f'(H_s^1) W_{LF_{sf}}^1$$

$$\frac{\partial f_{PF}}{\partial F} = \sum_{j=1}^{M_{PF}} W_{PF_j}^3 f'(H_j^2) \sum_{s=1}^{N_{PF}} W_{PF_{js}}^2 f'(H_s^1) W_{PF_{sf}}^1$$

- -

$$\frac{\partial f_{TW}}{\partial W} = \sum_{j=1}^{M_{TW}} W_{TW_j}^3 f'(H_j^2) \sum_{s=1}^{N_{TW}} W_{TW_{js}}^2 f'(H_s^1) W_{TW_{sw}}^1$$

● **Update weights between the 1st hidden layer and the 2nd hidden layer (next to the input layer):**

$$\Delta w_{jk}^2 = -\eta \frac{\partial E}{\partial w_{jk}^2} = \eta \delta_j^2 f(h_k^1) \qquad \delta_j^2 = f'(h_j^2) \sum_{s=1}^{3} w_{sj}^3 \delta_s^3$$

● **Update weights between input layer and the 1st hidden layer:**

$$\Delta w_{kl}^1 = -\eta \frac{\partial E}{\partial w_{kl}^1} = \eta \delta_k^1 Input_l \qquad \delta_k^1 = f'(h_k^1) \sum_{s=1}^{m} w_{sk}^2 \delta_s^2$$

for $t = 1, ...,$ number of samples, $l = 1, ...,$ number of inputs, $j = 1, ..., m$ (the number of neurons in the 2nd hidden layer next to the output layer), $k = 1, ..., n$ (the number of neurons in the 1st hidden layer close to the input layer). M_{LF} is the number of neurons in the 2nd hidden layer (next to the output layer) of the simulation model, $f_{LF}(.)$, and N_{LF} the number of neurons in the 1st hidden layer (next to the input layer) of the simulation model, $f_{LF}(.)$. The weights, w's, stand for the weights of the controller, and W_{LF}'s the fixed weights of the model, $f_{LF}(.)$. h_i^j the net input of the ith neuron in the jth layer of the neural network controller, H_i^j is the net input of the ith neuron in the jth hidden layer of the related simulation model. The same notation goes to other models.

Flexible Manufacturing Systems Scheduling Using Q-Learning

Luis C. Rabelo[1], Murat Sahinoglu[1], and Xavier Avula[2]

[1]Department of Industrial and Systems Engineering
Ohio University, Athens, Ohio 45701
[2] Mechanical Engineering and Engineering Mechanics Department
University of Missouri-Rolla, Rolla, Missouri 65401

ABSTRACT

The integration of Dynamic Programming and Artificial Neural Networks has very important characteristics which may provide efficient real-time learning mechanisms for manufacturing scheduling. This paper presents a system that achieves real-time learning using the mentioned integration for flexible manufacturing system (FMS) scheduling. The system is capable of operational mappings. In addition, it utilizes reinforcement signals of the environment (a measure of how desirable the achieved state is taking into consideration the performance criteria) due to the lack of an expert scheduler.

1. INTRODUCTION

Flexible manufacturing systems (FMS) are automated systems which combine computer numerical control (CNC) machine tools, material handling and storage systems, and a computational (hardware-software/processing-communications) scheme to provide an integrated environment.

1.1. Flexible Manufacturing System Scheduling

Flexible manufacturing system scheduling is a complex problem in nature that leads to a high level of uncertainty due to the limited number of feasible solutions in an extensive search space. Scheduling can be described as the allocation of resources over time to perform tasks. In this sense, three questions arise: what, when, and where [5]. A process, which solves these three questions, does scheduling:
 - The first question is what task must be done.
 - The second question is when each task will be performed.
 - The third question, where, defines the set of resources that the tasks occupy.

1.2. Real-Time Learning in Scheduling

A scheduling system requires effective decision making capabilities. Reinforcement learning algorithms could be utilized as the decision-making units. Reinforcement learning mimics the human brain's learning system. The past experiences are stored in a way that the actions taken are evaluated for the same or similar possible future experiences. The decision-making ability is improved with a long term optimality. The level of expertise in activities could be increased by experiencing more situations. Werbos [11] discusses the importance of real time learning and points out that "if one builds systems which can truly learn in real time, one can also achieve much greater flexibility in manufacturing, which is crucial to competitiveness in many economic sectors."

Real-time learning has several advantages over off-line learning. It is more robust because errors and omissions in the training set can be corrected during operation. Training data could be created easily and in great quantities when a system is in operation, whereas it isusually scarce in off-line learning. The most important advantage is the necessity of real-time learning in order to learn and track time varying functions, to continue to adapt to a changing environment. Real-time learning is needed as a component of reinforcement learning methods [1,2,7,8,10,12].

1.3. Problem Statement

The main purpose of this research is the development of a scheduler which has automatic learning and adaptive capabilities. Adaptive Critics concepts, which allocate reinforcement learning algorithms, are utilized in real-time to control the dynamic scheduling environment. Q-learning [8], and its extension, Q-learning with a discrete model are used to predict a scheduling policy to meet the required performance criterion for a given queue status and an undefined period of operation.

2. REAL-TIME LEARNING FOR DYNAMIC SCHEDULING

Most of the existing FMS scheduling methodologies arenot adaptive in real-time with respect to changes in system behavior at appropriate points in time. They either havecomplex and computationally expensive heuristics to make them adaptive, or use a single scheme at all times resulting in optimal degradation [3,6]. Furthermore, the problem of a dynamic decision-making process is not even considered.

In this paper, integration and utilization of scheduling techniques with Q-learning is accomplished to achieve desired performance levels. Two schemes were utilized in order to achieve this integration. The first one is based on the generic description of Q-learning and the second one is based on the utilization of Q-learning and a model.

2.1. Q-learning for Dynamic Scheduling

The key idea of Q-learning is to assign values to state-action pairs. Q-learning does not need an explicit model of the dynamic system underlying the decision problem. It directly estimates the optimal Q values for pairs of states and admissible actions. The optimal Q value for state i and action u is a cost of executing action u in state i. Any policy selecting actions that are greedy with respect to the optimal Q values is an optimal policy. Q values define an evaluation function in a way but they contain more information than an evaluation function. Actions can be ranked based on the Q values alone. On the other hand, ranking through an evaluation function requires more information like immediate costs of state action pairs and state transition probabilities. Instead of state transition probabilities Q-learning requires a random function to generate successor states. The Q-value of the successful action is updated with learning parameters, although the other admissible actions' Q values remain the same.

Q-learning learns to accurately model the evaluation function. For a given state x, the system chooses the action a, where the utility util(x,a) is maximal. Q-learning consists of two parts: a utility function and a stochastic action selector (see Figure 1).

The utility function works as both evaluation andpolicy networks. It tries to model the system by assigning values to action-state pairs. The utility function has multiple outputs, one for each action. In the utility function, neural networks are utilized to update the Q value of the selected action. The utilization of neural networks could be in two ways:
- One neural network with multiple outputs.
- Multiple neural networks (one for each action) with a single output.

In the first method, whenever the single network is modified with respect to an action, the whole behavior ofthe system is modified, since the actions share hidden units [4]. In other words, the reinforcement of an action results in modification of the Q values of other actions, although they should remain the same. This makes using multiple networks more desirable.

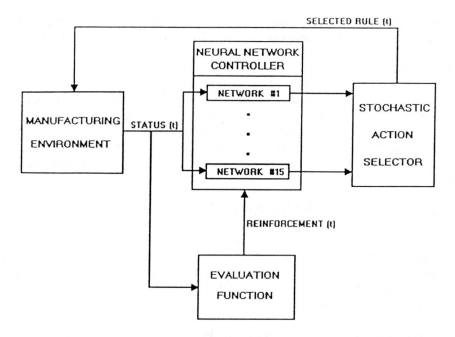

Figure 1. Q-Learning and the FMS Scheduling Problem

The stochastic action selector chooses the actions randomly according to a probability distribution function determined by the action's Q values. So, the actions with larger Q values have more chance to be selected than the ones with smaller Qvalues. Each action has a chance to be selected as much as it's Q value. In this research, the Q-learning algorithm is appliedto the scheduling problem to create pairs of queue status and dispatching rules to achieve a desired level of system performance. The algorithm assigns Q values to queue status for each action rule and then these Q values are updatedbased on the performance of the manufacturing system.

The admissible action set consists of dispatching rules. Backpropagation with dual subroutines [9] was utilized for the utility networks. Multiple neural networks (one for each action) were used with single outputs. The inputs to the networks are the representation of queue status based on the attributes of the tasks in the queue. The arrival times, processing times, setup times and due dates are the attributes of the tasks and determined stochastically. The output of each network is the Q value of the dispatching rule that the network belongs to. The Q values of all actions are processed in the stochastic action selector. The action selected by the stochastic action selector is then performed in the manufacturing environment. By the completion of the action, the performance of the system (e.g., work-in-process inventory) is evaluated. If the system's performance progresses in the desired direction, the network of the selected action is rewarded. Otherwise, it is punished. The punishment and reward mechanism are managed by adjusting the weights in the neural networks. In the punishment case, the weights are adjusted in a way that the network outputs a less Q value for the same state. In the reward case, theweights are adjusted to produce a higher Q value to increasethe chance of being selected. Since actions are selectedvrandomly, the system stores Q values for each network, and these Q values reach optimal in the long term. The algorithm of Q-learning could be described as follows:
  - Receive the current state x;
  - Calculate util(x,i), for each action i;
  - Select the action a;
  - Perform action a;
  - Receive new state y and reinforcement r;
  - Calculate the desired utility of action a based on the new state and reinforcement;

$$u = r + \delta \ \mathbf{Max} \ \{ \ \mathbf{util(y,k)} \ | \ k \ \varepsilon \ \mathbf{actions} \ \}$$ where r is the immediate payoff and δ is the discount factor.

- Adjust the utility network, by backpropagating the error ρU, where $\rho U = \mathbf{u} - \mathbf{util(x,a)}$;

2.2 Q-Learning With a Discrete Model

This is an extension of the Q-learning algorithm. Theproblem in the application of Q-learning to the scheduling problem occurs in the reinforcement stage. The system is not clear when to punish or reward. The reinforcement mechanism works based on the differences of the previous and current values. There could be some cases that, the stochastic action selector chooses an action with the best effect on the system, but, the difference in the system performance'scurrent and previous values might require a punishment.

In Q-Learning with a discrete model, a model is added to the system (see Figure 2).

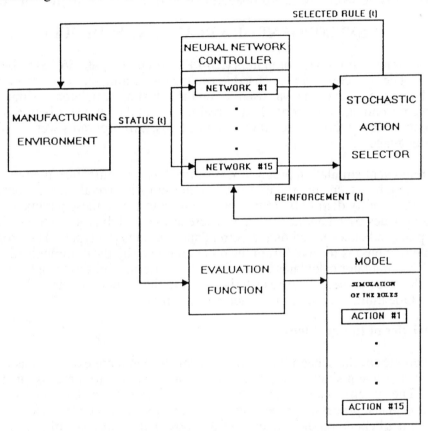

Figure 2. Framework of Q-learning with a Discrete Model

The model's job is to evaluate the effect of each action (not the actual one performed) through a simulator and tell the network whether there is a punishment or a reward. The procedure used here is different from on-line simulation techniques in real-time scheduling. In on-line simulation techniques, simulation is used to predict the system's behavior in the future, whereas in Q-learning with a discrete model, simulation is used for learning purposes (and therefore the behavior of the system during that period of time (past) is already known). The actions are simulated independently and thesystem performance is calculated for each action. According to the results of the simulation, the actions are ranked with respect to the difference calculated. The type of reinforcement is defined, as explained in the previous section, based on the relative difference of previous and current performance criteria. If there is a punishment case, but the

rule's rank is the highest, thereinforcement is switched to reward. This procedure is applied to the program in each iteration. The algorithm of Q-learning with a model is as follows:
- Receive the current state x;
- Calculate util(x,i), for each action i;
- Select the action a;
- Perform action a;
- Receive new state y and reinforcement r;
- Simulate all actions to predict their reinforcements;
- Calculate the desired utility of action a based on the new state, reinforcement and simulation

results; $u = r + \delta \cdot \textbf{Max} \{ \textbf{util(y,k)} | k \ \varepsilon \ \textbf{actions} \}$ (If action a is good according to simulation results, reward the network, otherwise punish the network.)

- Adjust the utility network, by backpropagating the error ρU, where $\rho U = u - util(x,a)$;

3. DEVELOPMENT OF A REAL-TIME SCHEDULER

This research required two computers (IBM PC compatible 80486/33) to be used simultaneously. The first computer was used to run the Q-learning and Q-learning with a discrete model, and the second one was used to run the job-shop simulator to simulate the manufacturing environment to be controlled in real time. All data transfer between these two systems has been achieved through serial communications. All programs were written in the C programming language.

A discrete-event simulation program was utilized as a manufacturing environment. In the simulator part, the jobs are created randomly with deterministic arrival times, processing times and due dates. Probability distribution functions are used to create these parameters with different characteristics based on the job type. There are seven job types in total. In addition, There are setup dependencies based on the current and previous job types. The proper dispatching rule (actions) is received from the other computer by the communication routine of the program. The simulator calculates the performance criteria after the completion of the process. Then the selected performance criteria is sent to the other computer. In the controller, Q-learning and Q-learning with a discrete model were utilized.

3.1 Characteristics of the Problem

The characteristics of the scheduling problem of this research are explained as follows:
- There are independent single-operation jobs that are available for processing at time zero and over time. The system creates seven types of jobs. Each job type has its own arrival behavior, process plans, processing time distributions, and setup dependencies .
- The setup times depend on the sequence of the jobs. Different types of jobs might have different setup times based on the job processed previously.
- The machine is continuously available and never kept idle while work is waiting. The machine never breaks down.
- Pre-emption (interruption of process for processing other jobs) is not allowed. Transportation times of the jobs are negligible.
- The maximum queue size for the machine is limited to ten. When there are ten jobs available in the queue, the jobs entering the system are rejected.
- The interarrival times, processing times and due dates are randomly assigned based on the job types (see Table 1).

3.2 Evaluation of a Schedule

In this paper minimization of work-in-process inventory (WIP: The average of the total number of jobs in the system) was chosen as the performance criterion.

Interarrival times

	1	2	3	4	5	6	7
Distribution Type	Poisson	Poisson	Poisson	Expo.	Expo.	Expo.	Expo.
Mean	25	50	45	22	75	70	100

Processing Times

	1	2	3	4	5	6	7
Distribution Type	Normal	Normal	Normal	Normal	Normal	Normal	Normal
Mean	4	6	5	3	10	8	15
Std. Deviation	0.2	0.3	0.2	0.1	0.6	0.4	0.75

Due Dates

	1	2	3	4	5	6	7
Distribution Type	Normal	Uniform	Uniform	Normal	Normal	Normal	Uniform
Mean/Min.	5	3	0	1	10	5	0
Std. Dev./Max	2	4	10	1	2	2	10

Table 1. Probability Distributions for each Job Type

3.3 Dispatching Rules (Actions)

Fifteen dispatching rules, reported in the scheduling literature, were selected for this research. The definitions of these rules are as follows:

SPT (Shortest Processing Time): The job with the least expected processing times has the highest priority.

LPT (Largest Processing Time):The job with the largest expected processing times has the highest priority.

FIFO (First In First Out): The highest priority is given to the job that arrived earliest.

LIFO (Last In Last Out): The highest priority is given to the job that arrived latest.

SST (Shortest Setup Time): The job with the least expected setup time has the highest priority.

LST (Largest Setup Time): The job with the largest expected setup time has the highest priority.

SPST (Shortest Processing and Setup Time): The job with least expected processing and setup time has the highest priority.

LPST (Largest Processing and Setup Time): The job with largest expected processing and setup time has the highest priority.

EDD (Earliest Due Date): The highest priority is given to the job with the earliest due date.

LDD (Latest Due Date): The highest priority is given to the job with the latest due date.

mSlack (Minimum Slack Time): The job with the least amount of slack time (available time before due date time for remaining operation) has the highest priority.

MSlack (Maximum Slack Time): The job with the largest slack time has the highest priority.

CR (Critical Ratio): The highest priority is given to the job with the smallest ratio, calculated at time t (current time), as follows: $CR(i) = (Due Date (i) - t) / processing time of job i$.

SSlack: The highest priority is given to the job with largest value found by the following formula: $Sslack = Due Date - Arrival Time - Process Time - Setup Time$

Slack / RT: The highest priority is given to the job with largest value found by the following formula: $Slack/RT = (Due Date - Current Time - Process Time - Setup Time) / (Due Date - Current Time)$.

3.4. Application of Q-Learning to the Manufacturing Problem

Fifteen independent neural networks (backpropagation with dual subroutines), one for each fifteen dispatching rules and each with the same inputs and one output, were built in the program.

3.5. Interaction of the Scheduling Problem and Q-learning in Real-Time

The programs and the interactions is managed as follows: First the queue status is transferred to the control from the monitor. Then the queue status is translated to the input form. Fifteen networks in the Q-learning use the same inputs, but, since they have different weights, all give different outputs. Each network's output is collected and processed by the Stochastic Action Selector. Each of the fifteen rules had a chance to be selected as much as its output value. The selected rule is then transferred to the monitor. The monitor applies the rule to the system. In other words, it processes the job required by the dispatching rule (like the job with earliest arrival for FIFO, the job with shortest processing time for SPT etc.) After the job is processed, the monitor sends the selected performance criteria back to the control. This information is needed for reinforcement of the networks: If the WIP has increased after applying the rule, the network which this rule belongs to is punished. If WIP has decreased after applying the rule, the network is rewarded. If it stayed the same, the weights are not adjusted.

3.6. Results

The results were compared against the utilization of a single dispatching rule all the times (a technique currently used in the industry). The time periods were chosen as 12,500 and 25,000 simulation units (1 simulation unit was equal to 1 minute), which were approximately equal to 1 daily shift working for one month and 2 daily shift working for one month (see Table 2). The results of the benchmarking are in for 12,500 time units, and in Table for 25,000 time units. Q-Learning with a model gave the best results for work in process (WIP) inventory (5.64 for 12500, and 5.63 for 25000).

4. CONCLUSIONS

In this research, a Dynamic Programming based reinforcement learning algorithm "Q-learning" and its extension, "Q-Learning with a model", were applied to the FMS scheduling problem. We also described a small example which demonstrates the methodology. By exploiting the parallel processing and modeling capabilities of neural networks and reinforcement based algorithms it has the potential to be extremely fast and highly adaptable to customer needs. This integration technique has the potential to solve real-world sequencing and scheduling problems in real-time.

REFERENCES
[1] A.G. Barto, R.S. Sutton, C.J.C.H. Watkins. "Learning and Sequential Decision Making. Learning and Computational Neuroscience: Foundations of Adaptive Networks," M. Gabriel and J. Moore ed. The MIT Press, 1990.
[2] A.G. Barto. Reinforcement Learning and Adaptive Critic Methods. Handbook of Intelligent Control: Neural, Fuzzy, and Adaptive Approaches. D.A. White and D.A. Sofge ed. Van Nostrand Reinhold Publication, 1992.
[3] J. Blackstone, D. Phillips, and G.Hogg, "A state-of-the-art survey of dispatching rules for manufacturing job shop operations," International Journal of Production Research, Vol. 20, No. 1, 1982, p. 27-45.
[4] Long-Ji Lin. Self-Improving Reactive Agents Based On Reinforcement Learning, Planning and Teaching. Reinforcement Learning (Machine Learning), Edited by R. Sutton.
[5] H. Van Dyke Parunak. "Characterizing the Manufacturing Scheduling Problem," Journal of Manufacturing Systems. Vol. 10, No. 3.
[6]. C. Rabelo, A Hybrid Artificial Neural Networks and Knowledge-Based Expert Systems Approach to Flexible Manufacturing Ststem Scheduling, Ph.D. Dissertation, University of Missouri-Rolla, 1990.

[7] R.S. Sutton. "Planning by Incremental Dynamic Programming," . In L.A. Birnbaum and G.C., eds., Machine Learning: Proceedings of the Eighth International Workshop, p. 353-357.

[8] Watkins 1989. C.J.C.H. Watkins. Learning From Delayed Rewards. PhD Thesis, University of Cambridge, England.

[9] P.J. Werbos. Beyond Regression. New Tools for Prediction and Analysis in the Behavioral Sciences. PhD Thesis, Harvard University.

[10] P.J. Werbos. Building and Understanding Adaptive Systems: A Statistical/Numerical Approach to Factory Automation and Brain Research. IEEE Transactions Systems, Man, and Cybernetics, Vol 17, No 1, January, February 1987.

[11] P.J. Werbos. Neurocontrol and Related Techniques. Handbook of Neural Computing Applications. A. Maren ed., Academic Press, New York.

[12] Werbos 1992d. P.J. Werbos. Approximate Dynamic Programming for Real Time Control and Neural Modelling. Handbook of Intelligent Control: Neural, Fuzzy, and Adaptive Approaches. D.A. White and D.A. Sofge ed. Van Nostrand Reinhold Publication.

	Simulation Time	
	12500	25000
SPT	8.985	8.662
LPT	7.181	7.144
FIFO	8.306	8.271
LIFO	7.465	7.640
CR	9.091	9.062
MSlack	7.046	7.078
mSlack	8.449	8.485
EDD	7.883	8.302
LDD	7.317	7.493
SST	5.743	5.778
LST	7.920	7.823
SPST	8.386	8.497
LPST	8.036	8.179
SSlack	8.909	8.809
Slack/RT	8.950	8.808
Q-Learning	7.421	7.368
Q-L+M(Training)	5.701	5.668
Q-L+M(Testing)	5.644	5.632

Minimum	5.644	5.632
Maximum	9.091	9.062
Average	7.691	7.706

* Q-L+M : Q-Learning with a discrete model

Table 2. Result for Work -In-Process-Inventory (Minimization)

REAL-TIME CONTROL OF SYNCHRONOUS MACHINES WITH NEURAL NETWORKS

Dennis T. Lee, Yoh-Han Pao and Kambiz Komeyli
Department of Electrical Engineering and Applied Physics
Case Western Reserve University
and AI WARE Inc., Cleveland, Ohio, 44106

Dejan J. Sobajic
EPRI
3412 Hillview Avenue
Palo Alto, CA 94303

Abstract

In this paper we present the principal features and modes of operation of a new real-time control system (RTCS) and demonstrate its use as PID Gain Scheduler for stabilization of synchronous machine transients. Brief overview of RTCS functionalities is provided and a numerical example is presented to illustrate its performance.

Introduction

Being able to accurately predict the behavior of a dynamic system is of essential importance in monitoring and control of complex processes. In this regard recent advances in neural-net based system identification represent a significant step toward definition and design of a new generation of control tools for increased system performance and reliability [1,2,3,4]. The enabling functionality is the one of accurate neural-net representation of a model of a nonlinear and nonstationary dynamic system. This functionality provides interesting new opportunities including:

(a) The ability to predict future system behavior on the basis of actual system observations
(b) On-line evaluation and display of system performance and design of early warning systems, and
(c) Controller optimization for improved system performance.

Most of the existing control methodologies depend largely on the historic information about the system performance. These methodologies operate on the premise that future control actions are going to be able to correct presently observed errors. Clearly, such control actions are inherently reactive. There are very few exceptions of this principle one of which is the derivative action of the PID controller. Derivative action is supposed to counteract the linear prediction of current control error. Unfortunately, the derivative action is turned off in most of real-world applications largely due to the difficulties in adjusting it manually. With the capability to predict system behavior accurately and hence predict the errors, PID tuning can be carried out with more confidence resulting in improved system performance.

Learning of a System Model

The task of critical importance is capturing a model of a dynamic system. This is accomplished through a learning process. A feedforward multilayered neural network is attached to an unknown dynamic system as shown in Figure 1. Same inputs (controls) are provided to the unknown system and to a neural-net and their outputs (responses) are obtained. The closed-loop prediction error is calculated as a mean-square-error over the prespecified time horizon. This error serves as on/off trigger for the learning process. Learning is carried out in real-time and has the incremental character. Each data point is processed once, hence the storage requirements are minimal. During the learning process the response of a neural-net model gradually approaches the actual system response at a rate (adjustment rate) that can be controlled. As the adjustment rate increases (faster learning) so does the amount of computing. In practice, the adjustment rate is controlled to suit behavior of a learning process as well as capabilities of computing equipment [5]. During learning the RTCS is in the closed-loop prediction mode.(Figure 2.)

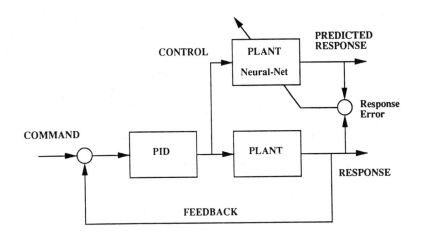

Figure 1. Learning a Model of Dynamic System

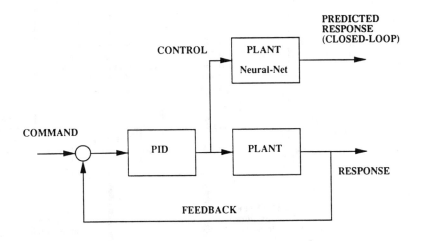

Figure 2. Closed-Loop Prediction of System Response

On-Line PID Gain Scheduling

In operation a copy of a neural-net model (of dynamic system) is used for open-loop prediction of system response (see Figure 3). Typically prediction rates are many times higher in comparison to the actual system response. In other words, in few seconds of real time the predicted response can be calculated for several minutes ahead. We use this capability to evaluate system performance through the comparison of predicted and desired response and consequently as a basis for optimal PID gain scheduling.

Gain scheduling is carried out on-line by suitably designed optimization procedure.(Figure 4.)

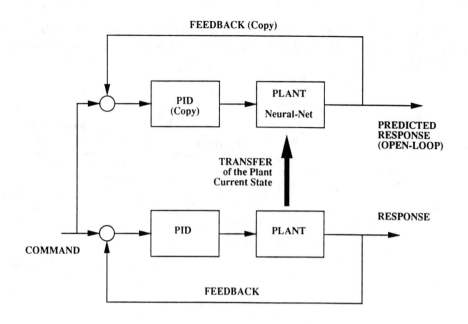

Figure 3. Open-Loop Prediction of System Response

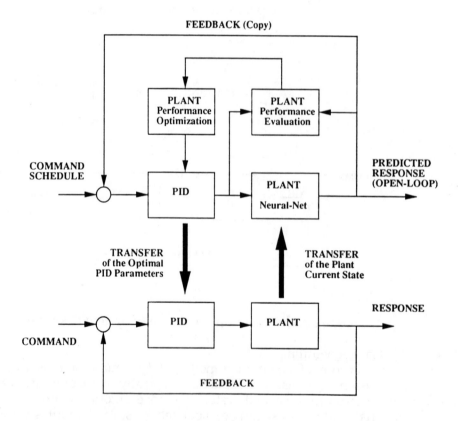

Figure 4. Schematic Depiction of On-Line PID Gain Scheduling Process

Synchronous Machine Control

In preceding sections we have described briefly the main characteristics of the proposed Real-Time Control System. Here we provide some results to illustrate the application of developed technology to a problem of stabilization of synchronous machine transients. For that purpose we consider an example of a nonlinear synchronous generator connected to a variable load [6].

Synchronous generator is equipped with two control mechanisms. One maintains nominal frequency ($f_{desired}$ = 60Hz) and the other one , the stabilizer, maintains nominal generator voltage ($V_{desired} = V_{nom}$). Frequency regulation is a slow electromechanical process due to large generator inertiae. On the other hand voltage regulation is considerably faster and can be effectively used to control electromagnetic transients.

The experiment is conducted in the following manner. First, a neural-net representation of the generator is obtained using the information gathered during normal system operation.(Figure 5.) During this process a slow adjustment rate was selected in order to minimize computing requirements. Successful learning is indicated by a small closed-loop prediction error and open-loop prediction mode is engaged.

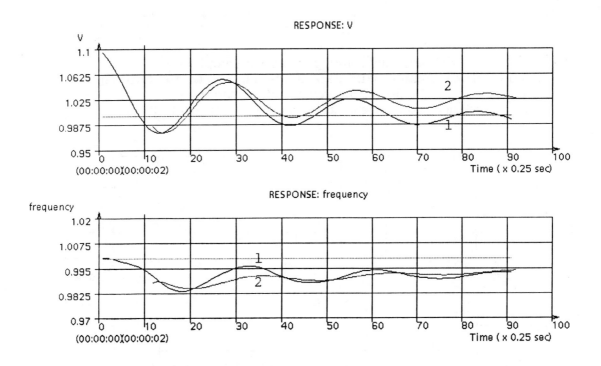

5a. Initial phase of the learning process
Figure 5. Time evolution of the generator terminal voltage and frequency
following 5% step load disturbance
1 - actual response (generator model)
2 - neural net response

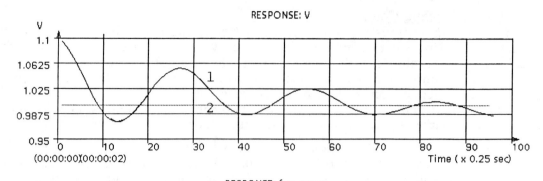

RESPONSE: V

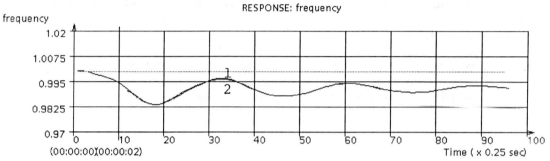

RESPONSE: frequency

5b. Successful learning has been accomplished
Figure 5. Time evolution of the generator terminal voltage and frequency
following 5% step load disturbance
1 - actual response (generator model), 2 - neural net response

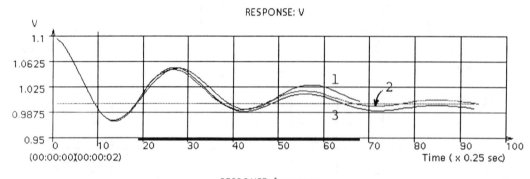

RESPONSE: V

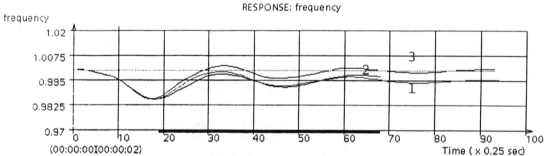

RESPONSE: frequency

Figure 3. Time evolution of the generator terminal voltage and frequency
following 5% step load disturbance
1 - actual response / Initial PID Parameters
2 - neural-net response / Final (Optimal) PID Parameters
3 - actual response / Final (Optimal) PID Parameters

I-390

The neural-net model and PID controller are coupled together to provide open-loop prediction of system transients (Figure 6a). Using the predicted response and comparing it to the desired one ($V_{desired} = V_{nom}$ and $f_{desired} = 60Hz$) system performance function is evaluated and optimal PID gains are determined. Figure 6b shows the response of the actual system controlled by the optimal PID controller.

Conclusion

In this paper we have presented main characteristics of a new real-time control system (RTCS). Its use as PID Gain Scheduler for stabilization of synchronous machine transients is illustrated with a numerical example.

References

1. Y.-H. Pao, S. Phillips and D.J. Sobajic, "Neural-Net Computing and the Intelligent Control of Systems", in the Special Issue on Intelligent Control of The International Journal of Control (IJC), Vol. 56, No. 2, Aug 1992, pp. 263-290.
2. D. J. Sobajic, Y.-H. Pao and D. T. Lee, "Autonomous Adaptive Synchronous Machine Control", In The Special Issue on Expert System Applications in Power Systems of The International Journal of Electrical Power and Energy Systems, Vol. 14, No. 2/3, April/June, 1992, pp. 166-174.
3. M. Djukanovic, D. Popovic, D. J. Sobajic and Y.-H. Pao, "Prediction of Power System Frequency Response After Generator Outages Using Neural Nets", The IEE Proceedings-C, Generation, Transmission and Distribution, Vol. 140, No. 5, September, 1993, pp. 389-398.
4. D. J. Sobajic (Editor), Neural Network Computing for the Electric Power Industry, Proceedings of The 1992 INNS Summer Workshop, Stanford, CA, August 17-19, 1992, INNS Press and Lawrence Erlbaum Associates, Inc., Hillsdale, New Jersey, 1993.
5. D. J. Sobajic, Y.-H. Pao and D. T. Lee, "Intelligent PID Scheduling for Stabilization of Power System Transients", World Congress on Neural Networks, 1993 International Neural Network Society Annual Meeting, Portland, OR, July 11-15, 1993.
6. D.J. Sobajic and Y.-H. Pao, Neural-net control in power systems, NSF Workshop on Applications of Artificial Neural Networks Methodology in Power Systems Engineering, Clemson, S.C, April 8-10, 1990.

On-Line Identification Using An ART2-BP Neural Net with Applications to Petroleum Reservoir Engineering

Wu-Yuan Tsai*, Heng-Ming Tai** and Albert C. Reynolds***

*Computer Science Department (tsai@euler.mcs.utulsa.edu)
**Electrical Engineering Department
***Petroleum Engineering Department

The University of Tulsa
600 S. College Ave.
Tulsa, OK 74104-3189

ABSTRACT

Backpropagation feedforward neural networks have been applied to pattern recognition and classification problems. However, under certain conditions the backpropagation net classifier can produce non-intuitive, non-robust and unreliable classification results. The backpropagation net is slower to train and is not easy to accommodate new data.

To overcome these difficulties, a novel neural net paradigm that integrates an adaptive resonance theory net (ART2) and a backpropagation net is proposed. ART2 is used to classify patterns into coarse classes and the latter is employed to recognize patterns within each class. This network is applied to a petroleum reservoir engineering problem for model identification and parameter estimation. A real-time model recognition system incorporating the proposed neural net is also implemented to demonstrate its measure-while-testing capability.

INTRODUCTION

Pattern recognition and classification are potentially useful approaches for interpreting data generated by industrial systems such as chemical, manufacturing, and well testing processes. Possible applications include sensor data interpretation, model identification and validation. Neural networks, especially backpropagation networks[1], have been applied to many pattern recognition problems including the classification of sonar targets[2] and sensor interpretation[3].

Application of back-propagation networks to well test model identification in reservoir engineering has been studied by several researchers[4,5]. These results have shown that the feedforward backpropagation network classifier has the ability to learn a set of pressure derivative curves and can often generalize to new cases of known models. Nevertheless, several difficulties were uncovered when more models are included in the net decision space and when more training curves are added to the training set[4]. For example, with 16 models and 30 pressure derivative data curves per model, it took more than 12 hours on a 486-PC for the backpropagation net to learn[6]. Moreover, it can not correctly distinguish models with similar features from each other. Furthermore, the backpropagation net is not robust since it is not easy to add new models.

~~~~~~

This work is partially supported by TUPREP at University of Tulsa funded by 12 major oil companies in the world.

In this paper, we propose a novel neural net to remedy the aformentioned difficulties. This network, called the *ART2-BP net*, uses an ART2 net[7] to sort a large number of input patterns into several classes. The one node that contains several similar patterns in the output layer of the ART2 net is then fed to a 2nd-order backpropagation net[8] for further classification. The advantages of the ART2-BP net include shorter training time, improved training and classification abilities, and capability of easily accomodating new models.

This paper illustrates the application of this new approach to identify well test interpretation models. A propotype module, which can be implemented in a pressure transient system for real-time application in the oil field, is also described.

The ART2-BP NEURAL NET

The ART2-BP neural network is shown in Figure 1. In this architecture, a backpropagation net is placed directly on top of an ART2 net for the bottom-up processing. First, top-down weights and bottom-up weights of ART2 are modified by the training examples. Then the three-layer BP net associated with each class node is trained using a 2nd-order backpropagation algorithm[8] for further classification. The training-recognition procedure can be described as follows. Input patterns are clustered into classes through the unsupervised learning process provided by ART2 layer. At this stage coarse classification was carried out such that patterns with similar features were clustered together. Patterns in each class are then forwarded to the BP layer for fine classification. In this phase, training is efficient because faster learning algorithm is employed. Furthermore, classification is effective since fewer patterns are used.

It is well known that ART2 is an unsupervised learning neural net[7]. Without any specified decision criterion, patterns can be categorized into classes. High vigilance parameter could be chosen to explicitly distinguish patterns with similar features, but the net will not be able to classify patterns corrupted with noise or distorted features. On the other hand, if the vigilance parameter value is too small, almost all patterns will be categorized as a single class.

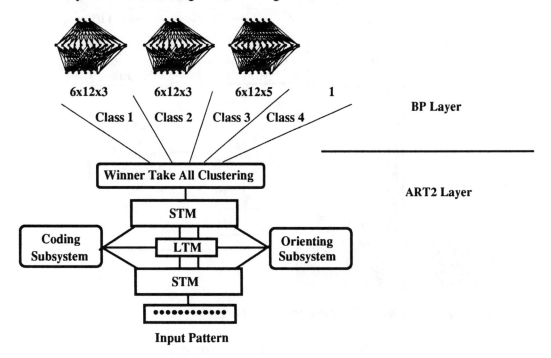

Figure 1. The ART2-BP neural net.

I-393

The backpropagation algorithm[1] reawakened the scientific and engineering world to model-free function estimation with neural networks. Though a great deal of applications using feedforward neural networks with the backpropagation algorithm have been reported, several disadvantages were also mentioned. These include slow training, convergence failure during training, and inability for the trained neural net to accurately distinguish patterns with similar features. More often than not, the algorithm converges to one of the local minima or the learning procedure stops prematurely. In the recalling phase, the neural networks being trained will be unable to produce satisfactory results.

To solve the difficulties mentioned above, an unsupervised/supervised type neural net, namely, ART2-BP net, is proposed. The idea is to use a low vigilance parameter in ART2 net to categorize input patterns into some classes and then utilize a backpropagation net to distinguish patterns in each class. Advantages of this ART2-BP neural net[6] are (1) improvement of recognition and classification capability, (2) enhancement of training convergence mechanism, and (3) easy to add new patterns. Detailed derivation and theoretical analysis on the ART2-BP net will be reported elsewhere.

Problem Setting and System Implementation

One major purpose of well testing in petroleum reservoir engineering is to determine the ability of a formation to produce reservoir fluids. Further it is important to determine the underlying reason for a well's productivity. Well test often can provide information about formation permeability, extent of wellbore damage or stimulation, reservoir pressure and boundaries, etc.

In a pressure transient test a signal of pressure vs. time is recorded. This signal is plotted as derivative curves which are used in the interpretation process. The signal on these curves is usually deformed and shaped by some underlying mechanisms in the formation and the wellbore. These mechanisms are known as well test interpretation models. Thus to identify these models from the signatures present on the derivative plot is of great importance.

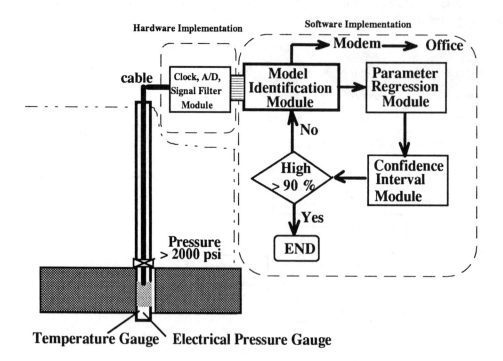

Fig. 2. A real time well testing recognition system.

The problem of identifying the well test interpretation model has been described as the inverse problem[9]. Inverse theory techniques (e.g. regression analysis) have been used to solve the inverse problem. Regression techniques can be used to estimate oil reservoir properties once the model reflected by the data has been identified. Since more than one interpretation model can produce the same signal, this approach can lead to misleading results. Further, without going through pattern recognition processing, wrong model may be selected by reservoir engineers who are not experts in the pressure transient analysis.

This problem has been effectively dealt with using backpropagation neural nets[4,5]. Results showed that the neural net approach is effective in identifying the well interpretation model. Nevertheless, several comments were also made. They include (1) selection of training examples having high quality data, (2) smaller nets can be trained efficiently and to correctly recognize one model, (3) the net can not learn new models, and (4) long training time as the size of the net and training examples become large. In this paper we show that the above four points can be resolved using the ART2-BP neural net.

A real-time well testing recognition system based on the ART2-BP neural net is depicted in Figure 2. Data collected from the two gauges are fed to clock, A/D and signal filter module to generate the time-dependent pressure curves. Model Identification Module is actually the ART2-BP neural net. After the model is identified, regression techniques such as the Levenber-Marquardt optimization technique in Laplace domain[10] are utilized for parameter estimation. In the Confidence Interval Module, statistical characteristics of the identified model are calculated to verify the results.

This system has the capability of measurement while testing. Therefore it can be put in oil field for real-time pressure transient analysis. Thus a complete set of high quality data can be obtained in a very short time during the testing. This on-site well test can reduce costs and enhance the prospect of correct interpretation.

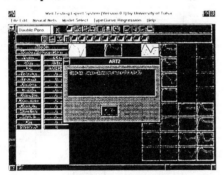

Fig. 3(a). Input pattern is clustered in Class 2.

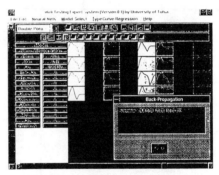

Fig. 3(b). Model identified.

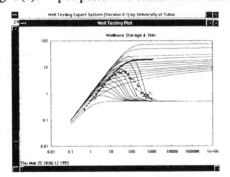

Fig. 3(c). Model recall.

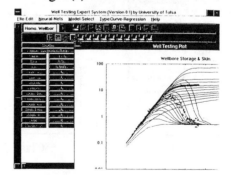

Fig. 3(d). Model regression.

A software package in C++ for the Software part in Fig. 2 has been implemented in a PC-486. This package is interactive and user-friendly. A sample recognition process is illustrated in Figures 3 (a-d). A time series pressure pattern is categorized in Class 2 which contains 4 models (Fig. 3(a)). Fig. 3(b) shows the pressure data matches Model 1 in Class 2 with very high activation value of 0.87 in comparison to other three models with low activation values (0.12, 0.15, 0.21). Fig. 3(c) shows the pressure data matches a wellbore storage/skin model. Once the model is identified, Fig. 3(d) shows the regression results after applying a Levenber-Marquardt optimization technique in Laplace domain.

ILLUSTRATIVE EXAMPLE

We applied the same well testing data used by Al-Kaabi and Lee[4] to demonstrate the better recognition capability exhibited by the ART2-BP neural net. Ten interpretation models as shown in Figure 4 were used in the training process.

The ART2-BP net consists of two training phases. One is the unsupervised clustering by ART2, the other is the supervised learning using the 2nd-order backpropagation algorithm. Each derivative curve in the training model was normalized between 0 and 1, and then was sampled at 12 points as the input pattern. Note that the same normalization method must be used for all curves including the training curves and the test unknown curves to avoid curves being shifted, enlarged or reduced. A vigilance parameter of value 0.9 was used in ART2.

There were seven classes formed at the output layer of ART2. Class 2 contains Models 2, 6, and 9; on the other hand, Models 4 and 5 were clustered together at Class 4 (see Fig. 4). Since each of these two classes needs one BP net, a $12 \times 24 \times 3$ BP net and a $12 \times 24 \times 2$ BP net were constructed for Classes 2 and 4, respectively. Both nets took less than 100 iterations for a satisfactory training. Note that this process can be executed in parallel. Compared with using a single BP net, training time is much shorter[4].

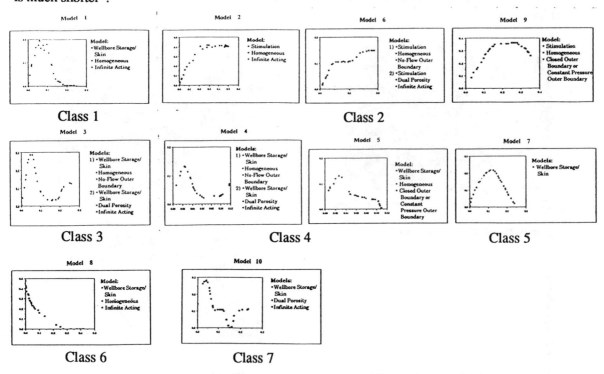

Fig. 4. Classes categorized by ART2 with vigilance parameter 0.9.

The recognition ability of the ART2-BP neural net was evaluated by applying an unknown pressure curve pattern (as shown in Fig. 7.) to the net. This new pattern was cluster into Class 2.

After going through a $12 \times 24 \times 3$ BP net, it was identified as Model 6 in that the output node representing Model 6 yields a high activation value of 0.811 compared with much lower activation values in the other two node. Table 1 shows the results. By contrast, when applying to the BP net alone, activation levels of two nodes (Model 2 and Model 6) were higher than 0.5. Because of the inherent nature of the sigmoid function, either one could be a matched model.

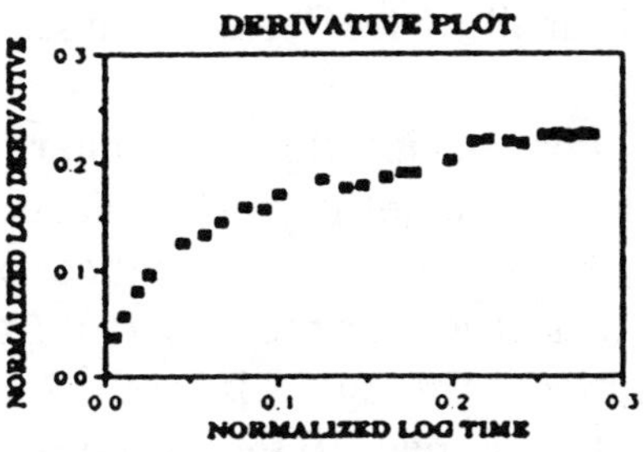

Table. 1 Recognition Capability Comparison.

Fig. 5. Unknown test pattern.

BP	ART2	-	BP
(Activation)	(Class)		(Activation)
0.075	1		
0.594	2		**0.010**
0.076	3		
0.079	4		
0.031	4		
0.936	2		**0.811**
0.068	5		
0.073	6		
0.079	2		**0.125**
0.079	7		

CONCLUSIONS

This paper has presented a new approach based on ART2 and BP neural nets to identify the well test interpretation model automatically from the pressure derivative curves. The ART2-BP net has better recognition capability and is easy to accommodate new models. Moreover it overcomes the drawback of the backpropagation network. This net can be implemented into an intelligent pressure transient analysis system suitable for real-time model idenfication.

REFERENCES

1.   Rumelhart, D.E., Hinton, G.E. and Williams, R.J., "Learning Internal Representations by Error Propagation," In Parallel Distributed Processing : Explorations in the Microstructures of Cognition, Vol. 1, pp. 318-362. Cambridge, MA : MIT Press, 1986.
2.   Gorman, R.P. and Sejnowski, T.J., "Analysis of hidden units in a layered network trained to classify sonar targets," *Neural Networks*, vol. 1, pp. 75-89, 1988.
3.   Naidu, S., Zafiriou, E. and McAvoy, T.J., "Use of neural networks for sensor failure detection in a control system," *IEEE Control Systems Magazine*, vol. 10, No. 3, pp. 49-55, 1990.
4.   Al-Kaabi ,A. U. and Lee W. J., "Using Artificial Neural Networks to Identify the Well Test Interpretation Model," paper SPE 20332, the *5th SPE Petroleum Computer Conference*, Denver, June 25-28, 1990.
5.   Houze, O.P. and Allain, O.F., "A hybrid artificial intelligence approach in well test interpretation," paper SPE 24733, the *67th SPE Annual Technical Conf. and Exhi.*, Washington, D.C., Oct. 4-7, 1992.
6.   Tsai, W.Y., "An Intelligent Well Testing Machine to Automate Pressure Transient Analysis," M.E. Report, Department of Petroleum Engineering, University of Tulsa, 1993.
7.   Carpenter, G.A. and Grossberg, S., "ART2 : Self-organization of Stable Category Recognition Codes for Analog Input Patterns," *Applied Optics*, Vol. 26, pp. 4919-4930, Dec. 1987.
8.   Moller, M.F., "A scaled conjugate gradient algorithm for fast supervised learning," Preprint, Computer Science Department, University of Aarhus, Denmark, 1990.
9.   Gringarten, A.C., "Computer-aided well test analysis," paper SPE 14099 presented at the *International Meeting*, Beijing, March 17-20, 1986.
10.   Carvalho, R., Redner, R., Thompson, L. and Reynolds, A.C., "Robust procedures for parameter estimation by automated type-curving matching," paper SPE 24732 presented at the *67th SPE Annual Technical Conf. and Exhi.*, Washington, D.C., Oct. 4-7, 1992.

Back-Propagation Algorithm for Refinement of Multilayer Dielectric Optical Interference Filter

Hyuek-Jae Lee, Jung Wook Cho, and Soo-Young Lee
Department of Electrical Engineering
Korea Advanced Institute of Science and Technology
373-1 Kusong-dong, Yusong-gu, Taejon 305-701, KOREA (South)
Tel: +82-42-869-3431, Fax: +82-42-869-3410, E-mail: sylee@ee.kaist.ac.kr

Abstarct: Analogy between multilayer dielectric optical interference filters and multilayer neural networks is investigated, and the former is efficiently refined from rough design by the adaptive learning algorithm for the latter.   Sensitivities of the filter response with respect to design parameters, i.e. dielectric thickness and refractive index, are efficiently calculated by back-propagation through layers for the gradient-base algorithm. Design examples for low and high pass filters are presented to demonstrate usefulness of the developed algorithm.

1. Introduction

The design of multilayer dielectric optical interference filters and anti-reflection coatings with complicated properties requires tedious parameter optimizations.[1-3] Some of the design methods, such as modified gradient method and damped least squares method, require the calculation of derivatives of the filter characteristics with respect to the design parameters.   Several attempts have been made to efficiently calculate the derivatives.   Recently an parameter optimization algorithm known as error back-propagation (EBP) was developed for adaptive training of feed-forward neural networks, i.e. multilayer Perceptron (MLP), with efficient calculation of the derivatives in layered architecture.[4,5] In this paper we have investigated analogy between light transmission in the multilayer dielectric thin films and signal feed-forward in the MLP, and developed a new refinement procedure for the multilayer dielectric interference filters and coatings.

2. Analogy between dielectric interference filter and neural networks

Lets consider an electromagnetic plane wave incident on a dielectric multilayer filter as shown in Fig.1.   Here n_l and h_l denote the index of refraction and thickness of the lth layer, respectively.   The electric field strength (E_{l+1}) and magnetic field strength (H_{l+1}) at $z=z_{l+1}-$ are related to the electric (E_l) and magnetic field strength (H_l) at $z=z_l-$ by a matrix equation $x_{l+1} = M_l \, x_l$, where $x_l = [\; E_l \quad H_l \;]^T$ and M_l is a 2 x 2 transmission matrix defined as [1]

$$M_l = \begin{vmatrix} \cos k_o d_l & -jZ_l \, \sin k_o d_l \\ -jY_l \, \sin k_o d_l & \cos k_o d_l \end{vmatrix}.$$

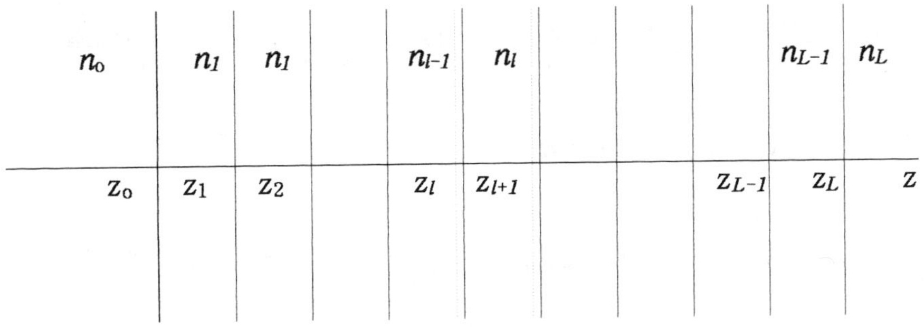

n_o	n_1	n_1		n_{l-1}	n_l			n_{L-1}	n_L	
z_o	z_1	z_2		z_l	z_{l+1}			z_{L-1}	z_L	z

Fig.1 Multilayer dielectric interference filter. Thickness of the lth dielectric layer is $h_l = z_{l+1} - z_l$. The electric and magnetic field strengths are evaluated at planes depicted by the dotted lines.

Here the k_o is free space wave number, d_l ($= n_l h_l \cos\phi_l$) is the effective optical thickness, and ϕ_l is the propagation direction angle in the lth layer and related to the angle of incidence ϕ_o by Snell's law. The optical characteristic impedance Z_l ($=1/Y_l$) is defined as $Z_o \cos\phi_l/n_l$ and $Z_o/n_l \cos\phi_l$ for transverse electric (TE) and transverse magnetic (TM) plane waves, respectively.

This matrix relationship is similar to that of feed-forward neural networks, where the nth element of the $(l+1)$th layer becomes $x_{(l+1)n} = S(\sum_m W^l_{nm} x_{lm})$.[3,4] However, unlike standard neural networks, the nonlinear function $S(.)$ is not shown here, and the matrix elements may have imaginary part. Now design of thin film dielectric filters, i.e. to find proper dielectric constants and thickness, becomes training of neural networks, i.e. to find the synaptic interconnection weights W^l.

3. Refinement Algorithm

We adopted the popular error back-propagation learning algorithm for the multilayer neural networks.[4,5] First a cost (or merit) function is defined at the output as $E \equiv \sum_s \sum_{n=1,2} \alpha_s (y^s_n - t^s_n)^2/2$, where the y and t are actual and target values of the frequency responses, and s is an index for different frequency. The α_s is weighting factor of the sth frequency component to the cost function. The cost function E is minimized by iterative gradient descent algorithm. However, unlike standard neural networks which optimize independent synaptic weight matrix elements, our matrix elements are all functions of dielectric index n_l and thickness h_l. Small modification of the learning rule is made to handle this difference as

$$h_l[p+1] = h_l[p] - \eta \, \partial E/\partial h_l \, [p],$$

$$\frac{\partial E}{\partial h_l} = \frac{\partial E}{\partial w_{11}^l}\frac{\partial w_{11}^l}{\partial h_l} + \frac{\partial E}{\partial w_{12}^l}\frac{\partial w_{12}^l}{\partial h_l} + \frac{\partial E}{\partial w_{21}^l}\frac{\partial w_{21}^l}{\partial h_l} + \frac{\partial E}{\partial w_{22}^l}\frac{\partial w_{22}^l}{\partial h_l} \, ,$$

$$\frac{\partial w_{11}^l}{\partial h_l} = -k_o n_l \cos\phi_l \sin k_o d_l, \qquad \frac{\partial E}{\partial w_{11}^l} = Re(\sum_s \delta_{l1}^s x_{l1}^s),$$

$$\frac{\partial w_{12}^l}{\partial h_l} = -k_o n_l Z_l \cos\phi_l \cos k_o d_l, \qquad \frac{\partial E}{\partial w_{12}^l} = -Im(\sum_s \delta_{l1}^s x_{l2}^s),$$

$$\frac{\partial w_{21}^l}{\partial h_l} = -k_o n_l Y_l \cos\phi_l \cos k_o d_l, \qquad \frac{\partial E}{\partial w_{21}^l} = -Im(\sum_s \delta_{l2}^s x_{l1}^s),$$

$$\frac{\partial w_{22}^l}{\partial h_l} = -k_o n_l \cos\phi_l \sin k_o d_l, \qquad \frac{\partial E}{\partial w_{22}^l} = Re(\sum_s \delta_{l2}^s x_{l2}^s),$$

where p is an index for iterative learning epoch and η is a learning coefficient. It is worth noting that the w_{mn}^l's are defined as real numbers from the complex transmission matrix elements M_{mn}^l by $M_{11}^l \equiv w_{11}^l$, $M_{12}^l \equiv j\, w_{12}^l$, $M_{21}^l \equiv j\, w_{21}^l$, $M_{22}^l \equiv w_{22}^l$. The mth element of the feed-forward signal at the lth layer with frequency s (x_{lm}^s) is recursively calculated from the input layer, i.e. $l=0$, as $x_{(l+1)n}^s = \sum_m M_{nm}^l x_{lm}^s$ ($l=0,1, \ldots,$ $L-1$). At the Lth and output layer the derivative of the cost function E with respect to the actual output $y_n^s \equiv x_{Ln}^s$ is defined as δ_{Ln}^s, i.e. $\delta_{Ln}^s \equiv \partial E/\partial x_{Ln}^s = \alpha_s(y_n^s - t_n^s)$, and back-propagates through layers to yield the other derivatives, i.e.

$$\delta_{ln}^s \equiv \frac{\partial E}{\partial x_{ln}^s} = \sum_{m=1,2} \frac{\partial E}{\partial x_m^{l+1}}\frac{\partial x_m^{l+1}}{\partial x_n^l} = \sum_{m=1,2} \delta_{(l+1)m}^s M_{mn}^{l+1} \ (l=L-1, \ldots, 1).$$

Although the above refinement rules are for the dielectric thickness only, similar rules can be easily derived for the index of refraction and incident angle.

At practical fabrications accurate control of the dielectric thickness is demanding. Since the sensitivity of the cost function with respect to the dielectric thickness, i.e. $\partial E/\partial h_l$, is calculated during refinement, low sensitivity restriction may be easily incorporated in the definition of the cost function E. Better performance at critical frequencies may be obtained by assigning high weight factor α_s. Since adding another layer to existing networks does not cause much difficulty, adaptive increase of dielectric layer may also be incorporated for better performance.

4. Results

In Fig.2 frequency responses are shown for low pass and high pass dielectric filters. The solid line and dotted line represent frequency responses for initial and refined

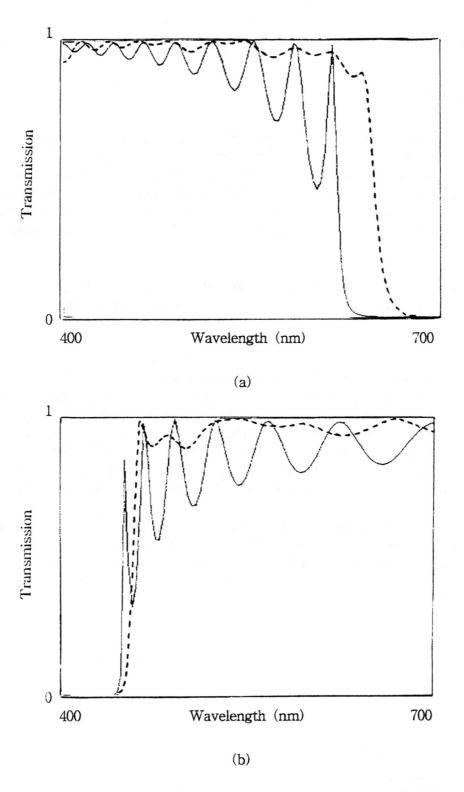

(a)

(b)

Fig.2 Transmission coefficient versus frequency of the designed multilayer dielectric filters. (a) low pass filter; (b) high pass filter. Solid lines for initial design, and dotted lines for the refined design by dielectric thickness only.

dielectric thicknesses, respectively.   Although the initial design was quite poor, the refined design show good frequency responses.

5. Conclusion

In this letter we have demonstrated a new refinement algorithm for design of multilayer dielectric optical interference filters and coatings.   Based on popular adaptive training algorithm for multilayer neural networks, the sensitivities of filter response with respect to the design parameters are efficiently calculated by back–propagation through layers. By assigning high weight factors for the cost function at critical frequencies and adaptively changing number of layers it will provide a powerful and efficient iterative design procedure.

Acknowledgement: This research was supported by Korean Ministry of Science and Technology through KAIST as an Advanced Essential Technology Project.

References

[1] H.A. Macleod, *Thin Film Optical Filters*, Macmillan, New York, 1986.
[2] C.J.v.d. Laan and H.J. Frankena, "Fast computation method for derivatives of multilayer stack reflectance," *Appl. Opt.*, **17**, pp. 538–541, 1978.
[3] J.A. Dobrowolski and R.A. Kemp, "Refinement of optical multilayer systems with different optimization procedures," *Appl. Opt.*, **29**, pp. 2876–2893, 1990.
[4] P.J. Werbos, "Beyond regression: New tools for prediction and analysis in the behavioral science," Doctoral Dissertation, Appl. Math., Harvard Univ., Boston, MA, 1974.
[5] D.E. Rumelhart, G.E. Hinton, and R.J. Williams, "Learning internal representations by error propagation," in *Parallel Distributed Processing: Explorations in the Microstructure of Cognition*, MIT Press, Camridge, MA, 1986.

Applications

Session Chairs: David Casasent
Robert Pap
Dejan Sobajic

POSTER PRESENTATIONS

Back Propagation Neural Network for American Sign Language Recognition

R.Erenshteyn, L.Messing, R.Foulds, G.Stern, and S.Galuska

Center for Applied Science and Engineering in Rehabilitation,
University of Delaware, Alfred I. duPont Institute
P.O.Box 269 Wilmington DE 19899
E-mail: erenshte@asel.udel.edu

ABSTRACT

The application of Back Propagation Neural Networks to gesture recognition in general, and to recognition of static representations of the American Sign Language (ASL) alphabet in particular is presented. Recognition system architecture, decomposition methods, data collection and neural network construction tools are discussed. An experimental study of ASL recognition is presented. The results achieved provide encouragement for the next stage of development: computer recognition and translation of dynamic signs and gestures.

1. INTRODUCTION

Approximately 300,000 Americans use American Sign Language as their primary language. [1]. Deaf and hearing people sometimes rely on a sign interpreter to facilitate communication by translating from ASL to spoken English and from spoken English to ASL. The global problem is to develop a computer recognition and translation system as a communication tool both for deaf and hearing people. Some papers describing different approaches to this problem have appeared in the past few years [2-6]. Some authors have tried to explore artificial neural networks [4-6].

We have developed a back propagation neural network (NN) system to recognize static representations of the ASL alphabet. Each letter in the alphabet is represented either by a handshape or by a handshape-movement pair. We used a CyberGlove to collect input data for NN training and testing. In this paper, we will discuss the features which were used to describe signs, the NN development problems, and our results.

We wish to apply what we have learned in developing these NNs to other NNs which would recognize dynamic fingerspelling, and, eventually, ASL signs and non-linguistic gestures. Such NNs have a potential to be useful in several fields; the most obvious one being applications involving a sign language. A few possible sign language applications are sign dictionaries (for example ASL-English, English-ASL, or ASL-ASL), sign language tutorials, translation programs, and aids to composing and recording sign literature and poetry.

Another group of applications are those for which gestures permit more efficient and/or natural computer input than do mice or keyboards. These applications include those which manipulate virtual realities or maneuver robots [7].

A third use of a sign or gesture recognition system would be to assist communication by people who are unable to speak, and who can not learn to sign, either because of cognitive or physical limitations, or because they don't know sign. A NN could be used to map movements which such

I-405

people are able to make onto linguistic elements (phonemes, syllables, morphemes, words, or phrases); and then to act as a personalized interpreter for the individuals.

2. SIGN RECOGNITION SYSTEM ARCHITECTURE

The characteristics of the recognition problem we solved are:
- $A = \{A_r\}$ - a set of recognized classes, $r = 1, 2, \ldots, R$. Each class A_r corresponds with a distinct letter from the ASL alphabet ($R = 26$). The set A is presented in Fig. 1.
- $X = \{x_i\}$ - features set or inputs, $i = 1, 2, \ldots, n$. The inputs are: degrees of flexion/extension of the joints in one hand, and degrees of abduction/adduction between fingers ($n = 18$).

Our first difficulty came with the discovery that the recognition problem is not linear, but is much more complicated. This was the main reason we decided to explore multi-layer back propagation NNs [8]. The simplest architecture of NN theoretically capable of solving this problem utilizes twenty six outputs and a varying number of hidden layers and number of nodes in the hidden layer(s). Unfortunately, our experiment with this architecture have not been completed successfully. Despite our using a fast SPARC10 Station and our manipulation of the NN architecture, learning rule and training parameters, we were unable to achieve any reasonable results in real time. Therefore we decided to decompose the problem into several simpler recognition problems. There are several different possible ways to decompose the problem. In our study we have limited the number of outputs for each developed NN to three. This made it possible to construct very simple and rapidly trained NNs. Another problem was the method of dividing recognized classes into subclasses. The most obvious way is to employ an alphabetic distribution: {abc, def, ghi, . . . , yz}. In the highest level of decision making each group of three subclasses has been joined into a single larger subclass. Therefore the decision making system for ASL alphabet recognition has three levels. However, this design requires greater accuracy on the highest tier. To solve this problem the subclasses on the highest level have to be more remote in the feature space, and we can't be sure that we achieved this using an alphabetic distribution. Another sign distribution was made by an ASL signer, who was experienced with several linguistic analyses of ASL. The linguistic-expert distribution, as we dubbed it, is shown in Fig. 2.

After making subclasses we developed thirteen NN (NN1, NN21, NN22, . . . , NN311, NN312, . . . , NN333). They have similar architecture: they all have three layers (an input layer, a hidden layer and an output layer) as shown in Fig. 3. Only the number of nodes in the hidden layer varies. The back propagation training algorithm with momentum and adaptive learning rate, and log-sigmoid transfer functions was used.

To improve initial conditions, we applied the Nguyen-Widrow NN initialization method [9]. We used two stop criteria: an acceptable level of sum squared error on the NN output, and a maximum number of epochs to train. We also employed recognition error probability estimation on the training set.

Two different methods have been used to make decisions for testing samples. Let us define NN outputs as O_j^1 - for the first level, O_j^{2k} - for the second level, and O_j^{3km} - for the third level ($j, k, m = 1, 2, 3$). The simplest method of making the decision is based on finding the maximum output in each level. The second way is to multiply the outputs for each letter, and then to make a decision also by finding the maximum and comparing it with definite threshold (Δ):

$$X \in A_{r*}, \text{ if } O_{r*} = \max_r O_r \text{ and } O_{r*} > \Delta;$$

$$r = 1, 2, \ldots, R; \quad \Delta = [0, 1]; \quad O_r = O_{jkm} = O_j^1 \, O_j^{2k} \, O_j^{3km}; \quad j, k, m = 1, 2, 3$$

3. DATA COLLECTION AND NEURAL NETWORK SOFTWARE

Data were collected using a CyberGlove - a special device with sensors that monitor the shapes of the signer's hand and fingers. There are 18 sensors on the CyberGlove including two bend sensors on each of the five fingers to measure joint flexion, four abduction sensors to measure the corresponding finger movement, an additional sensor which measures the thumb rotation across the palm toward the pinkie finger, another sensor which measures the pinkie rotation across the palm toward the thumb, and two wrist sensors to measure wrist pitch and yaw.
We used the CyberGlove Interface Unit to connect the CyberGlove to our Silicon Graphics Workstation and we also used special Virtual/Hand software to process the data received from the CyberGlove. An experienced signer produced 40 samples of each letter, either making pauses or coarticulating between letters. Then these data were randomly divided into training and testing sets (30 and 10 samples of each letter correspondingly). Additionally, a continuous sequence of samples of three letters which might be confused was recorded. This sequence was approximately 12 second long and included 357 frames (30 frames/sec).

NN software was designed with the Neural Network Toolbox for MatLab on the SPARC station [10]. NN Toolbox is a very powerful tool which permits access to all of the major neural network paradigms, including back propagation. The software allows one to change the paradigm, NN architecture and parameters, transfer functions, etc. and facilitates the design process.

4. EXPERIMENTAL STUDIES AND RESULTS

The experimental studies results are shown in Table 1. The recognition probability error was used as the criterion to indicate quality.

Table 1.

Linear Solving Rule		Back Propagation Neural Network				Number of training samples
Training	Testing	Training	Testing	Level 1	Level 2	
.293	.304	0	.096	.038	.024	260
		0	.065	.023	.020	520
		0	.035	.019	.008	780

The facts that NNs solve the problem much better than the linear solving rule and that the NN training results depend on the number of training samples have been proved. The number of nodes in the hidden layer is greatest for the highest level of decision making (20 - for level 1; 5-10 - for level 2; 2-5 - for level 3). Also the training of the highest levels requires more epochs to reach the acceptable level of sum-squared error (2500 - for level 1; 1200 - for level 2; 100-300 - for level 3). We also calculated an error matrix which showed us which signs were more frequently confused. For example, the NNs confused the letters 'b', 'c' and 'o'. The same signer then generated a sequence of these confused letters, including all possible transitions: b - c -o - b - o - c - b. Fig. 4 contains the result of this experiment is (frames: 95-155, $\Delta = .5$). These experiments provide initial evidence that back-propagation NNs can be used to solve gesture (ASL) recognition problems, and also to permit sign separation of a continuous sign sequence.

I-407

5. CONCLUSIONS

The experiments presented above demonstrate how useful back propagation neural networks are in solving the static sign recognition problem. Decomposition is also very important in making the system more applicable as part of an ASL translator. An attempt to extract static signs from a dynamic sign sequence shows one possible way to solve the dynamic gesture recognition problem.

We have taken the first steps in developing a gesture recognition package. Such a project will be difficult to accomplish, but it will pave the way for many types of useful applications.

ACKNOWLEDGEMENTS

The authors wish to thank the U.S. Department of Education for providing funding for this research under NIDRR grant number H133P300003-94.

REFERENCES

1. Stokoe,W.C., Gasterline,D., and Croneberg, C., A Dictionary of American Sign Language on Linguistic Principles, Linstok Press, Silver Spring MD, 1976
2. Peters,S.M., Coarticulation in American Fingerspelling and its Implication for Automatic Sign Recognition. Master's Thesis, University of Delaware, Newark DE, 1992
3. Takahashi,T., and Kishin,F., A hand gesture recognition method and its application. Systems and Computers in Japan, 23(2), 1992, 38-48
4. Murakami,K., and Taguchi,H., Gesture Recognition Using Recurrent Neural Networks, SIGCHI Proceeding, 1991, 237-242
5. Revesz,P.Z., and Veera,R.K., A Sign-to-speech Translation System Using Matcher Neural Networks. The Proceeding of Conference on Artificial Neural Networks in Engineering, St.Louis MO, 1993
6. Fels,S.S., Building Adaptive Interfaces Using Neural Networks: The Glove-Talk Pilot Study, Technical Report CRG-TR-90-1, University of Toronto, Toronto, Canada, 1990
7. Roy,D.M., Panayi,M., Harwin,W.S., and Fawcus R., The Enhancement of Interaction for People with Severe Speech and Physical Impairment through the Computer Recognition of Gesture and Manipulation, Proceedings of CSUN Conference on Virtual Reality and Persons with Disability, San Francisco, 1993
8. Rumelhart,D.E., and McClelland,J.L., Parallel Distributed Processing: Exploration in the Microstructure of Cognition, I,&II, MIT Press, Cambridge MA, 1986
9. Nguyen,D., Widrow,B., Improving the learning speed of 2-layer neural networks by choosing initial values of the adaptive weights, International Joint Conference of Neural Neworks, vol.3, 1990, 21-26
10. Neural Network Toolbox User's Guide, The MathWorks, Inc., 1992

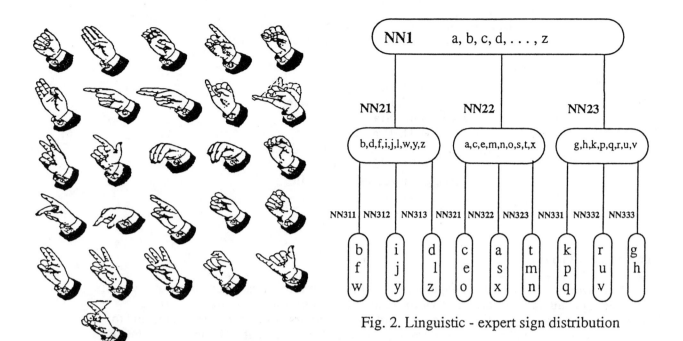

Fig. 1. American Manual Alphabet [1]

Fig. 2. Linguistic - expert sign distribution

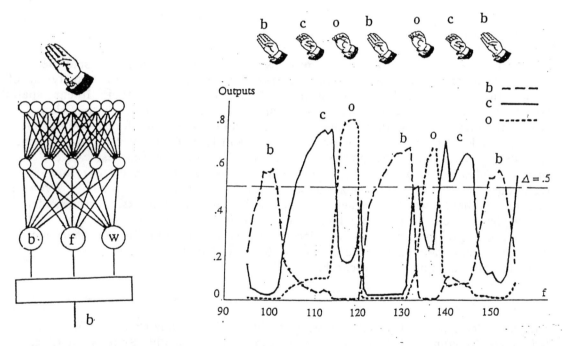

Fig. 3. Neural Network architecture

Fig. 4. Sign sequence recognition example

Using Artificial Neural Networks to Identify Roads in Satellite Images

Julian E. Boggess
Computer Science Department
Mississippi State University
P. O. Drawer CS
Mississippi State, MS 39762, U.S.A.
(601) 325-2756
gboggess@cs.msstate.edu

Introduction

Road networks in satellite images are generally readily discerned by the eye of the average human observer. Unfortunately, roads are difficult to extract automatically from satellite imagery, and many hours of work are required to extract them by hand. In the current world political climate, it is important be able to provide accurate, up-to-date maps of the road networks in any region of the world. For this reason, there is strong motivation to develop more powerful algorithms for automatic road identification.[1]

Background

Previous attempts to automate the process of identifying roads in satellite imagery generally have approached the problem by using one of two types of information about roads: their spectral characteristics, and their linear spatial structure. Unfortunately, roads share spectral characteristics with other types of terrain in satellite images (plowed fields, clear-cut forest areas, any bare ground), and thus cannot reliably be identified from spectral data alone. Moreover, many linear features occur in satellite images (barges, wakes, furrows, clearings for electrical transmission lines, etc.), and therefore techniques which identify linear features cannot reliably find roads. Even a merger of these two approaches can be misled by river banks, furrows, dry stream beds, field boundaries, levees, river meander scars, and the like. For this reason, previous attempts to identify roads in satellite images have met with only moderate success, and the problem continues to inspire a considerable amount of research.

---

[1]*Acknowledgements* - This work was supported by the U. S. Army Corps of Engineers Waterways Experiment Station, Geotechnical Laboratories, Mobility Systems Division, Analytical Studies Branch (Mr. Robert P. Smith, Chief; Mr. Cary D. Butler, project advisor) under the auspices of the U.S. Army Research Office Scientific Services Program administered by Battelle (Delivery Order 856, Contract No. DAAL03-91-C-0034). The views, opinions, and/or findings contained in this report are those of the author and should not be construed as an official Department of the Army position, policy, or decision, unless so designated by other documentation.

Artificial Intelligence algorithms derive their power from the use of domain-specific knowledge.   Several different types of Artificial Intelligence approaches to road detection are available, including Expert Systems, Fuzzy Set Theory, Heuristic Search, and Artificial Neural Networks.   This study extends previous work on finding roads using artificial neural network techniques by incorporating knowledge of spatial relationships (context) with the more-normally used spectral information.   Although useful results are obtained, it is probable that   a complete solution to the problem will require the integration of several AI techniques into a hybrid system.

Using Contextual Information with Neural Networks to Identify Roads

The scope of this study was to investigate the use of artificial neural networks in identifying roads in Landsat Thematic Mapper (TM) images.   Table 1 shows the spectral sensitivity of the seven TM bands.

BAND	BOUNDARIES (micrometers)	COLOR
1	0.45 - 0.52	blue
2	0.52 - 0.60	green
3	0.63 - 0.69	red
4	0.76 - 0.90	reflective-infrared
5	1.55 - 1.75	mid-infrared
6	10.40 -12.50	thermal (emission) infrared
7	2.08 - 2.35	mid-infrared

Characteristics of the Landsat Thematic Mapper Spectral Bands
(adapted from Jensen, 1986, p. 34, and   Richards, 1986, p. 13)
Table 1

One goal of the project, in order to have a method of visually determining whether the results were satisfactory, was to devise an automated process which could accept as input a multi-spectral TM image and produce as output an image of the road network suitable for overlaying on top of the original image.

A Landsat TM image of the Vicksburg, Mississippi, area taken on 1 April 1991 served as a testbed (See Figure 1).   This area was chosen due to its proximity to the investigator and the consequent ease with which ground-truthing could be performed.   A 400-by-400-pixel section of the original image was used for training and testing the network.

If the pixel to be classified as a road or non-road pixel is considered to be the target pixel, then, in order to include the local context as part of the input to the neural network, the pixels surrounding the target pixel would also have to be included as part of the input.   Consequently, it was decided to include both the 8 pixels directly contiguous to the target pixel, as well as the 16 pixels surrounding those 8 pixels, as part of the input, resulting in the input pixels consisting of a 5-pixel by 5-pixel square centered around the target pixel.

A backpropagation network with 175 input units, 50 hidden units, and 1 output unit was constructed; the input data consisted of values from all seven TM spectral bands for each of the pixels in the training set   (See Figure 2).

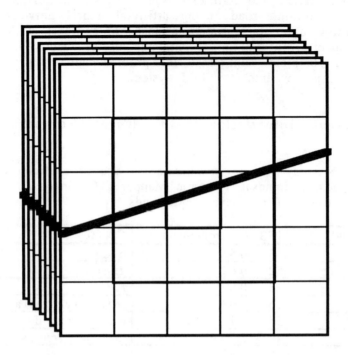

7-Band, 5 -by-5 Pixel Input Array for Context-sensitive Neural Network
(Showing Road Passing Through Center Pixel)
Figure   2

The image's pixel values (integer values from 0 to 255) were normalized to real numbers between 0.0 and 1.0 in order to be used as input to the neural network.   The network was trained by exposing it to the data for 450 (out of 500) pixels, half of which were road and half of which were non-road.   This process was repeated until the rate of improvement in the network's performance leveled off.

Once the network was trained, it was tested on the remaining 50 pixels.   The best-performing network scored 94% accuracy on the test set.   An image of the test area was produced using the trained network to identify road pixels; it is included as Figure 3.

Conclusion

Although humans can readily trace road networks in satellite images, it is difficult for computers to do so.   Current techniques have concentrated primarily on the use of spectral data alone; the results of the current report indicate that use of contextual or spatial information is essential.   The more traditional statistical and rule-based techniques produce images with many areas of soils identified as roads.   Although the neural network technique does not make many mistakes of commission (identifying non-road pixels as roads), it does omit many problematic road pixels. Consequently, additional work is needed to connect the road segments, generated by the neural network, into a coherent map of the road network structure. This will require information beyond that provided by the neural network; this information may be provided most easily by a hybrid system which utilizes several sources of information. Work is underway on such a hybrid system.

REFERENCES

Jensen, J. R. **Introductory Digital Image Processing: A Remote Sensing Perspective**. Prentice-Hall, Englewood Cliffs, New Jersey, 1986.

Richards, J. A. **Remote Sensing Digital Image Analysis: An Introduction**. Springer-Verlag, New York, 1986.

Figure 1   Landsat Thematic Mapper Image of Vicksburg, MS, 1
April 1991 - Band 1

Figure 9   Pixels Identified as Roads by Single-hidden-layer Back-propagation Neural Network

Neural Network Based Cancer Cell Classification

Y. Hu and K. Ashenayi
Electrical Engineering Department, University of Tulsa, Tulsa, OK 74135
R. Veltri
CytoDiagnostics Inc. Oklahoma City
R. Hurst and R. Bonner
Urology Department, Oklahoma University Health Sciences Center, Oklahoma City

Abstract
The investigation of bladder cancer cell classification by Neural Networks(NN) is reported. In this work, a single hidden layer feed-forward NN with error back-propagation training is adopted. Network configurations with various activation functions, namely sigmoid, sinusoid and gaussian, are studied. A set of features, including cell size, average intensity, texture, shape factor and pgDNA are selected as the input for the network. These features, in particular the texture information, are shown to be very effective in capturing the discriminate information in cancer cells. The experiments were conducted on 467 cell images from seven cases, normal and abnormal. The results show a classification accuracy of as high as 96.9%.

1. Introduction

Until recently, bladder cancer was diagnosed almost exclusively by either cystoscopy, wherein a fiber optic device is inserted into the bladder and lesions are detected visually by a urologist, or by conventional Papanicolaou staining of bladder cells obtained from urine or from a bladder wash(hereafter called "conventional cytology")[Koss1979]. The major use of cystoscopy is to detect tumors in patients expressing the symptom complex characteristic of bladder cancer, which do not occur until the tumor has progressed to a more dangerous grade or stage. The difficulty with conventional cytology is that its recognition rate to low grade lesions is highly sensitive to the training of the cytopathlogist. Human can learn to recognize bladder cancer cells visually, but the process of screening samples generally requires a high level of skill and knowledge [Koss1979], and the work is generally fatiguing and boring due to its repetitive nature, therefore results are sometime inconsistent. Automatic cell classification has been studied for decades by using conventional pattern recognition techniques [Noguchi1983, Zajicek1983], here we would like to look into the application of neural network(NN) for bladder cancer cell classification.

Neural network has been utilized in many areas due to its potential high speed inherent in its parallel architecture, learning ability and non-linear classification nature. Among various successful applications, pattern recognition is one in which NN has shown results comparable or superior to the conventional approaches.

From pattern recognition view point, neural network, to the essence, constructs a non-parametrical discriminate surface—boundary—in its often multidimensional input vector space. This surface is built up progressively by exploring the discriminate information from labeled patterns in the training process. The trained network is then used to classify future patterns by extrapolating the information learned. The discriminate surface is virtually coded into weights and activation function threshold values of the networks during training process. Fig. 1 shows a typical single hidden layer feed-forward neural network, which also has been used in this work.

Error back propagation training algorithm is chosen for our supervised learning processing. Back propagation algorithm is a gradient based learning procedure. Although it has the drawback of getting stuck into local optima, back propagation is by far the most popular method used and does perform well.

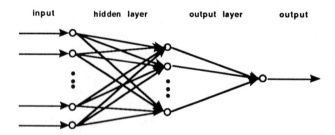

Fig. 1 Structure of a single hidden layer feed-forward NN

In section 2, we study various neural network configurations used in this work. Section 3 considers the feature extraction. Experiment results are presented in section 4. Section 5 is discussions and conclusion.

2. Network Configurations

In a multilayer neural network, hidden layers are of particular importance. How well and how quick the network converges to an approximation of the discriminate surface, to a large degree, depends on the number of hidden neurons and the type of the activation function used for each neuron. Too many hidden neurons will degrade the generalization capability of the network. The issue can be directly analogized to polynomial curve fitting. Allowing too few or too many parameters to be used in the polynomials will lead to under or over fitting. Therefore, there is an optimal hidden neural number for each individual recognition task. Works have been done in trying to quantify the generalization quality by using the concept of entropy or other complexity measurements.

Neural network can be perceived to have a underlying function decomposition mechanism [Nornick1989]. An arbitrary function, e.g. the discriminate surface in classification application, can be represented by a collection of simple primitive functions, which corresponds to the activation function associated with each neuron. It has been prove, meeting certain conditions, neural networks with many types of activation functions are convergent [Nornick1989]. Studies show the often used sigmoid activation function is not necessarily the optimal choice. It has been suggested in certain class of problems the use of sinusoid or gaussian activation functions reduces the training time substantially [Ashenayi1992a,b]. In this work, sigmoid, gaussian and sinusoid activation functions, denoted by $f_1(x)$, $f_2(x)$ and $f_3(x)$ respectively, are used in the network:

$$f_1(x) = \frac{1}{1 + \exp(-\frac{x}{a})} \tag{1}$$

$$f_2(x) = \exp(-\frac{x^2}{2\pi\sigma^2}) \tag{2}$$

$$f_3(x) = \frac{1+\sin(fx)}{2} \tag{3}$$

f_2 is not a gaussian function in the strict sense, but remains a bell shape. It is interesting to notice that if a sinusoid activation function is used, assuming a single hidden layer structure with linear output layer, the neural network can be made to resemble the fourier transformation. As fourier transformation is othogonal, there is reason to think that a network with sinusoid activation function will, in general, use fewer hidden neurons than either sigmoid or gaussian to approximate the same function.

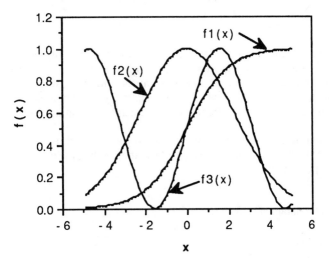

Fig. 2 Activation functions.

Fig. 2 denotes the three activation functions used in this work, with a, σ and f equal to 1, $(2\pi)^{-1/2}$ and 1 respectively. It is easy to notice that for a value outside region [-5,5] the function output of $f_1(x)$ and $f_2(x)$ will become saturated (close to 0 or 1). The discriminate nature of neural network mainly comes from the transition region on both sides of the origin, before entering the saturation areas. The change of the activation function slope will enable the network to deal with an input value of larger dynamic range. A scaling factor greater than 1 is used in this work.

3. Feature Extraction

The cell images are obtained through microscope and individually separated. Ideally, raw images (gray scale values) should be used directly as network input as they contain all original information. If the network can explore the discriminate information coming with the raw images itself, the hidden features will be revealed. However, the use of raw image as the input leads to a large input data size, and consequently increase substantially the complexity of the network as well as training time. Even for a moderate cell size of 60×60, there will be as many as 3,600 input data. Perhaps the more serious problems is the lacking of the invariant property in a trained network. Unless some special complex configuration of neural network is adopted [Spirkovska1993], or a large number of variations of original cell images in scale, rotation and location are used for training, the network will likely fail to classify cells not seen before.

In pattern recognition, only the discriminate information contributes to correct identification of objects, while the rest does not or even degrades the performance. Feature extraction is to map the raw data into feature domain, while at the same time preserve the discriminate information of the original data. The direct benefit of feature extraction is the substantial reduction of input data size. For object recognition, if the features are chosen to be invariant to geometrical transformations, the classification performance will be significantly improved.

By carefully observing the cell images it is revealed that the abnormal cells have either a larger size, irregular shape, rougher surface or darker appearance. Based on above observations and with hardware implementation in mind, a set of four simple visual features, including area, average intensity, shape factor(roundness) and texture, are identified. All of them can be realized in hardware without much difficulty. In addition, pgDNA value is also used, although this does not represent a visual property.

Shape Factor

As most non-cancer cells have a close to round shape, and the cancer cells look more irregular, roundness factor seems to be a simple and effective discriminate feature. This is calculated as

$$\text{Shape Factor} = \frac{\text{perimeter}^2}{\text{area}} \qquad (4)$$

An ideal circle will give a shape factor of 4π, while any shape other than a circle will produce a value greater than 4π.

Texture

Texture is an important visual feature for many pattern recognition tasks. Texture describes the interdependent characteristics of pixels within a neighboring area. Regular texture has more or less periodical patterns, while random texture is best described by its 'coarseness'. Various statistical models can be used for feature extraction from a random texture image [Reed1993]. To minimize the computation, only simple convolution by using a 3×3 mask is considered. This effectively extracts the high frequency information from an image.

Fig. 3 shows pixels in a small area of cell image and the convolution mask applied. From the configuration of kernel it can be found this mask has the effect of high pass filtering. In fact the mask resembles a Laplacian kernel, commonly used for edge sharpening.

The texture T_x for cell x can be obtained as follows,

$$T_x = \frac{\sum\limits_{(i,j)\in \text{ cell } x} (O(i,j))^2}{\text{Area}}$$

$$= \frac{\sum\limits_{(i,j) \in \text{cell x}} (8G(i,j) - \sum\limits_{(k,l) \in \eta} G(k,l))^2}{\text{Area}} \qquad (5)$$

$O(i,j)$ is the convolution output at location (i,j) on a cell image. $G(i,j)$ corresponds to the intensity value at location (i,j). η represents the 8 neighboring locations of (i,j).

As only texture information of the cell surface is of the interests, the high frequency information on the boundary between cell and background (zero pixel value) should be avoided. Above equation can be modified to

$$T_x = \frac{\sum\limits_{(i,j) \in \text{cell x}} O(i,j)^2}{\text{Area}}$$

$$= \frac{\sum\limits_{(i,j) \in \text{cell x}} (S \times G(i,j) - \sum\limits_{(k,l) \in \eta'} G(k,l))^2}{\text{Area}} \qquad (6)$$

η' represents the non-zero neighborhood region of (i,j), and S is the number of non-zero pixels. This effectively avoids the boundary problem by modifying the mask in those regions.

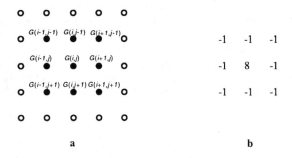

Fig. 3 a. pixel positions, **b.** the convolution mask applied

4. Experiments

All together 467 cell images from 6 cases are obtained. All cells have been labeled manually by experts as cancer or non-cancer. Among them 263 from two cases are abnormal (cancer) cells and 204 from the rest of four cases are normal cells. In order to restore the aspect ratio to 1:1, the original images are expanded horizontally by a factor of 1.78. After aspect ratio correction, the cell images are tailored into 60×60 pixel images. The cell image is centrally aligned in this area and used as input of network.

Four features, namely area, average intensity, texture and shape factor defined in previous section are extracted from images cell by cell. Based on these a feature vector list is formed. Apart from the raw images, also provided is additional non-perceptual feature information pgDNA. This supplementary information will be shown to be useful in enhancing the performance of classification.

As is often the case in pattern recognition certain features have substantially larger numerical values than others. To prevent those features from dominating the training process, all features are normalized by their corresponding standard deviations. Some cells, even after normalization, still have feature values out of transition region [-5,5], beyond which is a saturated region in a sigmoid activation function. To keep the feature value within the transition region, a scaling factor of 8 is identified and used in sigmoid activation function of Eq. (1). Similarly, a value 2.5 is also chosen as σ for gaussian activation function.

Shown in Fig. 4 is the input training data vectors in feature space. Non-cancer cells are symbolized by 'o' and cancer cells by '•'. One can see that non-cancer cells cluster tightly around origin of the feature space while cancer cells spread out along each axis. This spreading out manifests the irregular nature of cancer cells in shape, cell surface smoothness, intensity and size.

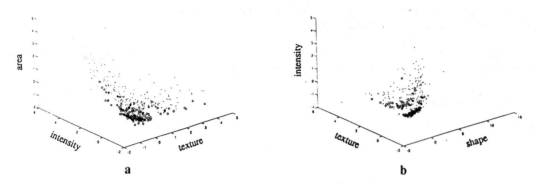

Fig. 4 Training data vectors plot in feature space
a. area-intensity-texture, **b.** intensity-texture-shape.

All cells (and feature vectors) are split into two groups for training and testing. Roughly 80% of the cells (normal and abnormal) are used for training. The rest is retained for testing.

First, the network is trained by raw images. The number of input neurons required is 3,600. A single hidden layer network structure is adopted. The number of neurons in the hidden layer was varied until an optimum number (20) was found. To ensure that the initial network configurations are different from experiment to experiment, each run was initialized randomly and different random seeds were used. Table 1 reports the test results for three networks with raw image input on a 98 test cell set. Values listed in Table 1 for each experiment are 1) classification rate, 2) iterations taken for the network to converge, and 3) total square error at the output layer for all test patterns. As is indicated by the results shown in Table 1, the network trained using raw image only classified about 70% of the test cell images correctly.

Table 1. Performance of networks for various input, activation functions.

Input Data	Networks	Classify Rate	Learning Speed	Output Error
Raw Image	Sigmoid	77.4%	1,000	20.09
	Sinusoid	62.3%	600	30.10
	Gaussian	64.5%	300	24.47
4 Features	Sigmoid	94.6%	8,500	5.58
	Sinusoid	86.7%	200	10.00
	Gaussian	91.8%	1,000	7.09
5 Features	Sigmoid	96.9%	10,000	2.98
	Sinusoid	90.8%	200	9.41
	Gaussian	95.9%	3,000	3.58

Utilizing the feature vectors from the same training and testing cell sets as before, classification by using feature vector trained networks were studied. Experiments with all four perceptual features were conducted under various conditions (hidden neuron number, random seeds). For the optimal number of hidden neurons 4, the classification score reaches 94.6% for sigmoid network, and 86.7% and 91.8% for sinusoid and gaussian networks respectively. Here, it is worth to point out that by using texture feature alone, with sigmoid network, a classification rate of 88% can be achieved. This demonstrates the rich information contained in cell surface texture.

When pgDNA is used in combination with the four perceptual features to train the network, there is a noticeable improvement for sigmoid network, from previous 94.6% to 96.9%. Sinusoid and gaussian networks archive 90.8 and 95.9 respectively. This indicates pgDNA does provide additional discriminate information. Table 1 shows the experiment results.

As long as the comparison of three networks are concerned, the sinusoid and gaussian networks seems to converge much faster than sigmoid network, but performances are somehow inferior. This is probably due to the rougher search space resulted from the activation function.

5. Discussions and Conclusion

Above described investigations present the results obtained by using different artificial neural networks for bladder cancer cell classification. Both raw data and feature vectors are used as input to the networks. Results indicate that feature extraction leads to a substantial computation saving and classification accuracy improvement. With feature vector as input, the neural network correct classification rate ranges from 86% to 97%, while with raw image input, the classification rate is just about 70%.

Comparison between networks with sigmoid, sinusoid and gaussian activation functions shows sigmoid network is able to archive higher classification rate, but sinusoid and gaussian networks converge faster. It is suggested this quicker convergence and lower classification rate are possibly due to the fact that sinusoid and gaussian network have higher degree of non-linearity. This allows the network to quickly fit the *given training data*. But also because of this non-linearity, the generalization ability suffers which can been seen from lower classification rate.

References

[Ashenayi1992a]   K. Ashenayi, J. Vogh and M. R. Sayeh, 1992, "Gaussian Perceptron Capable of Classifying "2N+1" Distinct Classes of Input Patterns," *IASTED Journal of Control and Computers*, Vol. 20, No. 2, pp. 54-60.

[Ashenayi1992b]   K. Ashenayi, J. Vogh, M. R. Sayeh, B. Karimi and T. Baradaaran, 1992, "Multiple Threshold Perceptron Using Sinusoidal Function," *IASTED Journal of Modelling and Simulation*, Vol. 12, No.1, pp.22-26.

[Hornick1989]   K. Hornick, M. Stinchcombe and H. White, 1989, "Multilayer Feedforward Networks are Universal Approximators," *Neural Networks*, Vol. 2, No. 5, pp.359-366.

[Koss1979]   L. G. Koss (Ed), 1979, "Diagnostic cytology and its histologic bases," Vol.2, pp.767.

[Noguchi1983]   Y. Noguchi, Y. Tenjin and T. Sugishita, 1983, "Cancer-cell detection system based on multispectral images," Anal. Quant. Cytol. Vol.5, pp.143-151.

[Reed1993]   T. Reed and J. Hans Du Buf, 1993, "A Review of Recent Texture Segmentation and Feature Extraction Techniques," *CVGIP:Image Understanding*, Vol.57, pp.359-372.

[Spirkovska1993]   L. Spirkovska and M. Reid, 1993, "Coares-Coded Higer-Order Neural Networks for PSRI Object Recognition," *IEEE Trans. on Neural Networks*, Vol.4, No.2, March, pp.276-283.

[Zajicek1983]   G. Zajicek, M. Shohat, Y. Melnick and A. Yegeuz, 1983, "Image analysis of nucleated red blood cells," Comp. Biomed. Res. Vol.16, pp.347-356.

A Preview I-PD Control System Using Neural Networks

Toshinobu Matsuoka, Kouichi Katsumata, Jun-ichi Shibuya,

Yoshihisa Ishida and Takashi Honda

Department of Electronics and Communication, Meiji University

Abstract

This paper presents a method to design a preview I-PD controller using neural networks. As is well known, I-PD controllers are widely used because they have good performance. However, if the controlled objects have long dead-times, the control performance of the I-PD controllers are limited. We propose a preview I-PD controller with dead-time compensation. The proposed method has the advantage of auto-tuning I-PD and feedforward gains.

1. Introduction

The I-PD controllers based on optimal control techniques are widely used for servomechanism systems because they have good performance [1]. They have also both good disturbance rejection and low sensitivity. However, if there are uncertainties of the process parameters and/or the controlled objects have long dead-times, I-PD gains should be adequately adjusted. Most process engineers tune manually I-PD (PID) gains by "trial and error" procedures. When the controlled objects have long dead-times, these gains are very difficult to tune manually [2]. In this paper, we present a method of auto-tuning I-PD gains using neural networks for such as controlled objects. The neural networks consist of three layers and are trained so as to minimize the error between the controlled object and the reference model outputs by using the conventional back-propagation algorithm [3].

At first, a preview I-PD controller using neural networks is explained. Then the network learning algorithm is precisely described. Finally, we show simulation results to demonstrate the effectiveness of the proposed method for the controlled object with long dead-time.

2. Preview I-PD control system using neural networks

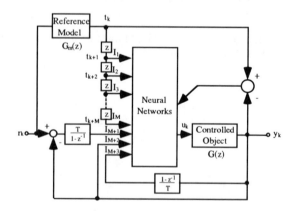

Figure 1. A preview I-PD Controller.

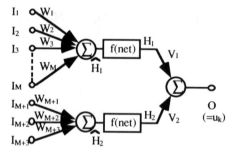

Figure 2. Neural networks.

Figure 1 shows the preview I-PD controller using neural networks. $G(z)$ is the pulse transfer function of the controlled object and $G_m(z)$ is that of the reference model. $I_1, I_2, \cdots, I_M$ are inputs for preview control. The neural networks are trained by using the conventional back-propagation algorithm to minimize the error between the controlled object and the reference model outputs. The neural networks consist of three layers as shown in Figure 2. The input layer has $M+3$ units, the hidden layer 2 units and output layer 1 unit. The output function of each unit is a linear neuron defined as follows:

$$f(x)=x \tag{1}$$

where x is the sum of the inputs. The control input u_k is derived as follows:

$$u_k=(W_1 t_{k+1}+W_2 t_{k+2}+\cdots+W_M t_{k+M})V_1+(W_{M+1}T\sum_{i=0}^{k} e_i+W_{M+2}y_k+W_{M+3}\frac{y_k-y_{k-1}}{T})V_2 \tag{2}$$

where $e_i(=r_i-y_i)$ is the control error and the integral gain K_i, the proportional gain K_p and the derivative gain K_d are respectively given as

$$K_i=W_{M+1}V_2, \quad K_p=W_{M+2}V_2, \quad K_d=W_{M+3}V_2 \tag{3}$$

3. Network learning algorithm [4]

In Figure 2, assuming that I_i is the output value of i-th node in the input layer, $\widehat{H}_j$ ($j=1, 2$), the output value of j-th node in the hidden layer, becomes

$$\widehat{H}_1=\sum_{i=1}^{M} W_i I_i \tag{4a}$$

$$\widehat{H}_2=\sum_{i=M+1}^{M+3} W_i I_i \tag{4b}$$

where W_i is the coupling coefficient between an input layer node and a hidden layer node. The outputs of the hidden layer, H_1 and H_2 are

$$H_1=\widehat{H}_1, \quad H_2=\widehat{H}_2 \tag{5}$$

Then O, the output value of an output layer node, becomes

$$O=\sum_{j=1}^{2} V_j H_j \tag{6}$$

and this equals the manipulating variable u_k.

Here, we define the error function E_k by the following equation.

$$E_k=\frac{1}{2}(t_k-y_k)^2 \tag{7}$$

The coupling coefficients between neurons are tuned by the following equations so as to minimize the error function.

$$V_j^{(k+1)}=V_j^{(k)}-\eta_1\frac{\partial E_k}{\partial V_j} \tag{8a}$$

$$W_i^{(k+1)}=W_i^{(k)}-\eta_2\frac{\partial E_k}{\partial W_i} \tag{8b}$$

where η_1 and η_2 are learning rates determining convergence speed. To process $\dfrac{\partial E_k}{\partial V_j}$ and $\dfrac{\partial E_k}{\partial W_i}$, we use the chain rule

$$\frac{\partial E_k}{\partial V_j} = \frac{\partial E_k}{\partial y_k} \frac{\partial y_k}{\partial O} \frac{\partial O}{\partial V_j} \tag{9}$$

where

$$\frac{\partial E_k}{\partial y_k} = -(t_k - y_k), \quad \frac{\partial O}{\partial V_j} = H_j$$

For simplicity, we assume that the partial derivative $\partial y_k / \partial O$ is constant.

Similarly, we have

$$\frac{\partial E_k}{\partial W_i} = \frac{\partial E_k}{\partial y_k} \frac{\partial y_k}{\partial O} \frac{\partial O}{\partial H_1} \frac{\partial H_1}{\partial \widehat{H_1}} \frac{\partial \widehat{H_1}}{\partial W_i} \quad \text{for } i = 1, 2, \ldots M \tag{10a}$$

and

$$\frac{\partial E_k}{\partial W_i} = \frac{\partial E_k}{\partial y_k} \frac{\partial y_k}{\partial O} \frac{\partial O}{\partial H_2} \frac{\partial H_2}{\partial \widehat{H_2}} \frac{\partial \widehat{H_2}}{\partial W_i} \quad \text{for } i = M+1, \, M+2, \, M+3 \tag{10b}$$

where

$$\frac{\partial O}{\partial H_j} = V_j, \quad \frac{\partial H_j}{\partial \widehat{H_j}} = 1, \quad \frac{\partial H_j}{\partial W_j} = I_j$$

4. Simulation results

Let the pulse transfer function of the controlled object be

$$G(z) = z^{-L} \frac{b_1 z + b_2}{z^2 + a_1 z + a_2} \tag{11}$$

In this simulation values of $L=4$, $a_1 = -1.529$, $a_2 = 5.323e\text{-}01$, $b_1 = 7.628e\text{-}02$ $b_2 = 6.168e\text{-}02$, M=5 and T=10msec were selected.

On the other hand, the pulse transfer function of the reference model is as follows:

$$G_m(z) = \frac{b_{m1} z^2 + b_{m2} z + b_{m3}}{z^3 + a_{m1} z^2 + a_{m2} z + a_{m3}} \tag{12}$$

where $a_{m1} = -2.71451\text{-}02$, $a_{m2} = 2.45619$, $a_{m3} = -7.40819e\text{-}01$, $b_{m1} = 1.54667e\text{-}04$, $b_{m2} = 5.74070e\text{-}04$ and $b_{m3} = 1.33047e\text{-}04$.

Figure 3 shows simulation results of the position control for the controlled object described by Eq.(11). (a) show the reference model output. (b) and (d) show the step resonse of the proposed method after the training of 1000 iterations and that before the training, respectively. (c) shows that by the I-PD controller without the preview input. Each simulation starts with an already pretuned controller. The target vector is a set of 200 training seguences. These figures illustrate the effectiveness of the proposed method.

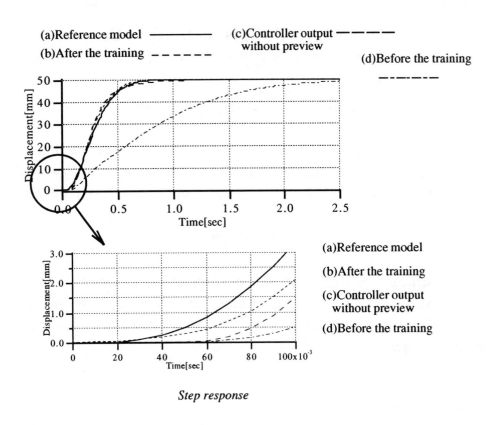

(a)Reference model ———
(b)After the training – – – – – –
(c)Controller output – – – –
without preview
(d)Before the training
– – – – – –

(a)Reference model
(b)After the training
(c)Controller output
without preview
(d)Before the training

Step response

Figure 3. Simulation results of the proposed method .

5. Conclusions

We have proposed a preview I-PD control system using neural networks. Simulation results have shown that the proposed method is effective to the position control of plants with long dead-times. This method is also effective to auto-tune I-PD gains and to the controlled objects with time-varying dead-times. We expect that this method has applicability to nonlinear systems with both unknown parameters and long dead-times by introducing a sigmoidal function.

Acknowledgments

This work is supported by the fund of the Institute of Science and Technology, Meiji University, under Intensive Research Grant for 1993-1994 Academic Year and partially by SMC Co., Ltd in Japan.

References

[1]G. F. Franklin, J. D. Powell and M. L. Workman, "*Digital Control of Dynamic Systems,*" Addison-Wesley, 1990.

[2]T. Hägglund, "*A Predictive PI Controller for Processes with Long Dead Times,*" IEEE Control Systems Magazine, Vol.12, No.1, pp.57, 1992.

[3]D. E. Rumelhart and J. L. McClelland, "*Parallel Distributed Processing: Explorations in the Microstructure of Cognition: Foundation,*" Vol.1, MIT Press, 1986.

[4]K. Endo, Y. Ishida and T. Honda, "*Gain Adjustment of I-PD Control System Using Neural Network,*" Trans. of IEE of Japan, Vol.113-C, No.6, pp.408, 1993(in Japanese).

NEURAL CONTROLLER FOR
PARALLEL CONNECTED SWITCHING FABRICS

A. García-Lopera, F. García-Oller, and F. Sandoval

Dpto. de Tecnología Electrónica; E.T.S.I. de Telecomunicación
Universidad de Málaga; Plaza El Ejido, s/n; 29013 Málaga, Spain
Telephone: 34-5-2131342, Fax: 34-5-2131447, E-Mail: AGL@ctima.uma.es

ABSTRACT

A centralized neural controller for parallel connected switching fabrics is presented. The system allows a substantial reduction in the input buffers length of the Banyan switching matrices for lossless Asynchronous Transfer Mode (ATM) communications. In addition, the architecture is fault-tolerant.

INTRODUCTION

The interconnection nodes of the Broadband Integrated Services Digital Network (B-ISDN) are based on space division multistage switching matrices. Usual software control of these switches appears inadequate to give a proper answer to the response times needed at Asynchronous Transfer Mode (ATM) frequencies (higher than 155 Mbit/s) [1]. For this reason, hardware control, which is based on application specific circuits, is used. However, this kind of control is not flexible, is not easily adapted to new conditions of the network, and even is more complex than the switching network itself. Recently, centralized control systems based on artificial neural networks (ANN) have been proposed [2]. These systems use massive parallel processing capacity and similar topology to the ANN. For an **NxN** switch (**N** inputs and **N** outputs), the neural controller proposed is a Hopfield network with **NxN** neurons, interconnected as multiple overlapping Winner-Take-All (WTA) circuits [2][3]. However, this controller suffers from two main deficiencies. First, the greater the value of **N**, the longer the input buffer queue needed. Second, the network is not fault-tolerant. In this paper, we present a centralized neural controller for parallel connected switching fabrics. The system allows a substantial reduction in the input buffers length of the Banyan switching matrices for lossless Asynchronous Transfer Mode communications, and is fault-tolerant.

PARALLEL ARCHITECTURES

The Banyan networks are self-routing networks, i.e., there is only one route through the switch for each pair of input-output addresses. This allowss the ATM cells to be routed at a high rate. However, as a drawback, the Banyan networks are blockrd either at the output or through the switch. In both cases, this may cause a non-admissible impact on the amount of ATM cells lost, specially in the case of a non-constant traffic.

To avoid the blocking problem while maintaining the self-routing capacity, we propose an architecture consisting of the parallel association of multistage interconnection networks under a centralized neural control. The neural controller analyzes the ATM cells waiting at the queues of the input buffers, selects a subset of them that does not present blocking either internal nor at the output, and guarantees that the cells do not pass through any wrong internal switch. Fig. 1 depicts the block diagram of the architecture proposed, where each switching matrix has its associated neural controller. The input buffers are common to all the switching matrices; in this way, the same ATM cell can reach the output through any of the switching matrices. Since several ATM cells can reach the same output from different inputs at the same time slot, it is necessary to establish output buffers with the appropriate minimal length. This length should not be lesser than the number of matrices in parallel.

The question is how to interconnect the individual neural controller associated to each matrix so that they behave like an unique neural controller of the association. In Fig. 2, we show the solution proposed in this paper, where the interconnection between each individual controller of the switching matrices parallel association is represented, together with the request matrices corresponding to each switch ($k=1$, $k=2$,....., $k=n$). The elements a_{ij1}, a_{ij2},...., a_{ijn}, correspond to the same input-output pair of the input matrix, which is common to all the switches. The ATM cell with the input-output addresses I_i/O_j must be directed through just one of the switches in parallel. In order to achive this, we connect all the corresponding neurons associated to the elements a_{ij1}, a_{ij2},...., a_{ijn} in a Winner-Take-All circuit, overlapped with the appropriate neuron of each individual controller. Thus, the output of each neuron inhibits all the others, and the winner neuron avoids that all the others win in their respective overlapped WTA circuits. In this way, the ATM cell is only selected by a controller.

The system operates in the following way. The request matrix is divided into **n** maximum disjoint sets which overlap with the set **C**, where **C** consists of the possible input/output addresses. Then, each neural controller sends an output matrix to its corresponding switching matrix. Therefore, the output, after the neural parallel computation, will be a maximum of **k** disjoint subsets of non-blocking ATM cells.

FAULT TOLERANCE

Since the system offers alternative routes for the same ATM cell, the proposed architecture presents a fault-tolerant scheme. A system is defined as **d-tolerant** if it maintains the same capacity to realize permutations from input addresses to output addresses when **d** internal switches are wrong. We implement this scheme by sending a excitatory signal from all those neurons associated to the internal routes that use the wrong switch, to the corresponding neurons in the parallel controllers. Thus, we guarantee that the last neurons will participate with advantage in the competition, and that the ATM cell may use any of the alternative routes. We could also get the same results if we apply an inhibitory signal to the neuron associated with the wrong internal switch.

STABILITY ANALYSIS

In a system composed of multiple switching matrices in parallel, the temporal evolution of the neurons that compose the neural controllers is governed by equation (1), which represents the neural controller state equation [4], including the external biases to the neurons, and where we have added the last two terms, $m(g(u_{ik-1}))$ and F_i, to take into account the two conditions we want our system to carry out: inhibition among neurons from different matrices and fault tolerance, respectively.

In (1), n is the number of neurons of each controller matrix in parallel; u_{ik} represents the state variable of the neuron **i**, in the matrix **k**; and w_{jik} is the weight between the neurons **j** and **i**, in the matrix **k**.

$$C_{ik}\frac{du_{ik}}{dt} = -\lambda_{ik} u_{ik} + \sum_{i=1}^{n} w_{jik} \, g(u_{jk}) + (I_i - t_i + F_i + m(g(u_{ik-1})))$$

$$where$$

$$g(x) = \begin{cases} 1 & if \ x > 1 \\ x & if \ -1 \le x \le 1 \\ 1 & if \ x < -1 \end{cases}$$

$$(1)$$

$$\lambda_{ik} = \sum_{j=1}^{n} |w_{jik}|$$

$$m(x) = \begin{cases} -2|I_i| & if \ x > -0.75|I_i| \\ 0 & otherwise \end{cases}$$

$$F_i = \begin{cases} -2|I_i| & if \ any \ switch \ of \ the \ neuron \ i \ is \ wrong \\ 0 & otherwise \end{cases}$$

The Lyapunov's energy functional associated with the system is of the form:

$$V = -\frac{1}{2} \sum_{k=1}^{p} \sum_{j=1}^{n} \sum_{i=1}^{n} w_{jik} \, g(u_{ik}) g(u_{jk}) - \sum_{i=1}^{n} \int_{0}^{u_{ik}} g'(\theta_{ik}) \theta_{ik} \, d\theta_{ik}$$

(2)

being

$$\theta_{ik} = (-\lambda_i \theta_i + I_i - t_i + F_i + m(g(\theta_{ik-1})))$$

The system is stable if the function **V** is stable, that is:

$$\dot{V} = \sum_{k=1}^{p} \sum_{i=1}^{n} \frac{\partial V}{\partial u_{ik}} \cdot \frac{du_{ik}}{dt} \leq 0 \quad ; \forall \dot{u}_{ik}$$

(3)

Since the two terms we have added in equation (1) are asynchronous, i.e., they do not depend on time, the system is stable.

SIMULATION RESULTS

For simulation purposes, we have used two different traffic models. The first one is a Constant Bit Rate (CBR) traffic model, which is a simple Bernoulli process, where one cell arrives at each time slot with a constant probability **p**. The input ATM cells are stored in the input buffers with variable length, i.e. queue depth. The second type of traffic is an ON-OFF model where the cells arrive at the ON period with a probability **p**, and the T_{ON}/T_{OFF} rate is variable. The destination addresses of the cells are uniformly distributed, being **1/N** the probability that a given output is chosen.

Each simulation was performed in three cycles of 1000 packets per cycle for each input for both types of traffic and different load conditions. We have considered individual switching matrices and parallel associations of two and three individual switching matrices. All of them were **16x16** self-routing Banyan matrices. To study the fault tolerance of the system when some internal switches fail, we have analyzed the new throughput of the system by measuring the increase of the input queues required to get zero loss.

In Fig. 3, the results obtained are shown. We observe the substantial reduction of the queue depth in the input buffers in the case of using parallel matrices. This reduction is independent of the type of traffic. The system shows its fault tolerance capacity, getting good results even in the case of five wrong internal switches; although in this case, the throughput decreases. The parallel analog process performed by the architecture indicates that the system will be able to manage the short times required in a real-time ATM network. The main drawback of the system proposed here is the need for more hardware to implement the system.

CONCLUSIONS

A centralized neural controller for the parallel association of Banyan switching matrices in an ATM network has been developed. The system reduces significantly the average queue depth of the input buffers for zero loss, as the parallel association of matrices increases. In addition, the architecture is fault-tolerant at the expense of some reduction in the throughput of the system. It has also been shown that the neural controller is stable using a Lyapunov functional.

ACKNOWLEDGMENTS

This work has been partially supported by the Spanish Plan Nacional de Banda Ancha, Project TEMA, and the CICYT project No. TIC91-0965.

REFERENCES

1. Wu, C.L. and Feng, T.Y., *Tutorial: Interconnection Networks for Parallel and Distributed Processing*, IEEE Computer Society Press, New York (N.Y.) 1984.
2. Brown, T.X., "Neural Networks for Switching", IEEE Communication Magazine, 1989, Vol. 27, No. 11, pp. 72-81.
3. Majani, E., Erlanson, R. and Abu-Mostafa, Y., "On the K-Winner-Take-All Networks", in Touretzky, D.S. (Ed.) *Advances in Neural Information Processing Systems 1*, (Morgan Kaufmann Publishers, San Mateo, CA, 1989), pp. 634-642.
4. Hopfield, J.J., "Neural Computation of Decisions in Optimization Problems", Biological Cybernetic, 1985, Vol. 52, pp. 141-152.

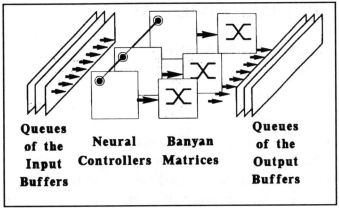

Figure 1: Parallel Conexion of the neural controllers

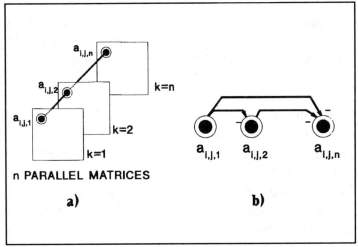

Figure 2: Conexion of neurons in the parallel controllers

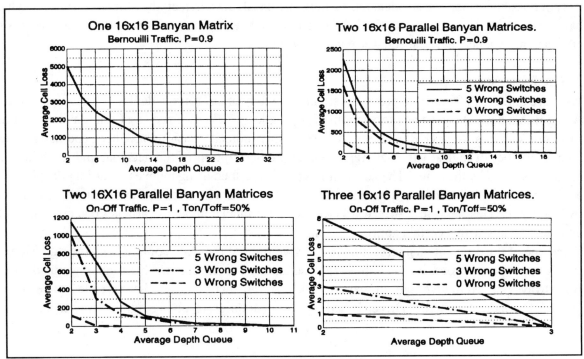

Figure 3: Simulation results

SIMULATION OF VERDICTS IN CIVIL LIABILITY

Francesco Romeo, Fabrizio Barbarossa

Dipartimento di Medodi Quantitativi, Università G. D'Annunzio, Viale Pindaro 42, 65100, Pescara, Italy.

Abstract

Using Neural Networks we have simulated judge's sentences in the field of Civil Liability Relating to Motor Vehicles. Our Neural model has been able to pass correct sentences which respect the laws and the principle of equity. The net has learnt how to judge. In fact, it has drawn out sentences equal to court precedents which were not in the training set. The back propagation procedure has calculated sets of weight which give out new information showing and quantifying the relevance of each element of guiltiness.

Our experiment demonstrates that the net is able to better manipulate the simbols than the expert systems do because it learns from training procedure both logical rules and analogical quantifications. In our opinion it is very difficult to simulate any subjective judgement without using both rules.

1. Introduction

With this experiment, we want to demonstrate the possibility of the neural nets to simulate human judgment. We would like to point out briefly that it is possible to use the nets to a symbolic manipolation (Kosko, B. 1992).

We have simulated a typical subjective judgment to prove it. One of the most typical subjective judgments is when the judge ascribes the liability for the car accidents. That judgement originates from observing the logical rules (Rules of the Road) and from a subjective method of appraisal which is unwritten result of experience.

In our opinion the application of the neural nets in that field is very appropriate. As a matter of fact, it is not possible to judge an accident basing only on logical rules. In fact, the other experiments, which have been trying to demonstrate the liability and have been carried out using the other systems of artificial intelligence, have failed (Reisinger,L.1981).

2. The Experimental Part

We have gathered 200 judicial precedents regarding judgement for accidents between two vehicles A and B that have occurred at intersections. They made up 70% of survey on Civil Liability Relating to Motor Vehicles (Alpa,G. & Bessone,M.,1982). Such judicial decisions have been codified through a large number of logical variables, representing the description of the accident and the following liability ascribed by the judge. The accident has been described using indexes regarding the place the accident occurs (intersection, stop signal, etc.) and the behaviour of the drivers involved (speed, overtaking, carelessness etc.). Afterwards we selected a small number of variables that could indicate all the accidents with a certain approximations.

Since one of the driver at an intersection has to give right of the way, coming from the right side, or from a minor priority road, in our simbolic representation, Driver A always has right of way and Driver B is always obliged to give right of way to vehicle A. Furthermore, another variable has been used (Stop B) to indicate whether Driver B had to stop in addition to giving right of way to vehicle A, according to the stop sign.

The behavior of each driver (A and B) involved has been represented by three variables. The first one (speeding) indicates whether the driver was speeding close to intersection, infringing art. 102 of Italian Higway Code.

The second variable (Carelessness) represents other breaches of the Highway Code (such as overtaking, driving off the carriageway) and elements of more general blame as resklessness and negligence of the driver (dangerous driving, carelessness, etc.). The third variable indicates the lack of skill of the driver, meaning his or her technical incapacity to prevent the accident from occurring using fitting emergency manoeuvres which a good driver could have been able to execute.

In description of the accident, seven variables have been sufficient, one indicating the presence or absence of stop signal, two group of variables respectively representing A's and B's offences.

Two numerical variables have been used to represent the judgement in terms of the quantitative attribution of blame and of liability. Such variables indicate the percentage of liability of each driver involved.

3. The Architecture and the Training of the Net

The neural net has been dividend into seven inputs, six hidden cells and two output cells [Fig. 1]. The input values represent the description of the accident and the output values the evaluation of the liability given in percentage to Driver A and B. The number of necessary hidden cells has been selected empirically. Each cell has been connected with all cells of the layer above with a sigmoid transfer function.

The net has been trained trought a set of eighty typical judgements, in which we supposed that the judge applied specifically to the field of C.L.M.V. not only the information contained in the legal provisions, but also af all the knowledge that is not included in them. The net has been trained with the back propagation procedure using the Delta Rule (Rumelhart, D.E. & McClelland, J.L. 1986) function for 8000 cycles with a learning rate of 0,2.

After training, the net has learned all the sample decisions with minimum error. This means that the backpropagation method has calculated a set of weight between the connections able to present all the given judgements.

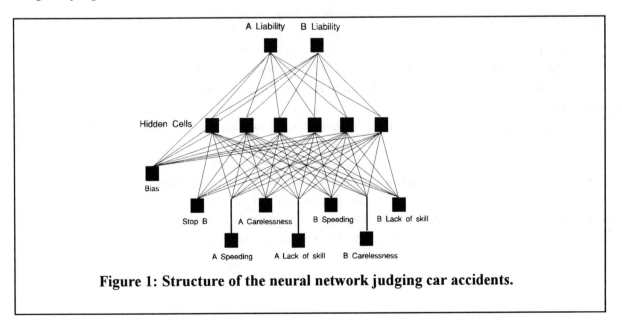

Figure 1: Structure of the neural network judging car accidents.

4. Experimental Results

The judgement meter calculated by the net allows us to judge all the possible accidents, that can be represented through the provisions with repetition of seven variables of class two (true-false).

The judgements given for the cases that have been foreseen in training appeared to be similar to case precedents and, anyway, were always reasonable acceptable.

Two phenomena can be underlined from the analysis of the judgements of the nets:

1) the net judges a case having one or more similar precedents, not by repeating or making an average of the judgements gathered (in training), but considers as more biased those precedents (even if a little different) in which the judge's evaluations appeared to be more suitable to the general evaluation principles of court precedents.

2) the net also draws out judgements in cases differing from the ones that have been gathered.

It is interesting the net verdict drawn out from the set of data representing accidents in which the driver of the vehicle with right of way is responsible only for lack of skill in his or her behaviour, basically meaning that he or she did not make the proper emergency manoeuvres an ''average driver'' would have performed. In this case whatever the offence Driver B committed (he or she had to give the way), the neural nets decides that Driver A has no liability whatsover.

The lack of skill alone of the driver is of no influence in determining liability, the same as court precedents unknown to the net (Court of Cassation, Rome, 6.3.1991).

This outcome shows that the net has learned ''legal knowledge'' that is unwritten and unforeseen in programming, and the actual relationship of importance that connect the rules one to the other depending on the described facts which are also unknown.

5. Analysis of the results

From the juridical point of view the net deducts extremely correct sentences. In fact, these nets respect every rule of the road and the net's solution does not seem to be unreasonable or incompatible with legislation or equity.

But how can the net reproduce all the judge's sentences without introducing all the logical rules (laws), used when a judge ascribes the liability to somebody ?

In our opinion, after the training, a set of weights is able to represent also a logical rules:

1)If the driver of the vehicle does not give right of way, he is liable.

2)If the driver of the vehicle drives at too high speed, he is liable.

3)If the driver of the vehicle lacks of skill in his behaviour, he is not liable.

4)If the driver of the vehicle does not respect the stop-sign, he is liable.

5)If the driver A lacks of skill in his behaviour and the driver B does not give him right of way, the driver B is liable. Etc.

These logical rules have not been taught expressly but the net has interiorized them through training.

The model is able to quantify the relative importance of the input elements. In fact, we can see in Fig. 2 the average of the weights which connects the input layer of the net with the hidden cells.

The picture shows us that the net has determined that the driver A is guiltier if he drives at too high speed than if he is careless in his behaviour. The lack of skill of the driver is of no importance.

This quantification associated with the interiorized logical rules allowes the net to infer the right quantity of liability in every possible accident which can be represented by a simple model.

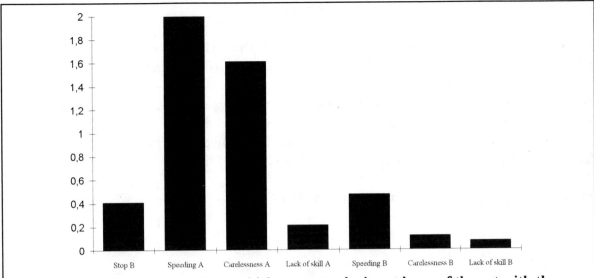

Fig.2: Average of the weights which connects the input layer of the net with the hidden cells.

6. Conclusion

We suppose to have reached two goals with our experiment:

Firstly, we have demonstrated the possibility that the judge can be replaced by a well-trained neural net. This net must respect laws, rules and a unit of value applicated by judges.

Such a neural judgement would be useful at least in the judgement of first instance and would guarantee the same judgement for every case. In fact, it is not very unusual that two different judges give two different evaluations for the same accident.

The computerization of the judgement proposed herein does not totally replace the judge's work, some points being difficoult to computerize and representing the limit of this research. These are:

1. Cases that have particular and complex aspects, involving several branches of law, the automation of which can be programmed only after the automation of all the field that are involved with the specific case.

2. Sometimes a judicial decision creates a precedent. This innovation is very important for legal regulations as it represents the alignment of already existing law to social reality. The neural net proposed herein is "conservative": it brings every new case back to the logic of his precedents.

Secondly, we think that our experiment has demonstrated that the neural nets constitute a model of a symbolic manipulation which is more powerful than the expert systems. Whereas the expert systems applicate a series of logical rules, the neural nets are able to calculate a function which represents both the logical rules and the analogical quantification (Phillips,L.1991).

First of all, we may say that the nets induce a rule from training. Such a rule, which is able to represent logical and analogical rules, will be codified in the weights of the neural net connections.

Afterwards, during the recall, they deduce the answers from the application of the rule induced by experience.

In our opinion the nets applicate a two degree process (induction-deduction) which can be used not only for a direct interpretation of the reality (video images, sounds and so on) but also for a manipulation and for a symbolic reasoning.

References

Kosko B. (1992) *Neural networks and fuzzy systems*, Prentice-Hall Inc. Englewood Cliffs, N.J.

Rumelhart, D.E. & MsClelland, J.L. (1986) *Parallel Distribuited Processing*, MIT Press, Cambridge, MA.

Reisinger L. (1981) *Legal Reasoning by analogy, a model applying fuzzy set theory* in Artificial Intelligence and legal information system, Ciampi C.(ed.), Amsterdam.

Phillips L. (1991) *Analogie und computer*, Archiv für Rechts und Sozialphilosophie, Stutgard.

Alpa G. Bessone M. (1982) *La responsabilità civile*, Giuffrè, Milano.

Acknowledgements. This research was supported by C.N.R.

SIMULATION OF HUMAN HEDONIC CHOICES

FRANCESCO ROMEO, MARIO GIACCIO

DIPARTIMENTO DI METODI QUANTITATIVI, UNIVERSITÀ G.D'ANNUNZIO, VIALE PINDARO 42, 65100 PESCARA, ITALY.

Abstract

Neural networks are able to learn structures by using typical examples of this structure as input, without necessarily knowing the rules of it, even if the data are fuzzy (Rumelhart, D.E. & McClelland, J.L.1986). Human like/dislike choices are the result of complex perceptions whose components are not known or quantifiable in their importance in decision making: this is the case for example when tasting foodstuffs (Frijters, J.E.R., 1988). Using neural networks we have simulated a human subjective choice of taste employing as input chemical data and as output the taster's choice of a Panel test about the quality of wines and oils. The nets, after training cycles with a few examples, were able to give responses to the quality of all samples with little percentage judgement difference compared to each taster and related to the average Panel's judgement. The nets worked out sets of weights that give out new information showing and quantifying the relevance of each set of input data for the individual taster's choice.

1 Introduction

Several tests have shown the particular ability of the nets, in comparison with normal algorithms, in simulating human perception (Churchland, P.S. & Sejnowski, T.J., 1992). The most researched field is that of visual cognition, where the computer should be able to recognize an object when there is a lack of information about its definition or if the bounds of it are not geometrically described (Lisberger, S.G. & Sejnowski, T.J.,1992). In a hedonic choice the computer can make a further perception step: on the basis of an already known perception, that is, of a classification already having occurred, the net should be able to work out a judgement of taste for each specific similar perception, at least saying whether the object is a good or a bad one.

The chemical analysis of foodstuffs alone generally doesn't allow inductive judgements about the individual taster's choice. The analysis performed by the sense evaluates those qualities that are not provided by the chemical analysis, even the most advanced, probably because the compound of sense information produced by the nervous system allows us to perceive those relations between sensations that are insignificant if considered separately (Wold,S. et al., 1983). Furthermore, the simulation of individual taste choices has not been sufficiently researched in AI, whereas the importance of such individual preferences is well known in decision making (Slovic, P., 1990).

The advantages of such applications are to be seen in an improvement of evaluation criteria of goods based on an increased objectivity of judgement. The computer in fact is not affected by those influences (i.e. tiredness, prejudice etc.) that can create errors in evaluation. Another advantage comes from the possibility of a standardization of judgement evaluation, because computers allow a better control of the experimental conditions and therefore a higher repeatability. This is especially true if we consider that the Panel test is now a fundamental criterion, at least in the European Community, for the trademark attribution of certain goods, as for example in the case of oil when attributing the ''extra virgin olive oil''. trade mark (Regulation EC,1987).

2 Model Description

Representative samples of wines (n°150) and olive oils (n°67) were submitted to net judgement using analytical data produced by official analysis methods. The analytical parameters we chose were for wines: Density, Alcoholic degree, Total alcoholic degree, Total reductor sugar, Dry extract, Total acidity, Volatile acidity, Ph, Ash, Total sulphur dioxide, Free sulphur dioxide, Methyl alcohol; for oils: Acidity, Polyphenols, Peroxides, $UV = K_{270}$ and $\Delta K = K_{268} - \left[\dfrac{(K_{262} + K_{274})}{2} \right]$

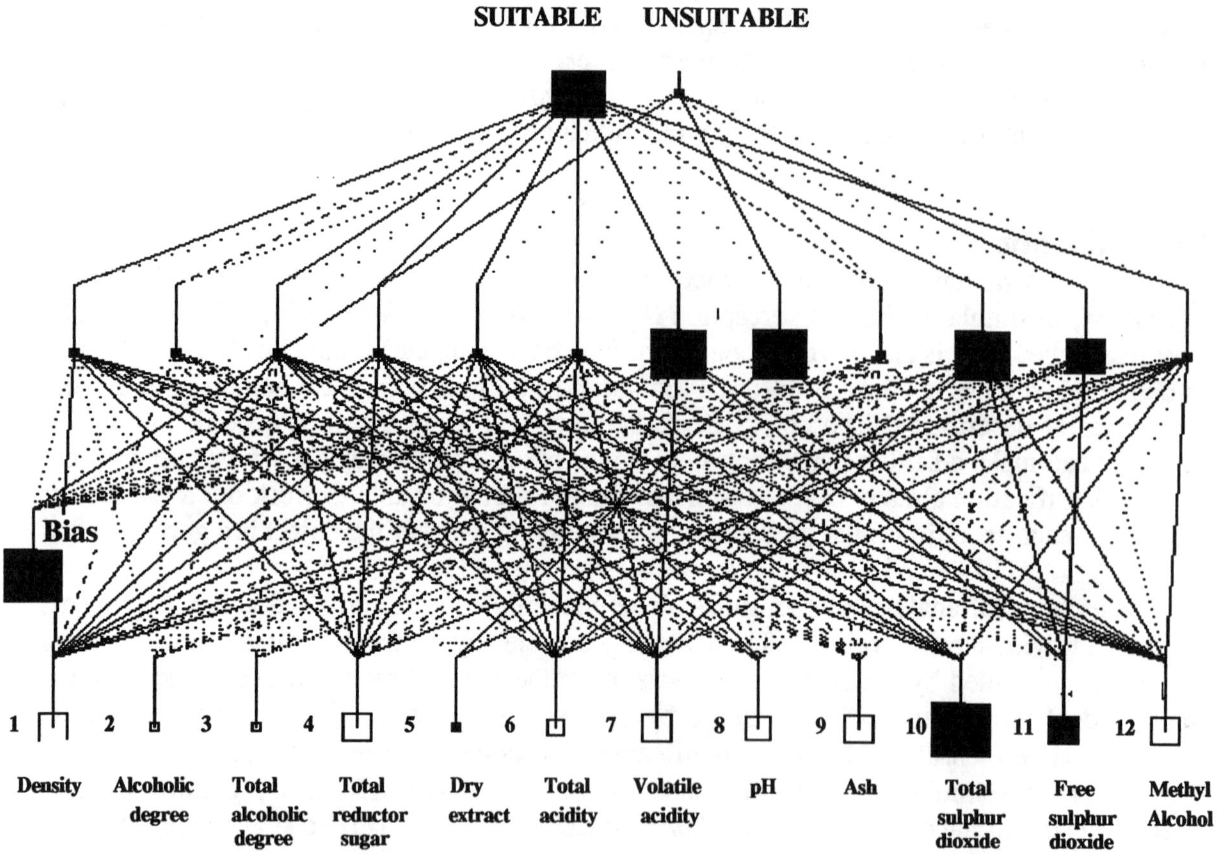

FIGURE 1: Structure of the neural network judging the suitability of a wine for the quality trademark. The 12 input units represent the chemical analisys of the wine, the two output units give out the suitability for the quality trade mark. The net is able to judge with a difference of 20% compared with the average judgements of a Panel, but with a percentage slightly over the one given by each Panel member.

The same samples were submitted to a Panel test. The wine net was made up of 12 nodes in input, 12 hidden and 2 nodes in output; and the net for oil of 5 nodes in input, 5 hidden and 1 node in output. The input data were given by the analytical values that have previously been indicated. The output data show a comparison with the judgements of the Panel of tasters and indicate whether that sample of wine or oil is suitable for the quality trademark.

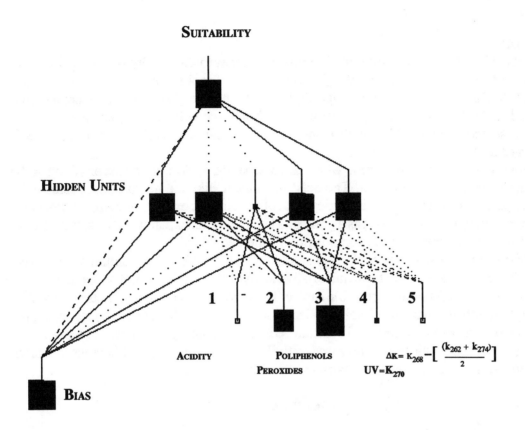

FIGURE 2: Structure of the network judging the suitability of a oil for the "extra virgin olive oil" trade mark. The net is able to judge with a difference of 6% compared with the average judgements of a Panel, but with a lower percentage compared to the one given by each Panel member.

The nets were trained through a set of 10 prototypical samples for the wines and 20 for the oils, with the back- propagation procedure using the 'delta rule' and sigmoid functions for 1,000,000 cycles.

Regarding wines, for the hedonic choice the net considers the following data important: Free sulphur dioxide, Total sulphur dioxide, Ash, pH. It is interesting to note that in commodity science a number of studies have attempted to show the existence of these correlations without however reaching an acceptable conclusion. Because this induction by the net of the principal components of the subjective judgement of a wine is interesting, we therefore tried to reproduce it in the field of olive oils where such correlations were in part already known.

The data that the net considers important for the subjective evaluation of oils are the polyphenols content and the value of peroxides. It is known that the polyphenols, natural anti-oxidants, preserve the aroma of the oils (Maga, J.A. 1978), while the peroxides are an index of the oxidation of the oils. It is interesting to note that this relationship is so reinforced in the net, that the cases in which the net was further from the taster's judgements are cases of oils in which the polyphenols and the peroxides gave a judgement that was opposite to the actual Panel one.

3 Discussion

The nets, after the training, were able to give responses to the quality or non quality of a sample with a judgement difference of 20% for wines and 6% for oils compared with the average judgement of the Panel, but with a percentage slightly over the one given by each Panel member for wines and lower for oils. The high level of correspondence with the judgements of tasters shows the non-accidental nature of the net's responses. It is certainly possible to improve the result by using larger samples.

The input data in the model used, when taken separately, do not permit anything to be inferred concerning sample evaluation. The nets' judgement, like the human one, seems to be based on the relationships between the analytical data of the sample, extracting those relationships that allow man to define a wine or a oil as a good or a bad one. This explains why a small number of analytical data is sufficient for the composition of the net.

This first result at least indicated that: 1) neural nets can simulate the qualitative subjective judgement of an individual starting from quantitative analytical data; 2) it is not necessary to have a large amount of data to obtain an acceptable subjective judgement, since neural nets process data analogically, building up a structure that is applicable to all similar information; 3) regarding the first point, a neural net is able to create information because the quantitative structure, that appears after the weights of the net have been configured by the learning procedure, simulates the unknown part of the human mental structure that causes the hedonic choice.

References

Rumelhart, D.E. & McClelland, J.L. (1986) *Parallel Distributed Processing* (MIT Press, Cambridge, MA.

Frijters, J.E.R. (1988) *in Food Acceptability* (ed.Thomson,D.M.H.) 11-25, Elsevier Applied Science, London & New York.

Churchland, P.S. & Sejnowski, T.J. (1992) *Nature* 360, 159 -161.

Lisberger, S.G. & Sejnowski, T.J. (1992) *The Computational Brain* MIT Press, Cambridge, MA.

Wold,S. et al. (1983) *in Food Research and Data Analysis, Proc. of the IUFoST Symp.* , 147-188 Applied Science Publishers.

Slovic, P. (1990) in *An invitation to cognitive science*, (eds.Osherson, D.N. & Smith E.E.) III, 89-116 MIT Press, Cambridge, MA.

Regulation EC 02.07.1987 n.1915.

Maga, J.A. (1978) *Crit. Rev. Food Sci. Nutr.* 10, 4, 332.

Acknowledgements. This research was supported by the C.N.R.

An open application framework for hybrid neural network research

Josef Mittendorfer and Alexander Berger

Cynex & HTC, A-4600 Wels Austria, Anton Brucknerstraße 6

Abstract:

In this paper NetTools, a set of tools optimised for research, evaluation and simulation in the field of artificial neural nets, fuzzy control and optimisation is presented. It is shown, that in an object oriented framework, the seamless integration of neural network components, fuzzy theory and genetic algorithms evolves naturally. The general architecture of NetTools is presented and fields of applications are reviewed.

1. Introduction

When moving from research projects to industrial strength applications the combination of different technologies becomes more and more important. There may be a neural net for noise reduction from a sensor, a fuzzy controller steering a plant or adaptive controllers optimised by an evolutionary algorithm.

Proof of concept studies, design and optimisation of such projects need a strong, versatile simulation tool, which combines ease of use and applicability to different environments.

Neural network research on the other hand requires a flexible, open and extensible framework to develop, test and evaluate new algorithms and architectures.

2. Basic architecture

The basic building block in NetTools is the network node, the basic entity of the simulation. For SimLib, the simulation engine, a node consists of three equations, which are in general represented by strings: the input function, which maps the input to the node output, an optional output function, which modifies the output and an training function which specifies the training in case of neurons.

Each node is addressed by an unique handle and stores the links to and from other connected nodes, together with the corresponding weights in its internal memory (Fig.1).

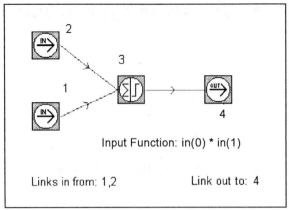

Input Function: in(0) * in(1)

Links in from: 1,2   Link out to: 4

Fig. 1

The input for SimLib is a simulation data file which consists of a header with general network informations and node characteristics mentioned above. The simulation sequence is determined by a vector, holding the node handles in the desired processing order.

There are two ways to build a simulation data file: NetMaker is a text oriented tool, which compiles network information input to the format readable by SimLib. Filter programs for established network definition languages are under development.
The second, more user friendly way is NetDesigner, a highly interactive, easy to user graphical network designer. Fig. 2 show a preliminary version of NetDesigner with a sample net loaded.

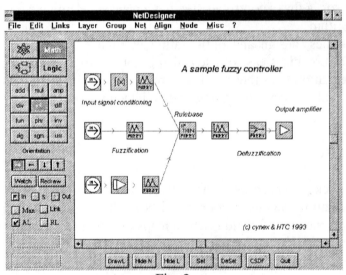

Fig. 2

For convenience 4 x 12 elements from neural networks, fuzzy and binary logic and classical control theory a predefined and represented by user editable icon. Their node functions can be globally preset, stored or individually altered in a project.
Network nodes are organised in a highly object oriented way. They can be combined to groups, which simplifies the design process enormously.
In neural network research the need for fully connected layers arises. To speed up the design of layers, a layer node object has been introduced. Layer elements are individually addressable and their input, output and training functions can be individually set.

To implement objects which are too complex for the simple three functions approach or to speed up the simulation of frequent used elements, device objects have been introduced. A device is a precompiled object, which is stored in a catalogue and retrieved from there to the current project. The design and handling process is equivalent to standard nodes. The device parameters are stored in a datafile and editable through an editor.

Fig. 3 shows the basic architecture of NetTools. Modules are project specific programs, which can be written in any language and work as interface between SimLib and project input/output (e.g. data entry modules, visualisation modules, real world interfaces,...)

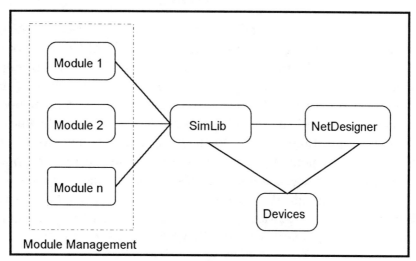

Project Management
Fig. 3

NetTools is currently implemented for the Windows 3.1 and Windows NT and written in C++ and Smalltalk. Unix platforms are under consideration.

3. Fields of applications

The open architecture of NetTools guarantees a wide range of applications (even process control). In projects neural nets, fuzzy logic, boolean logic and classical control theory can be mixed and simulated in common framework. Through modules NetTools can be adapted to any project specific task.

4. Conclusion:

Combining neural systems with fuzzy logic and classical systems simulation is easy and straight forward in an oriented framework like NetTools. The concept of network nodes is versatile enough to support different technologies and handle hybrid simulation tasks.

Adaptive Self-Organizing Concurrent Systems and their Applications

Andrew Bartczak
Department of Electrical Engineering
The University of Rhode Island
Kingston, RI 02881

Abstract

This paper overviews an adaptive self-organizing concurrent system (ASOCS) model for incremental supervised learning of boolean propositions. ASOCS is comprised of many boolean processing nodes, distributed throughout the system, to represent the presently acquired knowledge. ASOCS internal structure is effected by the training data provided by the user. ASOCS architecture synthesizes a reconfigurable network of boolean processing nodes using an adaptation unit to supervise consistency checking of the knowledge contained in the new boolean propositions relative to the existing nodes, and to minimize the system function representation. Depending upon the adaptation unit directives, boolean processing nodes interactively pass messages, add new nodes, delete redundant nodes from the network. These actions lead to self-modification and self-organization. The adaptivity issue is of major concern, as it determines the potential applications of the ASOCS model. This paper strongly emphasizes this point. In addition, actual ASOCS applications are discussed.

1   Introduction

ASOCS is a special-purpose parallel processor performing asynchronous and concurrent dataflow computations using boolean variables [1]. Self-organized learning and parallel execution form two separate phases of ASOCS operation [2]. ASOCS uses network structure modification as a means of adaptation to the new training data [3].

An instance is the atomic knowledge element used to train ASOCS. It is a boolean propositional logic rule whose antecedent is a conjunction of boolean variables representing input propositions and consequent is a single boolean variable representing output proposition, such as $AB' \Rightarrow Z$ for example, where B' is a complement of variable B, and $\Rightarrow$ is an implication operator to specify a partial boolean function. Instances, used to train ASOCS, allow arbitrary mappings of inputs to outputs and critical variable generalization [4]. Only a single presentation of an instance is necessary in ASOCS.

Adaptation phase begins with an introduction of the new instance (NI) to the system. Network structure evolves according to the changing system function. Learning proceeds using information contained in both the stored instances or old instances (OI) and the NI. During execution the system acts as a parallel network of boolean gates and returns binary output values in response to the input vector with only propagation delays of the functional nodes.

A propositional logic rule with m variables in its consequent is equivalent to the union of m instances with the same antecedents, as that of the original rule, and each containing unique output variable. ASOCS uses this paradigm to deal with multiple outputs.

The layout of this paper is as follows: section 2 discusses theoretical principles supporting ASOCS operation, section 3 describes ASOCS system architecture, section 4 presents AA2 adaptive algorithm, section 5 focuses on ASOCS applications, section 5 contains a summary and conclusions.

2   Theoretical Foundations

Based on classification criteria for intelligent computational models established by Khebbal and Goonatilake [5], ASOCS model is a sub-symbolic or adaptive system. At a higher level of abstraction though, ASOCS can be considered performing both sub-symbolic and symbolic processing depending upon responsibilities assigned to the adaptation unit. Artificial Neural Networks (ANN) and Genetic Algorithms (GA) are are representative of sub-symbolic processing. Expert systems and other machine learning paradigms exemplify symbolic processing. Verstraete discussed adaptive versus symbolic processing in more detail and talked about combinational rule-based inference systems [6]. Many researches proposed a hybrid approach to take advantage of of both adaptive and symbolic processing [5]. Using ASOCS in real-world applications should provide a fruitful ground for testing similar approaches.

Variables actually present in the instance are called critical variables, as opposed to 'don't care' variables that do not appear in the instance symbolic representation. For example,
A B C $\Rightarrow$ Z
is an instance whose critical variables are A, B, C, and 'don't' care variables are D, E. This boolean proposition is equivalent to the following set of training patterns:
A B C D' E' $\Rightarrow$ Z,
A B C D' E $\Rightarrow$ Z,
A B C D E' $\Rightarrow$ Z,
A B C D E $\Rightarrow$ Z,
each containing all the variables of the system. Hence, instance representation is a more general one than binary pattern representation typically used in discrete Artificial Neural Networks (ANN) [4].

ASOCS operation is predicated on the following principles:

Consistency.   A discriminant variable between two instances is a variable that appears in the antecedents of both instances simultaneously but with opposite polarity. Two instances, that have opposite polarity and do not have at least one discriminant variable between them, contradict each other. A set of instances that includes such pair is inconsistent. However, consistency in such a set can be restored by resolving all conflicts between the contradicting instances. To resolve such conflicts, ASOCS gives higher precedence to the newer instances. Discriminant Variable Addition (DVA) operation replaces the OI node by a node created by concatenating the OI variables with the complement of a variable that is present in the NI but not in the OI. A single node is created for every variable of this kind.

Minimization.   It is performed for the same polarity instances on a pairwise basis by applying Boolean identities [1], [7]. This leads to a more parsimonious network representation of the instance set and improves system's generalization capability. Also, network parsimony manifests critical variable generalization capability of ASOCS to handle novel input patterns from the environment [4]. Minimization is computationally demanding operation that results in drastically increased system complexity and less intuitive knowledge representation. In addition, redundant data representation may bring about inherent fault tolerance and robustness in ASOCS distributed computational system environment.

3 System Architecture

Block diagram. Figure 1 depicts ASOCS internal structure, including major functional units: Adaptation Unit (AU), Logic Network (LN), Input Binder and Router, Output Binder, and their unidirectional communication channels: Presentation Path, Test Path, Feedback Path, and a bidirectional communication channel called Broadcast Bus. Input and Output Binders connect the input and output variables to the LN. Normally, the AU and LN exchange messages via Broadcast Bus. Optionally, the AU can communicate with the LN using the Presentation Path and the Input Router. The Feedback Path is to be used in finite state machine applications.

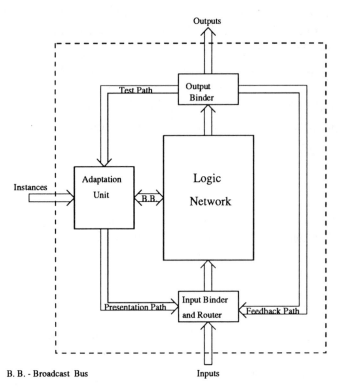

Figure 1: ASOCS block diagram

The AU receives new instances from the user and coordinates the adaptation process while learning proceeds. Processing nodes of the LN respond to the input stimulus during execution and are also active during learning to adapt the network structure to the changing instance set. The AU guides the LN through the adaptation process using global commands that specify actions the nodes perform concurrently and in a self-organizing fashion. The logic network can build itself from scratch with new interconnections being dynamically formed between nodes. For multiple outputs, ASOCS systems require separate logic networks to be associated with each output variable.

4 Adaptive Algorithm AA2

The AA2 adaptive algorithm [1], [3] represents a computed system function in a sum-of-products form with the product terms corresponding to the stored instances. This scheme relies on instances being stored implicitly in the logic network.

Hardware Support   ASOCS requires the following kind of nodes supporting AA2 adaptive algorithm operations:

1. Primitive nodes conjunct and store two variables, and indicate if these variables are present or absent in the NI.

2. Discriminant nodes of positive (negative) type represent the entire instance learned by the logic network. Critical variable list of the discriminant node is built by up by a layer of internal primitive nodes. The LN must support a dynamic interconnect between any primitive node and any discriminant node [1]. The outputs of all the positive (negative) discriminant nodes are connected to positive (negative) non-adaptive OR-plane located outside the logic network. During execution, if a positive (negative) OR-plane outputs a logic 1, the logic networks outputs a logic 1 (0). Otherwise, the output is a 'don't know' variable since the AA2 adaptive algorithm does not support generalization.

AA2 Adaptive Algorithm   It consists of four steps corresponding to global commands broadcast by the AU to the LN:

1. Instance Presentation - broadcasts the NI to the network. Only if the NI is matched by the network, indicating that ASOCS has already learned the information, adaptation is not needed and the the remaining steps of the algorithm are skipped.

2. Consistency Resolution - modifies the instances stored in the network that contradict each other. DVA operation is used to recover the uncontradicted portions of the stored instances. As a result, the number of nodes in the network may grow well beyond the number of instances actually presented in the step one of the algorithm.

3. New Node Addition - adds the NI to the LN. Since the NI contains new knowledge, a new processing node is allocated and connected to the logic network.

4. Self-Deletion - requires any portion of the network that is completely contradicted by the NI to be deleted. Redundant subnetworks, as determined by the minimization rules, may also be deleted from the logic network, optionally.

5 ASOCS Applications

Actual Applications.   The following illustrates a real world application of ASOCS system using AA2 adaptive algorithm [1]. It is a part of the flight control of an experimental aircraft tested by NASA. Based on the system specification, instances were created that expressed output variables as functions of the inputs variables utilizing a cyclic tree representation. This application used the instance data representation with a single-valued AA2 adaptive algorithm, i.e., the system was limited to instances of positive polarity only, such that the system output a logic 1 when a positive instance was matched, and a logic 0 otherwise. This positive value logic based implementation did not allow 'don't know' input or output variables. So the power of ASOCS paradigm was not fully utilized there. In fact, the activities of all the phases of the AA2 adaptive algorithm were not exercised in this case, e.g., the existing instances never contradicted each other so no consistency resolution was necessary. But most importantly, the incremental learning using instances still took place.

Other real-world application of ASOCS model include a system to perform adaptive real-time network routing in computer networks proposed by Campbell & Martinez in [8]. In addition, ASOCS model using AA1 adaptive algorithm has shown promising results when tested on standard machine learning databases requiring generalization capability, as reported in [9].

Potential Applications. Adaptivity in ASOCS model manifests its on-line learning ability. ASOCS can successfully deal with constantly varying conditions and learn in real-time in the presence of unstationary environments. In addition, ASOCS model has great promise in applications requiring critical variable generalization capability, such as:

- **Embedded Systems**, which require high speed and adaptivity to perform real-time decision making with input data obtained from the environment. ASOCS systems, by means of the concurrent combinational computing paradigm, could be successfully used to perform the desired control activities.

- **Robotics**, which falls into the category of the embedded systems and is considered its own research and application discipline. For the reasons discussed above, the ASOCS systems could speed up the adaptive activities performed by autonomous robots, such as visual tracking and navigation.

- **Pattern recognition and classification** problems lend themselves naturally to ASOCS applications because of the critical variables contained in the input data. Hence, adaptive pattern recognition should be possible with ASOCS and could be used in complex intelligent systems comprised of visual and auditory subsystems.

- **Adaptive logic devices** could be made using ASOCS systems. They, in turn, could be applied to fast prototyping of boolean circuits, that once verified could be implemented using standard fixed interconnection networks, such as programmable logic arrays, field programmable gate arrays and so on.

- **Adaptive Control and decision systems**, which output the information depending upon the input state, are within the domain of ASOCS system applications. The problems falling into this category are control of complex systems with multiple inputs and outputs, such as aircraft malfunction management and recovery system, collision avoidance, vehicle guidance, process control, and distributed traffic control. High-speed adaptive control could also be achieved in modern computers using ASOCS systems.

- **AI applications of logical inference** using ASOCS system. Specifically, a concurrent ASOCS mechanism could be applied in expert systems as an inference engine to concurrently fire rules. This would allow to process large rule bases without a noticeable slowdown in the system operation.

- **Standard ANN applications.** Training would need to be accomplished by means of rules introduced incrementally over time instead of the traditional training set methods typically applied in ANNs. As already indicated, there is an easy mapping between ASOCS instance representation and the training pattern representation used in ANN. However, substitution of instances for the training patterns would greatly diminish the critical generalization ability of ASOCS.

6   Conclusions

This paper discussed ASOCS model for incremental supervised learning. ASOCS can be trained to recognize categories in response to an arbitrary binary input vector. ASOCS enforces consistency of its instance set and minimizes internal data representation. The above abstract principles of ASOCS operation rely on message passing, adding new nodes to the network, removing old nodes from the network primitive activities, leading to self-modification and self-organization. ASOCS model supports adaptivity by means of self-modification and self-organization operations. Thus, ASOCS model has great promise in practical engineering applications.

Potential engineering applications of ASOCS model are abundant, and include embedded systems performing real-time decision making, adaptive pattern recognition, adaptive logic devices and AI applications of logical inference.

References

[1] Martinez T., "Adaptive Self Organizing Logic Networks", UCLA, Ph.D. Dissertation, 1986.

[2] Bartczak A. (1993) Distributed Knowledge Representation in Adaptive Self-Organizing Concurrent Systems. *Proceedings of the Workshop on Neural Architectures and Distributed AI*, USC, 1–6.

[3] Martinez T., Campbell D., "A Self-adjusting dynamic logic module", Journal of Parallel and Distributed Computing, Vol. 11, No. 4, pp. 303-313, 1991.

[4] Martinez, T., "Consistency and Generalization of Incrementally Trained Connectionist Models", Proceedings of the International Symposium on Circuits and Systems, pp. 706-709, 1990.

[5] Goonatilake S., Khebbal S., "Intelligent Hybrid Systems", Proceedings of the First Singapore International Conference on Intelligent Systems, Singapore, September 1992.

[6] Verstraete R., "Assignment of functional responsibility in Perceptrons", UCLA, Ph.D. Dissertation, 1986.

[7] Martinez, T., "Adaptive Self-organizing Concurrent Systems", Progress in Neural Networks, Ablex Publishing, Vol. 1, Ch. 5, pp. 105-126, 1990.

[8] McDonald K., Martinez T., Campbell D., "A Connectionist Method for Adaptive Real-Time Network Routing", Proceedings of the 4th International Symposium on Artificial Intelligence, pp. 371-377, Cancun, Mexico, 1991.

[9] Martinez T., A Generalizing Adaptive Discriminant Network", WCNN'93 Proceedings, pp. 303-313, October 1993.

Classifying Aphasic Syndromes By Means of Connectionist Models

M.-D. Soriano López
Institute for Medical Informatics and Biometry
Aachen University of Technology
maria@kolleg.informatik.rwth-aachen.de

K. Willmes
Department of Neurology of the Aachen University Hospital
Aachen University of Technology
willmes@rwth-aachen.de

Abstract—Since standard stochastic models were not successful in classifying subtypes of aphasic syndromes, the performance of modified Multilayer Perceptrons (MLP's) in solving this task is tested. The choice of an appropriate network structure and of a new training strategy (so called probabilistic learning) enabled the network to be trained for the classification of the whole sample of about thousand aphasia examinations according to the neurolinguistic coding. Like any other prognosis or classification procedure, however, the MLP is susceptible to capitalizing on chance. Cross-validation techniques must be applied to assess the generalization properties of the network. Their application during the learning phase leads to a new termination criterion which avoids overgeneralization. Nevertheless, for the classification of aphasia examinations this leads to a considerable drop in classification quality. It is recommended that the examination of classification and prognosis properties of connectionist network models should be carried out with the same rigor as for multivariate statistical procedures in order to prevent unrealistic expectations concerning the potentials of network algorithms. Finally, inversion of networks is used to detect the criteria for the classification decision. This is intended to serve as a tool for the analysis of knowledge representations in connectionist models such as MLP's.

1. Introduction

Aphasias are central language disorders caused by brain lesions acquired at an adult age. Linguistically, they can be described as disturbances in different components of the language system (phonology, lexicon, syntax and semantics). In most cases, they are the result of a cerebrovascular accident (stroke) affecting parts of the language areas of the brain located with most people (over 95%), in the left hemisphere of the brain. About 40% of patients suffering from stroke present with aphasia (Poeck 1987).

In clinical aphasia research, six major categories of aphasia syndromes are distinguished. Within each category, several (between six and eight) subtypes can be differentiated according to the quality of their aphasic symptoms. On the whole, 48 different subtypes can tentatively be distinguished.

At the Department of Neurology of the Aachen University of Technology the Aachen Aphasia Test (AAT), has been developed for the examination of German-speaking patients. With the aid of this test, a test profile consisting of 24 test variables is obtained for each patient (Huber et al. 1984). For standard diagnostic purposes this detailed test profile is reduced to 11 summary variables, serving as a basis for the identification of aphasia as well as for a statistical classification of aphasic syndromes.

Up to now, neurolinguists have arrived at a detailed classification of subtypes of aphasic syndromes on the basis of clinical impression. Descriptions of the characteristic features of each aphasia subtype have so far been lacking sufficient psychometric foundation. Attempts to use statistical methods for the classification of aphasias by subtypes and for the identification of their respective features have so far led to no satisfactory results, due to the large discrepancy in the occurrence of individual subtypes. For this reason we used connectionist models to tackle this problem. Multilayer perceptrons (MLPs) according to Rumelhart, Hinton and Williams (Rumelhart et al. 1986) were found to be of special interest.

Figure 1 describes the greatly varying frequency of subtypes in the set of 996 test profiles on which the analysis was based.

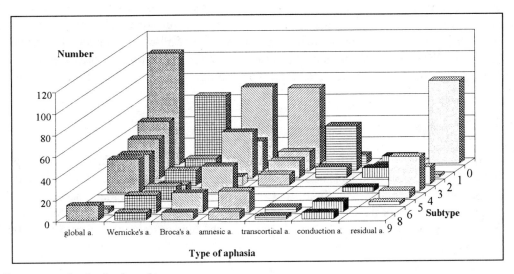

Fig. 1 Frequency of aphasias by subtypes

The features characterizing this classification problem are typical of many medical classification problems, especially for differential diagnosis:

- In the different categories, the incidence of objects differs considerably.
- The number of objects per category often is too small in relation to the respective number of object features.
- No multivariate normal distribution for the set of variables considered can be assumed.
- There is no homogeneity of variance-covariance matrices of feature vectors among the diagnostic categories.

Any solution for such a classification problem should accomplish correct classification of new cases not known to the system (**generalization capacity**). Furthermore, **discriminating features** should be identified which have been responsible for establishing an individual's classification.

2. Multilayer networks for the detailed diagnosis of aphasia by subtypes

The multilayer network is designed in two phases. The first phase aims at determining training strategy, network structure and network dimension leading to a correct classification of all cases in the sample. The general adequacy of the network for the solution of the classification problem under discussion is ensured in this way. Procedures such as weight-decay and choice of a suitable termination criterion are introduced only during the second phase to counteract overgeneralization.

Training with the aid of a MLP without a hidden unit layer was tried first. Elements from just two of the 48 categories were identified correctly. Accordingly, all further trials were made with MLP's comprising a hidden unit layer. For the determination of the number of hidden units, the upper limit established by Baum and Haussler (Baum 1990) was employed. Experiments were carried out with MLP's using this fixed dimension to find a suitable training strategy.

Probabilistic learning

Commonly used training strategies like sequential, periodical or batch learning did not lead to learning the entire set of samples in MLP's with one layer of hidden units. Elements from low-frequency categories in particular were classified incorrectly in each case. For this reason, a new probabilistic training strategy was introduced. The idea is to make the presentation rate of patterns proportional to the difficulty with which they are learned. During the training process calculation of the actual local error for all patterns to be learned is carried on continuously. Depending on the size of its local error, the probability of a pattern being presented to the network and of weights being adjusted increases. This training strategy made learning of 97% of all cases possible. The remaining 3% could not be learned even after different initialization of the system. It was found that they represented erroneous diagnoses due for instance to the confusion of syndrome and subtype coding. After correction, all cases could be classified correctly.

Network architecture

Once a suitable training strategy had been found, the number of hidden units was reduced as far as possible without reducing the number of cases that could be learned to prevent overgeneralization. The number of hidden units could thus be reduced from 67, the Baum-Haussler limit, to 45. Afterwards, complete-linkage hierarchical cluster analysis was carried out on the activations of the hidden units for all cases. Each cluster contained vectors belonging to two or three different and not just one aphasic syndrome. Apparently, the hidden units also served to distinguish aphasic syndromes from each other.

This observation led to the splitting of the network into sub-networks by cancelling links between hidden units and output units belonging to different aphasic syndromes. Thus, all subtypes of the same aphasic syndrome were learned in *one* sub-network and those belonging to different aphasic syndromes in different sub-networks. This network architecture consisting of sub-networks is shown in figure 2.

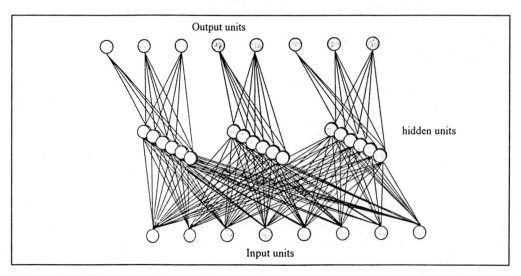

Fig. 2 Network architecture consisting of sub-networks

The dimensions of the sub-nets were then adjusted to the size of the corresponding sub-classification problem. The number of hidden units was determined for each sub-network separately, in order to obtain the lowest number of units still permitting a correct classification of all cases concerned. During the learning phase, the criteria for the assignment of an output vector to a specific subtype take into account only the output activations of subtypes of one aphasic syndrome. All output activations continue to be taken into account in evaluating the entire network, thus ensuring an unequivocal categorization. In structuring the network architecture in this way, the number of weights was reduced by two thirds although there was a slight increase in the overall number of hidden units needed.

The division of the network into sub-networks shortened the learning phase in two ways: on the one hand, less weights had to be adjusted, and on the other hand the parallel calculation of sub-networks using different processors was possible. The number of back-propagation-steps during the learning phase of each sub-network was reduced.

As expected, when analysing the learning phases of the different sub-networks, the training process within each net is concerned primary with the distinction between subtypes. It appears that, initially, all elements of the training set are chosen with similar frequency. The further advanced the learning phase, the greater is the frequency of presentation of sample elements belonging to the particular sub-network.

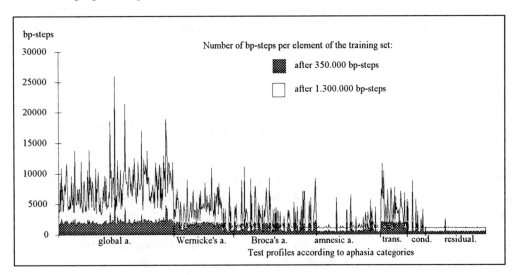

Fig. 3 Number of back-propagation steps executed within the sub-network for global aphasia per element of the training set after 1.300.000 bp-steps

With this, the first phase of designing the network is finished, determining training strategy, network structure and network dimension.

Overgeneralization

During the second phase of network design, only two thirds of all cases were used for training. The remaining third was taken for testing the generalization capacity of the network. Already during the first phase of network design, the number of hidden units has been reduced as far as possible. In this way we tried to avoid overgeneralization (Chauvin 1989) apart from acceleration of the learning phase. Weight-decay was used as a further means to counteract overgeneralization (Nowlan et al. 1991).

Already during the learning phase itself, the error rates for both the training and the test sets were calculated. During training the error rate for the test set first decreases but then starts to become bigger again whereas the error rate for the training set continues to go down. This point during the learning phase indicates when the network starts to overgeneralize. It was chosen as the suitable moment to stop the learning phase. The test set can then no longer be used for determination of the true generalization capacity of the network. Otherwise, the objection would be justified that the network has been trained on the test set. For this reason, the entire set is divided into three parts of the same size, the training set, the 'development' set and the actual test set.

For the determination of the expected error rate for this type of network and for the given set, the cyclic hold-out method was used for this threepartite partition and it was repeated for three different initializations. The result was an error rate of 0.72. Incorrect classifications were in two thirds of all cases due to a confusion between subtypes within an aphasic syndrome, resulting in an expected error rate of 0.3. Apparently, given this sample of aphasic patients networks of this type cannot be used successfully for the classification of aphasic subtypes.

Several reasons can be account for the high amount of generalization errors:
First, the very low number of cases for some subtypes must be mentioned. Furthermore, the boundaries between subtypes are poorly determined. A further reason may be seen in the quality of data obtainable from a clinical aphasia test. The different components of the test profile do not have proven metric properties. One realizes the basic difficulty of arriving at an exhaustive measurement of qualitative speech disturbances of an aphasic patient through the use of quantitative test scores. The question remains unanswered whether a classifier for a differential diagnosis of subtypes can be determined at all. Classification according to syndromes war however comparable to results obtained from nonparametric dicriminant analysis

3. Analysis of multilayer networks

To attain insight into the criteria on which any classification by means of a network is based, two questions should be answered:

- According to which criteria does the network assign a given feature vector to a specific category?
- Do criteria exists within the network which are decisive for the assignment of feature vectors to a given category, and if so, which?

Two procedures, 'contribution analysis' (Sanger 1989) and 'inversion of a network' (Linden et al. 1989), were examined. Only inversion led to satisfactory results. Through inversion, the input vector is reduced to the features decisive for classification. Only those input units which represent the discriminating features exceed a prespecified low threshold value (minimal positive discriminating features), or they remain below a particular high threshold value (minimal negative discriminating features). The classification of this decesive feature vector when taken as an input vector is identical to that of the original feature vector. Thus, the first question seems to be answered.

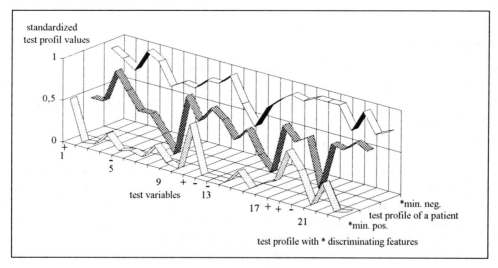

Fig. 4 Test profile with minimal positive and minimal negative discriminating features

Second, it becomes apparent that all elements of a class are reduced in a very similar manner. The ten most prominent features of each element of the set were ordered according to size. Calculating the average result for all elements of a category, one may interpret the features with the highest rankings to be criteria for each category responsible for the classification.

Even without using the actual cases from a subtype it is possible to obtain comparable results. To achieve this, the reduction of the input vector starts with each component being set to a maximum (or minimum) value. Both procedures lead to classification criteria bearing a strong resemblance to each other. They both provide an answer to the second question.

Conclusions about the measure of coincidence between the discriminating features defined here and the actual criteria pertaining to the assignment of feature vectors to a certain category are hardly possible on the basis of the example of aphasia diagnosis presented here. Throughout, the networks fail to be successful in terms of generalization.

Linden and Kindermann (1989) present the first type of inversion approach only for binary coded data. As far as the present classification problem is concerned, however, the value or rather the relationship of values of individual features respectively is decisive for a definite classification. Whether the definition of minimal positive and negative discriminating features is sufficient for characterizing the classification proposed by the network so far remains unanswered.

The assumption seems justified that discriminating features can be extracted from complex data sets on the basis of generalizing networks by means of the procedures discussed above. Negative discriminating features in particular were in good correspondence with the leading symptoms of the aphasia subtypes.

4. Application of the connectionist classifier

The program modules developed in this study were integrated with the existing system for the processing of AAT data (Willmes et al. 1987) already in existence at the Department of Neurology in Aachen. Thus, an additional tool for the classification of aphasia, apart from the procedure of nonparametric discriminant analysis can be used by clinical practitioners. Furthermore, it is possible to identify subtypes of aphasic syndromes and to analyze the respective criteria decisive for classification. Results, however, due to the high rate of generalization errors, can only be treated as preliminary as far as a definition according to subtypes is concerned.

Nonetheless, these criteria can help the neurologists and neurolinguists to check their own, partly intuitive criteria, which hopefully will lead to a clearer differentiation of subtypes of aphasic syndrome in the future.

Baum, E.B. (1990): When are k-nearest neighbour and backpropagation accurate for feasible sized sets of examples? In: L. B. Almeida & C. J. Wellekens (eds.): **Neural Networks**, 2-25. Berlin: Springer

Chauvin, Y. (1989): A back-propagation algorithm with optimal use of hidden units. In: D.S. Touretzky (ed.):**Advances in Neural Information Processing Systems I (Denver 1988)**, 519-526. San Mateo: Morgan Kaufmann

Huber, W., Poeck, K., Willmes, K. (1984): The Aachen Aphasia Test. In F.C. Rose (ed.): **Progress in aphasiology** (pp. 291-303). New York: Raven Press.

Linden, A., Kindermann, J. (1989): A correlative view on backpropagation. In: R. Pfeiffer, Z. Schreter, F. Fogelman-Soulie, L. Steels (eds.): **Connectionism in perspective** (pp. 377-384). New York: Elsevier science publishers

Nowlan, S.J., Hinton, G.E. (1991): **Simplifying neural networks by soft weight-sharing**. San Diego, CA: Computational Neuroscience Laboratory, The Salk Institute

Poeck, K. (1987): **Neurologie**. Heidelberg: Springer, 7. Auflage.

Rumelhart, D.E. Hinton, G.E., Williams, R.J. (1986): Learning internal representations by error propagation. In: D.E. Rumelhart & J.L. McClelland (eds.): **Parallel Distributed Processing: Explorations in the Microstructures of cognition Vol.I** (pp. 319-362). Cambridge, MA: MIT Press.

Sanger, D. (1989): Contribution Analysis: a technique for assigning responsibilities to hidden units in connectionist networks **Connection Science**, 1, 2, 115-138

Willmes, K., Ratajczak, H. (1987): The design and application of a data- and method base system for the Aachen Aphasia Test. **Neuropsychologia**, 25, 4, 725-733

THE COOPERATIVE - COMPETITIVE NETWORK:
A NEURAL NETWORK METHOD FOR MAKING ASSIGNMENTS

Alianna J. Maren and Robert Pap
Accurate Automation Corporation
7001 SHALLOWFORD Rd., Chattanooga, TN 37343

ABSTRACT

The multilayered COoPerative - COMpetitive (COPCOM) network is an assignment network; it determines which items in a given set have closest similarity across a set of relationships. It is possible to use this network to form a hierarchical cluster representation of a set of objects. This network has a wide range of applications uses, ranging from perceptual grouping for image understanding to target-to-track assignment. The generic, powerful, and yet simple nature of this network make it a reasonable choice for many assignment tasks.

1. ORIGINS OF THE COOPERATIVE-COMPETITIVE NETWORK

COPCOM operates as an assignment network. There are several ways in which it can be used. It can make the best one-to-one assignments between elements of one set to those in another, it can find the closest one-to-one matches within a given set of elements, or it can find "clusters" of related elements within a given set. When applied recursively, COPCOM can be used to build a hierarchical representation of the structure (clustering) of a set of elements.

Although the multilayer COoPerative-COMpetitive (COPCOM) network architecture was developed for use in image understanding, it has broad applications uses. It is historically related to the Boundary Contour System (BCS) [Grossberg & Mignolla, 1985a&b]. The primary difference between COPCOM and predecessor cooperative-competitive neural networks is that the predecessors such as BCS operate on the *spatial relationship between image points*, and the COPCOM network operates on the *feature relationships between distinct units*. The difference is one of level of abstraction. Because COPCOM can use different types of features as appropriate, it can be used for a wider range of applications than can the BCS network. It is able to create abstract clusters of most closely related units out of an ensemble of units.

2. OVERVIEW OF NETWORK STRUCTURE AND OPERATIONS

COPCOM operates by making the easiest assignments first, followed by progressively more difficult assignments. "Easiest" assignments are those which are characterized by both
- Greatest similarity (cooperation) between units that will be matched, and
- Least similarity (competition) with those units that will compete with, but will not be included in the match.

This means that the COPCOM process follows a form of iterative minimaxing operation.

COPCOM operates on a set of similarity metrics for pairwise relationships of units. COPCOM works best if there are multiple dimensions in which similarity metrics can be obtained. If there are l different types of relationships that will be used, then the cooperative-competitive network will use l different subnets at a certain layer of operation. Each of the l subnets will consider all the appropriate pairwise relationships between units. Interactions within and between the subnets produce values for pairwise relationships which, when aggregated, identify the best pairwise or clusters of matches.

2.1 Structure

In the multilayered COPCOM structure, the elements of the first "layer" refer to the units which are to be associated with each other. The nodes in all higher layers refer to the *pairwise relationships between these units.* For a set of n items, there would be n nodes in Layer 1. The nodes in Layers 2-5 represent the strength of pairwise relationships between items in the set, not to the individual items themselves. This means that for a set of n items, there are $n*(n-1)/2$ nodes in each subnet, to accommodate that number of pairwise relationships. When the COPCOM network is used to uniquely assign elements of set A to elements of set B, then a total of $n*m$ relationships can be considered, where n is the number of elements in set A, and m those in set B.

COPCOM consists of five conceptual layers, as illustrated in Figure 1. These layers perform the following major functions:

Layer 1: Stores information about each of the original units, which is used to create similarity metrics for relationships between the units.

Layer 2: Stores initial information about pairwise relationships between different units. Propagates this information to Layer 3, and passes cooperative and competitive signals proportional to relationship strengths to elements in Layer 3. Layers 2 and 3 are each composed of a set of isomorphic subnets, one subnet per relationship type.

Layer 3: Stores values which result from original values plus cooperative (positive) and competitive (negative) signals passed up from Layer 2.

Layer 4: Combines signals from all subnets in Layer 3.

Layer 5: Contains thresholded (winning) values from Layer 4. Only the strongest values from Layer 4 survive thresholding (whether histogram-based or winner-takes all) and propagate to Layer 5. These winning elements in Layer 5 correspond to the most closely-related possible pairwise matches.

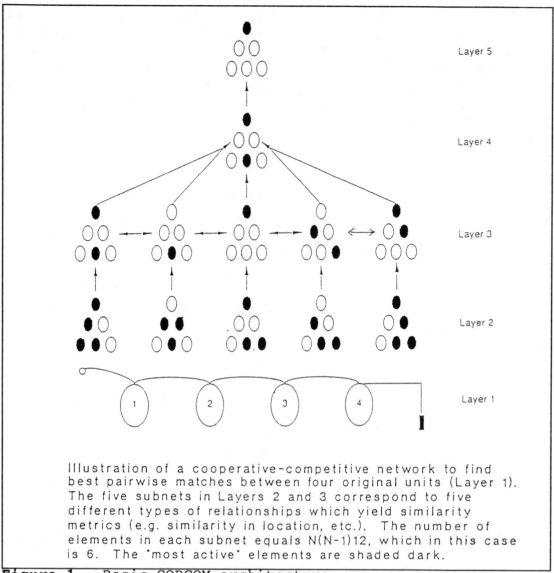

Illustration of a cooperative-competitive network to find best pairwise matches between four original units (Layer 1). The five subnets in Layers 2 and 3 correspond to five different types of relationships which yield similarity metrics (e.g. similarity in location, etc.). The number of elements in each subnet equals N(N-1)12, which in this case is 6. The 'most active' elements are shaded dark.

Figure 1. Basic COPCOM architecture.

The user must define his or her own metric for determining the initial strengths to load into the nodes in Layer 2. Typically, an exponential decay distance function is used. Thus, when the "distance" between two items in any dimension is 0, the strength of the node in the subnet for that dimension is 1. As the "distance" between two items increases, the strength value put into the Layer 2 subnet node decreases towards 0.

COPCOM has feedforward connections between all layers. The feedforward connections between most layers are strictly of like-node to like-node. For example, the feedforward connection of the Subnet A node for pair (i,j) at Layer 2 connects to the corresponding node in Subnet A in Layer 3. Similar connections hold between the nodes in Layer 4 to the nodes in Layer 5. In going from Layer 3 to Layer 4, each node in each of the subnets in Layer 3 goes to the single corresponding node in the single subnet at Layer 4.

There are lateral connections between the nodes at Layer 2. The connections between a subnet at Layer 2 (e.g. Subnet A) to a nodes in a different subnet at Layer 2 (e.g. Subnet B) are all inhibitory. For a node representing the item pair (i,j), there is an inhibitory connection to all nodes representing an item pair containing either i or j. The lateral connections from one subnet to another are all excitatory. For a node representing the item pair (i,j) in Subnet A at Layer 2, there is an excitatory connection to all item pair (i,j) nodes in all other subnets (e.g. Subnets B..N) at Layer 2.

This is illustrated in Figure 2, which shows how a single strong unit in a subnet in Layer 2 might influence the values in a subnet in Layer 3. In addition to receiving the cooperative and competitive inputs from Layer 2, each unit in Layer 3 also receives a direct copy of the value from its corresponding unit in Layer 2. This amounts to copying over the values from Layer 2 to Layer 3, and modifying those values with cooperative and competitive signals. This is done using two layers, so that the cooperative and competitive signals sent from Layer 2 to Layer 3 are based on the original values stored in Layer 2 and are not distorted in incoming signals.

2.2 Dynamics

When Layer 2 subnet nodes receive their input from Layer 1, they pass excitatory and inhibitory signals to each other, and sum each of these to their existing strength. The resultant is passed up to Layer 3 nodes. At Layer 3, the nodes are thresholded, and the nodes with surviving activations send signals to the single subnet in Layer 4, which sums (for each node representing a pairwise combination of items) each of the inputs. This is then again thresholded, and the resultant passed to Layer 5. Excited Layer 5 nodes represent the strongest pairwise combinations. They may be accessed in one of several ways; finding the maximal-strength winner, finding all nodes with excitations above a certain threshold, etc.

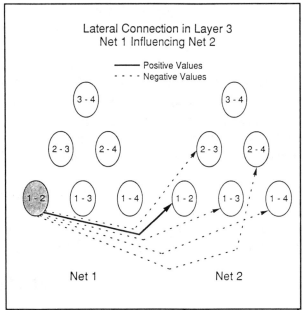

Figure 2. Cooperative (———) and competitive (- -) interactions.

2.3 Learning

Connections strengths are typically set before the network is used, and are not adapted during network use. The possibility of adapting the connection strengths is an open research issue, and would provide a means of generating context-sensitivity or sensitivity to *a priori* expectations. The parameters which should be set by the operator, and which remain fixed during network operation, are the relative strengths of the inter- and intra-net connections. Also, the thresholds for cutting off the transfer of activations from Layer 4 to Layer 5 can be set by the user.

3. COPCOM APPLICATIONS

COPCOM was originally designed to produce a Hierarchical Scene Structure (HSS) for use in image understanding. The HSS would be a structured representation of the segmented regions of an image. Regions which were related by proximity, boundary line continuation, similarity of intensity, and other factors would be grouped together. However, COPCOM's ability to create clusters based on similarity metrics across multiple relationship types makes this network useful for several different applications, including:

- Identifying best one-to-one matches out of a possible set of many-to-many matches which is useful for sensor data association and target-to-track assignments [Pap, 1990; Maren et al., 1992]
- Forming hierarchical data structures which represent the perceptual organization (identify most salient combinations of features) in an image or set of time-varying data, which is useful for image interpretation and automatic target recognition [Maren, 1988; Maren et al., 1989a&b; Maren & Minsky, 1990; Maren et al., 1990; Minsky, 1991], and
- Combining different votes to arrive at a 'best-choice' classifier from several different classifiers.

Because the COPCOM architecture is so intuitively obvious, we believe that applications for this new neural network have just begun. We find this network to be an excellent exemplar of the cooperative-competitive class of networks [Maren et al., 1990], and has as wide an application utility as exemplars of other main classes, such as the multilayer Perceptron and the Hopfield networks. We anticipate seeing a wide range of applications being developed in the future.

ACKNOWLEDGEMENTS

We would like to acknowledge support for this work under Phase I SBIR Contract N00014-93-C-0265, funded by the Office of Naval Research.

REFERENCES

Grossberg, S., & Mingolla, E. (1985a). "Neural dynamics of perceptual grouping: Textures, boundaries, and emergent segmentation," *Psychological Review*, **92**, 141-171.

Grossberg, S., & Mingolla, E. (1985b). "Neural dynamics of form perception: Boundary completion, illusory figures, and neon color spreading," *Psychological Review*, **92**, 173-211.

Maren, A.J. (1990). "Multilayer Cooperative / Competitive Networks," in A.J. Maren et al. (Eds.) *Handbook of Neural Computing Applications*. New York: Academic.

Maren, A.J., & Ali, M. (1988). "Hierarchical Scene Structure representations to facilitate image understanding," *Proc. First Int'l. Conf. Indus. & Eng. Appl. of AI & Expert Systems* (Tullahoma, TN; Jun. 1-3, 1988).

Maren, A.J., Harston, C.T., and Pap, R.M. (1989a), "A hierarchical data structure representation for fusing multisensor information," *Proc. SPIE Technical Symposia on Aerospace Sensing, Sensor Fusion Section* (Orlando, FA; March 27-31, 1989).

Maren, A.J., Lothers, M.D., Pap, R.M., & Akita, R.J. (1992), "Neural network sensor data fusion methods for air traffic control," *Proc. Fifth Nat'l. Conf. on Sensors and Sensor Fusion.* (Orlando, FL: Apr. 20-24, 1992.)

Maren, A.J., & Minsky, V.M (1990). "Representing the perceptual organization of segmented images using hierarchical scene structures," *J. Neural Network Computing*, **1** (Winter), 14-33.

Maren, A.J., Pap, R.M., & Harston, C.T. (1989b), "A hierarchical structure approach to multisensor information fusion," *Proc. Second Nat'l. Symposium on Sensors and Sensor Fusion* (Orlando, FA; March 27-31, 1989).

Minsky, V.M. (1990). *A Multilayer Cooperative / Competitive Method for Grouping and Organizing Related Image Segments*, Master's Thesis, The University of Tennessee Space Institute, Tullahoma, TN.

Pap, R.M., Harston, C.T., Maren, A.J., Parten, C., & Akita, R.J. (1990), "Target identification using neural networks for sensor fusion," *Proc. Third Nat'l. Conf. on Sensors and Sensor Fusion* (Orlando, FA; April 16-20, 1990).

Comparison of a Backpropagation Network and a Nonparametric Discriminant Analysis in the Evaluation of Sleep EEG Data.

M.Grözinger[a], B.Freisleben[b], J.Röschke[a]
[a]Department of Psychiatry, University of Mainz,
Untere Zahlbacher Straße 8, 55131 Mainz, Germany
and [b]FB12, University of Siegen, Hölderlinstraße 3
57068 Siegen, Germany

Abstract
As previously shown neural networks can successfully be used to detect
Rapid Eye Movement (REM) sleep stage from EEG data. The EEG signal
was preprocessed in time periods of 20 seconds and presented to a neural
network as a six dimensional vector of real numbers. Backpropagation was
used as the training algorithm. The percentage of correctly classified time
periods was 89% for data not belonging to the training set. In comparison to
the results of a classical nonparametric discriminant analysis algorithm the
network proved to be clearly superior for data not belonging to the calibration
data set resulting in a decrease of the average error rate between 19% and
30%. Different parameters and networks are compared.

Introduction
The course of sleep stages - the sleep architectur - is an important clinical
indicator in judging sleep disturbances. For manual evaluation EEG, EOG
and EMG information is used to determine the sleep profile from sleep EEG
data according to Rechtschaffen and Kales (1968). Some work has been
done on the automatic recognition of sleep stages (Ferri et al. 1989, Kubicki
et al. 1989). More recently other authors have applied neural networks to
solve this problem (Mamelak et al. 1991, Roberts and Tarassenko 1992,
Grözinger et al. 1993). Since a backpropagation algorithm worked very well
in detecting REM sleep in our clinical situation, we were curious to compare
these results with a more classical mathematical analysis. As we did not
expect the data to be normally distributed, a nonparametrical method seemed
appropriate.

Methods

Following an adaption night polysomnographic registrations were performed from five healthy volunteers in two separate nights each. The continous EEG data flow at P_Z and C_Z was analysed in 1440 consecutive time intervals each consisting of 2048 data points sampled with a precision of 12 bit and a frequency of f_S= 100 Hz. Thus the time intervals were about 20 seconds. The monopolar signal C_Z/A_1 was digitally filtered into 6 frequency bands as usually used in EEG analysis: 0.5 - 3.5 Hz, 3.5 - 7.5 Hz, 7.5 Hz -15 Hz, 15 Hz - 35 Hz, 35 Hz - 45 Hz and 0.5 - 45 Hz. The Root-Mean-Square (RMS)-variation of each frequency range over time was calculated. The result - a vector of 6 real numbers - was used as input to the network, which consisted of 6 input -, 4 hidden - and 1 output neuron. The different layers were totally connected. The input neurons were linear, the hidden and the output neurons had a sigmoid output function and were connected to a threshold neuron leading to 33 synapses. A generalized backpropagating algorithm was used as the learning rule for computer simulation. The software program was provided by the Neural Networks Research Group University of Kassel (Klöppel 1990).

The sleep profiles of the EEGs were evaluated manually by two independent raters according to Rechtschaffen and Kales. Each of the 1440 time periods that included a change of sleep stage were neglected. All others were assigned REM or non-REM as given by the sleep profile.

In order to determine the "fit" of the network output levels t_i in predicting the manually evaluated sleep stages t_i* the percentage of misclassified time periods were determined by using $t_i = 0,5$ as the cutoff point for the neural network to discriminate between "REM" ($t_i > 0,5$) and "non-REM" ($t_i <= 0,5$) periods.

Because of the smaller amount of REM in regards to non-REM periods in the course of the night - and in the training set - the `REM errors´ dominate the `non-REM errors´ unless the amount of REM periods is increased in the training set (another way would be to change the error function). To keep both options two networks were trained by data sets put together from input vectors as defined below and the sleep stage coded outputs.

PM1 :   Trainig data were pooled by taking every fifth time period of the first night - EEG-signals of each subject .

PM2 :   Like PM1, but substituting other sleep stages by REM periods equally for each subject, so that the precentage of REM time periods in the training set increased to 40%.

The EEG data of the second night were used as test data.

Starting from randomly chosen synaptic weights training was stopped, when QME improved less than 10^{-4} within 50 training loops, which was reached within a maximum of 2500 loops. Each learning cycle was repeated from at least three different starting points to avoid local minima.

As a classical method of discriminant analysis to compare with we chose the nonparametric k-nearest neighbor discriminant analysis (Mahalanobis distance) for k=1 and k=3 as provided by the SAS standard software. The calibration data set was exactly the training data sets of PM1 and PM2.

Results and discussion

Figure1 gives an example for the output of PM2 during the first third of a night of a subject in comparison to the manually evaluated sleep profile. For the lower part of the figure the network output was smoothened by moving average over a time period of one minute respectively.

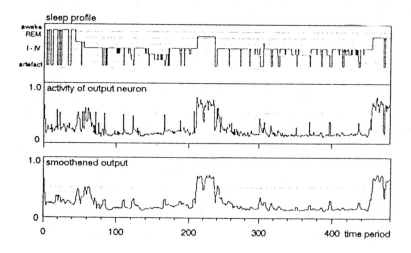

Figure 1: Example of the sleep profile in comparison to the network output.

Tables 1 and 2 show the error rates of the networks PM1 and PM2 as compared to the nearest neighbor discriminant analysis (k=1 and k=3). Looking at the average error rate of the different methods for the first night one can see hardly any difference, while there is a clear advantage for the neural network in the second night resulting in a decrease of the error rate between 19% to 30% as compared to the nearest neighbor methods. Additionally the error rate for the first night is lower than that for the second night in both tables. Both effects are caused by the fact that the training/calibration data set is pooled from EEG data from the first night. Thereby every test data set of the first night is containing one fifth of training/calibration data resulting in a lower and more equal error rate.

subject	Percentage of misclassified time periods		
	Neural Network	Discriminant Analysis	
		k = 1	k = 3
first night			
1	6.9	7.5	7.7
2	6.1	7.4	5.5
3	13.3	11.4	11.3
4	15.4	16.0	15.9
5	7.9	9.6	8.9
average	9.92	10.38	9.86
second night			
1	6.2	9.2	7.6
2	11.6	18.1	16.5
3	14.0	18.8	15.9
4	17.8	22.1	22.4
5	7.4	9.3	8.3
average	11.40	15.50	14.14

Table 1: Percentage of misclassified time periods for different discriminant procedures using calibration data as continuously recorded (PM1).

subject	Percentage of misclassified time periods		
	Neural Network	Discriminant Analysis	
		k = 1	k = 3
first night			
1	7.5	7.3	7.8
2	6.1	7.5	6.7
3	12.6	10.2	13.9
4	16.4	13.6	14.7
5	7.8	9.6	9.1
average	10.08	9.64	10.44
second night			
1	6.3	10.7	8.8
2	13.7	19.5	16.4
3	13.7	24.9	21.5
4	21.9	22.5	21.6
5	6.0	10.6	8.7
average	12.32	17.64	15.40

Table 2: Percentage of misclassified time periods for different discriminant procedures using equalized calibration data (PM2).

Literatur

Ferri,R., Ferri,P., Colognola,R.M., Petrella,M.A., Musumeci,S.A., Bergonzi,P.
Comparison between the results of an automatic and a visual scoring
of sleep EEG recordings. Sleep, 1989 12(4):354-362.

Grözinger,M., Klöppel,B. Röschke,J. Automatic recognition of Rapid Eye
Movement (REM) sleep by artificial neural networks.
(Submitted 1993).

Klöppel,B. Generalized backpropagating. In: Models of Brain Function &
Artificial Neuronal Nets: Proceedings of an Interdisciplinary
Symposium on Neural Networks, May 28-29, 1990, University of
Kassel, Germany, pp.187-212.

Kubicki,St., Höller,L., Berg,I.,Pastelak-Price,C., Dorow,R.
Sleep EEG evaluation: A comparison of results obtained by visual
scoring and automatic analysis with the Oxford sleep stager.
Sleep 1989 12(2):140-149.

Mamelak,A., Quattrochi,J., Hobson,J.
Automated staging of sleep in cats using neural networks.
Electroenceph.clin.Neurophysiol. 1991 79:52-61.

Rechtschaffen,A., Kales,A. A manual of standardized terminology, technics
and scoring system for sleep stages of human subjects. Public Health
Service. NIH publication 204 1968, Washington D.D.; US Government,
Printing Office.

Roberts,S., Tarassenko,L. A new method of automated sleep quantification.
Med. & Biol. Eng. & Comput. 1992.

Reengineering Software Modularity using Artificial Neural Networks

J Brant Arseneau and Tim Spracklen

University of Aberdeen, Electronic Research Group, Department of Engineering,
Fraser-Noble Building, Old Aberdeen, AB9 2UE, Scotland, U.K.

1. Introduction

Reengineering software modularity includes both discovering existing module structures and changing these structures to improve organisation (Arnold 1993). The overall success of most large systems is dependent on their organisation, because organisation affects understandability, modifiability, integratability, and testability (Schwanke 1991). Remodularisation activities become more and more necessary as software systems grow in size and age. As procedures are added to a system to meet new requirements, decisions must be made, by the programmer, as to where the new procedures should be placed; which module will the new procedure belong to? As systems grow large, programmers find it difficult to make these decisions because their view of the system is focused on the software they are working on, which is small with respect to the size of the entire system.

This paper describes a software reengineering tool which attempts to guide programmers in the remodularisation of software systems. The tool makes use of several technologies, which include an object-oriented information base for storing the original source code and an artificial neural network (ANN), which is used to cluster together procedures that share information. The remainder of this paper discusses the relations between software modularity and information hiding, suggesting a way that data and procedures could be organised into modules, and describes the reengineering tool, which attempts the remodularisation of existing code, with a presentation of results from several experiments.

2. Software Modularity and Information Hiding

It is almost certain that, at some point during a software system's lifecycle, there will be a need to reorganise its modularity following numerous changes to functionality and structure. Several methods exist defining criteria for remodularising software components, based on grouping procedures that call one another. However, since Parnas formulated his influential "information hiding" criterion (Parnas 1971), programmers have generally agreed that it is more important to group together procedures that share data, than to group procedures that call one another. Using the information hiding principle, as did Schwanke (Schwanke 1991), the process of remodularising existing code can be partially automated, helping programmers reorganise large systems.

A software module has two major roles which are: Providing organisation and scope. Organisation is achieved by dividing the system into logical modules which helps the programmer understand the overall structure, while scope refers to the region of a program where a particular variable may be used. For example in the C language, a name declared in a function (called a local name), has scope that extends from the point of declaration to the end of the block in which it is declared; for a name not in a function (called a global name), the scope extends from the point of declaration to the end of the module. In essence scope provides a way to group data and procedures so that system organisation can be achieved.

The information hiding principle can provide programmers with a guideline as to how data and procedures should be organised into modules within a system to provide "good" organisation. Information hiding occurs when a module's access to data, which is not needed by the module, is denied by using the scope rules of the programming language. One advantage of hiding such unnecessary information is that it can not be changed or deleted by units which are not supposed to use that information. David L. Parnas, a leader in software modularity research, formulated the information hiding criterion in 1971 which states a module should be

> "... characterised by a design decision which it hides
> from all others. Its interface or definition [is] chosen
> to reveal as little as possible about its inner
> workings" (Parnas 1971).

Good modularity is a subjective issue, however, using the information hiding principle a general heuristic for modularisation can be formulated which couples procedures together which share information (data): If two units use several of the same data, in a global scope, they may very well be sharing important design information, and should be grouped together. This heuristic can be implemented by a ANN, using information sharing features as input vectors.

3. The Remodularisation Tool

The software reengineering tool introduced in this paper is composed of several interacting programs which attempt to remodularise existing code. This section will describe the three major components of the tool (1) The decomposer, which is a parser and semantic analyser for breaking down the original code, (2) the information base, which is an object-oriented database representing information about the software, and (3) the composer, which is a combination of two translators. The first translator extracts information sharing features from each procedure, and the second uses these features as input vectors for a ANN which attempts to remodularise the original code, generating a new organised system.

3.1. The Decomposer and Information Base

Decomposition is the process of transforming a particular view of software into objects and relationships which are stored in an information base. Working with a decomposed view rather than on the source code directly saves the time and energy of parsing the code for each transformation. The challenge of decomposing views is not the issue of parsing because tools exist such as lex and yacc that eliminate a great deal of work. The challenge is, however, which decomposed views should be represented in the information base and how. Several papers introduce object based representations (Kozaczynski & Ning 1989 and Harandi & Ning 1990) which allow additional program abstractions to be derived or added to the existing hierarchy giving the information base great flexibility and extendability.

In this system the source code is originally decomposed, using lex and yacc, into an implementation language independent object-oriented information base, which will be referred to as the *source base*. The parser uses the programming language syntax to translate the source information; there is a corresponding parser for each source language. From the source base a set of views can be composed displaying different information about the original code.

3.2. The Composers

Composing views is the process of generating visual information about the software from the information base. A composer is a tool which inspects the information base, collects relevant objects and relationships, builds visual representations, and displays a view. This section describes two of the composers within the system, including first the software modularity feature view, which extracts the feature vectors from each procedure, and secondly the module view, which uses an ANN to display the reorganised modules.

3.2.1. Software Modularity Feature Views

Each procedure will have a unique signature which will distinguish it from other procedures. The signature is created by extracting the information sharing constructs of each procedure from the information base. These constructs can be recognised as non-local variables, which are defined as any variable whose scope includes two or more procedures. The feature view is used by the ANN as input for clustering procedures.

3.2.2. ANN Subsystem: Composing Module Views

The original modularity of a system is first broken down by placing each procedure in its own module. Each module has a corresponding feature vector, created by the feature view. A neural map is then generated by applying the feature vectors to a neural array without supervision, this is known as the process of self-organisation (Kohonen 1984). The array consists of a large number of neural elements; a 2-dimensional 20x20 array is used in this system. All the neurons have N inputs which are supplied with the same N-dimensional input vector $\mathbf{X}$. The output n_i, of the ith neuron in the array is a function, f, of similarity, S, between the input vector $\mathbf{X}$ and a prototype vector, or weight $\mathbf{W}_i$, uniquely associated with the neuron:

$$n_i = f\{S(X, W_i)\} \qquad (1)$$

The map can then be visualised by translating the trained prototype vector, $\mathbf{W}_i$, to a summary map (Whittington et al., 1992), see Figure 1. The modules, which the ANN produced, are represented on the map by wells. To establish which procedures were organised into each well, or module, the map is first calibrated using known input samples. The map units are labelled according to the majority of labels "hitting" a particular map unit. Secondly, a list of coordinates are generated corresponding to the best-matching unit in the map for each procedure.

Original	Expert		Reengineering Tool

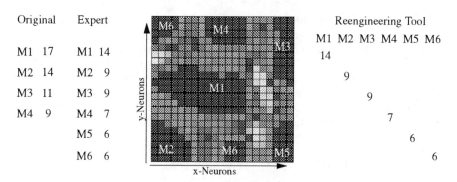

Original		Expert		Reengineering Tool						
				M1	M2	M3	M4	M5	M6	
M1	17	M1	14	14						
M2	14	M2	9		9					
M3	11	M3	9			9				
M4	9	M4	7				7			
		M5	6					6		
		M6	6						6	

Figure 1. The neural map's representation of a reorganised software system. The group labelled, Original, is the original structure of the system while the group labelled, Expert, is how an expert would remodularise the same system. The groups list the system's modules on the left and the number of procedures contained in each module on the right. In the middle is a Kohonen map generated by the tool with each well, or dark spot, representing a module. The map is translated to the representation on the far left, showing the number of procedures in each module.

4. Experimental Results and Summary

The reengineering tool was used to remodularise several software systems The systems were all written in C and COBOL, ranging in size from 10-50 modules. For each system an expert was contacted and ask to verify the quality of the remoduralisation.

One system written in C, which originally contained 51 procedures in 4 modules, was reorganised into 6 modules, see Figure 1. The remodularisation process required 43 choices (to reduce 45 groups to 6). Thirty five of the choices the tool made organised procedures together, which had originally been in the same module. Ten choices organised procedures originating in different modules. More importantly the expert agreed with the choices the tool made for remodularisation.

Through the experiments conducted, and advice from experts, the ANN based reengineering tool presented in this paper has proven that it has the capability to guide programmers in the modulation or remodularisation of existing code to improve its organisation.

References

Arnold, R.S. (1993) Software Engineering. IEEE Computer Society Press.

Harandi, T.H., Ning, J.Q. (1990) "Knowledge-Based Program Analysis". IEEE Software, Jan., 74-81.

Kozaczynski, W., Ning, J.Q. (1989) "SRE: A Knowledge-based Environment for Large-Scale Software Re-engineering Activites". Proceedings of the 11th Conference on Software Engineering, 113-122.

Kohonen, T. (1984) Self-Organization and Associative Memory. Springer-Verlag.

Parnas, D. (1971) "On the Criteria To Be Used In decomposing System into Modules". Tech. Report, Computer Science Department, Carnegie-Mellon University.

Schwanke, R.W. (1991) "An Intelligent Tool For Re-engineering Software Modularity". Proceedings of the 13th Conference on Software Engineering, 83-92.

Whittington, G., Spracklen, T. (1992) "Applying Visualisation Techniques to the Development of Real-World Artificial Neural Networks Applications". Proceedings of the International Conference on Artificial Neural Networks.

A Coupled Gradient Network for the Solution of the Static Unit Commitment Problem in Power Systems Planning

Paul B. Watta and Mohamad H. Hassoun
Computation and Neural Networks Laboratory
Department of Electrical and Computer Engineering
Wayne State University
Detroit, MI 48202

Abstract

This paper deals with a neural network solution for a problem specific to the power industry. In particular, the *static* unit commitment problem [1], [2] is addressed. The static problem is a special case of the unit commitment problem, where the planning horizon of unit commitment consists of only one hour. To represent the mixed-integer nature of the problem, a coupled gradient network is formulated. The dynamics of the network are defined by gradient descent on a global energy function, and hence the network converges to locally optimal solutions. After formulating the model, the parameter selection involved in actually simulating the network is discussed. Finally, this paper concludes with a discussion of some simulation results.

1. Introduction

In this section, the static unit commitment problem is formulated as a mixed-integer optimization problem. Following this introduction, a coupled gradient network is proposed as a method of solution for the static problem. A penalty function approach is used to construct an appropriate energy function and gradient-type network. Actually, to solve the static problem, two *coupled* gradient networks will be constructed that will represent the mixed-integer nature of the problem, operate in parallel, and converge to a locally optimal solution. After specifying the network architecture and energy function, the dynamics are defined by gradient descent. Finally, simulation results are presented and discussed.

Suppose we have a power system with n generators, or units. Let the generation level of each power plant be denoted by $P_1, P_2, ..., P_n$, and let the commitment of each generator be denoted by $u_1, u_2, ..., u_n$ where $u_i \in \{0, 1\}$. That is, $u_i = 1$ if unit i is on-line; otherwise, $u_i = 0$ and unit i is off-line. The static unit commitment problem is to determine optimal unit commitments such that the overall cost of operation of the power network is minimized, subject to some constraints. The cost of operation, which is the objective function to be minimized, is given as:

$$f(\mathbf{P}, \mathbf{u}) = \sum_{t=1}^{T} \sum_{i=1}^{n} (\gamma_i P_i^2 + \beta_i P_i + \alpha_i) u_i + sc_i (1 - u_i^0) u_i$$

where $\mathbf{P} = (P_1, ...P_n)$, $\mathbf{u} = (u_1, ...u_n)$, and for the ith unit, γ_i, β_i, and α_i are the cost parameters of generation, sc_i is the start-up cost, and u_i^0 is the initial commitment of the unit (the commitment of the unit at time $t = 0$). Note that start-up cost is only incurred if a unit is switched on-line, i.e., $u_i^0 = 0$ and $u_i = 1$.

The constraints of the problem include *unit constraints* and *generation constraints*. The unit constraints require each generator i to stay within its minimum power capacity, denoted m_i and its maximum power capacity, denoted M_i. So while on-line, unit i must not generate less than m_i units of power and must not generate more than M_i units of power:

$$m_i \leq P_i(t) \leq M_i \qquad i = 1, 2, ..., n,$$

The generation constraint requires that the total supply of power must meet the projected *load* or *power demand* L:

$$\sum_{i=1}^{n} P_i u_i = L$$

Also, we will require that at any given time, there is reserve power on hand. This reserve power is called *spinning reserve* and is denoted R. Such a reserve is necessary because at any time t, the actual demand is not known precisely; L then represents some projected value of the total power demand. Hence those units which are on-line should be able (if necessary) to aggregately supply an additional R units of power. This constraint can be expressed as: $\sum_{i=1}^{n} [M_i - P_i(t)] u_i \geq R$, and since the power balance equation gives $\sum_{i=1}^{n} P_i u_i = L$, then the spinning reserve constraint can be written as:

$$\sum_{i=1}^{n} M_i u_i \geq L + R$$

Finally, the static unit commitment problem may be concisely written as the following mixed-integer programming problem:

$$\text{Minimize } f(\mathbf{P}, \mathbf{u}) = \sum_{i=1}^{n} [\gamma_i P_i^2 + \beta_i P_i + \alpha_i + sc_i(1.0 - u_i^0)] u_i \qquad (1)$$

$$\text{subject to } m_i \leq P_i \leq M_i \quad i = 1, 2, ..., n \qquad (2)$$

$$\sum_{i=1}^{n} P_i u_i = L \qquad (3)$$

$$\sum_{i=1}^{n} M_i u_i \geq L + R \qquad (4)$$

$$u_i \in \{0, 1\}, \quad i = 1, 2, ..., n \qquad (5)$$

2. The Structure of the Coupled Gradient Network

The coupled network consists of two interacting recurrent networks: a network to represent the unit generation levels, called the p-network, and a network to represent the unit commitments, called the u-network. The p-network will have as node outputs (states) the power generation variables P_i, while the u-network's node outputs will correspond to the commitment variables u_i, $i = 1, ...n$. Hence the state space for this dynamical system will be the hypercube given by

$$\Omega = \prod_{i=1}^{n} [m_i, M_i] \times \prod_{i=1}^{n} [0, 1]$$

The input to the ith node in the p-network will be denoted by h_i^p, and the input to the ith node in the u-network will be denoted by h_i^u. Later, the dynamics of the coupled net will be defined in terms of these input variables. The network structure is shown schematically in Figure 1.

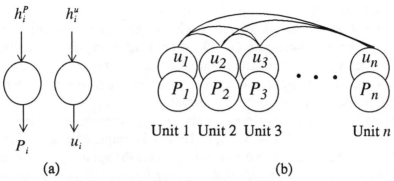

Figure 1. The structure of the coupled gradient net. (a) The input-output scheme for the neurons representing the ith unit. (b) The coupled structure of the two networks.

To ensure that $P_i \in [m_i, M_i]$ and $u_i \in \{0,1\}$, the activation functions shown below in Figure 2 will be used for the nodes of the coupled network. So for the nodes in the p-network, the activation function is given by a saturated linear function with slope λ_p in the linear region. The activation function for the commitment network takes the following sigmoidal form:

$$u_i = \sigma(h_i^u) = \frac{1}{1 + e^{-\lambda_u h_i^u}}$$

During computation, the integral constraints on the commitments are relaxed, and the commitment variables are allowed to assume intermediate values in the hypercube $[0, 1]^n$, but it is expected that the final values of these variables will saturate at either 0 or 1 upon convergence to a solution.

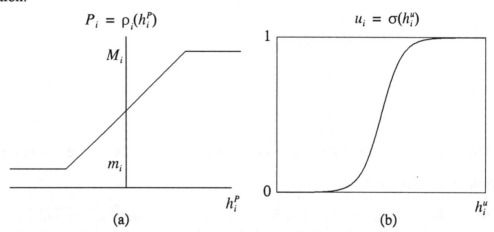

Figure 2. The activation functions for (a) the nodes of the p-network and (b) the nodes of the u-network.

This approach of allowing both the generation levels and commitment levels to continuously evolve is different from some previously defined neural net solutions of the unit commitment problem. For example, the network of Liu, et al. [3] searches for the optimal commitments in the discrete space $\{0, 1\}^n$ using a Boltzman machine. In the model of Sasaki, et al. [4], although the commitments evolve in the unit hypercube, the generation levels are held fixed during computation. Furthermore, their model uses a linear objective function, rather than the quadratic cost function given above.

The energy function for the coupled network will be constructed using a penalty function approach. That is, the energy function $E(\mathbf{P}, \mathbf{u})$ will consist of the objective function $f(\mathbf{P}, \mathbf{u})$ for the static problem plus a penalty function to enforce the constraints. In the case of the static unit commitment problem, there is only one equality constraint: the power balance constraint, and one inequality constraint: the spinning reserve constraint.

Also there are n combinatorial constraints on the commitment variables; these are the constraints $u_i \in \{0, 1\}$, for each $i = 1, ..., n$. Hence the required penalty function will consist of three terms: P_L for the power balance constraint, P_S for the spinning reserve constraint, and P_C for the combinatorial constraints. The resulting energy function $E = f(\mathbf{P}, \mathbf{u}) + P_L + P_S + P_C$ for the static unit commitment problem is given below:

$$E = A \sum_{i=1}^{n} (\gamma_i P_i^2 + \beta_i P_i + \alpha_i) u_i + B \sum_{i=1}^{n} sc_i (1 - u_i^0) u_i$$

$$+ C \left(\sum_{i=1}^{n} P_i u_i - L \right)^2 + D g\left(\sum_{i=1}^{n} M_i u_i - L - R \right) + K \sum_{i=1}^{n} u_i (1 - u_i)$$

where $g(\bullet)$ is the penalty function shown below in Figure 3. That is, $g(x) = x^2$ for all $x < 0$ and $g(x) = 0$ for all $x \geq 0$; so $g(\bullet)$ penalizes solutions which fail to meet the spinning reserve. In the above energy, A, B, C, D, and K are positive penalty coefficients. The selection of these coefficients will be discussed below.

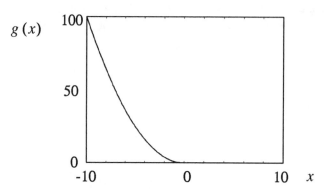

Figure 3. A graph of the penalty function used for the spinning reserve constraint.

3. The Dynamics of the Network

As usual, the dynamics for this Hopfield-type gradient network are obtained by gradient descent on the energy function. So for each node $i = 1, 2, ...n$ in the network, we have

$$\dot{h}_i^P = -\eta_P \frac{\partial E}{\partial P_i} = -A (2\gamma_i P_i + \beta_i) u_i - 2C u_i \left[\sum_{i=1}^{n} P_i u_i - L \right]^2 \tag{6}$$

$$P_i = \rho_i(h_i^P) \tag{7}$$

$$\dot{h}_i^u = -\eta_u \frac{\partial E}{\partial u_i} = -A\left(\gamma_i P_i^2 + \beta_i P_i + \alpha_i\right) - B\left(1 - u_i^0\right) sc_i$$

$$-2CP_i\left[\sum_{i=1}^{n} P_i u_i - L\right] - DM_i g'\left(\sum_{i=1}^{n} M_i u_i - L - R\right) - K\left(1 - 2u_i\right) \tag{8}$$

$$u_i = \sigma(h_i^u) \tag{9}$$

where η_p and η_u are positive coefficients which will be used to scale the dynamics of the two networks. Note that the derivative of the penalty function g is piece-wise linear: $g'(x) = -2x$ for $x < 0$ and $g'(x) = 0$ for all $x \geq 0$. The stability of the network may easily be verified by using the usual procedure of Hopfield and showing that E is decreasing along trajectories. Hence E is a Liapunov function for the coupled network. That is, by following the dynamics of Equations (6)-(9), the energy E always decreases until a local minimum of E is reached. But since E only contains cost terms and constraint satisfaction terms, then by following these dynamics we are lead to regions of the state space which represent lower cost and/or more constraint satisfaction. The balance between the cost optimality and constraint satisfaction critically depends on the choice of the penalty coefficients, which is discussed next.

4. Parameter Selection

To actually simulate the above coupled gradient network, values for the following parameters must be chosen:

1. The penalty coefficients: A, B, C, D, and K.
2. The activation function slopes: λ_p and λ_u.
3. The scaling factors: η_p and η_u.
4. Initial Conditions: (P_i^0, u_i^0)

Additionally, some method of numerical integration must be chosen to solve the coupled differential equations given in (6)-(9). In the simulations reported below, a simple forward Euler integration with sufficiently small step-size was used. The penalty coefficients were determined empirically by running trial simulations and observing the optimality and/or feasibility of the resulting equilibrium points of the system. A proper choice of A, B is critical to obtaining optimal and feasible solution, and the selection of these parameters will be discussed later. The other parameters were set as follows: $C = 1.0$, $D = 0.0001$, and $K = 10.0$, $\lambda_p = 1$, $\lambda_u = 0.5$, $\eta_p = 500$, and $\eta_u = 1$. The initial conditions of the network were chosen randomly near the center of state space Ω: $P_i^0 = \overline{P}_i \pm 10\delta$ and $u_i^0 = 0.5 \pm 0.2\delta$, where $\overline{P}_i$ is the midpoint of the range $[m_i, M_i]$, and δ is a random number chosen uniformly from the interval $[0, 1]$.

Once all the parameters have been chosen, a typical simulation of the coupled gradient network proceeds as follows. Starting from a random initial condition, Equations (6)-(9) are integrated using a forward Euler numerical integration. Upon convergence of the dynamics, the outputs of the commitment network are thresholded at 0.5 to yield the required binary values. This thresholding is required since the outputs of the commitment network may not have fully saturated upon convergence. Based on these binary commitment variables, an economic dispatch program is run to obtain the optimal generation levels.

5. Simulation Results

In this section, simulations are reported for the coupled gradient network for a 15-unit system. The solutions obtained by the coupled net are compared to the globally optimal solution, which, for this size problem, is possible to obtain by exhaustive search. To do this, we simply enumerated all possible commitment settings $\mathbf{u} = (u_1, u_2, \ldots u_n)$, from $\mathbf{u} = (0, 0, \ldots 0)$ to $\mathbf{u} = (1, 1, \ldots 1)$. For each such commitment vector, the economic dispatch problem is solved, and the lowest cost solution which also satisfies the constraints is retained.

For the 15-unit system, 20 different problems were formulated by varying the load and spinning reserve requirements (See Table 1). For each of these problems, 20 simulations were run, each time starting the coupled net at a different initial position in state space Ω. Upon convergence of the network for each such simulation, the cost optimality of the resulting solution is measured as the percentage *above* optimal cost:

$$\% \, above \, optimal \, = \, 100 \, (\frac{f(\mathbf{P}^*, \mathbf{u}^*) - f^*}{f^*}) \qquad (10)$$

where $f(\mathbf{P}^*, \mathbf{u}^*)$ is the cost of the local minimum solution found by the coupled network, and f^* is the globally optimal cost obtained by exhaustive search. Table 1 shows the results obtained for different values for the penalty coefficients A and B. For each Table entry, the first two values reported are: (1) the average cost of solution (averaged over the 20 runs); and, (2) the cost of the best solution (out of the 20 runs). Actually, the raw cost is not reported, rather, the percent above optimal cost [using Equation (10)] is shown. So an entry of 0.0 means that the network was able to produce the globally optimal solution. Since the coupled net does not always converge to a feasible solution, a third quantity is reported for each problem: the percentage of time that the network converged to a feasible solution.

6. Discussion

From Table 1, it is clear that the average performance of the coupled network improves as the penalty coefficients A and B increase. Unfortunately, though, with higher values of A and B, the network is more likely to produce solutions which are not valid. In this application, though, a high percentage of invalid solutions could be tolerated, if it could be shown that the network (run in a multi-start mode) could, with high probability, produce the globally optimal solution. The third column of Table 1 clearly indicates that this is possible with the coupled net. In this case, the global solution was found in 15 out of the 20 problems. For comparison purposes, the Lagrangian relaxation solution was able to produce the globally optimal solution in 12 out of the 20 problems.

The above network may be extended to handle the temporal unit commitment problem, where it is necessary to schedule the commitment of each unit over a planning horizon of, say T hours. In this case, there are additional unit constraints, such minimum up times, and minimum down times, which must be included in the problem formulation. A later paper will address this problem. Also, the percent convergence to valid solutions may be improved by using global search techniques, such as mean field annealing or stochastic gradient descent [5].

References

[1] F. Zhuang, "Optimal Generation Unit Commitment in Thermal Electric Power Systems," *Ph.D. Thesis*, McGill University, 1988.

[2] A. Cohen and V. R. Sherkat, "Optimization-Based Methods for Operations Scheduling," *Proceedings of the IEEE*, **75**(12) 1574-1591, 1987.

[3] Z. Liu, F. E. Villaseca, and F. Renovich, Jr., "Neural Networks for Generation Scheduling in Power Systems," *Proceedings of the International Joint Conference on Neural Networks*, Baltimore, MD, 233-238, 1992.

[4] H. Sasaki, M. Watanabe, J. Kubokawa, N. Yorino, R. Yokoyama, "A Solution Method of the Unit Commitment by Artificial Neural Networks," *IEEE Transactions on Power Systems*, **7** (3), 974-981, 1992.

[5] P. Watta, "A Neural Network Approach to Mixed-Integer Programming Problems," *Ph.D. Thesis*, Wayne State University, 1994.

$n = 15$	Load	Reserve	The Coupled Gradient Network % Above Optimal Cost: Average Solution/Best Solution								
			$A = B = 0.30$			$A = B = 0.32$			$A = B = 0.35$		
10% Reserve	1520.0	152.0	7.8	0.0	100%	7.6	0.0	95%	0.2	0.0	100%
	1590.0	159.0	8.1	0.7	95%	5.5	0.0	95%	1.1	1.1	30%
	1645.0	164.5	6.9	1.5	90%	6.0	0.9	100%	0.7	0.0	90%
	1700.0	170.0	7.8	4.7	95%	6.6	2.3	100%	1.0	0.0	95%
15% Reserve	1520.0	228.0	6.4	0.5	90%	4.5	0.0	100%	1.2	1.2	15%
	1590.0	238.5	7.6	2.3	90%	7.0	1.1	95%	1.0	1.1	35%
	1645.0	246.8	6.1	0.8	95%	5.2	0.0	90%	0.0	0.0	70%
	1700.0	255.0	6.9	2.3	95%	6.7	3.0	85%	0.4	0.0	65%
20% Reserve	1520.0	304.0	5.8	0.0	90%	6.9	0.0	80%	0.0	0.0	15%
	1590.0	318.0	4.9	0.6	85%	5.3	0.0	90%	0.0	0.0	75%
	1645.0	329.0	7.0	0.2	80%	7.5	2.9	80%	0.3	0.2	70%
	1700.0	340.0	4.3	0.8	90%	6.1	0.0	100%	0.5	0.0	40%
25% Reserve	1520.0	380.0	5.0	0.0	85%	4.9	0.0	65%	0.0	0.0	75%
	1590.0	397.5	5.9	0.0	80%	4.8	0.0	75%	0.0	0.0	75%
	1645.0	411.2	4.7	0.0	75%	4.0	0.0	85%	0.1	0.0	30%
	1700.0	425.0	4.5	3.0	75%	5.9	3.0	75%	0.1	3.0	85%
30% Reserve	1520.0	456.0	5.6	0.0	80%	5.1	0.0	50%	0.0	0.0	70%
	1590.0	477.0	5.7	0.0	65%	2.2	0.0	60%	0.1	0.0	30%
	1645.0	493.5	6.5	0.0	70%	4.2	0.8	65%	0.1	0.0	90%
	1700.0	510.0	2.3	0.0	60%	2.5	0.0	80%	0.0	0.0	20%

Table 1. A summary of the performance of the coupled gradient network for a 15-unit system with various load and spinning reserve constraints. The performance is shown for different settings of the penalty coefficients A and B. The first number in each table entry is the average cost of solution (averaged over 20 runs) measured as the percent above optimal cost [see Equation (10)]. The second number is the percentage above optimal cost of the best solution found. Third number is the percentage of time that the coupled net converged to a feasible (valid) solution.

Neural network processing improves the accuracy of a system dedicated to the automatic interpretation of antibiotic disk diffusion susceptibility tests

J. VILAIN[1], G. HEJBLUM[1], V. JARLIER[2], J. GROSSET[2], A. AURENGO[1] and B. FERTIL[1].

[1]*Unité de Recherche en Imagerie Biomédicale Morphologique et Fonctionnelle (INSERM U-66)* and [2]*Laboratoire Central de Bactériologie-Virologie , CHU Pitié-Salpêtrière*

mailing address: Gilles HEJBLUM, INSERM U66, CHU Pitié-Salpêtrière, 91 Bd de l' Hôpital, 75654 Paris CEDEX 13, France

Abstract

A neural network (NN) dedicated to the estimation of inhibition zone size of disk diffusion antibiotic susceptibility tests was developed and compared to previously described algorithm (ALGO) based on image processing. The biological sample was composed of 2552 drug-organism combination tests. Data were divided in two sets, a learning and a testing set. Neural networks were developed with PDP programs and supervised learning was performed with the back propagation module. On the testing set, neural networks corrected most of the inaccurate results obtained with the image processing algorithm. The discrepancies between two human readings were at the same level that those obtained between NNs and a reference estimate. Furthermore, the use of selection rules combining NNs and ALGO results allowed the automatic detection of a very reduced part of the sample (1%) that contained most of the severe errors of the system. In these rare difficult cases, a warning is issued by the system, asking for a human interpretation. This behavior meets clinical requirements. The developed method appears as a solid backbone for an automated system dedicated to the interpretation of disk diffusion antibiotic susceptibility tests.

I - Introduction

Many efforts have focused on the automation of antibiotic susceptibility tests and most of the commercial systems yet available are based on broth culture (1). Despite the availability of such systems, disk diffusion in agar media, a simple and inexpensive method (Fig 1), is still widely used all over the world for antibiotic susceptibility testing. The most critical step for an automated analysis of such tests lies in the estimation of the inhibition zone sizes. Recently, we proposed an image analysis-based automated method that performs such a task (2). Our results indicated that the efficiency of the proposed algorithm (ALGO) compares with most systems based on broth culture. However, the residual errors of the system are difficult to correct. Neural Networks (NNs) may be used to solve complex problems with no need of an explicit description of the decision processes. Since a comprehensive algorithm is quite hard to implement, we developed a NN processing as an alternative approach. The present work shows that the results obtained with NNs, when combined with those obtained with the efficiency of our conventional algorithmic method can be used to increase the accuracy of the system. Moreover, the comparison of different outputs obtained with different NNs and with the algorithmic method allows an automatic clustering of the sample in two parts: a large part where confidence in the results verges on certainty and a reduced part that contains most of the errors.

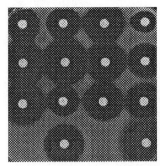

Figure 1. Disk diffusion tests. Bacteria are cultured on an Agar medium in Petri plates. Antimicrobial agents are applied to the test plates in the form of dried filter paper disks that are placed on the inoculated surface. The antimicrobial agent being free to diffuse through the adjacent agar medium, the result is a gradually changing of drug concentration and no bacterial growth will be observed in the circular area around the disk where inhibitory concentrations of the drug are present. In practice, the reading of the drug-organism test consists in determining the diameter of inhibition zone, after a 24 hour incubation. This measurement is compared to standard breakpoints to clinically categorize the organism as susceptible, intermediate or resistant to the tested drug. The collection of the tests performed with the various drugs is then interpreted by the clinician who then decides the best treatment strategy.

II Material and Methods

Computer system. The system was composed of a Macintosh Quadra 700 computer (Apple Computer Inc., Cupertino, CA), a Nubus image grabber board (Neotech Limited, Eastleigh, United Kingdom) and a CCD XC-77CE digitizing camera (Sony Inc., Japan). Programs were written in Object-Oriented MPW Pascal (Apple Computer Inc., Cupertino, CA). Neural Network processing was performed with PDP programs (Mac Version 1.1,©1989 J. L. Mc Clelland and D. E. Rumelhart).

Estimation of the inhibition zone diameters with the ALGO. The estimates of the inhibition zone size diameters were obtained according to an algorithm previously described (2). The algorithm can be summarized as follows: after digitization of the image of the Petri plate, the method generates and analyzes a pattern corresponding to each antibiotic disk tested. The pattern analysis is based on the examination of a profile (Fig. 2) representing the mean grey level value as a function of the distance from the disk, the latter being recognized and labeled in a preliminary step. The estimate of the inhibition zone size obtained with the profile analysis is finally compared to conventional breakpoints recommended for susceptibility categorization, resulting in an automatic categorization of the organism as susceptible, intermediate or resistant to the antibiotic tested.

a   b   c

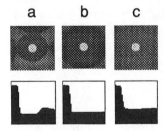

Figure 2. Extracting profiles from local zones around each antibiotic disk. After the recognition of each tested disk, the pixel constituting a local zone around each disk (top) is used to generate profiles (bottom). The profiles represent the mean grey-level (ordinate) as a function of the distance to the disk center (abscissa).

Three typical cases are shown. -a: an inhibition zone is observed and its diameter is ≤ 35 mm; within the 35 mm wide square zone of analysis, an inhibition zone appears as a circular spotless area. The corresponding radial profile pattern is formed by a U-shaped curve. The ascending slope corresponds to the edge of the inhibition zone. -b: an inhibition zone is observed but its diameter is > 35 mm; within the 35 mm wide square zone of analysis, the edge of the inhibition zone does not appear. Consequently, the profile shows a L-shape curve with a low grey-level of the plateau. The diameter of the inhibition zone is fixed to 35 mm. -c: no inhibition zone is observed; the profile shows a L-shape curve with a medium grey-level value of the plateau. The diameter of the inhibition zone is fixed to 6 mm, value of the antibiotic disk diameter.

Evaluating the accuracy of automated methods. Each Petri plate was examined at the naked eye by two independent human readers. They estimated a diameter corresponding to the inhibition zone for each test with a ruler. A reference diameter was built as follows: When the difference between the two measurements was greater than 3 mm, the measurement of a third human (a senior) was considered as RD. Otherwise, the mean of the two first human measurements was considered as RD. RD was used both as the target value in the learning phase of the neural network processing and as reference to evaluate the accuracy of the machine estimates.

Biological sample. The sample was composed of 107 unselected consecutive bacterial strains isolated from clinical specimens in a teaching hospital laboratory. The strains were tested for drug susceptibility in a routine process with no special care. For that purpose, square (165 x 165 mm) Petri plates containing Mueller-Hinton agar (Diagnostics Pasteur™, Marne-la-Coquette, France) were used. Because of limited growth resulting in poor image contrast, nine strains of *Enterococcus sp.* were excluded. Finally, the 98 strains included in the study belonged to the following staphylococci or gram negative rod bacterial species: *Staphylococcus aureus* (25 strains), *Staphylococcus epidermidis* (15), *Escherichia coli* (36), *Proteus mirabilis* (6), *Pseudomonas aeruginosa* (6), *Klebsiella sp.*(5), *Acinetobacter sp.*(2), *Enterobacter cloacæ* (2), *Serratia marcescens* (1). For each strain, drug susceptibility tests were performed with 22 to 28 distinct antibiotic disks made of blotting paper that were distributed onto two plates (six to sixteen disks per plate) according to a predefined standard scheme that depended on the tested species. In all, 2618 disk susceptibility tests of 40 distinct antibiotics were studied. Additionally, 8 plates were automatically excluded from the study because of a poor image contrast. They were automatically detected by the image processing program. The final sample was based on the 2552 remaining tests.

Estimation of the inhibition zone diameters with neural networks. Each processing unit was composed of 4 layers (Fig. 3): 1 input layer, 2 hidden layers, 1 output layer. The radial profile was given as input, the output being an inhibition zone diameter estimate or a derived value. In practice, different types of profiles representing the mean or the variance of the grey levels (raw data or calculated differences with the neighboring pixel values). The data set was split in two equal parts, a learning subset and a testing subset. During the learning phase, performed with the back propagation module of PDP programs, the weights were iteratively adjusted to minimize the distance (error) between the target (RD value) and the output. The testing subset was exploited to control the quality of learning. Specialized networks have been trained to deal with three different situations (Fig. 4): a "large" susceptibility (inhibition zone diameters greater than 27 mm), a full resistance (inhibition zone diameters equal to 6 mm), and finally the remaining cases (6 mm < inhibition zone diameters < 28 mm). Eight independent learning sessions were run in each case. Due to the stochastic nature of the learning process, different weight sets could be obtained, the corresponding networks having comparable efficiencies. For each new radial profile analyzed, a confidence index was defined as a function of the variability of the outputs of these different networks (see joined paper, reference 3). This index, combined with the mean value of the outputs, was used to decide whether to retain the mean value as the diameter estimate or to carry on the analysis. The neural network architecture is summarized in Fig. 4.

III Results

Table 1 presents the evaluation of the machine accuracy in terms of clinical categorization. The differences observed between RD and NNs categorizations closely approaches those observed between two human readers. When comparing the accuracy of NNs and ALGO, NNs appeared to remove most of the errors of the ALGO that led to major disagreements in the staphylococci sample. Most minor disagreements corresponded to tests where the true inhibition zone diameter is very close to a breakpoint value. Actually, 15% of the NNs estimates were at most distant from 2 mm of a breakpoint value, and this subset contained 28 among the 30 minor disagreements with RD estimates. More important is the detection of major and very major disagreements that may lead respectively to the non-prescription of an active drug and to the prescription of a non-active drug. The amount of such disagreements between NNs and RD compares to that observed between two human readers.

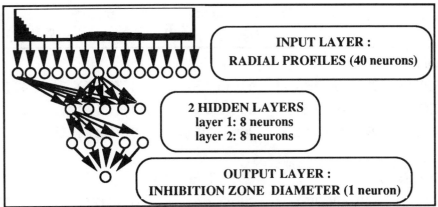

Figure 3. The neural network processing unit.

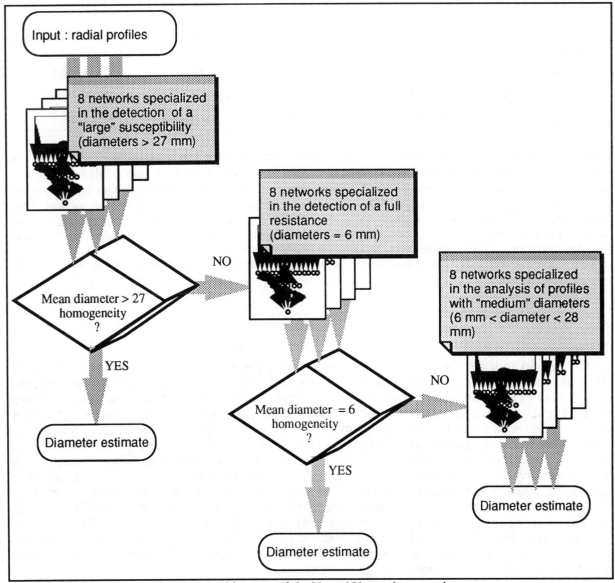

Figure 4: Architecture of the Neural Network processing.

	Agreement[a]	minor disagreements[b]	major disagreements[c]	very major disagreements[d]
Total test sample				
HR1/HR2[e]	1229 (95.7%)	47 (3.7%)	4 (0.3%)	4 (0.3%)
RD/ALGO	1230 (95.8%)	33 (2.6%)	14 (1.1%)	7 (0.5%)
RD/NNs	1244 (96.9%)	30 (2.3%)	3 (0.2%)	7 (0.5%)
Gram negative rods				
HR1/HR2	840 (96.7%)	29 (3.3%)	0 (0.0%)	0 (0.0%)
RD/ALGO	841 (96.8%)	25 (2.9%)	1 (0.1%)	2 (0.2%)
RD/NNs	844 (97.1%)	23 (2.6%)	1 (0.1%)	1 (0.1%)
Staphylococci				
HR1/HR2	389 (93.7%)	18 (4.3%)	4 (1.0%)	4 (1.0%)
RD/ALGO	389 (93.7%)	8 (1.9%)	13 (3.1%)	5 (1.2%)
RD/NNs	400 (96.4%)	7 (1.7%)	2 (0.5%)	6 (1.4%)

Table 1. Agreement and disagreements in SIR categorization for the test sample. [a]agreement: identical categorization; [b]minor disagreement: intermediate susceptibility with one method but susceptibility or resistance with the other. [c]major disagreements: susceptibility with the reference method but resistance with the test method. [d]very major disagreements: resistance with reference method but susceptibility with the test method. [e]The following codes correspond to: RD, reference value obtained with the combination of the three human readings (see material and methods); HR1, estimate of human reader n°1; HR2, estimate of human reader n°2; ALGO, estimate of the algorithmic method; NNs, estimate obtained with the Neural networks results.
HR1/HR2 corresponds to the comparison between the two first human readers where the first reader was arbitrarily chosen as the reference.

IV Discussion

Our results indicate that the neural networks are of great help in our biological application. First, they appear to be more accurate than a dedicated image processing algorithm. Second, the differences in the estimates of NNs and ALGO may also be used to cluster the sample in two parts, a reliable result sample (>95% of the tests) and a questionable result sample (<5% of the tests) spoiled with many errors. The detection of a very reduced part of the sample, that points out on the system errors may be investigated in two directions, the call for a human intervention and the development of special tools for automatically correcting the errors. Whereas about 95% of the tests could be automated, it is clear that a human intervention of a clinician expert is desired in practice to interpret difficult results obtained in rare cases. Among the criteria that may be used for automatically detecting the errors, the agreement between ALGO and NNs results (in terms of SIR categorization or diameter estimates) is helpful (Table 2). For instance, we show that, using the second criterion described in the Table 2, the examination of only 11 tests (only 1% of the test sample) allows the detection of 5 among the 10 severe (major and very major disagreements) errors made by the machine.

Although the results shown are very encouraging, they have to be further confirmed for two reasons. First, we used the testing subset to control the quality of learning, although this should be theoretically done with another independent subset. We did this because the number of tests available was too small for making three subsets. Indeed, in terms of drug-organism combinations, some situations are rarely encountered in our sample. Therefore, our objective is to perform a study with a very large sample. Provided that the results obtained with the neural networks are confirmed, the developed method constitutes a very solid backbone for an automaton dedicated to routine laboratory.

	Agreement	minor disagreements	major disagreements	very major disagreements
Total test sample				
(100%)	1244 (96.9%)	30 (2.3%)	3 (0.2%)	7 (0.5%)
criterion 1: agreement in SIR categorization between NNs and ALGO				
true (97.7%)	1223 (97.5%)	27 (2.1%)	1 (0.1%)	4 (0.3%)
false (02.3%)	21 (72.5%)	3 (0.2%)	2 (0.2%)	3 (0.2%)
criterion 2: difference between diameter estimates of NNs and ALGO is at most 10 mm				
true (98.7%)	1233 (97.3%)	29 (2.1%)	1 (0.1%)	4 (0.3%)
false (01.3%)	11 (64.7%)	1 (0.2%)	2 (0.2%)	3 (0.2%)

Table 2. Clustering the sample in two parts according to two criteria. Columns indicate the number of observations (and their rate, in parenthesis) for agreements and disagreements (see Table 1 for definitions) between RD and the NNs estimates. The first column indicates in parenthesis the proportion of sample satisfying (true) or not (false) the criterion.

References

1 Jorgensen, J. H. 1991. Antibacterial susceptibility tests: Automated or instrument-based methods, p. 1166-1172. *In* A. Balows, W. J. Hausler, Jr., K. L. Herrmann, H. D. Isenberg, H. J. Shadomy, (ed.), Manual of clinical microbiology, 5th ed. American Society for Microbiology, Washington, D.C.
2 Hejblum G., Jarlier V., Grosset J., and Aurengo A. 1993. Automated interpretation of disk diffusion antibiotic susceptibility tests with the radial profile analysis algorithm. J. Clin. Microbiol. 31:2396-2401.
3 Fertil B. and Vilain J. 1994. Multiple learning sessions to improve predictions and evaluate reliability of neural networks. Proceedings of the Wolrd Congress on Neural Networks. San Diego, USA. June 4-9, 1994.

PAVEMENT SURFACE EVALUATION USING NEURAL NETWORKS

Vinod K. Kalikiri
Graduate Research Assistant
Department of Civil Engineering
University of Connecticut

Norman W. Garrick
Assistant professor
Department of Civil Engineering
University of Connecticut

Luke E. K. Achenie
Assistant Professor
Department of Chemical Engineering
University of Connecticut

ABSTRACT

Neural network models are paradigms for performing cognitive tasks such as pattern recognition and classification. It has been established that neural networks are particularly well suited for pattern recognition tasks because of their inherent ability to generalize based only on a set of training data. The goal of our study at the University of Connecticut (UCONN) is to make use of this capability of neural networks for the development of an automated system for pavement condition evaluation. The system is expected to have the capacity to recognize and characterize distress patterns from pavement images that are recorded by the Connecticut photolog system.

In this paper we discuss the neural network model that we are developing at UCONN for the analysis of pavement images. Some of the topics addressed in the paper include the image processing methods that are used to isolate distress features, the input data used for analysis, the feed forward neural network model that forms the core processing unit of the system and the results obtained from the model.

So far, we found that our analytical system has a success rate of 91 % for pavement distress identification. Preliminary results show that the proposed approach of using neural networks for distress pattern recognition is viable and has real potential to be integrated into a fully automated system for pavement surface condition evaluation.

INTRODUCTION

Supervised neural networks have been successfully used for pattern recognition tasks because of their ability to generalize based on training data. These networks were also found to be capable of analyzing and classifying data that cannot be described by conventional data analysis techniques (1). This capability of neural networks has been successfully used in various fields of engineering to solve problems which could not be solved by the commonly available computer algorithms. One potential area of application is in the field of pavement engineering. The pattern recognition capabilities of neural networks can be used to characterize common pavement distress forms like cracks, patches and potholes.

The aim of the current research work at the University of Connecticut is to develop an automated system incorporating the concepts of image processing and pattern recognition for pavement condition surveys. Such an automated system is expected to give an accurate and reliable analysis of the pavement condition. The condition ratings of the pavements would serve as input to a pavement management system to assist decision makers in scheduling maintainance operations, projecting future funding requirements and allocating funds to the prioritized projects.

At present the Connecticut Department of Transportation (ConnDOT) uses a manual rating procedure to analyze pavement images recorded by a photolog vehicle. This rating procedure is both time consuming and labor intensive. In addition the evaluations obtained by this process are also highly subjective in nature. In this paper we will summarize the study being carried out at UCONN to mitigate these problems by using neural networks for pavement distress identification. The image data used in this project is taken from the photolog laser videodisc (PLV) collection at ConnDOT.

OVERALL STRATEGY

Our current project for the development of an automated pavement condition evaluation system is being carried out in two phases. The first phase involves the processing of images from the PLV collection. The objective is to use the principles of digital image processing to generate standard images of sufficient quality to serve as input for analysis (2). The second phase involves the use of artificial neural networks for analyzing the processed images. These two phases will be discussed in the following sections of this paper.

IMAGE PROCESSING

The images used in this project are taken from the ConnDOT PLV system. Images from this system are particularly difficult to process because of characteristic features of the ConnDOT photolog system like perspective views, non uniform illumination and shadows. The images must be treated to compensate for these factors before they can be used for analysis. The various elements of the strategy that we have developed for processing the images are outlined in the flowchart shown in Figure 5.

The first stage involves the use of a video digitizing software to capture and digitize a selected portion of the pavement image. Filters are then applied to this image to convert the color image to a gray scale image. The next stage, referred to as feature extraction, involves the processing of the gray scale image to isolate distress features. The two alternative processes that we have identified to achieve this objective are shown in the flow chart. Each of the alternatives involves a series of image processing techniques which are applied to the image to isolate distress features. Figures 1 and 2 illustrate the two series starting with the gray scale image in the first frame and ending with the processed binary image in the last frame. Figures 3 and 4 show the typical histograms with the corresponding optimum threshold values at which each of the gray scales were thresholded to obtain the binary images from the two series. The strategy outlined here was found to be capable of eliminating problems like shadows and variable contrasts which are characteristic of the Connecticut photolog system. The binary images obtained at the end of the process were of sufficient quality to serve as input to the neural network model for distress pattern recognition.

PREPARATION OF INPUT DATA FOR THE MODEL

The binary image file obtained at the end of image processing is first converted into an ASCII file to obtain a matrix of binary values. A zero in this matrix corresponds to a background pixel while a one corresponds to a distressed pixel. Parameters characteristic of each of the distress types are then calculated from the binary image matrix. We identified four attributes, listed below, which characterize the various types of distresses. These parameters (in various combinations), constitute the input matrix for each of the images. This matrix is stored in a batch file which serves as input to the neural network model for analysis.

D_x : Average pixel density along the X-axis
D_y : Average pixel density along the Y-axis
D_{xy} : Overall average pixel density
A : Angle of inclination of the distress feature (relevant only for linear cracks)

THE FEED FORWARD NEURAL NETWORK MODEL

A feed-forward neural network forms the core processing unit of the distress data analysis system. A typical feed forward multi-layer neural network (N-N) model consists of S layers of neural elements. Each neural element in a layer is interconnected with each of the elements in adjacent layers. The strength of each interconnection is characterized by its weight.

The four parameters listed previously constitute the input data to the network. Information propagates from the input layer to the output layer. Subsequently, the sum of the weighted inputs is filtered through a logistic function to produce an output from the output element. These outputs represent the final prediction of the neural network. Training of the neural network occurs through systematic adjustment of the interconnection weights so that the prediction output of the network will be as close as possible to the desired output.

Figure 6 shows a typical S layered Neural Network structure. In the j th layer, there are M_j processing elements which are interconnected with elements in the $(j-1)$ th and $(j+1)$ th layers. Associated with the interconnections between the k_{j-1} th element of layer $(j-1)$ and the k_j th element of layer j is the weighing factor W_{k_{j-1},k_j}. The transfer function, σ, maps the cumulative input X, to the output Y of a processing element. A generalized logistic function for σ is defined as follows (3) :

$$Y = \sigma(X) = (1 + e^{P(x)})^{-1} - c$$

For the present work $P(X)$ is restricted to the family of polynomials defined by $\sum_{q=0}^{m} \alpha_q X^q$. The commonly used values of $m = 1$, $\alpha_1 = -1$ and $C = 0.5$, corresponds to the conventional form of the logistic function (4). The term, α_0, corresponds to the bias term. A quasi Newton based training strategy was used for training the network. Details of the neural network training methodology are documented in reference (3).

PERFORMANCE OF MODEL

The training of the network is carried out in three stages. The first, second and third stages require three, twenty and twelve parameters respectively. It can be seen from the plots of number of iterations versus required training time (Figure 7) that as the number of parameters increases, the time required for training increases steeply. For example, the first stage requires only fifteen seconds of the CPU time before the training objective value gets close to zero. In contrast the second stage, involving twenty parameters, requires approximately eight hundred seconds.

The number of iterations required for training the network was independent of the number of data sets available for training and the number of parameters used. Forty five data sets involving twenty parameters required approximately the same number of iterations as thirty data sets with only twelve parameters. The plots of training objective versus number of iterations show that all the stages required approximately 50-60 iterations before a constant objective value was attained.

The third plot of objective versus iterations (Figure 7, Stage 3) indicate that the curve turns assymptotical at an objective value of 0.9 instead of zero. This problem is usually a result of multiple local minima and can be countered by reinitializing the training parameters and retraining the network.

At the end of the final stage, the network is trained to recognize four different types of distresses : patches, longitudinal cracks, transverse cracks and alligator cracks. The trained model was then used to validate a new data set of pavement images. We used a data set containing twenty three images, representing the four categories of distresses, for validating the network. The first two stages were validated with 100 % success. The final stage classified two images erroneously resulting in an overall success rate of 91 %. Better performance can be achieved by choosing a combination of parameters which more accurately characterize the distress types.

CONCLUSIONS

Neural networks have been found to perform robustly as pattern recognition tools in many different types of applications. The goal of our research work at the University of Connecticut is to make use of this capability of neural networks for the development of an automated system for pavement surface condition evaluation. We have developed an image processing strategy which can be used to process the pavement images before they are provided to the neural network model for analysis.

The pattern recognition system that we are developing at UCONN is based on a feed forward neural network model. We identified parameters, that we feel, adequately characterize various distresses based on the pixel density and the orientation angles of the distress feature. These parameters are used to train the feed forward neural network model. The model is then validated using a separate set of images.

So far, we have found that our analytical system has a success rate of 91 %. These results suggest that the methodology outlined has potential to be developed into a fully automated pavement distress analysis system.

REFERENCES

1. Mohamed S. Kaseko, Stephen G. Ritchie, "A Neural Network-Based Methodology for Pavement Crack Detection and Classification", Transportation Research - C, Vol.1, No. 4, 1993.

2. Vinod K. Kalikiri, Norman W. Garrick, Luke E. K. Achenie, "Processing Techniques for Evaluating Images Recorded by the Connecticut Photolog System", Transportation Research Board, TRB Preprint No. 940537, Washington, D.C., 1994.

3. Luke E. K. Achenie, "A Quasi Newton based Approach to the Training of the Multilayer Perceptron", Intelligent Engineering Systems Through Artificial Neural Networks, Volume 3, 1993.

4. D. E. Rumelhart, G. E. Hinton, R. J. Williams, "Learning Representations by Back-Propogation Errors", Nature, Volume 323, p. 533-536, 1986.

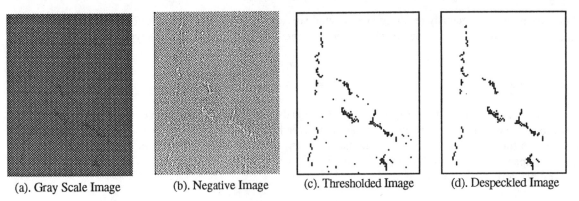

(a). Gray Scale Image   (b). Negative Image   (c). Thresholded Image   (d). Despeckled Image

Figure 1. Contrast Enhancement

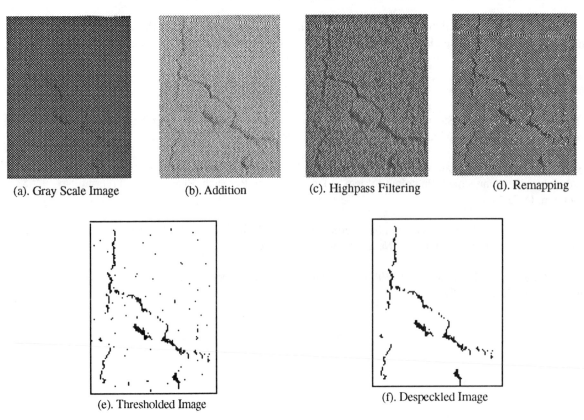

(a). Gray Scale Image   (b). Addition   (c). Highpass Filtering   (d). Remapping

(e). Thresholded Image   (f). Despeckled Image

Figure 2. Noise Supperssion

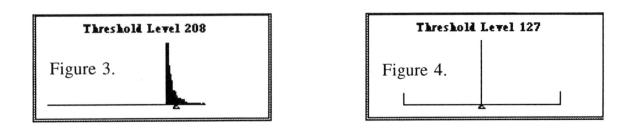

Threshold Level 208

Figure 3.

Threshold Level 127

Figure 4.

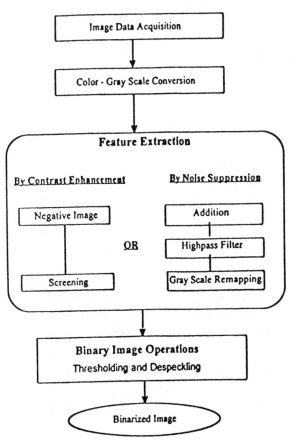

Figure 5.

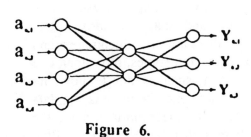

Figure 6.

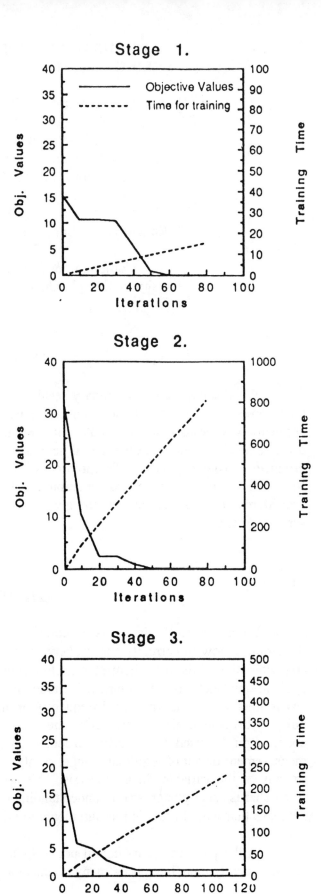

Figure 7.

A NEURAL NETWORK APPROACH TO PREDICT MISSING ENVIRONMENTAL DATA

I.W. Wong[1], D.C.L. Lam[1], A. Storey[2], P. Fong[2] & D.A. Swayne[2,3]

[1]National Water Research Institute
867 Lakeshore Road, Box 5050
Burlington, Ontario, CANADA L7R 4A6

[2]ESA Inc.
489 Enfield Road, Burlington, Ontario, CANADA L7T 2X5

[3]Computing & Information Sciences Dept.
University of Guelph, Guelph, Ontario, CANADA N1G 2W1

ABSTRACT

We discuss some preliminary results of a neural network approach to predict missing environmental data. One of the main problems in environmental modelling and expert system application is the lack of useful data. The neural network approach will no doubt provide more useful data. It is found that the neural network, when used with proper pre-screening processes, produces satisfactory results. The preprocessing techniques used here are the cluster analysis to filter noisy data and the transformation to align the data in the appropriate range. Design procedures for this application are given and its performance is discussed by means of a sensitivity analysis.

I. INTRODUCTION

Environmental science is a complex field and multidisciplinary in nature. When determining how to correctly analyze any collection of data, the first consideration must be the characteristics of the data themselves. After understanding the data, we can apply these data in applications such as environmental modelling, expert systems and statistics. Most often, environmental data are measured frequently or in real time, but others are often incomplete and noisy. Most statistical software permit the entry of the missing data. Sometimes, more than one code might be used to identify particular types of missing data, such as don't know, no measurement or out of legitimate range. Analytical packages typically exclude the missing data for any of the variables in an analysis. This approach is found to be inappropriate, since the researcher is usually interested in understanding the entire database, rather than the portion of the database that would provide measurements to all relevant variables in the analysis.

In the past few years neural networks have received a great deal of attention in many areas. Recently there have been many practical applications to apply neural networks techniques to environmental science [1]. Much of the success is contributed to the ability of neural networks to predict and draw conclusions when presented with complex, noisy, irrelevant, and even partial and missing information. In particular, we are interested in dealing with the data poor situation, i.e. finding the appropriate values of the missing data. As a result, a neural network can be trained to predict missing values from a network trained to examples.

II. NEURAL NETWORK APPROACH

We have developed a knowledge-based system, RAISON, using the C++ language [2]. This system is composed of a geographical information system (GIS), a database, a spreadsheet and most importantly, an artificial intelligence (A.I.) module. In this paper, we describe how to implement neural networks within the A.I. module.

The neural network that we have implemented is a variation of the back-propagation network model [3] because of its simplicity and flexibility required to interface with other modules in RAISON. In this network model, data from the input layer are fed into one or more hidden layers and a set of connections weights are continually adjusted under the supervised training mode. In particular, the feedforward output state calculation is combined with backward error propagation (e.g. using the conventional sum of squared errors based on the square of the difference between the output value and observed value). In addition, it is found that the back-propagation network is the most appropriate one in dealing with missing data. However, the training time tends to be very slow in this kind of network. Since environmental data sets are often very large, we have opted for a modified form of back-propagation network [4], called quickprop.

The following are some of the essential features of this neural network model:
(i)   The weight is updated based on the sum of the errors affected by that weight over the entire training set. This gives the gradient of the composite error function in the weight space.
(ii)   Different learning rates are prescribed for different weights in the network.
(iii)   We set the weight change proportional to the derivative of the sigmoid function and when a node output is close to the extremes of the function, the derivative is close to zero. When an output node's error is large, the small derivative allows a slight change to be propagated back, hence slowing down the convergence. To overcome this, a constant of 0.1 is added to the derivative value.
(iv)   While standard back-propagation takes the first derivative of the error surface with respect to the weights and adds a constant step size in that direction, quickprop uses the gradient of the error function at two consecutive points and the weight change between them, fits a parabola and sets the step size to the minimum of this parabola.
(v)   To further improve the performance, a weight decay term is added to the error function which optimizes the weights on this slightly changed error surface.

III. PREPROCESSING TECHNIQUES

It is not always necessary to have all the environmental parameters in the data set used in the neural networks. Some parameters have a stronger relationship than others. For example, pH and alkalinity measurements should be closely related. Therefore, it is desirable to pre-screen the parameters before feeding them into the neural network. One of the most commonly used preprocessing methods is cluster analysis.

Statistical methods are used to select clusters in order to examine whether significant differences exist between the objects of different clusters. One of the approaches is to consider a criterion for measuring the tightness of the clusters and to plot its value against the number of clusters [5]. A sudden marked flattening of the curve indicates a significant number of clusters since there is relatively little gain from a further increase of number of clusters. In our case, the correlation coefficients between parameters are used as a criterion to determine the number of significant clusters.

It is also found that the ranges of some environmental parameters vary over several orders of magnitude. In practice, careful treatment of the network representation is usually required to obtain an efficient network. When the range of a parameter is large (many orders of magnitude), the logarithm of the variable should be used. This transformation makes small changes in small inputs as important as large changes in large inputs. In addition, some of the parameters are logarithmic in nature, e.g. pH. We must deal with these parameters properly to achieve optimum results.

IV. AN EXAMPLE

We use a data set of water quality data (NAQUADAT) in the Great Lakes Ecoregions as an example. This set of data consists of the following parameters: Na, K, Ca, Mg, SO_4, Cl, alkalinity, pH, colour, specific conductivity, Al, Fe, NO_3, NH_4 and DOC. Some of the pH data are not available. The problem is to show how to make use of the existing known data for all parameters to predict the missing pH values.

First, we have to identify the parameters which have a close relationship with pH and use them as the input parameters in the neural network. This is done using the cluster analysis. A cluster distance is assigned to each pair of parameters and then the cluster process uses these distances to classify the parameters into different clusters and to determine the appropriate number of clusters. In this example, the cluster distance is based on the correlation coefficient from the regression analysis. Figure 1 shows the plot of cluster distance (regression coefficient) against the number of clusters. The significant value is identified when there is a abrupt change in slope. The results of the cluster analysis are summarized in Figure 1. By inspecting this figure, the appropriate number of clusters is 10. It is found that pH formed a cluster with Ca, specific conductivity and alkalinity.

Once we identify the parameters that are related to pH, we can set up a neural network to estimate the pH values from these parameters. To validate the preprocessing techniques, a

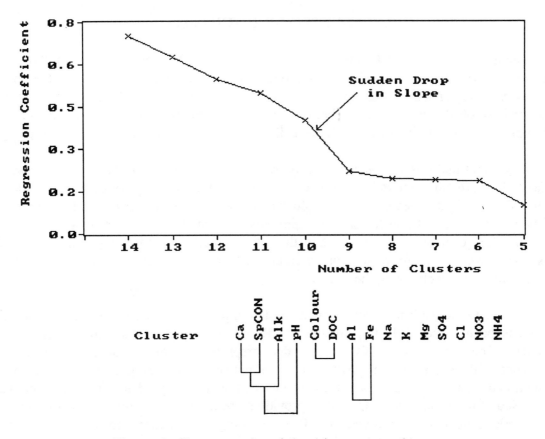

Figure 1: Cluster results of the 14 parameter data set

sensitivity analysis is performed. Three different network topologies are used. The first network uses all 14 parameters to predict pH. The second network uses seven randomly picked parameters that are unrelated with pH as determined from the cluster analysis as inputs. Finally, we use the three parameters from the cluster results as the input parameters. In addition, each topology has two variations: the output parameter pH is either normal or log-transformed. The number of hidden layers can be set to one to speed up the training. As a rule of thumb, the number of hidden nodes is set to the geometric mean of the sum of the inputs and outputs nodes [6]. Table 1 summaries the layout of the sensitivity analysis.

Case	Input Nodes	Hidden Nodes	Output Node	pH Tranform.	Relationship with pH	Median Rel. Error
a	14	4	1	Yes	Don't Care	1.8%
b	14	4	1	No	Don't Care	3.2%
c	7	3	1	Yes	Unrelated	4.5%
d	7	3	1	No	Unrelated	8.2%
e	3	2	1	Yes	Highly related	1.6%
f	3	2	1	No	Highly related	2.8%

Table 1: Layout of the sensitivity analysis

V. RESULTS AND DISCUSSION

There are a total of 2250 good records in the data set. We randomly select 400 records as our training set and the rest is for verification. Training is complete when either the network reaches one million epochs or the sum-squared error satisfies a prescribed threshold. We use the median values of the relative error between the predicted pH and the observed pH as a benchmark of the sensitivity analysis. Table 1 displays the results of the six network topologies.

It is found that cases (c) and (d) are the worst cases as expected. Although the results of case (a) and (e) are close, the training time on case (e) is about one-tenth of case (a). In addition, case (e) shows slightly better results. It confirms that cluster analysis based on regression coefficient is an essential tool for preprocessing environmental data. It is also found that cases (a), (c) and (e) generate better results than their counterparts, i.e. cases (b), (d) and (e). This shows that proper transformation on certain environmental parameters will yield vast improvement over simply using the data.

The neural network provides a new approach to predict missing values of environmental data. It has been successfully implemented in RAISON as part of the artificial intelligence component. The sensitivity analysis shows that preprocessing of the data is crucial to the performance of the neural network. Although neural networks require a great deal of training and computational resources, it is very fruitful when dealing with large data sets in environmental science. Neural networks can be applied to provide more information with reasonable accuracy. Future work include the improvement of the training time and in formulating imprecise measurements with fuzzy logic algorithm.

VI. ACKNOWLEDGEMENTS

The authors would like to thank Dr. William G. Booty, Jane Kerby and Kevin Hopkins for their helpful suggestions.

VII. REFERENCES

[1]   Schmuller, J. 1990, "Neural Networks and Environmental Applications", in J.M. Hushon (ed.) *Expert Systems for Environmental Applications*, ACS Symposium Series 431, pp. 52-68.

[2]   Lam, D.C.L. and D.A. Swayne, 1992. "Some experiences in applying the RAISON expert system to environmental problems. In (Eds. J.W. Brahan and G.E. Lasker) Advances in Artificial Intelligence - Theory and Applications, IIAS Publication, Windsor, Canada. pp. 59-64.

[3]   Rumelhart, D.E. and J.L. McCelland, 1986. "Parallel distributed processing, explorations in the microstructure of cognition. Vol. 1: Foundations", MIT Press, Cambridge, MA.

[4]   Fahlman, S.E., 1989, "Faster-learning variations on back-propagation: an empirical study", in Proceedings of the 1988 Connectionist Models Summer School, Morgan Kaufmann.

[5]   Massart, D.L. and L. Kaufman, 1983, "The interpretation of analytical chemical data by the use of cluster analysis", Wiley, pp. 147-149.

[6]   Maren, A.J., Harston, C.T. and R. M. Pap, 1990. Handbook of neural computing applications, Academic Press, pp.238-243.

ART-based Control Chart Pattern Recognizers

H. Brian Hwarng and Chu Wei Chong

Department of Decision Sciences
National University of Singapore
Singapore 0511
E-Mail: fbahhl@nusunix.nus.sg

Abstract

A control chart pattern recognizer (CCPR) which is based on Adaptive Resonance Theory (ART) is proposed. There are two major motives for using ART, that is, ART's ability to retain previously learned pattern classes while adaptively learning new ones and ART's capability of fast learning. To improve the ART-based CCPR's ability to discriminate patterns between pattern classes and, at the same time, to tolerate minor pattern variations within each pattern class, a synthesized layer is added on top of the recognition layer. To cater to the peculiar needs of control chart applications, a quasi-supervised training strategy is employed. The performance evaluation indicates that the ART-based CCPR can be readily integrated into an on-line, real-time manufacturing environment.

Introduction

The need of identifying patterns of data on statistical quality control charts was realized early in the 1950's [Western Electric, 1956]. In Western Electric's *Statistical Quality Control Handbook* a set of run rules were devised to detect some nonrandom patterns. These rules or variation of these rules are still quite popular in today's literature and practices. However, recently the utility of neural networks in identifying process nonrandomness exhibited on statistical quality control charts has been demonstrated by a number of researchers [Hwarng & Hubele, 1991, 1992, 1993; Lim et. al., 1991; Guo & Dooley, 1992]. While traditional run rules are useful in signaling if there is any structural change in the mean and/or variance of the process, the pattern recognition approach which explicitly identifies nonrandom patterns is more useful in recognizing what particular type of nonrandomness occurs in the process. Additional information about nonrandomness in the process then can be deduced through the identified nonrandom pattern. This approach is not only more effective in determining corrective actions but more flexible in a dynamic manufacturing environment.

In almost all of the published works, the major architecture used has been back-propagation neural networks. Although back-propagation algorithm has been widely used and well studied, two well known problems, namely, slowness in training and inability to perform adaptive learning without re-learning still pose some inconveniences for practical applications. In this paper, we use Adaptive Resonance Theory (ART) [Carpenter & Grossberg, 1987, 1988] to resolve the problems. ART-based neural networks are adopted for two distinguished features, that is, ART's ability to retain previously learned pattern classes while adaptively learning new ones and ART's capability of fast learning. Throughout this paper, we only refer to the binary version of ART, ART1.

Problems Encountered

While the ART architecture provides solutions for two major concerns of back-propagation networks, the use of ART does not guarantee a success in control chart pattern recognition. The first problem comes from ART's recoding instability. Ryan & Winter [1987] pointed out that ART1 networks had not entirely solved the code stability problems. For example, once a new category was learned in the recognition layer (or F2 layer in Carpenter & Grossberg's notation) the top-down weights can be gradually recoded in subsequent presentation of slightly varied new patterns. The recoding can be so substantial that eventually the network would not recognize the original pattern or patterns which are very close to the original pattern. Figure 1 illustrates how this problem occurs in control chart pattern recognition. In the figure each control chart pattern is represented by 1's in a 7 by 8 grid. A pattern is read from top to bottom of a grid. The network has been trained and encoded with two top-down templates which are sudden shift upward and cyclic patterns. Four inputs of noisy sudden shift upward are presented to the network. On the fourth input, the network fails to classify it as category 1 because the top-down template has been recoded by the previous noisy sudden shift upward patterns. The input pattern fails the vigilance test. As a result, it is classified into a new category.

The second problem arises from ART's inability to classify shifted or rotated patterns into the same category as the un-shifted or un-rotated patterns. Figure 2 shows two cyclic patterns. One was shifted downward by one row. The only vigilance value which could classify both of them into the same category is zero.

The third problem results from the unsupervised training environment. Under unsupervised training, when an input pattern fails to match the learned top-down templates during the vigilance test the network always learns a new category

```
                                 TOP DOWN TEMPLATES      vigilance=0.7
       Input pattern       1              2
                                                              3
  1    0 0 0 1 0 0 0    0 0 0 1 0 0 0    0 0 0 1 0 0 0
       0 0 0 1 0 0 0    0 0 0 1 0 0 0    0 0 1 0 0 0 0
       0 0 0 1 0 0 0    0 0 0 1 0 0 0    0 1 0 0 0 0 0
       0 0 0 1 0 0 0    0 0 0 1 0 0 0    0 0 1 0 0 0 0
       1 0 0 0 0 0 0    1 0 0 0 0 0 0    0 0 0 1 0 0 0
       1 0 0 0 0 0 0    1 0 0 0 0 0 0    0 0 0 0 1 0 0
       1 0 0 0 0 0 0    1 0 0 0 0 0 0    0 0 0 0 0 1 0
       1 0 0 0 0 0 0    1 0 0 0 0 0 0    0 0 0 0 1 0 0

  2    0 0 0 1 0 0 0    0 0 0 1 0 0 0    0 0 0 1 0 0 0
       0 0 0 1 0 0 0    0 0 0 1 0 0 0    0 0 1 0 0 0 0
       0 0 0 0 0 1 0    0 0 0 0 0 0 0    0 1 0 0 0 0 0
       0 0 0 1 0 0 0    0 0 0 1 0 0 0    0 0 1 0 0 0 0
       1 0 0 0 0 0 0    1 0 0 0 0 0 0    0 0 0 1 0 0 0
       1 0 0 0 0 0 0    1 0 0 0 0 0 0    0 0 0 0 1 0 0
       1 0 0 0 0 0 0    1 0 0 0 0 0 0    0 0 0 0 0 1 0
       1 0 0 0 0 0 0    1 0 0 0 0 0 0    0 0 0 0 1 0 0

  3    0 0 0 1 0 0 0    0 0 0 1 0 0 0    0 0 0 1 0 0 0
       0 0 0 1 0 0 0    0 0 0 1 0 0 0    0 0 1 0 0 0 0
       0 0 0 1 0 0 0    0 0 0 0 0 0 0    0 1 0 0 0 0 0
       0 0 0 0 1 0 0    0 0 0 0 0 0 0    0 0 1 0 0 0 0
       1 0 0 0 0 0 0    1 0 0 0 0 0 0    0 0 0 1 0 0 0
       1 0 0 0 0 0 0    1 0 0 0 0 0 0    0 0 0 0 1 0 0
       1 0 0 0 0 0 0    1 0 0 0 0 0 0    0 0 0 0 0 1 0
       1 0 0 0 0 0 0    1 0 0 0 0 0 0    0 0 0 0 1 0 0

  4    0 0 0 1 0 0 0    0 0 0 1 0 0 0    0 0 0 1 0 0 0    0 0 0 1 0 0 0
       0 0 0 0 1 0 0    0 0 0 1 0 0 0    0 0 1 0 0 0 0    0 0 0 0 1 0 0
       0 0 0 1 0 0 0    0 0 0 0 0 0 0    0 1 0 0 0 0 0    0 0 0 1 0 0 0
       0 0 0 1 0 0 0    0 0 0 0 0 0 0    0 0 1 0 0 0 0    0 0 0 1 0 0 0
       1 0 0 0 0 0 0    1 0 0 0 0 0 0    0 0 0 1 0 0 0    1 0 0 0 0 0 0
       1 0 0 0 0 0 0    1 0 0 0 0 0 0    0 0 0 0 1 0 0    1 0 0 0 0 0 0
       1 0 0 0 0 0 0    1 0 0 0 0 0 0    0 0 0 0 0 1 0    1 0 0 0 0 0 0
       1 0 0 0 0 0 0    1 0 0 0 0 0 0    0 0 0 0 1 0 0    1 0 0 0 0 0 0
```

Figure 1 Illustration of the Recoding Instability

provided sufficient capacity in the recognition layer. This might not be desirable in control chart pattern recognition. Because, in the actual application, we are interested in only a number of nonrandom patterns. When random patterns, which are anything other than the pre-specified nonrandom patterns, are presented to the network, they should not be classified as new nonrandom patterns. Nevertheless, under unsupervised training it is very likely that many random patterns would be classified as new categories in the recognition layer even a low vigilance value is used. Consequently, the network might grow very large in the recognition layer.

With the above three noted problems unsolved, the use of ART-based neural networks still can not provide satisfactory results for control chart pattern recognition. Some alternatives need to be devised.

Alternative Architecture and Training Strategy

Overcoming these problems would involve using some alternative architecture and training strategy. For the problem of recoding instability and that of inability to classify shifted or rotated patterns, adding one additional layer on top of the recognition layer would alleviate the dilemma. This layer is called synthesized layer. The

```
0 0 0 1 0 0 0      0 0 0 0 1 0 0
0 0 1 0 0 0 0      0 0 0 1 0 0 0
0 1 0 0 0 0 0      0 0 1 0 0 0 0
0 0 1 0 0 0 0      0 1 0 0 0 0 0
0 0 0 1 0 0 0      0 0 1 0 0 0 0
0 0 0 0 1 0 0      0 0 0 1 0 0 0
0 0 0 0 0 1 0      0 0 0 0 1 0 0
0 0 0 0 1 0 0      0 0 0 0 0 1 0
   cycle              shifted cycle
```

Figure 2 Shifted Patterns

synthesized layer is configured in such a way that one node is used to connect all similar learned categories, which are either shifted or slightly varied, in the recognition layer into one class. In other words, for any patterns which are shifted or slightly varied in the input, the network will be able to classify them into a same category even though they might belong to different categories in the recognition layer. Of course, this can only be done with some a priori knowledge about the data. Figure 3 shows the new ART architecture. As an illustration in the figure, the network has learned the shifted cycles and upward trend patterns. They are represented as distinguished categories in the recognition layer. However, the shifted versions of patterns are connected to one shared node in the synthesized layer. That is, three cyclic pattern categories are connected to node 1 and three upward trend categories are connected to node 2 in the synthesized layer.

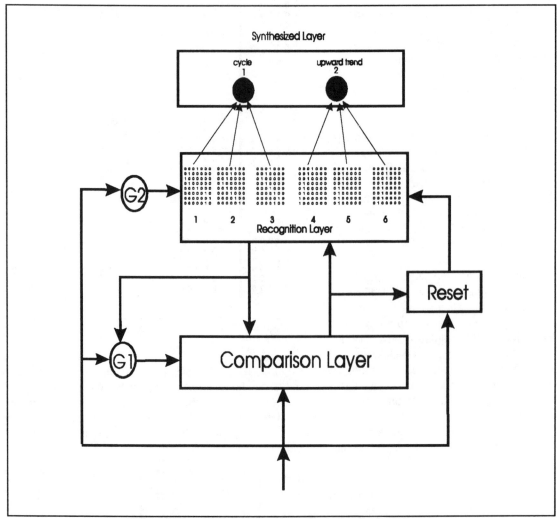

Figure 3 The ART Architecture with A Synthesized Layer

To resolve the problem of learning too many new categories at the recognition layer, some quasi-supervised training strategy based on prior knowledge about the process data should be employed. The strategy is as follows: (a) generate or collect a representative set of nonrandom patterns which covers the whole spectrum of patterns of interest and group them according to pattern classes; (b) configure the size of the recognition layer to be the number of nonrandom patterns in the training set plus one additional node denoted as "others"; (c) during training each pattern is presented to the network once according to the pre-arranged sequence and connection weights are adjusted accordingly; (d) upon completion of training the number of learned categories should be exactly the number of nonrandom patterns; (e) during testing (recalling) weights are not modified and any patterns that are not classified under any one of the learned categories will be placed under "other" category, i.e., random patterns; (f) in the synthesized layer one node is used to connect all similar categories in the recognition layer into one class, called a pattern class. Thus, the size of the synthesized layer should be configured to be the number of pattern classes of interest. The training time for this ART-based CCPR is rather brief because the training simple goes through a single pass of the training data set.

It should be noted that although the extent of the difficulties posed by the first two problems can be manipulated to a certain degree by the vigilance parameter, it is necessary to resort to alternatives such as the one mentioned above in order to eliminate the problems. With the additional synthesized layer which deals with looser boundary conditions tackling the second problem, the original recognition layer can remain at a more vigilant level such that the first problem of recoding instability can be alleviated.

Performance Evaluation

Here we present partial results from our simulation. The two performance measures are the detection rate (R_t) and the run length (ARL_t). R_t is the percentage of sequences of data in which the target pattern was detected within a sequence of data of a fixed length, i.e., measuring how frequently the CCPR detects the target pattern. ARL_t is the average run length of detecting the target pattern within a sequence of data, i.e., measuring how quickly the target pattern can be detected in a sequence of data [Hwarng & Hubele, 1993]. In Table 1, R_t is calculated based on 100 independent sequences of data. Each sequence consists of 30 observations. ARL_t is calculated in terms of the number of classifying attempts. We compared the performance with that of a back-propagation CCPR [Hwarng & Hubele, 1993]. The results based on two vigilance values, 0.6 and 0.7, for the ART-based CCPR and two activation cutoff values, 0.85 and 0.90, for the back-propagation CCPR are listed in Table 1. In general, two CCPRs performed comparably and they were able to detect most of patterns within an ARL_t of two at low noise levels. Even at high noise levels, the ART-based CCPR was able to detect cycles within an ARL_t of 8. The ART-based CCPR has better R_t for noisier cycles.

Table 1. Partial results of performance evaluation of ART-based CCPR: cyclic patterns with various amplitude and noise values

Amp (σ)	Noise (σ)	ART			Back-Propagation		
		Vig.	R_t(%)	ARL_t	Act. Cut.	R_t(%)	ARL_t
1.50	0.1	0.6	100	1.00	0.85	100	1.00
		0.7	100	1.00	0.90	100	1.00
2.00	0.1	0.6	100	1.00	0.85	100	1.00
		0.7	100	1.00	0.90	100	1.00
2.50	0.1	0.6	100	1.00	0.85	100	1.00
		0.7	100	1.00	0.90	100	1.00
1.50	0.3	0.6	98	1.57	0.85	100	1.56
		0.7	99	3.02	0.90	100	1.72
2.00	0.3	0.6	96	1.67	0.85	94	1.21
		0.7	97	3.64	0.90	91	1.17
2.50	0.3	0.6	100	1.24	0.85	86	1.00
		0.7	100	1.56	0.90	82	1.05
1.50	0.5	0.6	92	3.85	0.85	95	3.58
		0.7	72	5.78	0.90	96	5.35
2.00	0.5	0.6	93	3.26	0.85	71	1.73
		0.7	78	7.56	0.90	73	2.15
2.50	0.5	0.6	93	3.51	0.85	53	1.46
		0.7	81	5.84	0.90	49	1.98

Closing Remarks

Alternative architecture and training strategy were used to improve the performance of an ART-based control chart pattern recognizer. In general the ART-based CCPR performs comparably to the back-propagation CCPR but with better detection rates for noisier patterns. The major advantages of the ART-based CCPR are ART's ability to retain previously learned pattern classes while adaptively learning new ones and ART's capability of fast learning. With the inherent distinguished features and the improved capabilities, the ART-based CCPR can be readily integrated into an on-line, real-time manufacturing environment.

Acknowledgement

This research is supported in part by National University of Singapore research grant No. 3920070.

References

Carpenter, G. A. and Grossberg, S., 1987, A Massively Parallel Architecture for a Self-Organizing Neural Pattern Recognition Machine, *Computer Vision, Graphics, and Image Processing*, **37**, 54-115.

Carpenter, G. A. and Grossberg, S., 1988, Self-Organizing Neural Network Architectures for Real-Time Adaptive Pattern Recognition, *IEEE Computer*, **21**(3), 77-88.

Guo, Y. and Dooley, K. J., 1992, Identification of Change Structure in Statistical Process Control, *International Journal of Production Research*, **30**(7) 1655-1669.

Hwarng, H. B. and Hubele, N. F., 1991, X-bar Chart Pattern Recognition Using Neural Nets, *ASQC Quality Congress Transactions*, Milwaukee, WI, 884-889.

Hwarng, H. B., and Hubele, N. F., 1992, Boltzmann Machines That Learn to Recognize Patterns on Control Charts, *Statistics and Computing*, **2**(4) 191-202.

Hwarng, H. B., and Hubele, N. F., 1993, Back-propagation Pattern Recognizers for $\bar{X}$ Control Charts: Methodology and Performance, *Computers and Industrial Engineering*, **24**(2) 219-235.

Lim, M. H., Gwee, B. H. and Goh, T. H., 1991, Cause Associator Network for Fuzzily Deduced Conclusion in Process Control, *International Joint Conference on Neural Networks*, Singapore, November 18-21, **II**, 1248-1253.

Ryan, T. W. and Winter, C.L., 1987, Variations on Adaptive Resonance Theory, *International Joint Conference on Neural Networks*, **II**, 767-775.

Western Electric Co., Inc., 1956, *Statistical Quality Control Handbook*, Western Electric Co., New York.

A CONSENSUS-LEARNING COMMITTEE NETWORK[1]

Susan Garavaglia
Dun & Bradstreet Information Services, N. A.
Three Sylvan Way
Parsippany, New Jersey 07054-3896
Email: P01051@psilink.com

ABSTRACT: Neural Networks that employ a competitive learning layer are especially well suited to modeling organizational behavior. The Committee Machine of Nilsson (1965) and the Counterpropagation Network of Hecht-Nielsen are two examples that incorporate a majority rule and a winner-take-all rule, respectively. A variation on the Committee Machine is introduced that uses Kohonen learning and constructs a consensus based on the riskiness of the decision-making environment. The network adapts in real time to the risk profile by modifying the size of the consensus required to "approve" each case. The model proposed by Sah and Stiglitz (1985, 1988) serves as a theoretical framework for the economic consequences of increasing committee and/or consensus size and the costs of Type I and Type II errors. Experimental results show that increasing the consensus size reduced Type II errors but that the best overall performance was with a relatively small consensus. The implication is that there is "safety in numbers," i. e., the entire committee can protect itself from Type II errors, but the true optimal consensus size may be less than a majority.

Partial List of References:

Kohonen, Teuvo. 1989. Self-Organization and Associative Memory. 3d ed. Berlin: Springer-Verlag.

Nilsson, Nils J. 1990. The Mathematical Foundations of Learning Machines. (Previously published as: Learning Machines. 1965.) San Mateo, CA: Morgan Kaufman Publishers, Inc.

Sah, Rah Kumar, and Joseph E. Stiglitz. 1986. The architecture of economic systems: hierarchies and polyarchies. The American Economic Review. 76 No. 4 (September): 716-727.

_____ and _____. 1988. Committees, hierarchies, and polyarchies. The Economic Journal. 98 (June): 451-470.

_____ and _____. 1985. Economics of Committees. School of Organization and Management Working Paper No. D10. Yale University.

---

[1] Originally Published as Chapter Three of Ph.D. Thesis: Economic Rationality and Neural Networks, City University of New York Graduate Center, 1993.

An Information Theoretic Re-interpretation of the
Self Organizing Map With Standard Scaled Dummy Variables

Susan Garavaglia
Dun & Bradstreet Information Services, N. A.
Three Sylvan Way
Parsippany, New Jersey 07054-3896
Email: P01051@psilink.com

Abstract: The Self-Organizing Map (SOM) of Kohonen (1989) produces a two-dimensional topological ordering of data vectors. Data clustering and dimensionality reduction are two typical applications.of SOMs. In Garavaglia (1993), two versions of the same data vectors, the original with simple binary valued elements and the other having the elements transformed by standard scaling, were input as training sets to a SOM. The results were that the scaled vectors were concentrated in fewer and less topologically dispersed processing elements (PEs), as measured by the PE activation counts. Originally, it was proposed that this result could serve as some form of relative measure of homogeneity.. The statistical properties of the scaled version of the data are discussed and a more formal diversity index is proposed that draws its inspiration from Information theory.

1. Background

The Self-Organizing Map (SOM) of Kohonen (1989) produces an $n \times m$ (two-dimensional) topological ordering of data vectors using a special layer of $n \times m$[1] processing elements and Kohonen's mean-reverting competitive learning. A basic form of Kohonen learning is:

$$w'_i = w_i + c(x_i - w_i) \text{ or } \Delta w_i = c(x_i - w_i) \qquad (1)$$

$$\text{and} \qquad \lim_{t \to \infty} w'_i = \bar{x_i}$$

where w'_i is the updated connection weight, w_i is the initial weight at time t, c is a learning coefficient, and x_i is the input.

In Garavaglia (1993) a SOM was applied to clustering U. S. Census data after transforming the data elements into binary valued vectors. Each vector represented a single Census Tract and the individual elements represented factual information for each tract . One 8 x 8 SOM was trained with the binary data values and a second 8 x 8 SOM was trained with standard scale transformations of the binary data. Standard scaling produces values which are an index of deviation from the mean.[2] The number and location of activated processing units was compared for the two versions. The initial example, Census Division #6 - New England, yielded 33 active units for the unscaled data and 18 active units for the scaled data. The first experiment did not use normalized vectors. A macro-micro interpretation was proposed, the unscaled version being a micro analysis which reflected the diversity of the data and the scaled version reflecting the macro view of the data emphasizing the overall "sameness" or homogeneity of the data.

In the sections following, an overview of the statistical properties of the data, results on all 9 U. S. Census divisions, a SOM-derived Diversity Index, and theory of interpretation are given. The conclusion may appear to contradict the earlier result, but is, in fact, an information theoretic interpretation rather than a contradiction. The homogeneity described in the earlier work (Garavaglia 1993) reflected a view of the data that equated "sameness" with "amorphousness." The relationship between this quality and relative system entropy, i .e., that the homogeneity characteristic pertains to the

---

[1]In most applications $n = m$ producing a square layer.

[2] A standard scaled version of a variable x is $z = \dfrac{x - x}{\sigma}$

probabilities and not the data itself, is explained. In other words, *the ratio of unscaled active SOM units to scaled active SOM units gives information about the degree of equiprobability among data in a system.*

2. Statistical Properties of Binary Valued Data and the Relationship to System Entropy

Dummy variables allow the representation of qualitative information in quantitative modeling. If the information is a two-valued, i. e., a true-false proposition, then one dummy variable can be used to indicate the proposition is true with a value of 1, or 0 otherwise. More complicated qualitative information, such as the education level of a person, requires either reduction of the information to a two-valued proposition, or more than one dummy variable. For example, typical education categories (no high school diploma, high school diploma only, some college, undergraduate degree, or graduate school and beyond) would be represented in a traditional statistical model as four dummy variables, with one category, say, no high school diploma, represented by the 4 dummy variables having a value of zero. For simple transmission of the data in a noiseless channel, five equiprobable categories could be represented by an average of 1.609438 binary digits each.[3] The difference is that the collinearity of having two dummy variables assume the same value for any condition would threaten the statistical stability of a model, while the average of 1.609438 binary digits is used solely to transmit the information from a sender to a receiver or to efficiently store the data. For an explanation of the resulting collinearity when n conditions are represented by n dummy variables and a constant (intercept) is also present, see Maddala (1977).

The average or mean of a dummy variable is the proportion , p, of observations having the dummy variable value of 1. The statistic p is also the probability of obtaining a value of 1 in a random draw. Therefore, the distribution is neither continuous nor normal, but point binomial, or Bernoulli. Because of this, the standard deviation, **S**, (of the population) takes on a unique meaning because it depends on only p. It is at a maximum with $p = 0.5$ and approaches 0 when p approaches its extreme values 0 or 1.[4] Entropy has similar characteristics in that it is at its maximum when all events being measured have an equal likelihood. However, entropy increases with n and the population standard deviation does not depend on n (although the sample standard deviation does). Wiener's (1948) comparison of entropy with information is apropos here: "Just as the amount of information in a system is a measure of its degree of organization, so the entropy of a system is a measure of its degree of disorganization; and the one is simply the negative of the other."[5]

Thus, for binary valued data elements, a value of the standard deviation that is at its maximum indicates equal proportions of each value. In information theory, equal proportions mean "no bias," a maximum freedom of choice and maximum uncertainty. The measurement of "information, choice and uncertainty," [6] is the domain of entropy. The general formula (from Shannon and Weaver (1949)) is:

$$\mathbf{H} \quad = \quad - K \Sigma \, p_i \log p_i \qquad (2)$$

where **H** is the entropy, K is some constant for unit of measure, p_i is the probability of the event. For binary data, in which there are two possible values with probabilities p and $(1-p)$, entropy is calculated by

$$\mathbf{H} \quad = \quad - (p \log p + (1-p) \log (1-p)) \qquad (3)$$

Two of the properties that Shannon cited that make **H** a "reasonable" measure of choice or information also apply to the standard deviation in the case of dummy variables. **H** tends to 0 as the proportion of $p_i = 0$ increases reflecting a decrease in choices. The standard deviation tends to 0 as the variability of the data decreases. As stated above, both **H** and **S** are at a maximum when the probability or

---

[3] Based on $-(5(0.2 \log 0.2)) = 1.609438$.

[4] The population statistics are used in this example rather than the sample statistics. For more details on the distributions, see (Mood, Graybill, and Boes 1974).

[5] p. 11.

[6] See (Shannon and Weaver 1949), p. 50.

proportion = 0.5. Figure 2-1 shows the relationships between p, **H**, and **S**. This is relevant to the application because one goal of analyzing the U. S. Census data is to gain information about the relative diversity of each region and of the regions among themselves. Weaver thought that information theory and entropy might strike his reader as "disappointing and bizarre - disappointing because it has nothing to do with meaning, and bizarre because it deals not with a single message but rather with the statistical character of a whole ensemble of messages, bizarre also because in these statistical terms the two words information and uncertainty find themselves to be partners."[7]

As a brief digression to confirm the intuition of this idea: consider the following example as an illustration of the partnership between information and uncertainty. If the results of an election are predicted to favor one candidate by with 90% of the vote and there is confidence in this prediction, an observer may be tempted both: a) not to vote, and b) not to spend money on a newspaper the next day because: a) he or she does not perceive a free choice, and b) the money spent on the newspaper will not bring any extra information. Now if the results are predicted as "50-50" there is both an incentive to vote and to buy the newspaper, because the vote could effect the outcome and the newspaper will tell the reader something he cannot confidently infer from the predictions - the outcome. The point is that with a high degree of certainty, and the cost of information being fixed, there is less of a benefit in purchasing the information.

Figure 2-1

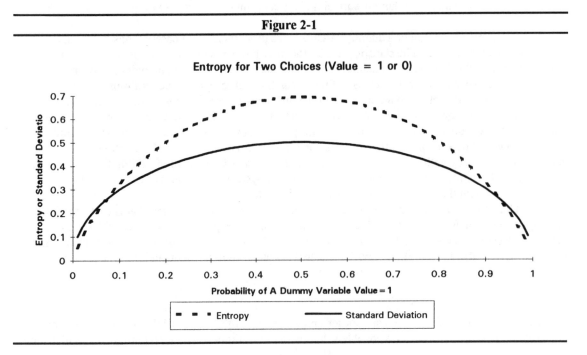

When standard scaling is applied to binary valued data, the results are *new binary values for the data that inherently contain the information about proportions.* Specifically, when binary data is represented as 0 or 1, the maximum absolute value distance between any two binary data elements is 1 regardless of the distribution of values. When the data is standard scaled, the maximum absolute value distance between any two binary data elements depends on the proportion of 1's. This distance is maximized when the proportion is minimized, i. e. $1/n$. Table 2-1 contains examples of these distances for a set of proportions (in deciles), and Figure 2-2 is a graph of these relationships.

---

[7]ibid., p. 27.

Table 2-1

Mean p p1	Scaled 1 z1	Scaled 0 z0	Scaled Distance (z1 - z0)	Non-Scaled (p1 - p0)
0.0	n/a	n/a	n/a	-1.0
0.1	3	-0.33333	3.333333	0.8
0.2	2	-0.5	2.5	0.6
0.3	1.527525	-0.65465	2.182179	0.4
0.4	1.224745	-0.8165	2.041241	0.2
0.5	**1**	**-1**	**2**	**0**
0.6	0.816497	-1.22474	2.041241	-0.2
0.7	0.654654	-1.52753	2.182179	-0.4
0.8	0.5	-2	2.5	-0.6
0.9	0.333333	-3	3.333333	-0.8
1.0	n/a	n/a	n/a	0.0

Figure 2-2

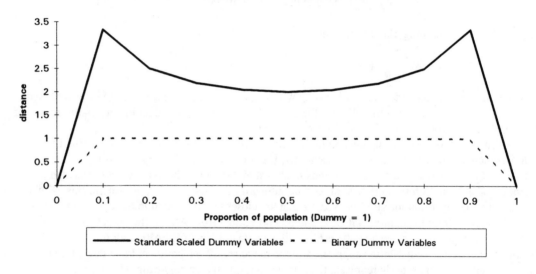

Distance between Dummy Variable Values

3. Relevance to SOMs and Kohonen Learning

In Kohonen learning, the competitive rule combined with the mean reverting learning algorithm will cause the weights to "imitate" the data vectors. Thus, a Kohonen layer processing element will output a 1 if its weights most closely resemble the input vector as measured by the Euclidean distance between the weights and the input vector. Thus, if the maximum absolute value (a. v.) distance is 1, as it is with unscaled and unnormalized vectors, the weights will organize themselves within these boundaries. For normalized vectors, in which each vector length is 1, the maximum distance between binary values will depend on the size of the vector, but is still bounded at 1. Under standard scaling, the maximum a. v. distance is attained when $p = 1/n$, i. e., only one observation out of n has a value of 1, and the minimum distance is attained when $p = n/2$ or 0.5. In the latter case, the a. v. distance between the scaled 1 and the scaled 0 is 2.

The formula for the standard deviation of the population when $p = \mu = 1/n$ is:

$$S = \frac{[(1 - n^{-1})^2 + (0 - n^{-1})^2(n - 1)]^{1/2}}{n} \quad (4)$$

$$z0 = \frac{(0 - n^{-1})}{S} \qquad z1 = \frac{(1 - n^{-1})}{S} \quad (5)$$

$$\lim_{n \to \infty} |z1 - z0| = \infty$$

The standard deviation of the population when $p = \mu = n/2$ is 0.5 is.

$$z0 = -1 = \frac{(0 - 0.5)}{0.5} \qquad z1 = 1 = \frac{(1 - 0.5)}{0.5} \quad (6)$$

where, in ( ) and ( ) above, z0 and z1 are the standard scaled values when the original binary values are 0, and 1, respectively.

From the above, we infer that $z1 \geq 1$ and $z0 \leq 0$. Hence, for any connection weight, w:

$$(z1 - w) \geq (1 - w) \text{ and } (z0 - w) \leq (0 - w). \quad (7)$$

In Kohonen learning, this means that:

$$\Delta w_z \geq \Delta w \quad (8)$$

i. e., the change in weights under standard scaling will be greater or equal to the change in weights with non-scaled data. These adjustments will have the effect of concentrating the data into a smaller region of the topology, just as what would occur in the case of an outlier vector.

Hecht-Nielsen (1990) comments on this characteristic with a geographic analogy which is paraphrased here: if the weight vectors represent, say, the continental U. S. and the first input vector represents a point in Africa, the processing element closest to Africa will have its weights adjusted to represent all of Africa, Europe, and most of Asia because after the first weight adjustment, this PE will win the learning competition for all of the vectors that are closer to Africa than to the continental U. S. If there are 50 vectors from the continental U. S. and 50,000 vectors from Africa, the 50 vectors will be spread out in the topology, but the 50,000 vectors will activate only one PE. Although for many applications, this is, as Hecht-Nielsen suggests, a problematic result, the point could be made that the vectors were not set up to properly represent the sample, and that the vectors from Africa were a "surprise" and the SOM's arrangement of weight vectors conveys information to that effect.

Even though it is a matter of representation, standard scaling has somewhat the same effect because of the larger adjustment of the weights and the more extreme values of the data. Any connection weight which wins the competition by matching a z0, will have its value adjusted by the learning algorithm to get closer to z0. That brings it further away from z1. Conversely, a connection weight that wins by being closest to z1 will be adjusted to be further away from z0. As these distances are greater than the unscaled maximum distance of 1, the vectors will organize themselves relatively further away. However, in a bounded space defined by the number of processing elements in the Kohonen layer, becoming further away from their opposites means getting closer to each other. Hence, the result of fewer activated elements with standard scaled elements. .The "clumps" of active units are created by nearest neighbor weight adjustments. This explains why, for any one census division, there are fewer active PE's with the standard scaled data. The other question is, what characteristics of the data determine the

I-506

relative differences in the number of active PEs from one census division to another. Section 4. summarizes the results and Section 5 proposes the SOM-derived Diversity Index.

4. The Complete Results for all Nine U. S. Census Divisions

Tables 4-1 and 4-2 contain the list of U. S. Census Divisions and the results for the entire 1990 U. S. Census, respectively. In all 9 cases, the standard scaled data produced relatively fewer activated units and denser spatial concentrations. The Pacific region showed the greatest difference in numbers of activated units while the Middle Atlantic region showed the least difference. This is illustrated by the ratio of unscaled data/ scaled data unit activations.

Table 4-1
The Nine U. S. Census Divisions

1. Pacific: Alaska, California, Hawaii, Oregon, and Washington
2. Mountain: Arizona, Colorado, Idaho, Montana, New Mexico, Nevada, Utah, and Wyoming
3. West North Central: Iowa, Kansas, Minnesota, Missouri, North Dakota, Nebraska, South Dakota
4. East North Central: Illinois, Indiana, Michigan, Ohio, Wisconsin
5. Middle Atlantic: New Jersey, New York, Pennsylvania
6. North East: Connecticut, Massachusetts, Maine, New Hampshire, Rhode Island, Vermont
7. West South Central: Arkansas, Louisiana, Oklahoma, Texas
8. East South Central: Alabama, Kentucky, Mississippi, Tennessee
9. South Atlantic: District of Columbia, Delaware, Florida, Georgia, Maryland, North Carolina, South Carolina, Virginia, West Virginia

Table 4-2
Summary of Results for the SOM Training
(in order by Diversity Index)

Census Div.	Raw Data Average	Raw Data Average Std. Dev.	Norm. Data Average	Norm. Data Average Std. Dev.	Diversity Index	Unscaled Active Units	Scaled Active Units	Vector Size	# Obs.
DIV5	0.6128	0.3269	0.1371	0.0784	**1.22**	22	18	8	9826
DIV4	0.4602	0.3384	0.1000	0.0751	**1.53**	29	19	10	10915
DIV2	0.2827	0.3645	0.0769	0.1226	**1.58**	52	33	13	3438
DIV7	0.3229	0.4136	0.1111	0.1659	**1.67**	45	27	9	6619
DIV8	0.3160	0.4341	0.1111	0.1773	**1.68**	42	25	9	3822
DIV6	0.4494	0.2921	0.0909	0.0666	**1.79**	25	14	11	3202
DIV3	0.3703	0.4085	0.0972	0.1247	**1.92**	50	26	12	4791
DIV9	0.3319	0.2770	0.1224	0.1080	**2.19**	35	16	14	9609
DIV1	0.3653	0.3682	0.1000	0.1199	**6.00**	42	7	10	7906

5. The SOM-derived Diversity Index Theory

A Diversity Index is proposed for SOMs that is the ratio of the number of active PEs after training on unscaled data to the number of active PEs after training with standard scaled data. The higher this ratio, the more diversity or relative equiprobability is implied in the data. The maximum amount of diversity in the data vectors is attained under the condition that the mean and standard deviation of each element is 0.5. As the distance between $z1$ and $z0$ is at its minimum when $p = 0.5$ the weight vectors have a smaller adjustment in learning the vectors and may organize themselves to activate for either z1 or z0 for some data elements. In addition, the mean of any standard scaled variable is 0, so the mean of all the data elements is zero.

Therefore, a higher relative compaction of the topology is expected when the average standard deviation of the vectors is closer to 0.5. When the size of the vectors is held constant, this is the result. Table 5-1 shows pairs of divisions in which the vector sizes were equal. A varying vector size will have an additional effect on the standard deviation. The information in Table 5-1 shows that, the Diversity Index increases as the average of the standard deviations of the vector elements approaches 0.5. The comparison cannot be made with vectors of unequal sizes because the average of all the standard deviations will be affected by the total number of elements in the vector.

Table 5-1

Census Div.	Raw Data Average	Raw Data Average Std. Dev.	Norm. Data Average	Norm. Data Average Std. Dev.	Diversity Index	Unscaled Active Units	Scaled Active Units	Vector Size	# Obs.
DIV7	0.3229	0.4136	0.1111	0.1659	1.67	45	27	9	6619
DIV8	0.3160	0.4341	0.1111	0.1773	1.68	42	25	9	3822
DIV4	0.4602	0.3384	0.1000	0.0751	1.53	29	19	10	10915
DIV1	0.3653	0.3682	0.1000	0.1199	6.00	42	7	10	7906

6. Summary and Conclusions

A SOM combined with a probability sensitive data transformation such as standard scaling is a useful tool for some aspects of data analysis. The results obtained with the U. S. Census data rely on the mean reverting quality of the Kohonen learning law and the information content of standard scaled dummy variables. An index of relative entropy or data diversity can be derived by taking the ratio of unscaled to scaled active PEs. The higher this ratio, the more entropy or diversity in the data, holding the vector lengths equal. Another way of stating this is that the higher this index, the more amorphous and "gray-valued" the data.

This application of SOM models presumes that either the entire population or an unbiased sample is available for calculation of the means and standard deviations. Therefore, the theory of the diversity index cannot be applied to deriving unknown distributions. Furthermore, only information which can be appropriately represented as dummy variables can be modeled in this framework. Nevertheless, a broad spectrum of applications still fits within these constraints.

This research has a number of applications in commerce and public policy. For product marketing, a diverse group presents challenges in a highly competitive environment where increasingly targeted messages are used to attract prospects. This targeting eliminates "noise" relative to the intended received but is noisier when transmitted to unintentional receivers. In public policy, the high-entropy areas are the focus of expected economic growth and an accompanying demand for public services such as roads and schools. Scaled and unscaled versions could be compared over time for trend analysis.

Future research points to tuning of SOMs by investigating different neighborhood sizes and configurations and different sizes of SOM. In addition, statistical measures of the significance of these topologies would be useful. There may also be some information if the training of a SOM could be observed by some graphic representation of the changes in weights over time. The SOM remains an attractive neural network paradigm because it is relatively simple to implement and can be applied to highly complex analytical tasks.

7. References:

Garavaglia, S. 1993. A Self-Organizing Map Applied to Macro and Micro Analysis of Data With Dummy Variables. Proceedings of the World Congress on Neural Networks - Portland, OR. July 10-13, 1993, Lawrence Erlbaum Assoc., Inc. and INNS Press.

Hecht-Nielsen, Robert. 1990. Neurocomputing. Addison-Wesley. Reading, MA.

Kohonen, T. 1989. Self-Organization and Associative Memory. Third Edition. Springer-Verlag. Berlin.

Maddala, G. S. 1977. Econometrics. McGraw-Hill, Inc. New York.

Mood, A. M., F. A. Graybill, and D. C. Boes. 1974. Introduction to the Theory of Statistics. Third Edition. McGraw-Hill, Inc. New York.

Shannon, Claude E. and Warren Weaver. 1949. The Mathematical Theory of Communication. U. of Illinois Press. Urbana, Ill. (reprinted as a paperbound book in 1972).

Wiener, Norbert. 1949. Cybernetics. Second Edition. The MIT Press. Cambridge, MA.

Computer System Performance Modeling using Neural Networks

Joseph P. Bigus
IBM Corporation
3605 Highway 52 North
Rochester, MN 55901

ABSTRACT

This paper presents results of empirical studies applying feedforward neural networks to modeling computer system performance. Experiments were performed on a simulated multiprogrammed computer system with a time-varying workload comprising four job classes. Key system performance measures such as device utilizations, mean queue lengths, and paging rates were collected and used to train several neural networks. Single-layer, multi-layer, and radial basis function feedforward neural networks were used to model the simulated computer system's performance characteristics, accurately predicting job class response times.

INTRODUCTION

Computer system performance is a function of four elements. First is the workload presented to the system. Second is the service level expected from the system. The service level is a measure of user satisfaction with the system, such as response times or throughput. Third is the processing capacity of the system in terms of hardware. Last is the system efficiency in processing the workload. This is called system tuning and is often a critical factor in the operation of a computer system. These four elements are dependent on each other and can interact in subtle (nonlinear) ways, complicating the performance modeling process.

Accurate computer system performance models are required to do initial system sizing, long range capacity planning, and system tuning. Typically, performance models are created using analytic models designed specifically for a particular system configuration, and for a particular workload. More generally applicable models can be created, but at the expense of model accuracy. A workload characterization study is also usually required. Building this type of performance model is expensive and requires skilled personnel not usually available at any but the largest computing centers.

Neural networks offer several advantages over analytic system performance models. A neural network model can be created for any system configuration, no matter how unique, by collecting data on the system using a performance monitor, and then training the neural network on that data. Because the neural network model is created specifically for the system, the model should be at least as accurate as the custom-built analytic models (5 to 10% for utilizations and throughputs, and 10 to 30% for response times) (Lazowska, et al.). Since the data inherently contains information on the workload, no workload characterization step is required. Also, the process of collecting the data and training the neural network can be largely automated, so that the model-building process can be performed by system operators.

This paper presents results of empirical studies applying feedforward neural networks to modeling computer system performance (see Bigus, 1993 for a more detailed treatment). Experiments were performed on a simulated multiprogrammed computer which is described in the next section. Next a series of experiments are detailed, in which single-layer, multi-layer, and radial basis function feedforward neural networks are trained to model the computer system's response times.

COMPUTER SYSTEM ARCHITECTURE

The system is a simulated, multiprogrammed system with a workload comprising four job classes: two closed queueing classes and two open queueing classes. A workload generator is used to provide the load to the system. The system consists of a CPU server using a priority first-come-first-served (FCFS) queueing discipline, and a composite I/O subsystem (made up of multiple (2) servers) with a single queue scheduled as FCFS without priority. The system memory is divided into four memory partitions in each of which jobs from a single job class can run. Entry into each partition is controlled by a multiprogramming level (MPL) blocking queue or gate. Figure 1 below shows the job flow for a single (closed) job class and partition.

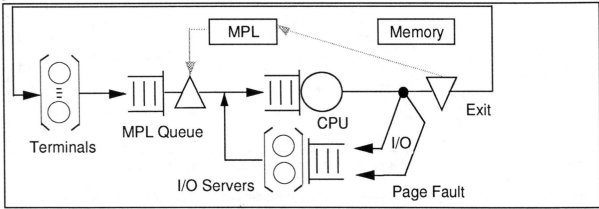

Figure 1. Computer System Model and Job Flow

A job enters the system and requests a multiprogramming slot. When one is available, it then enters the system and competes for memory, CPU and I/O resources with other jobs. Whenever a job enters or leaves a memory partition, the amount of real memory (in pages) available for each job is calculated by dividing the current poolsize by the number of jobs currently in that partition. Based on the amount of memory available, the mean or expected CPU time to the next page fault is calculated using a paging lifetime function (Chamberlin, Fuller, and Liu, 1973). Routing probabilities are calculated for CPU to program I/O, CPU to page fault, and CPU to exit transitions. If jobs in one memory partition start thrashing because the MPL is set too high for the amount of memory available then its paging rate will increase dramatically and throughput of jobs in that class will be lower. If thrashing occurs in one partition, it will impact the other job classes through more contention (queueing) for CPU and the I/O subsystem. A similar model was used by Ferguson in (Birman, Ferguson, & Kogan, 1992) to model the paging characteristics of an MVS system with multiple workloads and was shown to be quite accurate.

The input to the simulated computer system consists of four job classes. The job class definitions are parameterized to describe both the workload intensity and the CPU and I/O subsystem service demands. Job classes can be either open or closed chains. Open chains have infinite arrival populations while closed chains are limited to the number of jobs in the chain. The terminal and batch jobs are closed. The workload for these classes is adjusted by varying the population of these chains (workload intensity parameter N). For the two open classes, transactions and distributed I/O requests, the arrival rate (workload intensity parameter λ, which is the mean of an exponential distribution) determines the workload presented to the system. A smaller mean inter-arrival time corresponds to a heavier workload. The workload intensity is represented by a four element vector (N_{term}, N_{batch}, λ_{trans}, λ_{dist}) which changes over time, the other job class attributes are constant for each job class. The behavior of a job once it is in the system is defined by the rest of the job class attributes. The total CPU time is consumed in small pieces or bursts. Once a CPU service burst is complete, the job is routed to either a program I/O request, a page fault, or exit of the system (see Figure 1). After exiting the system, closed jobs simply recirculate back to the terminal and delay for the associated think time. The total number of program I/Os and page faults defines whether the program will be CPU or I/O bound (or neither).

The computer system is assumed to be in use 12 hours a day, and the workload is specified for each half hour increment, so that a complete day's workload can be specified by a set of 24 4-element vectors. This is a much more realistic workload representation than the more common, steady-state workload assumption. This workload is the "standard daily workload" used in the system performance prediction studies. The workload varies in both job mix and intensity more or less in keeping with a typical business office system.

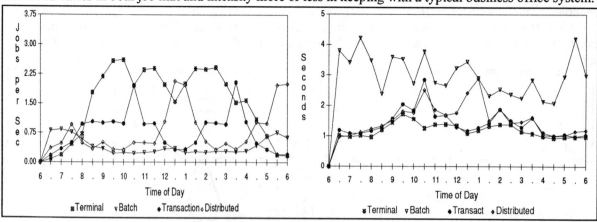

Figure 2. Job Class Throughputs and Response Times for the Standard Daily Workload

Figure 2a shows the average job class throughputs for the standard daily (12 hour) workload with a static system configuration. Performance measurements were taken at 30 minute intervals. Figure 2b shows the job class response times for the standard daily workload and a static system configuration.

The computer system model was implemented using an object-oriented discrete-event simulation environment, designed and developed by the author, and written in C++. The computer simulator was integrated with the IBM Neural Network Utility/2 (NNU), a commercial neural network application development environment. NNU allows integration with other application programs in the form of OS/2 or Windows dynamic link libraries (DLLs).

METHODS

In this series of experiments, neural networks are trained to predict the average response time of each job class based on the information given by the performance monitor. Figure 3 shows the workload presented to the computer system and resulting in some actual throughput and response time for each job class. As the computer system is running, the performance monitor provides internal workload measures to the neural network, along with information on the current achieved system performance. The neural network is trained to relate this internal performance (and workload) information to the achieved throughput. This technique makes no *a priori* assumptions about the computer system performance. The neural network is learning a mapping function from the current system load (as measured by device utilizations and mean queue lengths) to the actual response time measures. If the system performance is dependent on the workload, then the neural network will learn this dependency. Also, if the relationship between workload and response time is nonlinear, the neural network will account for that.

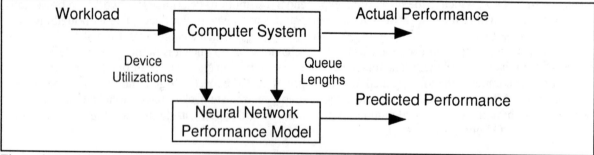

Figure 3. Modeling System Performance using Neural Networks

Experiment 1

In this experiment, 10 simulations were run with a static system configuration and the standard (12 hour) daily workload. Performance data was collected at 60 second intervals, resulting in 720 data points for each day. A feedforward neural network with 24 inputs, no hidden units, and 4 output units was trained using back propagation supervised learning (Rumelhart, Hinton, and Williams, 1986). The input vector consisted of the 8 configuration parameters (held constant), and the internal workload measures consisting of the 2 total device utilization values, the 10 queue length values (total and per job class), and the 4 page fault rates (per partition). The 4 outputs were the job class response times. The performance data was scaled to a range of 0.0 to 1.0. The networks were trained with a learn rate of 0.2, a momentum of 0.0. The error tolerance was set to 0.1 for the first 150 epochs, and then lowered to a value of 0.01 for the last 100 epochs. The logistic activation function (0.0 to 1.0) was used throughout. In all cases, connection weights were updated after each pattern was presented (i.e. not batch).

On average, after 250 training epochs, the average RMS error was 0.0540 on the training data set and the maximum RMS error was 0.1792. To see whether the neural network was predicting the response time equally well for all 4 classes, the RMS errors for the individual outputs were also calculated. These were 0.0531 for terminal, 0.0828 for batch, 0.0566 for transactions, and 0.0733 for distributed I/O jobs. An interesting fact is that the prediction accuracy corresponds exactly with the job class priorities. It would seem that the FCFS priority scheduling is responsible for these differences.

Next the generalization ability of the neural network system performance model was tested. Three different neural network architectures were tested, a back propagation network with no hidden units 24-4, a back propagation network with a single hidden layer 24-4-4, and a radial basis function network with 25 hidden units, 24-25-4. Simulation data was collected from 10 different simulation runs of the standard daily workload. Each network was trained on a subset of the data and then tested for prediction accuracy on the holdout subset. The training subsets ranged from 1, 5, and 8 days. The networks were trained first on the 1 day training set for 250 epochs, then locked and their predictive accuracy was checked. They were then unlocked (but weights were not reset) and trained on the enlarged training set for an additional 25 epochs. This was repeated until the training set contained all 10 days.

The radial basis function networks (Moody & Darken, 1989) were trained in a two step process. First a self-organizing feature map was trained with 24 inputs and 25 output units to cluster the input space (Kohonen, 1989). After the SOFM was trained, the connection weights were then loaded into the radial basis function (RBF) network centers array (which serve as the basis vectors for the hidden units). The RBF network was then trained multiple times (like the back propagation networks), but only the hidden to output layer weights were reset, not the centers. The test results are shown in Tables 1 2, and 3. In all cases the networks were locked (weights were frozen) when error measurements were taken.

Training Data	Avg. RMS Err	Max. RMS Err	Test Data	Avg. RMS Err	Max. RMS Err
Day 1	0.0530	0.2061	Days 2..10	0.05966	0.2683
Days 1..5	0.0510	0.2877	Days 6..10	0.06214	0.2763
Days 1..8	0.0549	0.3822	Days 9,10	0.0634	0.2293
Days 1..10	0.0584	0.3831	na	na	na

Table 1. BKP 24-4, System Performance Prediction

Training Data	Avg. RMS Err	Max. RMS Err	Test Data	Avg. RMS Err	Max. RMS Err
Day 1	0.0543	0.2001	Days 2..10	0.0627	0.2700
Days 1..5	0.0511	0.2929	Days 6..10	0.0640	0.2883
Days 1..8	0.0558	0.3872	Days 9,10	0.0660	0.2411
Days 1..10	0.0573	0.3923	na	na	na

Table 2. BKP 24-4-4, System Performance Prediction

Training Data	Avg. RMS Err	Max. RMS Err	Test Data	Avg. RMS Err	Max. RMS Err
Day 1	0.0590	0.2310	Days 2..10	0.0725	0.3386
Days 1..5	0.0581	0.4568	Days 6..10	0.0748	0.4119
Days 1..8	0.0710	0.4227	Days 9,10	0.0783	0.3671
Days 1..10	0.0715	0.4515	na	na	na

Table 3. RBF 24-25-4, System Performance Prediction

The results were that the 24-4 back propagation network was the best at predicting the system performance of the 9 succeeding days when they were trained on a single day's data. This result was surprising because it was assumed that the system performance function was highly nonlinear and so that at least 1 hidden layer of units was needed to learn the mapping. Apparently the computer system dynamics are such that for a fixed configuration the relationships are relatively linear. Another surprise was that the average prediction accuracy (average RMS error) did not improve as the training set grew, but got slightly worse. However, the prediction accuracy in the worst case (maximum RMS error) did improve as the trained set increased. It should be noted that all 3 neural network architectures produced results with well under 10% error rates, which is better than the 10-30% accuracy usually attributed to analytic models when predicting response times.

Experiment 2

In this experiment, we change the multiprogramming levels, while the workload intensity and poolsize are held constant. The terminal multiprogramming level was changed from 1 to 9 in increments of 1, while the other MPL were held constant. The simulation consisted of 30 minutes at each of the 9 terminal multiprogramming levels. Data was collected every 60 seconds, so there were 270 training vectors. Each type of neural network was trained 5 times using learn rate parameters of 0.2, momentum of 0.0, and an initial error tolerance of 0.1. After 150 epochs, the error tolerance was lowered to 0.01. All error measurements were taken with the neural network weights locked, and each network was trained for 250 epochs. The results shown in Table 4 are the average errors over the 5 training runs.

Architecture	Training Data (80%)		Test Data (20%)	
	Avg. RMS Error	Max. RMS Error	Avg. RMS Error	Max. RMS Error
BKP 24-4	0.0906	0.2381	0.0914	0.2019
BKP 24-4-4	0.0909	0.2331	0.0855	0.2750
RBF 24-25-4	0.0823	0.2798	0.0837	0.2134

Table 4. System Performance Prediction - Changing MPL

As in the previous experiment, our expectation was that the multilayer networks would perform better than the 24-4 network. This is the case, as the average RMS prediction error for the multilayer networks was compared to the RMS error for the linear networks with a planned contrast-of-means. The average RMS error for the linear networks was significantly larger, $F(1,12)=19.21$, $p < 0.01$. Although the worst case (maximum) RMS prediction error is lowest for the linear network, the maximum RMS errors were not significantly smaller than the radial basis networks, $F(1,12)=0.23$, $p > 0.01$. The multilayer networks can fit the performance function better than the linear network for most patterns.

Experiment 3

In this experiment, the system configuration was varied while presenting the system with the standard daily workload. The objective is to see whether a neural network can learn the complex dynamics of the multiple interactions between system configuration and workload on the system performance. A set of 5 days of simulations were run, with different multiprogramming levels and poolsize settings for each day. The performance measurements were made at 60 second intervals. The multiprogramming levels were held constant, while the poolsizes were adjusted before each day's run.

	Training Data (80%)		Test Data (20%)	
Architecture	Avg. RMS Error	Max. RMS Error	Avg. RMS Error	Max. RMS Error
BKP 24-4	0.0445	0.1625	0.0447	0.1843
BKP 24-4-4	0.0459	0.1966	0.0452	0.1868
RBF 24-25-4	0.0591	0.3390	0.0594	0.3272

Table 5. System Performance Prediction - Changing PoolSize

As shown in Table 5, the neural networks actually performed better on the changing poolsize and workload data than on the static configuration tests. The two back propagation networks had average RMS prediction errors of under 0.046, and under 0.187 in the worst case. The poor performance of the radial basis function network, especially in predicting some patterns (Max RMS error), indicates that perhaps more hidden (basis) units were required. Because the center vectors were found using a self-organizing feature map on 80% of the data, there is a chance that some of the patterns in the holdout data were not well represented. Thus, the RBF network would see patterns which produced no significant hidden unit activations, and so resulted in poor predictions on those patterns. Of course, this is always a concern when training neural networks. The training data must be representative of the total input space of the data.

CONCLUSION

In static predictions of response times, the neural networks were able to achieve average RMS prediction errors of less than 10%. The advantages of the neural network approach over traditional queueing theoretic approaches are that the neural network approach is at least as accurate, and is less expensive. It requires the use of a performance monitor to gather data and requires some scaling of the data (which could be automated), and the training of the neural network model.

This work shows that neural networks are a viable alternative to queueing theoretic models of computer systems. By using performance data collected during normal system operation, a neural network model can be generated to accurately model the system response times.

ACKNOWLEDGMENTS

This work was done while the author was on the IBM Ph.D. resident study program at Lehigh University in Bethlehem, PA.

REFERENCES

Bigus, J. P. (1993). Adaptive Operating System Control Using Neural Networks, Ph.D. Dissertation, Electrical Engineering and Computer Science Department, Lehigh University, Bethlehem, PA.

Birman, A., Ferguson, D., and Kogan, Y. (1992). Asymptotic Solutions for a Model of Large Multiprogramming Systems with Multiple Workloads, in Conference Proceedings, Performance Tools '92.

Chamberlin, D.D., Fuller, S.H., and Liu, L (1973). An analysis of page allocation strategies for virtual memory systems, IBM Journal of Research and Development, 17, 404-412.

IBM Corporation (1992), Neural Network Utility/2: User's Guide, SC41-0046, Neural Network Utility/2: Programmer's Reference, SC41-0045.

Kohonen, T. (1989). Self-Organization and Associative Memory, Springer-Verlag.

Lazowska, E.D., Zahorjan, J., Graham, J.S., & Sevcik, K.C. (1984). Quantitative System Performance: Computer System Analysis Using Queueing Network Analysis, Prentice Hall.

Moody, J. & Darken, C. (1989). Fast Learning in Networks of Locally-Tuned Processing Units, Neural Computation 1, 281-294.

Rumelhart, D.E. Hinton, G.E. and Williams, R.J. (1986). Learning Internal Representations by Error Propagation, in Parallel Distributed Processing (Rumelhart & McClelland, eds.), MIT Press, Vol. I.

The Application of the Artificial Neural Network in the Grading of Beer Quality

Yudong CAI

(Shanghai Research Center of Technology, Chinese Academy of Sciences, Shanghai, 200233, China)

Abstract

In this paper, a typical artificial neural network -- self-organization model was applied to establish computer expert system for grading the beer quality on the basis of physical and chemical indexes of beer. As a result, the grading was consistent with the fact.

Keywords: Grading for the Beer Quality, Physical and Chemical Indexes, Self-Organization Artifivial Neural Network, T.Kohonen Model

I. Introduction

In standard practice, the beer quality is evaluated according to the sensory indexes (outlook, beer head, smell and taste), the chemical indexes (the content of a alcohol, the actual concentration, the concentration of raw malt huice, the colour degree, the acidity, the content of CO_2?, the content of duel acetyl, the EBU value, the duration of beer head and the height of beer head, etc.) and the stability. However, the chemical indexes inter-related and inter-influenced with each other. In view of single index, there is not a clear grading criterion between the special grade and the ordinary grade. Especially those sensory indexes, which are comprehensive refliction of all kinds of chemical indexes, can only be assessed by experienced beer appraisers. So, the assessed results are anyway affected by subjective and other unstable factors. In this paper, with the application of a typical artificial neural network -- self-organization model, we establish a computer expert system for the grading of beer quality in an attempt to get more experience in the assessment of wine or other foods by computers. The study on this problem has not been reported yet.

II. Artificial Neural Network -- Self-Organization Model

Actificial Neural Network (ANN) is a non-linear science which began to rise quickly in the mid-1980's. It has been preliminarily applied to the fields of pattern recognition, data precessing, automatic control, etc., and obtained satisfactory results [1].

Kohonen's Self-Organization neural network is a two-layer network. Output nodes are arranged regularly on a planar mapping grid. Each input node is connected to every output node via a variable connection weight. Weights are adjusted interatively during training by input data and organized gradually such that topologically close nodes are sensitive to inputs which are physically similar. Self-Organization model is well known for its lowdimensional topology preserving mapping of high dimensional patterns and stable evolving properties. It is now widely applied in vector quantization, pattern recognition, associate memory, combinatorial optimization and motor control [1].

The structure and learning algorithm of self-organization model has been reported in literature [1].

III. T. kohonen Neural Network Applied to the Grading of Beer Quality

1. Source of information

It is reported in the literature some chemical indexes in sampling analysis of beer in the Shanghai Area in recent years.

In this research , the concentration of raw malt juice is omitted because it is relative with the concentration of alcohol and the actual concentration. And the Grade refers to the grade given by the beer factories.

2. The establishment of ANN recognition model

First, 14 samples in Table 1 are randomly selected and used as the "learning" material (class one: special; class two: ordinary) for the neural network. All those feature variables are taken as the input; the output nodes form a 2×7 lattice and the convergence of training set reaches the value 0.0001. After learning process, these samples can be perfectly recognized by neural network. In the meanwhile, the complicated relationship between the chemical indexes and its quality grade has been established. (See Figure 1, Table 1)

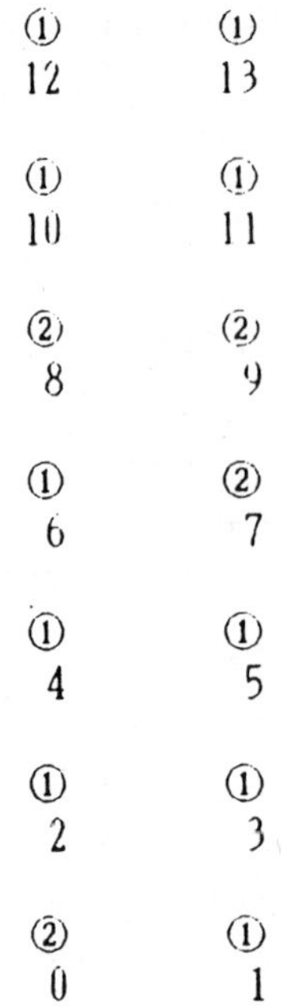

> ① ①
> 12 13
>
> ① ①
> 10 11
>
> ② ②
> 8 9
>
> ① ②
> 6 7
>
> ① ①
> 4 5
>
> ① ①
> 2 3
>
> ② ①
> 0 1

Figure 1   Results of Classfication

Table 1.   14 Learning Samples

Content of Alcohol (%)	Actual Conc (%)	Colour Degree	Total Acidity	Duel Acetyl (PPm)	EBU Value (EBU)	Calculation Results by ANN	Evaluated Grade
4.286	3.735	0.4	1.9	0.05	27.4	12	1
3.918	4.595	0.54	1.24	0.053	28	2	1
4.0588	4.0005	0.42	1.81	0.264	28.25	13	1
4.251	3.8099	0.52	2.105	0.8696	21.85	5	1
4.1689	3.9005	0.52	2.00	0.009	24.7	6	1
4.003	4.398	0.5	2.48	0.055	28.3	3	1
4.111	4.041	0.418	1.614	0.0400	28.6	11	1
4.00335	4.39775	0.5	2.404	0.0552	28.3	4	1
3.893	4.412	0.42	1.64	0.0656	25.25	10	1
3.698	4.83	0.58	1.31	0.066	37.9	1	1
4.72	4.133	0.48	1.74	0.3	25.25	8	2
3.9044	4.3873	0.5	2.2	0.1416	26	7	2
3.906	4.579	0.55	2.66	0.168	31.95	0	2
4.033	4.398	0.5	2.48	0.055	28.3	9	2

3. The results of assessment

Furthermore, in order to test the performance of the newly-est
ablished model, 8 samples which haven't been trained are recognized by th
e neural network which has grasped the knowledge information. And, the
samples will be classifid into a certain category in light of the class
of its closest output node(the max. value correspondingly, namely, th
e similar point with max. value). The predicting is totally in conformi
ty with the actual result(See Table 2).

Table 2. 8 Samples for Assessment

Content of Alcohol (%)	Actual Conc (%)	Colour Degree	Total Acidity	Duel Acetyl (PPM)	EBU Value (EBU)	Calculation Results by ANN	Evaluated Grade	Manufacturing Grade
3.627	4.649	8.12	1.5	8.847	24.5		1	1
3.686	4.554	8.52	1.1	1.998	27		1	1
3.5645	4.1758	8.43	1.5	8.1296	22.46	13	1	1
3.6388	4.7047	8.43	1.5	8.0464	33.45	1	1	1
3.6992	4.8258	8.58	1.31	8.0656	37.3	1	1	1
3.8822	4.4245	9.5	1.53	8.1249	27.1	4	1	1
4.019	4.3868	8.52	2.89	8.17	23.25	7	2	2
3.9856	4.5785	8.55	2.66	8.168	31.95	8	2	2

From Table 2, we can see that except for one sample, the grade of other samples aare completely consistent with that of the manufacturing factory. So, the neural network approach is also useful in differentiating fake wines.

IV. Conclusion

Because of its superior classifying and recognizing ability, the ANN approach is suitable to solve nonlinear multi-factor and multi-target pattern recognition problems, such as the grading of beer quality. Compared with ordinary multi-factor discrimination methods, this approach has the following advantages:

1. Stronger fault-tolerant ability.

Because any information which the model obtains is distributed over the whole network, the error of individual input signal of the sample turns large, no fault will be given rise to, namely, the neural network can associate a complete and clear picture stored in the memory even with an incomplete or ambiguous signal.

In this research, for example, 0.1 is added to the second input signal of each unkown sample. And prediction is given to the samples thus obtained by trained network. Comparison between the original and latter prediction results is shown in Table 3.

Table 3. Influence on the Performance of the
Network by the Increasing of Error
of Individual Input Signal

Position of the Closest Output Node (1)	Predicted Grade (1)	Position of the Closest Output Node	Predicted Grade
2	1	2	1
2	1	2	1

11	1	13	1
1	1	1	1
1	1	1	i
1	1	1	:
7	2	7	2
0	2	0	2

(1): Constructed Samples.

2. Grading speed

Because only some simple addition and multiplication are needed in the recognition of 'unknown' samples in trained neural network, so the recognition speed is very high.

If we prodfuce a particular hardware or make use of parallel processors, the speed will be further higher.

So, it may be expected that with the further development of the artificial neural network theory, it will pave a new way for the grading of beer quality.

References

[1] Yin Hongeng, etc. , Theory of Artificial Neural Network, Pattern Recognition and Artificial Intelligence, 1990. 3(1):1-12
[2] Xuchi, etc., 1986, Computer and Applied Chemistry, 3(1), 21-24.
[3] R. Hecht-Nielson, 'Theory of the Backpropagation Nueral Network', Int, J. Conf. on Neural Network, Washington D. C. June 1989.

Solving the Pure 0-1 Linear Programs with Inequality Constraints Using a Two-Step Method

Jianfei Chen   Shaowei Xia

Department of Automation, Tsinghua University, Beijing, 100084, P.R.China

National Laboratory of Pattern Recognition, Beijing, 100080, P.R.China

Abstract

More and more attention has been paid to the HNN algorithm since it [1] was used by Hopfield and Tank to solve TSP in 1985. However, the algorithm can only solve the pure 0-1 linear programs with equality constraints and many tests [2] showed that it is unreliable. In this paper we propose a two-step method, whose core is HNN-type algorithm. The method can solve all the pure 0-1 linear programs with inequality constraints and is guaranteed to obtain their "or-optimal" solutions. Finally, one example is given out.

Key words: neural network, the pure 0-1 linear program, or-optimal solution, simplex algorithm

1. Introduction

There have been several methods to solve the pure 0-1 linear programs, such as implicit enumeration method, dynamic programming method and etc.. But when the number of 0-1 variables increases, the computation quantity increases very fast, sometimes by exponential speed. So people would rather persue the "or-optimal" solutions than the optimal ones when the number of 0-1 variables is very large in many practical situations.

Hopfield and Tank [1] proposed to solve TSP using a neural network algorithm (called HNN algorithm for short) in 1985, which has been received more and more attention from people. However, the algorithm can only solve the pure 0-1 linear programs with equality constraints and many tests [2] showed that it is unreliable. In the paper we propose a two-step method which may be used to solve all the pure 0-1 linear programs with inequality constraints and is always reliable. At the end of the paper, one example is given out.

2. Introduce of the two–step method

The pure 0–1 linear program with inequality constraints may be depicted in following form:

$$\begin{cases} \min & C^T X \\ \text{s.t.} & AX \geqslant b, \quad X \in \{0,1\}^n \end{cases} \tag{2-1}$$

where

$$C = (c_1, c_2, \cdots, c_n)^T, \quad A = (a_{ij})_{m \times n},$$

$$b = (b_1, b_2, \cdots, b_m)^T$$

To solve (2–1) using the two–step method, the program must be modified as (2–2) by penalty method at first:

$$\begin{cases} \min & E(t) = C^T X(t) + \lambda \sum_{j=1}^{m} F\left(A_j^T X(t) - b_j \right) \\ \text{s.t.} & X(t) \in \{0, 1\}^n \end{cases} \tag{2-2}$$

where λ is a large positive number, $A_j = (a_{j1}, a_{j2}, \cdots, a_{jn})^T$,

$$F(z) = \begin{cases} 0, & \text{if } z \geqslant 0 \\ \dfrac{1}{2} z^2, & \text{else} \end{cases} \tag{2-3}$$

The added tag t denotates iteration step, so $E(t)$, $X(t)$ are respectively the value of E and X after the tth iteration step.

It's obvious that (2–2) is equivalent with (2–1) when λ is large enough.

In order to guarantee that the two–step method can always converge, add a term to $E(t)$ as (2–4):

$$\begin{cases} \min & E(t) = C^T X(t) + \lambda \sum_{j=1}^{m} F\left(A_j^T X(t) - b_j \right) + \dfrac{1}{2} X^T(t) U(e - X(t)) \\ \text{s.t.} & X(t) \in \{0, 1\}^n \end{cases} \tag{2-4}$$

The matrix e is a vector in R^n, all elements of e are 1. Assumping the diagonal elements of the matrix $A^T A$ are $a'a_{11}$, $a'a_{22}$, $\cdots$, $a'a_{nn}$,

$$U = \begin{bmatrix} \lambda a'a_{11} & & 0 \\ & \lambda a'a_{22} & \\ 0 & & \lambda a'a_{nn} \end{bmatrix} \tag{2-5}$$

When $x_i = 0$ or 1 for all i, the added term $\dfrac{1}{2} X^T U(e - X)$ gets the minimum value, zero. So (2–2) and (2–4) has the same global minimum point.

(2—4) may be solved through the following iteration (This paper merely introduces an asynchronous iteration that only one variable may change every step, assuming that the variable x_i may change at the tth step.):

$$\begin{cases} x_i(t+1) = sgn\left[-c_i - \frac{1}{2}e^T U_i + X^T U_i - \lambda \sum_{j=1}^{m} a_{ji} f(A_j X(t) - b_j) \right] \\ x_j(t+1) = x_j(t) \qquad j \neq i \end{cases} \qquad (2-6)$$

where $U_i = (u_{i1}, u_{i2}, \cdots, u_{in})^T$,

$$f(z) = \frac{dF(z)}{dz} = \begin{cases} 0, & \text{if } z \geq 0 \\ z, & \text{else} \end{cases} \qquad (2-7)$$

$$sgn(z) = \begin{cases} 1, & \text{if } z \geq 0 \\ 0, & \text{else} \end{cases} \qquad (2-8)$$

When X don't change, that is, $X(t+1) = X(t)$, the iteration (2—6) has converged and must be stopped. It will be proved that the iteration (2—6) converges certainly if (2—1) has a limited minimum objective value in the next section.

Unfortunately, the problem (2—4) is not completely equivalent with the original problem (2—1). The function $\frac{1}{2}X^T U(e - X)$ is a concave function, so E in (2—4) may not be a convex function and has a number of minimum points, among which only the global one is the minimum point of (2—1). It is all possible that the iteration (2—6) falls into any one of the local minimum points of E in (2—4) and stops. In order to get the minimum value of (2—1) at the greatest possibility, we propose a two—step method:

Firstly, to solve the following problem using simplex algorithm for linear programs with bounded variables:

$$\begin{cases} min & C^T X \\ \text{s.t.} & AX \geq b \\ & 0 \leq x_i \leq 1, \qquad i = 1, \cdots, n \end{cases} \qquad (2-9)$$

where A, b, C are similar with them in (2—1).

Assuming that the solution obtained by the first step is X', it's obvious that $0 \leq x_i' < 1, i = 1, \cdots, n$.

Secondly, to solve the problem (2—4) through the iteration (2—6), selecting X' as initial point. The iteration (2—6) is likely to take very little steps to fall into the minimum point of (2—1) because the initial point X' nears it.

In a word, the two—step method can always obtain the "or—optimal" solutions of the pure 0—1 linear programs with inequality constraints.

3. Proof of convergence of the iteration (2—6)

From (2–6) we know that at the tth step,

$$\Delta x_j(t) = x_j(t+1) - x_j(t) = 0 \quad \text{for all } j \neq i \tag{3-1}$$

By (2–4),

$$\Delta E(t) = E(t+1) - E(t)$$

$$= C^T \Delta X(t) + \lambda \sum_{j=1}^{m} \left[F\left(A_j^T X(t+1) - b_j \right) - F\left(A_j^T X(t) - b_j \right) \right]$$

$$+ \frac{1}{2} e^T U \Delta X(t) - X^T(t) U \Delta X(t) - \frac{1}{2} \Delta X^T(t) U \Delta X(t)$$

$$= \left(C^T + \frac{1}{2} e^T U - X^T U \right) \Delta X(t)$$

$$+ \lambda \sum_{j=1}^{m} \left[F\left(A_j^T X(t+1) - b_j \right) - F\left(A_j^T X(t) - b_j \right) \right] - \frac{1}{2} \Delta X^T(t) U \Delta X(t)$$

$$= \left(c_i + \frac{1}{2} e^T U_i - X^T U_i \right) \Delta x_i(t)$$

$$+ \lambda \sum_{j=1}^{m} \left[F\left(A_j^T X(t+1) - b_j \right) - F\left(A_j^T X(t) - b_j \right) \right] - \frac{1}{2} u_{ii} \Delta x_i^2(t) \tag{3-2}$$

The value of $F\left(A_j^T X(t+1) - b_j \right) - F\left(A_j^T X(t) - b_j \right)$ is discussed as follows in terms of (2–3), (2–7) and (3–1):

① $A_j^T X(t) - b_j \geq 0, \quad A_j^T X(t+1) - b_j \geq 0$:

$$F\left(A_j^T X(t+1) - b_j \right) - F\left(A_j^T X(t) - b_j \right)$$

$$= 0 - 0 = a_{ji} \Delta x_i(t) f\left(A_j^T X(t) - b_j \right)$$

$$\leq a_{ji} \Delta x_i(t) f\left(A_j^T X(t) - b_j \right) + \frac{1}{2} a_{ji}^2 \Delta x_i^2(t)$$

② $A_j^T X(t) - b_j \leq 0, \quad A_j^T X(t+1) - b_j \leq 0$:

$$F\left(A_j^T X(t+1) - b_j \right) - F\left(A_j^T X(t) - b_j \right)$$

$$= \frac{1}{2} \left(A_j^T X(t+1) - b_j \right)^2 - \frac{1}{2} \left(A_j^T X(t) - b_j \right)^2$$

$$= \frac{1}{2} \left(A_j^T (X(t) + \Delta X(t)) - b_j \right)^2 - \frac{1}{2} \left(A_j^T X(t) - b_j \right)^2$$

$$= A_j^T \Delta X(t) \left(A_j^T X(t) - b_j \right) + \frac{1}{2} \Delta X^T(t) A_j A_j^T \Delta X(t)$$

$$= a_{ji} \Delta x_i(t) \left(A_j^T X(t) - b_j \right) + \frac{1}{2} a_{ji}^2 \Delta x_i^2(t)$$

$$= a_{ji}\Delta x_i(t) f\left(A_j^T X(t) - b_j\right) + \frac{1}{2} a_{ji}^2 \Delta x_i^2(t)$$

③ $A_j^T X(t) - b_j \leqslant 0, \quad A_j^T X(t+1) - b_j \geqslant 0$:

$$F\left(A_j^T X(t+1) - b_j\right) - F\left(A_j^T X(t) - b_j\right)$$

$$= 0 - \frac{1}{2}\left(A_j^T X(t) - b_j\right)^2 = -\frac{1}{2}\left(A_j^T X(t) - b_j\right)^2 \tag{3-3}$$

$$a_{ji}^2 \Delta x_i^2(t) + 2a_{ji}\Delta x_i\left(A_j^T X(t) - b_j\right) + \left(A_j^T X(t) - b_j\right)^2$$

$$= \left(a_{ji}\Delta x_i(t) + A_j^T X(t) - b_j\right)^2 \geqslant 0,$$

so

$$-\left(A_j^T X(t) - b_j\right)^2 \leqslant a_{ji}^2 \Delta x_i^2(t) + 2a_{ji}\Delta x_i(t)\left(A_j^T X(t) - b_j\right)$$

$$= a_{ji}^2 \Delta x_i^2(t) + 2a_{ji}\Delta x_i(t) f\left(A_j^T X(t) - b_j\right) \tag{3-4}$$

By (3-2) and (3-4),

$$F\left(A_j^T X(t+1) - b_j\right) - F\left(A_j^T X(t) - b_j\right)$$

$$\leqslant \frac{1}{2} a_{ji}^2 \Delta x_i^2(t) + a_{ji}\Delta x_i(t) f\left(A_j^T X(t) - b_j\right)$$

④ $A_j^T X(t) - b_j \geqslant 0, \quad A_j^T X(t+1) - b_j \leqslant 0$:

$$F\left(A_j^T X(t+1) - b_j\right) - F\left(A_j^T X(t) - b_j\right)$$

$$= \frac{1}{2}\left(A_j^T X(t+1) - b_j\right)^2 - 0 = \frac{1}{2}\left(A_j^T X(t+1) - b_j\right)^2 \tag{3-5}$$

$$A_j^T X(t+1) - b_j = A_j^T X(t) - b_j + A_j^T \Delta X(t)$$

$$= A_j^T X(t) - b_j + a_{ji}\Delta x_i(t)$$

so

$$a_{ji}\Delta x_i(t) = \left(A_j^T X(t+1) - b_j\right) - \left(A_j^T X(t) - b_j\right)$$

$$\leqslant A_j^T X(t+1) - b_j \leqslant 0$$

Furthermore,

$$(a_{ji}\Delta x_i(t))^2 \geqslant \left(A_j^T X(t+1) - b_j\right)^2 \tag{3-6}$$

By (3-5) and (3-6),

$$F\left(A_j^T X(t+1) - b_j\right) - F\left(A_j^T X(t) - b_j\right)$$

$$\leqslant \frac{1}{2}\left(a_{ji}\Delta x_i(t)\right)^2 = \frac{1}{2}a_{ji}^2\Delta x_i^2(t) + a_{ji}\Delta x_i(t)f\left(A_j^T X(t) - b_j\right)$$

By conlusion, the following inequality always holds:

$$F\left(A_j^T X(t+1) - b_j\right) - F\left(A_j^T X(t) - b_j\right)$$

$$\leqslant \frac{1}{2}a_{ji}^2\Delta x_i^2(t) + a_{ji}\Delta x_i(t)f\left(A_j^T X(t) - b_j\right) \tag{3-7}$$

By (3–2) and (3–7),

$$\Delta E(t) = \left(c_i + \frac{1}{2}e^T U_i - X^T U_i\right)\Delta x_i(t)$$

$$+ \lambda \sum_{j=1}^{m}\left[F\left(A_j^T X(t+1) - b_j\right) - F\left(A_j^T X(t) - b_j\right)\right] - \frac{1}{2}u_{ii}\Delta x_i^2(t)$$

$$\leqslant \left[c_i + \frac{1}{2}e^T U_i - X^T U_i + \lambda\sum_{j=1}^{m}a_{ji}f\left(A_j^T X(t) - b_j\right)\right]\Delta x_i(t)$$

$$+ \left[\frac{1}{2}\lambda\sum_{j=1}^{m}(a_{ji})^2 - \frac{1}{2}u_{ii}\right]\Delta x_i^2(t) \tag{3-8}$$

From (2–5), we know $u_{ii} = \lambda\sum_{j=1}^{m}(a_{ji})^2$ (3 – 9)

$$\Delta x_i(t) = \begin{cases} 0 & \text{if } x_i(t) = x_i(t+1) \\ 1 & \text{if } x_i(t) = 0, \ x_i(t+1) = 1 \\ -1 & \text{if } x_i(t) = 1, \ x_i(t+1) = 0 \end{cases}$$

whereas

$$x_i(t+1) = sgn\left(-c_i - \frac{1}{2}e^T U_i + X^T U_i - \lambda\sum_{j=1}^{m}a_{ji}f(A_j X(t) - b_j)\right) \tag{2-6}$$

so

$$\left(c_i + \frac{1}{2}e^T U_i - X^T U_i + \lambda\sum_{j=1}^{m}a_{ji}f(A_j X(t) - b_j)\right)\Delta x_i(t) \leqslant 0 \tag{3-10}$$

By (3–8), (3–9) and (3–10), $\Delta E(t) \leqslant 0$.

If the original (2–1) has a limited minimum objective value, $E(t)$ must have a low bownd, so the iteration (2–6) convergences certainly.

4. One example

$$\begin{cases} min & C^T X \\ \text{s.t.} & AX \geqslant b, \ X \in \{0, 1\}^{16} \end{cases} \tag{4-1}$$

where

$$A = \begin{bmatrix}
1 & 1 & 1 & 1 & 0 & 0 & 0 & 0 & 0 & 0 & 0 & 0 & 0 & 0 & 0 & 0 \\
0 & 0 & 0 & 0 & 1 & 1 & 1 & 1 & 0 & 0 & 0 & 0 & 0 & 0 & 0 & 0 \\
0 & 0 & 0 & 0 & 0 & 0 & 0 & 0 & 1 & 1 & 1 & 1 & 0 & 0 & 0 & 0 \\
0 & 1 & 0 & 0 & 0 & 1 & 0 & 0 & 0 & 1 & 0 & 0 & 0 & 1 & 0 & 0 \\
0 & 0 & 1 & 0 & 0 & 0 & 1 & 0 & 0 & 0 & 1 & 0 & 0 & 0 & 1 & 0 \\
0 & 0 & 0 & 1 & 0 & 0 & 0 & 1 & 0 & 0 & 0 & 1 & 0 & 0 & 0 & 1 \\
-1 & -1 & -1 & -1 & 0 & 0 & 0 & 0 & 0 & 0 & 0 & 0 & 0 & 0 & 0 & 0 \\
0 & 0 & 0 & 0 & -1 & -1 & -1 & -1 & 0 & 0 & 0 & 0 & 0 & 0 & 0 & 0 \\
0 & 0 & 0 & 0 & 0 & 0 & 0 & 0 & -1 & -1 & -1 & -1 & 0 & 0 & 0 & 0 \\
0 & 0 & 0 & 0 & 0 & 0 & 0 & 0 & 0 & 0 & 0 & 0 & -1 & -1 & -1 & -1 \\
-1 & 0 & 0 & 0 & -1 & 0 & 0 & 0 & -1 & 0 & 0 & 0 & -1 & 0 & 0 & 0 \\
0 & -1 & 0 & 0 & 0 & -1 & 0 & 0 & 0 & -1 & 0 & 0 & 0 & -1 & 0 & 0 \\
0 & 0 & -1 & 0 & 0 & 0 & -1 & 0 & 0 & 0 & -1 & 0 & 0 & 0 & -1 & 0 \\
0 & 0 & 0 & -1 & 0 & 0 & 0 & -1 & 0 & 0 & 0 & -1 & 0 & 0 & 0 & -1
\end{bmatrix}$$

$$b = (1, 1, 1, 1, 1, 1, -1, -1, -1, -1, -1, -1, -1, -1)^T$$

$$C = (2, 15, 13, 4, 10, 4, 14, 15, 9, 14, 16, 13, 7, 8, 11, 9)^T$$

The first step solves out that the value of X' is (0.00, 0.00, 0.02, 0.98, 0.00, 0.99, 0.01, 0.00, 0.00, 0.01, 0.97, 0.02, 0.00, 0.00, 0.00, 0.00)

The second step firstly modifies (4–1) as follow:

$$\begin{cases} min \quad E = C^T X + \lambda \sum_{j}^{m} F(A_j X - b_j) + \frac{1}{2} X^T U(e - X) \\ \\ X \in \{0, 1\}^n \end{cases} \tag{4-2}$$

where $\lambda = 200$, A, b, C are similar with them in (4–1), then solves (4–2) through the iteration (2–6). If selecting X' as initial point, the final solution is $(0, 0, 0, 1, 0, 1, 0, 0, 0, 0, 1, 0, 0, 0, 0, 0)^T$, which coresponds to the global minimum objective value, 24 of (4–1). When selecting $(0, 0, 0, 0, 0, 0, 0, 0, 0, 0, 0, 0, 0, 0, 0, 0)^T$ or $(1, 1, 1, 1, 1, 1, 1, 1, 1, 1, 1, 1, 1, 1, 1, 1)^T$ as initial point, both the obtained solutions are $(0, 1, 0, 0, 0, 0, 1, 0, 0, 0, 0, 1, 0, 0, 0, 0)^T$, which is one local minimum solution of (4–2) and one feasible solution of (4–1), but not the minimum solution of (4–1).

5. Conclusion

The paper proposes a two–step method which may be used to solve all the pure 0–1 linear programs with inequality constraints. The core of the method is the HNN algorithm. The method can always get the "or–optimal" solutions of the pure 0–1 linear programs with inequality constraints.

References

[1] Hopfield, J.J. & Tank, D. W., Neural computation of decisions in optimization problems, Biol. Cybern., Vol.52, 141−152, 1985.

[2] Wilson, G. V. & Pawley G. S., On the stability of the Travelling Salesman Problem Algorithm of Hopfield and Tank, Biol. Cybern., Vol.58, 63−70, 1988.

ATM TRAFFIC MODELS GENERATION BY NEURAL NETWORKS

Antonio Jurado, A. Díaz-Estrella and F. Sandoval

Dpto. Tecnología Electrónica, E.T.S.I. Telecomunicación,
Universidad de Málaga, Plaza El Ejido, s/n, 29013 Málaga, Spain

ABSTRACT

In this paper, it is shown how complex mathematical models can be replaced by artificial neural networks to determine the superposition model parameters of many ON-OFF sources of ATM traffic. The model is adjusted using multilayer perceptrons (MLPs) with a backpropagation learning. The architecture proposed allows to obtain the superposition parameters of any Markov chain models with any number of states, just changing its dimension.

INTRODUCTION

The broadband integrated services digital network (B-ISDN) seems to be the most suitable architecture for supporting multimedia (data, voice and video) applications in telecommunications. The transfer technique proposed for its implementation is the asynchronous transfer mode (ATM) due to its efficiency and flexibility. The ATM networks have to support a wide variety of services, each with different characteristics such as: interactive or distributed, broadband or narrowband, constant or variable traffic, etc. In addition, each service requires a different quality of service (QOS) [1].

To analyze and develop ATM networks, mathematical models are used to simulate the traffic sources. These models try to imitate the system with maximum accuracy and avoiding arduous computation times. Usually, the models used are Markov chains where the process rate depends on the state. The process is a Poisson or determinist distribution, and the time in each state follows an exponential distribution.

An easy way to model an ATM traffic source is via a simple ON-OFF model, which is a renewal process with an exponentially distributed duration between states. Therefore, the simulation of ATM network traffic may be realized with the superposition of many different ON-OFF models. However, the mathematical models that resolve this superposition are not so simple. The superposition of ATM sources can be modeled just like an equivalent ON-OFF process [2]. This model has poor accuracy, but presents a simple computational solution. A model widely used is the Markov modulated Poisson process (MMPP) [3]; this is a double stochastic Poisson process, consisting of a continuous time Markov chain with two states. This model is accurate enough, but its solution takes much computational time.

Lately there is a great interest in the application of artificial neural networks (ANNs) in the telecommunication world [4,5], assuming they may have some advantages over traditional methods: a) knowing acquisition through observation of real systems (adaptive learning) and identification of nonlinear complex functions; b) high velocity of computation due to the massive parallelism of the ANNs hardware implementation; computation time is independent of the ANN dimension and of the number of control variables; c) generalization capacity, i.e., ANNs may learn with just a subset of training patterns; d) ANN is fault tolerant because of its distributed process.

In this paper we show how complex mathematical models can be replaced by artificial neural networks to determine the superposition model parameters of many sources of ATM traffic. In addition, our system can determine the main parameters of any unknown superposition of ATM traffic, and model it. These parameters will depend on the number of connected sources of each class. The model is adjusted using multilayer perceptrons with a backpropagation learning [6].

SYSTEM DESCRIPTION

The most simple model to simulate the traffic of an ATM network is an ON-OFF process. This model is a two-state Markov chain, with an active state (ON) where ATM cells arrive with a constant rate, and a silent state (OFF). The time in each state is exponentially distributed. The model is characterized by three parameters: the rate of arriving cells in the ON state, R, the mean sojourn time in the ON state, a, and the mean sojourn time in the OFF state, b. Therefore, ATM network traffic can be defined through the vector $k = (R, a, b)$. The traffic statistical characteristics of this model must be equal to those of the real traffic.

The system is composed of four modules (see figure 1). The S module is an ATM Network

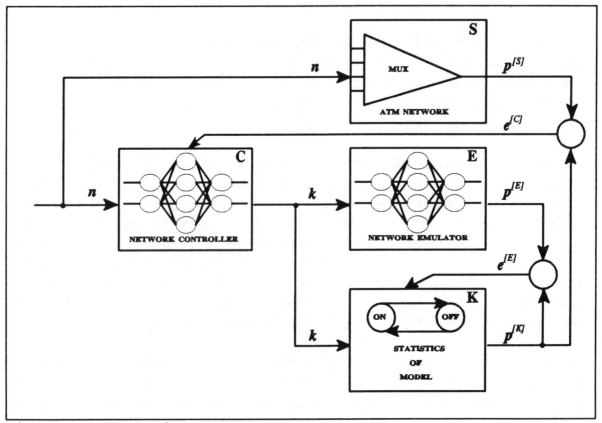

Figure 1. Block diagram of the system.

link, which for this purpose, has been simulated. From this module, in function of the connected sources in a given instant, we can find out a set of traffic statistic parameters of the ATM network[3], defined by the vector $p^{[S]} = (m^{[S]}, v_1^{[S]}, v_2^{[S]})$, with:

$$m^{[S]} = \frac{E[N(t)]}{t}$$

$$v_1^{[S]} = \left.\frac{var[N(t)]}{E(N(t))}\right|_{t=\frac{1}{m}} \qquad (1)$$

$$v_2^{[S]} = \left.\frac{var[N(t)]}{E(N(t))}\right|_{t\to\infty}$$

where $N(t)$ is the number of arriving cells along the time, m is the mean arrival rate over a long time, and v_1 and v_2 are the variance-to-mean ratios of the number of arrivals in $t = 1/m$ and $t \to \infty$, respectively.

The **C** module is the Network Controller, which estimates the parameters of the model in function of the number of connected sources of each class at its input; this module calculates the vector $k = F(n, W)$, being the vector $n = (n_1, \ldots, n_i, \ldots, n_N)$ where n_i is the number of sources of the class i ($i = 1, 2, \ldots, N$), and W the weights matrix of the multilayer perceptron. Unfortunately, we do not know the components of the vector k, and so it is not possible to perform the learning phase of the Network Controller module. To overcome this difficulty, we introduce two new modules (**K** and **E**).

The **K** module calculates the statistic parameters of an ON-OFF model, defined by the vector $p^{[K]} = (m^{[K]}, v_1^{[K]}, v_2^{[K]})$. For an OFF-ON model, the estimated values of these statistic parameters in function of the model parameters (R, a, b) are [7]:

$$m^{[K]} = \frac{Ra}{a+b}$$

$$v_1^{[K]} = \frac{2R^2(ab)^2}{(a+b)^3}\left[t + \frac{ab}{a+b}\left(\exp\left(-\frac{a+b}{ab}t\right) - 1\right)\right] \qquad (2)$$

$$v_2^{[K]} = \frac{2Rab^2}{(a+b)^2}$$

The **E** module is the Network Emulator, which is another MLP and calculates the statistic parameters of the ON-OFF model, defined through the vector k, i.e., this module gives at its output the vector $p^{[E]} = (m^{[E]}, v_1^{[E]}, v_2^{[E]})$, with the same statistic parameters as the real system (**S** module). The Network Emulator will learn to identify the **K** module, estimating a vector $p^{[E]} = G(k, V)$, being V the weights matrix of the Network Emulator module. This module adjusts its weights to minimize the error $e^{[E]} = \frac{1}{2}(p^{[K]} - p^{[E]})(p^{[K]} - p^{[E]})^T$, using the gradient:

$$\frac{\partial e^{[E]}}{\partial V} = -(p^{[K]} - p^{[E]}) \frac{\partial p^{[E]}}{\partial V}$$

The Network Emulator is necessary to backpropagate the error to the Network Controller

[8,9]. This module must minimize the error $e^{[C]} = \frac{1}{2}(p^{[S]}-p^{[K]})(p^{[S]}-p^{[K]})^T$, by means of the gradient:

$$\frac{\partial e^{[C]}}{\partial W} = -(p^{[S]}-p^{[K]})\frac{\partial p^{[K]}}{\partial W} = -(p^{[S]}-p^{[K]})\frac{\partial p^{[E]}}{\partial W}$$

where $\partial p^{[K]}/\partial W$ is replaced by $\partial p^{[E]}/\partial W$ as $p^{[E]}$ tends asymptotically to $p^{[K]}$. When the learning process finishes, the Network Controller will calculate the vector k, in function of the number of traffic sources (vector n); this vector will identify an ON-OFF model that will have similar characteristics than the real traffic of the ATM network.

SIMULATION AND NUMERICAL RESULTS

For simulation purposes we have used the neural network development system Nworks, by NeuralWare Inc. The ATM Network was simulated with C-language software; we have assumed that the transfer rate at the output link is 150 Mbit/s, and the cell length is 53 byte (424 bit). The service time for each cell (slot) is 2.83×10^{-6}s (424 bit/150 Mbit/s). For the sake of simplicity, only two classes of sources were selected, each modeled via an ON-OFF process, whose characteristics are shown in Table I.

We have obtained 50 training patterns introducing 50 different n vectors into the ATM Network, and measuring at its output the corresponding $p^{[S]}$ vector. The n vectors are random combinations of n_1 class 1 sources and n_2 class 2 sources, with $n_1 = \{0,1,...,75\}$ and $n_2 = \{0,1,...,25\}$. The Network Controller has 2, 15 and 3 neurons in its input, hidden and output layers, respectively, therefore, its dimension is (2,15,3). The dimension for the Network Emulator is (3,15,3). Using the error propagation shown above, both MLPs converge in less than 100.000 iterations. After the learning phase, the mean quadratic errors for the Controller and Emulator Networks are 3.8×10^{-5} and 1.8×10^{-5}, respectively. The MLPs outputs have been normalized between 0 and 1. The backpropagation learning algorithm of both MLPs uses a learning rate of 0.1, and a momentum of 0.075.

Once the learning phase is finished, the system is tested with 9 new patterns, obtained as a set of combinations of sources n_1 and n_2. Table II shows the parameters of the calculated model by the Network Controller (vector k) for a combination set of sources n_1 and n_2. Tables III, IV and V, compare the estimated and simulated statistic parameters of our system with the new 9 patterns. These results are good enough since the starting ON-OFF model is rather simple. More complex models, for instance the MMPP model, should give better results.

CONCLUSIONS

We have achieved through MLPs a procedure that calculates the model parameters for the superposition of ON-OFF ATM traffic sources, in function of the number of connections of each class. With this procedure we obtain the parameters of a simple model, which simulates some statistic characteristics, previously selected, of the traffic of the ATM network. Since the simplicity of the selected model, to get more accuracy certainly needs to increase the number of statistic parameters. In fact, our architecture allows to obtain the superposition parameters of Markov chain model with any number of states, just changing its dimension.

ACKNOWLEDGMENT

This work has been partially supported by the Spanish Comisión Interministerial de Ciencia y Tecnología (CICYT), Project No. TIC92-1325-PB.

REFERENCES

[1] J.J. Bae and T. Suda, "Survey of Traffic Control Schemes and Protocols in ATM networks", *Proceedings of the IEEE*, Vol. 79, No. 2, pp. 170-189, February 1991.

[2] E.D. Sykas, K.M. Vlakos and E.N. Protonotarios, "Mathematical tools for analysis of ATM systems", in *Teletraffic and Data Traffic (A. Jensen and V.B. Iversen, Eds)*, pp. 781-786, Elsevier Science Publishers 1991.

[3] H. Heffes and D.M. Lucantoni, "A Markov Modulated Characterization of Packetized Voice and Data Traffic and Related Statistical Multiplexer Performance", *IEEE Journal on Selected Areas in Communications* , Vol. 4, No. 6, pp. 856-868, September 1986.

[4] A. Hiramatsu, "ATM Communications Network Control by Neural Networks", *IEEE Trans. Neural Networks*, Vol. 1, No. 1, pp. 122-130, March 1990.

[5] R.J.T. Morris, "Prospects for Neural Networks in Broadband Networks Resource Management", in *Teletraffic and Data Traffic (A. Jensen and V.B. Iversen, Eds)*, pp. 335-340, Elsevier Science Publishers 1991.

[6] B. Widrow and M.A. Lehr, "30 years of Adaptive Neural Networks: Perceptron, Madaline and Backpropagation", *Proceedings of the IEEE*, Vol. 78, No. 9, pp. 1415-1442, September 1990.

[7] W. Burakowski, J. Andrade Parra and L. Fernández Alvarez, "Characterization of traffic sources in ATM networks", *Comunicaciones de Telefónica I+D*, Vo. 1, No. 2, July-December 1990 (in Spanish).

[8] K.S. Narendra and K. Parthasarathy, "Identification and Control of Dynamic Systems Using Neural Networks", *IEEE Trans. Neural Networks*, Vol. 1, No. 1, pp. 4-27, March 1990.

[9] X. Chen and I.M. Leslie, "Neural Adaptive Congestion Control for Broadband ATM Networks", *IEE Proceeding-I*, Vol. 139, No. 3, pp. 233-244, June 1992.

CHARACTERISTICS	CLASS 1	CLASS 2
R	0.01333 cells/slot	0.06666 cells/slot
a	884 slots	177 slots
b	884 slots	708 slots

Table I. Characteristics of the traffic sources

n_1/n_2	R	$a(slots)$	$b(slots)$
25/20	0,3502	32,358	35,286
16/5	0,3628	51,301	54,954
15/23	0,7836	35,103	31,929
3/18	0,5145	53,137	53,412
6/21	0,6247	44,995	43,102
6/6	0,2285	112,684	104,818
0/4	0,1126	205,208	257,353
47/11	0,9355	18,056	18,214
52/0	0,7343	14,932	16,84

Table II. Parameters of the model

n_1/n_2	$m^{[K]}$	$m^{[S]}$	$(m^{[K]}-m^{[S]})^2$
25/20	0,1664	0,1675	0,0000
16/5	0,1731	0,1751	0,0000
15/23	0,4056	0,4100	0,0000
3/18	0,2590	0,2566	0,0000
6/21	0,3194	0,3190	0,0000
6/6	0,1196	0,1183	0,0000
0/4	0,0599	0,0499	0,0001
47/11	0,4593	0,4657	0,0000
52/0	0,3463	0,3451	0,0000

Table III. Estimated and simulated m

n_1/n_2	$v_1^{[K]}$	$v_1^{[S]}$	$(v_1^{[K]}-v_1^{[S]})^2$
25/20	0,9676	0,9725	0,0000
16/5	0,9839	0,9981	0,0002
15/23	0,8135	0,8669	0,0029
3/18	0,9905	0,9578	0,0011
6/21	0,9393	0,9140	0,0006
6/6	0,8938	0,8837	0,0001
0/4	1,1845	1,1839	0,0000
47/11	0,8866	0,9336	0,0022
52/0	1,0094	1,0018	0,0001

Table IV. Estimated and simulated v_1

n_1/n_2	$v_2^{[K]}$	$v_2^{[S]}$	$(v_2^{[K]}-v_2^{[S]})^2$
25/20	6,3035	6,1673	0,0186
16/5	9,7365	9,9564	0,0484
15/23	12,285	12,483	0,0392
3/18	13,666	13,741	0,0056
6/21	14,028	13,458	0,3249
6/6	12,067	11,960	0,0114
0/4	14,280	14,314	0,0012
47/11	8,5015	8,5100	0,0001
52/0	5,9940	6,1611	0,0279

Table V. Estimated and simulated v_2

DEVELOPMENT OF A NEOCOGNITRON SIMULATOR FOR GROUP TECHNOLOGY

Fuat Kulak and Luis Carlos Rabelo
Department of Industrial and Systems Engineering
Ohio University
Athens, Ohio 45701

ABSTRACT

The neocognitron, a neural network paradigm, is selected by comparisons with other neural networks families due to its characteristics of recognizing patterns without being affected by the shifts in the position and distortions for a group technology (GT) implementation. Two-dimensional Computer Aided Design(CAD) representations are input to a neocognitron neural network to produce groups of similar parts. This system demonstrates the feasibility of training a neocognitron neural network to develop templates, and then to recall a family of similar parts (based on the templates).

1. INTRODUCTION

A part family is a collection of parts that are similar in geometry and size, or in the processing steps that are required in their manufacture. The identification of part families forms a major prerequisite for the implementation of group technology (GT). The objective of GT, as a total manufacturing philosophy, is to exploit these similarities and achieve economies in the entire manufacturing cycle [1,12,13]. A wide range of benefits are made possible, which include design rationalization and variety reduction in the engineering design stage, setup times, lead times, labor needs, and work-in-process inventory in the shop floor.

The visual examination involved in part geometry-based classification is similar to the process involved in pattern recognition, character recognition and image processing. Due to this fact, several studies have been carried in the possible use of neural networks to accomplish GT [2,3]. In this paper, a neocognitron implementation for GT is studied. Neocognitron has the capability of scale, rotation-invariant recognition of parts. Neocognitron also acquire the ability to handle large amount of deformation on the patterns. These are essential elements to develop an effective GT implementation driven by computer-aided design (CAD).

2. DESCRIPTION OF THE NETWORK

The neocognitron is an example of a hierarchical neural network in which there are many layers with a very sparse and localized pattern of connectivity between layers [4,5,6,7,8,9,1011].

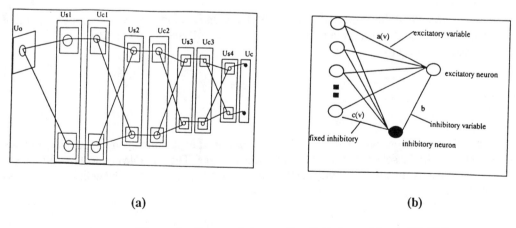

(a)   (b)

Figure 1. Connections to a S-cell (Adapted from [10,11])

The first layer of the network is the input layer called Uo (see Figure 1). Uo consist of a two-dimensional array of receptor cells. The layers of S-cells (i.e., simple cells) and C-cells (complex cells) at the l th stage are denoted by Usl and Ucl. The notation Usl(n,k), for example, is used to denote the output of an S-cell in layer Usl, where n is a two dimensional coordinates (x,y) indicating the position of the cell's receptive field center in the input layer Uo, and k is the serial number of the cell-plane. (1< k < Kl).

The output of an S-cell is :

$$U_{sl}(n,k) \; \gamma \; \times \; \varphi\left[\frac{1 + \sum_{k=1}^{K_{l-1}} \sum_{v \in A_l} a_l(v,K,k) \times U_{c_{l-1}}(n+v,K)}{1 + \frac{\gamma_l}{1+\gamma_l} \times b_l(k) \times U_{vl}(n)} - 1\right]$$

$$\varphi[X] = X, \text{ IF } X \geq 0$$

$$\varphi[X] = 0, \text{ IF } X < 0$$

al (v+ K, k) is the strength of the variable excitatory connection coming from C-cell Ucl-1(n+v,K) of the preceding stage. al denotes the summation range of v, that is the size of the spatial spread of the input connections to one S-cell. bl (k) is the strength of the variable inhibitory connection coming from subsidiary V-cell Uvl(n). All the S-cells in a S-cell plane have identical sets of input connections. Hence, equation do not contain argument n representing the position of the receptive field of the cell Usl. The positive constant 1 determines the efficiency of the inhibitory input to this cell.

The output of an subsidiary V-cell :

$$U_{vl}(n) = \sqrt{\sum_{K=1}^{K_{l-1}} \sum_{v \in A_l} c_l(v) \times U_{cl-1}(n+v,K)^2}$$

where cl and is a monotically decreasing function of ‖v‖

$$\sum_{k_{l-1}}^{K_{l-1}} \sum_{v \in S_l} c_{l-1}(n) = 1$$

The output of a C-cell inserted in the network to allow for positional errors, is :

$$U_{cl}(n,k) = \Psi\left[\sum_{v \in D_l} d_l(v) \times U_{sl}(n+v,k)\right]$$

Parameter dl(v) denotes the strength of the fixed excitatory connections, and is monotically decreasing function of ‖v‖. Dl is the area to which these connections spread. ψ[x] is a function specifying the characteristics of saturation of the C-cell, and is defined by

$$\psi[x] = \frac{\varphi[x]}{1 + \varphi[x]}$$

During learning, the variable connections al(v, k, K) and bl(k) are reinforced depending upon the intensity of the input to the seed cell. Let Usl(n,k) be selected as a seed cell at a certain time. The variable connections al(v,k,K) and bl(k) to this seed cell, and consequently to all the S-cells in the same cell plane as the seed cell, are reinforced by the following amounts :

$$\Delta a_l(\upsilon, K, k) = q_l \times c_l(\upsilon) \times U_{cl-1}(n + \upsilon, K)$$

$$\Delta b_l(k) = q_l \times U_{vl}(n)$$

Where q is a positive constant determining the speed of reinforcement.

3. GT Application

The objective was to develop a classification system that places the parts into groups based upon the observable similarities in the part design. When these types of similarities exist, it is very obvious that similar production operations and plans are used to produce the parts. This basic similarity fact is based purely upon a visual judgment of the commonalties. The neocognitron is intended to detect these similarities and classify them into correct part families.

A simulator was written in the C programming language on a SUN \Sparc workstation (see Figure 2). Five part families were created in an INTERGRAPH workstation. These part families are shown in Figure 3. Then, pixel representations of the part drawings were generated. Bitmaps of the drawings were then utilized as the inputs to the neocognitron. Then, the hierarchy of the network would be as followed layer by layer:

16x16   Uo, 13x13x10 Us1,
12x12x10 Uc1, 9x9x10 Us2,
8x8x10   Uc2, 5x5x10 Us3,
4x4x10   Uc3, 2x2x10 Us4
1x1x5   Uc4.

Receptive fields for simple cells are 3x3, and for the complex layers are 2x2 for this specific simulator.

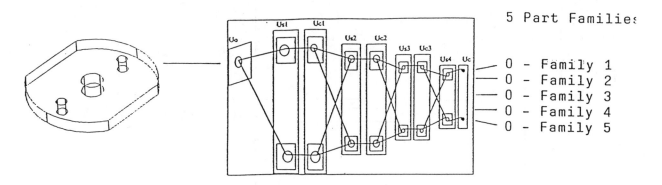

Figure 2. Schematic of the system

For both training and testing, only one geometric view of parts were used. This could be any geometric view. The network could also be trained with six possible views of parts. Indeed, this should be the way in practical life. Because, this method does not require any part orientation before classification. This means that parts can be traveling on a conveyor or any material handling device at any position. Hypotethically, the neocognitron will give different responses for each different view. Then by using other supervised classifier these six views could be combined into one part family.

The network was trained layer by layer with the repeated presentations of five training patterns. Each layer was trained sequentially (i.e., with the completion of training of the preceding layer). Details of the training iterations process are given below:

Layer No.	Number of Training Pattern Presentations
Layer 1	8 times
Layer 2:	4 times
Layer 3:	13 times
Layer 4:	8 times

At the end of training, one C-cell in the final C-layer (4) was fired.

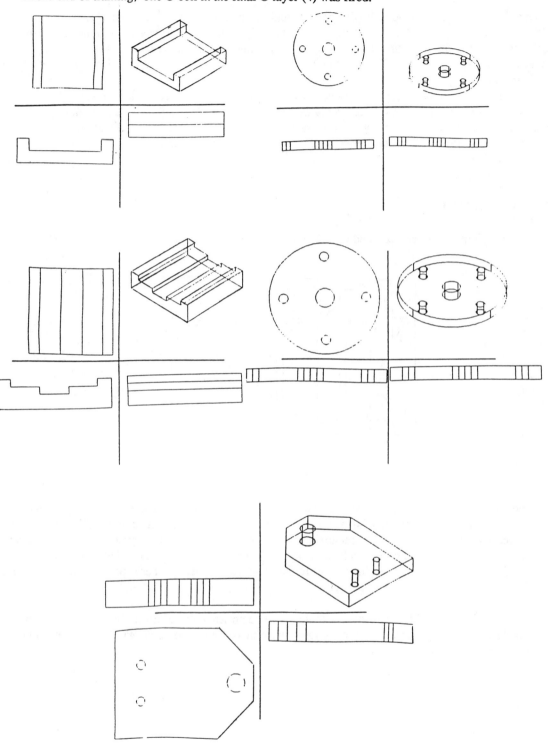

Figure 3.. Training Patterns

Different parts were developed to test the trained network (see Figure 4). These patterns were coded the same way as those used for training. Parameters and network structure were kept the same. The performance of the network on these testing patterns was 100% correct. Each testing pattern from the same part family activated the same C-cell at the final layer.

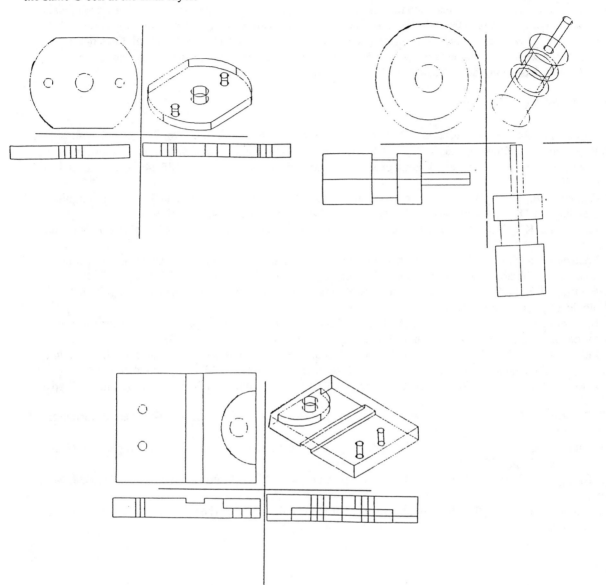

Figure 4. Samples of Testing Patterns

CONCLUSION AND ONGOING RESEARCH ISSUES

In this research, a neocognitron with only feed forward connections was built. A variation with backward connections could provide a more flexible structure. Another important point is that all the engineering design parts for this experiment were encoded for one certain view and tested with the same view. The development of a system that could be trained from six possible views of the same part which forms a part family is under construction. However, for future developments, it is very important to determine the capabilities of the neocognitron when more group families are needed (e.g., 1000 - the literature available does not describe neocognitron-based systems that could handle a great number of categories.)

REFERENCES

1. Ingram, F., 1982, "Group technology", Production and Inventory Management, vol.23(2), pp. 19-34.

2. Kamarthi, S.V., Kumara, S.R.T., Yu, F.T.S, and Ham, I., "Neural networks and their applications in component design data retrieval", Journal of Intelligent Manufacturing, vol.1, pp. 125-140, Chapman and Hall Ltd, 1990.

3. Caudell, T.P., Smith, D.G., Escobedo, R., Jonhson, G.C., "A neural database system for reusable engineering", Proceedings of The International Joint Conference on Neural Networks, Singapore, Nov. 1991.

4. Fukushima, K. (1975). "Cognitron : A self-orginizing multi-layered neural network," Biological Cybernetics, vol.20(3/4), pp. 121-136

5. Fukushima, K. (1980), Nocognitron: A self-orginizing neural network model for a mechanism of pattern recognition unaffected by shift in position, Biological Cybernetics, vol.36(4), pp. 193-202.

6. Fukushima, K. (1986), "A neural network model for selective attention in visual pattern recognition," Biological Cybernetics, vol.55(1), pp.5-15.

7. Fukushima, K., and Miyake, S. (1982), "Neocognitron: A new algorithm for pattern recognition tolerant of deformations and shifts and shifts in position," Pattern Recognition, vol.15(6), pp.455-469.

8. Fukushima, K., Miyake, S. and Ito, T. (1983), "Neocognitron: A neural network model for a mechanism of visual pattern recognition," IEEE Transactions on Syst. Man Cybernetics, SMC-13(5), pp. 826-834.

9. Fukushima, K. (1988a). "A neural network for visual pattern recognition," IEEE Computer, vol.21(3), pp. 65-75.

10. Fukushima, K.(1988b), "Neocognitron: A hierarchical neural network capable of visual pattern recognition," Neural Networks, vol.1(2), pp.119-130.

11. Fukushima, K. (1989), "Analysis of the process of visual pattern recognition by the neocognitron," Neural Networks, vol.2, pp.413-420.

12. Chang,Tien C., Wysk, Richard A., Wang, Hsu p., **Computer-Aided Manufacturing**,, Prentice Hall, New Jersey, 1991

13. Kevin Hooks (1993), Thesis Study, Department of Industrial and Systems engineering, Ohio University, Athens, Ohio.

A Neural Network Approach to Estimating Material Properties

Thomas Martinetz and Thomas Poppe
Siemens AG
Corporate Research and Development
Otto-Hahn-Ring 6
81730 München, Germany

A neural network approach to the problem of estimating physical properties of a material based on the material's chemical composition is presented. The network, a multilayer perceptron, consists of sigmoidal hidden units and a linear output unit arranged in a feedforward architecture. As a component of a process optimization system which is applied in production processes with a priori unknown and eventually drifting characteristics, fast on-line adaptation of the network is performed. A first application has been the estimation of the "relative yield stress" of different steel qualities, which is necessary for optimizing the rolling process at a hot line rolling mill. On an independent test data set the neural network approach achieved a reduction of the average estimation error of about 15% compared to the current state-of-the-art method.

1. Introduction

Process optimization requires knowledge about the relevant properties of the processed material. Depending on the material transformation process to be controlled, physical properties of the material like its heat capacity, its viscosity, its heat conductivity, or its hardness (just to mention a few) determine the optimal choice for the control parameter values. In most cases, however, the respective material property cannot be measured directly but must be estimated based on the thermodynamic state of the material, i.e., its chemical composition, its temperature, the given pressure, and eventually geometric quantities. The quality of the estimation result determines to a great extent the cost effectiveness and the product quality of the production process.

To be able to estimate material properties based on the thermodynamic state variables, the respective physical relationship has to be known. A common approach is to try to describe this relationship through physical models. However, in most cases the underlying physics is too intricate and/or not understood sufficiently to allow the design of feasible physical models which yield satisfying estimation results. In addition, the development of physical models is time consuming, requires precise knowledge about the usually very complex physical processes, and each model is specific for each material and each material transformation process.

To increase cost effectiveness and product quality also of intricate material transformation processes, an approach is necessary which *learns* the underlying physical relationship instead of modeling it based on specific prior knowledge. In addition, it would be highly desirable to have an approach which is generic and can be applied to a variety of materials and transformation processes. In the following we demonstrate that neural networks as adaptive modeling schemes have the desired capabilities. We describe the application of a neural network to the problem of estimating the *relative yield stress* (plasticity) of steel plates based on the steel plates' chemical composition, temperature, and shape. Knowledge about the relative yield stress is necessary for optimizing rolling processes, in our case the rolling of steel at a hot line rolling mill.

2. The Neural Network Architecture

The neural network has to model the relation

$$\alpha = F(C, Si, Mn, P, S, Al, N, Cu, Cr, Ni, Sn, V, Mo, Ti, Nb, B, d, b, T_i, T_f)$$

between the relative yield stress α of the steel plate and the concentrations of the sixteen chemical additives $C, Si, ..., B$, the steel plate's thickness d and its width b. T_i and T_f denote the temperature of the steel plate before and after the rolling, respectively. These two temperatures serve as a measure for the actual rolling temperature T, which cannot be determined explicitly. The concentration of the sixteen chemical additives $C, Si, ..., B$ is obtained from a material analysis during the steel cooking.

Figure 1 shows the neural network architecture, a three-layer feedforward network consisting of ten sigmoidal hidden units and one linear output unit. Each hidden unit receives the same twenty-dimensional input vector $\mathbf{x} = (C, Si, ..., Nb, B, d, b, T_i, T_f)$. The weights of the hidden units i, $i = 1, ..., 10$, are denoted by $\mathbf{w}_i = (w_{i1}, ..., w_{i20})$, and the weights of the linear output unit are denoted by $\mathbf{w} = (w_1, ..., w_{10})$. The thresholds of the hidden units and the output unit are denoted by θ_i and θ, respectively. Hence, when the network receives the input $\mathbf{x}$ which carries the information about the steel plate to be rolled, the network generates the output

$$\mathcal{N}_{\mathcal{W}}(\mathbf{x}) = -\theta + \sum_{i=1}^{10} w_i \, \sigma \left(\sum_{j=1}^{20} w_{ij} x_j - \theta_i \right)$$

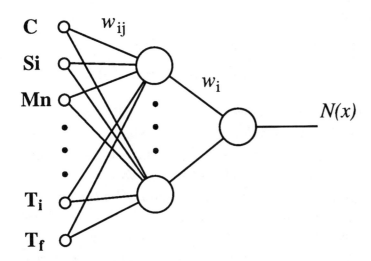

Figure 1: The architecture of the neural network. The network receives 20 inputs and consists of 10 sigmoidal hidden units plus one linear output unit.

as an estimation for the relative yield stress of the steel plate, with $\sigma(.) = 1/(\exp(-.) + 1)$ forming the sigmoidal output of the hidden units. The index $\mathcal{W}$ denotes the dependence of the network output $\mathcal{N}_{\mathcal{W}}(\mathbf{x})$ on the set $\mathcal{W} = (\mathbf{w}_i, \theta_i, \mathbf{w}, \theta)$ of all network weights and thresholds.

The estimation error of the network has to be minimized by adapting the network weights $\mathcal{W} = (\mathbf{w}_i, \theta_i, \mathbf{w}, \theta)$. This is achieved through pattern-by-pattern training, i.e., with each pattern μ through gradient descent on the square error

$$E(\mathcal{W}) = (\alpha^\mu - \mathcal{N}_{\mathcal{W}}(\mathbf{x}^\mu))^2 \,.$$

$\mathbf{x}^\mu$ comprises the chemical composition, thickness, width, and temperature of the μ-th steel plate, the actual relative yield stress of which was α^μ. With each new data pairs $(\mathbf{x}^\mu, \alpha^\mu)$ the network weights are adjusted through gradient descent on $E(\mathcal{W})$, which yields, by calculating

$$\Delta \mathcal{W} = -\eta \frac{\partial E(\mathcal{W})}{\partial \mathcal{W}}, \tag{1}$$

the backpropagation learning rules [1, 2].

3. The Performance

For testing the performance of the neural network approach and comparing it with the current state-of-the art method, 38442 measured data pairs $(\mathbf{x}^\mu, \alpha^\mu)$ from a rolling mill were made available by the steel manufacturer. The data pairs were ordered chronologically, corresponding to the order the steel plates were rolled. The first 10000 data pairs formed the training set which was used for a preadaptation of the network. The following 28442 data pairs were used for on-line testing and training.

$\langle E_{cur} \rangle$	$\langle E_{net} \rangle$	Δ
39.57%	33.70%	14.9%

Table 1: The relative RMS error of the neural network and the current method.

The on-line performance of the network was tested by sequentially presenting data pairs $(\mathbf{x}^\mu, \alpha^\mu)$ from the test set, in the same chronological order as the steel plates were rolled. With each steel plate the estimation error of the neural network and the current-state-of-the-art method, respectively, was recorded, and an adaptation step of the network weights was performed. Then the next data pair was presented, etc.. After 28442 data pairs the average estimation error of the neural network and the current-state-of-the-art method on these 28442 steel plates was calculated. The test was performed in the laboratory, however, the result is equivalent to the average estimation error the neural network would have achieved if it had really been applied at the rolling mill.

The achieved estimation performance is shown in Table 1. $\langle E_{net} \rangle$ denotes the root mean square (RMS) estimation error of the neural network on the data of the test set, relative to the standard deviation of the test data. $\langle E_{cur} \rangle$ denotes the relative RMS estimation error of the current state-of-the-art method on the test set, and Δ is the achieved improvement. The neural network approach achieves an improvement of 14.9% over the current state-of-the-art method.

4. Discussion

The results obtained with the straight-forward neural network approach are very promising. In the application described, the estimation of the relative yield stress of steel, the improvement of the estimation quality is so significant that the neural network approach will replace the current method and soon be a component of a commercially available process optimization system for rolling mills.

There are a couple of reasons for the favorable results with the neural network approach. The main reason is the on-line adaptation of the network. The network weights are permanently adjusted to the changing characteristics of the rolling mill and the drifts of the measuring devices for the chemical composition, thickness, width and temperature of the steel plate. Particularly the calibration of the measuring devices is not very reliable because of the very hazardous environment at a hot line rolling mill. The presented approach based on a neural network is able to compensate for these drifts due to its adaptability.

References

[1] Werbos P (1974) "Beyond Regression: New Tools for Prediction and Analysis in the Behavioral Sciences." Ph.D. thesis, Harvard Univ. Committee on Applied Mathematics.

[2] Rumelhart DE, Hinton GE, Williams RJ (1986) "Learning Representations by Back-Propagating Errors." Nature, 323:533–536.

Electricity Demand Prediction Using Discrete-Time Fully Recurrent Neural Networks

Santiago Rementeria, Josu Oyanguren and Gurutze Marijuán
LABEIN Research Centre
Parque Tecnológico 101
48016 Zamudio, Spain

Abstract: Despite their more complex dynamics and the computational cost demanded to train them, recurrent networks are potentially better suited than traditional feedforward layered perceptrons for time-series prediction problems. In this paper we present some results obtained in power demand forecasting using such architectures. It is also shown how vector implementations on supercomputers may help to improve the experimental design of artificial neural networks.

I. INTRODUCTION

There are lots of natural and artificial processes in which observations are collected sequentially in time. Predicting the values that such observations will take in the future is an important problem in areas like production planning, marketing, quality control, stock management and matereology. By the very nature of prediction, with all the risks involved in extrapolating concrete assumptions to the future, no single method is infallible for all types of problems. Nonetheless, neural networks have been shown to be a robust alternative to already existing forecasting methods in applications like electric load forecasting. On the other hand, vector and parallel supercomputers offer the storage size and speed required to get maximum performance in numeric applications like neural network training and operation. Supercomputing lends itself naturally to neural network research because most of the operations involved in the simulation of such devices are vector and matrix-oriented. Such powerful machines can exploit the fine-grained parallelism inherent in neural architectures speeding up their computationally costly training process.

This paper shows the results obtained in a series of experiments aimed at testing the usefulness of fully interconnected feedback neural networks in an industrial demand forecasting application. It also provides an example of the way supercomputers can help in the development of computationally intensive simulations of artificial neural systems. In the following section we will introduce fully recurrent neural networks. Section III focuses on the electric load forecasting problem, describing the experiments carried out and the results obtained. Section IV explains how the original implementation was ported to a CONVEX computer and section V2orffne concludes the paper by bringing out a few summary ideas.

II. STATE NOTION THROUGH RECURRENCE

In our research we tested *feedforward* and *fully recurrent* networks. Feedback or recurrent networks, unlike the formers, contain inter and intralayer feedback loops. In particular, each unit in a fully recurrent network is connected with all the other units -including itself-, and so the network loses its layer structure. A crucial difference between multilayer perceptrons (the feedforward paradigm tested) and recurrent networks is that the latters are characterized by dynamic node behavior. In contrast to other neural paradigms with dynamic node equations, like Hopfield networks, recurrent networks have learnable weights. Feedback connections allow the units in a recurrent network to process information about past states of the system i.e. they provide a certain memory capability. Previous systematic experimental research has shown that the good performance of such networks in time-series forecasting applications stems from the notion of *context* incorporated in them [11]. Figure 1 shows one fully recurrent architecture with two input units and three fully recurrent ones, including one external, observable output.

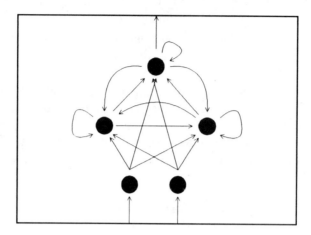

Figure 1. An example of a fully recurrent network

In this paper we will focus on the discrete-time approximation [13] to the continuous-time network described, for example, in [10].

III. ELECTRICITY DEMAND FORECASTING

We chose electric energy consumption forecasting as a practical problem to test the potential of recurrent neural networks. Predicting tomorrow's load as accurately as possible is a task performed daily by engineers in power generating and distributing companies worldwide. Such short-term forecasts play an important role for a reliable, safe and economic operation of power systems. However, electricity consumption is highly unpredictable as it is influenced by factors like the hour of the day, the weather and random disturbances whose effect on the load is uncertain. Artificial neural networks are an alternative to conventional statistical techniques like regression, exponential smoothing or time-series modelling that are normally used in this task [5]. Most experiments described in the literature are based on the multilayer perceptron. There are very few references proposing partial recurrent networks [8,9] and we have found a single one considering full recurrence [3]. In contrast to the approach proposed there, we used a single network to forecast hourly loads for all days of the year.

3.1 Experimental setting

Before starting the experimentation stage the set of available load data was divided in two sets. The *training set* consisted of total hourly load information in Northern Spain between 1987 and 1990 (35,064 examples), whilst the hourly consumptions during 1991 constituted the *test set* (8,760 cases).

Two different series of experiments were carried out. Experimentation began assuming a one hour ahead prediction problem. This means trying to predict the consumption of the following hour having hourly information of past consumption values. Additional information like past temperatures or the day of the week was also used in later experiments. Although the most useful short-term forecasts are the ones done the day before, the predictions done with a lead time of one hour constitute a best-case situation useful to set the performance limits of neural nets for more realistic time horizons. The second series of experiments assumed a lead time of 48 hours, which can be considered the most unfavourable situation in one day ahead forecasting.

For the one hour ahead problem we compared the performance of multilayer networks trained through backpropagation and discrete-time fully recurrent networks trained using a more general but conceptually similar gradient search algorithm seeking to minimize a sum of squared error criteria [13]. After extensive experimentation it was concluded that the latter type behaves better in this kind of applications. Hence, for 48 hours ahead forecasting only fully recurrent networks were considered. All the software was written in C language and run on a Sun Sparc II station.

3.2 Results

Table I shows the performance achieved with the best fully recurrent neural network for each of three different input vectors. The error measures reported refer to the *mean absolute percentage error (MAPE)*:

$$MAPE = \frac{1}{N} \sum_{i=1}^{N} \frac{|o(i) - d(i)|}{d(i)}$$

where o(i) is the forecast value computed by the neural network, d(i) is the expected value and N is the size of the test set.

Table I.   Neural network performance
(correctness on the test set: 100%-MAPE)

Forecasting horizon	Input: L_{t-1}, L_{t-2}	Input: L_i(ARIMA)	Input: L_i(ARIMA), T_t(forecast), Q_i(qualitative)
1 hour	96.5%	98%	98.2%
48 hours	--	91%	94%

Using only information relative to previous loads it was observed that knowing the load values of the preceding two hours suffices to achieve a MAPE of 3.5% in the test set. Being this a pure time-series problem, ARIMA modelling was used to reveal the features which are statistically more relevant [2]. The most relevant past demand values in the best models were, in decreasing order, L_{t-1}, L_{t-169}, L_{t-168}, L_{t-2} and L_{t-170}, where L_{t-x} denotes the demand X hours before the prediction time (note the obvious weekly period). Taking such features as input of the neural network the MAPE decreased to around 2%.

It was observed that, for the one hour ahead problem, adding qualitative information like the month, day and time of the prediction and whether the current day is a holiday or not, and quantitative one like the temperature forecast do not contribute much to decreasing the MAPE (only about 0.2%). Demand and thermal inertia prevent from sudden changes in periods of just one or two hours, being most relevant information already contained in the last elements of the time series.

The situation is a bit more complex in the 48 hour ahead forecasting problem. Having a wider prediction horizon increases the uncertainty and so the results are necessarily worse than in the previous problem. Statistical methods determined L_{t-168}, L_{t-48}, L_{t-216}, L_{t-49} and L_{t-217} to be the most relevant input features in this case. The recurrent network trained with those features as inputs attained a 91% of correctness in the test set. In contrast to what was observed in the one hour ahead problem, additional information is quite helpful in this case and the MAPE is reduced in about 3%. This is because the information contained in the load values of 48 hours before the value to be forecast is much less than the one implicit in the load value of the immediately preceding hours. Thus the importance of additional information in realistic load forecasting problems.

It must be noted that, at least with the data available for the experiments, there was little room for improvement of the results achieved in the next-hour forecasting problem by considering separate networks to model different hours, days or seasons. As the lead time increases, the performance of the network worsens, and splitting the problem into several networks could result in a better fit to cyclic load variations.

IV. LEARNING PHASE SPEED-UP

Unfortunately, neural network building is practically an *ad hoc* procedure for which an extensive experimentation may be required. Moreover, the *training* times required by learning algorithms for multilayer perceptrons or fully recurrent networks can result too long for them to be practical in complex applications on conventional computers. Huge databases have to be processed in the training phase involving lots of time-consuming vector and matrix operations. High-performance hardware allows to broaden the training stage experimentation in order to get a (near-)optimal neural network design much faster. After having been trained off-line e.g. on a supercomputer, the network may be efficiently operated on a smaller machine, typically a workstation or even a personal computer.

Artificial neural networks are well suited for simulations on supercomputers [4]. By the term *supercomputer* we refer to a class of computers supporting not only large and high-speed memories and input/output operations, but mostly some degree of parallelism understood as the capability to simultaneously process tasks ranging from jobs and programs to loops or statements. Some combination of multiprocessing, vector processing and concurrent scalar processing will be therefore expected from such machines.

The relevance of parallel computing in this context stems from the fact that neural architectures and learning algorithms are also parallel in nature. Each neural unit is assumed to process information independently. At the implementation level collections of neurons could be associated with individual computer processors. Alternatively, neuron arrays can be represented as vectors and the connections between these arrays of units (i.e. weights) can be represented as matrices. Vectorization converts loops performing scalar operations on array elements into equivalent vector operations. Vector operations use special vector registers to operate on hundreds of array elements with a single machine instruction. Obviously, optimizing loop handling is crucial to accelerate typical neural network training. A second degree of parallelism refers to the processing of training examples. Several steps of typical neural net training algorithms can be vectorized or parallelized, thus bringing a considerable reduction in computation time. Weight matrix and unit activation updating, for example, are inherently parallel procedures. Assuming a *batch* updating of weights (that is, following the strict gradient) individual contributions made by each training pattern to the adjustment of the network weights can be linearly combined so, in principle, patterns could be processed independently and concurrently. Moreover, most supercomputers have resources like floating point processing or fast multiply-accumulate operations (a majority of neural computations is of the type multiply-and-add) that provide additional support for efficient neural network simulations. The processing, memory and input/output speed provided by supercomputers can thus be advantageously exploited for neural network *design*. Other researchers have also reported a favourable performance of neural networks implemented on supercomputers [1,6,7,12].

We tested this working procedure for assessing the potential advantages provided by supercomputers in neural network design by vectorizing the learning algorithms mentioned in section III and measuring the training phase speed-up. In our experiments we used a CONVEX C-3820 computer with two processors providing a computational rate of 200 Mips and 250 Mflops and with 256 Mbytes of crossbar memory with three access channels (500 Mbytes/s). A CONVEX C compiler was used. Having the source code running on this computer was almost straightforward, but the first small optimization efforts did not yield as good results as expected. Although compilers are far from providing a neural network optimally designed for vector processing, the information generated at compile time was found useful to detect parts of the code like, for example, dynamic memory allocation, that required a special treatment. The original programs required several changes, mostly to break the data dependencies that inhibit the utilization of special vector registers and pipelined multiplications and additions. Figure 2 shows the average improvement obtained over a workstation by using different compiler optimization levels and after recoding the training algorithm for fully recurrent networks:

- no :   default scalar optimization
- O0 : no + scalar optimization within basic blocks
- O1 : O0 + scalar optimization within functions
- O2 : O1 + vector optimization

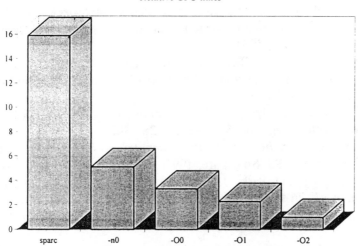

Figure 2. Training speed optimization

V. CONCLUSIONS

In view of the preliminary results obtained there are several conclusions that can be drawn from the current line of investigation. In what concerns neural networks, they seem to be a robust black-box approach in forecasting applications like the one considered here. Ordinary multilayer perceptron performance can be improved in short-term electric power demand modelling and prediction by considering feedback connections and discrete time delays within the neural architecture. Given the sensitivity of the network performance to the inputs of the system, we relied on traditional statistical methods to decide what particular features are more relevant.

Although operation speed is an unarguable asset of neural networks, their training slowness may become an inconvenience. As an alternative -or better a complement- to theoretical research aiming at faster algorithms, we tested an empirical procedure consisting of training sufficiently complex artificial neural networks on supercomputers and then porting the resulting best solution to other machines in order to be integrated with the computing environment of the application. High-speed processing has beneficial effects on neural network design and makes working methodology more flexible. Fast training times improve productivity and contribute to more reliable solutions. We are currently trying to obtain more accurate and faster predictions by testing adequate data preprocessing methods, considering alternative neural architectures and having multitasking implementations across several processors.

This project was supported by a grant from the Department of Industry of the Basque Government. We are grateful to Félix Alonso from Iberdrola S.A. for having provided us with data for the experiments.

REFERENCES

[1]   Ahalt, S.C., Chen, P., Chou, C-T. and Jung, T-P., *Implementation of a vector quantization codebook design technique based on a competitive learning artificial neural network*, The Journal of Supercomputing, vol. 5, 1992, pp. 307-330.

[2]   Box, G.E.P and Jenkins, G.M., *Time Series Analysis: Forecasting and Control*, Holden-Day, 1976.

[3]   Connor, J.T., Atlas, L.E. and Martin, D., *Recurrent neural networks and load forecasting*, in Proceedings of the First International Forum on Applications of Neural Networks to Power Systems, Seattle, WA, 1991, pp. 22-25.

[4]   DARPA, *DARPA Neural Network Study*, AFCEA Press, Washington, DC, 1988.

[5]   Highley, D.D. and Hilmes, T.J., *Load forecasting by ANN*, IEEE Computer Applications in Power, vol. 6, no. 3, July 1993, pp. 10-15.

[6]   Hung, S.L. and Adeli, H., *Parallel backpropagation learning algorithms on CRAY Y-MP8/864 supercomputer*, Neurocomputing, vol. 5, 1993, pp. 287-302.

[7]   Koike, N., *Neuro-computing and its application in supercomputer*, in Proceedings of the Singapore Supercomputing Conference '90, Singapore, 1991, pp. 260-265.

[8]   Lee, K.Y., Choi, T.I., Ku, C.C. and Park, J.H., *Short-term load forecasting using diagonal recurrent neural network*, in Proceedings of the Second International Forum on Applications of Neural Networks to Power Systems, Yokohama, Japan, 1993, pp. 227-232.

[9]   Mori, H. and Ogasawara, T., *A recurrent neural network approach to short-term load forecasting in electric power systems*, in Proceedings of the World Conference on Neural Networks, Portland, OR, 1993, vol. I, pp. 342-345.

[10]   Pineda, F.J., *Dynamics and architecture for neural computation*, Journal of Complexity, vol. 4, 1988, pp. 216-245.

[11]   Ulbricht, C. and Dorffner, G. (Eds.), *Neural Networks for Processing Sequences*, in preparation.

[12]   Wang, C-J., Wu, C-H and Sivasundaram, S., *Neural network simulation on shared-memory vector multiprocessors*, in Proceedings of the 16th Annual International Symposium on Computer Architecture, Baltimore, MD, 1989, pp. 197-204.

[13]   Williams, R.J. and Zipser, D., *A learning algorithm for continually running fully recurrent neural networks*, Neural Computation, vol. 1, 1989, pp. 270-280.

Hardware Tradeoffs for Boolean Concept Learning

Ashok V. Krishnamoorthy, Ramamohan Paturi, Matthias Blume, Gregory D. Linden*, Lars H. Liden*, and Sadik C. Esener*

Department of Electrical & Computer Engineering, UCSD, La Jolla CA 92093
*Department of Computer Science & Engineering, UCSD, La Jolla CA 92093

Abstract

Valiant has suggested a polynomial-time algorithm that can learn disjunctions of conjunctions (DNF) from a suitable training set using simple threshold gates. Each conjunction has up to k literals. The input layer is randomly connected to the hidden layer, where conjunctions are learned in an unsupervised mode; the disjunctive output layer is trained in a supervised mode. We perform theoretical and empirical studies of the learning performance of the boolean concept learning algorithm. We confirm that the method provides a fast, efficient means for learning k-DNF concepts. We examine hardware tradeoffs in the structure of these learning networks, in terms of the number of hidden neurons required versus the fan-in per neuron. Finally we investigate 3-dimensional optically-interconnected architectures well suited to implement k-DNF learning.

1. Introduction

Acquisition of discrete knowledge by learning is one of the central issues in artificial intelligence. One approach to this issue is to study boolean concept learning by induction. In this approach, acquisition of knowledge amounts to acquiring representations of boolean concepts. A boolean concept is a boolean function of boolean attributes. A concept learning algorithm takes a sequence of examples of an unknown boolean function as input, and outputs a hypothesis which is an approximation to the unknown boolean function. More often than not, we insist that the learning algorithm have the on-line property, i.e. the algorithm updates its hypothesis between the successive presentations of the examples. We typically assume that the unknown function belongs to a certain class of boolean functions. The complexity measures of interest are the costs of each update and the rate of convergence, i.e. the rate at which the hypothesis approaches the unknown function as a function of the number of examples. For an implementation, the hardware resources required to represent the hypothesis and for the updating process are also of interest. Usually the choice of representation for the hypothesis strongly influences these complexity measures.

The importance of Boolean functions to represent knowledge and the inductive acquisition of knowledge is supported by the success of expert systems [1]. Valiant [2] studied the learnability of a class of Boolean functions represented as disjunctions of conjunctions, otherwise known as disjunctive normal form (DNF); he presented an algorithm for learning a class of DNF formulae in polynomial time. Moreover, he showed that this algorithm can be implemented using networks of linear threshold devices. In this paper, we study the neural network implementation for learning DNF functions. The focus of our study is the scalability of hardware resources and the rate of convergence. We take Valiant's paper as our starting point and study the neural implementation of the DNF learning algorithm in detail. In particular, we view his idea of random interconnections as a means of efficiently allocating storage. We theoretically and empirically determine the relationship between the number of threshold gates and the fan-in, given the number of monomials, length of the monomials, and the number of boolean variables. We use these results in the design of a hardware-efficient optoelectronic neural network. In section 2, we analyze Valiant's algorithm for learning DNF under the assumption of randomly chosen conjunctions. In section 3, we describe the simulations we performed to study the scalability issue, present our empirical results, and compare it to our theoretical predictions. In section 4 we discuss several optoelectronic neural system designs for DNF learning. A brief summary constitutes section 5.

2. Learning k-DNF Formulae

Valiant [2] proposed a network architecture for learning a disjunction of conjunctions, where each conjunction consists of exactly k literals. The network consists of t input nodes, N hidden layer nodes and one (or more in case of multiple disjunctions) output node. Each hidden node is connected randomly to f input nodes (the hidden layer fan-in is f), and the output node is fully connected to the hidden layer. In this section we derive the probability that randomly chosen conjunctions can be learned by the hidden layer.

A particular conjunction (or monomial) can only be learned if all of the corresponding input nodes are connected to some hidden node and if the distribution of training examples satisfies certain requirements [2]. Each hidden unit learns at most one conjunction using an unsupervised learning algorithm. Thereafter, the output unit learns the disjunction of the conjunctions using a supervised algorithm.

The following analysis deals with the probability that a network generated according to the above rules has the connections required for learning some particular disjunction of conjunctions.

There are $\binom{t}{f}$ possible sets of inputs to a hidden unit. Of these, $\binom{t-k}{f-k}$ include any particular set of k inputs. Thus the probability that the inputs of a particular hidden unit include any particular set of k inputs is given by:

$$P = \frac{\binom{t-k}{f-k}}{\binom{t}{f}} = \frac{(t-k)! \ f!}{t! \ (f-k)!}$$

(1)

If $f >> k$ and $t >> k$, Stirling's approximation may be used to obtain:

$$P \cong \frac{f^k}{k!} \Big/ \frac{t^k}{k!} = \left(\frac{f}{t}\right)^k$$

(2)

The probability that at least one of the N hidden units can learn a given monomial is $P_1 = 1 - (1-P)^N$. If $f >> k$ and $t >> k$, then:

$$P_1 \cong 1 - \left(1 - \left(\frac{f}{t}\right)^k\right)^N$$

(3a)

Also, if $f < t$ and $N >> 1$, then:

$$P_1 \cong 1 - e^{-N\left(\frac{f}{t}\right)^k}$$

(3b)

Given k, t, and N, the desired fan-in is:

$$f = tN^{-\frac{1}{k}}\left[-\ln(1-P_1)\right]^{\frac{1}{k}} \cong tN^{-\frac{1}{k}}$$

(4)

If N is approximately equal to t, then for a large value of P_1 (close to 1), each input node should be connected to a random set of about $t^{1-\frac{1}{k}}$ hidden nodes.

An upper limit on the probability, P_K, that such a network can learn the disjunction of K conjunctions is $(P_1)^K$. However, under the assumption that the conjunctions to be learned are randomly chosen, a more exact expression may be obtained. In this case, the probability that a hidden unit is connected to the inputs corresponding to exactly one of the K monomials (exactly one of K k-sets) is:

$$P_e = \binom{K}{1}P(1-P)^{K-1} = KP(1-P)^{K-1}$$

(5)

The probability that i of N hidden units are each connected to exactly one of K k-sets and the remaining $N-i$ units are each connected to none or more than one k-set is $\binom{N}{i}P_e^i(1-P_e)^{N-i}$. Finally, the probability that K k-sets are each connected to at least one distinct hidden unit is

I-552

$$P_K = \binom{N}{K} P_e^K (1-P_e)^{N-K} P_D(K,K) + \binom{N}{K+1} P_e^{K+1} (1-P_e)^{N-(K+1)} P_D(K,K+1) + \dots$$

$$+ \binom{N}{N-1} P_e^{N-1} (1-P_e)^1 P_D(K,N-1) + \binom{N}{N} P_e^N (1-P_e)^0 P_D(K,N)$$

(6)

where $P_D(K,i)$ is the probability that K of i monomials are distinct. Equation 6 may be rewritten:

$$P_K = \sum_{i=K}^{N} \binom{N}{i} P_e^i (1-P_e)^{N-i} P_D(K,i)$$

(7)

The term $P_D(K,i)$ may be calculated recursively from $P_D(K,i\text{-}1)$ for a given value of K :

$$P_D(K,i) = \begin{cases} P_D(2,i) = 1 - \left(\frac{1}{2}\right)^{i-1} \\ \\ P_D(3,i+1) = P_D(3,i) + \dfrac{2^i - 1}{3^i} \quad \text{with} \quad P_D(3,3) = 0.22\overline{2} \\ \\ \vdots \end{cases}$$

(8)

A general expression for $P_D(K,i)$ may be obtained by reformulating it as the well-known coupon collection problem [3]. Equation 7 gives the probability that the given network will be able to learn the randomly chosen conjunctions. Learning at the second layer proceeds according to the single-layer perceptron rule [4], that converges assuming the DNF formula is comprised of the conjunctions learned by the hidden layer.

3. Investigation of DNF Learning Performance & Scaling Behavior

For large networks, it becomes increasingly difficult to fully connect the input layer to the hidden layer due to the large number of connections (fan-out and fan-in) required. Furthermore, an exhaustive network that explicitly provides a hidden unit for each possible conjunction requires an exorbitant amount of hardware. The contention is that a randomly connected hidden layer with a small number of hidden units and a limited fan-in can efficiently learn *k-DNF* . However, as the fan-in is reduced more hidden units may be needed. The goal of the software simulation was to develop an accurate software model of the circuit and to use this model to investigate the relationship between the number of hidden units and the fan-in of the hidden units. The simulation, written in C, was used to empirically determine optimal values for these variables.

3.1 Methodology of DNF Learning Study

The DNF circuit can be simulated by a three-layer network (figure 1). The input to the network is a locally represented bit string. The hidden layer, which is partially connected to the input layer, learns to recognize fixed-length bit strings. The number of connections between the hidden and input layer is determined by the fan-in; connections are randomly selected. The output layer, which is fully connected to the hidden layer, contains one node for each function, and learns to detect the presence of specific functions in the input bit string.

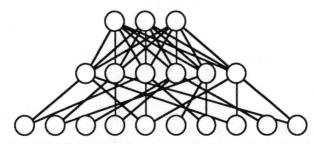

Figure 1: DNF Circuit with 3 functions, 6 hidden units, 10 literals, and fan-in of 3.

As discussed in section 2, the DNF circuit attempts to learn boolean functions that are disjunctions of conjunctions. Here we assume every conjunction contains the same number of literals. The number of conjunctions in each function is variable. The following is an example of a DNF training set:

$$X_1X_2X_3 + X_1X_3X_4 + X_3X_4X_8 + X_0X_1X_2 \qquad \textit{Function \#1}$$
$$X_1X_2X_3 \qquad \textit{Function \#2}$$
$$X_3X_4X_8 + X_4X_5X_9 \qquad \textit{Function \#3} \qquad (9)$$

The network was presented with uncorrupted information about each conjunction to be learned. The training set consisted of a list of conjunctions presented in random order. For the training of the output layer, the training set also contained the desired output function.

Unsupervised learning was used for the hidden layer, according the method suggested by Valiant [2]. Weights were updated according to the following method, in which w_{ij} represents the weight from input unit j to hidden unit i, and y_n represents the activation value of hidden unit n. ∂ and ∂^{-1} are continuous, strictly monotone functions.

$$w_{ij} = \begin{cases} \partial(w_{ij}) & \text{if } y_j = 1 \text{ and } y_i = 1 \\ \partial^{-1}(w_{ij}) & \text{if } y_j = 0 \text{ and } y_i = 1 \end{cases} \qquad (10)$$

$$\partial(w_{ij}) = 2(w_{ij}) - (w_{ij})^2 \quad ; \quad \partial^{-1}(w_{ij}) = 1 - \sqrt{1 - (w_{ij})} \qquad (11)$$

This learning algorithm ensures that a given hidden unit will learn to ignore inputs which do not contribute to the unit's firing. The learning algorithm increments the weights to inputs which are active when the unit fires, and decrements weights to inactive inputs. When learning is complete, the weights of irrelevant inputs to a hidden unit will be set to near-zero values; in essence, irrelevant inputs are disconnected. Each hidden unit is given a threshold value of one. The initial and maximum weights are related to the number of literals per conjunctions, k:

$$Initial\ Weight = \frac{1}{k - \frac{1}{4}} \quad ; \quad Final\ Weight = \frac{1}{k - \frac{1}{2}} \qquad (12)$$

The initial weights ensure that at least k connected input units must be on to fire a given hidden unit. During learning, the maximum-weight limit prevents the weights from becoming large enough for less then k inputs to fire the node. Note that the specific form of the increment and decrement functions in equation 11 are not important, as long as they are continuous and monotonic. This fact can be used to advantage when designing custom hardware.

Output learning proceeds after hidden layer learning is complete. The output layer learning was governed by the perceptron learning rule [4]. In equation (13), w_{kj} represents the weight from hidden unit j to output unit k, y^* is the desired output, and y_k and y_j are the activations of hidden units k and j respectively.

$$w_{kj}(t+1) = w_{kj}(t) + (y_k^*(t+1) - y_k(t+1))\, y_j(t) \qquad (13)$$

It was necessary to devise a means of determining when learning in the hidden layer was complete. This was accomplished by examining the weights of the connections to the hidden layer. When every weight was equal to the initial weight or within a specified threshold of either the maximum weight or zero, learning was complete. Connections that remain at the initial weight for hidden units are unused by the network. These units can be ignored. Due to the nature of the DNF learning rule, weights within the specified threshold can be considered to be at their extremes. The threshold was determined by the number of inputs to the network. It must be low enough so that negative examples of a conjunction do not fire the node. Otherwise, a large number of irrelevant inputs with small weights may cause the node to fire for a negative example. The following formula specifies the maximum threshold, θ, where w_o is the initial weight, i is the number of input units and k is the number of literals per conjunction:

$$\theta = \frac{w_o}{i - k} \qquad (14)$$

After learning was complete, the hidden layer was tested to determine if every conjunction was exclusively represented by at least one hidden unit.

3.2 Simulation Results

The performance of the network was influenced by the random selection of hidden layer connections. Networks with a small number of hidden units were particularly sensitive to this random selection. In order to collect data that accurately represented the performance of a particular network, it was necessary to measure the average performance of a large number of networks with different random connections. Averaging over one hundred runs was sufficient to eliminate swings in the data caused by the random hidden layer connections for a particular set of conjunctions. In all cases, the fan-in and the number of hidden units were varied, and the specific performance statistic was measured. The number of hidden units was based on a pseudo-logarithmic scale ranging from 1 to 100. Four performance statistics were collected:

- *Percent Success*
  The percentage of the networks that successfully learned all the conjunctions. Due to the random connections, some percentage of the networks will always fail to learn the given conjunctions. This statistic reveals the probability of selecting a network with the specified fan-in and number of hidden units that will successfully learn the conjunctions.
- *Number of Trials to Learning*
  The number of presentations of training set examples required for the network to reach the stopping criteria. Only networks succeeding in identifying all conjunctions were averaged into this statistic.
- *Percentage of Redundant Hidden Units*
  Only one hidden unit should represent a given conjunction. All other hidden units representing that conjunction are redundant.
- *Percentage of Unused Hidden Units*
  The percentage of hidden units which remain in their initial state. This occurs when the selection of fan-in connections for a given hidden unit fails to include any of the conjunctions.

A number of runs were performed with various values of t, k, and K. In each case, a series of simulations were run with increasing overlap between the chosen conjunctions. As the number of conjunctions and the overlap between conjunctions were increased, a larger number of hidden units were needed. For example, figure 2a-b shows the results for $k=3$, $t=10$, and $K=2$ and $K=8$, respectively. A fan-in of 6 or higher gave good results for no overlap (or small values of overlap) between conjunctions (figure 2a); For 8 conjunctions with an overlap of two literals between any two conjunctions, a fan-in of six gave the best result (figure 2b).

Figure 3a-b shows the average number of trials required to learn the conjunctions. Again this was dependent on the number of conjunctions and the overlap between conjunctions. For a given set of conjunctions, the network was able to quickly learn the conjunctions if the necessary fan-in and number of hidden units were provided.

In Figure 4a-d, the result for $k=5$, $t=10$, and $K=2$, are plotted for fan-ins of 6-9 respectively. On each graph five different simulations with varying amounts of overlap between conjunctions are presented along with the theoretical prediction of equation 7. For a fan-in of seven or larger, the network provides a means of efficiently learning (with high probability) the chosen conjunctions. Note that an exhaustive network (one unit for each possible conjunction) would require over 250 units. For large fan-ins the predicted probability of success, which is valid for *randomly* chosen conjunctions, is consistently lower than the simulation result, particularly for conjunctions with low overlap. This issue is addressed later.

As figures 2-4 reveal, the ability of a given network to learn a set of functions depends on the following characteristics of the training set:

- Number of inputs (t)
- Number of literals per conjunction (k)
- Total number of conjunctions (K)
- Overlap between conjunctions

Increasing the number of literals per conjunction, the number of inputs, or the number of shared inputs between conjunctions (overlap) requires more hidden units for a given fan-in to satisfy the success criteria. Increasing the overlap decreases the number of inputs that can be used to distinguish the conjunctions and thereby decreases the probability of selecting connections that can represent the conjunction. In this case the choice of correct fan-in is critical.

Next, the relationship between the fan-in and number of hidden units required for a given probability of success was investigated. This is an important issue in determining the scalability of a hardware implementation of the DNF learning algorithm. In another series of experiments, random conjunctions were created, and data was averaged over one thousand runs. The effect of overlap was thus eliminated by averaging network runs over randomly selected conjunctions. Network performance reflected the average overlap typical of functions with the given number of conjunctions, literals per conjunction, and number of inputs. This is precisely what equation 7 assumes, so we expect good agreement with the simulation result. This is verified in figure 5a-b, which plots the number of hidden units required for a given probability of success, versus the fan-in. The minimum fan-in for any set of conjunctions is equal to the number of literals per conjunction. At the other extreme, a fully-connected hidden layer can only learn one conjunction. The network was configured with the fan-in ranging from the minimum fan-in to a nearly fully connected network. For each fan-in value, the number of hidden units required for the given probability of success was determined.

Note that increasing the number of functions only adds more conjunctions to the training set; the number of functions does not otherwise effect the learning of the hidden layer. Once the hidden layer is correctly learned, the output layer will converge when using the single-layer perceptron learning rule. Therefore, varying the number of functions has the same effect on the network as increasing the number of conjunctions. For a given probability of success, figure 6a-b indicates a relatively linear growth for the number of hidden units required (at the optimum fan-in) as the number of conjunctions is increased.

A final issue is the redundancy and fault tolerance of the network. A potential concern for any learning mechanism that relies on a local representation for learned concepts is the low tolerance to degraded or faulty hidden units. As depicted in figure 7a-b, the DNF learning algorithm discussed above typically provides a high degree of redundancy among the hidden units. Large fan-in typically results in many hidden units learning the same function and a low percentage of unused hidden units. Again, a judicious choice of fan-in will provide the required level of redundancy without under-utilizing or wasting the network resources.

4. Design of Optoelectronic Systems for Boolean Concept Learning

Scalable hardware implementations of the DNF learning algorithm described above must possess several properties: a large number of hidden units (neurons), a large fan-out from the input layer and large fan-in to each hidden neuron, and an efficient interconnection system that can provide random, non-local interconnnects between the input and hidden layers. Such implementations may be classified as to whether they provide a *reconfigurable* interconnect topology or a *fixed* one. In the former case, it may be allowable to use a smaller network with a lower probability of success and run the unsupervised learning algorithm several times (reconfiguring the network between tries) until the conjunctions have been learned. In the latter case, a larger, network may be needed to ensure successful, one-shot application of the unsupervised learning rules.

Free-space optical interconnects have been widely recognized as a means of providing high-density interconnects [5]. We have previously presented a scalable 3-dimensional optoelectronic neural architecture, the dual-scale topology optoelectronic processor (D-STOP), that provides efficient, fixed optical interconnection between silicon-based neural processing elements [6]. We have built and tested a 64-synapse prototype feed-forward D-STOP neural system with a maximum sustained rate of 640 million interconnects-per-second [7]. The D-STOP neural system [8] nominally provides full interconnection (or limited regular interconnection) between layers of neurons using space-invariant computer-generated holograms (CGH). However, using special encoding algorithms, arbitrary space-variant computer-generated holograms can be generated to provide fixed random interconnections between processing elements [9]. The modified, randomly-connected D-STOP system would be one possible means of achieving a fixed topology DNF learning system.

The potential for random, reconfigurable optical interconnects has also been investigated [10]. In one method, a fourth-rank tensor, that provides arbitrary interconnection between two 2-dimensional arrays, is stored in a photorefractive crystal [11]. By appropriately populating the tensor, random optical interconnects with arbitrary fan-in can be achieved. In fact, it has been shown that the interconnection system achieves a high SNR when the fan-in per output is large, i.e. it scales with the number of inputs.

A third alternative is to provide a fixed optically interconnected system, such as D-STOP, with a means of electronically reconfiguring the network topology. This can be achieved, for instance by combining the optoelectronic neural network with an optoelectronic multistage interconnection network [12]. The resulting system combines the advantages of a fixed, mature optical interconnect technology (e.g. CGH technology) with the flexibility and efficiency of a reconfigurable network.

5. Conclusions and Future Work

In this paper we investigated hardware-tradeoffs for implementing *k-DNF* Boolean concept learning as suggested by Valiant. The importance of this class of functions stems from the fact it is learnable in polynoimial time and provably tolerant to noisy data. We performed theoretical and empirical studies of the learning performance and hardware costs of the unsupervised conjunctive learning algorithm. We confirmed that the method can provide a fast, efficient means of learning *k-DNF* concepts. We investigated tradeoffs in the structure of these learning networks, in terms of the number of hidden neurons required versus the fan-in per neuron. Finally we suggested 3-dimensional optically-interconnected architectures well suited to implement *k-DNF* learning. Our studies so far have assumed only positive literals. Future work will consider the internal implementation of negated literals, the investigation of the noise tolerance of the learning rules, and the design of the learning circuitry.

References:

[1]   S. Muggleton, "Inductive Acquisition of Expert Knowledge", Turing Institute Press, 1990.
[2]   L.G. Valiant, "Learning Disjunctions of Conjunctions", *Proc. 9th IJCAI*, pp. 550-556, August 1985.
[3]   see for example P. Hoel, S. Port, and C. Stone, *Introduction to Probability Theory*, Houghton Mifflin (Boston), 1971.

[4] F. Rosenblatt, *Principles of Neurodynamics: Perceptrons and the Theory of Brain Mechanisms*, Spartan Books (Washington, D. C), 1962.

[5] J. W. Goodman, F. J. Leonberger, S. Y. Kung, and R. A. Athale, "Optical interconnections for VLSI systems," *Proceedings IEEE*, vol. 72, pp. 850, 1984.

[6] A. V. Krishnamoorthy, G. Yayla, and S. C. Esener, "A scalable optoelectronic neural system using free-space optical interconnects," *IEEE Transactions on Neural Networks*, vol. 3, no. 3, pp. 404-413, May 1992.

[7] G. Yayla, A. Krishnamoorthy, G. Marsden, and S. Esener, "Prototype optoelectronic neural system using free-space optical interconnects," *Proc. Govt. Microchip Applications Conf. 92*, (Las Vegas), November 1992.

[8] A. Krishnamoorthy, J. Mercklé, G. Yayla, G. Marsden, B. Mansoorian, J. Ford, and S. Esener, "New dimensions in D-STOP neural systems," *Proc. SPIE Intl. Symp. Opt., Imag. and Instrum.*, Paper 2026-35, July 1993.

[9] B. Kress and S. H. Lee, "Iterative design of computer generated fresnel holograms for free-space optical interconnections", *Proc. OSA Topical Meeting on Optical Computing*, pp. 22-25, (Palm Springs), March 1993.

[10] R. Paturi, D. T. Lu, J. Ford, S. Esener and S. H. Lee, "Parallel algorithms based on expander graphs for optical computing," *Applied Optics*, vol. 30, no. 8, pp. 917, 1991.

[11] J. E. Ford, Y. Fainman, and S. H. Lee, "Array Interconnection by phase-coded optical correlation," *Opt. Lett.*, vol.15, no. 19, pp. 1088-1090, October 1, 1990.

[12] A. Krishnamoorthy, P. Marchand, F. Kiamilev, and S. Esener, "Grain-size considerations for optoelectronic multistage interconnection networks," *Applied Optics*, vol. 31, no. 26, pp. 5480-5507, September 1992.

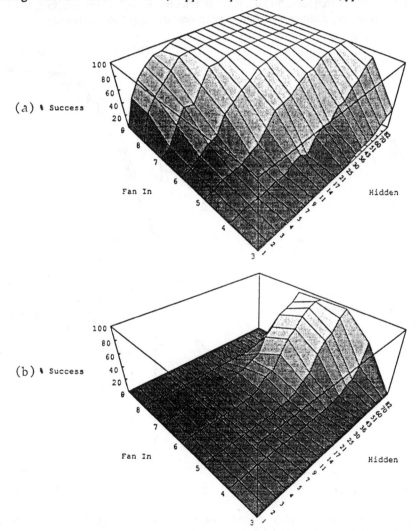

Figure 2ab: Percent success versus number of hidden units and the fan-in per hidden unit [k=3, t=10]: (a) K=2 conjunctions with no overlap (b) K=8 conjunctions with two overlap between any two conjunctions.

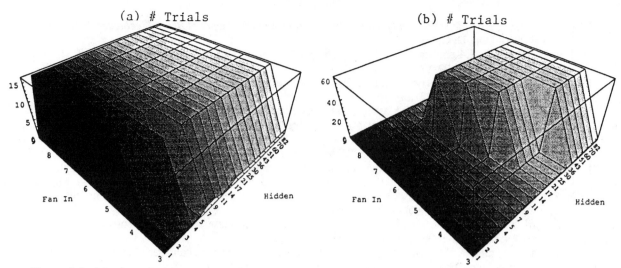

Figure 3ab: Number of trials versus number of hidden units and the fan-in per hidden unit[k=3, t=10]: (a) K=2 conjunctions with no overlap (b) K=8 conjunctions with two overlap between any two conjunctions.

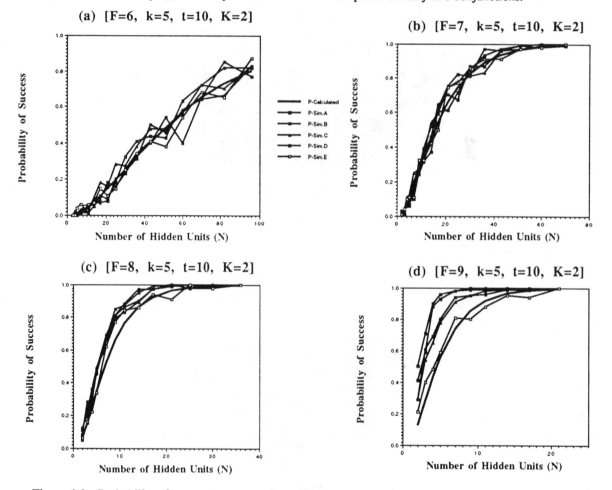

Figure 4ab: Probability of success versus number of hidden units [k=5, t=10, K=2]: (a) fan-in=6 (b) fan-in=7 (c) fan-in=8 (d) fan-in=9. Solid line shows predicted value. SimA has no overlap, SimB has one literal overlap, SimC and SimD have two literals overlap, and SimE has three literals overlap.

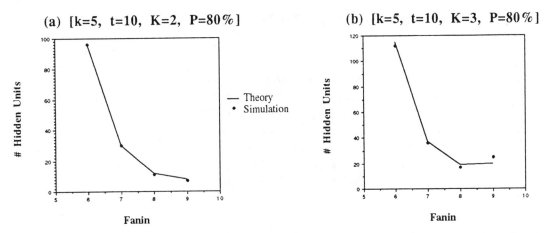

Figure 5ab: Number of hidden units required versus the fan-in for 80% success [k=5, t=10]: (a) K=2 conjunctions (b) K=3 conjunctions. Conjunctions were randomly chosen. Solid line shows predicted value.

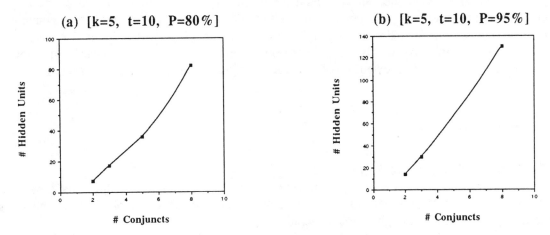

Figure 6ab: Number of hidden units required versus the number of conjunctions at the optimal fan-in [k=5, t=10]: (a) P=80% success (b) P=95% success. Conjunctions were randomly chosen.

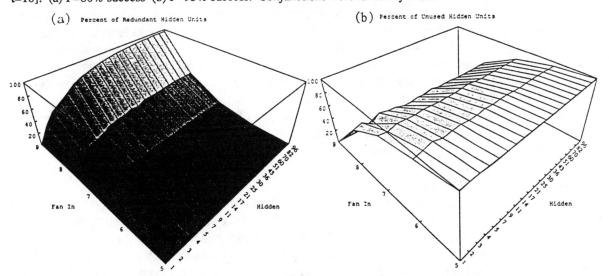

Figure 7ab: (a) Percent redundant hidden units and (b)Percent unused hidden units for K=2 conjunctions with no overlap [k=5, t=10, K=2].

I-559

Visualization of Evolution of Genetic Algorithms

B. Nassersharif, D. Ence, and M. Au
National Supercomputing Center for Energy and the Environment
University of Nevada Las Vegas
Las Vegas, Nevada 89154-4028
Email: bn@nye.nscee.edu
ence@nye.nscee.edu
aym@nye.nscee.edu

Abstract

Genetic Algorithms (GAs) operate on problems with a complex feature space. Each member of the population can contribute to the overall knowledge about the feature space. Visualization of the evolution of the gene population is an effective mechanism to increase user understanding of the complex problem space. Information about the problem space, population size suitability for the problem, and rate of convergence can be quickly and efficiently understood through the visualization. The visualization is also a great tool for teaching or debugging GAs. In this work, visualization experience with a two dimensional problem space is presented. A method for extension of this work to higher-dimensional problem spaces is described.

1. Introduction

1.1. Introduction to Genetic Algorithms

Genetic Algorithms (GAs) are powerful generalized search and optimization procedures that are based on natural laws of genetics. Natural selection is a phenomenon that is observed in biological systems as they adapt to their environments through several generations.

Genetic Algorithms have a basic cycle. The cycle starts with a given population, or gene pool, and yields a new, more fit pool. The algorithm begins with an initially random gene pool which is made up of individuals, and a fitness function that must be optimized. The optimization does not have to be exact but must represent "suitable" choices. The individuals of the gene pool are composed of a set of values which are parameters of the function. Each individual is then evaluated by the fitness function which yields a measure of fitness. The individuals which are most fit are then allowed to reproduce. Reproduction involves an exchange of genetic material between two selected individuals. After the exchange there is a chance that one of the genes of an individual may be mutated. Application of these procedures creates a new more fit gene pool. One iteration through this cycle is termed a generation. After several generations, the system converges to a pool of most fit individuals.

1.2. Introduction to MPGS

Our visualization for this research uses the Multi-Purpose Graphics System (MPGS) version 5.1 from Cray Research, Inc. MPGS provides engineers and scientists a powerful graphics post processing package. The power of MPGS comes from the marriage of high-end workstations and high speed supercomputers. Graphics output and manipulations, like translations and rotations, are handled by local hardware in a graphics workstation while more memory intensive tasks and complex calculations, like isosurface generation and particle traces, are performed by a supercomputer.

Some of the key features of MPGS are the ability to visualize transient data and to create keyframe animations. We treat the data from the genetic algorithm as a system of particles in three dimensions with each generation being a time step. Animating through the generations with MPGS shows a distinct migration of the genes to the maxima of the function. We select key frames by rotating the particle system to interesting points of view and then animating not only through the transient data, but also through the motion of the particle system. This allows us to see depth throughout the system providing more information about the performance of the GA.

2. Implementation

2.1. Implementation of The Genetic Algorithm

2.1.1 Gene Representation
In our implementation, genes are represented by real numbers. Our GA algorithm was implemented on the Cray Y-MP2/216 at the National Supercomputing Center for Energy and the Environment (NSCEE). The Cray Y-MP stores real numbers as a packed representation of a binary mantissa and an exponent with two sign bits, one for the mantissa and for the exponent [1]. The programming language of implementation is C. Since C does not allow bitwise manipulation of real numbers, a union, consisting of an integer field and float field was used. This allowed bitwise manipulations on the integer field which also facilitated use of masks in the implementation of the crossover procedure. When bitwise operations are performed on reals, there is a chance of producing an invalid real number. This is a side effect of the GA operations. All invalid real numbers are discarded and not allowed to reproduce.

By using logical operations and a gather-scatter technique we were able to take advantage of vectorization on the Cray Y-MP2/216 for performing crossover. This reduced execution time.

2.1.2 Selection
A roulette wheel algorithm [2] was used to select the fit genes from the gene pool. The fitness of each gene in the pool is summed, giving the total pool fitness. Each gene fitness is then divided by the total pool fitness, giving a normalized value (a value between 0 and 1) which indicates how much any individual contributes to the total pool fitness. A table of ranges is then created based on these normalized values. A random real number is selected on the interval between 0 and 1. That number is then applied to the table. The gene corresponding to the range in which the number falls is selected for the next generation. The genes with the largest fitness would have the greatest ranges and thus the greatest chance of being selected. Only the fittest survive.

2.1.3 Crossover
Crossover is a procedure that takes two individuals of a gene pool and combines their genetic material to create two new individuals. There are a number of different implementations of crossover. Both one and two-point crossover is implemented in our GA. The user can select which one to use. The crossover point defines where the genetic material of each gene is split among the two selected genes.

2.1.3.1 One-Point Crossover
In the one point crossover strategy, both genes are split at the same random spot. Figure 1 shows two genes (gene A and gene B) before and after crossover. A random point to split the genes is selected. The gene code to the right of the split point of gene A is joined with the gene code to the left of the split point of gene B. Also, The gene code to the left of the split point of gene A is joined with the gene code to the right of the split point of gene B, thereby yielding two different genes.

Figure 1: One-point cross over.

2.1.3.2 Two-Point Crossover

When two-point crossover is implemented both genes are split at two points, although these points are the same for both genes. Figure 2 illustrates the two-point crossover. The gene code to the left of the first split point of A is joined with the gene code to the right of the first point and to the left of the second point of gene B. This is also joined with the gene code to the right of the second split point of gene A.

The gene code to the left of the first split point of B is joined with the gene code to the right of the first point and to the left of the second point of gene A. This is also joined with the gene code to the right of the second split point of gene B. Again yielding two different genes. The two-point crossover has been shown to be superior to one-point crossover [3].

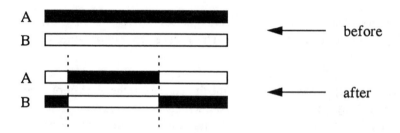

Figure 2: Two-point cross over.

2.1.4 Mutation

Each bit in a gene has a probability of mutation (usually a very small number). If a bit is mutated, then its value is changed. If the bit is a zero it is changed to one. If it is one it is changed to zero. Fig. 3 illustrates the mutation process (the top gene is the original and the gene on the bottom is the mutated gene). The 12th bit from the left has been mutated (its value was changed from zero to one).

In the absence of mutation, there is a chance that a genetic algorithm could converge to a gene pool where all individuals are clones. Thus, the GA would enter a steady state where it neither converges nor diverges. Mutation adds the necessary variability (new genetic material) in the population for continued progress of the algorithm towards the maxima (or minima). This feature gives the GA a great advantage over other search and optimization algorithms.

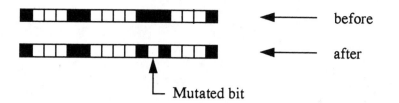

Figure 3: Mutation.

2.2. Sample Problem

In order to produce a visualization, an "interesting" sample problem had to be selected. We arbitrarily developed the following function

$$f(x, y) \;=\; \sin(3x) + \sin(5y) + \cos(2x) + \cos(y) \,.$$

This function has many local minima and maxima on the (x,y) plane.

2.3. Implementation with MPGS

The ordered triple (x,y, f(x,y)) of the Sample Problem is treated as the location of a particle (an individual) in three dimensional space. Collectively, several individuals can be represented as a particle system. After each generation, a file of these positions is written in a format suitable for importing into MPGS. Each file, therefore, is a particle system that can be visualized by MPGS. The largest and smallest ordered triples are used to determine a bounding box for this problem. This box helps the user position the particle system and camera and also quickly determine the size occupied by the system.

MPGS can read several of these particle system files, buffer them, and then play them back to create an animation. As MPGS animates through the files, the user can see the particles migrate toward the highest peaks. The user can also rotate, translate, and zoom in and out of the system as the particles are animating which gives the user more control over what can be seen. The animation can be paused at any frame to allow for screen capture of images. The figures in this paper were generated in this fashion.

3. Results

The four snapshots in Fig. 4 were produced by MPGS. They are snapshots of the initial, second, fourth and tenth generations of a GA calculation of the sample function discussed in section 2.2. Where x and y are bounded by the interval (10,15). The fitness of any individual was based on the z value it yielded after function evaluation.

The GA was run for 20 generations with 4000 individuals. There was a 60% chance of crossover and 0.1% chance of mutation. The two-point crossover procedure was used.

The visualization demonstrates the convergence of the individuals to the maxima of the function. MPGS has a tool that allows animation of particle files. Particle files are created for each generation. Animation of the evolution is accomplished by flipping through particle files. During the animation, the individuals appear to migrate to the peaks of the function.

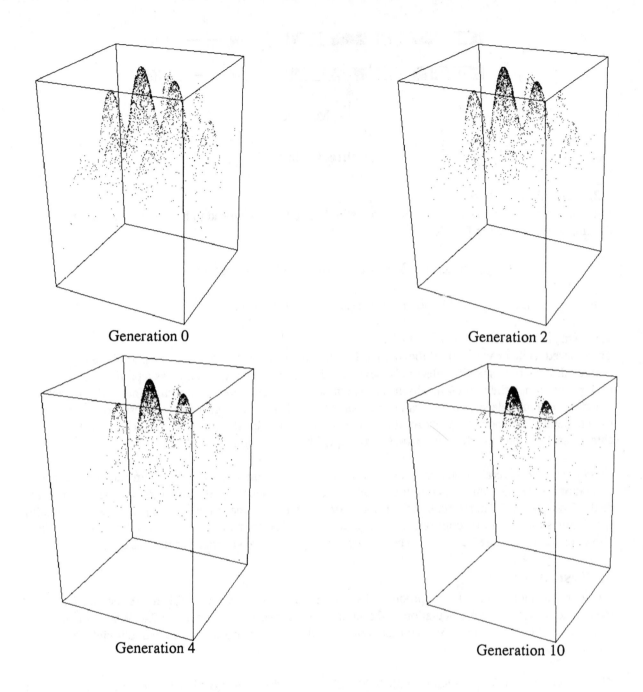

Figure 4: Snapshots of the sample problem evolution.

4. Conclusions

Visualization of a GA is a powerful vehicle for increasing a user's understanding of the complex problem terrain. The GA search procedure is better understood by observing the evolution of the generations from their initial random distributions towards the optimal values. Furthermore, detailed information about the objective function is displayed in a visual form. The enhanced insight gained through visualization can also be used as an effective tool for teaching GA and debugging.

Visualization of the evolution demonstrates the concept of convergence and the robust nature of the GA. Visualization can also be used for testing new reproduction rules or other new procedures. Visualization may also help in the running and optimizing of these procedures.

4.1. Future Work

As the GA converges, the population at the peek becomes increasingly dense. It may be useful to delineate the number of individuals at or around the peek. One method would be to use a color map to indicate the population density.

In our implementation, we used a two dimensional feature space. Most problems of interest for GA application will have many dimensions in the feature space. This situation would require more sophisticated visualization techniques. We plan to experiment with a nested coordinate systems as a method of breaking down the problem dimensionality. A hyperspace of n independent variables can then be visualized.

5. References

1. Cray Research Inc. "CF77 FORTRAN Language Reference Manual," SR-37772 6.0.

2. Goldberg, David E. "Genetic Algorithms in Search, Optimization, and Machine Learning", Addison-Wesley Publishing Company, Inc.

3. Liepins, G.E. and Hillard, M.R. "Genetic Algorithms: Foundations and Applications", Annals of Operations Research, 21 (1989) 31 - 58.

A TASK DECOMPOSITION NEURAL NETWORK APPROACH TO NON-DESTRUCTIVE TESTING PROBLEMS.

Francesco Carlo Morabito - Maurizio Campolo
Dipartimento Ingegneria Elettronica e Matematica Applicata
Università degli Studi di Reggio Calabria
Via E.Cuzzocrea,48, 89127 Reggio Calabria (Italy)
Tel.+39 965 875224 , Fax +39 965 875220

Abstract

In this paper an artificial neural network technique to treat inverse problems, typically encountered in Non-Destructive Testing applications, is introduced. The basic architecture is proposed for an electrostatic test problem. We also address the case of plural defect recognition, and we also show how the method here described could be useful for more realistic NDT problems, commonly known as eddy current testing. Simulations show that our method can be very effective, particularly when a high accuracy of the identification procedure is required.

1. INTRODUCTION.

The interaction of electric and magnetic fields with conducting materials can reveal both their properties and the presence of defects. Non-Destructive Testing (NDT) is an interdisciplinary science aimed at providing methods, hopefully completely automated, and techniques which allow to decide about the soundness of a specimen under test. In some research areas, such as nuclear fusion, there are significant financial incentives to prolong the useful life of operating plants and NDT plays a central role in pursuing this goal. Of course, this aim has to be achieved preserving safety, particularly near the end of the design life of the plant.

In this paper we consider a special problem which, though not necessarily realistic, presents the major characteristics of standard electromagnetic testing, as well as the formulation of a real problem. Actually, the decision about each specimen is carried out by analysing the perturbations of a potential map generated by an exciting source placed close to the zone where a defect is suspected. By measuring potentials and/or fields in properly selected points one can have informations about the location, size and shape of the defects. Research in NDT focuses attention on methods for in-service inspection. Another significant aspect of modern NDT is concerned with saving inspection time. Neural Networks (NNs) can have an impact in NDT, particularly considering both these two aspects. In recent years NNs have emerged as important numerical tools in a number of multi-sensor analyses and data fusion problems. Moreover, the speed of NNs in the recall phase make them ideally suited to processing patterns of data very rapidly as requested by modern NDT applications. In NDT problems the goal is to find the configuration of the sources generating the pattern of measurements. This is an inverse problem usually solved by minimising a cost function and taking into account some constraints on the system parameters.

NNs have already been proposed for the classification of NDT signals [1]. Examples of NNs applications for identification of both size and locations of defects have been presented in [2,3]. In this paper we introduce the concept of task decomposition to reduce the ill-posedness of the test problem, and to discriminate between defect detection and defect characterisation. Moreover, the concept of fuzzy set is introduced at various stages . The problem under study is extended to consider the possibility of having more defects on a same plate. Finally, an eddy current testing problem is presented.

2. A SAMPLE NDT ELECTROSTATIC PROBLEM.

An earthed ($v=0$) conducting plane has a hemispherical boss of radius a. The centre of the sphere lies on the plane. A point charge q is placed close to the plane at a distance $b>a$ from it. Let P be a point exterior to the metallic plate. The electric potential $v(P)$ can be determined by using the method of images and the inversion transformation as follows:

$$v(P) = (q/r_1 - q'/r_2 + q'/r_3 - q/r_4) / 4\pi\varepsilon_0 \qquad (1)$$

where $q'=qa/b^*$, $b'=a^2/b^*$, and b^* is the distance from the inducing point charge to the centre of the boss, i.e. the centre of the inversion. The remaining symbols are explained in fig.1.

The attempt of the present work is to solve the identification problem of inverting (1) to recover the location and size of the defect of known shape from potential and field measurements. Aim of the work is to achieve a processing architecture which guarantees a good identification accuracy. The hypothesis of considering a pre established shape of the boss seems not too restrictive. In fact, in [4] it is shown that an NN can successfully discriminate among different defect shapes. Actually, by knowing a pattern of measurements which represent a proper sampling of a continuous function, we do not aim to reconstruct the entire function, rather to infer some geometrical quantities related to the object that generate the distribution.

The inverse problem under study can be viewed as a pattern recognition task. Actually, by considering the map of the electric potential generated by the point source in presence of the metallic plate, the existence of a defect is pointed out by the perturbation of this pattern (see fig.2).

The extent of the perturbation is, in turn, related to size and location of the defect. By possessing a large database of simulated experiments one can, in principle, approximately solve the identification problem by means of a search within the library of cases. As a matter of fact, a dataset which guarantees to reach the user's required accuracy could be impractically large. Moreover, the search within such a dataset would be very hard. Today's research are then oriented toward the development of methods based on computational intelligence. Among these, the use of NNs appears appealing particularly considering two features of these systems:

i) the generalisation capability, which allows to interpolate between the available limited number of cases;

ii) the data fusion capabilities, which suggest the possibility of using a multi-sensors approach and/or of incorporating a linguistic (rule based) approach which can exploit the know how of human experts.

To set up the database required for the learning process, exact synthetic data are calculated using (1). The radius of the boss, *a*, can vary between *15* and *35 mm*. The region over which the boss could be present is a rectangular grid of size 10 cm along *x* and *5 cm* along *y*. All of the sensors are placed along this rectangular contour at a fixed height. A suitable choice of the locations' measurements within the inspected window is a prerequisite to good detection. Concerning the number of measurements, our analyses show that at least three sensors per quadrant are needed. In fact, in the case of small bosses only sensors in the vicinity of the defect are expected to contribute to the identification, and then three measurements are just needed to saturate the three parameters to be estimated. The selected pattern of sensors is shown in fig.3.

3. A NEURAL SYSTEM FOR NDT PROBLEMS.

In this section we show how it is possible to solve the proposed problem by means of a complex structure composed of specialised neural sub-systems.

3.1 Analysis of the multilayer NN approach.

The first step of our work has been using a NN which acts as a mapping between input and output. The selected model of NN has been a multilayer feed forward one with a single hidden layer and sigmoidal activation functions for both hidden and output layers. The input layer only distributes the measurements to the adjacent layer. Several experiments of training have been carried out aiming to obtain an appropriate set of weights. These experiments have been conducted varying the number of hidden nodes, the number of training patterns, and the initial seeding of the weights.

Moreover, the learning rate and the "momentum" coefficient of the backpropagation procedure have been varied according to a proper schedule. It is worth noting that the initial choice of these two parameters strongly affect the successive training. Again, this choice derives from the designer's experience, and depends on the architecture of the network. For example, for a linear output the learning rate of the output layer has to be chosen different and generally smaller than the one selected for a sigmoidal layer. Finally, when the involved gradient descent procedure reaches a minimum, the learning rate must decrease to avoid oscillation around the minimum. In any case, the behaviour of a single NN cannot be considered accurate enough to solve the problem. Table 1 reports the performance of a fully sigmoidal NN, a linear output NN, and a network modified by adding a layer of direct connections between input and output [5]. It is worth noting that by considering special pattern of connections rather than a fully connected NN , one can enforce the network to distribute the knowledge embodied in the training set in useful ways.

NN Topology	Fully Sigmoidal	Linear Output	Modified
#input sensors	12	12	12
#hidden nodes	8	10	6
#conn.+biases	131	163	99
%xb train./test	13 / 15	13 / 15	11 / 12
%yb train./test	13 / 15	12 / 14	10 / 12
%a train./test	18 / 24	16 / 22	12 / 14

Table 1 - Performance of three different NNs in terms of full scale root mean square error (measurements of potential only). Training and test sets contains both 300 cases.

Even considering unsuccessful the behaviour of the NN, a detailed study of the weights' patterns carried out, for example, by Hinton diagrams [6], can yield important hints about how to decompose our problem. Indeed, the internal representation of the hidden layer suggests some elemental rules of behaviour. There is at least one hidden node which roughly recognises the vertical position of the boss, i.e. $yb \gtrless 0$ and another one which specialises itself to decide $xb \gtrless 0$. Finally, there are two hidden nodes sensitive to the differences between measurements of sensors located at opposite corners of the plate (sensors 1-7, 6-12, fig.3). By combining such elemental decisions, the global NN can easily determine the region containing the boss. The NN is so strongly sign-sensitive with respect to *xb, yb*. A very interesting technique that can help to recognise the behaviour of each HN is the one of the *localised damage*. Briefly in these procedure, we damage the trained NN by randomly changing the weights of a processing element, and as a result the NN loses some properties and it continues to work if the special feature represented by the damaged HN is not of interest.

Note that the size of the boss does not affect this kind of processing. It is to be noted that such a processing lends itself to difficulties in estimating bosses located in correspondence of the axes of the structure. Another interesting question posed by the analysis of the trained NN concerns the difficulties to discern between a small boss located in the vicinity of a sensor and a medium-sized boss located near the inducing charge. Indeed, these two configurations can give similar electric potential drops in correspondence of the sensor. Because of the scarce contribution of other sensors, it is hard to decide what configuration has given rise to that pattern of measurements. The discussed problem remains unsolved and it reduces to getting stuck in a poor local minimum in the training phase.

Another interesting topic is that training a NN on a set of cases of fixed radius, a, strongly improves the accuracy in estimating xb, yb. Again, by considering a restricted range of variability for a, we achieve better results. Studies carried out on sensory systems of animal species show that the perceptual processing is often separate into task-specific sensory channels. In our case, it's clearly impossible to separate the estimate of a from that of xb, yb. However, it seems possible to define some general rules which allow, for example, to qualitatively discriminate among bosses of small or large size starting from the pattern of measurements. Furthermore, we have seen how simple for a NN is the task of deciding the region where the boss is expected to be. All these capabilities can also be improved either by properly processing the absolute measurements to obtain useful differences of potential, or by using field measurements. In the last case we deal with a different mathematical formulation of the problem but the neural approach is not affected by this aspect.

3.2 Task decomposition of the identification problem.

In what follows, it is shown how a special neural architecture can incorporate all the preceding considerations. We train a NN to classify the pattern of examples into four categories: 1) no boss, 2) small boss, 3) medium boss, 4) large boss. Such a NN is not expected to yield a completely correct classification. In fact, the decision is also related to the location of the boss. However, it's relatively easy to define generic expressions about the identification like the following:

1) a large boss located near a sensor produces a significant reduction of the electric potential measured by this sensor;
2) the neighbouring sensors are affected by the boss in dependence of the boss size;
3) a small boss produces a negligible effect if not located in the vicinity of a sensor: in any case, the perturbation regards a limited region.

Then, it seems reasonable to teach a NN to cope with this problem. We have so trained a NN of 12 inputs, 8 hidden neurons, and 4 outputs with sigmoidal activation function both for hidden and output layer. The training set consists of 300 cases. Because of the nature of the output, in correspondence of some values of a, it's hard to decide whether a pattern belongs to either one class or another. In our model we admit that a pattern may belong to more than one class with a finite degree of confidence. This means that the boss radius, a, is treated as a fuzzy variable which admits four fuzzy values (No Boss, Small, Medium, Large). Each fuzzy value of the fuzzy variable is a subset of the entire domain (universe of discourse) and is characterised by a membership function. This function maps the universe of discourse to the real interval [0,1]. The degree to which a measured value belongs to a particular class is its grade of membership. This framework provides a natural way of dealing with problems where the source of imprecision is the absence of sharp cut-off between classes. To set-up the training dataset we have selected the membership functions reported in fig.4.

Of course, due to the nature of the data the membership functions resulting from the training process may be quite different. In particular, in our case, both the Small and Large classes are characterised by the presence of special features, whereas the Medium class is associated to the absence of them. Once detected the boss, and given a fuzzy estimate of its size, we have to characterise it. To do so, we need three different NNs trained on datasets corresponding to the three above mentioned classes. To entirely exploit the concept of fuzzy variable as well as that of overlapping membership functions, we decide to train the three network on datasets generated by considering, respectively: $a \in 15 \div 23\ mm$ (Small), $a \in 20 \div 30\ mm$ (Medium), $a \in 28 \div 35\ mm$ (Large). In case of uncertainties about the membership of a pattern to a precise class, as happens in the regions of overlap, there are two NNs switched on: the outputs of the identification process are then obtained properly combining the two NNs output. The weights of the combination are related to the degree of membership to the involved classes as estimated by the detection NN. By considering the symbols reported in fig.5, the estimation of the defect's parameters is carried out according to the following logic (post-processing):

```
IF S>0.8 THEN p=p_s
IF L>0.8 Then p=p_l
IF M=max(S,M,L) THEN p=p_m
IF S=max(S,M,L) AND S<0.8 THEN p=S*p_s+M*p_m
IF L=max(S,M,L) AND L<0.8 THEN p=M*p_m+L*p_l
```

with S, L, M preliminarily normalised so that either S+M=1 or M+L=1 for the last two cases.

Of course, each NN continues to work as previously described, that is by implicitly dividing the identification process into two contextual stages: i) rough determination of the plate's region containing the boss; ii) tuning of the estimation.

Notice that the number of hidden neurons carrying out the above described processing and their efficiency is a matter of design. In particular, the size of the hidden layer(s) have to be related to the complexity of the mapping to be interpolated as well as to the available number of examples. In this respect, the use of an example problem is beneficial. A simple trick to speed up the training process is again to separate the two conceptual steps: the area to be inspected is subdivided into five overlapping regions (see fig.6). A classification NN (or a properly designed rule-based logic) selects the region and then switch on the identification NN specifically trained by examples concerning only the presence of a boss in that region.

As previously discussed, the topology here introduced allows to incorporate possible uncertainties about the region containing the boss. In particular, it is possible to consider vague (fuzzy) boundaries between classes. In such a way, a boss located in correspondence of a boundary may be considered lying in two regions with different degree of membership: in this case the resulting estimate derives from the cooperation of two identification NNs properly trained.

It is worth noting that once detected the region of interest, it would be possible to subsequently change the map of the sensors. On the other hand, it can be of more interest to obtain a completely automatic system without having to repeat the measurements. For this reason, the training of each specialised NN is carried out by considering the same configuration of sensors. Fig.5 details the proposed architecture showing that for each fuzzy value of the fuzzy variable we have a module composed of five specialised NNs. Table 2 reports the results of the identification process in terms of full scale root mean square errors, of maximum absolute errors, as well as of misclassification error for the two classification NNs.

3.3. Location of plural defects.

When the above-mentioned conducting plate can present more defects of hemispherical shape, the analytical formulation of the problem must change to cope with an infinite series of images. However, if the centres of the two bosses are located so that $d >> max(a',a'')$, where d is the distance between the centres, we can consider a finite number of terms of the expansion [7], fig.7. By limiting ourselves to the discrimination between one or two bosses, the identification process can be carried out as follows:

i) decision about the presence of defects:

ii) in case of presence, decide about the number of defects;

iii) in the case of one boss, determine its size and location by means of the above described neural system;

iv) in the case of two bosses, determine their location, in the hypothesis of considering bosses of equal size.

Misclassification error %	Training	Test
Size detection NN	2.0	3.0
Region detection NN	1.0	1.6

NN Topology	Fully Sigmoidal	Linear Output	Modified
%xb train./test	4.2 / 5.1	4.2 / 5.0	3.9 / 4.5
%yb train./test	4.0 / 4.8	4.3 / 5.1	3.7 / 4.1
%a train./test	7.0 / 7.5	6.8 / 7.1	4.5 / 5.2
Max abs error	xb = 8mm	yb = 4mm	a = 0.3mm

Table 2 - Performance of the task decomposing neural system.

When admitting bosses of different sizes, it is awkward to discriminate between the presence of a large boss and two near smaller bosses: this problem of ambiguity is now under study. In particular, work is underway aimed at determining the minimal distance of correct detection w.r.t. the ratio a'/a''.

3.4. Identification of circular holes in thin plates.

A more realistic NDT problem concerns the evaluation of eddy currents at low frequency in thin plates with the aim of finding size and shape of defects. In this case a time-varying magnetic field induces eddy currents in the metallic structure under test: the presence of defects can modify the pattern of fields. Also in this electromagnetic inspection problem we have to cope with an inverse problem. We can generate the cases required by the training phase by means of a finite element code , but it seems useful to derive treat again a closed form solution to have at our disposal a simple and practical pattern generator. The analytical formulation of the problem for circular holes is reported elsewhere [3]. However, we can say that the approach above considered yields a good accuracy also in the estimation of the hole location.

4. CONCLUDING REMARKS.

It seems clear that the usefulness and flexibility of future neural systems will depend in large part on the integration of simple NNs into more complex architectures, perhaps emulating biological sensory systems. In this work we have shown that NNs can have an important impact on the development of improved tools for NDT applications. An open question regards the noiseless nature of the data used in our work: an important aspect of neural computing is the robustness to additive noise. It can be said that the injection of noise in the training dataset can improve the generalisation capabilities of the NN showing a regularising effect, nevertheless we have to consider the sensitivity of the NDT processing to such a noise.

ACKNOWLEDGMENT
The authors thank F. Cirianni for tecnical assistance.

REFERENCES

[1] L.Udpa, S.S.Udpa, "Neural Networks for the Classification of Nondestructive evaluation signals", IEE Proceedings, Vol.138, No.1, February 1991.

[2] E.Coccorese, R.Martone and F.C.Morabito, 1993, "A Neural Network Approach for the Solution of Electric and Magnetic Inverse Problems", submitted to IEEE Trans. on Magn.

[3] F.C.Morabito, et al., 1993, "Identification of Circular Holes in Thin Plates Using a Neural Networks Approach", to be published.

[4] M.Enokizono, T.Todaka, M.Akita, "Rotational Magnetic Sensor with Neural Network for Non-Destructive Testing", INTERMAG 1993, Stockholm.

[5] F.C.Morabito, "Multilayer Neural Network for Identification of Non-Linear Electromagnetic Systems", 1993, WCNN, I-428,432, Portland, OR.

[6] Rumelhart, D.E., Hinton, G.E. and Williams, R.J., "Learning Representation by Back-propagating errors", Nature 323, 533-536, 1986 ,in :Anderson, J.A., Neurocomputing, 1988

[7] E.Durand, Electrostatique, tome II, Masson, Paris, 1966.

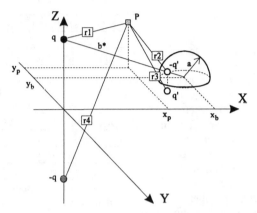

Fig 1 - A pictorial representation of the NDT problem.

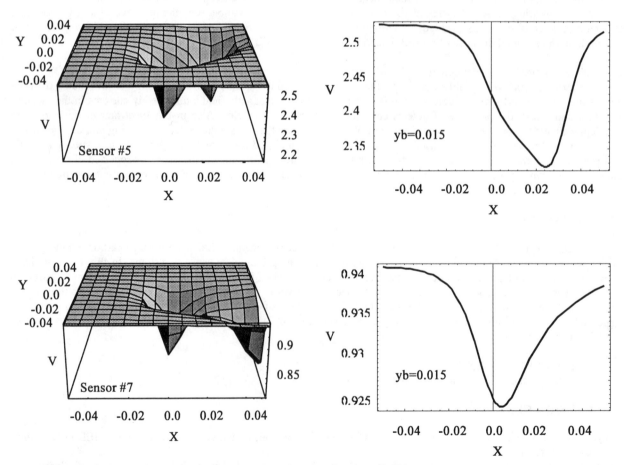

Fig 2 - The electric potential measured by sensor #5 and sensor #7 (a=0.5mm).

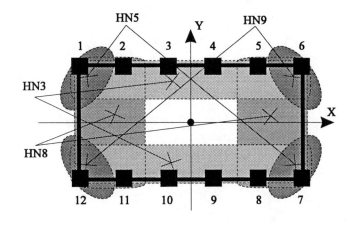

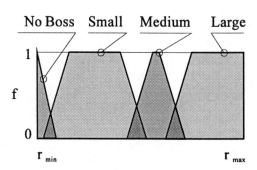

Fig. 3 - Configuration of the sensors and implicit subdi-
vision of the inspected area carried out by NN.

Fig. 4 - Membership functions selected for the
fuzzy values of the fuzzy variable.

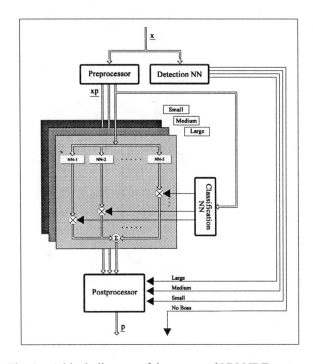

Fig. 5 - A block diagram of the proposed NN-NDT system.

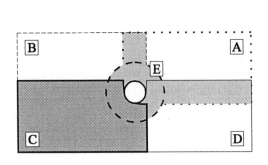

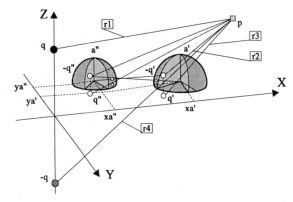

Fig. 6 - Decomposition of the inspected plate
into 5 overlapping regions

Fig. 7 - The two-bosses case.

Machine Vision

Session Chairs: Kunihiko Fukushima
Robert Hecht-Nielsen

ORAL PRESENTATIONS

Visual Pattern Recognition with Selective Attention

Kunihiko Fukushima,   Hayaru Shouno

Faculty of Engineering Science, Osaka University,   Toyonaka, Osaka 560, Japan

Abstract

The "selective attention model" proposed previously by Fukushima is a neural network model that has the ability to segment patterns, as well as the function of recognizing them. In order to increase the ability of the model, bend-processing circuits have been introduced in the network. The search controller in the network has also been modified, and backward signals as wells as forward signals are used to control the search area. Using the principles of the new model, a cursive word recognition system has been developed. The system can recognize and segment connected characters in cursive handwriting of English words. The ability to recognize and segment each individual character has been greatly improved by these modifications of the model, compared to the previous system proposed by Fukushima and Imagawa.

1   Introduction

The "selective attention model" proposed by Fukushima [1] is a neural network model that has the ability to segment patterns, as well as the function of recognizing them. Using the principles of the model, a cursive word recognition system [2] was developed. The system was able to recognize and segment connected characters in cursive handwriting of English words.

On the other hands, from previous work on the neocognitron, it was found that the introduction of bend-extracting cells greatly improves its generalization ability for pattern recognition [3]. The neocognitron with bend-extracting cells can easily be trained to robustly recognize deformed patterns.

Therefore, we have introduced bend-extracting cells in the connected character recognition system [4]. Following the introduction of the bend-extracting circuit in the forward paths, an identical circuit has been added also to the backward path, through which the backward signals are made to flow, retracing the same route as the forward signals.

A new idea is introduced also in the search controller. A search controller produces a so-called "search light effect" and restricts the number of patterns to be processed simultaneously. The system mainly processes the input patterns contained in a small "search area", which is moved by the search controller. The new search controller uses not only forward but also backward signals to control the search area.

The ability to recognize and segment each individual character has been greatly improved by these modifications of the system, and the error rate for word recognition has been reduced. The new system is discussed in detail in this paper.

2   Basic Function of the Network

The selective attention model used for connected character recognition is a hierarchical multilayered network, which has backward (i.e., top-down) as well as forward (i.e., bottom-up) connections between layers. Figure 1 illustrates how the cell layers are connected in the network.

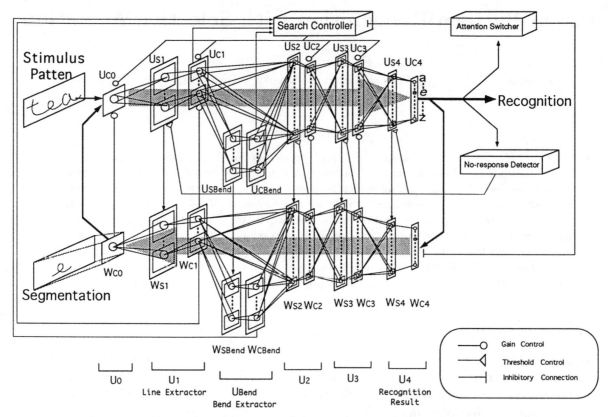

Figure 1: Network architecture of the cursive word recognition system.

A stimulus pattern, or an image of a cursive word, is presented to the input layer U_{C0} shown at the upper left of Figure 1. The result of recognition of each individual character in the input word appears in turn in the recognition layer U_{C4} at the highest stage of the forward path. The character that is now recognized is segmented and appears in the recall layer W_{C0} at the lowest stage of the backward path.

This section explains the basic idea of the system, which is similar to that of the old system [2] with some modifications. Various large modifications applied to the new system will be discussed in the following sections.

The signals through the forward paths manage the function of pattern recognition. If we consider the forward paths only, the model has almost the same architecture and function as the neocognitron [5]. Cells u_S are feature-extracting cells. Cells u_C have the function of tolerating positional errors of the features extracted by the u_S cells. By the blurring operation by the u_C cells, the network acquires robustness against deformation in the patterns during recognition. The u_C-cells at the highest stage work as the recognition cells.

The signals through the backward paths manage the function of selective attention, segmentation and associative recall. The cells and connections in the backward paths of the network are arranged in a mirror image of those in the forward paths. Cells w_S and w_C in the backward path correspond to cells u_S and u_C in the forward paths, respectively.

The output signal of the recognition layer U_{C4} is sent through the backward paths, and reaches the recall layer W_{C0} at the lowest stage. Guided by the gate signals from the forward cells, the backward signals reach exactly the same positions at which the input pattern is being presented. Since backward signals are sent from the active recognition cell only, only the signals corresponding to the recognized pattern reach the recall layer W_{C0}. Even if the input pattern, which is now recognized, is a deformed version of a training pattern, the deformed pattern is segmented from the other patterns and emerges with its deformed shape.

A backward cell w_C sends a gain control signal to the corresponding forward cell and increases the gain of the cell. Thus, only the forward signal flow in the paths in which backward signals are flowing is facilitated. This has the effect of focusing attention on only one of the patterns in the stimulus.

There are cells that monitor the situation that a w_C-cell in the backward paths is active but that feature-extracting u_S-cells around it are all silent. This occurs when some part of the input pattern is missing or contaminated by noise and a feature that is supposed to exist there fails to be extracted in the forward paths. If a monitoring cell detects such a situation, it sends a threshold control signal to these u_S cells and lowers their thresholds. Thus, the u_S-cells come to extract even faint traces of the undetected feature. This is useful for repairing imperfect patterns: Even if the input pattern is an imperfect one, a complete pattern, in which defective parts are interpolated, emerges in the recall layer W_{C0}.

A threshold-control signal is sent also from the no-response detector shown at far right in Figure 1. If all the recognition cells are silent, the no-response detector sends the threshold-control signal to the feature-extracting cells in all stages, and lowers their thresholds until at least one recognition cell responds.

The attention switcher shown at the top right in Figure 1 monitors the response of the recognition layer U_{C4}, and determines the timing of attention switching. When the response of U_{C4} reaches a steady state, the attention switcher sends inhibitory signals and cuts off the backward signal flow for a short period. This causes the gain control signal from the backward cells to disappear, and the gain of the forward cells decreases because of fatigue of the cells. The search controller again seeks a place in which a larger number of line- and bend-extracting cells are active, and shifts the search area to the new place.

3   Bend-Processing Circuits

Layer U_{SBend} consists of bend-extracting cells. These cells detect bend-points and endpoints of lines. A u_{SBend}-cell receives antagonistic inputs from two adjoining areas in a cell-plane of the preceding layer U_{C1}. These two areas are aligned in parallel with the preferred orientation of the cell-plane. The u_{SBend}-cell is strongly activated, if the input signal comes from the excitatory area only, and not from the inhibitory one. Therefore, it responds to an endpoint of a line in the input pattern. When a curved line is presented, the u_{SBend}-cells' response represents bend-points of the curved line.

Layer U_{S2} receives input connections not only from U_{C1} but also from U_{CBend}. This means that layer U_{S2} integrates the information of not only the existence of line components but also the bend-points and endpoints of the lines. Generally speaking, the important information required to recognize a pattern is concentrated around these points. Therefore, the utilization of bend-extracting cells can easily increase the feature extraction ability of U_{S2}.

Following the introduction of the bend-extracting circuit (layers U_{SBend} and U_{CBend}) in the forward paths, an identical circuit (layers W_{SBend} and W_{CBend}) has been added also to the backward paths. Similarly to other W_S layers, W_{SBend} receives gate signals from U_{SBend} in the forward path and regenerates signals at the exact places where the bend-points and endpoints of the attended pattern exist.

This circuit is useful not only for recalling a perfect pattern in W_{C0}, but also for improving the ability to segment individual characters. As shown in Figure 2, the inhibitory signal from W_{SBend}

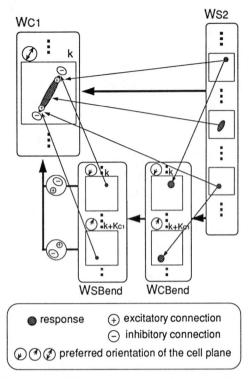

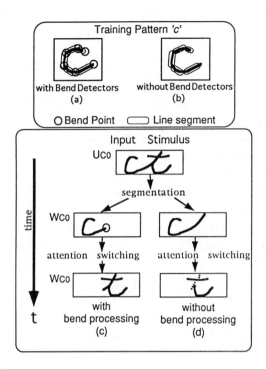

Figure 2: The bend-processing circuit in the backward path.

Figure 3: An effect of the bend-processing circuit on the result of segmentation.

to W_{C1} prevents the unlimited extension of a connecting stroke from a segmented character, and the border of the character can be correctly delimited. Figure 3 illustrates this situation.

4 Search Controller

A new idea is introduced also in the search controller, which is shown at the top center in Figure 1. A search controller restricts the number of patterns to be processed simultaneously. The system mainly processes the input patterns contained in a small "search area", which is moved by the search controller. The gain control signal from the search controller produces the search area by decreasing the gain of the forward cells situated outside the search area.

The search controller monitors the response of layers U_{C1} and U_{CBebd} at first, and shift the position of the search area to the place in which a larger number of line-extracting and bend-extracting cells are active. However, the position of the search area is not fixed during the whole period of recognizing one character.[1] It is adaptively moved as shown in Figure 4. When one of the characters in the input pattern is once recognized, the search controller now starts monitoring the response of the backward cells, that is, layers W_{C1} and W_{CBend}, instead of U_{C1} and U_{CBend}. The search area is now shifted to the place that exactly coincides with the character that is now recognized and segmented. This process of adaptive shifting the search area is useful, when the initial position of the search area happens to be misplaced, say, in the middle of two characters. If the position of the search area is not adjusted, there is a chance that the segmented character has a missing part near the border of the search area. In the present system, however, the search area

---

[1] In the old model [2], the position of the search area was determined from the response of U_{C1} only, and was not moved afterward.

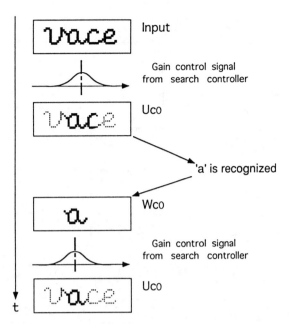

Figure 4: Shift of search area using not only forward but also backward signals.

is moved adaptively, and a missing peripheral part rarely occurs.

The search controller works not only in the recognition phase, but also in the training phase. Incidentally, in the old system [2], the search controller was stopped working during the training phase.

5   Computer Simulation

The performance of the system has been simulated on a computer. The system has been trained using ten alphabetical characters shown in Figure 5(a). Although we used ten characters instead of twenty-six because of the limitation of the computer power, we chose characters whose shapes are similar to each other and difficult to be segmented when they are connected in handwriting. In other words, a character set difficult to discriminate have been chosen intentionally so that the performance can be tested with a small number of test patterns.

Figure 5(b) shows how the characters in cursive words have been recognized and segmented. Most of the characters have been recognized correctly, but few of them are erroneously recognized or failed to be correctly segmented. In Figure 5(b), the letter written below the image of an input pattern indicates how the corresponding character in the word was erroneously recognized by the system. No such letters are written for characters recognized correctly. When one character in a word was recognized twice by mistake, the two results are indicated by letters enclosed in parentheses. A question mark shows the character could not be recognized.

As can be seen from Figure 5(b), most of the characters were recognized and segmented correctly. Even in the words in which some characters were erroneously recognized, the rest of the characters were usually recognized correctly.

Acknowledgments: This work was supported in part by Grant-in-Aid #02402035 and #05267103 for Scientific Research from the Ministry of Education, Science and Culture of Japan; and by a grant for Frontier Research Project in Telecommunications from the Ministry of Posts and Telecommunications of Japan.

(a) Training patterns

(b) Test patterns

Figure 5: Computer simulation of cursive word recognition.

References

[1] K. Fukushima: "A neural network model for selective attention in visual pattern recognition and associative recall", *Applied Optics*, **26**[23], pp. 4985–4992 (Dec. 1987).

[2] K. Fukushima, T. Imagawa: "Recognition and segmentation of connected characters with selective attention", *Neural Networks*, **6**[1], pp. 33–41 (1993).

[3] K. Fukushima, N. Wake: "Improved neocognitron with bend-detecting cells", *IJCNN'92-Baltimore*, Baltimore, MD, U.S.A., Vol. IV, pp. 190–195 (June 1992).

[4] H. Shouno, K. Fukushima: "Character recognition in cursive handwriting using selective attention model with bend detectors", (in Japanese), *Tech. Report IEICE*, No. **NC92**-105 (1993).

[5] K. Fukushima: "Neocognitron: A hierarchical neural network capable of visual pattern recognition", *Neural Networks*, **1**[2], pp. 119–130 (1988).

Why Synchronization? An Attempt to Show Quantitative Advantages[1]

G. Hartmann, S. Drüe
Fachbereich 14 Elektrotechnik, Universität-GH Paderborn
Warburger Straße 100, D 33098 Paderborn, Germany

Abstract

There is a lot of evidence that cortical neurons show synchronized activity. There is also a variety of synchronization-based models and simulations, but there are almost no arguments excluding the possibility that the investigated phenomena could also be explained without synchronization. Our results from comparison of two alternative models show quantitatively the superiority of a synchronization-based mechanism. The simulated contour representations proved to be successful in our robot vision system, but we can also give strong arguments for similar representations in the biological visual system.

Introduction

The hypothesis of dynamical links [1], and the experimental confirmation of synchronized activity in the visual cortex [2], [3] caused a lot of enthusiasm in this field of research. It was argued that temporal labels could be dynamic links, binding elements of coherent contours, regions, or moving backgrounds. Models were provided and supported by simulations showing that synchronization ist able to provide the desired mechanisms. On the other hand there are almost no arguments excluding the possibility that the investigated phenomena could also be explained without synchronization and there are also models [4] treating the observed cortical acitivity as sheer oscillations of a control loop.

Our contribution is focussed on the comparison of two alternative models for one phenomenon, and the results show clearly that the synchronization-based architecture is less expensive by orders of magnitude. We look at the problem from a vision system designer's point of view, and we pursue the following line of argumentation: Our robot vision system is based on a holistic approach [5] assuming that objects up to a relativly high degree of complexity like faces, traffic signs, or written syllables are recognized by matching of suitable neural representations. Region based representations including colour representations are very robust against minor errors in foveation, and against errors due to parametric mappings [6] providing invariances. Region based representations are also very helpful for discriminating objects of different size and colour, but they are not very sensitive to shapes. So we had to include contour representations in our system, and we could achieve reliable and selective recognition. However, matching of contours requires special representations which are significantly less expensive on the base of synchronization mechanism.

The Problem of Contour Matching

An active vision system learning and recognizing normalized representations is subject to errors in position, size, and shape of retinal images and has even to interpolate between perspective distortions. Associative networks with error back-propagation or networks of the Hopfield type can tolerate these deviations, but only at the expense of long training sequen-

[1] Supported by the German Minister of Research and Technology (BMFT), ITN 910 506

ces. In our robot vision system we decided to use one step learning [7] for practicability, and so we have to tolerate these errors by reducing the demands on the similarity measure. This strategy works well in the case of region based features, but at the expense of shape selectivity. Equal sized areas of circular or hexagonal shape can not be distinguished by region based features as soon as the similarity measure is reduced in order to tolerate the system-related errors.

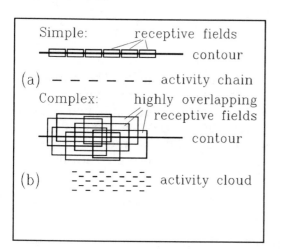

Fig. 1: Simple model neurons (a) with small oriented receptive fields provide chains of activity in response to a contour. Complex model neurons with large, highly overlapping receptive fields (b) respond to the contour with a cloud of activity.

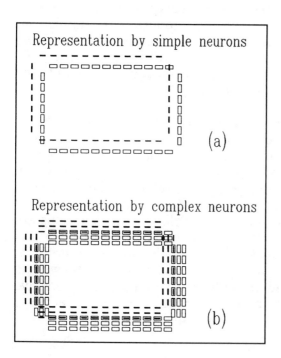

Fig. 2: Activity pattern of simple (a) and complex (b) model neurons in response to a rectangular contour. Overlap between activity pattern (-) and learnt pattern (□) of simple neurons is completely lost (a) due to a diagonal shift of the image by only one pixel. In a representation by complex neurons (b) overlap is only reduced.

We could significantly improve shape sensitivity by including contour representations. Spatial tolerance could not be achieved, however, by only changing the similarity measure, we also had to change the contour representation. Model neurons with oriented receptive field [8] similar to simple cortical neurons provide chains of acitivity in response to a contour structure (fig. 1a). Model neurons with enlarged, highly overlapping receptive fields like complex cortical cells (fig. 1b), however, respond to contours with a cloud of activation. If we learn the representation e. g. of a rectangle (fig. 2), and present the image in a diagonally shifted position, there will be decreased overlap in the case of complex neurons, but no overlap in the case of simple neurons. Though there is a local overlap at two crossing points in fig. 2a, please note that there is no overlap in the components of the feature vector, as the neurons at the crossing points are differently oriented. Clouds of orientation in the representation by complex neurons still provide overlap also in the feature vector, and recognition is again possible with reduced demands on the similarity measure.

At the moment we have investigated two types of complex model neurons with receptive fields of double and quadruple size compared to our simple neurons, but in principle all sizes are possible. There is an equal number of simple and complex neurons per unit area and so the large sized fields have high overlap, necessary for cloud representation. The shapes of the receptive fields are similar to those of the simple cells [8] and allow response to contours with orientations of $\pm 15°$ related to the field axis. Field axes are oriented at $\varphi = 0°$, $15°$, $30°$ ... $180°$ related to a hexagonal pixel matrix. Our complex neurons respond to all types of continous contours and are not sensitive to the phase (bright/dark).

All these features are very similar to those of biological complex cells, but they are also indispensable for our system. They provide spatial tolerance and orientation selectivity necessary for representation of contours by orientation clouds. Insensitiveness against contrast phase helps to cope with changing contrasts due to ilumination [9]. Finally, response to only continuous uninterrupted contours provides a clean up effect, showing only essential parts of contour structures in the oriented cloud. By verification of continuity recognition becomes more reliable, as noise and oriented textures are not learnt together with the contour structure of an object. So continuity is an essential point in our model of a complex neuron.

Alternatives for Implementation of Complex Model Neurons

There are actually two alternatives for implementing all the features of our complex model neuron: one using synchronization, the other one using only an appropriate interconnection scheme in a straightforward way.

In both cases we define size and position of the complex receptive field, and within this area we select all the combinations of simple cells which may be simultaneously activated by any contour, matching to the receptive field of the complex cell. So the condition for activation of the complex neurons is the simultaneous acitivity of one of these combinations of simple neurons. In a straightforward model we could use linking neurons for verification of simultaneous activity. A linking neuron l_1 should only become supraliminal if all the neurons a, b, c, d of combination c_1 are active (fig. 3a) and another linking neuron l_n should be acitvated by neurons s, t, u, v of combination c_n. The complex neuron itself should be activated by only one out of the linking neurons due to a very low threshold adjustment. The interconnection scheme is very simple (Fig. 4a) and no synchronization is necessary.

The real problem with this architecture is the tremendous number of linking neurons. In order to allow arbitrary contours to be encoded, small parts of the visual field are encoded by complete sets of simple neurons with receptive fields of different position, orientation, and shape. There is a detailed description of this set in [8] and fig. 3b shows only a simplified scheme. But the graph in fig. 3b will clearly show that a contour entering at point p will have 5^4 possibilities to cross the complex field. So already in our small sized example there are more than 5000 combinations and a corresponding number of linking neurons l_n

if all possible entering points are considered . An architecture, however, which needs 5000 useless interneurons in order to connect about 100 simple neurons to one complex neuron is evidently unaceptable expensive, and so we did not really realize it.

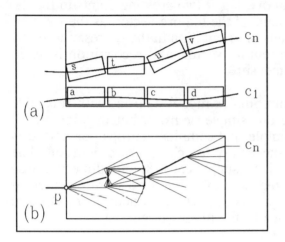

Fig. 3: Continuous contours matching to the receptive field of the complex model neuron activate combinations of simple neurons. The receptive fields of the contributing simple neurons form sequences in this case (a) and the high number of possible combinations can be estimated on the base of these sequences (b).

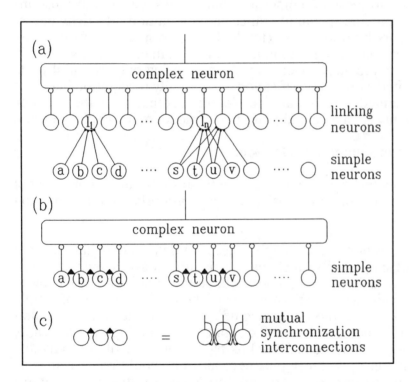

Fig. 4: Due to a tremendous number of linking neurons the straightforward architecture (a) is very expensive compared with the synchronization-based architecture (b). The symbols for synchronizing interconnections (b) are explained in (c).

The alternative architecture is based on synchronization between pulse coded model neurons [10]. All pairs of simple neurons in the visual field with adjacent in-line receptive fields, like (a, b) or (t, u) in fig. 3a, are mutually interconnected via excitatory synapses (fig. 4c). We could previously show [11] that all neurons responding to an arbitrary continuous contour are synchronized by this interconnection scheme. Consequently, the combinations c_n (Fig. 3a), the building blocks of our complex neuron, are also synchronized by continuous contours. Vice versa, continuity of a contour can easily be verified by sensing synchronized activity.

This leads to the very simple and inexpensive architecture in fig. 4b. All those simple neurons contributing to valid combinations c_n of a complex neuron are interconnected to it by excitatory synapses. These synapses have a short time constant in the range of 1 ... 3 ms, and so the membrane potential can only become supraliminal, if more than three spikes pile up within a short time slot. This occurs as soon as a combination c_n of simple neurons is simultaneously activated and synchronized.

This simple architecture obviously provides all the features of our model neuron. Only simple neurons contributing to valid combinations are interconnected to the complex neuron, and so only contours are represented if they are matching to the receptive field of the complex neuron in orientation and space. Interrupted contours or textures with correct orientation can also activate but not synchronize simple neurons. So the spikes can not pile up and the complex neuron remains subliminal.

Biological Aspects and Conclusion

Our actual research is in the field of robot vision systems, and our model neurons sucessfully provide clouds of activation (Fig. 5). The above results, however, could also support the assumption that sychnronization provides superior solutions in biology. Our complex model neurons show all the features of biological complex neurons, and as far as we know there is no experimental evidence speaking aginst this architecture. Especially, we would like to discuss two points. Hubel and Wiesel have already proposed a model of complex neurons receiving input from simple neurons. The spikes of the simple neurons are not synchronized in this model and so the synapses of the complex neuron must have longer time constants and smaller weights in order to integrate the uncorrelated rates. This leads to a delayed activity of the complex model neuron which is not observed in biology. This delay was one of the strongest objections against this model, but this delay does not occur in our synchronization based model. The first set of synchroneous spikes will immediatelly cause a spike of the complex neuron, and there is almost no delay. Moreover, the complex model neuron is synchronized to the simple neurons in accordance with recent experimental results.

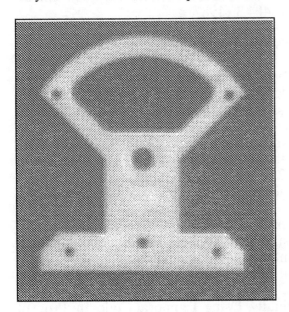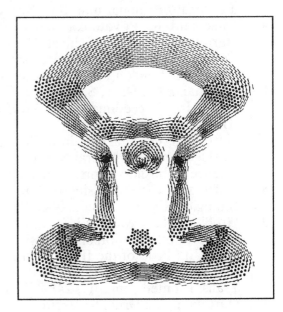

Fig. 5: Contour representation of workpiece (b) by "activity" cloud of complex neurons (a).

The second point which should be included into the discussion deals with the fast direct inputs to biological complex neurons. These additional inputs are not considered in our simulations. However, it would be compatible with our model, if fast inputs would prepare a complex neuron by rising the membrane potential. Sychronized spikes from simple cells could then more easily add the missing part of the membrane potential.

On the other hand, on can almost exclude that biology uses a straightforward interconnection like that in fig. 4a. Due to the additional interneurons delay would be still increased. The additional "linking neurons" should repond to a piece of contour acitivating a combination of simple cells with in-line receptive fields, and so they should have extremely elongated receptive fields. Due to the tremendous number of these neurons they should have been found. Finally, synchronization between simple and complex neurons could never be interpreted on the base of this straightforward model.

For completeness, we should not omit to discuss a third possibility by which biology could realize complex cells without snchronization, and without additional interneurons. The logical AND-function of the linking neurons (fig. 4a) could also be executed within the dendritic tree itself between neighbouring synapses. In this model the tremendous number of interneurons can be avoided, but not the time delay due to integration of uncorrelated spike trains. Again, the observed synchroneous activity of simple and complex neurons could not be explained at the base of this model.

References

[1]   Von der Malsburg, C.: The correlation theory of brainfunction. Internal Report 81-2, Dpt. Neurobiology, Max Planck Institute for Biophysical Chemistry (1981)
[2]   Eckhorn, R. et al.: Feature linking via stimulus-evoked oscillations: Experimental results from cat visual cortex and functional implications from a network model. Proc. IJCNN89, IEEE, 1.723-1.730 (1989)
[3]   Gray, C. M., Singer, W.: Stimulus specific neuronal oscillations in the cat visual cortex: a cortical functional unit. Soc. Neurosc. abstr. 404.3 (1987)
[4]   Kirschfeld, K.: Private communications
[5]   Hartmann, G.: Hierarchical Neural Representation by Synchronized Activity: A Concept for Visual Pattern Recognition. In: Taylor, J. G. et al. (Hg.): Neural Network Dynamics. London et al. (Springer-Verlag) 1991, S. 356-370
[6]   Hartmann, G.; Drüe, S.; Kräuter, K. O.; Seidenberg, E.: Simulations with an artificial retina. In: Proceedings of the World Congress on Neural Networks. WCNN 1993. S. III-689-III-694
[7]   Hartmann, G.: Learning in a Closed Loop Antagonistic Network. In: Kohonen, T. et al. (Hg.) Artificial Neural Networks. Proc. of the ICANN-91. Amsterdam u.a. (Elsevier Science Publishers/North-Holland) 1991, S. 239-244
[8]   Hartmann, G.: Processing of Continuous Lines and Edges by the Visual System. In: Biological Cybernetics 47 1983, S. 43-50
[9]   Großberg, S. & Marshall, J. A.: A computational model of how cortical complex cells multiplex information about position, contrast, orientation, spatial frequency, and disparity. In: Proc. of the IEEE First Intern. Conf. on Neural Networks, 4 203-214 (1987)
[10] French, A. S., Stein, R. B.: A flexible neural analog using integrated circuits. IEEE Trans. Biomed. Eng., 17, 248-253 (1970)
[11] Hartmann, G.; Drüe, S.: Verification of Continuity, Using Temporal Code. In: Proc. of the International Joint Conference on Neural Networks (IJCNN), II, San Diego 1990, S. 459-464

An Improved High Order Neural Network for Invariant Recognition of Human Faces in Gray Scale

Rafał Foltyniewicz and Sławomir Skoneczny

Institute of Control & Industrial Electronics,
Warsaw University of Technology,
00–662 Warszawa, ul. Koszykowa 75, Poland
tel. (+48–2) 6280665, fax. (+48–2) 6256633
e–mail: rfoltyn@plwatu21.bitnet or
foltyniewicz@nov.isep.pw.edu.pl

Abstract

The problem of binary pattern recognition invariant over translation, scale and in–plane rotation is very often encountered in many practical situations. Recently high order neural networks (especially third order) were proposed to solve this task. However this approach was successful only for distinguishing between two simple binary objects. In our paper we propose an efficient solution for recognizing real world images (human faces) because of elaboration of effective coding algorithm for gray level images and new neural network structure. Theoretical investigations and practical results are described.

1 Introduction

For many years a problem of invariant pattern recognition draws attention of many researchers in this field. One of the very interesting tools for solving such problems is an artificial neural network. It seems to be reasonable to use a high order neural network of the third order since the required invariances can be incorporated into its structure and do not have to be taught. In this contribution we present the classical concept of the high order neural network (of third order) and efficient improvements which enable to classify complicated gray level objects. The method described in this paper is very effective and gives high recognition rates (over 96% correctly classified patterns).

2 Third Order Network for Binary Images

The output y_i of the neuron i in a general high order network is given by:

$$y_i = f \left(\sum_j w_{ij} x_j + \sum_j \sum_k w_{ijk} x_j x_k + \sum_j \sum_k \sum_l w_{ijkl} x_j x_k x_l + \ldots \right) \tag{1}$$

where f is a nonlinear threshold function (hardlimiter or sigmoid), the $x_{(.)}$ is the pixel value equal 1 or 0. $w_{i,\ldots}$ is an element of the interconnection matrix. In order to achieve invariant recognition over all three considered transformations it is sufficient to use a third order neural network (TONN) [1]. The output signal of a strictly TONN is given by the function:

$$y_i = f \left(\sum_j \sum_k \sum_l w_{ijkl} x_j x_k x_l \right) \tag{2}$$

For our purposes consider a binary pattern represented by a pixel map. Each triplet of different input pixels forms a triangle. The idea of building invariances into structure of TONN takes advantage of the well known fact that three included angles in a triangle are unchanged despite the translation, scaling or in-plane rotation the triangle is subjected to. The connections architecture must be design in such a way that the output signals are the same for the object independently of the mentioned transformations. Therefore before the learning phase of the network we must connect triplets belonging to one class of similar triangles to one weight. This synaptic weight is related to one equivalence class (EC)[3]. Instead of having one weight for each triangle we have only one weight $w_{k,}$ for each triangle class. Taking it into account we can reformulate equation (2):

$$y_i = f\left(\sum_k w_{ki} I_k\right) \tag{3}$$

where k is the equivalence class index and I_k denotes the effective input given by equation:

$$I_k = \sum_{(j_1 j_2 j_3) \in C_k} x_{j_1} x_{j_2} x_{j_3}. \tag{4}$$

C_k is a set of pixels triplets of class k.

Because of the multiplications of pixels values in (4) the TONN is capable of supplying nonlinear separation using only a single layer. During learning phase typically a simple perceptron learning rule is used:

$$\Delta w_{ijkl} = (t_i - y_i) x_j x_k x_l \tag{5}$$

where t_i and y_i are desired and actual outputs respectively and $x_{(.)}$ is an input binary signal.

3 Reducing the Complexity of TONN

In order to take advantage of a third order neural network for invariant pattern classification we must overcome the problem of combinatorial increase of the number of weights with the size of the input field. This is the reason why we cannot use described in the previous section algorithm directly for real size images. Even if we consider small input field, for instance 16×16 pixels, the number of connections between pixel triplets and multiplying elements is very high (2 763 520 interconnections). Building invariances into the structure of this network partially solves this problem, since we can substitute all weights related to one EC by just one synaptic weight. Thus we can reduce the number of weights but we still must store the same number of connections or to evaluate them on-line during simulation experiments on a sequential machine.

The more pattern resolution is the higher number of triangle classes we have. In order to control the number of EC independently of the image size a method for dividing triangles into "approximately similar triangle" (AST) classes will be used [3]. AST are characterized by the same values of their two smallest angles. We denote these angles by α, β and γ which satisfy: $\alpha \leq \beta$, $0 \leq \alpha \leq \pi/3$, $0 \leq \beta < \pi/2$ and $0 \leq \beta + \alpha/2 \leq \pi/2$. Furthermore we choose an angular tolerance ω, so that $W = \pi/3\omega$ and $Q = \pi/2\omega$ are integers. Finally we partition the set of possible values of α and β into following subsets:

$$(k-1)\omega \leq \alpha < k\omega, \quad (l-1)\omega \leq \beta < l\omega \tag{6}$$

with $k \in [1, W]$ and $l \in [1, Q]$. All triangles whose angles satisfy (6) for given (k, l) are in the same EC. The number of EC (effective inputs) can be calculated from:

$$N_I = \frac{\pi(4\omega + \pi)}{6\omega^2} \tag{7}$$

which is independent of pattern size. This reduces significantly the number of weights, for instance for an 16×16 pixels image normally we have 7414 EC (angle calculation with tolerance 1°) and with $\omega = 10^o$ only 66.

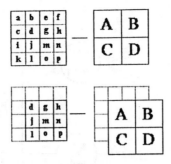

Figure 1: Illustration of coarse coding technique.

The controllability of the number of EC helps alleviate the problem for hardware realization but we are still limited to relatively small input fields. Another simple scheme applied to solve this problem was inspired by coarse coding (CC) [2] and described in [4]. In the latter the technique was successfully implemented for simple binary images and such problems as T/C or distinguishing between two object. We present here our view at efficient coarse coding technique for TONN.

Consider a small binary input field of size 4×4 pixels. All pixel numbers are denoted by letters $a \ldots p$ as in figure 1. In order to reduce the size of an image we encode it into two plains of size 2×2. Elements of the first plane (see first row in Fig. 1) are evaluated from:

$$A = a \vee b \vee c \vee d, \quad B = e \vee f \vee g \vee h, \ldots \tag{8}$$

The second plane (see second row in Fig. 1) is shifted one pixel right and one pixel down and its elements are given by

$$A = d \vee g \vee j \vee m, \quad B = h \vee n, \quad C = l \vee o, \quad D = p \tag{9}$$

If the plain exceeds boundaries of the input field we do not consider the values outside this field which results in (9).

After this procedure we must compute effective inputs of each plain separately using (4) and sum them up. This simple example can be generalized to higher image dimensions (more plains).

4 Efficient High Order Network for Gray Level Images

The described in the previous sections TONN with CC technique and angular tolerance is designed only for binary images and can be easily implemented for invariant recognition of such objects. However it is not always sufficient to have at one's disposal such classifying system, since many real world pictures are represented in a gray level scale and transforming them into binary space means loosing essential information. In this section we propose a neural network structure developed especially for invariant recognition of gray level (GL) images.

Consider a binary 2-D pattern formed by pixels which can have values equal 0 or 1. This means that the output of a multiplying element (eq. (4)) is taken into consideration only if all three pixels building a triangle are set. In order to generalize this for GL images, which pixel values ranges from 0 to some N_{max} (maximum gray level) we utilize a linear transformation that changes integer into real numbers uniformly dividing the $[0, 1]$ interval.

After this transformation we must apply a coarse coding technique similar to this dedicated for binary images (eq. (8.9)) but instead of logical operations we will take advantage of an average value of pixels in defined neighborhood. We can reformulate now CC for GL images, which gives us following formulae:

$$A = \frac{1}{4}(a + b + c + d), \quad B = \frac{1}{4}(e + f + g + h), \ldots \tag{10}$$

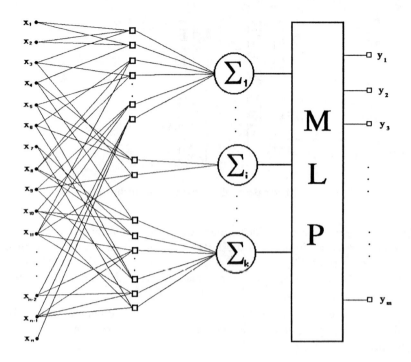

Figure 2: Neural network structure for gray level images (description in text).

and for second plane:

$$A = \frac{1}{4}(d + g + j + m), \quad B = \frac{1}{2}(h + n), \quad C = \frac{1}{2}(l + o), \quad D = p \qquad (11)$$

For letter assignment see figure 1.

Finally we must calculate effective inputs for each plane separately using formula (4) and sum them up for all EC. The result forms a vector which has the number of elements equal the number of EC. This vector is then an input vector presented for classification to a reliable neural network classifier - the multi layer perceptron (MLP). The algorithm is reproduced in form of a neural network structure in figure 2, where $x_1, \ldots, x_n$ denotes all elements of plane coming out of coarse coding, $\square$ is a multiplying element, $\sum_1, \ldots, \sum_k$ are summation elements (one for each equivalence class), and $y_1, \ldots, y_m$ are the outputs of the MLP (one for each pattern).

5 Implementation Details

As a result of theoretical investigations a TONN implementation was developed. A complete software package for testing and estimating usefulness of proposed algorithms was coded in C language for a 32-bit compiler. All experiments were done on i486DX2/66 based machine with 64MB of RAM.

Two different network structures were utilized: a TONN with a simple perceptron–like learning rule (described in sections 2 and 3) and a new TONN equipped with a MLP with two hidden layers (see fig. 2). In both cases two different angular tolerance values ω were chosen: $\omega = 1^\circ$ and $\omega = 10^\circ$ defining 7414 and 66 equivalence classes respectively. This results in four different network structures for testing.

In all experiments 64×64 pixels images of human faces as input patterns were taken. In order to make computer simulations possible we were forced to reduce the complexity of TONN: each input pattern was first normalized, so that all pixels values were transformed into $[0, 1]$ interval and then coded using CC

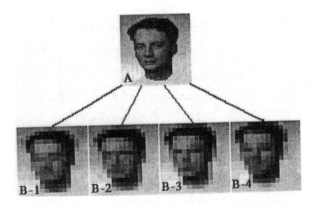

Figure 3: A – input image, B – coded planes.

technique (eq. (10,11)). After this step, 4 planes each 16×16 elements were taken for calculation of effective inputs. An example of an original image used for training the neural networks and its 4 planes is pictured in figure 3.

In order to measure and compare the recognition abilities of traditional algorithm (TONN with perceptron–like learning rule) the same experiments as for GL images (new network model) were done for binary images. The black and white pictures were obtained with threshold technique from original GL images. With these pictures equations (8, 9) were used for CC purposes.

6   Simulation Results

For each experiment (both binary and GL images) two sets of eight human faces were used. After learning the network to distinguish between patterns from training set transformed patterns of all images were utilized for testing:

- scaled to 90%, 95%, 105% and 110% of its size, and

- rotated by $\pm 2^{o}$, $\pm 5^{o}$, $\pm 10^{o}$, $\pm 15^{o}$, $\pm 20^{o}$, $\pm 30^{o}$, $\pm 45^{o}$ and $\pm 90^{o}$.

The origin of all transformation was in the geometrical centre of the input field. The translation case was not considered, since while rotating or changing size of an object we simultaneously move the object in reference to defined origin (the origin is not in the gravity centre of a face). It would not be the case if we have rotated or scaled the image with the origin in the gravity centre of it. We have also done experiments with translation separately and it was not a problem for a network to classify properly all objects. The same refers to rotation by $\pm 90^{o}$, when all faces were correctly recognized.

All results are summarized in figures 4 and 5.

7   Conclusions

In recent literature it has been shown that third order neural networks are able to distinguish between two binary objects regardless of their position, in–plane rotation or changes in size. Although the problem of combinatorial increase of the number of weights with the size of the input field seems to be under control utilizing angular tolerance and coarse coding techniques, during experiments one can observe that with the increase of patterns (number of faces in the learning set) the perceptron–like learning rule is not sufficient for proper class separation. This is partially caused by the fact that exact transformation by

image form/classifier type	Number of EC (Tolerance)	
	7414 ($\omega = 1°$)	66 ($\omega = 10°$)
Binary / simple perceptron	53.6%	89.1%
Gray Scale / simple perceptron	64.3%	72.3%
Gray Scale / MLP	82.3%	96.0%

Figure 4: Recognition rates for rotated images.

image form/classifier type	Number of EC (Tolerance)	
	7414 ($\omega = 1°$)	66 ($\omega = 10°$)
Binary / simple perceptron	65.6%	71.9%
Gray Scale / simple perceptron	53.4%	68.8%
Gray Scale / MLP	65.6%	96.9%

Figure 5: Recognition rates for scaled images.

arbitrary vectors, rotation by arbitrary angles and scaling by arbitrary factors are not realizable on a square lattice. Another problem inherent in HONN is the necessity of applying various techniques for reducing the complexity of connections which cause another information losses. For this two reasons we are obliged to use a better classifier – a multi layer perceptron, which has better separation abilities.

Next improvement can be achieved using the angular tolerance. The distribution of triangles based on the "approximately similar triangle" approach causes that mild distortions of the shape of a triangle as a result of transforming images on a square lattice will not push it out of equivalence class to which it originally belongs.

Another benefit can be utilized with the generalization of coarse coding technique for gray level images. The results are better then those for binary images and the recognition rates for proposed network structure is very high and promising.

The simplicity of described neural network structure allows possible hardware implementation which would speed up the learning and classifying process. Further research should concentrate upon finding new methods for increasing input plane size, minimizing interconnections number and testing robustness against pixel noise.

References

[1] C.L. Giles and T. Maxwell. Learning, Invariances, and Generalization in High–Order Neural Networks. *Appl. Opt.*, 26:4972–4978, 1987.

[2] G.E. Hinton, McClelland, and D.E. Rumelhart. *Distributed Representations. In D.E. Rumelhart and J.L.McClelland, editors, Parallel Distributed Processing*, volume 1, chapter 3. The MIT Press, Cambridge, MA, 1986.

[3] S. Perantonis and P. Lisboa. Translation, Rotation, and Scale Invariant Pattern Recognition by High-Order Neural Networks and Moment Classifiers. *IEEE Transactions on Neural Networks*, 3(2):241–251, Nov 1992.

[4] L. Spirkovska and B. Reid. Coarse-Coded Higher-Order Neural Networks for PSRI Object Recognition. *IEEE Transactions on Neural Networks*, 4(2):276–283, March 1993.

Incremental ART: A Neural Network System for Recognition by Incremental Feature Extraction

J. Mario Aguilar[1] and William D. Ross[2]

Center for Adaptive Systems and Cognitive and Neural Systems Dept.

111 Cummington St. Rm 240 , Boston University, Boston, MA 02215

Abstract

Incremental ART extends adaptive resonance theory (ART) by incorporating mechanisms for efficient recognition through incremental feature extraction. The system achieves efficient confident prediction through the controlled acquisition of only those features necessary to discriminate an input pattern. These capabilities are achieved through three modifications to the fuzzy ART system: (1) A *partial feature vector complement coding rule* extends fuzzy ART logic to allow recognition based on partial feature vectors. (2) The addition of a F_2 *decision criterion* to measure ART predictive confidence. (3) An *incremental feature extraction layer* computes the next feature to extract based on a measure of predictive value. Our system is demonstrated on a face recognition problem but has general applicability as a machine vision solution and as model for studying scanning patterns.

Introduction

Classification algorithms including K-means, nearest neighbor, self-organizing feature maps, backpropagation and ART systems (Carpenter and Grossberg, 1987) all require that the entire input or feature vector be presented before confident prediction can be made. This requirement demands that preprocessing of a scene be completed prior to recognition despite that fact that much of that preprocessing may be unnecessary or irrelevant. For typical applications such preprocessing demands feature extraction by either expensive parallel or time-consuming sequential implementations. One common remedy is to determine and extract a set of task specific features off-line. By contrast, human visual recognition acquires scenic features incrementally through the intelligent deployment of the spatially limited foveal resource by automatically determining which scenic features are important for a range of tasks (Rojer and Schwartz, 1992; Seibert and Waxman, 1993). Our model extends fuzzy ART (Carpenter, Grossberg, and Rosen 1991) both as a pattern recognition device and as a model of human recognition through the incorporation of three modifications which interactively allow recognition through incremental feature evaluation and extraction.

Our control strategy results in an efficient system in which the status of the recognition process guides the deployment of acquisition and preprocessing resources offering the potential for real-time affordable operation even in very complex input environments.

The operation of Incremental ART is illustrated on a face recognition problem. In this example, Incremental ART was trained on a set of complete feature vectors extracted from

---

[1]Supported in part by ARPA (ONR N00014-92-J-4015) and the Office of Naval Research (ONR N00014-92-J-1309).

[2]Supported in part by the Air Force Office of Scientific Research (AFOSR 90-0083), the National Science Foundation (NSF IRI 90-00530), and the Office of Naval Research (ONR N00014-91-J-4100).

12 faces taken from the MIT Eigenfaces database (Turk and Pentland 1991). Each complete feature vector consisted of a coarse spatial coding of local boundary activations concatenated with a much longer fine spatial coding of local boundary activations.

Testing was then carried out using the faces corrupted by noise. During testing, only the coarsely coded portion of the feature vector was initially presented. The system then extracted finely coded features incrementally from predictive regions of the face until confident recognition was achieved.

Feature extraction was accomplished by a minimal scheme for discounting the effects of variable illumination and detecting boundaries (Contreras-Vidal and Aguilar, 1993). Gabor filters were used to detect boundaries of 4 orientations, the resulting boundaries were sharpened by techniques inspired by the Boundary Contour System (BCS) (Grossberg and Mingolla 1985a,b), and then orientation activations were summed and normalized within both coarse and fine regions. The details of preprocessing are not relevant since the system is compatible with any preprocessing scheme.

Incremental ART

Incremental ART is a departure from conventional feedforward approaches in which the system only processes that information which is initially supplied. A more efficient approach is to reduce the amount of information preprocessed at any one time provided that the system can actively control from which areas in the environment it will next extract features. This sequential acquisition process allows for a reduction in the complexity of initial preprocessing and for confident recognition based on minimal feature extraction.

Figure 1 presents a diagram of the Incremental ART system. The Incremental ART system dynamically guides the feature extraction process to accomplish face recognition. Algorithmically, the operation of the system can be summarized as a three step process in which each step incorporates one of the extensions to fuzzy ART. The three steps repeat until the decision criterion is met and confident recognition occurs.

Step 1: The incrementally completed feature vector is input to the F_1 layer. This vector activates the F_2 layer according to the fuzzy ART activation equation augmented by the *partial feature vector complement coding rule*. Step 2: The distributed pattern of F_2 activation is then contrast enhanced and a winner is chosen if a *decision criterion* is met. Step 3: Otherwise the *incremental feature extraction* layer determines which feature to next extraction.

Partial feature vector complement coding rule

In order for a partial feature vector to activate F_2 categories in a way that accurately reflects the partial information represented some distinction must be made between the absence of feature due to the fact that it has not yet been extracted and the absence of a feature due to an actual absence in the scene.

The complement coding preprocessing strategy provides a means of expressing this distinction. In complement code, each feature is represented by both on and off channels so that the on channel codes a measure of the feature's presence and the off channel codes a measure of the feature's absence (Carpenter, Grossberg and Rosen 1991). Thus, in both categorization and learning both the presence and the absence of a feature can be predictive.

The partial feature vector complement coding rule states that in a complement coded feature vector, the absence of a feature due to an actual absence in the scene (after extraction) is coded as a 0 in the on channel and a 1 in the off channel, whereas the absence of a feature due to the fact that it has not yet been extracted is coded as a 0 in the on channel and a 0 in the off channel.

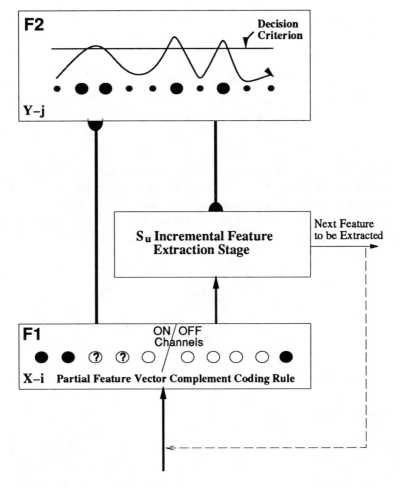

Figure 1: System diagram of incremental ART.

This rule allows informative activation of recognition categories at F_2 by a partial feature vector. Since in the current implementation, learning is prevented when only a partial feature vector is present, the rule does not result in spurious decrease in weights for features that have not yet been extracted. However, a given partial feature vector may not yield an unambiguous winner among F_2 categories.

Decision criterion

An alternative to the standard ART F_2 winner-take-all choice rule uses a *decision criterion* (DC) at the field F_2. The decision criterion is introduced in ART-EMAP to achieve efficient 3-D object recognition (Carpenter, and Ross 1993a,1993b). The decision criterion permits ART choice only when the most active F_2 category J becomes a minimum proportion more active than the next most active F_2 category. Thus if z_j codes system prediction and y_j codes F_2 node activation:

$$z_J = \begin{cases} 1 & \text{if } y_J > (DC)y_j \quad \text{for all } j \neq J \\ \\ 0 & \text{otherwise,} \end{cases} \tag{1}$$

where DC $\geq$ 1. When DC = 1, the decision criterion rule reduces to the F_2 winner-take-all choice rule used in previous ART systems. When DC > 1, the decision criterion prevents prediction in cases in which multiple F_2 categories are about equally activated, representing ambiguous predictive evidence. For computational convenience, activity at F_2 can be contrast enhanced prior to application of the DC by a normalized power rule:

$$y_j = \frac{(y_j)^q}{\displaystyle\sum_{n=1}^{N_{F_2}} (y_n)^q}. \tag{2}$$

When the decision criterion fails more features must be extracted to disambiguate.

Incremental feature extraction

The determination of which features of the input environment, in this example a face, to process next to best disambiguate between potential recognition categories requires some measure of the discriminating power of one portion of the feature vector versus others. The variation across the weights between a single feature and likely categories provides a good indication of the predictive value of extracting that feature, since it is a measure of the variation in y_j activation that would result. Therefore, in this implementation, we use, S_u, where u is the index of an unaccessed F_1 feature, to be the sum of the biased differences between the template weights and the template weight of the maximally activated category. Each difference is biased according to the likelihood of that category as given by y_j. Thus, if the most active F_2 category is J, the F_1 features are x_i, and the $F_1 \rightarrow F_2$ weights are w_{ij} then the feature to be extracted next, U, will be given when;

$$S_U > S_u \text{for all } u \neq U \tag{3}$$

where,

$$S_u = \sum_{j=1}^{N_{F_2}} y_j |w_{uj} - w_{uJ}|. \tag{4}$$

This incremental feature extraction layer determines each unaccessed features predictive value dynamically since after each extraction y_j changes. It should also be noted that the

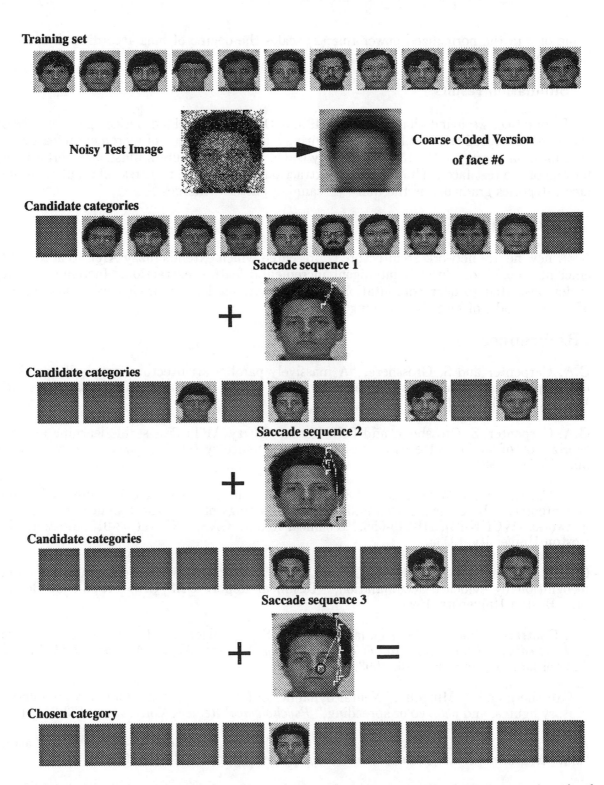

Figure 2. Simulation of recognition sequence for noisy version of face 6. The system is trained with the faces shown in the first row. The sequence of feature as exctracted by the system are shown after each new reduction in the number of candidate categories. Clean images are used to show the scanning patterns. The actual test input was noisy as shown.

value of q in the normalized power rule (2) scales the degree of bias according to category likelihood.

Simulation results

In practice, we found that using $q = 4$, and DC = 1.25 yielded perfect performance on the noise-corrupted face test set while requiring a minimal number of incremental feature extractions, on average 10% (15) of the finely coded features. Figure 2 illustrates performance for one of the test faces. The sequential extraction of predictive features rules out candidate face categories gradually as the marked scanning pattern emerges.

Conclusion

A new neural network architecture is presented which extends fuzzy ART to accomplish efficient recognition through intelligent incremental feature extraction. Incremental ART is demonstrated to offer computational savings without loss of predictive accuracy while offering a model of saccadic scanning pattern.

References

G.A. Carpenter and S. Grossberg, "A massively parallel architecture for a self-organizing neural pattern recognition machine," *Computer Vision, Graphics, and Image Processing*, Vol. 37, pp. 54–115, 1987.

G.A. Carpenter, S. Grossberg, and D.B. Rosen, "Fuzzy ART: Fast stable learning and categorization of analog patterns by an adaptive resonance system," *Neural Networks*, Vol. 4, pp. 759-771, 1991.

G.A. Carpenter and W.D. Ross, "ART-EMAP: A neural network architecture for learning and prediction by evidence accumulation," Proceedings of the World Congress on Neural Networks (WCNN-93), III-649-656. Technical Report CAS/CNS-TR-93-015, Boston, MA: Boston University, 1993a.

G.A. Carpenter and W.D. Ross, "ART-EMAP: A neural network architecture for object recognition by evidence accumulation," Technical Report CAS/CNS-TR-93-035, Boston, MA: Boston University, 1993b.

J.L. Contreras-Vidal and M. Aguilar, A fast BCS/FCS algorithm for image segmentation. In *Proceedings of the International Conference on Artificial Neural Networks (ICANN-93)*, Amsterdam, September 13-16, 1993.

S. Grossberg and E. Mingolla, "Neural dynamics of form perception: Boundary completion, illusory figures, and neon color spreading," *Psychological Review*, Vol. 92, pp. 173-211, 1985.

A.S. Rojer and Schwartz, "A quotient space hough transform for space-variant visual attention," *Neural networks for vision and image processing*, pp. 408-436, 1992.

M. Seibert and A.M. Waxman, "An Approach to Face Recognition Using Saliency Maps and Caricatures," In Proceedings of the World Congress on Neural Networks (WCNN-93), III-661-664. M.A. Turk and A.P. Pentland, "Face Recognition using Eigenfaces," *Journal of Cognitive Neuroscience*, March 1991.

A Parallel Channel Binocular Vision Neural Network Model

Thomas Y.P. Lee and Clark C. Guest
Department of Electrical and Computer Engineering
University of California, San Diego, La Jolla, CA 92093-0407

ABSTRACT

Stereo vision, which creates the sensation of visual depth, results from the neural response to dissimilarities in the images seen by the two retinas. Psychophysical studies have strongly suggested that stereo disparity exists in the human visual system, and forms the basis for three-dimensional depth perception in the brain. This subject has been studied by many scientists using various approaches. Recently, several vision biologists have proposed a human binocular neural interaction model. Base on their discovery, we modify Neocognitron's mathematical equations proposed by K. Fukushima, and simulate this multilayer neural network model with binocular images on a digital computer. This model provides binocular depth performance close to the biological data.

1. INTRODUCTION

The scene input through the two eyes is segregated from the retinas up to the visual cortex. Cortical neurons and the lateral geniculate body neural interconnections are organized in two sets of ocular dominance columns that each receive input from one of the eyes. Neurophysiologists studying this structure have concluded that binocular interaction neuron cells exist in the visual cortex of the brain. Hubel and Wiesel [1] were the first to discover binocular interaction cells in the upper and lower layers of the cortex that receive input from both eyes. The two most important conclusions of their discovery, are: (1) The cells of receptive fields in the visual cortex consist of "simple" cells and "complex" cells and (2) Several types of simple receptive fields exist, differing in the spatial distribution of excitory and inhibitory regions. Other biological experimental reports have been contributed by G.F. Poggio [2]; P.O. Bishop, et al. [3]; C.Blakemore [4]; and I. Ohzawa and R.D. Freeman [5]. G.F. Poggio [2] concluded that in the macaque monkey, a substantial portion of both complex and simple neurons are differentially sensitive to horizontal binocular disparity. Different subsets of excitory or inhibitory neurons respond to a small disparity range. P.O.Bishop [3] discovered that binocular interaction fields in the cat striate cortex consist of some neurons with weak monocular responses, binocular gate neurons interconnection types, and binocular opposite direction selective neurons. C.Blakemore [4] provided evidence of constant depth columns and constant direction columns for disparity detecting neurons. More recently, I. Ohzawa and R.D. Freeman [5,6] studied the binocular organization of simple cells and complex cells in the cat's visual cortex. They concluded that most of the simple cells show phase-specific binocular interaction, and the complex cells combine outputs from a small number of simple type receptive fields. The results of these studies suggest that the binocular interaction neurons are capable of forming a depth solution and that they extract stereoscopic features. The disparity-detecting neuron interconnection of our model is primarily based on these biological data.

In the field of computational vision, binocular stereo vision has also been studied by scientists. B. Julesz [7] used random-dot stereograms to demonstrate that the stereo module is separated from other vision modules. D. Marr [8] suggested feature-based matching algorithms. T.D.Sanger [9] used the differences in the complex phase of local spatial frequency components of Gabor filters for stereopsis computation. C.C.Chang [10] used the Markov Random Field (MRF) theory and Simulated Annealing (SA) to model the disparity field from image data. Although these approaches demonstrate stereo computation capability, none is related to the neural network model. Y.Hirai and K.Fukushima [11,12] previously proposed a binocular depth-perception neural network model that can find binocular correspondence predicted by neurophysiologists. These neurons are selectively sensitive to a particular orientation and position of the stimulus. More recently, M.Nomura, et al. [14] proposed a mathematical model for simple cell response based on G.F.Poggio's [13] experiments. It uses two Gabor-type receptive fields that have the same spatial frequency and orientation, then integrates input from both eyes and performs a nonlinear threshold operation. Their binocular disparity cell model consists of tuned excitory, tuned inhibitory, near and far cells. As of this date, the full functionality of excitory and inhibitory connection has not been explored in the above models.

2. STEREO NEURAL VISION AND STEREO DISPARITY

Figure 1 illustrates the geometry for a binocular stereo-imaging system consisting of stereo cameras that have a common focal length f, and a baseline distance D. Assume an object is located at P. The relative difference in positions between the image points corresponding to its projections onto the left and right image planes is defined as the stereo disparity associated with the pair of image points.

$$d = (x^r, y^r) - (x^l, y^l) \tag{1}$$

If we use one of the stereo image pairs as the reference image and the other as the target image, the goal of the stereo matching process is to locate the corresponding points in the target image for the points in the reference image. Although the stereo matching process is usually characterized as an ill-posed problem in early vision studies, and many methods have been suggested before [8], our goal is to demonstrate a neural network stereo matching process to compute the stereo disparity.

In the next section, we propose a binocular neural vision model to compute the binocular disparity (depth). We will summarize our computer simulation results in Section 4 and present the conclusion in Section 5.

3. BINOCULAR NEURAL INTERACTION MODEL

Figure 2 shows the complete neural interconnection structure. This model primarily consists of two parallel neural channels. The first layer of each is a monocular feature extraction layer; there are several simple cell planes in this layer. Each of these planes extracts preferred orientation features of the stereo image pairs. On the left monocular feature extraction layer, the right image is used as an inhibitory input to extract the features from the left image. The same principle applies to the right feature extraction layer. At the next stage, the binocular complex gate neural layer combines input from both the left monocular feature extraction neural layer and the right monocular feature extraction neural layer using two pairs of asymmetric excitory and inhibitory weight connection matrices. The output response of this layer forms the input to the binocular integration neural layer. A mutual inhibitory connection is applied to both the left and right binocularly opposite direction selective neural layer. Each of these binocularly opposite direction selective neural layers are connected by a pair of symmetric excitory and inhibitory weight connection matrices. The outputs of these layers are summed into the binocular integration neural layer. The symmetric and asymmetric excitory and inhibitory weight connection matrices used in our model are taken directly from the biological data obtained by P.O. Bishop, et al., [3] and G.C. DeAngelis et al. [15]. P.O. Bishop's data indicate that for binocularly opposite direction-selective neurons, each eye has a receptive field which is excitory for one direction of stimulus movement and inhibitory for the other direction. G.C. DeAngelis provides strong evidence to show that the optimal stimulus disparity is determined by the difference in phase between the excitory and the inhibitory profile.

In Figure 3, we show the connection diagram for the left and right image planes to the monocular feature extraction neural layer. The neural interconnection between the left and right image planes to these feature planes is expressed in Eqns (2) and (3) which have both modifiable excitory weight matrices and inhibitory inputs. Equation (2) defines the

feature plane representation of the j-th plane in the left monocular feature extraction layer., where, in the equation $a^j_{l\,1}(v)$ and $b(r_1)$ represent the modifiable weight matrices, and $d_{r\,l}(v)$ represents the inhibitory weight connection matrix. The strength of connection can be modified through control of the constant in the equation. We modify the equations previously published by K. Fukushima [16] for this layer. The difference is that while Fukushima uses this equation for monocular input image feature extraction, we use it for binocular input image pair feature extraction. The numerator of equation (2) stands for the excitory input from the left image plane, and the denominator of equation (2) stands for the inhibitory input from the right image plane. The same principles apply to the right monocular feature extraction layer which is represented in Eqn (3).

$$S^j_{l\,1}(\mathbf{n}) = r_{l\,1} \cdot \varphi \left[\frac{1 + \sum\limits_{v \in A_{l\,1}} a^j_{l\,1}(v) * i_l(\mathbf{n}+v)}{1 + \dfrac{2r_{l1}}{1+r_{l1}} \cdot b(r_1) \cdot \sqrt{\sum\limits_{v \in D_{r1}} d_{r\,l}(v) * i_r{}^2(\mathbf{n}+v)}} - 1 \right] \quad \text{where} \quad \varphi(x) = \begin{cases} x & \text{if } x \geq 0 \\ 0 & \text{if } x < 0 \end{cases} \tag{2}$$

$$S^j_{r1}(\mathbf{n}) = r_r 1 \cdot \varphi \left[\frac{1 + \sum\limits_{v \in A_{r1}} a^j_{r\,1}(v) * i_r(\mathbf{n}+v)}{1 + \dfrac{2r_{r1}}{1+r_{r1}} \cdot b(l_1) \cdot \sqrt{\sum\limits_{v \in D_{l\,l}} d_{l\,l}(v) * i_l{}^2(\mathbf{n}+v)}} - 1 \right] \tag{3}$$

The binocular gate neural layer acts as a gate for visual depth or disparity features. Stimulus passes through this layer only if it is located at the precise depth in space where the excitory region of one input image is congruent with the inhibitory region of the other input image [3,5]. The connection diagram from the monocular feature extraction simple neural layer to binocular gate neural layer is shown in Figure 4. The output of this layer, which comes from multiple cell planes is described in Equation (4). The matrix $S_{l1}^j(\mathbf{n+v})$ represents the left monocular feature extraction neural layer, $S_{r1}^j(\mathbf{n+v})$ represents the right monocular feature extraction neural layer. $a_{l\,g}^j(v)$ and $a_{r\,g}^j(v)$ are the fixed synaptic weight connection matrices for the left monocular feature extraction neural layer and the right monocular feature extraction neural layer respectively. Matrix $a_{l\,g}^j(v)$ is symmetric with respect to the horizontal axis of the weight connection matrix. The disparity sensitivity d is built into these weight connection matrices. The constant α determines the saturation of the feature output response of the cell planes.

$$C_{g1}^j(\mathbf{n}) = \Psi\left[\frac{1+\sum\limits_{v\in A_{l\,g}} a_{l\,g}^j(v)*S_{l\,1}^j(\mathbf{n+v})}{K_g}\cdot\frac{1}{1+\frac{1}{K_g}\cdot\sum\limits_{j=1}^{}\sum\limits_{v\in A_{l\,g}} a_{l\,g}^j(v)*S_{l\,1}^j(\mathbf{n+v})} - 1\right] + \Psi\left[\frac{1+\sum\limits_{v\in A_{r\,g}} a_{r\,g}^j(v)*S_{r1}^j(\mathbf{n+v})}{K_g}\cdot\frac{1}{1+\frac{1}{K_g}\cdot\sum\limits_{j=1}^{}\sum\limits_{v\in A_{r\,g}} a_{r\,g}^j(v)*S_{r1}^j(\mathbf{n+v})} - 1\right] \quad (4)$$

where $\Psi(x) = \begin{cases} \dfrac{x}{x+\alpha} & \text{if } x\geq 0 \\ 0 & \text{if } x<0 \end{cases}$ and $a_{l\,g}^j(v) = a_{l\,g}^j(x\text{-}d,y;\lambda,\theta)$, $a_{r\,g}^j(v) = a_{r\,g}^j(x\text{+}d,y;\lambda,\theta)$

The interconnection from the monocular feature extraction neural layer to the binocularly opposite direction selective neural layer is shown in Figure 5. The binocularly opposite direction selectivity neural layer [3] is similar to the neural interconnection mechanism in the monocular feature extraction layer except that the inhibitory input is averaged before convergence from the left and right monocular feature extraction layers. The outputs of this layer, $C_{l\,2}^j(\mathbf{n})$ and $C_{r\,2}^j(\mathbf{n})$, consist of multiple cell planes described in Eqns (5) and (6). $a_{l\,2}^j(v)$ and $a_{r2}^j(v)$ are the fixed synaptic weight connection matrices for the left monocular feature extraction neural layer and the right monocular feature extraction neural layer, respectively. The matrix $a_{l\,2}^j(v)$ is asymmetric with respect to the horizontal axis of the weight connection matrices. These matrices are similar to $a_{l\,g}^j(v)$, in which the disparity sensitivity d is built into the weight connection matrices. These equations show that the interconnections are different from the binocular gate neural layer in the sense of asymmetric excitory and inhibitory weight connection matrices.

$$C_{l\,2}^j(\mathbf{n}) = \Psi\left[\frac{1+\sum\limits_{v\in A_{l\,2}} a_{l\,2}^j(v)*S_{l\,1}^j(\mathbf{n+v})}{1+\frac{1}{K_2}\cdot\sum\limits_{j=1}^{K_2}\sum\limits_{v\in A_{r\,2}} a_{r\,2}^j(v)*S_{r\,1}^j(\mathbf{n+v})} - 1\right] \quad (5)$$

$$C_{r\,2}^j(\mathbf{n}) = \Psi\left[\frac{1+\sum\limits_{v\in A_{r\,2}} a_{r\,2}^j(v)*S_{r\,1}^j(\mathbf{n+v})}{1+\frac{1}{K_2}\cdot\sum\limits_{j=1}^{K_2}\sum\limits_{v\in A_{l\,2}} a_{l\,2}^j(v)*S_{l\,1}^j(\mathbf{n+v})} - 1\right] \quad (6)$$

The binocular integration neural layer is constructed according to principles found in I. Ohzawa, et al., [6,17] and Y. Hirai, et al [11,12]. They concluded that binocular non-phase-specific complex cells have subunits whose optimal relative phases are random or monocular. Additionally, they discovered the linearity of binocular summation in receptive field subunits. Equation (7) describes the principle of this layer. In the equation, $a_{b3l}^j(v)$ and $a_{b3r}^j(v)$ are the synaptic weight connection matrices from the left and right binocularly opposite direction selective neural layer. $a_{b3g}^j(v)$ is the synaptic weight connection matrix from the output of binocular gate neural layer. Both the excitory and the inhibitory synaptic weight connection matrices are non-phase specific. The modifiable strength is set up according to the same principle used by the left and the right monocular feature extraction layer.

I-601

$$S_{b3}^{j}(n) = r_{b3} \cdot \varphi \left[\frac{1 + \sum\limits_{v \in A_{b3l}} a_{b3l}^{j}(v) * C_{l\,2}^{j}(n+v) + \sum\limits_{v \in A_{b3r}} a_{b3r}^{j}(v) * C_{r\,2}^{j}(n+v)}{1 + \frac{2r_{b3}}{1+r_{b3}} \cdot b(b3) \cdot \sqrt{\sum\limits_{v \in A_{b3g}} a_{b3g}^{j}(v) * C_{g1}^{j\,2}(n+v)}} - 1 \right] \tag{7}$$

4 . COMPUTER SIMULATION

Using the same tree stereo images as C.C. Chang[10], we show by computer simulation that the computation of horizontal disparity achieves using this neural network model. The simulation results of our model are shown in Figures 7. The disparity responses of each of the cell planes in each layer are coded as image intensity.

5. DISCUSSION AND CONCLUSIONS

The neural stereo vision model will have many commercial and military applications. Examples include automatic vision systems for extracting 3-D information, autonomous vehicle navigation, and automatic parts inspection used by industrial assembly lines.

In this paper, we have presented a binocular visual neural network model to compute the disparity response for real stereo pairs of images. The model and its performance closely match the performance predicted by some of the biological data. Although this model is extremely complex, our data only show a preliminary result.

The authors wish to thank Dr. C.C. Chang and Dr. S. Chatterjee for the use of their stereo image data.

6. REFERENCES

1. D.H. Hubel, T.N. Wiesel," Stereoscopic Vision in Macaque Monkey," *Nature*, Vol. 225, pp. 41-42, 1970.
2. G.F. Poggio, " Processing of Stereoscopic Information in Primate Visual Cortex," in Dynamic Aspects of Neocortical Function, G.M. Edelman, W. Einer Gall, W. Maxwell Cowan, eds.; John Wiley and Sons, New York, 1984.
3. P.O. Bishop, G.H. Henry and C.J. Smith, "Binocular Interaction Fields of Single Units In The Cat Striate Cortex," *Journal of Physiol.* 216, pp. 39-68, 1971.
4. C. Blakemore," The Representation Of Three-Dimensional Visual Space In The Cat's Striate Cortex", *Journal of Physiol.* Vol. 209, pp. 155-178, 1970.
5. I. Ohzawa, R.D. Freeman, "The Binocular Organization Of Simple Cells in the Cat's Visual Cortex," *Journal of Neurophysiology*, Vol. 56, No. 1, pp. 221- 242, July 1986.
6. I. Ohzawa, R.D. Freeman, "The Binocular Organization Of Complex Cells in the Cat's Visual Cortex", *Journal of Neurophysiology*, Vol. 56, No. 1, pp. 243-259, July 1986.
7. B. Julesz. "Binocular Depth Perception," *Bell System Technical J.*, Vol. 39, pp. 1125-1162, 1960.
8. D.Marr,T.Poggio."A Computational Theory of Human Stereo Vision,"*Roy. Soc. of London*, B-204,pp.301-328, 1979.
9. T.D. Sanger, "Stereo Disparity Computation Using Gabor Filters,"*Biological Cybernetics*, Vol.59, pp. 405-418, 1988.
10. Chienchung Chang, "Area Based Methods for Stereo Vision: Computational Aspects and Their Applications," Ph.D disseration, University of California, San Diego, CA, 1991.
11. Y. Hirai, K. Fukushima, " An Inference Upon Neural Network Finding Binocular Correspondence," *Biological Cybernetics*, Vol 31, pp. 209-217, 1978.
12. Y. Hirai, K. Fukushima, "A Model of Neural Network Extracting Binocular Parallax," *Biological Cybernetics*, Vol. 18, pp. 19-29, 1975.
13. G.F. Poggio, B. Fischer, "Binocular Interaction and Depth Sensitivity in Striate and Srestriate Cortex of Behaving Rhesus Monkey," *Journal of Neurophysiology*, Vol. 40, pp. 1392-1405, 1977.
14. M. Nomura, G. Matsumoto, and S. Fujiwara, "A Binocular Model for the Simple Cell," *Biological Cybernetics*, Vol. 63, pp. 237-242, 1990.
15.G.C. DeAngelis, I.Ohzawa, R.D. Freeman, "Depth is Encoded in the Visual Cortex by a Specilized Receptive Field Structure," *Nature*, Vol. 352, pp. 157-159, July 1991.
16. K. Fukushima, S. Miyake, and Takayuki Ito, " Neocognitron: a Neural Network Model for a Mechanism of Visual Pattern Recognition,", *I.E.E.E. Transactions on Systems, Man and Cybernetics*, Vol. SMC-13, pp. 826-834, 1983.
17. A. Macy, I. Ohzawa, R.D. Freeman, "A Quantitative Study of the Classification and Stability of Ocular Dominance in the Cat's Visual Cortex," *Exp. Brain Research*, Vol. 48, pp. 401-408, 1982.
18. M. R.M. Jenkin, A.D. Jepson, " The Measurement of Binocular Disparity," in Computational Processes in Human Vision: an interdisciplinary perspective," edited by Z.W. Pylyshyn, Norwood, N.J., Albex Pub. Corp., 1988.

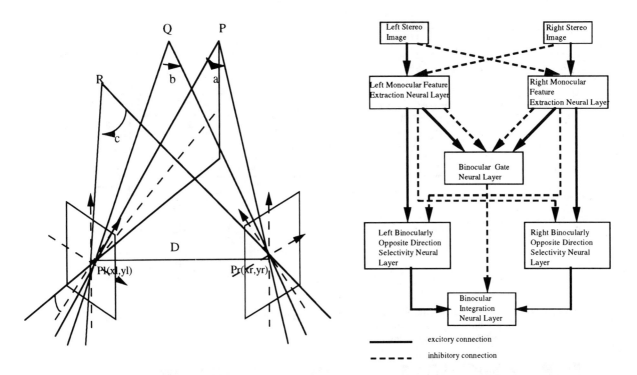

Figure 1. Epipolar geometry of a binocular neural image system

Figure 2. The binocular neural interaction channel derived from left channel to right channel and right channel to left channel,the final result is the combination of these channels.

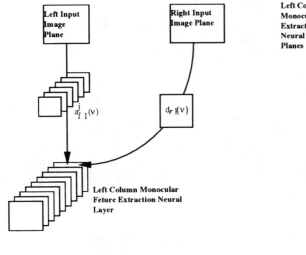

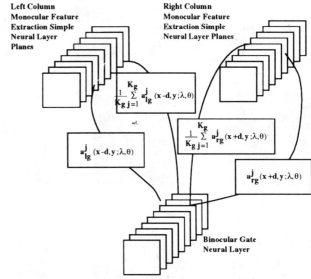

Figure 3. The connection diagram from the left and right image plane to the monocular feature extraction neural layer

Figure 4. The connection diagram from monocular feature extraction neural layer to binocular gate neural layer. The binocular feature response planes are detected by the summation of disparity detected filters.

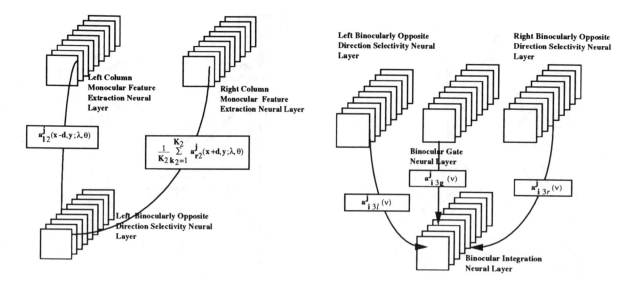

$$a^j_{l2}(x-d,y;\lambda,\theta)$$

$$\frac{1}{K_2}\sum_{k_2=1}^{K_2}a^j_{r2}(x+d,y;\lambda,\theta)$$

Left Column
Monocular Feature
Extraction Neural
Layer

Right Column
Monocular Feature
Extraction Neural Layer

Left Binocularly Opposite
Direction Selectivity Neural
Layer

Left Binocularly Opposite
Direction Selectivity Neural
Layer

Right Binocularly Opposite
Direction Selectivity Neural
Layer

Binocular Gate
Neural Layer

$$a^j_{i3g}(v)$$

$$a^j_{i3l}(v)$$

$$a^j_{i3r}(v)$$

Binocular Integration
Neural Layer

Figure 5. The connection diagram from monocular feature extraction neural layers to binocularly opposite direction selectivity neural layer.

Figure 6. The connection diagram for binocular integration neural layer

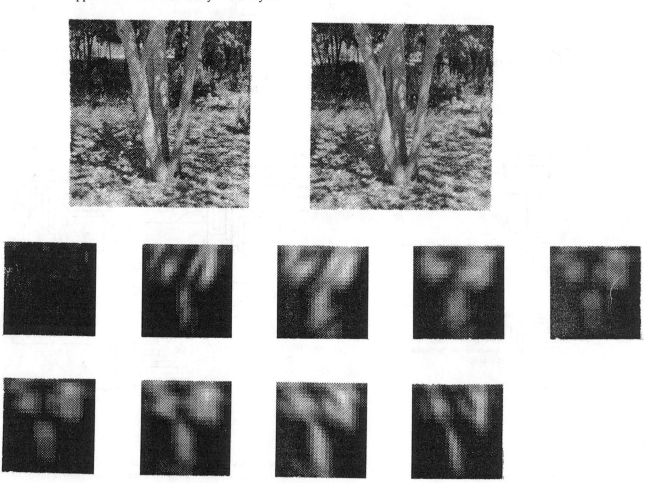

Figure 7. The simulation results with binocular parallel channel neural network model for tree stereo image pairs: the disparity planes coded as image intensity on binocular integration neural layer.

Selectivity of Feature Detection Weights for a Neocognitron-like, Image Analysis Neural Network

Peter Soliz
John P. DiTucci
Applied Sciences Laboratory, Inc.
P.O.Box 21158 Albuquerque, NM 87154

Mark Culpepper
Greg Tarr
Phillips Laboratory (AFMC)
Kirtland AFB, NM 87117

Abstract

The neocognitron, proposed and pioneered by N. Fukushima, has inspired vision-based neural network research at a number of centers throughout the world. The self-organizing approach to feature selection and pattern classification is often plagued with long training times and selection of features which may or may not have significance to the application. For the more interesting image classification problems, the neocognitron has extremely large memory requirements to accommodate connecting weights. Pre-training feature selectivity can lead to a closed form solution to Fukushima's neocognitron, which in turn can result in the elimination of the tedious training requirement of the lowest layer. When combined with a clustering type of neural network, which takes advantage of the neocognitron feature selection, this hybrid neural network performs image analysis and classification of complex objects in a much more efficient manner than Fukushima's traditional neocognitron. The hybrid neural network loses none of the highly desirable features of the neocognitron. It is shift invariant, distortion tolerant, and has been extended to extract complex, gray-scale features. A neocognitron inspired neural network is suggested which runs significantly faster and with significantly less memory requirements. The Phillips Laboratory has embarked on an aggressive research program to assess vision-based neural networks in a number of applications, including automatic image analysis..

1.   Introduction.

The Air Force Phillips Laboratory is researching techniques for automatic, near real-time processing of optically-sensed images of a variety of man-made objects. To take advantage of the rich possibilities offered by a neural network which detects and extracts physical features, the Phillips Laboratory sponsored research has selected the neocognitron for its vision-like approach to image analysis. The hybrid ANN's approach for pattern recognition at higher levels is based on "feature discovery" implemented through a neocognitron-like algorithm at the lower levels. The success in using a multi-step procedure that extracts features before attempting a pattern recognition has been demonstrated by a number of researchers[1,2,3]. There are aspects of the vision problem that an implementation of a pattern/object recognition system using only the neocognitron does not perform readily. A hybrid approach has been implemented successfully by the aforementioned researchers who employ the neocognitron for feature extraction and a network like adaptive resonance theory (ART) for the classification problem.

Instead of the computationally intensive approach employed by the researchers for feature extraction and image analysis, an alternative approach is being studied. Features will be extracted from new images with a directed training approach which will not require large weight fields or laborious iterative training. Data for feature characterization and weight determination are provided by the computer-aided model database. Object identification can be performed with simpler and more appropriate neural networks. Similar hybrid approaches have been successfully demonstrated.

2.   Background

Although it is not known with total certainty how the human performs pattern recognition, it is generally understood that it involves a matching of the visual stimulus with stored memory. A number of pattern-recognition theories have been advanced to explain the processes involved in the matching of the long-term memory information with the visual stimulus. Among them are feature theories and that advanced by Gestalt psychologists [4]. The framework within which the human vision system processes the visual stimulus and corresponding computational analogs is described especially well by D. Marr [5] and Grossberg [6]. Pattern or object recognition is performed through a process which is highly dependent on our ability to extract primitives or tokens which are representative of shapes. Visual stimuli are processed in successive stages, where the first stage extracts features like edges, and the final stage involves advanced vision processes like spatial organization of complex 3-D features.

Marr contends that this representational framework for deriving shape involves three levels:

- Primal Sketch - which extracts geometric and intensity information from a two-dimensional image.

- 2 1/2-D Sketch - which describes the orientation and rough depth, and discontinuities.

- 3-D Sketch - which represents the pattern with spatially organized shapes.

In the primal sketch, where many of today's pattern recognition applications are focused, the primitives which are being analyzed are the pixel intensities, edge segments, blobs, zero crossings, and there is some analysis of groups, boundaries and curvalinear organization. The more difficult primitives in the primal sketch, such as virtual lines, groups, terminations and discontinuities, are often not treated with the same attention as the former list of primitives. The primitives in 2 1/2-D sketch, which include local surface orientations, depth, and discontinuities in depth and surface orientation, are rarely treated explicitly in most pattern recognition systems.

Implementations of vision-based artificial neural networks have addressed only narrow aspects of Marr's ideas on computational vision. This situation has led to neural networks which are limited in their application to image recognition problems. For example, Fukushima's neocognitron has demonstrated extremely good capability in character recognition problems where the pixel data contain binary images [7]. The neocognitron has been used successfully in extracting features from an image plane containing a complex object, such as a vehicle. Researchers, including the authors, have repeatedly shown the neocognitron to be shift invariant and distortion tolerant. Issues related to training time for features in complex scenes and objects with any possible 4-π steradian orientation have also been mentioned and solutions attempted..

Fukushima [8] proposes a neural network paradigm that models some aspects of the architectural theme of human vision. He achieves the objective of feature extraction through a series of localized feature detectors in his implementation of the neocognitron. The neocognitron is a hierarchical neural network, where the input layer is a two-dimensional array of pixels (the image). Each layer has a number of planes, consisting of two-dimensional arrays of S-cells and C-cells. The purpose of the S-layer is to detect the presence of a particular feature in the preceding C-layer. Through the presentation of sample patterns, the neocognitron is trained so that S-cells respond (highest output) to certain features. As the training proceeds, each S-plane becomes selectively sensitive to a feature in the image pattern. Details on how neocognitrons are trained and a background on their development will not be presented in this paper, but are given by Fukushima [9]. The C-planes in the last layer contain a single C-cell each. If one were training the neocognitron on the ten numerals, then the neocognitron would be constructed such that the last layer would have ten C-planes. Each of the planes would train to recognize a different numeral. When activated, the plane would signify recognition of the number it had learned to recognize. A similar behavior would be exhibited for a neocognitron trained, for example, to differentiate between two or more objects. There would be at least as many C-planes in the last layer as there were objects.

Conceptually, the neocognitron extracts features by scanning an image plane with a receptive field of finite size, seeking to match a certain feature with a number of feature planes in the first layer. This process is illustrated in Figure 1. The letter "A" can be thought of as having three simple features: a horizontal line and two lines slanted in opposite directions. Each feature is detected in a number of places in the image planes, as depicted by the activation of the cells in the second layer. Each successive layer operates in the same manner, except that in the higher layers (layers 2 and greater), the receptive field scans for patterns in the features detected by the previous layer. The result is an integration of features by the higher layers until classification occurs. This concept has been demonstrated by a number of researchers, including the authors, in a number of applications.

Because for most applications the patterns to be recognized are not presented as block letters in the center of the field of view, the algorithm for feature detection must be insensitive to translation (object off-center in the field of view) and tolerant of distortions (for example, handwritten letters). Figure 1 shows how the neocognitron solves these problems. Since the algorithm scans the entire image plane with its receptive field, the feature may occur anywhere and the neocognitron will find the feature. As with the mammalian vision system, the neocognitron was developed to account for distortions. The weights (excitatory and inhibitory) will illicit a response in the S-cells for patterns that are not exactly the learned pattern. The tolerance for accepting distorted features can be tuned by the "similarity term" in the neocognitron.

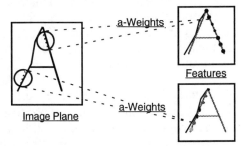

Figure 1. Feature Detection and Integration in a Neocognitron.

The "learning" of combined features in the higher layers of the neocognitron is often a computer intensive process. To overcome this problem, a popular approach has been to exploit the neocognitron's aptitude for feature extraction, then apply a different type of neural network, usually a clustering paradigm, to combine features into a higher level pattern recognition system.

3.   Closed-form Approach to Feature Selectivity

The principal equations for Fukushima's neocognitron are given below. Equation [1] gives the activation of a cell in the feature detection planes of the first layer, l. As one can see, the activation is a function of the a-weights, the input image (U_c), the b-weights, the inhibitory plane (V_c) and the similarity constant, r_l. In Fukushima's scheme, his goal is to train the network to recognize unspecified features in the input plane by allowing the a- and b-weights to learn a set of features through a competitive learning process. For the first layer, only the a- and b-weights are unknown and must be solved for unspecified features through Fukushima's iterative process.

For some applications, as with a mature human, recognition of an object or a pattern is not a learning process which starts with "random features". Humans learn to distinguish between classes of objects by comparing previously learned (therefore pre-selected) features. If one were to specify all the features one wished the neocognitron to detect, then the equations could be solved for a unique set of b-weights. If, for the moment, the calculation of weight values for the remaining layers is not of concern, a cognitron can be developed to detect features in the input plane without the time-consuming iterative process of Fukushima.

$$U_{sl}(k_l, \mathbf{n}) = r_l \bullet \phi \left[\frac{1 + \sum \sum a_l (k_{l-1}, v, k_l) \bullet U_{c l-1} (k_{l-1}, \mathbf{n}+v)}{1 + \dfrac{r_l}{1 + r_l} \bullet b_l(k_l) \bullet V_{c l-1} (\mathbf{n})} - 1 \right]$$
[1]

$$V_d(\mathbf{n}) = \sqrt{\sum \sum c_{l-1} (v) \bullet U_{c l-1}^2 (k_{l-1}, \mathbf{n}+v)}$$
[2]

$$\Delta a_l(k_{l-1}, v, \widehat{k_l}) = q_l \bullet c_{l-1} (v) \bullet U_{c l-1} (k_{l-1}, \mathbf{n}+v)$$
[3]

$$\Delta b_l(\widehat{k_l}) = q_l \bullet c_{l-1} (v) \bullet V_{c l-1} (\mathbf{n})$$
[4]

The first step in this directed training process is to select the features which one wishes the neocognitron to detect. The a-weights are adjusted so that there is an orientation of the weights toward the selected feature. This process specifies the excitatory weights. The calculation of the inhibitory weights can also be performed knowing the input image, U_c, and the c-weights. The b-weights are calculated using Equation [4]. In a single scan of the image plane, U_{c0}, the activation fields for the first layer, U_{s1}, for each feature (set of weights) can be calculated explicitly without an iterative algorithm.

A directed feature pre-selection version of the neocognitron has been developed based on the same general formalisms originally proposed by Fukushima [7]. Because of the highly structured nature of the problem which is being addressed in this application, where it is highly desirable to be able to pre-select manually the features of greatest interest, it is possible to prescribe excitatory- and inhibitory-weights analytically. An algorithm which combines the feature detection process popularized by Fukushima with a modification of his excitatory-inhibitory functions and the technique for calculating these functions has been developed and tested on imagery of a variety of geometrical objects.

Using Fukushima's notation, the activation for a plane is shown in equation [5] to be a function of an excitatory function, f_{ex} and an inhibitory function, f_{in}. The excitatory contribution to the activation is given by equation [6] as the dot product of the weight field and the receptive field on the image plane, normalized by the weight field. This means that a value of unity will result when there is a perfect match of the pixels in the image plane and the weight vector. If one allows arbitrary values of pixel values, i.e. gray levels, then values greater than one are possible. An inhibition function is needed to suppress activity when a receptive field in the image plane causes too much activity due to high pixel values in areas where there is a positive but lower value in the weight vector. Similarly, the activation should be inhibited when there are high pixel levels where no activity exists in the weight field. Calculating cell activation in this manner is not unlike Grossberg's [10] approach for determining resonance in his adaptive resonance theory neural network (ART-1). Equation [7] shows how the effects of these two situations on the activation of a cell may be mitigated.

$$U_s \propto f_{ex}(\vec{U}_c, \vec{A}) \bullet f_{in}((\vec{U}_c, \vec{A})$$
[5]

$$f_{ex}(\vec{U}_c, \vec{A}) = \frac{\vec{A} \bullet \vec{U}_c}{\vec{A} \bullet \vec{A}}$$
[6]

$$f_{in}(\vec{U}_c, \vec{A}) = \exp\left(\frac{\left|\vec{A}\cdot\vec{A} - \vec{A}\cdot\vec{U}_c\right| + \left|\vec{A}\cdot\vec{A} - \vec{U}_c\cdot\vec{U}_c\right|}{(\vec{A}\cdot\vec{A})\cdot r}\right)$$

[7]

Processing time and memory requirements have been reduced significantly by employing this directed training approach for extracting the first level features from the image plane. A desirable consequence of the use of the above activation functions has been applicability either to binary images, such as character recognition, or to multi-gray-scale images. At this stage, one can proceed using Fukushima's learning algorithm, or one may choose a more suitable neural network paradigm for integrating the spatial and intensity extent of the extracted features. This is the approach of a number of researchers including Moya[1], Hush[2], Pulito[3], McKinstry[11], Lincoln[12], and others.

Although the vision-based neocognitron neural network has performed well in feature discovery and object recognition, its strength is in performing the former, and it is less efficient in integrating the features in the final recognition step. For the integration of the features detected by the neocognitron, a neural network has been implemented which can more easily take advantage of knowledge about the relative importance of key features. The parallel in humans would be their ability to recognize a partially obscured object or target based on the detection of a single but unique feature. In the second stage, an adaptive resonance theory (ART) neural network is being used to form the final recognition. A two-stage self-organizing neural network architecture was used to recognize an object at any arbitrary azimuthal angle. The first stage performs feature extraction and implements a one-layer neocognitron. The resulting feature vectors are presented to the second stage, a clustering-type neural network like an ART [13] classifier network, which clusters the features into multiple target categories. The aforementioned researchers (Moya[1], Hush[2], McKinstry[11], and Pulito[3]) are meeting with extremely good success using this architecture.

4.   Application in Feature Detection and Classification

Ultimately, the objective of this research will be to determine the pose of a 3-D object by extracting object features from a single 2-D image. Features will be selected from a number of representative orientations. The feature selection approach described above will be used to search and extract these features when they appear in an image. Since these features often are not unique and may in fact be blurred, noisy, or distorted due to the sensors limitations and atmospheric effects, the detection of the features will have some uncertainty. As was mentioned earlier, because of the large number of possible orientations of an object, viewing geometry and illumination angles, all cases cannot be searched sequentially. Using representative features is essential, as for the human standing on a street corner looking for a particular type of automobile. He will discount trucks and buses at a distance because they lack many of the distinguishing features of automobiles. Once he recognizes an automobile, the search narrows and focuses on more specific features, such as the difference between a sports car and a sedan, *etc.* In a similar manner, a hierarchical approach is being implemented to make orientation determination of any 3-D object.

To date the hybrid neural network system described has bee used successfully in a number of target recognition applications. With the strong emphasis within the Department of Defense and other government organizations, it is encouraging that the neural network system which has been developed, in part through Phillips Laboratory sponsorship, is applicable to a number of pattern classification problems. Below are two examples of the potential for transferring the vision-based technology to law enforcement as well as cell biology. Figure 2 shows a set of figure prints which are easily distinguishable by the hybrid neural network. In Figure 3, a microscope image showing cells from amniotic fluid. The vision-based neural network has been applied successfully in detecting the cells which display the DNA in a manner suitable for analysis.

At this time other applications of a vision-based neural network are being explored. Figure 2 shows a sample of the set of fingerprints used in the training of the vision-based neural network for a personnel identification security system. Figure 2a shows the left thumbprint used as the pattern to be matched by the neural network. Figure 2b and 2c are examples of other prints presented that were not the left thumbprint in question. The vision-based neural network rejected all these other prints. Experiments showed that the vision-based neural network was capable of identifying correctly a fingerprint with noise. The vision-based neural network recognized the pattern with as much as 30 percent occlusion (or loss of data). Automated analysis of cell patterns in amniotic fluid for DNA pattern matching is being conducted. A sample of the imagery for analysis is presented in Figure 3. The vision-based system consistently detected the "open" cell pattern that is sought for cytogenetics.

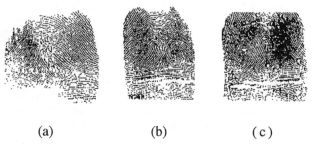

(a)   (b)   (c)

Figure 2. Fingerprint samples.

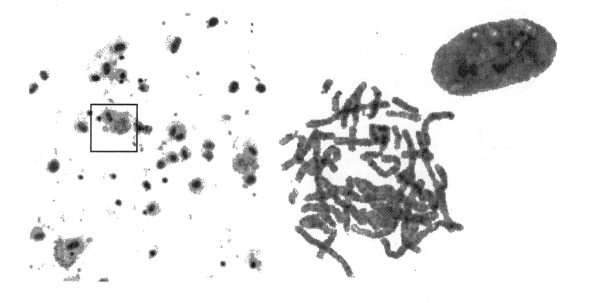

Figure 3.   (a) 10 x magnification display of a typical view of amniotic fluid through a microscope. Cell structure sought is given in (b) at 100 x magnification.

<u>Summary</u>

In this study a technique for feature selection was demonstrated which eliminates the need for an iterative search technique to train the sets of excitatory and inhibitory weights for a neocognitron-type of network. Since many researchers are not using the higher layers of the neocognitron, but rather are turning to neural networks like the ART, the need to train for feature weights is eliminated altogether.

References

1.   Moya, M. M., M.W. Koch, and L.D. Hostetler. "One-class classifier networks for target recognition applications." *World Congress on Neural Networks*, Portland, OR, 1993.
2.   Hush, D. R., M.M. Moya, and S-Y. Clark. "Constrained Neural Network Architectures for Target Recognition. "*Proc. SPIE Aerospace Sensing Symposium*, Apr. 1992 (INVITED PAPER).
3.   Pulito, B. L., T.R. Damarla, and S. Nariani. "A two-dimensional shift invariant image classification neural network which overcomes the stability/plasticity dilemma." *International Joint Neural Network Conference* II-825-833, 1990.
4.   Wertheimer, M. *Productive Thinking* (2nd Ed.). New York: Harper & Row, 1958.
5.   Marr, D. *Vision..* San Francisco: W.H. Freeman and Company.
6.   Grossberg, S. *The Adaptive Brain I: Cognition, Learning, Reinforcement, and Rhythm, and the Adaptive Brain II: Vision, Speech, Language, and Motor Control.* Elsevier/North-Holland, Amsterdam, 1986.
7.   Fukushima, K. "Neocognitron: A Hierarchical neural network capable of visual pattern recognition." *Neural Networks*, 1:119-130, 1988.
8.   Fukushima, K. "Neocognitron: A self-organizing neural network model for a mechanism of pattern recognition unaffected by shift in position." *Biological Cybernetics*, 36:193-202, 1980.
9.   Fukushima, K. "Neural network model for selective attention in visual pattern recognition and associative recall." *Applied Optics*, 26(23), 1987, pp 4985-4992.
10.   Grossber, S. "Competitive learning: From interactive activation to adpative resonance, Cognitive Science, 11:23-63.
11.   McKinstry, J., T. Ruff, and A. Ott. "The neocognitron for viewpoint invariant automatic target recognition." *Government Neural Network Applications Workshop*. Wright-Patterson AFB, OH, 1:39-43, Aug. 1992.
12.   Lincoln, W. P., C.E. Daniell, W.A. Tackett, and G. A. Baraghimian. "The SAHTIRN™ System for ATR." *Government Neural Network Applications Workshop*. Wright-Patterson AFB, OH, 1:105-109, Aug. 1992.
13.   Carpenter, G. A., S. Grossberg, and D.B. Rosen. "ART 2-A: An adaptive resonance algorithm for rapid category learning and recognition." *Neural Networks*, 4, 1991.

Cortical Perceptual Processing Mapped into an Active Resistor Network

Luigi Raffo, Silvio P. Sabatini, Giacomo Indiveri
Daniele D. Caviglia and Giacomo M. Bisio

Department of Biophysical and Electronic Engineering
University of Genova-Via all'Opera Pia 11/A-16145 Genova-ITALY
ph: +39 10 3532163, fax: +39 10 3532795, e_mail: luigi@dibe.unige.it

Abstract

Recently an isotropic resistive network that performs a Gaussian filtering of an image for pre-processing tasks in image analysis has been proposed. In this paper, starting from biological considerations on cortical organization, we propose an anisotropic resistive network able to extract local features of an image, that can be used to detect variations of texture and to perform higher level visual tasks.

1 Introduction

A great deal of visual tasks is solved by animals and humans in a preattentive phase, without focusing of attention. In this phase, vast arrays of intercommunicating, identical processes carry out low-level vision tasks such as perceiving edges by texture differences, depth mapping, computing optical flow, recovering local surface structure, segmenting images, etc. To extract information relevant to movement or action (e.g. of a robot) it is fundamental that such low-level processes can be performed in real time. Thus, analog hardware devices, with embedded image sensing, are of great interest in machine vision. In such devices, information, indeed, is really distributed, being mapped directly in the electrical variables, and computation is carried out massively in parallel with high efficiency and speed. In the perceptual phase, the brain analyzes the scene and extracts symbolic information to form an abstract representation of the external environment [1]. Hence, the tasks involved in this phase are 1) to map from the original pattern of light intensities to intermediate abstract representation by means of appropriate receptive fields and 2) to arrange information in functional mapping apt to help all subsequent processes to come up with useful image descriptors.

In this paper we present an active resistor network in which different orientation-selective neurons, are simultaneously realized on the same layer, according to a simulated orientation domain of the mammalian visual cortex. Each neuron (or node) has a receptive field that is characterized by an elongated two-dimensional Gabor-like profile. Network performance is evaluated to test its potential use in compact machine-vision systems.

2 Neurophysiological basis for complex stimulus perception

Computational solutions evolved by nature, are particularly valuable in designing neural devices for optimal feature extraction, and neuromorphic architectures to solve perceptual tasks.

At first stages of perception, retinal ganglion cells provide local contrast information to higher stages. Combining such information, receptive fields of striate cortex become complex enough to handle symbolic information. In the striate cortex a wide class of cortical cells are characterized by elongated receptive fields with parallel subregions alternately driven by stimuli of opposite contrast, that can be closely fitted by two-dimensional Gabor functions. The properties of these functions in maximizing the joint selectivity in space and frequency domain, and their efficacy in optimal image filtering have been widely investigated [4][9].

I-612

The characteristics of such operators guarantee the extraction of information on both the orientation and the spatial frequency of the local visual stimulus and allow a multi-channel approach for image analysis. However, to solve simple visual tasks, we need blending information from different channels [5]. More specifically, a simultaneous analysis of small areas of the image by multiple differently oriented filters, compatibly with the sensor resolution, and functional interactions among them, are required to enhance their selectivity to orientation contrast. To fulfill these demands, the mammalian visual system resorts to two computational principles, embodied in its structure. First, the existence of a retinotopic mapping preserves topological relations of the input images so that two nearby points in the retinal image activate nearby points on the cortical surface. Second, orientation-selective neurons are horizontally arranged in an ordered fashion (orientation map) to help cooperation and competition among different orientations with minimal wiring demand.

The organization of the orientation-selective cells in the visual cortex fulfills two golden rules: (1) all orientations are well-represented in a small area, (2) in a more restricted area neurons have similar orientation preference. Several models, driven by functional considerations [2] or mathematical description of real orientation maps [10], have been presented and simultaneously, experimental research provided new insights on the organization of the orientation maps. Two examples of biological-plausible maps are depicted in Fig.1.

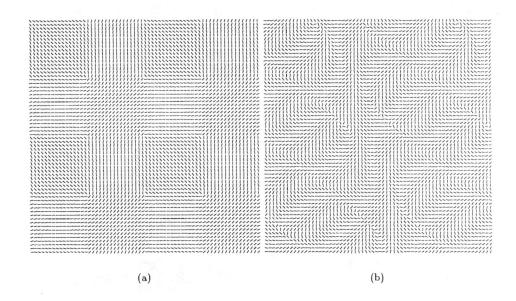

(a)   (b)

Figure 1: Examples of biological plausible orientation maps: (a) a plaid-like map and (b) a more realistic one.

3   The Architecture of the Resistive Network

The starting point is the schema shown in Fig. 2 for an isotropic square grid network: g_1 is the conductance value of positive interconnected resistors; $g_2 = -g_1/4$ is the value of negative resistors, and g_0 is the value of node-to-ground resistors. The 2D distribution of the current sources represents the input image. The output image is represented as the node voltage distribution of the array. The steady-state signal processing functionality of the network is completely described by the shape of the node voltage response to a constant current excitation at a single node. For the mesh in Fig. 2, such a response is similar to a Gaussian function centered around in the excited node; the width of the Gaussian function depends on the (g_1/g_0) ratio.

To generate elongated Gaussian functions, we consider an extra positive resistor of conductance G from the node, in the direction of the orientation selectivity we need [7].

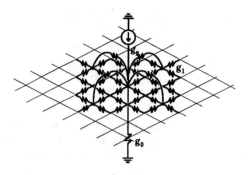

Figure 2: The basic schema of the connections from a node: an input current proportional to the luminous intensity is provided by a photoreceptor, that is here represented by a generator.

To improve the spatial frequency selectivity, a Gabor-like convolution kernel should be used. Following the approach described [7], we add two negative resistors for each node, arranged in the direction orthogonal to the one to which the node is selective and at a distance related to the width of the modulating Gaussian function (see Fig. 3a for the case $\pi/4$ and inhibition radius 3). In Fig. ??b, a Gabor-like operator with the orientation preference $\pi/4$ is depicted: it has been obtained by a 31×31 grid, and by inhibition radius 6.

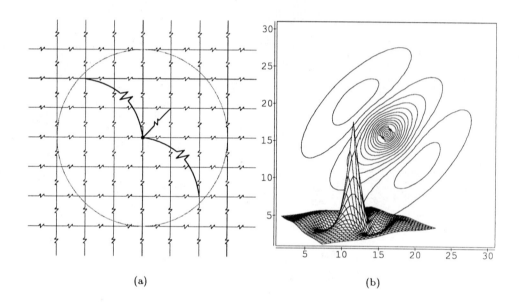

(a)   (b)

Figure 3: (a)Connections to obtain a Gabor-like operator oriented along $\pi/4$ with inhibition radius 3. (b) Perspective and contour plots for the Gabor-like operator oriented along $\pi/4$ with radius 6 for a 31×31 node.

This result can be extended to the implementation of orientation maps by varying the pattern of interconnections of the resistor mesh in a continuous fashion [8].

Among all the biological plausible orientation maps that are in accordance with the above-mentioned golden rules, we will refer here to the two shown in Fig. 1 which allow us to have uniform areas, large enough to obtain well shaped and well-oriented convolution kernels. The minimal portion of the array containing nodes selective to all the orientations present in the map will be refered in the following as the basic *module* of the map.

4 Experimental results

Our network is able to detect texture differences in an image by different responses of cells selective to different orientations, as other networks based on biological considerations do [9][3]. Indeed, if the test image is composed of repeated oriented elements, the cells in the regions of the map selective to that orientation have the strongest output.

For testing network performances we have considered at first a synthetic image containing four different oriented textures (see Fig. 4a. In Fig. 4b the output of the network that implements the cortical map on the left shown in Fig. 1a is depicted subdivided in domains (collecting all considered orientations). Ignoring the border effect, we can note that regions with uniform texture lead neurons to have similar domain responses. More generally different texture structures correspond to different patterns of excitation on the cortical map. The output of the orientation map can be used as the basis for a post-processing phase to provide a texture classification. This is not sufficient on its own to solve segmentation processes and an efficient strategy to bind features must be introduced.

There is a strong evidence that in real visual cortex, the average characteristics of local-field potentials may aggregate local information of small assemblies of neurons selective to a complete set of orientations. The spatio-temporal characteristics of such local-field potentials yield global perception about edges separating one region from another and determine regions on the basis of continuity of structure.

The development of a suitable algorithm to solve on the same devices the binding problem will be argument of a future work. However, to show that global coding is conceptually feasible, we made an effective color display of texture information assigning different colors to different orientations and modulating the luminous intensity according to the activity of the neurons. In order to consider a global coding the color-merging is simulated with an average operation. The value of each component is obtained by averaging the output over an array portion centered in the node of the same size as the map's module.

Under this assumptions it is possible to discriminate a number of textures equal to all the nuances of the color palette. In the last image of Fig. 4c the result of this operation subjected to the constraints of the gray-level representation is shown. Network performances on natural texture image (Fig. refnata) have been evaluated and the results obtained with the two maps in Fig. 1 are shown in Fig. 5bc.

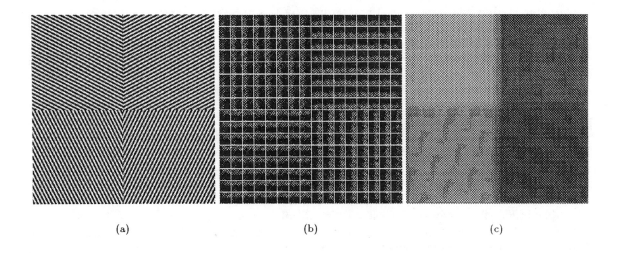

(a)　　　　　　　　　　(b)　　　　　　　　　　(c)

Figure 4: (a) the synthetic textured pattern image, (b) the output of the network subdivided into orientation domains, (c) the global coding of textural information (see text).

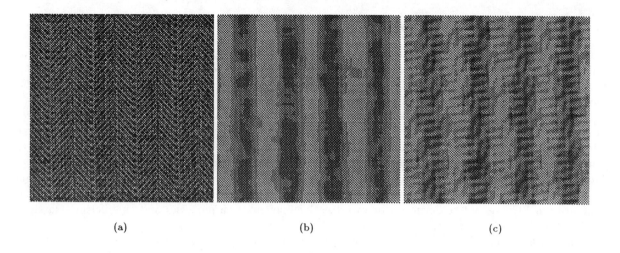

(a)   (b)   (c)

Figure 5: From left to right: a natural textural image and the segmentated images for the cortical maps of Fig. 1.

5 Discussion and Conclusions

The active resistor network presented in this paper, provides an efficient hardware solution to real-time low-level visual tasks. The topology of the network allows, indeed, an efficient feature extraction and image representation, but should also provide an effective solution for subsequent local symbolic interactions, particularly useful for texture segregation.

Moreover, we have shown how complex operators for low-level image processing can be mapped, with low effort, directly in the structure of a resistor network. Such network reveals itself particularly robust, indeed, the choice of the value of the resistances is not critical since the final orientation of the convolution kernels is more a consequence of the topology of connections than of a proper choice of these values.

Concerning the implementability on VLSI hardware of this network, we have to express it in terms of a set of computational primitives, representing the resources available for the realization of the system, and of the rules that determine the interactions among the blocks implementing those primitives. While in a digital system the primitives are simple logical operators (AND, OR, NOT, . . .), in analog neural system the functionalities of the primitives present higher complexity, even if the rules are represented by Kirchoff's laws. In particular, in the network here presented, we can identify three basic primitives: resistors, active resistors and photoreceptors.

Various choices are available to the circuit designer for the implementation of such primitives: fixed resistors can be implemented in silicon with paths of diffusions with assigned resistivity; properly biased MOS transistors can act as variable resistors; active resistors can be implemented by more complex circuitry, such as operational amplifiers or negative impedance converters; finally, photoreceptors can be implemented through p-n junctions (photodiodes or phototransistors), being its reverse current proportional to the incident light intensity. The previous choices determine the number of nodes (i.e. pixels) the network is able to process. By example, in [6] on a silicon area of $8mm \times 9mm$ using a $2\mu m$ CMOS technology and phototransistors that take up a $26\mu m \times 54\mu m$ silicon area, an exagonal grid of simmetrical gaussian operators 45×40 is proposed. In such implementation the dimensions of the operators are controlled by a variable resistor (g_0), which is responsible of the 75% of the power dissipation.

The network we propose considers additional resistors to implement Gabor-like oriented receptive-fields for higher level processing; though we disregard the variability of the resistors in order to dissipate less power and increase operator density. It is not so easy (or, at least, not possible on a cost basis) to meet constraints on power dissipation and area occupation, with present commercially available technologies, for a network of 256×256 nodes, however the design of a smaller network is under development.

I-616

References

[1] M.A. Arbib and A.R. Hanson. *Vision, Brain, and Cooperative Computation*. MIT Press, 1987.

[2] W.T. Baxter and B.M. Dow. Horizontal organization of orientation-sensitive cells in primate visual cortex. *Biol. Cybern.*, 61:171–182, 1989.

[3] G.M. Bisio, D.D. Caviglia, G. Indiveri, L. Raffo, and S.P. Sabatini. A neural model of cortical cells characterized by Gabor-like receptive fields-Application to texture segmentation. In I.Aleksander and J. Taylor, editors, *Artificial Neural Networks 2*, volume 2, pages 917–920. Elsevier Science, 1992.

[4] J.G. Daugman. Uncertainty relation for resolution in space, spatial frequency, and orientation optimized by two-dimensional visual cortical filters. *J. Opt. Soc. Amer.*, A/2:1160–1169, 1985.

[5] S. Grossberg, E. Mingolla, and D. Todovoric. A neural network architecture for preattentive vision. *IEEE Trans. Biomed. Eng.*, 36:65–83, 1989.

[6] H. Kobayashi, J.L. White, and A.A. Abidi. An active resistor network for Gaussian filtering of images. *IEEE J. on Solid State Circuits*, 26:738–748, May 1991.

[7] L. Raffo, S.P. Sabatini, D.D. Caviglia, and G.M. Bisio. Anisotropic active resistor meshes for implementing image processing operators. *Electronics Letters*, 29(11):960–961, May 1993.

[8] L. Raffo, S.P. Sabatini, D.D. Caviglia, and G.M. Bisio. Artificial visual orientation map implemented as inhomogeneous active resistor mesh. *Electronics Letters*, 29(11):963–964, May 1993.

[9] M.R. Turner. Texture discrimination by Gabor functions. *Biol. Cybern.*, 55:71–82, 1986.

[10] F. Wörgötter, E. Niebur, and C. Koch. Isotropic connections generate functional asymmetrical behavior in visual cortical cells. *J. Neurophysiol.*, 66:444–459, 1991.

NEUROEXPERT – An Automatic Neural Network Based System for Image Blur Identification

Sławomir Skoneczny and Rafał Foltyniewicz

Institute of Control & Industrial Electronics,
Warsaw University of Technology,
00–662 Warszawa, ul. Koszykowa 75, Poland
tel. (+48–2) 6280665, fax. (+48–2) 6256633, e–mail: skonecz@plwatu21.bitnet or
rfoltyn@plwatu21.bitnet

Abstract

The first step in restoring a degraded image is the identification of the type of degradation the image has suffered. A fundamental issue for image restoration is blur removal. Blur can be introduced by an improperly focused lens, relative motion between the camera and the visual scene or atmospheric turbulence. The more accurate, we can describe blur phenomenon of degraded image the more precisely we can construct the proper filter, which results in high quality restoration. In this paper we present a very efficient and robust method of blur identification by applying a combined neural classifier called NEUROEXPERT built of three separated networks (basic classifiers). This system learns power cepstra, SVD cepstra and high order spectra (bispectra) of blurred images during the training period and the basic classifiers vote in recognizing phase. This assures a very high reliability of degradation identification (98% of correctly identified blurs for single encountered case and about 90% for mixture of different blurs in one image), which allows to build completely automatic image restoration system. Theoretical investigations and practical result are presented.

1 Introduction

The problem of deblurring images with a known point spread function (PSF) has been dealt extensively in the image processing literature. The blurred image is modeled as the output of a noncasual unknown linear impulse response. A model of the system that causes, the degradation could be obtained analytically from the physical nature of the problem if there is sufficient *a priori* information. In most real-life situations, however, it is not possible to have enough *a priori* information to determine the PSF analytically and the blur must be identified from the blurred image itself. In this situation it is helpful to have a parametric description of blurring function. Lee in [2] showed that, it is possible to parameterize the PSF with a few parameters knowing only the type of blur. This is an attractive alternative in blur identification, especially when the number of these parameters is less than the number of the PSF coefficients. For linear motion blur it is only necessary to estimate the direction of blur and blurring distance. With the simplified model for an out–of–focus blur it is sufficient to estimate the radius of the circle of confusion. Because both of these blurs have an oscillatory frequency response with a characteristic zero–crossing pattern, it is advantageous to identify them in the spectral or cepstral domain under the assumption that the blur is locally space invariant, which is often encountered in practice. We have successfully solved this difficult blur identification problem by applying neural network multiclassifier called NEUROEXPERT.

2 Problem Statement

A degradation process of image can be expressed by using an equation

$$\mathbf{g} = [h]\mathbf{f} + \mathbf{v} \qquad (1)$$

where $\mathbf{f}$ and $\mathbf{g}$ are column matrices containing the samples from the original object and the degraded image respectively. The blur matrix [h](also called point spread function or PSF) is derived from the impulse response of the degrading system and $\mathbf{v}$ is a column matrix (vector) containing noise samples (for example due to the detector). The problem is: given $\mathbf{g}$ estimate $\mathbf{f}$. The necessary condition for image restoration is $[h]$ identification.

Another possibility is to formulate discrete model for each pixel

$$g(x,y) = h(x,y) * f(x,y) + v(x,y) \qquad (2)$$

where $*$ denotes convolution.

The effects of blurs can be better interpreted in the frequency domain. Then we have

$$G(u,v) = H(u,v) \cdot F(u,v) + V(u,v) \qquad (3)$$

So we have to identify the PSF function $[h]$. In our paper we restrict ourselves to the most often encountered blur types: camera motion blur (CM), out of focus blur (OOF) and atmospheric turbulence blur (AT).

3 Neural Method of Blur Identification by Cepstral Techniques

A well-known approach to identify h(x,y) is to compute the cepstrum by g(x,y). The cepstrum is defined as

$$C_g(p,q) = \mathcal{F}\{log|G(u,v)|\} \qquad (4)$$

where $\mathcal{F}$ denotes the Fourier transform. One of the most important features of the cepstrum is that if two signals are convolved, their cepstra add. Thus, neglecting the effects of noise

$$C_g(p,q) = C_f(p,q) + C_h(p,q) \qquad (5)$$

If we express (3) in terms of power spectra we obtain

$$\Phi_g(k,l) = \Phi_f(k,l)|H(k,l)|^2 + \Phi_v(k,l) \qquad (6)$$

It is more efficient to apply power cepstrum instead defined as

$$P_g(p,q) = \mathcal{F}\{log[\Phi_g(k,l)]\} \qquad (7)$$

and neglecting the noise

$$P_g(p,q) = P_f(p,q) + 2C_h(p,q) \qquad (8)$$

The multilayer perceptron with backpropagation learning algorithm was apply to teach the cepstra of the observed images (training set). During the recognizing phase the network is able to identify the blur with 90.5% correctly classified for one blur in image only and 82% for two types of blur in one image.

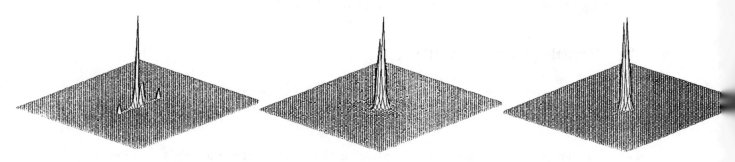

Figure 1: The Power Cepstra for CM, OOF, AT Blurred Image

4   Neural Identification of Blur Using the cepstra of SVD expansion

An blurred image given by $\mathbf{A}$ can be represented using Singular Value Decomposition (SVD) as:

$$\mathbf{A} = \mathbf{U}\mathbf{\Lambda}\mathbf{V}^{T} \tag{9}$$

The unitary nature of $\mathbf{U}$ and $\mathbf{V}$ implies the following relations:

$$\mathbf{U}\mathbf{U}^{T} = \mathbf{I}$$
$$\mathbf{V}\mathbf{V}^{T} = \mathbf{I} \tag{10}$$

We represent blurred image $\mathbf{A}$ by its SVD expansion taking the sum of maximally 10 eigenimages.

$$\mathbf{A}_{10} = \sum_{i=1}^{10} \lambda_{ii}\mathbf{u}_i\mathbf{v}_j^{T} \tag{11}$$

and the mean–square truncation error becomes

$$||\mathbf{A} - \mathbf{A}_{10}||^2 = \sum_{i=10}^{R} \lambda_{ii} \tag{12}$$

where R is the rank of $\mathbf{A}$ and the matrix norm is the Euclidean measure, $\mathrm{tr}\mathbf{A}^T\mathbf{A} = ||\mathbf{A}||^2$. The motivation for utilizing the SVD expansion is that such a small number of eigenimages provides a good representation of $\mathbf{A}$. In a noiseless case (or almost noiseless after prefiltering) the rank of the blur image $\mathbf{A}$ is determined by the minimum of the ranks of blurring matrix and original image matrix. But the blurring matrix is sparse and of low rank. So the truncation error is small. We can take advantage of the fact that if we compute the power cepstrum of such expanded image we generalize it and make decreasing the ideal image part (by rejecting some higher eigenimages) in cepstrum and emphasizing the blur contribution which is easy automatically recognized by neural network. We apply backpropagation algorithm presented in ([4]).

5 Neural Network Blur Identification Using the Bispectrum

Instead of identifying PSF using cepstra we can take advantage of high-order statistics of the degraded image. Chang [1] suggested an interesting method of blur estimation. This method proposes inspecting the zero crossing in the central slice of the bispectrum [3] of the observed image.

It is assumed again that the blurring process, in the exposure domain, can be modeled by a linear, shift–invariant system as

$$g(m,n) = \sum_{(i,j) \in S_h} h(i,j) f(m-i,n-j) + v(m,n) \tag{13}$$

where $g(m,n)$ and $f(m,n)$ are the observed and the ideal images respectively, $h(m,n)$ denotes the PSF function of the blur, S_h is the support of the PSF, and $v(m,n)$ denotes additive, Gaussian observation noise.

The bispectrum of the observed 2–D image $g(m,n)$ in 13 is given by

$$
\begin{aligned}
B_g(\omega_1,\nu_1;\omega_2,\nu_2) &= H(\omega_1,\nu_1)H(\omega_2,\nu_2)H^*(\omega_1+\omega_2,\nu_1+\nu_2)B_f(\omega_1,\nu_1;\omega_2,\nu_2) \\
&+ B_v(\omega_1,\nu_1;\omega_2,\nu_2)
\end{aligned} \tag{14}
$$

Since $v(m,n)$ is Gaussian, $B_v(\omega_1,\nu_1;\omega_2,\nu_2)$ is identically zero, and can be dropped from (14). Then setting $\omega_2 = 0$ and $\nu = 0$ in (14), we consider a 2–D cross section, or a central slice, of the bispectrum of the observed image, given by

$$B_r(\omega_1,\nu_1;0,0) = |H(\omega_1,\nu_1)|^2 H(0,0) B_s(\omega_1,\nu_1,0,0) \tag{15}$$

Assuming that $H(0,0)$, and there are no periodic zero crossings in $B_f(\omega_1,\nu_1;0,0)$, the zeros of $|H(\omega_1),\nu_1|^2$ can be observed as the "central slice" $B_g(\omega_1,\nu_1;0,0)$ of the bispectrum of the output image.

The estimation procedure is as follows. The observed image has been segmented into N segments, which are possibly overlapping. The segments are rectangular, where the dimensions of the rectangle can be chosen according to the type and expected extent of the blur. Discretizing the frequencies ω_1 and ν_1, the estimate of the central slice of the i–th segment, using the direct method [3], is given by

$$B_g^{(i)}(k,l;0,0) = G_i(k,l) R_i(0,0) G_i^*(k,l) \tag{16}$$

where $G_i(k,l)$ is the Discrete Fourier Transform of the ith segment of the observed image. It is important to note that the mean of the entire observed image is removed before it is segmented, which implies that the average of $G_i(0,0)$ over all i is zero, although $G_i(0,0)$ is, in general, not zero for each i. The estimate of the "central-slice" $B_g(k,l;0,0)$ is taken as the average of the "central-slices" of the bispectra of each segment

$$B_g(k,l;0,0) = \frac{1}{N} \sum_{i=1}^{N} B_g^{(i)}(k,l;0,0) \tag{17}$$

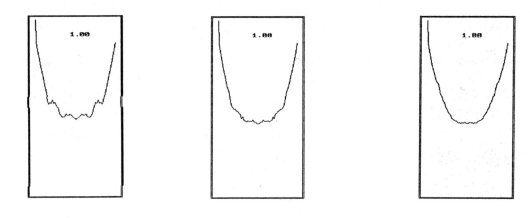

Figure 2: The Central Slices of Bispectra for CM, OOF,AT Blurred Image

The multilayer perceptron network is taught the estimate of the "central slice" of the bispectrum of the observed image (blur training set). After the learning phase the network is able to recognize camera motion, out of focus and atmospheric turbulence blurs (testing set different from learning set) with about 91% efficiency for simple blur but only with about 55% correctly classified patterns for the mixture of two blurs in one picture. It is clear that we need more complicated classifying system (with voting classifiers at least for two blurs at once).

6   Computer Simulation Results

All the experiments were done for 32×32 images with 64 grey levels on IBM compatible i486 DX-2 /66Mhz based computer. The software package has been built in C language.

We have built a NEUROEXPERT system based on three voting neural network classifiers (parallel classification). This idea seems to be very fruitful. Three multilayer perceptron networks are used each being taught different transform (different feature vector), having different number of neurons and requiring different number of learning epochs.

- FIRST EXPERIMENT –SINGLE BLUR
  The training set consisted of 27 blurred images (27 human faces blurred by one of three types of blur camera motion, out of focus and atmospheric turbulence). The testing set consisted of 162 blurred images. Each blur had three different parameter values indicating blur severity.

- SECOND EXPERIMENT –MIXTURE OF TWO BLURS IN ONE IMAGE
  The training set consisted of 27 blurred images with two blurs in each image and the testing set of 162 images of the same kind.

First neural network has 1024 neurons in the input layer, 50 and 30 neurons in first and second hidden layers, 3 neurons in the output layer. It uses cepstral transform for learning and recognizing. While working as a separate classifier it has 90.5% of correct classification in the first experiment and 82.1% in the second experiment.

Second neural network consists of 1024 neurons in the input layer, 50 and 25 neurons in hidden layers, 3 neurons in the output layer. It uses SVD cepstral transform (10 eigenimages

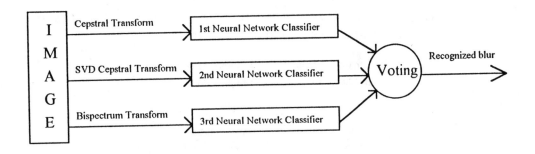

Figure 3: NEUROEXPERT System for Blur Classification

is taken into account). In separate classification it has 93.7% of correctly classified blurs in the first experiment and 81.5% in the second one.

Third classifier has only 32 neurons in the input layer (it needs to learn only a short feature vector), 40 and 20 neurons in the hidden layers and also 3 neurons in the output layer. It uses a "central slice" of bispectrum transform. As a separate classifier it reaches 91% in the first experiment and 55% for two blurs at once.

All these three neural networks vote (their votes are equally important) making this way an efficient automatic blur classification systems. The final rate of correctly classified blurs for NEUROEXPERT is 97.7% for simple blur indentification problem (first experiment) and 90% for two blurs in one image (second experiment).

It is interesting to note that even if one classifier seems to be inefficient in some experiment (bispectrum classifier in the second experiment) if it votes together with other classifiers (a little bit more efficient) **it increases the performance of the whole system significantly** so that the NEUROSYSTEM is **more efficient** than any separate classifier and because of this high efficiency can be use as a part of completely automatic image restoring system.

References

[1] M.M. Chang and A.M. Tekalp. Blur Identification Using the Bispectrum. *IEEE Transaction on Signal Processing*, 39:2323–2325, 1991. no. 10.

[2] H.C. Lee. Review of Image Blur Models in a Photographic System Using the Principles of Optics. *Optical Engineering*, 29, 1990. no. 4.

[3] Ch.L. Nikias and M.R. Raghuveer. Bispectrum Estimation: A Digital Signal Processing Framework. *Proceedings of the IEEE*, 75:869–891, 1987. no. 7.

[4] D.E. Rumelhart and J.L. McClelland. *Parallel Distributed Processing*. MIT Press, 1986.

An Ensemble Approach to Automatic Masking of Clouds in AVIRIS Imagery Using BCM Projection Pursuit

Charles M. Bachmann *, Eugene E. Clothiaux †, John W. Moore ‡,

Keith J. Andreano ◇ and Dong Q. Luong *

* Airborne Radar Branch
Radar Division,Code 5362
Naval Research Laboratory,
Washington, D. C. 20375
e-mail: bachmann@radar.nrl.navy.mil

† Department of Meteorology
Pennsylvania State University
University Park, Pennsylvania 16802
e-mail: cloth@essc.psu.edu

‡ Martin Marietta Services
2231 S. Crystal Park Dr.
Arlington, VA 22202-3735

◇ SWL
1900 Gallows Rd.
Vienna, VA 22182

Abstract- We describe the first-phase of an investigation into techniques for automatic cloud masking in remote sensing data. BCM Projection Pursuit (BCM) networks are explored as a method of unsupervised feature extraction from AVIRIS images. Search vectors in this method discover directions in the data in which the projected data is skew or multi-modal, by minimizing a Projection Index which depends on higher moments of the projected data distribution. We compare this approach against backward propagation (BP). In addition, we explore the use of ensemble techniques, which allow smoothing of the estimation process for more robust classification of image pixels. Predicted cloud masks are compared against cloud masks derived from human interpretation.

Introduction

The automatic identification of clouds and cloud type in remote sensing data poses a significant technical challenge to researchers in climate modelling. Human analysis of images is time-consuming, and automatic methods of scene-level and pixel-level identification are needed to cope with large volumes of image data. A number of researchers have investigated multi-class scene- and pixel-level identification of cloud type based on textural and spectral features [6], [7], [28], [26] using AVHRR (Advanced Very High-Resolution Radiometer) [10], [17] images. Examples of such features are moments of gray-level difference vector (GLDV) statistics [29], [4], sum and difference histograms (SADH) [27], [4] and gray-level run length (GLRL) [29]. Neural network techniques based on backward propagation (BP) [23], the probabilistic neural network (PNN), [25] and Kohonen's Learning Vector Quantization (LVQ) [18] have been used successfully to find meaningful information in these features and their inter-relationship for classification [28], [26] ; results compare favorably to traditional statistical analysis of the same textural features [28].

The present study examines techniques for pixel-level classification in AVIRIS (Airborne Visible and Infra-Red Imaging Spectrometer) imagery. In the first phase of our investigation, we looked only at the raw intensity data without textural and spectral pre-processing steps; a future paper will describe ensemble methods which simultaneously examine both raw data inputs and textural and spectral inputs as found in [7], [28], [26]. In this paper, we describe ensemble techniques which incorporate both unsupervised feature extraction networks, in this case BCM Projection Pursuit, as well as a supervised learning algorithm, BP, for mapping BCM features to a final classification. These results are compared against backward propagation alone. Classification results are generated for low-level cloud masks which only distinguish between pixels containing cloud and those containing no cloud. The problem of identifying cloud-type will be addressed in a future publication.

Unsupervised Feature Extraction Using BCM Projection Pursuit

Recent treatments of the BCM model [3] [5] [24] have shown its relation to the statistical approach known as Projection Pursuit [15] [16]. A Lyapunov function (cost function) for the modification rule can be defined for BCM; minimization of this function will favor directions where the projection distribution (projection onto the search vector) is statistically skew, i.e bi-modal or multi-modal (Figure 1).The BCM model uses a semi-local learning rule: search vectors are modified based on the information available within a single layer without reference to training labels; in

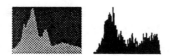

Figure 1: BCM Cell Response Histograms from two cells in networks trained with 16x16 pixel patches from AVIRIS Imagery.

contrast, supervised networks such as BP modify network connections in all layers based on a global error measure in the last layer.

The ith cell in layer n of a multi-layer BCM network responds according to: [1] [2]

$$\tilde{c}_i^{(n)} = \sigma(\sum_j L_{ij}^{(n)} c_j^{(n)}) \tag{1}$$

$with$

$$c_j^{(n)} = \vec{w}_j^{(n-1)} \cdot \vec{\tilde{c}}^{(n-1)} + b_j^{(n)} \tag{2}$$

$$L_{ij}^{(n)} = \begin{pmatrix} 1, for\ i = j \\ -\mu, for\ i \neq j \end{pmatrix} \tag{3}$$

where $L_{ij}^{(n)}$ is the fixed lateral inhibition [3] matrix of weights in layer n, $\vec{w}_j^{(n-1)}$ is the vector of connections to cell j in layer n from the prevous layer, $(n-1)$, and $b_j^{(n)}$ is the bias of cell j in layer n. The Lyapunov function in layer n is a statistical function emphasizing skewness of cell responses, or projections, in that layer: [4]

$$E[\xi^{(n)}] = -(\sum_i \frac{E[(\tilde{c}_i^{(n)})^3]}{3} - \gamma \frac{E^2[(\tilde{c}_i^{(n)})^2]}{4}) \tag{4}$$

This leads to a learning rule of the form:

$$\Delta \vec{w}_k^{(n-1)} = -\eta \frac{\partial E(\xi^{(n)})}{\partial \vec{w}_k^{(n-1)}} = -\eta \sum_i \frac{\partial E[\xi_i^{(n)}]}{\partial \tilde{c}_i^{(n)}} \frac{\partial \tilde{c}_i^{(n)}}{\partial c_k^{(n)}} \frac{\partial c_k^{(n)}}{\partial \vec{w}_k^{(n-1)}}$$

$$= \eta E[\sum_i \phi(\tilde{c}_i^{(n)}, \tilde{\theta}_i^{(n)})(\tilde{c}_i^{(n)})' L_{ik}^{(n)} \vec{\tilde{c}}^{(n-1)}] \tag{5}$$

with:

$$\phi(\tilde{c}_i^{(n)}, \tilde{\theta}_i^{(n)}) = \tilde{c}_i^{(n)}(\tilde{c}_i^{(n)} - \gamma \tilde{\theta}_i^{(n)})\ and\ \theta_i^{(n)} = E[(c_i^{(n)})^2] \tag{6}$$

$\gamma \theta_i^{(n)}$ is the dynamic modification threshold which separates regions where the ϕ-function yields Hebbian reinforcement and anti-Hebbian weakening in the single-cell theory. For a small and decreasing step-size, Equation 5 can be well approximated by stochastic gradient descent (see [16] for further details). The presence of the lateral inhibition means that the fixed points of the synaptic vectors of individual cells are coupled (Equation 5). Therefore, in a trained network, cells may find directions for which the projection distribution is not just bi-modal, but perhaps even multi-modal (Figure 1). The inhibition also promotes cell differentiation, so that features are less likely to be redundant.

Ensemble Methods

---

[1]The sigmoidal function is typically of the form: $\tilde{c}(x) = a \tanh(a\lambda x)$, which has the derivative: $\tilde{c}'(x) = \lambda(a - \tilde{c}(x))(a + \tilde{c}(x))$.

[2]Superscripts denoting layer indices appear in parentheses.

[3]The choice of $L_{ij}^{(n)}$ places each cell in a field proportional to the average response of the other cells in the layer. Other choices could be used to establish different fixed influence fields, for instance the Mexican Hat [18].

[4]$E[]$ represents the expectation value.

A number of researchers have explored the use of ensemble methods for the purpose of enhancing overall performance of neural network classifiers [12], [19], [13], [20], [21], [22]. The notion of pooling a set of "experts" is by no means confined to research in adaptive neural network algorithms. Whatever the nature of the underlying estimation process, ensemble methods can be employed profitably [11], [14], [20]. We illustrate the general framework for ensembles of estimators in Figure 2.

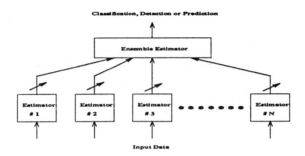

Figure 2: Schematic diagram of an ensemble of estimators. Each individual estimator may have a very large number of parameters as in non-parametric estimation proceedures such as neural networks, and the input data to each may be identical data sets or different representations of the same problem such as in sensor fusion. The ensemble estimator weights the estimates of members of the ensemble, and the relative weighting may be adapted.

Cloud Masking for AVIRIS Images: Experimental Design (First Phase)

In the initial phase of our research as described in this paper, we investigated aof ensemble networks. In one version of these ensembles, multiple BCM Projection Pursuit networks performed low-level, unsupervised feature extraction from input patches of AVIRIS images. Inputs to these networks were vectors containing the pixel values as a percentage of the dynamic range over the entire image. In some cases, we used a unit vector representation, which preserved the direction of the high-dimensional vector in input space, but normalized the length of the vector onto the unit sphere. The ouput of the BCM networks was fed to the input layer of a BP network which performed the mapping to pixel-level predictions. Error correction in the BP networks was done by comparing network pixel predictions against a ground truth mask generated by human interpretation. The unsupervised BCM networks were trained independtly before being attached to the BP networks. As a baseline, results were also obtained for 3-level BP networks operating directly on the input patches. A third experiment consisted of pooling the ensembles in the first set of ensembles and the single BP network to obtain an ensemble of ensembles. This last experiment is closer in spirit to the ensemble concept in [13] and [22], in which the actual output classifications of estimators are pooled. Network configurations for the experiments described here are reported in Table 1. LIBP [1] refers to BP run with fixed lateral inhibition, as in the feedforward rule for the BCM network; inhibition in the BP networks was found to be important for obtaining reasonable performance with 3-layer networks.

Table 1 Network Configurations: Single & Ensemble Nets					
Experiment	Net Type		Configuration		
BP1	Single	Level : 1	LIBP: (256-100-16)		
		Input:	Band 17		
Ens9	Ensemble	Level 2:	BP (256-100-16)		
		Level 1:	BCM80 (256-20)	BCM123 (256-40)	BCM134 (256-40)
		Preprocess:	None	None	Unit Vector
		Input:	Band 17	Band 52	Band 52
Ens10	Ensemble	Level 2:	BP (256-100-16)		
		Level 1:	BCM80 (256-20)	BCM123 (256-40)	BCM134 (256-40)
		Preprocess:	None	None	Unit Vector
		Input:	Band 17	Band 52	Band 52
Ens11	Ensemble	Level 2:	BP (256-100-16)		
		Level 1:	BCM80 (256-20)	BCM123 (256-40)	BCM134 (256-40)
		Preprocess:	None	None	Unit Vector
		Input:	Band 17	Band 52	Band 52
Ens12	Ensemble	Level 2:	BP (256-100-16)		
		Level 1:	BCM80 (256-20)	BCM123 (256-40)	BCM134 (256-40)
		Preprocess:	None	None	Unit Vector
		Input:	Band 17	Band 52	Band 52
Supens1	Ensemble of Ensembles	level 2:	LIBP (48-100-16)		
		level 1:	ens9 (2 level BCM-BP ensemble)	ens10 (2 level BCM-BP ensemble)	BP1 (256-100-16)
Supens2	Ensemble of Ensembles	level 2:	LIBP (32-100-16)		
		level 1:	ens9 (2 level BCM-BP ensemble)	ens10 (2 level BCM-BP ensemble)	

The AVIRIS data used in this set of experiments were comprised of 10 different images derived from 6 different locations under a variety of weather conditions; they included a variety of terrain, for example a land-sea interface, or agricultural areas; a number of different cloud types were also present. For each location, 4 bands were made available to us, three in the visible and one in the near infra-red, although the experiments in this phase only used two bands, Band 52 (near infra-red), and Band 17 (visible). Eight images were used for training and two for testing. More complete statistics using the bootstrap method will be obtained in the future. Note that in general setting a single threshold for the entire image will not suffice since this would lead to unacceptably high levels of false alarms in many of the images 3(a). Even if a single threshold were used, it would not be the same for each image(Figures 3(b) and 3(c). Each image contained 614x512 pixels.

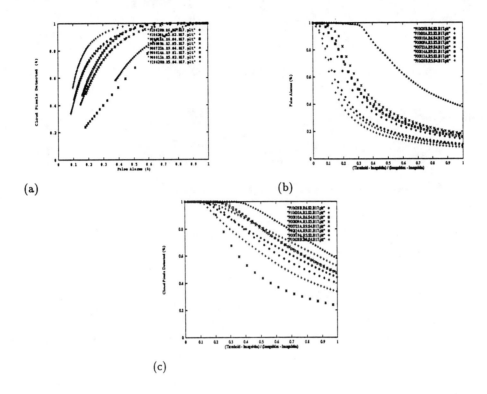

(a)   (b)

(c)

Figure 3: The results of trying to use a global threshold for cloud-masking in AVIRIS Band 17: in many of the images, good detection rates would come at the expense of a high false-alarm rate (a); even if a global threshold were used, it would be impossible to set a single threshold which would translate into the same level of performance across different images: (b) false-alarm rate vs. threshold (c) rate of cloud-pixel detection vs. threshold.

During training, images in the training set were selected at random and from each image, 16x16 patches were sampled at random as input to the networks. A number of different input patch sizes have been explored (8x8, 16x16, 32x32 and 64x64) to examine the qualities of the BCM feature vectors on different scales of area, although in the experiments described here for prediction input patches were all 16x16. An example of BCM feature vectors obtained from experiments with different input patch sizes is shown in Figure 4. The figure shows some particular network solutions which were strong edge detectors. Notice that local structure found in smaller patch vectors appears as a sub-component of the larger patch feature vectors. Feature vector structure in BCM takes on a variety of different forms depending on the control parameters η, γ, τ (τ is the temporal width of the sampling window for the sliding threshold $\gamma E(c^2)$ in the BCM rule). Other factors such as dwell-time on each image may also play a role. In experiments with larger values of τ, feature vectors may be banded or speckled (Figure 5) in appearance compared with those in Figure 4.

In the prediction experiments described in the Results section, the final prediction of the network ensembles and single networks was the identity of the pixels in the 4x4 sub-patch in the upper left corner of the input patch. Prediction masks were generated for the training and testing sets by scanning the entire image with the 16x16 pixel

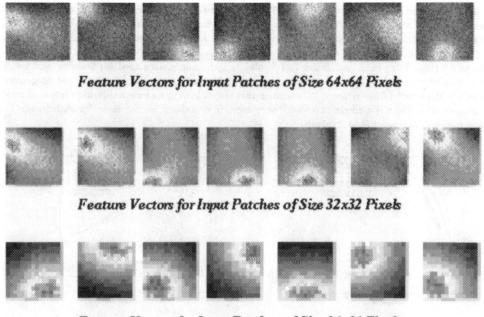

Feature Vectors for Input Patches of Size 64x64 Pixels

Feature Vectors for Input Patches of Size 32x32 Pixels

Feature Vectors for Input Patches of Size 16x16 Pixels

Figure 4: BCM feature vectors trained with AVIRIS Images (three networks with different patch sizes). These particular networks developed strong edge detection vectors.

input box. The box was moved in 4 pixel increments to obtain a complete prediction mask. This procedure meant that predictions were obtained for all pixels with the exception of a small strip on the bottom and right edges of the AVIRIS images. These strips comprised only $\sim$ 2% of the whole image. The results in Table 2 were generated by comparing network prediction masks against masks generated through human interpretation.

Results

BP Performance: Magnitude Sensitivity

The results of the phase 1 experiments are given in Table 2. BP has a high degree success on the first test image because it is fairly similar to some of the training images on which it was also successfully trained; this testing image and some of the images on which BP were the most successful are those for which fairly simple magnitude filtering might have fairly good results. However, BP does have some notable failures which are cause for concern; these are for training images 5, 6 and 7, for which the magnitude sensitivity of BP is a real drawback. Image 5 contains a lot of high magnitude land return which is confounded for cloud cover by BP; image 6 has thin cirrus over a land-sea interface, for which backprop fails to detect much of the cloud cover because it has a low return. In both of these cases, the required features vectors need to encode textural

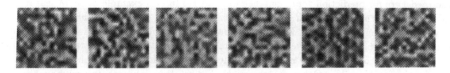

Figure 5: BCM feature vectors trained with AVIRIS Images; patch size is 16x16. These vectors appear to be sensitive to texture of the input patch; the feature vector has been smoothed to emphasize peaks and valleys. τ for the BCM sliding threshold was 29 times larger than that of the feature vectors for the 16x16 patch size in figure 4; the learning rate was also

information. Similarly, image 7 has bright land as seen through a diffuse layer of smoke from a forest fire. Mistakenly, this image is completely identified as cloud by BP1.

BCM-BP Ensemble Performance

What is notable about the ensembles incorporating both BCM and BP is that some of them appear to find solutions which achieve considerably greater classification accuracy than BP alone for images 5, 6 and 7. Ens9, for instance, has a respectable level of performance on both images 5 and 6; Ens10 has a strong performance on image 7. Ens9 and Ens10, incorporating BCM for low-level feature extraction, appear to have found textural information sufficient for performing some of these more difficult classifications. Ens9 has a respectable level of performance on all of the other images as well, but does not perform as optimally on the images for which a more simple magnitude thresholding might be sufficient; Ens10 has a respectable level of performance on all but three of the images. The other ensemble runs, Ens11 and Ens12, did not perform as well as Ens9 and Ens10.

Ensembles of Ensembles

The best ensemble of ensembles run was Supens2, which received input from Ens9 and Ens10. Across all of the images, it achieved the most consistent performance and the highest overall classification rate for the two classes for Image 5. For Image 6, it was only fractionally less accurate than Ens9 which achieved the highest level accuracy on this image. It achieved the second highest classification rate on Image 7; however,on Image 7 the only network achieving acceptable performance was Ens10. The ensemble of ensembles run, Supens1, is a low false-alarm classifier, receiving input from BP1, Ens9 and Ens10. Its overall performance on Image 5 is an improvement over the individual performances of the networks from which it is receiving input; for image 7, its performance is only slightly better than the mean of its components, for image 6, its performance was slightly worse than its subcomponents.

Table 2 Pixel-Level Classification of AVIRIS Images								
	Cloudiness	BP1	Ens9	Ens10	Ens11	Ens12	Supens1	Supens2
Training Images				% Cloud Pixels Correct % Non-Cloud Pixels Correct				
910628B.R6.S2	12 %	91.3 % 96.9 %	92.2 % 87.9 %	80.0 % 90.5 %	91.8 % 80.0 %	85.4 % 93.8 %	79.6 % 98.8 %	87.6 % 92.9 %
910620A.R2.S2	39 %	76.8 % 99.2 %	82.7 % 90.2 %	70.5 % 93.0 %	84.3 % 85.0 %	75.9 % 93.6 %	68.4 % 98.1 %	75.0 % 94.4 %
900810A.R6.S4	33.8 %	98.8 % 94.0 %	98.6 % 79.8 %	72.2 % 94.4 %	98.4 % 78.5 %	95.1 % 92.7 %	89.4 % 98.7 %	91.2 % 91.3 %
900809A.R3.S5	21.4 %	96.2 % 93.9 %	93.1 % 92.2 %	71.8 % 95.9 %	95.2 % 83.2 %	88.8 % 95.3 %	83.3 % 98.9 %	87.4 % 96.4 %
900723A.R9.S4	4.9 %	100.0 % 2.3 %	93.6% 73.8 %	73.4 % 92.2 %	99.2 % 8.5 %	93.4 % 76.9 %	85.1 % 85.8 %	89.5 % 82.5 %
900814A.R9.S1	51.0 %	36.7 % 96.8 %	75.7 % 74.0 %	45.0 % 89.6 %	62.1 % 81.8 %	33.0 % 96.7 %	32.1 % 98.6 %	75.0 % 75.4 %
900813A.R9.S3	0.0 %	— 0.0 %	— 6.4 %	— 93.3 %	— 2.1 %	— 6.3 %	— 37.2 %	— 48.5 %
900813A.R5.S2	53.6 %	79.0 % 99.4 %	83.2 % 92.5 %	55.2 % 93.8 %	85.0 % 89.4 %	71.9 % 96.5 %	61.1 % 99.1 %	76.0 % 95.1 %
Testing Images								
910628B.R5.S4	23.2 %	94.7 % 97.6 %	95.0 % 80.0 %	79.7 % 90.2 %	95.2 % 71.7 %	91.7 % 87.5 %	87.5 % 98.0 %	91.7 % 88.9 %
900814B.R12.S2	100 %	100.00 % —	99.7 % —	14.6 % —	98.3 % —	98.3 % —	68.3 % —	71.5 % —

Conclusions and Future Directions

BCM Projection Pursuit in an ensemble configuration (Supens2, Ens9 ,Ens10) is capable of discovering textural features which may be useful in separating bright land from cloud, as well as detecting cirrus over a land-sea interface. The ensemble of ensembles run Supens2 achieved the most consistent performance across the images. BP solutions tended to be vary sensitive to overall intensity of return and had notable failures on the training set for these difficult cases. Further experimentation with ensemble configurations of BCM-BP and other hybrid networks to optimize classification performance will be explored in a future publication; we will also study the performance of ensembles receiving inputs from statistical measures derived from GLDV, SADH and GLRL distributions as well as the raw data.

Acknowledgement C. Bachmann gratefully acknowledges the support of Dr. Thomas McKenna of the Office of Naval Research (ONR) through ONR Grant # N0001494WX23060 and also wishes to thank Fred Lee, AEW Section Head, Airborne Radar Branch, Naval Research Laboratory (NRL), for internal funding of this research under ONR Grant #N0001494WX35052. This work was also supported by NRL core funds (53-1501-04). E. E. Clothiaux is supported by an appointment to the Global Change Distinguished Postdoctoral Fellowships sponsored by the U.S. Department of Energy, Office of Health and Environmental Research, and administered by the Oak Ridge Institute for Science and Education.

References

[1] C. M. Bachmann, S. Musman, D. Luong, and A. Schultz, Unsupervised BCM Projection Pursuit Algorithms for Classification of Simulated Radar Presentations, to appear in Neural Networks.

[2] C. M. Bachmann, S. A. Musman, A. Schultz, Classification of Simulated Radar Imagery Using Lateral Inhibition Neural Networks, in Neural Networks for Signal Processing II - Proceedings of the 1992 IEEE Workshop, Aug. 31 - Sept. 2, 1992, Copenhagen, Denmark, pp. 279 - 288.

[3] E. L. Bienenstock, L. N. Cooper, P. W. Munro, Theory for the Development of Neuron Selectivity: Orientation Specificity and Binocular Interaction in Visual Cortex, The Journal of Neuroscience, Vol. 2, No. 1, pp. 32-48, 1982.

[4] D. W. Chen, S.K. Sengupta, and R.M. Welch, Cloud Field Classification Based upon High Spatial Resolution Textural Features: 2. Simplified Vector Approaches, J. Geophys. Res., 94, No. D12, 14749-14765, 1989.

[5] E. E. Clothiaux, M. F. Bear, L. N. Cooper, Synaptic Plasticity in Visual Cortex: Comparison of Theory with Experiment, Journal of Neurophysiology, Vol. 66, No. 5, pp. 1785 - 1804, 1991.

[6] E. Ebert, A Pattern Recognition Technique for Distinguishing Surface and Cloud Types in the Polar Regions, J. Climate Appl. Meteor., 26, 1412-1427, 1987.

[7] E. E. Ebert, Analysis of Polar Clouds from Satellite Imagery Using Pattern Recognition and a Statisitical Cloud Analysis Scheme, Journal of Applied Meteorology, Vol. 28, pp. 382 - 399, 1989.

[8] J. H. Friedman, J. W. Tukey, A Projection Pursuit Algorithm for Exploratory Data Analysis, IEEE Transactions on Computers, Vol. c-23, No. 9, pp. 881 - 890, 1974.

[9] J. H. Friedman, Exploratory Projection Pursuit, Journal of the American Statistical Association, Vol. 82, No. 397, Theory and Methods, pp. 249 - 266, March 1987.

[10] L. Garand, Automated Recognition of Oceanic Cloud Patterns. Part I: Methodology and Application to Cloud Climatology. J. Climate, 1, 20-39, 1988.

[11] C. Genest, J. V. Zidek, Combining Probability Distributions: A Critique and Annotated Bibliography, Statistical Science, Vol. 1, No. 1, pp. 114 - 148, 1986.

[12] L. K. Hansen, P. Salamon, Neural Network Ensembles, IEEE Transactions on Pattern Analysis and Machine Intelligence, Vol. 12, No. 10, pp. 993 - 1001, October, 1990.

[13] L. K. Hansen, C. Liisberg, P. Salamon, Ensemble Methods for Handwritten Digit Recognition, in Neural Networks for Signal Processing II - Proceedings of the 1992 IEEE Workshop, Aug. 31 - Sept. 2, 1992, Copenhagen, Denmark, pp. 333 - 342.

[14] T. K. Ho, J. J. Hull, S. N. Srihari, On Multiple Classifier Systems for Pattern Recognition, Proceedings of the 11th IAPR International Conference on Pattern Recognition, Vol. II., Conference B: Pattern Recognition Methodology and Systems, pp. 84 -87, 1992.

[15] N. I. Intrator, (1990). Feature Extraction Using an Unsupervised Neural Network, in Proceedings of the 1990 Connectionist Models Summer School, D. S. Touretzky, J. L. Ellman, T. J. Sejnowski (eds.), Morgan Kaufmann, San Mateo, CA, 1990.

[16] N. Intrator, L. N. Cooper, Objective Function Formulation of the BCM Theory of Visual Cortical Plasticity: Statistical Connections, Stability Conditions, Neural Networks, Vol. 5, pp. 3-17, 1992.

[17] J. Key, Cloud Cover Analysis with Arctic Advanced Very High Resolution Radiometer Data. 2. Classification with Spectral and Textural Measures, 95, No. D6, 7661-7675, 1990.

[18] T. Kohonen, Self-Organization and Associative Memory, Springer-Verlag, Berlin, 1984, pp. 128 - 133.

[19] R. A. Jacobs, M. I. Jordan, S. J. Nowlan, G. E. Hinton, Adaptive Mixtures of Local Experts, Neural Computation, Vol 3., pp 79-87, 1991.

[20] M. P. Perrone, Improving Regression Estimation: Averaging Methods for Variance Reduction with Extensions to General Convex Measure Optimization, Ph.D. Dissertation, Department of Physics, Brown University, May, 1993.

[21] M. P. Perrone, L. N. Cooper, Learning from What's Been Learned: Supervised Learning in Multi-Neural Network Systems, to appear in: Proceedings of the World Congress on Neural Networks, Portland, OR, July 11 - 15, 1993.

[22] M. P. Perrone, L. N. Cooper, When Networks Disagree: Ensemble Methods for Hybrid Neural Networks, to appear in Artificial Neural Networks for Speech and Vision, R. J. Mammone, ed., Chapman-Hall, 1993.

[23] D. E. Rumelhart, G. E. Hinton, R. J. Williams, Learning Internal Representations by Error Propagation, in Parallel Distributed Processing, Explorations in the Microstructure of Cognition, Vol. 1, Rumelhart, D. E., McClelland, J. L. (eds.), MIT Press, Cambridge, MA, 1986, pp. 318-362.

[24] B. S. Seebach, Evidence for the Development of Phonetic Property Detectors in a Modified BCM Neural Network without Innate Knowledge of Linguistic Structure, Ph. D. Dissertation, Brown University, Program in Neural Science, 1990.

[25] D. F. Specht, Probabilistic Neural Networks, Neural Networks, Vol. 3, pp. 109-118, 1990.

[26] V. R. Tovinkere, M. Penaloza, A. Logar, An Intercomparison of Artificial Intelligence Approaches for Polar Scene Identification, Journal of Geophysical Research, Vol. 98, No. D3, pp. 5001-5016, March, 20, 1993.

[27] M. Unser, Sum and Difference Histograms for Texture classification. IEEE Trans. Pattern Anal. Mach. Intell., PAMI-8, 118-125, 1986

[28] R. M. Welch, S. K. Sengupta, A. K. Goroch, P. Rabindra, N. Rangaraj, M. S. Navar, Polar Cloud and Surface Classification Using AVHRR Imagery: An Intercomparison of Methods, Journal of Applied Meteorology, Vol. 31, pp. 405-420, May, 1992.

[29] J. S. Weszka, C.R. Dyer, and A. Rosenfeld, A comparative Study of Texture Measures for Terrain Classification, IEEE Trans. Syst., Man, Cybern., SMC-6, 269-285, 1976.

Foreign object detection using an unsupervised neural network

D. Patel, I. Hannah and E.R. Davies

Royal Holloway, University of London
Machine Vision Group, Department of Physics
Egham, Surrey, TW20 0EX, United Kingdom.

e-mail: d.patel@uk.ac.rhbnc

Abstract

In this paper, we illustrate the use of an artificial neural network using an unsupervised learning strategy for detecting contaminants in food packets. The rare occurrence of foreign objects such as glass, rubber or wood in the food bags is worrying to both the consumer and the food industry. This research aims to automatically detect and segment any foreign objects that might be present in the bags. Artificial neural networks using unsupervised learning have an advantage that they do not require much *apriori* information of the pattern recognition task. Nodes representing both the food substrate and foreign objects need to be characterised in the training phase. However, no training data is used for learning the features of the foreign objects, because the knowledge of the various types of foreign objects cannot be assumed.

1. Introduction

Foreign objects (FOs) such as stone, glass or wood occurs rarely in food packets; however, when they are found it causes considerable alarm to both the consumer and manufacturer. The purpose of our research is to develop an image analysis system that will automatically detect these FOs in food bags. We deal with the analysis of the contents of packaged frozen food such as corn or peas, and consequently in order to view the contents we use X-ray imaging. X-ray imaging makes hard contaminants such as stone or metal appears darker and soft contaminants such as wood or plastics appear lighter against the background food substrate. However plastics or rubbers that are generally known as soft contaminants can have a darker appearance as will be seen in the paper. Whilst the detection of hard contaminants is a relatively easy task, soft contaminants pose a problem due to the fact that the X-rays get absorbed through them at a very similar rate as for the food substrate itself. The detection of hard contaminants is presented elsewhere [Hannah, Patel and Davies, 1993 and Patel, Hannah and Davies, 1994]. Whereas, this paper deals with the automatic detection of soft contaminants. Sample X-ray images containing FOs are shown in figure 1.

There exists an infinite number of FOs in various shapes and sizes. It would be impractical to build a network or an array of sub-networks to learn the numerous possible FOs. The detection of a specific FO - wood, via texture recognition and a Multi-Layer Perceptron topology using the supervised Back Propagation learning rule has been previously suggested [Patel, Hannah and Davies, 1993]. The method used in this paper is based on characterising the food substrate that contains no FOs and then detecting any anomalies in the food substrate. These anomalies can then be classed as either FO or a defect in the food bag. The application uses an artificial neural network (ANN) comprised of a few nodes and is shown to successfully detect FOs.

2. Artificial neural network for foreign object detection

The simplest method to detect the possible presence of the FOs is human inspection. However, the use of human operators is unreliable, slow and expensive. The existing system that is currently being used is based on a simple thresholding technique. Detection based on these techniques cannot be relied upon for a stringent quality control process.

Research into artificial neural networks (ANNs) is undertaken in the hope of achieving human-like performances for pattern recognition tasks. The pattern recognition application addressed in this study is concerned with the detection of foreign contaminants in food bags. Several ANN architectures exist [Simpson, 1990], each characterised by the particular connection topology of their nodes (processing elements) and learning rule. Learning is a task whereby the connection weights between the nodes are adapted such that the network can undertake a specific task. There are two categories of learning: supervised and unsupervised. In supervised learning, there is a supervisor to teach the system how to classify a known set of training patterns, i.e. both the training patterns and the associated desired output patterns are available. In unsupervised learning on the other hand, all one has is a collection of patterns and the network usually categorises them according to some pre-specified measure of similarity between them. The unsupervised approach is attractive because the network learns without assuming much knowledge about the data. In a previous paper we have investigated the segmentation of images based on textural features and a logical ANN paradigm using an unsupervised learning rule [Patel, Tambouratzis and Stonham, 1993]. Visa [1992], also segments images using texture features in an unsupervised mode using a Kohonen self-organising topological feature map. Hsiao and Sawchuk (1989) presented a method using the Laws (1980) texture masks and the conventional K-means clustering method. ANNs have an overall advantage over the conventional methods such as the nearest neighbour approaches and a comparison between the two unsupervised methods can be found in Lo and Bavarian (1991). The unsupervised learning rule in our ANN is similar to Kohonen's vector quantisation methodology [Kohonen, 1990] and briefly is as follows:

Step 1. Select a pattern $X_p = (x_1, x_2, ... x_N)$ from the training set; $p \in (1, 2, ... P)$ and feed into input layer. N is the dimension of the pattern vector.

Step 2. Find node $W_j; j = (1, ... J)$ closest to X_p using:
$$\|X_p - W_i\| = \underset{j=1}{\overset{J}{Min}} \|X_p - W_j\|,$$
where W_i is the closest node to X_p and the measure of similarity is the Euclidean distance.

Step 3. Move W_i closer to X_p using:

$$W_i(t+1) = W_i(t) + \alpha(t)[X_p(t) - W_i(t)],$$

where $\alpha(t)$ is the learning rate at time t.

Step 4. Repeat steps 1 to 3 for successive instants of time t until convergence.

The ANN consists of a topology of nodes that represent both the areas on the bag that does not contain any FOs and the FOs. Although the proposed method analyses textured images, it is not dependant on a mathematical measure for texture and therefore eliminates the long processing times that might be needed to characterise the texture. All the images are pre-processed using an averaging filter to remove spot noise and cluster the grey levels; this tends to connect neighbouring pixels. The training data for the node that represents the part of the bag that is free from contaminants is acquired from a 3×3 mapping window and is represented by a 9-element vector. The variation within such images over a small neighbourhood can be substantial because the X-rays penetrate an uneven layer of food. In order to accommodate such a variation, more than one node is used to represent the food substrate. The vector quantisation learning procedure is used to adapt the data, until the nodes sufficiently represent the food substrate. After the nodes representing the food substrate have learnt the essential features, nodes representing the FOs need to be characterised. There exists a large number of different kinds of impurities that might be found in the food bags and therefore no *apriori* knowledge of the FOs can be used. However, using X-ray imaging we know that hard and soft contaminants appear at either the darker or lighter end of the grey level spectrum (this difference is not always distinct enough for detection using simple thresholding techniques). We therefore have two nodes at each end of the spectrum representing the hard and soft contaminants.

After the nodes have been sufficiently adapted, the test images are scanned by a 3×3 window and the 9-element data vectors are passed through the network. The vectors are assigned the label of the node that best matches the input. The Euclidean distance is used as a measure of similarity between the pattern sample under test and the nodes. The clusters of regions formed around the nodes representing the food substrate can be merged into one homogeneous region. Here unsupervised networks can reveal regions on an image that might otherwise have been unobserved using supervised networks. These clusters can be of considerable significance as they can indicate the presence of insufficiently filled bags. The method has been tested on several images and works well. An example of the detection of a small rubber grommet, an eraser and a splinter of wood embedded in bags of frozen corn kernels is illustrated in figures 1 a, b and c. In the example of the wood FO in figure 1a, the contrast between the wood and the food substrate is small and consequently at the edge of the bag where the layers of corn kernels decrease, they get mistakenly classified as FO. This is because X-ray absorption by the thin layers of corn at the edge of the bag is similar to that of the wood. The decision unit that signals to indicate the presence of FO can cope with any border anomalies and a rigid blob removing algorithm can remove the spurious regional discrepancies in the post-processing stage. An algorithm to locate any FOs on the edge of the bags is also currently being developed. In figure 1b it must be stated that the segmentation of the eraser can also be achieved by simple thresholding. However, thresholding methods for other categories of soft contaminants are not entirely reliable and have only had limited success.

3. Concluding remarks

This paper shows that an artificial neural network operating in an unsupervised mode can detect FOs in food packets without assuming any knowledge about the FOs. The results show that the segmentations achieved are in good agreement with the perceived ones. There is marked improvement on the capabilities of the existing system which cannot cope with the detection of soft FOs such as wood.

In general the detection of soft FOs is difficult because the contrast arising between the food and the FO by X-ray attenuation is small. These small differences are difficult to discriminate due to the presence of system noise such as X-ray detector variations or density fluctuations in homogeneous food. Differences can only be detected if large volume FOs are present. The size of the wood piece used in the experimentation reported earlier is $48 \times 18 \times 17$ mm. Smaller pieces and certain plastics could not be discriminated from the food substrate. Several techniques such as iodine doping, to increase the contrast between the FO and the food substrate are being investigated.

References

I. Hannah, D. Patel and E.R. Davies (1993), *"The use of variance and entropic thresholding methods for image segmentation"*, Journal of Pattern Recognition, [paper submitted].

J.Y Hsiao and A.A Sawchuk (1989), *"Unsupervised textured image segmentation using feature smoothing and probabilistic relaxation techniques"*, Computing Vision Graphics and Image Processing, vol. 48, pp. 1-21.

T. Kohonen (1990), *"The self-organising map"*, Proc. of the IEEE, vol. 78, no. 9, pp. 1464-1480.

K.I. Laws (1980), *"Textured image segmentation,"* Ph.D. dissertation, University of Southern California, U.S.A.

Z-P. Lo and B. Bavarian (1991), *"Comparison of a neural network and a piecewise linear classifier"*, Pattern Recognition Letters, vol. 12, no. 11, pp. 649-655.

D. Patel, I. Hannah and E.R. Davies (1993), *"Foreign object detection via texture recognition and a neural classifier"*, Proc. SPIE Conf. on Visual Communication and Image Processing, Cambridge, USA, pp. 1291-1299.

D. Patel, I. Hannah and E.R. Davies (1994), "Foreign object detection via texture analysis", 12th Int. Conf. on Pattern Recognition, [paper submitted].

D. Patel, G. Tambouratzis and T.J. Stonham (1993), *"A logic neural network-based segmentation system with variable-sensitivity characteristics"*, Proc. SPIE Conf. on Visual Communication and Image Processing, Cambridge, USA, pp 769-776.

P.K. Simpson (1990), *"Artificial neural systems"*, McGraw-Hill, NY.

A. Visa (1992), *"Unsupervised image segmentation based on a self-organising feature map and a texture measure"*, Proc. 11th Int. Conf. on Pattern Recognition, ICPR-92, The Hague, The Netherlands, pp. 101-104.

Acknowledgements

The authors are grateful to the ACME Directorate of the UK Science and Engineering Research Council for financial support during the course of this research.

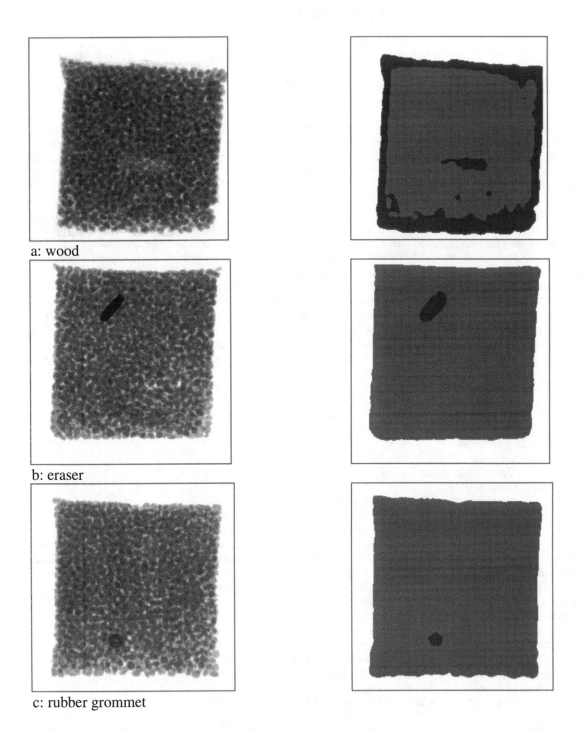

a: wood

b: eraser

c: rubber grommet

Figure 1: Original X-ray images imbedded with FOs (a) wood, (b) eraser, (c) rubber grommet and the resulting segmentations in an unsupervised mode.

"Multispectral Neural Network Camouflaged Vehicle Detection Using Flight Test Imagery"

Dr. Christopher Bowman
Ball Aerospace Systems Division
P.O. Box 1062
Boulder, Colorado 80306

Dr. Mark DeYong
Intelligent Reasoning Systems, Incorporated
P.O. Box 30001, Dept. 3 ARP
Las Cruces, NM 88003-0001

Abstract
The primary role for Neural Network (NN) image processing is in achieving a thousand-fold increase in the number of pixels interpreted per watt. In doing so, data driven learning will be necessary to maintain solution development costs. This paper introduces a biologically motivated NN image processing design and an associated pulse stream NN architecture. Also, the ability of an inner-product NN to learn multispectral vehicle signatures using flight test imagery is described.

1.0 Introduction
NN's have experienced a resurgence in activity during the last decade due to the availability of higher speed parallel processing and the need for data driven adaptive non-linear pattern recognition. Cost effective applications have driven the development of classic inner-product NN's (e.g. backpropagation) software simulations and hardware accelerators including DSP boards (~$10K; 5 million connections per second CPS), Single Instruction Multiple Data (SIMD) NN learning machines (~$60K; 5 Billion CPS), digital CMOS chips (1GCPS/watt), and analog CMOS chips (100 GCPS/watt). The payoff of NN's is in applying this speed/watt processing close to the sensor to learn problem solutions based upon available data. Progress is also being made on developing more biologically motivated NN architectures (e.g. pulse-stream NNs) which will achieve a Tera CPS/watt (still over a thousandth of the brain). Based upon their very high speed per watt and their data driven learning, NNs have secured a place in high performance hybrid computing (HPHC) as a method of choice for fast solutions to pattern recognition problems such as image processing. HPHC architecture technologies include:
• Computing architectures
  - Processors (SIMD, MIMD, vector, neural)
  - Memory (shared, distributed, connectionist)
  - Interconnection (bus, ring, hypercube, local fan in/out, direct)
• Computing hardware
  - Electrical (digital, analog, hybrid)
  - Optical (analog, digital, hybrid)
• Computational models/algorithms
  - Numerical analysis (Bayesian, possibilistic)
  - Symbolic (knowledge representation, inferencing)
  - Neural networks (Supervised, scored, and clustered learning)
These components are combined (see Figure 1) and then matched to the various parts of a large problem in order to optimize its solution. NN's are a key enabling technology which provides orders of magnitude increase in speed per size, weight, and power, as well as reduced solution development cost. This is accomplished by processing data nearer the focal plane using analog massively parallel processing which is trained on the data instead of a "programmed solution". As such, the NN automatically tailors its architecture parameters to fit each problem. The benefits of NN's for image processing include:
• Thousand-fold reduction in power per operation,
• Sensors and processing circuitry integrated together (e.g. both in silicon),
• Massively parallel analog computation for speed with low power and volume,
• Biologically motivated computations that map naturally to electronics,
• Computational methods that do not require high precision, and
• No "up-front" long-term storage (via fast processing and connectivity).

Section 2 summarizes our NN-based image processing and control functional flow. A volt-nanosecond pulse stream NN architecture is described in Section 3. The results of applying NNs for multispectral, pixel-level detection is given in Section 4.

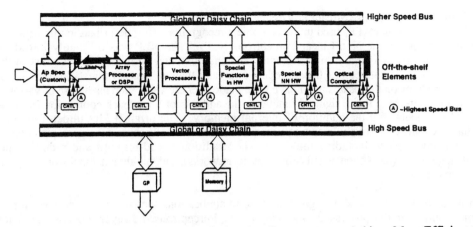

Figure 1. HPHC Architecture Enables Tailoring of Computing Components to Achieve More Efficient Solutions

2.0 NN Image Processing Functional Partitioning Reference Design

The NN image processing functional partitioning (given in Figure 2) expands upon the Seibert-Waxman[1], SAHTIRN[2], constrained BPN [3] and biologically-motivated pulse stream NN designs[Section 3]. It is summarized as follows:

- Detect areas of interest
    - Use NN analog difference networks for motion detection with coarse coding for brightness and contrast detection.
- Edge segmentation
    - Use cellular (iconic) NNs with oriented fields, Gabor center-surround, and diffuse-enhance codings.
- Feature extraction
    - Centroid shift and scale.
    - Using edge boundary centroid and known range.
- Classify/recognize 2-D objects
    - Train a constrained (iconic) NN to determine objects. (new aspect = new object).
- Aspect classification
    - Train a recurrent NN to recognize viable aspect transitions (all steps allow feedback from later steps).

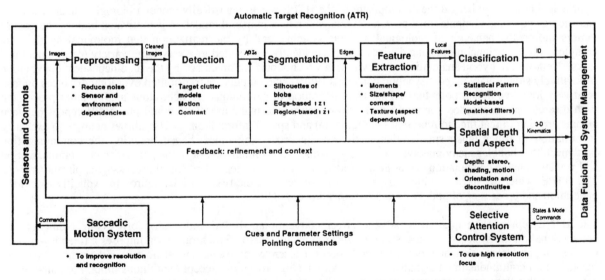

Figure 2. A Biologically-Motivated Image Processing and Control Functional Partitioning

I-637

3.0 Biologically-Motivated Pulse Stream Processing Elements

The basic Processing Element (PE) used in the NN object recognition effort described in this paper and the majority of all NN applications is the Non-Linear Perceptron (NLP). The NLP was originally introduced in 1943 by McCulloch and Pitts [4] as a binary threshold unit. The unit computes an inner product between the current input vector and an internal weight vector. If the product is greater than an internal threshold, the unit output becomes active. Many variations on this basic model have been made over the years such as the use of various non-linearities (e.g. step function, threshold logic, sigmoid function), the addition of a feedback connection from the output of the unit to one of its inputs, and the addition of internal memory. The original McCulloch-Pitts model and all its variations have become collectively known as *perceptrons*. Additionally, numerous perceptron-based architectures have also been investigated including multilayer (i.e. traditional feed-forward and recurrent networks), two-dimensional single layer (i.e. Kohonen and cellular style networks), and one-dimensional single layer (i.e. Carpenter-Grossberg style networks).

Perceptron-based networks have shown great promise in applications such as image and speech processing which benefit from highly-parallel processing and adaptivity. Perceptrons, however, do not adequately capture the characteristic behaviors of the biological neurons they attempt to model; perceptrons are greatly abstracted from biological neurons. The primary reason for this abstraction is the motivation behind perceptrons. Perceptrons were intended as a primitive neuron model which could be used to study different parallel computing architectures and adaptation mechanisms without the computational complexity associated with biologically-realistic neuron models. Perceptron-based networks typically operate on spatial relations (i.e. the relationships between the elements of the input vector). Even if the input vector elements represent a temporal feature, the processing is based on spatial relationships. Recurrent and time-delay NNs have extended traditional NN processing to include discrete temporal relationships but, the capabilities of the individual PE have remained unchanged. As an alternative, consider the spatiotemporal processing performed by the VLSI Hybrid Temporal Processing Element (HTPE, patent pending) which explicitly models the processing performed by biological neurons.

Development of the HTPE was initiated in 1989 with support from the NASA Innovative Research Program (Grant NAGW 1592). The goals of the project were to develop realistic models of the electrophysiological behavior of typical spiking neurons at a level of description that allowed investigation of different time-dependent models of channel conductances, and to use these models to investigate processing of time-dependent signals. Scaling to the volt-nanosecond operating domain and modeling both passive membrane conductances and channel populations with discrete MOS devices allowed flexible models with minimal device counts to be developed and simulated using SPICE. This modeling methodology can be contrasted with that of Mead and colleagues, who have employed primarily operational transconductance amplifiers to model neurons, neuron components, and small circuits in the mV - ms operating domain. Circuits developed with the HTPE are generally smaller, lower-power, less noise-sensitive, and much faster than circuits developed with operational amplifiers.

A principal motivation behind the development of the HTPE was to realistically model a biological neuron without sacrificing speed and computational power. Biological realism in neural modeling is motivated both by the goal of understanding the behavior of biological nervous systems, and by the realization that biological neurons are complex, versatile signal processing devices that are evidently well-suited to a very large variety of computational tasks. Neurons are hybrid analog/discrete devices, in which inputs are processed by the time-dependent convolution of relatively slowly-varying post-synaptic potentials (PSPs), and outputs are transmitted over long distances by fast, relatively loss-free action potentials APs. The integration of continuous, asynchronous analog input processing with discrete, pulse-encoded communication allows neurons to make use of time and phase differences between signals arriving in real time to represent both temporal and spatial information. It also allows neurons to exchange information in times much smaller than their internal processing times, hence breaking the communication bottleneck that hobbles many massively parallel systems. The combination of high-speed, discrete communication and versatile analog computation makes neurons ideal for many time-dependent signal processing applications [5-7]. The HTPE, which we have developed over the past five years, is the first artificial neuron to explicitly model the generation and processing of both PSPs and APs in hardware [8,9].

The HTPE represents a qualitative advance over conventional digital and analog processing elements. In conventional digital systems, all processing is synchronous (clocked). Synchronization imposes a fixed lower limit on the temporal resolution of processing, and forces a discrete representation at no better than the processing resolution on continuous input signals. Conventional analog processors accept continuous input, but embody the assumption that transient responses to inputs can be neglected. In the most common hardware PE, incoming signals are summed and then convolved with a sigmoidal transfer function, as is done in standard software simulations of

ANNs. By only using steady-state responses in processing, these systems impose an effective upper limit equal to the relaxation time of transients on the overall temporal resolution of the system. Biological neurons are sensitively dependent on transient responses of ion channels to fluctuations in membrane potential - the AP itself can be viewed as a transient response - and both accept and generate signals asynchronously. The HTPE is similarly a fully asynchronous PE that allows information to be encoded in both the transient and steady-state components of time-varying signals [5-9].

While many of the properties of biological neurons are important in developing robust NNs, some are artifacts of the neuron's implementation in organic matter. The HTPE has been designed to model the computationally advantageous properties of neurons while making full use of the speed and compactness of silicon implementation. Signal timing in the HTPE has been linearly scaled to take advantage of this speed while maintaining the relative shapes and timing of both APs and PSPs. VLSI input voltages are typically on the order of a volt; therefore the signal voltages have been scaled from the millivolt range of neural signals to the volt range of MOS devices. The operating range of a typical neuron is roughly -80mV, just below the Nernst potential for K^+ ions, to roughly +60mV, just above the Nernst potential of Na^+ ions. This range has been scaled linearly to the [0,5] volt range of MOS devices. This maps the resting potential of approximately -60mV to 1 volt and the typical threshold voltage of -40mV to 1.7 volts. The operating range for temporal relations in neurons, which is in the ms range, has also been scaled to the ns range of VLSI devices (approximately 1ms per 10ns in the current implementation). Figure 4 shows a typical AP (pulse), Excitatory PSP (positive going analog waveform), and Inhibitory PSP (negative going analog waveform). AP streams are analogous to the non-linear output functions of the NLP and PSPs are analogous to the weights of the NLP.

Neurons are generally highly specialized, both electrochemically and geometrically, to particular signal processing functions. The HTPE, in contrast, is a "generic" model neuron that can be customized either by adjusting device sizes at the fabrication stage or by adjusting DC control voltages during operation. The design of the HTPE reflects a computational interpretation of neural architecture that views modulatory connections between neurons as the primary mechanism of real-time programming in neural circuits, and supports a flexible set of modulatory and learning mechanisms.

The primary advantage of the HTPE is its capability to process temporal information. Conventional NNs are based on the assumptions that each input vector is independent of other inputs, and the job of the NN is to extract patterns contained within the input vector that are sufficient to characterize it. For problems of this type, which amount to local spatial pattern recognition, a network that assumes time independence will provide acceptable performance. However, in a large class of signal analysis problems the input vectors are not independent and the network must process each vector with respect to both its own temporal characteristics and its relations to previous vectors. Network architectures that assume time independence are typically unwieldy when applied to a temporal problem, and require additional inputs, neuron states, and/or feedback structures. Although temporal characteristics can be converted into activation levels, this is difficult to do without losing information that is critical to solving the problem efficiently. Networks that assume time dependence have the advantage of being able to handle both time dependent and time independent data. The HTPE is ideal for developing networks of this type. Particular advantages of the HTPE for time-dependent signal processing include the following:

- The modeling of the continuous/asynchronous dynamics of biological neurons allows the HTPE to detect ultrafine temporal characteristics of the input signals, such as frequency and phase differences, less than the minimum switching time of the MOSFET devices on which it is based.
- The HTPE is designed to exploit the full nonlinear range of the MOSFET devices on which it is based. This has two consequences: first, the HTPE has an extremely wide temporal behavior range resulting from the use of all four modes of MOSFET operation (i.e., cutoff, sub-threshold, saturation, and ohmic); second, the additional circuitry used in conventional systems for biasing and non-linearity compensation is not required, thus reducing the device count and VLSI area of the HTPE. Custom VLSI layout further reduces the HTPE layout area by ensuring that each MOSFET device performs a necessary function and that it is the minimal size required to provide adequate drive capabilities.
- The behavior of the HTPE is fully controllable through DC biases, which makes systems of HTPEs easily configurable. Neural systems typically require locally-dense globally-sparse interconnection schemes, which make them ideal for VLSI implementation.
- Parallel systems are inherently noise immune. This in conjunction with built-in adaptation mechanisms allows the HTPE and its systems to be very robust by absorbing system noise and imperfections.
- Several HTPE characteristics make it a very low power device: first, the system is asynchronous, which reduces the peak power requirements of the HTPE with respect to conventional digital systems in which all devices switch

same time; second, sincethe quiescent state of the HTPE is rest it has much less static power dissipation than conventional analog systems, which constantly dissipate power to maintain a particular quiescent state; and third, minimal device count and size reduces the overall power requirements of the HTPE.

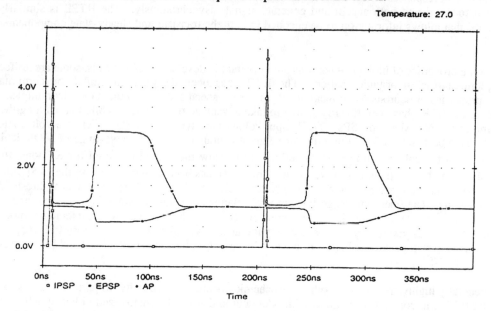

Figure 3. Typical AP and PSP Waveforms Produced by the HTPE.

HTPE networks can be applied to any task to which NLP networks are applicable. In addition, HTPE networks can be used to extract and directly process the temporal information in the input signal. The application of HTPE based networks to the multispectral object recognition effort described in this paper is currently underway. The results of this effort will be reported in subsequent publications.

4.0. Initial Neural Net Multispectral Vehicle Detection Results

The imagery was gathered in flight tests over Ft. Huachuca, AZ. Overlapping data in the UV, Vis, MWIR, LWIR, and SAR was gathered using the sensors described in Bowman [10]. Over 25 hours of raw sensor video was collected on military staged targets (e.g. tanks, trucks, BMP's) and targets of opportunity in wooded and open fields, with natural camouflage, radar transmission camo, and no camo. Data was gathered on targets with engines on/off, in morning and afternoon conditions, at slant ranges of 4K and 8K feet. The imagery is highly cluttered with object-like regions in all bands. The vehicles were approximately 6-12 pixels lengthwise depending upon the band and orientation. The approach is summarized in Figure 4.

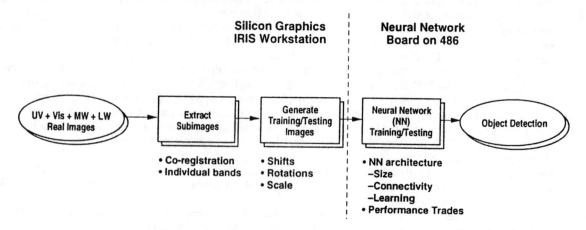

Figure 4. NN's Have Identified Patterns in Multispectral Images for Vehicle Detection

The following training and testing process for NN object detection was used in each of 4 bands. First, extracted 9x9s of targets, random clutter, and "target-like" clutter. Second, trained then tested BPN feed-forward NNs on ± 2 pixel shifts of 9x9s for individual bands, pairs of bands, triples of bands, and all four bands. Third, analyzed performance sensitivity to training/testing sets, number of layers, nodes per layer, learning rate and type (i.e. batch, sequential), activation function type, and training iterations. The IDL-based IRIS image processing bench was enhanced with a user friendly (button based) data preparation and extraction tool that allowed the user to work with up to 4 (512x512) images simultaneously while selecting zoom extractions (area, magnification).

The NN performance sensitivity results are summarized as follows: direct weighted connections from input to output with minimal net size improved results, scaled learning rate by 6^n for the nth layer of BPN improved training, and generalization best when training stopped at knee-of-curve in error[11]. The object detection results are summarized as follows:

- Individual bands (81-9-3-1) [8 inputs, 9 & 3 nodes in hidden layers, 1 output node]
  - UV and Vis achieved 97% accuracy (1750/1800 9x9s correct).
  - LW and MW performed poorly at 80% and 85% respectively.
- Multiple bands
  - Pairs (62-9-1) UV+Vis and Vis+MW best with both achieving 97%
  - Triples (243-9-1) UV+Vis+MW performed best with 99% accuracy
  - All four (324-5-1) achieved 93% due to larger net size memorization
  - Hierarchy of NNs using V, UV, and MW single band NN outputs as inputs to a 3-2-1 NN achieved 99% accuracy with a much smaller net size.

5.0 Summary

NN and traditional parallel (MIMD/SIMD) object recognition comparisons have shown a rough equivalence of the connection per sec (CPS) and the operation per sec (OPS) per pixel. However, NN's have over a thousand-fold power advantage with MIMD and SIMD computational capability of 20 to 200 MOPS/watt, respectively, and analog NN's at 100 to 1000 GCPS/watt. This is significant for the 300 ops/pixel (per frame) required for space-based and UAV-based image processing needed for theater missile defense. This paper has presented an image processing architecture for applying NN's, an analog pulse stream NN paradigm for simultaneous spatial and temporal processing with a Tera CPS/watt capability, and results on flight test imagery showing the potential for multispectral, pixel-level vehicle detection in clutter.

6.0 References

[1] Siebert, Michael and Waxman; Allen, M.; "Spreading Activation Layers, Visual Saccades, and Invariant Representations for Neural Pattern Recognition Systems," Neural Networks, Vol. 2, pp. 9-27, January, 1989.

[2] Lincoln, William P.; Daniell, Cindy E.; Tackett, Walter A; and Baraghimian., Gregory A. ; "The SAHTIRN System for ATR"; Government Neural Network Applications Workshop 24-26 August 1992, GACIAC PR 9 02.

[3] LeCun, Y.; Bose, B.; Denker, J.S.; Henderson, D.; Howard, R.E.; Hubbard, W.; Jackel, L.D.; "Backpropagation Applied to Handwritten Zip Code Recognition", Neural Computation, 1, 541-551, 1989.

[4] McCulloch, W.S.; Pitts, W.; "A logical calculus of ideas immanent in nervous activity," Bulletin of Mathematical Biophysics, Vol. 5, pp. 115-133, 1943.

[5] DeYong, M.; Findley, R.; and Fields, C.; "The design, fabrication, and test of a new hybrid analog-digital neural processing element," IEEE Transactions on Neural Networks, Vol. 3, No. 3, 1992.

[6] DeYong, M.; Eskridge, T.; and Fields, C.; "Temporal signal processing with high-speed hybrid analog-digital neural networks," Jour. of Analog Integrated Circuits and Signal Processing, Vol. 2, pp. 367-388. Boston: Kluwer Academic Publishers, 1992.

[7] DeYong, M.; "VLSI Hybrid Temporal neural networks for signal processing," Ph.D. Dissertation in Electrical Engineering, New Mexico State University, 1992.

[8] DeYong, M.; Findley, R.; and Fields, C.; "Computing with fast modulation: experiments with biologically-realistic model neurons," Proc. 5th. Rocky Mountain Conference on AI, Las Cruces, NM, pp. 111-116, 1990.

[9] Findley, R.; DeYong, M.; and Fields, C.; "High speed analog computation via VLSI implementable neural networks," Proc. 3rd. Microelectronic Education Conference and Exposition, San Jose, CA, pp. 113-123, 1990.

[10] Bowman, C.L.; "Neural Networks Image Processing" Ball Aerospace Systems Division VHPP-93-02.

[11] Bowman, C.L.; "Artificial Neural Network Adaptive Systems Applied to Multisensor ID", The Second Tri-Service Data Fusion Symposium, May 1988.

VISUAL MOTION TRACKING: A NEURAL APPROACH

Davide Anguita, Filippo Passaggio, and Rodolfo Zunino

DIBE - Department of Biophysical and Electronic Engineering
University of Genoa - V.Opera Pia 11a - 16145 GENOVA - Italy

Abstract

The paper considers visual motion tracking from a connectionist perspective; the described approach aims at showing how the flexibility of neural networks can provide a tracking system with adaptiveness and effectiveness. The method first performs an elementary mapping of sensorial data into a lower-dimensional representation ("messages") tractable by neural structures, hence motion information is inferred from differences between consecutive messages. The described tracking structures range from single-network schemata, which demonstrate the basic principle of operation, to multinetwork architectures, whose estimation-averaging mechanism greatly increases tracking stability. The approach validity is assessed on a simple domain to ensure generality, yet a difficult testbed has been chosen and satisfactory results confirm the method's effectiveness.

I. INTRODUCTION

The paper addresses motion tracking (i.e., the evaluation of an object's motion properties) by a fully connectionist perspective, where neural networks (NNs) perform visual information processing at a subsymbolic level. As a result, the described schemata operate as stimulus-response devices, and would lie at a pre-attentional cognitive level. The proposed approach appears consistent with some biological evidence, in which tracking precedes recognition; anyway, it allows integration with higher-lever representation paradigms, to which it can contribute with fast, data-driven attention-focusing mechanisms.

In related approaches, classical methods achieve generality and effectiveness by sophisticated mathematics (e.g., filtering [13], regularization [18], optical flow [8,4]), but may also prove computationally heavy and noise-sensitive. The approach here described offers greater simplicity in both design and implementation. Other methods implicitly assume some higher-level analysis of perceived information (e.g., by feature-extraction) [1,15]; they lie at an attentional level but might lack general applicability. Connectionist visual systems usually involve specific signal pre-processing steps to facilitate a network task by reducing data dimensionality; in vehicle-guidance applications, a neural visual subsystem aims to accomplish some critical subtask (e.g., following road edges) [6]. Concerning the tracking process, the neural schema described in [10] focuses on biological congruence, and the approach presented in [9] bridges the gap between optical-flow models and connectionist structures.

The method described in this paper aims at exploiting the generalisation power of neural networks in those complex domains (like active Vision) for which explicit and analytic approaches would prove inefficient or difficult to apply. The specific system's task is to maintain a visual sensor continuously centered on and aligned with an observed moving object. The resulting schemata show a wide range of applicability; in addition, distributed implementations on (neuro)computing architectures inherently allow fast performances in real-time applications.

Tracking is performed in two steps: first, visual data are mapped into an intermediate representation ("messages"); thus a sequence of images maps into a sequence of messages. The lower-dimensional message space can then be handled by neural networks, which can extract motion information from message differences and drive tracking accordingly. The visual testbed includes binary images representing object shapes. The choice of binary images aims at preventing domain-dependent techniques from affecting the evaluation validity, even though they may improve the system's performance; at the same time, the specific testbed can demonstrate the method's accuracy. As to the method's generality, the motion-tracking schema applies to pictorial images, as well; moreover, in case "target" implementations should involve dedicated processing, the proposed structures are inherently compatible with any application-dependent module.

Section II presents the basic research framework, including the dimensionality-reduction mechanism and the neural component. Section III illustrates the neural tracking architectures, covering single- and multinetwork schemata. Section IV reports experimental results, whereas some concluding remarks are made in Section V.

II. NEURAL FRAMEWORK

II.1 - Message-based reduction in dimensionality

Generalization theory [5] and practical training limit the data dimensionality that neural networks can process effectively. For this impossibility of neural networks to handle visual patterns directly, an image, **I**, is mapped into an intermediate, lower-dimensional representation ("messages"). This message-based approach proved effective in previous applications of associative models to image understanding, such as classification and stimulus-response behaviour [3]. Reduction in dimensionality is modelled by a general image-message mapping function, **M()**; in practice, a message is represented by an K-dimensional vector of real numbers.

We chose a straightforward implementation of M() to enhance the method's generality and fast response. In the basic schema, row-wise and column-wise sums of image pixels yield a message for each coordinate axis (Fig.1). The representation of the **M()** function can be formally expressed as follows:

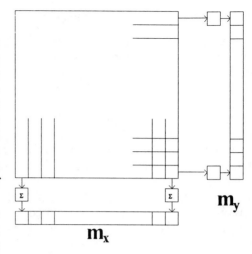

Fig.1 - Sample of message generation

$$\mathbf{M(I)} \overset{def}{=} \left(\mathbf{m}_x, \mathbf{m}_y\right) \;;\quad m_x^{(k)} = \sum_{i=1}^{N} \mathbf{I}_{i,k}; \quad k = 1,...,K \;;\quad m_y^{(k)} = \sum_{j=1}^{N} \mathbf{I}_{k,j}; \quad k = 1,...,K \tag{1}$$

In spite of this apparently simple characteristics, the resulting structures proved quite effective, and would not prevent the application of other more sophisticated message-generation schemata.

II.2 - The neural component

The use of a neural network (NN) for motion estimation offers the possibility of training the system by examples; under some conditions, the generalization power of the NN can improve effectiveness. A connectionist structure does not require any explicit model of the message-motion relationship; in addition, training flexibility makes the schema adaptive to different implementations of **M()**.

All the described schemata involve classical feedforward networks; the input layer has the same dimensionality of messages; analog units in the output layer provide motion evaluation (Fig.2). The meaning of output information depends on the implemented schema, and may express, for example, an object shift in the image plane, or its object rotation angle. The number of neurons in the (unique) hidden layer is set experimentally for each configuration. Such a number can be first assessed using generalization theory, which relates the number of connections to the cardinality of the training set, whereas necessary

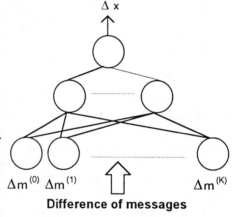

Difference of messages

Fig.2 - The neural structure

adjustments follow practical experience. The training algorithm is an improved version of the back-propagation, named SuperSAB [14], where adaptiveness is provided by a specific learning rate, η_{ij}, for each weight dimension:

$$\Delta w_{ij}^{(r)} = -\eta_{ij} \frac{\partial E}{\partial w_{ij}} + \alpha \cdot \Delta w^{(r-1)} \tag{2}$$

where α is a momentum term, and $\Delta w_{ij}^{(r)}$ represents the weight variation from the i-th to the j-th units at the training iteration r. An optimized version of this algorithm on a RISC-based workstation [2] made it possible to cope with the huge computational load involved in all experiments.

III. NEURAL ARCHITECTURES FOR TRACKING

III.1 - The differential estimation schema

The principle of operation of the basic tracking mechanism is to infer an object's motion from the differences between two consecutive messages; for this property, this estimator is denoted as a "differential" estimator. This schema implicitly assumes rigid object and translational motion, but these assumptions can be relaxed without loss of generality provided the time difference between two consecutive frames is small enough.

As described earlier, row-wise and column-wise summations of pixel values result in two messages. The neural networks (one for each coordinate axis) process the information contained in time-consecutive messages and work out the corresponding estimates of the object shift in the image plane.

Training is performed by showing the network differences in messages for several shifts of several objects at different scales. The eventual training steps consist in an experimental measurement and compensation of the estimator's constant error (if any) to improve stability. As a result, the network generalizes an implicit procedural rule to associate differences in the message space with differences in the image space. The conditions for the network's proper learning are based on both generalization theory [5] and practical criteria [16], which set the cardinality of the training set in order to achieve reliable generalization. The differential estimator can be formally defined as:

$$\mathcal{E}_d(\Delta\mathbf{m}) \overset{def}{=} \mathcal{E}_d : \{\mathbf{m}'' - \mathbf{m}'\} \rightarrow \{(\Delta x, \Delta y)\} \tag{3}$$

where $\mathbf{m}'$ and $\mathbf{m}''$ denote the messages associated with two consecutive frames, and $(\Delta x, \Delta y)$ indicate the corresponding object shift in the image. Figure 3 presents the basic differential-tracking architecture.

An additional advantage of the row-wise and column-wise approach is the possibility of controlling the dimensionality of the message space to comply with generalization requirements. For example, a further compression in the experiments was obtained by summing up rows and columns into groups of four elements; thus images consisting of 128x128 pixels can be mapped into two messages of 32 elements each.

The above schema enhances performance and generality, as the differential mechanism extracts from image sequences only motion-relevant information and removes insignificant information (e.g., the background). Focusing the network on tracking-essential information strongly facilitates the generalization task. As to the training-set cardinality, it can be tailored by controlling, for example, the number of objects shown or the number of different object shifts.

III.2 - The multinetwork schema

The differential schema may, in critical situations, exhibit an intrinsic drawback: processing differential information inherently increases noise-sensitivity. Techniques to overcome this limitation may include, for example, low-pass processing of neural inputs to remove spikes and high-frequency noise. Although such additional modules have full compatibility with the overall methodology here described, we followed a different and more straightforward approach, which exploits recent achievements in neural network theory.

The integrated structure we developed includes several networks, each contributing to motion-evaluation independently of the others. The final average over the outputs provided by all members will correspond to the actual motion estimate. For this mechanism, the structure is called the "multinetwork" schema; Figure 4 gives its schematic representation.

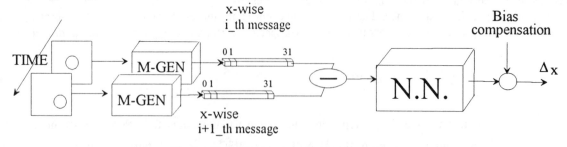

Fig.3 - The differential tracking schema

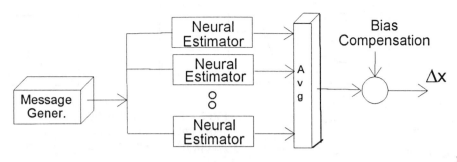

Fig.4 - The multinetwork schema

To obtain several independent contributors, one can just perform several network-training runs, with different and independent weight initializations. A more accurate estimator can be obtained by using different training sets for each network. This procedure can increase the estimator's generality by removing possible bias that may be introduced by a specific training set; on the other hand, the practical feasibility of such an approach will depend on the availability of huge amounts of training data.

The integrated approach makes it possible to exploit the statistical properties of network ensembles [11,7] to improve the whole system's robustness. Multinetwork approaches recently received increasing attention. Although an in-depth theoretical investigation of their basic properties (e.g., generalization ability) has not been carried out,, network ensembles have proved very effective in practical applications [17]. The formal expression for a multinetwork schema including N members can be the following:

$$\mathscr{V}(\Delta \mathbf{m}) = \frac{1}{N} \sum_{n=1}^{N} \mathscr{E}_d^{(n)}(\Delta \mathbf{m})$$
(4)

In this paper, we exploits two results of research on network ensembles, which has shown that network averaging 1) does not affect estimation bias, and 2) reduces error variance. Indeed, one can make error variance arbitrarily small by including a sufficient number of networks. A formal demonstration of these properties [11] involves notions from statistics and approximation theory, and goes beyond the scope of this paper. Very briefly, property 1) follows from the linearity of the average operator: the bias of $\mathscr{V}()$ is equal to the average bias of members, and the members' biases are all equal (averaged over data on a statistical basis) because they relate to equivalent estimation structures. Variance reduction (property 2) follows from modelling estimation as a regression problem: if MSE() indicates the mean square error averaged over data of a regression module, it has been proved in [11] that:

$$\mathrm{MSE}(\mathscr{V}) \leq \frac{1}{N} \sum_{n=1}^{N} \mathrm{MSE}(\mathscr{E}^{(n)})$$
(5)

which demonstrates that the multinetwork estimator performs better than the average individual member of the ensemble. When applied to prediction tasks, the variance reduction provided by multinetwork structures improves the second-order statistics of the estimator, and the ultimate result is to increase the tracking system's stability.

IV. EXPERIMENTAL RESULTS

IV.1 - The experimental testbed

Images of shapes belonging to 7 different classes form the testbed for this research. The simplicity of using binary images is countervailed by the complexity inherent in the specific testbed considered. Training shapes are different from test ones; in addition, the nature and composition of training and test sets have been intentionally chosen to stress the system's accuracy and effectiveness. Figure 5 (top) presents the shape classes used for training and test. Each class includes a set of thirteen 128x128-pixel images, representing shapes at increasing scales; scale factors range in the interval [1,13]. The neural networks have been trained using only images at three scales: 3,7,and 11; all 13 scale factors are instead used for test shapes. This training strategy implements a sparse sampling in the scale space (Fig.5, bottom); this makes it possible to verify the method's scale-invariance, which is provided by the network's generalization power.

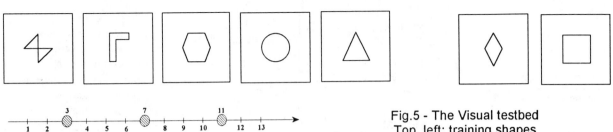

The scale-sampling strategy for training and test

Fig.5 - The Visual testbed
Top, left: training shapes
Top, right: test shapes

In each experiment, the network training set was built up as follows: the object was initially placed at a reference (leftmost or bottom) position, and increasingly shifted (when possible) by 10, 20, and 30 pixels in both the positive and the negative directions. The network's analog output ranged from -0.9 to 0.9 and represented the shift amplitude with the related sign. The difference between the shifted-object message and the "unshifted-object" message was combined with the desired output value, and formed a single element of the network's training set.

The object's reference position was then increased until the whole axis range was covered. As a result, the network learned to map differences in messages into object shifts, independently of the object's actual position in the image. The whole software environment (tracking system and neural model) has been implemented with the C language on a IBM 6000 RISC workstation.

IV.2 - Accuracy results on differential and multinetwork estimation

A massive experimentation involved more than 400 evaluation runs, and provided reliable sample results for using unobserved shapes at unobserved scales. The graphs in Fig.6 present sample results for horizontal shifts of ± 10 and ± 20 pixels of test shapes with scale factor =6; similar results have been obtained for other scales and for vertical shifts. In the graphs, the x-axis indicates the object's reference position in the image, the y-axis gives the network's output, and the straight line indicates the object's actual shift.

The training and test strategies for the multinetwork schema were the same used for differential estimation. In each experiment, the ensemble was made up of three members, chosen from a set of independently trained networks. The choice privileged the networks with the minimum error variance (averaged over training data). Two different ensembles were used, one for each image coordinate. Table I shows statistic measurements of prediction quality for one such ensemble; the individual performance of each member was measured on the training set, whereas the ensemble's behaviour was evaluated on the test set. Results fully confirm expectations from ensemble theory (bias invariance and reduction in error variance).

IV.3 - Tests on the method's stability

When closed-loop systems (like trackers) have to be set up, stability represents a crucial issue, too. Stability here means the method's capacity to compensate for errors (in other words, to avoid error accumulation). As mentioned previously, a rough stability mechanism is bias compensation to remove constant errors. Run-time stability is difficult to prove formally, due to the network's nonlinear behaviour. Stability can hardly be predicted by

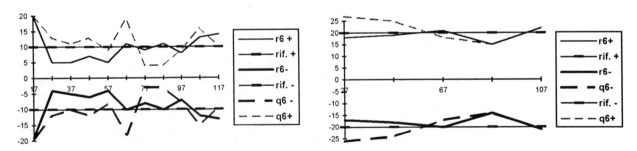

Fig. 6 - Sample results from differential estimation

ID	SHIFT	AVG.ERROR	ABS. ERROR	VARIANCE
#2	10	1.851	3.255	12.766
	20	1.818	4.227	34.597
	30	-3.038	3.654	15.499
#72	10	1.861	3.436	15.515
	20	-0.136	4.181	39.841
	30	-3.961	4.653	29.419
#291	10	2.521	3.372	9.840
	20	2.227	3.545	12.264
	30	-3.846	4.615	17.355

	SHIFT	AVG.ERROR	ABS. ERROR	VARIANCE
☐	10	1.882	2.968	3.097
	20	0.863	3.000	3.653
	30	-4.153	4.692	4.571
◇	10	-0.904	4.585	5.968
	20	-2.340	3.750	4.111
	30	-4.000	4.153	2.660

Table I - The effect of multinetwork averaging
Top: individual behaviours of three networks (Training set)
Bottom: behaviour of their ensemble (Test set)

observing the experimental charts on accuracy; in the present research, it was evaluated experimentally. Using the same test shapes at several scales, we simulated a random path of an object within a 1024x1024 visual field. While moving in the image, the object takes random steps of amplitude ranging from 2 to 30 pixels along each axis.

At several positions along this path, the object's scale varies, thus mimicking radial motion. This makes it possible to stress the method's scale invariance.

At each (fixed) time, the tracker evaluates the object's shift and moves the centre of the camera (here modelled as a 128x128 pixel region) toward the estimated object's centre. The reference camera view for the next evaluation step is this new estimated position (which differs from the actual object centre because of estimation errors). Figure 7 displays the tracking result for the multinetwork schema, demonstrating the method's stability.

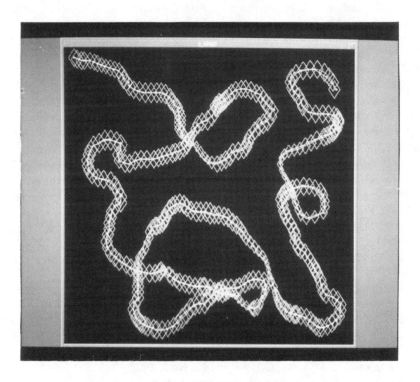

Fig.7 - Stability test for multinetwork estimation
The continuous line connects estimated object centers; shapes indicate actual positions and scales

V. CONCLUDING REMARKS

The research aimed to show how elementary schemata, when supported by the representation power of connectionist structures, can accomplish complex tasks in difficult but interesting domains like that of active vision. Results show a satisfactory balance between the effectiveness needed in practical applications and the generality requirement to be met by scientific methodologies. The confirmed validity of multinetwork structures, whose expected theoretical performance have always been supported by experimental evidence, represents another major achievement of the present research. The described methods can be further improved in several respects. Rotation tracking can be easily accomplished by the same message-based mechanism here described. Removing simplifications increases the method's practical impact and allows one to tailor the general principle to final applications. For example, the differential schema can be directly extended to handle pictorial images and inherently solves the problem of background elimination. In addition, the simplicity of the dimensionality-reduction mechanism opens new interesting vistas for using specific signal-processing techniques, which may help benefit from particular sensors (e.g., IR, etc.). A promising aspect of the present research is the possibility of easy implementation on dedicated hardware. Indeed, the realization of the neural component (i.e., the core of a tracking schema) by using (neuro)chips makes it possible to tackle real-time applications at a relatively low cost.

REFERENCES

[1] Aggarwal JK, Nandhakumar N "On the computation of motion from sequences of images - A review", *Proc. IEEE*, vol. 76, no. 8, Aug. 1988

[2] Anguita D, Parodi GC, Zunino R "An efficient implementation of BP on RISC-based workstations" *Neurocomputing*, No.5, 1993, pp.1-9

[3] Anguita D, Parodi GC, Zunino R "Associative structures for Vision" *Multidimensional Systems and Signal Processing*, vol.5, No.1, in press in Jan 1994

[4] Ballard B, Kimbal O "Rigid body motion from depth and optical flow", *Computer Graphics and Image Processing*, vol. 22, 1983, pp.95-115

[5] Baum EB, Haussler D "What size net gives valid generalization?" *Neural Computation*, No.1, 1989, pp.151-160

[6] Del Bimbo A, Landi L, Santini S "Determination of road directions using feedback neural nets" *Signal Processing*, vol. 32, 1993, pp.147-160

[7] Hansen LK, Salamon P "Neural network ensembles" *IEEE Trans. on Pattern Anal. and Machine Intell.*, vol.12, No.10, Oct. 1990, pp.993-1000

[8] Horn B, Schunck B "Determining optical flow" *Artificial Intelligence*, vol. 17, 1981, pp. 185-203

[9] Lee JC, Shen BJ, Fang WC, Chellappa R "VLSI neuroprocessors for video motion detection" *IEEE Trans. on Neural Networks*, Vol.4, No.2, March 1993, pp.178-191

[10] Missler J, Kamangar F "A neural network for moving object detection and tracking inspired by the fly visual system" *Proc. World Conference on Neural Networks*, July 1993, pp.I 62-I 67

[11] Perrone MP, Cooper LN "Learning from what's been learned: supervised learning in multi-neural network systems" *Proc. World Conference on Neural Networks WCNN'93*, July 1993, pp. III 354-III 357

[12] Rumelhart D E, Hinton G H, Williams R J "Learning internal representation by error propagation" in D E Rumelhart, J L McClelland (Eds) *Parallel Distributed Processing - Explorations in the Microstructure of Cognition voll.1-2*, MIT Press, 1986

[13] Sworder DD, Singer PF, Doria D, Hutchins RG "Image-enhanced estimation methods" *Proc. of the IEEE*, vol.81, No.6, June 1993, pp.797-814

[14] Tollenaere T "SuperSAB: fast adaptive back propagation with good scaling properties" *Neural Networks*, vol.3, 1990, pp.561-573

[15] Tsai RY, Huang TS "Uniqueness and estimation of three-dimensional motion parameters of rigid objects with curved surfaces", *IEEE Trans. Pattern Anal. Machine Intell.*, vol. PAMI-6, no.1, pp. 3-27, Jan. 1984.

[16] Widrow B, Lehr M A "30 years of adaptive neural networks: perceptron, madaline, and backpropagation" *Proc. of the IEEE*, vol.78, No.9, Sept. 1990, pp.1415-1442

[17] Xu L, Kryzak A, Suen CY "Methods of combining multiple classifiers and their applications to handwriting recognition" *IEEE Trans. on Sys., Man, and Cybern.*, vol.22, No.3, 1992

[18] Yasumoto Y, Medioni G "Robust estimation of three-dimensional motion parameters from a sequence of image frames using regularization", *IEEE Trans. Pattern Anal. Machine Intell.*, vol. PAMI-8, no. 4, pp. 464-471, July 1986.

SEJONG-NET with Analysis-by-Synthesis

Kwanyong Lee* and Yillbyung Lee†

*† Department of Computer Science, Yonsei University
Seoul, 120-749, KOREA
† Center for Artificial Intelligence Research, KAIST, Daejeon, KOREA

E-mail : kylee@comsci.yonsei.ac.kr, yblee@comsci.yonsei.ac.kr

Abstract

SEJONG-NET, inspired by the visual system of vertebrate animals, has been designed to recognize on-line characters, and initially applied to Hangul(Korean alphabet) characters. Later, the model was modified to recognize various other character sets such as Roman characters, Chinese sub-characters and numerals.

In this paper, we propose the extended SEJONG-NET model based on the on-line SEJONG-NET model to recognize both on-line Hangul patterns and off-line Hangul patterns through a common mechanism of recognition. We treat the process of off-line character recognition as a special case of on-line character recognition through selectively scanning over strokes according to the remembered writing sequence.

In the case of complicated characters as Hangul, contacts between parts that compose a character is a major factor of confusion by the off-line recognition system. We use human-like process of analysis-by-synthesis to solve the problem of contacts by extracting strokes on the basis of the writing sequence.

1 Introduction

SEJONG-NET(_SE_lective _J_udgement _O_f _N_umerous _G_rapheme-neural _NET_work), inspired by the visual system of vertebrate animals, is a neural network model to provide a comprehensive paradigm to explain visual character pattern recognition. This model composed of multilayer extracts spatial and temporal features in parallel, and then combines the two modes of information to recognize a given pattern.

This artificial neural network model has been designed originally for the recognition of on-line Hangul characters[1][2], and then modified to recognize Roman characters[3] and Chinese radicals[4]. An integrated model for the on-line recognition of several sets of characters mentioned above has been developed with a single mechanism[5].

The main difference between the existing SEJONG-NET and most of the pattern recognition neural network designed so far lies in that the input of the existing SEJONG-NET is not of a static visual pattern but of a dynamic one. Thus the extraction of temporal features through multistage transformations of 2-dimensional visual input is taken as an equally important problem as the extraction of spatial features.

The field of character recognition can be classified into two classes, on-line recognition and off-line recognition. On-line recognition is characterized by the use of dynamic information to recognize a character, on the other hand off-line recognition can use only the x-y coordinates of each pixel. Thus on-line recognition has produced much more encouraging results than off-line recognition. So far, most of the recognition system has been developed only for one of the two classes of input pattern.

Now, we propose the extended SEJONG-NET with backward paths on the basis of the on-line model for Hangul to recognize off-line characters as well as on-line characters using a common mechanism. This model can take both a static visual pattern and a dynamic one as the input, while the existing models can recognize only a dynamic pattern. In this paper, we recognize off-line characters by treating the process of off-line character recognition as a special case of on-line character recognition through selectively scanning over strokes according to the writing sequence of a character.

Several studies related to the use of on-line information have been made. Pan[6] uses a heuristic-rule-based tracing algorithm to get the temporal relationship among the strokes in a numeral. Rosenfeld[7] provides a taxonomy of local, regional, and global temporal clues to recover temporal information from the image.

Marcelli[8] presents a method based on a suitable implementation of good continuity criteria which take into account direction, length and width of the strokes making up characters to recover part of the lost script dynamics.

The major factor of confusion by the recognition system for complicated characters as Hangul have been the contact problems that occur between strokes/graphemes that compose an individual syllabic character. Several attempts have been made to solve the contact problem[9][10]. Most of them use bottom-up approaches and result in systems that consume inappropriate amount of time to handle all the possible cases of contact. In this paper we use human-like process of "analysis-by-synthesis"[11][12][13] to extract strokes on the basis of the writing sequence which is already remembered. By using the process, Halle and Stevens[11] described computer program that attempted to recognize spoken language and Eden[12] developed the system to recognize handwritten cursive script.

Hence SEJONG-NET can be considered as a more general model of problem solving for the tasks of visual pattern recognition.

In this paper, we describe the details of the structures and functions of the proposed model and report the results of applying the extended SEJONG-NET as a recognizer for both off-line and on-line Hangul characters.

2 Structures and Functions

SEJONG-NET has the feed-forward local connections between two adjacent layers. Each layer may contain several planes, each extracting different features. Signal flows from input layer to output layer(feed-forward), and when the system fails to get the proper information from the previous layers, it transmits feedback signals to the previous layers. (The structure of the model is identical to that of on-line Hangul model[1][2] except for the addition of backward paths)

This model receives binary input patterns and recognizes individual strokes using spatial and temporal information extracted from the previous layers, and then combines the strokes to compose graphemes. Finally these graphemes are combined in sequence to form a particular character. ⟨Figure 1⟩ shows the functional structure of the extended SEJONG-NET.

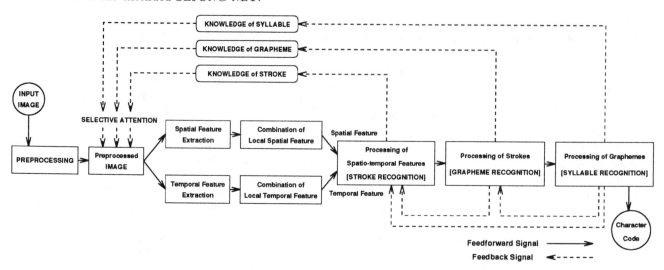

Figure 1: The functional structure of the extended SEJONG-NET

After getting an input image through on-line input device or scanner, the model thins/relaxs the input pattern, and then the input pattern is transferred to IN(_IN_put) layer to represent the presence of visual stimulus by binary value. Next in REC(photo_REC_eptor) layer, each pixel from IN layer is converted into a real value to represent its spatio-temporal information. The outputs of REC layer are supplied to two paths to extract spatial and temporal features at the same time. One path is SSF(_S_imple _S_patial _F_eature) and CSF(_C_omplex _S_patial _F_eature), the other is STF(_S_imple _T_emporal _F_eature) and CTF(_C_omplex _T_emporal _F_eature). STR(_STR_oke) layer extracts strokes utilizing these spatial and temporal features of CSF and CTF layer, and GRA(_GRA_pheme) layer combines several extracted strokes to recognize a specific grapheme. In SYL(_SY L_lable) layer, these graphemes are combined to form a particular character. ⟨Figure 2⟩ shows the overall structure and the signal flow of the proposed SEJONG-NET in this paper.

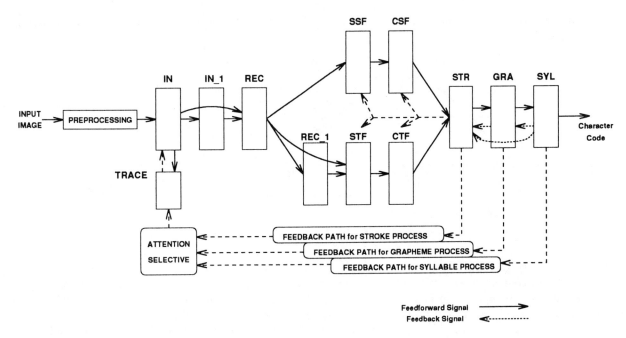

Figure 2: The overall structure of SEJONG-NET

2.1 Basic Idea for Off-line Recognition through On-line Mechanism

Basically, the model is based on the on-line Hangul model. The main structural difference between the model and the on-line Hangul model is that the model have backward paths to take the adequate actions on the lower layers when the system fails to get the valid outputs in the higher levels, STR, GRA, and SYL layers.

This model can recognize on-line characters through feed-forward paths like the on-line Hangul model. However for example, if an input image has inappropriate strokes unsupported by STR layer of the model, these strokes are split into several small strokes and then the system continues to recognize along the backward paths. Thus we can say the model is more general and powerful than the existing on-line model.

It is well known that on-line recognition is relatively easier than off-line recognition, mainly due to the fact that stroke dynamics is known. Unfortunately, because we can't directly get temporal information from off-line characters, in this paper we present the method to recover dynamic information from a static images. We get the writing sequence information of an off-line character through attending selectively on images according to the remembered writing sequence of a character. By following the remembered sequence, we can trace a character in the natural order which human follows generally.

To trace from the first stroke of a given character, first of all we have to identify the start point of the first stroke. Generally, the writing direction follows top to bottom and left to right. According to this rule, we can easily decide the start point of the first stroke of the first grapheme through scanning the input image diagonally from the top-left corner. (A start point should be a termination point.) If several points are found as the candidates of the start point, we select only one point by comparing the positional relationship among these points. We define a line-segment as a string of pixels sequenced according to their tracing order, and each line-segment is separated by a start point, a termination point, or a branch. Trace starts with a selected start point and continues until all the line-segments connected with the point are traversed. By tracing point by point from the start point, we find line-segments, and then make strokes by combining these line-segments with the same directional properties. The process for merging line-segments is always guided and induced by stroke knowledge of Hangul represented by automata.

After processing all the line-segments connected with the first stroke of the first grapheme, we continue to find start points, and to trace all the line-segments related to each start point. Note, the number of the start point to be processed varies because of the contacts between strokes/graphemes.

After recognizing strokes through merging line-segments, we can extract graphemes by combining the extracted strokes according to the automata on the graphemes of Hangul.

Feedback signals are generated if there are some violations against automata when merging line-segments or strokes, and then the system continues the process of recognition until it reaches a stable state, which means the system no longer generates any feedback signals.

We can't get the correct temporal information and the recognition result of a character until the system reaches the stable state.

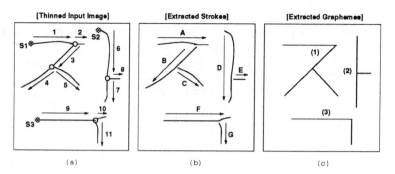

Figure 3: The basic idea for off-line recognition

In ⟨Figure 3⟩(a), there are three start points('S1', 'S2', 'S3'), and 11 line-segments. After the line-segments ('1','2','3','4','5') connected with 'S1' are processed first, the line-segments connected with 'S2' and 'S3' will be processed respectively. Line-segment '1' and '2' can be merged into the stroke 'A' of ⟨Figure 3⟩(b), while line-segment '1' and '3' can't be merged into a stroke because automata on Hangul stroke don't support such stroke. In ⟨Figure 3⟩(b), stroke 'A', 'B', and 'C' are merged into the grapheme '(1)' of ⟨Figure 3⟩(c), and so on.

We can classify the types of contact between strokes/graphemes into 2 types. One is the branch form, and the other is the extension form of horizontal or vertical line.

While merging line-segments into strokes or the extracted strokes into graphemes according to automata on stroke/grapheme, we can solve the contact problem. Because a guessed stroke with inappropriate strokes and a hypothesized grapheme with inadequate strokes can't be recognized correctly by each automata, alternative strokes/graphemes are generated and tested until correct strokes/graphemes are found.

2.2 Details of Each Layer

The structures and functions of each layer are described briefly as follows. (Refer [1][2] to get more details of the structures and functions of each layer)

Preprocessing : In the case of the on-line character recognition, we accomplish the spatio-temporal relaxation to remove discontinuity between points. In the case of off-line character recognition, a thinning process[14] is applied to skeletonize a given character, and the processing stage of the system identifies the start point of the first stroke of the first grapheme to proceed trace pixel by pixel through scanning an image diagonally from the top-left corner.

IN layer and IN_1 layer : Each element of IN layer can have a binary value and indicates whether input exists currently at each position in coordinates. Each element of IN_1 layer marks whether there was input before one unit time at each position. Each stroke is stored in each plane. In the first stage of off-line character recognition, line-segments instead of strokes are stored in each plane, and the number of plane varies as the line-segments are merging/splitting to form strokes.

TRACE layer : Each non-zero element of this layer shows the order of positions written over the input character. In the case of off-line character recognition, this sequence may be considered as the sequence of tracing a off-line character through time. This layer detects the end point of a stroke and then activates the stroke to be processed the next time according to this sequence when receiving the signal from STR layer. This stroke-based computation can be regarded as the basic processing unit, works to facilitate character recognition, and helps to solve the contact problem.

REC layer and REC_1 layer: Elements of REC layer represent spatial information of points entered into IN layer as the strength of steady state as well as represent the time of their appearance as the strength of transient state. REC_1 layer represents the state of each element of REC layer at one unit time before.

SSF layer : Elements of SSF layer extract various simple local spatial features. 8 filters with different orientation are currently used. SSF layer consists of sublayers called planes each of which extracts a given local feature within the receptive field.

STF layer : This layer represents temporal changes in the respective positions of the visual image. Each element of this layer activates when the corresponding element of REC layer changes above threshold.

CSF layer : Elements of CSF layer represent more complex spatial features constructed from features gathered from SSF planes. The window size and the thresholding value used in this layer are adjusted by the feedback signal of the higher layers to control the tolerance degree of distortions and variations whe the recognition fails.

CTF layer : Elements of CTF layer represent termination of a stroke gathering their information from STF layer. Through this layer, we can get the information of the start point and the end point of a stroke by only visual information, not using pen-down/pen-up information obtained from input device. Especially, this layer is useful for off-line character recognition.

STR layer : Elements of STR layer combine elements of CSF layer and of CTF layer and then discriminate a particular stroke according to the start and the end of the stroke and the different types of connectivity. In the case of off-line character recognition, a stroke such as 'ㄱ' and 'ㄴ' is split into two strokes, a horizontal stroke and a vertical stroke because of the hook and the contact of a stroke. Thus, we first extract sub-strokes and then combine them to find a particular stroke.

If STR layer fails to form a stroke, the system generates the feedback signal to reanalyze a pattern. According to the cause of the recognition failure, one of the following actions is taken.

- Reverse the direction of a stroke to follow top to bottom and left to right
- Adjust the window size or the thresholding value of CSF layer to control the tolerance degree of distortions and variations.
- Split a stroke into the smaller strokes.
  Note we should be careful of selecting points to be cutted. In the case of the contacts with the branch form, a stroke is split at the corresponding branch point. On the contrary in the case of the contacts with the extension form of a straight line, a point to be cutted have to be decided by referencing the information of the neighboring strokes.
- Merge several strokes with the same directional properties into a larger stroke

And then STR layer sends a control signal to TRACE layer to process the next stroke, or to continue the process of recognition after feedback process.

GRA layer : Elements of GRA layer combine recognized strokes at various positions in the previous STR layer and then recognize a particular grapheme.

The process of combining recognized strokes is always guided/induced by the knowledge of grapheme represented as automata. This automata continually monitor the output of STR layer, remember what has gone on before, and predict what will come next. Thus the automata use much information than conventional automata to recognize a particular grapheme.

One of the following actions according to the current state of automata on grapheme is taken if this layer can't find a particular grapheme.

- Adjust the sequence between strokes
- Split a stroke into the smaller strokes

SYL layer : Elements of SYL layer combine recognized graphemes in sequence to recognize an initial consonant, a vowel and a final consonant(if any) to form the syllable according to the automata on Hangul syllables. This layer is the final output layer for Hangul recognition.

3 Experimental Results

3.1 Simulation Environment

This extended SEJONG-NET is implemented in C language on Sparc-1 Workstation(SDT-200). For off-line recognition, we used 2350 printed Hangul syllabic data obtained from a font file of Macintosh because the data obtained through scanner have too many complex contacts to handle properly at this stage of the research. Also, we used 600 handwritten syllabic characters for on-line recognition experiment.(most frequently used 200 syllables by 3 persons).

3.2   Recognition Result

Although we used off-line data obtained form a font file to tackle the contact problems between strokes/graphemes with ease, data have many contacts. In this circumstance the model recognized 90.8 % of data described. In the on-line recognition, the recognition rate is 94.5 %.

In the case of off-line character recognition, most of misrecognition are caused by the contacts between strokes/graphemes. In the case of on-line character recognition, many data are misrecognized because the variations of the shape of strokes and the connectivity among strokes.

The test patterns could be classified into the 6 types of Hangul according to the arrangement of graphemes.(See ⟨Figure 4⟩). According to these types, the result of the recognition are shown in ⟨Table 1⟩.

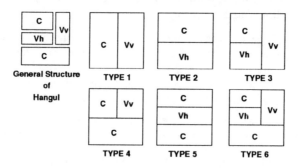

Figure 4: The 6 types of Hangul

The average recognition time is about 13 second per character for the recognition of off-line characters, and about 4 second per character for the recognition of on-line characters.

In the case of off-line character recognition, it took too much time to reanalyze a given pattern when the recognition on a guessed target fails. On the other hand the model recognized on-line characters easily and most of on-line data could be recognized only using feed-forward paths because the temporal information is available.

		No of data	No of Reco	No of Misreco	Reco Rate(%)
Type 1	Off-line	148	132	16	89.2
	On-line	148	142	6	95.9
Type 2	Off-line	94	87	7	92.6
	On-line	77	76	1	98.7
Type 3	Off-line	101	95	6	94.1
	On-line	26	25	1	96.2
Type 4	Off-line	1070	971	99	90.8
	On-line	215	200	15	93.0
Type 5	Off-line	587	523	64	89.1
	On-line	113	106	7	93.8
Type 6	Off-line	350	326	24	93.1
	On-line	21	18	3	85.7
Total	Off-line	2350	2134	216	90.8
	On-line	600	567	33	94.5

Table 1: The result of the recognition according to the structure of Hangul

⟨Figure 5⟩ and ⟨Figure 6⟩ show the example of correctly recognized character. As you can see in ⟨Figure 5⟩ and ⟨Figure 6⟩ the sequence of extracted strokes is identical to that of human writing.

4   Conclusions

From the described experiment, we can say that the model is valid for off-line character recognition. This model recovers temporal informations from a off-line character through scanning selectively over strokes according to the remembered writing sequence, and then the on-line recognizer uses the off-line character together with the recovered temporal information as its input. In on-line recognition case the temporal information on a given pattern is already known, the model can readily recognize the pattern. Because the model is a superset of

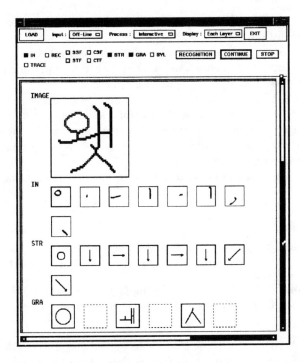

Figure 5: The example of correctly recognized character (1)

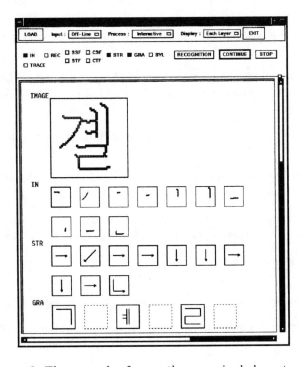

Figure 6: The example of correctly recognized character (2)

on-line Hangul recognition model, the model can recognize both off-line characters and on-line characters using a common mechanism of recognition.

When contacts occur, the system guesses a target based on the remembered writing sequence, and then tests it by using knowledge of the higher processing stages. Through this experiment we have solved some of the inter-grapheme contact problems by analysis-by-synthesis approach.

Current implementation of the model did not obtain a high recognition rate in recognizing both on-line and off-line Hangul characters, but it has presented plausible model of reading/recognizing off-line characters through the same recognition mechanism using temporal information from the perspective of cognitive science. To obtain better recognition rate, more knowledge of contacts and the variations of stroke informations such as shape, connectivity, and sequence should be added.

In the near future, we are planning to test the model with handwritten off-line characters.

References

[1] Y. Lee and A-Yeon Chung, "Sejong-Net: A Dynamic Visual Pattern Recognition Neural Net," *Proc. of Int. Joint Conference on Neural Networks 90 WASH. DC*, Vol.1, pp.412-415, 1990

[2] Cho H.J., J.Kim, A-Yeon Chung and Y.Lee, "Sejong-Net: A Neural Net Model for Dynamic Character Recognition," *Proc. of Int. Conference on Fuzzy Logic and Neural Networks IIZUKA '90*, Vol.1, pp.315-318, 1990.7

[3] J.Kim and Y.Lee, "Handwritten English Alphabet Recognition using SEJONG-NET," *Proc. of 1990 Fall Conference of SIG-AI of Korean Information Science Society*, pp.107-111, 1990 (in Korean)

[4] S.Kim, "On-line Recognition of Handwriting Chinese Character(Radical) using SEJONG-NET," Master thesis of Yonsei Univ., SEOUL, KOREA, 1991 (in Korean)

[5] S.Lee, K.Lee and Y.Lee, "A Generalized Character Recognition using SEJONG-NET," *Proc. of the 2nd Pacific Rim Int. Conference on Artificial Intelligence*, Vol.2, pp.947-952, 1992

[6] Sukhan Lee and Jack C. Pan, "Handwritten Numeral Recognition based on Hierarchically Self-Organizing Learning Networks with Spatio-Temporal Pattern Representation," *Proc. of 1992 IEEE Computer Society Conference on Computer Vision and Pattern Recognition*, pp.176-182,1992

[7] David S. Doermann and Azriel Rosenfeld, "Recovery of Temporal Information from Static Images of Handwriting." *Proc. of 1992 IEEE Computer Society Conference on Computer Vision and Pattern Recognition*, pp.162-168, 1992

[8] A. Marcelli et.al, "Recovering Dynamic Information From Static Handwriting," *Jour. of Pattern Recognition*, Vol.26, No.3, pp.409-418, 1993.3

[9] H.Kang, et.al, "Hangul Recognition using Syntax Analysis and Pattern Classification," *Proc. of Conference on Hangul and Korean Language Processing*, pp.197-202,1989 (in Korean)

[10] K.Lee, Y.B.Kwon and Y.Lee, "A Novel Hangul Recognition Algorithm based on Stroke Extraction," *Proc. of the 1st Int. Conference on Document Analysis and Recognition*, pp.272-280, Saint Malo, France, 1991

[11] M.Halle and K.N.Stevens, "Analysis by Synthesis," *Proc.of the Seminar on Speech Compression and Processing*, Bedford,

[12] M.Eden, "Handwriting and pattern recognition," *Trans. Information Theory*, IT-8, pp.160-166, 1962

[13] ULRIC NEISSER, "Cognitive Psychology," Prentice-Hall INC., Englewood Cliffs, New Jersey, 1961, pp.101-102

[14] Jin-Whan Kim, et.al, "A Study for ASIC Chip Implementation of the Noise Elimination and the Thinning," *Proc. of 1991 Spring Conference of SIG-AI of Korean Information Science Society*, pp.164-168, 1991 (in Korean)

Machine Vision

Session Chairs: Kunihiko Fukushima
Robert Hecht-Nielsen

POSTER PRESENTATIONS

Neural Network Power Density Filter for Image Filtering

Sławomir Skoneczny Jarosław Szostakowski and Rafał Foltyniewicz

Control Division,
Institute of Control & Industrial Electronics (ISEP),
Warsaw University of Technology,
00–662 Warszawa, ul. Koszykowa 75, Poland
e-mail: skonecz@plwatu21.bitnet

November 26, 1993

Abstract

In this paper we present neural network implementation of the power density filter for image restoration purpose. Two performance indices are utilized by the neural network: minimum square error and minimum of error absolute value. This filter assumes that the power density after restoration is equal to power density of original image. The autocorrelation estimate of power density is used. The filter proved its fast convergence (below 50 iterations) controlled by the learning factor in conjugate gradient method, which was applied both in continues and discrete filter realization, presented in this paper.

1 Introduction

The problem of restoring noisy - blurred images is a very important in early vision processing for a large number of applications [1]. Restoration techniques are applied to remove:

1. system degradation such as blur due to optical aberrations, atmospheric turbulence, motion, and diffraction,

2. statistical degradation due to noise.

Over the last 20 years, various methods such as the inverse filter [1], Wiener filter [1], homomorphic filter [1], Kalman filter [5], [4], SVD pseudoinverse [3], and many other approaches have been proposed for image restorations. Also methods using neural nets approach have been proposed [6], [2].

2 Problem formulation

In many practical situation, the image degradation can be adequately modelled by a linear blur (motion, defocusing, turbulence, or others) and the additive white Gaussian process. Then the degradation model is given by

$$y = Hx + n \qquad (1)$$

where y, z, and n represent, respectively, the lexicographically ordered original and degrade images and the additive noise. Matrix H represents the linear spatially invariant or spatially varying distortion. It has as elements samples of the point spread function (PSF) of the imaging system. H can have special structure depending on the properties of the PSF. In the following we assume that the size of the images is $M \times N$, resulting in x and y being $MN \times 1$ vectors and H an $MN \times MN$ matrix.

With this model, the purpose of digital image restoration is to operate on the degraded image y to obtain an improved image that is close to the original image x as possible, subject to a suitable optimality criterion.

3   Multilayer Perceptron Realization of Autocorelation Filter

Another interesting idea of taking the advantage of neural network in image restoration is the usage of the multilayer perceptron as a autocorrelation or power density filter (homomorphic).

Writing equation (1) in an equivalent form of

$$y_i = \sum_{j=0}^{N-1} H_{i,j} x_j + n_i \qquad (2)$$

and denoting

$$z_i = \sum_{j=0}^{N-1} H_{i,j} x_j \qquad (3)$$

we obtain noise autocorrelation function expressed as

$$e_l = \sum_{k=0}^{N-1} y_{l-k} y_k - \sum_{k=0}^{N-1} z_{l-k} z_k = \sum_{k=0}^{N-1} (y_{l-k} y_k - z_{l-k} z_k) \qquad (4)$$

$$\frac{\partial e_l}{\partial x_i} = \sum_{k=0}^{N-1} \frac{\partial}{\partial x_i} [y_{l-k} y_k - z_{l-k} z_k] = -\sum_{k=0}^{N-1} \left[\frac{\partial z_{l-k}}{\partial x_i} z_k + \frac{\partial z_k}{\partial x_i} z_{l-k} \right] \qquad (5)$$

If we take into account that

$$\frac{\partial z_k}{\partial x_i} = \frac{\partial}{\partial x_i} \sum_{j=0}^{N-1} H_{kj} x_j = H_{ki} \qquad (6)$$

then the equation (5) can be expressed as

$$\frac{\partial e_l}{\partial x_i} = \sum_{k=0}^{N-1} [H_{l-k,i} z_k + H_{k,i} z_{l-k}] \qquad (7)$$

In order to be used as a homomorphic (squared autocorrelation) filter the neural network should minimized a proper performance index (energy function) i.e.

$$E = \frac{1}{2} \sum_{l=0}^{N-1} e_l^2 \qquad (8)$$

Minimizing this energy leads to the next step

$$\frac{\partial E}{\partial x_i} = \sum_{l=0}^{N-1} e_l \frac{\partial e_l}{\partial x_i} = - \sum_{l=0}^{N-1} e_l \left[\sum_{k=0}^{N-1} (H_{l-k,i} z_k + H_{k,l} z_{l-k}) \right] \qquad (9)$$

The filtering rule for continuous case (state updating rule) uses the steepest descent method. Therefore we have

$$\frac{dx_i}{dt} = -\mu \frac{\partial E}{\partial x_i} = \mu \sum_{l=0}^{N-1} e_l \left[\sum_{k=0}^{N-1} (H_{l-k,i} z_k + H_{k,l} z_{l-k}) \right] \qquad (10)$$

Sometimes it is more convenient (especially when simulating neural network on a discrete, sequential computer) to use a discrete representation of equation (10). So we have

$$x_{i+1} = x_i + \epsilon \sum_{l=0}^{N-1} e_l \left[\sum_{k=0}^{N-1} (H_{l-k,i} z_k + H_{k,l} z_{l-k}) \right] \qquad (11)$$

Alternative performance index possible to minimize is

$$E = \sum_{i=0}^{N-1} |e_l| \qquad (12)$$

then

$$\frac{\partial E}{\partial x_i} = \frac{\partial}{\partial x_i} \sum_{l=0}^{N-1} |e_l| = \sum_{l=0}^{N-1} \frac{\partial}{\partial x_i} |e_l| = \sum_{l=0}^{N-1} sign(e_l) \frac{\partial e_l}{\partial x_i} \qquad (13)$$

Continuing the minimization procedure we compute

$$\frac{\partial e_l}{\partial x_i} = \frac{\partial}{\partial x_i} \left[\sum_{k=0}^{N-1} (y_{l-k} y_k - z_{l-k} z_k) \right] = - \sum_{k=0}^{N-1} \frac{\partial}{\partial x_i} (z_{l-k} z_k) = - \sum_{k=0}^{N-1} \left[\frac{\partial z_{l-k}}{\partial x_i} z_k + \frac{\partial z_k}{\partial x_i} z_{l-k} \right] \quad (14)$$

and

$$\frac{\partial z_k}{\partial x_i} = \frac{\partial}{\partial x_i} \sum_{j=0}^{N-1} H_{kj} x_j = H_{ki} \qquad (15)$$

Therefor we have another continues filtering rules:

Figure 1: Degraded (left) and restored (right) Lena image

$$\frac{dx_i}{dt} = -\mu\frac{\partial E}{\partial x_i} = \mu \sum_{l=0}^{N} sign(e_l)\left[\sum_{k=0}^{N-1}(H_{l-k,i}z_k + H_{k,l}z_{l-k})\right] \tag{16}$$

and discrete one

$$x_{i+1} = x_i + \epsilon \sum_{l=0}^{N-1} sign(e_l)\left[\sum_{k=0}^{N-1}(H_{l-k,i}z_k + H_{k,l}z_{l-k})\right] \tag{17}$$

4   Experimental Results and Conlusion

A neural network implementation of power density filter seems to be very promising and effective tool for gray level image processing and restoration. The sizes of tested images varied from 16×16 to 128×128. For both performance indices i.e. minimum square error and minimum of the absolute values error, neural network converges to the stable state (equilibrium point) significantly reducing this way the degradation of the image increasing a signal to noise ratio and performing filtering task. By applying the varying learning factor ϵ in conjugate gradient method we can speed up the converges of the algorithm (30 iterations is usually enough to be in stable state). We replace then a long period of training time for multilayer perceptron and backpropagation algorithm (many thousands of lessons by just 30 iteration.) In our case the training phase is actually a filtering phase. It is worth mentioning that in order to reduce the computation burden of algorithm and to speed it up we use Fast Fourier Transform (FFT) for calculating convolution while computing autocorrelation function of the images. It allowed us to simulate filtering of real size images on a 386/486 PC computer. However, this implementation would by much more efficient while using neural hardware. Example of the filtering by neural power density filter is presented on Lena image (see figures 1 and 2).

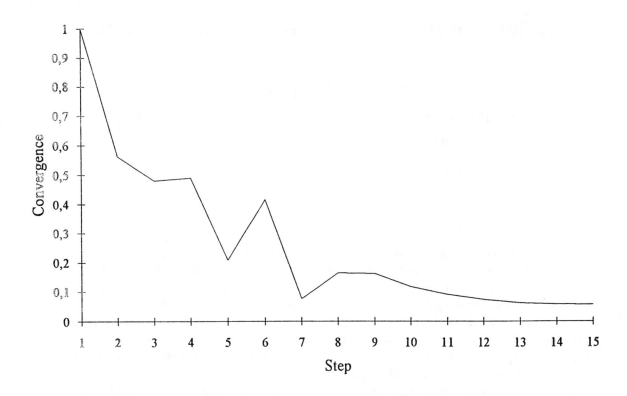

Figure 2: Covergence of Neural Network Filter for Lena Image

References

[1] H. C. Andrews and B. R. Hunt. *Digital Image Restoration*. Prentice-Hall, Englewood Cliffs, NJ, 1977.

[2] Joon K. Paik and Aggelos K. Katsaggelos. Image restoration using a modified hopfield network. *IEEE Trans. on Image Processing*, 1(1):49–63, January 1992.

[3] William K. Pratt. *Digital Image Processing*. John Wiley & Sons, second edition, 1991.

[4] S. Skoneczny and A. Dzieliński. Image Processing by Neural Network Implementation of 2–D Kalman Filter. In T. Kohonen, K. Mäkisara, O. Simula, and J. Kangas, editors, *Proceedings of International Conference on Artificial Neural Networks*, pages 1075–1078, Helsinki–Espoo, Finland, 1991.

[5] J. W. Woods and V. K. Ingle. Kalman filtering in two dimensions: Further results. *IEEE Trans. Acoustics, Speech, and Signal Processing*, ASSP-29(4):188–197, April 1981.

[6] Yi-Tong Zhou, Rama Chellappa, Aseem Vaid, and B. Keith Jenkins. Image restoration using a neural network. *IEEE Trans. Acoustics, Speech, and Signal Processing*, 36(7):1141–1151, July 1988.

Motion analysis with recurrent neural nets

A. Psarrou†,H. Buxton‡

† School of Computer Science, Uni. of Westminster, London, U.K.

‡ COGS, Uni. of Sussex, Brighton, U.K.

Abstract

During this work we show how observed trajectories can be mapped on recurrent neural networks in order to resolve the problem of temporal prediction in visual tasks as diverse as the interpretation of cell images and the recognition of moving vehicles. As it is noted, objects move purposely in an environment and effective prediction on their trajectories can be achieved by modelling the spatio-temporal regularities associated with their moving purposes. Such hidden regularities can be represented by a finite state machine where the location of the regularities correspond to the states of the machine and the orientation and dispacement vectors correspond to the transition arcs. Such a representation can be modelled on a neural network based on Elman's architecture that learns the significant locations of the trajectory of a moving object and encodes such information in its hidden units.

1   Introduction

Visual tasks such as the interpretation of cell images (Psarrou and Buxton, 1993) and the recognition of moving vehicles require to track objects along their trajectory and to predict their future position in their environment. It was noted that objects move purposely in an environment and effective prediction on their trajectories can be achieved by modelling the spatio-temporal regularities associated with their moving purposes with visually augmented hidden Markov Models (Gong and Buxton, 1992). Temporal prediction and recognition require (a) a short-term memory that retains aspects of the input sequence relevant to prediction and recognition, (b) the specification of a function that combines the current memory and the current input in order to form a new temporal context (Mozer, 1993), (c) to identify and learn the regularities from the temporal sequence. Feedforward neural networks (Figure 1a) can be trained with the backpropagation algorithm to represent, predict and recognise temporally ordered events since (a) they are capable of extracting "common features" from a temporal sequence, (b) can encode such features in the hidden units of the network and (c) these features encode information that relates past events with future input values. However, this approach requires the spatial representation of events by parallelising time which involves several drawbacks: (a) only allows fixed window size on the event representation, (b) large memory consumption and (c) the network cannot easily distinguish the relative temporal position of an element in a sequence from its absolute temporal position (Elman, 1990). In this paper we explore the work of (Elman, 1990), (Cleeremans et al, 1989) and (Mozer, 1993) to show how recurrent neural networks can be used to address the problem of temporal prediction in computer vision applications.

2   Why Recurrent Neural Networks

A popular way to recognise and predict sequences is to use partially recurrent networks. In these architectures the connections are mainly feedforward, but include a carefully chosen set of feedback connections either from the hidden layer or the output layer (Figure 1b). The feedback or context units remember some aspects of the recent past, and so the state of the whole network at time t depends on the aggregate of previous states as well as on the current state. In both cases, feedback is easily implemented by extending the input field with an additional feedback vector containing the hidden or output unit values generated by the preceding input. In most cases the feedback connections are fixed, so standard back-propagation may easily be used for training. Elman suggested the architecture shown in Figure 1b in which the context units hold a copy of the activations of the hidden units from the previous time step. As it is pointed out, the hidden unit patterns of activation represent an "encoding" of the features of the input patterns that are relevant to the task. The context units patterns of activation represent an "encoding" of the relevant features of the past input elements (Elman, 1990). Thus, a hidden layer pattern now can encode information about the relevant features of two consecutive input elements. Furthermore, (a) the event can now be processed sequentially without the need of a buffer and (b) there is not an absolute temporal position of an element. Such a network is able to recognise and produce short continuations of known sequences. Cleeremans (Cleeremans et al, 1989) has shown that when this network is trained with strings from a particular finite-state grammar, it can learn to be a perfect finite-state recognizer for the grammar (Figure 2b).

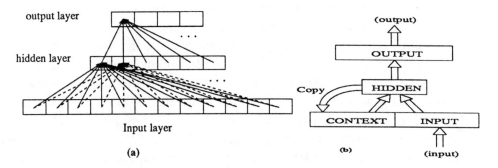

Figure 1: (a) Feedforward network (b) Recurrent network

Prediction using Recurrent Neural Networks: Trajectories that include hidden regularities can be represented by a finite state machine where the location of these regularities correspond to the states of the machine and the orientation and dispacement vectors correspond to the transition arcs. Such a representation can be modelled on a neural network based on Elman's architecture that learns the significant locations of the trajectory of a moving object and encodes such information in its hidden units (Figure 2c). Figure 2b shows a finite state machine representation of a circular trajectory. The states of the machine correspond to the locations in a cyclic trajectory where the orientation changes suddenly, namely at 0, 90, 180 and 270 degrees from the horizontal. The symbols on the transition arcs correspond to the set of possible displacement the object may exhibit. The object may either tranverse to the next state or loop on the same state. Their course of direction can be described by eight qualitative directional states that denote the next possible movement of the object and are shown in Figure 2a.

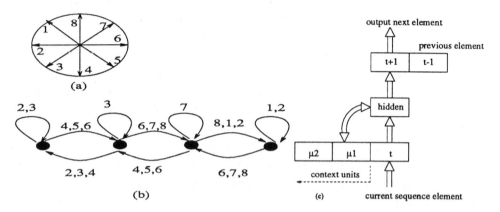

Figure 2: (a) Qualitative directional states. (b,c) A finite-state machine modeled by a recurrent neural network is used to model and predict the trajectory of purposively moving vehicles.

3 Architecture and Experimental Results

When mapping object trajectories on recurrent neural networks the following issues should be addressed: (a) the representation of the object's trajectory in terms of data elements and (b) the representation of the trajectory in the short-term memory. In our experiments the object trajctory was represented using only displacement vectors. The displacements were presented as normalised real values in the input units. Trajectories are mapped in the short-term memory using an exponential function (Mozer, 1993) of the past hidden unit activations. The architecture used is shown in Figure 2c. In comprises of: (1) *input layer* of one unit and represents the element of the sequence at time t; (2) *hidden layer* of four units; (3) *output layer* of two units representing the element of the sequence at time $t + 1$ and $t - 1$; (4) *context layer* of eight units. The value of the context units is an exponential encoding of the hidden unit activation values. They maintain moving averages of past hidden value activations according to the equation $x_i(t) = (1 - \mu_i)x(t) + \mu_i x_i(t - 1)$, where μ_i lies in the interval $[1, -1]$ and allows for the representation of averages spanning various intervals of time, $x(t)$ represents the vector of the hidden units activation values at time t and, $x_i(t)$

represents the memory vector i at time t. An exponential trace memory is formed using the kernel function $c_i(t) = (1 - \mu_i)\mu_i^t$. Figure 3 shows the expected and predicted cyclic trajectory of a moving vehicle. As it is shown the trajectory predicted from the network follows the pattern of the expected orientation along the trajectory. The results show that (a) there may be a scaling factor between the expected and predicted displacement value (b) a different data representation where the displacement values are encoded in the gradient of the input sequence may be prefered.

4 Discussion

In this paper we described how observed trajectories can be mapped on recurrent neural networks. During our experiments we showed that the network was able to learn the sequence that was presented to it and produce continuations of the observed sequence given the initial element. Investigation of the hidden unit activation values showed that they exhibit characteristic patterns associated with the orientation pattern of the trajectory, however a cluster analysis on the hidden unit values did not yet provide any conclusive evidence of state representation. This is mainly attributed to the absolute displacement value predicted by the network. Past experiments have shown that the (a) the number of memory elements in the context units and (b) the data representation of the input sequence may affect considerably the recovery of quantitative results. Our work currently is to (a) exploit further the parameter setting of our network architecture and especially the structure of the context layer, (b) exploit alternative data representation of our input sequence as suggested in the previous section and apply this network to a real world scenario.

5 References

Cleeremans, A. et. al. (1989), "Finite State Automata and Simple Recurrent Networks", *Neural Computation*, 1, 372-381.

Elman, J. (1990), "Finding structure in time", *Cognitive Science*, 14, 179-211.

Gong, S., Buxton, H. (1992), "On the Expectations of Moving Objects", ECAI-92, Vienna, Austria.

Mozer, M. (1993) "Neural net architectures for temporal sequence processing", *Predicting the future and Understanding the past* A. Weigend & N. Gershenfeld (eds), Redwood City, CA: Addison-Wesley.

Psarrou, A., Buxton, H. (1993), "Hybrid architecture for understanding motion sequences", *Neurocomputing*, 5, 221-241.

A Computational Model for Texton-based Preattentive Texture Segmentation

Mehdi N. Shirazi, Mitsuo Hida and Yoshikazu Nishikawa

Elec. Eng. Dept., Kyoto University Yoshida-Honmachi, Sakyoku, Kyoto, Japan

Abstract- A hierarchical Markov random field with two layers is proposed as a computational model for texton-based preattentive texture segmentation. Different textures are assumed to be different arrangements of bars (textons) with different orientations.

1 Introduction

A fundamental property of human visual system is its ability to discriminate between textures. A systematic approach to texture discrimination was pioneered and pursued by Julesz [3]. Julesz has made it clear that human visual system operates in two distinct modes called "preattentive vision" and "attentive vision." In preattentive vision, texture differences are perceived by an observer almost instantaneously and effortlessly whereas in the attentive vision, they are perceived by a time-consuming serial search and scrutiny. Julesz and his colleagues have hypothesized that a preattentive texture discrimination is done instantaneously and effortlessly based on a few local conspicuous features, which they called textons, [4]. On the other hand, there have, in parallel, been efforts to describe the preattentive texture discrimination in terms of linear filter models and their nonlinear extensions (see the references given in [8].)

The texton theory is not a computational theory. The texton theory has been proposed to explain, as closely as possible, the psychophysical findings regarding the ability of the human preattentive visual system. On the contrary to the texton theory, the linear spatial filtering theory is a computational theory constructed in such a way to be in consistent with the known physiological findings regarding the early vision of primates. The linear filtering theory cannot fully explain the psychophysical findings and there have been some efforts to to extend it by adding some nonlinear elements in order to explain quantitatively the psychophysical data regarding the human preattentive vision. Nevertheless, the filtering theory is not still capable of explaining some psychophysical findings which can be explained by the texton theory [8].

Our main goal is to construct a computational model for preattentive texture discrimination (segmentation) based on texton theory. In this paper, we propose a hierarchical Markov random field with two layers as a preliminary computational model for texton-based preattentive texture segmentation.

2 Test Images

We assume that test images (images displayed to an observer for a brief time for a preattentive segmentation or to the preattentive segmentation system which we are going to make)

consist of $N \times N$ texton subimages. Each subimage might consists of $n \times n$ pixels, where n is an integer which its actual value is not important. We assume that the subimages are located on an $N \times N$ rectangular lattice $\mathcal{L} = \{(i,j)\}$, $1 \leq i, j \leq N$. Each subimage is assumed to be either empty or depicts a texton. In this paper, we only consider textures consisting of bars (texton) with $0°$, $45°$, $90°$ and $135°$ angles and encode them by 2, 3, 4, and 5, respectively and keep 1 as a code for empty subimages. We associate a random variable Y_{ij} to the (i,j)-subimage and treat test images as realizations of the random field $Y_{\mathcal{L}} = \{Y_{ij}\}$, $(i,j) \in \mathcal{L}$, where Y_{ij} takes a value from the set $\{1,2,3,4,5\}$. In Fig. 1, we display the possible states of the (i,j)-subimage and their codes.

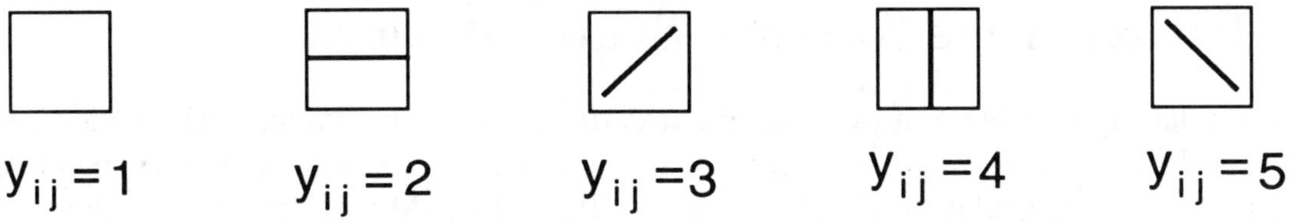

$$y_{ij} = 1 \qquad y_{ij} = 2 \qquad y_{ij} = 3 \qquad y_{ij} = 4 \qquad y_{ij} = 5$$

Figure 1: The subimages' possible states and their associated codes.

3 Modeling of the Test Images

We model test images consisting of regions of different textures (texton arrangements) by a hierarchical Markov random field (HMRF) with two layers. The first layer consists of an MRF [2] which is considered as a model for the underlying unobservable regions while the second layer incorporates MRFs which are assumed to generate the observable distinct textures.

3.1 A Hierarchical Markov Random Field with Two Layers

We assume that a test image consisting of regions of different textures is a realization of a collection of interacting random variables $(X_{\mathcal{L}}, Y_{\mathcal{L}})$. The image process $Y_{\mathcal{L}} = \{Y_{ij}\}$, $(i,j) \in \mathcal{L}$ is assumed to be a function of the underlying region process $X_{\mathcal{L}} = \{X_{ij}\}$, $(i,j) \in \mathcal{L}$. The interacting processes $(X_{\mathcal{L}}, Y_{\mathcal{L}})$ can be characterized completely by a joint probability density function $P(x_{\mathcal{L}}, y_{\mathcal{L}})$ or equivalently, according to Bayes' rule, by $P(x_{\mathcal{L}})$ and $P(y_{\mathcal{L}} \mid x_{\mathcal{L}})$. In the following, we precisely describe $(X_{\mathcal{L}}, Y_{\mathcal{L}})$ in terms of $P(x_{\mathcal{L}})$ and $P(y_{\mathcal{L}} \mid x_{\mathcal{L}})$.

We consider test images consisting of M different textures (textons with different arrangements), i.e., we assume that X_{ij} is a discrete-valued random variable taking a value from the set $Q_X = \{1, \ldots, M\}$. We further assume that $X_{\mathcal{L}}$ is an MRF characterized by local conditional distributions $P(x_{ij} \mid x_{\eta'_{ij}X})$, where η'_{ij} denotes η_{ij} with the (i,j)-subimage deleted. For details see [6].

The conditional joint distribution $P(y_{\mathcal{L}} \mid x_{\mathcal{L}})$ is given by

$$P(y_{\mathcal{L}} \mid x_{\mathcal{L}}) = (Z^{Y|X})^{-1} e^{-\mathcal{E}(y_{\mathcal{L}}|x_{\mathcal{L}})} \tag{1}$$

where the global conditional energy function is

$$\mathcal{E}(y_{\mathcal{L}} \mid x_{\mathcal{L}}) = \sum_{(i,j) \in \mathcal{L}} \sum_{C \in \mathcal{C}_{ij}^Y(x_{\eta_{ij}^Y(x_{ij})})} \mathcal{E}(y_C \mid x_{ij}) \qquad (2)$$

and the conditional partition function is given by

$$Z^{Y|X} = \sum_{y_{\mathcal{L}} \in \Omega_Y} e^{-\mathcal{E}(y_{\mathcal{L}} \mid x_{\mathcal{L}})}. \qquad (3)$$

In (3), $\Omega_Y(x_{\mathcal{L}}) = \prod_{(i,j) \in \mathcal{L}} Q_Y$, where $Q_Y = \{1, 2, 3, 4, 5\}$. For details see [6].

4 Preattentive Texture Segmentation

We formulate the problem of preattentive texture segmentation as an optimization problem. Let $P(x_{\mathcal{L}})$ and $P(y_{\mathcal{L}} \mid x_{\mathcal{L}})$ be given. We assume that the preattentive segmentation is carried out by calculating the Maximum A Posteriori (MAP) estimate of the region process $X_{\mathcal{L}}$, when a target image $y_{\mathcal{L}}$ is given as a realization of $Y_{\mathcal{L}}$. By definition, the MAP estimate of $X_{\mathcal{L}}$ is

$$\hat{x}_{\mathcal{L}} = \arg \max_{x_{\mathcal{L}} \in \Omega_X} P(x_{\mathcal{L}} \mid y_{\mathcal{L}}). \qquad (4)$$

We have already proposed a parallel deterministic relaxation algorithm based on the mean field approximations to solve the above large scale optimization problem [7]. The local deterministic updating rule of the algorithm is given by

$$\hat{x}_{ij}^{(p+1)} = \arg \max_{x_{ij} \in Q_X} P(y_{ij} \mid x_{ij}, x_{\eta_{ij}'^Y}^{(p)}, y_{\eta_{ij}'^Y}) P(x_{ij} \mid x_{\eta_{ij}'^X}^{(p)}) \qquad (5)$$

at the $(p+1)$-th iteration.

5 Simulation Result

To test our computational model, we applied it to the test image shown in Fig. 2(a). It is well known that the human preattentive vision segments the test image into two regions of tilted Ts and upright Ts and Ls. As it is shown in Fig. 2, our computational model shows the same behaviour. For the region process, we used a 2nd-order MRF model with the following local conditional distribution [1]

$$p(x_{ij} \mid x_{\eta_{ij}'^X}) = \frac{e^{\beta \mathcal{E}_{\eta_{ij}'^X}(x_{ij})}}{\sum_{k=1}^M e^{\beta \mathcal{E}_{\eta_{ij}'^X}(k)}}$$

where $\mathcal{E}_{\eta_{ij}'^X}$ denotes the number of x_{ij}-valued pixels in $\eta_{ij}'^X$, $M = 3$ and $\beta = 0.8$. For the texture processes, we used 2nd-order MRF models with singleton and doubleton (pairwise) cliques only, given respectively as follows

$$\mathcal{E}(y_{ij} \mid x_{ij}) = \begin{cases} -\alpha_0(x_{ij}) & \text{when } y_{ij} = 0 \\ 0 & \text{otherwise} \end{cases}$$

and

$$\mathcal{E}(y_C \mid x_{ij}) = \begin{cases} -\alpha_C(y_{ij}, x_{ij}) & \text{if pixels in C have the same value} \\ \alpha_C(y_{ij}, x_{ij}) & \text{otherwise} \end{cases}$$

where C denotes a pair-wise clique. If we assume that the MRF models are homogenous and isotropic then it is easy to see that our model has sixty four parameters in total. In our simulation study, we set the horizontal and vertical bonding parameters to 1.0 for the textures consisting of upright Ts and Ls, the diagonal bonding parameters to 1.5 for the texture consisting of tilted T's, the singleton parameters to 10.0 and the rest of parameters to 0.0. The segmentation is initialized by an image consisting of three regions (white, black and crossed squares) scattered randomly as shown in Fig. 2 (b).

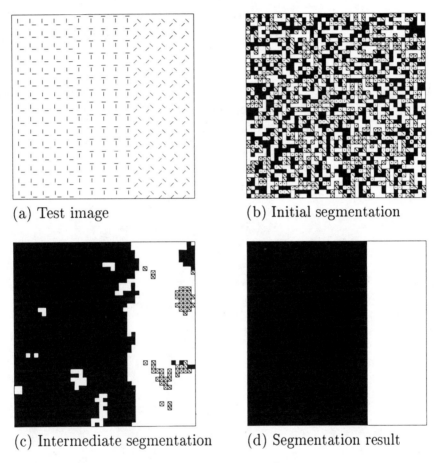

(a) Test image

(b) Initial segmentation

(c) Intermediate segmentation

(d) Segmentation result

Figure 2: Segmentation result after 20 iterations

References

[1] J. E. Besag, "On the Statistical Analysis of Dirty Pictures", J. Roy. Statis., Soc. B, 48, No. 3, pp.259-302, 1986.

[2] S. Geman and D. Geman, "Stochastic relaxation, Gibbs distributions, and the Bayesian restoration of images," IEEE Trans. on Pattern Analysis and Machine Intelligence, PAMI-6, pp. 721-741, 1984.

[3] B. Julesz, "Visual Pattern Discrimination," IRE Trans. Info. Theory, IT-8, pp. 84 92, 1962.

[4] B. Julesz and J. R. Bergen, "Textons, the Fundamental Elements in Preattentive Vision and Perception of Textures," Bell System Technical Journal 62(6), pp. 1619-1645, 1983.

[5] J. Malik and P. Person, "Preattentive Texture Discrimination with Early Vision Mechanisms," J. Opt. Soc. Am. A, Vol., No., pp.923 932, 1990.

[6] Mehdi N. Shirazi and H. Noda, "Textured Image Segmentation: Hierarchical Markov Random Fields and Mean Field Approximations," submitted to IEEE Transactions on Image Processing.

[7] Mehdi N. Shirazi and H. Noda, "A Deterministic Iterative Algorithm for HMRF-Textured Image Segmentation," Proceedings of IJCNN'93-NAGOYA, Japan, October 1993.

[8] D. Williams and B. Julesz, "Filters Versus Textons in Human and Machine Texture Discrimination," in Neural Networks for Perception Vol. 1, Human and Machine Perception edited by H. Wechster, pp. 145 175, 1992.

A General Purpose Model for Image Processing based on Multilayer Perceptrons

Jenlong Moh and Frank. Y. Shih
Department of Computer and Information Science
New Jersey Institute of Technology
Newark, NJ 07102

Abstract

In this paper, we investigate the use of multilayer perceptrons with recurrent connections as general purpose processing modules in a parallel architecture for image processing. The networks are trained to learn classification rules in order to determine the output of their corresponding pixels in the processed image. The training patterns can be obtained from existing algorithm of well-defined transformations or can be extracted by loading sample image along with its target image. The latter is meaningful if the operation applied to an image is an unknown operation because we may find the input-output association by using input patterns and its desired output for training multilayer perceptron. The potential application of the model includes image smoothing, enhancement, edge detection, noise removal, morphological operations, image filtering, etc. By providing different sets of training patterns the system may adapt itself to corresponding operations. With a number of stages stacked up together we may apply several different operations on the image. Besides, recurrent connections from the output of last stage to the input of the first stage also allow repeated sequence of operations to be used.

I. INTRODUCTION

A typical vision system requires many *low-level* capabilities we often take for granted; for example, our ability to extract intrinsic images of *lightness*, *color*, and *range*. To extract interesting parts of an image, we have to apply some low-level image operations, such as smoothing, enhancement, edge detection, noise removal, morphological operations, etc. Low-level processing deals with functions that may be viewed as automatic reactions, requiring no intelligence on that part of the image analysis system [3]. A number of algorithms for these operations has been developed [3][8]. Most of these algorithms need to check the values of neighboring pixels to determine the new value of a pixel. The computation of the algorithm for pixel values are usually independent to that for other pixels. Therefore, parallelism of the computation is highly expected in order to achieve higher performance. The introduction of neural network models has been an exciting approach for most of the image analysis tasks due to their highly parallelism and good learning performance.

Some efforts in developing morphology neural networks have been found in literatures. Davidson [1][2] redefined the weighted-sum activation function with additive maximum operation, which is in fact the original definition of gray-scale dilation in mathematical morphology [11]. Shih and Moh [12] developed a neural architecture to extract the maximum or the minimum value among nine input by parallelly compare every pair of the inputs in one stage. Morales and Ko [7] proposed an efficient implementation of neural training algorithm and defined an overall equality index related fuzzy implication, *Lukasiewicz &-conjunction*, as a performance index. In [5], a parallel implementation of Rosenfeld-Kak thinning [9] algorithm and Wang-Zhang thinning algorithm are proposed using recurrent multistage multilayer neural networks. The proposed architectures may learn the deletion rule to determine if an object pixel should be eliminated during skeletonization. All of them contribute the implementation of architecture performing a special operation only.

Our goal is to design a general purpose architecture which can adapt itself to different sets of operations. We adopt the multilayer perceptrons (MLPs) as processing modules so that no special neural net has to be defined. Such an architecture promises the feasibility of learning different operations and applying an operation parallelly to all pixels in the image. The proposed MLP modules may learn transformation rule in two different ways: using training patterns obtained from existing algorithm of well-defined transformations and using training patterns extracted from sample images and the target images. The former is significant in processing binary images and the latter is meaningful for unknown operation and/or for gray-scale images. With a number of stages stacked up together we may apply several different operations on the image. Besides, recurrent connections from the output of last stage to the input of the first stage allow repeating a sequence of operations.

In this paper, section II discusses how a multilayer perceptron can be used as processing modules for low-level image operations. Section III elaborates the system architecture proposed for adaptive image processing. Section IV shows an example of system design and explain the idea in determining good training parameters. Section V concludes the paper and points out some directions of future researches.

II. MULTILAYER PERCEPTRON AS PROCESSING MODULES

Multilayer perceptrons are feed-forward nets with one or more layers, called hidden layers, of neural cells, called hidden neurons, between the input and output layers. The learning process of MLPs is conducted with back-error propagation learning algorithm derived from *generalized delta rule* [10]. The more hidden layers we use, the more complicated discriminant regions it forms in the domain space spanned with input vectors. There is some tradeoff between the complexity of MLP connections and the time for the MLP to converge. A discussion on limits of the number of hidden neurons in multilayer perceptrons can be found in [4]. Since we are interested in general purpose MLP module, reasonably short training time to adapt the MLP to a new task and big capacity of connection weights are expected. An example of determining the required number of hidden neurons in MLP with one hidden layer is discussed in Section IV.

The back-propagation training algorithm is defined in [10]. The neurons calculate the activation value with the equation

$$x_j^{(n+1)} = f\left[\sum_i w_{ji}^{(n)} x_i^{(n)} - \theta_j\right] \quad \text{where} \quad f(\alpha) = \frac{1}{1 + e^{-(\alpha-\theta)}} \tag{1}$$

The superscript (n) is the label for the layer the neuron is in, and θ serves as the bias or threshold. The sigmoid logistic nonlinearity in Eq.(1) is used as the output function of neurons. The major part of the algorithm is to adjust the connection weights according to the difference between the actual output from Eq. (1) and the desired output provided in training patterns. The equations for weight adjustment (from neuron i in a lower layer to neuron j in next higher layer) is given as follows [6].

$$w_{ji}^{(n)}(t+1) = \begin{cases} w_{ji}^{(n)}(t) + \eta x_i^{(n)} y_j (1 - y_j)(d_j - y_j) & \text{if neuron } j \text{ is in the output layer} \\ w_{ji}^{(n)}(t) + \eta x_i^{(n)} x_j^{(n+1)} (1 - x_j^{(n+1)}) \sum_k \delta_k w_{jk}^{(n)}(t) & \text{if neuron } j \text{ is a hidden layer} \end{cases} \tag{2}$$

where η is the gain term (or called learning rate) and δ_j is the error term for neuron j.

Most of the low-level operations applied in image preprocessing, such as smoothing, enhancement, edge detection, noise removal, morphological operations, etc., require to check the values of neighboring pixels. The sizes of neighboring area may vary depending on the algorithms designed for the operations. Eight-neighbor, of course, along with the center pixel itself is the most common choice. A number of algorithms for these operations are designed to evaluate the values of neighboring pixel and the center pixel to determine whether and/or how the value of the center pixel should be changed. For binary images, the values of center and neighboring pixels forms an input vector of binary values. The expected output is usually a single binary value indicating the resulting value of the center pixel. These algorithms can be used to generate look up tables to associate the relationship between the set of original values and the resulting value.

The input-output association can be realized by neural network models with nine input neurons (assumed that 8-neighbor area is used) and one output neuron with one or more layers of hidden neurons in between. By iteratively presenting input vector to the input neurons and the expected output from the look up table for determining the magnitude of error. The error will then be used to adjust the weights of connections (see the learning algorithm) so that the neural nets can gradually learn the input-output association. If the neural net converges after learning, it can be used as a neural module to determine the value of a pixel after applying the same algorithm.

The training patterns can be generated with the algorithms expected for the specified low-level image operations. In the case of binary image processing with a 3×3 neighboring area, there are up to $2^9 = 512$ training patterns, with a vector of 9 binary values and one desired output. For instance, morphological erosion operation with the structuring element shown in Fig. 1 should have desired output 1 at the center pixel for only the 16 input patterns shown in Fig. 1. and 0 at center pixel for all other input patterns do not contain the structuring elements.

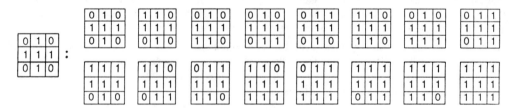

Fig. 1 Erosion structuring element with 16 possibly activating input patterns.

By exhausting all (512) possible combinations of input vectors for training, the MLP module is guaranteed to respond a 1 when the structuring element is contained in the 3×3 window after the training achieves convergence.

III. SYSTEM ARCHITECTURE

Fig. 2 shows the overall architecture consisting of MLP modules for low level image operations. There is one MLP module constructed for each pixel in the input image. Every MLP module applies the trained operation to the pixel and its $m \times m$ neighboring pixels where m means the width of neighborhood window. The neighborhood size may change depending upon the operations to learn.

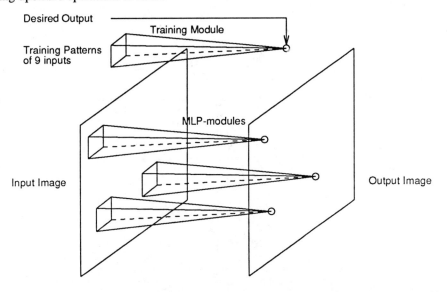

Fig. 2   Overall system architecture with MLP modules for low-level image operations. Each pyramid represents an MLP module and receives m^2 inputs from its $m \times m$ neighboring pixels. To make the figure clear, only some MLP modules are shown in the figure. The separated pyramid, called training module, is used for training task and for storing the trained weights. To simplify the figure, we show only some sample pyramids in between the input and the output images.

Since the same operation is simultaneously applied to all the modules for the pixels in the input image, all MLP modules in the same stage can share the same set of trained connection weights during the operating phase. Thus, no local memory are required for individual MLP modules in between the input and output images to hold the connection weights. This will significantly reduce the required number of local memory for connections weights in MLP modules. In Fig. 2, the separated pyramid shown at the top represents the training module which provides shared memory for connection weights. The training phase is first turned up at the training module. As soon as the training module converges, the connection weights are frozen and are shared and retrieved by all the MLP modules to compute the activation value of each pixel.

The proposed architecture is similar to the one proposed in [12] except the pixel-based operating modules are substituted with MLP modules because MLP modules are capable of adapting themselves to the expected operations. It is also more flexible than those designed for dilation and erosion operations only [5].

During the experiments of different image operations, we found out that the training sets for some operations, such as dilation, erosion, and noise removal, have a small number of patterns with desired 1 or 0 output. For example, erosion operation with structuring element in Fig. 3 has only 16 patterns expecting output 1 and erosion with the following structuring element

1	1	1
1	1	1
1	1	1

Fig.3 A structuring element with all 1's in pixels.

expects an output 1 only if all nine inputs are 1's. By checking the training patterns, we figured out that the value of some of the m^2 inputs do not even affect the output. Without considering for a certain value of the center pixel, the training pattern set can, then, be reduced. The same effect can be achieved by connecting the output neuron directly with the center input and the MLP module operation is bypassed when the center pixel equals 0 or 1. For instance, applying erosion operation to a center pixel with value 0 will never generate an output 1. Also, a dilation operation applied to a center pixel of value 1 will always have output 1. Such bypassing connections can be specified with the desired output as weight in the training MLP module for shared weights. For all the MLP modules in the architecture, the bypassed connections implement an exclusive NOR operation between the center pixel and the memorized connection weight from the training module. The operation of an MLP is disable if the exclusive NOR gets output 1, which mean the center pixel has the same value as specified in the shared module. Fig. 4 illustrates the bypass connection and expresses how it affects the operation of an MLP module.

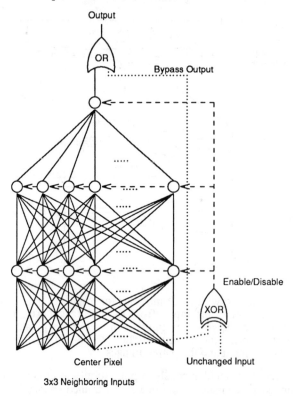

Fig. 4   MLP module with a bypass control to enable/disable the activation of neurons in the modules. The dashed lines with arrows show the enable/disable controls to neurons, while the dotted lines indicate the bypassed connection for passing the value of the center pixel to the output.

We may stack up with more than one stage of the proposed architecture in Fig. 2. By training the stages with different set of patterns, we can provide and apply a sequence of image operations to the input image. The outputs of the last stage may be connected to the inputs of the first stage to form a recurrent architecture so that the same operation sequence can be applied to the image for more than one iteration. See Fig. 5 for the overall architecture.

In the case of gray-scale images, it is impossible to enumerate all $2^{m \times m}$ combinations of training patterns. Thus, we may provide a certain number of sample training patterns to define the discriminant regions in the input space. Such training patterns can be extracted at each pixel location from the sample training images for $m \times m$ inputs and the corresponding pixel in the desired image. The MLP modules can learn input-output association by self-adjusting connection weights based on the error between the actual and the expected pixel values. Fortunately, for most applications, some factors, like environment lights and background materials and colors, can be fixed so that images in the same problem domain are usually limited in a certain number of characteristics. For instance, a vision system designed for a manufacturing plant may only process images containing a finite set of mechanical tools. Representative images chosen from a problem domain can then be used as training images. Their desired output image should also be provided during the training phase so that the training module can associate the input-output mapping. Therefore, automatic training phase can be achieved.

IV. TRAINING EXAMPLES

In determination of number of hidden neurons in MLP modules, we depict the following example. We investigate the training iterations and convergence condition in training MLP module with patterns obtained from morphological dilation and erosion with structuring element shown in Fig. 3, edge detection with Sobel operators, and

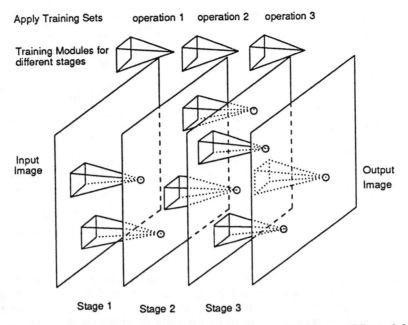

Apply Training Sets   operation 1   operation 2   operation 3

Training Modules for different stages

Input Image

Output Image

Stage 1   Stage 2   Stage 3

Fig. 5   Stacked MLP-based architecture for multiple image operations. Only some MLP-modules are shown to simplify the figure. The separated pyramids at the top of the figure are the training modules for different stages. There may be more stages stacked on the architecture.

noise removal for binary images. The MLP module used in this investigation has nine inputs, 1 output neuron, and one layer of hidden neurons. With a fixed momentum ($\alpha = 0.2$), we change the learning rate, η, (varying from 0.01 to 0.05) and the number of hidden neurons in the hidden layer (varying from 1 to 20) to determine the number of iterations for convergence. Table 1, 2, 3, and 4 show the result of training patterns for morphological dilation operation, morphological erosion operation, edge detection, and noise removal, respectively. A "×" symbol in the table entry represents that the training did not converge in 30,000 iterations. The same set of random weights is used as initial connection weights for all these training experiments.

Table 1. Dilation ($\alpha = 0.1$)					
number of hiddens	η				
	0.01	0.02	0.03	0.04	0.05
20	130	97	85	71	64
19	143	138	102	105	93
18	134	140	91	72	70
17	156	138	88	76	59
16	114	61	51	48	41
15	125	99	94	80	64
14	120	96	81	65	59
13	139	92	72	62	53
12	114	59	44	40	40
11	124	63	42	34	31
10	121	61	43	40	43
9	117	74	70	62	52
8	193	139	115	102	71
7	160	100	75	57	44
6	136	72	52	44	40
5	153	94	77	59	47
4	195	111	75	63	46
3	181	92	62	49	41
2	192	99	67	53	50
1	203	108	76	62	53

Table 2. Erosion ($\alpha = 0.1$)					
number of hiddens	η				
	0.01	0.02	0.03	0.04	0.05
20	141	90	71	80	125
19	130	59	73	81	83
18	119	73	65	81	78
17	123	87	57	77	73
16	212	64	77	98	298
15	140	91	64	78	92
14	142	96	73	67	91
13	137	95	64	69	105
12	174	102	72	87	421
11	163	103	107	145	145
10	188	90	89	111	131
9	196	111	85	79	99
8	139	94	83	78	74
7	164	126	102	91	116
6	201	100	112	110	122
5	119	125	86	89	105
4	156	119	121	174	1041
3	204	96	118	272	×
2	250	129	95	118	101
1	224	169	138	133	157

We may determine certain ranges for both the number of hidden neurons and the learning rate so that the MLP-training module is guaranteed to converge in a small number of tarining iterations. For instance, in the training examples, the number of hidden neurons can be chosen in between 10 and 18 and the learning rate can be set to any value from 0.01 to 0.02. For each operation we create and store a look-up table like this along with training patterns. A signal representing a certain operation will load a good choice of (number of hidden neurons, learning rate) pair from the table, load the training patterns, and start the training phase.

I-677

Table 3. Sobel Edge Detection ($\alpha = 0.1$)					
number of hiddens	η				
	0.01	0.02	0.03	0.04	0.05
20	783	1602	×	×	×
19	905	×	1578	×	×
18	862	1787	×	×	×
17	921	1468	2901	×	×
16	895	534	534	×	×
15	978	2158	×	×	×
14	946	×	×	×	×
13	1190	3762	×	×	×
12	887	1371	×	×	×
11	1080	1390	×	×	×
10	1334	3376	×	×	×
9	1650	×	×	×	×
8	1407	2486	×	×	×
7	6656	×	×	×	×
6	2065	17039	×	×	×
5	4220	2312	×	×	×
4	×	×	×	×	×
3	×	×	×	×	×
2	×	×	×	×	×
1	×	×	×	×	×

Table 4. Noise Removal ($\alpha = 0.1$)					
number of hiddens	η				
	0.01	0.02	0.03	0.04	0.05
20	100	120	162	247	243
19	106	77	157	219	×
18	90	106	241	219	215
17	107	101	148	302	260
16	97	121	295	962	×
15	103	133	216	136	145
14	108	143	164	138	121
13	102	147	226	186	206
12	94	112	342	×	714
11	109	104	194	253	353
10	96	119	4331	×	×
9	95	142	1798	×	×
8	103	133	194	×	×
7	103	131	213	115	×
6	93	108	232	×	×
5	128	138	307	259	150
4	110	111	848	×	×
3	116	122	1125	298	1162
2	122	160	637	×	×
1	100	93	316	×	×

V. CONCLUSION

An architecture incorporating MLP's as fundamental modules is proposed for low-level image preprocessing. This model is flexible — it can adapt itself with training process to most of the low-level image operation. Experiments have been done to show the feasibility of the proposed architecture and the results are given. Since the training patterns are generated with existing algorithms for the specified operations, it is guaranteed that the architecture obtains the same result as applying the same algorithm to the same image.

The training phase of a MLP module takes a long time to converge for some complicated operations. This could be a major drawback in the implementation of the proposed architecture. An extended experiment of training MLP-modules with gray-scale images is in progress. A further research of choosing or developing another neural net model as the pixel-based operating modules is expected. Also, self-determining the window size of pyramid modules is another interesting field to study.

REFERENCES

[1] J. L. Davidson and F. Hummer, "Morphology Neural Networks: An Introduction with Applications," *Circuits, Systems, Signal Processing*, vol. 12, no. 2, pp. 177-210, 1993.

[2] J. L. Davidson and K. Sun, "Template Learning in Morphological Neural Nets," in *SPIE vol. 1568 Image Algebra and Morphological Image Processing II*, 1991.

[3] R. C. Gonzales and R. E. Woods, *Digital Image Processing*, Addison-Wesley, 1992.

[4] S. C. Huang and Y. F. Huang, "Bounds on the Number of Hidden Neurons in Multilayer Perceptrons," *IEEE Trans. on Neural Networks*, vol. 2, no. 1, Jan. 1991.

[5] R. Krishnapuram and L. F. Chen, "Implementation of Parallel Thinning Algorithms Using Recurrent Neural Networks," *IEEE Trans. on Neural Networks*, Vol.4, no.1, pp.142-7, 1993.

[6] R. P. Lippmann, "An Introduction to Computing with Neural Nets," *IEEE ASSP Magazine*, pp. 4-22, 1987.

[7] A. Morales and S. J. Ko, "Efficient Neural Network Implementation of Morphological Operations," in *SPIE vol. 1658 Nonlinear Image Processing III*, 1992.

[8] W. K. Pratt, *Digital Image Processing*, 2nd Edition, John Wiley & Sons, 1991.

[9] A. Rosenfeld and A. C. Kak, *Digital Image Processing*, vol. 2, chap.11, Academic Press, Orlando, FL, 1982.

[10] D. E. Rumelhart, G. E. Hinton, and R. J. Williams, "Learning Representations by Back-Propagating Errors," *Nature*, vol. 323, pp. 533-6, Oct. 9, 1986.

[11] S. Sternberg, "Gray-Scale Morphology," *Computer Vision, Graphics, and Image Processing*, vol. 35, pp.333-55, 1986.

[12] Frank Y. Shih and Jenlong Moh, "Implementing Morphological Operations Using Programmable Neural Networks," *Journal of Pattern Recognition*, vol. 25, no. 1, pp. 89-99, Jan. 1992.

A HYBRID NEURAL NETWORK ARCHITECTURE FOR SENSOR FUSION

Kiran Gelli and Robert A. McLauchlan   Rajab Challoo and Syed Iqbal Omar
Mechanical and Industrial Engrg.Dept. Computer Sc.and Electrical Engrg.Dept.
Texas A&M University-Kingsville, Kingsville,Tx 78363

ABSTRACT

An unsupervised neural network has been developed to fuse multisensory information for a multilink robotic arm/hand system for target detection. The network consists of a feature extractor for each sensor used in the robotic system and a single classifier which takes input from all the feature extractors. The network is a hybrid network which combines the following: (a) a modified backpropagation learning rule in a self-organizing fashion, for extracting the features, and (b) the Kohonen linear vector quantization (LVQ) method to classify the objects based on the extracted features. The feature extractor detects the important features of the input image in different subelement groups of its hidden layer(s) by reproducing the input image in its output layer. The features obtained from each of the feature extractors are then fused and fed into a classifier which classifies the object based on these features. The overall hybrid network is totally unsupervised because it does not need the intervention of a human operator to provide the desired outputs during learning. Weight sharing is incorporated in each of the feature extractors to reduce the number of free parameters. Also, the modified backpropagation learning rule presented in [Ref.1] has been used to improve the rate of convergence of the network.

INTRODUCTION

Multiple sensors are used in an intelligent system to obtain redundant and complementary information about the environment at low cost and in less time and to improve the confidence factor of the sensory information [Ref.4]. But, the use of multiple sensors entails integration and fusion of multisensory information. An artificial neural network which mimics the architecture and dynamics of a biological neuronal system can be used to integrate and fuse multisensory information. This approach gains inspiration from the fact that multisensory fusion occurs in every living organism to a varying degree of complexity during its perception of the environment. The advantages of using a neural network include the following: (a)real time operation, (b)adaptability to unstructured environments, (c)robustness to noise, (d)fault tolerance, (e)parallel processing of sensor data and (f)feasibility in hardware implementation.

ARCHITECTURE OF THE NETWORK

The network consists of a feature extractor for every sensor and a single classifier (see figure 1). The feature extractor is a three layer feedforward neural network whose output layer is the mirror image of the input layer. The input layer and the output layer consist of a 16X16 array of units. The hidden or the second layer consists of twelve groups, each group containing 144 units (12X12). Each unit in a group has connections to a 5X5 square in the input array, with the location of the square shifting by one pixel between neighbors in the 12 groups of units of the hidden layer (see figure 1). In this manner the entire input image of size 16X16 is thoroughly scanned by every group in the hidden layer to detect the features relevant to each of them. All the 144 units in a group have the same 25 weight values, so they all detect the same feature in different places of the input image. This weight sharing, and the 5X5 receptive fields, reduce the number of free parameters (excluding the independent thresholds for all the units) for the network from 4,42,368 to 300, between the input layer and hidden layer. The same reduction in the number of free parameters occurs between the hidden layer and the output layer. The connection matrix between the input layer and the hidden layer C1 (see figure 1) and that between the hidden layer and the output layer C1' are both of size [12]X[25]. Functionally, C1 and C1' are inverses of each other. This is in the sense that the input to one is the output to the other and vice versa. So, during learning, only one weight matrix can be updated and the other updated weight matrix obtained by finding the inverse of the updated first one.

The classifier consists of a two layer Kohonen network which takes input from the 12 groups of each of the feature extractors. So, the number of neurons in the input layer of the classifier is twelve times the number of sensory images being considered for fusion. The number of units in the output layer of the classifier is proportional to the number of classes of patterns that the robotic system has to differentiate to detect its target. Both the layers are fully connected with every node in the input layer having connection with every node in the output layer. There are no lateral connections between the neurons of the output layer.

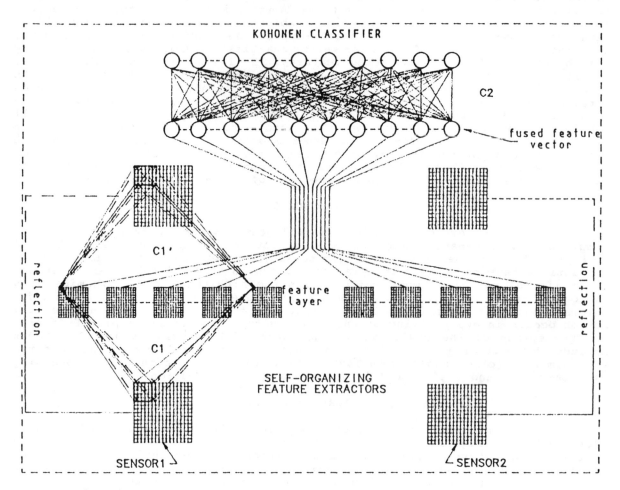

Figure 1: Hybrid Neural Network Architecture for Sensor Fusion

LEARNING RULE USED

The learning rule used in the feature extractors is a modified backpropagation learning rule used in an unsupervised and self-organizing fashion.

The activation to the input layer is the input image itself. The activations for the hidden layer and the output layer are given by

$$h_i^m = \sum_j w_{ij}^m V_j^{m-1}$$

where 'm' is the layer number, 'V' is the input and 'h' represents the activation above the threshold. The sigmoidal function $g(h) = 1/(1+\exp(-h))$ is used to find the output for each layer.

A new energy function is used to find the error of the output layer which can eliminate the occurrence of local minima. In the standard backpropagation network, the output error signal is propagated back through the network for every iteration and is used to modify the weight values. But, the output unit $(t_{pj}-o_{pj})(1-o_{pj})o_{pj}$ can be zero not only when $t_{pj} = o_{pj}$ but also when $o_{pj} = 0$ or $o_{pj} = 1$. This leads to zero error signal for internal units as well. Therefore all the derivatives are zero, and the network loses its learning ability at this state.

A new energy function was presented in [Ref.1] which resolves this problem of local minima. The energy function is given by

$$E_p = -\sum_j \left((1-t_{pj}) \ln(1-o_{pj}) + t_{pj} \ln o_{pj} \right)$$

The above function can be used to evaluate the errors for the output layer as

$$\delta_{pj} = -\left(-t_{pj}\frac{1}{o_{pj}} + (1-t_{pj})\frac{1}{1-o_{pj}}\right)(1-o_{pj})o_{pj} = (t_{pj}-o_{pj})$$

Thus, the term $(1-o_{pj})o_{pj}$ is eliminated and the problem of local minima is removed. The errors for the remaining layers are given by

$$\delta_i^{m-1} = g'(h_i^{m-1})\sum_j w_{ji}^m \delta_j^m$$

The weights are updated using the equation

$$\Delta w_{ij}^m = \eta\, \delta_i^m V_j^{m-1}$$

in which η, the learning parameter lies in the range $0<\eta<1$.

During updating of the synaptic connection matrices, a small portion of the previous synaptic matrix values is added to the new values of the connection matrices for faster learning. The learning parameter is different for different synaptic connection matrices and is inversely proportional to the fan-in of the nodes for that matrix. The initial values of the synaptic matrices are defined randomly and scaled proportional to the fan-in of the nodes at that matrix.

The classifier is also unsupervised and learns using the Kohonen's linear vector quantization algorithm [Ref.14]. In this algorithm, $w_{ij}(t)$ ($0\leq i\leq n-1$) is defined to be the weight from input node i to output node j at time t (or iteration). The input is $x_0(t)$, $x_1(t)$, $x_2(t)\ldots x_{n-1}(t)$ where $x_i(t)$ is the input to node i at time t.

The distance d_j between the input and each output node j, is given by

$$d_j = \sum_{i=0}^{n-1} (x_i(t) - w_{ij}(t))^2$$

The output node with the minimum distance d_j is designated to be $j*$. Then, the weights for the node $j*$ and its neighbors, defined by the neighborhood size $N_{j*}(t)$, are updated by

$$w_{ij}(t+1) = w_{ij}(t) + \eta(t)(x_i(t) - w_{ij}(t))$$

The term $\eta(t)$ is a gain term $(0<\eta<1)$ that decreases in time, thereby slowing the weight adaptation. For **j** in the neighborhood size $N_{j*}(t)$, $0<i\leq n-1$, in which '**n**' is the input vector dimension. The neighborhood size $N_{j*}(t)$ is initially set to a large value so as to include every other node in the output layer in the neighborhood. The neighborhood $N_{j*}(t)$ decreases in size as time goes on, thus localizing the area of maximum activity. The final size is determined depending on the number of different input patterns that have to be classified.

In brief, Kohonen's competitive learning paradigm tries to find the closest matching unit to a training input and then increases the similarity between this unit and those in the neighborhood which are in close proximity to the input.

COMPUTER IMPLEMENTATION

The network has been implemented on a Sun SPARC Workstation 2 using ANSI 'C'. The network was tested on two sets of visual data. This is similar to using two visual sensors or viewing with the right and left eye to identify the same object. The visual images considered are binary images of numerical characters from zero to nine. The binary images of the numerical characters are of size 16X16 which are fed into the input layer of the network.

Before the learning process is begun, the weight matrices are initialized to small random values. The weights for each group in the feature layer are initialized to different values so that they detect different features in the input image. Even the threshold values for the units in a group are initialized to different values which lends uniqueness to the feature they detect.

The twelve 12X12 feature groups obtained in the hidden layer of each of the feature extractors are reduced to a one dimensional result in order to obtain a 12-D feature vector. This is done as follows. First, the output of each unit is multiplied by the sum of its row and column number in the 12X12 group. This incorporates the spatial distribution of the different features detected in the given image. Then the mean of the new values of the outputs of all the units in the group is considered as the reduced feature for the feature group. In this way, a 12 dimensional feature vector is obtained for each sensor image. The 12-D feature vectors obtained for both the sensors are concatenated to give a 24-D fused feature vector for the given object.

The 24 dimensional feature vector is then fed into the input layer of the Kohonen classifier. The connection matrix between the input and output layer is initialized to values such that each output neuron vector is close to one of the character feature vectors before the learning is started. This helps in speeding up the learning process. The neighborhood is set to zero because the patterns are totally unique.

Learning is continued until the neurons in the output layer respond to the feature vectors of different characters. Ultimately, each output neuron exemplifies one character.

DISCUSSION OF THE RESULTS AND RECOMMENDATIONS

The network is successful in extracting unique features for different characters presented to it. The behavior of the mean squared error varies with the type of the character. In case of characters like 0,5,6,8,9, the error fluctuates a lot before decreasing steadily. Characters like 1,7 are learned relatively fast with the mean squared error falling steeply. The behavior of the mean squared error with the number of iterations for each character pattern used is shown in Figures 2a-2j. The feature extractor learns to detect the features of each character in about 180-250 iterations. The features generated in the feature layer by the data compression are unique for each character. The feature vectors obtained by reducing the two-dimensional features to one dimension are also unique for every character.

The classifier is able to classify the characters based on their fused feature vectors. The output neurons of the Kohonen network learn to respond to different character feature vectors. After learning, each output neuron exemplifies one character.

The network's performance could be better evaluated by considering real data obtained by actual measurement of the object's features by different sensors. It is proposed to use multiple views of solid models of objects generated by the IDEAS software (an integrated design package from SDRC) as input to the network to test its performance. This involves developing an interface between the IDEAS software and the neural network. It is also proposed to test the network for fusing data from two different sensors as e.g, using vision and range map data. Injecting noise in the input patterns by translation, rotation and shape distortion will be an efficient way to further test the performance and capability of the network.

The network's speed could be further improved by pruning the unnecessary units in the hidden layer of its feature detectors. The network generates similar features in different groups of the hidden layer of the feature extractor. This implies that more than one group of the hidden layer detect the same feature in the input image thus necessitating the removal of some groups from the hidden layer. However, determining an optimal number of feature detectors in the hidden layer is of vital importance. This is highly dependent on the complexity of the patterns to be recognized. Also, determining the number of units in each group of the hidden layer is an important aspect to be looked at.

REFERENCES

[1] A. Kryzyzak, W.Dal and C.Y. Suen, "Classification of Large Set of Handwritten Characters Using Modified Backpropagation Model", Intl. Conference on Neural Networks, Vol.III, 1993.

[2] Kiran Gelli, Robert A. McLauchlan, Iqbal S. Omar and Rajab Challoo,"A Fast Method of Teaching Character Recognition to a Five Layered Backpropagation Neural Network", Proceedings of the 1993 World Congress on Neural Networks,Portland, Oregon, 11-15 July, 1993.

[3] John C. Pearson, Jack J. Gelfand, W.E. Sullivan, Richard M. Peterson and Clay D. Spence, "Neural Network Approach to Sensory Fusion", SPIE Vol. 931, Sensor Fusion, 1988.

[4] Ren C. Luo and Michael G. Kay, "Multisensory Integration and Fusion in Intelligent Systems", IEEE Transactions on Systems, Man and Cybernetics, Vol. 19, No. 5, 1989.

[5] Dennis W. Ruck, Steven K. Rogers, Matthew Kabrisky and James P. Mills, "Multisensory Target Detection and Classification", SPIE, Vol. 931, Sensor Fusion, 1988.

[6] Michael C. Roggeman, James P. Mills, Steven K. Rogers and Matthew Kabrisky, "Multisensory Information Fusion for Target Detection and Classification", SPIE, Vol.931, Sensor Fusion,1988.

[7] Michael C. Roggeman, James P. Mills, Matthew Kabrisky, Steven K. Rogers and Joseph A. Tatman, "An Approach to Multiple Sensor Target Detection", SPIE, Vol. 1100, Sensor Fusion II, 1989.

[8] Robert M. Kuczewski, Michael H. Myers and William J. Crawford, "Exploration of Backward Error Propagation as a Self-Organizational Structure", 1993 World Congress on Neural Networks, INNS, 1993.

[9] Greg Duane, "Pixel-level Sensor Fusion for Improved Object Recognition", SPIE, Vol.931, Sensor Fusion, 1988.

[10] Jack J. Gelfand, John C. Pearson and Clay D. Spence, "Neural Network

Approach to Sensor Fusion", <u>SPIE, Vol. 931, Sensor Fusion,</u> 1988.

[11] Eric I. Knudsen and Masakazu Konishi, "Mechanisms of Sound Localization in the Barn Owl(Tyto alba)", <u>Journal of Comparative Physiology.A,</u> Vol.133, pp 13-21, 1979.

[12] Phillip John Mckerrow, <u>Introduction to Robotics,</u> Addison-Wesley Publishing Company, Reading, Massachusetts, 1986.

[13] Bart Kosko, <u>Neural Networks and Fuzzy Logic,</u> Prentice Hall, Englelwood Cliffs, NJ, 1992.

[14] R. Beale and T. Jackson, <u>Neural Computing: An Introduction,</u> Adam Higler, NY 1990.

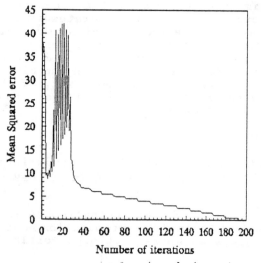

Figure 2a: Behavior of MSQE for character 0

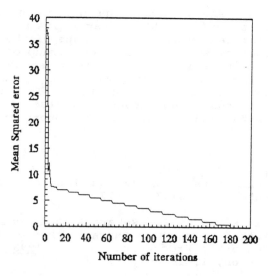

Figure 2b: Behavior of MSQE for character 1

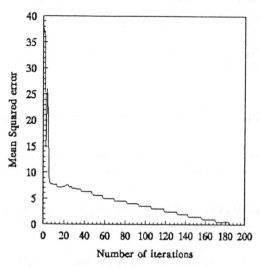

Figure 2c: Behavior of MSQE for character 2

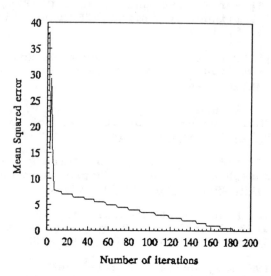

Figure 2d: Behavior of MSQE for character 3

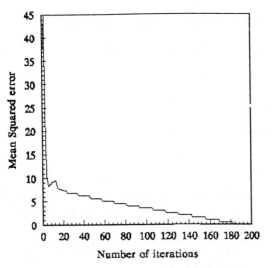

Figure 2e: Behavior of MSQE for character 4

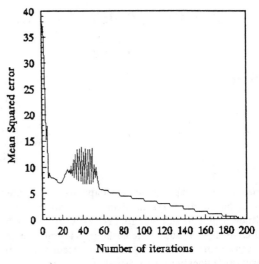

Figure 2f: Behavior of MSQE for character 5

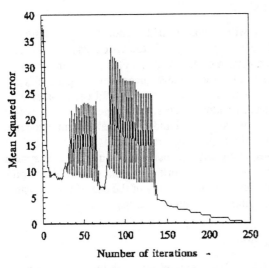

Figure 2g: Behavior of MSQE for character 6

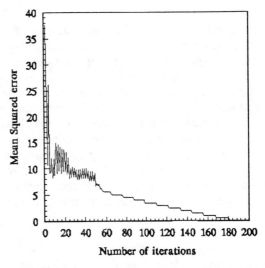

Figure 2h: Behavior of MSQE for character 7

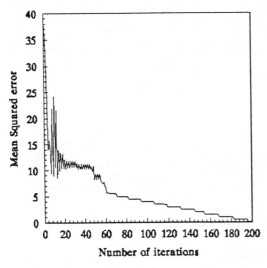

Figure 2i: Behavior of MSQE for character 8

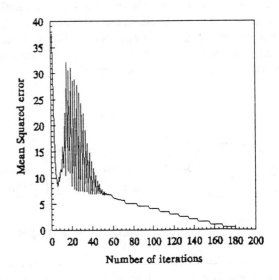

Figure 2j: Behavior of MSQE for character 9

An Interpolated Counterpropagation Approach for Determining Target Spacecraft Attitude

Bradley L. Vinz

INNS Member

Computer Science Department
University of Alabama in Huntsville
Huntsville, AL 35899

Abstract— This paper presents an approach that integrates a small cluster of counterpropagation neural networks into a video-based vision system designed for automatic spacecraft docking. First, the docking phases, the docking target attitude problem, and potential rewards attributed from an automated docking system are discussed. Then, the issues and challenges of automatic docking, relevant to machine vision processing, are addressed. Following a brief review of the counterpropagation network architecture and training, an approach for determining the relative attitude of a spacecraft's docking target, based on an interpolated counterpropagation net, is described.

I. INTRODUCTION

THE capability to identify the relative attitude of a target vehicle with unconstrained motion has special significance, particularly to the autonomous docking of spacecraft. In a video-based method, the vision system must capture an analog instance of the target scene and transform it into a pattern of pixels. Within the procedure that analyzes this pattern is the key to determining the relative attitude of the target. Thus, successful recognition is dependent on the pixel-arrangement interpretation. Artificial neural networks, with their powerful pattern-matching and pattern-mapping skills, can play an important role in the determination process. This paper will demonstrate how a small cluster of counterpropagation neural nets can be constructed, trained and integrated into an automatic docking system for the purpose of determining the relative attitude of a target spacecraft.

In Section II, automatic docking basics, issues, and challenges, along with the benefits of an automated system are delineated. Section III provides a brief review of the counterpropagation network architecture and training procedure. An interpolation mode is included. Finally, Section IV depicts the functionality of the chaser vision system components and presents a counterpropagation approach for determining the attitude of a spacecraft.

II. AUTOMATIC DOCKING

The automatic docking process between two orbiting spacecraft is a delicate venture involving interactive cooperation and adeptness. Upon rendezvous to the proximity of the target, the chaser spacecraft executes successive coordinated maneuvers to achieve the mechanical interlocking with the target spacecraft. Success is dependent upon the effectiveness of the chaser's video-based vision system to accurately distinguish the target within a scene and then provide valid attitude and position data to the control system (Fig. 1). This data is then analyzed by the controller to determine the correct six degree-of-freedom maneuvering commands to be performed by the propulsion system for attaining proper docking alignment.

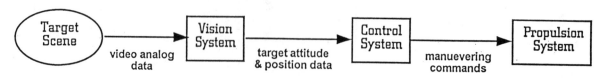

Fig. 1. Recognition/analysis/action pipeline process of chaser spacecraft.

The research of Bradley L. Vinz is supported by a grant provided by the NASA Graduate Student Researchers Program, Contract No. NGT-50679.

A. Issues, Challenges and Potential Rewards

As discussed above, the effectiveness of a video-based target recognition system depends on its ability to accurately identify a target infixed in a scene. Scenes containing structured background clutter, foreground visual obstruction, and/or varying pixel intensities proliferate the recognition task, particularly when the system requires automation [1]. An additional challenge is incurred for automatic docking due to the possible dynamic behavior of the target vehicle. For example, the target spacecraft may lose its attitude stabilization and start to cone, spin or tumble [2]. Since the automated system must function in a realistic environment (e.g., sun shadows, tumbling target, embedded objects in the background, etc.), it follows that rapid and reliable responses become imperative for success.

Although the U.S. space program currently lacks experience in automated docking systems [3], studies have resulted in a desire by NASA to develop this capability [4]. Potential benefits of such systems include decreased risk liabilities, reduced expenditures, and expanded operational versatility [5]. Automated docking systems permit safety restrictions — incurred for manned missions — to be relaxed, resulting in substantial cost savings. Operational capabilities can be broadened beyond manned spacecraft altitudes so that repair of inoperable satellites, space debris capture, and reboosting of satellites to higher orbits [5] can be accomplished autonomously. Other payoffs include resupply [6], orbital assembly [7], and the prevention of hazardous materials from entering Earth's atmosphere [8].

B. Docking Phases and The Docking Target Attitude Problem

The chaser spacecraft proximity and closure maneuvers may be partitioned into two sequential phases [9], permitting possible optimization of automated tasks: approach maneuvers and final docking maneuvers. Approach maneuvers provide closure of the chaser from a range of approximately 200 meters from the target to a distance of about 10 meters — the point at which the final docking maneuvers commence. A three-dimensional docking target, affixed near the target spacecraft's docking port (latching mechanism), will function as a visual alignment marker [10]. Upon inception of the final docking maneuvers phase, the docking target is required to be within the field of view of the chaser vision system. Docking maneuvers conclude when the mechanical latches of the two spacecraft are securely coupled.

Before mechanical latching of the two docking spacecraft can become realized, proper alignment of the chaser spacecraft with the docking target must be maintained. As the final docking maneuvers phase commences, the problem of determining the attitude of the docking target relative to the chaser must be continuously solved to allow the chaser to perform correction maneuvers for sustaining alignment. This paper provides a neural network approach for determining docking target attitude during the final docking maneuvers phase.

III. THE COUNTERPROPAGATION NETWORK

The streamlined feed-forward version of the counterpropagation network [11] couples the Grossberg outstar with the Kohonen self-organizing competitive network, creating a three-layer paradigm possessing functionality that exceeds the individual capabilities of the Grossberg and Kohonen models. Of special interest to target recognition is the network's capability to generalize [12], even when presented with a partially incomplete or partially incorrect input vector. Counterpropagation permits successful recognition of a target within a degraded image scene — perhaps one resulting from a sudden change in the environment (e.g., target is partially casted with sun shadows producing intensified regions within the digitized image).

A. Training The Three-Layer Network

Information progresses forward through a succession of three interconnected layers of neurons [11]: the input (distribution) layer, the middle (Kohonen) layer, and the output (Grossberg) layer. Before the network can be employed for recognition tasks, it must first be trained using a representative collection of input-target pattern vector pairs (training set). During training, the net learns to correlate similar input patterns to distinct output (target) patterns. The Kohonen layer processing divides the input patterns into distinct classes or categories. The Grossberg layer associates each class with a precise output pattern by storing a reference vector. When the network is continually subjected to pattern pairs from the training set, learning evolves over time through selective modification of the weights associated with each neuron of the Kohonen and Grossberg layers [11]. After the net memorizes the correct input-to-target pattern mapping, the training process is halted and learning is complete. During recall, a trained counterpropagation network will classify an input pattern into the most suitable matching class. The stored pattern (reference vector) associated with this class is then produced as network output.

For the purpose of discussion, assume the network comprises of n input layer neurons, p Kohonen layer neurons, and m Grossberg layer neurons. The collection of weights affiliated with Kohonen neuron i, $1 \le i \le p$, constitute the weight vector $W_i = (w_{i1}, w_{i2}, ..., w_{in})$, where w_{ij} denotes the connection strength between input neuron j and Kohonen neuron i. Similarly, the collection of weights affiliated with Grossberg neuron j, $1 \le j \le m$, constitute the weight vector $U_j = (u_{j1}, u_{j2}, ..., u_{jp})$, where u_{ji} denotes the connection strength between Kohonen neuron i and Grossberg neuron j. Each input-target pattern pair comprises of an input vector $X = (x_1, x_2, ..., x_n)$ and a target vector $Y = (y_1, y_2, ..., y_m)$. When a pattern pair is presented to the network, the input vector is delivered to the input layer and the target vector to the Grossberg layer. In due time, the network output from the Grossberg layer will be compared for accuracy with the (correct) target vector. The input layer's sole function is to distribute the input vector entries to the Kohonen layer, where a winner-take-all competition is undertaken.

During competition [11], each Kohonen neuron calculates a Euclidean distance metric, $\| W_i - X \|$, which establishes the distance each neuron's weight vector W_i lies from the input vector X. The neuron having the smallest distance wins the competition and sets its output signal z_i to 1.0. All other neurons set their output to zero. After competition, only the winning neuron's weight vector is adjusted (using the Kohonen learning rule):

$$W_i^{new} = W_i^{old} + \alpha(X - W_i^{old})z_i$$

where α is the learning rate $(0.0 \le \alpha \le 1.0)$ and $z_i = 1$ is the winner's output. In the next level of processing, the network output vector is computed [11]. Each Grossberg layer neuron j, $1 \le j \le m$, computes the summation of inbound weighted signals:

$$y_j' = \sum_{i=1}^{p} u_{ji}^{old} z_i$$

resulting in the network output $Y' = (y_1, y_2, ..., y_m)$. In the comparison of output vector Y' to the target vector Y, the Grossberg layer weights are adjusted according to:

$$u_{ji}^{new} = u_{ji}^{old} + \mu(y_j - y_j')$$

where μ is a learning rate, $0.0 \le \mu \le 1.0$. The training process repeats with the next pattern pair until the correct input-to-target pattern mapping is memorized.

B. Interpolation Mode

The feed-forward version of the counterpropagation net permits only one winner in the Kohonen competitive layer. However, a variation to the method maintains the same training procedure as described above, but, during recall, more than one Kohonen neuron is allowed to share in the winning [11]. This relaxation, in effect, influences the resulting value at the output layer. The winners split the (1.0) output signal. Each winner's share in the output signal is inversely proportional to the winner's Euclidean distance metric.

As an example [13], take the case where two winners are permitted, Kohonen neurons i and k. The 1.0 output signal is then distributed such that $z_i + z_k = 1.0$. The output vector can then be calculated as follows:

$$y_j' = u_{ji} z_i + u_{jk} z_k$$

This variation is known as interpolation mode, since the resulting output pattern appears as a compromise between the (stored) target patterns for which the net learned to output during training.

This section explains the coordinate reference systems used for orbital docking and the method of image construction used in training the counterpropagation cluster. The functionality of the chaser vehicle vision system components is discussed and an approach for determining docking target attitude based on an interpolated counterpropagation network is offered.

A. Coordinate Systems and Training Set Construction

An unrestricted orbital spacecraft can demonstrate 6 degrees-of-freedom: 3 degrees-of-freedom in linear translation (X_T, Y_T, Z_T) and 3 degrees in attitude or body rotation (X_R, Y_R, Z_R). A coordinate reference system provides a way of representing a spacecraft's position and attitude. Each spacecraft operates within its own coordinate system. For successful docking to be realized, the chaser and target coordinate systems must be aligned in some prearranged orientation.

In order for the counterpropagation network to be employed within the automated docking target attitude determination method, a suitable training set is required. It is assumed that a ground-based facility will be available to capture image views of the target vehicle. The collection acquired will comprise views attained by translating and rotating a video camera about the target in various translations and attitudes. The amount of image collection coverage needed for the final maneuvering phase can be restricted to a volume in the shape of a cone [10]. This cone projects from the center of the docking target to the range of the maneuvering phase (approximately 10 to 15 meters should be adequate) and projects 30 degrees out from the docking alignment axis (i.e., 30 degrees in all three dimensions from the target's line-of-sight to the camera).

B. System Components

The chaser vision system (Fig. 2) for the final maneuvering phase consists of five components: 1) video camera, 2) digitizer, 3) image compression component, 4) image normalization component, and 5) docking target attitude determination component. The following discussion exemplifies the interaction of these components. Upon capturing a target image (frame) from the analog video stream, the digitizer transforms it into a 256×256 pixel image. Image compression reduces the image to a 32×32 binary pixel image. The (X_T, Y_T, Z_T) translation misalignment of the target is then calculated by an image normalization procedure. The image region representing the target is centered and scaled to conform to images used during the training of the cluster of counterpropagation networks. The docking target attitude determination component uses the 32×32 normalized binary image to determine the (X_R, Y_R, Z_R) rotation misalignment (attitude dispersions) of the docking target. The (X_T, Y_T, Z_T) and (X_R, Y_R, Z_R) misalignment data is input to the control system, where appropriate thruster maneuvering commands are determined for the propulsion system.

C. Docking Target Attitude Determination

Recall that before mechanical docking between the two spacecraft can occur, the chaser spacecraft must properly align itself with the target spacecraft. The docking target located on the target spacecraft will serve as a visual cue for sustaining alignment as the chaser accomplishes the closure. During the final closing maneuvers, the chaser's vision system must continually determine the attitude of the docking target — that is, must compute the rotational displacement (in all three dimensions) of the docking target from a known reference orientation. Once the docking target attitude is determined, the control system issues the appropriate maneuvering commands to the propulsion system to perform the correct adjustment.

The function of the docking target attitude determination component is to accept a 32×32 normalized binary image as input and produce the rotation misalignment of the docking target. The rotation misalignment (or attitude displacements) relative to the chaser can be expressed as a three-dimensional vector (X_R, Y_R, Z_R), where

X_R = rotation displacement about X-axis of target
Y_R = rotation displacement about Y-axis of target
Z_R = rotation displacement about Z-axis of target

are angular offsets from a standard reference position such as $(0°, 0°, 0°)$.

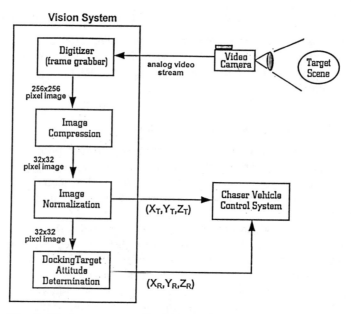

Fig. 2. Chaser spacecraft vision system.

The attitude determination can be approximated using a single counterpropagation network operating in single (Kohonen layer neuron) winner mode. During training, the network is presented with a collection (training set) of input-target pattern pairs. Each pair consists of a 32×32 normalized binary image (input pattern) and the correct attitude displacements, (X_R, Y_R, Z_R), as the target pattern. As training proceeds, the Kohonen layer learns to categorize each input pattern into a distinct class. The Grossberg (output) layer associates the correct target pattern with this class. The network requires 1024 (or 32x32) neurons in the input layer and 3 neurons in the output layer. One Kohonen neuron is needed for each distinct class established. The number of Kohonen neurons is determined by the number of input-target pattern pairs, or equivalently, the number of target attitudes used to obtain the training set.

Target analysis and simulation experience indicate that training sets for attitude misalignments between ± 30 degrees for each target axis will be sufficient for the final docking maneuvers [10]. The centering and scaling processes of the image normalization component will determine the translation displacements, (X_T, Y_T, Z_T), of the target relative to the chaser. These calculations will greatly reduce the number of Kohonen neurons needed. Since the normalization uses a reference distance to compute the range and a reference center point for centering, all training images can be acquired from a fixed range with the target centered in the field of view.

Suppose the training images are obtained with the attitude dispersions varying by $10°$ increments in each dimension. Then, for a single dimension, the attitude dispersions vary from $-30°$ to $+30°$, resulting in 7 dispersions. For all three dimensions, the number of combinations total 7x7x7 or 343. Thus, using this approach, 343 neurons are needed in the Kohonen layer.

The single network, single winner mode is likely to function adequately if only approximations (of attitude displacements) are required. For example, suppose the network is subjected to the training set described above. During recall, when presented with an image corresponding to the attitude displacements $(-26°, 24°, 16°)$, the net would likely respond with an output of $(-30°, 20°, 20°)$. However, in order to minimize the possibility of vehicular collision and avoid the risk of mission failure, a higher degree of precision in deriving the attitude displacement calculations is essential.

One approach [13] is to simply keep adding more neurons in the Kohonen layer until an acceptable level of precision is reached. This can dramatically increase the number of training images required. A more accurate approach is take advantage of the interpolation mode, i.e., two Kohonen neuron winner of the counterpropagation net [13]. To allow a simple linear interpolation scheme to be implemented, a separate network is constructed for each degree of rotational freedom (Fig. 3). Each counterpropagation net accepts the same 32×32 normalized binary image as input. However, each network is trained to output the attitude displacement for a single, distinct dimension.

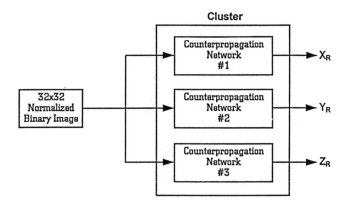

Fig. 3. The Docking Target Attitude Determination Component.

During recall, each net performs the 2-winner interpolation, resulting in a greater degree of accuracy in the calculated output.

V. CONCLUSION

The determination of the relative attitude of a target spacecraft can be a demanding problem. In this paper, we investigated how a counterpropagation network, integrated into a spacecraft vision system, can provide a potential solution to determining the attitude. The interpolated counterpropagation net, with its ability to add precision in the calculated output., can provide reliability to a delicate procedure.

Neural nets, with their robustness and generalization ability have potential for many applications. Future research will concentrate on developing neural net methods for image normalization.

REFERENCES

[1] Roth, M.W. (1990). "*Survey of Neural Network Technology for Automatic Target Recognition*". Institute of Electrical and Electronics Engineers (IEEE). IEEE Transactions on Neural Networks, Vol. 1, Issue 1, March 1990, p. 28-43.

[2] Vinz, F.L., L.L. Brewster, L. D. Thomas (1984). "*Computer Vision for Real-Time Orbital Operations - Center Directors Discretionary Fund Final Report (Project No. 82-27)*". National Aeronautics and Space Administration (NASA). NASA Technical Memorandum 86457, Marshall Space Flight Center (MSFC), Huntsville, AL, August 1984.

[3] Berenji, H.R. and T. Castellano (1991). "*Hybrid Neural Network and Fuzzy Logic Approaches for Rendezvous and Capture in Space*". In *NASA Automated Rendezvous and Capture Review: A Compilation of Abstracts*. National Aeronautics and Space Administration (NASA). Williamsburg, VA, November 19-21, 1991.

[4] Shannon, E.J. [editor] (1993). "Team to Develop Automated Rendezvous and Capture Technology", National Aeronautics and Space Administration (NASA). Marshall Star, Marshall Space Flight Center (MSFC), Huntsville, AL, Vol. 33, No. 16, January 1993.

[5] Vinz, F.L. (1989). "*Computer Vision for Space Applications*". In *Intelligent Robots and Computer Vision VIII: Systems and Applications*. Proceedings of the Meeting, Philadelphia, PA, November 9-10, 1989. Society of Photo-Optical Instrumentation Engineers (SPIE), Vol. 1193, p. 100-110.

[6] Bergmann, E. (1991). "*An Automated System for Spacecraft Proximity Operations*". In *NASA Automated Rendezvous and Capture Review: A Compilation of Abstracts*. National Aeronautics and Space Administration (NASA). Williamsburg, VA, November 19-21, 1991.

[7] Bittel, M.A. (1991). "*Six-Degree of Freedom Test Facility*". In *NASA Automated Rendezvous and Capture Review: A Compilation of Abstracts*. National Aeronautics and Space Administration (NASA). Williamsburg, VA, November 19-21, 1991.

[8] Buden, D. and J.A. Angelo, Jr. (1991). "*Automated Technologies Needed To Prevent Radioactive Materials From Reentering The Atmosphere*". In *NASA Automated Rendezvous and Capture Review: A Compilation of Abstracts*. National Aeronautics and Space Administration (NASA). Williamsburg, VA, November 19-21, 1991.

[9] Vinz, B.L. (1993). "*An Automated DBMS Approach To The Target Orientation Problem*". [Graduate Student Paper, Dr. Sara J. Graves, Advisor]. ACM Mid-Southeast Chapter Fall Conference, Gatlinburg, TN, November 11-12, 1993, 12 pages.

[10] Dabney, R.W. (1992). "*Application of Neural Networks to Autonomous Rendezvous and Docking of Space Vehicles*". American Institute of Aeronautics and Astronautics (AIAA) Paper 92-1516. Space Programs and Technologies Conference, Huntsville, AL, March 24-27, 1992.

[11] Hecht-Nielsen, R. (1990). *Neurocomputing*. Addison-Wesley, 1990.

[12] Wasserman, P.D. (1989). *Neural Computing: Theory and Practice*. Van Nostrand Reinhold, 1989.

[13] Freeman, J.A. (1988). "*Neural Networks for Machine Vision: The Spacecraft Orientation Demonstration*". e^{x}ponent: Ford Aerospace Technical Journal, Fall 1988, p. 16-20.

IMAGE TRANSFORMATION BY RECOGNISING FACIAL CONTROL POINTS

T.D. Gedeon & S.K. Chan

School of Computer Science and Engineering
The University of New South Wales
PO Box 1, Kensington 2033, AUSTRALIA

Abstract:

A sequence of images which change slowly can be recognised as a transformation from the starting image to the final image. This transformation can then be used to generate further images in the sequence, either interpolating to produce extra images during the sequence, or extrapolating to continue beyond the final image.

This has application in a number of domains, such as real world image understanding, where the sequence of images involve the movement of some object, or matching facial features for identification purposes; in tracing connected paths on geographical data, where the sequence is a series of nearby patches of the overall image containing some sizeable geographic feature; in medical imaging, for example following blood vessels in scan data, where the sequence is adjacent 3D patches of voxels.

We have experimented with morphing two faces successfully using a neural network to discover the appropriate control points of the target face. This process can be made fully automatic with the incorporation of minor domain knowledge.

Neural Fuzzy Systems

Session Chairs: Lotfi A. Zadeh
Bart Kosko

ORAL PRESENTATIONS

March 22, 1994

Fuzzy Logic and the Calculi of Fuzzy Rules, Fuzzy Graphs and Fuzzy Probabilities

L. A. Zadeh*

Abstract

It is important to recognize that the term "fuzzy logic" is currently used in two different senses. In its narrower sense, fuzzy logic, or simply FLn, is a logical system which underlies approximate reasoning. But in a much wider sense — which is the prevalent sense at this juncture — fuzzy logic, or simply FL, is fuzzily synonymous with fuzzy set theory, FST, that is, a theory of classes with unsharp boundaries. In this perspective, FLn is but one of many branches of FL, with other important branches including possibility theory, fuzzy data analysis and probability theory, fuzzy arithmetic, fuzzy relations and the calculi of fuzzy rules, CFR, fuzzy graphs, CFG, and fuzzy probabilities, CFP.

The calculi of fuzzy rules and fuzzy graphs play a particularly important role in the applications of fuzzy logic, especially in the realms of control and the enhancement of MIQ (Machine IQ) of consumer products and industrial systems. As its name suggests, the calculus of fuzzy rules, CFR, is concerned with the representation and manipulation of fuzzy if-then rules. The core of CFR is what is called the Fuzzy Dependency and Command Language, FDCL. The syntax of FDCL is concerned with the taxonomy and format of fuzzy if-then rules. The semantics of FDCL is focused on the meaning of individual rules and their collections.

The calculus of fuzzy graphs, CFG, is a subset of CFR. Its importance stems from the fact that CFG is largely self-contained and is sufficient for most practical applications.

The point of departure in CFG is the concept of a fuzzy graph, that is, an approximation to a function or a relation by a disjunction of cartesian products of fuzzy sets. Such approximations differ from conventional approximations in that (a) the approximant is a fuzzy relation or a possibility distribution; and (b) the use of linguistic variables results in data compression. A version of fuzzy Prolog, FA-Prolog, provides a convenient as well as effective way of representing fuzzy graphs and performing operations on them.

In fuzzy logic, probabilities are assumed to be fuzzy numbers. The motivation for this assumption is that most real-world probabilities cannot be estimated as real numbers. A typical example is the probability that my car may be stolen, with the understanding that the information that can be obtained from insurance companies is not specific enough to apply to my car.

In dealing with fuzzy probabilities, there are two major issues. First, how can fuzzy probabilities be estimated; and second, how can fuzzy probabilities be computed with? We explore an application of the calculus of fuzzy rules to the first problem and describe methods derived from the extension principle of fuzzy logic for computing with fuzzy probabilities and fuzzy utilities.

The calculi of fuzzy rules, fuzzy graphs and fuzzy probabilities provide a widely applicable methodology for exploiting the tolerance for uncertainty and imprecision. We describe the basic ideas which underlie these calculi and illustrate their use by examples.

*Computer Science Division and the Electronics Research Laboratory, Department of EECS, University of California, Berkeley, CA 94720; Telephone: 510-642-4959; Fax: 510-642-5775; E-mail: zadeh@cs.berkeley.edu.

representation, stability analysis, signal processing and data compression.

Today, most of the applications of fuzzy logic relate to control in the context of industrial systems and consumer products. This is the case because such applications are easy to make and result in systems and products with a higher level of MIQ (Machine Intelligence Quotient). What is discernible, however, is (a) the trend toward the use of fuzzy logic in task-oriented — rather than set-point-oriented — control; and (b) the incorporation of fuzzy logic and neural network techniques in the conception and design of complex systems in which control and expert system techniques are used in combination. Among the examples of such systems are power plants, cement kilns, elevator systems, air traffic control systems and, more generally, those systems in which there is an interaction between local control and higher level decision-making.

Viewed in a broader perspective, fuzzy logic may be viewed as a constituent of what might be called *soft computing* (SC). In contrast to traditional, hard computing, soft computing is tolerant of imprecision, uncertainty and partial truth. In addition to fuzzy logic, the principal constituents of soft computing are neurocomputing (NC) and probabilistic reasoning (PR), with PR subsuming belief networks, genetic algorithms, chaotic systems and parts of learning theory.

In the partnership of FL, NC and PR, FL is concerned in the main with imprecision and approximate reasoning, NC with learning and curve-fitting, and PR with uncertainty and propagation of belief. In large measure, FL, NC and PR are complementary rather than competitive. It is becoming increasingly clear that in many cases it is advantageous to employ FL, NC and PR in combination rather than exclusively. A case in point is the growing number of neurofuzzy consumer products and systems which make an effective use of a combination of fuzzy logic and neural network techniques.

In the final analysis, it may be argued that it is soft computing — rather than the traditional, hard computing — that should be viewed as the foundation for artificial intelligence. In the years ahead, this may well become a widely held position.

OPTIMAL FUZZY RULES COVER BUMPS

Bart Kosko

Department of Electrical Engineering

Signal and Image Processing Institute

University of Southern California

Los Angeles, California 90089-2564

Abstract

A fuzzy system approximates a function by covering the graph of the function with fuzzy rule patches and averaging patches that overlap. But the number of rules grows exponentially with the total number of input and output variables. The best rules cover the extrema or bumps in the function. For mean-squared approximation this follows from the mean value theorem of calculus. Optimal rules can help reduce the computational burden. To find them we can find or learn the zeroes of the derivative map and then center input fuzzy sets at these points. Neural systems can then both tune these rules and add rules to improve the function approximation.

Fuzzy Function Approximation and the Curse of Dimensionality

A fuzzy system needs too many fuzzy rules to approximate most functions. The number of rules grows exponentially with the number of input and output variables. In the end this "curse of dimensionality" can defeat an expert who guesses at the rules or a neural system that tries to learn the rules from data.

The rule geometry shows the problem. The rules define fuzzy patches that can cover part of the graph of the function. An additive fuzzy system adds or averages patches that overlap and can always approximate a continuous function on a compact set with a finite number of rules [1]. For $f: R \to R$ it takes k rule patches in the plane to cover the graph. For $f: R^2 \to R$ it takes on the order of k^2 rules to cover the surface in some 3-D rectangle. In general for $f: R^n \to R^p$ it takes on the order of k^{n+p-1} rules to cover the graph of f.

Optimal rules can reduce the number of rules used to approximate a function. Neural learning tends to find some of these rules and so can prune the rule set as well as tune it. In theory we can find the best rules by minimizing the mean-squared error of the approximation for a given fuzzy architecture. A complete closed-form solution depends on the shape of the fuzzy sets and how the system converts inputs to outputs.

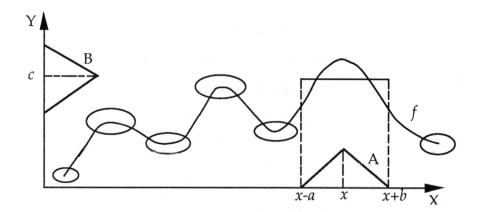

Figure 1. Optimal fuzzy rule patches cover the extrema of a function. Lone rules define a flat line segment that cuts the graph of the local extremum in at least two places. The mean value theorem implies that the extremum lies between these points.

A natural place to put the rule patches is at the extrema or bumps of the function (including its endpoints). We show in [2] that this is the best place in the mean-squared sense. Figure 1 shows how the rules might cover the bumps in a smooth function.

This result gives a new way to approximate $f: X \rightarrow Y$. First find the zeroes of the derivative map f'. Neural or direct methods can estimate f' from the difference of noisy samples $(x, f(x))$. Then Newton's method or other iterative or contraction maps can find some or all of the root values $\hat{x}$ such that $f'(\hat{x}) = 0$. Then center the input fuzzy sets at these roots and perhaps add fuzzy sets centered between the roots. Supervised or unsupervised learning can further tune the rules.

[1] Kosko, B., "Fuzzy Systems as Universal Approximators," *IEEE Transaction on Computers*, 1994; an earlier version appears in the *Proceedings for the 1st IEEE International Conference on Fuzzy Systems (IEEE FUZZ-92)*, 1153 - 1162, March 1992.

[2] Kosko, B., "Optimal Fuzzy Rules Cover Extrema," *International Journal of Intelligent Systems*, to appear, 1994.

Adaptive Fuzzy-Rule-Based Classifier

YoungJun Lee[1]   Vladimir Cherkassky[2]   James R. Slagle[1]
lee@cs.umn.edu   cherkass@ee.umn.edu   slagle@cs.umn.edu
Department of Computer Science[1]   Department of Electrical Engineering[2]
University of Minnesota   University of Minnesota
Minneapolis, MN 55455   Minneapolis, MN 55455

Abstract

We present the architecture and learning procedure for a fuzzy-rule-based classifier that can reject outliers and minimizes the cost of misclassification instead of the error rate. The fuzzy-rule-based system can be interpreted as an adaptive kernel method where each fuzzy rule corresponds to a kernel. Each kernel is asymmetric, and its center and and span(width) are adaptively determined from the training data. The fuzzy-rule-based classifier has been applied to synthetic data and two real data sets: Iris data and Heart Disease data. The performance of the system compares favorably with that of other methods.

1 Introduction

Many previous learning algorithms measure the quality of a learned model in terms of classification error rate. However, in practical applications, other aspects of classifier performance, such as the ability to reject classes on which it has not been trained and minimizing the cost instead of the error rate, can become critically important. We can obtain the classifier with those abilities by learning generative models for each of the classes. In the generative model, each rule states the properties that are true for all objects in the concept rather than stating the properties that discriminate a given concept from the other concepts. The goodness-of-fit of the model is defined in terms of how the features vary as a function of the classes. Fuzzy classifiers provide a soft decision, i.e., a value that describes the degree to which a pattern fits within a class. In this paper, we incorporate the cost function into the classification decision in a manner similar to optimal Bayes decision rule. We also present an architecture and a learning procedure to generate a set of simple fuzzy rules with appropriate membership functions for a fuzzy-rule-based classifier.

A learn-by-example mechanism is desirable to automate the construction of a fuzzy classifier. The fuzzy logic system can be represented as multi-layer feedforward networks. A back-propagation training algorithm can be used to adjust the parameters of the fuzzy logic system to make it match the desired input-output pairs[7]. However, this back-propagation fuzzy system may be trapped in a local minimum and it converges very slowly. Also, a user has to specify the system structure, i.e., number of rules, the number of membership functions, etc. We thus want a learning method that is more computationally efficient, as well as able to generate a structure of the system. There is an adaptive RBFN-like fuzzy systems[2]. However, the performance of radial basis function based classifiers deteriorates rapidly in the presence of noise and irrelevant input variables, while elliptical basis variants can adapt to extraneous input components robustly[1]. The elliptical basis function implements the local feature selection through the different variance for each feature of a rule.

In this paper, we propose an architecture for a fuzzy-rule-based classifier and a learning procedure automatically generates fuzzy rules to perform complex classification tasks. The distinct feature of the proposed system is its ability to learn fuzzy rules from high-dimensional training data. Learning fuzzy rules amounts to selection of locally important features. This is achieved by learning centers and widths of asymmetric kernels corresponding to fuzzy rules.

2 Fuzzy Classifier Systems

Fuzzy Systems

This research was supported in part by 3M Corp. and by Center for Urban and Regional Affairs(CURA) at the University of Minnesota.

We consider a set of simple fuzzy if-then rules in the following form:

$$\text{Rule } \mathbf{i}: \ \text{If } \mathbf{x_1} \text{ is } \mathbf{A_{i1}} \text{ and } \mathbf{x_2} \text{ is } \mathbf{A_{i2}} \cdots \text{ and } \mathbf{x_N} \text{ is } \mathbf{A_{iN}}, \text{ Then } \mathbf{y} \text{ is } \mathbf{B_i} \tag{1}$$

where $i = 1, 2, ..., M$, $x_k (k = 1, 2, ..., N)$ are the input variables to the fuzzy system, y is the output variable of the fuzzy system, and B_i is a crisp value. The membership function is Gaussian:

$$\mu_{A_{ik}}(x_k) = \exp\left(-\frac{(x_k - c_{ik})^2}{b_{ik}}\right) \tag{2}$$

where b_{ik} and c_{ik} are parameters for the membership function of the i-th rule, k-th variable. The singleton fuzzifier is used for fuzzification. The inference method is a multiplication(product inference). For aggregation of output of each rule, the centroid crispification method is widely used. The centroid crispification realizes a normalization of rule activation and every input signal causes the same total activation of fuzzy rules. Therefore, input signals that are arbitrarily far away from all fuzzy rules can activate them considerably. It is somewhat questionable to generalize over patterns which are very different from all patterns seen during training. Therefore, we may want no normalization. This has the advantage that "outliers" do not activate any rules very much, and can therefore be identified easily. It is particularly beneficial for fault detection applications, since we usually do not have data for every possible fault state of the system. We thus propose to use a Dynamic Ordered Weighted averaging Aggregation(DOWA) operator. It is an Ordered Weighted averaging Aggregation(OWA) operator[10] in which weights are dynamically changed according to the rule activation during both training and classification stages of the system's operation. The OWA operator has the property of lying between the "and," requiring all the criteria to be satisfied, and the "or," requiring at least one of them to be satisfied. Denote the crisp output $y = F(R_1(x), R_2(x), \cdots, R_M(x))$, where R_i is the i-th rule. A mapping F is called an OWA operator if it is associated with a weighting vector W such that $W_i \in [0, 1]$ and $\sum_i W_i = 1$, and where $F(r_1, r_2, \cdots, r_M) = W_1 D_1 + W_2 D_2 + \cdots + W_M D_M$, where D_i represents the i-th largest element in the collection of rule activation $r_1, r_2, ..., r_M$. The DOWA operator has weights W_i:

$$W_i = \frac{\prod_{k=1}^{N} \mu_{A_{ik}}(x_k)}{\sum_{j=1}^{M} \prod_{k=1}^{N} \mu_{A_{jk}}(x_k)} \tag{3}$$

where M is the number of fuzzy rules, and N is the number of input variables. Note that W_i is changed according to the rule's activations. We thus call it a Dynamic Ordered Weighted averaging Aggregation(DOWA) operator. If we use this DOWA operator as a crispification method, the fuzzy system can be represented as a function of the form:

$$f(\vec{x}) = \sum_{i=1}^{M} B_i W_i \prod_{k=1}^{N} \mu_{A_{ik}}(x_k) \tag{4}$$

where M is the number of fuzzy if-then rules, and N is dimension of the input data.

Approximation capability of the proposed fuzzy system can be established under the usual assumption that the input data is sampled from the closed and bounded domain. Similar to the proof in [8], we can prove the proposed fuzzy system is a universal approximator by applying the Stone-Weierstrass theorem[6]. This representation problem is important, because, if the chosen system could give only a poor representation of the mapping to be learned, even with optimal parameter values, then there would be little point in trying to learn the system.

Architecture of a Fuzzy Classifier System

The fuzzy classifier can handle both continuous and symbolic input variables. If a symbolic variable is fuzzy, each symbolic value has the fuzzy value of that feature. For a crisp symbolic variable, each symbolic value is "1" if the input pattern has that feature, otherwise it is "0". Although it is possible to use an input pattern that has an arbitrary range of values in any dimension, this paper will use values that range from 0 to 1 along each dimension; hence the pattern space will be an n-dimensional unit cube. These ranges of values were selected because they made the computations simpler and some sort of normalization on pattern value is necessary in order to prevent a certain variable from dominating the distance measure.

In our construction of the fuzzy classifier, we use m fuzzy systems for m-class classification. Each system is to represent the *possibility distribution* of a class. In learning the p-th system, if the data are fuzzy, the training data of the p-th class are targeted to have the fuzzy value of that class. If the given data are crisp, the training data of the p-th class are targeted to have the output "1" and those of the rest of the classes are targeted to have the output "0". During the test phase, the decision rule could be a "winner takes all" scheme. If a cost is associated with the classification, we can use that information to minimize the cost. Both fuzziness and randomness represent a matter of degrees. The fuzziness comes from the variety among the properties of the instance while the randomness comes from the variety among the instances. Consider a sentence "X is A". The probability of "X is A"(randomness) is the ratio of the number of the instances that are A over the total number of instances. The possibility of "X is A" (fuzziness) is the ratio of the

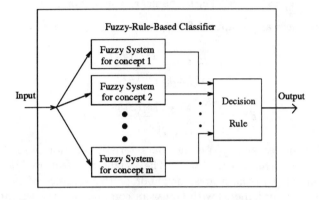

Figure 1: Fuzzy-Rule-Based Classifier

number of the properties possessed by A over the total number of the properties of X. Both probability and possibility are the ratio of the weight of all positive evidence over the weight of all relevant evidence. This frequency interpretation allows us to use Bayes decision rule approach: *choose class k if*

$$\sum_{i=1}^{m} C(i,k)p(i|x) \leq \sum_{i=1}^{m} C(i,j)p(i|x) \quad for\ all\ j,\ j \neq k, \tag{5}$$

where $C(i,j)$ is the cost of selecting the class j while the true class is i, and $p(i|x)$ is the *possibility* of class i for the given example x.

Learning Procedure

The number of fuzzy rules determines the complexity of the fuzzy system. For many rules, we have a more sophisticated system at the price of more computation to evaluate it. The performance of the system is improved as more rules are used. However, with too many rules, the performance of the system deteriorates, as the system overfits the training data. In order to identify the proper number of rules, we use a constructive method, *i.e.* we construct a system with a small number of rules and then add rules until certain performance criteria are satisfied. The constructive learning algorithm is described as follows.

1. Initialize the system, *i.e.*, assign one initial rule to each class, set termination conditions, and divide the training samples into a training set X_1 and a validation set X_2.
2. For all $x \in X_1$, execute the learning algorithm described in the next section.
3. Evaluate the classifier on the validation set X_2.
4. If termination conditions are reached, stop. Otherwise continue.
5. Add a rule and goto (2).

To avoid over-learning, the cross validation method is used to estimate the error rate of the system. In this approach, the available data is divided into two parts - a training set and a validation set. Only the training set is used to determine the system parameters, and the performance on the validation set is continuously monitored. If we know the model error ϵ, then the termination condition is "the error rate is less than ϵ" If we do not know the model error, training is stopped when performance on the validation set ceases to improve. If the number of the available data is small, we may use leave-one-out method to estimate the error rate of the system.

Learning kernel centers and widths

The fuzzy-rule-based system can be interpreted as an adaptive kernel method where each fuzzy rule corresponds to a kernel. The centers and widths of the kernels are adaptively determined from the training data as discussed below. Then, weight B_i for each rule i in equation (4) is determined by a supervised LMS algorithm.

We allocate one kernel per each cluster. For each class, the centers of the clusters are determined by stochastic competitive learning techniques analogous to statistical clustering. The competitive learning algorithm [4] is used to find the cluster centers of each class. The Voronoi region set V_j associated with the center $\vec{c}_j$ is defined as

$$V_j = \{\vec{x} \in R^N \mid \vec{c}_j \text{ is the nearest neighbor of } \vec{x}\}.$$

The cluster centers and variances are computed from a set of examples as:

$$\vec{\mu}_j = \frac{\sum_{k=1}^{K} \vec{x_k} \delta_j(\vec{x_k})}{\sum_{k=1}^{K} \delta_j(\vec{x_k})}, \tag{6}$$

$$\vec{\sigma}_j^2 = \frac{\sum_{k=1}^{K} \vec{x_k} * \vec{x_k} \delta_j(\vec{x_k})}{\sum_{k=1}^{K} \delta_j(\vec{x_k})} - \vec{\mu}_j \vec{\mu}_j, \tag{7}$$

where K is the number of examples, and $\delta_j(\cdot)$ is the characteristic function of set V_j.

The $\vec{\mu}$ is the center of a kernel(rule), i.e., $\vec{c} = \vec{\mu}$. The weight of a feature $1/b_k$ may not be determined by simple heuristics, the distance to the nearest neighbor or the variance of the feature. Because, if the distance or variance goes to zero in a model with Gaussian components, the weight of a certain feature can be infinitely large. This is likely to happen with the relevant features (especially discrete features). One ad hoc approach to solve this problem is to constrain the value greater than some minimum variance/distance. More systematic solution to this problem is discussed below. The weight of a feature $1/b_k$ are estimated as follows.

$$\sum_{k=1}^{N}(x_k - c_k)^2/b_k = \sum_{k=1}^{N} \xi \rho_k (x_k - c_k)^2 \tag{8}$$

where $\xi \rho_k = 1/b_k$. That is, the kernel width parameters b_k are estimated by two parameters ρ_k (to specify locally important features), and ξ (to specify the effective widths of the fuzzy rules).

The ρ_k is a attribute weight that determines the importance of attribute k for a rule. The attribute weight ρ_k are defined in $[0, 0.5]$ rather than $[0, 1]$ because an irrelevant attribute's weight is expected to be half of its total weight and we wanted each irrelevant attribute to have a zero attribute weight. Recall that input data have been normalized to have values that range from 0 to 1 along each dimension; hence the maximum σ is 0.5. Thus, ρ_k is determined by $\max(\mid 1 - \sigma_k \mid -0.5, 0)$. The parameter ξ, which determines the slope of the exponential decay, is determined based on the number of rules, on the distribution of the input data, and on the dimensionality of the input data, since the distribution of $\sum_{k=1}^{N}(x_k - c_k)^2/b_k$ is χ^2 with N degrees of freedom. The value of ξ is chosen so that the total activation of the kernels (fuzzy rules) for any input is approximately 1. Then, the kernel width parameters b_k in equation (8) are determined by $b_k = 1/(\xi \rho_k)$.

3   Comparisons

This section presents the simulation results of the system. Three data sets have been used to illustrate operation and properties of the fuzzy classifier. The first data set, an overlapping class problem, with known optimal Bayes boundary, will illustrate the fuzzy classifier's performance on overlapping class data. The second data set is the Fisher's Iris data, which is perhaps the best known database to be found in the pattern recognition literature. One class is linearly separable from the other two classes. The others are not linearly separable from each other. This is used to illustrate the fuzzy classifier's performance on linearly separable as well as non-linearly separable classes. The third data set comprises Heart Disease Data[3]. This will illustrate the fuzzy classifier's performance on a mixed type attribute, high-dimensional data set. All of the data sets have been published, and we performed the analyses in a manner consistent with those previously reported.

Synthetic data

This data set[5] has two classes. Each class is an equal mixture of two two-dimensional normally distributed populations, and the two populations are equally likely. The centers are (-0.7,0.3) and (0.3,0.3) in class 0 and (-0.3,0.7) and (0.4,0.7) in class 1, and variances are 0.03 for both classes. The boundary of the Bayes's rule is known. The error rate has been estimated on the 1000 samples of test data after the classifier was trained on 250 training samples. Table 1 compares the performance of the fuzzy classifier with several other methods. Error rates of the other methods were previously reported in [5]. It achieved an 8.7 % error rate with 4 rules. The fuzzy classifier achieves very good performance, but not the optimal result, because the competitive learning algorithm that was used to find cluster centers can be trapped in local minima. We may get better a result with a better cluster-center-learning algorithm.

Methods	Error Rate %
Bayes rule	8.0
K-Nearest Neighbor	13.0
LVQ	9.5
BP	9.4
Classification tree	10.1
Fuzzy Classifier	8.7

Table 1: Classification Performance on Synthetic Data

Iris Data

The iris data set has three classes and four continuous features. It consists of 150 cases, 50 for each class. One class is linearly separable from the other two classes and the latter are not linearly separable from each other. The error rate has been estimated by the leaving-one-out method. The fuzzy classifier achieved a 2.7% error rate with 9 rules. Error rates of the other methods were previously reported in [9].

Methods	Error Rate %
Bayes	6.7
K-Nearest Neighbor	4.0
BP	3.3
C4.5	4.7
CART	4.7
Fuzzy Classifier	2.7

Table 2: Classification Performance on the IRIS Data

Heart Disease Data

The heart disease data set[3] has two classes (absence or presence of heart disease) and 13 mixed type attributes. It consists of 270 examples. It has a cost matrix that is useful when different classification errors have different costs. For a user, the most important evaluation criterion for this data set is the minimization of cost instead of error rate. Table 3 shows the cost matrix for the Heart Disease Data, where the rows represent the true values and the columns represent the predicted values. Note that misclassifying a presence of heart disease as an absence of heart disease will result in a high cost. The average cost is calculated through dividing the total cost of misclassification by the total number of examples tested. For

class	absence	presence
absence	0	1
presence	5	0

Table 3: Cost matrix for the Heart Disease Data

the heart disease data, the 9-fold cross-validation testing strategy is used. The misclassification cost of the fuzzy classifier is compared with those of the other methods that were previously reported in [3].

Some algorithms can incorporate a cost matrix into its training phase and/or testing phase. Backpropagation makes use of the cost matrix in both phases. The algorithms that can include a cost matrix in their testing phase include K-Nearest Neighbor and CART. However, machine learning algorithms, such as C4.5, can not incorporate cost in either phase. Therefore, it may not be useful on a domain where minimizing cost is more important. The fuzzy classifier can incorporate cost in the testing phase by using decision rule (Equation 5). With the cost matrix, the fuzzy classifier achieved an average cost of 0.43 with 12 rules. C4.5 and RBFN performed very poorly since they did not incorporate the cost matrix. Note that BP, C4.5, and RBFN achieve worse performance than the simple scheme that always chooses the class "presence", which has an average cost of 0.55.

Methods	Avg. Cost
K-Nearest Neighbor	0.48
BP	0.57
CART	0.45
RBFN	0.78
C4.5	0.78
Fuzzy Classifier	0.43

Table 4: Classification Performance on the Heart Disease Data

4 Concluding Remarks

We have described the architecture and learning procedure of the fuzzy-rule-based system. By using a learning procedure, the proposed architecture can learn fuzzy if-then rules to perform complex classification tasks. The fuzzy classifier can be used in various practical applications, since it has the ability to reject classes that it has not been trained on, and to minimize the cost instead of the error rate.

Simulation results demonstrate that the fuzzy classifier system can find a reasonable decision boundary for an overlapping class, can handle non-linearly separable classes, and can incorporate the cost associated with the classification. The fuzzy classifier performance appears to be competitive against popular AI, neural network, and statistical classifiers.

In this paper, the number of fuzzy rules in the fuzzy system, which determines the complexity of the system, is determined by the cross-validation method. Possible improvements to the proposed system include incorporating better methods for determining the number of kernels/fuzzy rules, as well as better procedures for determining kernel centers.

References

[1] S. Beck and J. Ghosh. Noise sensitivity of static neural network classifiers. In *Applications of Artificial Neural Networks III, SPIE Vol. 1709*, pages 770–779, 1992.

[2] H. R. Berenji and P. Khedkar. Clustering in product space for fuzzy inference. In *IEEE International Conference on Fuzzy Systems*, 1993.

[3] C. Feng, A. Sutherland, R. King, S. Muggleton, and R. Henery. Comparison of machine learning classifiers to statistics and neural networks. In *Fourth Int'l Workshop on AI & Statistics*, pages 41–52, January 1993.

[4] B. Kosko. Stochastic competitive learning. *IEEE Trans. on Neural Networks*, 2(5):522–529, Sep. 1991.

[5] B. D. Ripley. Neural networks and related methods for classification. *Submitted to the Royal Statistical Society Research Section*, 1993. Available by anonymous ftp from markov.stats.ox.ac.uk.

[6] W. Rudin. *Principles of Mathematical Analysis*. McGraw-Hill, New York, 3rd edition, 1976.

[7] L. X. Wang and J. M. Mendel. Back-propagation fuzzy systems as nonlinear dynamic system identifiers. In *Proc. of the International Conference on Fuzzy Systems*, pages 1409–1418, San Diego, 1992.

[8] L. X. Wang and J. M. Mendel. Fuzzy basis function, universal approximation, and orthogonal least squares learning. *IEEE Trans. on Neural Networks*, September 1992.

[9] S. Weiss and C. Kulikowski. *Computer systems that learn: classification and prediction methods from statistics, neural networks, machine learning, and expert systems*. Morgan Kaufmann, 1991.

[10] R. R. Yager. On ordered weighted averaging aggregation operators in multicriteria decision making. *IEEE Trans. on System, Man, and Cybernetics*, 18(1):183–190, January/February 1988.

Neural Network Based Fuzzy Logic Decision System

A. D. Kulkarni, Praveen Coca, G. B. Giridhar, Y. Bhatikar
University of Texas at Tyler, Tyler, TX 75701

ABSTRACT

During the last few years there has been a large and energetic upswing in research efforts aimed at synthesizing fuzzy logic with neural networks. This combination of neural networks and fuzzy logic seems natural because the two approaches generally attack the design of "intelligent" systems from quit different angles. Neural networks provide algorithms for learning, classification, and optimization whereas fuzzy logic often deals with issues such as reasoning on a high (semantic or linguistic) level. Consequently the two technologies complement each other (Bezdek, 1993). In this paper, we combine neural networks with fuzzy logic techniques. We propose an artificial neural network (ANN) model for a fuzzy logic decision system. The model consists of six layers. The first three layers map the input variables to fuzzy set membership functions. The last three layers implement the decision rules. The model learns the decision rules using a supervised gradient descent procedure. As an illustration the model is used to classify multispectral satellite image data.

1. Introduction

ANN models have been used for pattern recognition since the 1950 (Rosenblatt, 1958). ANN models are preferred for pattern recognition tasks because of their parallel processing capabilities as well as learning and decision making abilities. ANN models consists of a large number of highly interconnected processing units. ANN models with learning algorithms such as the backpropagation are being used as supervised classifiers, and self organizing networks with learning algorithms such as the competitive learning and Kohonen's feature maps are being used as unsupervised classifiers. Recently many neural network based fuzzy logic decision systems have been suggested for pattern recognition tasks. ANN models essentially provide algorithms for problems such as optimization, classification, and clustering, whereas fuzzy logic is a means for representing and utilizing data and information that posses non-statistical uncertainty. Thus fuzzy methods often deal with issues such as reasoning on a higher (semantic or linguistic) level. Fuzzy sets were introduced by Zadeh (1965) as means of representing and manipulating data that were not precise but rather fuzzy. A fuzzy set is an extension of a crisp set. Crisp sets allow only full membership or no membership at all, whereas fuzzy sets allow partial membership. In a crisp set, the membership or non membership of an element x in set A is described by a characteristic function $\mu_A(x)$, where $\mu_A(x)$ = 1 if $x \in A$, and $\mu_A(x) = 0$ if $x \notin A$. Fuzzy logic techniques in the form of approximate reasoning provide decision-support and expert systems with powerful reasoning capabilities bound by a minimum of rules. The permissiveness of fuzziness in human thought processes suggest that much of the logic behind human reasoning in not traditional two valued or even multi-valued logic, but a logic with fuzzy truths, fuzzy connectives, and fuzzy rules of inference (Zadeh, 1973). During the past decade fuzzy logic has found a variety of applications in various fields ranging from process control (Lee, 1990) to medical diagnosis (Hall et al., 1992).

There are many neural network based fuzzy logic decision and control systems proposed in literature. Lin and Lee (1991) have suggested a fuzzy logic control/decision network. In their network input/output nodes represent the input states and output control/decision signals, respectively, and in the hidden layers there are nodes functioning as membership functions and rules. The learning algorithm for their network combines unsupervised learning and supervised gradient descent learning procedures. As an illustration they have considered two problems- the scheduling problem as a decision making problem and the fuzzy control of unmanned vehicle as a control problem. Berenji and Khedkar (1992) have developed a neural network based fuzzy control system wherein the learning and tuning fuzzy logic controllers is achieved through reinforcement. In reinforcement learning the teacher's response is not as direct, immediate, and informative as in supervised learning and serves more to evaluate the state of the system. Learning in their network is implemented by integrating fuzzy inference into a five-layer feed-forward network. They have used a gradient descent method to improve performance adaptively, and the fuzzy membership functions used in the definition of the labels are modified (tuned) globally to improve performance. They have considered the cart-pole problem. Pal and Mitra (1992) have developed a fuzzy neural network model using the backpropagation learning algorithm. They have used the model to classify Indian Telugu vowel sounds. Newton et al. (1992) have developed an adaptive fuzzy leader clustering algorithm. They have used the concept of ART-1 (Carpenter and Grossberg, 1987). This modification of ART-1 type neural network can be used for classification of discrete or analog patterns without prior knowledge of the number of clusters in data sets. Hall et al. (1992) used approximate fuzzy c-means clustering algorithms for segmenting magnetic resonance images (MRIs) of the brain. In this paper we suggest an architecture for a neural network based fuzzy logic decision system. The model consists of six layers. The first three layers are used for fuzzification wherein input feature values are mapped to membership functions and the last three layers implement the fuzzy inference rules. Units in the input and output layers represents input features and output decisions, respectively. We have used triangular shaped membership functions. The learning algorithm for this network is a supervised gradient descent procedure. The decision rules are automatically determined from the training samples. As an illustration the model is used to classify multispectral images.

2. Fuzzy Sets and Fuzzy Logic Decision Systems

Fuzzy sets allow partial membership. In a crisp set the membership or non membership of an element x in a set is described by a characteristics function $\mu_A(x)$ where $\mu_A(x) = 1$ if $x \in A$, and $\mu_A(x) = 0$ if $x \notin A$. Fuzzy set theory extends this concept by defining partial membership. A fuzzy set A in a universe of discourse U is characterized by a membership function μ_A which takes values in the interval [0,1]; that is, $\mu_A : U \to [0,1]$. Thus a fuzzy set A in U may be represented as a set of ordered pairs. Each pair consists of a generic element x and its grade of membership function; that is, $A = \{(u, \mu_A(u)) | u \in U\}$, u is called a support value if $\mu_A(u) > 0$. A linguistic variable x in the universe of discourse U is characterized by $T(x) = \{T_x^1, T_x^2, ..., T_x^k\}$ and $\mu(x) = \{\mu_x^1, \mu_x^2, ... \mu_x^k\}$, where $T(x)$ is the term set of x; that is the set of names of linguistic values of x with each T_x^i being a fuzzy number with membership function $\mu x i$ defined on U. For example, if x indicates reflectance value then $T(x)$ may be *low, medium, high*. A general model of a fuzzy logic decision system is shown in Figure 1. The input vector x which includes the input state linguistic variables x_is and the output state vector y which includes the output linguistic variables y_is can be defined as

$$x = \{ (xi, Ui, \{ T_{xi}^1, T_{xi}^2, ..., T_{xi}^{ki} \}, \{ \mu_{xi}^1, \mu_{xi}^2, ..., \mu_{xi}^{ki} \}) \ / \ i = 1 ...n\}$$

$$y = \{ (yi, Ui', \{ T_{yi}^1, T_{yi}^2, ..., T_{yi}^{li} \}, \{ \mu_{yi}1, \mu_{yi}^2, ..., \mu_y^{li} \}) \ / \ i = 1 ..m \} \tag{1}$$

The fuzzifier in Figure 1 is a mapping from an observed feature space to fuzzy sets in certain input universe of discourse. A specific value x_i is mapped to the fuzzy set T_{xi}^1 with degree μ_{xi}^1 and the fuzzy set T_{xi}^2 with degree μ_{xi}^2 and so on. We can use triangular or bell shaped membership functions for mapping. The triangular shaped membership functions are shown in Figure 2. The fuzzy rule base contains a set of fuzzy logic rules R. For a multi-input and multi-output system,

$$R = \{R_1, R_2, ... R_n\}$$

where the ith fuzzy logic rule is

$$R_i = \quad \text{IF} (x_1 \text{ is } T_{x1}, \text{ and } ... \text{ and } x_p \text{ is } T_{xp}),$$
$$\text{THEN} (y_1 \text{ is } T_{y1} \text{ and } ... \text{and } y_q \text{ is } T_{yq}) \tag{2}$$

The p preconditions of R_i form a fuzzy set $T_{x1} \times ... \times T_{x2}$ and the consequence of R_i is the union of q independent outputs. The inference engine is to match the preconditions of rules and perform implication. For example if there are two rules

$$R_1: \quad \text{IF } x_1 \text{ is } T_{x1}^1 \text{ and } x_2 \text{ is } T_{x2}^1 \quad \text{THEN } y \text{ is } T_y^1$$
$$R_2: \quad \text{IF } x_1 \text{ is } T_{x1}^2 \text{ and } x_2 \text{ is } T_{x2}^2 \quad \text{THEN } y \text{ is } T_y^2 \tag{3}$$

Then the firing strengths of rules R_1 and R_2 are defined as $\alpha 1$ and $\alpha 2$ and are given by

$$\alpha_i = \mu_{x1}^i \wedge \mu_{x2}^i \tag{4}$$

where $\wedge$ is the fuzzy *AND* operation and is defined as

$$\alpha_i \quad = \quad \min(\mu_{x1}{}^i, \ \mu_{x2}{}^i) \tag{5}$$

The above two rules, R_1 and R_2, lead to the corresponding decision with membership function $\mu_y{}^i$, $i = 1, 2$, which is defined as

$$\mu_y{}^i \quad = \quad \alpha_i \ \wedge \ \mu_y{}^i \tag{6}$$

The output decision can be obtained by combining the two decisions

$$\mu_y \quad = \quad \mu_y{}^1 \ \vee \ \mu_y{}^2 \tag{7}$$

where $\vee$ is the fuzzy *OR* operation, which is defined as

$$\mu_y \quad = \quad \max(\mu_{y1}, \ \mu_{y2}) \tag{8}$$

Equations 5 and 8 describe the commonly used fuzzy *AND* and *OR* functions. However, these functions can be defined in many other alternative ways. The defuzzification block is required only for control systems. The most commonly used defuzzification method is the center of area method.

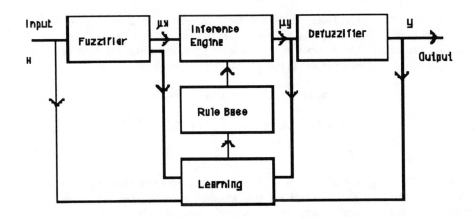

Fugure 1. Fuzzy logic decision system

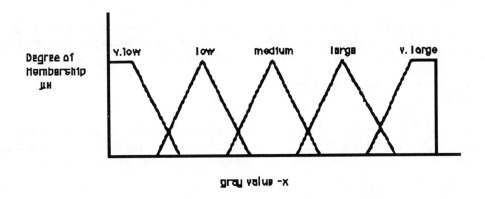

Figure 2. Fuzzy membership functions

3. Artificial Neural Network (ANN) Model

The ANN model for a fuzzy logic decision system is shown in Figure 3. The model consists of six layers. Each layer consists of a number of simple processing units. Layer L_1 is the input layer and layers L_2, L_3, L_4 perform the functions of the fuzzifier block shown in Figure 1. We have used triangular shaped membership functions. However membership functions with other shapes such as bell shape functions or the standard $\prod$ functions can be used. These functions can be predetermined or can be adaptive. Layers L_4, L_5, and L_6 represent the inference engine and the knowledge base. The connection strengths connecting these layers encode the decision rules used in decision making. In order to encode the decision rules we have used a backpropagation learning algorithm which essentially uses a gradient search technique (Pao, 1989). The algorithm minimizes the mean squared error obtained by comparing the desired output with the actual output. The model works in two phases the training phase and the decision making phase. During the training phase the model is trained using the training set data. The layers in the model are described below.

Layer L_1. The number of units in this layer is equal to the number of input features. Units in this layer correspond to the input features and they just transmit the input vector to the next layer. The net-input and the activation function for this layer is given by

$$
\begin{aligned}
net_i &= x_i \\
out_i &= net_i
\end{aligned}
\tag{9}
$$

where net_i indicates the net-input for unit i and out_i represents the output of unit i.

Layers L_2, L_3, and L_4. These layers implement the membership function. Units in layer L_2 represent the linguistic term variables. In this model we have used five term variables {*very low, low, medium, high, very high*} for each input feature value. The number of units in layer L_2 is five times the number of units in layer L_1. We have chosen triangular shaped membership functions, which are given by

$$
\mu_{xi} = \begin{cases}
1 - (x_i - m_i)/\rho_i & \text{for } m_i \leq x_i \leq \rho_i + m_i \\
1 - (m_i - x_i)/\rho_i & \text{for } m_i - x_i \leq x_i < m_i \\
0 & \text{otherwise}
\end{cases}
\tag{10}
$$

where μ_{xi} indicates the membership value for a given linguistic term veritable, m_i and ρ_i correspond to the center and the width of the triangular shaped membership functions. The net-input and activation functions for units in these layers are chosen so as to implement the membership functions given above. The net-input and output for units in layer L_2 are given by

$$
\begin{aligned}
net_i &= x_i / m_i \\
out_i &= net_i
\end{aligned}
\tag{11}
$$

Each of the units in layer L_2 is connected to two units in layer L_3. The two units in layer L_3 represent the left and right sides of a triangular shaped membership function. The weights connecting these units are +1 and -1. The net-input and output for each of the two units in layer L_3 are given by

$$
\begin{aligned}
net1_i &= (m_i - x_i)/\rho_i \\
out1_i &= 1 - net1_i
\end{aligned}
\tag{12}
$$

where $net1_i$ and out_i represent the net-input and the output, respectively of the unit that corresponds to the left side of the triangular membership function, and i represents the ith input feature. Similarly the net-input and output of units that correspond to the right side of a triangular membership function are given by

$$
\begin{aligned}
net2_i &= (x_i - m_i)/\rho_i \\
out2_i &= 1 - net2_i
\end{aligned}
\tag{13}
$$

Each unit in layer L_4 combines the outputs of the corresponding two units in L_3. The outputs of units in layer L_4 represent the membership values. The output of layer L_4 is used the input to layer L_5.

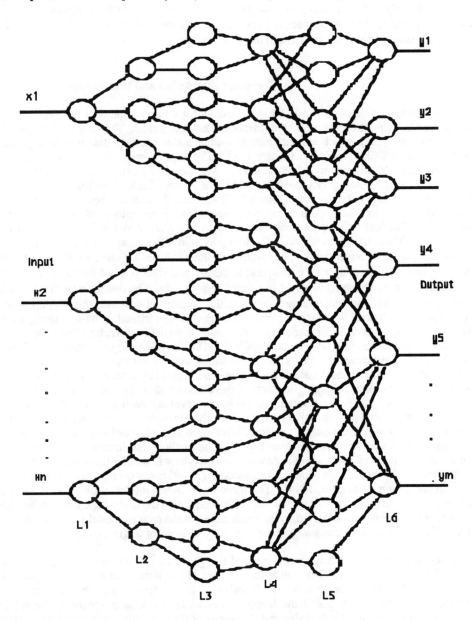

Figure 3. ANN model for a fuzzy logic decision system

Layers L_5 and L_6. Layers L_5, and L_6 implement the inference engine. Layers L_4, L_5, and L_6 represent a simple three layer feed-forward network with a backpropagation learning algorithm. Layer L_4 serves as the input layer, layer L_5 is the hidden layer, and layer L_6 represents the output layer. The number of units in the output layer is equal to the output decisions. The net-input and output for units in layers L_5 and L_6 are given by

$$net_i \quad = \quad \sum_j out_j \ w_{ij} \tag{14}$$

where net_i is the net-input and out_j is the output of the unit j in the preceding layer, w_{ij} is the represents the weight between the units i and j.

$$out_i \quad = \quad 1 / \{ 1 + \exp [-(net_i + \emptyset)] \} \tag{15}$$

where out_i is the output of unit i and $\emptyset$ is a constant. The network works in two phases the training phase and the decision making phase. During the training phase the weights between layers $L_4 - L_5$ and $L_5 - L_6$ are adjusted so as to minimize the error between the desired and the actual output.

4. Computer Simulation and Discussions

We have developed software to simulate the ANN model for a fuzzy logic decision system. As an illustration the model was used to recognize objects in a multispectral satellite image. The data are obtained from a sensor called the thematic mapper (TM), which is a multispectral scanner that captures data in seven spectral bands. We have considered a scene (#Y4018116055) of January 1983. The original image for spectral band 5 is shown in Figure 4. The scene represents Mississippi river bottom land. We used five linguistic term values {*very low, low, medium, high, very high*} to represent a gray value of a pixel in the scene. Each of the pixel was represented by a vector of five gray values. We used only five bands (bands 2, 3, 4, 5, and 7), because these bands showed maximum variance and contained information. that separates various classes. During the training phase the network was trained using training set data. The four training set areas were selected which are shown in Figure 4. In our model we used five units in layer L_1. These units correspond to the five gray values that represent a pixel. Layers L_2 and L_3 contain twenty five and fifty units respectively. The twenty five units in layer L_2 correspond to the twenty five term values, five for each band. Units in layer L_3 correspond to the left and right sides of the triangular membership functions. Layers L_5 and L_6 contained thirty five and five units, respectively. The five units in the output layer represent five output categories. The four categories are shown in the training set data, and the fifth unit for a data sample that does not belong to any one of the four categories. The network was trained with the training set data and the training set data was reclassified to check the accuracy The training set data was reclassified with 99.5% accuracy. In the decision making phase the entire scene was classified. The classified output is shown in Figure 5. We have also analyzed the data using conventional statistical classifier such as the maximum likelihood classifier. The main disadvantage of conventional statistical methods is they are sequential in nature that is here for each pixel we obtain the probability of that pixel belonging to each of the classes and assign the pixel to the class with the greatest probability. This process is time consuming as we have to evaluate each pixel for all the possible classes. ANN models are preferred as they work in parallel and once the network is trained, we present the input sample and a feed-forward network yields the output category. We have also analyzed the data using only a three-layer feed-forward network with a backpropagation learning algorithm without the fuzzification layers. The classified output with the three-layer network is shown in Figure 6. ANN model without the fuzzification takes a large amount CPU time for training. The model took about 88,155 seconds (24.48) hours on a PC and about ten minutes on a CRAY-Y/MP computer system (Kulkarni, 1994). The three-layer ANN model took 2000 iterations for each training sample to minimize the mean squared error. The ANN model with the fuzzy logic could minimize the mean squared error only in 30 iterations. Thus learning was much easier in the case of model with the fuzzy logic. Also with a fuzzy logic decision system we can interpret decision rules in terms of linguistic variables.

In the present case we used predetermined triangular shaped membership functions with 25% overlap. However, other functions such as Gaussian or the standard Π functions with different overlaps can also be used for fuzzification. The are two approaches in learning. In the first approach the fuzzification functions are predetermined and the system learns the mapping rules. In the second approach the inference rules can be predetermined from the expert's knowledge and the shapes of the fuzzy functions are adjusted during the training. In our model we have followed the first approach. It is also possible to determine the ranges of the membership functions from the histograms obtained from training set data. Neural networks represent a powerful and reasonable alternative to conventional classification methods. Our experiment suggest that by combining fuzzy logic with neural networks we can develop more efficient decision systems.

5. References

Berenji, H. R., and Khedkar, P., (1992). Learning and tuning fuzzy logic controllers through reinforcements. *IEEE Transactions on Neural Networks*, vol 3., no. 5, pp 724-740.

Bezdek, J. C., (1992). Computing with uncertainty. IEEE *Communications Magazine*, vol 30, no. 9, pp 24-36.

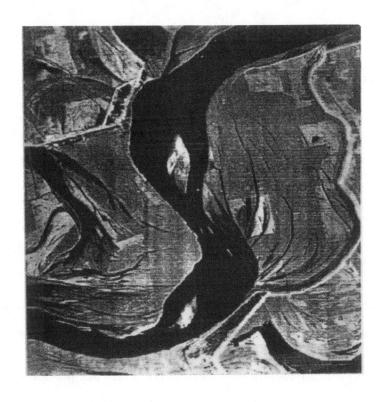

Figure 4. Original image (band 5)

Figure 5. Classified output - neural network
based fuzzy logic decision system

Figure 6. Classified output - neural network
with backpropagation learning algorithm

Bezdek, J., (1993). Editorial-fuzzy models-what are they and why. *IEEE Transactions on fuzzy systems, vol 1, no. 1,* pp 1-5.

Carpenter, G. A., and Grossberg, S. (1987). A massively parallel architecture for a self organizing neural pattern recognition machine. *Computer Vision Graphics and Image Processing,* vol 37, pp 54-115.

Hall, L. O., et al. (1992). A comparison of neural network and fuzzy clustering techniques in segmenting magnetic resonance images of the brain. *IEEE Transactions on Neural networks,* vol 3, no. 5, pp 672-682.

Kulkarni, A. D., (1994). *Artificial neural networks for image understanding.* Van Nostrand Reinhold. New York, NY.

Lee, C. C. (1990). Fuzzy logic in control systems: Fuzzy logic controller Part I. *IEEE Transactions on Systems, Man, Cybernetics,* vol 20, no. 2, pp 404-418.

Lin, Chin-Teng, and Lee George C. S., (1991). Neural network based fuzzy logic control and decision system. *IEEE Transactions on Computers,* vol 40, no. 12, pp 1320-1336.

Newton, S. C., Pemmaraju, S., and Mitra, S., (1992). Adaptive fuzzy leader clustering of complex data sets in pattern recognition. *IEEE Transactions on Neural Networks,* vol 3, no. 5, pp 794-800.

Pal, S. K., and Mitra, S., (1992). Multilayer perceptron, fuzzy sets, and classification. *IEEE Transactions on Neural Networks,* vol 3, no. 5, pp 683-697.

Pao, Y. H., (1989). *Adaptive pattern recognition and neural networks.* Addison-Wesley, Reading, MA.

Rosenblatt, F. (1958). The perceptron: A probabilistic model for information storage and organization in brain. *Psychology Review,* vol 65, pp 368-408.

Zadeh, L. A., (1965). Fuzzy sets. *Information and Control,* vol 8, pp 338-352.

Zadeh, L. A., (1973). Outline of a new approach to analysis of complex systems and decision processes. *IEEE transactions on Systems, Man, and Cybernetics,* vol 3, pp 28-44.

Fuzzy ART Choice Functions

Gail A. Carpenter and Marin N. Gjaja

Center for Adaptive Systems and Department of Cognitive and Neural Systems
Boston University, 111 Cummington Street, Boston, Massachusetts 02215 USA

Abstract

Adaptive Resonance Theory (ART) models are real-time neural networks for category learning, pattern recognition, and prediction. Unsupervised fuzzy ART and supervised fuzzy ARTMAP networks synthesize fuzzy logic and ART by exploiting the formal similarity between the computations of fuzzy subsethood and the dynamics of ART category choice, search, and learning. Fuzzy ART self-organizes stable recognition categories in response to arbitrary sequences of analog or binary input patterns. It generalizes the binary ART 1 model, replacing the set-theoretic intersection ($\cap$) with the fuzzy intersection ($\wedge$), or component-wise minimum. A normalization procedure called complement coding leads to a symmetric theory in which the fuzzy intersection and the fuzzy union ($\vee$), or component-wise maximum, play complementary roles. A geometric interpretation of fuzzy ART represents each category as a box that increases in size as weights decrease. This paper analyzes fuzzy ART models that employ various choice functions for category selection. One such function minimizes total weight change during learning. Benchmark simulations compare performance of fuzzy ARTMAP systems that use different choice functions.

ART and ARTMAP

Adaptive Resonance Theory (ART) was introduced as a theory of human cognitive information processing (Grossberg, 1976). The theory has led to an evolving series of real-time neural network models for unsupervised and supervised category learning and pattern recognition. These ART models form stable recognition categories in response to arbitrary input sequences with either fast or slow learning. Unsupervised ART networks include ART 1 (Carpenter and Grossberg, 1987a), which stably learns to categorize binary input patterns presented in an arbitrary order; ART 2 (Carpenter and Grossberg, 1987b), which stably learns to categorize either analog or binary input patterns presented in an arbitrary order; and ART 3 (Carpenter and Grossberg, 1990), which carries out parallel search, or hypothesis testing, of distributed recognition codes in a multi-level network hierarchy. Many of the ART papers are collected in the anthology *Pattern Recognition by Self-Organizing Neural Networks* (Carpenter and Grossberg, 1991).

A supervised network architecture, called ARTMAP, self-organizes categorical mappings between m-dimensional input vectors and n-dimensional output vectors. ARTMAP's internal control mechanisms create stable recognition categories of optimal size by maximizing code compression while minimizing predictive error in an on-line setting. Binary ART 1 computations are the foundation of the first ARTMAP network (Carpenter, Grossberg, and Reynolds, 1991), which therefore learns binary maps. Fuzzy ART (Carpenter, Grossberg, and Rosen, 1991) generalizes ART 1 to learn stable recognition categories in response to analog and binary input patterns (Figure 1). The domain of fuzzy ART is thus the same as that of ART 2, but fuzzy ART

Acknowledgments: This research was supported in part by ARPA (ONR N00014-92-J-4015), the National Science Foundation (NSF IRI 90-00530), and the Office of Naval Research (ONR N00014-91-J-4100).

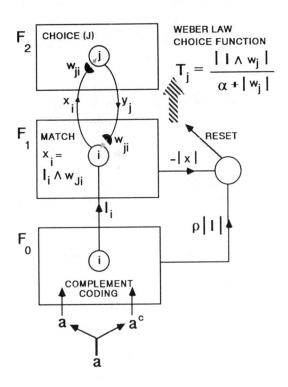

Figure 1: Fuzzy ART module.

measures pattern similarity by the city-block metric, while ART 2 is based on the Euclidean metric. When fuzzy ART replaces ART 1 in an ARTMAP system, the resulting fuzzy ARTMAP architecture (Carpenter, Grossberg, Markuzon, Reynolds, and Rosen, 1992) self-organizes categorical mappings between analog or binary input and output vectors that are stable with fast or slow learning (Figure 2).

This article analyzes fuzzy ART systems that employ various choice functions for category selection. One such network is shown to be optimal in the sense that it minimizes total weight change during learning. Simulations of supervised ARTMAP networks illustrate computational properties of the different fuzzy ART choice functions. The following section outlines the fuzzy ART algorithm with complement coding preprocessing. The limiting case of conservative choice is then examined, along with several alternative choice functions for bottom-up category selection. The function that minimizes the total weight change during learning is more truly conservative than other choice functions. A geometric interpretation of fuzzy ART represents categories as boxes that grow as weights shrink during learning. Benchmark simulations show that alternative choice functions minimally affect system performance. Various choice functions may therefore be selected for their individual computational properties while maintaining the demonstrated utility of ART 1, fuzzy ART, and ARTMAP networks. These studies indicate that when alternative choice functions are selected for reasons such as computational ease or generalizability, the basic ART and ARTMAP dynamics are retained.

Fuzzy ART Algorithm

Normalization by complement coding: Complement coding is a preprocessing step that normalizes fuzzy ART input while preserving amplitude information. When $\mathbf{a} = (a_1, \ldots, a_M)$ is

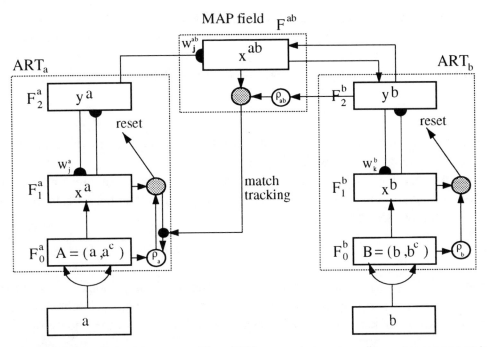

Figure 2: Fuzzy ARTMAP architecture. The ART_a complement coding preprocessor transforms the M_a-vector **a** into the $2M_a$-vector $\mathbf{A} = (\mathbf{a}, \mathbf{a}^c)$ at the ART_a field F_0^a. **A** is the input to the ART_a field F_1^a. Similarly, the input to F_1^b is the $2M_b$-vector $(\mathbf{b}, \mathbf{b}^c)$. When ART_b disconfirms a prediction of ART_a, map field inhibition induces the match tracking process. Match tracking raises the ART_a vigilance ρ_a to just above the F_1^a-to-F_0^a match ratio $|\mathbf{x}^a|/|\mathbf{A}|$. This triggers an ART_a search which leads to activation of either an ART_a category that correctly predicts **b** or to a previously uncommitted ART_a category node.

the network input, with $a_i \in [0, 1]$, the complement coded input **I** is the 2M-dimensional vector

$$\mathbf{I} = (\mathbf{a}, \mathbf{a}^c) \equiv (a_1, \ldots, a_M, a_1^c, \ldots, a_M^c), \tag{1}$$

where

$$a_i^c \equiv 1 - a_i \tag{2}$$

(Figure 1). Complement coding implies that $|\mathbf{I}| = M$, with the city-block norm $|\cdot|$ defined by:

$$|\mathbf{I}| \equiv \sum_{i=1}^{2M} I_i. \tag{3}$$

ART field activity vectors: Each ART system includes a field F_0 of nodes that represent a current input vector and a field F_1 that receives both bottom-up input from F_0 and top-down input from a field F_2 that represents the active code, or category. With complement coding, **I** $\equiv (I_1, \ldots, I_{2M})$ denotes F_0 activity, $\mathbf{x} \equiv (x_1, \ldots, x_{2M})$ denotes F_1 activity, and $\mathbf{y} \equiv (y_1, \ldots, y_{2M})$ denotes F_2 activity. The number of nodes in each field can be arbitrarily large.

Weight vector: Associated with each F_2 category node j $(j = 1, \ldots, N)$ is a vector $\mathbf{w}_j \equiv (w_{j1}, \ldots, w_{j,2M})$ of adaptive weights, or long-term memory (LTM) traces. Initially each category is *uncommitted*. After a category codes its first input it becomes *committed*. Each component

w_{ji} can decrease but never increase during learning. Thus each weight vector $\mathbf{w}_j(t)$ converges to a limit. The fuzzy ART weight, or prototype, vector $\mathbf{w}_j$ subsumes both the bottom-up and top-down weight vectors of ART 1.

Initial values: With complement coding, initial values of the weights are:

$$w_{j1}(0) = \ldots = w_{j,2M}(0) = 1. \tag{4}$$

Parameters: A choice parameter $\alpha > 0$, a learning rate parameter $\beta \in [0, 1]$, and a vigilance parameter $\rho \in [0, 1]$ determine fuzzy ART dynamics.

Category choice: The system makes a *category choice* when at most one F_2 node can become active at a given time. A *choice function* $T_j(\mathbf{I})$ determines the selected category. The index J denotes the chosen category, with:

$$T_J = \max\{T_j : j = 1 \ldots N\}. \tag{5}$$

If more than one T_j is maximal, the category with the smallest j index is chosen, so nodes become committed in order $j = 1, 2, 3, \ldots$. When the Jth category is chosen, $y_J = 1$ and $y_j = 0$ for $j \neq J$. In a choice system, the F_1 activity vector $\mathbf{x}$ obeys the equation:

$$\mathbf{x} = \begin{cases} \mathbf{I} & \text{if } F_2 \text{ is inactive} \\ \mathbf{I} \wedge \mathbf{w}_J & \text{if the } J^{th} F_2 \text{ node is chosen,} \end{cases} \tag{6}$$

where the fuzzy intersection $\wedge$ (Zadeh, 1965) is defined by:

$$(\mathbf{p} \wedge \mathbf{q})_i \equiv \min(p_i, q_i). \tag{7}$$

Weber law choice function: ART 1 (Carpenter and Grossberg, 1987a) and fuzzy ART (Carpenter, Grossberg, and Rosen, 1991) employ a Weber law choice function defined by:
Weber law choice

$$T_j(\mathbf{I}) = \frac{|\mathbf{I} \wedge \mathbf{w}_j|}{\alpha + |\mathbf{w}_j|}, \tag{8}$$

for each F_2 node j.

Resonance or reset: *Resonance* occurs if the chosen category meets the vigilance criterion:

$$|\mathbf{x}| = |\mathbf{I} \wedge \mathbf{w}_J| \geq \rho|\mathbf{I}|. \tag{9}$$

Learning then ensues, as defined below. *Mismatch reset* occurs if:

$$|\mathbf{x}| = |\mathbf{I} \wedge \mathbf{w}_J| < \rho|\mathbf{I}|. \tag{10}$$

Then the value of the choice function T_J is set to 0 for the duration of the input presentation to prevent the persistent selection of the same category during search. A new index J represents the active category, selected again by (5) and (8). The search process continues until the chosen J satisfies the matching criterion (9).

Learning: Once search ends, the weight vector $\mathbf{w}_J$ learns according to the equation:

$$\mathbf{w}_J^{(\text{new})} = \beta(\mathbf{I} \wedge \mathbf{w}_J^{(\text{old})}) + (1 - \beta)\mathbf{w}_J^{(\text{old})}. \tag{11}$$

Fast learning corresponds to setting $\beta = 1$.

Conservative Choice

The linkage between fuzzy subsethood and ART choice/search/learning forms the foundation of the computational properties of fuzzy ART. Vector $\mathbf{w_j}$ is a *fuzzy subset* of $\mathbf{I}$ if:

$$\mathbf{I} \wedge \mathbf{w}_j = \mathbf{w}_j \tag{12}$$

(Zadeh, 1965), i.e., $w_{ji} \leq I_i$ for $i = 1, \ldots, 2M$. When the choice parameter $\alpha = 0^+$, the Weber law choice function $T_j(\mathbf{I})$ (8) measures the *degree* to which $\mathbf{w}_j$ is a fuzzy subset of $\mathbf{I}$ (Kosko, 1986). When $\alpha = 0^+$, $T_j(\mathbf{I})$ is maximized by vectors $\mathbf{w}_j$ that are fuzzy subsets of $\mathbf{I}$, since then $T_j(\mathbf{I}) = 1^-$. A category J for which $\mathbf{w}_J$ is a fuzzy subset of $\mathbf{I}$ will therefore be selected first, if such a category exists. Specifically, the fuzzy subset category J that maximizes $|\mathbf{w}_j|$ will be chosen since then:

$$T_j(\mathbf{I}) = \frac{|\mathbf{w}_j|}{\alpha + |\mathbf{w}_j|}, \tag{13}$$

which is an increasing function of $|\mathbf{w}_j|$. If $\mathbf{w}_J$ is a fuzzy subset of $\mathbf{I}$, learning does not change weights, since then:

$$\mathbf{w}_J^{(\text{new})} = \beta \mathbf{w}_J^{(\text{old})} + (1 - \beta) \mathbf{w}_J^{(\text{old})} = \mathbf{w}_J^{(\text{old})}. \tag{14}$$

Because, when $\alpha = 0^+$, the chosen category J conserves weight values whenever possible, this parameter range is called the fuzzy ART *conservative limit*.

While fuzzy ART choice depends on the degree to which $\mathbf{w}_j$ is a fuzzy subset of $\mathbf{I}$, resonance depends on the degree to which $\mathbf{I}$ is a fuzzy subset of $\mathbf{w}_J$, by (9) and (10). When J is a fuzzy subset choice, then the match function value is:

$$\frac{|\mathbf{I} \wedge \mathbf{w}_J|}{|\mathbf{I}|} = \frac{|\mathbf{w}_J|}{|\mathbf{I}|}. \tag{15}$$

Choosing J to maximize $|\mathbf{w}_j|$ among fuzzy subset choices thus maximizes the opportunity for resonance in (9). If reset occurs for the node that maximizes $|\mathbf{w}_J|$ among fuzzy subset choices, then reset will also occur for all other subset choices.

Fuzzy ART Choice Functions

The choice function $T_j(\mathbf{I})$ in (8) describes a Weber law form factor that scales the degree of match between the input $\mathbf{I}$ and a weight vector $\mathbf{w}_j$ ($|\mathbf{I} \wedge \mathbf{w}_j|$) relative to the size, or degree of specificity, of $\mathbf{w}_j$. The choice parameter α modulates the scaling process. In the conservative limit, where $\alpha = 0^+$, the rule:

Choice-by-ratio

$$T_j(\mathbf{I}) \cong \frac{|\mathbf{I} \wedge \mathbf{w}_j|}{|\mathbf{w}_j|} \tag{16}$$

determines J, with the largest subset category chosen by (13) when such a category exists. At the opposite extreme, as $\alpha \to \infty$, the rule:

Choice-by-intersection

$$T_j(\mathbf{I}) \cong |\mathbf{I} \wedge \mathbf{w}_j| \tag{17}$$

determines J. Since $\mathbf{I} \wedge \mathbf{w}_j = \mathbf{I}$ for any uncommitted node j, by (4), choice-by-intersection will always select an uncommitted node, unless $\mathbf{I} = \mathbf{w}_J$ for some J. Thus, at this parameter limit, the system's memory consists of exact copies of all input exemplars. As α moves from 0 to ∞, the network becomes progressively more biased in favor of selecting an uncommitted node rather than a coded node with a low match ratio (16). The effect of parametrically raising the choice parameter α from 0 to ∞ is hereby similar to raising the vigilance parameter ρ from 0 to 1.

An alternative to the choice-by-ratio rule (16) *minimizes* the function:

$$T_j(\mathbf{I}) = (|\mathbf{w}_j| - |\mathbf{I} \wedge \mathbf{w}_j|). \tag{18}$$

This function is related to the membership function used by Simpson (1992). However, Simpson's *fuzzy min-max classifier* does not permit overlapping categories and so does not require a factor, such as (13), to differentiate fuzzy subset categories.

An extension of the rule (18) that is analogous to the Weber law rule (8) minimizes the function $T_j(\mathbf{I})$ defined by:

Choice-by-difference

$$T_j(\mathbf{I}) = (|\mathbf{w}_j| - |\mathbf{I} \wedge \mathbf{w}_j|) + \epsilon (|\mathbf{I} \vee \mathbf{w}_j| - |\mathbf{w}_j|). \tag{19}$$

In (19), $\vee$ denotes the fuzzy union, or component-wise maximum (Zadeh, 1965).

Parameter ϵ in (19) is analogous to the fuzzy ART choice parameter α. When $\epsilon = 0^+$, the category J is chosen to minimize the function (18), unless some $\mathbf{w}_j$ is a fuzzy subset of $\mathbf{I}$. Then, the first term in (19) equals 0, so:

$$T_j(\mathbf{I}) = \epsilon (|\mathbf{I} \vee \mathbf{w}_j| - |\mathbf{w}_j|) = \epsilon (|\mathbf{I}| - |\mathbf{w}_j|). \tag{20}$$

The function $T_j(\mathbf{I})$ is therefore minimized by the largest subset category J, if such a category exists. Thus, as in (14), the choice rule approaches a conservative limit as $\epsilon \to 0^+$.

Compared to the Weber law rule (8) with $\alpha = 0^+$, the choice-by-difference rule (19) with $\epsilon = 0^+$ holds a superior claim to the label *conservative*. Both rules make a fuzzy subset choice when possible, so both conserve weights if the fuzzy subset choice J satisfies the vigilance criterion (9). In addition, however, the choice-by-difference rule with $\epsilon = 0^+$ selects the category that *minimizes total weight change* during learning, whether or not $\mathbf{w}_j$ is a fuzzy subset of $\mathbf{I}$, as follows.

Suppose that $\mathbf{w}_j$ is not a fuzzy subset of $\mathbf{I}$. Then choice-by-difference minimizes the function:

$$\begin{aligned} T_j(\mathbf{I}) &= (|\mathbf{w}_j| - |\mathbf{I} \wedge \mathbf{w}_j|) + \epsilon (|\mathbf{I} \vee \mathbf{w}_j| - \mathbf{w}_j) \\ &\cong (|\mathbf{w}_j| - |\mathbf{I} \wedge \mathbf{w}_j|) > 0 \end{aligned} \tag{21}$$

when $\epsilon = 0^+$. Suppose that the chosen category J satisfies the vigilance criterion (9). Then the learning law (11) implies that the total weight change during learning is:

$$\begin{aligned} \Delta \mathbf{w}_J &\equiv |\mathbf{w}_J^{(old)} - \mathbf{w}_J^{(new)}| \\ &= \beta \left(|\mathbf{w}_J^{(old)}| - |\mathbf{I} \wedge \mathbf{w}_J^{(old)}| \right). \end{aligned} \tag{22}$$

Thus selecting J to minimize the choice-by-difference function leads to minimal weight change among all categories that satisfy the vigilance criterion, and to no weight change if $\mathbf{w}_J$ is a fuzzy subset of $\mathbf{I}$.

At the other extreme, as $\epsilon \to \infty$, choice-by-difference minimizes the function:

$$T_j(\mathbf{I}) \cong \epsilon \left(|\mathbf{I} \vee \mathbf{w}_j| - |\mathbf{w}_j| \right). \tag{23}$$

$T_j(\mathbf{I})$ is minimal at uncommitted nodes or when $\mathbf{w}_j = \mathbf{I}$, since then

$$\begin{aligned} T_j(\mathbf{I}) &\cong \epsilon \left(|\mathbf{I} \vee \mathbf{w}_j| - |\mathbf{w}_j| \right) \\ &= \epsilon \left(|\mathbf{w}_j| - |\mathbf{w}_j| \right) = 0. \end{aligned} \tag{24}$$

Thus, like fuzzy ART with Weber law choice as $\alpha \to \infty$, choice-by-difference reduces to exemplar memorization as $\epsilon \to \infty$. Correspondingly, as ϵ moves from 0 to ∞, the degree of code compression generally decreases, as it does when the vigilance parameter ρ moves from 0 to 1.

Alternative choice functions have similar properties in the limit as $\epsilon \to 0^+$. One such function is:

$$T_j(\mathbf{I}) = \left(|\mathbf{w}_j| - |\mathbf{I} \wedge \mathbf{w}_j| \right) + \epsilon \left(|\mathbf{I}| - |\mathbf{w}_j| \right), \tag{25}$$

as in (20). With complement coding, this function is equivalent to:

$$T_j(\mathbf{I}) = \left(|\mathbf{w}_j| - |\mathbf{I} \wedge \mathbf{w}_j| \right) + \epsilon \left(M - |\mathbf{w}_j| \right), \tag{26}$$

since $|\mathbf{I}| \equiv M$. However, choice-by-difference maintains an aesthetic symmetry as well as a form factor that is similar to the difference function that determines resonance (9) or reset (10).

Benchmark simulations will now show that fuzzy ART with the Weber law choice rule (8) has performance characteristics similar to those of a system that is the same except for a choice-by-difference rule (19) determining category selection.

Fuzzy ART Geometry

A geometric interpretation of fuzzy ART represents each category as a box in M-dimensional space, where M is the number of components of input **a**. Consider an input set that consists of 2-dimensional vectors **a**. With complement coding,

$$\mathbf{I} = (\mathbf{a}, \mathbf{a}^c) = (a_1, a_2, 1 - a_1, 1 - a_2). \tag{27}$$

Each category j then has a geometric representation as a rectangle R_j. Following (27), a complement-coded weight vector $\mathbf{w}_j$ takes the form:

$$\mathbf{w}_j = (\mathbf{u}_j, \mathbf{v}_j^c), \tag{28}$$

where $\mathbf{u}_j$ and $\mathbf{v}_j$ are 2-dimensional vectors. Vector $\mathbf{u}_j$ defines the lower left corner of a category rectangle R_j and $\mathbf{v}_j$ defines the upper right corner (Figure 3). The size of R_j is:

$$|R_j| \equiv |\mathbf{v}_j - \mathbf{u}_j|, \tag{29}$$

which is equal to the height plus the width of R_j. In fact, for any M, $|R_j| = M - |\mathbf{w}_j|$.

In a fast-learn fuzzy ART system, with $\beta = 1$ in (11), $\mathbf{w}_J^{(\text{new})} = \mathbf{I} = (\mathbf{a}, \mathbf{a}^c)$ when J is an uncommitted node. The corners of $R_J^{(\text{new})}$ are then **a** and $(\mathbf{a}^c)^c = \mathbf{a}$. Hence $R_J^{(\text{new})}$ is just the point **a**. Learning increases the size of R_J, which grows as the size of $\mathbf{w}_J$ shrinks. Vigilance ρ determines the maximum box size, with $|R_j| \le 2(1 - \rho)$. During each fast-learning trial, R_J

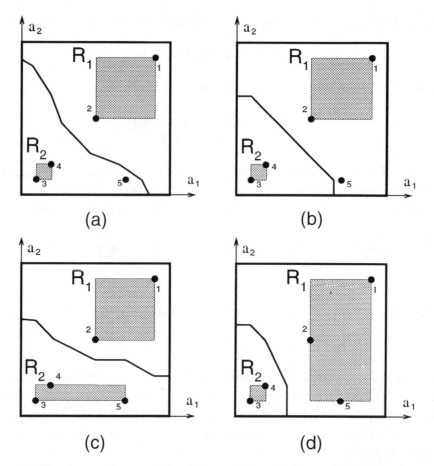

Figure 3: Fuzzy ART category boxes. Simulations (a) and (c) use the Weber law choice function (8), with $\alpha = 0^+$, and (b) and (d) use the choice-by-difference function (19), with $\epsilon = 0^+$. Plots (a) and (b) show category boxes and decision boundaries at the time input 5 is presented. Plots (c) and (d) show the system state after learning. Parameters $\beta = 1.0$ and $\rho = 0.4$.

expands to $R_J^{(\text{old})} \oplus \mathbf{a}$, the minimum rectangle containing $R_J^{(\text{old})}$ and $\mathbf{a}$, with corners $\mathbf{a} \wedge \mathbf{u}_J^{(\text{old})}$ and $\mathbf{a} \vee \mathbf{v}_J^{(\text{old})}$. However, before R_J can expand to include $\mathbf{a}$, reset chooses another category if $|R_J \oplus \mathbf{a}|$ is too large. With fast learning, R_j is the smallest rectangle that encloses all vectors $\mathbf{a}$ that have chosen category j without reset.

Figure 3 illustrates fuzzy ART category boxes at the start (a,b) and end (c,d) of an interval in which input 5 is presented. Plots (a) and (c) use the Weber law choice function (8) and plots (b) and (d) use the choice-by-difference function (19), both in the conservative limit. Vigilance $\rho = 0.4$, so reset occurs if $|R_J \oplus \mathbf{a}| > 1.2$ for a chosen category J. Each plot shows the decision boundary between the set of points $\mathbf{a}$ that would first select box R_1 and the set of points that would select box R_2. In plots (a) and (b), the boxes are the same and the decision boundaries are similar for the two choice functions. However, some points, including input 5, lie on different sides of the boundary. With Weber law choice (a), input 5 chooses $J = 2$, expanding the size of R_2 by 0.5 units during learning (c). With choice-by-difference (b), input 5 chooses $J = 1$, expanding the size of R_1 by 0.4 units during learning (d). This demonstrates the choice-by-difference property of minimal total weight change. Plots (c) and (d) show the different category

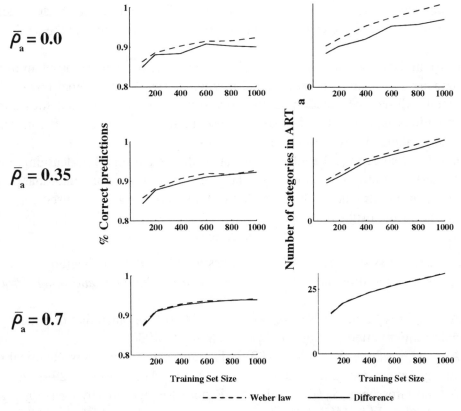

$\bar{\rho}_a = 0.0$

$\bar{\rho}_a = 0.35$

$\bar{\rho}_a = 0.7$

% Correct predictions

Number of categories in ART$_a$

Training Set Size

Training Set Size

----- Weber law ——— Difference

Figure 4: Fuzzy ARTMAP circle-in-the-square simulations for the Weber law choice function (8) (- - - - -) and the choice-by-difference function (19) (———). ART$_a$ baseline vigilance $\bar{\rho}_a = 0.0, 0.35,$ and 0.7, in the conservative limit ($\alpha = 0^+$, $\epsilon = 0^+$), with fast learning ($\beta = 1$).

structures and diverging decision boundaries that can result if a training set input falls near the boundary.

Fuzzy ARTMAP Simulations

An ARPA benchmark simulation, circle-in-the-square (Wilensky, 1990), illustrates fuzzy ARTMAP dynamics. The simulation task is learning to identify which points lie inside and which lie outside a circle. During training, components of the ART$_a$ input **a** are the x- and y-coordinates of a point in the unit square; and ART$_b$ input equals 0 or 1, identifying **a** as inside or outside the circle. When ARTMAP makes a predictive error during training, *match tracking* raises the ART$_a$ vigilance ρ_a (Figure 2) just enough to trigger search for another F_2^a category. This variable vigilance leads to variable category box sizes as the system balances the competing requirements of code compression (large boxes) and predictive accuracy (small boxes for exceptional cases).

Figure 4 shows fuzzy ARTMAP circle-in-the-square simulation results for the Weber law choice function (dotted lines) and the choice-by-difference function (solid lines), each in the conservative limit with fast learning. Performance is nearly identical for the two choice functions for baseline vigilance parameters $\bar{\rho}_a$ ranging from 0.0 to 0.7 and for training set sizes ranging from 100 to 1000 inputs. Since choice-by-difference minimizes weight change, that system creates slightly fewer categories when $\bar{\rho}_a = 0.0$ and has slightly more test set errors. Even this difference disappears as higher $\bar{\rho}_a$ itself creates more ART_a categories for both choice functions. Similarly, no consistent or significant differences persist for larger values of the choice parameters α and ϵ.

The mushroom database (Schlimmer, 1987) generated the benchmark problem of the original ARTMAP network (Carpenter, Grossberg, and Reynolds, 1991). The Weber law choice function and the choice-by-difference function again show similar performance statistics across a wide range of simulations that use this database. These include on-line and off-line learning with varied baseline vigilance levels and training set sizes.

Performance statistics, plus the added advantage of true conservative learning, argue for the use of the choice-by-difference function (19) when this function has computational properties that are needed for a fuzzy ART network embedded in larger architectures or used for computations beyond the scope of the original system.

References

Carpenter, G.A. and Grossberg, S. (1987a). A massively parallel architecture for a self-organizing neural pattern recognition machine. *Computer Vision, Graphics, and Image Processing*, **37**, 54–115.

Carpenter, G.A. and Grossberg, S. (1987b). ART 2: Stable self-organization of pattern recognition codes for analog input patterns. *Applied Optics*, **26**, 4919–4930.

Carpenter, G.A. and Grossberg, S. (1990). ART 3: Hierarchical search using chemical transmitters in self-organizing pattern recognition architectures. *Neural Networks*, **3**, 129–152.

Carpenter, G.A. and Grossberg, S. (Eds.) (1991). Pattern Recognition by Self-organizing Neural Networks. Cambridge, MA: MIT Press.

Carpenter, G.A., Grossberg, S., Markuzon, N., Reynolds, J.H., and Rosen, D.B. (1992). Fuzzy ARTMAP: A neural network architecture for incremental supervised learning of analog multidimensional maps. *IEEE Transactions on Neural Networks*, **3**, 698–713. Technical Report CAS/CNS-91-016. Boston, MA: Boston University.

Carpenter, G.A., Grossberg, S. and Reynolds, J.H. (1991). ARTMAP: Supervised real-time learning and classification of nonstationary data by a self-organizing neural network. *Neural Networks*, **4**, 565–588. Technical Report CAS/CNS-TR-91-001. Boston, MA: Boston University.

Carpenter, G.A., Grossberg, S., and Rosen, D.B. (1991). Fuzzy ART: Fast stable learning and categorization of analog patterns by an adaptive resonance system. *Neural Networks*, **4**, 759–771. Technical Report CAS/CNS-TR-91-015. Boston, MA: Boston University.

Grossberg, S. (1976). Adaptive pattern classification and universal recoding, II: Feedback, expectation, olfaction, and illusions. *Biological Cybernetics*, **23**, 187–202.

Kosko, B. (1986). Fuzzy entropy and conditioning. *Information Sciences*, **40**, 165–174.

Schlimmer, J.S. (1987). Mushroom database. UCI Repository of Machine Learning Databases (aha@ics.uci.edu).

Simpson, P. K. (1992). Fuzzy min-max neural networks – Part 1: Classification. *IEEE Transactions on Neural Networks*, **3**, 776-786.

Wilensky, G. (1990). Analysis of neural network issues: Scaling, enhanced nodal processing, comparison with standard classification. DARPA Neural Network Program Review, October 29–30.

Zadeh, L. (1965). Fuzzy sets. *Information and Control*, **8**, 338–353.

Retrieval of Images Using Fuzzy Interactive Activation Neural Networks

Sing Chai Chan, Chai Lian Choo
Dept. of Information Systems and Computer Science
Jian Kang Wu
Institute of Systems Science
National University of Singapore
Singapore 0511

1   Introduction

Our world has always been called the "information society", and great of effort has been devoted to the handling, storing, processing and analyzing of information. More than 70% of information we perceive is in visual form such as images, pictures, graphics, etc. We also realize that our world is filled with uncertainty, with problems that are often not clearly defined, and with imprecise and vague descriptions that may not be quantifiable. It is especially true for image information. Many of our real world problems constituted by two main factors: immense amounts of information and massive uncertainty of information. Research works have been undertaken for the management and processing of huge amount of image information [8, 9]. Recently, fuzzy logic techniques have been applied to retrieve image information from image database and to process images [12, 14]. It is believed that neural networks with the capability of massively parallel computations would be suitable to handle huge volume of images.

Interactive Activation and Competition model (IAC) [1] was proposed for information retrieval. IAC implies that the activation of output units is due to interaction and competition. There are several groups of units in the output layer. Each group represents certain concept. Units in example layer and units in the concept layer interact each other through bidirectional links. That was how name *interactive activation and competitive model* came from. In this paper, we propose a fuzzy IAC neural network model that is capable handle fuzzy queries for accessing to the stored images.

To demonstrate the ideas and capabilities of the proposed fuzzy IAC neural network model, we use facial images as a sample case. To describe a person, statements such as "she has big eyes and sharp chin" or "his face is so round" are often heard. What do we mean by "big eyes"? How big the eyes are considered "big"? Where do we draw the line? Fuzzy set theory founded by Zadeh [11] provides a theoretical basis for these questions and Wu has implemented these fuzzy concepts for facial images in [12]. In this paper we

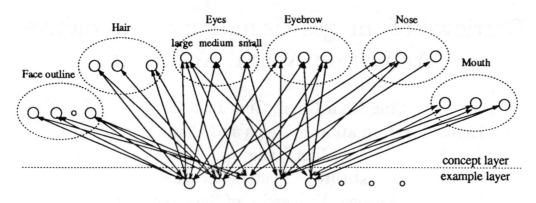

Figure 1: IAC network for members of organizations

present the fuzzy image retrieval approach in the neural networks. Section 2 is devoted to the general description of the problem and solution. Detailed discussion of fuzzy IAC will be appeared in section 3. Experimental results are presented in section4, and followed by the conclusion.

2   General Description

In the IAC model for facial image retrieval, the whole facial images are described by six facial features: chin, hair, eyes, eyebrow, nose, and mouth. When a facial image is captured, it is first normalized to a standard size. Possible skew is also removed by the normalization process. Numerical feature measures are then extracted using image analysis techniques for six facial features, namely, chin, hair, eyes, eyebrow, nose, and mouth. There are two type of feature measures, one is landmark coordinates, and the other is principle component analysis coefficients. They are all vectors in multi-dimensional feature (vector) space.

To enable fuzzy description of faces, fuzzy subsets defined for six facial features are shown in Table 1:

Table 1: Fuzzy subsets for facial description

chin	pointed, rounded, tapered, squared, bony cheek, short-chin, long-chin, jowls
hair	thin, normal, thick
eyes	small, medium, large
eyebrow	sparse, medium, thick
nose	short, medium, long
mouth	narrow, medium, wide

These fuzzy subsets are defined in the multi-dimensional feature space (or universe of discourse in terms of fuzzy terminology) by multi-dimensional fuzzy membership functions. Here, fuzzy membership functions relate fuzzy descriptions (subsets) and facial image (visual) through multi-dimensional feature measures. However, the relation between descriptions and images is not one-to-one, but rather complicated by the fact that there are six facial features and each feature has multi-dimensional measures.

When developing the fuzzy retrieval of facial images stored in image database [12], we found that the difficulties are due to incompleteness of query definitions. Detailed description of a particular person is usually not available. For example, a witness for a crime may say that the suspected criminal has long hair and wide face. Apart from these, at that time, he was too frightened to take note for anything else. It is very difficult to process these incomplete queries for a database. It might be relatively easy to retrieve the image information using the resonance mechanism and competitive interaction in neural networks.

The diagram of Fuzzy-IAC network for facial image retrieval is depicted in Fig. 1. The network has two main layers: concept layer and example layer. The units in the concept layer represent fuzzy subsets defined in table 1. They are grouped into six groups which correspond to six facial features.

The network can be activated either from example units or from concept units. When an example unit is activated, as the result, some concept units will be turned on with certain activation, which represent the classification result of the example. For example, if unit "medium" in the mouth group has activation value of 0.8, we say that the mouth of this example face is medium in width with certainty of 0.8.

In order to retrieve a face with round chin, small eyes, we can clamp the activation of unit "round" in chin group and unit "small" in eye group to some certainty, and let the network run for several cycles. As the result, some face examples will be activated with certain activation level representing the certainties.

In the situation when a person meets many people, examples are accumulated in his brain. Names of these examples might be blurred to him and he might mixed up people having the same or similar appearances. As time passes, some examples are forgotten by him, new examples are added to his brain. These phenomena can be simulated by adding an experience record to example units. In this case an example unit does not only represent a specific person but also represents a specific group of persons who have the same data. The experience record reflects the number of persons the example unit represents. This experience record is attenuated as time passes to simulate the forgetting process. The activation of example unit is proportional to its experience record. In this case, the higher the experience record, the higher the probability of recognition.

3 Structure of the Fuzzy-IAC

We have described the configuration of the Fuzzy-IAC. In this section, we will cover topics on unit structure, connection weight, and their initialization.

All example units have the same structure: activation, input, output, feature measures of six facial features, pointer to the incoming links from all concept units, pointer to the inhibitory links from other example units, and pointer to image data.

Different from example units, concept units contain category information to indicate the group it belongs, and the template feature measures and deviation which define the fuzzy subset membership function.

The certainty measure of a category is represented by the activation of the concept units. The weight of a link represent the relative importance of the facial feature (chin, eye, etc.).

Let us now concentrate at the situation without learning. Initially, all example facial image entries will be loaded to fill the items of the example units. The activation of example units will be initialized with 0. Because the structure of example units is different from all other concept units, there is no category information included.

Concept units are initialized with fuzzy subset label, template feature measure, and deviation. The activation of the units represent the certainty of the fuzzy subset. The relative importance of a feature is represented by the weight of the link from the feature group to all example units. That means that links from concept units of the same group have the same weight.

3.1   Interaction between Concept Units and Example Units

The interaction between concept units and example units is bi-directional. Let us now take mouth as an example. For mouth, we consider here only width, and three units are created and labeled as "narrow", "medium", and "wide". The membership functions for these three concepts are shown in Fig. 2. Each membership function will require three or four parameters for its definition. These parameters will be stored in the template vector. The function will be pointed by the function pointer defined in the unit data structure. Let us denote the function by $f_{narrow}()$, $f_{medium}()$, $f_{wide}()$ for the three fuzzy subsets. For any example image, there will be a number actually specifying the width of the mouth. If we denote it by x, then the interaction between these three concepts and this example will be $f_{narrow}(x)$, $f_{medium}(x)$, $and f_{wide}(x)$. Suppose the weight of the links between these three units and the example units are w, the total input from the example units to the unit "narrow" would be

$$s_{narrow} = \sum_j o_j f_{narrow}(x_j) w^{mouth} \tag{1}$$

Care should be taken when calculating the total input from various concept units to an example unit. It is quite often that someone says "the eyes of the guy is big, but not so big". This can be represented in our network in terms of certainties to the user and in terms of activation for both units "big" and "medium". The definition of the query is fuzzy. Here internal interactions between units are not fuzzy. Or in the other words, the concept units are fuzzy units. They need defuzzification. Unfortunately, our internal representations here are multi-dimensional. That means the fuzzy set membership functions are also multi-dimensional. This leads to very complicated, if not impossible, defuzzification. However, the retrieval is based on providing a set of most likely candidates, instead of defuzzification, we define the input to an example unit from units of a group (for example, eyes group) as simple summation. The difference is: defuzzification tries

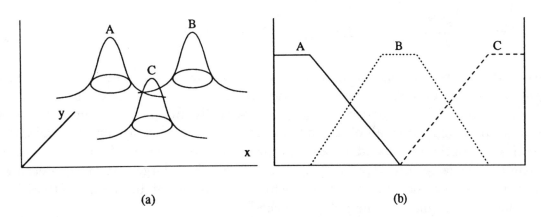

(a)   (b)

Figure 2: Membership functions

to recover the actual value, and then compare with values from the examples. Direct summation compares the value of examples with the template of concepts to generate the certainty which represent possibility the example image belongs to the fuzzy subset, and then sum them up with weights of certainties. Both method will produce the same results if the membership functions are equivalent.

3.2 Activation Function

Now let us discuss the activation function for IAC network. Each concept unit receives excitatory input from all example units, and example unit receives excitatory input from all concept units. All example units send inhibitory signal to each other. The competition comes from inhibitory lateral connections between concept units in the same gourd and example units, while resonance originates from mutual excitatory connections. Let us denote the total input, excitatory input, inhibitory input by s^{total}, s^{exc}, s^{inh}, respectively. The activation updating formula in [1] is written as follows:

$$
\begin{aligned}
if(s^{total} > 0) \quad & \Delta\, a_i = (a_{max} - a_i)\, s^{total} - \lambda_{decay}(a_i - a_{rest}) \\
Otherwise \quad & \Delta\, a_i = (a_i - a_{min})s^{total} - \lambda_{decay}(a_i - a_{rest})
\end{aligned}
\tag{2}
$$

where a_{max} and a_{min} are maximum and minimum of activations, a_{rest} is the resting activation level to which activations tend to settle in the absence of external input. λ_{decay} defines decay rate, which determines the strength of the tendency to return to resting level. Generally we choose $a_{max} = 1, a_{min} \le a_{rest} \le 0, 0 \le \lambda_{decay} \le 1$ so that a_i is assumed to be within the interval $[a_{min}, a_{max}]$. The decay term in the equation can be viewed as a kind of restoring force or leakage that tends to bring the activation of the unit down to a_{rest}, in the general case. The large the value of the decay term, the stronger this force is. The decay term can be also considered as a kind of leakage, which attenuates the activation of the unit to rest if there is no input signal to this unit.

The equilibrium can be found by setting $\Delta\text{-}a_i$ to zero and solving for a_i:

$$
a_i = \frac{a_{max}\, s^{total} + a_{rest}\, \lambda_{decay}}{s^{total} + \lambda_{decay}}
\tag{3}
$$

$$a_i = \frac{s^{total}}{s^{total} + \lambda_{decay}} \qquad for \; a_{max} = 1, \; a_{rest} = 0 \qquad (4)$$

Notice that s^{total} is changing for each iteration due to activation changes of other units. In general total input keeps unchanged for all iterations in one phase of running. Input signal due to lateral interconnections changes continually. Suppose that an unit receives inhibitory input signal from all other units in the same level or group, and that all lateral connection strengths are the same, an unit receiving largest signal from input pattern will tend to have large total input s^{total} and therefore to have large activation. Because it sends large inhibitory signal to other units while receives less inhibitory signal from other units. This is a phenomena "the rich gets richer".

Grossberg [2] treats the excitatory and inhibitory inputs separately. The excitatory inputs drive the activation of the unit up towards the maximum, whereas the inhibitory inputs bring the activation back down towards the minimum. The formulation is as follows:

$$\Delta a_i = (a_{max} - a_i) s^{exc} - (a_i - a_{min}) s^{inh} - \lambda_{decay}(a_i - a_{rest}) \qquad (5)$$

Resonance is a phenomena opposite to competition. If a group of units has mutually excitatory connections, then once one of the units becomes active, they will tend to keep each other active. For example, assume that between two units, u_a and u_b, there is bidirectional excitatory connection with weight of $2 \times \lambda_{decay}$, and that initial activation of these two units are 0.5. If we remove all external input, and if there is not other internal input to these two units, the activations of these two units will stay at 0.5. We can show this phenomena using evolution formula 2. In our brain such a resonance phenomena often happens to mutually consistent concepts, propositions. As the result of resonance, these concepts, propositions are reinforced. In IAC network resonance sustains consistent input patterns by mutually excitatory connections between units in different pools. For those input patterns which are not consistent, there will not be any excitatory links, corresponding units then decay away rapidly in the absence of continuing input.

Competitive networks and IAC networks update their states parallel. For each iteration following computations are parallel performed for all units: The program first computes three kind of input: total external input, total internal excitatory input, and inhibitory internal input. With three scaling parameters the total input is obtained. Finally, activation is updated.

How many iterations are required to complete an evolution when a new input pattern is presented? Principally, the evolution stops when the network reaches its equilibrium state. At the equilibrium state the delta of activations of units is negligible. An alternative way is to pre-define the number of interactions.

3.3 Learning by Categorization

In the situation when a person meets many people, examples of these people are accumulated in the brain. The names of these examples might be blurred to him, and he might mixed up people having the same or similar appearances. As time passes, some examples are forgotten by him, new examples are added to his brain. These phenomena can be simulated by adding an experience record to example units. In this case an example unit does not only represent a specific person, but also represents a specific group of persons who have the same data. The number of persons in the example unit is kept in the experience record. This experience record is attenuated as time passes. The activation of example unit is proportional to its experience record. In this case the number of example units will be all possible combinations of units from concept groups in the second layer.

In this case, an example no longer represents a particular person, but a category of people. A self-organization network is invoked to dynamically learning categories. Here we use a neural network model LEP (Learning based on Experience and Perspectives). The details of the model can be found in [7].

4 Experimental Results

The fuzzy retrieval network was implemented using C programming language and X-window. There are 88 example facial images. Fig. 3 shows the interface panel and the menu to input to the concept units. The function buttons on the first row in the panel provide tools to edit the neural network parameters, input to the concept units and example units, view concept units and example units, edit feature measures and network weights.

Fuzzy queries are defined by inputing to the concept units certainty values. This is done by shifting the scale widget in the input menu window. The certainty is in the range of 0 to 1. Having defined the query, press "run" menu bar under the "parameter" button to run the network, and then press "view node" button to view the images of the most active example units. Fig. 4 shows 9 images retrieved for query "rounded chin (0.8), short rounded chin (0.4), normal hair (0.7), and thin hair (0.3)". From top-left to the bottom-right are images with the highest activation to less high activation. The activation here has the meaning of possibility.

Learning and forgetting processing has not been implemented because this needs more facial images.

REFERENCES
[1] J. L. McClelland, D. E. Rumelhart, *Explorations in parallel distributed processing*, the MIT press, Cambridge, Massachusetts, (1986)

[2] Grossberg S., Competitive Learning: From Interactive Activation to Adaptive Resonance, *Cognitive Science*: 11, 23-63 (1987)

[3] T. Kohonen, *Self-Organization and Associative Memory*, Springer-Verlag, Berlin, (1988)

[4] J. K. Wu, LEP - Learning based on Experiences and Perspectives, *ICNN-90* Paris, (1990)

[5] J. L. McClelland, Retrieving General and Specific Knowledge From Stored Knowledge of Specifics, *Proc. the Third Anual Conference of the Cognitive Science Society*, (1981)

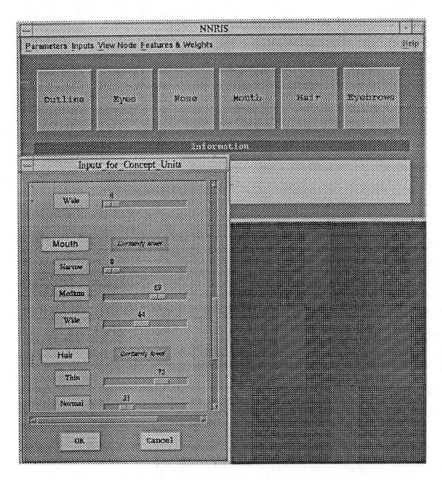

Figure 3: Interface panel of Fuzzy-IAC neural network.

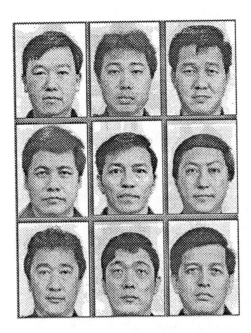

Figure 4: Fuzzy retrieval results for "rounded chin (0.8), short rounded chin (0.4), normal hair (0.7), and thin hair (0.3)".

[6] G. A. Carpenter and S. Grossberg, ART2: Self-organization of stable category recognition codes for analog input patterns, *Applied Optics* 26: p4919-4930 (1987).

[7] J. K. Wu, Neural Networks: Principles and Simulation, Marcel Dekker, New York, (1994).

[8] J. K. Wu, et al., Facial Image Retrieval, Identification, and Inference System, *ACM Multimedia Journal*, (1994)

[9] Bach J, Paul S, Jain R (1993) An interactive image management system for face information retrieval, *IEEE Trans. on Knowledge and Data Engineering*, Special Section on Multimedia Information Systems

[10] V. Bruce and M. Burton, *Processing Images of Faces*, Ablex Publishing, Norwood, New Jersey, (1992)

[11] L. A. Zadeh, Fuzzy sets as a basis for a theory of possibility, *J. FSS, 1*: pp 3-28 (1978)

[12] J. K. Wu, A. Desai Narasimhalu, Fuzzy Retrieval of Image Databases *Proc. First Asian Fuzzy Systems Symposium*, Nov. 23-26, (1993)

[13] H. Bandemer, W. Nather, *Fuzzy Data Analysis*, Kluwer Academic Publishers, Dordrecht, (1992)

[14] E. Binaghi, I. Gagliardi, and R. Schettini, Indexing and fuzzy logic-based retrieval of color images, *2nd Working Conference on Visual Database Systems*, 84-97, Budapest, Hungary, Oct. (1991)

Fuzzy Self-Organizing Map

John Sum and Lai-Wan Chan
Dept. of Computer Science, Chinese University of Hong Kong
Shatin, N.T., Hong Kong

December 8, 1993

Abstract

In this paper, we present a novel fuzzy neural network model called fuzzy self-organizing map (FSOM). Its algorithm will be elucidated. This model combines the properties of fuzzy c mean and topological mapping in self-organizing map. The limitation and capability of this model will be discussed in detail. Simulation will be given for illustration.

1   Introduction

As the well-development of fuzzy c mean (FCM) [1] and the simplicity of competitive learning (CL) network, some researchers have attempted to merge them together to form a class of fuzzy neural network. Jou[2] and Sum[3] recently derived the stochastic gradient descent algorithm for FCM and embedded it into competitive learning network to form fuzzy CL (FCL). Bezdek et.al. [4] [5] proposed a sequential update equation as an alternative. In their algorithm, they defined a kind of decreasing fuzziness scheme which is analogue to the size decreasing scheme in self-organizing map (SOM) [6]. As their model resumes LVQ, they called it Fuzzy Kohonen Clustering Network (FKCN).

Amongst all these models, only FKCN has taken into account of the update behavior of NN and put it back into the fuzzified training procedure. However, FKCN is suffered from two disadvantages:*(i) the algorithm is too complicated to be embedded into neural network architecture, and (ii) it does not actually take into the account of the concept of neighborhood interaction.* Though the algorithm derived by Jou[2] and Sum[3] are simpler but their algorithms do not consider the concept of neighborhood interaction. As neighborhood interaction leads to the property of ordering[1].

In this paper, we take this neighbor interaction concept into account. The paper is organized as follow. In the next section, we will derive a simple algorithm for one dimensional array of FSOM and illustrate its capability through examples. Besides, we will also discuss about its limitation and improvement. The proof of its convergence will be outlined. Then we extend the algorithm to two dimensional array. As well as the illustrative examples are given in section 3. Section 4 will be devoted to describe the linkages of our algorithm to CL, SOM and FCL. It aims at showing that our model is a generalization of CL, SOM and FCL. Besides, we explain how our algorithm can be converted to them. A conclusion will follow afterward.

2   Algorithm of FSOM: 1D Array

FSOM is similar to that of SOM in neural network. During each update, it is needed to find the winner node, v_I, and its neighborhood, N_I. In order to ease the discussion in the later section, let us define some notations.

2.1   Basic Notation

Definition 1: While data x is input, the winner node[2], $1 \leq I \leq c$, is defined by the one which global membership value (definition 5) is greatest, $\mu_I(x) > \mu_j(x)$ for all $j \neq I$. c is the number

---

[1]Since the definition of ordering is not well-defined, the present meaning of ordering is in a vague sense. We refer to those map which looks like Figure 1(a) (8x1map without twist) or Figure 3(b) (16x16 map without twist) is well ordered.

[2]It is just the same as nearest neighbor clustering.

of output node.

Definition 2: The neighborhood interacting set is denoted by, N_I, and it is defined as $N_I = \{ max(1, I - 1), I, min(I + 1, c)\}$.

Definition 3: The ith cluster set is denoted by Ω_i which obeys that $x \in \Omega_i$, $\mu_i(x) > \mu_j(x)$ for all $j \neq i$.

Definition 4: The local membership function is defined as follow[3]. For $m \geq 1$,

$$\beta_i(x) = \begin{cases} \left[\sum_{k \in N_I} \left(\frac{\|x - v_i\|^2}{\|x - v_k\|^2} \right)^{1/m-1} \right]^{-1} & \textbf{if } i \in N_I \textbf{ and } x \neq v_i \textbf{ where } i = 1, 2, \ldots, c \\ 1 & \textbf{if } x = v_i \\ 0 & \textbf{if } x = v_j \textbf{ where } j \neq i \\ 0 & \textbf{otherwise} \end{cases} \tag{1}$$

Definition 5: The global membership function is defined as follow. For $m \geq 1$.

$$\mu_i(x) = \begin{cases} 1 & \textbf{if } x = v_i \\ 0 & \textbf{if } x = v_j \textbf{ where } j \neq i \\ \left[\sum_{k=1}^{c} \left(\frac{\|x - v_i\|^2}{\|x - v_k\|^2} \right)^{1/m-1} \right]^{-1} & \textbf{otherwise} \end{cases} \tag{2}$$

2.2 Algorithm

With the aids of the above definition, we can define the algorithm as following. Suppose there are c code vectors which are indexed in one dimension.

S1. *Select randomly one sample, x, from the stationary sample space.*

S2. *Evaluate the winner node[4] I, i.e. finding I such that $\mu_I(x) > \mu_j(x)$ for all $j \neq I$.*

S3. *For all $i \in N_I$, update $v_i(t + 1)$ according to the following equation[5]*

$$v_i(t+1) = \begin{cases} v_i(t) + \alpha(t)\beta_i^m(x)(1 - \frac{m}{m-1}\beta_{i-2}(x))(x - v_i) & \textit{if } I = i - 1 \\ v_i(t) + \alpha(t)\beta_i^m(x)(x - v_i) & \textit{if } I = i \\ v_i(t) + \alpha(t)\beta_i^m(x)(1 - \frac{m}{m-1}\beta_{i+2}(x))(x - v_i) & \textit{if } I = i + 1 \\ v_i(t) & \textit{otherwise} \end{cases} \tag{3}$$

S4. *Decrease $\alpha(t)$[6]*

S5. *Goto S1.*

Obviously, one difference between our algorithm and FCL is in step 3. Moreover, there are three major differences: *(i) not all code vectors are needed to update. (ii) each of the update requires only local information, i.e. $\|x - v_k\|$ for all $k \in N_I$. (iii) topological map can be preserved through the above algorithm.* As the term $\beta_i^m(x)(1 - \frac{m}{m-1}\beta_{i-2}(x))$ exists inside the update equation, it is necessary to check its value. It is because topological map may be erased if it is greater than one[7]. Figure(1) plots two views of that function. m is set to be 2. It can easily see that

$$\beta_i^m(x)(1 - \frac{m}{m-1}\beta_{i-2}(x)) \leq 1.$$

---

[3] m is corresponding to the degree of fuzziness.

[4] Actually, the equivalent condition is $\|x - v_I\| < \|x - v_j\|$, for all $j \neq I$.

[5] These equations are actually obtained by taking the partial derivative of an objective functional with respect to v_i. This will be discussed later in section 2.4.

[6] According to [7], it has to be descreasing sequence in order to ensure that the convergence to minima is almost sure.

[7] It can be verified by considering the case when the input dimension is one.

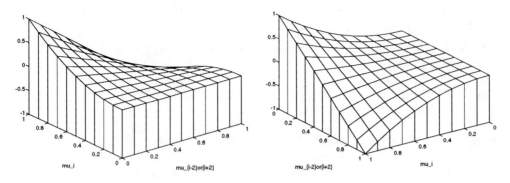

Figure 1: Two views of $\beta_i^2(1 - 2\beta_{i-2})$.

2.3 Limitation, Improvement and Simulation

This model though can be applied to give topological code map, it cannot be guarantee if the initial map is not ordered. Besides, the convergence rate of the above algorithm is rather slow especially when the size of the map is small compared with the size of the data. In order to lift up these problem, we suggest a **two phases update**. In phase one, the code vectors are updated based on SOM. Once the map converges (it goes to phase two) the map is updated based on above algorithm. Figure(2) shows four examples illustrating the idea[8]. In all four examples, the input data is drawn from the square which probability density is uniform.

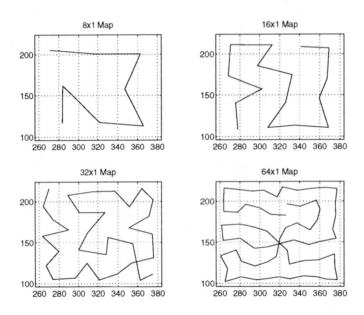

Figure 2: Examples of 1-D maps

By inspection, global topological map is not guarantee for 16x1 map and 32x1 map. However, local map is still established.

---

[8] Throughout the paper, m is set to be 2.

2.4 Convergence

Similar to that of neural network, convergence is also an important issue. Consider the following objective functional.

$$L = \sum_{i=1}^{c} L_i \tag{4}$$

where L_i is defined as follow, for all $i \neq 1$ or $i \neq c$.

$$
\begin{aligned}
L_i &= \int_{\Omega_{i-1}} \left[\sum_{k \in N_{i-1}} \left(\frac{\|x - v_i\|^2}{\|x - v_k\|^2} \right)^{1/m-1} \right]^{-m} \|x - v_i\|^2 f(x) dx \\
&+ \int_{\Omega_i} \left[\sum_{k \in N_i} \left(\frac{\|x - v_i\|^2}{\|x - v_k\|^2} \right)^{1/m-1} \right]^{-m} \|x - v_i\|^2 f(x) dx \\
&+ \int_{\Omega_{i+1}} \left[\sum_{k \in N_{i+1}} \left(\frac{\|x - v_i\|^2}{\|x - v_k\|^2} \right)^{1/m-1} \right]^{-m} \|x - v_i\|^2 f(x) dx
\end{aligned}
\tag{5}
$$

For $i = 1$,

$$
\begin{aligned}
L_i &= \int_{\Omega_i} \left[\sum_{k \in N_i} \left(\frac{\|x - v_i\|^2}{\|x - v_k\|^2} \right)^{1/m-1} \right]^{-m} \|x - v_i\|^2 f(x) dx \\
&+ \int_{\Omega_{i+1}} \left[\sum_{k \in N_{i+1}} \left(\frac{\|x - v_i\|^2}{\|x - v_k\|^2} \right)^{1/m-1} \right]^{-m} \|x - v_i\|^2 f(x) dx
\end{aligned}
\tag{6}
$$

For $i = c$,

$$
\begin{aligned}
L_i &= \int_{\Omega_{i-1}} \left[\sum_{k \in N_{i-1}} \left(\frac{\|x - v_i\|^2}{\|x - v_k\|^2} \right)^{1/m-1} \right]^{-m} \|x - v_i\|^2 f(x) dx \\
&+ \int_{\Omega_i} \left[\sum_{k \in N_i} \left(\frac{\|x - v_i\|^2}{\|x - v_k\|^2} \right)^{1/m-1} \right]^{-m} \|x - v_i\|^2 f(x) dx
\end{aligned}
\tag{7}
$$

It has no difficulty to show that **(3) is the necessary condition for the minimization of objective function**[9] L. Furthermore, it can also show that **the convergence of above algorithm is almost sure as the input dimension is one and the input data is between 0 and 1.** The outline of the proof is as follow. As the input is scalar value between 0 and 1, Ω_i can be specified as following open interval. $\Omega_1 = [0, s_1)$, $\Omega_i = [s_{i-1} + s_i)$ for $i \in \{2, 3, \ldots, c\}$, where, $s_i = \frac{v_i + v_{i+1}}{2}$ for all $i \in \{1, 2, \ldots, c-1\}$ and $s_c = 1$. Taking the derivative of (4) with respect to t, we obtained the following equation.

$$\frac{dL}{dt} = \sum_{i=1}^{c} \left(\frac{\partial L}{\partial v_i} \right)^T \frac{dv_i}{dt} + \sum_{i=1}^{c-1} \left(\frac{\partial L}{\partial s_i} \right)^T \frac{ds_i}{dt}$$

As $s_i = \frac{v_i + v_{i+1}}{2}$, $\frac{ds_i}{dt} = \frac{1}{2}\left(\frac{dv_i}{dt} + \frac{dv_{i+1}}{dt} \right)$. In addition, the expectation of (3) is the negative of the stochastic gradient of L with respect to v_i, $\frac{dL}{dt} \leq 0$. Therefore, (3) can converge to one of the local minima of L with probability one.

3 Algorithm of FSOM: 2D Array

While higher dimensional map is considered, the above algorithm is difficult to be extended[10]. Instead, we propose another algorithm stated as following.

---

[9] The proof can be accomplished by following the same approach as given by Tsypkin in section 4.3 of [8]

[10] We have tried to derive such algorithm but we fail. In so far, we still could not find out a suitable objective function which can lead to an equation as nice as equation (3).

S1. *Select randomly one sample, x, from the stationary sample space.*

S2. *Evaluate the winner node I, i.e. finding I such that $\mu_I(x) > \mu_j(x)$ for all $j \neq I$.*

S3. *For all $i \in N_I$, update $v_i(t+1)$ according to the following equation.*

$$v_i(t+1) = \begin{cases} v_i(t) + \alpha(t)\beta_i^m(x)(x - v_i) & \text{if } i \in N_I \\ v_i(t) & \text{otherwise} \end{cases} \quad (8)$$

S4. *Decrease $\alpha(t)$.*

S5. *Goto* **S1**.

Obviously, this algorithm is similar to SOM and it is simpler than the algorithm in section 2. Though it lacks of theoretical backup, it is simple and intuitive. Figure(3) illustrates two simulation results, 8x8 map and 16x16 map. In both simulations, m is set to be 2. Two phases update is employed. Input data is drawn randomly from a square. It is shown that global ordering is established by 16x16 map. However twisted map is established by 8x8 map.

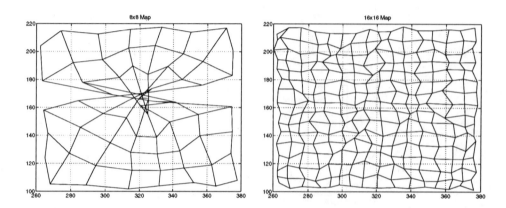

Figure 3: Examples of 2-D maps

4 Linkage with CL, SOM and FCL

Apart from treating FSOM as an algorithm alone, it can also be considered as a generalized model of CL, SOM and FCL. Review the algorithm defined in section 2, *the model is actually governed by two parameters, the size of the neighborhood interacting set N_I and the degree of fuzziness m*. Denotes the size of N_I by $S(N_I)$. Obviously, $0 \leq S(N_I) \leq c$. Then we can have the following special cases.

When $m \to 1$, no matter what $S(N_I)$ is, (3) reduces to CL.
When $m > 1$, if $S(N_I) = 1$, (3) reduces to CL.
When $m > 1$, if $S(N_I) = c$, (3) reduces to FCL.
When $m \to \infty$ and $1 < S(N_I) < c$, (3) reduces to SOM.

So it is clear that FSOM has a close relationship with other unsupervised learning algorithms.

5 Conclusion

This paper describes a model of fuzzy neural network called fuzzy self-organizing map. This model combines the property of fuzzy clustering and topological mapping. As a result, we can obtain not just the result comparable with fuzzy c mean, but also a topological relationship amongst these fuzzy cluster centers. Let us summary the advantages of FSOM.

a. *Topological fuzzy clustering map can form.*

b. *The update algorithm is simple.*

c. *The complexity of each update is low as only neighborhood of winner will be update.*

d. *Local membership function is introduced which further reduces the complexity of algorithm due to the evaluation of global membership value.*

e. *The update is sequential. The update can then continue even when the input is non-stationary, as long as the step size $\alpha(t)$ is fixed to a small constant.*

f. *It is flexible to reduce to other model as the parameters, including $S(N_I)$ and m, are changed appropriately.*

Though our algorithm provides a number of advantages, it lacks of a vigorous analytical proof on its property. So far, the convergence proof can only be success for a very special case, when both input and map dimension are one. For the input dimension or the map dimension is higher than one, the convergence proof is not established. We can only show that equation (3) satisfies the necessary condition for minimum. Besides, we encounter the same problem as SOM, the proof on the ordering preservation is not resolved. It is due to the fact that "order" has not been well-defined. Some other disadvantages are listed following.

a. *The convergence rate of FSOM is slow. So, a two phase update is suggested.*

b. *The order map cannot been usually form as the map is initially not in order. Even the map is initially in order, it may form a disorder map.*

References

[1] J.Bezdek, *Pattern Recognition with Fuzzy Objective Function Algorithms.* NY:Plenum,1981.

[2] C.C.Jou, "Fuzzy CounterPropagation Networks," Presented in the *Workshop on the Future Directions of Fuzzy Theory and Systems*, organized by faculty of engineering, CUHK, 27 Oct, 1993.

[3] J.Sum, "An Alternative Membership Function for Sequential Fuzzy Clustering and Fuzzy Competitive Learning," unpublished manuscript.

[4] J.Bezdek, E.Tsao and N.Pal, "Fuzzy Kohonen clustering networks,", *Proceeding of First IEEE Conf. on Fuzzy Systems*, 1035-1043, 1992.

[5] J.Bezdek, "A Review of Probabilistic, Fuzzy, and Neural Models for Pattern Recognition," *Journal of Intelligent and Fuzzy Systems*, VOL.1(1), 1-25, 1993.

[6] T. Kohonen, *Self-Organization and Associative Memory.* Springer-Verlag, 3rd Ed., 1989.

[7] L. Ljung, "Analysis of Recursive Stochastic Algorithms', *IEEE Transactions on Automatic Control*, Vol. AC-22, No.4, 551-575, 1977.

[8] Y.Z.Tsypkin, *Foundations of the Theory of Learning Systems*, Academic Press, 1973.

Edge Detection and Image Enhancement
Using Neuron-like Networks and Fuzzy Rules

Woon-Tack Woo

Department of Electrical Engineering-System
University of Southern California
Los Angeles, CA 90089-2564

Abstract

In this paper, I construct an Edge Detection System using neuron-like networks and Fuzzy Rules. First, neuron-like networks enhances the noisy image and finds rough edges using neuron-like networks. Then, the fuzzy system determines edges using the fuzzy knowledge. After several iterations, an enhanced image and edge can be found. Edge Detection is an essential step in the various applications because the results of later stages deeply depend on performance of this first step. This approach based on neuron-like networks and fuzzy system can be extended to vaarious vision problems. Neuron-like network offers good performance in low level signal processing and fuzzy theory may provide useful means to uncertain information processing. Experimental results for synthetic and natural images show the advantages of this system.

I. Introduction

The use of fuzzy theory is growing in the field of image processing and computer vision because of its flexibility[2][7][10]. An edge in an image is a boundary or contour at which a significant change of intensity occurs. In general, edges of the 2-D image contain limited information of the 3-D scene. This lack of information makes edge detection an ill-posed problem[11]. That is, the solution may not be unique, or it does not depend continuously on the data. It can be made unique only by adding information or assumptions. In this point of view, a priori edgei nformation can be used as fuzzy rules in the edge detection process. A good edge detector should correctly identify edge and have only one response to a single edge. In addition, the edge points should be close to the center of the true edges[1].

Edge detection process is one of the most important parts in the image processing and analysis. It is an essential step of segmentation, registration, and object identification as well as motion or stereo. The results of later stages of applications depend on performance of this edge detection step.

The aim of this paper is to verify the possibilities of Fuzzy Theory in the field of image processing and computer vision. This approach based on neuron-like networks and fuzzy system is meaningful because neuron-like network offer good performance in low level signal processing and fuzzy theory may help in processing uncertain information. Fuzzy logic can give clues for using high level information on the low level signal processing. The usefulness of this approach in the edge detection will be shown through experimental results. Fuzzy rules can help find edges in natural and systhetic images.

II. Image Space and Neuron-like Networks

Geman considered a given image as a realization of a stochastic process that is made up of an observable noise process and a hidden edge process[4]. With these stochastic models, we can represent the strength and structure of interactions between neighboring pixels and edges in an image[6].

Consider a random field of image $G=\{G_{ij}:(i,j) \in L\}$ defined on a discrete, finite, rectangular lattice $\Omega = \{(i,j) : 0 \le i \le N_1-1, 0 \le j \le N_2-1\}$. G is a Gibbs Random Field(GRF) with respect to a neighborhood system $\eta = \{ \eta_{ij} : (i,j) \in \Omega \}$, and consequently a Markov Random Field(MRF) according to the Clifford-Hammersley theorem, such that

$$\Pi(G_{ij} = g_{ji} \mid G_{kl} = g_{ij}, (k,l) \in L, (k,l) \neq (i,j)) \qquad (1)$$
$$= \Pi(G_{ij} = g_{ij} \mid G_{kl} = g_{ij}, (k,l) \in \eta_{ij})$$

where $\Pi(a \mid b)$ is conditional probability. For image processing applications, the first or second order neighborhood is used. Commonly used neighborhood are shown in Figure 1(a). Similarly, we can define edge neighborhood system $E = (E^h, E^v)$ which represent horizontal and vertical edge. The associated edge neighborhood systems are shown in Figure 1 (b) and (c).

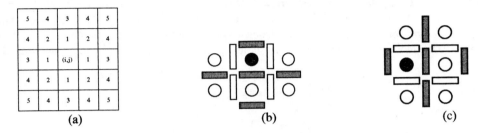

(a)   (b)   (c)

Figure 1. Neighborhood Systems of
(a) Pixels (b) Vertical Edges (c) Horizontal Edges

The filled circle stands for (i,j) pixel of G and rectangles are edges. In this paper, the edge strength has a continuous value between 0 and 1.

From the MRF model of image, we can construct neuron-like networks as shown Figure 2.

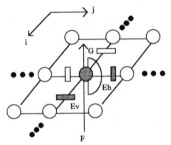

Figure 2. Neuron-like Networks

where output value of the filled circle is enhanced image intensity. The neuron-like networks involve two types of neurons[3][6][13]. The first type simply adds input after some weight multiplication. The output G of the first type of neuron can be computed as

$$G(i,j)^{n+1} = G(i,j)^n + \lambda\{F(i,j) - G(i,j)^n\} \qquad (2)$$
$$- (1-\lambda)\{(1-E^h(i,j))(G(i,j)^n - G(i,j+1)^n)$$
$$+ (1-E^h(i,j-1))(G(i,j)^n - G(i,j-1)^n)$$
$$+ (1-E^v(i,j))(G(i,j)^n - G(i+1,j)^n)$$
$$+ (1-E^v(i-1,j))(G(i,j)^n - G(i-1,j)^n)/k\},$$

where

$$k = 4 - E^h(i,j) - E^h(i,j-1) - E^v(i,j) - E^v(i-1,j),$$

where F is an observation of the ideal image G, λ is weighting factor and n is time state. The second type what we called edge or line process has sigmoidal response and modulates the summation neuron. It acts as a switching device between neighbor pixels. After computation of G, the edge E is determined as

$$E'(i,j) = \frac{1}{1 + \exp(\phi - (G(i,j) - G(i+1,j))^2)}, \qquad (3)$$

$$E^{h}(i,j) = \frac{1}{1 + \exp(\phi - (G(i,j) - G(i,j+1))^{2})}$$

(4)

where E^{h} and E^{v} are the horizontal and vertical edges and   is a thresholding value. The results are used as inputs of fuzzy system.

III. Fuzzy System

A new system based on a neuron-like network and fuzzy theory is shown in figure 3. First, the neuron-like network removes noise from the image. Then it generates an enhanced image and rough edges based on the intensity difference of neighboring pixels. In the second stage, the fuzzy system determines a set of edges using fuzzy rules in the MRF model. Finally, using the thresholding operation, binary edge can be determined.

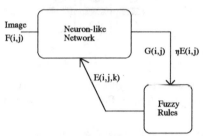

Figure 3. Overall structure

$F(i,j)$ and $G(i,j)$ are represent the noisy image and the enhanced image. $E(i,j,k)$ shows the edge and k is the direction of edges.

In fuzzy edge detection, the degree of intensity difference G_{ij} and neighbor edge state E_{ij} are used as inputs. The fuzzy edge E_{ij} is the output. First, each input is classified into three fuzzy classes represented by L(large), M(middle), and S(small) respectively.

> Input :   X: $(\Delta G_{ij}, \eta E_{ij})$
> $\Delta G_{ij} = \{$ Small, Middle, Large $\}$
> $\eta E_{ij} = \{$ Small, Middle, Large $\}$
> Output: Y: (E_{ij})
> $E_{ij} = \{$ Small, Middle, Large$\}$

The fuzzy membership functions for the inputs and the output are shown in figure 4. To determine the degree of neighbor edge states, I used good edge constraints as common-sense fuzzy rules. For example, I allocated *Large* to the edge types that have high occurrence frequency in the image. I allocated *Small* to double edge or isolated edge.

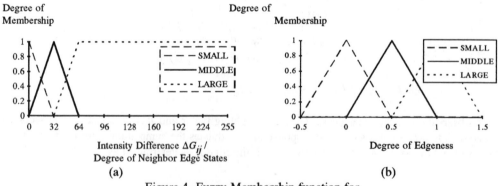

Figure 4. Fuzzy Membership function for
(a) Input (b) Output(Edge)

Fuzzy associative memory(FAM) rules encode structured knowledge as fuzzy associations[9]. The fuzzy association *(SMALL,SMALL ;SMALL)* represents the linguistic rule " *IF* G_{ij} *is Small AND* E_{ij} *is Small, THEN* E_{ij} *is Small."* Figure 5 show the fuzzy rule space used to find the edges.

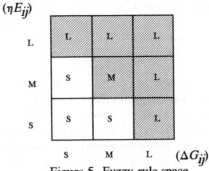

Figure 5. Fuzzy rule space

The output fuzzy set can be calculated using correlation-product encoding[9].

$$\omega_i = \min(m_{\sigma}(\Delta G_{ij}), m_{\eta B}(\eta E_{ij})) \tag{5}$$

where *m()* indicates the membership function of fuzzy set. The fuzzy system activates each FAM rule consequent set to a different degree. The *k*th FAM rule yields the output fuzzy set O_k

$$O_i = \omega_i L_i \tag{6}$$

where L_k stands for linguistic representation of output. The system then sums the O_k to form the combined output fuzzy set *O*. The superimposing of all rules is performed by

$$O = m_B(E_{ij}) = \sum_i O_i = \sum_i \omega_i L_i \tag{7}$$

Finally, I used centroidal defuzzification to get a crisp output *E*[9].

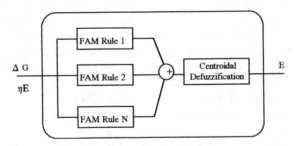

Fig 6. Additive Fuzzy System

A correlation-product inference is used to compute the centroid c_k of L_k from only three samples of the combined output fuzzy set *O*. The three sample points are the centroid of the output fuzzy set value because the three fuzzy sets are systematic and unimodal.

VI. Results

In general, Finding edge information largely depends on the pixel value itself. Consequently, high pass filtering not only enhances edge properties but also emphasizes noise. On the other hands, Smoothing operation or low pass filtering can be used to remove granularity but it can also blur edge. To over come this, Jeong et al[5] proposed adaptive filtering algorithm but high computation cost is need for this kind of algorithm. The proposed system can overcome these problems easily using adaptive filtering operation of neuron-like networks with fuzzy rules.

To show the effectiveness of this new system, three kinds of images are used. Figure 7 shows artificial image with additive Gaussian noise and its results computed by neuro-fuzzy system and Laplacian of Gaussian(LOG) operation respectively. Figure 8 shows the original peppers image and the edge maps. Figure 9 shows image included additive Gaussian noise and its resulting edge maps.

V. Conclusions

Early vision is mostly considered as a bottom-up process that does not rely upon specific high level information about the scene to be analyzed. However, it is unnatural. In this paper, thus, I have suggested a neuro-fuzzy cooperating system to build a rigorous basis of Human-like Computer Vision System. The efforts for unification of neuron-like network and fuzzy theory are needed because they may provide significant clues for using high level information on the low level signal processing. For example, neuron-like network offer good performance in low level signal processing and fuzzy theory may provide significant means uncertain information processing. The usefulness of using neuron-like networks with the fuzzy knowledge in the edge detection was shown through experiment results. There are lots of works to be done at all levels of computer vision. For example, it can be extended in the problem of texture, motion and stereo.

Acknowledgment

I would like to thank to Julie A. Dickerson and Bart Kosko for their useful advice and guidance.

Reference

[1] J. Canny, "A Computational Approach to Edge detection," *IEEE trans. on Pattern Analysis and Machine Intelligence*, vol. PAMI-8, no. 6, pp. 679- 698, Nov. 1986.

[2] R.J. Dave,"Boundary Detection through Fuzzy Clustering" *Proceeding of the IEEE International Conference on Fuzzy System*, San Diego, pp.127-134, 1992

[3] S. Geman and D. Geman, " Stochastic relaxation, Gibbs distribution, and Bayesian Restoration of Images," *IEEE Tran. on PAMI*, vol. 6, pp. 721-741, 1984.

[4] S. Geman and C. Graffing, " Markov Random Field Image Models and Their Applications to Computer Vision," *Proceedings of the International Congress of Mathematicians 1986*, pp. 1496- 1517, 1987

[5] H. Jeong, C. Kim, and W. Woo, " Determining Optical Scales for Edge Detection Using Regularization," *Proceedings of IEEE Inter. Conf. on Robotics and Automation*, vol. 2, no. 1, pp. 1596- 1601, 1991.

[6] H. Jeong, W. Woo, C. Kim, and G. Kim, " A Unification Theory for Early Vision," *Proceedings of First Korea-Japan Joint Conf. on Computer Vision*, vol. 1, no. 1, pp. 298- 311, Oct., 1991.

[7] R. Krishnapuran and J.M. Keller, "Fuzzy Set Theoretic Approach to Computer Vision: An Overview," *Proceeding of the IEEE International Conference on Fuzzy System*, San Diego, 1992, pp.135-142

[8] S. Kong and B. Kosko,"image Coding with Fuzzy Image Segmentation," *Proceeding of the IEEE International Conference on Fuzzy System*, San Diego, pp.213-220, 1992

[9] B. Kosko, Neural Networks and Fuzzy Systems, Prentice Hall, 1992.

[10] S.K. Pal, "Fuzzy Sets in Image Processing and Recognition," *Proceeding of the IEEE International Conference on Fuzzy System*, San Diego, pp.119-126, 1992

[11] T. Poggio and V. Torre, and C. Koch," Computational Vision and Regularization Theory," *Nature* , vol. 317, no,6035, pp. 314-319, 1985.

[12] T. Poggio and F. Girosi," Networks for Approximation and Learning," *Proceeding of the IEEE* , vol. 78, no,9, pp. 1481-1497, 1990.

[13] A. L. Yuile, " Energy Functions or Early Vision and Analog Networks," *Biological Cybernetics*, vol. 61, pp.115-123, 1989.

Learning Fuzzy Rules with Competitive Hebbian Learning 2

Ray H. White
Departments of Physics and Computer Science
University of San Diego
5998 Alcalá Park
San Diego, California 92110
white@teetot.acusd.edu

Abstract

Competitive Hebbian Learning 2, a very simple and very general unsupervised learning rule, is applied in this paper to the problem of finding fuzzy rules to approximate a function. In order to make CHL 2 effective in grouping adjacent points, and also to "fuzzify" a training-set point, the system is trained using a Gaussian region of input activity around a training-set point to train the neural network. Demonstrations show that CHL 2 learns a set of nodes, representing a set of fuzzy rules, which generate very good approximations to the training functions.

1 Introduction

An aspect of Fuzzy Systems which relates naturally to Neural Networks is the learning of fuzzy rules. For many systems appropriate fuzzy rules are not known *a priori*; for such systems an important step is that of finding good fuzzy rules. Such rules may be found based upon experience with the system using an unsupervised learning algorithm to generate the rules. A variety of unsupervised learning methods have been applied to the learning of fuzzy rules, for example see Dickerson and Kosko (1993) and Khedkar and Berenji (1993).

It is the purpose of this paper to show how Competitive Hebbian Learning 2 (CHL 2) may be applied to the learning of fuzzy rules. CHL 2 is an unsupervised learning rule which uses a simple modification of basic Hebbian learning to develop a set of competing units which each respond distinctly, but which collectively respond strongly to the input vectors in a training set, see White (1993). CHL 2 should be be able to train a set of nodes each to respond strongly to inputs in a distinct regions of the input space whenever there are exemplars included in the training set in those regions. In this paper the general method of applying CHL 2 to the learning of fuzzy rules is presented and then applied to a pair of demonstration problems.

2 CHL 2 Applied to the Learning of Fuzzy Rules

CHL 2 is an effective unsupervised learning rule when the system is monopolar, that is when inputs, outputs, and connection strengths are non-negative. (For systems in which the node outputs may be either positive or negative a bipolar learning rule such as CHL, see White (1992a,b), should be used instead.) The neural network to be trained consists of N nodes, which respond to a set of I inputs as:

$$y_i = f(\sum_{j=1}^{I} w_{ij}x_j). \tag{1}$$

Each w_{ij} is the connection strength, or weight, connecting input x_j to node y_i. The function $f(\cdot)$ is in principle a squashing function, but in the examples considered below y_i is simply a linear function of the x_j.

The CHL 2 learning rule is based upon the modified Hebbian rule

$$\Delta w_{ij} = \alpha x_j (y_i - \lambda \sum_{k \neq i} \overset{\circ}{y_k}).$$

(2)

In equation 2, α is a learning-rate parameter and λ is the competition parameter which determines the strength of the competitive learning interaction between the nodes, an adjustable parameter which is varied to optimize the learning of the system. In CHL 2 the learning determined by equation 2 is limited to non-negative learning, and the summation of the squared weights into each node is constrained to a constant value, *i.e.* $\sum_{j=1}^{I} w_{ij}^2 = W_{sum}^2 = Constant$.

One characteristic of CHL 2 is that the system learns to group together for any one node strong weights from input components which are *ON* simultaneously. In the demonstrations which follow, the natural training-set input vectors are points in a multi-dimensional input space which are on the surface which defines the function which is to be approximated. Such points would not produce contiguous regions of simultaneously *ON* inputs, nor would they produce a fuzzy boundary between inputs which are included and excluded from the training set.

A method to solve both of these problems at once is to use for training-set input-vectors input components which are partially *ON* in a region surrounding a point which is on the function surface. For each point which is chosen to produce a training vector, the components of the input vector are turned *ON* by an amount which decreases with distance from the point. In principle a variety of functions might be used to produce these turned-on input regions; in this paper a Gaussian function of the distance from the point is used. This choice of "fuzzifying" function means that the demonstrations presented below are extensions of the "Gaussian spots in two dimensions" demonstration, which was included in White (1992a) for CHL and in White (1993) for CHL 2.

3   Fifth-Order Polynomial

This demonstration is analogous to the one considered in Dickerson and Kosko (1993). The function to be approximated is a curve in a two-dimensional space, where the second variable, y, is a fifth-order polynomial of the first variable, x. The function is shown in figure 1, and is similar in form to the function approximated in the Dickerson and Kosko paper. Here we use CHL 2 to find sets of first 10 and then 20 nodes, each set representing a set of fuzzy rules to approximate this function.

Figure 1

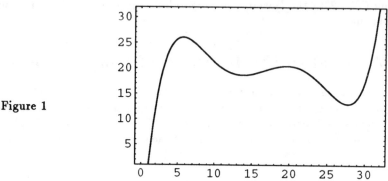

The input space for this case has 1024 components, which are treated as a 32×32 array. Training-set input-vectors are found by first choosing a point at a random position on the curve of the function. Then the value of each input component is given by $exp[-((i - x_0)^2 + (j - y_0)^2)]$, where x_0 and y_0 are the x

and y components of the random point on the curve, and i and j are the indices of an input component in the input array. A contour plot of the weights learned by 10 nodes is shown in figure 2a and a similar plot for 20 nodes in figure 2b, along with the original function.

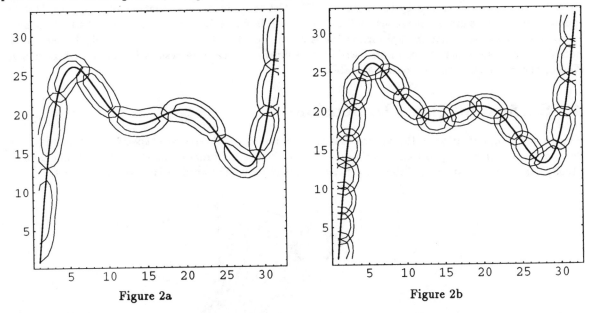

| Figure 2a | Figure 2b |

The nodes obviously learned to respond strongly in distinct regions along the curve of the function. For this training α was given a rather arbitrary value of 0.15, and λ was varied during the training to produce good results. Specifically, for the training of the ten-node set training started with $\lambda = 0.11$ for 5000 cycles, followed by 10000 cycles with $\lambda = 0.17$. Training continued with 5000 cycles at $\lambda = 0.25$, and thereafter with $\lambda = 0.50$. Changes in weights were small after 50000 cycles of training. Figure 2a shows weight contours after a total of 150000 training cycles, with very little change occurring during the final 100000 cycles.

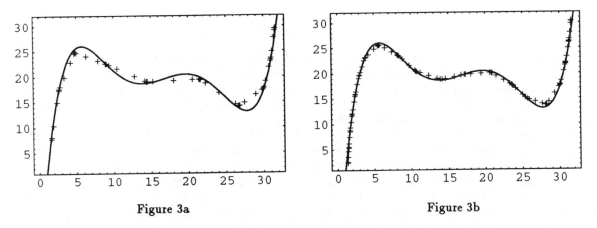

| Figure 3a | Figure 3b |

For the set of 20 nodes, training was started with 10000 training cycles using $\lambda = 0.056$, followed by 5000 training cycles with $\lambda = 0.20$. Further training used $\lambda = 0.50$, and changes in the weights became very small after an additional 20000 cycles. The contours shown in figure 2b show results after the learned weights had very thoroughly settled with 200000 cycles of additional training. but the changes over those additional training cycles were extremely small.

To check how well the nodes represented the original function, the centroids of the weight matrices of the nodes were used to reconstruct the function, using as the test set 100 points spaced uniformly along the function. For the test set only the four input components surrounding the test point on the curve were *ON*, as determined by the distance of the test-set point from the lattice point on the 32×32 input-array. The results of the reconstructions are shown in figure 3a and figure 3b for 10 and 20 nodes, respectively. One sees that the approximation is quite good for 10 nodes and noticeably better for 20 nodes. These results may be compared with the unsupervised-learning results found in Dickerson and Kosko, and obviously compare quite favorably.

4 Surface in Three Dimensions

The second demonstration is the approximation of a surface in three-space; specifically the surface is defined by $z(x,y) = 9.0/(1.0 + exp[1.11(x + y - 9.0)])$. This is the function used in Khedkar and Berenji (1993), rescaled so that the variables run between 0.0 and 9.0. The surface is shown in figure 4.

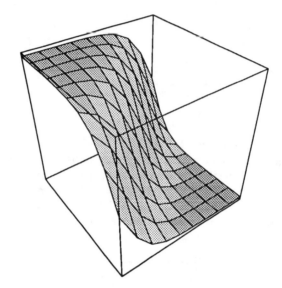

Figure 4

As in the previous demonstration, training-set input-vector are generated by placing a "Gaussian spot" of input activity around a point on the training function. In this case the "Gaussian spot" is three-dimensional, the input array consists of 1000 inputs treated as a $10 \times 10 \times 10$ array, and the training points are chosen by selecting a random point in the $x - y$ plane between 0.0 and 9.0 in both x and y and projecting that point onto the function surface.

Sets of first four and then nine nodes were trained. For the four-node run the initial value of the competition parameter, λ, was 0.33 for 5000 training cycles, and training continued with $\lambda = 0.50$. Weights were well settled after a total of 25000 training cycles, and further training for 100000 cycles produced extremely little further change. As in the previous demonstration, the learning-rate parameter, α, was set rather arbitrarily to 0.15. A contour plot of the learned weights for four nodes, projected onto the $x - y$ plane, is shown in figure 5a, and the four-node reconstruction of the function in figure 5b, again using centroids of the weight-arrays of each node to reconstruct the function.

Similarly, the projected contour-plot of the weights learned by the nodes, and the reconstruction of the function surface using nine nodes are shown in figure 6a and figure 6b. For nine nodes, training started with $\lambda = 0.125$ for 5000 cycles, followed by 5000 cycles with $\lambda = 0.25$, 5000 cycles with $\lambda = 0.33$, and then further training with $\lambda = 0.50$. The nodes were quite well trained after a total of 35000 cycles, but the figures show results after 100000 additional training cycles.

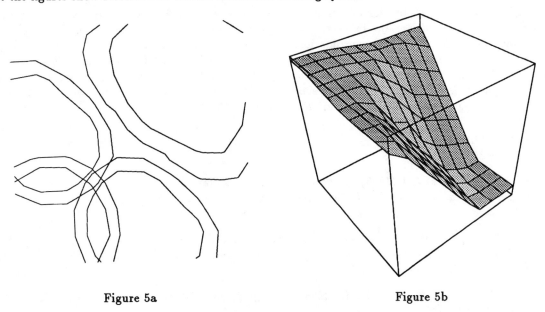

Figure 5a   Figure 5b

The reconstructions are very good, and indeed excellent for nine nodes except near the $x = 0$, $y = 9$ and $x = 9$, $y = 0$ corners, right on the transition of the surface and at the edges of the training region. These regions are outside the centroids of all the nodes as well as on the function transition from near $z = 9$ to near $z = 0$, and the approximation is noticeably poorer there. One should note that a comparison with the results of Khedkar and Berenji is not really appropriate, since the goals of these papers are distinct; Khedkar and Berenji were demonstrating fast unsupervised extraction of very rough fuzzy rules, whereas here we are demonstrating the use of a very simple and a very general unsupervised learning system to find good fuzzy rules.

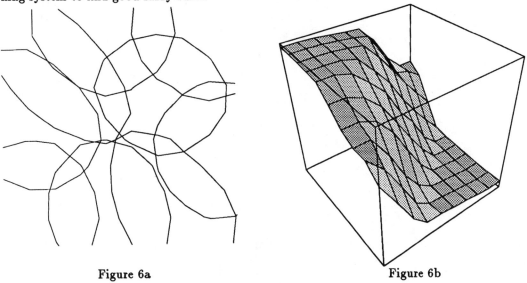

Figure 6a   Figure 6b

5 Conclusions

This paper outlines the application of Competitive Hebbian Learning 2, a very simple and very general method for unsupervised learning in neural networks with non-negative responses, to the problem of finding fuzzy rules for function approximation. In applying CHL 2 to the finding of fuzzy rules, a "Gaussian Spot" of activity is used around each point selected for the training set. This region of activity exploits the fundamental grouping property of CHL 2 and simultaneously serves to "fuzzify" the training-set point. The demonstrations show that CHL 2 is well-suited to such tasks, and that the fuzzy rules generated produce very good approximations to the training functions.

References

Dickerson, J. A. & Kosko, B. (1993). Fuzzy Function Approximation with Supervised Ellipsoidal Learning, in *Proceedings of the World Congress on Neural Networks, Portland*, (II:9 - II:17). Hillsdale, NJ: Lawrence Erlbaum Associates, Inc.

Khedkar, P. S. & Berenji, H. R. (1993). Generating Fuzzy Rules with Linear Consequents from Data, in *Proceedings of the World Congress on Neural Networks, Portland*, (II:18 - II:21). Hillsdale, NJ: Lawrence Erlbaum Associates, Inc.

White, R. H. (1992a). Competitive Hebbian learning: Algorithm and Demonstrations. *Neural Networks*, 5, 261 - 275.

White, R. H. (1992b). Recurrent Competitive Hebbian Learning, in *Proceedings of the International Joint Conference on Neural Networks, Baltimore*, (IV:767 - IV:772). Piscataway, NJ: IEEE Press.

White, R. H. (1993). Competitive Hebbian Learning 2: an Introduction, in *Proceedings of the World Congress on Neural Networks, Portland*, (II:557 - II:561). Hillsdale, NJ: Lawrence Erlbaum Associates, Inc.

3-D Object Recognition by the ART-EMAP Evidence Accumulation Network

Gail A. Carpenter[1] and William D. Ross[2]

Center for Adaptive Systems and Department of Cognitive and Neural Systems

111 Cummington Street, Boston University, Boston, MA 02215 USA

Abstract

ART-EMAP synthesizes adaptive resonance theory (ART) and spatial and temporal evidence integration for dynamic predictive mapping (EMAP). The network extends the capabilities of fuzzy ARTMAP in four incremental stages. Stage 1 introduces distributed pattern representation at a view category field. Stage 2 adds a decision criterion to the mapping between view and object categories, delaying identification of ambiguous objects when faced with a low confidence prediction. Stage 3 augments the system with a field where evidence accumulates in medium-term memory (MTM). Stage 4 adds an unsupervised learning process to fine-tune performance after the limited initial period of supervised network training. Simulations of the four ART-EMAP stages demonstrate performance on a difficult 3-D object recognition problem.

Object recognition by spatial and temporal evidence accumulation

ART-EMAP (Figure 1) is a neural network architecture that uses spatial and temporal evidence accumulation to recognize target objects and pattern classes in noisy or ambiguous input environments (Carpenter and Ross, 1993a, 1993b). During performance, ART-EMAP integrates spatial evidence distributed across recognition categories to predict a pattern class. When a decision criterion determines the pattern class choice to be ambiguous, additional input from the same unknown class is sought. Evidence from multiple inputs accumulates until the decision criterion is satisfied and the system makes a high confidence prediction. Accumulated evidence can also fine-tune performance during unsupervised rehearsal learning.

In four incremental stages, ART-EMAP improves predictive accuracy of fuzzy ARTMAP (Carpenter, Grossberg, Markuzon, Reynolds, and Rosen 1992) and extends its domain to include spatio-temporal recognition and prediction. ART-EMAP applications include a vision system that samples 2-D perspectives of 3-D objects. In this scenario, a sensor generates an organized database of inputs that are views of each object from different perspectives or noisy samples of fixed views. Evidence accumulation has been successfully used in neural network machine vision applications, as in the aspect network (Baloch and Waxman, 1991; Seibert and Waxman, 1990). ART-EMAP further develops this strategy.

---

[1]Supported in part by ARPA (ONR N00014-92-J-4015), the National Science Foundation (NSF IRI 90-00530), and the Office of Naval Research (ONR N00014-91-J-4100).

[2]Supported in part by the Air Force Office of Scientific Research (AFOSR 90-0083), the National Science Foundation (NSF IRI 90-00530), and the Office of Naval Research (ONR N00014-91-J-4100).

ART – EMAP

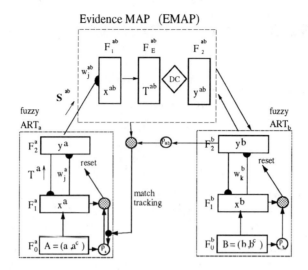

Figure 1: ART-EMAP architecture. The ARTMAP map field F^{ab} is replaced with a multi-field EMAP module. During testing, a distributed F_2^a output pattern $\mathbf{y}^a$, resulting from partial contrast enhancement of $F_1^a \to F_2^a$ input $\mathbf{T}^a$, is filtered through EMAP weights w_{jk}^{ab} to determine the F_1^{ab} activity $\mathbf{x}^{ab}$. If a predictive decision criterion is not met, additional input can be sought.

3-D object recognition

Simulations illustrate performance of fuzzy ARTMAP and ART-EMAP (Stages 1 - 4), on a recognition problem that requires a system to identify three similar 3-D objects (pyramid, prism, house). Inputs consist of ambiguous 2-D views taken from various angles (Figure 2). The problem is made difficult by the similarity of views across objects and by several test set views that do not resemble any training set view of the same object. Fuzzy ARTMAP correctly identifies only 64.7% of the objects from noise-free test set images. Stage 1 ART-EMAP raises performance accuracy to 70.6%, while Stage 2 and Stage 3 both boost performance to 98.0%.

Database inputs: The simulation database was constructed using Mathematica to generate shaded 2-D projections of 3-D objects illuminated by an achromatic point light source. For each of the three objects, 24 training set views were obtained from perspectives spaced 30° to 60° apart around a viewing hemisphere (Figure 2a). For each object, 17 test set views, spaced at 45° intervals, were obtained from perspectives between those of the training set (Figure 2b). Each 2-D view was then preprocessed, using Gabor filters (Gabor, 1946; Daugman, 1988) to recover boundaries, competitive interactions to sharpen boundary locations and orientations (Grossberg and Mingolla, 1985), and coarse coding, to yield a 100-component input vector **a**. The preprocessing algorithm is a typical feature extractor, chosen to illustrate comparative performance of different recognition systems, and was not selected to optimize performance of any one of these systems.

Training regime: Fuzzy ARTMAP and ART-EMAP Stage 1 through Stage 4 were evaluated using both a noise-free test set and a noisy test set. The noisy test set was constructed by adding Gaussian noise (SD = 0.2) to each input component. Each system was initially trained under one standard supervised learning protocol, with the training set presented once. Since the training set views were selected to be sparse and nonredundant, a situation of minimal code compression was simulated during training. This was achieved by assigning a high value to the ARTMAP baseline vigilance ($\bar{\rho}_a = 0.9$), which established 58 ART_a recognition categories for the 72 training set pairs (Figure 1).

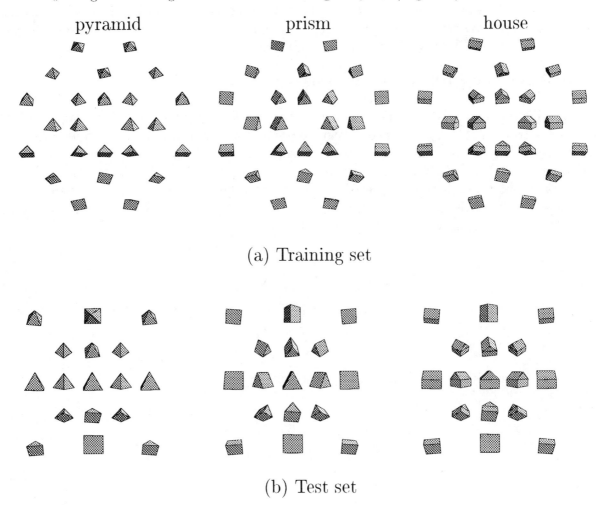

(a) Training set

(b) Test set

Figure 2: 3-D object database images. (a) The training set consists of 24 views spaced 30°-60° degrees apart within the front viewing hemisphere of each object. The topmost training images for each ordered set are views taken from above the object, the bottommost from beneath the object, etc. (b) The test set includes 17 new views of the front hemisphere, spaced 45° apart.

Fuzzy ARTMAP simulation: Performance measures of fuzzy ARTMAP and ART-EMAP on the 3-D object recognition database are summarized in Figure 3, for noise-free test set inputs (plots a-c) and for noisy test set inputs (plots d-f). The prediction of each test set view is represented graphically, on shaded viewing hemispheres. Each hemisphere shows 17 faces, which correspond to the 17 test set viewing angles (Figure 2b). For each simulation, three hemispheres show object class predictions made by the system in response to the corresponding input, with shading of a face indicating a prediction of pyramid (black), prism (gray), or house (white).

Fuzzy ARTMAP made only 64.7% correct object class predictions on the noise-free test set (Figure 3a), and 60.8% correct predictions on the noisy test set (Figure 3d). This poor performance indicates the difficult nature of the problem when prediction must be made on the basis of a single view. Note, for example, that many of the test set inputs from the lower left part of the pyramid view hemisphere were incorrectly identified as prism views. The reason for these errors can be inferred from the similarity between the corresponding pyramid and prism 2-D views in the test set (Figure 2b).

ART-EMAP Stage 1: Spatial evidence accumulation

ART-EMAP employs a spatial evidence accumulation process that integrates a distributed pattern of activity across coded category nodes to help disambiguate a noisy or novel input. In contrast, previous ART (Carpenter and Grossberg, 1987; Carpenter Grossberg, and Rosen, 1991) and ARTMAP (Carpenter, Grossberg, and Reynolds, 1991; Carpenter *et al.*, 1992) simulations chose only the most highly activated category node at the field F_2^a as the basis for recognition and prediction.

In the fast-learn fuzzy ARTMAP system, the input from F_1^a to the jth F_2^a node is given by:

$$T_j^a = \frac{|\mathbf{A} \wedge \mathbf{w}_j^a|}{\alpha + |\mathbf{w}_j^a|} \tag{1}$$

(Figure 1). Fuzzy ARTMAP uses a binary choice rule:

$$y_J^a = \begin{cases} 1 & \text{if } T_J^a > T_j^a \quad \text{for all } j \neq J \\ 0 & \text{otherwise.} \end{cases} \tag{2}$$

Then, only the F_2^a category J that recieves maximal $F_1^a \rightarrow F_2^a$ input predicts the ART_b output.

ART-EMAP also uses the binary choice rule (2) during the initial period of supervised training. However, during performance, F_2^a output $\mathbf{y}^a$ is determined by less exteme contrast enhancement of the $F_1^a \rightarrow F_2^a$ input pattern $\mathbf{T}^a$. Limited contrast enhancement extracts more information from the relative activations of F_2^a categories than does the all-or-none choice rule (2).

Power rule: Raising the input T_j^a of the jth F_2^a category to a power $p > 1$ is a simple way to implement contrast enhancement. Equation (3) defines a normalized power rule:

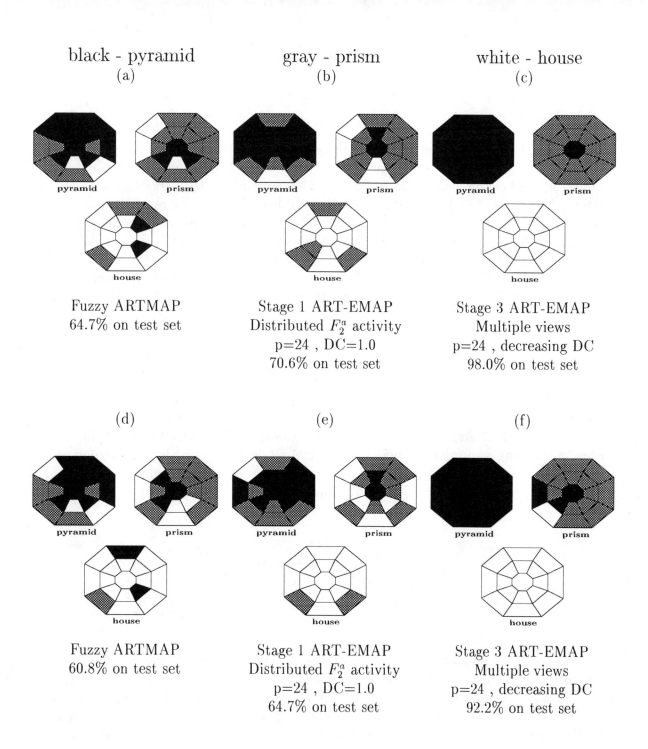

black - pyramid
(a)

gray - prism
(b)

white - house
(c)

pyramid   prism   house

Fuzzy ARTMAP
64.7% on test set

pyramid   prism   house

Stage 1 ART-EMAP
Distributed F_2^a activity
p=24 , DC=1.0
70.6% on test set

pyramid   prism   house

Stage 3 ART-EMAP
Multiple views
p=24 , decreasing DC
98.0% on test set

(d)

(e)

(f)

pyramid   prism   house

Fuzzy ARTMAP
60.8% on test set

pyramid   prism   house

Stage 1 ART-EMAP
Distributed F_2^a activity
p=24 , DC=1.0
64.7% on test set

pyramid   prism   house

Stage 3 ART-EMAP
Multiple views
p=24 , decreasing DC
92.2% on test set

Figure 3: 3-D object simulations. Response viewing hemispheres for each object show predictions from each test set view. A window in the hemisphere corresponds to one of the 17 test views (Fig. 2b). Plots (a), (b), and (c) show noise-free test set results and plots (d), (e), and (f) show noisy test set results. Plots (a) and (d) show fuzzy ARTMAP performance, using the F_2^a choice rule. Plots (b) and (e) show Stage 1 ART-EMAP performance using the power rule (3) with $p = 24$. Plots (c) and (f) show Stage 3 ART-EMAP performance with $p = 24$ plus temporal evidence accumulation with the decreasing decision criterion (10) and multiple views.

$$y_j^a = \frac{(T_j^a)^p}{\sum\limits_{n=1}^{N_a} (T_n^a)^p}. \tag{3}$$

Normalization constrains the F_2^a output values to a manageable range without altering relative values or subsequent predictions. The power rule (3) approximates the dynamics of a shunting competitive short-term-memory (STM) network that contrast-enhances its input pattern (Grossberg, 1973). The power rule is equivalent to the choice rule (2) when p is large. For smaller p, the distributed activity pattern (3) uses information from the relative F_2^a category activations to improve test set predictive performance at ART_b. In all ART-EMAP 3-D object simulations, $p = 24$.

After contrast enhancement, the F_2^a output $\mathbf{y}^a$ is filtered through the weights w_{jk}^{ab} to activate the EMAP field F_1^{ab}. The input S_k^{ab} from F_2^a to the kth F_1^{ab} node obeys the equation:

$$S_k^{ab} = \sum_{j=1}^{N_a} w_{jk}^{ab} y_j^a. \tag{4}$$

Since distributed F_2^a activity generally determines distributed EMAP field F_1^{ab} input, some means of choosing a winning prediction at the EMAP field is required. The simplest method is to choose the EMAP category K that receives maximal input from F_2^a. This can be implemented by letting $x_k^{ab} = S_k^{ab}$ and defining F_2^{ab} activity by:

$$y_K^{ab} = \begin{cases} 1 & \text{if } x_K^{ab} > x_k^{ab} \text{ for all } k \neq K \\ \\ 0 & \text{otherwise.} \end{cases} \tag{5}$$

Other methods for predicting an ART_b category will be discussed below.

Stage 1 simulation: Like fuzzy ARTMAP, Stage 1 ART-EMAP, with its spatially distributed activity pattern at F_2^a, is required to make a prediction from each single test set view. Nevertheless, predictive accuracy improves significantly, from 64.7% to 70.6% on the noise-free test set (Figure 3b) and from 60.8% to 64.7% on the noisy test set (Figure 3e).

Stage 2: EMAP predictive decision criterion

An alternative to the Stage 1 predictive choice rule (5) uses a *decision criterion* (DC) at the EMAP field F_2^{ab}. The decision criterion permits ART_b choice only when the most active category K becomes a minimum proportion more active than the next most active EMAP category. Thus:

	Noise-free test set		Noisy test set	
DC	Percent	Average # views	Percent	Average # views
5	98.0	4.8	90.2	6.8
4	92.2	4.3	96.1	6.0
3	92.2	4.2	94.1	4.1
2	88.2	2.7	80.4	3.2
1	70.6	1.0	64.7	1.0

Table 1: Stage 2 ART-EMAP 3-D object recognition simulation results as the fixed decision criteria (DC) decrease from 5 to 1. When DC=1, Stage 2 reduces to Stage 1.

$$
y_K^{ab} = \begin{cases} 1 & \text{if } x_K^{ab} > (DC)x_k^{ab} \quad \text{for all } k \neq K \\[2mm] 0 & \text{otherwise,} \end{cases} \tag{6}
$$

where $DC \geq 1$. With $DC = 1$, the Stage 2 decision criterion rule (6) reduces to the Stage 1 F_2^{ab} choice rule (5). With $DC > 1$, the decision criterion prevents prediction when multiple EMAP categories are about equally activated at F_1^{ab}, representing ambiguous predictive evidence. As the DC increases, both accuracy and the number of required input samples per decision tend to increase. For computational convenience, activity at F_1^{ab} can also be contrast enhanced by a normalized power rule:

$$
x_k^{ab} = \frac{(S_k^{ab})^q}{\sum\limits_{n=1}^{N_b}(S_n^{ab})^q}. \tag{7}
$$

Setting $q = 3$ in (7) makes performance less sensitive to the DC value than in the case $q = 1$ (no contrast enhancement at F_1^{ab}). The value of q does not change system function.

When the decision criterion fails, and (6) implies that $y_k^{ab} = 0$ for all k, additional input is sought to resolve the perceived ambiguity. In an application, additional inputs might correspond to multiple views or to multiple samples of a single view.

Stage 2 simulation: Stage 1 spatial evidence accumulation improves performance by causing a novel view to activate categories of two or more nearby training set views, which then strongly predict the correct object. However, many single view errors, caused by similar views across different objects, remain. Stage 2 or Stage 3 corrects most of these errors, when multiple views of the unknown object are available. With a high fixed decision criterion (DC=5.0) and an average of 4.8 test set views, Stage 2 ART-EMAP achieves 98.0% accuracy on the noise-free test set. Even on the noisy test set, object identification remains at 90.2% accurate, with an average of 6.8 test set views. Table 1 shows how both performance and the average number of views decrease as the fixed decision criterion decreases from 5 to 1.

Stage 3: Temporal evidence accumulation

The predictive decision criterion strategy (Stage 2 ART-EMAP) searches multiple views or samples until one input satisfies the decision criterion. However any single noisy input vector **a** might produce map field activity that satisfies a given decision criterion but still make an incorrect prediction. The Stage 2 strategy does not benefit from the partial evidence provided by all the views that failed to meet the decision criterion. Further performance improvement in a noisy input environment is achieved through the application of a decision criterion to *time-integrated* predictions that are generated by multiple inputs. Stage 3 ART-EMAP accumulates evidence at a *map evidence accumulation field* F_E^{ab} (Figure 1). The time scale of this medium-term memory (MTM) process is longer than that of the STM field activations resulting from the presence of a single view, but shorter than the long-term memory (LTM) stored in adaptive weights.

Additive evidence integration: A straightforward way to implement evidence accumulation at the EMAP module is to sum a sequence of F_1^{ab} map activations at the evidence accumulation field F_E^{ab}:

$$(T_k^{ab})^{(new)} = (T_k^{ab})^{(old)} + x_k^{ab}. \tag{8}$$

At F_E^{ab}, evidence accumulating MTM (T_k^{ab}) starts at zero and is reset to zero when the decision criterion is met. Activities y_k^{ab} at field F_2^{ab} obey:

$$y_K^{ab} = \begin{cases} 1 & \text{if } T_K^{ab} > (DC)T_k^{ab} \quad \text{for all } k \neq K \\ 0 & \text{otherwise.} \end{cases} \tag{9}$$

A decision will eventually be made if the DC starts large and gradually decreases toward 1. As in Stage 2 (Table 1), larger DC values tend to covary with both greater accuracy and longer input sequences. In simulations, the DC decreased exponentially form 6 to 1:

$$DC(l) = 5(1.0 - r)^{l-1} + 1, \tag{10}$$

where $\mathbf{a}(l)$ is the lth input in a same-class sequence ($l = 1,2, ...$). The decay rate (r) was set equal to 0.2. Additive integration is equivalent to applying the decision criterion to a running average of map field activations $\mathbf{x}^{ab}$ rather than to $\mathbf{x}^{ab}$ itself.

Stage 3 simulation: For a two-class prediction problem, evidence accumulation improves performance primarily by averaging across noisy inputs (Carpenter and Ross, 1993a, 1993b). Stage 3 ART-EMAP becomes increasingly useful as the number of predicted classes increases, since evidence accumulation can also help solve the difficult problem of disambiguating nearly identical views of different objects. With three or more object classes, when equal predictive evidence may exist for both the correct object and an incorrect one, the identity of the erroneous class tends to vary from one input to the next. As the sequence of views grows, erroneous evidence is quickly overwhelmed by evidence for the correct object. In the Stage 3 ART-EMAP three-object simulations, with the decreasing DC function (10), an average of 9.2 views were needed to reach 98.0% correct performance on the noise-free test set (Figure 3c). On the noisy test set, an average of 11.3 views allowed the system to reach 92.2% correct performance (Figure 3f).

Stage 4: Unsupervised rehearsal learning

Temporal evidence accumulation allows the Stage 3 ART-EMAP system to recognize objects from a series of ambiguous views. However the system learns nothing from the final outcome of this decision process. If, for example, an input sequence $\mathbf{a}^{(1)}$, ..., $\mathbf{a}^{(L)}$ predicts an ART_b category K, by (8)-(9), the entire sequence would need to be presented again before the same prediction would be made.

Unsupervised rehearsal learning (Stage 4) fine-tunes performance by feeding back to the system knowledge of the final prediction. Specifically, after input $\mathbf{a}^{(L)}$ allows ART-EMAP to choose the ART_b category K, the sequence $\mathbf{a}^{(1)}$, ..., $\mathbf{a}^{(L)}$ is re-presented, or rehearsed. Weights in an adaptive filter u_{jk}^{ab} from F_2^a to F_E^{ab} are then adjusted, shifting category decision boundaries so that each input $\mathbf{a}^{(l)}$ in the sequence becomes more likely, on its own, to predict category K.

Stage 4 simulation: Unsupervised rehearsal learning improves single view test set performance only marginally on the 3-D object simulations. Stage 4 rehearsal learning was conducted on the 51 noise-free test set views. Temporal evidence accumulation drew from an enlarged test set that included 72 additional views. Accessing exemplars from this larger test set allows stable fine-tuning by decreasing the percentage of ambiguous test views. After this fine-tuning, performance on individual views from the original 51 test set inputs was 73%, compared to 70.6% at Stage 1 (Figure 3b).

Conclusion

Spatial and temporal evidence accumulation by ART-EMAP have been shown to improve fuzzy ARTMAP performance on both the ARPA benchmark circle-in-the-square problem (Carpenter and Ross, 1993a, 1993b; Wilensky, 1990) and on the 3-D object recognition problem described here. Unsupervised rehearsal learning illustrates how self-training can fine-tune system performance. ART-EMAP is a general purpose algorithm for pattern class prediction based on the temporal integration of predictive evidence resulting from distributed recognition across a small set of trained categories. The system promises to be of use in a variety of applications, including spatio-temporal image analysis and prediction as well as recognition of 3-D objects from ambiguous 2-D views.

References

A.A. Baloch and A.M. Waxman, "Visual learning, adaptive expectations, and behavioral conditioning of the mobile robot MAVIN," *Neural Networks*, Vol. 4, pp. 271-302, 1991.

G.A. Carpenter and S. Grossberg, "A massively parallel architecture for a self-organizing neural pattern recognition machine," *Computer Vision, Graphics, and Image Processing*, Vol. 37, pp. 54–115, 1987.

G.A. Carpenter, S. Grossberg, and D.B. Rosen, "Fuzzy ART: Fast stable learning and categorization of analog patterns by an adaptive resonance system," *Neural Networks*, Vol. 4, pp. 759-771, 1991.

G.A. Carpenter, S. Grossberg, N. Markuzon, J.H. Reynolds, and D.B. Rosen, "Fuzzy ARTMAP: A neural network architecture for incremental supervised learning of analog multidimensional maps," *IEEE Transactions on Neural Networks*, Vol. 3, pp. 698-713, 1992.

G.A. Carpenter, S. Grossberg, and J.H. Reynolds, "ARTMAP: Supervised real-time learning and classification of nonstationary data by a self-organizing neural network," *Neural Networks*, Vol. 4, pp. 565-588, 1991.

G.A. Carpenter and W.D. Ross, "ART-EMAP: A neural network architecture for learning and prediction by evidence accumulation," Proceedings of the World Congress on Neural Networks (WCNN-93), III-649-656. Technical Report CAS/CNS-TR-93-015, Boston, MA: Boston University, 1993a.

G.A. Carpenter and W.D. Ross, "ART-EMAP: A neural network architecture for object recognition by evidence accumulation," Technical Report CAS/CNS-TR-93-035, Boston, MA: Bosotn University, 1993b.

J. G. Daugman, "Complete discrete 2-D Gabor transforms by neural networks for image analysis and compression," *IEEE Transactions on Acoustics, Speech, and Signal Processing*, Vol. 36, pp. 1169-1179, 1988.

D. Gabor, "A theory of communication," *Journal of the Institute of Electrical Engineers*, Vol. 93, pp. 429-457, 1946.

S. Grossberg, "Contour enhancement, short term memory, and constancies in reverberating neural networks," *Studies in Applied Mathematics*, Vol. LII, pp. 213-257, 1973.

S. Grossberg and E. Mingolla, "Neural dynamics of form perception: Boundary completion, illusory figures, and neon color spreading," *Psychological Review*, Vol. 92, pp. 173-211, 1985.

M. Seibert and A.M. Waxman, "Learning aspect graph representations from view sequences," *Neural Information Processing Systems 2*, Proceedings of the NIPS Conference, Denver, 1989, San Mateo, CA: Morgan Kaufmann Publishers, 1990, pp. 258-265.

G. Wilensky, "Analysis of neural network issues: Scaling, enhanced nodal processing, comparision with standard classification," DARPA Neural Network Program Review, October 29-30, 1990.

CONVENTIONAL CONTROLLERS IN FUZZY FORM

John A. Johnson and Herschel B. Smartt
Idaho National Engineering Laboratory
P.O. Box 1625
Idaho Falls, ID 83415-2209

Abstract

A specific formulation of fuzzy logic is shown to be exactly equivalent to conventional proportional-integral (PI), proportional-differential (PD), or proportional-integral-differential (PID) controllers under certain conditions. This formulation uses multiplication rather than finding the minimum to determine the conjunction between antecedents. This product is then multiplied by a crisp consequent membership function or output action for that rule and the sum of products determines the net output of the system. Only four rules are required for PI and PD controllers and only eight rules are required for PID controllers. With linear analytic antecedent membership functions, control is obtained through a single analytic expression which is equivalent to the analytic expressions for the conventional controllers.

Introduction

This paper presents a formulation of fuzzy logic that makes the relation to PD, PI, and PID controllers transparent, allowing the application of these technologies to fuzzy logic controllers and providing a deeper understanding of how these classical controllers operate. This formulation also greatly simplifies the calculations required for implementation. The complex and sometimes ambiguous methods of defuzzification are completely eliminated. In this formulation the conjunction operation on antecedents is accomplished by multiplication. The control action for each rule is determined by multiplying the antecedent truth value by a crisp consequent membership function. Since normalize input membership functions are used, a simple sum of the control actions for each rule determines the final, net control action. Sugeno[1] has previously used this formulation of fuzzy logic and is discussed in the context of other methods by Lee [2] in general terms. Neither has related the method to standard control theory.

Antecedent Membership Functions

For generality normalized scales are used for the membership functions, so all antecedent and consequent variables are in the interval [0,1]. Two membership functions for each antecedent or input variable are defined as "negative" which has a value of 1 when the input variable is 0, and "positive", which has a value of 1 when the input variable is 1. To derive the relationship between fuzzy controllers and conventional controllers, linear membership functions for one input variable are required:

$$
\begin{aligned}
m_{negative}(x) \quad &= 1 \quad \text{for } x < 0 \\
&= 1 - x \quad \text{for } 0 < x < 1 \\
&= 0 \quad \text{for } 1 < x \\[1em]
m_{positive}(x) \quad &= 0 \quad \text{for } x < 0 \\
&= x \quad \text{for } 0 < x < 1 \\
&= 1 \quad \text{for } 1 < x
\end{aligned}
\tag{1}
$$

For the general case of n antecedents, each with two membership functions, $m = 2^n$ rules are required:

If x_1 is negative and x_2 is negative and ... and x_n is negative,
　　　then z is z_1.
If x_1 is positive and x_2 is negative and ... and x_n is negative,
　　　then z is z_2.
・
・
・

If x_1 is positive and x_2 is positive and ... and x_n is positive,
　　　then z is z_m.

The output of the system is found by multiplying the antecedent membership values together for each rule, and finding the sum with each rule weighted by its output action, z:

$$z =$$
$$m_{negative}(x_1) * m_{negative}(x_2) *...* m_{negative}(x_n) * z_1 +$$
$$m_{negative}(x_1) * m_{negative}(x_2) *...* m_{positive}(x_n) * z_2 +$$
$$\bullet$$
$$\bullet \tag{2}$$
$$\bullet$$
$$+m_{positive}(x_1) * m_{positive}(x_2) *...* m_{positive}(x_n) * z_m$$

A Fuzzy PID Controller

A proportional-integral-differential controller works on the principle that an error correcting control signal should depend linearly on how large the error is, how large the integral of the error is, and how fast the error is changing. In the linear case this is equivalent to a three-input, eight-rule fuzzy logic system. In this case x_1 is the normalized error, with $m_{negative}(x_1)$ corresponding to the case where the variable is below the desired set point and $m_{positive}(x_1)$, above the set point. The normalized integral of the error is the variable x_2. If x_3 is the derivative of x_1, then $m_{negative}(x_3)$ corresponds to the case where x_1 is decreasing and $m_{positive}(x_3)$, where x_1 is increasing.

The formulation is more general if the physical variables themselves, rather than the errors, are used. The error signals are then just differences between a set point value and the actual physical value, which comes out naturally in the formulation. A subtle complication arises depending on whether the derivative of the physical variable is fed back and compared to a set point value (often equal to zero) or the derivative of the error signal itself is calculated. The complication is moot if the set point of the derivative is zero, but can confuse the comparison to standard controllers, in other cases. This is an especially important point for the integral part of the controller.

In the case of the linear membership functions given in (1) and eight rules, it is straight forward to derive an algebraic relationship for z, the output, as a function of the inputs, x_1, x_2, and x_3 by substituting into (2) and expanding:

$$z =$$
$$z_1 +$$
$$x_1*(z_4 - z_1) +$$
$$x_2*(z_3 - z_1) +$$
$$x_3*(z_2 - z_1) +$$
$$x_1*x_2*(z_1 - z_3 - z_4 + z_7) + \tag{3}$$
$$x_1*x_3*(z_1 - z_2 - z_4 + z_6) +$$
$$x_2*x_3*(z_1 - z_2 - z_3 + z_5) +$$
$$x_1*x_2*x_3*(-z_1 + z_2 + z_3 + z_4 - z_5 - z_6 - z_7 + z_8)$$

Note that this equation is valid only when x_1, x_2, and x_3 are within the range [0,1]. Outside that range, the membership functions are either 0.0 or 1.0.

Now we take a linear mapping of the physical variables onto the normalized variables:

$$x_1 = a_1*X_1 + b_1$$
$$x_2 = a_2*X_2 + b_2$$
$$x_3 = a_3*X_3 + b_3 \tag{4}$$
$$z = a_z*Z + b_z$$

where X_1, X_2, X_3, and Z are the physical variables that map onto the normalized variables x_1, x_2, x_2, and z, and a's and b's are constants that may be chosen as described below.

To compare to a conventional PID controller we must eliminate all the nonlinear terms in (3). This means that the output actions must obey these relations:

$$z_1 - z_3 - z_4 + z_7 = 0$$
$$z_1 - z_2 - z_4 + z_6 = 0$$
$$z_1 - z_2 - z_3 + z_5 = 0 \tag{5}$$
$$-z_1 + z_2 + z_3 + z_4 - z_5 - z_6 - z_7 + z_8 = 0$$

We may substitute the relations (4) into (3), leaving out the nonlinear terms:

$$a_z*Z + b_z =$$
$$z_1 +$$
$$(a_1*X_1 + b_1)*(z_4 - z_1) +$$
$$(a_2*X_2 + b_2)*(z_3 - z_1) + \tag{6}$$
$$(a_3*X_3 + b_3)*(z_2 - z_1)$$

When the system to be controlled is at the set point, (6) holds with the values $Z = Z_{set}$, $X_1 = X_{1set}$, etc. Subtracting (6) with the set point values from the general case, we obtain:

$$Z =$$
$$Z_{set} +$$
$$(X_1 - X_{1set}) * a_1/a_z*(z_4 - z_1) +$$
$$(X_2 - X_{2set}) * a_2/a_z*(z_3 - z_1) + \tag{7}$$
$$(X_3 - X_{3set}) * a_3/a_z*(z_2 - z_1) +$$

Thus the control is proportional to the error $(X_1 - X_{1set})$, the integral error $(X_2 - X_{2set})$, and the derivative error $(X_3 - X_{3set})$ and the exact, analytic equivalence of this formulation of fuzzy logic and conventional PID controllers is shown.

The values of the proportional, integral, and derivative gains are directly related to the output actions (z's) and the mapping constants. In particular, by varying the values of a_2 and a_3, the integral and derivative gains can be determined for a particular set of output actions. Curiously, the gains do not depend directly on z_5, z_6, z_7, or z_8. However, these variables are not superfluous and must be set to satisfy the conditions in (5) for a linear PID controller, required to eliminate the nonlinear terms.

The values of a and b can be chosen so that the range of the physical variable to be controlled, X (or Z), maps into the range [0,1]. Thus we have

$$a = 1./(X_{max} - X_{min})$$
$$b = -a * X_{min} \tag{8}$$

where X_{min} and X_{max} define the expected range of the physical variable X_1.

Comparison to Standard PD and PI Controllers
In a standard PD controller the control signal is proportional to the error and the derivative of the error. By setting the x_2 terms to zero in (3) or equivalently keeping only rules 1, 2, 4, and 6, we obtain:

$$Z = Z_{set} + (X_1 - X_{1set})*a_1/a_f*(z_4 - z_1) + (X_3 - X_{3set})*a_3/a_f*(z_2 - z_1) \tag{9}$$

that is, the control is proportional to the error and its derivative. The relationships (5) reduces to only the second relationship.

Similarly the PI controller is found by setting the x_3 terms in (3) to zero or equivalently keeping only rules 1, 3, 4, and 7:

$$Z = Z_{set} + (X_1 - X_{1set})*a_1/a_f*(z_4 - z_1) + (X_2 - X_{2set})*a_2/a_f*(z_3 - z_1) \tag{10}$$

The restriction on the output actions reduces to the first relationship in (5).

Inverted Pendulum Example

As an example consider the standard control problem of balancing an inverted pendulum. We use a formulation taken from Barto, Sutton, and Anderson (BSA) [3], which has also been used by other investigators to test neural network and fuzzy logic systems. In their formulation, the inverted pendulum sits on a movable cart and control is obtained by applying a force on the cart to the left or to the right. (Due to a typographical error in their paper, the value of gravity is given the wrong sign, so that the pendulum is in fact, not inverted. The equation they give is correct if g=+9.8. We use the correct sign in our calculations.) For this example we ignore the motion of the cart and only worry about balancing the pendulum.

Fuzzy PD Controller

We find it more convenient and intuitive to rewrite the rules with a slightly different notation for the output actions of the PD controller:

If x_1 is negative and x_3 is negative, then z is positive large = z_{pl}.	Rule 1
If x_1 is negative and x_3 is positive, then z is positive small = z_{ps}.	Rule 2
If x_1 is positive and x_3 is negative, then z is negative small = z_{ns}.	Rule 4
If x_1 is positive and x_3 is positive, then z is negative large = z_{nl}.	Rule 6

Here it is assumed that z is a corrective action which is called "positive" when it serves to increase a negative error, x_1, toward zero and "negative", to decrease a positive error toward zero. The terms "positive large", etc., are specific values for z, which correspond to the output actions required to produce an appropriate change in x. The first and fourth rules then correspond to the case where x is off the set point and moving in the wrong direction. The second and third rules correspond to the case where x is off the set point but moving in the correct direction.

The physical parameter to be controlled, X_1, is just the angle of the pendulum from the vertical. The range of motion of the angle of the pendulum is taken to be from -20^0 to +20^0. This defines the values of a_1 and b_1 to be 0.025 and 0.5 respectively. The set point is $X_{1set} = 0^0$. The output value, Z, the force applied to the cart, ranges from -10.0 to +10.0, so the value of a_f is chosen to be 0.05. The values of Z_{ps} and Z_{ns} are both taken to be 0.0 in this example, corresponding to z = 0.5. The values of Z_{pl} and Z_{nl} are taken to be the minimum and maximum values of the range of Z (-10 and +10), which correspond to $z_{pl} = 0.0$ and $z_{nl} = 1.0$. These are reversed from what might be expected since the force must be negative when a positive change in the angle is required, and vice versa, to put the pendulum at equilibrium. (The subscripts on Z refer to the effect on X_1, not on the numerical values of Z.) These values correspond to the conditions in (5, second equation) for the standard PD controller.

In Figure 1 are shown the results for several choices of a_3, the slope of the derivative mapping for identical starting conditions with the pendulum at the unstable equilibrium (X_1=0) and moving at 10^0/s (X_2=10.0). For a large value of the slope, the system is severely overdamped, resulting in a long time to reach the set point after recovery. As the slope is decreased, the time to the set point decreases until finally the value is too small and the system overshoots, indicating that it is underdamped.

Standard PD Controller

We can compare these results with those of the standard PD controller by first linearizing the equations for the pendulum, adding the controller, and calculating the effect of that controller. The original equation for the angular acceleration from BSA is

$$\ddot{\theta} = \frac{g\sin\theta + \cos\theta \dfrac{-F - ml\dot{\theta}^2\sin\theta + \mu_c \text{sgn}(\dot{x})}{m_c + m} - \dfrac{\mu\dot{\theta}}{ml}}{l\left(\dfrac{4}{3} - \dfrac{m\cos^2\theta}{(m_c + m)}\right)} \tag{11}$$

The notation is given in [3].

The linearized expression becomes:

$$\ddot{\theta} = \frac{g\theta + \dfrac{-F}{m_c + m} - \dfrac{\mu\dot{\theta}}{ml}}{l\left(\dfrac{4}{3} - \dfrac{m}{(m_c + m)}\right)} \tag{12}$$

The forcing function, F, is made proportional to the angle and the angular velocity using the equivalent coefficients for the gains from (9). The responses of the system for the same initial conditions are identical to those shown in Figure 1. Using the parameters from BSA and standard control theory, the value of a_3 for critically damped control is found to be 0.0054. Using fuzzy control with a value of $a_3 = 0.005$ (Figure 1) the system is observed to be very close to being critically damped.

Fuzzy PI Controller

The fuzzy PI controller has been implemented for the control of heat and mass input to a weld in gas metal arc welding (GMAW) [4]. A system had been developed which used a standard PI controller implemented in software. The error in the welding current is calculated from the actual measured current and that calculated from a model of the system three times a second. The integral of the error is calculated numerically by averaging the current error over a fixed time window. The standard PI controller was replaced with a fuzzy controller and the GMAW system operated identically, which is not really surprising since (10) shows the fuzzy system to be algebraically identical to the standard PI system. "The same equations have the same solutions." [5]

Comparison to the MacVicar-Whelan [6] Controller

MacVicar-Whelan showed that a fuzzy controller could emulate a standard PI controller by taking the limit as the number of rules approaches infinity or as the limit of the level of quantization of the input variables becomes infinitely fine. This is necessary primarily because of the discontinuities between the rules in the standard fuzzy logic theory and the defuzzification process. Using MacVicar-Whelan's design, Tang and Mulholland [7] had to use computer simulations to compare a fuzzy PD controller to a standard PD controller. The formulation of fuzzy logic in this paper, on the other hand, provides an analytic relationship between standard PI and PD controllers and fuzzy controllers.

Discussion

This method of implementing a conventional controller provides an alternative to formulating an analytical solution and designing a controller. In our uses of this method, we calculated the mapping constants based on (8) and guessed values for the output actions. Actually the "guesses" were based on expert knowledge of how the system operates based on empirical data or crude estimates or models. Then we tested the system which in our experience always worked reasonably well the first time. Following that we knew exactly which mapping constants to increase or decrease to change the integral or differential gains to tune the controller to our exact requirements. Here we were able to use our expert knowledge on conventional controllers. We have also investigated reinforcement learning techniques based on BSA [3] to change the output actions [8]

Acknowledgments

We appreciate the many discussions on this topic with Kevin Moore of Idaho State University, Gail Cordes and Carolyn Einerson of INEL. This work was supported by the U.S. Department of Energy, Office of Energy Research, Office of Basic Energy Sciences under DOE Contract No. DE-AC07-76ID01570.

1. M. Sugeno and G.T. Kang, "Structure identification of fuzzy model," **Fuzzy Sets and Systems 28**, 15-33, 1988.

2. C.-C. Lee,. "Fuzzy logic in control systems: fuzzy logic controller-parts 1 and 2," **IEEE Trans. on Systems, Man, and Cybernetics 20**, 404-435, 1990.

3 A.G. Barto, R.S. Sutton, C.W. Anderson, "Neuronlike adaptive elements that can solve difficult learning control problems," **IEEE Transactions on Systems, Man, and Cybernetics SMC-13**, 834-846, 1983.

4. H. B. Smartt, J. A. Johnson, C. J. Einerson, and G. A. Cordes, Intelligent Engineering Systems Through Artificial Neural Networks, New York, NY: ASME Press, pp. 711-716, 1991.

5. R. P. Feynman, R. B. Leighton, and M. Sands, <u>The Feynman Lectures on Physics Vol. II</u>, Addison-Wesley, pp. 12-1, 1963.

6. P.J. MacVicar-Whelan, "Fuzzy sets for man-machine interaction," **Int. J. Man-Machine Studies 8**, 697-697, Nov. 1976.

7. K.L Tang and R.J. Mulholland, "Comparing Fuzzy Logic with Classical Controller Designs," **IEEE Transactions SMC-17**, no. 6, 1085-1087, Nov. 1987.

8. J. A. Johnson and H.B. Smartt, "Fuzzy Logic and the Associative Search Element," <u>World Congress on Neural Networks</u>, Lawrence Erlbaum, New Jersey, II52-55, 1993.

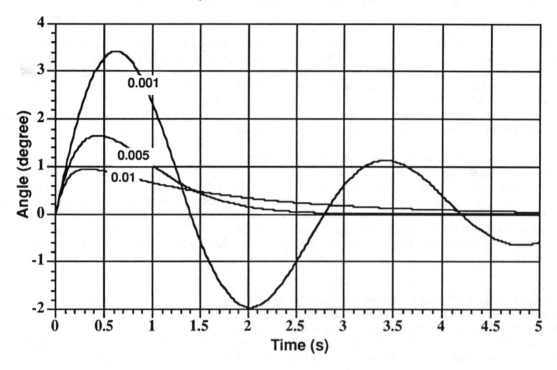

Figure 1. Fuzzy control of an inverted pendulum, show underdamped and overdamped solutions.

Modeling Complex Human Social Dynamics

Using Neural Networks of Fuzzy Controllers

Myron S. Karasik, Sutter Corporation, San Diego and
Paul Williamson, Correlates of War Project, University of Michigan, Ann Arbor

ABSTRACT

We are proposing a macro-model that will successfully capture the complexity of large-scale human interactions. The concept is based on distributed intelligent systems embedded in an environment whose own complexities are captured in various subsystems representing major natural forces at work on our planet. We therefore have:

1)   the world is represented as a system of interactions (flows or movements of information, energy, commodities, materials, persons, and other living things) among distinct "actors" (regions, nations, provinces, localities, communities, associations or other social groupings); and

2)   each actor is represented as a separate set of computational sub-routines corresponding to a distinct sub-model within the overall model.

In addition to representing social entities and their behaviors, the proposed model will capture the environment in which they function. Many environmental aspects correspond to more "physical" aspects of the modeling problem, in which variables are more operationally defined and relationships among them are understood structurally. For instance, clearly climate and geological forces and conditions are mutually affected. Each has different time frames of processes, one has to do with atmospheric and cosmological sources (sunspots) which can shift radically in days, the other has long-term forces which define the mineralogical wealth and soil characteristics. Both drive biological forces by defining ecological possibilities. Climate and geology interact with economics and technology when it comes to conversion of physical resources to goods and waste products. Each affects the other; consider acid rain, water pollution, over-farming/desertification, etc. as examples of such cross-linking. We can utilize individual models for climate, biological relationships, etc., to provide the matrix in which the actions of our 'actors' can be played out and where the effects (intentioned or unintentioned) can evolve.

The representation of these comparatively more deterministic factors will provide part of the environmental background (context) within which the societal components of the model interact. In addition, for many social and other processes not understood deterministically, nevertheless there are 'hard' statistics that can provide probability or population distribution functions for per capita wealth, education, health, etc. These comparatively tractable deterministic and probabilistic factors will provide the context within which the modeling activity will address, in ways we discuss below, the 'softer', more complex aspects of human and other global system behavior.

Together, these elements can be driven by a 'Monte Carlo' simulation engine to effectively explore the range of possible states and their likelihood. Overall the model will integrate probabilistic and deterministic aspects to explore the range of possible states within, and connections among, elements. One of the uses of these capabilities will be to simulate the interactions of the actors under the perturbations of various events.

Model Description

Our premise is, simple cybernetic feedback systems and statistical forecasting techniques cannot adequately capture, by themselves, the full range of interactions of all elements subject to policy decisions and other social actions on a large scale. Instead we have found every action creates in its wake a largely unforeseen range of results largely due to the fact that every 'problem' represents the culmination of a long history of events. This historical aspect is an important part of the complexity problem.

In reality, the nominally independent 'trajectories' of sub-system histories commingle and interact, changing each other in various ways. Previous experiences with other entities drives potential future experiences [Williamson 1985,1989]. Our way of meeting this requirement is that the sub-models of our distributed network will represent the actors as "intelligent." This means they possess memory of past events and are capable of acting based on the contents of their memory plus current information. Through this approach, we will seek to emulate present attitudes and behavioral traits (including dysfunctional traits such as ethnic prejudices in Bosnia and resistance to change in General Motors or IBM) as the product of evolution from past conditions and experiences.

We can organize the huge variety of human and environmental information necessary to support the above modeling approach, into nine major types. These concern:

- Geological forces and conditions

- Climatic, oceanic, and cosmological conditions

- Biological factors - non human species (physical and behavioral traits)

- Biological - human factors (physical and behavioral traits, including health, epidemiological, reproductive, and metabolic)

- Social structures that define the actors of the model (cultural, social, and ethnic groups; and provincial, national, international, and transnational political and economic units)

- Culture (language and value systems)

- Human artifacts, technologies, and wealth creation potential (including capital and capital infrastructure)

- Economic-political organization and behavior (including distribution of wealth and other resources)

- Interactions (material, energy, and information flows among relevant structures and elements)

Fuzzy Sets and Cultural Modeling

The problem of finding a computationally tractable way to represent human culture is important to the tasks of describing human values and perceptions (i.e. our cultural 'lenses'); these, in turn, may be essential to understanding the learning process central to the fact of history. Attempts in the past, such as Factions [Feder86], used utility function estimates and game theory models of voting with weightings based on salience and influence. This type of model has limited durability since it does not capture trends in the underlying cultural matrix. **The salient characteristics of a culture define normative behavioral patterns for its members. These patterns are based on social structures, historically catalytic events, and traditional teachings filtered through authoritative figures. Information of this type is often describable in linguistic terms and can be measured effectively by statistical measures such as percentage of population responding in a characteristic way. Periodic opinion surveys (assays) in combination with historical and demographic data can allow us to track these salient characteristics.**

Integrating linguistic data to determine relative frequencies with other 'hard' data can be accomplished through use of fuzzy sets and neural networks. The 'fuzzy' sets [Mamdani 1981] correspond to adjectives such as 'slightly agree', 'strongly agree', 'slightly disagree', 'strongly disagree', etc.

which are associated with phrases categorizing the preferred response to or desirability of a certain situation. For example, a questionnaire containing the following questions:

"I believe everyone has the right to make personal moral decisions', "I believe in the literal truth of the received word of God as taught by our Leader Y,", "Our present leader represents the values of our community properly", " Country X (or people X) are enemies of our country (or faith, etc.), "Violence is an acceptable means of resolving disputes"., etc.

In our case, an assay would ask demographic data to help assign membership into groups based on age, sex, religion, education, etc. The other questions would relate to behavioral propensities to answers as to how they would respond to given scenarios where values are at stake. We are after the relative frequencies of common behavior. Thus we may determine from analyzing the assay results that there are a certain number of groups based on behavior (having the same answers to the same sets of questions). Then, knowing the relative frequency of these behaviors among a particular demographic group, we can determine the overall likelihood of a behavior in the society at large. Care must be made in using a consistent of terms for each cultural group when framing our questions so that answers are comparable.

Our membership sets are developed by analyzing the assay results into a minimal grouping of non-overlapping patterns. In finite-state automata theory, we use 'Karnaugh' maps to produce the minimum number of discrete states necessary to describe a finite state machine. In this case our states represent all individuals whose answer patterns '1' 's for the selected choices and '0' elsewhere are the same. Sameness may be 'fuzzy' in that 'close' patterns are grouped together. The resulting finite set of distinct membership states then defines the 'interacting' agents whose distinct behaviors result in overt group behavior. The weights of 'influence' and combinatorial thresholds is factored by demographic and structural descriptions of the society.

We can then represent a social system as a combination of behavioral traits based on the relative proportions of the population espousing them. Thus if 63% of a population are illiterate and 88% of them strongly agree that one must defeat their enemies at all costs, while only 23% of the 37% of educated people believe so then we can see a great dissonance between these two groups. Today, the economic and political control might belong to the educated, but a popular movement could upset it and lead to a sharp change in that society's overt behavior. On the other hand, a program of adult education might make a permanent shift in the underlying behavior.

Thus every individual is the member of one or more communities; each community has a common history, culture (language, prescribed behaviors, taboos), and an accepted political structure to determine authority. At least one such community will have economic components and provide a means of livelihood; and at least one will provide the primary social matrix (usually family, kin system, clan, tribe or people). Our demographic description vector places us into a particular set of memberships. Each such membership group has a certain set of propensities for behavior. By combining the membership and behavior frequency data, **we can predict probable behaviors by population segments and relative contribution to total. These 'memberships' define the clustering of actor-elements of our distributed network model.** See Figure 1 below for examples of demographic categories and value / behavior laden questions used to determine classes of distinct behavioral groupings.

Every individual attempts to integrate the various communities into a personally congruent and fulfilling life. Sometimes this is easy, more often these days, not, because in this shrinking world, we find ourselves more likely to belong to more groups having less in common. For example, the Bosnian Muslim Biophysicist and Musician might have more in common with a Pakistani Muslim Poet or a Hindu Biophysicist than a Bosnian Serb Musician (even though the last and the first may have two things in common rather than one). This sort of non additive combination is the stuff of 'fuzzy' systems where degrees of membership and relative weights can be accurately modeled. In particular, the attribute of 'strongly agree' would characterize the identification with "Serbness" while the other attributes would have slight or no components, thereby driving the behavioral function to most closely resemble the 'optimal Serb behavior profile', i.e.., sense of historical injustice and acceptance of violence as means of rectifying it.

Example of Male Demographics

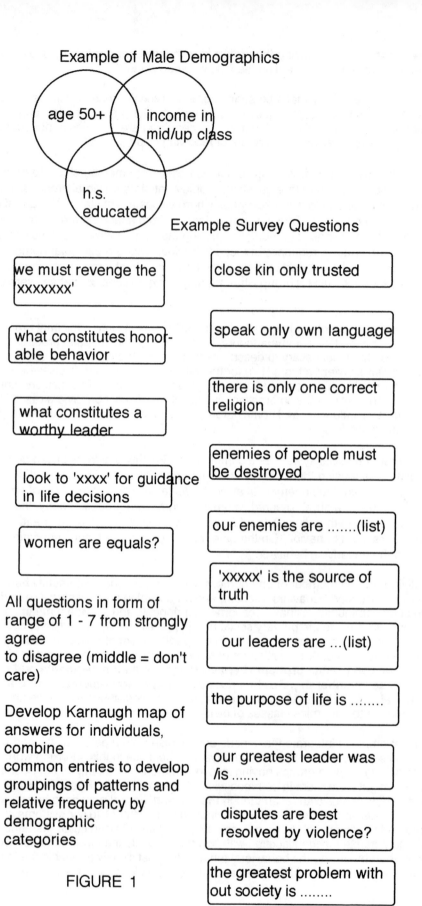

age 50+

income in mid/up class

h.s. educated

Example Survey Questions

we must revenge the xxxxxxx'

what constitutes honor-able behavior

what constitutes a worthy leader

look to 'xxxx' for guidance in life decisions

women are equals?

close kin only trusted

speak only own language

there is only one correct religion

enemies of people must be destroyed

our enemies are ....(list)

'xxxxx' is the source of truth

our leaders are ...(list)

the purpose of life is ....

our greatest leader was /is ....

disputes are best resolved by violence?

the greatest problem with out society is ....

All questions in form of range of 1 - 7 from strongly agree
to disagree (middle = don't care)

Develop Karnaugh map of answers for individuals, combine
common entries to develop groupings of patterns and relative frequency by demographic categories

FIGURE 1

Neural Networks to Model Interconnected Agents in a Common Domain of Interest

Per [Karasik 1992] we can embed the individual actor in a matrix of other actors to interconnect with each other in a neural network. Each acts as a simple 'neuron' processor which takes many inputs (environmental and other actor outputs) and has a single output (choice of behavior or null response). The 'on' signal is achieved if the linearly weighted sum of the input signals exceeds a certain threshold value. The output in turn can be fed into any number of subsequent stage neurons to be factored together to produce next stage outputs, etc., until we get a final level which generates an overt behavioral change at the global level. Weights can change over time as the model spontaneously 'learns' from past mistakes. Weights in essence are the 'memory' of the system and define the degree of interaction among the elements during the subsequent cycle of processing.

When we look at the model of the individual agent (person or grouping of like persons), we see the following: We have a means of representing personal history (memory) recording the results of previous encounters with reality. We also have a comparator function evaluating difference between existing state of the world and internal ideal (note, dissonance is a cumulative function). Finally, the agent is equipped by nature (through biological and physical resources and limitations) to perform a set of actions subject to cultural propensities (group history, values, behavioral paradigms). The agent has the ability to sense and filter events and messages from various sources (other agents, etc.) to determine an appropriate action which will affect its domain. An action taken will impact both the agent, through learning how its domain behaves when acted upon, as well as other agents linked through the common domain.

We are interested in modeling the dynamics of interacting social entities whose component agents are population categories having various behavioral propensities. At the agent level we can model the various strengths (or weights) of direct environmental signals and signals from other agents that reinforce or inhibit certain responses. The degree of contribution from the other agents depends on prior experiences. **These can be modeled using the concepts of proximity and credibility. Proximity would indicate a stronger weight, while credibility would indicate the sign or direction of influence.** The links between the agents are incorporated in an 'interconnection matrix'. Proximity and credibility of source signals are factored in the weights of the signals. The opinion-making process is then structurally described by this matrix. The elements of the weights can change over time as new sources arise and perceived credibility is reduced or enhanced based on history and evaluation of state.

Thus, messages from nearby friends are important, as well as those from nearby enemies; casual strangers have little influence; while culturally authoritative sources (pope, imam, etc.) could have a significant contribution as well. We can model the strengths as normalized to the set [-1, 1] for simplicity and ability to use Markovian methods in modeling time evolution. The thresholds can be modeled using a vector whose individual component values are in the set [-1, 1]. The individual component represents the degree of dissonance allowed for a given environmental variable of concern. Thus each agent acts as if it seeks to maintain some acceptable dissonance between its desired state and actual perceived state. The measures of each of these objectives can then be ranked. Similarly, we can perform the same structural analysis at the entity level.

In our model, our agents are 'neurons' representing disjunctive demographic components whose outputs are the relative frequencies of behavior. These are input into a second level 'agent' or actor that represents the behavior / preferred environment state in question. The voting logic triggers the threshold of the behavior when cumulative frequencies exceed a certain percentage. Threshold can change or be set based on actual structural factors as to how much 'weight' members of different groups might have. It is possible for us to have multiple conflicting behaviors triggered by adjusting the thresholds, thus modeling conflicts among agents. A simple, incomplete example is shown in Figure 2 below.

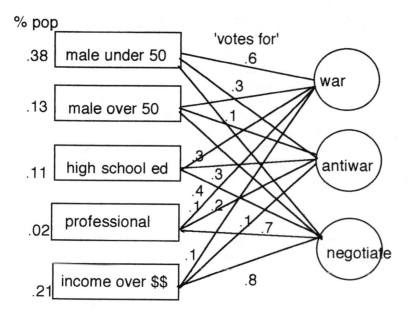

Figure 2   Superposition of behaviors / goals of communities

The common domain shared by the behavioral agents can 'expand' depending on timeframes of delays to incorporate larger numbers of agents who are indirectly affected or loosely coupled to the domain. For example, a town which has a plant that generates wastes into a nearby river can affect many other communities downstream and also, through ground water, even communities not on the river. The plant may generate important economic goods that impact the livelihood of many other communities and play a significant role in international trade, engineering research, etc. The recognition that domains cannot be narrowly construed is crucial to obtain the requisite linkages to make forecasting accurate.

Within this model, **conflict between entities is a result of the computed difference between the normalized "objective" vectors of the network of agents that compose the entity. The goals of each agent are a component of a set of all goals of the entity. The strengths within the range [-1,1] indicate the relative desirability or non desirability of a particular state of affairs in one's environment.** Values of zero or nearly so indicate a 'do not care' situation. Each social system can be described as a combination of a number of communities (kin, tribe, clan, people, nation-state, religion, economic class, political party, etc.) There is a combination of goals from each of these source group memberships leading to an overall goal set of the social entity. In some cases, the ranking of certain goals from one source will override that of another. Thus a strong desire from one group will override weak desires. On the other hand, opposing tendencies might either cancel as a way of avoiding internal conflict or might go with one or the other. Similarly, the net objective vectors of entities can be compared to determine conflictual propensities.

We can therefore project physical scenarios using climatic, geological and biological information, to forecast agricultural and economic occurrences and then model the results of these perturbations on the social/cultural/political matrix of human societies. Similarly we can model the human impacts on our physical environment and project its ramifications as well. Most of all, we can model the likelihood that given strategies will be pursued by differing communities under various economic, political and social stresses, based on the historical/cultural continuities and our ability to detect dissonance between actual domain states and desired ones for each community. Dissonance is the metric that measures the difference in value of the existing state of affairs versus the desired state of affairs. For a Bosnian Serb whose goal of being a member of a Serbian political entity is ranked at +1 (most important), living in a non-Serbian political entity is ranked as (-1) and thus the dissonance is 2. The value, indicating maximum difference between the vectors, will indicate that actions to redress the state of affairs is highly likely: when combined with other members of the same political entity who are adverse to a Serbian dominated political entity, one has then the makings of a serious conflict. Modeling strategies to allow multiple communities to reduce dissonance simultaneously is the art we are attempting, to validate them before they become policies inflicted on the communities in question.

Conclusions

We therefore hold that modern computational and visualization technologies are as last capable of being used to accumulate the raw polling data (after all, we even poll the peoples of the former Soviet system now) along with the demographic and other crucial physical data to build a tractable engine for effectively modeling the complex dynamics of interacting human social groups at various levels. By capturing the structural relationships and changes over time (opinions, demographics, etc.), we have a scientifically valid model of ever increasing accuracy as refinements accumulate and community leaders and authorities come to rely on it for evaluating prospectively the response of affected populations.

Bibliography:

Casti, John (1992) "Reality Rules", Volumes 1 and 2, Wiley Interscience
Feder, Stanley (1986) "FACTIONS and Policon: New Ways to Analyze Politics", 1993 CIA Released
         Paper for Historical Review Program
Gelernter, David (1991) "Mirror Worlds". New York, Oxford:, Oxford Univ. Press .
Goldstein, Joshua S. (1988) "Long Cycles: Prosperity and War in the Modern Age", Yale Univ. Press.
Hammerstrom, D. (1993) Neural Networks at Work, IEEE Spectrum Vol 30, No. 6, June, p 26 ff.
Iberall, Arthur S. (1975) "On Nature, Man, and Society: a Basis for Scientific Modeling."
         Annals of Biomedical Engineering 3: 344-385.
Kaiser, David (1990), "Politics and War" Harvard University Press.
Karasik, Myron (1983) "Conservation Laws and the Dynamics of Economic Systems",
         IEEE Systems, Man and Cybernetics Conference Proceedings 1983 p 756 - 762
Karasik, Myron (1984) "Conflict, Cooperation and Differentiation", IEEE Systems, Man
         and Cybernetics Conference Proceedings 1984, p 12 - 17.
Karasik, Myron (1986) "Dynamics of Ensembles of Autonomous Systems", Pergamon
         Press (Proceedings of Fifth Annual Conference on Mathematical Modelling)
Karasik, Myron (1992) " Distributed Intelligent Systems", Proc. of IFAC 1992 Workshop on Supp. Ways
         to Improve International Stability, Pergamon Press (in press).
Kosko, Bart (1991), "Neural Networks and Fuzzy Systems", Prentice-Hall
Kosko, Bart and Isaka, Satoru (1993) "Fuzzy Logic", Scientific American, June
Mamdani, E. and Gaines, B. (1981) "Fuzzy Reasoning and its Applications" Academic Press
Negoita C., and Ralescu, D. (1987) "Simulation, Knowledge-Based Computing and Fuzzy Statistics",
         Van Nostrand
Rich, E. and Knight , K. (1991) "Artificial Intelligence", McGraw Hill, Ch 16-21.
Richardson, Lewis F. (1960) Arms and Insecurity. Pittsburgh: The Boxwood Press and
         Chicago: Quadrangle Books, pp. 12-36, 95-97, 145-148.
Singer, J. David (1980) "Accounting for International War: The State of the Discipline." Annual Review
         of Sociology, 6:249-367.
Small, Melvin and J. David Singer (1982) Resort to Arms: International and Civil Wars,
         1816 -1980. Beverly Hills, CA: Sage.
Taagepera, Rein (1968) "Growth Curves of Empires." General Systems XIII: 171-175.
Wilkinson, David (1980) "Deadly Quarrels". Berkeley, CA: Univ. of California Press.
Wilkinson, David (1987) "Central Civilization." Comparative Civilizations Review 17 (Fall): 31-59.
Williamson, Paul: (1985) "A 'Physical' Model of World Politics," Systems Research, 2 , (October):
         221-235. Abridgement in Proceedings, Society for General Systems Research: 1110-1119.
Williamson, Paul (1989) "Modeling International Linkages," in Manfred Kochen
         (ed.) The Small World. Ablex Pub., Norwood, NJ: 108-127.
Williamson , Paul (1992) "The Need for an Integrated Global System Approach,"
         Proceedings, International Federation of Automatic Control/Scientists for Peace
         Workshop on Supplementary Ways of Improving International Stability," Bolton, Ontario.

Fuzzy Membership Functions in Soft Computing Models

Antony Satyadas and H. C. Chen

Department of Computer Science, The University of Alabama

Tuscaloosa, AL 35486-4983. email: antony@cs.ua.edu, chen@cs.ua.edu

Abstract— **Soft computing models use fuzzy membership functions and the associated operators to qualify and quantify uncertainties in diverse domains. This include dynamic multiple inferencing using high level fuzzy connectionist designs which combines the symbolic and sub-symbolic paradigms. The mechanics of modeling and choosing appropriate membership functions and their parameters, the relationship between linguistic variables and membership functions, the significance of membership functions in fuzzy reasoning, and the evolution of optimal membership functions and fuzzy rules in soft computing models are topics of active research. These topics form the theme of this paper. Concepts of soft computing and membership function are overviewed in the introduction. Representational categories and properties of membership functions are then explored. This is followed by a discussion on qualitative, empirical, and evolutionary modeling techniques. Learning schemes for associating membership functions with appropriate linguistic variables and the optimization choices are studied. The paper concludes with a discussion on future research directions.**

I. Introduction

A. Soft Computing

Soft computing models use fuzzy logic [1,2,3], artificial neural networks [4], approximate reasoning, genetic algorithms [5], possibility theory, fuzzy clustering, and so on to discover relationships in dynamic, nonlinear, complex, and uncertain environments [6]. These techniques often borrow mechanics of cognitive processes and laws of nature to provide us with a better understanding of, and solutions to, real world problems. A typical application is the development of hybrid intelligent systems [7]. Multicriteria Group Decision making techniques in conjunction with soft computing models and similarity and commonsense based reasoning form Flexible Intelligent Systems [4]. All these systems rely on fuzzy membership functions with associated linguistic terms and variables to manage uncertainty.

B. Fuzzy Membership Function

Fuzzy membership functions allows us to quantify the extend to which objects which are instances of a concept belongs to the concept. The concept is often a linguistic term T (e.g., tall woman) of a linguistic variable V(e.g., height of women in USA) [8,9,10]. The word *tall* is an example of a fuzzy predicate which may have associated quantifiers such as *kind of* and fuzzy truth values such as *quite true, very true, more or less true* . The linguistic variable is a label for an attribute of elements $\theta \, \epsilon \, \Theta$ (e.g., woman in women) with a measurable numerical assignment interval $X \, \epsilon \, [-\infty, \infty]$ called the referential set (e.g., [0,7] feet). $\mu_T(\theta)$, a subjective numerical assignment then represents the degree of membership of θ (e.g., a particular woman, say Mary) in T (e.g., tall woman). $V : \Theta \rightarrow X$ [11,12,13].

The relevance of context may be noted. The concept of Mary being tall is not only subjective with respect to individual opinion, but also dependent upon the universe of discourse. For example, height of basketball players or the height of a ten year old girl. The following may also be noted. Even if I know that the height of Mary is 5ft10in, my concept of tall and my visual image of a length of 5ft10in is still fuzzy. Uncertainties if any concerning the actual height of Mary (whether it is 5ft10in plus or less than 5ft6in are represented by fuzzy measures $(g:\wp(X) \rightarrow [0,1])$. Another point concerns the fact that the degree or grades of membership are not probabilities. An apparent difference is that, on a finite universal set, the summation of the membership grades need not be 1 where as the summation of probabilities must be 1.

There are several options for choice of the membership function. It includes qualitative modeling using methods such as fuzzy c-means clustering, empirical modeling, evolutionary learning using genetic algorithms or artificial neural networks, and using predetermined membership function. The mapping between the membership function and the linguistic variable may be pre or post determined depending upon whether subjective (use expert experience) or objective model building technique is used. The same applies to the membership function parameters. You have a choice of point-valued and interval-valued. You also have an option to choose from static and dynamic membership functions. The membership functions may be used in various fuzzy reasoning models including fuzzy neurons [14,15]. Various aggregation operators may be used to obtain conjoint measurement by performing fuzzy arithmetic operations such as max, min, t- norm and t-conorm. For example, *happy* could be a composite linguistic variable of its component linguistic variables *rich* , *love* , *education*. Monotonicity is of concern here.

The upcoming sections are organized as follows. Representational categories and properties of membership functions are explored. This is followed by a discussion on qualitative, empirical, and evolutionary modeling techniques. Learning schemes for associating membership functions with appropriate linguistic variables and optimization choices are then enumerated followed by the conclusion.

II. FUZZY MEMBERSHIP FUNCTION REPRESENTATION

Vertical, horizontal, and convex representational categories will be discussed here [9].

- Vertical:
$$\mu_T : X \rightarrow [0,1] \tag{1}$$
where $x \, \epsilon \, X$ belongs to T to a degree $\mu_T(x)$.
- Horizontal: Here, a fuzzy set T is represented in terms of its α-cuts level sets $\{T_\alpha \mid \alpha\epsilon[0,1]\}$, where $T_\alpha = \{x \mid \mu_T(x) \geq \alpha\}$, such that
$$\mu_T(x) = sup\{\alpha | x \, \epsilon \, T_\alpha\} \tag{2}$$
- Convex Combination: Given a finite discrete fuzzy set T with its level sets $\{T_\alpha \mid \alpha \, \epsilon \, [0,1]\}$, such that $\{T_{\alpha_1} \subseteq T_{\alpha_2} .. \subseteq T_{\alpha_n}\}$ and $\{\alpha_1 > \alpha_2 .. > \alpha_n\}$ where $m_i = \alpha_i - \alpha_{i+1}$, and $\alpha_{n+1} = 0$
$$\mu_T(x) = \sum_i (m_i \mid x \, \epsilon \, T_{\alpha_i} \text{ and } x \ni T_{\alpha_{i-1}}) \tag{3}$$

This is a probabilistic way of representing a fuzzy set.

III. FUZZY MEMBERSHIP FUNCTION PROPERTIES

Fuzzy membership functions are characterized by their unique properties. Scale type, membership function shapes, and aggregation operators will be discussed in this section.

A. Scale Type

Nominal scale (one-to-one function, e.g, student number), Ordinal scale (monotonic increasing function, e.g., grades), Interval scale (affine function, e.g., Temperature C,F), Ratio scale (Similarity function, e.g., Weight kg, lbs), and Absolute (Identity, e.g., Frequency) are options for scale types [16]. The interval scale is considered as the most adequate.

B. Shape

We have a choice of membership functions including triangular, trapezoidal, and gaussian, gamma, exponential, with their associated parameters. Each membership function may relate to a linguistic variable. For example, given a,b,c,d as real numbers, fuzzy triangular (Figure 1. a) and trapezoidal (Figure 1. b) membership function are defined as follows:

$$f(x) = \begin{cases} (x-a)/(b-a) & a \leq x \leq b \\ (x-c)/(b-c) & b \leq x \leq c \\ 0 & \text{otherwise} \end{cases} \tag{4}$$

$$f(x) = \begin{cases} (x-a)/(b-a) & a \leq x \leq b \\ 1 & b \leq x \leq c \\ (x-d)/(c-d) & c \leq x \leq d \\ 0 & \text{otherwise} \end{cases} \tag{5}$$

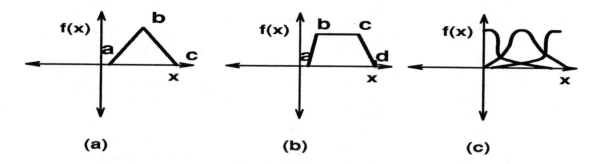

Figure 1. Membership Functions

The gaussian and exponential membership functions are given in (Figure 1. c).

$$f(x_i) = \frac{1}{\sigma\sqrt{2*\pi}} e^{\frac{-0.5}{\sigma^2}(x_i - \mu)^2}$$

(6)

where μ is the mean and σ is the standard deviation, the two parameters for the gaussian membership function. A particular value of σ and μ corresponds to a specific linguistic variable. Another example is the generalized bell function with three parameters a, b, and c.

$$f(x_i) = \frac{1}{1 + [(x_i - c)/a]^{2b}}$$

(7)

An exponential membership function with parameters a, b, and c may be of the form:

$$f(x_i) = 1 - e^{-(\frac{a}{|b - x_i|})^c}$$

(8)

The relationship between physical measure and subjective perception is highlighted by the exponential model. A linear function can be generated from this using transformation techniques. Static or dynamic hedge operations such as intensification, dilution, and inflection may be performed on these membership functions.

C. Aggregation Operators

The aggregation operation could be simple summation, some logical operation, fuzzy aggregation operations such as min and max proposed by Yager, Dombi, Sklar, Schweizer, and so on. Axioms such as monotonicity, continuity, idempotentcy, commutativity, associativity, distributive, symmetry, and involution are of concern. One commonly used aggregation operator is the monotonic nondecreasing, continuous, and symmetric, generalized means averaging operator given by

$$h_\alpha(a_1, a_2, .., a_n) = (\frac{a_1^\alpha + a_2^\alpha + .. + a_n^\alpha}{n})^{\frac{1}{\alpha}}$$

(9)

where $\alpha \, \epsilon \, \Re(\alpha \neq 0)$. Values of 0, -1, and 1 for α gives us the geometric, harmonic, and arithmetic means respectively. For an OR and AND neuron [12,13], given the input signals $x_1, x_2, .., x_n$ and the weights $w_1, w_2, .., w_n$ and $v_1, v_2, .., v_n$ respectively,

$$y(OR) = \bigvee_{i=1}^{n} (w_i \wedge x_i)$$

(10)

$$y(AND) = \bigwedge_{i=1}^{n} (v_i \vee x_i)$$

(11)

which corresponds to the max min and min max operations respectively.

IV. MEMBERSHIP FUNCTION MODELING

This section explores the membership function modeling aspects of fuzzy modeling. Qualitative, empirical, and evolutionary modeling techniques will be discussed. Interpretation of the generated membership function and their associations with linguistic variables is an important step towards explaining an inference. We will address this in a later section. The modeling options offer choices for developing suitable membership functions.

A. Qualitative Modeling

This is an objective modeling technique that includes

- structure identification (rule construction): At first the clusters are generated using fuzzy c-means method, followed by the selection of variables associated with input-output relations [17].
- parameter identification (parameter selection of antecedents and consequent in each rule) [18].

B. Empirical Modeling

This involves the experimental acquisition of membership values using direct rating, reverse rating, set valued statistics, and polling [8,9].

- Direct Rating: Randomly selected elements $\theta \epsilon \Theta$ with values $V(\theta) \epsilon X$ are presented to subjects with the following questions and responses.
    - *How T is θ (V(θ).* For example *How* **tall** *is* **Mary** *considering the* **height of women basketball players**. The response is a value y ϵ a sliding scale $[\mu_L, \mu_U]$.
    - Randomly asked to identify θ_{min} (V(θ_{min}) = X_{min}), corresponding to μ_L and similarly θ_{max} for μ_U in order to identify $[X_{min}, X_{max}]$.

  Memorization is avoided by repeatedly presenting the same $\theta(V(\theta))$ between other random presentations of $\theta \epsilon [\theta_{min}, \theta_{max}]$. The responses y/x generate a conditional distribution.
- Reverse Rating: Randomly selected membership values $y \epsilon [\mu_L, \mu_U]$ are presented with the following question: *Identify $\theta(V(\theta))$ that possess the yth degree of membership in the fuzzy set T.* The response is $\theta \epsilon \Theta(V(\theta) X)$. The memorization avoidance technique employed in direct rating is applied. Responses are recorded as x/y.
- Set Valued Statistics: A fuzzy set can be defined as an inner or outer approximation of a convex combination set.
- Polling: This is a probability model. The subject is randomly presented with elements $\theta \epsilon \Theta$ and an yes/no question *Do you agree that θ is T.*

$$P_T(x) = \frac{\#ofyes}{\#ofyes + \#ofno} \tag{12}$$

C. Evolutionary Modeling

In a fuzzy reasoning system, the membership functions are used to build fuzzy rules. Evolutionary modeling makes use of techniques such as genetic algorithms [5] and artificial neural networks to learn the membership function parameters and rules. Simulations with a variety of reasoning methods allow us to identify the most appropriate reasoning method. Preferences can be requested using an appropriate weighting scheme in a multicriteria decision making framework. A hierarchy can be established for choices. This eliminates the limitations of dependencies brought about by the choice of a particular membership function. We will now look at the options for evolutionary modeling.

- Genetic Algorithms(GA): An objective function and a suitable performance index measure are identified. GA selects appropriate membership function parameters through evolutionary learning. The rules and their number may also be learned by GA [5]. This gives an objective flavor by not depending upon experts for the choice of rules. It also solves the brittleness problem. Moreover, we have the option to consider expert rules for comparison, learning, and verification. Computational complexity is reduced by being able to make reliable inferences using a minimal rule set. Optimization of this learning curve is important for ensuring efficient and robust performance of the system.

- Artificial Neural Networks(ANN): Adaptive learning models using ANN also makes use of an objective function and performance index to train the neural network. Several fuzzy neural systems have been proposed [19 - 23]. Ideas such as simulated annealing may also be considered. Associated with these models are specialized architectures such as time series memory modules and learning techniques.

V. MEMBERSHIP FUNCTIONS AND LINGUISTIC VARIABLES

The relationship between the membership function and linguistic variable may be established through empirical measures. Often pre-established relationships are used. Appropriateness of this method is in question. This may be attributed to the uniqueness and context dependencies of diverse relationships. Post-determination of the relationship is one of our current topics of research. Questions include how a membership function relates to one's perception, the cognitive and linguistic aspects of human decision making. Similarity and commonsense based reasoning techniques may be considered [24]. Moreover, in the case of membership function parameters, the meaning of the parameters in the context of cognitive relationships is important. For example, in the case of Gaussian membership function, the parameters are the mean and standard deviation, a statistical dependency. Often other parameters such as skewness may be more significant in a relationship.

VI. OPTIMIZATION OF MEMBERSHIP FUNCTIONS

Optimization of membership functions can be addressed at the following levels.
- Choice of the type of membership function
- Membership function parameters
- Fuzzy rules formed using the membership functions

Computational complexity, robustness, reliability, specificity, validity, and efficiency are of concern here. The importance of these features may vary with the domain and the type of problem being addressed. Examples are classification, pattern completion and matching, optimization, and control problems.

- Computational complexity is important for implementation and practical application. Optimization directly improves computational complexity by making available a minimal rule set build using the membership functions. It may be noted that often there is a trade off between computational complexity and specificity.
- Robustness signify the extend to which the model can successfully handle internal disturbances and is a measure of the extend to which the system has learned the relationship.
- Reliability relates to robustness and consistency.
- Specificity relates to the principle of minimum specificity. Optimization helps to identify more appropriate matches of membership functions with the linguistic variables.
- The optimization technique should ensure the validity of the membership function parameters and the fuzzy rules. Other concerns include the validity of the match between the membership function and the linguistic variable.
- Optimization should increase the efficiency of the model. Efficiency relates to the speed of the system, and correctness of the solutions. Non-duplication in learning is also a matter of concern here.

Consider the case of an evolutionary model which learns the membership function parameters as well as the fuzzy rules. Unless appropriate optimization techniques are employed, you may end up with duplicate rules. There could be exceptions where the validity itself is in question. Thus the optimization employed should be capable of weeding out invalid membership functions and rules. Options such as simulated annealing, clustering, commonsense reasoning, and integer programming are currently being considered.

VII. CONCLUSION AND FUTURE DIRECTIONS

We have discussed the mechanics of modeling and choosing appropriate membership functions and their parameters, the relationship between linguistic variables and membership functions. This paper gives an overview of the properties of soft computing and fuzzy membership function. Fuzzy modeling techniques were explored. The flexibility of soft computing models permit computational freedom in managing uncertainties. Evolutionary learning and optimization of membership function parameters and fuzzy rules are currently being studied. This includes identifying the optimal fuzzy rule set, and explaining the rules which gives us a better understanding about the relationships between the concerned variables.

The importance of optimal membership functions and fuzzy rules has been established. Options for combining expert rules with the newly learned rules are being studied. Future research directions include development of parallel algorithms and analysis of the cognitive elements.

REFERENCES

[1] Satyadas Antony, Iran-nejad Asghar, Chen, H. C., Chissom Brad, "Intelligence: exact computation or biofunctional cognition." *Bulletin of the Psychonomic Society*, Vol. 31(3), 1993, pp. 175-178.

[2] Zadeh, L. A., "A theory of approximate reasoning, Memo "UCB/ERLM 77/58, University of California, Berkeley , 1977.

[3] Zadeh, L. A., "Fuzzy Sets," *Information Control*, Vol. 8, 1965, pp. 338-353.

[4] Satyadas Antony, Chen, H. C., "Flexible Intelligent Systems for Soft Computing: An Application to Economy Prediction," The Third International Fuzzy Systems and Intelligent Controls Conference, Louisville, March 15, 1994.

[5] Satyadas Antony, Krishnakumar, K., "GA-optimized Fuzzy Controller for Spacecraft Control," 3rd IEEE International Conference on Fuzzy Systems WCCI 1994, submitted.

[6] Sombe Lea, Reasoning under incomplete information in artificial intelligence, John Wiley & Sons, Inc., N.J, U.S.A, 1990.

[7] Rocha, A. F., and Yager, R., "Neural Nets and Fuzzy Logic," Kandel, A., Langholz Gideon (Ed.), Hybrid Architectures for Intelligent Systems, CRC Press, FL, U.S.A, 1992.

[8] Turksen, I. B., "Conjoint Measurement of Membership Functions," Proceedings of NAFIPS '90, pp. 326-329, Toronto, Ontario, June 6-8, 1990.

[9] Norwich, A., and Turksen, I. B., "The Construction of Membership Functions," in R. R. Yager (ed) Fuzzy Sets and Possibility Theory: Recent Developments, Pergamon Press, Oxford, pp. 61-67, 1982.

[10] Turksen, I. B., "Measurement of Membership Functions," in W. Karwowski, and A. Mital (ed) Application of Fuzzy Set Theory in Human Factors, Elsevier Publishers, Amsterdam, The Netherlands, pp. 55-67, 1986.

[11] Hisdal, E. (Guest Editor), "Special Issue - Interpretation of Grades of Membership," *Fuzzy Sets and Systems*, Vol. 25, 3, pp. 271-379, 1988.

[12] Santamarina, J. C., and Chameau, J. L., "Membership Functions II: Trends in Fuzziness and Implications," *International Journal of Approximate Reasoning* Vol. 1, pp. 303-317, 1987.

[13] Zysno, P., "Modeling Membership Functions," in B. B. Rieger (ed) Emperical Semantics, Studienverlag Brockmeyer, Bochum, Vol. 1, pp. 350-375, 1981.

[14] Satyadas Antony, "Fuzzy Neuron Formalism," World Congress on Neural Networks, WNN/FNN, San Diego, 1994, submitted.

[15] Gupta, M. M., and Rao, D. H., "On the principles of fuzzy neural networks," *Fuzzy Sets and Systems* Vol. 61, pp. 1-18, 1994.

[16] Zimmermann, H. J., "Fuzzy Set Theory - and Its Applications," Kluwer-Nijhoff Publishing, Boston, U.S.A, 1988.

[17] Sugeno Michio and Yasukawa Takahiro, "A Fuzzy-Logic-Based Approach to Qualitative Modeling," *IEEE Transactions on Fuzzy Systems* Vol. 1, No. 1, pp. 7-31, 1993.

[18] Nakanishi, H., Turksen I. B., and Sugeno M., "A review and comparison of six reasoning methods," *Fuzzy Sets and Systems*, Vol. 57, pp. 257-294, 1993.

[19] Pedrycz Witold, "Fuzzy neural networks and neurocomputations," *Fuzzy Sets and Systems* 56, pp. 1-28, 1993.

[20] Pedrycz, Witold and Rocha, F. Armando, "Fuzzy-set Based Models of Neurons and Knowledge-Based Networks." *IEEE Transactions on Fuzzy Systems*, Vol. 1, No. 4, pp. 254-266, 1993.

[21] Keller, James, M., Yager, Roland, R., Tahani Hossein, "Neural network implementation of fuzzy logic." *Fuzzy Sets and Systems*, Vol. 45, pp. 1-12, 1992.

[22] Yager, Roland, R., "Implementing fuzzy logic controllers using a neural network framework," *Fuzzy Sets and Systesm* Vol. 48, pp. 53-64, 1992.

[23] Jang, R. Jyh-Shing, "ANFIS: Adaptive-network-based fuzzy inference system." University of California, Berkley, 1992.

[24] Thanassas Dimitrios, "The Phenomenon of Commonsense Reasoning: Nonmonotonicity, Action and Information ," Ellis Horwood, N.Y, U.S.A, 1992.

Setting the Initial Weights in a Neural Network Using Fuzzy Curves

Yinghua Lin
Department of Computer Science
New Mexico Institute of Mining and Technology
Socorro, NM 87801

George A. Cunningham, III
Department of Electrical Engineering
New Mexico Institute of Mining and Technology
Socorro, NM 87801

Abstract

We introduce a simple fuzzy-neural network and prove that it can represent any continuous function over a compact set. We introduce "fuzzy curves" and use them to set the initial weights in the fuzzy-neural network. We show that our choice of initial weights and network structure yields networks that train very rapidly.

1 Introduction

Bello [1], Drago [3], Narazaki [6], and Wessels [9] have published work on obtaining the proper network structure and initial weights to reduce training time. We introduce a simple back propagation network to implement a fuzzy model. We also introduce the concept of a "fuzzy curve," and we use fuzzy curves to determine the initial weights in the neural network. Finally, we give several examples to show that our method produces adequate models that train very rapidly.

2 The Architecture of the Fuzzy-Neural Network

Figure 1 shows the architecture of our four layer (input, fuzzification, inference, and defuzzification) fuzzy-neural network. Referring to Figure 1, we see that there are N inputs, with N neurons in the input layer, and R rules, with R neurons in the inference layer. There are $N \times R$ neurons in the fuzzification layer. Hence, once we determine the number of inputs N and the number of rules R, we know the structure of the network. The first N neurons (one per input variable) in the fuzzification layer incorporate the first rule, the second N neurons incorporate the second rule, and so on.

Every neuron in the second or fuzzification layer represents a fuzzy membership function for one of the input variables. The output of the fuzzification layer is $o_{ij} = \exp\left(-|w_{ij1}x_i + w_{ij0}|^{l_{ij}}\right)$ where o_{ij} is the value of fuzzy membership function of the ith input variable corresponding to the jth rule and l_{ij} is typically in the range $1 \leq l_{ij} \leq 6$ and initially equals 2. We label the set of weights between the input and the fuzzification layer by $W = \{\{w_{ij0}, w_{ij1}\} : i = 1, \ldots, N; j = 1, \ldots, R\}$.

We use multiplicative inference, and the output of the inference layer is $o_j = \prod_i^N o_{ij}$. The connecting weights between the third layer and the fourth layer are the central values, v_j, of the fuzzy membership functions of the output variable. We label the set of weights $\{v_j\}$ by $V = \{v_j : j = 1, \ldots, R\}$. Note that the weights in V and W determine the fuzzy membership functions. We use the weighted sum defuzzification. The equation for the output is

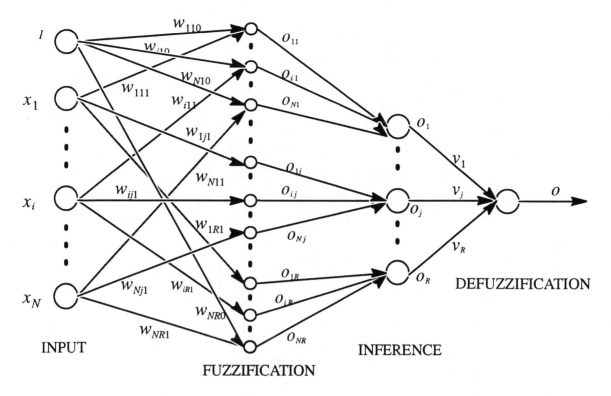

Figure 1: The architecture of the fuzzy-neural network.

$$o = \sum_j^R o_j v_j = \sum_j^R v_j \prod_i^N \exp\left(-|w_{ij1} x_i + w_{ij0}|^{l_{ij}}\right) \tag{1}$$

It is a straightforward to show using the Stone-Weierstrass Theorem [5] that any continuous function $f : \Re^N \to \Re$ over a compact set can be approximated as closely as we desire by Equation 1.

3 An Introduction to Fuzzy Curves

We consider a multiple-input, single-output system. We call the input candidates x_i $(i = 1, 2, \ldots, n)$, and the output variable y. Assume that we have m training data points available and that x_{ik} $(k = 1, 2, \ldots, m)$ are the ith coordinates of each of the m training points. Table 1 shows an example with $n = 3$ and $m = 20$. For each input variable x_i, we plot the m data points in x_i–y space. Figure 2 illustrates the data points from Table 1 in the x_1–y, x_2–y, and x_3–y spaces. For every point in x_i–y space, we draw a fuzzy membership function defined by

$$\mu_{ik}(x_i) = \exp\left(-\left(\frac{x_{ik} - x_i}{b}\right)^2\right) \tag{2}$$

We typically take b as about 10% of the length of the input interval of x_i. Figure 3 shows the fuzzy membership functions for the points in Figure 2. In Figure 3, the point where $\mu_{ik} = 1$ coincides with x_{ik}. We use centroid defuzzification to produce a fuzzy curve c_i for each input variable x_i by

$$c_i = \frac{\sum_k^m \mu_{ik}(x_i) \cdot y_k}{\sum_k^m \mu_{ik}(x_i)} \tag{3}$$

No.	x_1	x_2	x_3	y	No.	x_1	x_2	x_3	y	No.	x_1	x_2	x_3	y
1	14.9	2.0	9.3	3.8	8	6.9	2.3	10.3	3.3	15	18.1	2.5	5.9	2.5
2	16.6	1.7	5.8	3.7	9	7.4	1.9	9.4	2.8	16	26.4	2.2	8.1	4.4
3	21.3	2.1	9.1	3.0	10	11.3	2.0	8.4	3.0	17	13.7	2.8	7.9	3.3
4	24.3	2.9	7.0	4.7	11	17.6	2.0	8.2	2.7	18	23.1	3.8	4.9	2.2
5	26.6	1.7	4.8	4.1	12	19.5	2.4	6.5	3.3	19	7.7	2.6	9.3	2.3
6	23.2	1.3	4.7	3.1	13	21.6	2.5	5.1	4.9	20	21.1	2.5	5.1	1.8
7	22.2	2.5	4.5	3.1	14	26.5	1.9	6.3	4.8					

Table 1: Data points used in An Introduction to Fuzzy Curves.

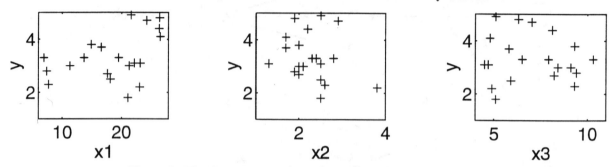

Figure 2: The data points plotted in x_1–y, x_2–y, and x_3–y spaces.

Figure 4 shows the fuzzy curves c_1, c_2, and c_3 for the data in Table 1.

4 Setting the Initial Weights

We set the initial weights in V, we divide the range of the desired output data into R intervals, and we set the initial v_j ($j = 1, 2, \ldots, R$) to be the central value of these R intervals. If, using the data in Table 1, we choose $R = 4$, then we make $v_1 = 2.19, v_2 = 2.96. v_3 = 3.74$, and $v_4 = 4.51$.

We set the initial weights in W by dividing the domain for each fuzzy curve c_i into R intervals corresponding to the R intervals in the output space. For the fuzzy curve c_i, we label the centers of the intervals x_{ij} ($j = 1, 2, \ldots, R$). We order the x_{ij} ($j = 1, 2, \ldots, R$) by the value of c_i at the center of each interval. x_{iR} corresponds to the interval containing the largest central value of c_i. The interval containing the point x_{iR} is associated

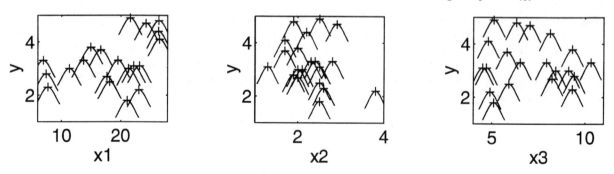

Figure 3: Fuzzy membership functions in x_1–y, x_2–y, and x_3–y spaces.

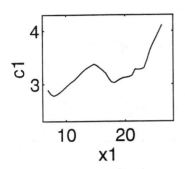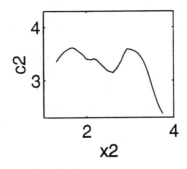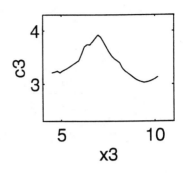

Figure 4: Fuzzy curves c_1, c_2, and c_3.

with the output interval whose center is at v_R. In a similar fashion, x_{iR-1} is the center of the interval which contains the next largest central point on the curve c_i, and x_{iR-1} is associated with v_{R-1}, and so on for $j = R - 2, R - 3, \ldots, 1$.

The length of the interval over which a rule applies in the domain of c_i is denoted as Δx_i. We define the initial fuzzy membership function of x_i for rule j to be $\exp\left(-\left|\frac{(x_{ij}-x_i)}{a \cdot \Delta x_i}\right|^{l_{ij}}\right)$, where a is typically in the range of $[0.5, 2]$. Hence, we see that the initial weights w_{ij0} and w_{ij1} are $w_{ij0} = \frac{1}{a \cdot \Delta x_i}$ and $w_{ij1} = \frac{x_{ij}}{a \cdot \Delta x_i}$.

5 Training the Model

We define the performance index for our model as

$$PI = \frac{\sqrt{\sum_{k=1}^{m}(o_k^d - o_k)^2}}{\sum_{k=1}^{m}|o_k^d|} \tag{4}$$

where $o_k^d, (k = 1, 2, \ldots, m)$, are the actual or desired output values and $o_k, (k = 1, 2, \ldots, m)$, are the outputs from the model. We train the neural network with a back-propagation technique to modify the variables v_j, w_{ij0}, w_{ij1}, and l_{ij}. We choose a maximum number of iterations I_{max} and some small number $\epsilon > 0$. The training is continued until, for some i, $\sum_{j=i}^{i+100} PI_j - \sum_{j=i+100}^{i+200} PI_j \leq \epsilon$ or the number of iterations reaches I_{max}. All of the examples in this paper used $I_{max} = 5000$. The choice of ϵ depends on the problem.

6 Performance Comparisons

Our performance comparisons are summarized in Table 2. We see that our models are almost always simpler than previously proposed models, they usually yield equivalent or better performance, and they train very rapidly. The details for the various comparison tests are enumerated below. The performance measures differ from author to author, but a lower number means better performance in every case. We have used the performance measure of the original authors in all cases. Hence, the performance figures are comparable across a line, but not vertically. A blank space in the table indicates that the data was not provided in the reference. In cases where the original author did not quote a performance measure, we use Equation 4. The item numbers refer to the test number in Table 2.

1. This is the non-linear equation $y = (1 + x_1^{-2} + x_2^{-1.5})^2$ taken from [7].

TEST	PRIOR WORK				OUR RESULTS			
NUMBER	RULE	NEUR	PERF	ITER	RULE	NEUR	PERF	ITER
1. Sugeno NL	6	na	0.010	na	3	9	0.004	1900
2. Box & Jenkins	6	na	0.190	na	4	23	0.081	4300
3. Narazaki NL	na	22	3.19	468	4	9	0.987	2200
4. COD	2	79	3.5/1.6		4	19	2.8/1.8	5000
5. Chem Plant	6	na		na	7	28	0.002	1700
6. Stock Price	5	na		na	5	31	0.018/0.126	3000

Table 2: Comparison with prior work. The RULE column is the number of rules, NEUR is the number of neurons, PERF is a performance measure, and ITER is the number of iterations to train.

2. This is Box and Jenkins gas furnace data taken from [2] and [7]. We compare our performance with a model developed in [7].

3. This is the non-linear equation $y = 0.2 + 0.8(x + 0.7sin(2\pi x))$ taken from [6].

4. This is data came from the Chemical Oxygen Demand in Osaka Bay example in [4] and [8]. A Group Method Data Handling algorithm was used for analysis in [4]. They train on 33 data points, and predict 12. The performance measure from [4] on the training data is 3.63, and the performance measure on the checking data is 2.04. [8] uses a fuzzy-neural to model the system and obtain performance measures of 3.5 and 1.6 on the training and checking data respectively.

5. This is data for operating a chemical plant originally appeared in [7].

6. This is data on daily stock prices for stock A from [7]. We trained on 80 data points and predicted on the next 20. The outputs are shown in Figure 5.

7   Conclusions

We create simple and effective fuzzy-neural models of complex systems from a knowledge of the input-output data. We introduce the concept of a fuzzy curve and use it to set the initial weights for the fuzzy-neural network model. Because the initial structure and weights of the neural network are set properly, our networks train rapidly.

References

[1] M. G. Bello, "Enhanced Training Algorithms, and Integrated Training/Architecture Selection for Multilayer Perceptron Networks," *IEEE Trans. on Neural Networks*, vol. 3, no. 6, November 1992, 864-875.

[2] G. E. P. Box and G. M. Jenkins, *Time Series Analysis, Forecasting and Control*. San Francisco: Holden Day, 1970.

[3] G. P. Drago and S. Ridella, "Statistically Controlled Activation Weight Initialization (SCAWI)," *IEEE Trans. on Neural Networks*, vol. 3, no. 4, July 1992, 627-628.

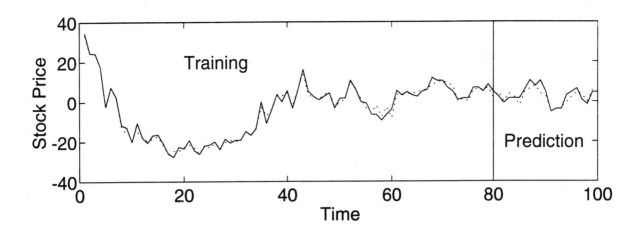

Figure 5: Performance on the stock price data. We build the model on the first 80 points and predict the next 20. Actual is shown by the solid line —, model by the dotted line ⋯.

[4] S. Fujita and H. Koi, Application of GMDH to Environmental System Modeling and Management, in *Self-Organizing Methods in Modeling: GMDH Type Algorithms*, (S.J. Farlow, Ed.), Statistics Textbooks Monographs Ser., Vol. 54, Marcel Dekker, New York, 1984, p. 257-275.

[5] E. Hewitt, *Real and Abstract Analysis*. Berlin, New York: Springer-Verlag, 1965.

[6] H. Narazaki and A. L. Ralescu, "An Improved Synthesis Method for Multilayered Neural Networks Using Qualitative Knowledge," *IEEE Trans. Fuzzy Systems*, vol. 1, no. 2, 1993, 125-137.

[7] M. Sugeno and T. Yasukawa, "A Fuzzy-Logic-Based Approach to Qualitative Modeling," *IEEE Trans. Fuzzy Systems*, vol. 1, no. 1, 1993, 7-31.

[8] H. Takagi, I. Hayashi, "NN-Driven Fuzzy Reasoning," *Int'l. J. Approximate Reasoning*, vol. 5, no. 3, 1991, 191-212.

[9] L. F. A. Wessels and E. Barnard, "Avoiding False Local Minima by Proper Initialization of Connections," *IEEE Trans. on Neural Networks*, vol. 3, no. 6, November 1992, 899-905.

Neural Fuzzy Systems

Session Chairs: Lotfi A. Zadeh
Bart Kosko

POSTER PRESENTATIONS

AN APPROACH FOR CONTROLLING NONLINEAR DYNAMIC SYSTEMS USING NEURO-FUZZY NETWORKS

EDILBERTO TEIXEIRA & GILSON LAFORGA & HAROLDO AZEVEDO
UNIVERSIDADE FEDERAL DE UBERLÂNDIA - CAMPUS SANTA MONICA
UBERLÂNDIA - MG 38400-902 - BRAZIL

Phone: (34) 235 2888 / 166   FAX: (34) 236 5099
email: EDILBERT@BRUFU.BITNET
BRAZIL

Key words: Fuzzy Systems, Nonlinear Systems, Process Control

ABSTRACT

Nonlinear systems are becoming an area of great interest in the control engineering community. Many interesting problems such as controllability [14], input-output decoupling [15], feedback linearization, have been approached with success. On the other hand, not to many results have been achieved in the solution of the problem of identification and control of unknown nonlinear systems. In general, linear methods are being applied to nonlinear systems, when only narrow ranges of adjustments are allowed in the neighborhood of the set point. Non-conventional methods are being investigated for systems that are inherently nonlinear and when wide control ranges are necessary. Narendra [16] proposed a method for identifying some classes of nonlinear systems using neural networks. Teixeira [10] developed a feedback linearization procedure for unknown nonlinear systems, using two feedforward neural networks, and applied the method for motor control. On the other hand the recent success on the application of fuzzy logic in industry automation has motivated its use in the control of nonlinear systems. Its simplicity and the fact that is not a time consuming method, make it a very promising approach for this kind of control problems. Some difficulties arise, such as, the adjustment of the rule base and the choice of the membership functions [5]. A new approach that combines the learning capability of the neural networks with the simplicity of fuzzy logic is been identified as neuro-fuzzy systems [12]. Initially, this paper presents an overview of the various neuro-fuzzy approaches, including their special features. Secondly, a dc motor with a nonlinear load is controlled and the paper is concluded with an analysis of the simulation results.

1. INTRODUCTION

Since 1946 some research groups have been involved in studying the basic principles of the intelligent information processing. Mc Cullow & Pitts, established the basic principles of the neural computation [4]; Hebb [4] developed the rule for storing orthogonal patterns which is considered the basis for the development of the Perceptron Neural Network [4]. The development of the Back-propagation algorithm [4] for training the Feedforward Multi-Layer Neural Network, contributed for the wide use of Artificial Neural Networks (ANN) in many different areas. Another important theory occurred in parallel to the neural network development, becoming known as "Fuzzy Logic" (FL). The basic principles of FL were introduced by Zadeh [1] in 1965, having its first application to the area of control systems in 1975 [2]. The analysis of the different ANN proposals and the basic principles of FL shows that there are many points where the two areas can be put together, specially in control applications. Multi-layer Neural Networks are very good for estimating nonlinear maps and the approaches used in Fuzzy Logic can be applied for controlling complex systems, by using the information given by a system expert. This information is used to create a rule base associated to membership functions describing how elements are related to a set. In FL the membership functions can assume values varying continuously from 0 to 1. Neuro-Fuzzy Networks (NFN) [12-13] which are attempts to combine the advantages of FL and ANN, are the main object of analysis in this paper. More specifically, different proposals of NFN are analyzed and used in the control of DC motor with a non-linear load. Initially, an analysis of the many ways that one can put together neural networks, and fuzzy logic is carried out.The following approaches are analyzed: -Fuzzy logic control, -Fuzzy logic with neural membership functions, -Fuzzy logic with neural rule base, -Fuzzy logic with neural membership functions and neural rule base. Each one of the approaches are then applied to the control of a DC motor. Finally, the results are analyzed and compared with the results obtained from the use a PID controller.

2.FUZZY CONTROL

Basically, vague information can be used and processed in a fuzzy controller in such a way that industrial plants can be actually controlled. A control algorithm is prepared based in the plant control program that is used by the control operators. In general, it consists of a set of IF-THEN-ELSE statements that are used to compose the fuzzy rule base. One could organize the development of a fuzzy controller [5] in the following steps:

STEP 1- The rule base is established based on the linguistic information that involves, for the control case, the actions to be taken as a function of the output error and its variation. These values define the universe of discourse, i. e., the range of application of the rule base.

STEP 2- This is the fuzzyfication stage, i. e., the transformation of the numerical and linguistic values in fuzzy values. Basically, an inference rule is applied to the output error set **E**, to the output error variation set **VE**, and to the control reference **R**:

$$U = (E \; x \; VE) \cdot R \quad (1)$$

where the symbols **x** and • represent the cartesian product and the dot product, respectively. For the case of fuzzy sets, these operations include the application of the membership functions related to each element of the sets [5,7].

STEP 3- This is the defuzzyfication stage where the output values of the fuzzy controller is transformed in actuating signal that is introduced in the plant through conventional devises like digital-analogic converters, transducers, etc. There are many ways of performing the defuzzyfication process [5], including the max, the gravity center, the indexed max, and the indexed gravity center.

Considering that the membership functions denote how much the elements are related to the sets, and that, in most of the cases, their equations are not known but only some plant input-output samples, the use of any kind of estimation becomes necessary. Considering also that multi-layer feedforward neural networks are excellent estimators of nonlinear maps, they are considered a good choice as membership function estimators. Next section, deals with this subject.

3.   THE USE OF FEEDFORWARD NEURAL NETWORKS FOR THE IMPLEMENTATION OF THE MEMBERSHIP FUNCTIONS

The definition of fuzzy sets and the choice of the membership functions are usually done in a very subjective way depending on many factors. There are some well known methods for defining the membership functions [5] such as Saaty comparison method. In this section we describe the use of a feedforward neural network, for the estimation of the membership functions. In this kind of neural networks the input layer receives the samples of the universe of discourse. In the output layer there is one element for each linguistic value. Therefore, during the neural network training session, numerical values obtained from simulation or from the information of an expert are used as desired neural network output values. The number of elements in the hidden layer influences the trainability and the accuracy of the neural network [9,8]. Therefore, this number must be chosen in a convenient way for the cases where a large number of partitions is defined for the universe of discourse.

It is important to notice that this kind of neural network makes the functional approximation by superposition of sigmoidal functions, making the membership function differentiable. This certainly contributes for the robustness of the overall control system. In the next section, the use of a neural network is also analyzed for the implementation of the rule base.

4. THE USE OF FEEDFORWARD NEURAL NETWORKS FOR THE IMPLEMENTATION OF THE BASE RULE

The rule base is defined based on the information obtained from a system expert and from simulation. In this kind of rule base, it is not possible to take into account situations not considered in the formulation of the rule base. A common solution is to use the relational matrix [2] based on the linguistic rules and some logical operators. The output of the fuzzy controller in then obtained using the Zadeh inference rule[6]. Another solution is to use the inherent generalizing capacity of the feedforward neural networks.

Basically, the neural network makes an approximation of the mapping having its domain represented by the rule conditions and the range represented by the rule consequents. In this paper, we first adjust a PID controller and then use its control

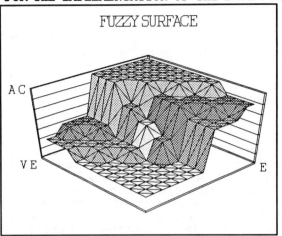

Figure 1 - Fuzzy surface (E, VE and AC are the control error, variation, and control action)

performance to obtain a first fuzzy rule base. This way, we accomplish the fuzzyfication stage. The phase surface involving the control error, the error change, and the control action becomes discontinuous due to the quantization levels used during the fuzzyfication stage (figure 1). The use of a neural network to assimilate the rule base makes this surface continuous as seen in figure 2. From this explanation, the following options can be proposed for the implementation of fuzzy controllers:
·Conventional fuzzy controller;
·Fuzzy controller with neural membership functions;
·Fuzzy controller with neural rule base;
·Fuzzy controller with neural membership functions and neural rule base.

One of the purposes of this paper is to analyze the performance of each one of these approaches. This is done in the next section through the simulation of a DC motor with a nonlinear load torque.

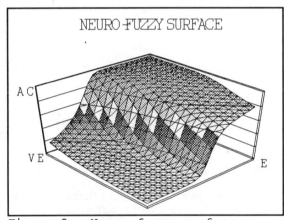

Figure 2 - Neuro-fuzzy surface

5. SIMULATION

In this simulation, the speed of a DC motor is controlled by each the methods mentioned in the previous section. A computer program was developed including the dynamic system simulation and the training of the neural networks. The motor data are the following:

Ra=4.67 Ω (Armature resistance), La=0.170 H (Armature inductance), J=42.6e-6 Kg.m (Moment of inertia), f=47.3e-6 Nm/rad/s (Viscous damping coefficient), K=14.7e-3N-m/A (Armature current constant), Kb=14.7e-3 V-sec/rad (Motor speed constant) Vmp=15 V (Maximum armature voltage), Vmn=-15 V (Maximum armature voltage), ΔVmp=1.5 V (Maximum voltage variation), ΔVmn=-1.5 V (Minimum voltage variation).

The transfer function describing the motor dynamics is shown in equation (2).

$$W(s) = \frac{K}{(JLa)\,s^2 + (fLa + JRa)\,s + (fRa + KKb)\,s} \quad (2)$$

The load torque is considered as a three order polynomial as in equation (3).

$$T = A_0 + A_1 \omega + A_2 \omega^2 + A_3 \omega^3 \quad (3)$$

where: $A_0 = 0.01$, $A_1 = 0.001$, $A_2 = 0.0001$, $A_3 = 0.00001$.

Initially a PID controller was adjusted with the following parameters that produced the best possible performance: $Kp=0.8$, $Ki=0.3$, $Kd=0.1$. The system is then simulated to obtain the rule base from the results of the PID simulation. Figure 3 shows the results of this simulation. A better performance is not possible due to the nonlinear characteristics of the load.

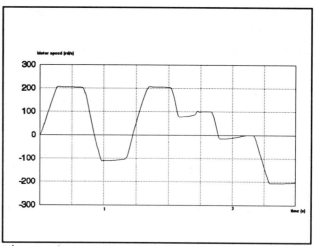

Figure 3 - PID controller step response

The simulation of the fuzzy controller

The control error E and the variation of the control error VE are the variables chosen for the implementation of the of the fuzzy controller [5]. In this case:

$$VE_k = E_k - E_{k-1} \quad (4)$$

$$E = \omega_r - \omega \quad (5)$$

where ω is the motor speed in radian and ω_r is the reference. E_k and $E_{(k-1)}$ are the values of the control error at the instants K and K-1, respectively. An open loop simulation was first performed. The control action, in this case, is the increment in the motor armature voltage. An open loop simulation was performed for determining the universe of discourse of the control error E, obtaining a maximum velocity of 500 rd/s. The maximum control error and control error change was considered 1000 rd/s and 6 rd/s, respectively. On the other hand, the maximum increment in the armature voltage was 1.5 volts. The universe of discourse was divided in 7 partitions. For the determination of the rule base, we used the PID simulation, resulting in 49 rules. The results of several step perturbations, for the PID controller and for the fuzzy controller are shown in figures 3 and 4, respectively. A better performance of the fuzzy controller could be achieved by expanding the rule base for values close to zero.

Fuzzy controller with neural membership functions

This approach is accomplished in two steps. The first step consists of training two neural networks with the membership functions corresponding to the control error and the control error change, respectively. In the second step, the same procedure used for the fuzzy controller is applied using the neural networks as membership functions. The advantage of this approach is the use of the generalizing capacity of the neural networks, for values not included in the discrete universe of discourse. The step functions were applied, resulting in a better performance, with very small overshoots and very few oscillations (see fig. 5).

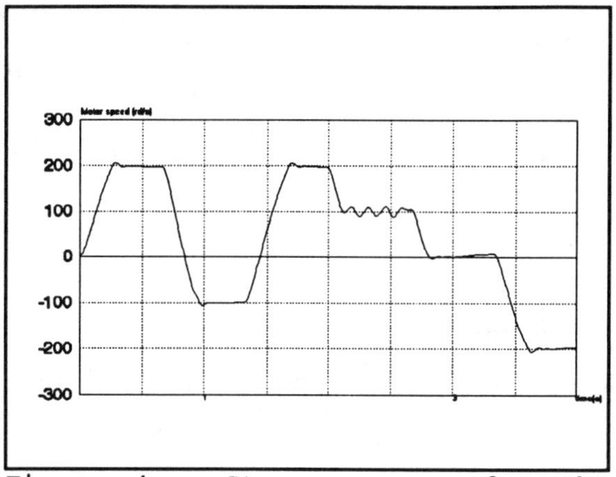

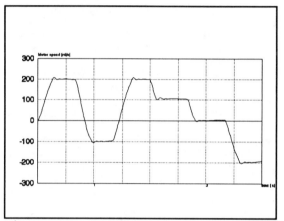

Figure 4 - Step response for the fuzzy control

Fuzzy controller with neural rule base.

In this case, a neural network is trained with the rule base, and then the same procedure used for the fuzzy controller is used. The basic difference is that a smooth surface is obtained as shown in figure 2. An investigation of how much this could improve the control robustness is going to appear in a future publication. In the case of this simulation, there is not a great improvement in the controller performance (see figure 6).

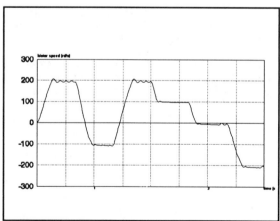

Figure 5 - Step response for the neural membership function controller

Fuzzy controller with neural membership functions and neural rule base

Two feedforward neural networks are used in this case: one for the membership functions and another for the rule base. Again, no great improvement could be observed, in comparison with the other approaches, although it should be expected an improvement of the overall system robustness due to the fact that the neural networks are composed of differentiable functions.

Conclusions

This paper presents an analysis of three neuro-fuzzy approaches. The basic improvement resulting from the use

figure 6 - Step response for neural rule base controller

of feedforward neural networks to approximate the membership functions and/or the rule base, comes from the generalizing capacity of feedforward neural networks. The system nonlinearities are taken into account by using simulation results and expert knowledge that are introduced in the rule base. An investigation of the overall system robustness is been prepared to analyze the implications of the use of feedforward neural networks in conjunction with the conventional fuzzy control.

REFERENCES

[1] Zadeh L.A., "Fuzzy Sets", Information and Control, 8, pp. 338-353, 1965.

[2] Mandani E. H. & Assilian S., An experiment in linguistic Synthesis with a fuzzy logic controller", Internat. J. Man-Machine Studies, nº 7, pp. 1-13, 1975.

[3] Yasunobu S. & Miyamoto S., "Automatic train operation system by predictive fuzzy control", Industrial Applications of fuzzy control, North Holland, 1985.

[4] Rumelhart, D. McClelland, J., "Parallel Distributed Processing", Vol. 1, MIT Press, Cambridge, MA, 4th Edition, 1987.

[5] Pedrycz W., "Fuzzy Control & Fuzzy Systems", Research Studies Press, 1989.

[6] Zadeh L. A., "Outline of a new approach to the analysis of complex systems and decision processes", IEEE Trans. S.M. & Cyber., v.3, nº 1, pp. 28-44, 1973.

[7] Lee C. C., "Fuzzy Logic in Control Systems: Fuzzy Logic Controller", IEEE Transactions Systems, Man & Cybernetics, vol. 20, nº 20, pp. 404-435, 1990.

[8] Loparo K. & Teixeira E., "A new approach For Adaptive Control of Nonlinear Systems Using Neural Networks", IEEE Int. Conf. Sys. Man Cyb., Los Angeles, 1990.

[9] Teixeira E, Loparo K, Gomide F, "Design Multi-layer Neural Networks for Accurate Identification of Nonlinear Mappings", American Cont C., Boston, 1991.

[10] Teixeira E., Loparo K., Gomide F., "Feedback Linearization of Dynamic Nonlinear Systems Using Neural Networks", 9º Cong. Bras. Autom., Vitória, 1992.

[11] Nie J. & Linkens D., "Neural Network-based approximate reasoning: principles and implementation", Int. Journal of Control, vol. 56, nº 2, pp. 399-413, 1992.

[12] Kong S. & Kosko B., "Adaptative Fuzzy Systems for Backing up a Truck-and-Trailer", IEEE Transactions on Neural Networks, v. 3, nº 2, pp. 211-223, 1992.

[13] Dote Y., "Fuzzy and Neural Networks Controller", Proceedings of the second workshop on Neural Networks, Auburn University, A.L., USA, February 1991.

[14] Stefani G. "On the Local Controllability of a Scalar-Input Control System", Theory and Application of Nonlinear Control Systems, Elsevier Science, 1986.

[15] Singh R. & Rugh W. "Decoupling Class of Nonlinear Systems by State Variable Feedback", Transactions ASME J.D.Syst.M.Cont, V.21, pp. 651-654, 1975.

[16] Nguyen D. & Widrow B. "Neural Networks for Self-Learning Control Systems", IEEE Control Magazine Systems, April 1990.

Neural Fuzzy Logics as a tool for design Ecological Expert Systems

Paulo Bernardo Blinder

Logic and Epistemology Center
Universidade Estadual de Campinas
Caixa Postal 6065
13081 Campinas, SP, Brasil
BITNET: blinder ime.unicamp.br

Keywords: Neural Fuzzy Logics, Feed-Forward ANN, Expert Systems, Theoretical Ecology

1 Introduction

Expert Systems in Theoretical Ecology reach a few applications, mainly because the uncertainty and the dificulties to represent and describe ecological fenomena.

Lately there appeared some applications of fuzzy expert systems intended to solve the representational problem in Biology (Salsky, 1991 [16]), and others isolated works using fuzzy technics [14,13,21]. Some of them are based on other special propriety owned by a fuzzy operator (like the anti-commutative fuzzy operator in Roberts's work).

Neverthless, is a problem to choose adequate implication operator when developing fuzzy expert systems, and this problem was underestimed in some application work. There are a lot of work on this problem, after problems begans to appear (see [7]) and too much discussions about the choose of the fuzzy implication operator (like, e.g. [17]).

In this context neural fuzzy logics, which uses the implementation of fuzzy implication operator through a feed-forward neural network, sounds better.

Neural fuzzy logics has recently appeared [4,2,1], and its ecological applications may fit well also when traditional fuzzy logics operators doesn't work properly [12].

Solving the problems of appropriate representation of uncertain ecological data and finding right operators, also possibiliting to the Ecologist to choose the intuitive desired proprieties of the implication is the main aim of Neural fuzzy logics based systems applied to ecology. We will do a brief review on Traditional fuzzy logics and about the topology of feed-forward network used, and about the Neural implementation on fuzzy logics. Ecological applications and numerical results will appear in the last sections.

2 Traditional Fuzzy Logics

2.1 Fuzzy Sets and its Sintatic rules

We are using here discrete fuzzy sets, denoted by the pair $(u, \mu_A(u))$, where $u \in U$, U is a domain and A is a proposition. We are using also the usual fuzzy conectives as follow

set operator	formula	logical equivalent
$\mu_{A^C}(u)$	$1 - \mu_A(u)$	$\neg A$
$\mu_{A \cup B}$	$\max(\mu_A(u), \mu_B(u))$	$\tilde{A} \vee \tilde{B}$
$\mu_{A \cap B}$	$\min(\mu_A(u), \mu_B(u))$	$\tilde{A} \wedge \tilde{B}$

2.2 Semantic Overview

Classical Logic uses boolean proposition (who are about to be false or true) and uses traditional inference engine, called *Modus Ponens*, who states: "*If I know thats true an Proposition A and an implication $A \Rightarrow B$, then I can infer the truth value of a proposition B*".

It can be thought as a function, where B's truth value should be derived as a function of $B = A \circ I(A, B)$ and $I(A, B)$ denote a formula for the implication used[1].

Many valued logics uses many-valued truth values[2] and I(A,B) depends on the choice of semantic used. There are a lot of "semantically coherent" implication operators, eventhough they are valid depending on the case. What's the case, is really an empirical matter (see, for e.g.,[17]).

Operator	Formulae
Lukasiewicz	$\min(1, 1 - a + b)$
Zadeh	$\max(1 - a, \min(a, b))$
Kleene-Dienes	$\max(1 - a, b)$

Table 1. More frequently used Implication Operators in Fuzzy Logics

Traditional Fuzzy Logics is based on some premisses:

- It uses fuzzy sets to represent their propositions and use fuzzy sets operators as logical conectives.

- Relations of attributes and objects by partial membership can "encode" information about observable reality.

---

[1] In Classical First Order Logic it whold be took as derived by the Logic equivalence between $A \Rightarrow B$ or $\neg A \, and \, B$, whose formula could be $\max(1 - v(A), v(B))$, where $v(P) \in \{0, 1\}$.

[2] Here, a should denote the partial truth value of an proposition A, whose values range between 0 (absolutely false) to 1 (absolutely true)

- Operators (Modifiers) can chage the "meaning" of the information in a fuzzy set, giving it a gracefull representation in a linguistic-fashioned way.

- The inference engine (implication) is based on a *Generalized Modus Ponens* Principle (**GMP**), who states:

> "If x is A then y is B"
> and knowing that "x is A' "
> _____
> We can infer: "x is B'"

where B' is computed based on fuzzy propositions A, A' e B; where A and A', B e B' are elements of same domain, respectively.

GMP[3] give an *Approximate Reasoning* capability to Fuzzy Logics, concerning it the possibility to make inference with only partially true premisses (partial knowledge of the reality, which is very common in decision-making and nature, obviously thinking that we aren't Gods...).
The traditional **GMP** semantic example is:

> Having the follow rule in mind: "*If the tomato is red then its ripe*"
> and knowing that: "the tomato is *more or less ripe*"
> we readily infer that the "tomato is *more or less ripe*, even when we can't exactly describe what state is "*more or less res*" or "*more or less ripe*".

There are some *intuitive* proprieties required by a fuzzy GMP, like:

Propriety	Premisses	Deduction
GMP1	x is A	y is B
GMP2a	x is *very* A	y is *very* B
GMP2b	x is *very* A	y is B
GMP3	x is *more-or-less* A	y is *more-or-less* B
GMP4a	x is *not* A	y is *unknown*
GMP4b	x is *not* A	y is *not* B
GMP5	x is *not* B	y is *not* A

Table 2. Desired proprieties for *Generalized Modus Ponens*

They must to be choosen knowing beforehand the mathematical proprieties of fuzzy relational implication operators (like continuity, classic logical equivaleces, etc.).
Since earlier uses of Fuzzy Logics, some implication operators (including the first one proposed by the pioneer Zadeh) was demonstrated to work only in restrited and natural cases, do not working in generical ones. There are a lot of proposed implication operators and also there are at least four great groups (there is a need of taxonomy !) of implicators. We well show how FFNN can offer an graceful implemantation of that proprieties.

---

[3]**GMP** can be thinked as an natural extension of classic deductive rule *Modus Ponens*, by extending it to fuzzy atributes in a linguitic way, as we can see further on.

3   Feed-Forward Neural Networks

The ANN's used in this work are a standard back-propagation one with sigmoidal activation function and one hidden layer. The number of elements in the hidden layer are equal to the entry layer for simplicity (with was demonstred to have no influence in results but in the number of epoch training). The program used to do numerical simulation was the one found in [15]. The number of units at input and output layers will be explained in the next section.

4   Neural Fuzzy Logics

It was noticed that implication operators could be thought as a relation $I(A, B)$ between the antecedent and the consequent premisses (A and B). As is known [5], FFNN can represent any $\mathbb{R}^m \to \mathbb{R}^n$ non-linear function, the vector $|I$ at inputs can be took as its elements are the partial ("fuzzy") membership $\mu_{\tilde{A}}(x)$ of x, where x are the elements of the domain U and in the output is $\mu_{\tilde{B}}(y)$, $y \in U$. But, what about $\tilde{A}$ and $\tilde{B}$? They're linguistic modified values of fuzzy sets A and B, to represent statements in Table 2, and a set P composed by pairs of $(\tilde{A}, \tilde{B})^4$ will be our training set. The modification rules are the same found in section 2. It should operate well (as can be saw in [4,2,1] for theoretic point of view and [12] for practical purposes). Then, one can choose the more adequate proprieties for represent one's problem, in a specific situation (May be there is no "*world general rules*", but it cannot be proved true or false, only empirically observed in particular cases[5]). It would be useful, particulary in ecological systems, that are complex and, in general, have local knowledge about the governing rule of the problem.

5   An Theoretical Ecology example of uncertainty: Phyto Sociology

Phyto Sociology may be the case when we deal with ecological uncertainty and linguistic description, as we can see [11]

> ... the group of diagnostic species is not always represented in full in any relevé. In fact, we may find a continuous series of relevés with a sucessively decreasing number of diagnostic spieces, from those with the higest number, which represent the nucleus of the sintaxon, towards poorly characterized relevés at sintaxon's margin, which is no sharp.

and by the following practical example [Polakowski 1968]

> ...discussed **community** <u>resembles the most</u> *Salicetum albo-fragilis.*

---

[4] One for each Fuzzy proprieties (found also in Table 2).

[5] Although it can be, I have not yet noticed about by God or anyone's...

It can be shown [9] that the *sintaxa*[6] can be represented as a fuzzy set of *taxas*[7] and linguistic descriptors can be states also as linguistic modified fuzzy sets pretty well.

6 Case Study: Production System for Phyto-indication based on Neural Fuzzy Logics

Using Phyto-Sociological informations, one can infer proprieties of the soil and anothers, by a process called *Phyto-indication*, as can be seen in the follow description [8]

> Phytocoenosys of this association [*Potentillo albae-Quercetum*] grow on moderately fertely and relatively dry soils ...; substratum is easily permeable ... and has a nearly neutral reaction, while the topmost layers can be **rather strongly acid**.

Its clear that the above statement can be paraprased as conjunctions of condictionals, who uses strongly linguistic variables like "rather strongly acid", fact that can be represented by a fuzzy set in an pH scale in $U = [0, 14]$.

Based in this kind of statement, we can construct an Expert System who can do inferences about soil acidity, based on observed community of plants, like [10], using the rules

$$(S_1 \Rightarrow \text{rather alcaline}) \wedge (S_2 \Rightarrow \text{acid}) \wedge (S_3 \Rightarrow \text{strongly acid}) \tag{1}$$

7 Numerical Results and comments

We shall not present here tables of numerical results (it can be found in [3]), but we have to mention that all patterns in the training set reach less than 1% error in their outputs of the network using only 150 training epochs. Other patterns have worked as expected. Generally, we found at least 6% error at each element using fuzzy implication operators [1].

As quoted by Moraczevicz itself

> However, its clear that in all applications the result will depend on thje degree of adequacy of transition from linguistic values to fuzzy sets. Some methods of acquision of membership functions associated with vague terms were proposed (e.g. Labov, 1973; Hersh and Caramazza, 1976; Turksen 1988, 1991). As there is no general and simple solution to this problem, in any serious application the membership functions which are used to represent meanings of some terms should be regarded with extreme caution to ensure **genuine**[8] representation.

May be Neural Fuzzy Logics is the case for representing local ("case by case") knowledge using fuzzy sets, tipically found in Ecological Systems.

---

[6]Comunity's descriptor set

[7]The vegetal spieces in it.

[8]My emphasis.

8 Acknowledgements

We wish to thanks the help, comments and corrections made by the following Professors: George Sheppard (IB-UNICAMP), Henrique S. del Nero (IEA-USP), Rodney C. Bassanezzi (IMECC-UNICAMP), Eduardo T. Paes (IO-USP), Benny Z. Yanga and Eduardo Passos Pereira and for the Cognitive Science Group of the Institute for Advanced Studies of USP.

References

[1] P.B. Blinder R.C. Bassanezi. Modelagem em ecologia teórica através de sistemas especialistas fuzzy. In *XVI CNMAC - Uberlândia*, 1993.

[2] P.B. Blinder. *Implementação da Lógica Fuzzy em Redes Neurais e suas aplicações em Biologia*. Campinas, 1993.

[3] P.B. Blinder E.T.Paes. An improvement in fuzzy logic for phytosociology. *Vegetatio (submitted)*.

[4] J.M.Keller H.Tahani. Backpopagation neural networks for fuzzy logic. *Information Sciences*, 62, 1992.

[5] A.N. Kolmogorov. Dolk. arad. navk. *A.M.S. Translations*, 2(55), 1957.

[6] B. Kosko. *Neural Networks and Fuzzy Systems: A dynamical systems approach to machine intelligence*. Prentice-Hall International, 1992.

[7] M. Mizumoto S. Fukami K.Tanaka. Some methods of fuzzy reasoning. In M.M. Gupta R.K. Ragade R.R.Yager, editor, *Advances in Fuzzy Set Theory and Applications*, North Holland, Amsterdam, 1979.

[8] W. Matuszkiewicz. *A guide for identification of the plant comunities of Poland*. PWN, 1981.

[9] I.R. Moraczewski. Fuzzy logic for phytosociology: 1. sintaxa as a vague concept. *Vegetatio*, 106, 1993.

[10] I.R. Moraczewski. Fuzzy logic for phytosociology: 2. generalizations and predictions. *Vegetatio*, 106, 1993.

[11] J. Moravec. Influences in individualistic concepts of vegetation on syntaxonomy. *Vegetatio*, 81, 1989.

[12] P.B. Blinder E.T. Paes. Regulação da abundância de comunidades de peixes pelo número de predadores utilizando a implementação da lógica fuzzy em redes neurais. In *XVI CNMAC - Uberlândia*, 1993.

[13] D.W. Roberts. Fuzzy systems vegetation theory. *Vegetatio*, 83, 1989.

[14] D.W. Roberts. Ordination based on fuzzy set theory. *Vegetatio*, 66, 1986.

[15] J.L. McClelland D.E. Rumelhart. *Exploration in Parallel Distribuited Processing: A Handbook of Models, Programs and Exercises*. Bradford Book, 1988.

[16] A. Salski. Fuzzy knowledge-based models in ecological research. *Ecological Modelling*, 63, 1992.

[17] T. Whalen B. Schott. Alternative logics for approximate reasoning in expert systems: a comparative study. *Int.J.Man-Machine Studies*, 22, 1985.

[18] L.A. Zadeh. Fuzzy logic. *IEEE Magazine*, Abril 1988.

[19] L.A. Zadeh. Fuzzy sets. *Information Control*, 8, 1965.

[20] L.A. Zadeh. A theory of approximate reasoning. In e L.I. Mikulich J. Hayes, D. Michie, editor, *Machine Intelligence*, Halstead Press, New York, 1979.

[21] E. Feoli V. Zuccarello. Syntaxonomy: a source of useful fuzzy sets environmental analysis? *Coenoses*, 3, 1988.

æ

Human-Motion Recognition using Fuzzy Associative Memory System

Hirohide USHIDA*, Atsushi IMURA*, Toru YAMAGUCHI**, and Tomohiro TAKAGI***

* Laboratory for International Fuzzy Engineering Research,
Siber Hegner Buil. 3F, 89-1 Yamamashita-cho,
Naka-ku, Yokohama, 231 JAPAN
e-mail: ushida@fuzzy.or.jp

** Faculty of Engineering, Utsunomiya University
2753 Ishii-cho, Utsunomiya, 321 JAPAN

*** Multimedia Software Development Office, Matsushita Electric Industrial Co., LTD
1-1-2, Shibakoen, Minato-ku, Tokyo, 105 JAPAN

Abstract

A real-time human-motion recognition method is proposed that uses a fuzzy associative memory system. It transforms space-time patterns into state-transition patterns, which are then recognized by means of fuzzy associative inference using associative memories. The tracking data is given as time-series data, from which the characteristic states are extracted. Each human motion has a specific state-transition pattern that consists of characteristic states. To recognize these motions, the specific state-transition patterns of the motions are defined as fuzzy rules and these fuzzy rules are implemented in a fuzzy associative memory system. This method is independent of the person being measured and the speed of the motion. In real-time experiments, this method was able to recognize three basic tennis motions (forehand stroke, backhand stroke, and smash) for six unspecified people. The recognition ratio of the fuzzy associative memory system is better than that of conventional fuzzy inference and a multi-layer perceptron.

1. Introduction

Human beings communicate with one another using motion as well as language. The recognition of human motion in human-machine interfaces is expected to improve the efficiency of communication between human beings and machines. Human-motion recognition systems will require a technique for extracting human motion from moving images. Many tracking techniques have been developed, which extract specific colors and/or specific shapes in images, but the knowledge representation and the ability to recognize human motion are not yet sufficiently developed. More research into knowledge representation and processing is needed.

Murakami et al. [1] has studied recognizing gestures by using data gloves to detect finger angles. These angles are used by a recurrent neural network to recognize human gestures. Data gloves, however, are not a practical detector because they are wired and require human touch. Also, the recurrent neural network is a kind of multi-layer perceptron (MLP) so that it is difficult to understand the meaning of each neuron in the hidden layers. In other words, the knowledge representation is not clear enough for human understanding.

A typical system for human-motion recognition using moving images is a spotting recognition system, which uses a dynamic programming method [2]. This method also has two problems. One is difficulty in recognizing the motions of unspecified people because it compares an input pattern with standard patterns in its memory. The other problem is that the knowledge representation in the dynamic programming is also not clear. It is therefore difficult to analyze the knowledge when the system does not perform. Human-motion recognition systems require (1) a technique to extract features from a motion image, (2) clear knowledge representation, and (3) independence from specified people.

This paper proposes a human-motion recognition method that satisfies these requirements. The basic idea of the proposed method is to transform space-time patterns into state-transition patterns and then to recognize them by means of fuzzy associative inference [3]. The tracking data is given as time-series data and the characteristic states are extracted from the data.

Each human motion has a specific state-transition pattern consisting of characteristic states. To recognize a motion, the specific state-transition patterns for human motions are defined as fuzzy rules, which are then implemented in the fuzzy associative memory system. The memory system performs fuzzy associative inference and converges to the most likely human motion. Ushida et al. showed the robustness of fuzzy associative inference by applying it to the recognition of facial expressions [4]. He demonstrated that fuzzy associative memory can recognize facial expressions by a combination of top-down and bottom-up processing, even if some information is lacking. Our proposed method is so effective that it is independent of the person being measured and the speed of the motions.

2. FAMOUS: Fuzzy Associative Memory Organizing Units System

Human movements are not exact because the speed and sizes of each movement depends on the person and other variables. While fuzzy inference [5] is effective in recognizing vague objects, such as human motions, the degree of fuzziness increases and the conclusions becomes more fuzzy because the fuzziness is permitted as a precondition. To solve this problem, fuzzy associative inference, driven by fuzzy associative memories, has been proposed [3].

We use fuzzy associative inference in our recognition system. Fuzzy associative memory is a kind of associative memory network, consisting of several bidirectional associative memories (BAMs) [6]. The fuzzy associative inference is driven by node activations propagation in the associative memory. This section describes the Fuzzy Associative Memory Organizing Units System (FAMOUS) [3] which was proposed as a method for carrying out fuzzy associative inference.

FAMOUS is used to develop fuzzy rules, as shown in Fig. 1. These rules consist of three elements: the if-part, the if-then-rule-part, and the then-part. Fuzzy rules represent knowledge describing relationships between "conditions" and "conclusions." The if-part has membership functions that abstract and characterize the conditions of the rule set. The then-part has membership or input-output functions of the rule set.

FAMOUS uses associative memories to create relationships between the if-part conditions and the then-part conclusions using the BAMs. Each BAM stores x_i-y_i pattern pairs in terms of the correlation matrix M and its transposition matrix M^T. For an x-y pair ($x, y \in \{0,1\}$) stored in a BAM, and given x'' (which implies a noisy x) in the x-layer, the BAM recalls the x-y pair on the x, y -layer. The BAM recalls from memory by using reverberation, which is given by Eq. (1).

$$Y_t = S(MX_t), \quad X_{t+1} = S(M^T Y_t) \tag{1}$$

In Eq. (1), $X_t = [ax_1, ax_2, ..., ax_p]^T$ and $Y_t = [ay_1, ay_2, ..., ay_q]^T$ are activation vectors on the x, y-layer at reverberation step t, and $S(\cdot)$ is the sigmoidal function of each node. The correlation matrices M and M^T are given by Eq. (2).

$$M = \beta \sum_{i=1}^{n} y_i x_i^T, \quad M^T = \beta \sum_{i=1}^{n} x_i y_i^T \tag{2}$$

In Eq. (2), x_i, y_i (i =1 to n) are stored pairs in a BAM, β is an association parameter, and each element x_i, y_i {0, 1}^{n} is usually converted to a bipolar element $\{-1, 1\}^n$ based on the BAM energy function. The BAM recalls the pair best matching the input conditions by using decreasing fuzzy entropy.

Fuzzy entropy describes the degree of fuzziness in the inference output. This feature is used to control fuzziness during fuzzy inference. Fuzzy rules can be implemented using associative memories such as BAMs because of its memory ability. Figure 1 shows how a fuzzy rule is implemented by means of associative memories. Each node on the x-layer represents the if-part membership function given by the fuzzy rules as conditions. Each node on the y-layer represents the then-part given by the fuzzy rules. Each node on the r-layer represents a fuzzy rule.

The BAM connects the x-layer to the r-layer and the r-layer to the y-layer. M_{xr} and M_{ry} are the resulting correlation matrices. There are mutual, negatively weighted connections on the r-layer to recall the most suitable rule for the input conditions. There are also minor positively weighted recessive connections on the r-layer to retain each activation. M_{rr} is the r-layer correlation matrix, it is called the coordinator.

During fuzzy inference, reverberation is performed with the correlation matrices M_{xr}, M_{rr}, M_{ry}, and each transposition correlation matrix. This fuzzy associative inference improves one of the weak points of conventional fuzzy inference, which is the increasing fuzziness of the inference output, this association controls increasing fuzziness. Some fuzzy inference methods can be simulated without this weakness because each activation value is used before it sufficiently converges.

3. Human-motion recognition system

The proposed recognition system (Fig. 2) consists of three modules: a tracking module, a feature extraction module, and a fuzzy associative inference module. This section describes these modules.

<u>Tracking module</u> The tracking module detects the positions of moving objects by extracting their colors and/or shapes. The color extractor and the color image tracker are products of Emtec Co., Ltd. in Japan. The color extractor extracts the specific colors of the hands, face, and other parts of the human body from moving images. The color image tracker determines the position of the extracted color by calculating its center of gravity. These processes are carried out every 1/60 second and create a time-series pattern of the detected positions. This pattern represents the movements of the parts of the body being tracked. The data is transferred to a computer via interface devices. The computer determines the features of the data and carries out fuzzy associative inference.

<u>Feature extraction module</u> The position movement of an object in a moving image creates a space-time pattern. The feature extraction module extracts the characteristic states from this space-time pattern, it is transforming into a state-transition pattern. The states in the state-transition pattern are inputs to the associative inference process. Human beings track human motion as a series of states. For example, a tennis racket stroke consists of six states: ready position, take-back, forward swing, impact, follow-through, and finish. In our research, we simulate this by extracting the characteristic states as a wave that is a space-time pattern.

From the space-time pattern, processed values, such as velocity and angle, are available. Our system extracts three characteristic shapes, mountain shapes, valley shapes, and stable states, from the space-time pattern. The extracted shapes are the features used by the fuzzy associative memory system.

The feature extraction procedure is as follows.
1. Define a threshold Θ (>0) to be compared with values obtained from a pattern.
2. Compute difference $\delta1$ between data(t) and data(t+1), where data(t) is the value at each point in time t (t = 1/60, 2/60, 3/60, ... [sec]).
3. If $|\delta1| < \Theta$, then the present state is a stable state and the standard value σ is defined as data(t+1). A stable state means that no motion occurs.
4. If $|\delta1| \geq \Theta$ and $\delta1>0$, then the present state is a candidate for a mountain shape. If $|\delta1| \geq \Theta$ and $\delta1<0$, then the present state is a candidate for a valley shape.
5. If the state is a candidate for a mountain shape (or valley shape), the point in the wave is moved forward along time t in order to find the top of the mountain (or the bottom of the valley).
6. If the top (or the bottom) is found, the height of the mountain (or the depth of the valley) is calculated. This height (or depth) is defined as Λ.
7. After passing the top (or the bottom), the point in the wave goes down (or up) the slope. The system calculates the difference $\delta2$ between the point's height and Λ at every point on the slope.
8. When $\delta2> (\alpha\%$ of $\Lambda)$ ($0<\alpha<100$), the point is regarded as the end position of the mountain (or valley) candidate from step 4.
9. In step 8, if $\delta2$ is less than Θ, the candidate from step 4 is not regarded as a mountain (or a valley).
10. When a mountain (or a valley) is detected, $\delta2$ is extracted as a characteristic value and is used as an input to the membership functions in the fuzzy associative inference process.

<u>Fuzzy Associative Inference Module</u> The fuzzy associative inference module recognizes human motions by using the fuzzy associative memory system FAMOUS described in section 2. Membership functions are defined as

suitable features of motions and are embedded within fuzzy inference rules in FAMOUS. The characteristic value extracted by the feature extraction module is input to the membership functions. The associative memory system then performs associative inference to determine the motion of the object.

4. Experimental results

Three basic tennis motions (forehand stroke, backhand stroke, and smash (Fig. 3)) were used in our real-time experiment. Their characteristic values and membership functions were obtained as follows. As the first value for the space-time pattern, the angle θ under the right arm is used. It is obtained from the positions of the right hand and the right shoulder (Fig. 4). This position is extracted by the tracking module every 1/60 second. The space-time pattern $\theta(t)$ (t = 1/60, 2/60, ... [sec]) generates a velocity vector for every point. When the direction of the vector changes, a characteristic state appears in the space-time pattern. For example, a mountain or a valley of wave $\theta(t)$ appears when the direction of the swing of the right arm changes. The top of the mountain or the bottom of the valley in the swing corresponds to "take-back" and "finish". The height of the mountain and the depth of the valley are thus used as characteristic values. The characteristic value of "take-back" is defined as x1 and that of "finish" is defined as x2. There are three membership functions for each characteristic value. These membership functions are "FO" (forehand stroke), "BA" (backhand stroke), and "SM" (smash) in each state. To define these membership functions, a subject person was tracked while he swung his arm six times for each motion. Each membership function was produced by averaging the values for each set of six samples.

The fuzzy rules are as follows.

R1: IF x1 is FO and x2 is FO, THEN the motion is a Forehand stroke.
R2: IF x1 is BA and x2 is BA, THEN the motion is a Backhand stroke.   (3)
R3: IF x1 is SM and x2 is SM, THEN the motion is a Smash.

In the if-part, the values of x1 and x2 are estimated by using the membership functions, and the then-part concludes a motion (forehand stroke, backhand stroke, or smash). These fuzzy rules are embedded in FAMOUS (Fig. 5). FAMOUS consists of three layers (x-layer, r-layer, and y-layer). The x-layer corresponds to the if-parts of the rules. The x-layer has six nodes representing FO, BA, and SM for x1 and FO, BA, SM for x2. Each node in the x-layer is activated by a grade that is the output of each membership function. A node in the r-layer represents a rule (R1, R2, or R3). The then-parts are assigned to the y-layer. The y-layer has three nodes representing forehand stroke, backhand stroke, and smash. The association matrices in FAMOUS are obtained by transforming the fuzzy rules into binary values according to Eq. (2).

The fuzzy associative inference is carried out as follows. The nodes in the x-layer are activated by the membership functions grades and the BAMs reverberate according to Eq. (1). Node activations propagate in the FAMOUS network and finally the activations distribution converges into a stable state. After convergence, the most activated node in the y-layer represents the recognized motion.

In the experiment, the six subject people swung their arms six times for each tennis motion, producing 108 samples. To examine robustness for unspecified people, the original subject, whose data was used to obtain the membership functions, was not included in the test group. The recognition performance of the proposed system was compared with that of conventional fuzzy inference and a three-layered perceptron. The membership functions and fuzzy rules in the conventional fuzzy inference were the same as in the fuzzy associative inference. The three-layered perceptron learned the ranges of the membership functions with a back-propagation algorithm. The testing was done in real time.

The fuzzy associative inference system produced the highest total correct recognition ratio (Table 1). It was particularly better at recognizing a smash. The values in Table 2 represent the membership grades of a sample "smash" which could not be recognized by the conventional fuzzy inference. The fuzzy inference does not select the rule when it has a grade 0 in its if-part. In the example in Table 2, the grade for SM(x1) is 0.7243, but the grade for SM(x2) is 0 in R3. Therefore, R3 is not selected. With fuzzy associative inference, when the grade for SM(x2) is 0, the grade for SM(x1) takes the activation of the R3 node of the r-layer to a higher value as a result of reverberation in the network. Finally, the activation of the "smash" node in the y-layer converges to a higher value. This is the effect of BAM inductivity. Thus, fuzzy associative inference can obtain an inference result even when conventional fuzzy inference cannot be performed because of the lack of a membership grade. With a three-layered perceptron, it has to learn all of the input space and thus cannot recognize data in a region which is not learned. Fuzzy associative inference can use the nearest learned region from input data even if the data exists in a region which is not learned, and thus can obtain a recognition result. These results show that the proposed associative inference system can overcome a lack of information to recognize the motions of unspecified people and is thus more robust than other inference systems.

5. Conclusion

We have developed a system that can recognize human motion in real time by using a fuzzy associative memory system. The system transforms space-time patterns into state-transition patterns and then recognizes them by means of fuzzy associative inference using associative memories. The tracking data is given as time-series data and the characteristic states are extracted from the data. The fuzzy associative memory system recognizes human motion by using state-transition patterns consisting of these extracted characteristic states. The proposed method can recognize three basic tennis motions about 84% on average for unspecified people. This recognition rate is better than that of conventional fuzzy inference and a multi-layer perceptron. The proposed method will be improved to recognize more complex human motion.

References

[1] K. Murakami and H. Taguchi : Gesture Recognition using Recurrent Neural Networks, Proc. of Conference on Human Factors in Computing Systems 1991, pp. 237-242 (1991)
[2] K. Takahashi, S. Seki, and R. Oka : Spotting Recognition of Human Gestures from Motion Images, Technical Report of IEICE., IE92-134, PRU92-157, pp. 9-16 (1993) (in Japanese)
[3] T. Yamaguchi, K. Goto, and T. Takagi : Two-Degree-of-Freedom Fuzzy Model Using Associative Memories and Its Applications, Information Sciences, 71, pp. 65-97 (1993)
[4] H. Ushida, T. Takagi, and T. Yamaguchi : Recognition of Facial Expressions using Conceptual Fuzzy Sets, Proc. of the 2nd IEEE International Conference on Fuzzy Systems, pp. 594-599 (1993)
[5] E.H. Mamdani: Applications of Fuzzy Algorithms for Control of Simple Dynamic Plant, Proc. IEE, Vol. 121, No. 12, p. 1585 (1974)
[6] B. Kosko : Adaptive Bidirectional Associative Memories, Applied Optics, Vol. 26, No. 23, pp. 4947-4960 (1987)

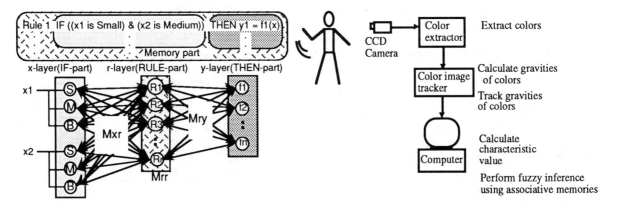

Fig. 1 *Fuzzy rule representation in FAMOUS*   Fig. 2 *The proposed system*

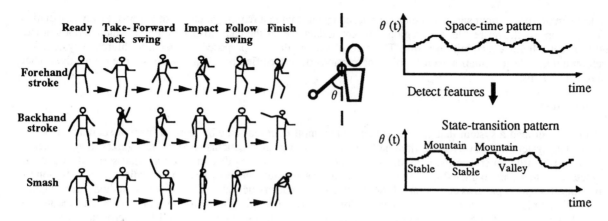

Fig. 3 *Three basic tennis motions* Fig. 4 *Characteristic value and its time-space pattern*

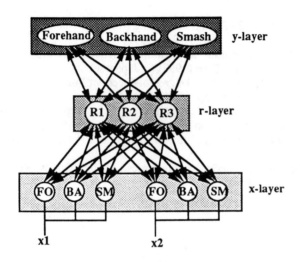

Fig. 5 *Using FAMOUS to recognize human tennis motion*

Table 1 *Correct recognition ratio (%)*

	FAMOUS	MLP	Fuzzy
Forehand	86.1	88.9	75.0
Backhand	77.8	77.8	72.2
Smash	88.9	69.4	66.7
Total	84.2	78.7	71.3

Number of samples : 108
FAMOUS: Inference by FAMOUS
MLP: Multi-layer perceptron trained by back-propagation
Fuzzy: Conventional fuzzy inference

Table 2 *Membership grades of a sample which could not be recognized by conventional fuzzy inference.*

	$x1$	$x2$
Forehand	0.0000	0.1222
Backhand	0.0000	0.0000
Smash	0.7243	0.0000

I-804

The Fuzzy Polynomial Rules

Lai-Wan CHAN

Computer Science Department, The Chinese University of Hong Kong
Shatin, HONG KONG
Email : lwchan@cs.cuhk.hk

Abstract

We examine the properties of function approximation using polynomial rules in a fuzzy system. We show that this kind of fuzzy function approximation is equivalent to Lagrange polynomial interpolation between turning points when normalized fuzzy function memberships are used. The fuzzy inference procedure combines two polynomials of degree n and m in x into one single polynomial of at most degree $\max(n, m) + 1$ which passes through the points of intersections of the original polynomials. We present the cases for linear and quadratic polynomials and then generalize it into polynomials of degree n.

1 Introduction

Approximating an unknown function has been a research topic for a long time. One commonly used model-based approach in numerical methods is to evaluate a polynomial which passes through some given data points of the unknown function. It is assumed *in priori* that the unknown function is of the form of a $n - 1$ degree polynomial in x, $P_n(x) = \sum_{i=0}^{n-1} a_i x^i$. *Lagrange's polynomial interpolation method* is a classical method of this approach to compute the coefficients, a_i, of this polynomial. Recently, some model-free approaches have been suggested, such as the use of neural networks [4], [11] or fuzzy systems [9], [7] to approximate a function. Hornik *el al* shows that multilayer feedforward networks with one hidden layer is a class of universal approximators [4]. Similarly, Kosko shows that fuzzy systems can approximate any real continuous function on a compact domain to any degree of accuracy [9]. These two model-free approaches have more attractions than the model-based methods because of their high degree of flexibility. Unlike the model-based approach, both neural networks and fuzzy systems provide only frameworks for the function approximation. From these frameworks, we can build up various approximators for the unknown functions. In multi-layer feedforward networks, any arbitrary bounded and nonconstant activation function can be used for the function mapping [3]. In fuzzy systems, we can define the "if-then" fuzzy rules, and as well as the membership functions, in various forms. However, both neural networks and fuzzy systems suffer from the same criticism. Their operations can be understood in the microscopic level. Whereas, in the macroscopic level, it is relatively hard to visualize their operations. In microscopic level, neural networks are computational methods based on a massively interconnection of processing nodes. Fuzzy systems are operated by inference systems with a collection of fuzzy rules. In this paper, we look at the fuzzy function approximation system at the macroscopic level. We examine a fuzzy system using polynomial rules and show that this system combines polynomial rules to form piecewise polynomials for function approximation. The resultant polynomial has a degree no more than one degree higher than the highest degree of the polynomial rules.

2 The Additive Fuzzy Systems

Kosko showed that any real continuous function, $f : X \to Y$, can be approximated by additive fuzzy systems [8]. The basic idea is to cover the graph of the continuous function by fuzzy patches. These fuzzy patches are equivalent to fuzzy rules of the form "If X is A, then Y is B". The input, x, is fuzzified into fuzzy subsets A_i. Then the fuzzy rules associate and inference the fuzzy input A_i to the output B_i. Weighted sum is used to add the out fuzzy sets B_i to form B and a defuzzifier transforms B into y. This approximation can be achieved to any degree of accuracy by using finite number of fuzzy patches [9].

3 Lagrange's form of Interpolation

Suppose we want to construct a $n-1$ degree polynomial which passes through the points (x_i, y_i), $i = 1, 2, \ldots, n$. Assuming the polynomial as in the form of $P_n(x) = \sum_{i=0}^{n-1} a_i x^i$, we substitute all the data points in $P_n(x)$, and solve these n linear equations to obtain the coefficients, a_i, of the polynomial. Alternatively, Lagrangian form of interpolation obtains the coefficients of the polynomial without the need to solve a set of linear equations. This method expresses the polynomial, $P_n(x)$, of degree $n-1$, in the following form

$$P_n(x) = L_1(x)y_1 + L_2(x)y_2 + \cdots + L_n(x)y_n \tag{1}$$

with

$$L_k(x) = \prod_{\substack{i=1, \\ i \neq k}}^{n} \frac{x - x_i}{x_k - x_i} \qquad k = 1, 2, \ldots, n \tag{2}$$

$L_k(x)$ in equation 2 has an interesting property that $L_k(x_k) = 1$ and $L_k(x_i) = 0$, for any $i \neq k$, and $i, k = 1, 2, \ldots, n$. Consequently, combining equations 1 and 2, we have $P_n(x_i) = y_i$ for $i = 1, 2, \ldots, n$. Therefore, $P_n(x)$ is a polynomial which passes through all data pairs of (x_i, y_i).

4 The Approximation Using Functional Rules

4.1 The Polynomial Rules

The rules in the form of "Rule i : IF **X** $= A_i$, THEN **Y** $= B_i$" are used in the additive fuzzy function approximation systems [9]. In these rules, A_i and B_i are fuzzy sets defined on the input and output universe of discourse respectively. An example of the rule is "IF **X** is Negative Small, THEN **Y** is Positive Small". In our paper, we replace the linguistic variables in the consequences by some functional variables [10], [12]. Hence, the general form of the rules is "**Rule i** : **if** x is A_i, **then** $y = f_i(x)$" where A_i remains a fuzzy set, and $f_i(x)$ is a function of x.

In particular, functions in the form of polynomials are investigated in this article. An example of this type of rules is "IF **X** is Negative Small, THEN **Y** is equal to $5x^2 + 3x - 1$". Each individual rule can now be regarded as using a polynomial to approximate the unknown function within the support of the linguistic variable, A_i, associated with the rule. The final stage of the fuzzy system is to combine the inferred output of the rules and to give a crisp estimation for the unknown function. The inferring mechanism of this type of fuzzy rules is given by

$$y = \frac{\sum_i w_i * f_i(x)}{\sum_i w_i} \tag{3}$$

where $f_i(x)$ is the output from the rule i, w_i is the degree of satisfaction of the rule i.

4.2 The Membership Functions

The antecedent of our rules is in the form of fuzzy sets. These sets partition the continuous input universe of discourse into fuzzy subsets. In this paper, we specify the membership functions, μ_i, to be in triangle-shaped or in trapezoid-shaped, with $\max_x \mu_i(x) = 1$. These functions can be asymmetrical or unevenly distributed in the universe, but we restrict to the normalized degree of memberships, $i.e. \sum_i \mu_i(x) = 1$ at any x. This can also prevent the overlapping of more than two rules in the input space.

We define the *turning point* (or also called "edges" [5]), a, of the input variable, x, on any triangular or trapezoidal membership functions to be

$$\mu_i(a) = 1 \quad \text{and} \quad \text{the derivative of } \mu_i(x) \text{ is discontinuous at } a.$$

An example of the membership functions we used is shown in Figure 1, which x_1, x_2 and x_3 are turning points, and these turning points partitions the input space into intervals. Within each interval, the input space is a subset of the support of one or two fuzzy sets defined in the input space. Thus, we have two types of partitions in the input space; one is the space covered by one rules and the other one is the space covered by two rules. In the first type (*e.g.* in Figure 1, $x_1 < x < x_2$), the output is solely determined by

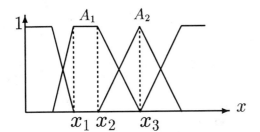

Figure 1: Fuzzy Membership Functions

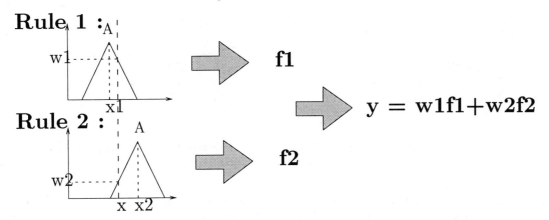

Figure 2: Fuzzy Inference System

the consequence of one rule. Thus, the unknown function is approximated by the polynomial involved in this rule. This is a trivial case and it reduces into a bivalent rule-base system. In the second case, (*e.g.* in Figure 1, $x_2 < x < x_3$), x is under the support of two sets, A_1 and A_2. Apart from the rules using A_1 and A_2 as their antecedents, other fuzzy rules have zero degree of satisfaction, and hence their outputs have no effect on the final outcome. It is our interest to see how the fuzzy inference mechanism to composite the output of the active rules and to produce a smooth transition within this interval.

The subsequence of this article will focus on the analysis of the inferencing of fuzzy rules. Figure 2 is a simplified view of the composition. When $x_1 < x < x_2$, Rule 1 and Rule 2 are involved and the other rules are not shown. Let w_1 and w_2 be the firing strength of these rules respectively, and their relation to x is

$$w_1 = \frac{x - x_2}{x_1 - x_2}, \qquad w_2 = \frac{x - x_1}{x_2 - x_1} \qquad \text{and} \qquad w_1 + w_2 = 1 \tag{4}$$

According to equation 3, the final output from this system is

$$y(x) = \frac{w_1 * f_1(x) + w_2 * f_2(x)}{w_1 + w_2} \tag{5}$$

4.3 The Linear Case

Let us consider the interval between two turning points x_1 and x_2. Any input x within this interval is under the support of two sets; A_1 and A_2. Here in this section, we assume that the consequence of the corresponding rules are zero-degree polynomials as

Rule 1 : **if** x is A_1, **then** $y = f_1(x) = y_1$

Rule 2 : **if** x is A_2, **then** $y = f_2(x) = y_2$

where y_1 and y_2 are constants and $y_1 \neq y_2$. [1]

Substituting equation 4 into the weighted average in equation 5, the final output becomes

$$y(x) = \frac{(x - x_2)}{(x_1 - x_2)}y_1 + \frac{(x - x_1)}{(x_2 - x_1)}y_2 \tag{6}$$

---

[1] If $y_1 = y_2$, these two rules are redundant, and the resultant output will simply be $y = y_1$.

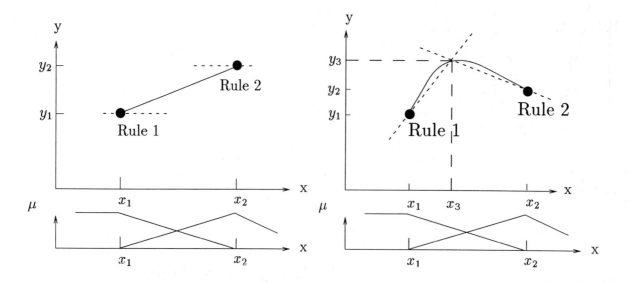

Figure 3: Results of inferencing of two zero degree polynomials.

Figure 4: The polynomial generated by the fuzzy system

From equation 6, this results in a first-order polynomial in x. In graphical terms, the rules use horizontal line segments to approximate part of the function and the fuzzy system joins the segments by having a linear interpolation between the virtual point pairs of (x_1, y_1) and (x_2, y_2) (Fig 3).

In the case of Lagrangian Polynomial Interpolation, suppose we want to construct a first degree polynomial to pass through the points (x_1, y_1) and (x_2, y_2). From equation 1, the constructed polynomial is the same as equation 6.

4.4   The Quadratic Case

Now, instead of using fixed constants as the consequence of the rules, we consider the case of using linear polynomials in x in the fuzzy rules as shown below.

$$\textbf{Rule 1}: \quad \textbf{if } x \textbf{ is } A_1, \quad \textbf{then } y = px + q$$

$$\textbf{Rule 2}: \quad \textbf{if } x \textbf{ is } A_2, \quad \textbf{then } y = rx + s$$

where p, q, r and s are constants and $p \neq r$. Applying these rules into equation 5, the output becomes

$$y(x) = \frac{(x - x_2)}{(x_1 - x_2)}(px + q) + \frac{(x - x_1)}{(x_2 - x_1)}(rx + s) \tag{7}$$

Now the fuzzy system forms a second-order polynomial. Here the combination of two first degree polynomials extends into a second degree polynomial. Graphically, individual rules produce separate line segments to approximate the unknown function. A fuzzy approximation system combines these linear segments by joining them smoothly between the turning points (Fig 4).

We let $y_1 = px_1 + q$, $y_2 = rx_2 + s$ and let the point (x_3, y_3) be the intersection of the lines $y = px + q$ and $y = rx + s$, and x_3 is distinct from both x_1 and x_2. The coefficients of the polynomial rules can be expressed in terms of x_1, y_1, x_2, y_2, x_3 and y_3 as

$$p = \frac{y_1 - y_3}{x_1 - x_3}, \qquad q = \frac{y_3 x_1 - y_1 x_3}{x_1 - x_3}, \qquad r = \frac{y_2 - y_3}{x_2 - x_3} \qquad \text{and} \qquad s = \frac{y_3 x_2 - y_2 x_3}{x_2 - x_3} \tag{8}$$

Substituting equation 8 into equation 7 gives

$$y(x) = \frac{(x - x_2)(x - x_3)}{(x_1 - x_2)(x_1 - x_3)} y_1 + \frac{(x - x_1)(x - x_3)}{(x_2 - x_1)(x_2 - x_3)} y_2 + \frac{(x - x_1)(x - x_2)}{(x_3 - x_1)(x_3 - x_2)} y_3 \tag{9}$$

Equation 9 shows that the output, $y(x)$, given by this fuzzy approximation system is a second degree polynomial passing through the points (x_1, y_1), (x_2, y_2) and (x_3, y_3) (Figure 4). This equation is exactly the same as the Lagrange's polynomial obtained by interpolating (x_1, y_1), (x_2, y_2) and (x_3, y_3). Again this case shows the equivalence to the Lagrange's polynomial of degree two.

4.5 Generalization to Degree n Polynomials

The above shows particular results for the equivalence of fuzzy approximation using polynomial rules and the the Lagrange's polynomial in linear and quadratic cases. Now we show that this equivalence can be extended to any degree of polynomials.

Theorem : In a fuzzy function approximation system using normalised membership functions and polynomial rules of the form "**Rule i** : if x is A_i, then $y = P_{n_i}^{(i)}(x)$" where $P_{n_i}^{(i)}(x)$ is a polynomial in degree $n_i - 1$, if A_i and A_{i+1} are two fuzzy sets with x_i and x_{i+1} being their respective turning points such that A_i and A_{i+1} are monotone between x_i and x_{i+1}, the output of this system between x_i and x_{i+1} is equivalent to a polynomial in degree of less than or equal to $\max(n_i, n_{i+1})$, and this polynomial passes through the points of intersection of $P_{n_i}^{(i)}(x)$ and $P_{n_{i+1}}^{(i+1)}(x)$.

Proof. For simplicity, let us consider two polynomial rules

$$\textbf{Rule 1}: \quad \textbf{if } x \text{ is } A_1, \quad \textbf{then } y = P_n^{(1)}(x)$$
$$\textbf{Rule 2}: \quad \textbf{if } x \text{ is } A_2, \quad \textbf{then } y = P_m^{(2)}(x)$$

with A_1 and A_2 are two fuzzy sets with x_1 and x_2 being their respective turning points such that A_1 and A_2 are monotone between x_1 and x_2. Now for any x between x_1 and x_2, the resultant output is

$$y(x) = \frac{(x - x_2)}{(x_1 - x_2)} P_n^{(1)}(x) + \frac{(x - x_1)}{(x_2 - x_1)} P_m^{(2)}(x) \tag{10}$$

which is a polynomial in degree $\max(n, m)$ at most.

If (x_i, y_i) is an intersection point of $y = P_n^{(1)}(x)$ and $y = P_m^{(2)}(x)$, $P_n^{(1)}(x_i) = P_m^{(2)}(x_i) = y_i$. Substitute $x = x_i$ into equation 10, we have $y(x) = y_i$. **Q.E.D.**

Suppose $y_1 = P_n^{(1)}(x_1)$, $y_2 = P_m^{(2)}(x_2)$ and we assume that $P_n^{(1)}(x) = 0$ and $P_m^{(2)}(x) = 0$ have $n - 1$ intersection points which labeled as (x_3, y_3), (x_4, y_4), $\ldots (x_n, y_n), (x_{n+1}, y_{n+1})$, and that all (x_i, y_i), $i = 1, 2, \ldots, n + 1$ are distinct.

Since $P_n^{(1)}(x) = 0$ passes through (x_1, y_1), (x_3, y_3), (x_4, y_4), $\ldots (x_n, y_n), (x_{n+1}, y_{n+1})$. We can express $P_n^{(1)}(x) = 0$ in the form of Lagrangian Polynomial

$$P_n^{(1)}(x) = L_1^{(1)}(x)y_1 + L_3^{(1)}(x)y_3 + L_4^{(1)}(x)y_4 + \cdots + L_n^{(1)}(x)y_n + L_{n+1}^{(1)}(x)y_{n+1} \tag{11}$$

where

$$L_1^{(1)}(x) = \prod_{i=3}^{n+1} \frac{x - x_i}{x_1 - x_i}, \qquad L_k^{(1)}(x) = \frac{x - x_1}{x_k - x_1} \prod_{\substack{i=3, \\ i \neq k}}^{n+1} \frac{x - x_i}{x_k - x_i} \qquad k = 3, 4, \ldots n, n + 1$$

Similarly, $y = P_m^{(2)}(x)$ passes through the points (x_2, y_2), (x_3, y_3), (x_4, y_4), $\ldots (x_n, y_n), (x_{n+1}, y_{n+1})$, and thus we can express $P_m^{(2)}(x)$ as

$$P_m^{(2)}(x) = L_2^{(2)}(x)y_2 + L_3^{(2)}(x)y_3 + L_4^{(2)}(x)y_4 + \cdots + L_n^{(2)}(x)y_n + L_{n+1}^{(2)}(x)y_{n+1} \tag{12}$$

where

$$L_2^{(2)}(x) = \prod_{i=3}^{n+1} \frac{x - x_i}{x_2 - x_i}, \qquad L_k^{(2)}(x) = \frac{x - x_2}{x_k - x_2} \prod_{\substack{i=3, \\ i \neq k}}^{n+1} \frac{x - x_i}{x_k - x_i} \qquad k = 3, 4, \ldots n, n + 1$$

Equation 12 appears to be a degree $n - 1$ polynomial instead of degree $m - 1$. However, the higher order terms in this polynomial cancel out and this polynomial is actually reducible to degree $m - 1$.

Substituting equations 11,12 into equation 10 gives

$$P_{n+1}(x) = L_1(x)y_1 + L_2(x)y_2 + \cdots + L_n(x)y_n + L_{n+1}(x)y_{n+1} \tag{13}$$

with

$$L_k(x) = \prod_{\substack{i=1, \\ i \neq k}}^{n+1} \frac{x - x_i}{x_k - x_i} \qquad k = 1, 2, \ldots, n, n + 1 \tag{14}$$

which is the Lagrangian polynomial that interpolates the points (x_i, y_i) for $i = 1, 2, ...n+1$. Thus, the output polynomial is uniquely defined in this way. When some of the intersection points do not exist or are not distinct, there have fewer points for us to define the output polynomial. However, the output polynomial of this type has some interesting properties [1].

5 Discussion and Conclusions

This article reviews the equivalence between the output of fuzzy function approximation using polynomial rules and the Lagrangian polynomial interpolation. We show that the inference of the fuzzy system combines the polynomial rules into a single polynomial with a degree of no more than one degree higher than the polynomials defined in the rules.

Apart from their fundamental difference of belonging to different categories of approaches; namely, model-free approach and model-base approach, these two methods of function approximation have other major difference in the interpretation. Firstly, Lagrangian polynomial requires *exact given data pairs* and the constructed polynomial passes through the data points exactly. The points that the fuzzy system interpolates are *virtual* and they are the coordinates of the turning points and the intersection points of the corresponding polynomial rules. In other words, only the fuzzy rules and the membership functions have to be provided to the fuzzy systems. No data points are needed. The virtual data points that the system is interpolating are embedded in the fuzzy polynomial rules. At present, the fuzzy rules are usually obtained from human expert or via learning mechanism from numerical data. For examples, the ellipsoidal fuzzy rules can be constructed from supervised and/or unsupervised competitive learning [2], the premise parameters of the bell-shaped function can be obtained by gradient descent learning [6]. Suppose the polynomial rules can be constructed from a learning mechanism with a set of training data. The training data are not necessarily the same as the interpolating points. Besides, it is possible that the training data are noisy or inexact, and this depends on the detail mechanism of the learning algorithm.

Within each interval between two turning points, the fuzzy inference mechanism combines the rules and generates a new polynomial. The domain of the constructed polynomial is between two turning points only. Polynomials in different partitions are unrelated. This makes the fuzzy polynomial system a piecewise function approximation. Any discontinuous functions can therefore be easily accommodated. For continuous functions, the bell-shaped membership functions seem to be a better candidate.

References

[1] L. W. Chan. The fuzzy system using polynomial rules as function approximator. Technical Report CS-TR-93-07, The Chinese University of Hong Kong, 1993.

[2] J. A. Dickerson and B. Kosko. Fuzzy function approximation with supervised ellipsoidal learning. In *World Congress on Neural Networks Networks 1993, Portland*, volume 2, pages II9–II17, 1993.

[3] K. Hornik. Approximation capabilities of multilayer feedforward networks. *Neural Networks*, 4(2):251–257, 1991.

[4] K. Hornik, M. Stinchcombe, and H. White. Multi-layer feedforward networks are universal approximators. *Neural Networks*, 2:359–366, 1989.

[5] S. Isaka. On neural approcimation of fuzzy systems. In *International Joint Conference on Neural Networks 1992, Maryland*, volume 1, pages I263–I268, 1992.

[6] J-S. R. Jang. Self-learning fuzzy controllers based on temporal back propagation. *IEEE Transactions on Neural Networks*, 3(5):714–723, September 1992.

[7] C. C. Jou. On the mapping capacity of fuzzy inference systems. In *International Joint Conference on Neural Networks 1992, Maryland*, volume 2, pages II708–II713, 1992.

[8] B. Kosko. Fuzzy function approximation. In *International Joint Conference on Neural Networks 1992, Maryland*, volume 1, pages I209–I213, 1992.

[9] B. Kosko. Fuzzy systems as universal function approximators. In *IEEE International Conference on Neural Networks and Fuzzy Systems*, pages 1153–1162, 1992.

[10] C. C. Lee. Fuzzy logic in control systems : Fuzzy logic controller – part i. *IEEE Transactions on Systems, Man & Cybernetics*, 20(2):404–418, 1990.

[11] T. D. Sanger. A tree-structured adaptive network for function approximation in high-dimensional space. *IEEE Transactions on Neural Networks*, 2(2):285–293, March 1991.

[12] M. Sugeno. An introductory survey of fuzzy control. *Information Sciences*, 36:59–83, 1985.

Can Possibility Functions Directly Enter A Fuzzy Neural Network ?

Li Chen   Don Cooley   Jianping Zhang
Department of Computer Science
Utah State University
Logan, UT 84322-4205

Extended Abstract

1. INTRODUCTION

Fuzzy neural networks have been applied to many areas in control systems, patter n recognition, image processing, and fuzzy reasoning [1-5]. Almost all fuzzy neural networks are based on typical neural networks(e.g. Backpropagation), and the connection weights have the particular meanings. Pal and Mitra proposed a fuzzy neural network, each element of which input vector is a triple vector *(low, medium, high)* of a membership function[5].

In this note, we try to describe a reasonable fuzzy neural network, which can accept a group of possibility functions as an input vector. In order to use fuzzy arithmatic operations, each of weights in first layer is also assigned as a possibility function. Its output is a fuzzy set.

The Fuzzy neural network is proposed for classification of complicated images and data. The fuzzy neural network has been used to satellite image classification. For a satellite image data, the 79.1 percent correctness for the traning set and 79.32 percent correctness for the test set have been attained combining with a fuzzy system method for weight initialization.

Some reasons for building a neural network of this kind fuzzy neural network could be:
(1) Possibility function have been used to almost every where in fuzzy system and its application.
(2) In image classification, when we not only consider a pixel but also consider its surroundings for an image unit. We can use possibility functions to represent the features of the unit[7,8].

2. A NEW FUZZY NEURAL NETWORK

In this section, we introduce the new fuzzy neural network. Its model is described below:

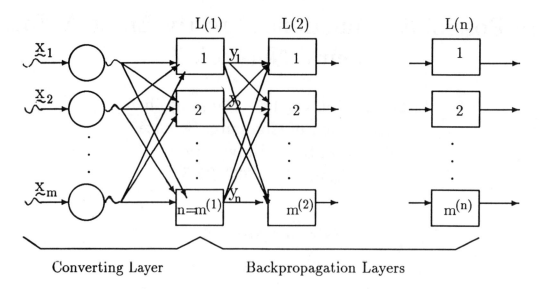

Fig. 1 The Fuzzy Neural Network Model

We will only discuss the computation and training of the model in the first layer.

For this model, $\mathbf{x}(i)$ is a possible fuction but not a value. Without loss the generality, the domain is assigned as always $[0,1]$. Where each $\mathbf{w}_{ij}$ is a possibility function.

(I)Computation Formulas

The input_output relationship of the first layer are defined as:

$Input = (\mathbf{x}_1, \mathbf{x}_2, ..., \mathbf{x}_m)$, where each $\mathbf{x}_i : [0,1] \to [0,1]$ is a possibility function. $\mathbf{x}_i(t)$ represents the value t_th sample of domain $[0,1]$ of function $\mathbf{x}_i$.

$Output = (y_1, y_2, ..., y_n)$.

the weights is $\{\mathbf{w}_{ij} : i = 1,...,m; j = 1,...,n\}$, where each $\mathbf{w}_{ij} : [0,1] \to [0,1]$ is a possibility function. $\mathbf{w}_{ij}(t)$ represents the value t_th sample of domain $[0,1]$ of function $\mathbf{w}_{ij}$. We define the output as:

$$y(j) = \sum_{i=1}^n (Max_{t=1}^T (Min(\mathbf{x}_i(t), \mathbf{w}_{ij}(t))))/n. \quad \text{j=1,...n.}$$

(II)Training

Training this fuzzy neural network in first layer is different from training the traditional model. Let $Target = (tar_1, ..., tar_n)$ be a target vector, the training procedure is designed below:

(1) Let $\Delta = Target - Output = (\Delta_1, ..., \Delta_n)$.

(2) For all j,

If $\Delta_j > 0$ then for all $t = 1, ..., T$ do:

If $\mathbf{x}_i(t) > \mathbf{w}_{ij}(t)$ then let $\mathbf{w}_{ij}(t) = \mathbf{w}_{ij}(t) + \Delta_j * y(j)$.

If $\Delta_j < 0$ then for all $t = 1, ..., T$ do:

If $\mathbf{x}_i(t) < \mathbf{w}_{ij}(t)$ then let $\mathbf{w}_{ij}(t) = \mathbf{w}_{ij}(t) + \Delta_j * y(j)$.

The training method may be varied in different cases.

3. AN APPLICATION

As a case study, we have applied the fuzzy neural network without using Backpropagation layers to satellite image classification.

We use the satellite data was public domain data and published by Ross King [6]. Each sample concerns with 3×3 pixels, and there are 4 band values for each pixel. The goal is to category the every sample into seven classes. There are two data sets; one has 4436 samples (Data_4436) and another one has 2001 samples (Data_2001).

We use the method described in [7,8] to get possibily functions of inputs and initialize the weights in the fuzzy neural network. We have got a 79.1 percent of accuracy for training set Data_2001 and got a 79.32 percent of accuracy for test set Data_4436. It is so interesting that when we apply the trained weights to the fuzzy system described in [7,8], we get a 83.3 percent correctness for the test data.

Acknowledgments. We are deeply indebted to Dr. J. Bezdek, Dr. R. King and Dr. C. Feng for discussion and providing their papers and results.

REFERENCES

[1] B. Kosko, Neural Networks and Fuzzy Systems. A Dynamical Systems Approach to Machine Intelligence, Prentice-Hall, 1992.

[2] D. Kerr and J. Bezdek, Edge detection using a fuzzy neural network, SPIE vol 1710,1992.

[3] P. Simpson, Fuzzy Min-Max neural networks: part 1: Classification, *IEEE Trans. Neural Network*, vol 3, No 5,1992.

[4] S. Horikawa, T. Furuhashi, and Y. Uchikawa, On fuzzy modeling using fuzzy neural networks with the Back-Propagation algorithm, *IEEE Trans. Neural Network*, vol 3, No 5,1992.

[5] S.K. Pal and S. Mitra, Multilayer perceptron, fuzzy sets, and classification, *IEEE Trans. Neural Network*, vol 3, No 5,1992.

[6] C. Feng, A. Sutherland, R. King, and B.Henery, Comparing machine learning classifiers to statistics and neural networks. *Proceedings of the International Conference on Artificial Intelligence and Statistics*, Florida 1993

[7] L. Chen, D. Cooley and J. Zhang. A new fuzzy classification te chnique and its application to remote sensing. *Proc. of the North American Fuzzy Image Processing Meeting 93*, Bethlehem,PA. 1993.

[8] L. Chen, D. Cooley and J. Zhang, Genetic algorithm application to fuzzy classification in remote sensing, *Proc. of International Simulation Technology Multiconference*, 1993.

Selection of Fuzzy Rules Using a Genetic Algorithm

Jerry J. Cupal and Bogdan M. Wilamowski
Department of Electrical Engineering
University of Wyoming
Laramie, Wyoming, USA

Abstract

A genetic algorithm was used to modify the members of a population of rules for a fuzzy controller. In this work, the example of a truck backing toward a ramp was solved by the controller. An error function was used to rank the members of the population, and the best members became the parents of the next generation. Crossovers were done to further mix the new members, with additional mutations done on individual rules of randomly chosen members. The algorithm proved to converge toward suitable solutions of this problem, starting from 100 randomly chosen sets of fuzzy rules. The technique shows great promise for the automatic synthesis of rules for fuzzy controllers.

Introduction

Fuzzy systems require expert intuition to define the membership functions and the fuzzy rules. Most fuzzy controllers are robust enough to work amazingly well, despite the fact that often this expert intuition is far from optimum. Because it is often necessary and/or desirable to operate a fuzzy controller in an optimum mode, there is an interest in developing techniques for the optimum design of these controllers. Many researchers are attempting to find the optimum solutions for systems whose input-output relations are known [1][2]. For these systems, the fuzzy controller can be trained in a similar way as neural networks [3][4][5] or more advanced methods based on orthogonal least-squares learning algorithms[6]. One possible approach is to use quasi random search techniques through the fuzzy rule tables looking for some optimum performance [7].

In this paper, a genetic search is used to find the best performance. The example of backing up a truck to a ramp is used in this study. The problem is stated the same way as presented in [7] and [8], including the same membership functions. The goal of the genetic search is to find the optimum set of fuzzy rules. In fact, the search algorithm described here can be used to automatize the synthesis process of fuzzy systems.

Problem statement

In the example of backing a truck to ramp, there is no predefined path for each truck location and therefore the optimum steering angle is likewise unknown. Furthermore, a controlled object such as the truck has a certain "inertia", so the correctness of the assumed control variables and not known for some time. In our example, the truck could drive out of the parking lot or crash because of the effect of a wrong set of rules.

The truck is moving back toward the ramp as shown in Figure 1. The motion of the truck can be described by the following set of equations:

$$
\begin{aligned}
x_{i+1} &= x_i - r\sin(\alpha_i) \\
y_{i+1} &= y_i + r\cos(\alpha_i) \\
\alpha_{i+1} &= \alpha_i + \beta_i
\end{aligned}
\qquad (1)
$$

where α is the truck angle, x and y are coordinates of the back of the truck, ß is the steering angle, and r is the incremental driving distance. A fuzzy controller for this problem would have three input variables (α, x and y). However, it can also perform its' function if the variable y is ignored since it is enough to direct truck on the correct track toward the ramp. When truck is directed to the state with x = 0 and α = 0, then it is only matter of time until it will reach the ramp (y = 0). The same approach was used in [8], where y was not used as the input variable for controller. That is, its membership function was not specified.

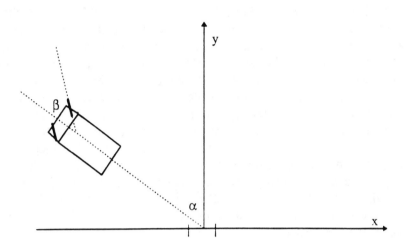

Figure 1.   Top view of a truck backing toward a ramp. The ramp is located at the origin.

The membership functions for the inputs and the outputs are the same as in [8]. There are five membership functions for the x input, and seven for both the α input and the β output variables. As a result, the fuzzy rule table consists 35 rules and each rule may has seven different levels. Consequently, there are $35^7 \approx 10^{30}$ possible combinations of rules. It is obvious that a random search is not practical. Even a quasi random search as it was proposed in [7] would require a very long search time. The genetic algorithm seems to be the proper method to obtain a solution to this problem. A genetic search is capable of doing a parallel search of solution space, as opposed to a point-by-point search. By using a population of trial solutions the genetic algorithm can effectively explore many regions of the search space simultaneously, and therefore, it is less sensitive to becoming trapped in a local minima [9].

The genetic algorithm consists of recursively performing the following steps:

1. A given population is tested to rank the members of the population. Ranking is done on certain criterium, usually some error function the measures how well the fuzzy system performs its' task.

2. The population is separated into winners and losers and the losers eliminated. The winners are then reproduced to reestablish the population.

3. The new population is subjected to "Crossovers" where parts of the winners are randomly exchanged.

4. The members of the population are then mutated, where some randomly chosen rules are perturbed slightly.

As the algorithm converges, a population of better and better parents reproduce even better children. The best of these, based upon the error criteria, is then used in the final fuzzy controller.

Experiments

In the experiments done here, a population of 100 members was maintained in each new generation. The members of a given generation were ranked using a cost or error function as follows:

$$Er - \sum_{j-1}^{N_{runs}} \left(x_{end_j}^2 + 0.1\, \alpha_{end_j}^2 \right) + \sum_{j-1}^{N_{runs}} D_j \qquad (2)$$

where N_{runs} is the total numbers of trial runs make on a member of the population, x_{end} and α_{end} are the ending positions of the truck, and the driving distance D_j is a measure of how far the truck travels as it approaches the ramp. A particular run was terminated when the position error (the term within the first summation) became less than unity. From Equation 2, it can be seen that the genetic algorithm attempted to align the truck directly in front of the ramp, keeping the driving distance to a minimum.

The cost function was totaled for selected starting points of the truck. For the training process, it was logical to choose values of input variables which correspond to the center values of membership functions. Using the inputs x and α, a training set of 5 * 7 = 35 possible starting points were selected. Because each starting point corresponded to the center of a membership function, initially only one fuzzy rule was applicable. In this way, the rules that started the truck in the correct direction were quickly determined. Each member of the population was ranked using the cost or error function.

After the population of a given generation was ranked, the losers were eliminated and a group of the best individuals were recreated to reestablish a population of 100 members. Several cases were tested; one group that recreated the top 10% of the original population; in another group, 20%. These then became the parents of the next generation.

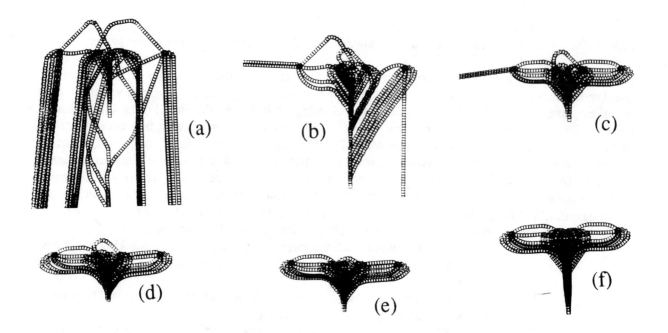

Figure 2.   Paths of the truck as the genetic algorithm converges. The truck starts at 35 different positions. In this test, 10% of a population is retained, with 300 mutations in each generation. Shown are the paths of the best member of the initial population(a) and then after 10(b), 20(c), 30(d) and 40(e) generations. Also shown (in (f)) is the solution from [8].

This new population was further altered by randomly crossing over (exchanging) one half of the rules between members of the population. A total of 150 such exchanges were made. Then, a given numbers of the individual rules were randomly changed one position in the membership function to add further mutations in the new population. This number varied, in various experiments, from 100 to 3000 to investigate the effect on the convergence of the genetic algorithm.

Many different tests were run. In each, the same original population was passed through the genetic algorithm, with only different number of children retained after each generation, and different number of mutations within each population. The algorithm was allowed to run for 200 generations.

Discussion of results

All of the tests produced sets of fuzzy rules that did guide the truck to the ramp, although some of the paths were certainly not the most direct. A plot of the best set of rules after 0, 10, 20, 30, and 40 generations for the best of these are shown in Figure 2. In this case, 10 members of the population were used in recreation, and 300 individual rules were mutated in each new generation. After about 40 generations, the error did not drop significantly and the algorithm was for all practical purposes converged. For comparison, the paths for the truck when the fuzzy rules are designed by an expert [8] are also shown in Figure 2(f).

Figures 3 and 4 show the error of the best fuzzy sets after each generation. The algorithm seems to converge rather slowly, reaching a steady-state error after 40 generations. The best solutions for all eight tests after the algorithm reached its' 200th generation are shown in Figures 5 and 6. It can be seen that in most cases, the genetic algorithm can find a solution to this fuzzy controller problem.

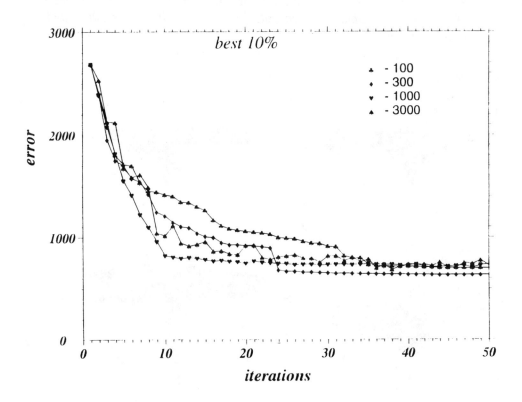

Figure 3.   *Error function of the population for passes through the genetic algorithm. In these tests, 10% of a given population is retained, with 100, 300, 1000, and 3000 random mutations given to each generation.*

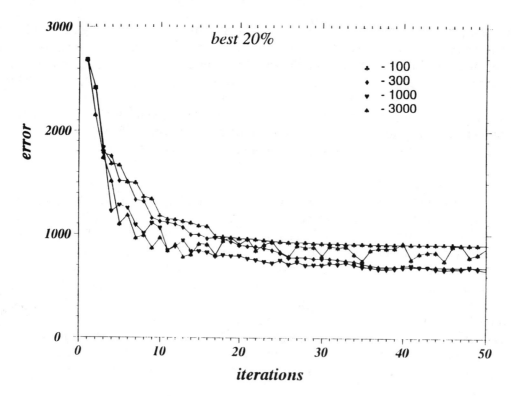

Figure 4. *Error function of the population for passes through the genetic algorithm. In these tests, 20% of a given population is retained, with 100, 300, 1000, and 3000 random mutations given to each generation.*

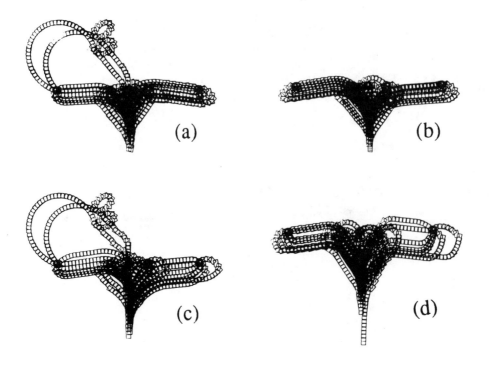

Figure 5. *Paths of the truck for the best member of the 200th generation through the genetic algorithm. In these tests, 10% of a given population is retained, with 100(a), 300(b), 1000(c), and 3000(d) random mutations given to each generation.*

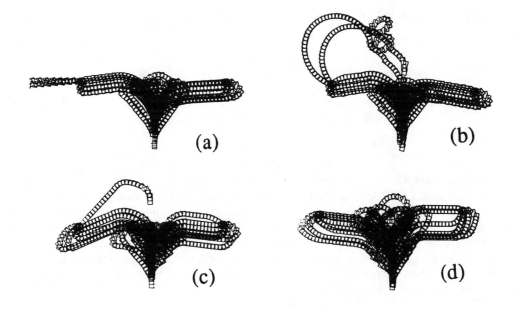

Figure 6.   *Paths of the truck for the best member of the 200th generation through the genetic algorithm. In these tests, 20% of a given population is retained, with 100(a), 300(b), 1000(c), and 3000(d) random mutations given to each generation.*

Conclusion

It has been shown that the genetic algorithm can be used successfully for automatic rule finding in fuzzy systems. It was found from experiment that each time a good solution was found, but not the necessarily the best one. Apparently, the algorithm converges to local minimas not far from the global minimum. A disadvantage of the algorithm was that relatively long time was required for convergency.

References

1.   J. Bezdek, "Fuzzy models - What are they, and Why," *IEEE Trans. on Fuzzy Systems*, vol. 1, pp. 1-6, Feb. 1993.

2.   M. Sugeno, T. Yasukawa, "A fuzzy-logic-based approach to qualitative modeling," *IEEE Trans. on Fuzzy Systems*, vol. 1, pp. 7-31, Feb. 1993.

3.   S. Horikawa, T. Furuhashi, Y. Usikawa, "On fuzzy modeling using fuzzy neural network with the back-propagation algorithm," *IEEE Trans. on Neural Networks* vol. 3, pp. 801-806, Sept. 1992.

4.   D. B. Hertz, Q. Hu, "Fuzzy-neuro controller for backpropagation networks," *Proceedings of WNN 92*, pp 474-478, Auburn, AL, Feb. 10-12, 1992.

5.   J. R. Jang, "Self-learning fuzzy controllers based on temporal back propagation," *IEEE Trans. on Neural Networks* vol. 3, pp. 714-723, Sept. 1992.

6.   L. X. Wang, J. M. Mendel, "Fuzzy basis function, universal approximation, and orthogonal least-squares learning," *IEEE Trans. on Neural Networks*, vol. 3, pp. 807-814, Sept. 1992.

7.   B. M. Wilamowski, R. S. Sandige, "Trainable Fuzzy Controller", presented at *ANNIE'93 - Artificial Neural Networks in Engineering*, St. Louis, Missouri, November 14-17, 1993; also *Intelligent Engineering System Through Artificial Neural Networks*, ASME Pres, vol 3, pp. 561-566.

8.   S. Kong, B. Kosko, "Adaptive fuzzy system for backing up a truck-and-trailer," *IEEE Trans. on Neural Networks*, vol. 3, pp. 211-223, March 1992.

9.   David Goldberg, *Genetic Algorithms in Search, Optimization, and Machine Learning*, Addison-Wesley, 1989.

A SELF-LEARNING FUZZY INFERENCE SYSTEM

R. J. KUO

Department of Industrial and Management Systems Engineering
The Pennsylvania State University
207 Hammond Building, University Park, PA 16802, U.S.A.
Phone: (814)8633909 E-mail: RENK@ECL.PSU.EDU

ABSTRACT

In this paper, we propose a novel learning method, self-learning fuzzy modeling (SLFM), for inference rules. Basically, the input data should be divided into several groups in advance. Then, Gaussian distribution function is employed as the standard form of the membership function. Methods of statistics are used to determine the center and width of the membership function for each group. Regarding the consequences, the linear regression method is used. After the above procedures, we can decide the initial parameters of fuzzy system. Then, the error backpropagation-type learning method is used to fine-tune the parameters. An example system is identified as fuzzy inference rules. The simulation results show that the proposed method is better than the conventional artificial neural networks in both accuracy and speed.

1 INTRODUCTION

Artificial neural networks (ANNs), fuzzy logic, and genetic algorithm are three independent researches regarding sixth generation systems. In this paper, the author would like to propose a method which shows the fusion between ANNs and fuzzy logic. The basic idea of this method is to apply the learning capability of ANNs to improve the performance of fuzzy logic which has been widely applied in many areas, such as control. Applying fuzzy logic to improve the training speed of error backpropagation (EBP) learning algorithm can be found in [Kuo 1993].

Applying ANN's learning algorithm to improve the performance of the fuzzy system is very new and promising research. Lately, Takagi et al. [1991] introduced feedforward ANN into fuzzy inference. Each rule is represented by an ANN while all the membership functions are represented by only one ANN. The algorithm is divided into three major parts: (1) the partition of inference rules; (2) the identification of IF parts; and (3) the identification of THEN parts. Since each rule and all the membership functions are represented by the different ANNs, they are trained separately. In other words, the parameters can not be updated concurrently. Jang [1992], Wang et al. [1992], Shibata et al. [1992], Nakayama et al. [1992], and Fukuda et al. [1992] also presented the similar methods.

Though there already has been some literature reported to apply ANNs to fuzzy systems just as mentioned above, none of them can successfully solve two main problems of fuzzy systems at the same time. One is the lack of design for a membership function and the other is the lack of adaptability for possible changes in the reasoning environment. The reason is that some of them only concern the second problem, the others concern the both problems but the parameter learning for each problem is independent. Therefore, in the following section, a novel architecture, the self-learning fuzzy modeling (SLFM), is proposed to solve the above two serious problems concurrently.

2 METHODOLOGY

In this section, we would like to propose a method, the self-learning fuzzy modeling (SLFM) to solve the above two mentioned problems. Basically, SLFM will determine a decision making action by using ANNs which implement fuzzy system. Such an architecture is able to determine the inference rules by using the real data without the experts' knowledge.

In order to decide the shapes and positions of the membership functions, the training data should be divided into several groups in advance. Several different membership functions can be chosen for such domain. In this research, Gaussian distribution function is used. Thus two parameters, center and width, of Gaussian function should be determined. For each group, or rule, the Euclidean distances E between the training data and the desired center is minimized in order to determine the center of the group. The width of the group is then determined by the method of statistics. The consequence, which is the control action of each inference rule, is determined for each group, or rule, by using the linear regression method.

After the above procedures, we can obtain the initial parameters for SLFM. The basic idea of SLFM is to employ the learning capability of ANNs to update the parameters, which have already been predetermined, of fuzzy system. Because of this purpose, the fuzzy system should be represented as the form of ANN. Before discussing the proposed architecture, the used fuzzy system, based on Takagi's method [1983], is discussed first.

2.1 Takagi's Fuzzy System

In order to clearly explain Takagi's system, a simple example is used in the following. For instance, two rules are illustrated below.

> *Rule 1 : IF X is Small(A1) and Y is Small(B1)*
> *THEN Z is $f_1 = a_{11}x + a_{12}y + b_1$.*
> *Rule 2 : IF X is Large(A2) and Y is Large(B2)*
> *THEN Z is $f_2 = a_{21}x + a_{22}y + b_2$.*

It is assumed that the membership functions for X and Y have been determined. Each rule has a premise, or IF, part which contains several preconditions. The number of preconditions is corresponding to the number of the inputs. And a consequent, or THEN, part which describes the value of one or more output actions. Now suppose there are two inputs, x and y, for fuzzy variables X and Y, respectively. Then the truth values are represented as $\mu_{A1}(x)$ and $\mu_{B1}(y)$ for rule 1 where μ_{A1} and μ_{B1} represent the membership function for A_1 and B_1, respectively. Similarly for rule 2, we have $\mu_{A2}(x)$ and $\mu_{B2}(y)$ as the truth values. Hence the firing strength of rule 1 is obtained as $w_1 = \mu_{A1}(x)\mu_{B1}(y)$ and $w_2 = \mu_{A2}(x)\mu_{B2}(y)$.

The overall output O is determine by using centroid defuzzification where

$$O = \frac{\sum_i w_i f_i}{\sum_i w_i} = \frac{x_1 \times y_2 \times f_1 + x_2 \times y_1 \times f_2}{x_1 \times y_2 + x_2 \times y_1} \tag{1}$$

and f_i is the consequence, or control action, value of rule i.

2.2 Self-Learning Fuzzy Modeling (SLFM)

Based on the above fuzzy system the corresponding ANN structure can be represented. The proposed fuzzy ANN, which is shown in Figure 1, consists of five layers.

a. Layer 1

Layer 1 is the input layer which consists of the real-valued input variables.

b. Layer 2

Every node in this layer is the value of the membership function:

$$\mu_A(x) = e^{-\frac{1}{2}(\frac{x-c}{\sigma})^2} \tag{2}$$

where x is the input variable and c and σ are the parameters. A is the linguistic term. Just as mentioned, the shape and position of membership function will change while any of c or σ are changed.

c. Layer 3

Every node in this layer possesses the capability of multiplication. It is equivalent to the meaning of the firing strength in fuzzy system.

d. Layer 4

This layer calculates the ith firing strength proportional to the sum of all the firing strengths.

e. Layer 5
This is the output layer which combines all the control action values from all the inference rules.

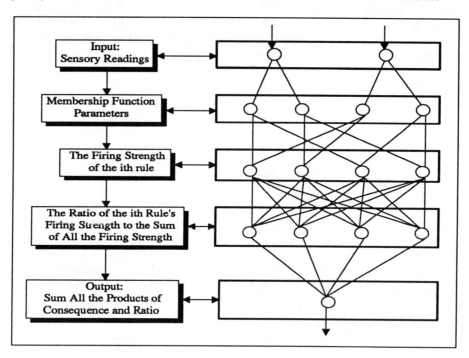

Figure 1. Self-learning fuzzy modeling (SLFM) structure.

All the weights connecting two nodes are 1 except the weights between layer 4 and 5. They are control actions for each rule which is denoted as f_i,

$$f_i = (\sum_j a_{i,j} x_j) + b_i \qquad (3)$$

where j is number of input and a_{ij} and b_i are the parameters. The proposed learning algorithm for fuzzy system is trained by using the EBP-type algorithm. Since the structure is much different from the standard EBP, the modification should be make. In order to clearly describe the learning algorithm, the variables used are defined in the following in advance.

Nomenclature
e   = the example number
μ_{ij}^e = the ijth membership function value for example e.
c_{ij} = the center of the ijth membership function.
σ_{ij} = the variance or width of the ijth membership function.
$w_{[j]}^e$ = the intersection of the membership function values for rule [j], example e.
n   = the number of the input variables.
m   = the number of the categories of each input variable.
ζ^e = the desired output for example e.
$f_{[j]}^e$ = the firing strength of rule [j] for example e.
$a_{[j],i}$ = the coefficient of input x_i.
$b_{[j]}$ = the coefficient of input rule j.
x_i^e = the ith input of example e.
E   = the cost function.
O^e = the actual output of example e.

η = the training rate.

The fuzzy system, in the form of ANN, can be derived from the following equations:

$$\mu_{i,j}^{e} = e^{-\frac{1}{2}(\frac{x_i^e - c_{i,j}}{\sigma_{i,j}})^2} \tag{4}$$

$$w_{[j]}^{e} = \prod_{i=1, j \in [1,m]}^{i=n} \mu_{i,j}^{e} \tag{5}$$

$$O^e = \frac{\sum_{[j]} w_{[j]}^{e} f_{[j]}^{e}}{\sum_{[j]} w_{[j]}^{e}} \tag{6}$$

$$f_{[j]}^{e} = (\sum_i a_{[j],i} x_i^e) + b_{[j]} \tag{7}$$

Since the EBP-type algorithm is employed to self-learning the parameters, the inference rules are updated so as to minimize the cost function E which is defined as:

$$E = \frac{1}{2} \sum_e (\zeta^e - O^e)^2 \tag{8}$$

where e is the training example number. Each parameter of control action function is updated by an amount proportional to the partial derivative of E with respect to that parameter. For the layer 4-to-output parameter a_{ij}, the gradient descent rule gives:

$$\Delta a_{[j],i} = -\eta \frac{\partial E}{\partial a_{[j],i}} = \eta(\zeta^e - O^e) \frac{w_{[j]}^{e}}{\sum_{[j]} w_{[j]}^{e}} x_i^e \tag{9}$$

For parameter b_j, the gradient descent rule gives:

$$\Delta b_{[j]} = -\eta \frac{\partial E}{\partial b_{[j]}} = \eta(\zeta^e - O^e) \frac{w_{[j]}^{e}}{\sum_{[j]} w_{[j]}^{e}} \tag{10}$$

For the layer 2, the scaled Gaussian function parameters are updated by an amount portional to the partial derivative of E with respect to that parameter. For c_{ij}, the gradient descent rule gives:

$$\Delta c_{i,j} = -\eta \frac{\partial E}{\partial c_{i,j}} = \eta \sum_{\mu_{i,j}^{e} \in w_{[j]}^{e}} (\zeta^e - O^e) \frac{w_{[j]}^{e}}{\sum_{[j]} w_{[j]}^{e}} (f_{[j]}^{e} - O^e)(\frac{x_i^e - c_{i,j}}{\sigma_{i,j}^2}) \tag{11}$$

For σ_{ij}, the gradient descent rule gives:

$$\Delta \sigma_{i,j} = -\eta \frac{\partial E}{\partial \sigma_{i,j}} = \eta \sum_{\mu_{i,j}^{e} \in w_{[j]}^{e}} (\zeta^e - O^e) \frac{w_{[j]}^{e}}{\sum_{[j]} w_{[j]}^{e}} (f_{[j]}^{e} - O^e)(\frac{(x_i^e - c_{i,j})^2}{\sigma_{i,j}^3}) \tag{12}$$

The update learning rule is of the form

$$w_{i,j}^{(t+1)} = w_{i,j}^{(t)} - \eta \frac{\partial E}{\partial w_{i,j}} \tag{13}$$

where w_{ij} is the changed parameter.

3 SIMULATION RESULTS

In order to demonstrate the validity of the proposed method, an example system is identified as fuzzy inference rules. The input and output data are shown in Figure 2. Totally, there are 30 input-output pairs. The system has one input and one output. Basically, the input and output variables are normalized within [0, 1]. The membership functions before and after fine-tuning for each rule are shown in Figure 3. In order to really show the advantages of the proposed method, only three membership functions are used for input variables. Therefore, only three inference rules are used in this case. The fine-tuning stops the learning when the inference error E for the identification data is less than 0.03. The comparison between conventional ANN and the proposed method is shown in Table 1, which shows that the inference error obtained from the proposed method is less than error obtained by the conventional ANN. Moreover, SLFM can learn in a substantially shorter period than the conventional ANNs. The control actions for three rules are shown in Appendix.

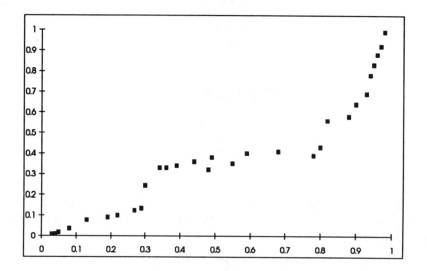

Figure 2. Simulation data.

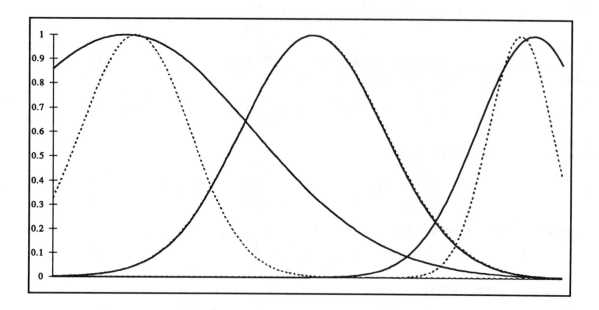

Figure 3. Membership functions before and after fine-tuning, where dash line represents the membership functions before fine-tuning and solid line represents the membership functions after fine-tuning.

4 CONCLUSIONS

A learning method, SLFM of fuzzy inference rules is proposed. The parameters in both the antecedent part and the consequent part can be fine-tuned simultaneously. The simulation results also show that SLFM has the high-speed learning capability, generalization capability, and capability to express acquired knowledge. In the future, SLFM will be applied in multi-sensor integration for tool wear monitoring.

	Table 1. Comparison between ANN and SLFM.	
	ANN	SLFM
Error	0.184	0.03
Iteration	3000	56

APPENDIX

Rules Before Learning
Rule 1: IF x is small THEN y = 0.62x - 0.0159
Rule 2: IF x is medium THEN y = 0.177x + 0.271
Rule 3: IF x is large THEN y = 2.73x - 1.76

Rules After Learning
Rule 1: IF x is small THEN y = 0.63x - 0.028
Rule 2: IF x is medium THEN y = 0.202 + 0.303
Rule 3: IF x is large THEN y = 2.769x - 1.781

REFERENCES

Fukuda, T. and Shibata, T., "Hierarchical Intelligent Control for Robotic Motion by Using Fuzzy, Artificial Intelligence, and Neural Network," *Proc. of IJCNN'92*, pp. I-269-I-274.

Jang, J.-S. R., "Fuzzy Controller Design without Domain Expert," *IEEE International Conference on Fuzzy Systems*, 289-296, 1992.

Kuo, R. J., Chen, Y. T., Cohen, P. H., and Kumara, S., "Fast Convergence of Error Backpropagation Algorithm through Fuzzy Modeling," *Proc. of ANNIE'93*, pp. 239-244.

Nakayama, S. Horikawa, S., Furuhashi, T., and Uchikawa, Y., "Knowledge Acquisition of Strategy and Tactics Using Fuzzy Neural Networks," *Proc. of IJCNN'92*, pp. II-751-II-756.

Shibata, T., Fukuda, T., Kosuge, K., and Arai, F., "Skill Based Control by Using Fuzzy Neural Network for Hierarchical Intelligent Control," *Proc. of IJCNN'92*, pp. II-81-II-86.

Takagi, T. and Sugeno, M. "Derivation of Fuzzy Control Rules from Human Operator's Control Actions," *Proc. of the IFAC Symposium on Fuzzy Information, Knowledge Representation and Decision Analysis*, pp. 55-60, Marseilles, France, July 1983.

Takagi, H. and Hayashi, I., "NN-Driven Fuzzy Reasoning," *International Journal of Approximate Reasoning* 5, pp. 191-212, 1991.

Wang, L.-X. and Mendel, J. M., " Back-Propagation Fuzzy System as Nonlinear Dynamic System Identifiers," *IEEE International Conference on Fuzzy Systems*, pp. 1409-1418, 1992.

Fuzzy Functional-Link Net for Seismic Trace Editing

Kou-Yuan Huang
Institute of Computer and Information Science
National Chiao Tung University
Hsinchu, Taiwan, R.O.C

Abstract

A higher-order neural net incorporated with fuzzy concept in learning procedure is proposed. This net is called fuzzy functional-link net. Fuzzy functional-link net is applied to the seismic trace editing to determine the good or bad recording. Perceptron with pocket learning algorithm and multi-layer perceptron are also applied to the seismic trace editing. Compared with the classification results, fuzzy functional-link net has good performance in learning time and recognition rate.

Introduction

The widely used model of neural network for seismic pattern recognition in seismic trace editing is the back-propagation learning model [1, 2, 3]. But there are two major drawbacks of back-propagation learning model: one is that the training time is sometimes too long to accept, the other is that it can not assure a successful learning due to the local minimum problem.

In this paper, we propose the fuzzy functional-link net to seismic trace editing to determine the good or bad recording in seismic traces. Since patterns with higher-order terms contain more separable power than original patterns do, we can expect that higher-order neural network can give better recognition rate. Next, we propose the learning algorithm by using the fuzzy weights in perceptron learning algorithm. The adjusted fuzzy weights can reduce the influence of the uncertain patterns in adjusting the decision boundary.

Learning Algorithm of Fuzzy Functional-Link Net

Functional-link net was mentioned by Pao [4]. It is a single-layer perceptron and a higher-order neural network. Here, we use the tensor form (outerproduct form) to be the higher-order term. Before presented to functional-link net, the original pattern must be enhanced to tensor form. By training with tensor form, the functional-link net can solve some nonlinear separable problem such as XOR problem. Here, the tensor form of a set of components $\{x_i\}$ would be $\{x_i, x_i x_j \ (j > i)\}$.

Keller [5] proposed a fuzzy weights updated rule which can be incorporated into perceptron-based learning algorithm. Such a rule can reduce the influence of the uncertain training patterns in adjusting the linear decision boundary. We try to incorporate fuzzy set theory into learning algorithm of the functional-link net.

Learning Algorithm of Fuzzy Functional-Link Net

Input: Given a set of P training patterns. Each pattern belongs to class A or class B. Two classes are linear separable.

Output: A linear decision boundary.

Methods:

> **Step 1. Enhance the original features to higher-order terms for all training patterns. New pattern vector has form $X = [x_1, x_2, ..., x_{N'}]^t$.**

Step 2. Initialize weights and threshold

Set $w_i(0)$ $(1 \leq i \leq N')$ and θ $(= w_{N'+1})$ to small random values. Here $w_i(t)$ is the weight from input i at step t and θ is the adaptive threshold. N' is the number of features in tensor form. Set K, η, and m.

Step 3. Present new input and its desired output

Present new input pattern vector X and its desired output d.

Step 4. Calculate the membership degree of each pattern X in each classe

If X belongs to class A, then

$$\mu_1(t) = 0.51 + (n_1/K) * 0.49$$
$$\mu_2(t) = (n_2/K) * 0.49$$

else (i.e. X belongs to class B)

$$\mu_1(t) = (n_1/K) * 0.49$$
$$\mu_2(t) = 0.51 + (n_2/K) * 0.49$$

where n_1 is the number of nearest neighbors of input pattern X in class A, n_2 is the number of nearest neighbors of X in class B. Note that $n_1 + n_2 = K$ and $1 \leq K \leq P$.

Step 5. Calculate actual output

$$y(t) = f_h \left(\sum_{i=1}^{N'} w_i(t) \, x_i - w_{N'+1}(t) \right)$$

where $f_h( )$ is the hard-limiting function.

Step 6. Adapt weights incorporated with fuzzy membership degree.

$$w_i(t + 1) = w_i(t) + \eta \, |\mu_1(t) - \mu_2(t)|^m \, [d(t) - y(t)] \, x_i$$

$$1 \leq i \leq N' + 1$$

$$d(t) = \begin{cases} +1, & \text{if input is from class A} \\ -1, & \text{if input is from class B} \end{cases}$$

Step 7. Repeat by going to Step 3.

Application to Seismic Trace Editing

Four features of each seismic trace are generated as follows. Assume that each seismic trace is the current time function $f^{(i)}(t)$, where i is the index of the seismic trace.

(1) Average trace frequency $F^{(i)}$:

If the sample number of a trace is $S^{(i)}$, and the number of peaks in a trace is $N^{(i)}$, then

$$F^{(i)} = N^{(i)}/S^{(i)} \tag{2}$$

(2) Sum of absolute amplitude $A^{(i)}$:

$$A^{(i)} = \sum_{j=1}^{S^{(i)}} \left| f_j^{(i)} \right| \tag{3}$$

(3) Average trace power $P^{(i)}$:

$$P^{(i)} = (1/S(i)) \sum_{j=1}^{S(i)} (f_j^{(i)})^2 \tag{4}$$

(4) Maximal crosscorrelation $C^{(i)}$ with two adjacent seismic traces:

$$C^{(i)} = \max\left(\int f^{(i)}(\tau)\, f^{(i-1)}(\tau - t)\, d\tau, \int f^{(i)}(\tau)\, f^{(i+1)}(\tau - t)\, d\tau \right) \tag{5}$$

where $f^{(i-1)}(t)$ and $f^{(i+1)}(t)$ (if $i-1$ or $i+1$ exists) are time functions of two adjacent seismic traces.

Experiments of determining the good or bad seismic trace recording are implemented by the perceptron with pocket learning algorithm [6], the fuzzy functional-link net, and two-layer perceptron here. Four features are generated from each seismic trace and enhanced to the two feature product terms. So there are 10 input nodes. For the two-layer perceptron, the network is 10(input nodes)-5(hidden nodes)-1(output node).

In training phase, several good recording seismic traces are selected as training traces. Three networks are adopted in the trainig first, and then the whole seismic traces are tested.

Process of Seismic Trace Editing by the Neural Network
Input: Seismogram
Output: Classification result to indicate that each seismic trace output is accepted (good recording trace) or rejected (bad recording trace).
Methods:
   Step 1. Present one neural network model which has been trained.
   Step 2. Present a new trace.
       Calculate four features of the input trace and enhance to the two feature product terms. Total input nodes are 10 terms.
   Step 3. Calculate actual output y and assign to the class.
   Step 4. Repeat by going to step 2.

Now, we select trace number 3, 4, 5, 6, 21, 22 from Figure 1 as the training traces of the good recording, and select 11, 12, 13, 14, 17, and 18 as the training traces of the bad recording. Note that the trace number from 1 to 10 and 21 to 32 are good traces. After training, all traces are tested to acquire the number of correct classification by the above three models. Finally, we list the correct rates of each model in Table 1. We also find that the training time of fuzzy functional-link net runs in PC 486 are less than 4 seconds, and two-layer perceptron with back-propagation training needs over 5 minutes. Compared with the classification results, fuzzy functional-link net has better performance in learning time and recognition rate.

Neural Network Models	Perceptron with Pocket Algorithm	Fuzzy Functional-Link Net	Two-layer Perceptron
Correct Recognition Rate	96.88%	100%	100%

Table. 1 Correct recognition rate of each model.

Conclusions

The fuzzy functional-link net is proposed and applied to the seismic trace editing. The performance is good in recognition rate and learning time. The fuzzy neural networks may apply to other problems of the seismic pattern recognition.

References

[1]. M. D. McCormack, D. E. Zaucha, and D. W. Dushek, "First-Break Refraction Event Picking and Seismic Data Trace Editing Using Neural Networks", Geophysics, Vol. 58, no. 1, pp. 67-78, January 1993.

[2]. J. Veezhinathan and D. Wagner, "A Neural Network Approach to First Arrival Picking", IJCNN, Vol. 1, pp. 235-240, 1990.

[3]. J. Veezhinathan, D. Wagner and J. Ehlers, "First Break Picking Using a Neural Network", In Expert Systems in Exploration, ed. Fred Aminzadeh and Marwan Simaan, pp. 179-202, SEG, 1991.

[4]. Yoh-Han Pao , Adaptive Pattern Recognition and Neural Networks, Addison-Wesley, 1989.

[5]. J. M. Keller, D. J. Hunt, " Incorporating Fuzzy Membership Functions into the Perceptron Algorithm", IEEE Trans. Pattern Anal. Machine Intell., Vol. PAMI-7, no. 6, pp. 693-699, November 1985.

[6]. Gallant S.I., "Perceptron-Based Learning Algorithms", IEEE Trans. Neural Networks, Vol. 1, no. 2, pp. 179-191, June 1990.

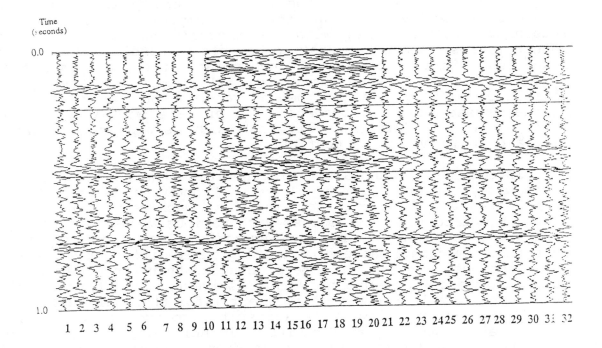

Fig. 1 Seismogram for seismic trace editing.

A REAL-TIME NEAR NEIGHBOR TYPE FUZZY PATTERN RECOGNITION NEURAL NETWORK

M. E. Ulug

Intelligent Neurons Inc., 1537 E. Hillsboro Blvd., #342
Deerfield Beach, Florida 33441

ABSTRACT

This paper describes a PC-based real-time neural network for fuzzy pattern recognition. A near neighbor type architecture is used. The training consists of a set of computations. Hence the number of cycles is zero. It is a single layer network that uses seven π functions for input fuzzification. For output fuzzification parametric representation is used . A user can select granularity by choosing a 5, 9 or 13 element term set. The numerical data about the membership function is also supplied. Two fuzzy pattern recognition systems that we built are discussed.

1. INTRODUCTION

It is well known that the pattern recognition problems are solved more easily by humans than by computers. Yet the human reasoning involves dealing with many imprecisions, ambiguities, and uncertainties. For a computer to be able to handle uncertain data like humans it is necessary to incorporate into the system design fuzzy set theory [8] and fuzzy logic [1]. Many patterns used in pattern recognition systems belong to more than one class with a finite degree of belongingness [4], or have widely overlapping regions [7]. In addition, their input signals may possess features with a certain degree of confidence.

In the past decade artificial neural networks have been used to classify patterns in many fields. However, problems have been encountered in Intelligent Systems, e.g., machine vision platforms that attempt to interpret scenes with various kinds of sensors and contextual information, by the incorrect classification of test patterns. Imagine a pattern indicating three different signatures. The first one, however, is more pronounced than the other two. In such a case a crisp neural network will identify the first signature because it achieved the minimum error for this particular class and ignore the other two. As a result, the expert system of the Intelligent System may either fail to identify or wrongly interpret the situation and make the wrong decision. The use of fuzzy rather than crisp classification can avoid these problems.

2. ARCHITECTURE OF FUZZY NEURAL NETWORK

The training times of fuzzy neural networks using the backpropagation learning rule are exceptionally slow. Moreover, convergence of the network cannot always be guaranteed. This is due to the fact that the target values represent the membership values of the training samples. Therefore, they are dynamic. For this reason the use of PC-based fuzzy near neighbor [3] networks, or for short FN[4], shows great promise for small to medium size applications. This is because the training consists of a set of computations and involves zero number of cycles. For large applications the training/computation for each output node/class can be done on a separate microprocessor mounted on a PC-based accelerator card. Therefore, the real-time training capability a FN[4] can be maintained for large systems by training the output nodes in parallel. In Figure 1 We show the architecture of FN[4].

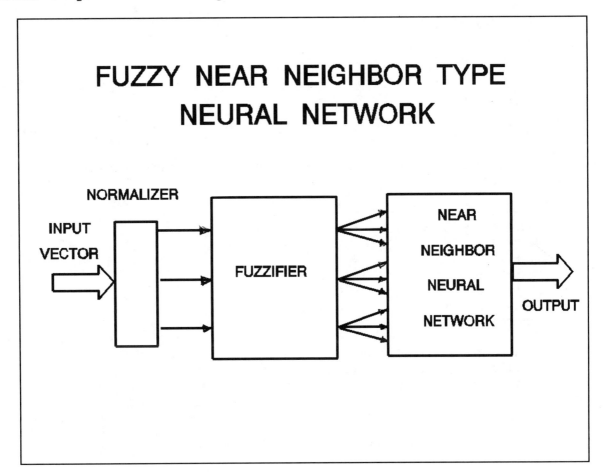

Figure 1

As shown we use a normalizer and a π fuzzifier before the FN[4].

2.1. Fuzzification of Input Signals:

For the fuzification of input signals we used the following technique in our software system:

(i) we normalized the input signals, and

(ii) we placed seven π functions at the entrance to the ONN.

Our π functions were given by the following equations [5]:

x = distance from origin
c = center of the π function
r = radius of the π function

for r/2<= |x-c| <= r

$$\pi = (x;c;r) = 2(1 - \frac{|x-c|}{r})^2 \qquad \textbf{(1)}$$

for 0.0<= |x-c| <= r/2

$$\pi(x;c;r) = 1 - 2(\frac{|x-c|}{r})^2 \qquad \textbf{(2)}$$

Otherwise

$$\pi = (x;c;r) = 0.0 \qquad \textbf{(3)}$$

After normalizing the input signal, we placed the medians of our π functions as follows:

```
Extremely low  (EL)      = 0.125
Very low  (VL)           = 0.250
Low  (L)                 = 0.375
Midpoint  (M)            = 0.5
High  (H)                = 0.625
Very high  (VH)          = 0.750
Extremely high  (EH)     = 0.875
```

The advantage of this approach is that as long as the input signals are normalized these π functions can be used in all applications. For this normalization process we determine the minimum and the maximum values of the input signals. We then subtract from each signal the minimum value. After that divide them with the difference between the maximum and the minimum values. This process makes the minimum value zero and the maximum value one.

2.2. Fuzzification of the Output Signals:

For the fuzzification of the output signals we used the triangular norms and conorms of Schweizer and Sklar [6] to handle conjunctions and disjunctions [2],[8] respectively. A user could choose the uncertainty granularity by selecting a 5, 9, or 13 element term set. Below we show the a, b, c, and d parameters of a 5 element term sets. In this representation we have: un[*][1]=a, un[*][2]=b un[*][3]=c, un[*][4]=d, and me[*] = median of the membership function, where * is the number of the term set, i.e., for a five element term set we have the following notation:

1 = impossible, 2 = unlikely, 3 = maybe, 4 = likely, 5 = certain.

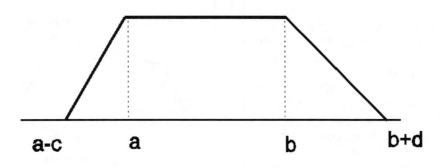

PARAMETRIC REPRESENTATION OF A MEMBERSHIP FUNCTION

a-c   a   b   b+d

Figure 2

IMPOSSIBLE
un[1][1]=0;
un[1][2]=0;
un[1][3]=0;
un[1][4]=0;
me[1]=0;

UNLIKELY
un[2][1]=0.01;
un[2][2]=0.25;
un[2][3]=0.01;
un[2][4]=0.10;
me[2]=0.1532;

MAYBE
un[3][1]=0.40;
un[3][2]=0.60;
un[3][3]=0.10;
un[3][4]=0.10;
me[3]=0.5;

LIKELY
un[4][1]=0.75;
un[4][2]=0.99;
un[4][3]=0.10;
un[4][4]=0.01;
me[4]=0.8467;

CERTAIN
un[5][1]=1;
un[5][2]=1;
un[5][3]=0;
un[5][4]=0;
me[5]=1;

3. OPERATION OF FN[4]

The membership function for the input vector of the pattern i, x_i, is calculated using the following equation which is a simplified version of the equation introduced by S.K. Pal [4]:

$$\mu(\boldsymbol{x_1}) = \cfrac{1}{1 + \sqrt{\sum_{j=1}^{n} [x_{ij} - mean_{kj}]^2}} \quad \textbf{(4)}$$

for k=1, ... ,m and where x_{ij} = j'th component of the i'th sample, $mean_{kj}$ = j'th component of the mean vector of the k'th class,

The calculation of the membership values is shown in Figure 3. We first calculate a mean vector for each class. We then calculate a membership value for all the training samples of all the classes with respect to a given mean vector. We then repeat the process for all the mean vectors. This computation completes the training process. In classification of an unknown sample, we calculated the vectorial differences between the vector representing the sample and all the mean vectors. In Figure 3 we only show two classes. For clarity

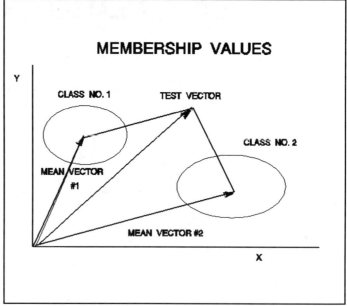

Figure 3

we did not show all the vectors used in training. As can be seen from Equation 4, the membership value of a sample in a class is inversely proportional to the sum of 1 and the vectorial difference between the sample vector and the mean vector of this particular class.

4. APPLICATIONS

We tried our FN[4] on two different applications. The first one used data taken from a map reading neural network. There were seven classes, i.e., output nodes, and 25 samples from each class. Each output node was trained with 7x25=175 samples. The input signals were 27 dimensional vectors. In the second application we used data taken from a curve recognition neural network. There were four classes/output nodes and 5 samples from each class. Each output node was trained with 4x5=25 samples. The input signals were 10 dimensional vectors. The four classes had small areas of overlap. This can be seen by observing the test results on an object from class #1. In this test we used a nine element term set with the following notation Mm = membership value, Md = median of the membership value, and a, b, c, and d are the parameters of the membership function as shown in Figure 2.

Belongingness of Object # 1 to Class # 1 is **CERTAIN**
Mm=1.000000 Md=1.000000 a=1.000000 b=1.000000 c=0.000000 d=0.000000

Belongingness of Object # 1 to Class # 2 is **SMALL CHANCE**
Mm=0.370852 Md=0.292600 a=0.220000 b=0.360000 c=0.050000 d=0.060000

Belongingness of Object # 1 to Class # 3 is **VERY LOW CHANCE**
Mm=0.200000 Md=0.137300 a=0.100000 b=0.180000 c=0.060000 d=0.050000

Belongingness of Object # 1 to Class # 4 is **SMALL CHANCE**
Mm=0.216331 Md=0.292600 a=0.220000 b=0.360000 c=0.050000 d=0.060000

These real-time training and testing results were obtained using a 486 PC. The programs were written in "C" language.

5. CONCLUSIONS

The architecture and operation of a PC-based near neighbor type real-time neural network, FN^4, designed for fuzzy pattern recognition is described. It is shown that π functions and parametric representations are used for input and output fuzzification respectively. It is believed that because of the extreme slowness of fuzzy backpropagation neural networks, the use of FN^4 shows great promise in providing real-time training and testing for small to medium size applications. It is further believed that the real-time training capability of FN^4 can be extended to large systems by training the output nodes in parallel using a PC-based accelerator card.

6. REFERENCES

[1] Bellman R.E. and Zadeh L.A. (1976), "Local and Fuzzy Logic", Mem. No. ERL-M584, University of California, Berkeley.
[2] Bonissone, P.P., Decker, K.S., "Selecting Uncertainty Calculi and Granularity: An Experiment in Trading-off Precision and Complexity," in Uncertainty in Artificial Intelligence, 2217-247, North Holland, 1986.
[3] Reilly D.L., Cooper, L.N., Elbaum, C. (1982), "A neural model category learning," Biol. Cybern. 45, 35-41.
[4] Pal K.S. and Mitra S. (1992), "Multilayer Perceptron, Fuzzy Sets, and Classification", IEEE Transactions on Neural Networks, Vol. 3, No. 5.
[5] Pal K.S., Pramanic, P.K. (1986), "Fuzzy measures determining seed points in clustering," Pattern Recognition Lett., vol. 4, page 159-164.
[6] Schweizer B., Sklar A. (1963), "Associative Functions and Abstract Semi-Groups," Publicatione Mathematicae Debrecen, Vol. 10, pp.69-81.
[7] Ulug, M.E.,"A Single Layer Fuzzy and Fuzzy-Like ANN for Parallel Electro-Optical Implementation," Proceedings of 1993 International Neural Networks Society, WCNN 93, Portland, Oregon. [8] Zadeh L.A. (1965), "Fuzzy Sets", Information and Control, 8, 338-353
[8] Zadeh L.A.(1965), "Fuzzy Sets," Information and Control,8, pp. 338-353.

ACKNOWLEDGMENT

This work was funded by SBIR SDIO Contract No: DASG60-93-C-0095. The author would like to thank Dr. C. McCullough of USASSDC for her helpful suggestions.

CAUSAL STRUCTURE, MODEL INFERENCES, AND FUZZY COGNITIVE MAPS: HELP FOR THE BEHAVIORAL SCIENTIST

Philip Craiger
Navy Personnel Research and Development Center[1]
San Diego , CA

Abstract

A fuzzy cognitive map (FCM) is a heuristic alternative to causal modeling; a graphical means of representing arbitrarily complex causal networks, the implications of which can be calculated via matrix algebra. This paper discusses the use of FCMs for providing *qualitative* causal information in behavioral science research.

I. Causal Modeling in the Behavioral Sciences

One of the most widely used statistical techniques in the behavioral sciences is causal modeling. Causal modeling allows researchers to define and test statistically relationships represented as causal networks among a set of latent variables. The underlying statistical model for this technique is:[5-6]

$$\eta = \beta\eta + \Gamma\xi + \zeta \tag{1}$$

$$x = \Lambda_x \eta + \Theta_\varepsilon \tag{2}$$

$$y = \Lambda_y \xi + \Theta_\delta \tag{3}$$

The *structural* model (Eq. 1) specifies how latent endogenous variables (η), latent exogenous variables (ξ), and errors in equations (ζ) combine to form a causal network. The *measurement* models (Eq. 2 and 3), are confirmatory factor analysis models that partition each measured variable into common (true) variance (η and ξ, modified by factor loadings Λ_x and Λ_y, respectively) and associated error of measurement (θ_ε and θ_δ). Computer software implementing various parameter estimation procedures (commonly maximum likelihood and generalized least squares) allows the specification and testing of the (putatively) causal relationships among the latent variables defined in a causal model.

II. Limitations of Causal Modeling

A contributing factor to the popularity of causal modeling has been its capacity for representing complex networks of relationships. Representing psychological phenomena in terms of *networks* of variables more closely resembles real-world systems. Its use, however, is often problematic. For instance, non-convergence of solutions and impossible parameter estimates, such as negative error variances and standardized correlations greater than unity, are not uncommon, and their occurrence can often be attributed to problems with model identification. *Identification* concerns the question of whether the model and data constraints are sufficient to determine a unique set of parameter estimates.[2] *Empirical* underidentification occurs when the data are such that a unique set of parameter estimates is unobtainable, whereas *theoretical* underidentification occurs when the model specified does not allow for a determination of a unique set of parameter estimates[1]. One cause often associated with underidentification are reciprocal (bi-directional) causal links.[4]

Causal modeling has greatly expanded the potential for studying complex systems of latent variables in the behavioral sciences. Below I describe fuzzy cognitive maps (FCM), an alternative to causal modeling that does not suffer from some of the limitations described

---

1 The views expressed in this paper are those of the author, and are not necessarily official Navy policy.

above.[3] The primary difference between the two techniques is that FCMs (1) provide *qualitative* information regarding model implications, (2) facilitate pattern prediction, as opposed to parameter estimation, and (3) facilitate the modeling of *dynamic* processes. FCMs may be used in conjunction with causal modeling --- as a precursor in the initial modeling building phase --- or in place of causal modeling --- when it is desirable to explore a causal network, but conditions are such that the use of causal modeling is impossible or inappropriate.

III. Fuzzy Cognitive Maps

Developed by Kosko[7-8], a FCM is a graphical means of representing causal knowledge that can be used to evaluate the time-varying effects of patterns of causal connections represented in a model. The "fuzzy" indicates that FCMs are often comprised of concepts that can be represented as *fuzzy sets*. Fuzzy set theory was originally developed by Zadeh as a means of representing and reasoning with vague and ambiguous information.[10] The reader is referred to Zadeh[10] and Kosko[8] for information on fuzzy set theory.

IV. A FCM of Job Turnover

A FCM is comprised of nodes (concepts) and edges (directional arrows). Figure 1 is a FCM representing an elaboration of a model of job turnover[9].

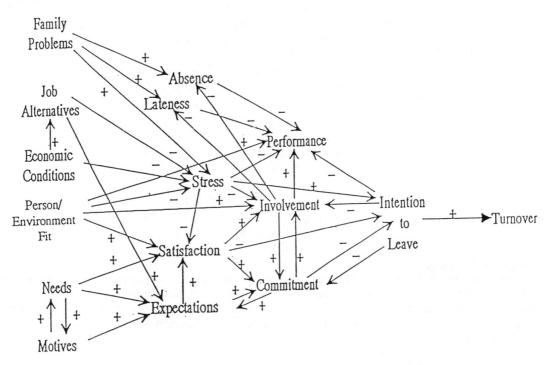

In contrast to causal models, FCMs lack "traditional" statistical parameter estimates; real numbers estimated from sample data that indicate the strength of relationships between concepts. In a FCM causal links take on values in {-1,+1}, where a -1 indicates a negative relation, and +1 a positive relation. Because the causal links are represented as all-or-none relationships, FCMs provide qualitative as opposed to quantitative causal information

V. Causal Network Complexity

Behavioral scientists commonly ignore the global implications of his or her model. Model implications are determined by the *patterns* of the causal links represented in a model. To illustrate a simple case, the necessary implications of the causal network $A{\rightarrow}B{\rightarrow}C$ are that a change in A results in a change in B and a change in C. Now consider the turnover FCM. What are the implications of an increase in person/environment fit? A decrease? What are the implications of increases in stress and commitment, and concomitant decreases in satisfaction and involvement? It is difficult to determine the effects because of the reciprocal causal links and the complexity of the patterns of causal connections, the two ingredients that determine a model's "complexity".[3]

It may be difficult to determine the consequences of the spreading causal activation of complex causal models. In general, there is a negative relationship between the complexity of a causal network and our ability to determine the implications of the model; however, FCMs provide the ability to determine consequences of a causal network regardless of complexity.[8]

VI. Determining Causal Network Implications

In FCM nomenclature, model implications are determined by *clamping* variables and using an iterative vector-matrix multiplication process to assess the effects of these perturbations on the state of the causal network. As such, an analogy can be drawn between clamping nodes and manipulating independent variables in a psychological experiment.

If we designate exogenous (independent) variables as the rows and the endogenous (dependent) variables as the columns, we can transform a FCM into a *connection matrix*. A connection matrix is a specification of the causal links represented in matrix form; a square matrix with the number of cells equal to the number of latent variables squared. Below is the connection matrix for the turnover model.

$$c = \begin{pmatrix}
0 & 0 & 0 & 0 & 0 & 0 & 1 & 1 & 1 & 0 & 0 & 0 & 0 & 0 & 0 & 0 \\
0 & 0 & 0 & 0 & 0 & 0 & 0 & -1 & 0 & 1 & 0 & 0 & 0 & 0 & 0 & 0 \\
0 & 1 & 0 & 0 & 0 & 0 & 0 & -1 & 0 & 0 & 0 & 0 & 0 & 0 & 0 & 0 \\
0 & 0 & 0 & 0 & 0 & 0 & 0 & -1 & 1 & 0 & 1 & 1 & 0 & 0 & 0 & 0 \\
0 & 0 & 0 & 0 & 0 & 1 & 0 & 0 & 0 & 1 & 1 & 0 & 0 & 0 & 0 & 0 \\
0 & 0 & 0 & 0 & 1 & 0 & 0 & 0 & 0 & 0 & 1 & 0 & 0 & 0 & 0 & 0 \\
0 & 0 & 0 & 0 & 0 & 0 & 0 & 0 & -1 & 0 & 0 & 0 & 0 & 0 & 0 & 0 \\
0 & 0 & 0 & 0 & 0 & 0 & 0 & 0 & -1 & 0 & 0 & 0 & 0 & 0 & 0 & 0 \\
0 & 0 & 0 & 0 & 0 & 0 & 0 & 0 & 0 & -1 & 0 & -1 & -1 & 0 & 1 & 0 \\
0 & 0 & 0 & 0 & 0 & 0 & 0 & 0 & 0 & -1 & 0 & 1 & 1 & 1 & -1 & 0 \\
0 & 0 & 0 & 0 & 0 & 0 & 0 & 0 & 0 & -1 & 0 & 0 & 0 & 1 & 0 & 0 \\
0 & 0 & 0 & 0 & 0 & 0 & 0 & 0 & 0 & 0 & 0 & 0 & 0 & 0 & 0 & 0 \\
0 & 0 & 0 & 0 & 0 & 0 & -1 & -1 & 0 & 0 & 0 & 1 & 0 & 0 & 1 & 0 \\
0 & 0 & 0 & 0 & 0 & 0 & 0 & 0 & 0 & 0 & 0 & 0 & 1 & 0 & 1 & 0 \\
0 & 0 & 0 & 0 & 0 & 0 & 0 & 0 & 0 & 0 & 0 & 0 & -1 & -1 & 0 & 1 \\
0 & 0 & 0 & 0 & 0 & 0 & 0 & 0 & 0 & 0 & 0 & 0 & 0 & 0 & 0 & 0
\end{pmatrix}$$

VII. Inference Equation

Say we wish to evaluate the effect of family problems and person/environment fit on the state of our model. That is, in our causal model we posit that family problems exist and there is a positive person/environment fit, and we want to evaluate these effects on the other variables (intention to quit, turnover, satisfaction, and so on). The equation employed in the to ascertain model implications is:

$$I_{[i+1]} = O_{[i]} = \sum_{n=1}^{k} \sum_{m=1}^{k} I_{[m]} C_{[m.n]} \tag{4}$$

I is an input vector of k elements, and C is a connection matrix of order k x k. This equation calculates the inner (dot) product for each variable (column) of the connection matrix. The dot product defines the cosine of the angle between two (normalized) vectors, or in statistical terms, is the correlation between the vectors.

Computed elements of the output vector often lie outside {-1, 1}. We transform the out-of-range output vector elements ($O_{[i]}$) into an acceptable input (bit) vector ($I_{[i+1]}$) using the following transformation rule:

$$I_{[m]} = \begin{cases} -1 & \text{if } x < 0 \\ 0 & \text{if } x = 0 \\ 1 & \text{if } x > 0 \end{cases} \quad (5)$$

Thus, to transform the output vector into an acceptable input (bit) vector we (1) clamp any nodes turned on in the initial input vector, and (2) transform elements outside {-1, 1} into valid vector elements (bits) using the transformation rule (Eq. 5).

VIII. Hidden Patterns = Model Implications

In FCM nomenclature, a model implication or inference is a global stability --- an equilibrium in the state of the system represented as a set or sets of repeated patterns.[8] Repeating patterns can be *hidden patterns* or *limit cycles*. A hidden pattern is a single recurring pattern, such as the *C* in *ABCCCC*..., whereas a limit cycle is a sequence of (multiple) repeating patterns, such as the pattern *BC* in *ABCBCBCBC*... *Hidden patterns and limit cycles are model inferences.* Note that this equilibrium can be likened to the global minima of the maximum likelihood estimation procedure commonly employed in causal modeling. Hidden patterns/ limit cycles and global minima reveal the minimum energy state of the of the system (model).

IX. Vector/Matrix Multiplication = Inference Process

We represent the effect of family problems and person/environment fit by the following bit vector:

$$I_{[1]} = \{1\ 0\ 0\ 1\ 0\ 0\ 0\ 0\ 0\ 0\ 0\ 0\ 0\ 0\ 0\}$$

Each element of the vector represents the state of one of the latent variables in our model. Thus, $I_{[1]} = 1$ indicates that the family problem variable is clamped, $I_{[2]} = 0$ and $I_{[3]} = 0$ indicate that job alternatives and economic conditions are off, $I_{[4]} = 1$ indicates that person/environment fit is clamped, and so on.

We begin the inference process by applying the inference equation (Eq. 4)], resulting in the output vector:

$$O_{[1]} = \{0\ 0\ 0\ 0\ 0\ 0\ 0\ 0\ 0\ 1\ \text{-}1\ 0\ 2\ 1\ 0\}$$

This output vector is interpreted as a "snapshot" of the global state of the causal network after the first iteration; it indicates that the initial effect of person/environment fit and family problem is an increase in expectations, commitment, and intentions to leave, and a decrease in job performance. Note that $I_{[14]} = 2$ is outside {-1, 1}, the range of valid bit values for input vectors. Recall that to transform this output vector into an acceptable input vector, we (1) apply the transformation rule (Eq. 5) to this output vector (affecting $I_{[14]}$ only), and (2) clamp any nodes on in the original input vector (nodes one and four). This results in $I_{[2]}$:

$$I_{[2]} = \{1\ 0\ 0\ 1\ 0\ 0\ 0\ 0\ 1\ \text{-}1\ 0\ 0\ 1\ 1\ 0\}$$

Employing this process for four more iterations results in the following output vectors (model inferences):

$$O_{[2]} = \{0\ 0\ 0\ 0\ 0\ 0\ 0\ 0\ 1\ 0\ 1\ 1\ 0\ \text{-}1\ 0\}$$
$$O_{[3]} = \{0\ 0\ 0\ 0\ 0\ 0\ 0\ 0\ 1\ \text{-}1\ 1\ 1\ 0\ 0\ \text{-}1\}$$
$$O_{[4]} = \{0\ 0\ 0\ 0\ 0\ 0\ 0\ 0\ 1\ 0\ 1\ 1\ 0\ \text{-}1\ 0\}$$
$$O_{[5]} = \{0\ 0\ 0\ 0\ 0\ 0\ 0\ 0\ 1\ \text{-}1\ 1\ 1\ 0\ 0\ \text{-}1\}$$

The process reveals the model's implications on the fifth iteration by the sequence of repeating patterns $O_{[2]}$ ($O_{[4]}$) and $O_{[3]}$ ($O_{[5]}$). This two-stage limit cycle is repeated *ad infinitum*. Note that it took only three iterations for the system to equilibrate. Research indicates that FCMs come quickly to an equilibrium, regardless of the complexity of the model.[8]

The model's implications and inferences are represented in the following two-stage limit cycle:

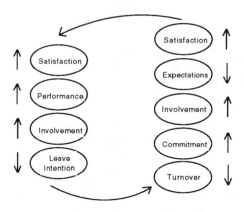

X. Results

The two-stage limit cycle can be interpreted as a reciprocal causal connection between the two sets of latent variables. The result is a more realistic reflection of real-world causal systems than the simple static results representative of causal modeling because the limit cycle implies a *time* component. Thus, unlike causal modeling, FCMs facilitate the modeling of dynamic processes.

Given our model, one would expect that the presence of family problems would have a deleterious effect on job performance (family problems increases absence and lateness, which decrease job performance). The model implications calculated using the inference equation, however, suggests otherwise. Why might this be? One cause appears to be a *blocking* effect. Note that the effect of person/environment fit on job performance is mediated through four variables; satisfaction, involvement, commitment, and stress (and numerous combinations thereof). The effect of family problems on job performance is mediated through absence, lateness, and stress. Note, however, that there is an apparent blocking effect of person/environment fit on absence and lateness through involvement. Thus, although family problems does increase absence and lateness (which decreases performance), person/environment fit has a greater effect on the state of the causal network by virtue of the way we have represented the relationships among the variables. If we had clamped the family problems node *only*, job performance would have decreased; however, clamping both variables results in person/environment fit moderating the effect of family problems on job performance by blocking (reducing) absence and lateness. The blocking effect is not obvious because of the complexity of the causal network. The model implication is that the effect of family problems on job performance is moderated by person/environment fit. Thus, FCMs have the ability of modeling both mediator and moderator effects.

XI. Discussion

FCMs exhibit a number of desirable properties that make it attractive as a supplemental process in model building for behavioral scientists, including:

- providing qualitative information about the (hidden, nonapparent) inferences in complex causal matrices,
- providing a means of quickly mapping out and testing the implications of a model,
- can represent an unlimited number of reciprocal causal links,
- do not require data,
- facilitate "thought experiments" through the interactive manipulation of independent variables and evaluation of concomitant effects,
- relationships need not be linear,

- can model both mediator and moderator relationships,
- it is impervious to problems with empirical or theoretical identification,
- can be easily calculated by hand,
- and facilitates the modeling of dynamic processes.

A limitation of FCMs is that they provide only qualitative information regarding the predictions of emerging patterns; no real-value parameter estimates or statistical tests of significance are available. Thus for the traditional methodologist, FCMs may not be an acceptable alternative. FCMs, however, are ideal for situations where traditional statistical techniques are inappropriate, as when a model is so complex that there are problems with identification (e.g., when too many reciprocal causal links are modeled), when statistical assumptions are severely violated (variables evidence highly skewed and kurtotic distributions), or when data are not available. FCMs should prove useful for all behavioral scientists in regards to prototyping models, and for assessing the global implications of complex causal models.

[1]   Brannick, M. T., & Spector, P. "Estimation Problems in the Block-Diagonal Model of the Multitrait-Multimethod Matrix," Applied Psychological Measurement, vol. 14, 325-339, 1990.

[2]   Coovert, M. D., Penner, L. A., & MacCallum, R. "Covariance Structure Modeling in Personality and Social Psychological Research: An Introduction," In Review of Personality and Social Psychology: Research Methods in Personality and Social Psychology, C. Hendrick and M. Clark, Eds., Sage, 1989.

[3]   Craiger, J. P. "Fuzzy Cognitive Maps and Causal Modeling," Paper to be presented at the Ninth Annual Meeting of the Society for Industrial and Organizational Psychology, Nashville, TN, April, 1994.

[4]   Hayduk, L. Structural Equation Modeling with LISREL: Essentials and Advances, Johns Hopkins Press, 1987.

[5]   Jöreskog, K. "A General Approach to Maximum Likelihood Factor Analysis," Psychometrika, vol. 34, 183-202, 1969.

[6]   Jöreskog, K. "A General Method for Analysis of Covariance Structures," Biometrika, vol. 57, 239-251, 1970.

[7]   Kosko, B. "Fuzzy Cognitive Maps," International Journal of Man-Machine Studies, vol. 24, 65-75, 1986.

[8]   Kosko, B. Neural Networks and Fuzzy Systems: A Dynamical Systems Approach to Machine Intelligence, Prentice Hall, 1992.

[9]   Koslowsky, M. "Antecedents and Consequences of Turnover: An Integrated Systems Approach," Genetic, Social, and General Psychology Monographs, vol. 113, 271-292, 1987.

[10]   Zadeh, L. "Fuzzy Sets," Information and Control, vol. 8, 338-353, 1965.

AUTOMATED SURFACE PROPERTY INSPECTION USING FUZZY NEURAL NETWORKS AND TIME SERIES ANALYSIS

R. J. Kuo

Department of Industrial and Management Systems Engineering
The Pennsylvania State University
207 Hammond Building, University Park, PA 16802, U.S.A.
Phone: (814)8633909 E-mail: RENK@ECL.PSU.EDU

ABSTRACT

The ability to inspect the surface property in reasonable time plays a very important role for manufacturing processes. Basically, the surface properties can be divided into three categories: pass, re-grinding, and fail, for by-products. Thus, in this paper, we propose an automated inspection system, which consists of three components, data acquisition, feature extraction, and pattern recognition, to on-line inspect the surface properties. In the first component, the surface information, sensory signals, are collected. The features of sensory signals are extracted for each inspected by-product by using the time series model in the second component, while the features extracted are fed to a feedforward artificial neural network (ANN) trained with fuzzy error backpropagation (FEBP) learning algorithm for property recognition in the last component. In order to select an appropriate time series model for this application, some tests of statistics are made for model determination. The classification accuracy is over 80% for most of the surfaces and the time required to implement the inspection is shorter enough for on-line inspection.

1 INTRODUCTION

The ability to inspect the surface property plays a very important role for manufacturing processes. Especially to inspect the by-products instead of the finished products provides more economical alternative. In addition, the surface property of working material can be used to indicate the cutting tool conditions, fresh or worn out. Basically, the surface properties are divided into three categories: pass, re-grinding, and fail. On the basis of the types of surface property, the system decides the next operation and makes the decision for tool change. However, in order to efficiently apply this concept, the inspection time should be very short and automatically implemented. Otherwise, the total production time becomes very long. Under such consideration, the inspection system used should be able to make the decision in reasonable time.

Therefore, in this paper, an automated inspection system, which consists of three components: (1) data acquisition; (2) feature extraction; and (3) pattern recognition; is presented. Firstly, the surface information, sensory signals, are collected. Due to large amounts of values for each surface information, it turns out to be very important to extract the features for each surface information. In this research, the features of sensory signals are extracted by using the time series model. Since there are some choices of time series models, to make an accurate model determination becomes very significant. Thus, some tests of statistics are employed to make the decision. Finally, the features extracted are fed to a feedforward artificial neural network (ANN) trained with fuzzy error backpropagation (FEBP) learning algorithm for property recognition. The classification accuracy is over 80% for most of the surfaces and the time required to implement the inspection is very short.

2 METHODOLOGY

The basic scheme of the proposed automated inspection system is shown in Figure 1. The detailed discussions are as follows.

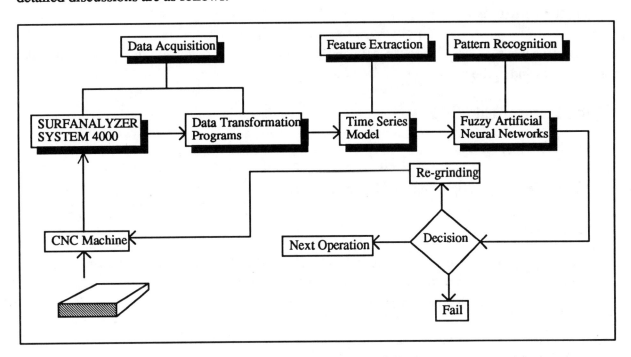

Figure 1. The automated inspection system.

2.1 Data Acquisition

For data acquisition, SURFANALYZER SYSTEM 4000 can be used to measure the surface roughness in this application, since the surface roughness indicates the surface property. Basically, SURFANALYZER SYSTEM 4000 is connected to PC which already has the data transformation programs. Then, all the data is transferred to time series analysis package, MINITAB, for parameter determination. This procedure will be discussed more detailed in the following section.

2.2 Feature Extraction

Different sensory signal patterns correspond to different surface properties. In order to analyze the relationship between the signal patterns and the surface properties, it is critical to extract the features of the sensory signal patterns. Using the features extracted from the surface information instead of the whole surface information can save a lot of training time for ANNs which will be used in the next component. Intuitively, the sensory signals obtained from sensors are a time series. By analyzing the time series data, we can construct a simple system, usually of a more or less mathematical kind, which describes its behavior in a concise way. There are three kinds of time series models which are as follows for stationary data [Kendall 1990, Wei 1990].

Autoregressive Model (AR)

The pth-order AR(p) is written as:
$$y_t = \delta + \phi_1 y_{t-1} + \ldots + \phi_p y_{t-p} + \varepsilon_t, \tag{1}$$
where coefficients $\phi_1, \ldots, \phi_p$ being the AR coefficients for y_t on y_{t-1}, ..., y_{t-p} with δ denoting the constant term and ε_t the error term.

Moving Average Model (MA)

The general MA(q) form is
$$y_t = \mu - \theta_1 \varepsilon_{t-1} - \ldots - \theta_q \varepsilon_{t-q} + \varepsilon_t. \tag{2}$$
where coefficients $\theta_1, \ldots, \theta_p$ being the MA coefficients.

ARMA Model

By combining the above two models, AR and MA, a mix ARMA model can be represented as:
$$y_t = \delta + \phi_1 y_{t-1} + \ldots + \phi_p y_{t-p} - \theta_1 \varepsilon_{t-1} - \ldots - \theta_q \varepsilon_{t-q} + \varepsilon_t. \tag{3}$$
Since there are the following concerns:

a. Trend removal,
b. The choice of AR, MA, ARMA, and
c. Order of the selected model,

it is necessary to determine which model is more suitable for the current data. In Figure 2, a general paradigm for univariate time series modeling is shown. The first step is to analyze the data. If there are trends or seasonal effects, the adjustments should be made. Then find the most suitable model for the data which has been adjusted. Finally, the model can be used to do the estimation.

2.3 Pattern Recognition

ANN is applied with the features extracted from the training data to identify the surface properties to determine whether the by-product should be re-ground or not. The results will suggest whether the ANN could successfully classify the surface properties by using the features extracted from time series model. Three-layer feedforward ANN trained with EBP learning algorithm is employed in this application.

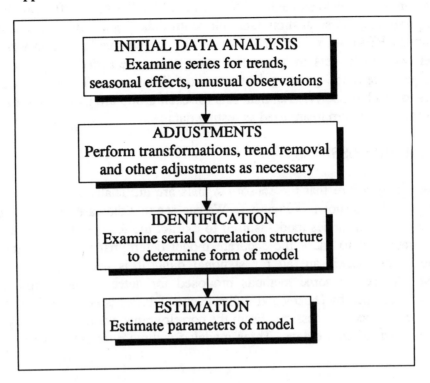

Figure 2. The procedures of model determination.

However, EBP learning algorithm generally lacks the ability to produce an effective network for a given task within a reasonable time. Thus, it is necessary to overcome this problem for practical applications. In this research, fuzzy models are employed to speed up the convergence of the EBP learning algorithm by dynamically updating the training parameters. Though Xu et al. (1992) and Choi et al. (1992) have applied fuzzy modeling to accelerate the training speed, the proposed fuzzy models are not suitable for all the different structures of ANNs. The reason is that the ranges of linguistic variables for different ANN structures are different. Therefore, the standard EBP learning algorithm with adjustable training parameters proposed by Kuo et al. [1993] is used. In Kuo's fuzzy EBP (FEBP) learning algorithm, the factors used to determine the change of the parameters are performance index (PI), which is defined as error divided by maximum error, and change of PI (CPI). Since PI is the error proportional to maximum error and CPI is the error change proportional to the maximum error, both of them can be treated as the general information for all the different ANN structures. In other words, E and CE should be normalized before being used. Moreover, all the three training parameters, training rate, momentum, and steepness of activation function, are updated simultaneously.

3 SIMULATION

In this research, the proposed system will be evaluated by using an example system. Due to communication problem between SURFANALYZER SYSTEM 4000 and PC with data transformation programs, the simulation data will be artificially generated. Because sort of data can be read from SURFANALYZER SYSTEM 4000, the generated data can well represent the real data. After twenty data sets are generated, some noises are added to the above twenty data sets in order to generate the re-grinding data sets and fail data sets. Therefore, totally, there are twenty data sets for each property. Ten data sets for each group are used as the training sets, the other ten data sets for each group are used as testing data sets.

4 RESULTS AND DISCUSSIONS

It has been mentioned before that the sensory signals are artificially generated. Two different kinds of surface signals are shown in Figure 3. We can see that they are really very difficult to be recognized. Thus, the time series model is used to extract the features from them. But, it turns out to be very important to make the accurate model determination. Since the above three mentioned time series models are all for stational data, it is necessary to detect the non-stationarity first. There are some methods proposed for detecting non-stationarity. In this research, the test developed by Dickey and Fuller (Kendall 1990) is employed. The results show that only the first difference is necessary. From the correlograms, we find that ARMA(4, 4) is the best model for the first-difference data. Three models for three different properties are shown in Table 1.

Therefore, the network architecture consists of nine input units which were connected to sixteen hidden units which were connected to three output units. The task is considered solved when the cost function for an epoch is below 0.01. Error backpropagation (EBP) learning algorithm is used for training. The testing results show that the classification accuracy is over 80% for 30 testing surfaces.

Table 1. Time series model parameters								
	∇y_{t-1}	∇y_{t-2}	∇y_{t-3}	∇y_{t-4}	ε_{t-1}	ε_{t-2}	ε_{t-3}	ε_{t-4}
Pass	-0.288	0.17	-0.31	-0.98	-0.246	0.377	-0.073	-0.517	-0.321
Re-grinding	-0.983	0.221	1.137	0.622	-0.463	0.459	0.59	0.41	0.516
Fail	-0.547	0.217	-0.466	0.972	-0.338	0.562	-0.032	0.846	0.333

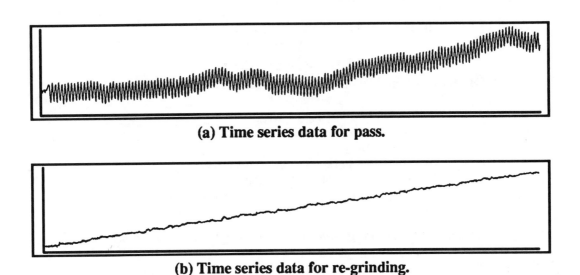

(a) Time series data for pass.

(b) Time series data for re-grinding.

Figure 3. Two different time series data.

5 CONCLUSIONS

An automated inspection system is proposed. It has been shown that parameters of the time series data can be treated as the features of that data set. The simulation results also show that the proposed system can recognize the surface properties in a very short time. In the future, real data sets collected from SURFANALYZER SYSTEM 4000 will be used to evaluate the proposed system instead of the artificial generated data sets.

REFERENCES

Choi, J. J., Arabshahi, P., Marks II R. J., and Caudell, T. P., "Fuzzy Parameter Adaptation in Neural Systems," *Proc. of IJCNN'92*, pp. I-232-I-238.

Kendall, S. M. and Ord, J. K., *Time Series*, Third Edition, Oxford University Press, New York, 1990.

Kuo, R. J., Chen, Y. T., Cohen, P. H., and Kumara, S., "Fast Convergence of Error Backpropagation Algorithm through Fuzzy Modeling," *Proc. of ANNIE'93*, pp. 239-244 1993a.

Kuo, R. J., Chen, Y. T., Cohen, P. H., and Kumara, S., "Fast Convergence of Error Backpropagation Algorithm through Fuzzy Modeling," *Industrial and Management Systems Engineering Working Paper 93-117*, The Pennsylvania State University, 1993b.

Wei, W. W. S., *Time Series Analysis*, Addison-Wesley Publishing Company, Inc., 1990.

Xu, H.Y., Wang, G.Z., and Baird, C.B., "A Fuzzy Neural Networks Technique with Fast Back Propagation Learning," *Proc. of IJCNN'92*, pp. I-124-I-219.

HOLOGRAPHIC NEURAL MANIFOLDS
AND
GENETIC SYSTEMS
EMBEDDED WITHIN A CLASSICAL DISTRIBUTED RDBMS

Robert J. Nixon
Director of Research and Development
The Heuristic Automation Laboratories
Konsult Data Systems Corporation
Oshkosh, WI 54901
EMAIL: NIXONR@Delphi.Com   (INNS:3734)

"Not only is everything changing, but all is flux..." - David Bohm

Abstract

With the introduction of Holographic Neural Networks we find ourselves looking out on an entirely new, virtually unexplored terrain. We propose to partially connect Holographic Neurons (HNs) or Clusters of Holographic Neurons (CHNs) to each other via a Classical Distributed RDBMS where the relationship rules are evolved (in a genetic sense) by the informational and temporal content of the neurons themselves. The synergy of the these technologies should allows us to create systems of enormous potential.

Introduction

The Holographic Neural Method pioneered by Sutherland allows us to enfold extremely large numbers of stimulus-response associations into a single complex vector the size of a single input pattern. The process is roughly analogous to the process of [2,3]Bohm's Holomovement, which is the continuous enfolding into the Implicate Order (the complex vector representation) and extraction out to the Explicate Order (what we consider to be the world we see around us or a data record). The modulating relationships of a classical RDBMS system may be encoded into the holographic neurons that are themselves part of the data that is linked 'relationally'. A series of relationship rules may themselves be evolved over time based on daemon processes that extract metrics from within this domain.

While HNs have tremendous associative capabilities, not all data (or Objects) that we wish to deal with are best suited to being represented within them. However, the relationships of various data records or objects can be encoded within them to great effect. If we also enfold the execution sequence of a series procedural threads within dedicated HNs the system can modify and adapt its behavior based on its informational input history. A typical data record (or table) within the RDBMS framework may consist of a small HN, a tag, and the actual fields (text, numeric, etc.) which we wish to store. The HN within the record could hold all of the relationships of that data to the related records throughout the system. This would allow us to more tightly couple the information within the database, while substantially shortening any search time required to find related data within the system. This should even allow us to incorporate 'Hypertext' style access to a traditional RDBMS system. Another approach would have us disassociate the HN(s) from the data record and externally modulate the relationships via some daemon (or agent) process outside of the traditional functions of the RDBMS. While this would reduce the necessary data storage requirements in proportion to the total number of records stored, we may loose some flexibility in retrieval and associative linking. This will require further investigation.

Fuzzy Relationships

By incorporating Holographic Neurons within a traditional RDBMS, we can add aspects of fuzziness to the data relationships which may also include temporal dependencies and even [1]dynamic memory decay (if desired). Over time we can follow how the relationship of the associated data elements change. This in itself is an incredibly powerful tool. With the HNs we can encode the entire historic picture of precisely how the relationship has evolved over time. The system should be able to on a continuous basis via daemon processes update its internal model of the relationship of two or more data elements in such a way as to do a ' N-dimensional surface fit' on the deltas in order to interpolate possible future (or past) behaviors . As long as the change is not chaotic we should be able to extract powerful predictive models. If the process turns out to be chaotic, we will have to modify the approach so as to approximate a semi-stable topology down to a chosen resolution. Instead of a single 'Snap Shot' probability based on the current configuration, we now have access to the entire historical probability of the enfolded relationships. We may find very interesting patterns in the first and second partial derivatives of the generated functions.

Adding Genetic Processes

Let us assign a set of algorithms to a series of tags (equivalent to [4,5]Koza's chromosomes). As time and experience progress, the simple algorithms that we started out with could evolve into more sophisticated ones based on recurrent patterns of complex relations. The relationship functions generated previously may be built up out of these genetic functions. By doing this we allow the system to create a summarizing ability based on a arbitrary resolution that in itself may be modified. In essence the system should be able to generate or 'teach' another system or us what it knows, without an exhaustive temporal run through of all relationships (which probably would not be feasible).

If we asked the system to tell us what it knew, it would have to query us as to what we were interested in, else pick a fairly random data set to start with and proceed in an associative fashion from that point on. However, since the temporal relationships can be encoded with in the HNs, we could also proceed in a past to future path through the data, where many connections may be affected by a single probability within a series of associative links. We may find ourselves traveling down a particular associative path in a positive time-wise fashion (at least within our frame of reference) only to find that the general path that we have been following leads to a point that we have traversed in the past due to the systems associative functions. We might find ourselves in associative 'vortices' more often then we might suspect. If you envision a river of water with thousands of small eddies, pools, vortices, and an overall current, you will begin to grasp the picture. Since an associative path may also evolve, the path may be semi-recurrent, just as a small particle in the flow of our 'river' may temporarily be caught in an eddy. Each time the particle orbits the vortex, it's path is modified, and with Chaos playing a role, our particle's path is modified by the entire state of the system. Every molecule of H_2O in the ocean is affected by every other molecule in the ocean. It is viewed by many that because of an apparent 'chaotic' relationship, reversal of the process would lead you to a different past path. If however the whole process is analogous to [2,3]Bohm's Holomovement, it should be possible to reverse the process and view the state of the system as it existed in the past. I refer to the example Bohm offered which described two clear concentric cylinders filled with a very viscous fluid into which is introduced small ink droplets in various configurations, which are then drawn out or enfolded as the central cylinder is rotated. When the cylinder is reversed the ink drops become explicate or manifest. We could in essence 'hypnotize' the system and regress it to any point we wished to examine. This process is analogous to the enfolding of the stimulus response patterns within the holographic neurons. In this model we have the totality of all of the information ever manifest in the system along with how its relationships have changed throughout its existence. The system may very well generate very complex procedural structures whose linked tags roughly resemble (cybernetic) DNA sequences.

Manifest Object Encoding and Recognition

If we use real time (30 frames/sec) video frame digitizing in combination with audio sampling of vocal (or sound) wave forms as the stimulus portions of two closely linked holographic neurons, and in turn set the response patterns equal to an identifying structure such as the ASCII representation of a person's name, the system over time would build a very detailed internal model of an object or person. Since tens of thousands of video frames (or audio wave forms) of the object (or person) at different orientations and scales may be collected over time and encoded into a complex vector the size of a single stimulus pattern, the system should be able to, when presented with an arbitrary input image, identify the object within a single decode operation. And here again the notion of fuzziness comes into play. The neurons will automatically produce the closest fit to the input pattern; and allow us to state, for example, 'There is a 87% chance that it is a picture of X'. By linking a set of holographic neurons which perform object recognition functions to related information within the data bases, we would have the basis of a security system, or perhaps it could assist a physician in diagnosing a patients condition based on subtle changes detected over time in their body's appearance.

Natural Language Interface

It should be possible to create a system that could learn to read and understand spoken language much in the way that we appear to, based on holographic neural associations. I believe that a system presented with a large body of human readable, and sensable text, would be able to build most of the necessary semantic relationships needed for natural language recognition.

There are many others who are far more versed in this area, and I leave it to them to apply these new tools to the task. It seems to me that the holographic neural method is perfectly suited to this application. [6]Levesque and Mylopoulos's 'Procedural Semantic Networks' and [7]Hendrix's 'Partitioned Semantic Networks' should benefit greatly by including holographic principles.

Inferential Data Base Management Systems (IDBMS)

Developmental psychologists [8]Piaget and Inhelder forward the hypothesis that human learning is not one-pass learning. The stages of learning appear to be:

1. *Sensomotoric Intelligence;* direct associations between sensory stimuli and motor responses. (I define data retrieval as a type of motor response...)

2. *Imaginative Intelligence;* concrete, unidirectional, imagination-based mental operations. (Identification and classification of metrics within the information domain, by free progression.)

3. *Formal Operations;* closed system bi-directional abstract operations. (The process of genetic rule construction via holographic neural methods...)

It appears at the moment that Human learning is a mixture of two learning types as indicated by [8]Hrycej:

1. *Unsupervised, non-specific, and undirected learning, or self-organization.* (Free form holographic neural association trials.)
2. *Supervised, specific, and goal-oriented learning.* (Building rules or solving goals using genetically assembled modules.)

If we structured a set of objects so that their linking relationships were 'Concepts' (where a *concept* is defined as a set of relations.) or learned associations built up through the interactions of Holographic Neurons, Genetic processes, and Fuzzy sets, the system should develop the capacity to not only infer relationships between the objects with in our data base, but also greatly abstract those relationships.

Conclusion

Please forgive me for any over simplifications, and the lack of formal proofs. The main objective of this paper was to point out new areas for exploration, and not to rigorously address any particular one.

Acknowledgments and Dedication

This small work in the scheme of things is dedicated to the memory of **David Bohm**, a physicist of the highest caliber and revolutionary thinker whose contributions to science and philosophy won't truly be understood for many years. And to **Karl H. Pribram**, another revolutionary whose work has led the way. **Kwang-Ming Wu**, Philosopher and my second father, 'May you reach Te by the Tao'. To the memory of **George Payne**, Physicist and mentor. And **John G. Sutherland** of AND Corp., for making <u>much</u> better toys then St. Nick...

Thank you.

References

[1] Sutherland, John G., (1992) *Fuzzy, Holographic, and parallel Intelligence* by Branko Soucek, Chap 2. The Holographic Neural Method, 7-92

[2] Bohm, David, (1980) *Wholeness and The Implicate Order*, Chap 3. 48-64

[3] Bohm, David, Basil Hiley , (1993) *The Undivided Universe*, Chap 15. 357-363

[4] Koza, John R., (1992) *Dynamic, Genetic, and Chaotic Programming* by Branko Soucek, Chap 10. The Genetic Programming Paradigm: Genetically Breeding Populations of Computer Programs to Solve Problems, 203-352

[5] De Garis, Hugo, (1991) *Neural and Intelligent Systems Integration* by Branko Soucek, Chap 8. Genetic Programming: Building Artificial Nervous Systems with Genetically Programmed Neural Network Modules, 207-218

[6] Levesque, Hector, John Mylopoulos (1985) *Introduction To Natural Language Processing* by Mary Dee Harris, Chap 7. 238-242

[7] Hendrix, Gary, (1985) *Introduction To Natural Language Processing* by Mary Dee Harris, Chap 7. 227-238

[8] Hrycej, Tomas, (1992) *Modular Learning in Neural Networks*, 5-7, series ed. B. Soucek

Naming the Unmeasurable
Using a Neural-Fuzzy Approach
William M. Pulice
12472 Taylor Cir.
Garden Grove, California 92645

Abstract:
This paper reports on a neural-fuzzy technique to identify and name a mathematically
nondescript image, an image of a person's eye. An unsupervised artificial neural network
algorithm, the Self-Organizing Feature Map, is used to perform discrimination and a
supervised fuzzy clustering algorithm, the Fuzzy c-Means, is used to perform the
identification (naming). This study was done as an inexpensive home-project and used: a
video camcorder, an AT class PC, an inexpensive video frame grabber, and software
developed by the author.

Introduction:
In this study, image processing, artificial neural network discrimination, and fuzzy pattern
recognition combine to discriminate facial features and thereby identify the image of one
subject over the images of others. This effort uses the combination of two powerful
algorithms, the Kohonen's Self-Organizing Feature Map neural network [3] and the
Bezdek's Fuzzy c-Means clustering [1].

The neural network discriminates the images in an unsupervised manner. Then, the fuzzy
c-Means clusters the neural network's output in a supervised manner so that selection and
labeling (naming) can be accomplished through a set of fuzzy rules.

The neural network mimics the parallel processing of biological sensory systems and
produces an output map (layer) which preserves the topology of the input images [3].
This means the ordering of the neural network's output is along a continuum. Attempting
to characterize or give meaning to information contained in this continuum is not
necessary as this is an intermediate stage in the process. It is only important that training
samples are able to be discriminated and that there is an order in the pattern. Performing
clustering along this continuum breaks the data into classes but the fact that all the data
points are still in the continuum remains.

Fuzzy logic is well suited for situations in which elements of a set of classes transition
from membership to non-membership in a gradual rather than abrupt manner [7]. So a
fuzzy approach to clustering is appropriate and the c-Means algorithm is well suited for
this.

Algorithms:
The Kohonen algorithm is an unsupervised neural network and it consists of two layers,
the input and the output. The algorithm orders its output layer based on the patterns

contained in the images. This ordering occurs in a manner that is difficult to characterize and understand as it is a function of the parallel dynamics of the processing elements in the network.

Data is presented to the input layer of the network, and the network forms internal clusters that compress the input data onto a dimensioned-reduced set space, the output layer.

The Kohonen neural network can be trained to classify input vectors while preserving the inherent topology of the training set. In topological preserving maps, the nearest neighbor relationships in the training set are preserved in the network in such a manner that input images presented to the network which have not been previously "learned" will be categorized by its nearest neighbor in the training set.

The ordered, activated elements of the output layer of the neural network are presented to the fuzzy algorithm as the data samples to be clustered.

The Bezdek fuzzy c-Means algorithm is a supervised clustering technique. It groups data samples into clusters or classes, and assigns a fuzzy grade of membership to each of the data points with respect to each of the classes. Fuzzy c-Means also determines the cluster centers.

Recognition of Facial Features:
To test how the combination of the Kohonen and the Bezdek algorithms work together, digitized video images of the right and left eyes of three subjects were taken at three different poses. The poses were facing straight ahead toward the camera, and facing approximately thirty degrees to the left and to the right.

The digitized image of the faces were 512 by 512 pixels with a 64 gray level resolution. Image edge detection was then done using the Robert's Cross edge detection algorithm [6]. The images of the right and left eye from each of the subjects' poses were each stored in 16 by 20 pixel data arrays.

The data files with the eye images were arranged into left and right eye training sets. The training sets were each processed through the Kohonen neural network and the right and left eye networks were allowed to self organize on these images.

The Kohonen network mapped an output pattern onto the network's output layer, an 8 by 8 array. As the network stabilized, each presentation of an eye image activated a particular output element on the network's output layer.

The main question was how will the neural network arrange the clusters? Will the images of the same eye presented at different poses map to the output layer in a orderly manner?

As hoped, the unsupervised network did discriminate in an orderly manner between the images of the eyes and thereby caused different output elements to be activated as different input images were presented.

Then fuzzy c-Means was performed using the output layer as the set space. For this application, three classes were assumed.

After the c-Means algorithm iterated and reached a solution, the algorithm provided the cluster centers and fuzzy membership grades for the data points corresponding to the activated output elements from the Kohonen algorithm.

Based on the results of the fuzzy clustering, fuzzy logic rules were established. They were three straight-forward fuzzy rules for this application, one rule for each of the original subjects. The rules were built along the lines of logic such as "(in left eye class X or in left eye class Y) and (in right eye class A or in right eye class B)". The winner was the subject (name) in which the related fuzzy rule had the highest value.

Not only did paired left eyes and right eye images (that is eye images from the same video frame) give the correct subject (name) but unpaired left and right eyes images (left and right eyes from the same subject but from different video frames) identified the correct subject. There were sixteen of sixteen correct selections. Chance would predict only a third would be correct.

This technique appears to be robust. The quality of the images could have been improved by further image preprocessing, such as noise removal. Also information is lost in the edge detection operation. Even with these limitations the technique was able to name the objects correctly.

In this example with the small number of samples, identification could have been done simply with just the output of the neural network, but as more subjects and images are added the need for the fuzzy processing becomes more apparent.

Real-Time Naming Operation:
Learning time is considerable due to the time it takes the self-organizing neural network to stabilize its output. Also, the fuzzy clustering is a supervised approach and training images must be labeled in the learning phase.

However, application of this technique, once learning has been done, will be quite rapid as only simple calculations [1], [4] are required and there are a relative small number of neural network processing elements. The introduction of parallel neural network type processors or accelerator boards will also speed execution.

Conclusion:

While only one example was explored, it appears that the neural network and the fuzzy clustering combine to provide a simple way to categorize complex patterns and identify (name) them without having to mathematically describe these patterns.

The strengths of the neural network and fuzzy approach were utilized. The neural network for adaptation and discrimination and the fuzzy for clustering, labeling and decision making.

This investigation was accomplished by using a household camcorder, a personal computer and an inexpensive video frame grabber, all at a minimum cost.

References

1. J.C. Bezdek, Pattern Recognition with Fuzzy Objective Function Algorithms, Plenum Press, New York (1981)

2. V. Bruce, Recognizing Faces, Lawrence Erlbaum Associates, London (1988)

3. T. Kohonen, Self-Organization and Associative Memory, Springer-Verlag, Berlin (1984)

4. R.P. Lippmann, An Introduction to Computing with Neural Nets, IEEE ASSP Magazine, April 1987

5. W. Pedryez, Fuzzy Control and Fuzzy Systems, John Wiley & Sons, New York (1989)

6. R.J. Schalkoff, Digital Image Processing and Computer Vision, John Wiley & Sons, New York (1989)

7. L.A. Zadeh, Outline of a New Approach to the Analyses of Complex Systems and Decision Processes, IEEE Transactions on Systems, Man, and Cybernetics, January, 1973

A Machine with "Feelings": System Models of Emotional Behavior

Irwin Marin and Jeanne Sappington
The Emblematics Corporation
P.O. Box 81809
Pittsburgh, Pennsylvania 15217-0809
Phone: 412-242-5732
Fax: 412-242-5381

ABSTRACT:

Fifty years have elapsed since the pioneering work by McCulloch and Pitts--forty years of cybernetics. Emotional behavior has been studied by many scientists from Darwin on. Emotions have characterized in biological, psychological, physiological and even everyday physical terms. Recently cognitive mapping technologies have been available to view some of the processes by related mapping and imaging of physiological activity in the brain. However, no unified theory for emotional behavior exists.

A possible reason for this difficulty is that emotions are composite and complex integrative behavior processes consisting of interacting cognitive, perceptual and physiological components. With the advances in non-linear dynamics (including chaotic processes and fractal science) techniques and tools have arrived which allow the construction of biologically realistic and psychologically plausible mathematical models realizable in computer architectures such as neural networks. These models can be of help in: (1) constructing realistic physical analogues of non-linear behavioral systems exhibiting emotional behavior, (2) examining the feasibility of applying such "machines with feelings" as "emotional components" in the design of future deterministic and non-deterministic computer operating systems, and (3) evolving a new generalization of "passionate processors" which, if found effective in clinical trials, would be applicable to constructing a new generation of Clinically Usable Psychoanalytic Simulation tools for the diagnosis and treatment of affective disorders, providing useful extensions to the pioneering psychoanalytic work of cognitive scientists, R. Abelson and K. Colby.

In this paper, it is argued that using the approach of non-linear dynamics can provide a physical basis for constructing models of an operational unified theory of emotion. Toward this end, a prototype for "A Machine with Feelings" - is introduced; based upon the first author's Theory of Affect Linkages, modelled as a self-organizing system, with its initial mathematical models realized in MATHEMATICA$_{tm}$. In addition, simple behavior ensuing from its coupling to a simple effector-receptor system is examined, and implications for its applicability to constructing an operational theory of emotional behavior are explored.

Connectionist Production Systems for Approximate Reasoning

Nikola K. Kasabov
Department of Information Science,
University of Otago, Dunedin, New Zealand
Phone:+64 3 4798319, Fax: +64 3 4798311,
email: nkasabov@otago.ac.nz

Abstract

Production systems (PS) are one of the most used AI techniques as well as a widely explored model of cognition. The problem of connectionist realization of PS is very important because it could bring all the benefits of the connectionist approach to the AI symbolic computation (Toretzky & Hinton, 1988; Lange & Dyer, 1989; Sun, 1992). If properly designed, connectionist PS could make possible massive parallelism, typical for the neural networks (NN); partial match; reasoning with inexact, missing and/or corrupted data; graceful degradation; fault tolerance; robustness; learning and adaptation, thus overcoming the two main problems in the present-day expert systems - approximate reasoning, and knowledge acquisition.

In this presentation, the main principles of building **connectionist production systems (CPS)** for approximate reasoning and their current applications are discussed. The presentation is based on two recently published papers (Kasabov, N. and Shishkov, S. ,1993a and 1993b).

To illustrate the main principle of CPS a **Neural Production System** (NPS) and its third realization - NPS3 designed to facilitate approximate reasoning, are presented (Kasabov, N. and Shishkov, S., 1993a). NPS3 facilitates partial match between facts and rules, variable binding, different conflict resolution strategies, chain inference. Facts are represented in a working memory by so called certainty degrees. Different inference control parameters are attached to every production rule. Some of them are known neuronal parameters, receiving an engineering meaning here. Others, which have their context in knowledge engineering, have been implemented in a connectionist way. The partial match implemented in NPS3 is demonstrated on the same test production system as used by other authors. NPS3 allows negated condition elements and introduces two new inference control coefficients: a relative degree of importance attached to every condition element in the left-hand side of each production, and a certainty degree attached to its right-hand side.

CPS have enormous abilities for **approximate reasoning**. Some of them, illustrated by reasoning in NPS3 are:
• reasoning over a set of simple diagnostic production rules;
• reasoning over a set of decision support fuzzy rules (Lim et al, 1991);
• reasoning over fuzzy rules for solving ambiguity problems in speech recognition;
• solving planning problems on the example of the "Monkey and bananas problem" when fuzzy terms are used;
• solving optimization problems on the example of the "Travelling Salesman Problem".

We consider approximate reasoning as a process of inferring new facts and achieving conclusions when inexact facts and uncertain rules are presented. The reasoning process in NPS3 for example is non-monotonic, i.e. processing of new facts may decrease the certainty degree of an already inferred fact. The main idea of controlling the approximate reasoning in NPS3 is that by tuning the inference control parameters we can adjust the reasoning process for a particular PS to the requirements of the expert. Approximate reasoning in NPS3 is a consequence of its partial match. For example by using the noise tolerance coefficients, NPS3 can separate facts which are relevant to the decision process, from irrelevant facts. Rules with different sensitivity coefficients react differently to a same set of relevant facts. NPS3 can work with missing data. One rule may fire even when some facts are not known. Adjusting the degrees of importance we declare that some condition elements are more important than another, and rules can fire if only the important supporting facts are known. In NPS3 fuzzy propositions are represented by unary predicates of "attribute (value)" type. This shows that even unary predicates, and not only n-ary ones, may be successfully used to represent complex concepts (fuzzy concepts in particular). By adjusting different values for the inference control parameters attached to a PS in NPS3, different fuzzy inference methods (Terano et al, 1992) could be realized. This is an interesting characteristic of CPS which needs further investigation.

The connectionist environment, in which CPS is realized, makes possible building of **parallel production systems** in the sense that all the rules which are satisfied above a set threshold fire in parallel and make a parallel update of the working memory (Kasabov, N. and Shishkov,S., 1993b). The same examples of approximate reasoning are discussed in the parallel version of NPS.

The **analysis** of the CPS developed so far suggests that even though having limited abilities for knowledge representation (for example a limited number of variables in the production rules) CPS can be widely used in knowledge engineering (see also Sun, 1992) and can also be hardware implemented as a new generation computer architectures along the current implementations (Yamakawa et al, 1992).

References

1. Kasabov, N. and Shishkov, S. (1993a) A Connectionist Production System with Partial Match and Its Use for Approximate Reasoning, "Connection Science", vol.5, 3-4, pp.275-305
2. Kasabov, N. and Shishkov, S. (1993b) Approximate Reasoning with Parallel Connectionist Production Systems, in:Proceedings of IJCNN'93, 2963-2966
3.Kosko, B. (1992) Neural networks and fuzzy systems: A dynamical approach to machine intelligence. Prentice-Hall.
4.Lange, T. & Dyer, M. (1989) High-level inferencing in a connectionist network. Connection Science, 1 (2), 181-217.
5.Lim, M. & Takefuji, Y. (1990) Implementing fuzzy rule-based systems on silicon chips. IEEE Expert, February, 31-45.
6.Sun, R. (1992) On variable binding in connectionist networks. Connection Science, 4 (2), 93-124.
7.Terano, T., Asai, K. & Sugeno, M. (1992) Fuzzy systems theory and its applications. NY: Academic Press.
8.Touretzky, D.S & Hinton, G.E. (1988) A distributed connectionist production system. Cognitive Science, 12, 423-466.
9.Yamakawa, T., Uchino, E., Miki, T. & H. Kusanagi (1992) A neo fuzzy neuron and its application for system identification and prediction of the system behaviour. Proceedings of the 2nd International Conference on Fuzzy Logic and Neural Networks. Iizuka, Japan, July 17-22, 477-483.
10.Zadeh, L. (1985) The role of fuzzy logic in the management of uncertainty in expert systems. In Gupta, M., Kandel, A., Bandler, W. & Kiszka, J. (eds), Approximate reasoning in expert systems, 3-31.

Addendum

A Net Program for Natural Language Comprehension

Jacob Weiss

CUNY University Center, Computer Science Dept.

33 W 42nd St. New York, NY 10036-8099

JAC@cunyvms1.gc.cuny.edu

Abstract

The Natural language comprehension problem is being approached in this work by using a "net program". The net program is a programmable network of cooperative neural nets and procedural functions. Its goal is to bridge the gap between connectionist-sub symbolic and symbolic processing in AI by forming a fusion between neural nets and classical programming. We devised a language, C^{+NET}, for "neural programming" as an enhancement to the procedural language C. We used C^{+NET} to write a net program for language comprehension. The model and program presented here were developed from a preliminary version presented in [8].

1. Introduction

We believe that it is appropriate to solve language comprehension issues with a computational scheme that can combine connectionist and procedural, inductive and deductive methods, such as the Net Program scheme which we are presenting here. To achieve comprehension of natural language, it is necessary to deal and experiment with much structure of which little is known. A flexible structure would be useful. Clues for understanding natural language texts may come in many forms. There is a combination of structural, contextual, lexical, transformational and rational-logical processing and the exact border lines are blurred. A preferred way to approach such a domain seems to be with a scheme that enables a flexible interaction of procedural, lexical and "neural knowledge", where "neural knowledge" is both *structure and* experience. *Structure* and *experience* can perhaps be associated with *innate* and *learned* knowledge when modeling natural understanding of language. Symbolic processing can be associated with both innate mechanisms (perhaps inaccessible rules) and learned ones (perhaps conscious rules). The presented scheme is meant to harness all of the above functional elements to reach solutions, rather than fixate on one of them.

2. Net Programs

We view simulated neural nets as programmable software modules to which programming methods are applied. This enables consolidation of nets and programs into a net program. The net program uses both connectionist and procedural methods. It inherits the advantages of neural nets: the abilities to generalize, approximate, guess and search solutions, the versatility and the graceful degradation of quality of solutions. But, conversely to plain neural nets it can accept descriptions of problems and solutions as they are known to the user - with symbols, algorithms, rules and prior and axiomatic knowledge as well as sample data, and process and utilize all the above. It can blur the distinction between procedural knowledge and the knowledge acquired from the data, by having structure and procedural assertions help reach a solution without dictating it, much like human reasoning. It can permit a variable level of control of structure and learning. It can use strictly computer-like processes where accuracy is needed. Its solutions can be justifiable. It enables reuse of knowledge and skills as it can be structured, created, tested, refined and used like a high-level language, compounding modules by structure and functionality, distributing tasks to modules, and reusing and re-invoking modules. It can do so for both functions and neural nets. It may have a better chance than straight forward neural nets to solve problems of large scale and complexity.

The net program is composed of procedural functions and neural nets. Each of the neural nets is (currently but not necessarily) a back propagation net that follows [2]. A net node may be of one or more layers of one or more neurons. A net program is composed of these basic elements or of other net programs. The connections among nets are not restricted - nodes can be connected to any number of any other nodes and cycles are permitted.

Neural net nodes and function nodes can be connected by way of invocation - a net can invoke a function to get input or transform the output, a function can use a net to do a subtask. Neural nets can be connected to each other by arrays of connection weights. Connected nets, therefore, need not be of matching input and output layer size. The back propagation mechanism is extended accordingly. The connection weights can be manipulated to set default correlations. Subnets can be trained separately or jointly. Connected nets may be pre-trained.

Function calls can be recursive. When active nets are reinvoked by a function, they can have a different context and activation values; the weights are the same.

A more detailed discussion of the net program scheme was provided in [8].

3. The Net Program Language - C^{+NET}

The net program scheme is underlying a programming language which we call C^{+NET} ,an enhanced version of ANSI C implemented by the development of a collection of subroutines to be used as an extension to C. A current implementation runs on a PC using MS-DOS and MS-C (and/or MS-Windows).

C^{+NET} supplies facilities that can be invoked in a statement-like manner from within C programs. The basic objects upon which C^{+NET} operated are net lists: lists of one or more net (node) names. Most statements (facilities), therefore accept as their main operand (argument) a list of net names.

The basic five facilities that are used to create a basic multinode net program, train it and run it are:

CreateNeuNets	to create backpropagation nets and name them
connets	to create connections among the nets
setinpat	to set external inputs and patterns
	and to connect input functions to net nodes
learn	to train one or more nodes with or without those connected to them
run	to activate a list of nodes and those connected to them

A more detailed discussion of the net program scheme was provided in [8].

4. Usage of Net Programs in Natural Language Comprehension

Jean Piaget and Noam Chomsky are debating [3] the manner of acquiring language. Piaget's view is, very generally, that the knowledge of language is constructed in necessary stages, that develop from each other by way of abstraction and generalization. Chomsky, contrarily, assumes an innate fixed nucleus for the language knowledge. Both assume some initial mechanisms and some learning and both agree that a certain fixed nucleus of knowledge is achieved. They differ, mostly, in assuming what is innate (or learned by an evolutionary process) and what is learned. If we were to create a model for language acquisition that follows either one, or maybe tries to experiment with finding a compromise, we would want to be able to manipulate structure easily, and enable the employment of rules upon it conveniently and flexibly. We would need to facilitate creation of and experimentation with structure, training and logical reasoning. For these, the net program scheme might be appropriate.

Connectionist models have been applied to problems relating to language comprehension. However, Current systems that do work limit either their domain as [4, 5] which have an inherently limited vocabulary, or their range, as [6] that associates a limited number of responses (actions) with unrestricted input. We want to contribute to devising integratable parts of a solution to a large problem, rather than solutions to reduced problems. Our intent is to try to create a system that may be in actuality expandable to deal with real texts.

It may well be that the natural language problem requires joining all of the means that we have, connectionist and symbolic. Classical systems do not have the flexibility, adaptability, fuzziness, robustness, graceful degradation and associativity that are needed for the task. Connectionist models do not have the capacity to process representations of structures and their compositions, nor can they do acceptable logical reasoning [2, 7]. As there probably are not any serious advocates of strict behaviorism left, there should not be a serious reason for anyone to believe that a backpropagation type net can somehow learn to behave as if it knows the grammar of a natural language, without appropriate representations and reasoning mechanisms. We hope to contribute to natural language comprehension in doing what is doable by each of the tools available, and avoiding forcing upon any of the mechanisms what is not feasible for it. We are not aiming at full understanding of meaning as [4] and [5] do, it may be impossible at this stage. We will not train for every possible word and every possible structure as [4] may have to. We will try to learn syntax and be aided by "light" semantics. We are trying to build a system that can learn to handle many forms of sentences by training on examples containing frequent building blocks, so that it can induce recurring and composable sentence structures.

Our approach is to parse sentences employing an interaction between a procedural parser and a decision making neural net. The net takes care of the parts of the domain that do not have a good known tractable deductive algorithm. It derives its "wisdom" from its own structure and the inductions and experience coming from the data presented to it. With the net's help, the parser's task is much simplified. The structure of the net is such that it can receive an encoding of the partial parse tree, create reusable internal representations for its constituents, and output a decision. The parser keeps the codes created by the net for words and phrases, to re-present them to the net as parts of larger phrases. The parser therefore, does the programmatic work, the nets do the decisions and encoding.

4.1 The Parser

The engine of the language comprehension program is the parser. The parser is directed by the input text, the directives intermingled in the input text and the decisions of the neural network. The parser maintains a structure of phrase elements which contains all the information that is known about them (e.g. their lexical value and their function in the phrase). The information can either come explicitly from the input or be induced by the nets. The structure also defines the parse tree. Initially, the first element (word) in the phrase is considered against the sentence level, and then the parser decides the relation of each next element, in its turn, to the position held in the tree. This process is not necessarily sequential - during parsing, as phrases are constructed, the parser can be called to decide the relations of phrases at various levels.

When the parser is called to decide a relation it checks to see whether lexical information about the element considered (from the input or the dictionary) and the parsing directives are available. If it is, the parser trains the net with it, otherwise it tries to extract the missing information from the net.

The information about the lexical value of words is taken from a dictionary, but the net is trained to give that information while encoding it. The same complex of nets learns to give the parsing decisions and lexical information about words and phrases. The net does not learn to encode words as such, but to output some information as a response to descriptors of words and give an encoding for that information. Since the network has as input the spelling of a word and its context, it can give some intelligent codes for words that do not appear in the dictionary. This means that the parser is not limited to a fixed vocabulary, it can have the "feel" for new words.

4.2 The Input

The input to the system is continuous text with intermingled optional directives. The directives relate to meaning, i.e. lexical values, of words and to the strucure of phrases. The net learns to reproduce both meaning and structure. Lexical values are kept in a dictionary as well as taught to the net. The dictionary is managed according to word level directives. A (most basic) example text is:

You [pronoun noun gend(anim) num(singular plural)] (start pivot,noun)

bake [verb tran form(finite) sem(food)] (start cont pivot)

a [article] (start push)

cake [noun gend(inanim) sem(food)] (cont pivot) . [punct] (fullstop)

Dictionary instructions are optional. When a word is followed by a dictionary instruction(s), its lexical value is determined by the instructions and the system uses the value for its training. If there is no lexical instruction but there already is a lexical value kept for the word in the dictionary, then the value in the dictionary will be used, otherwise the system will extract it from the neural nets. A lexical value, consists of speech part(s) and qualifiers. They are not pre defined but some basic ones are assumed. Speech parts are terms like noun, verb, article etc. Qualifiers are variables with values such as gend(male) sem(young). Multiple values are allowed Values can be negated. The qualifiers and values given in the input cause the creation of corresponding net nodes. The coding is not done accross a fixed set of micro features, it uses relevant and possibly introduced ones.

A phrase level directive determines how to construct the parse tree and what is the function of the immediate word or phrase within its context. It relates to the current entity being considered which may be a word received from the input or a previously constructed phrase or a phrase "under construction".

The parse instruction consists of combinations of operators:

start Start a new phrase.

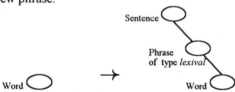

cont   The entity belongs to current phrase, put it in its continuation

Pivot   The current entity serves as a head in its phrase, the phrase will get (the relevant parts of) its lexical value. (cont,pivot) would look

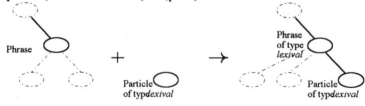

I-866

pop	Close the open phrase, recheck the entity in relation to upper level

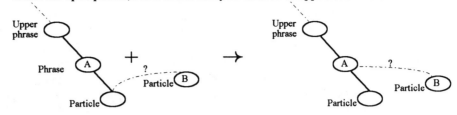

start cont	Start a new phrase at the same level of the open one, close the open one.

start push	Start a new phrase as part of the open one

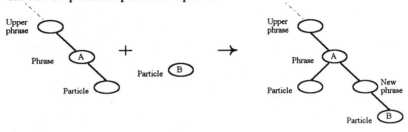

start pop	Close the open phrase, start a new phrase, recheck the new phrase in relation to upper level

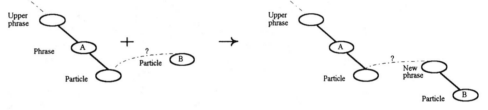

start cont enclose

Close the open phrase, start a new one at the same level and
enclose the two of them within a new higher level phrase.

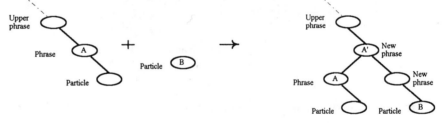

start push enclose

Start a new phrase within the open one and enclose both within a new phrase.

adjoin	The entity is part of a bigger one (an expression).
lookahead	Withhold decision. Read and encode the next few words, then redo the parsing.
record	Learn to encode the last element, but ignore it as part of the phrase
fullstop	finish parsing the sentence, display it.

4.3 The Language Comprehension Net

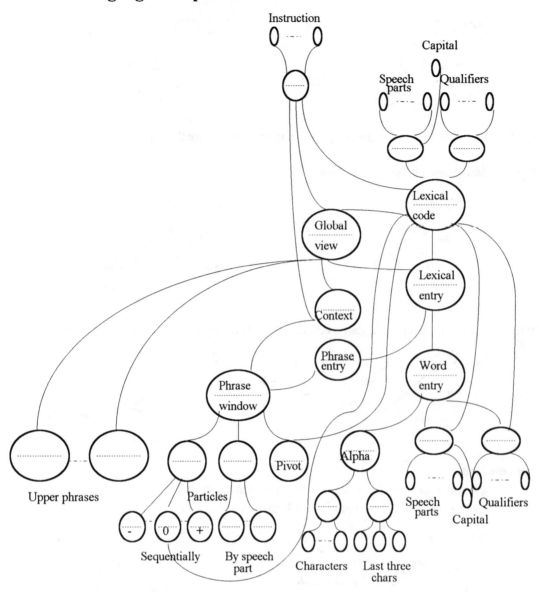

4.3.1 Subnets, Connections and Usage

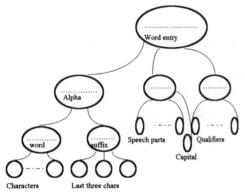

The subnet (left) for word entry, which appears in the lower right part of the net overview above, enables entry of multiple aspects of the word. The coded characters of the word are the input to the little nets in the bottom left. The three last characters are also given to the next subnet called suffix, as the word ending may be of importance to its meaning. Each speech part that appears in the input causes the creation of a one neuron subnet connected to the speech part net. Each unknown value of each qualifier that appears in the input, causes the creation of a one neuron node connected to the qualifier subnet.

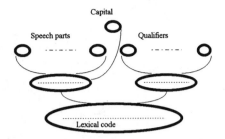

The subnet that outputs a lexical value (upper right part of the global view and repeated here in the left) has nodes that correspond to components of lexical value, similarly to the previously discussed subnet that serves to enter a lexical value. Once the net learns a lexical value, which means that it learns to output the proper activation for the output lexical nodes, the activation of the **lexical code** subnet serves to represent a coded word to the system for further reference.

Phrases too have lexical values, which are encoded by the same subnet, so that they are represented in the same way as words. Phrases are entered to the system both for encoding and as context, The ground level nodes in the phrase entry subnet receive as input codes that are created by the lexical code subnet described above. These represent parts of a phrase which may be words or phrases. The pivot node is activated with the code of the phrase head (if there is one). The system can (be trained to) determine while parsing that a given part of a phrase is its pivot, which could help tell the function of the whole phrase. The **"particles sequentially"** subnet is a window to the current phrase, the nodes connected to it correspond to the last few elements in the phrase and (when needed) a few lookahead elements. They are activated with the codes of the phrase parts.

The **"speech part"** subnet has nodes that correspond to elements in the phrase by speech part e.g. if the phrase has a noun, the noun node would be activated with its code. The inclusion of entities of certain speech parts in the phrase is induced during parsing.

The leftmost nets in the overview are the **upper phrases** nets:

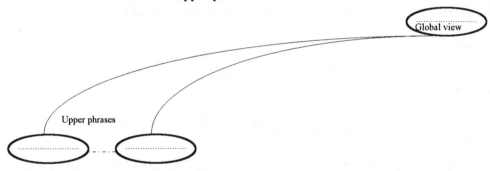

These are the codes of the upper level phrases of which the current phrase is a part, that is the immediate phrase to which the current phrase belongs, the phrase to which the latter belongs, etc. which give *a complete context in which the phrase is set*.

The nets described so far can represent phrases within a parse tree and produce an encoding. We can now add the top of the edifice which is the production of a parsing instruction.

The instruction subnet decides what to do when presented with a parsing state. The state is characterized by a partial parse tree on one hand and a word or phrase on the other hand. The instruction determines the connection of the element that is being considered to the partial tree.

The instruction subnet is a straightforward addition to the net we have so far, it simply has to know the global state of the parsing and details about the next element. The output nodes of the instruction subnet are a set of one neuron nodes, one node for each possible component (operator) of the parse instruction. They are activated as an integral part of the global net: When the net is presented with a new element to be encoded or to extract knowledge upon, it is also presented with its context, which is the partial parse tree. The output would be the activation of the lexical value nodes telling the lexical value of the element considered, and the instruction

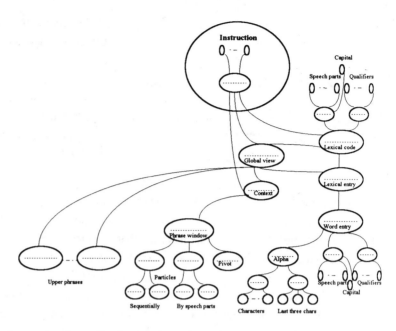

in the form of the activation of the instruction nodes that tells the relation of an element to its context or the parsing tree.

5. Conclusion

The implemented model has proven capable of learning to parse some quite elaborate sentences. With the same software tools, but better (than PC) hardware tools it may be a promising methodolgy.

References

[1]   D. E Rumelhart,. G.E. Hinton, & R. J. Williams, Learning internal distributed processing, Cambridge, Mass: MIT Press, 1986

[2]   P. Smolensky, Tensor product variable binding and the representation of symbolic structures in connectionist networks, Artificial Intelligence, Vol 46, 1990

[3]   Massimo Piattelli-Palmarini, Editor, Language and Learning, The Debate between Jean Piaget and Noam Chomsky, Harvard University Press, Cambridge Mass., 1980.

[4]   M.F. St. John & J.L. McClelland, Learning and Applying Contextual Constrains in Sentence Comprehension, in Artificial Intelligence 46 1990, 217-257

[5]   Risto Miikulainen and M.G. Dyer, Encoding Input/Output in connectionist Cognitive Systems, in Proceeding of the 1988 Connectionist Model Summer School, Morgan Kaufmann, 1989

[6]   A.L. Gorin, S.E. Levinson, A. N. Gertner and E. Goldman, Adaptive Aquisition of Language, Computer Speech and Language 5, 1991, Pages 101-132

[7]   J.A. Fodor & Z.W. Pylyshyn, Connectionism and cognitive architecture, Cogntion: International Journal of Cognitive Science, vol 28, 1988

[8]   Jacob Weiss, Neural Programming, Proceeding of the International Joint Conference on Neural Networks, Baltimore 1992, Vol 1, Pages 781-7

Journal of Autism and Developmental Disorders, Vol. 23, No. 3, 1993

A Neural Network Approach to the Classification of Autism[1]

Ira L. Cohen[2] and Vicki Sudhalter
New York State Office of Mental Retardation and Developmental Disabilities, New York State Institute for Basic Research in Developmental Disabilities, Staten Island

Donna Landon-Jimenez
Queens College and the Graduate Center of the City University of New York and CSI/IBR Center for Developmental Neuroscience

Maryellen Keogh
New York State Office of Mental Retardation and Developmental Disabilities, New York State Institute for Basic Research in Developmental Disabilities, Staten Island

ABSTRACT
A nonlinear pattern recognition system, neural network technology, was explored for its utility in assisting in the classification of autism. It was compared with a more traditional approach, simultaneous and stepwise linear discriminant analyses, in terms of the ability of each methodology to both classify and predict persons as having autism or mental retardation based on information obtained from a new structured parent interview: the Autistic Behavior Interview. The neural network methodology was superior to discriminant function analysis both in its ability to classify groups (92 vs. 85%) and to generalize to new cases that were not part of the training sample (92

vs. 82%). Interrater and test–retest reliabilities and measures of internal consistency were satisfactory for most of the subscales in the Autistic Behavior Interview. The implications of neural network technology for diagnosis, in general, and for understanding of possible core deficits in autism are discussed.

Ira L. Cohen
New York State Office of Mental Retardation and Developmental Disabilities
New York State Institute for Basic Research in Developmental Disabilities
Staten Island, New York

Neural Network Analogue of Autism

Abstract

An artificial neural network is simulated that shares formal qualitative similarities with the selective attention and generalization deficits seen in people with autism. The model is based on neuropathological studies which suggest that affected individuals have either too few or too many neuronal connections in various regions of the brain. In simulations where the model was taught to discriminate children with autism from children with mental retardation, having too few simulated neuronal connections led to relatively inferior discrimination of the two groups in a training set and, consequently, relatively inferior generalization of the discrimination to a novel test set. Too many connections produced excellent discrimination but inferior generalization because of over-emphasis on details unique to the training set. It is concluded that, within the context of the current model, the neuropathological observations that have been described in the literature are sufficient to explain some of the unique pattern recognition and discrimination learning abilities seen in some people with autism as well as their problems with generalization and concep acquisition. The model generates testable hypotheses which have implications fc understanding the pathogenesis, treatment and phenomenology of autism.